Lecture Notes in Computer Science 16351

The series Lecture Notes in Computer Science (LNCS), including its subseries Lecture Notes in Artificial Intelligence (LNAI) and Lecture Notes in Bioinformatics (LNBI), has established itself as a medium for the publication of new developments in computer science and information technology research, teaching, and education.

LNCS enjoys close cooperation with the computer science R & D community, the series counts many renowned academics among its volume editors and paper authors, and collaborates with prestigious societies. Its mission is to serve this international community by providing an invaluable service, mainly focused on the publication of conference and workshop proceedings and postproceedings. LNCS commenced publication in 1973.

Yongdae Kim · Atsuko Miyaji · Mehdi Tibouchi
Editors

Cryptology and Network Security

24th International Conference, CANS 2025
Osaka, Japan, November 17–20, 2025
Proceedings

Editors
Yongdae Kim
Korea Advanced Institute of Science and Technology
Daejeon, Korea (Republic of)

Atsuko Miyaji
The University of Osaka
Osaka, Japan

Mehdi Tibouchi
NTT Social Informatics Laboratories
Tokyo, Japan

ISSN 0302-9743 ISSN 1611-3349 (electronic)
Lecture Notes in Computer Science
ISBN 978-981-95-4433-2 ISBN 978-981-95-4434-9 (eBook)
https://doi.org/10.1007/978-981-95-4434-9

This Springer imprint is published by the registered company Springer Nature Singapore Pte Ltd.
The registered company address is: 152 Beach Road, #21-01/04 Gateway East, Singapore 189721, Singapore

Preface

CANS 2025, the 24th International Conference on Cryptology and Network Security, was held in Osaka, Japan on November 17–20 2025. The conference covered all theoretical and practical aspects of cryptology and network security, and its extended domains in modern computing systems.

We received a total of 81 submissions from all over the world, among which the Program Committee (PC) selected 26 full papers and 7 short papers for publication in the proceedings of the conference. The two program chairs were supported by a PC consisting of 69 leading experts in all aspects of applied cryptography and security. The review process was conducted using double-blind peer review. Each submission received an average of 4 reviews from the committee. Strong conflict of interest rules ensured that papers were not handled by PC members with a close personal or professional relationship with the authors. The two program chairs were not allowed to submit a paper. There were approximately 75 external reviewers, whose input was critical to the selection of papers.

Alongside the presentations of the accepted papers, the program of CANS 2025 featured two excellent invited talks by Shweta Agrawal and Surya Nepal.

Two particularly well-regarded submissions, one on the cryptology side and the other on the security side, were selected to receive the CANS 2025 *best paper award*: "Efficient Fuzzy Labeled PSI from Vector Ring-OLE" by Dung Bui and Kelong Cong, and "Synthetic Lateral Movement Data Generation for Azure Cloud: A Hopper-Based Approach" by Mohammad Mamun, Hadeer Ahmed, Sherif Saad and Anas Mabrouk.

Many people contributed to the success of CANS 2025. We would like to thank the authors for submitting their research results to the conference. We are very grateful to the PC members and external reviewers for contributing their knowledge and expertise, and for the tremendous amount of work involved in reviewing papers and contributing to the discussions. We are greatly indebted to Atsuko Miyaji, the General Chair, for her efforts and overall organization, as well as to the entire organizing committee. We thank the steering committee for their direction and valuable advice throughout the preparation of the conference. We also the staff of at Springer for handling the publication of these conference proceedings, as well as Yuta Kodera and Hiroki Sudo for preparing the proceedings volume.

November 2025

Yongdae Kim
Atsuko Miyaji
Mehdi Tibouchi

Organization

Committee

General Chair

Atsuko Miyaji	University of Osaka, Japan

Program Committee Chairs

Mehdi Tibouchi	NTT Social Informatics Laboratories, Japan
Yongdae Kim	Korea Advanced Institute of Science and Technology, South Korea

Program Committee

Akiko Inoue	NEC, Japan
Angelos Stavrou	Virginia Tech, USA
Armando Faz-Hernández	Cloudflare, USA
Avik Chakraborti	Institute for Advancing Intelligence, India
Barbara Fila	Irisa, France
Bernardo David	IT University of Copenhagen, Denmark
Bogdan Carbunar	Florida International University, USA
Byoungyoung Lee	Seoul National University, South Korea
Calvin Abou Haidar	NTT Social Informatics Laboratories, Japan
Chao Sun	Southwest University, China
Christoph Striecks	AIT Austrian Institute of Technology, Austria
Claudio Soriente	NEC Laboratories Europe, Germany
Cristina Onete	University of Limoges, France
Damien Vergnaud	Sorbonne Université, France
Dave Singelee	Katholieke Universiteit Leuven, Belgium
Dieter Gollmann	Hamburg University of Technology, Germany
Eiichiro Fujisaki	JAIST, Japan
Fareena Saqib	University of North Carolina at Charlotte, USA
Hikaru Tsuchida	Saitama Institute of Technology, Japan
Hiroshi Onuki	University of Tokyo, Japan
Hyoungshick Kim	Sungkyunkwan University, South Korea
Insu Yun	KAIST, South Korea

Jacob C.N. Schuldt	AIST, Japan
Jeongeun Park	Norwegian University of Science and Technology, Norway
João P. Vilela	University of Porto, Portugal
Jooyoung Lee	KAIST, South Korea
Jorge Chavez-Saab	Technology Innovation Institute, UAE
Jorge Guajardo	Robert Bosch LLC, USA
Jun Han	KAIST, Korea
Katerina Mitrokotsa	University of St. Gallen, Switzerland
Kazue Sako	Waseda University, Japan
Kazuo Sakiyama	University of Electro-Communications, Japan
Keita Emura	Kanazawa University, Japan
Keita Xagawa	Technology Innovation Institute, UAE
Ky Nguyen	Ecole normale superieure, France
Lejla Batina	Radboud University, Netherlands
Liqun Chen	University of Surrey, UK
Michael Roland	Johannes Kepler University Linz, Austria
Miguel Ambrona	Input Output Global (IOHK), Spain
Miran Kim	Hanyang University, South Korea
Miyako Ohkubo	NICT, Japan
Murtuza Jadliwala	University of Texas at San Antonio, USA
Naofumi Homma	Tohoku University, Japan
Nils Ole Tippenhauer	CISPA, Germany
Noboru Kunihiro	University of Tsukuba, Japan
Octavio Perez Kempner	NTT Social Informatics Laboratories, Japan
Omid Mir	AIT Austrian Institute of Technology, Austria
Panos Papadimitratos	KTH Royal Institute of Technology, Sweden
Patrick Derbez	Inria Rennes, France
Peeter Laud	Cybernetica AS, Estonia
Ravishankar Borgaonkar	SINTEF Digital, University of Stavanger, Norway
René Mayrhofer	Johannes Kepler University Linz, Austria
Ryo Kikuchi	NTT Social Informatics Laboratories, Japan
Serge Vaudenay	École Polytechnique Fédérale de Lausanne, Switzerland
Sherman S. M. Chow	Chinese University of Hong Kong, China
Sofia Celi	Brave, Portugal
Sokratis Katsikas	Norwegian University of Science and Technology, Norway
Somitra Sanadhya	IIT Jodhpur, India
Sooel Son	KAIST, South Korea
Stjepan Picek	Radboud University, Netherlands
Takaaki Mizuki	Tohoku University, Japan

Willy Susilo	University of Wollongong, Australia
Xiaoyu Ji	Zhejiang University, China
Xiapu Luo	Hong Kong Polytechnic University, China
Yang Yu	Tsinghua University, China
Yanjun Pan	University of Arkansas, USA
Yiannis Tselekounis	Royal Holloway, University of London, UK
Yingying Chen	Rutgers, USA
Yongsoo Song	Seoul National University, South Korea

Organizing Committee

Technical Support

Masaaki Shirase (Web Chair)	Future University Hakodate, Japan
Hiroshi Koide	Kyushu University, Japan
Ruka Yoshida	Aisin Software Co., Ltd., Japan
Shingo Yasuda	National Institute of Information and Communications Technology, Japan

Publicity and Publication

Chen-Mou Cheng (Publicity Chair)	Chang Gung University, Taiwan
Yuta Kodera (Publication Chair)	Okayama University, Japan
Baojun Liu	Tsinghua University, China
Hiroki Sudo	NTT Social Informatics Laboratories, Japan
Keita Emura	Kanazawa University, Japan
Tetsushi Ohki	Shizuoka University, Japan

External Relations

Akira Otsuka	Institute of Information Security, Japan
Kazumasa Omote	University of Tsukuba, Japan
Minoru Kuribayashi	Tohoku University, Japan
Rui Tanabe	Juntendo University, Japan

Logistics

Daisuke Kotani	Kyoto University, Japan
Hideaki Miyaji	Ritsumeikan University, Japan

Hiroyuki Inaba	Kyoto Institute of Technology, Japan
Naoto Yanai	Panasonic Corporation, Japan
Yuya Tarutani	University of Osaka, Japan
Yuji Suga	Internet Initiative Japan Inc., Japan

Financial Management

Akira Yamada	University of Hyogo, Japan
Atsuo Inomata	University of Osaka, Japan
Masaki Hashimoto	Kagawa University, Japan
Shinya Okumura	University of Osaka, Japan
Takeshi Chikazawa	Information-Technology Promotion Agency, Japan

Registration

Fukutomo Nakanishi	Toshiba Corporation, Japan
Takashi Hatashima	NTT Social Informatics Laboratories, Japan
Tomoaki Mimoto	KDDI Corporation, Japan

Additional Reviewers

Aysajan Abidin
Hiroaki Anada
Marcus Botacin
Cintia Maja Bódi
Adina Carapostol
Keng-Yu Chen
Alessandro Colombo
Dipayan Das
Julien Devevey
Xiaohui Ding
Max Duparc
Subhranil Dutta
Sayon Duttagupta
Reo Eriguchi
Tako Boris Fouotsa
Lewis Glabush
Catarina Gomes
Masanari Gotoh
Scott Griffy
Jincheol Ha
Jinguang Han
Keitaro Hashimoto
Yituo He
Atsunori Ichikawa
Ryoma Ito
Hyungrok Jo
Xuan Thanh Khuc
Elena Kirshanova
Ricardo Jose Menezes Maia
Omid Mirzamohammadi
Shigeo Mizuno
Kohei Morita
Munkenyi Mukhandi
Takeshi Nakai
Christopher Newton
Kazuma Ohara
Ying-Yu Pan
Florias Papadopoulos
Sebastian Ramacher
Yusuke Sakai

Kosei Sakamoto
Shingo Sato
Pedro Sousa
Hiroki Sudo
Koutarou Suzuki
Yangguang Tian
Rei Ueno
Jiafan Wang
Yalan Wang
Tsuata Wilson
Shota Yamada
Liujun Yu

Organizers

Organized by

In Cooperation with:

Sponsoring Institutions

公益財団法人
セコム科学技術振興財団
SECOM Science and Technology Foundation

FORTINET

CISCO

TOSHIBA

Contents

Post-Quantum Cryptography

Compressed Verification for Post-quantum Signatures with Long-Term Public Keys

Gustavo Banegas(✉), Anaëlle Le Dévéhat(✉), and Benjamin Smith(✉)

Inria and Laboratoire d'Informatique de l'Ecole polytechnique, Institut Polytechnique de Paris, Palaiseau, France

gustavo@cryptme.in, anaelle.le-devehat@inria.fr, smith@lix.polytechnique.fr

Abstract. Many signature applications—such as root certificates, secure software updates, and authentication protocols—involve long-lived public keys that are transferred or installed once and then used for many verifications. This key longevity makes post-quantum signature schemes with conservative assumptions (e.g., structure-free lattices) attractive for long-term security. But many such schemes, especially those with short signatures, suffer from extremely large public keys. Even in scenarios where bandwidth is not a major concern, large keys increase storage costs and slow down verification. We address this with a method to replace large public keys in GPV-style signatures with smaller, private verification keys. This significantly reduces verifier storage and runtime while preserving security. Applied to the conservative, short-signature schemes Wave and Squirrels, our method compresses Squirrels-I keys from 665 kB to 20.7 kB and Wave822 keys from 3.5 MB to 207.97 kB.

Keywords: Post-quantum cryptography · Digital Signatures · Lattice-based cryptography · Code-based cryptography · Compressed GPV

1 Introduction

Post-quantum signatures are a primary requirement for the transition towards quantum-resistant cryptography. Post-quantum lattice- and code-based signatures can be roughly classified as *conservative* or *structured*, according to whether their underlying hard problems involve general codes and lattices, or involve special algebraic structure. These structures facilitate important practical improvements (often, much smaller public keys); but they also allow the possibility of specialized attacks, so structured schemes generally have weaker security arguments (i.e., their assumptions are stronger).

This work was supported by the HYPERFORM consortium, funded by France through Bpifrance, and by the France 2030 program under grant agreement ANR-22-PETQ-0008 PQ-TLS.

Y. Kim et al. (Eds.): CANS 2025, LNCS 16351, pp. 3–26, 2026.
https://doi.org/10.1007/978-981-95-4434-9_1

For example: compare the structured lattice scheme FALCON [13] with the conservative lattice scheme SQUIRRELS [11]. Both are based on the same GPV design [14]. At NIST post-quantum security level 1, FALCON and SQUIRRELS have comparable signature sizes: 666 and 1019 bytes, respectively. But while the structured lattices of FALCON give 897-byte public keys, the unstructured lattices of SQUIRRELS push public-key sizes up to 665 *kilo*bytes.

Signature schemes with large public keys are unsuitable for applications where public keys are regularly transmitted, such as TLS certificates. They are better-suited to applications where

- the public key is pre-installed on the verifier's device (for verifying signed software updates, for example, or root certificates), or
- the public key is transmitted, but the cost of transmission is amortised over many subsequent verifications (in `ssh` authentication, for example).

These applications often involve public keys with *very* long lifetimes: 20–30 years for root certificates like ISRG Root X1 and GlobalSign Root R1, for example, and a decade or more for IoT code-signing certificates and government-issued digital IDs.

The long-term nature of keys in these applications makes conservative security assumptions reassuring, but working with very large public keys remains expensive and inconvenient. This makes hash-based signatures like SLH-DSA (SPHINCS+) [3,21] an interesting choice: they offer conservative security assumptions *and* very small public keys—but at the cost of large signatures and computationally intensive verification. SQUIRRELS offers shorter signatures and faster verification, but its 665 kB public keys make long-term storage impractical.

1.1 Compressed Verification

We want to reduce public key storage for conservative GPV-style signatures. The core idea is that the verifier can (pre-)process the public key PK once to derive a much smaller verification key VK (private to the verifier), which they can then use in place of PK for confident—and often much faster—signature verification.

More formally: suppose we are given a signature scheme defined by three algorithms, with an implicit security parameter λ:

- `KeyGen`: returns a private key SK and a public key PK.
- `Sign`: given a private key SK and a message m, returns a signature σ.
- `Verify`: given a putative signature σ on m under a public key PK, returns Accept or Reject.

We will define three additional algorithms to be used by the verifier:

- `CKeyGen`: returns a (private) compression key CK.
- `VKeyGen`: given a public key PK and a (private) compression key CK, return a private verification key VK.
- `CVerify`: given a putative signature σ on m and a verification key VK, returns Accept or Reject.

The goal is to define these functions such that if $\mathsf{VK} = \texttt{VKeyGen}(\mathsf{CK}, \mathsf{PK})$ for some public key PK and some CK output by $\texttt{CKeyGen}$, then

1. if $\texttt{Verify}(\sigma, m, \mathsf{PK}) = \mathsf{Accept}$ then $\texttt{CVerify}(\sigma, m, \mathsf{VK}) = \mathsf{Accept}$;
2. if $\texttt{Verify}(\sigma, m, \mathsf{PK}) = \mathsf{Reject}$ then $\texttt{CVerify}(\sigma, m, \mathsf{VK}) = \mathsf{Reject}$ with probability $\geq 1 - 1/2^{\mu}$ for a second security parameter μ; and
3. the size of VK is much smaller than the size of PK.

In terms of storage, CK is generated randomly and—once it has been used in $\texttt{VKeyGen}$—need not be stored. Therefore, the verifier only needs to retain VK.

The verifier is free to choose μ; our goal is that the probability that $\texttt{CVerify}$ accepts one forgery after Q attempts is on the order of $Q/\#\mathcal{S}$, where $\mathcal{S}$ is the verifier's compression-keyspace. We will generally take $\#\mathcal{S} \approx 2^{\mu}$ with $\mu \approx \lambda$, assuming Q is relatively small (in any case, $Q \leq 2^{64}$). The verifier may force a limit on Q by refreshing VK after a given number of rejections.

Figure 1 illustrates the signature protocol with compressed verification. CK and VK are private *to the verifier* and are derived only from the signer's public key PK, and not the signer's private key SK. Additionally, the verification algorithm $\texttt{CVerify}$ does not require PK or CK. From the signer's point of view, the original signature scheme is unchanged.

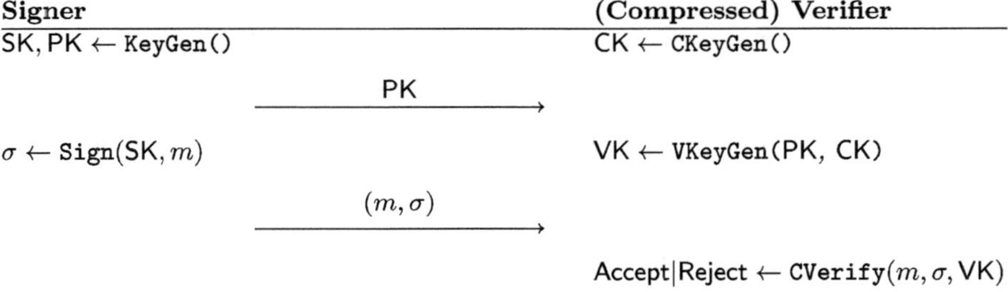

Fig. 1. Compressed verification as a protocol.

1.2 Results

We introduce a framework for *compressed verification* in GPV-style signatures. The verifier chooses a private homomorphism ϕ and uses it to compress incoming public keys to compact *private verification keys*. We give security arguments for the general construction, and consider two conservative instantiations: SQUIRRELS [11], a lattice-based signature, and WAVE [1,9], a code-based signature.

SQUIRRELS and WAVE both have little special algebraic structure. This builds confidence in their security, but it comes at an important practical cost: as we see in Table 1, their public keys are *very* big. Indeed, among the submissions to the NIST Postquantum Signatures on-ramp with no vulnerabilities found during Round 1, SQUIRRELS and WAVE had the largest public keys at most security levels.[1] These oversized public keys would be a major factor in the non-selection of these schemes for Round 2 of the standardization process. They also make SQUIRRELS and WAVE prime candidates to demonstrate the effectiveness of our technique.

We developed two implementations of both SQUIRRELS and WAVE:

1. A comprehensive implementation in Python, and
2. A C implementation, based on the reference implementations of SQUIRRELS [27] and WAVE, used to measure performance improvements.

Table 1 shows the significant reduction in verifier storage achieved for both SQUIRRELS and WAVE while maintaining security levels (and backward compatibility with the original schemes). Specifically, we achieve a **compression ratio of up to 34x** for WAVE at higher security levels, and **over 26x** for SQUIRRELS at comparable levels. Compressed verification can also reduce verification time: verification is **up to 9.26% faster** than ordinary verification for SQUIRRELS and **up to 30% faster** for WAVE.

Table 1. Signature scheme parameters and verification times. All sizes are in bytes. Compressed verification parameters are chosen such that $\mu \approx \lambda$ (see Sect. 4 and Sect. 5 for details). Verification times are cycle counts on an Intel Core i7-1365U processor running Arch Linux Kernel 6.11.5-arch1. "Reference" refers to C reference implementations, and "Compressed" to our own C code. WAVE signatures are variable-length; sizes here are upper bounds, and WAVE signature length roughly doubles for compressed verification.

	Reference		Compressed verification			Verification time (kCycles)		
	$\lvert\sigma\rvert$	$\lvert$PK$\rvert$	$\lvert$VK$\rvert$	($\lvert$CK$\rvert$)	$\lvert$PK$\rvert$/$\lvert$VK$\rvert$	Reference	Compressed	*Speedup*
NIST PQ Security Level 1, classical $\lambda = 128$								
SQUIRRELS-I	1 019	**681 780**	**20 700**	(3 360)	*32.9*×	280	254	*9.3%*
WAVE822	822	**3 677 390**	**171 594**	(83 822)	*21.4*×	1 101	762	*30.8%*
SPHINCS+-SHAKE-128 s	7 856	32	—	—	—	3 285	—	—
XMSS^{MT}-20-2	4 963	64	—	—	—	2 868	—	—
NIST PQ Security Level 3, classical $\lambda = 192$								
SQUIRRELS-III	1 554	**1 629 640**	**49 824**	(8 480)	*32.7*×	551	520	*5.69%*
WAVE1249	1 249	**7 867 598**	**266 188**	(183 134)	*29.6*×	2 330	1 865	*19.9%*
SPHINCS+-SHAKE-192 s	16 224	48	—	—	—	5 374	—	—
XMSS^{MT}-40-4	9 893	64	—	—	—	5 729	—	—
NIST PQ Security Level 5, classical $\lambda = 256$								
SQUIRRELS-V	2 025	**2 786 580**	**90 598**	(15 048)	*30.8*×	916	898	*1.9%*
WAVE1644	1 644	**13 632 308**	**370 436**	(321 507)	*36.8*×	3 911	3 198	*18.2%*
SPHINCS+-SHAKE-256s	29 792	64	—	—	—	7 567	—	—
XMSS^{MT}-60-6	14 824	64	—	—	—	8 743	—	—

[1] The *classic* parameters of UOV, a conservative multivariate scheme, had larger public keys than SQUIRRELS at NIST PQ Security Level 5, but other UOV variants had smaller keys. In any case, WAVE is the undisputed super-heavyweight champion: its Level I public keys were larger than even the Level V keys of any other scheme.

As a baseline for conservative signatures, Table 1 includes the hash-based schemes SPHINCS+ and XMSS^{MT} [15]. For SPHINCS+, the authors provide a benchmark script, which we ran in our environment; in the table we report the fastest result produced by that script [26]. For XMSS^{MT}, we used the reference code [16] with the smallest parameters for each security level.

Remark 1. Compressed verification may also benefit schemes like Ajtai-based hash-and-sign [7, 19], which offer strong SIS-based security. The benefit is limited for structured GPV-style schemes such as FALCON [13]: public keys are already compact, and compressed verification requires the full (s_1, s_2) signature rather than just s_2, thus doubling signature size.

Remark 2. Our method is compatible with the PS-3 [24] and BUFF [8] transforms, which strengthen security in certain attack models. However, both require hashing PK with the message—a costly step when PK is large. We suggest storing the much smaller $\mathsf{Hash}(\mathsf{PK})$ and hashing that with the message instead.

1.3 Related Work: Flexible Signatures and Progressive Verification

Fischlin's *progressive verification* for MACs [12] can probabilistically Reject early or Accept with reduced confidence; [12, §4] suggests an extension to signatures. Le, Kelkar, and Kate's *flexible signatures* [17], verified up to a real "confidence level" $0 \leq \alpha \leq 1$, quantify "partial" verification when expensive verification operations are interrupted voluntarily by the user or forcibly by the OS. This can improve fault-tolerance and reduce the cost of verification in embedded applications, but it does not reduce public-key or signature sizes. Indeed, the main targets in [17] are hash-based signatures, where public keys are already extremely compact; but extensions to GPV signatures are projected in [17, §5.3].

Taleb and Vergnaud revisit progressive verification in [28], analyzing Bernstein's RSA trick (see Sect. 2) and GPV signatures (including WAVE). They propose verifying GPV signatures using a small set of linear combinations of columns based on a random linear code, achieving exponential confidence growth with runtime, unlike the linear growth in [12] and [17]. However, their approach significantly increases public key size, which is the opposite of our goal.

Boschini, Fiore, Pagnin, Torresetti, and Visconti [6] propose an *efficient verification* for signatures which verify using a matrix-vector product $\mathbf{M}\mathbf{v}^\top$. In an "offline" phase they compute a matrix $\mathbf{M}'$ formed by k random linear combinations of the n rows of $\mathbf{M}$; then, in an "online" phase, they verify using $\mathbf{M}'\mathbf{v}^\top$, with reduced confidence but with a speedup of n/k. This is very similar to what we do with WAVE in Sect. 5, but they repeat the offline phase for every verification rather than maintaining the same $\mathbf{M}'$; indeed, their focus is minimising online verification latency, rather than reducing overall verification time or key sizes.

2 Warmup: Bernstein's Trick for Rabin–Williams

As a warmup, we recall Bernstein's fast Rabin–Williams signature verification [2]. We write $\textsc{Primes}(\mu)$ for the set of (exactly) μ-bit primes: that is,

$$\textsc{Primes}(\mu) := \{2^{\mu-1} < p < 2^{\mu} \mid p \text{ is prime}\}.$$

2.1 Verifying Rabin–Williams Signatures

A Rabin–Williams signature [25,30] on a message m under a public key $N = pq$ is a tuple $\sigma = (e, f, \mathsf{salt}, s)$ such that

$$efs^2 \equiv \mathsf{Hash}(\mathsf{salt} \parallel m) \pmod{N} \tag{1}$$

where $1 < s < N$, salt is a salt value, and $e \in \{-1, 1\}$ and $f \in \{1, 2\}$ are chosen such that s exists for the given salt, m, and N. That is: given $\sigma = (e, f, \mathsf{salt}, s)$, m, and $\mathsf{PK} = N$, $\mathtt{Verify}(\sigma, m, \mathsf{PK})$ returns Accept if and only if (1) holds.

If (1) is satisfied, then there is a unique integer $-2N < t < 2N$ such that

$$efs^2 - tN = \mathsf{Hash}(\mathsf{salt} \parallel m). \tag{2}$$

(The sign of t is equal to e.) Note that (2) holds over $\mathbb{Z}$, not just over $\mathbb{Z}/N\mathbb{Z}$; and any solution to (2) yields a solution to (1) and vice versa, so verifying (1) or (2) is mathematically (though not algorithmically) equivalent.

Bernstein suggested speeding up verification by including t in σ and verifying (2) modulo a random λ-bit prime ℓ (with λ the security parameter). The verifier picks $\ell \in \textsc{Primes}(\lambda)$, computes $N_\ell := N \bmod \ell$, and upon receiving $\sigma = (e, f, \mathsf{salt}, s, t)$, checks

$$efs_\ell^2 - t_\ell N_\ell \equiv h_\ell \pmod{\ell}, \tag{3}$$

where $s_\ell := s \bmod \ell$, $t_\ell := t \bmod \ell$, and $h_\ell := \mathsf{Hash}(\mathsf{salt} \parallel m) \bmod \ell$. Since $\ell \ll N$, this is faster than computing $s^2 \bmod N$; the speedup increases with λ. The trade-off: including t doubles the size of σ, and generating ℓ is relatively costly. However, as Bernstein notes, ℓ can be reused across multiple verifications—even for different public keys—if kept secret, amortizing the cost.

This trick was proposed to speed up verification. We observe that it also saves space if many signatures are verified under the same N, since N_ℓ can be stored instead of N (and this saves even more time, since N_ℓ need not be recomputed).

In terms of our framework above,

- $\mathtt{CKeyGen}$ samples a random λ-bit prime ℓ;
- $\mathtt{VKeyGen}(\mathsf{CK} = \ell, \mathsf{PK} = N)$ returns $\mathsf{VK} = (\ell, N_\ell := N \bmod \ell)$;
- $\mathtt{CVerify}(m, \sigma = (e, f, \mathsf{salt}, s, t), \mathsf{VK} = (\ell, N_\ell))$ returns Accept if and only if $efs^2 - tN_\ell \equiv \mathsf{Hash}(\mathsf{salt} \parallel m) \pmod{\ell}$.

As Bernstein observes, the same technique applies to RSA signatures. However, if e is the public exponent, the resulting integer t is roughly N^{e-1}, making the signature e times longer than a standard RSA signature.

2.2 Security Argument for Bernstein's Trick

Let's say that an ℓ-forgery on a message m for a public key $\mathsf{PK} = N$ is a vector $(e, f, \mathsf{salt}, s, t)$ such that (2) (and hence (1)) fails, but (3) holds. That is: an ℓ-forgery is a putative expanded Rabin–Williams signature that `Verify` with $\mathsf{PK} = N$ would safely reject, but `CVerify` with $\mathsf{VK} = (\ell, N \bmod \ell)$ would accept. (We assume that forging a signature for (1) or (2) is infeasible.)

An adversary that knows ℓ can easily construct ℓ-forgeries for any m and N. Take a random salt, and find a t such that $x := \mathsf{Hash}(\mathsf{salt} \parallel m) + tN$ is a square modulo ℓ; then, compute $s := x^{1/2} \pmod{\ell}$ (which is easy because ℓ is prime); finally, set $e := 1$ and $f := 1$.

Conversely, if we can find an ℓ-forgery $\sigma = (e, f, \mathsf{salt}, s, t)$ for (m, N) then

$$\ell \mid \Xi(\sigma, m, N) \qquad \text{where} \qquad \Xi(\sigma, m, N) := efs^2 - tN - \mathsf{Hash}(\mathsf{salt} \parallel \mathrm{m}) .$$

At just λ bits, the prime ℓ is sufficiently small (for cryptographic values of λ) to be recovered from $\Xi(\sigma, m, N)$ with ECM [18,20,31].[2]

An adversary $\mathcal{A}$ who can compute an ℓ-forgery can therefore find ℓ, and vice versa. But $\mathcal{A}$'s interaction with the verifier is limited to submitting tuples (σ, m, N), and observing whether they are accepted or rejected: that is, whether the unknown ℓ divides $\Xi(\sigma, m, N)$ or not. Let

$$\mu := \log_2 \ell \qquad \text{and} \qquad \kappa := \lfloor (\log_2 N)/\mu \rfloor .$$

Observe that $\mathcal{A}$ learns nothing from an ℓ-forgery attempt (σ, m, N) such that $\Xi(\sigma, m, N)$ is not divisible by at least one μ-bit prime, and that if $\Xi(\sigma, m, N) \neq 0$, then it is divisible by at most 2κ μ-bit primes (because $|\Xi(\sigma, m, N)| < 2N^2$). Therefore, if an adversary makes at most Q forgery attempts against a verifier using a μ-bit prime ℓ for VK, then their success probability is at most

$$P(N, \mu, Q) := \frac{2\kappa Q}{\#\textsc{Primes}(\mu)} . \tag{4}$$

It follows from [10, Corollary 5.3] that

$$0.975 \frac{2^{\mu-1}}{(\mu - 1)\log 2} < \#\textsc{Primes}(\mu) < \frac{2^{\mu-1}}{(\mu - 1)\log 2} . \tag{5}$$

Thus, $P(N, \mu, Q) \approx Q \cdot (\log N)/2^{\mu-2}$. For $\mu \approx \lambda$, this bound remains negligible even across more verifications than could feasibly be generated, without needing to refresh ℓ or track rejections.

3 The General Approach

3.1 GPV Signatures

Consider a general GPV-style signature. Let $\mathcal{M}$ be a finitely generated module over an integral domain $\mathcal{R}$: in practice, $\mathcal{M}$ is either a lattice (with $\mathcal{R} = \mathbb{Z}$) or

[2] Further: if we can find two ℓ-forgeries σ_1 and σ_2—*not* necessarily for the same m and N—then $\ell \mid g := \gcd(\Xi(\sigma_1, m_1, N_1), \Xi(\sigma_2, m_2, N_2))$, and in fact probably $\ell = g$.

a code (with $\mathcal{R} = \mathbb{F}_q$). Fix a cryptographic hash function $\mathsf{Hash} : \{0,1\}^* \to \mathcal{M}$. A public key is a random-looking $\mathbf{M} = (\mathbf{M}_0, \ldots, \mathbf{M}_{n-1}) \in \mathcal{M}^n$ for some system parameter n. A signature on a message m under $\mathbf{M}$ is a tuple $\sigma = (\mathsf{salt}, \mathbf{s})$ with $\mathsf{salt} \in \{0,1\}^\lambda$ (a random salt) and $\mathbf{s} \in \mathcal{R}^n$ such that

$$\textsc{Constraint}(\mathbf{s}) \qquad \text{and} \qquad \mathbf{sM} := \sum_{i=0}^{n-1} s_i \mathbf{M}_i = \mathsf{Hash}(\mathsf{salt} \parallel m) \tag{6}$$

where $\textsc{Constraint}(\mathbf{s})$ is a predicate on $\mathbf{s}$ such as having small norm (in SQUIRRELS) or a fixed number of nonzero entries (in WAVE). An important variant has Hash mapping into (a subset of) $\mathcal{R}^n$ instead of $\mathcal{M}$, and (6) is replaced by

$$\textsc{Constraint}(\mathbf{s}) \qquad \text{and} \qquad \big(\mathsf{Hash}(\mathsf{salt} \parallel m) + \mathbf{s}\big)\mathbf{M} = \mathbf{0}\,. \tag{7}$$

Example 1. In SQUIRRELS, $\mathcal{R} = \mathbb{Z}$ and $\mathcal{M} = \mathbb{Z}/\Delta$ for some large Δ (though later we lift to $\mathcal{M} = \mathbb{Z}$); verification uses (7) where $\textsc{Constraint}(\mathbf{s})$ is $\|\mathbf{s}\|_2^2 \le \lfloor \beta^2 \rfloor$ for a small system parameter β. For example, SQUIRRELS-I has $n = 1034$, Δ a 5048-bit modulus formed as the product of 165 31-bit primes, and $\lfloor \beta^2 \rfloor = 2026590$.

Example 2. In WAVE, $\mathcal{R} = \mathbb{F}_3$ and $\mathcal{M} = \mathbb{F}_3^{n-k}$ for system parameters n and k; verification uses (6) where $\textsc{Constraint}(\mathbf{s})$ is $\#\{i \mid s_i \neq 0\} = w$ for some (large) $w < n$. For example: WAVE822 has $n = 8576$, $k = 4288$, and $w = 7668 \approx 0.9n$.

3.2 Compressed Verification

Let Σ be a general GPV-style signature on an $\mathcal{R}$-module $\mathcal{M}$ as described above, and fix a set $\mathcal{S}$ of $\mathcal{R}$-submodules of $\mathcal{M}$. We define a compressed-verification signature scheme Σ_{comp} with the same `KeyGen` and `Sign` as in Σ, but with `Verify` replaced by the following `CKeyGen`, `VKeyGen`, and `CVerify`:

- `CKeyGen`: samples a random $\mathcal{K}$ from $\mathcal{S}$, and returns the quotient homomorphism $\mathsf{CK} := \phi : \mathcal{M} \to \overline{\mathcal{M}} := \mathcal{M}/\mathcal{K}$ (which is unique up to isomorphism, and has kernel $\ker\phi = \mathcal{K}$).
- `VKeyGen`: takes $\mathsf{PK} = \mathbf{M}$ and returns $\mathsf{VK} := (\phi, \overline{\mathbf{M}} := (\phi(\mathbf{M}_1), \ldots, \phi(\mathbf{M}_n)))$.
- `CVerify`: given m, $\sigma = (\mathsf{salt}, \mathbf{s})$, and VK, let $\mathbf{h} = \mathsf{Hash}(\mathsf{salt} \parallel m)$. If σ would normally be verified with (6), then `CVerify` returns Accept if and only if $\textsc{Constraint}(\mathbf{s})$ and $\phi(\mathbf{sM}) = \phi(\mathbf{h})$; and since ϕ is a homomorphism of $\mathcal{R}$-modules, this means

$$\textsc{Constraint}(\mathbf{s}) \qquad \text{and} \qquad \sum_{i=0}^{n-1} s_i \overline{\mathbf{M}}_i = \phi(\mathbf{h}) \quad \text{in } \overline{\mathcal{M}}\,. \tag{8}$$

  If verification normally uses (7), then `CVerify` returns Accept if and only if

$$\textsc{Constraint}(\mathbf{s}) \qquad \text{and} \qquad \sum_{i=0}^{n-1} (s_i + h_i)\overline{\mathbf{M}}_i = \mathbf{0} \quad \text{in } \overline{\mathcal{M}}\,. \tag{9}$$

If (9) is used for verification, then $\mathsf{CK} = \phi$ need not be included in VK.

If the verifier verifies many signatures from the same signer, then the cost of `CKeyGen` and `VKeyGen` is amortised over the many subsequent `CVerify` calls. A good choice of ϕ can also reduce the time required for each verification.

3.3 Correctness and Security

The correctness of the signature scheme Σ_{comp} described above follows from ϕ being a homomorphism: (6) implies (8) and (7) implies (9). Our security goal is EUF-CMA (Existential unforgeability under adaptive chosen-message attacks). Recall that a signature scheme $\Sigma = (\mathsf{Gen}, \mathtt{Sign}, \mathsf{Verify})$ is said to be EUF-CMA if for all probabilistic polynomial-time (PPT) adversaries $\mathcal{A}$, the probability that $\mathcal{A}$ wins the following game is negligible in the security parameter λ:

1. The challenger gets $(\mathsf{pk}, \mathsf{sk}) \leftarrow \mathsf{Gen}(1^\lambda)$ and gives pk to the adversary $\mathcal{A}$.
2. The adversary $\mathcal{A}$ has access to a signing oracle $\mathcal{O}_{\mathtt{Sign}}$ and a verification oracle $\mathcal{O}_{\mathtt{Verify}}$. It may adaptively query $\mathcal{O}_{\mathtt{Sign}}$ on messages $m_1, \ldots, m_q$ and receive valid signatures σ_i for each. It also may query $\mathcal{O}_{\mathtt{Verify}}$ on signatures σ_i and know if it is valid signature or not.
3. $\mathcal{A}$ outputs a pair (m^*, σ^*).
4. $\mathcal{A}$ wins the game if:
   (a) $\mathsf{Verify}_{\mathsf{pk}}(m^*, \sigma^*) = 1$ (i.e., the signature is valid), and
   (b) $m^* \notin \{m_1, \ldots, m_q\}$ (i.e., m^* was not queried to the signing oracle).

We want to relate the EUF-CMA security of a GPV signature with compressed verification to the assumed EUF-CMA security of the original scheme. We model forgery attempts as attempts at solving a hidden-structure problem:

Definition 1 (Submodule Element Guessing Problem $\mathsf{SEGP}(\mathcal{S}, \mathcal{T})$). *Let $\mathcal{M}$ be an $\mathcal{R}$-module, $\mathcal{T}$ a finite subset of $\mathcal{M}$, and $\mathcal{S}$ a set of $\mathcal{R}$-submodules of $\mathcal{M}$. The* ***Submodule Element Guessing Problem*** *$\mathsf{SEGP}(\mathcal{S}, \mathcal{T})$ is: given a membership oracle $\mathcal{O}_{\mathcal{K}}$ for an unknown submodule $\mathcal{K} \in \mathcal{S}$ taking input in $\mathcal{T}$ (i.e.: $\mathcal{O}_{\mathcal{K}}$ takes $\mathbf{t} \in \mathcal{T}$ and returns* True *if $\mathbf{t} \in \mathcal{K}$ and* False *otherwise), find an element $\mathbf{t}^* \neq \mathbf{0} \in \mathcal{T}$ such that $\mathcal{O}_{\mathcal{K}}(t^*) = \mathsf{True}$, i.e., $\mathbf{t}^* \in \mathcal{K}$.*

The set $\mathcal{S}$ in Definition 1 represents the set of possible kernels of the secret homomorphism ϕ, and $\mathcal{T}$ represents the vectors constructed by forgery attempts before input to ϕ. We remark that, in the SEGP game, the kernel K is sampled uniformly at random from $\mathcal{S}$.

Definition 2. *Let Σ be a general GPV signature scheme as above. We define*

$$\mathcal{T}(\Sigma) := \left\{\mathbf{sM} - \mathbf{h} : \mathbf{h} \in \mathrm{Im}(\mathsf{Hash}), \mathbf{s} \in \mathcal{R}^n \mid \textsc{Constraint}(\mathbf{s})\right\}$$

if Σ uses (6) for verification, or

$$\mathcal{T}(\Sigma) := \left\{(\mathbf{h} + \mathbf{s})\mathbf{M} : \mathbf{h} \in \mathrm{Im}(\mathsf{Hash}), \mathbf{s} \in \mathcal{R}^n \mid \textsc{Constraint}(\mathbf{s})\right\}$$

if Σ uses (7) for verification.

Theorem 1. *Let Σ be a general GPV-style signature scheme on an $\mathcal{R}$-module $\mathcal{M}$, and fix a set $\mathcal{S}$ of $\mathcal{R}$-submodules of $\mathcal{M}$. For each $\mathcal{K}$ in $\mathcal{S}$, let $\Sigma^{\mathcal{K}}_{comp}$ be the instance of Σ_{comp} where* `CKeyGen` *samples uniformly random $\mathcal{K}$ from $\mathcal{S}$. If $\mathcal{A}$ is an algorithm running in time T that wins the EUF-CMA game for $\Sigma^{\mathcal{K}}_{comp}$ with probability P, then there exists an algorithm $\mathcal{B}$ running in time $T + O(1)$ that succeeds with probability P in winning the EUF-CMA game for Σ, or solving the $\mathsf{SEGP}(\mathcal{S}, \mathcal{T}(\Sigma))$ instance corresponding to $\mathcal{K}$.*

Proof. The challenger for EUF-CMA game of Σ gives $\mathsf{PK} = \mathbf{M}$ to the algorithm $\mathcal{B}$. $\mathcal{B}$ has access to a signing oracle $\mathcal{O}_{\mathtt{Sign}}$, a verification oracle $\mathcal{O}_{\mathsf{Verify}}$ both associated to Σ and a submodule membership oracle $\mathcal{O}_K$ associated to $\mathsf{SEGP}(\mathcal{S}, \mathcal{T}(\Sigma))$. $\mathcal{B}$ calls $\mathcal{A}$ on $\mathsf{PK} = \mathbf{M}$. $\mathcal{B}$ answers a signing oracle query m from $\mathcal{A}$ by $\mathcal{O}_{\mathtt{Sign}}(m)$ as the signing process is the same for Σ and $\Sigma^{\mathcal{K}}_{\text{comp}}$. If $\mathcal{A}$ makes a query to the verification oracle for $\Sigma^{\mathcal{K}}_{\text{comp}}$ on a signature $\sigma = (\mathsf{salt}, \mathbf{s})$, $\mathcal{B}$ queries $\mathcal{O}_{\mathsf{Verify}}(\sigma)$. If $\mathcal{O}_{\mathsf{Verify}}(\sigma) = 1$ then $\mathcal{B}$ answers 1 to $\mathcal{A}$. Otherwise, If Σ verifies with (6) then $\mathcal{B}$ sets $\mathbf{t} := \mathbf{sM} - \mathsf{Hash}(\mathsf{salt} \parallel m)$; if Σ verifies with (7) instead, then $\mathcal{B}$ sets $\mathbf{t} := (\mathsf{Hash}(\mathsf{salt} \parallel m) + \mathbf{s})\mathbf{M}$. $\mathcal{B}$ answers the verification oracle query by $\mathcal{O}_K(\mathbf{t})$.

If $\mathcal{A}$ fails, then $\mathcal{B}$ fails. Otherwise, it receives a $(m^*, \sigma^* = (\mathsf{salt}^*, \mathbf{s}^*))$ such that $\textsc{Constraint}(\mathbf{s}^*)$ holds and $\mathtt{CVerify}(m^*, \sigma^*, \mathsf{VK}) = \mathsf{Accept}$. $\mathcal{B}$ computes $\mathbf{t}^*$, if $\mathbf{t}^* = \mathbf{0}$, then $\mathtt{Verify}(m^*, \sigma^*, \mathsf{PK})$ would return Accept, so $\mathcal{B}$ returns (m^*, σ^*) and wins the EUF-CMA game associated to Σ. Otherwise, $\mathbf{t}^*$ is a nonzero element of $\mathcal{K}$, so $\mathcal{B}$ returns $\mathbf{t}^*$ and finds a solution to $\mathsf{SEGP}(\mathcal{S}, \mathcal{T}(\Sigma))$. □

Theorem 1 tells us that if Σ is EUF-CMA secure, then forging a signature for $\Sigma^{\mathcal{K}}_{\text{comp}}$ is *at least as hard* as solving the $\mathsf{SEGP}(\mathcal{S}, \mathcal{T}(\Sigma))$ instance corresponding to $\mathcal{K}$. We can therefore choose secure parameters for Σ_{comp} by choosing the set $\mathcal{S}$ of compression keys such that random instances of $\mathsf{SEGP}(\mathcal{S}, \mathcal{T}(\Sigma))$ are hard.

3.4 The Hardness of SEGP

The hardness of $\mathsf{SEGP}(\mathcal{S}, \mathcal{T})$ depends on the choice of $\mathcal{S}$ and $\mathcal{T}$, and also on the properties of $\mathcal{R}$ and $\mathcal{M}$ (and $\mathcal{M}/\mathcal{K}$ for $\mathcal{K}$ in $\mathcal{S}$). There are a few general things that we can say before returning to the problem in the concrete cases of Squirrels and Wave later. Let $\mathcal{O}$ be a membership oracle for a secret $\mathcal{K}$ sampled uniformly random from $\mathcal{S}$, and accepting only queries from $\mathcal{T}$; and let $\phi : \mathcal{M} \to \mathcal{M}/\mathcal{K}$ be the quotient homomorphism. We can assume $\phi(\mathcal{T}) = \mathcal{M}/\mathcal{K}$. The adversary's goal is to find some $\mathbf{t} \neq \mathbf{0}$ in $\mathcal{T}$ such that $\mathcal{O}(\mathbf{t}) = \mathsf{True}$: implicitly, $\mathbf{t} \in (\mathcal{K} \setminus \{\mathbf{0}\}) \cap \mathcal{T}$.

The adversary makes a series of adaptive queries $\mathbf{t}^{(1)}, \mathbf{t}^{(2)}, \ldots$ to $\mathcal{O}$. Suppose $\mathcal{O}(\mathbf{t}^{(i)}) = \mathsf{False}$ for $1 \leq i \leq Q$. The adversary wants $\phi(\mathbf{t}^{(Q+1)}) \neq \phi(\mathbf{t}^{(i)})$ for $1 \leq i \leq Q$, because none of the $\phi(\mathbf{t}^{(i)}$ were $\mathbf{0}$. In the best case for the adversary all these values are distinct,[3] so if the adversary chooses $\mathbf{t}^{(Q+1)}$ arbitrarily then

$$P\big[\mathcal{O}(\mathbf{t}^{(Q+1)})\big] \leq \frac{1}{\#(\mathcal{M}/\mathcal{K}) - \mathrm{Q}}\,.$$

(If the adversary can choose $\mathbf{t}^{(Q+1)}$ such that it maps into a proper submodule $\mathcal{N} \subset \mathcal{M}/\mathcal{K}$ then we can replace $\#(\mathcal{M}/\mathcal{K})$ with $\#\mathcal{N}$ and Q with the number of prior queries landing in $\mathcal{N}$, but this is not significant in our applications.)

In the meantime, the adversary has also learned that

$$\mathcal{K} \notin \bigcup_{i=1}^{Q} \mathcal{S}_{\mathbf{t}^{(i)}} \quad \text{where} \quad \mathcal{S}_{\mathbf{t}} := \{\mathcal{K} \in \mathcal{S} \mid \mathbf{t} \in \mathcal{K}\} \subset \mathcal{S}\,.$$

[3] Note that collisions $\phi(\mathbf{t}^{(i)}) = \phi(\mathbf{t}^{(j)})$ are not useful to the adversary, because they cannot detect them without querying $\mathcal{O}$ on all the $\mathbf{t}^{(i)} - \mathbf{t}^{(j)}$.

In our applications $\mathcal{S}$ is finite, so there exists an integer

$$\kappa_{\mathcal{T}} := \max\{\#\mathcal{S}_{\mathbf{t}} : \mathbf{t} \in \mathcal{T}\};$$

each unsuccessful query eliminates up to $\kappa_{\mathcal{T}}$ candidate kernels from consideration. The adversary must choose $\mathbf{t}^{(Q+1)}$ such that $\mathcal{S}_{\mathbf{t}^{(Q+1)}} \not\subset \bigcup_{i=1}^{Q} \mathcal{S}_{\mathbf{t}^{(i)}}$ to have any chance of success. If $\mathbf{t}^{(Q+1)}$ is chosen arbitrarily among the elements of $\mathcal{T}$ such that $\mathcal{S}_{\mathbf{t}^{(Q+1)}} \setminus \bigcup_{i=1}^{Q} \mathcal{S}_{\mathbf{t}^{(i)}}$ is maximal, then the probability of success is

$$P\big[\mathcal{O}(\mathbf{t}^{(Q+1)})\big] \leq \frac{\#\big(\mathcal{S}_{\mathbf{t}^{(Q+1)}} \setminus \bigcup_{i=1}^{Q} \mathcal{S}_{\mathbf{t}^{(i)}}\big)}{\#\mathcal{S} - \#\bigcup_{i=1}^{Q} \mathcal{S}_{\mathbf{t}^{(i)}}} \leq \frac{\kappa_{\mathcal{T}}}{\#\mathcal{S} - \kappa_{\mathcal{T}} Q}\,. \tag{10}$$

For EUF-CMA security with parameter μ against this adversary, we need to ensure the success probability after Q queries is $\leq 2^{-\mu}$, so

$$\min(\#\mathcal{S}/\kappa_{\mathcal{T}}, \#(\mathcal{M}/\mathcal{K})) \geq 2^{\mu} + Q\,. \tag{11}$$

We should therefore sample $\mathcal{K}$ from an $\mathcal{S}$ chosen such that (at least)

$$\#\mathcal{S}/\kappa_{\mathcal{T}} \geq 2^{\mu} \qquad \text{and} \qquad \#(\mathcal{M}/\mathcal{K}) \geq 2^{\mu} \text{ for each } \mathcal{K} \in \mathcal{S}\,, \tag{12}$$

and we should replace the verification key when the number of (failed) compressed verifications approaches 2^{μ}.

Heuristically, we will suppose that the adversary cannot improve on any strategy that simply enumerates queries $\mathbf{t}^{(i+1)}$ while maximising $\#\mathcal{S}_{\mathbf{t}^{(i+1)}} \setminus \bigcup_{j=1}^{i} \mathcal{S}_{\mathbf{t}^{(j)}}$. Indeed, to do so they would need more information on $\phi(\mathbf{x})$ for unqueried $\mathbf{x}$. Our heuristic is that this information has to come from exploiting the $\mathcal{R}$-module structures of $\mathcal{M}$ and $\mathcal{M}/\mathcal{K}$, but these structures generally do not help.

First, $(\phi(\mathbf{x}) \neq \mathbf{0}) \wedge (\phi(\mathbf{y}) \neq \mathbf{0}) \not\Rightarrow \phi(\mathbf{x}+\mathbf{y}) \neq \mathbf{0}$ unless $\mathbf{y} \in \mathcal{R}\mathbf{x}$ or $\mathbf{x} \in \mathcal{R}\mathbf{y}$. This tells us that given the results of $\mathcal{O}(\mathbf{t}^{(i)})$ for $1 \leq i \leq Q$, we cannot predict the result of $\mathcal{O}(\mathbf{t}^{(Q+1)})$ for general linear combinations $\mathbf{t}^{(Q+1)} = \sum_{i=1}^{Q} \alpha_i \mathbf{t}^{(i)}$.

Looking at scalar multiplication, there are two cases.

1. If $\alpha \neq 0 \in \mathcal{R}$ is invertible on $\mathcal{M}/\mathcal{K}$, then $\phi(\mathbf{x}) = \mathbf{0} \iff \phi(\alpha\mathbf{x}) = \mathbf{0}$ for all $\mathbf{x}$. In this case, if we know $\mathcal{O}(\mathbf{x}) = \mathsf{False}$, then we can predict that $\mathcal{O}(\alpha\mathbf{x}) = \mathsf{False}$ *without* querying $\mathcal{O}$ on $\alpha\mathbf{x}$ (and vice versa). But these "virtual" queries cannot not help the adversary, because $\mathcal{S}_{\alpha\mathbf{x}} = \mathcal{S}_{\mathbf{x}}$ for all such α.
2. If $\alpha \neq 0 \in \mathcal{R}$ is *not* invertible on $\mathcal{M}/\mathcal{K}$, then $\phi(\mathbf{x}) = \mathbf{0} \implies \phi(\alpha\mathbf{x}) = \mathbf{0}$ for all $\mathbf{x}$, but the converse does not hold; likewise, $\mathcal{S}_{\mathbf{x}} \subset \mathcal{S}_{\alpha\mathbf{x}}$ but the inclusion may be strict. If such elements α are known, then the adversary should query on $\alpha\mathbf{x}$ instead of $\mathbf{x}$ to maximise $\#\mathcal{S}_{\alpha\mathbf{x}}$ (and hence $\#\mathcal{S}_{\mathbf{t}^{(i+1)}} \setminus \bigcup_{j=1}^{i} \mathcal{S}_{\mathbf{t}^{(j)}}$). If these α exist but are *not* known to the adversary, then they should try to guess them in order to approach the ideal bound of (10).

In our application to Wave, $\mathcal{R} = \mathbb{F}_3$ is a field, so we are always in the first situation. For Rabin–Williams and Squirrels, $\mathcal{R} = \mathbb{Z}$ and $\mathcal{M}/\mathcal{K} = \mathbb{Z}/d\mathbb{Z}$ for some d unknown to the adversary. Every query is $\alpha \cdot 1$ for some α, and the adversary's goal is precisely to find $\alpha \neq 0$ divisible by the unknown d: that is, they are (or are trying to be) in the second situation.

Remark 3. The bounds in (12) may be overly pessimistic: even if $\mathsf{SEGP}(\mathcal{S}, \mathcal{T}(\Sigma))$ is hard, forging signatures in $\Sigma_{\text{comp}}^{\mathcal{K}}$ for random $\mathcal{K}$ in $\mathcal{S}$ may be significantly harder. With GPV-style signatures, a solution $\mathbf{t}$ to the $\mathsf{SEGP}(\mathcal{S}, \mathcal{T}(\Sigma))$ instance for $\mathcal{K}$ gives a forgery against $\Sigma_{\text{comp}}^{\mathcal{K}}$ only if we can construct $(m, \sigma = (\mathsf{salt}, \mathbf{s}))$ mapping to $\mathbf{t}$; and this is made difficult by the need to satisfy CONSTRAINT($\mathbf{s}$). After all, if we could find (m, σ) for arbitrary $\mathbf{t}$ then we could find them for $\mathbf{0}$, and thus construct forgeries in the original scheme Σ. For a computationally bounded adversary, it may be infeasible to construct (m, σ) yielding implicit queries $\mathbf{t}$ with large $\#\mathcal{S}_{\mathbf{t}}$, which means the success probability is actually much lower—and then we can make $\mathcal{S}$ (and thus, potentially, $|\mathsf{VK}|$) much smaller. Hence, while setting parameters to make SEGP hard will guarantee unforgeability, these parameters may also be much larger than what is required for EUF-CMA in practice.

4 Compressed Verification for SQUIRRELS

Now we turn our attention to SQUIRRELS. The challenge here is to define compressed verification algorithms that, like SQUIRRELS, avoid multiprecision arithmetic. To simplify presentation, we use the following notation:

Definition 3. *Given a list of primes* $\mathbf{m} = (m_1, \ldots, m_s)$*, we write*

$$[[x]]_{\mathbf{m}} := \big(x \bmod m_1, \ldots, x \bmod m_s\big) \quad \textit{for all } x \in \mathbb{Z}\,.$$

4.1 The SQUIRRELS Signature Scheme

SQUIRRELS is a GPV signature on unstructured lattices. More precisely, it uses co-cyclic lattices: n-dimensional lattices $\mathcal{L}$ such that $\mathbb{Z}^n/\mathcal{L} = \mathbb{Z}/\Delta\mathbb{Z}$ for some Δ. Co-cyclic lattices are dominant among full-rank integer lattices [22]: their natural density is $\approx 85\%$. SQUIRRELS works with co-cyclic lattices $\mathcal{L}$ of determinant

$$\Delta := p_1 \cdots p_s$$

where $\mathbf{p} = (p_1, \ldots, p_s)$ is a fixed tuple of 31-bit primes (the length s depends on the security parameter). Table 2 gives the SQUIRRELS parameter sets.

Table 2. Parameters for SQUIRRELS instances.

NIST Security Level	1	2	3	4	5
Lattice dimension n	1034	1164	1556	1718	2056
Hash space size q	4096	4096	4096	4096	4096
Max. signature square norm $\lfloor\beta^2\rfloor$	2 026 590	2 442 439	4 512 242	3 659 372	5 370 115
Number s of small primes	165	188	262	275	339
Bitlength of Δ	5048	5738	8017	8402	10347
Signature Size (B)	1019	1147	1554	1676	2025
Public Key Size (B)	681 780	874 576	1 629 640	1 888 700	2 786 580

SQUIRRELS is built on the one-way function

$$f : D_n \longrightarrow \mathbb{Z}/\Delta\mathbb{Z} \qquad \mathbf{x} \longmapsto \mathbf{x}\mathbf{A}^T \pmod{\Delta}, \tag{13}$$

where $\mathbf{A}$ is the matrix defining $\mathcal{L}$ and $D_n = \{\mathbf{e} \in \mathbb{Z}^n \mid \|\mathbf{e}\| \leq \beta\}$. One-wayness depends on the hardness of $GSIS_{n,\Delta,\beta}$, that is, finding a vector $\mathbf{x}$ such that $\mathbf{x}\mathbf{A}^T \equiv 0 \pmod{\Delta}$ and $\|\mathbf{x}\| \leq \beta$ for some small β.

Suppose $\mathcal{L}$ is co-cyclic of dimension n and determinant Δ. We can specify $\mathcal{L}$ with the row-HNF of its generating matrix, which is determined by a vector

$$\mathbf{v}_{\text{check}} = (\mathbf{v}_{\text{check},1}, \dots, \mathbf{v}_{\text{check},n}) \in (\mathbb{Z}/\Delta\mathbb{Z})^n \quad \text{with} \quad \mathbf{v}_{\text{check},n} = -1\,.$$

The public key encodes $\mathbf{v}_{\text{check}}$ as a list of lists of residues mod the small primes:

$$\mathsf{PK} = \left((v_{i,j} := \mathbf{v}_{\text{check},i} \bmod p_j)_{i=1}^{n-1} \right)_{j=1}^{s}$$

(since $\mathbf{v}_{\text{check},n} = -1$ by convention, there is no need to store it or any of the $v_{n,j}$). The $v_{i,j}$ are encoded as *signed* twos-complement 32-bit integers, but they are all non-negative (except the $v_{n,j}$, which are all -1 and not stored anyway); in particular, $0 \leq v_{i,j} < 2^{31}$ for all $1 \leq i < n$ and $1 \leq j \leq s$.

The private key encodes a "good" basis for $\mathcal{L}$, which allows sampling short vectors in $\mathcal{L}$ following a Gaussian distribution using Klein's trapdoor sampler. `KeyGen` ensures that each $\mathbf{v}_{\text{check},i}$ looks like a uniform random integer modulo Δ.

We now focus on SQUIRRELS verification (`KeyGen` and `Sign` are detailed in [11]). The verifier accepts $\sigma = (\mathbf{s}, \mathsf{salt})$ if two conditions are met:

1. The vector $\mathbf{s}$ is short: $\|\mathbf{s}\| \leq \beta$, which is more easily checked as

$$\text{CONSTRAINT}(\mathbf{s}) : \|\mathbf{s}\|^2 \leq \lfloor \beta^2 \rfloor\,.$$

2. The vector $\mathbf{c} := \mathbf{s} + \mathbf{h}$ (where $\mathbf{h} := \mathsf{Hash}(\mathsf{salt} \parallel \mathbf{m})$) is in $\mathcal{L}$. That is,

$$\sum_{i=1}^{n} c_i \mathbf{v}_{\text{check},i} \equiv 0 \pmod{\Delta}\,, \tag{14}$$

or equivalently (by the CRT)

$$\sum_{i=1}^{n} c_i v_{i,j} \equiv 0 \pmod{p_j} \qquad \text{for all } 1 \leq j \leq s\,. \tag{15}$$

We can thus verify by checking (15) for each of the p_j in turn, as in Algorithm 1.

Algorithm 1: Verification algorithm for SQUIRRELS.

Parameters : q, n, $\lfloor \beta^2 \rfloor$, and $P_\Delta = (p_1, \dots, p_m)$
Input: Signature $\sigma = (\mathsf{salt}, \underline{\mathbf{s}})$, message m, public key $\mathsf{PK} = ((v_{i,j})_{i=1}^{n-1})_{j=1}^{m}$ with $v_{i,j} = \mathbf{v}_{\text{check},i} \bmod p_j$
Output: Accept if σ is a valid signature on m under PK, otherwise Reject.

$\mathbf{s} \leftarrow \mathsf{Decompress}(\underline{\mathbf{s}})$
if $\mathbf{s} = \perp$ ***or*** $\|\mathbf{s}\|_2^2 > \lfloor \beta^2 \rfloor$ **then**
  return Reject
$\mathbf{c} \leftarrow \mathbf{s} + \mathsf{HashToPoint}(m \parallel \mathsf{salt}, q, n)$
foreach $1 \leq j \leq m$ **do** // Trivially parallelizable
  $S \leftarrow \sum_{i=0}^{n-1} c_i v_{i,j} \bmod p_j$
  if $S - c_n \neq 0 \mod p_j$ **then** // Uses $\mathbf{v}_{\text{check},n} = -1$
    return Reject
return Accept

4.2 Homomorphisms for SQUIRRELS Verification

SQUIRRELS is an instance of our general framework with $\mathcal{R} = \mathbb{Z}$ and $\mathcal{M} = \mathbb{Z}/\Delta\mathbb{Z}$. But the only homomorphisms from $\mathbb{Z}/\Delta\mathbb{Z}$ map through $\mathbb{Z}/\Delta'\mathbb{Z}$ for $\Delta'|\Delta$, and while a verifier could choose a secret ϕ by choosing a secret subset of the p_j, an adversary who could forge a signature for a large subset of the p_j would fool many verifiers. There are many more homomorphisms from $\mathbb{Z}$, and we can lift SQUIRRELS trivially to $\mathcal{M} = \mathbb{Z}$ if we replace (14) with the equivalent condition

$$\sum_{i=1}^{n} c_i \cdot \mathbf{v}_{\text{check},i} = k\Delta \qquad \text{for some integer } k\,. \tag{16}$$

Let the verifier choose a secret list of secret 31-bit primes $\mathbf{r} = (r_1, \ldots, r_t)$, each prime to Δ. The parameter t is a function of the desired verification security level, to be determined later in Sect. 4.5. Now the verifier could check

$$\sum_{i=1}^{n} c_i \cdot (\mathbf{v}_{\text{check},i} \bmod r_j) \equiv k(\Delta \bmod r_j) \pmod{r_j} \quad \text{for } 1 \le j \le t \tag{17}$$

—but k is not included in the signature, and re-computing it is the same computation as a full SQUIRRELS verification. Instead, we will verify by implicitly recovering k modulo $\prod_j r_j$, and checking that it is in the appropriate range.

First, we need to compute each of the $[[\mathbf{v}_{\text{check},i}]]_{\mathbf{r}}$ from the $[[\mathbf{v}_{\text{check},i}]]_{\mathbf{p}} = (v_{i,j} = \mathbf{v}_{\text{check},i} \bmod p_j)_{j=1}^{s}$. In the spirit of SQUIRRELS, we want to avoid multiprecision integer arithmetic, so we need to compute the $[[\mathbf{v}_{\text{check},i}]]_{\mathbf{r}}$ *without reconstructing* any of the integers $\mathbf{v}_{\text{check},i}$. Our main tool is the *explicit* CRT.[4]

Definition 4. *With the notation above: for each $1 \le i \le s$, we write Δ_i for Δ/p_i, and let q_i be the the unique integer in $(1, p_i)$ such that $q_i\Delta_i \equiv 1 \pmod{p_i}$.*

We will never explicitly compute with the Δ_i (they are a notational convenience). We *will* need the q_i, and these can be precomputed in advance (using e.g. Algorithm 7 in Appendix A). Each is a positive 31-bit integer.

Lemma 1 (Explicit CRT). *If $0 \le x < \Delta$ and $(x_1, \ldots, x_s) = [[x]]_{\mathbf{p}}$, then*

$$x = \alpha\Delta - \lfloor \alpha \rfloor \Delta \quad \textit{where} \quad \alpha = \sum_{i=1}^{s} x_i q_i / p_i\,. \tag{18}$$

Proof. Observe that α is a rational number, but $\alpha\Delta$ is an integer. The CRT says $x \equiv \alpha\Delta \pmod{\Delta}$, so obviously $\alpha\Delta - \lfloor\alpha\rfloor\Delta \equiv x \pmod{\Delta}$. But $0 \le \alpha - \lfloor\alpha\rfloor < 1$ by construction, so $0 \le \alpha\Delta - \lfloor\alpha\rfloor\Delta < \Delta$, so $\alpha\Delta - \lfloor\alpha\rfloor\Delta = x$. □

Lemma 1 gives an exact expression for $0 \le x < \Delta$ in terms of $[[x]]_{\mathbf{p}}$ that we can use to compute $[[x]]_{\mathbf{r}}$ by computing the integers $\alpha\Delta$ and $\lfloor\alpha\rfloor\Delta$ modulo each r_j. We precompute the q_i, $[[\Delta_i]]_{\mathbf{r}}$, and $[[\Delta]]_{\mathbf{r}}$. Computing $\alpha\Delta = \sum_i x_i q_i \Delta_i$ modulo r_j is straightforward. The interesting part is determining $\lfloor\alpha\rfloor$, and thus computing $\lfloor\alpha\rfloor \bmod r_j$, without computing α. We will do this using fixed-point approximations, as in [4]. Lemma 2, an adaptation of [4, Lemma 3.1], shows that with a relatively low precision we can determine $\lfloor\alpha\rfloor$ up to a possible error of 1.

[4] This is similar to the modular reduction in RNS arithmetic in [4], but there, $\mathbf{p}$ can be freely chosen to optimise computations on the operands; here, $\mathbf{p}$ is fixed.

Lemma 2. *Let* $\alpha_1, \ldots, \alpha_s$ *be non-negative real numbers, and set* $\alpha := \sum_{j=1}^{s} \alpha_j$*. Fix some integer* $a \geq \log_2 s + 1$*. Then*

$$f := \left\lfloor \frac{s}{2^a} + \frac{1}{2^a} \sum\nolimits_{j=1}^{s} \lfloor 2^a \alpha_j \rfloor \right\rfloor \quad \text{is either } \lfloor \alpha \rfloor \text{ or } \lfloor \alpha \rfloor + 1\,.$$

Further, if $\alpha - \lfloor \alpha \rfloor < 1 - s/2^a$ *then* f *is exactly* $\lfloor \alpha \rfloor$*.*

Proof. Note that $2^a \geq 2s$, so $s/2^a \leq 1/2$. Let $q := (1/2^a) \sum_j \lfloor 2^a \alpha_j \rfloor$. By construction, $0 \leq 2^a \alpha_j - \lfloor 2^a \alpha_j \rfloor < 1$ for each $1 \leq j \leq s$. Summing over j gives $0 \leq 2^a \alpha - 2^a q < s$, so $0 \leq \alpha - q < s/2^a$; so $\lfloor \alpha \rfloor < s/2^a + q \leq s/2^a + \alpha$. Taking floors gives $\lfloor \alpha \rfloor \leq f \leq \lfloor s/2^a + \alpha \rfloor$. But $\lfloor s/2^a + \alpha \rfloor$ is either $\lfloor \alpha \rfloor$ or $\lfloor \alpha \rfloor + 1$, because $0 < s/2^a \leq 1/2$, proving the first statement. For the second, if $\alpha - \lfloor \alpha \rfloor < 1 - s/2^a$ then $\alpha + s/2^a < \lfloor \alpha \rfloor + 1$, so $\lfloor \alpha + s/2^a \rfloor = \lfloor \alpha \rfloor$, and thus $f = \lfloor \alpha \rfloor$. □

Theorem 2. *Fix an integer* $a \geq \log_2(s) + 1$*. Given* $\mathbf{r}$*,* $[[\Delta]]_{\mathbf{r}}$*,* $([[\Delta_i]]_{\mathbf{r}})_{i=1}^{s}$*, and* $[[x]]_{\mathbf{p}}$ *for some* $0 \leq x < \Delta$*, Algorithm 2 returns* $[[z]]_{\mathbf{r}}$ *where* z *is either* x *or* $x - \Delta$*. Further: if* $x < (1 - s/2^a)\Delta$*, then* $z = x$*.*

Proof. Algorithm 2 evaluates (18) modulo r_j for $1 \leq j \leq t$, computing the floor using Lemma 2 with $\alpha_i = x_i q_i / p_i$ for $1 \leq i \leq s$. □

Algorithm 2: Explicit CRT: computing $[[x]]_{\mathbf{r}}$ or $[[x - \Delta]]_{\mathbf{r}}$ from $[[x]]_{\mathbf{p}}$

Parameters : Squirrels prime vector $\mathbf{p} = (p_1, \ldots, p_s)$ and CRT coefficients $(q_1, \ldots, q_s)$; an integer $a \geq \log_2 s + 1$ (fixed-point precision)
Input: Secret prime list $\mathbf{r}$; $[[\Delta]]_{\mathbf{r}}$, $([[\Delta_i]]_{\mathbf{r}})_{i=1}^{s}$, and $[[x]]_{\mathbf{p}}$ for $0 \leq x < \Delta$
Output: $[[z]]_{\mathbf{r}}$, where $z = x$ or $x - \Delta$ (if $x < (1 - s/2^a)\Delta$, then $z = x$)

1 **function** `ModECRT`($\mathbf{r}$, $[[\Delta]]_{\mathbf{r}}$, $([[\Delta_i]]_{\mathbf{r}})_{i=1}^{s}$, $[[x]]_{\mathbf{p}}$)
2 $\quad (z_1, \ldots, z_t) \leftarrow (0, \ldots, 0)$
3 $\quad f \leftarrow s$
4 $\quad$ **foreach** $1 \leq j \leq s$ **do**
5 $\quad\quad y_j \leftarrow x_j \cdot q_j$
6 $\quad\quad f \leftarrow f + \lfloor 2^a y_j / p_j \rfloor$ `// See Remark 5`
7 $\quad\quad$ **foreach** $1 \leq k \leq t$ **do**
8 $\quad\quad\quad y_{j,k} \leftarrow y_j \bmod r_k$
9 $\quad\quad\quad z_k \leftarrow (z_k + y_{j,k} \cdot \Delta_{j,k}) \bmod r_k$
10 $\quad f \leftarrow \lfloor f / 2^a \rfloor$ `// Right-shift f by a`
11 $\quad$ **foreach** $1 \leq k \leq t$ **do**
12 $\quad\quad z_k \leftarrow (z_k - f \cdot \Delta_k) \bmod r_k$
13 $\quad$ **return** $(z_1, \ldots, z_t)$

Remark 4. Theorem 2 recovers $[[x]]_{\mathbf{r}}$ or $[[x - \Delta]]_{\mathbf{r}}$ from $[[x]]_{\mathbf{p}}$. To guaranteee a result of $[[x]]_{\mathbf{r}}$ requires increasing the precision to $a \sim \log_2 \Delta$, which means working with integers the size of Δ; but then we may as well reconstruct x.

Remark 5. As noted in [4], the floors in Line 6 of Algorithm 2 can be computed by repeatedly doubling y_j modulo p_j and counting overflows.

4.3 Compressed Verification for Squirrels

Recall that our goal is to verify (16) by evaluating (17), namely

$$\sum_{i=1}^{n} c_i \cdot \mathbf{v}_{\text{check},i} \equiv k\Delta \pmod{r_j} \quad \text{for each } 1 \le j \le \text{ t},$$

but *without* knowing k. Given a public key PK and a compression key $\mathsf{CK} := (\mathbf{r}, ([[\Delta_i]]_{\mathbf{r}})_{i=1}^{s}, [[\Delta]]_{\mathbf{r}}, (I_1, \ldots, I_t))$, for each $1 \le i \le n$ we use `ModECRT` to compute

$$\begin{aligned} [[\bar{v}_i]]_{\mathbf{r}} &:= \texttt{ModECRT}(\mathbf{r}, [[\Delta]]_{\mathbf{r}}, ([[\Delta_j]]_{\mathbf{r}})_{j=1}^{s}, [[\mathbf{v}_{\text{check},i}]]_{\mathbf{p}} = (v_{i,j})_{j=1}^{s}) \\ &= [[\mathbf{v}_{\text{check},i} - \epsilon_i \Delta]]_{\mathbf{r}} \quad \text{where } \epsilon_i \in \{0,1\} \text{ is unknown.} \end{aligned}$$

The r_j are chosen such that $r_j \nmid \Delta$, so if we let

$$k'_j := \Big(\sum_{i=1}^{n} c_i \bar{v}_{i,j}\Big) I_j \bmod r_j \quad \text{where} \quad I_j := \Delta^{-1} \bmod r_j \quad \text{for } 1 \le j \le t\,,$$

then the system of verification equations (17) becomes

$$k'_j \equiv k' \pmod{r_j} \quad \text{where} \quad k' := k + \sum_{i=1}^{n-1} \epsilon_i c_i\,. \tag{19}$$

Lemma 3 below shows that

- If (16) holds, then k' is a small integer (Table 3 gives bounds on k' for each Squirrels instance), small enough that $k'_j = k'$ *as an integer* for each j.
- If (16) does not hold, then k' does not exist, and the k'_j look like random (and generally large) values modulo each of the r_j.

This distinction is the basis of our `CVerify` for Squirrels: we compute $(k'_1, \ldots, k'_t)$, and Accept if $k'_1 = \cdots = k'_t$ and k'_1 is within the bounds on k'; otherwise, we Reject. Note that even if the adversary has full control over the c_i, they cannot control the k'_j, because $\mathbf{r}$ and the I_j are unknown.

Lemma 3. *With* Squirrels *parameters $q \ll \Delta$ and $\lfloor \beta^2 \rfloor \ll \Delta$: if $\|\mathbf{s}\|_2^2 \le \lfloor \beta^2 \rfloor$, then the integer k' of* (19) *satisfies*

$$k'_{\min} \le k' \le k'_{\max} \quad \textit{where} \quad \begin{cases} k'_{\min} := -\lfloor 2\sqrt{n\lfloor \beta^2 \rfloor} \rfloor - 1\,, \\ k'_{\max} := 2(n-1)(q-1) + \lfloor 2\sqrt{n\lfloor \beta^2 \rfloor} \rfloor + 1\,. \end{cases}$$

Proof. By definition,

$$k' = \left(\sum_{i=1}^{n-1} c_i \beta_i\right) - \frac{c_n}{\Delta} \quad \text{with} \quad \beta_i = \frac{\mathbf{v}_{\text{check},i}}{\Delta} + \epsilon_i$$

for $1 \le i < n$, so

$$k' + E = H + S$$

where

$$H = \sum_{i=1}^{n-1} h_i \beta_i, \quad S = \sum_{i=1}^{n-1} s_i \beta_i, \quad E = \frac{c_n}{\Delta}.$$

For $1 \leq i < n$, we have $0 \leq \mathbf{v}_{\text{check},i} < \Delta$, so $0 \leq \beta_i < 2$.

Thus,

$$-S' - E < k' < H' + S' + E$$

where

$$H' = 2\sum_{i=1}^{n-1} h_i \quad \text{and} \quad S' = 2\sum_{i=1}^{n} |s_i|$$

(note: we include $|s_n|$ in S').

But $0 \leq |E| \leq \frac{h_n + |s_n|}{\Delta} < 1$ because

$$h_n < q \ll \Delta \quad \text{and} \quad |s_n| \leq \lfloor \beta^2 \rfloor \ll \Delta,$$

so

$$-S' - 1 < k' < H' + S' + 1.$$

Now,

$$0 \leq S' \leq 2\sqrt{n}\|\mathbf{s}\|_2 \leq 2\sqrt{n\lfloor\beta^2\rfloor}, \quad 0 \leq H' \leq 2(n-1)(q-1)$$

and k' is an integer, so

$$\left\lceil -2\sqrt{n\lfloor\beta^2\rfloor} \right\rceil - 1 \leq k' \leq 2(n-1)(q-1) + \left\lfloor 2\sqrt{n\lfloor\beta^2\rfloor} \right\rfloor + 1,$$

and the result follows. □

Table 3. Values of $k'_{\min}$ and $k'_{\max}$ from Lemma 3 for the SQUIRRELS instances in [11]. Note that $k'_{\max} - k'_{\min}$ is a 24-bit integer except for SQUIRRELS-V, where it is 25 bits.

Instance	SQUIRRELS-I	SQUIRRELS-II	SQUIRRELS-III	SQUIRRELS-IV	SQUIRRELS-V
$k'_{\min}$	−91554	−106640	−144446	−15879	−210152
$k'_{\max}$	8551824	9631610	9603896	14220809	17040602

The verification key VK is $\left(\mathbf{r}, (I_1, \ldots, I_t), ([[\bar{v}_i]]_{\mathbf{r}})_{i=1}^{n-1}\right)$, so

$$|\mathsf{VK}| = 4(n+1)t \text{ bytes} \quad \text{and} \quad |\mathsf{PK}| = 4(n-1)s \text{ bytes}.$$

The key-compression ratio is $|\mathsf{PK}| : |\mathsf{VK}| \approx s : t$. See Table 4 for sample values.

The compression key CK requires $4(s+3)t$ bytes. The values of $([[\Delta_i]]_{\mathbf{r}})_{i=1}^{s}$, $[[\Delta]]_{\mathbf{r}}$, and $(I_1, \ldots, I_t)$ may be left out of CK, thus reducing $|\mathsf{CK}|$ to $4s$ bytes, but this implies recomputing them from $\mathbf{r}$ and $\mathbf{p}$ for every verification key generation.

4.4 The Algorithms

Algorithms 3, 4, and 5 formalise `CKeyGen`, `VKeyGen`, and `CVerify` for Squirrels.

Algorithm 3: `CKeyGen` (compression key generation) for Squirrels.

Parameters : n, s, Δ, $\mathbf{p}$, $(\Delta_1, \ldots, \Delta_s)$, $[[\Delta_i]]_{\mathbf{p}}$, t
Output: CK
Sample a list $\mathbf{r} = (r_1, \ldots, r_t)$ of random 31-bit primes // Use Lemma 4
Compute $([[\Delta_i]]_{\mathbf{r}})_{i=1}^{s}$ and $[[\Delta]]_{\mathbf{r}}$ from $\mathbf{p}$ // Using e.g. Algorithm 8 in App. A.
for $1 \leq j \leq t$ **do**
  $I_j \leftarrow \Delta^{-1} \bmod r_j$ // Use $I_j = (\Delta \bmod r_j)^{-1} \bmod r_j$
return CK $:= (\mathbf{r}, ([[\Delta_i]]_{\mathbf{r}})_{i=1}^{s}, [[\Delta]]_{\mathbf{r}}, (I_1, \ldots, I_t))$

Algorithm 3 requires randomly sampling 31-bit primes, which is easy using the criteria of [23]. Recall that an odd integer $r = d2^u + 1$ is a *strong pseudoprime to the base* a if $a^d \equiv 1 \pmod{r}$ or $a^{d2^v} \equiv -1 \pmod{r}$ for some $0 \leq v < u$.

Lemma 4. *Let* $2^{30} < r < 2^{31}$ *be odd. If* r *is a strong pseudoprime to the bases* 2, 3, *and* 5, *then either* r *is prime or* $r = 1157839381 = 24061 \cdot 48121$.

Proof. See [23, Page 1022]. □

Algorithm 4: `VKeyGen` (verification key generation) for Squirrels.

Parameters : n, s, Δ, $\mathbf{p}$, $(\Delta_1, \ldots, \Delta_s)$, $[[\Delta_i]]_{\mathbf{p}}$, t
Input: CK $= (\mathbf{r}, ([[\Delta_i]]_{\mathbf{r}})_{i=1}^{s}, [[\Delta]]_{\mathbf{r}}, (I_1, \ldots, I_t))$, PK $= (\mathbf{v}_{\text{check},i})_{i=1}^{n-1}$
Output: VK
foreach $1 \leq i < n$ **do** // May be parallelized
  $[[\bar{v}_i]]_{\mathbf{r}} \leftarrow$ `ModECRT`$(\mathbf{r}, [[\Delta]]_{\mathbf{r}}, ([[\Delta_i]]_{\mathbf{r}})_{i=1}^{t}, \mathbf{v}_{check,i})$ // $=[[\mathbf{v}_{\text{check},i} + \epsilon_i \Delta]]_{\mathbf{r}}$
return $(\mathbf{r}, (I_1, \ldots, I_t), (\bar{v}_{i,1}, \ldots, \bar{v}_{i,t})_{i=1}^{n-1})$

Algorithm 5 defines `CVerify`. Lines 6–13 must be implemented with constant-time techniques to ensure no information on $\mathbf{r}$ is leaked in the event of rejection[5].

---

[5] The implementation can be made constant-time by using constant-time arithmetic routines (e.g. multiplication/modular reduction [5]) and replacing any conditional branches with bit-masking operations.

Algorithm 5: `CVerify` (compressed verification) for SQUIRRELS.

Parameters : n, s, Δ, $\mathbf{p}$, $(\Delta_1, \ldots, \Delta_s)$, $[[\Delta_i]]_{\mathbf{p}}$, t
Input: $\sigma = (\mathsf{salt}, \underline{\mathbf{s}})$, m, $\mathsf{VK} = (\mathbf{r}, (I_1, \ldots, I_t), (\bar{v}_{i,1}, \ldots, \bar{v}_{i,t})_{i=1}^{n})$
Output: Accept or Reject

$\mathbf{s} \leftarrow \mathsf{Decompress}(\underline{\mathbf{s}})$
if $\mathbf{s} = \perp$ ***or*** $\|\mathbf{s}\|_2^2 > \lfloor \beta^2 \rfloor$ **then**
  return Reject
$\mathbf{c} \leftarrow \mathbf{s} + \mathsf{HashToPoint}(m \parallel \mathsf{salt}, q, n)$
$(a_1, \ldots, a_t) \leftarrow (\mathsf{True}, \ldots, \mathsf{True})$
foreach $1 \leq j \leq t$ **do** `// May be parallelized`
  $k'_j \leftarrow \left((\sum_{i=1}^{n} c_i \bar{v}_{i,j}) I_j - k'_{\min} \right) \bmod r_j$ `//` $k'_{\min}$`: see Lemma 3`
  if $k'_j > k'_{\max} - k'_{\min}$ **then** `//` $k'_{\max} - k'_{\min}$`: see Lemma 3`
    $a_j \leftarrow$ False
if $(a_1 \wedge \cdots \wedge a_t) \wedge (k'_1 = \cdots = k'_t)$ **then**
  return Accept
else
  return Reject

4.5 Security Argument

If Σ is SQUIRRELS, then $\mathcal{R} = \mathcal{M} = \mathbb{Z}$. Compressed SQUIRRELS samples $\mathcal{K}$ from

$$\mathcal{S} = \{\Delta'\mathbb{Z} : \Delta' \text{ is a product of } t \text{ 31-bit primes}\}.$$

Theorem 1 ensures EUF-CMA security for compressed SQUIRRELS provided $\mathsf{SEGP}(\mathcal{S}, \mathcal{T}(\Sigma))$ is hard. For SQUIRRELS parameters, $\mathcal{T}(\Sigma) \subset [0, 2q\sqrt{n}\lfloor \beta^2 \Delta \rfloor] \subset [0, 2^{30}\Delta)$: at most s 31-bit primes can divide any $\mathbf{t} \in \mathcal{T}(\Sigma)$, so $\kappa_{\mathcal{T}} \approx s!/(t!(s-t)!)$. Now $\#\mathcal{S} = P_{31}!/(t!(P_{31}-t)!)$ where $P_{31} := \#\text{PRIMES}(31)$, and $\#(\mathcal{M}/\mathcal{K}) \approx 2^{31t}$. When $t \ll s$, we have $s!/(s-t)! \sim s^t$ and $P_{31}!/(P_{31}-t)! \sim P_{31}^t$. Looking at [29, Table 3], we find that

$$P_{31} := \#\text{PRIMES}(31) = 105097565 - 54400028 \approx 2^{25.6}.$$

The heuristic of Sect. 3.4 therefore suggests taking $t \approx \mu/(25.6 - \log_2(s))$, where μ is the targeted security level.

In reality, it is computationally infeasible to construct forgery attempts (m, σ) that yield $\mathbf{t}$ with $\#\mathcal{S}_{\mathbf{t}} \approx \kappa_{\mathcal{T}}$: this would mean constructing (m, σ) such that $\mathbf{t}$ is divisible by another product Δ' of s 31-bit primes, and this is essentially as hard as forging a full SQUIRRELS signature: that is, solving $\text{GSIS}_{n,\Delta,\beta}$. If we want an (m, σ) mapping to a $\mathbf{t}$ with k 31-bit prime factors, and thus $\#\mathcal{S}_{\mathbf{t}} = \binom{k}{t}/\#S$, we must solve a single GSIS instance with modulus $\Delta^\star \ll \Delta$. Indeed, it requires a nontrivial computational effort to even construct a forgery attempt (m, σ) yielding $\mathbf{t}$ with $\#\mathcal{S}_{\mathbf{t}} > 0$. In our security estimates, we therefore model the expected value of $\#\mathcal{S}_{\mathbf{t}}$ as a small constant, and hence we choose t such that $P_{31}!/(t!(P_{31} - t)!$ is on the order of 2^λ, which suggests taking t as in Table 4. While the resulting security level μ is slightly smaller than λ in some cases, it should be remembered that each forgery attempt requires an interaction with the verifier, and is therefore substantially more expensive than (e.g.) the AES circuit evaluations used to model post-quantum cryptographic attack costs.

Table 4. Suggested values for the number t of secret primes in $\mathbf{r}$.

Instance	Original scheme				Compressed verification				
	λ	s	$\|\mathsf{PK}\|$	$\|\sigma\|$	t	μ	$\|\mathsf{CK}\|$	$\|\mathsf{VK}\|$	$\|\mathsf{PK}\| : \|\mathsf{VK}\|$
SQUIRRELS-I	128	165	681780	1019	5	121.1	3360	20700	32.94
SQUIRRELS-II	128	188	874576	1147	5	121.1	3820	23300	37.54
SQUIRRELS-III	192	262	1629640	1554	8	189.5	8480	49824	32.71
SQUIRRELS-IV	192	275	1888700	1676	8	189.5	8896	55008	34.34
SQUIRRELS-V	256	339	2786580	2025	11	256.3	15048	90508	30.79

5 Compressed Verification for WAVE

WAVE is a GPV-style signature based on hard problems in ternary linear codes. Very briefly: a WAVE public key is a matrix $\mathsf{PK} = \mathbf{R} \in \mathbb{F}_3^{k\times(n-k)}$ such that $\mathbf{M} = (\mathbf{I}_{n-k}|\mathbf{R})^\top$ in $\mathbb{F}_3^{n\times(n-k)}$ is a parity-check matrix for a permuted generalized $(U|U+V)$-code C; knowledge of the relation between C and the component codes U and V is a trapdoor allowing the signer to generate vectors $\mathbf{s}$ in $\mathbb{F}_3^n$ such that

$$\textsc{Constraint}(\mathbf{s}) \quad \text{and} \quad \mathbf{sM} = \mathsf{Hash}(\mathsf{salt}, m)\,, \tag{20}$$

where $\textsc{Constraint}(\mathbf{s})$ is that $\mathbf{s}$ have a fixed, high weight w. An "original" WAVE signature (as in [9]) is $\sigma = (\mathsf{salt}, \mathbf{s})$. In the WAVE NIST submission [1], $\mathbf{s}$ is truncated to its last k entries (the other $n-k$ entries are implicitly recovered in verification). The special form of $\mathbf{M} = (\mathbf{I}_{n-k}|\mathbf{R})^\top$ allows us to rewrite (20) as

$$\textsc{Constraint}(\mathbf{s}) \quad \text{and} \quad \mathbf{tM} = \mathbf{0} \quad \text{where} \quad \mathbf{t} := \mathbf{s} - (\mathsf{Hash}(\mathsf{salt}, \mathbf{s})|\mathbf{0}_k)\,. \tag{21}$$

WAVE has exceptionally large public keys: for example, WAVE822, WAVE1249, and WAVE1644 require 3.5 MB, 7.5 MB, and 13 MB, respectively. This motivates the use of *compressed verification*, where the verifier privately replaces the large matrix $\mathbf{M}$ with a much smaller secret key VK derived via a compression matrix.

`VKeyGen` computes $\mathsf{VK} := (\mathbf{I}_{n-k} \mid \mathbf{R})^\top \mathbf{C}$, where $\mathbf{C}$ is the verifier's compression matrix. Only the bottom $n-k-c$ rows of VK need to be stored, yielding a total size of $c(n-c)/4$ bytes. `CVerify` then replaces the full-rank check $\mathbf{tM} = \mathbf{0}$ with a lower-dimensional test $\mathbf{t}\mathsf{VK} = \mathbf{0}$ over $\mathbb{F}_3^c$, as detailed in Algorithm 6. Compressed verification requires "original" WAVE signatures (as in [9]) and is incompatible with the truncated versions from [1]. Although full signatures can be recovered from truncated ones using the public key, doing so during verification defeats compression by reintroducing computational and storage overhead.

Algorithm 6: `CVerify` (compressed verification) for WAVE

Input: message m, signature $\sigma = (\mathsf{salt}, \mathbf{s})$, and verification key VK
Output: Accept or Reject

```
if Weight(s) ≠ W then
    return Reject
t ← s − (Hash(salt ‖ m) ‖ 0_k)
r ← tVK
if r ≠ 0 then
    return Reject
return Accept
```

The security argument for compressed WAVE is particularly simple. Theorem 1 ensures that $\Sigma^{\mathcal{K}}_{\text{comp}}$ is EUF-CMA secure if $\mathsf{SEGP}(\mathcal{S}, \mathcal{T}(\Sigma))$ is hard, where $\mathcal{S}$ is the set of codimension-c subspaces of $\mathcal{M} = \mathbb{F}_3^{n-k}$ and $\mathcal{T}(\Sigma) = \mathcal{M}$. We have $\#\mathcal{S} = \begin{bmatrix} n-k \\ n-k-c \end{bmatrix}_3$, where $\begin{bmatrix} \cdot \\ \cdot \end{bmatrix}_3$ is the 3-binomial coefficient, $\#(\mathcal{M}/\mathcal{K}) = 3^{n-k-c}$, and $\#\mathcal{S}_{\mathbf{t}} = \kappa_{\mathcal{T}(\Sigma)} = \begin{bmatrix} n-k-1 \\ n-k-c-1 \end{bmatrix}_3$ for *every* $\mathbf{t} \neq \mathbf{0} \in \mathcal{M}$. This tells us that a naive adversary that simply tries random forgery attempts (m, σ) is already close to optimal. Intuitively: since $\mathbf{C}$ is a random projection, if $\mathbf{t} \neq \mathbf{0}$ then $\mathbf{tC}$ is a random element of $\mathbb{F}_3^c$, which is $\mathbf{0}$ (leading to an Accept) with probability $1/3^c$.

Indeed, if we admit the heuristic of Sect. 3.4 then we can take $2^\mu \approx 3^c$: that is, $c \approx \log_3(2)\mu$. Taking c to be a multiple of 8 simplifies implementation. Table 5 lists suggested values of c and corresponding sizes of CK and VK for WAVE822, WAVE1249, and WAVE1644.

Table 5. Parameters for (compressed) WAVE. Sizes are in bytes. WAVE signatures are variable-length: the values of $|\sigma|$ here are upper bounds, and $|\sigma|$ roughly doubles for the "original" (non-truncated) signatures required for compressed verification.

Instance	Security level		Original scheme		Compressed verification				
	NIST PQ	λ	$\|\sigma\|$	$\|\mathsf{PK}\|$	c	μ	$\|\mathsf{CK}\|$	$\|\mathsf{VK}\|$	$\|\mathsf{PK}\| : \|\mathsf{VK}\|$
WAVE822	1	128	822	3 677 390	80	126.8	83 822	171 594	21.4
WAVE1249	3	192	1249	7 867 598	120	190.2	183 134	266 188	29.6
WAVE1644	5	256	1644	13 632 308	160	253.6	321 507	370 436	36.8

A Subroutines for the Explicit CRT

We maintain the notation of Sect. 4: $\mathbf{p} = (p_1, \dots, p_s)$ is a list of distinct primes, $\Delta := \prod_{i=1}^{s} p_i$ is their product, $\Delta_i := \Delta/p_i$ and $q_i := \Delta_i^{-1} \pmod{p_i}$ for $1 \le i \le s$. Algorithm 7 computes $(q_1, \dots, q_s)$. Algorithm 8 computes $([[\Delta_i]]_{\mathbf{r}})_{i=1}^{s}$ and $[[\Delta]]_{\mathbf{r}}$. given another list of primes $\mathbf{r} = (r_1, \dots, r_t)$ (all prime to Δ). These algorithms are not optimal, but they avoid multiprecision arithmetic.

Algorithm 7: Explicit Modular CRT setup: q-coefficients.

Input: $\mathbf{p} = (p_1, \ldots, p_s)$

Output: $(q_1, \ldots, q_s)$ s.t. $0 < q_i < p_i$ and $q_i(\Delta/p_i) \equiv 1 \pmod{p_i}$ for $1 \leq i \leq s$

function `qCoefficients`($(p_1, \ldots, p_s)$)
  $(q_1, \ldots, q_s) \leftarrow (1, \ldots, 1)$
  foreach $1 \leq i \leq s$ **do**
    foreach $1 \leq j \leq s$, $j \neq i$ **do**
      $q_i \leftarrow q_i \cdot p_j \bmod p_i$
    $q_i \leftarrow q_i^{-1} \bmod p_i$
  return $(q_1, \ldots, q_s)$

Algorithm 8: Explicit Modular CRT setup.

Input: $\mathbf{p} = (p_i)_{i=1}^{s}$ and $\mathbf{r} = (r_j)_{j=1}^{t}$.

Output: $([[\Delta_i]]_{\mathbf{r}})_{i=1}^{s}$ and $[[\Delta]]_{\mathbf{r}}$.

function `ModECRTSetup`($\mathbf{p}$, $\mathbf{r}$)
  $\mathbf{m} \leftarrow [[1]]_{\mathbf{r}}$
  $(\mathbf{c}^{(1)}, \ldots, \mathbf{c}^{(s)}) \leftarrow ([[1]]_{\mathbf{r}}, \ldots, [[1]]_{\mathbf{r}})$
  foreach $1 \leq i \leq s$ **do**
    $\mathbf{u} \leftarrow [[p_i]]_{\mathbf{r}}$ // $u_j = p_j$ or $p_j - r_j$
    $\mathbf{m} \leftarrow (m_1 u_1 \bmod r_1, \ldots, m_t u_t \bmod r_t)$
    foreach $1 \leq j < i$ ***and*** $i < j \leq s$ **do**
      $\mathbf{c}^{(j)} \leftarrow (c_1^{(j)} u_1 \bmod r_1, \ldots, c_t^{(j)} u_t \bmod r_t)$
  return $(\mathbf{c}^{(1)}, \ldots, \mathbf{c}^{(s)})$, $\mathbf{m}$

References

1. Banegas, G., et al.: WAVE – submission to NIST post-quantum signatures project (2023). https://wave-sign.org/
2. Bernstein, D.J.: RSA signatures and Rabin–Williams signatures: the state of the art (2008)
3. Bernstein, D.J., Hülsing, A., Kölbl, S., Niederhagen, R., Rijneveld, J., Schwabe, P.: The SPHINCS+ signature framework. In: Proceedings of the 2019 ACM SIGSAC Conference on Computer and Communications Security, CCS 2019, pp. 2129–2146. Association for Computing Machinery (2019)
4. Bernstein, D.J., Sorenson, J.P.: Modular exponentiation via the explicit Chinese remainder theorem. Math. Comput. **76**(257), 443–454 (2007)
5. Bos, J.W., Kleinjung, T., Page, D.: Efficient modular multiplication. Cryptology ePrint Archive, Paper 2021/1151 (2021)
6. Boschini, C., Fiore, D., Pagnin, E., Torresetti, L., Visconti, A.: Progressive and efficient verification for digital signatures: extensions and experimental results. J. Cryptogr. Eng. **14**(3), 551–575 (2024)
7. Chen, Y., Genise, N., Mukherjee, P.: Approximate trapdoors for lattices and smaller hash-and-sign signatures. In: Galbraith, S.D., Moriai, S. (eds.) ASI-

ACRYPT 2019. LNCS, vol. 11923, pp. 3–32. Springer, Cham (2019). https://doi.org/10.1007/978-3-030-34618-8_1

8. Cremers, C., Düzlü, S., Fiedler, R., Fischlin, M., Janson, C.: Buffing signature schemes beyond unforgeability and the case of post-quantum signatures. In: IEEE Symposium on Security and Privacy, pp. 1696–1714 (2021)
9. Debris-Alazard, T., Sendrier, N., Tillich, J.-P.: Wave: a new family of trapdoor one-way preimage sampleable functions based on codes. In: Galbraith, S.D., Moriai, S. (eds.) ASIACRYPT 2019. LNCS, vol. 11921, pp. 21–51. Springer, Cham (2019). https://doi.org/10.1007/978-3-030-34578-5_2
10. Dusart, P.: Explicit estimates of some functions over primes. Ramanujan J. **45**, 227–251 (2018)
11. Espitau, T., Niot, G., Sun, C., Tibouchi, M.: SQUIRRELS - Square Unstructured Integer Euclidean Lattice Signature (2023)
12. Fischlin, M.: Progressive verification: the case of message authentication. In: Johansson, T., Maitra, S. (eds.) INDOCRYPT 2003. LNCS, vol. 2904, pp. 416–429. Springer, Heidelberg (2003). https://doi.org/10.1007/978-3-540-24582-7_31
13. Fouque, P.-A., et al.: Falcon: fast-fourier lattice-based compact signatures over NTRU – submission to NIST post-quantum cryptography project (2018). https://falcon-sign.info/
14. Gentry, C., Peikert, C., Vaikuntanathan, V.: Trapdoors for hard lattices and new cryptographic constructions. In: Proceedings of the 40th Annual ACM Symposium on Theory of Computing, pp. 197–206. ACM (2008)
15. Hülsing, A., Rausch, L., Buchmann, J.: Optimal parameters for $XMSS^{MT}$. In: Cuzzocrea, A., Kittl, C., Simos, D.E., Weippl, E., Xu, L. (eds.) CD-ARES 2013. LNCS, vol. 8128, pp. 194–208. Springer, Heidelberg (2013). https://doi.org/10.1007/978-3-642-40588-4_14
16. Hülsing, A., Rijneveld, J.: XMSS reference implementation (2024). https://github.com/XMSS/xmss-reference
17. Le, D.V., Kelkar, M., Kate, A.: Flexible signatures: making authentication suitable for real-time environments. In: Sako, K., Schneider, S., Ryan, P.Y.A. (eds.) ESORICS 2019. LNCS, vol. 11735, pp. 173–193. Springer, Cham (2019). https://doi.org/10.1007/978-3-030-29959-0_9
18. Lenstra Jr, H.W.: Factoring integers with elliptic curves. Ann. Math. 649–673 (1987)
19. Micciancio, D., Peikert, C.: Trapdoors for lattices: simpler, tighter, faster, smaller. In: Pointcheval, D., Johansson, T. (eds.) EUROCRYPT 2012. LNCS, vol. 7237, pp. 700–718. Springer, Heidelberg (2012). https://doi.org/10.1007/978-3-642-29011-4_41
20. Montgomery, P.L.: Speeding the Pollard and elliptic curve methods of factorization. Math. Comput. **48**(177), 243–264 (1987)
21. National Institute of Standards and Technology. Stateless hash-based digital signature standard. Technical Report Federal Information Processing Standards Publications (FIPS PUBS) 205, NIST (2004)
22. Nguyen, P.Q., Shparlinski, I.E.: Counting co-cyclic lattices. SIAM J. Discret. Math. **30**(3), 1358–1370 (2016)
23. Pomerance, C., Selfridge, J., Wagstaff Jr., S.S.: The pseudoprimes to $25 \cdot 10^9$. Math. Comput. **35**(151), 1003–1026 (1980)
24. Pornin, T., Stern, J.P.: Digital signatures do not guarantee exclusive ownership. In: Ioannidis, J., Keromytis, A., Yung, M. (eds.) ACNS 2005. LNCS, vol. 3531, pp. 138–150. Springer, Heidelberg (2005). https://doi.org/10.1007/11496137_10

25. Rabin, M.O.: Digitalized signatures and public-key functions as intractable as factorization. Technical Report 212, MIT Laboratory for Computer Science (1979)
26. SPHINCS+ Team. SPHINCS+ reference implementation (2024). https://github.com/sphincs/sphincsplus
27. Squirrels team. Squirrels reference implementation (2024). https://squirrels-pqc.org/ with sha256sum `c4fd2a961f177a2f49970ca1758bde1a676a2fd7b3e62ea0e0c0593955902ab7`
28. Taleb, A.R., Vergnaud, D.: Speeding-up verification of digital signatures. J. Comput. Syst. Sci. **116**, 22–39 (2021)
29. Wagstaff, S.S.: Is there a shortage of primes for cryptography? Int. J. Netw. Secur. **3**, 296–299 (2006)
30. Williams, H.C.: A modification of the RSA public-key encryption procedure. IEEE Trans. Inf. Theory **26**, 726–729 (1980)
31. Zimmermann, P., Dodson, B.: 20 years of ECM. In: Algorithmic Number Theory, ANTS-VII, pp. 525–542 (2006)

Generalizing Key Recovery Attacks Against NTRU with Multiple Keys and Its Application in NTRUReEncrypt

Qingjie Hu[1], Zhen Liu[1(✉)], Yuchen Cao[2], Guanju Xiao[1(✉)], and Jianhua Wang[3]

[1] School of Cyber Science and Technology, Key Laboratory of Intelligent Sensing System and Security, Ministry of Education, Hubei University, Wuhan 430062, China
qingjie_hu@stu.hubu.edu.cn, liuzhen@hubu.edu.cn, gjXiao@amss.ac.cn
[2] Wuhan Maritime Communication Research Institute, Wuhan 430205, China
[3] School of Cryptology, University of Chinese Academy of Sciences, Beijing, China
wangjianhua@ucas.ac.cn

Abstract. The NTRU problem with multiple keys arises when a user generates multiple distinct NTRU public keys $\boldsymbol{h}_i = \boldsymbol{g}_i/\boldsymbol{f} \bmod q$ by keeping its private key $\boldsymbol{f}$ fixed, and an adversary tries to recover the user's private key $\boldsymbol{f}$ by collecting multiple instances of public keys $\boldsymbol{h}_i$. At DCC 2023, Kim et al. introduced a polynomial-time algorithm to address this problem. Subsequently, at ICICS 2024, Song et al. identified a weakness in Kim et al.'s approach and proposed their own method. There are various versions of the NTRU algorithm, resulting in different ways of selecting the parameter $\boldsymbol{f}$. For instance, in the NIST PQC standardization process, the NTRUEncrypt in Round 1 and NTRU-HPS in Round 3, chooses the private key $\boldsymbol{f}$ in the form $\boldsymbol{f} = 1 \bmod p$ to improve efficiency. However, previous studies focus on the scenario where the private key $\boldsymbol{f}$ is a ternary polynomial with a fixed Hamming weight.

In this paper, we propose a polynomial time attack against NTRU with multiple keys, assuming that $\boldsymbol{f} = 1 + p * \boldsymbol{F}$, where $\boldsymbol{F}$ is a ternary polynomial of degree at most $N-1$ with a fixed Hamming weight and $p = 3$. Given the fixed Hamming weight of $\boldsymbol{g}_i$, we can derive the initial modular equations from different $\boldsymbol{h}_i$. By employing linearization techniques and exploiting the relationships between the coefficients of the equations, we can establish a system of linear modular equations with $\lfloor \frac{N}{2} \rfloor$ variables that possesses a unique solution. Using this solution, we can effectively recover the private key $\boldsymbol{f}$. We conducted experiments using the parameters of NTRU scheme in NIST PQC Competition and achieved successful results with an overwhelming probability. As a by-product, we can naturally extend the multi-key attack scenario to the NTRU-based proxy re-encryption scheme NTRUReEncrypt proposed by Nuñez et al. at AsiaCCS 2015, and successfully recover the user's private key.

Z. Liu and G. Xiao—Corresponding authors.

Y. Kim et al. (Eds.): CANS 2025, LNCS 16351, pp. 27–45, 2026.
https://doi.org/10.1007/978-981-95-4434-9_2

Keywords: NTRU · NTRUReEncrypt · Key Recovery Attack · Multiple Keys

1 Introduction

NTRU is a famous public key cryptosystem introduced by Hoffstein et al. in 1996 [10] and has been standardized as IEEE 1363.1 [22] and ANSI X9.98 [2]. The security of the NTRU scheme is based on the NTRU problem. That is, given the public key $\boldsymbol{h}$ in the ring $\mathcal{R}_q = \mathbb{Z}_q[x]/(P(x))$, where $P(x)$ is a polynomial of degree N, it is difficult to find small polynomials $\boldsymbol{f}, \boldsymbol{g}$ such that $\boldsymbol{h} = \boldsymbol{g}/\boldsymbol{f} \bmod q$. Typically, the polynomials $\boldsymbol{f}$ and $\boldsymbol{g}$ are tied to the private keys, while the polynomial $\boldsymbol{h}$ represents the public key in the cryptosystem. Since its invention, the NTRU problem has been used in various cryptographic constructions such as the encryption scheme NTRUEncrypt [7], NTRU-HRSS [14], NTRU-Prime [4], proxy re-encryption scheme NTRUReEncrypt [21], and many others [1,5]. Pellet-Mary and Stehlé [23] demonstrated a reduction from the worst-case approximate shortest vector problem over ideal lattices to an average-case search variant of the NTRU problem, thereby proving the hardness of this variant of the NTRU problem. Nevertheless, the original NTRU problem has withstood nearly three decades of cryptanalysis, and the NTRU encryption scheme continues to be one of the fastest candidates for public-key cryptography in the post-quantum era.

Throughout the development, many different types of attacks against NTRU have been proposed, such as key mismatch attacks [20,26] and broadcast attacks [8,17]. These attack methods primarily aim to recover the private key or plaintext using ciphertexts. For example, in the broadcast attack against NTRU [17], the attacker first translates a ciphertext $\boldsymbol{c} = \boldsymbol{h} * \boldsymbol{r} + \boldsymbol{m} \bmod q$ into $\boldsymbol{c} * \hat{\boldsymbol{h}} - \boldsymbol{m} * \hat{\boldsymbol{h}} = \boldsymbol{r} \bmod q$, where $\hat{\boldsymbol{h}}$ is the pseudo inverse of $\boldsymbol{h}$ satisfying that $\boldsymbol{h} * \hat{\boldsymbol{h}} * \boldsymbol{r} = \boldsymbol{r}$, $\boldsymbol{m}$ is a plaintext, and $\boldsymbol{r}$ is an unknown small polynomial. Based on prior knowledge of the Hamming weight of $\boldsymbol{r}$, the equation is formulated as $(\hat{\boldsymbol{H}} \cdot \phi(\boldsymbol{c}) - \hat{\boldsymbol{H}} \cdot \phi(\boldsymbol{m}))^T(\hat{\boldsymbol{H}} \cdot \phi(\boldsymbol{c}) - \hat{\boldsymbol{H}} \cdot \phi(\boldsymbol{m})) = \phi(\boldsymbol{r})^T \cdot \phi(\boldsymbol{r}) \bmod q$, where $\phi(\cdot)$ is a function that maps a polynomial to a column vector of its coefficients and $\hat{\boldsymbol{H}}$ is the circular matrix of $\hat{\boldsymbol{h}}$. By applying a linearization technique, this equation can be transformed into a linear form. The message $\boldsymbol{m}$ can then be recovered by gathering enough ciphertexts corresponding to the same plaintext.

Another approach is to consider the scenario for the multikey NTRU problem, which involves one party fixing its private key $\boldsymbol{f}$ and using the NTRU key generation algorithm to produce multiple different public keys $\boldsymbol{h}_i = \boldsymbol{g}_i/\boldsymbol{f} \bmod q$ and send them to a public channel. In DCC 2023, Kim et al. [15] proposed a polynomial-time algorithm for the multikey NTRU problem. The attacker collects multiple instances of the public keys $\boldsymbol{h}_i$ from the public channel and uses the first row of $\boldsymbol{H}_i \cdot \overline{\boldsymbol{H}}_i \cdot \phi(\boldsymbol{f} * \overline{\boldsymbol{f}}) = \phi(\boldsymbol{g}_i * \overline{\boldsymbol{g}}_i) \bmod q$ to build a full-rank linear equation system with N variables, where $\bar{\boldsymbol{g}}_i$, $\bar{\boldsymbol{f}}$ are conjugates of $\boldsymbol{g}_i, \boldsymbol{f}$, respectively, and $\boldsymbol{H}_i$ is the circular matrix of $\boldsymbol{h}_i$. Since $\boldsymbol{g}_i$ is a ternary polynomial sampled from a fixed Hamming weight space, the first term of $\phi(\boldsymbol{g}_i * \overline{\boldsymbol{g}}_i)$ is known. By solving the system, the unknown part $\phi(\boldsymbol{f} * \overline{\boldsymbol{f}})$ can be obtained and then the private key $\boldsymbol{f}$ is recovered using the Gentry-Szydlo (GS) algorithm [9]. However, later at ICICS 2024, Song et al. [25] pointed out that the coefficient matrix of the modular equation system constructed by Kim et al. is not full-rank and provided a method to fix this issue. By utilizing the fixed Hamming weight property of the private key $\boldsymbol{g_i}$ (i.e., $\phi(\boldsymbol{g_i})^\top \cdot \phi(\boldsymbol{g_i}) = 2d_g$), a new modular equation $\phi(\boldsymbol{f})^\top \cdot (\boldsymbol{H}_i^\top \cdot \boldsymbol{H}_i) \cdot \phi(\boldsymbol{f}) = \phi(\boldsymbol{g_i})^\top \cdot \phi(\boldsymbol{g_i}) \bmod q$ can be derived. Similarly, the adversary can gather sufficient instances of public keys $\boldsymbol{h_i}$ from the public channel to create a system of modular equations. By applying a linear technique as described in [17], the number of variables in the equation system can be reduced from the original N to $\lfloor \frac{N}{2} \rfloor + 1$, enabling the adversary to successfully determine the value of $\phi(\boldsymbol{f} * \overline{\boldsymbol{f}})$. In addition, Bai et al. [3] proposed another algebraic algorithm to break the multikey NTRU problem based on kernel reduction techniques. Compared to Kim-Lee's algorithm, their algorithm does not require prior knowledge of the Hamming weight of the key.

In the original NTRU scheme, decryption involves two steps. First, the ciphertext $\boldsymbol{c}$ is multiplied by the private key $\boldsymbol{f}$ to obtain an intermediate value $\boldsymbol{c} * \boldsymbol{f} \bmod q = p * \boldsymbol{g} * \boldsymbol{s} + \boldsymbol{m} * \boldsymbol{f}$. Then, the inverse of $\boldsymbol{f}$ modulo p is used to multiply this intermediate value modulo p to obtain $\boldsymbol{m} * \boldsymbol{f} * \boldsymbol{f}^{-1} \bmod p$, thereby recovering the plaintext $\boldsymbol{m}$. It can be seen that when the inverse of $\boldsymbol{f}$ modulo p is 1, the second step of decryption only requires a direct modulo p operation. Hence, the formula $\boldsymbol{f} = 1 + p * \boldsymbol{F}$ can streamline the decryption process and accelerate the key generation process. This approach to selecting the private key has been implemented in several versions of NTRU [6,7,11,13]. However, the attacks proposed by Song et al. [25] can not be directly applied for $\boldsymbol{f} = 1 + p * \boldsymbol{F}$. The reason is that the solution of the linear modular equations is $\phi(\boldsymbol{f} * \overline{\boldsymbol{f}}) \bmod \frac{q}{2}$. When $\boldsymbol{f}$ is a ternary polynomial with a fixed Hamming weight, we have $\phi(\boldsymbol{f} * \overline{\boldsymbol{f}}) \bmod \frac{q}{2} = \phi(\boldsymbol{f} * \overline{\boldsymbol{f}})$. However, if we consider $\boldsymbol{f} = 1 + p * \boldsymbol{F}$, where $\boldsymbol{F}$ is a ternary polynomial with a fixed Hamming weight and $p = 3$, this equivalence may not hold. Therefore, we cannot directly apply the GS algorithm to derive the private key $\boldsymbol{f}$. On the other hand, if we treat $\boldsymbol{h} * \boldsymbol{f} = \boldsymbol{g} \bmod q$ as an instance $\boldsymbol{h} + p * \boldsymbol{h} * \boldsymbol{F} = \boldsymbol{g} \bmod q$ in the broadcast attack against NTRU [17], it seems that we can recover $\boldsymbol{f}$. However, the special relation between $\boldsymbol{h}$ and $p * \boldsymbol{h}$ results in a correlation between the coefficients of the equation, indicating that their method cannot be directly applied to solve the problem. Therefore, how to solve the case for $\boldsymbol{f} = 1 + p * \boldsymbol{F}$ needs to be further investigation.

Our Contributions. In this paper, we propose an efficient key recovery attack against NTRU using multiple keys. We consider the case where $\boldsymbol{f} = 1 + p * \boldsymbol{F}$, $\boldsymbol{F}$ is sampled from a fixed Hamming weight space, and $p = 3$. Moreover, in our linear modular equations, the number of variables is $\lfloor \frac{N}{2} \rfloor$. We then apply this approach to introduce a new perspective for the key recovery attack against NTRUReEncrypt, by leveraging the collection of sufficient re-encryption keys. In contrast, previous cryptanalysis of NTRUReEncrypt primarily focused on collecting a large number of re-encrypted ciphertexts [18,19,24].

In our attacks against NTRU, we first use $\boldsymbol{h} + p * \boldsymbol{h} * \boldsymbol{F} = p * \boldsymbol{g} \bmod q$ to construct an equation $(\phi(\boldsymbol{h}) + p \cdot \boldsymbol{H} \cdot \phi(\boldsymbol{F}))^T (\phi(\boldsymbol{h}) + p \cdot \boldsymbol{H} \cdot \phi(\boldsymbol{F})) = p^2 \cdot \phi(\boldsymbol{g})^T \cdot$

$\phi(\boldsymbol{g})$ mod q, where the public key has the form of $\boldsymbol{h} = p * \boldsymbol{g}/\boldsymbol{f}$ mod q and $\boldsymbol{H}$ is the circular matrix of $\boldsymbol{h}$. By applying the linearization technique from [17], we reduce the number of variables in the equation to $N + \lfloor \frac{N}{2} \rfloor + 1$. Through analysis of the coefficients, we transform it into a new linear equation with $\lfloor \frac{N}{2} \rfloor$ variables. By collecting $\lfloor \frac{N}{2} \rfloor + 4$ public keys and solving the new system of linear modular equations, we obtain a unique solution $\boldsymbol{z}$. Using $p \cdot \boldsymbol{z}$, we can reconstruct $\phi(\boldsymbol{f} * \overline{\boldsymbol{f}})$. This approach yields a smaller solution $\boldsymbol{z}$ compared to Song et al.'s method for restoring $\phi(\boldsymbol{f} * \overline{\boldsymbol{f}})$. Finally, the GS algorithm can be employed to recover $\boldsymbol{f}$.

This attack can be applied to the NTRUReEncrypt, as we observe that the proxy is able to collect various re-encryption keys, enabling the launch of such attacks. As an extension of NTRU, NTRUReEncrypt incorporates both re-encryption and re-encryption key generation algorithms. According to the proxy re-encryption key generation algorithm, we know that for users i, j, the re-encrypted key $\boldsymbol{rk}_{i \to j} = \boldsymbol{f}_i * \boldsymbol{f}_j^{-1}$ mod q, where $\boldsymbol{f}_i, \boldsymbol{f}_j$ are the private keys of users i, j, respectively. The proxy can continuously collect re-encryption keys $\boldsymbol{rk}_{1 \to i} = \boldsymbol{f}_1 * \boldsymbol{f}_i^{-1}$ mod q between a fixed user (e.g., User 1) and other different users i. In this scenario, the proxy can then compute $\boldsymbol{f}_1{}^{-1} * \boldsymbol{f}_i * \boldsymbol{h}_i$ mod q (denoted by $\tilde{\boldsymbol{h}}_i$) with the public key $\boldsymbol{h}_i$ of the user i, which is equal to $p * \boldsymbol{g}_i * \boldsymbol{f}_1{}^{-1}$ mod q. Furthermore, the proxy can obtain $\tilde{\boldsymbol{h}}_i * \boldsymbol{f}_1 = p * \boldsymbol{g}_i$ mod q. Since $\boldsymbol{g}_i$ is a ternary polynomial with a fixed Hamming weight and $\boldsymbol{f}_1 = 1 + p * \boldsymbol{F}$, this equation has the same form in our above attack against NTRU. As a result, the private key $\boldsymbol{f}_1$ will be recovered, which in turn leads to the recovery of $\boldsymbol{f}_i$.

To validate our idea, we conducted experiments using the parameters of NTRUEncrypt [7] and NTRU-HPS [6] in the NIST PQC Competition on both NTRU and NTRUReEncrypt. The probability of successfully recovering the private key is approximately 100%. Furthermore, our attack's running time is reasonable, rendering it practically effective.

Organization. The structure of the remaining sections is as follows: In Sect. 2, we introduce the preliminaries, specific NTRU, as well as a review of the attacks by Kim et al. and Song et al.. In Sect. 3, we describe our key recovery attack for multikey NTRU under the condition $\boldsymbol{f} = 1 + p * \boldsymbol{F}$. In Sect. 4, we first introduce the NTRUReEncrypt, and then apply our attack against NTRU to it. In Sect. 5, we present the experimental results of our attacks against NTRU and NTRUReEncrypt, respectively. Finally, we give our conclusion in Sect. 6.

2 Preliminaries

2.1 Notations

Let $\mathcal{R}$ denote the ring $\mathbb{Z}[X]/(x^N - 1)$, where N is a prime. For positive integers p, q, we assume that $p \ll q$, and $\gcd(p, q) = 1$. Let $\mathcal{R}_q$ denote the ring $\mathbb{Z}_q[X]/(x^N - 1)$ and $\mathcal{R}_p$ denote the ring $\mathbb{Z}_p[X]/(x^N - 1)$. In this paper, all computations are made in the quotient ring $\mathcal{R}$, where the symbols "$*$" represents multiplication of polynomials. For convenience, we use bold letters to represent polynomials, vectors, and matrices. We use $\boldsymbol{1}$ to represent a vector whose entries are all 1. The symbol "$\cdot$" is used to denote multiplication between matrices as well as between integers, while the symbol "+" denotes addition between polynomials, matrices, and integers. Let $\|\boldsymbol{v}\|_\ell$ represent the ℓ-norm of the polynomial (or vector) $\boldsymbol{v}$. We denote the Hamming weight of a polynomial $\boldsymbol{v} \in \mathcal{R}$ by $hw(\boldsymbol{v})$.

For a polynomial $\boldsymbol{v} = \sum_{i=0}^{N-1} v_i x^i \in \mathcal{R}$, we use $\phi(\boldsymbol{v}) = (v_0, v_1, \cdots, v_{N-1})^T$ to denote the coefficient representation of $\boldsymbol{v}$. Let $\phi(\boldsymbol{v})_i$ denote the i-th coefficient of $\boldsymbol{v}$,that is, $\phi(\boldsymbol{v})_i = v_i$. We also denote the circular matrix form related to $\boldsymbol{v}$ by $rot(\boldsymbol{v}) \in \mathbb{Z}^{N\times N}$:

$$rot(\boldsymbol{v}) = [\phi(\boldsymbol{v})|\phi(\boldsymbol{v} * x)| \cdots |\phi(\boldsymbol{v} * x^{N-1})] = \begin{pmatrix} v_0 & v_{N-1} & \cdots & v_1 \\ v_1 & v_0 & \cdots & v_2 \\ \vdots & \vdots & \ddots & \vdots \\ v_{N-1} & v_{N-2} & \cdots & v_0 \end{pmatrix}.$$

We define the conjugation of the polynomial $\boldsymbol{v}$ as $\overline{\boldsymbol{v}} := \boldsymbol{v}(x^{-1})$. Thus, we have $\phi(\overline{\boldsymbol{v}}) = (v_0, v_{N-1}, \cdots, v_1)^T$ and the circular matrix form related to $\overline{\boldsymbol{v}}$ is denoted as $rot(\overline{\boldsymbol{v}}) \in \mathbb{Z}^{N\times N}$:

$$rot(\overline{\boldsymbol{v}}) = \begin{pmatrix} v_0 & v_1 & \cdots & v_{N-1} \\ v_{N-1} & v_0 & \cdots & v_{N-2} \\ \vdots & \vdots & \ddots & \vdots \\ v_1 & v_2 & \cdots & v_0 \end{pmatrix}.$$

For the production of two circular matrices, we give the following lemma.

Lemma 1. [16] If $\boldsymbol{G}, \boldsymbol{H} \in \mathbb{Z}_q^{N\times N}$ are both circular matrices, then $\boldsymbol{G} \cdot \boldsymbol{H}$ is also a circular matrix. In particular, $\boldsymbol{H}^\top \cdot \boldsymbol{H}$ is a symmetric circular matrix.

For polynomials $\boldsymbol{f}, \boldsymbol{g} \in \mathcal{R}$, the polynomial multiplication of $\boldsymbol{f} * \boldsymbol{g}$ can be represented in matrix form as:

$$rot(\boldsymbol{f}) \cdot \phi(\boldsymbol{g}) = \begin{pmatrix} f_0 & f_{N-1} & \cdots & f_1 \\ f_1 & f_0 & \cdots & f_2 \\ \vdots & \vdots & \ddots & \vdots \\ f_{N-1} & f_{N-2} & \cdots & f_0 \end{pmatrix} \cdot \begin{pmatrix} g_0 \\ g_1 \\ \vdots \\ g_{N-1} \end{pmatrix}.$$

We now introduce the concept of a ternary polynomial. For positive integers d_1, d_2, the polynomial set $\mathcal{T}_{(d_1,d_2)}$ is defined as follows:

$$\mathcal{T}_{(d_1,d_2)} = \left\{ \begin{array}{c} \text{ternary polynomials of } \mathcal{R} \text{ with } d_1 \text{ entries} \\ \text{equal to 1 and } d_2 \text{ entries equal to } -1 \end{array} \right\}.$$

2.2 NTRU Cryptosystem

The NTRU cryptosystem consists of three parts, and the specific details are given in [10]. Let

$$\mathcal{L}_m = \left\{ \boldsymbol{m} \in \mathcal{R}\text{: every coefficient of } \boldsymbol{m} \text{ lies between } -\tfrac{p-1}{2} \text{ and } \tfrac{p-1}{2} \right\}.$$

- **KeyGen**(1^κ): Given the security parameter κ, the key generation algorithm first randomly selects $\boldsymbol{f} \in \mathcal{T}_{(d_f,d_f-1)}$, where $\boldsymbol{f}$ has inverses $\boldsymbol{f}_q^{-1}$ and $\boldsymbol{f}_p^{-1}$ in $\mathcal{R}_q$ and $\mathcal{R}_p$ respectively. Then, a polynomial $\boldsymbol{g} \in \mathcal{T}_{(d_g,d_g)}$ is randomly chosen and $\boldsymbol{h} = p * \boldsymbol{g} * \boldsymbol{f}_q^{-1} \bmod q$ is calculated. The public key $\boldsymbol{pk} = \boldsymbol{h}$ and the private key $\boldsymbol{sk} = (\boldsymbol{f}, \boldsymbol{g})$ are then output.
- **Enc**($\boldsymbol{pk}, \boldsymbol{m}$): Given the public key $\boldsymbol{pk}$ and the message $\boldsymbol{m} \in \mathcal{L}_m$, a random disturbance polynomial $\boldsymbol{r} \in \mathcal{T}_{(d_r,d_r)}$ is selected, and the ciphertext $\boldsymbol{c} = \boldsymbol{h} * \boldsymbol{r} + \boldsymbol{m} \bmod q$ is computed and output.
- **Dec**($\boldsymbol{sk}, \boldsymbol{c}$): Given the private key $\boldsymbol{sk}$ and the ciphertext $\boldsymbol{c}$, the value $\boldsymbol{a} = \boldsymbol{c} * \boldsymbol{f} \bmod q$ is calculated, and the plaintext $\boldsymbol{m} = \boldsymbol{a} * \boldsymbol{f}_p^{-1} \bmod p$ is output.

In the decryption process, it first computes $\boldsymbol{a} = \boldsymbol{c} * \boldsymbol{f} \bmod q$ and then computes $\boldsymbol{m} = \boldsymbol{a} * \boldsymbol{f}_p^{-1} \bmod p$ to recover the plaintext $\boldsymbol{m}$. Notice that the coefficients of the polynomials $\boldsymbol{f}$, $\boldsymbol{g}$, $\boldsymbol{r}$, and $\boldsymbol{m}$ are small, so the coefficients of the polynomial $\boldsymbol{a} = \boldsymbol{c} * \boldsymbol{f} = p * \boldsymbol{g} * \boldsymbol{r} + \boldsymbol{m} * \boldsymbol{f} \bmod q$ are most likely between $-\frac{q}{2}$ and $\frac{q}{2}$, which ensures the correctness of the NTRU algorithm. Finally, we have that $\boldsymbol{a} * \boldsymbol{f}_p^{-1} \bmod p = p * \boldsymbol{g} * \boldsymbol{r} * \boldsymbol{f}_p^{-1} + \boldsymbol{m} * \boldsymbol{f} * \boldsymbol{f}_p^{-1} \bmod p = \boldsymbol{m}$.

Note that the second step for the decryption process is redundant if the polynomial $\boldsymbol{f}$ is selected congruent to 1 modulo p. Therefore, to improve the efficiency of the decryption, a form of the private key $\boldsymbol{f}$ is chosen as $\boldsymbol{f} = 1 + p * \boldsymbol{F}$, which has been widely used in the different versions of NTRU, such as NTRU-2001 [11] for $p = x + 2$, NTRU-2005 [13] for $p = 2$, and NTRUEncrypt [7] for $p = 3$. This ensures that $\boldsymbol{f}_p^{-1} \equiv 1 \bmod p$, and the calculation for the plaintext during decryption becomes $\boldsymbol{m} = \boldsymbol{c} * \boldsymbol{f} \bmod q \bmod p$.

Remark 1. In the analysis conducted by Kim et al. [15] and Song et al. [25] , the public key is represented as $\boldsymbol{h} = \boldsymbol{f}/\boldsymbol{g} \bmod q$, and the ciphertext $\boldsymbol{c}$ is defined as $p * \boldsymbol{h} * \boldsymbol{r} + \boldsymbol{m} \bmod q$. Their objective in these studies is to recover $\boldsymbol{g}$. In this paper, we follow the notations in the description of NTRU in [10]. Therefore, for the sake of consistency, we will continue to use the symbols introduced in this section to describe their operation in the next section.

2.3 Known Attacks Against NTRU with Multiple Keys

In this section, we first provide the definition of NTRU with multiple keys. Then, we review the work of Kim, Lee [15], and the result proposed by Song et al. [25].

Definition 1. (NTRU with multiple keys [25]) Suppose a ring $\mathbb{Z}[X]/(X^N - 1)$ and a modulus q are given. Choose $\boldsymbol{g_i} \in \mathcal{T}_{(d_g,d_g)}$ and $\boldsymbol{f} \in \mathcal{T}_{(d_f,d_f-1)}$ for $0 \le i \le k-1$ such that $\gcd(\boldsymbol{g_i}, \boldsymbol{f}) = \gcd(\boldsymbol{g_i}, \boldsymbol{g_j}) = 1$ for $i \ne j$. Let $\boldsymbol{h_1}$, $\boldsymbol{h_2}$, $\cdots$, $\boldsymbol{h_k}$ be the instances of the form $\boldsymbol{h_i} = \boldsymbol{g_i}/\boldsymbol{f} \bmod q$. Then, the NTRU encryption with multiple keys problem is to recover $\boldsymbol{f} * x^j$ for some j from given $\{\boldsymbol{h_i}\}$.

Based on the works of Kim et al. and Song et al., their attack framework can be generally divided into the following two steps.

1. Find a method to obtain $\boldsymbol{f} * \overline{\boldsymbol{f}}$.

2. Apply Gentry-Szydlo(GS) algorithm to obtain $\boldsymbol{f}$.

In 2002, Gentry and Szydlo proposed the GS algorithm [9] to obtain the $\boldsymbol{v}$ from $\boldsymbol{v} * \overline{\boldsymbol{v}}$. We summarize their results in the following lemma.

Lemma 2. [9] Let $\boldsymbol{v} \in \mathcal{R}$. Given $\boldsymbol{v} * \overline{\boldsymbol{v}}$ and the Hermite normal form basis $\boldsymbol{B}$ for the ideal lattice $\langle \boldsymbol{v} \rangle$, we can compute $\boldsymbol{v} * x^i$ for some i in polynomial time N and the bit-length of $\boldsymbol{v}$.

The main difference between the works of Kim et al. and Song et al. lies in the first step. The process in Kim et al.'s work to recover $\boldsymbol{f} * \overline{\boldsymbol{f}}$ is roughly as follows:

1. Compute the first row of the matrix $\boldsymbol{H}_i \cdot \overline{\boldsymbol{H}}_i$, denoted as $\boldsymbol{A}_i$, where $0 \leq i \leq k-1$, where $\boldsymbol{H}_i$ denotes the matrix $rot(\boldsymbol{h}_i)$ and $\overline{\boldsymbol{H}}_i$ denotes the matrix $rot(\overline{\boldsymbol{h}}_i)$;
2. Construct the linear system $\boldsymbol{A} \cdot \boldsymbol{x} = m * \mathbf{1} \bmod q$, where the i-th row of $\boldsymbol{A}$ is $\boldsymbol{A}_i$, and m is $hw(\boldsymbol{g}_i)$.
3. Solve the linear system to obtain $\boldsymbol{f} * \overline{\boldsymbol{f}}$.

Since $\boldsymbol{g}_i \in \mathcal{T}_{(d_g,d_g)}$, step 1 utilizes the fact that the constant term of $\boldsymbol{g}_i * \overline{\boldsymbol{g}}_i$ is m, which is a constant. From k instances $\boldsymbol{h}_i = \boldsymbol{g}_i / \boldsymbol{f} \bmod q$, we obtain $(\boldsymbol{h}_i * \overline{\boldsymbol{h}_i}) * (\boldsymbol{f} * \overline{\boldsymbol{f}}) = (\boldsymbol{g}_i * \overline{\boldsymbol{g}_i}) \bmod q$. Further, its linear form is $(\boldsymbol{H}_i \cdot \overline{\boldsymbol{H}}_i) \cdot \phi(\boldsymbol{f} * \overline{\boldsymbol{f}}) = \phi(\boldsymbol{g}_i * \overline{\boldsymbol{g}_i}) \bmod q$, where the first term of $\phi(\boldsymbol{g}_i * \overline{\boldsymbol{g}_i})$ is m. Steps 2–3 construct and solve a linear system with N variables, where the coefficient matrix $\boldsymbol{A}$ should be full-ranked. Therefore, the rank of the matrix $\boldsymbol{A}$ is crucial for successfully solving for $\phi(\boldsymbol{f} * \overline{\boldsymbol{f}})$.

However, Song et al. pointed out that the matrix $\boldsymbol{A}$ has $\lfloor \frac{N}{2} \rfloor$ pairs of equal columns, which indicates that the coefficient matrix $\boldsymbol{A}$ constructed by Kim et al. is not invertible. Therefore, they proposed their strategies on building full rank linear equations.

For one instance, the sample $\boldsymbol{h}_i * \boldsymbol{f} = \boldsymbol{g}_i$ is transformed into a matrix form, i.e., $\boldsymbol{H}_i \cdot \phi(\boldsymbol{f}) = \phi(\boldsymbol{g}_i)$, and we can also obtain its transpose form $\phi(\boldsymbol{f})^\top \cdot \boldsymbol{H}_i^\top = \phi(\boldsymbol{g}_i)^\top$. Multiplying the two equations gives a new equation:

$$\phi(\boldsymbol{f})^\top \cdot \boldsymbol{H}_i^\top \cdot \boldsymbol{H}_i \cdot \phi(\boldsymbol{f}) = \phi(\boldsymbol{g}_i)^\top \cdot \phi(\boldsymbol{g}_i) = m. \tag{2.1}$$

Based on the Eq. (2.1), they use a linearization technique, which has been used in the cryptanalysis of NTRU [8,17], NTRUReEncrypt [19,24], to transform a non-linear variable into a linear variable. Since $\boldsymbol{H}_i^\top \cdot \boldsymbol{H}_i$ is symmetric, the number of variables in the final system of equations can be reduced to $\lfloor \frac{N}{2} \rfloor + 1$ to recover $\boldsymbol{f} * \overline{\boldsymbol{f}}$. The procedure of their recovery is as below:

1. For each $0 \leq i \leq k-1$, compute $\boldsymbol{H}_i^\top \cdot \boldsymbol{H}_i$, and use the linearization technique to adjust the element positions in a certain order, and denote it by $\boldsymbol{M}_i$.
2. Construct the linear system $\frac{1}{2}\boldsymbol{M} \cdot \boldsymbol{x} = \frac{m}{2} * \mathbf{1} \bmod \frac{q}{2}$, where the i-th row of $\boldsymbol{M}$ is $\boldsymbol{M}_i$.

3. Solve the linear system to obtain $\boldsymbol{f} * \overline{\boldsymbol{f}}$.

When solving the system of equations, it is crucial to ensure that the equations corresponding to the samples are as linearly independent as possible. This helps to avoid redundancy and ensures that the system has a unique solution with a high probability. Li et al. [17] predicted the probability that a matrix in $\mathbb{Z}_q^{(d+l)\times d}$ is of full rank, and the related theorem is as follows:

Theorem 1. *Let $\mathbb{F}_q$ be the finite field with q elements, where q is the prime of power. The proportion of matrices of rank d in the set of $(d+l)\times d$ matrices with entries in $\mathbb{F}_q$ is equal to:*

$$\prod_{i=l+1}^{d+l}(1-q^{-i}).$$

Based on Theorem 1, Song et al. chose $l=4$ to ensure that the linear system of equations has a unique solution with high probability. Therefore, Song et al.'s attack requires at least $\lfloor \frac{N}{2} \rfloor + 5$ samples or equations.

3 Key Recovery Attack on NTRU with Multiple Keys in the Case of $\boldsymbol{f} = 1 + \boldsymbol{p} * \boldsymbol{F}$

The attacks by Kim et al. [15] and Song et al. [25] focus on the scenario that the private key $\boldsymbol{f}$ is a ternary polynomial with a fixed Hamming weight. However, in practice, the private key $\boldsymbol{f}$ is usually set to have the form of $\boldsymbol{f} = 1 + p * \boldsymbol{F}$ to simplify the decryption. In this section, we will introduce how to break the NTRU scheme with multiple keys for $\boldsymbol{f} = 1 + p * \boldsymbol{F}$, $\boldsymbol{F} \in \mathcal{T}_{(d_f,d_f)}$, and $p = 3$.

It is important to note that in the work of Song et al., by constructing modular equation systems, the value of $\phi(\boldsymbol{f} * \bar{\boldsymbol{f}}) \bmod \frac{q}{2}$ can be obtained, and then the value of $\phi(\boldsymbol{f} * \bar{\boldsymbol{f}})$ can be obtained to call the GS algorithm. When $\boldsymbol{f}$ is a ternary polynomial with a fixed Hamming weight, one has $\|\phi(\boldsymbol{f} * \bar{\boldsymbol{f}})\|_\infty = hw(\boldsymbol{f}) < \frac{q}{4}$. Although the system of linear equations is established under modulo $\frac{q}{2}$, one can first construct equations to recover $\phi(\boldsymbol{f} * \bar{\boldsymbol{f}})$ modulo $\frac{q}{2}$, then directly obtain $\phi(\boldsymbol{f} * \bar{\boldsymbol{f}})$. However, when $\boldsymbol{f} = 1 + p * \boldsymbol{F}$, the coefficient of $\boldsymbol{f} * \bar{\boldsymbol{f}}$ will increase, causing $\boldsymbol{f} * \bar{\boldsymbol{f}} \bmod \frac{q}{2} = \boldsymbol{f} * \bar{\boldsymbol{f}}$ to no longer hold. This will prevent the GS algorithm from being applied to recover the private key $\boldsymbol{f}$.

To illustrate the feasibility of this concept, we will begin with a simple example. Let's consider $N = 13$, $q = 64$, $d_f = 3$, and take $\boldsymbol{f} = 3x^{11} - 3x^{10} + 3x^7 - 3x^4 + 3x^2 - 2$. When we compute $\boldsymbol{f} * \bar{\boldsymbol{f}}$, we get $-9x^{12} - 21x^{11} - 12x^{10} + 24x^9 - 6x^7 - 6x^6 + 24x^4 - 12x^3 - 21x^2 - 9x + 49$. However, when we reduce this result modulo 32, we obtain $-9x^{12} + 11x^{11} - 12x^{10} - 8x^9 - 6x^7 - 6x^6 - 8x^4 - 12x^3 + 11x^2 - 9x - 15$, which is not equivalent. In the NTRUEncrypt scheme [7], the private key $\boldsymbol{f}$ is chosen as $\boldsymbol{f} = 1 + p * \boldsymbol{F}$, where $\boldsymbol{F} \in \mathcal{T}_{(d_f,d_f)}$ and $p = 3$. For our experiment, we select the parameter set ntru-743 with $N = 743$ and $d_f = 247$. Following the approach of Song et al., we conduct 100 experiments, resulting in a success rate of nearly 0%. However, we observe that by utilizing the Hamming weight of $\boldsymbol{F}$ to eliminate the constant term of $\boldsymbol{f} * \overline{\boldsymbol{f}}$ in the equations, we can improve the success rate to approximately 50%.

We propose a new attack targeting $\boldsymbol{f} = 1+p*\boldsymbol{F}$ to improve performance. Our method constructs modular linear equations modulo $\frac{q}{2}$ with a unique solution $\boldsymbol{z} = (z_1, z_2, \cdots, z_{\lfloor \frac{N}{2} \rfloor})$. The equations ensure that $p \cdot z_i = \phi(\boldsymbol{f}*\overline{\boldsymbol{f}})_i = \phi(\boldsymbol{f} * \overline{\boldsymbol{f}})_{N-i}$ for $i = 1, 2, \cdots, \lfloor \frac{N}{2} \rfloor$. This approach results in a smaller solution compared to Song et al., reducing the impact of the operation on the modulo $\frac{q}{2}$.

Given k instances $\{p * \boldsymbol{h_i} * \boldsymbol{F} + \boldsymbol{h_i} = p * \boldsymbol{g_i} \bmod q\}_{i=0}^{k-1}$, here is the framework of our attack.

1. For each $0 \leq i \leq k-1$, compute $\tilde{\boldsymbol{H}}_i^\top \cdot \tilde{\boldsymbol{H}}_i$ and $\phi(\boldsymbol{h}_i)^\top \cdot \tilde{\boldsymbol{H}}_i$, where $\tilde{\boldsymbol{H}}_i = p \cdot rot(\boldsymbol{h}_i)$.
2. For each i, use linearization techniques to adjust the order of the elements in $\tilde{\boldsymbol{H}}_i^\top \cdot \tilde{\boldsymbol{H}}_i$, $\phi(\boldsymbol{h}_i)^\top \cdot \tilde{\boldsymbol{H}}_i$, and denote it by $\tilde{\boldsymbol{M}}_i$.
3. Construct a linear system $\tilde{\boldsymbol{M}} * \boldsymbol{x} = \boldsymbol{u} \bmod q$, where the i-th row of the coefficient matrix $\tilde{\boldsymbol{M}}$ is $\tilde{\boldsymbol{M}}_i$, and the i-th element of $\boldsymbol{u}$ is related to $\phi(\boldsymbol{g}_i)^\top \cdot \phi(\boldsymbol{g}_i)$, $\phi(\boldsymbol{h}_i)^\top \cdot \phi(\boldsymbol{h}_i)$.
4. Use the relationships between the coefficients of $\tilde{\boldsymbol{M}}$, combine the unknowns, and construct new equations $\boldsymbol{B} * \boldsymbol{z} = \boldsymbol{u'} \bmod \frac{q}{2}$.
5. Solve the linear system $\boldsymbol{B} * \boldsymbol{z} = \boldsymbol{u'} \bmod \frac{q}{2}$ to obtain the unique solution $\boldsymbol{z}$.
6. Use the relation between $\phi(\boldsymbol{f} * \overline{\boldsymbol{f}})$ and $\boldsymbol{z}$ to obtain the value of $\phi(\boldsymbol{f} * \overline{\boldsymbol{f}})$.
7. Given the instance $\{\boldsymbol{h}_i\}_{i=0}^{k-1}$ and $\boldsymbol{f} * \overline{\boldsymbol{f}}$, compute $p^{-1} * \overline{\boldsymbol{h_i}} * \boldsymbol{f} * \overline{\boldsymbol{f}}$.
8. Use the GS algorithm to recover the exact value of $\boldsymbol{f}$.

Note that steps 7 and 8 are the utilization of the GS algorithm. From the procedure, we have

$$\begin{aligned} p^{-1} * \overline{\boldsymbol{h_i}} * \boldsymbol{f} * \overline{\boldsymbol{f}} &= \frac{\overline{\boldsymbol{g_i}}}{\overline{\boldsymbol{f}}} * \overline{\boldsymbol{f}} * \boldsymbol{f} \bmod q \\ &= \overline{\boldsymbol{g_i}} * \boldsymbol{f} \bmod q. \end{aligned}$$

Since $\boldsymbol{g}_i \in \mathcal{T}_{(d_g,d_g)}$, we know $\|\phi(\overline{\boldsymbol{g_i}} * \boldsymbol{f})\|_\infty \leq \|\phi(\boldsymbol{f})\|_1$. For the parameters in NTRU, such as NTRUEncrypt [7], we have $2d_f = (2/3)N$. This implies $\|\phi(\overline{\boldsymbol{g_i}} * \boldsymbol{f})\|_\infty \leq \|\phi(\boldsymbol{f})\|_1 \leq 2pd_f + 1 < q/2$. Therefore, we can get $\overline{\boldsymbol{g_i}} * \boldsymbol{f}$ without modulo q. In addition, since $\overline{\boldsymbol{g_i}}$ and $\boldsymbol{f}$ are relatively prime, we can obtain multiples of $\boldsymbol{f}$ and a basis for the ideal lattice $\langle \boldsymbol{f} \rangle$ by computing the Gaussian echelon form of $\phi(\overline{\boldsymbol{g_i}} * \boldsymbol{f})$. To apply the GS algorithm, we also need to calculate the value of $\phi(\boldsymbol{f} * \overline{\boldsymbol{f}})$. Our contributions focus on how to construct and solve linear equations related to $\phi(\boldsymbol{f} * \overline{\boldsymbol{f}})$.

3.1 Constructing the Primitive Linear Modular Equations

For simplicity, we consider the case with only one instance $\boldsymbol{h} * (1 + p * \boldsymbol{F}) = p * \boldsymbol{g} \bmod q$ to construct one equation. Then we have

$$\tilde{\boldsymbol{H}} \cdot \phi(\boldsymbol{F}) + \phi(\boldsymbol{h}) = p \cdot \phi(\boldsymbol{g}) \bmod q.$$

We can also obtain its transposed form. Multiplying the two equations gives a new equation:

$$\phi(\boldsymbol{F})^\top\cdot(\tilde{\boldsymbol{H}}^\top\cdot\tilde{\boldsymbol{H}})\cdot\phi(\boldsymbol{F})+(2\phi(\boldsymbol{h})^\top\cdot\tilde{\boldsymbol{H}})\cdot\phi(\boldsymbol{F}) = p^2\phi(\boldsymbol{g})^\top\cdot\phi(\boldsymbol{g})-\phi(\boldsymbol{h})^\top\cdot\phi(\boldsymbol{h}) \quad (3.1)$$

Since the right-hand side of the equation is $p^2\cdot 2\cdot d_g - \phi(\boldsymbol{h})^\top\cdot\phi(\boldsymbol{h})$, which is known, we can eliminate the private key $\boldsymbol{g}$, leaving only variables related to $\boldsymbol{F}$.

Let $\phi(\boldsymbol{F}) = (f'_0,\cdots,f'_{N-1})^\top$, $\phi(\boldsymbol{h})^\top\cdot\tilde{\boldsymbol{H}} = (k_0,k_1,\cdots,k_{N-1})^\top$,

$$\tilde{\boldsymbol{H}}^\top\cdot\tilde{\boldsymbol{H}} = \begin{pmatrix} c_0 & c_{N-1} & \cdots & c_1 \\ c_1 & c_0 & \cdots & c_2 \\ \vdots & \vdots & \ddots & \vdots \\ c_{N-1} & c_{N-2} & \cdots & c_0 \end{pmatrix}.$$

According to Lemma 1, $\tilde{\boldsymbol{H}}^\top\cdot\tilde{\boldsymbol{H}}$ is a symmetric circular matrix, i.e., $c_i = c_{N-i}$, $i\in\{1,2,\cdots,N-1\}$. Equation (3.1) can be further written as

$$\begin{aligned} u = {} & c_0({f'_0}^2+{f'_1}^2+\cdots+{f'_{N-1}}^2) \\ & + c_1(f'_1f'_0+f'_2f'_1+\cdots+f'_0f'_{N-1}) \\ & +\cdots \\ & + c_{N-1}(f'_{N-1}f'_0+f'_0f'_1+\cdots+f'_{N-2}f'_{N-1}) \\ & + 2k_0f'_0+2k_1f'_1+\cdots+2k_{N-1}f'_{N-1} \bmod q \end{aligned} \quad (3.2)$$

where $u = p^2\cdot 2\cdot d_g - \phi(\boldsymbol{h})^\top\cdot\phi(\boldsymbol{h})$. To construct the linear equation, we apply the linearization technique, which has been used in [17,19,24]. Let

$$x_i = f'_if'_0+f'_{i+1}f'_1+\cdots+f'_{N-1}f'_{N-i-1}+f'_0f'_{N-i}+\cdots+f'_{i-1}f'_{N-1},$$

where $i=0,1,\cdots,N-1$. It can be easily seen that $x_i = x_{N-i}$, $i=1,2,\cdots,N-1$. Therefore, based on $c_i=c_{N-i}$ and $x_i=x_{N-i}$, we can derive:

$$\begin{aligned} u = {} & c_0x_0+2c_1x_1+\cdots+2c_{\lfloor\frac{N}{2}\rfloor}x_{\lfloor\frac{N}{2}\rfloor} \\ & + 2k_0f'_0+2k_1f'_1+\cdots+2k_{N-1}f'_{N-1} \bmod q \end{aligned} \quad (3.3)$$

At this stage, there are $N+\lfloor\frac{N}{2}\rfloor+1$ variables in the equation. However, it is important to emphasize that there is a strong relationship between c_i and k_i, which results in a connection between the columns of the coefficient matrix in the constructed system of linear equations. Therefore, we reconstruct the linear equations by utilizing the relationship between c_i and k_i, which can further reduce the number of variables.

3.2 Reducing the Number of Variables

In this section, we will introduce how to construct linear equations with fewer variables. Before that, we first present some relationships between the coefficients of the equations.

Theorem 2. *In the Eq.* (3.3) *constructed through linearization techniques, the following linear relationships exist:*

1. $k_i = k_{N-i}$, $i = 1, 2, \cdots, N-1$;
2. $c_j = p \cdot k_j$, $j = 0, 1, \cdots, N-1$;
3. u, c_0, *and* k_0 *are all even.*

Proof. 1. Given that $\tilde{\boldsymbol{H}} = p \cdot rot(\boldsymbol{h})$, we have:

$$\begin{aligned}\phi(\boldsymbol{h})^\top \cdot \tilde{\boldsymbol{H}} &= p \cdot \phi(\boldsymbol{h})^\top \cdot [\phi(\boldsymbol{h})|\phi(\boldsymbol{h} * x)|\cdots|\phi(\boldsymbol{h} * x^{N-1})] \\ &= p \cdot [\phi(\boldsymbol{h})^\top * \phi(\boldsymbol{h})|\phi(\boldsymbol{h})^\top \cdot \phi(\boldsymbol{h} * x)|\cdots|\phi(\boldsymbol{h})^\top \cdot \phi(\boldsymbol{h} * x^{N-1})] \\ &= (k_0, k_1, \cdots, k_{N-1})\end{aligned}$$

Since $\phi(\boldsymbol{h})^\top \cdot \phi(\boldsymbol{h} * x^i) = \phi(\boldsymbol{h})^\top \cdot \phi(\boldsymbol{h} * x^{N-i})$, for $i = 1, 2, \cdots, N-1$, it follows that $k_i = k_{N-i}$, for $i = 1, 2, \cdots, N-1$.
2. We have:

$$\begin{aligned}\tilde{\boldsymbol{H}}^\top \cdot \tilde{\boldsymbol{H}} &= p^2 \cdot \begin{pmatrix} \phi(\boldsymbol{h})^\top \\ \phi(\boldsymbol{h} * x)^\top \\ \phi(\boldsymbol{h} * x^2)^\top \\ \vdots \\ \phi(\boldsymbol{h} * x^{N-1})^\top \end{pmatrix} \cdot [\phi(\boldsymbol{h})|\phi(\boldsymbol{h} * x)|\phi(\boldsymbol{h} * x^2)|\cdots|\phi(\boldsymbol{h} * x^{N-1})] \\ &= p^2 \cdot \begin{pmatrix} \phi(\boldsymbol{h})^\top \cdot \phi(\boldsymbol{h}) & \cdots & \phi(\boldsymbol{h})^\top \cdot \phi(\boldsymbol{h} * x^{N-1}) \\ \phi(\boldsymbol{h} * x)^\top \cdot \phi(\boldsymbol{h}) & \cdots & \phi(\boldsymbol{h} * x)^\top \cdot \phi(\boldsymbol{h} * x^{N-1}) \\ \vdots & \ddots & \vdots \\ \phi(\boldsymbol{h} * x^{N-1})^\top \cdot \phi(\boldsymbol{h}) & \cdots & \phi(\boldsymbol{h} * x^{N-1})^\top \cdot \phi(\boldsymbol{h} * x^{N-1}) \end{pmatrix} \\ &= \begin{pmatrix} c_0 & c_{N-1} & \cdots & c_1 \\ c_1 & c_0 & \cdots & c_2 \\ \vdots & \vdots & \ddots & \vdots \\ c_{N-1} & c_{N-2} & \cdots & c_0 \end{pmatrix} \bmod q.\end{aligned}$$

Thus, $c_i = p \cdot k_i, i = 0, 1, 2, \cdots, N-1$.
3. Let $\boldsymbol{h} = p * \boldsymbol{g} * \boldsymbol{f}_q^{-1}$, and $\boldsymbol{G} = rot(\boldsymbol{g})$. In the matrix form, we have

$$\phi(\boldsymbol{h}) = p \cdot rot(\boldsymbol{g}) \cdot \phi(\boldsymbol{f}_q^{-1}) = p \cdot \boldsymbol{G} \cdot \phi(\boldsymbol{f}_q^{-1}).$$

Then we know:

$$\phi(\boldsymbol{h})^\top \cdot \phi(\boldsymbol{h}) = p^2 \cdot \phi(\boldsymbol{f}_q^{-1})^\top \cdot \boldsymbol{G}^\top \cdot \boldsymbol{G} \cdot \phi(\boldsymbol{f}_q^{-1}) \bmod q.$$

Assuming that $\phi(\boldsymbol{f}_q^{-1} * \overline{\boldsymbol{f}_q^{-1}}) = \{y_0, y_1, \cdots, y_{N-1}\}^\top$, and $y_i = y_{N-i}$, for $i = 1, 2, \cdots, N-1$, we obtain:

$$\begin{aligned}\phi(\boldsymbol{h})^\top \cdot \phi(\boldsymbol{h}) = p^2 \cdot [&\phi(\boldsymbol{g})^\top \cdot \phi(\boldsymbol{g}) \cdot y_0 \\ &+ 2 \cdot \phi(\boldsymbol{g})^\top \cdot \phi(\boldsymbol{g} * x) \cdot y_1 \\ &+ \cdots \\ &+ 2 \cdot \phi(\boldsymbol{g})^\top \cdot \phi(\boldsymbol{g} * x^{\lfloor \frac{N}{2} \rfloor}) \cdot y_{\lfloor \frac{N}{2} \rfloor}] \bmod q.\end{aligned}$$

Since $\phi(\boldsymbol{g})^\top \cdot \phi(\boldsymbol{g}) = 2d_g$ is an even number, $\phi(\boldsymbol{h})^\top \cdot \phi(\boldsymbol{h})$ is also an even number. Furthermore, since $c_0 = p^2 \cdot \phi(\boldsymbol{h})^\top \cdot \phi(\boldsymbol{h})$, $k_0 = p \cdot \phi(\boldsymbol{h})^\top \cdot \phi(\boldsymbol{h})$, and $u = p^2 \cdot 2d_g - \phi(\boldsymbol{h})^\top \cdot \phi(\boldsymbol{h})$, it follows that c_0, k_0, and u are also even numbers.

According to the Theorem 2, Eq. (3.3) can be further written as:

$$\begin{aligned} u = & k_0(px_0 + 2f'_0) \\ & + 2k_1(px_1 + f'_1 + f'_{N-1}) \\ & + \cdots \\ & + 2k_{\lfloor \frac{N}{2} \rfloor}(px_{\lfloor \frac{N}{2} \rfloor} + f'_{\lfloor \frac{N}{2} \rfloor} + f'_{N-\lfloor \frac{N}{2} \rfloor}) \bmod q \end{aligned} \tag{3.4}$$

where $x_0 = {f'_0}^2 + {f'_1}^2 + \cdots + {f'_{N-1}}^2 = 2d_f$. Thus, Eq. (3.4) can also be written as:

$$\begin{aligned} u - pk_0x_0 = & 2k_0f'_0 \\ & + 2k_1(px_1 + f'_1 + f'_{N-1}) \\ & + \cdots \\ & + 2k_{\lfloor \frac{N}{2} \rfloor}(px_{\lfloor \frac{N}{2} \rfloor} + f'_{\lfloor \frac{N}{2} \rfloor} + f'_{N-\lfloor \frac{N}{2} \rfloor}) \bmod q \end{aligned} \tag{3.5}$$

Since both u and k_0 are even and $q = 2^k$, dividing both sides of Eq. (3.5) by 2 gives:

$$\begin{aligned} \frac{1}{2}(u - pk_0x_0) = & k_0f'_0 \\ & + k_1(px_1 + f'_1 + f'_{N-1}) \\ & + \cdots \\ & + k_{\lfloor \frac{N}{2} \rfloor}(px_{\lfloor \frac{N}{2} \rfloor} + f'_{\lfloor \frac{N}{2} \rfloor} + f'_{N-\lfloor \frac{N}{2} \rfloor}) \bmod \frac{q}{2} \end{aligned} \tag{3.6}$$

Since $f'_0 \in \{0, 1, -1\}$, we can guess the value of f'_0, which allows us to rewrite the above equation as follows.

$$\begin{aligned} \frac{1}{2}(u - pk_0x_0) - k_0f'_0 = & k_1(px_1 + f'_1 + f'_{N-1}) \\ & + \cdots \\ & + k_{\lfloor \frac{N}{2} \rfloor}(px_{\lfloor \frac{N}{2} \rfloor} + f'_{\lfloor \frac{N}{2} \rfloor} + f'_{N-\lfloor \frac{N}{2} \rfloor}) \bmod \frac{q}{2} \end{aligned} \tag{3.7}$$

To further reduce the number of variables, we introduce new variables $z_1, \cdots, z_{\lfloor \frac{N}{2} \rfloor}$. Now, let us consider an equation of the following form:

$$\frac{1}{2}(u - pk_0x_0) - k_0f'_0 = k_1z_1 + \cdots + k_{\lfloor \frac{N}{2} \rfloor}z_{\lfloor \frac{N}{2} \rfloor} \bmod \frac{q}{2}$$

where u, k_i, x_0, f'_0 is known, and $(px_1 + f'_1 + f'_{N-1}, \cdots, px_{\lfloor \frac{N}{2} \rfloor} + f'_{\lfloor \frac{N}{2} \rfloor} + f'_{N-\lfloor \frac{N}{2} \rfloor})$ is a solution. The number of variables in the equation is reduced from $N + \lfloor \frac{N}{2} \rfloor + 1$ to $\lfloor \frac{N}{2} \rfloor$.

Suppose that we have collected enough samples to construct the system of linear equations $\boldsymbol{Bz} = \boldsymbol{u}' \bmod \frac{q}{2}$, where $\boldsymbol{z}$ contains $\lfloor \frac{N}{2} \rfloor$ variables. From Theorem 1, we know that with overwhelming probability, selecting $\lfloor \frac{N}{2} \rfloor + 4$ samples ensures that the coefficient matrix $\boldsymbol{B}$ is of full rank. As a result, we can uniquely recover the solution $(px_1 + f_1' + f_{N-1}', \cdots, px_{\lfloor \frac{N}{2} \rfloor} + f'_{\lfloor \frac{N}{2} \rfloor} + f'_{N-\lfloor \frac{N}{2} \rfloor}) \bmod \frac{q}{2}$ by choosing $\lfloor \frac{N}{2} \rfloor + 4$ samples.

Note that for $\boldsymbol{F} \in \mathcal{T}_{(d_f,d_f)}$, $\phi(\boldsymbol{F} * \overline{\boldsymbol{F}})$ has one term x_0 of size $2d_f$, while the other terms are of size $\mathcal{O}(\|\phi(\boldsymbol{F})\|_2)$ as discussed in Sect. 5.1 of [12]. For $1 \le i \le \lfloor \frac{N}{2} \rfloor$, we have $x_i \approx \sqrt{2d_f}$, and $f_i' \in \{0, 1, -1\}$. Therefore, we know that $|px_i + f_i' + f_{N-i}'| \approx p\sqrt{2d_f} + 2$, $1 \le i \le \lfloor \frac{N}{2} \rfloor$. Based on the parameter selection strategy of NTRU, such as $2d_f = (2/3)N$ in NTRUEncrypt [7], it can be verified that $|px_i + f_i' + f_{N-i}'| \approx p\sqrt{2d_f} + 2 < q/4$. Thus we can finally recover the value of $(px_1 + f_1' + f_{N-1}', \cdots, px_{\lfloor \frac{N}{2} \rfloor} + f'_{\lfloor \frac{N}{2} \rfloor} + f'_{N-\lfloor \frac{N}{2} \rfloor})$.

3.3 Recovering the Value of $\phi(\boldsymbol{f} * \overline{\boldsymbol{f}})$

In this section, we will explain that if we can recover the unique solution $(px_1 + f_1' + f_{N-1}', \cdots, px_{\lfloor \frac{N}{2} \rfloor} + f'_{\lfloor \frac{N}{2} \rfloor} + f'_{N-\lfloor \frac{N}{2} \rfloor})$ of the above system of linear equations, we can further recover $\phi(\boldsymbol{f} * \overline{\boldsymbol{f}})$.

Theorem 3. *Let* $\boldsymbol{z} = (z_1, \cdots, z_{\lfloor \frac{N}{2} \rfloor}) = (px_1 + f_1' + f_{N-1}', \cdots, px_{\lfloor \frac{N}{2} \rfloor} + f'_{\lfloor \frac{N}{2} \rfloor} + f'_{N-\lfloor \frac{N}{2} \rfloor})$, *the value of* $\boldsymbol{z}$ *is related to* $\phi(\boldsymbol{f} * \overline{\boldsymbol{f}})$ *by the following relation:*

$$p \cdot z_i = \phi(\boldsymbol{f} * \overline{\boldsymbol{f}})_i = \phi(\boldsymbol{f} * \overline{\boldsymbol{f}})_{N-i}, i = 1, 2, \cdots, \lfloor \frac{N}{2} \rfloor.$$

Proof. Let $\phi(\boldsymbol{f}) = (\lambda_0, \lambda_1, \cdots, \lambda_{N-1})^\top$, and according to $\boldsymbol{f} = 1 + p * \boldsymbol{F}, \phi(\boldsymbol{F}) = (f_0', f_1', \cdots, f_{N-1}')^\top$, we have $\lambda_0 = 1 + pf_0'$, $\lambda_1 = pf_1'$, $\lambda_2 = pf_2'$, $\cdots$, $\lambda_{N-1} = pf_{N-1}'$.
From the definition, when $1 \le i \le \lfloor \frac{N}{2} \rfloor$, we obtain:

$$\begin{aligned}
\lambda_i \lambda_0 &= p^2 f_i' f_0' + pf_i' \\
\lambda_{1+i} \lambda_1 &= p^2 f_{1+i}' f_1' \\
\lambda_{2+i} \lambda_2 &= p^2 f_{2+i}' f_2' \\
\lambda_{3+i} \lambda_3 &= p^2 f_{3+i}' f_3' \\
&\cdots \\
\lambda_{j+i} \lambda_j = \lambda_0 \lambda_j &= p^2 f_0' f_j' + pf_j', \quad j = N - i \\
\lambda_{j+1+i} \lambda_{j+1} = \lambda_1 \lambda_{j+1} &= p^2 f_1' f_{j+1}' \\
&\cdots \\
\lambda_{N-1+i} \lambda_{N-1} = \lambda_{i-1} \lambda_{N-1} &= p^2 f_{i-1}' f_{N-1}'
\end{aligned}$$

Summing these equations gives:

$$\begin{aligned}&\lambda_i\lambda_0 + \lambda_{1+i}\lambda_1 + \cdots + \lambda_0\lambda_j + \lambda_1\lambda_{j+1} + \cdots + \lambda_{i-1}\lambda_{N-1}\\ &= p^2(f'_i f'_0 + f'_{i+1}f'_1 + \cdots + f'_{i-1}f'_{N-1}) + p(f'_j + f'_i)\\ &= p(px_i + f'_i + f'_{N-i})\end{aligned}$$

Since $z_i = px_i + f'_i + f'_{N-i}$ and $\phi(\boldsymbol{f} * \overline{\boldsymbol{f}})_i = \lambda_0\lambda_i + \lambda_1\lambda_{i+1} + \cdots + \lambda_{N-1}\lambda_{i-1}$, we have $\phi(\boldsymbol{f} * \overline{\boldsymbol{f}})_i = p \cdot z_i$, for $1 \le i \le \lfloor \frac{N}{2} \rfloor$. On the other hand, for $1 \le i \le \lfloor \frac{N}{2} \rfloor$, we have $\phi(\boldsymbol{f} * \overline{\boldsymbol{f}})_i = \phi(\boldsymbol{f} * \overline{\boldsymbol{f}})_{N-i}$.

From the above theorem, we can recover $\phi(\boldsymbol{f} * \overline{\boldsymbol{f}})_i$, for $i = 1, \cdots, N-1$. The only remaining value to determine is $\phi(\boldsymbol{f} * \overline{\boldsymbol{f}})_0$, which is $\lambda_0^2 + \lambda_1^2 + \cdots + \lambda_{N-1}^2$. Given $\boldsymbol{f} = 1 + p * \boldsymbol{F}$ and $\boldsymbol{F} \in \mathcal{T}_{(d_f, d_f)}$, we can establish the following relation.

- If $f'_0 = 0$, we have $\lambda_0 = 1$, $\lambda_0^2 + \lambda_1^2 + \cdots + \lambda_{N-1}^2 = 2d_f p^2 + 1$.
- If $f'_0 = 1$, we have $\lambda_0 = p + 1$, $\lambda_0^2 + \lambda_1^2 + \cdots + \lambda_{N-1}^2 = 2d_f p^2 + 2p + 1$.
- If $f'_0 = -1$, we have $\lambda_0 = -p + 1$, $\lambda_0^2 + \lambda_1^2 + \cdots + \lambda_{N-1}^2 = 2d_f p^2 - 2p + 1$.

Therefore, when we guess the value of f'_0, we can determine the value of $\phi(\boldsymbol{f} * \overline{\boldsymbol{f}})_0$ and the solution $(px_1 + f'_1 + f'_{N-1}, \cdots, px_{\lfloor \frac{N}{2} \rfloor} + f'_{\lfloor \frac{N}{2} \rfloor} + f'_{N-\lfloor \frac{N}{2} \rfloor})$. By combining these two parts, we can ultimately recover the original $\phi(\boldsymbol{f} * \overline{\boldsymbol{f}})$. Once $\boldsymbol{f} * \overline{\boldsymbol{f}}$ has been successfully recovered, we can use the GS algorithm to determine the exact value of $\boldsymbol{f}$.

Remark 2. In NTRU-HPS, it also mentioned to use $\boldsymbol{f} = 1 + p * \boldsymbol{F}$, where $\boldsymbol{F}$ is a random ternary polynomial and the Hamming weight is unknown. In order to successfully utilize our method, it is necessary to guess the values of x_0 and f'_0 first.

4 Key Recovery Attack Against NTRUReEncrypt

In this section, we introduce a key recovery attack on the proxy re-encryption scheme for NTRU, which primarily exploits the conclusions from the previous section. Before that, we will first introduce this scheme.

In [21], Nuñez et al. proposed a proxy re-encryption scheme NTRUReEncrypt based on NTRU. Below, we describe the single-hop re-encryption process between the delegator, Alice, and the delegatee, Bob. In this process, the proxy assists in transforming the ciphertext generated by Alice into a new ciphertext for the delegatee, Bob.

- **KeyGen**($\boldsymbol{1}^\kappa$): Given the security parameter κ, output the public and private key pair $(\boldsymbol{sk}_A, \boldsymbol{pk}_A)$, where $\boldsymbol{sk}_A = (\boldsymbol{f}_A, \boldsymbol{g}_A)$ and $\boldsymbol{pk}_A = \boldsymbol{h}_A = p * \boldsymbol{g}_A * \boldsymbol{f}_A^{-1} \bmod q$.
- **ReKeyGen**($\boldsymbol{sk}_A, \boldsymbol{sk}_B$): Given the private keys $\boldsymbol{sk}_A$ and $\boldsymbol{sk}_B$ of the communication parties, compute and output the re-encryption key $\boldsymbol{rk}_{A\to B} = \boldsymbol{f}_A * \boldsymbol{f}_B^{-1} \bmod q$.

- $\mathbf{Enc}(\boldsymbol{pk_A}, \boldsymbol{m})$: Given Alice's public key $\boldsymbol{pk_A}$ and the plaintext message $\boldsymbol{m}$, randomly select a disturbance polynomial $\boldsymbol{r} \in \mathcal{T}_{(d_r,d_r)}$, compute and output the ciphertext $\boldsymbol{c_A} = \boldsymbol{h_A} * \boldsymbol{r} + \boldsymbol{m} \bmod q$.
- $\mathbf{ReEnc}(\boldsymbol{rk_{A\to B}}, \boldsymbol{c_A})$: Given the re-encryption key $\boldsymbol{rk_{A\to B}}$ and the ciphertext $\boldsymbol{c_A}$, randomly select a disturbance polynomial $\boldsymbol{e} \in \mathcal{T}_{(d_r,d_r)}$, compute and output the ciphertext $\boldsymbol{c_B} = \boldsymbol{c_A} * \boldsymbol{rk_{A\to B}} + p * \boldsymbol{e} \bmod q$.
- $\mathbf{Dec}(\boldsymbol{sk_B}, \boldsymbol{c_B})$: Given Bob's private key $\boldsymbol{sk_B}$ and the re-encrypted ciphertext $\boldsymbol{c_B}$, compute and output the plaintext $\boldsymbol{m} = \boldsymbol{c_B} * \boldsymbol{f_B} \bmod q \bmod p$.

Note that the private key $\boldsymbol{f_A}(\boldsymbol{f_B})$ has to be congruent to 1 modulo p, not for efficiency, but because it is essential for decrypting re-encrypted ciphertexts accurately. Therefore, according to the proxy re-encryption key generation algorithm, it is natural to adapt the attack framework for NTRU with multiple keys to NTRUReEncrypt, where $\boldsymbol{f} = 1 + p * \boldsymbol{F}$ with $\boldsymbol{F} \in \mathcal{T}_{(d_f,f_f)}$. For the proxy, the process of key recovery is as below:

1. for each re-encryption key $\boldsymbol{rk_{1\to i}}$ between user 1 and user i, compute $\boldsymbol{rk_{1\to i}^{-1}} * \boldsymbol{h_i} \bmod q$ and denote it by $\tilde{\boldsymbol{h}}_i$. We have $\tilde{\boldsymbol{h}}_i = p * \boldsymbol{g_i} * \boldsymbol{f_1}^{-1} \bmod q$.
2. collect enough $\tilde{\boldsymbol{h}}_i$, we can use the equation $\tilde{\boldsymbol{h}}_i * \boldsymbol{f_1} = p * \boldsymbol{g_i} \bmod q$ to recover $\boldsymbol{f_1}$, where $\boldsymbol{g_i}$ is a ternary polynomial with a fixed Hamming weight.
3. compute $\boldsymbol{rk_{1\to i}^{-1}} * \boldsymbol{f_1} \bmod q$ to obtain $\boldsymbol{f_i}$.

Hence, when the proxy accumulates a sufficient number of re-encryption keys between user 1 and other users, it can initially reconstruct $\boldsymbol{f_1}$ using the approach outlined in Sect. 3, followed by the recovery of the private keys of the remaining users.

Remark 3. The NTRUReEncrypt has the characteristic of multi-hop, which means that the message $\boldsymbol{m}$ is encrypted, then re-encrypted by one or more intermediate parties before reaching the final recipient. To be more precise, suppose we have a certain amount of users, labeled $1, 2, \cdots$, in the re-encryption chain, excluding the proxy, the ciphertext $\boldsymbol{ct_i}$ of the user i is generated as:

$$\boldsymbol{ReEnc}(\boldsymbol{rk_{i-1\to i}}, \boldsymbol{ReEnc}(\boldsymbol{rk_{i-2\to i-1}}, \boldsymbol{ReEnc}(\cdots, \boldsymbol{ReEnc}(\boldsymbol{rk_{1\to 2}}, \boldsymbol{ct_1})))),$$

where $\boldsymbol{rk_{j\to j+1}}$ represents the re-encryption key between two users j and $j+1$ generated by $\boldsymbol{RekeyGen}(\boldsymbol{sk_j}, \boldsymbol{sk_{j+1}})$, with $\boldsymbol{sk_j}$ and $\boldsymbol{sk_{j+1}}$ are the private keys of j, $j+1$, respectively, generated by the $\boldsymbol{KeyGen}(1^\kappa)$. Additionally, $\boldsymbol{ct_1} = \boldsymbol{Enc}(\boldsymbol{pk_1}, \boldsymbol{m})$ is the ciphertext corresponding to the message $\boldsymbol{m}$, generated by the first user using its public key $\boldsymbol{pk_1}$. It can be seen that the ciphertext $\boldsymbol{ct_i}$ can be transformed into a new ciphertext $\boldsymbol{ct_{i+1}}$ with the help of the proxy's re-encrypted key $\boldsymbol{rk_{i\to i+1}}$ for each hop. Therefore, for every user i in the re-encryption chain, it applies the decryption algorithm $\boldsymbol{Dec}(\boldsymbol{sk_i}, \boldsymbol{ct_i})$ to recover the original message $\boldsymbol{m}$.

Based on the property of multi-hop, the proxy can collect re-encryption keys in a different way. He can first compute

$$\boldsymbol{h_i} * \boldsymbol{rk_{1\to 2}}^{-1} * \boldsymbol{rk_{2\to 3}}^{-1} * \cdots * \boldsymbol{rk_{i-1\to i}}^{-1} \bmod q,$$

which is equal to $p * \boldsymbol{g_i} * \boldsymbol{f_1}^{-1} \bmod q$. Then he can use the method in step 2–3 to finish the key recovery of $\boldsymbol{f_1}, \boldsymbol{f_2}, \ldots..$

It is important to note that the number of hops determines the number of samples that can be collected. However, increasing the number of hops also raises the probability of decryption failure for re-encrypted ciphertext. Therefore, our results suggest that the selection of parameters for the actual scheme should consider both of these factors.

5 Experimental Results

In this section, we present the detailed experimental results for our attacks against NTRU and NTRUReEncrypt under the condition $\boldsymbol{f} = 1 + p * \boldsymbol{F}, \boldsymbol{F} \in \mathcal{T}_{(d_f, d_f)}$, and $p = 3$. All experiments were implemented on a Windows 11 system using SageMath 9.3, with hardware configuration of an AMD Ryzen 7 6800H processor (equipped with a Radeon graphics card, clocked at 3.20 GHz) and 16 GB of memory.

To verify our ideas, we utilize the parameters of NTRUEncrypt. Additionally, we incorporate the parameters of NTRU-HPS, setting $\boldsymbol{f} = 1+p*\boldsymbol{F}$ and $d_f = d_g$ Table 1.

Table 1. Parameter Settings for Sampling $\boldsymbol{f}$

Paramemter Set	N	p	q	$d_f = d_g$
ntru-hps2048509	509	3	2048	127
ntru-hps2048677	677	3	2048	127
ntru-hps4096821	821	3	4096	255
ntru-443	443	3	2048	143
ntru-743	743	3	2048	247

For each parameter set, we conducted 100 experiments to solve the system of linear equations and recover the value of $\phi(\boldsymbol{f} * \overline{\boldsymbol{f}})$. We evaluated the algorithm's average execution time and success ratio. Table 2 presents the experimental results for the key recovery attack on NTRU with multiple keys under the condition $\boldsymbol{f} = 1 + p * \boldsymbol{F}$, while Table 3 presents the experimental results applied to the NTRUReEncrypt scheme.

Based on the experimental results, the success rate of our algorithm is observed to be close to 100%, which strongly demonstrates the effectiveness of our method.

Table 2. Experimental Results for NTRU Attack with $\boldsymbol{f} = 1 + p * \boldsymbol{F}$

Paramemter Set	N	p	q	Time	Success Ratio
ntru-hps2048509	509	3	2048	19.71 s	99/100
ntru-hps2048677	677	3	2048	46.37 s	98/100
ntru-hps4096821	821	3	4096	84.32 s	96/100
ntru-443	443	3	2048	14.07 s	98/100
ntru-743	743	3	2048	64.67 s	99/100

Table 3. Experimental Results for NTRUReEncrypt Attack with $\boldsymbol{f} = 1 + p * \boldsymbol{F}$

Paramemter Set	N	p	q	Time	Success Ratio
ntru-hps2048509	509	3	2048	20.68 s	97/100
ntru-hps2048677	677	3	2048	46.96 s	97/100
ntru-hps4096821	821	3	4096	86.32 s	96/100
ntru-443	443	3	2048	13.92 s	99/100
ntru-743	743	3	2048	61.31 s	98/100

6 Conclusion

In this paper, we propose a polynomial time key recovery attack for NTRU with multiple keys, under the condition that $\boldsymbol{f} = 1 + p * \boldsymbol{F}, \boldsymbol{F} \in \mathcal{T}_{(d_f, d_f)}$, and $p = 3$. By using linearization techniques and correlations between coefficients, we can construct a system of linear equations with only $\lfloor \frac{N}{2} \rfloor$ unknowns. By collecting $\lfloor \frac{N}{2} \rfloor + 4$ equations, we ensure that there is a unique solution. Furthermore, the size of this unique solution is $1/p$ of $\phi(\boldsymbol{f} * \overline{\boldsymbol{f}})$. We can use this unique solution to obtain the desired $\phi(\boldsymbol{f} * \overline{\boldsymbol{f}})$, and ultimately recover $\boldsymbol{f}$. In addition, we also extend this attack to the NTRUReEncrypt scheme to reveal its potential security risks.

Our attack ultimately relies on the GS algorithm to fully recover the private key. Therefore, how to efficiently construct equations with fewer unknowns and solve them directly, without relying on the GS algorithm, remains an open problem worth further investigation.

Acknowledgments. The authors would like to thank the anonymous reviewers for their valuable comments to improve the quality of this paper. This work was supported by the National Natural Science Foundation of China (No. 12201193, No. 12201637), the Innovation Group Project of the Natural Science Foundation of Hubei Province of China (No. 2023AFA021), and the China Postdoctoral Science Foundation (No. 2025M771675).

References

1. Albrecht, M.R., Cocis, C., Laguillaumie, F., Langlois, A.: Implementing candidate graded encoding schemes from ideal lattices. In: International Conference on the Theory and Application of Cryptology and Information Security, pp. 752–775. Springer (2015)
2. ANSI, X.: 98: lattice-based polynomial public key establishment algorithm for the financial services industry. Tech. rep., Technical report, ANSI (2010)
3. Bai, S., Jangir, H., Ngo, T., Youmans, W.: An algebraic algorithm for breaking NTRU with multiple keys, pp. 1–24. Designs, Codes and Cryptography pp (2024)
4. Bernstein, D.J., Chuengsatiansup, C., Lange, T., Van Vredendaal, C.: NTRU prime: reducing attack surface at low cost. In: Selected Areas in Cryptography–SAC 2017: 24th International Conference, Ottawa, ON, Canada, August 16-18, 2017, Revised Selected Papers 24, pp. 235–260. Springer (2018)
5. Bos, J.W., Lauter, K., Loftus, J., Naehrig, M.: Improved security for a ring-based fully homomorphic encryption scheme. In: Cryptography and Coding: 14th IMA International Conference, IMACC 2013, Oxford, UK, December 17-19, 2013. Proceedings 14, pp. 45–64. Springer (2013)
6. Chen, C., et al.: Algorithm specifications and supporting documentation. Brown University and Onboard security company, Wilmington USA (2019). https://csrc.nist.gov/Projects/post-quantum-cryptography/post-quantum-cryptography-standardization/round-3-submissions
7. Chen, C., Hoffstein, J., Whyte, W., Zhang, Z.: Ntruencrypt: a lattice based encryption algorithm. In: Proc. NIST CSRC Post Quant. Cryptography (Round Submissions), pp. 1–9 (2017). https://csrc.nist.gov/Projects/post-quantum-cryptography/post-quantum-cryptography-standardization/round-1-submissions
8. Ding, J., Pan, Y., Deng, Y.: An Algebraic Broadcast Attack against NTRU. In: Susilo, W., Mu, Y., Seberry, J. (eds.) ACISP 2012. LNCS, vol. 7372, pp. 124–137. Springer, Heidelberg (2012). https://doi.org/10.1007/978-3-642-31448-3_10
9. Gentry, C., Szydlo, M.: Cryptanalysis of the Revised NTRU Signature Scheme. In: Knudsen, L.R. (ed.) EUROCRYPT 2002. LNCS, vol. 2332, pp. 299–320. Springer, Heidelberg (2002). https://doi.org/10.1007/3-540-46035-7_20
10. Hoffstein, J.: Ntru: A ring based public key cryptosystem. Algorithmic Number Theory (ANTS III) (1998)
11. Hoffstein, J., Silverman, J.H.: Optimizations for NTRU. In: Proceedings the Conference on Public Key Cryptography and Computational Number Theory, Warsaw, pp. 77–88 (2000)
12. Howgrave-Graham, N., et al.: The impact of decryption failures on the security of NTRU encryption. In: Annual International Cryptology Conference, pp. 226–246. Springer (2003)
13. Howgrave-Graham, N., Silverman, J.H., Whyte, W.: Choosing parameter sets for ntruencrypt with naep and sves-3. In: Cryptographers' Track at the RSA Conference, pp. 118–135. Springer (2005)
14. Hülsing, A., Rijneveld, J., Schanck, J., Schwabe, P.: High-speed key encapsulation from NTRU. In: International Conference on Cryptographic Hardware and Embedded Systems, pp. 232–252. Springer (2017)
15. Kim, J., Lee, C.: A polynomial time algorithm for breaking NTRU encryption with multiple keys. Des. Codes Crypt. **91**(8), 2779–2789 (2023)
16. Kra, I., Simanca, S.R.: On circulant matrices. Notices of the AMS **59**(3), 368–377 (2012)

17. Li, J., Pan, Y., Liu, M., Zhu, G.: An efficient broadcast attack against NTRU. In: Proceedings of the 7th ACM Symposium on Information, Computer and Communications Security, pp. 22–23 (2012)
18. Liu, Z., Pan, Y., Zhang, Z.: Cryptanalysis of an NTRU-based proxy encryption scheme from asiaccs'15. In: Post-Quantum Cryptography: 10th International Conference, PQCrypto 2019, Chongqing, China, May 8–10, 2019 Revised Selected Papers 10, pp. 153–166. Springer (2019)
19. Liu, Z., Pan, Y., Zheng, J.: Polynomial-time key-recovery attacks against ntrureencrypt from asiaccs'15. J. Syst. Sci. Complexity **37**(3), 1308–1325 (2024)
20. Liu, Z., Vishakha, Ding, J., Cheng, C., Pan, Y.: An improved practical key mismatch attack against NTRU. In: International Conference on Post-Quantum Cryptography, pp. 322–342. Springer (2024)
21. Nuñez, D., Agudo, I., Lopez, J.: Ntrureencrypt: an efficient proxy re-encryption scheme based on NTRU. In: Proceedings of the 10th ACM symposium on information, computer and communications security, pp. 179–189 (2015)
22. P1363.1TMD, I.: IEEE p1363.1 draft 10: draft standard for public key cryptographic techniques based on hard problems over lattices. IACR Cryptol. ePrint Arch. **2008**, 361 (2008). https://api.semanticscholar.org/CorpusID:7040165
23. Pellet-Mary, A., Stehlé, D.: On the Hardness of the NTRU Problem. In: Tibouchi, M., Wang, H. (eds.) ASIACRYPT 2021. LNCS, vol. 13090, pp. 3–35. Springer, Cham (2021). https://doi.org/10.1007/978-3-030-92062-3_1
24. Song, Z., Xu, J., Li, Z., Ye, D.: An efficient key recovery attack against ntrureencrypt from asiaccs 2015. In: International Conference on Cryptology in India, pp. 644–657. Springer (2022)
25. Song, Z., Xu, J., Xiang, B., Li, W., Ye, D.: New result for breaking NTRU encryption with multiple keys in polynomial time. In: International Conference on Information and Communications Security, pp. 25–39. Springer (2024)
26. Zhang, X., Cheng, C., Ding, R.: Small leaks sink a great ship: an evaluation of key reuse resilience of PQC third round finalist NTRU-HRSS. In: Information and Communications Security: 23rd International Conference, ICICS 2021, Chongqing, China, November 19-21, 2021, Proceedings, Part II 23, pp. 283–300. Springer (2021)

Strong Designated Verifier Signatures from Isogeny Assumptions

Xuan Thanh Khuc[1(✉)], Willy Susilo[1], Dung Hoang Duong[1], Yannan Li[1], Partha Sarathi Roy[1], Kazuhide Fukushima[2], and Shinsaku Kiyomoto[2]

[1] Institute of Cybersecurity and Cryptology, School of Computing and Information Technology, University of Wollongong, Wollongong, Australia
{xtkhuc,wsusilo,hduong,yannan,partha}@uow.edu.au

[2] Advanced Technology Laboratories, KDDI Research, Inc., Fujimino, Japan
{ka-fukushima,sh-kiyomoto}@kddi.com

Abstract. Designated verifier signatures (DVS) enable a signer to create a signature that only a specific verifier can authenticate, thereby ensuring both message authenticity and signer privacy. Strong designated verifier signatures (SDVS) further enhance the security of the signer's identity. In particular, they guarantee that it is computationally infeasible for any third party, even those possessing the secret keys of the signer or the designated verifier, to determine the public key under which the signature was produced. In this paper, we introduce a novel construction of a strong designated verifier signature scheme based on isogeny assumptions. Our scheme leverages the computational difficulty of finding isogenies between supersingular elliptic curves, a problem believed to be resistant to quantum attacks. Our construction achieves strong off-the-record security, unforgeability, and privacy of the signer's identity in the random oracle model. Furthermore, we employ optimized techniques to substantially reduce key sizes without compromising signature compactness. The resulting public keys are only 16 kB, and the secret keys are 128 bits, while a signature achieving 128-bit classical security is 862 bytes, which is smaller than those in lattice-based or code-based SDVS proposals.

Keywords: Digital Signatures · Isogeny-Based Cryptography · Strong Off-the-Record · Privacy of the Signer's Identity

1 Introduction

In the field of cryptography, digital signatures serve as essential tools for ensuring authenticity, integrity, and non-repudiation in digital communications. Traditional digital signature schemes allow any verifiers to confirm the validity of a

This work is partially supported by the ARC Linkage Project LP220100332. Willy Susilo is supported by the ARC Australian Laureate Fellowship FL230100033.
Yannan Li is supported by the ARC Discovery Early Career Researcher Award DE230100001.

Y. Kim et al. (Eds.): CANS 2025, LNCS 16351, pp. 46–69, 2026.
https://doi.org/10.1007/978-981-95-4434-9_3

signature using the signer's public key. This feature benefits public verifiability, while it is inadequate in scenarios where confidentiality is paramount.

Designated Verifier Signatures (DVS) [24] were introduced to address the need for selective verification. In a DVS scheme, a signer can generate a signature that only a designated verifier is able to authenticate. This guarantees message authenticity for the designated verifier while preventing any third party from verifying the signature or being convinced of its validity. Building upon this foundation, Strong Designated Verifier Signatures (SDVS) [24,30] enhance the privacy guarantees of DVS by ensuring that, even if an adversary corrupts the secret keys of all potential signers, they still cannot determine which public key was used to generate the signature.

The unique structure of strong designated verifier signatures (SDVS) distinguishes them from other cryptographic signature schemes. Unlike traditional digital signatures, which allow any party to verify the authenticity of a signature, SDVS limits this capability to a specific verifier, thereby preserving confidentiality. In comparison, ring signatures provide anonymity for the signer within a group, but they do not offer strong protections for off the record communication. SDVS allows the designated verifier to validate the signature without being able to convince others of its validity. Similarly, group signatures offer anonymity within a group and support identity tracing by a group manager, but they still permit third-party verification, which makes them less suitable for scenarios where privacy is a primary concern.

In the realm of confidential communications, SDVS enables a sender to authenticate messages privately, ensuring that only the intended recipient can verify the signature. This capability is particularly valuable in sensitive diplomatic or business exchanges. In secure authentication protocols, SDVS allows users to authenticate themselves to a server without exposing their credentials to intermediaries, thereby enhancing both privacy and security. Additionally, SDVS proves valuable in digital rights management, where content providers can distribute digital content that only authorized users can access, thus preventing unauthorized redistribution and verifying the legitimacy of access.

As quantum computing advances, many classical cryptographic schemes based on problems like integer factorization and discrete logarithms are becoming vulnerable to quantum attacks [38]. This vulnerability has prompted the development of post-quantum cryptography, which aims to create cryptographic systems that are secure against quantum adversaries. Within this domain, isogeny-based cryptography emerges as a promising area. It relies on the computational difficulty of determining isogenies between elliptic curves. An isogeny is a morphism between elliptic curves that preserves the group structure, and finding such isogenies is believed to be computationally hard even for quantum computers.

A well-known example is the Supersingular Isogeny Diffie–Hellman (SIDH) protocol [26], a key exchange scheme based on a relaxed isogeny assumption. However, recent advances in polynomial-time attacks [10,31,34] have completely broken SIDH, thereby undermining the security of several cryptosystems built upon it [19,42]. Despite these developments, the core hardness of the general isogeny problem remains unbroken, and several cryptographic constructions continue to rely securely on this assumption [2,17]. A notable variant is the Commutative Supersingular Isogeny Diffie–Hellman (CSIDH) protocol, introduced by Castryck et al. [11]. Although its evaluation is limited to small generating sets, CSIDH enables the first practical, secure, and non-interactive post-quantum key exchange. While subexponential attacks have been identified [4,12,14,33], ongoing research continues to demonstrate the flexibility and competitiveness of isogeny-based cryptography. Applications span a wide range of primitives, including digital signatures [3,7,20], threshold signatures [18], (linkable) ring signatures [6], group signatures [5], blind signatures [27], and adaptor signatures [25]. Moreover, recent optimization techniques [7,13,21] have further improved the efficiency and scalability of isogeny assumptions.

Despite these advances, the design of SDVS schemes from isogeny assumptions remains largely unexplored. Prior constructions [35,39] rely on SIDH and have become insecure in light of recent attacks [10,16,31,34]. This leads to an important open question: *"Can we construct a Strong Designated Verifier Signature scheme securely from isogeny assumptions?"*

1.1 Our Contribution

We address the open problem of constructing strong designated verifier signatures (SDVS) from isogeny-based assumptions. Our main contributions are as follows:

We propose the first SDVS scheme whose security relies on the hardness of the Group Action Inverse Problem (GAIP) over supersingular elliptic curves. The core technique is an OR-proof that combines the secrets of both the signer and the designated verifier, ensuring that a valid signature can be generated by either party but is verifiable only by the designated verifier.

We formally prove that our construction achieves strong unforgeability under adaptive chosen-message attacks (SU-CMA), strong off-the-record security (SOTR), and privacy of the signer's identity (PSI) in the random oracle model.

To reduce the soundness error without significantly increasing communication cost, we adopt a multi-key optimization strategy and exploit public key reuse via quadratic twists, inspired by techniques used in isogeny-based schemes.

Our SDVS construction achieves significantly reduced key sizes while maintaining compact signatures. In contrast to lattice-based approaches, which often require megabytes public and secret keys [32,41,43], our scheme employs a 128-bit secret key and a 16 kB public key for both signer and designated verifier. Although some code-based schemes achieve short signatures [37], they typically suffer from large keys. In comparison, our isogeny-based SDVS strikes a strong balance between key and signature size (See Table 1).

It is important to note that, since our scheme is instantiated with CSIDH-512, it offers approximately 128-bit classical security. However, our scheme currently achieves a lower quantum security level (approximately 64–70 bits) compared to SIS/LWE-based schemes, which offer around 100–110 bits of quantum security.

Table 1. Comparison of our SDVS with other schemes.

SDVS Schemes	Hardness Assumption	Signer Key Size		Designated Verifier Key Size		Signature Size
		Secret Key	Public Key	Secret Key	Public Key	
Zhang et al. [43]	SIS[c], LWE[d]	819 kB	120.5 MB	329.2 MB	67.9 GB	643 kB
Wang et al. [41]	SIS[b], LWE[c]	561.9 MB	8.02 MB	561.9 MB	8.02 MiB	65.1 MiB
Noh et al. [32]	SIS[b], LWE[c]	52 MB	1.35 MB	52 MB	1.35 MB	130 kB
Shooshtari et al. [37]	SD[d]	175 MB	165 MB	175 MB	165 MB	950 B
Cai et al. [9]	RSIS[c]	400 kB	800 kB	3.1 MB	6.25 MB	6.45 kB
Our Scheme	GAIP[a]	0.016 kB	16 kB	0.016 kB	16 kB	862 B

[a] GAIP: Group Action Inverse Problem.
[b] SIS: Short Integer Solution, RSIS: Ring Short Integer Solution.
[c] LWE: Learning with Errors.
[d] SD: Syndrome Decoding.

1.2 Technical Overview

In this section, we provide a detailed explanation of our constructions. We begin by reviewing the basic version of the isogeny-based signature scheme CSI-FiSh [7] and discuss its shortcomings in meeting the requirements for a strong designated verifier signature when directly applied to the isogeny setting. Subsequently, we present our SDVS construction, which employs an OR relation.

Consider a group action defined as $\star : G \times \mathcal{E} \rightarrow \mathcal{E}$, where G is an ideal class group and $\mathcal{E}$ is a set of elliptic curves. We assume that the structure of G is known and can be expressed as $G = \langle [\mathfrak{g}] \rangle \cong \mathbb{Z}_N$ for some $N \in \mathbb{N}$, where $\mathfrak{g}$ is the generator. The signer samples $a \leftarrow\!\!\$\, \mathbb{Z}_N$, computes $A^1 = [\mathfrak{g}^a] \star E_0$, and sets the secret key $\mathsf{ssk} = a$ and public key $\mathsf{spk} = (A^1, A^0 = E_0)$. Next, the signer samples $y \leftarrow\!\!\$\, \mathbb{Z}_N$ and computes $Y = [\mathfrak{g}^y] \star E_0$. The signer then computes $c = \mathsf{H}(Y \| \mathsf{m}) \in \{0, 1\}$ and computes $r = y - a \cdot c$. The signature on message m is $\sigma = (r, c)$. To verify the signature σ, the verifier computes $Y' = [\mathfrak{g}^r] \star A^c$ and checks whether $c \stackrel{?}{=} \mathsf{H}(Y' \| \mathsf{m})$. The correctness of this scheme can be verified as follows. If $c = 0$, then $r = y$, and we have $Y' = [\mathfrak{g}^y] \star E_0 = Y$. If $c = 1$, then $r = y - a$, and $Y' = [\mathfrak{g}^{y-a}] \star A^1 = [\mathfrak{g}^{y-a}] \star [\mathfrak{g}^a] \star E_0 = Y$. However, this scheme does not satisfy the *designated verifier* property, since anyone can verify the signature σ using the signer's public key.

To address the aforementioned issue, we adopt a fundamentally different approach by employing an OR relation and shared value to construct an SDVS. An OR relation enables a prover to demonstrate knowledge of at least one secret among multiple statements without revealing exactly which secret is known. In the context of SDVS, using an OR relation allows the signer to create a signature that could have been produced either by the signer or by the designated verifier, thereby ensuring the designated verifier property.

In our setting, the designated verifier has a pair of public and secret keys similar to the signer. Denote the signer's key pair as $(\mathsf{ssk}, \mathsf{spk}) = (a_0, (A_0^1, A_0^0))$, where $A_0^1 = [\mathfrak{g}^{a_0}] \star E_0$ and $A_0^0 = E_0$. The designated verifier's keys are $(\mathsf{vsk}, \mathsf{vpk}) = (a_1, (A_1^1, A_1^0))$, where $A_1^1 = [\mathfrak{g}^{a_1}] \star E_0$ and $A_1^0 = E_0$, with $a_0, a_1 \leftarrow\!\!\$\, \mathbb{Z}_N$. To sign a message m, the signer samples $y_0 \leftarrow\!\!\$\, \mathbb{Z}_N$ and computes $Y_0 = [\mathfrak{g}^{y_0}] \star E_0$. Then, the signer samples $c_1 \leftarrow_{\$} \{0,1\}$, $r_1 \leftarrow_{\$} \mathbb{Z}_N$, and computes $Y_1 = [\mathfrak{g}^{r_1}] \star A_1^{c_1}$. The signer also computes a shared value K using the secret key a_0 and the designated verifier's public key, i.e., $\mathsf{K} = \mathsf{H}'([\mathfrak{g}^{a_0}] \star A_1^1) \in \{0,1\}^\lambda$. Next, the signer computes $c = \mathsf{H}(Y_0 \| Y_1 | \mathsf{K} \| \mathsf{m})$ and sets $c_0 = c \oplus c_1$. The signer then computes $r_0 = y_0 - a_0 \cdot c_0$. Finally, the signer returns the signature $\sigma = (c_0, c_1, r_0, r_1)$.

To verify the signature, the designated verifier computes $Y_0' = [\mathfrak{g}^{r_0}] \star A_0^{c_0}$ and $Y_1' = [\mathfrak{g}^{r_1}] \star A_1^{c_1}$. The shared value K' is computed as $\mathsf{K}' = \mathsf{H}'([\mathfrak{g}^{a_1}] \star A_0^1)$. Since $[\mathfrak{g}^{a_1}] \star A_0^1 = [\mathfrak{g}^{a_0+a_1}] \star E_0 = [\mathfrak{g}^{a_0}] \star A_1^1$, the verifier can compute $\mathsf{K}' = \mathsf{K}$. The verifier then computes $c' = \mathsf{H}(Y_0' \| Y_1' \| \mathsf{K}' \| \mathsf{m})$ and checks whether $c_0 \oplus c_1 \stackrel{?}{=} c'$. Thus, only the designated verifier, who can recover K, can verify the signature.

To simulate a signature, the designated verifier uses their secret key a_1 to produce a signature indistinguishable from one generated by the signer. The designated verifier samples $y_1 \leftarrow_{\$} \mathbb{Z}_N$ and computes $Y_1 = [\mathfrak{g}^{y_1}] \star E_0$. They choose a random $c_0 \leftarrow_{\$} \{0,1\}$ and $r_0 \leftarrow_{\$} \mathbb{Z}_N$, and compute $Y_0 = [\mathfrak{g}^{r_0}] \star A_0^{c_0}$. The shared value K is computed as before: $\mathsf{K} = \mathsf{H}'([\mathfrak{g}^{a_1}] \star A_0^1)$ The designated verifier then computes $c = \mathsf{H}(Y_0 \| Y_1 \| \mathsf{K} \| \mathsf{m})$ and sets $c_1 = c \oplus c_0$. Next, the designated verifier computes $r_1 = y_1 - a_1 \cdot c_1$. The simulated signature is $\sigma = (c_0, c_1, r_0, r_1)$. Since only the designated verifier knows a_1, they can compute r_1 appropriately. This signature is valid under the verification algorithm and is indistinguishable from one generated by the signer, ensuring the strong designated verifier property of the scheme.

Since $c \in \{0,1\}$, the soundness error is 1/2. To reduce the soundness error, we increase the challenge space. Here, we adopt the multi-public-key technique from [7] in our construction. Specifically, the signer now has S public keys instead of one. That is, the signer's public key consists of the $(S+1)$-tuple $(A_0^0 = E_0,\ A_0^1 = [\mathfrak{g}^{a_0^1}] \star E_0,\ \ldots,\ A_0^S = [\mathfrak{g}^{a_0^S}] \star E_0)$. The designated verifier also holds a tuple of $S+1$ public keys $(A_1^0 = E_0,\ A_1^1 = [\mathfrak{g}^{a_1^1}] \star E_0,\ \ldots,\ A_1^S = [\mathfrak{g}^{a_1^S}] \star E_0)$. The signer then generates a signature proving knowledge of $a \in \mathbb{Z}_N$ such that $[\mathfrak{g}^a] \star E_0 = A_1^i$ or $[\mathfrak{g}^a] \star E_0 = A_1^j$ for some $i, j \in [S]$.

To generate the signature, the signer chooses a random exponent $y_0 \leftarrow_{\$} \mathbb{Z}_N$ and computes $Y_0 = [\mathfrak{g}^{y_0}] \star E_0$. Then, it chooses $c_1 \leftarrow_{\$} \{0, \ldots, S\}$ and $r_1 \leftarrow_{\$} \mathbb{Z}_N$, and computes $Y_1 = [\mathfrak{g}^{r_1}] \star A_1^{c_1}$. Next, the shared value K is computed using all secret keys $(a_0^1, \ldots, a_0^S)$ along with the verifier's public keys, i.e., $\mathsf{K} = \mathsf{H}'\left([\mathfrak{g}^{a_0^1}] \star A_1^1 \| \ldots \| [\mathfrak{g}^{a_0^S}] \star A_1^S\right) \in \{0,1\}^{2\lambda}$. The challenge value is computed as $c = \mathsf{H}(Y_0 \| Y_1 \| \mathsf{K} \| \mathsf{m})$. The signer sets $r_0 = y_0 - a_0^{c_0}$, where $a_0^0 := 0$ and outputs the signature $\sigma = (c_0, c_1, r_0, r_1)$.

In the verification algorithm, the designated verifier computes $Y_0' = [\mathfrak{g}^{r_0}] \star A_0^{c_0}$, $Y_1' = [\mathfrak{g}^{r_1}] \star A_1^{c_1}$, and $\mathsf{K}' = \mathsf{H}'([\mathfrak{g}^{a_1^1}] \star A_0^1 \| \ldots \| [\mathfrak{g}^{a_1^S}] \star A_0^S)$. It then computes $c' = \mathsf{H}(Y_0' \| Y_1' \| \mathsf{K}' \| M)$. We see that if $c_0 = i \in [1, S]$, then $r_0 = y_0 - a_0^i$, and $Y_0' = [\mathfrak{g}^{y_0 - a_0^i}] \star A_0^i = [\mathfrak{g}^{y_0 - a_0^i}] \star ([\mathfrak{g}^{a_0^i}] \star E_0) = Y_0$. The value Y_1' is computed in the same way as Y_1, hence $Y_1' = Y_1$. Therefore, the signature is valid and will be accepted by the verification algorithm.

The designated verifier can simulate signatures in the same way as the signer. Since the challenge space now contains $S+1$ elements, the soundness error is reduced to $1/(S+1)$. To further increase the challenge space, we exploit the fact that given a curve $A = [\mathfrak{g}^a] \star E_0$ for some unknown $a \in \mathbb{Z}_N$, we can efficiently compute its quadratic twist $A^{-1} = [\mathfrak{g}^{-a}] \star E_0$. Therefore, we can almost double the set of public key curves for both the signer and the verifier, going from $A_b^0, A_b^1, \ldots, A_b^S$ to $A_b^{-S}, \ldots, A_b^0, \ldots, A_b^S$ for all $b \in \{0,1\}$, where $A_b^{-i} = [\mathfrak{g}^{-a_b^i}] \star E_0$, without increasing communication cost. With this extension, we make a small change in the computation of r_0 in the signature σ. Specifically, we set $r_0 = y_0 - \mathsf{sgn}(c_0) \cdot a_0^{|c_0|}$. For instance, if $c_0 = -i$ for some $i \in [1, S]$, then $r_0 = y_0 + a_0^i$, and $Y_0' = [\mathfrak{g}^{r_0}] \star A_0^{c_0} = [\mathfrak{g}^{y_0 + a_0^i}] \star ([\mathfrak{g}^{-a_0^i}] \star E_0) = Y_0$. Thus, the challenge space increases to $[-S, S]$, and the soundness error drops to $\frac{1}{2S+1}$.

1.3 Related Works

Classical SDVS Schemes. In 2004, Laguillaumie and Vergnaud [30] presented an SDVS scheme utilizing bilinear pairings on elliptic curves. Their construction leveraged the properties of bilinear maps to achieve efficient signature generation and verification processes. The scheme demonstrated practical efficiency with relatively small key and signature sizes compared to other classical schemes. Huang et al. [23] developed an identity-based SDVS scheme using bilinear pairings. This approach simplified key management by allowing public keys to be derived from user identities. The scheme maintained efficiency similar to other pairing-based constructions and reduced the overhead associated with key distribution. Huang et al. [22] proposed an SDVS scheme without relying on random oracles, enhancing security in the standard model. Their method also utilized bilinear pairings, achieving reasonable efficiency while providing stronger security assurances.

Post-quantum Secure SDVS Schemes. There exist SDVS schemes [35,39] based on SIDH. However, subsequent attacks in [10,31] severely undermined SIDH's security, implying that it is no longer secure. Shooshtari et al. [37] and Assidi et al. [1] presented code-based SDVS schemes based on the McEliece cryptosystem. Their methods offered post-quantum security but were characterized by large key sizes. These factors impacted the schemes' practicality, making them less suitable for applications with strict efficiency requirements. Wang et al. [41] introduced a lattice-based SDVS scheme utilizing the hardness of the LWE and SIS problems. Later, Wang et al. [40] extended their work to identity-based SDVS schemes. Zhang et al. [43] proposed further improvements. However, these schemes suffered from large key sizes and high computational complexity.

2 Background

2.1 Notation

We use $\mathbb{N}$ and $\mathbb{Z}$ to represent the sets of natural numbers and integers, respectively. The ring of integers modulo N, denoted by $\mathbb{Z}_N$, is defined with representatives in the range $[-q/2, q/2) \cap \mathbb{Z}$. For any positive integer n, we let $[n]$ represent the set $\{1, 2, \ldots, n\}$. Given a distribution X, we use $x \leftarrow_{\$} X$ to indicate that x is sampled according to X. When sampling uniformly at random from a finite set U, we write $x \leftarrow_{\$} U$. The symbol $\oplus$ denotes the component-wise XOR operation for vectors in $\mathbb{R}$, while $\|$ is used for concatenating two strings. For an element g and a vector $\mathbf{a} = (a_1, \ldots, a_n)$, we use $g^{\mathbf{a}}$ as shorthand for $(g^{a_1}, \ldots, g^{a_n})$. The symbol sgn denotes the mathematical sign of a value. For a vector $\mathbf{a} = (a_1, \ldots, a_n)$, the sign function is applied element-wise, $\mathsf{sgn}(\mathbf{a}) = (\mathsf{sgn}(a_1), \ldots, \mathsf{sgn}(a_n))$. Furthermore, if an operation $\star$ is defined between two elements g and h and vectors $\mathbf{a} = (a_1, \ldots, a_n)$ and $\mathbf{b} = (b_1, \ldots, b_n)$, we write $g^{\mathbf{a}} \star h^{\mathbf{b}}$ as shorthand for $(g^{a_1} \star h^{b_1}, \ldots, g^{a_n} \star h^{b_n})$.

2.2 Elliptic Curves and Isogenies

Let E be a supersingular elliptic curve defined over the finite field $\mathbb{F}_p$, where $p \equiv 3 \pmod 4$ is a large prime. Denote by $\mathbf{0}_E$ the point at infinity. In our setting, the curve E is supersingular if and only if $\#E(\mathbb{F}_p) = p + 1$, which holds for the curves considered in CSIDH. Supersingularity can be efficiently verified using point-counting algorithms such as the Schoof–Elkies–Atkin (SEA) algorithm [36]. A curve that does not satisfy this condition is referred to as ordinary.

Given two elliptic curves E and E', an *isogeny* $\varphi : E \to E'$ is a non-constant morphism of algebraic curves that is also a group homomorphism and satisfies $\varphi(\mathbf{0}_E) = \mathbf{0}_{E'}$. An *isomorphism* is an isogeny of degree 1; equivalently, a morphism admitting a two-sided inverse over the algebraic closure. Two curves are isomorphic over $\overline{\mathbb{F}}_p$ if and only if they share the same j-invariant. There is a bijection between finite subgroups (over $\overline{\mathbb{F}}_p$) of E *of order not divisible by* p and separable isogenies from E, up to post-composition with isomorphisms. Specifically, for any finite subgroup $S \leq E(\overline{\mathbb{F}}_p)$ with $p \nmid \#S$, there exists a separable isogeny $\varphi : E \to E'$ with kernel S, such that $E' = E/S$. If $S \subseteq E(\mathbb{F}_{p^k})$, then φ is defined over $\mathbb{F}_{p^k}$. Given S, Vélu's formulas compute both E' and φ in time polynomial in $\log p$ and linear in $\#S$. Consequently, only isogenies with small kernels are practically computable.

The endomorphism ring $\mathrm{End}(E_{\overline{\mathbb{F}}_p})$ consists of all isogenies from E to itself over the algebraic closure, and $\mathrm{End}_{\mathbb{F}_p}(E)$ denotes those defined over $\mathbb{F}_p$. When $E/\mathbb{F}_p$ is supersingular, $\mathrm{End}(E_{\overline{\mathbb{F}}_p})$ is isomorphic to a maximal order in the definite quaternion algebra $B_{p,\infty}$ ramified at p and ∞ (Deuring). By contrast, $\mathrm{End}_{\mathbb{F}_p}(E)$ is *commutative*: it is an order in the imaginary quadratic field $\mathbb{Q}(\pi_E)$ generated by the Frobenius endomorphism π_E (satisfying $\pi_E^2 - t\pi_E + p = 0$ with $t = p + 1 - \#E(\mathbb{F}_p)$), namely $\mathbb{Z}[\pi_E]$ or $\mathbb{Z}\left[\frac{1+\pi_E}{2}\right]$. Let $\mathcal{O}$ be such an (imaginary quadratic) order and consider its ideal class group $\mathcal{C}\ell(\mathcal{O})$, consisting of invertible $\mathcal{O}$-ideals modulo principal ideals. This group is finite and abelian.

Let

$$\mathcal{E} = \{\, E/\mathbb{F}_p \mid \mathrm{End}_{\mathbb{F}_p}(E) \cong \mathcal{O} \,\}$$

denote the set of supersingular elliptic curves over $\mathbb{F}_p$ with endomorphism ring isomorphic to $\mathcal{O}$. By the Deuring correspondence, $\mathcal{C}\ell(\mathcal{O})$ acts freely and transitively on $\mathcal{E}$ via $[\mathfrak{a}] \star E := E'$, where E' is obtained by applying the (ideal–) isogeny associated with the ideal $\mathfrak{a}$ to E. This action is defined only on curves with $\mathrm{End}_{\mathbb{F}_p}(E) \cong \mathcal{O}$ and not on all supersingular curves over $\mathbb{F}_p$ [7,11].

In our instantiation, we adopt the CSIDH framework [11], where $p \equiv 3 \pmod 4$ and the class group is derived from $\mathcal{O} = \mathbb{Z}[\sqrt{-p}]$ (equivalently, $\mathbb{Z}[\pi]$ with $\pi^2 = -p$). In this setting, the action is by an abelian group and is defined over $\mathbb{F}_p$, enabling efficient evaluation of $[\mathfrak{a}] \star E$ using ideals from $\mathcal{C}\ell(\mathcal{O})$.

The quadratic twist of a curve $E : y^2 = f(x)$ is $E^{(d)} : dy^2 = f(x)$, where $d \in \mathbb{F}_p^\times \setminus \mathbb{F}_p^{\times 2}$. Since $p \equiv 3 \pmod 4$, -1 is a non-square, thus, for $E_A : y^2 = x^3 + Ax^2 + x$ the (-1)-twist is $E_A^{(-1)} : -y^2 = x^3 + Ax^2 + x$. These curves are not isomorphic over $\mathbb{F}_p$; they become isomorphic over $\mathbb{F}_{p^2}$ via $(x, y) \mapsto (x, iy)$, where $i^2 = -1$. The substitution $(x, y) \mapsto (-x, y)$ transforms $E_A^{(-1)}$ into $y^2 = x^3 - Ax^2 + x$, but it is not an $\mathbb{F}_p$-isomorphism and, in odd characteristic, is not an isogeny.

For the remainder of this paper, we assume that the class group has known structure $G = \langle \mathfrak{g} \rangle \cong \mathbb{Z}_N$ for some $N \in \mathbb{N}$, as suggested by the Cohen–Lenstra heuristics. For each $i \in [N]$, the group action $[\mathfrak{g}^i] \star E$ can be efficiently evaluated [7]. Let $E_0 \in \mathcal{E}$ be a fixed supersingular curve with j-invariant 1728. Our cryptosystem relies on the hardness of reversing this class group action.

Definition 1 (Group Action Inverse Problem (GAIP)). *Given* $(E_0, E') \in \mathcal{E}^2$ *where* $E' = [\mathfrak{g}^a] \star E_0$ *and* $a \leftarrow\!\!\$\, [N]$, *the* Group Action Inverse Problem *is to find* $[\mathfrak{g}^{a'}] \in G$ *such that* $[\mathfrak{g}^{a'}] \star E_0 = E'$.

The best-known classical algorithm for solving GAIP has a time complexity of $O(\sqrt{N})$, where $N = |\mathcal{C}\ell(\mathcal{O})|$. In the quantum setting, the most efficient known algorithm is Kuperberg's algorithm, which addresses the hidden shift problem [28,29]. This algorithm has subexponential complexity; however, concrete security estimates for its performance remain subject to ongoing debate [4,8,12,33].

Definition 2 (Multi-Target Group Action Inverse Problem (MT-GAIP)). *Given* S *curves* $(E_1, \ldots, E_S)$ *with each* $(E_0, E_i) \in \mathcal{E}^2$, *where* $E_i = [\mathfrak{g}^{a_i}] \star E_0$ *and* $a_i \leftarrow\!\!\$\, [N]$, *the* Multi-Target Group Action Inverse Problem *is to find* $[\mathfrak{g}^a] \in G$ *and* $i, j \in \{0, \ldots, S\}$ *with* $i \neq j$, *such that* $E_i = [\mathfrak{g}^a] \star E_j$.

Relation Between GAIP and MT-GAIP. The two problems are polynomial-time equivalent. First, GAIP $\leq_P$ MT-GAIP: given (E_0, E') with $E' = [\mathfrak{g}^a] \star E_0$, form the MT-GAIP instance with indices $\{0, 1\}$ (where index 0 denotes E_0 and index 1 denotes E'); any MT-GAIP solver returns $[\mathfrak{g}^a]$ with $(i, j) = (1, 0)$. Second, MT-GAIP $\leq_P$ GAIP: given $(E_1, \ldots, E_S)$ with $E_i = [\mathfrak{g}^{a_i}] \star E_0$, query a GAIP oracle on each pair (E_0, E_i) to obtain group elements $[\mathfrak{g}^{a_i}]$. For any $i \neq j$, output $[\mathfrak{g}^{a_i}]\,[\mathfrak{g}^{a_j}]^{-1}$ together with (i, j); this satisfies $E_i = ([\mathfrak{g}^{a_i}]\,[\mathfrak{g}^{a_j}]^{-1}) \star E_j$. Thus any solver for one problem yields a solver for the other with only polynomial overhead.

3 Strong Designated Verifier Signatures

In this section, we present the definition and security models for the SDVS scheme, initially introduced by Jakobsson et al. [24] and later formalized by Laguillaumie and Vergnaud [30]. An SDVS scheme requires the use of the designated verifier's private key during the verification process. This ensures that only the designated verifier can verify the signature, thereby preventing third parties from doing so and protecting the signer's identity. Specifically, during the signing process, the signer S generates a valid designated verifier signature σ for a message $\mathsf{m} \in \mathcal{M}$, using the public key of the designated verifier vpk and the signer's private key ssk. In the verification phase, only the designated verifier V can validate the signature σ using their private key vsk, while others cannot. Additionally, a simulation algorithm is required to achieve off-the-record security. This ensures that V can use their private key vsk to create a simulated signature σ, indistinguishable from one that S would have generated for a different message $\mathsf{m}' \in \mathcal{M}$.

Definition 3 (Strong Designated Verifier Signature). *A strong designated verifier signature* SDVS *consists of* PPT *algorithms* (SDVS.Setup, SDVS.SKGen, SDVS.VKGen, SDVS.Sign, SDVS.Verify, SDVS.Sim) *defined as follows:*

- $\mathsf{SDVS.Setup}(1^\lambda) \rightarrow \mathsf{pp}$: *On input a security parameter 1^λ, it returns public parameters* pp.
- $\mathsf{SDVS.SKGen}(\mathsf{pp}) \rightarrow (\mathsf{ssk}, \mathsf{spk})$: *On input public parameters* pp, *it outputs a pair of public and secret keys* $(\mathsf{ssk}, \mathsf{spk})$ *for the signer.*
- $\mathsf{SDVS.VKGen}(\mathsf{pp}) \rightarrow (\mathsf{vsk}, \mathsf{vpk})$: *On input public parameters* pp, *it outputs a pair of public and secret keys* $(\mathsf{vsk}, \mathsf{vpk})$ *for the verifier.*
- $\mathsf{SDVS.Sign}(\mathsf{vpk}, \mathsf{ssk}, \mathsf{spk}, \mathsf{m}) \rightarrow \sigma$: *On input the verifier's public key* vpk, *the signer's secret key* ssk, *the signer's public key* spk, *and a message* $\mathsf{m} \in \mathcal{M}$, *it outputs a signature* σ.
- $\mathsf{SDVS.Sim}(\mathsf{vpk}, \mathsf{vsk}, \mathsf{spk}, \mathsf{m}) \rightarrow \sigma$: *On input the verifier's public key* vpk, *the verifier's secret key* vsk, *the signer's public key* spk, *and a message* $\mathsf{m} \in \mathcal{M}$, *it outputs a simulated signature* σ.
- $\mathsf{SDVS.Verify}(\mathsf{vsk}, \mathsf{vpk}, \mathsf{spk}, \sigma, \mathsf{m}) \rightarrow 1/0$: *On input the verifier's secret key* vsk, *the verifier's public key* vpk, *the signer's public key* spk, *a signature* σ, *and a message* $\mathsf{m} \in \mathcal{M}$, *it (deterministically) outputs either 1 (accept) or 0 (reject).*

The correctness of an SDVS scheme ensures that any valid designated verifier signature σ generated for a message m will be successfully verified by the verification algorithm.

Definition 4 (Correctness). *A strong designated verifier signature* SDVS *is correct if, for all* $\lambda \in \mathbb{N}$, $\mathsf{pp} \leftarrow \mathsf{SDVS.Setup}(1^\lambda)$, *for all public and secret key pairs of the signer* $(\mathsf{ssk}, \mathsf{spk}) \leftarrow \mathsf{SDVS.SKGen}(\mathsf{pp})$, *for all public and secret key pairs of the verifier* $(\mathsf{vsk}, \mathsf{vpk}) \leftarrow \mathsf{SDVS.VKGen}(\mathsf{pp})$, *for every message* $\mathsf{m} \in \mathcal{M}$, *and for signatures* $\sigma \leftarrow \mathsf{SDVS.Sign}(\mathsf{vpk}, \mathsf{ssk}, \mathsf{spk}, \mathsf{m})$ *and* $\sigma \leftarrow \mathsf{SDVS.Sim}(\mathsf{vpk}, \mathsf{vsk}, \mathsf{spk}, \mathsf{m})$, *we have:* $\Pr[\mathsf{SDVS.Verify}(\mathsf{vsk}, \mathsf{vpk}, \mathsf{spk}, \sigma, \mathsf{m}) = 1] = 1 - \mathsf{negl}(\lambda)$.

There are multiple definitions of security properties for SDVS, with some overlapping in scope. In this paper, we use the clear definitions outlined in [15]. However, since the definitions in [15] were originally designed for multi-designated verifier signatures, we have modified them to align with the requirements of strong designated verifier signatures.

A practical SDVS scheme should satisfy several key security properties: Unforgeability, Off-the-Record, and Privacy of the Signer's Identity.

- Unforgeability ensures that only the signer S and the designated verifier V can produce a valid designated verifier signature, preventing any outsider from forging a valid signature between S and V.
- Off-the-Record [15] guarantees that a malicious designated verifier cannot convince any outsider that a given signature σ originates from the signer. It means that it is impossible to distinguish between a legitimate signature created by the signer S and a simulated signature generated by the designated verifier V. In this paper, we use a stronger property named Strong Off-the-record. Now, the adversary cannot tell whether the message was signed by the signer or the designated verifier even if the adversary can know both the secret of the signer and the designated verifier.
- Privacy of the Signer's Identity (PSI) ensures that, without collusion with the designated verifier V, no third party can verify the signature or identify the actual signer.

The concept of existential unforgeability for an SDVS scheme asserts that no polynomial-time adversary, without knowledge of the private keys of the signer or designated verifier, can produce a valid designated verifier signature for a message that has not been requested from the signing or simulation oracles. We present a stronger security notion, called Strong Unforgeability under adaptive Chosen-Message Attacks (SU-CMA).

Definition 5 (SU-CMA). *A strong designated verifier signature is* SU-CMA *if, for all security parameters $\lambda \in \mathbb{N}$, any probabilistic polynomial-time (*PPT*) adversary $\mathcal{A}$ has at most a negligible advantage in the following game played against a challenger $\mathcal{C}$:*
$\mathsf{Exp}^{\mathsf{SU\text{-}CMA}}_{\mathsf{SDVS}}(\mathcal{A})$:

1. *The challenger runs* $\mathsf{pp} \leftarrow \mathsf{SDVS.Setup}(1^\lambda)$*, generates a signer key* $(\mathsf{ssk}, \mathsf{spk}) \leftarrow \mathsf{SDVS.SKGen}(\mathsf{pp})$ *and a verifier key* $(\mathsf{vsk}, \mathsf{vpk}) \leftarrow \mathsf{SDVS.VKGen}(\mathsf{pp})$*. It keeps* $(\mathsf{ssk}, \mathsf{vsk})$ *and provides* $(\mathsf{spk}\ \mathsf{vpk})$ *to* $\mathcal{A}$*.*
2. *The adversary $\mathcal{A}$ can make signing, verification, and simulation queries an arbitrary polynomial number of times:*
   - $\mathcal{O}_{\mathsf{Sign}}(\mathsf{vpk}, \mathsf{spk}, \mathsf{m})$: *The challenger runs* $\mathsf{SDVS.Sign}(\mathsf{vpk}, \mathsf{ssk}, \mathsf{spk}, \mathsf{m})$ *to obtain a signature σ and sends it to $\mathcal{A}$.*
   - $\mathcal{O}_{\mathsf{Sim}}(\mathsf{vpk}, \mathsf{spk}, \mathsf{m})$: *The challenger runs* $\mathsf{SDVS.Sim}(\mathsf{vpk}, \mathsf{vsk}, \mathsf{spk}, \mathsf{m})$ *to obtain a simulated signature σ and sends it to $\mathcal{A}$.*
   - $\mathcal{O}_{\mathsf{Verify}}(\mathsf{vpk}, \mathsf{spk}, \mathsf{m}, \sigma)$: *The challenger runs* $\mathsf{SDVS.Verify}(\mathsf{vsk}, \mathsf{vpk}, \mathsf{spk}, \sigma, \mathsf{m})$ *to obtain a bit $b \in \{0, 1\}$ and sends it to $\mathcal{A}$.*

3. The adversary $\mathcal{A}$ outputs (m', σ'). We say $\mathcal{A}$ wins if:
   - $\mathsf{SDVS.Verify}(\mathsf{vsk}, \mathsf{vpk}, \mathsf{spk}, \sigma', \mathsf{m}') = 1$, *and*
   - *The pair (m', σ') is not equal to any pair (m, σ) previously output by $\mathcal{O}_{\mathsf{Sign}}$ or $\mathcal{O}_{\mathsf{Sim}}$.*

The advantage of $\mathcal{A}$ is defined as $\mathsf{Adv}^{\mathsf{SU\text{-}CMA}}_{\mathsf{SDVS}}(\mathcal{A}) = \Pr[\mathcal{A}\ wins]$. The probability is taken over the random choices of all probabilistic algorithms.

Strong off-the-record (SOTR) says that given a message-signature pair (m, σ) which is accepted by the designated verifier, it is infeasible for any probabilistic polynomial-time distinguisher to tell whether the message was signed by the signer or the designated verifier even if the adversary can know both the secret of the signer and designated verifier. Formally, we consider the following definition.

Definition 6 (SOTR). *A strong designated verifier signature* SDVS *is* SOTR *if, for all $\lambda \in \mathbb{N}$, any* PPT *adversary $\mathcal{A}$ has at most a negligible advantage in the following game played against a challenger $\mathcal{C}$.*
$\mathsf{Exp}^{\mathsf{SOTR}}_{\mathsf{SDVS}}(\mathcal{A})$:

1. *The challenger $\mathcal{C}$ runs $\mathsf{pp} \leftarrow \mathsf{SDVS.Setup}(1^\lambda)$, generates a signer key $(\mathsf{ssk}, \mathsf{spk}) \leftarrow \mathsf{SDVS.SKGen}(\mathsf{pp})$, and a verifier key $(\mathsf{vsk}, \mathsf{vpk}) \leftarrow \mathsf{SDVS.VKGen}(\mathsf{pp})$. It provides spk and vpk to $\mathcal{A}$.*
2. *The adversary $\mathcal{A}$ chooses a message $\mathsf{m}^* \in \mathcal{M}$ and sends it to $\mathcal{C}$.*
3. *$\mathcal{C}$ tosses a coin $b \in \{0,1\}$. If $b = 0$, it computes $\sigma^* \leftarrow \mathsf{SDVS.Sign}(\mathsf{vpk}, \mathsf{ssk}, \mathsf{spk}, \mathsf{m}^*)$. If $b = 1$, it computes $\sigma^* \leftarrow \mathsf{SDVS.Sim}(\mathsf{vpk}, \mathsf{vsk}, \mathsf{spk}, \mathsf{m}^*)$. The challenger provides σ^* to $\mathcal{A}$.*
4. *The challenger provides ssk and vsk to the adversary.*
5. *Finally, the adversary outputs a bit b'. We say $\mathcal{A}$ wins if $b' = b$.*

The advantage of $\mathcal{A}$ is defined as $\mathsf{Adv}^{\mathsf{NT}}_{\mathsf{SDVS}}(\mathcal{A}) = |\Pr[\mathcal{A}\ wins] - \frac{1}{2}|$. The probability is taken over the random choices of all probabilistic algorithms.

Privacy of the signer's identity (PSI) ensures that an adversary cannot distinguish between signatures produced by two different signers, provided that they do not possess the secret key of any signer or designated verifier.

Definition 7 (PSI). *A strong designated verifier signature* SDVS *is* PSI *secure if, for all $\lambda \in \mathbb{N}$, any* PPT *adversary $\mathcal{A}$ has at most a negligible advantage in the following game played against a challenger $\mathcal{C}$.*
$\mathsf{Exp}^{\mathsf{PSI}}_{\mathsf{SDVS}}(\mathcal{A})$:

1. *The challenger runs $\mathsf{pp} \leftarrow \mathsf{SDVS.Setup}(1^\lambda)$, and generates the key pairs for signers $\mathsf{S}_0, \mathsf{S}_1$ using $\mathsf{SDVS.SKGen}(\mathsf{pp})$, i.e., $(\mathsf{ssk}_0, \mathsf{spk}_0)$, $(\mathsf{ssk}_1, \mathsf{spk}_1)$, and a verifier key $(\mathsf{vsk}, \mathsf{vpk}) \leftarrow \mathsf{SDVS.VKGen}(\mathsf{pp})$. It provides spk_0, spk_1, and vpk to $\mathcal{A}$.*
2. *The adversary $\mathcal{A}$ can make signing, verification, and simulation queries an arbitrary polynomial number of times for signer S_i for all $i \in \{0,1\}$.*

- $\mathcal{O}_{\mathsf{Sign}}(\mathsf{vpk}, \mathsf{spk}_i, M)$: *The challenger runs* $\mathsf{SDVS.Sign}(\mathsf{vpk}, \mathsf{ssk}_i, \mathsf{spk}_i, M)$ *to obtain a signature* σ *and sends it to* $\mathcal{A}$.
- $\mathcal{O}_{\mathsf{Sim}}(\mathsf{vpk}, \mathsf{spk}_i, M)$: *The challenger runs* $\mathsf{SDVS.Sim}(\mathsf{vpk}, \mathsf{vsk}, \mathsf{spk}_i, M)$ *to obtain a simulated signature* σ *and sends it to* $\mathcal{A}$.
- $\mathcal{O}_{\mathsf{Verify}}(\mathsf{vpk}, \mathsf{spk}_i, M, \sigma)$: *The challenger runs* $\mathsf{SDVS.Verify}(\mathsf{vsk}, \mathsf{vpk}, \mathsf{spk}_i, \sigma, M)$ *to obtain a bit* $b \in \{0,1\}$ *and sends it to* $\mathcal{A}$.

3. *The adversary* $\mathcal{A}$ *chooses a message* $\mathsf{m}^* \in \mathcal{M}$ *and sends it to* $\mathcal{C}$.
4. *The challenger tosses a coin* $b \in \{0,1\}$, *then computes the challenge signature* $\sigma^* \leftarrow \mathsf{SDVS.Sign}(\mathsf{vpk}, \mathsf{ssk}_b, \mathsf{spk}_b, \mathsf{m}^*)$, *and sends it to* $\mathcal{A}$.
5. *The adversary* $\mathcal{A}$ *continues to issue queries as in Step 2, except that it may not query* $\mathcal{O}_{\mathsf{Verify}}$ *with input* (m^*, σ^*) *for any* $i \in \{0,1\}$.
6. *Finally, the adversary outputs a bit* b'. *We say* $\mathcal{A}$ *wins if* $b' = b$.

The advantage of $\mathcal{A}$ *is defined as* $\mathsf{Adv}^{\mathsf{PSI}}_{\mathsf{SDVS}}(\mathcal{A}) = |\Pr[\mathcal{A}\ wins] - \frac{1}{2}|$. *The probability is taken over the random choices of all probabilistic algorithms.*

4 Our Isogeny-Based Strong Designated Verifier Signature Scheme

Let (p, N, E_0) denote the public parameters, where p is the prime field characteristic, $N = |\mathcal{C\ell}(\mathcal{O})|$ represents the order of the ideal class group, and E_0 is a specific supersingular elliptic curve. Let $\mathfrak{g}$ be a generator for the ideal class group $\mathcal{C\ell}(\mathcal{O})$. These parameters are assumed to be accessible to all algorithms in the protocol. Additionally, let $H : \{0,1\}^* \to \{0,1\}^n$ and $H' : \{0,1\}^* \to \{0,1\}^{2\lambda}$ be secure hash functions, treated as a random oracle for the security analysis. The our algorithms are summarized in Fig. 1.

$\mathsf{SDVS.SKGen}(\mathsf{pp})$: On input the public parameters pp, this algorithm samples $a_0 \leftarrow_\$ \mathbb{Z}_N$, computes $A_0^1 = [\mathfrak{g}^{a_0}] \star E_0$ and sets $A_0^0 = E_0$. It outputs the public key $\mathsf{spk} = (A_0^1, A_0^0)$ and the secret key $\mathsf{ssk} = a_0$.

$\mathsf{SDVS.VKGen}(\mathsf{pp})$: On input the public parameters pp, this algorithm samples $a_1 \leftarrow_\$ \mathbb{Z}_N$, computes $A_1^1 = [\mathfrak{g}^{a_1}] \star E_0$ and sets $A_1^0 = E_0$. It outputs the public key $\mathsf{vpk} = (A_1^1, A_1^0)$ and the secret key $\mathsf{vsk} = a_1$.

$\mathsf{SDVS.Sign}(\mathsf{vpk}, \mathsf{ssk}, \mathsf{spk}, \mathsf{m})$: To sign a message m, the signer first parses $a_0 \leftarrow \mathsf{ssk}$, $(A_0^1, A_0^0) \leftarrow \mathsf{spk}$, and $(A_1^1, A_1^0) \leftarrow \mathsf{vpk}$. It then samples $\mathbf{y}_0 \leftarrow_\$ \mathbb{Z}_N^n$ and computes $\mathbf{Y}_0 = [\mathfrak{g}^{\mathbf{y}_0}] \star E_0$. Next, it samples $\mathbf{c}_1 \leftarrow_\$ \{0,1\}^n$ and $\mathbf{r}_1 \leftarrow_\$ \mathbb{Z}_N^n$, then computes $\mathbf{Y}_1 = [\mathfrak{g}^{\mathbf{r}_1}] \star A_1^{\mathbf{c}_1}$ and $\mathsf{K} = \mathsf{H}'([\mathfrak{g}^{a_0}] \star A_1^1)$, where the superscript $\mathbf{c}_1$ in $A_1^{\mathbf{c}_1}$ denotes a label (component index). The challenge $\mathbf{c}$ is computed as $\mathbf{c} \leftarrow \mathsf{H}(\mathbf{Y}_0 \| \mathbf{Y}_1 \| \mathsf{K} \| \mathsf{m})$. The signer sets $\mathbf{c}_0 = \mathbf{c} \oplus \mathbf{c}_1$ and computes $\mathbf{r}_0 = \mathbf{y}_0 - a_0 \cdot \mathbf{c}_0$. The final signature is $\sigma = (\mathbf{c}_0, \mathbf{c}_1, \mathbf{r}_0, \mathbf{r}_1)$.

$\mathsf{SDVS.Verify}(\mathsf{vsk}, \mathsf{vpk}, \mathsf{spk}, \sigma, \mathsf{m})$: To verify a signature $\sigma = (\mathbf{c}_0, \mathbf{c}_1, \mathbf{r}_0, \mathbf{r}_1)$ on message m, the verifier parses $a_1 \leftarrow \mathsf{vsk}$ and the components of σ. It then computes $\mathbf{Y}_0 = [\mathfrak{g}^{\mathbf{r}_0}] \star A_0^{\mathbf{c}_0}$ and $\mathbf{Y}_1 = [\mathfrak{g}^{\mathbf{r}_1}] \star A_1^{\mathbf{c}_1}$. The value K is computed as $\mathsf{K} = \mathsf{H}'([\mathfrak{g}^{a_1}] \star A_0^1)$, where . Next, the verifier computes the challenge $\mathbf{c}' \leftarrow \mathsf{H}(\mathbf{Y}_0 \| \mathbf{Y}_1 \| \mathsf{K} \| \mathsf{m})$. If $\mathbf{c}_0 \oplus \mathbf{c}_1 = \mathbf{c}'$, the verifier accepts the signature (returns 1); otherwise, it rejects (returns 0).

$\mathsf{SDVS.Sim}(\mathsf{vpk}, \mathsf{vsk}, \mathsf{spk}, \mathsf{m})$**:** To simulate a signature for message m, the designated verifier first parses $a_1 \leftarrow \mathsf{vsk}$, $(A_1^1, A_1^0) \leftarrow \mathsf{vpk}$, and $(A_0^1, A_0^0) \leftarrow \mathsf{spk}$. It samples $\mathbf{y}_1 \leftarrow_\$ \mathbb{Z}_N^n$ and computes $\mathbf{Y}_1 = [\mathfrak{g}^{\mathbf{y}_1}] \star E_0$. It then samples $\mathbf{c}_0 \leftarrow_\$ \{0,1\}^n$ and $\mathbf{r}_0 \leftarrow_\$ \mathbb{Z}_N^n$, computes $\mathbf{Y}_0 = [\mathfrak{g}^{\mathbf{r}_0}] \star A_0^{\mathbf{c}_0}$ and $\mathsf{K} = [\mathfrak{g}^{a_1}] \star A_0^1$. The designated verifier then computes the challenge $\mathbf{c} \leftarrow \mathsf{H}(\mathbf{Y}_0 \| \mathbf{Y}_1 \| \mathsf{K} \| \mathsf{m})$, sets $\mathbf{c}_1 = \mathbf{c} \oplus \mathbf{c}_0$, and computes $\mathbf{r}_1 = \mathbf{y}_1 - a_1 \cdot \mathbf{c}_1$. Finally, it outputs the simulated signature $\sigma = (\mathbf{c}_0, \mathbf{c}_1, \mathbf{r}_0, \mathbf{r}_1)$.

Theorem 1 (Correctness). *Our isogeny-based* SDVS *scheme is correct.*

Proof. To prove correctness, we need to show that if σ in the signing algorithm and in the simulation algorithm are valid signatures, then the verification algorithm will accept them. Specifically, we need to show that $\mathbf{c}_0 \oplus \mathbf{c}_1 = \mathbf{c}'$, where $\mathbf{c}' = \mathsf{H}(\mathbf{Y}_0 \| \mathbf{Y}_1 \| \mathsf{K} \| \mathsf{m})$. Here, we only provide the proof for σ in signing algorithm since it is the same with simulation one.

For each $j \in [1, n]$, the signer samples $\mathbf{y}_{0,j} \in \mathbb{Z}_N$ and computes: $\mathbf{Y}_{0,j} = [\mathfrak{g}^{\mathbf{y}_{0,j}}] \star E_0$. In the verification algorithm, we have $\mathbf{r}_{0,j} = \mathbf{y}_{0,j} - a_0 \cdot \mathbf{c}_{0,j}$ and $\mathbf{Y}_{0,j} = [\mathfrak{g}^{\mathbf{r}_{0,j}}] \star A_0^{\mathbf{c}_{0,j}}$. We need to show that $\mathbf{Y}_{0,j} = [\mathfrak{g}^{\mathbf{y}_{0,j}}] \star E_0$ holds under the two cases for $\mathbf{c}_{0,j}$. If $\mathbf{c}_{0,j} = 0$, then $A_0^{\mathbf{c}_{0,j}} = A_0^0 = E_0$ and $\mathbf{r}_{0,j} = \mathbf{y}_{0,j}$. Thus, we get: $\mathbf{Y}_{0,j} = [\mathfrak{g}^{\mathbf{r}_{0,j}}] \star E_0 = [\mathfrak{g}^{\mathbf{y}_{0,j}}] \star E_0$.

If $\mathbf{c}_{0,j} = 1$, then $A_0^{\mathbf{c}_{0,j}} = A_0^1 = [\mathfrak{g}^{a_0}] \star E_0$ and $\mathbf{r}_{0,j} = \mathbf{y}_{0,j} - a_0$. Then we have: $\mathbf{Y}_{0,j} = [\mathfrak{g}^{\mathbf{r}_{0,j}}] \star A_0^1 = [\mathfrak{g}^{\mathbf{y}_{0,j} - a_0}] \star ([\mathfrak{g}^{a_0}] \star E_0) = [\mathfrak{g}^{\mathbf{y}_{0,j}}] \star E_0$. Therefore, in both cases, we have $\mathbf{Y}_{0,j} = [\mathfrak{g}^{\mathbf{y}_{0,j}}] \star E_0$ as required.

Since $\mathbf{r}_1$ and $\mathbf{c}_1$ are the same in both signing and verification, and $A_1^{\mathbf{c}_1}$ remains unchanged, we have: $\mathbf{Y}_1 = [\mathfrak{g}^{\mathbf{r}_1}] \star A_1^{\mathbf{c}_1}$. Moreover, the value of K is computed as $\mathsf{K}' = \mathsf{H}'([\mathfrak{g}^{a_1}] \star A_0^1) = \mathsf{K}$. Indeed, $[\mathfrak{g}^{a_0}] \star A_1^1 = [\mathfrak{g}^{a_0}] \star ([\mathfrak{g}^{a_1}] \star E_0) = [\mathfrak{g}^{a_0 + a_1}] \star E_0 = [\mathfrak{g}^{a_1}] \star A_0^1$. Finally, the verifier checks if $\mathbf{c}_0 \oplus \mathbf{c}_1 = \mathbf{c}' = \mathbf{c}$. From the signing algorithm, we have $\mathbf{c}_0 = \mathbf{c} \oplus \mathbf{c}_1$. Therefore, $\mathbf{c}_0 \oplus \mathbf{c}_1 = (\mathbf{c} \oplus \mathbf{c}_1) \oplus \mathbf{c}_1 = \mathbf{c} \oplus (\mathbf{c}_1 \oplus \mathbf{c}_1) = \mathbf{c} \oplus \mathbf{0} = \mathbf{c}$. This shows that $\mathbf{c}_0 \oplus \mathbf{c}_1 = \mathbf{c}$. Hence, the verification algorithm will accept the signature σ.

5 Security Analysis

Theorem 2 (SU-CMA). *Our isogeny-based* SDVS *scheme is* SU-CMA *secure in the random oracle model.*

Proof. Assume there exists a PPT adversary $\mathcal{A}$ that can forge a signature in the SDVS scheme with non-negligible probability ϵ. We construct a simulator $\mathcal{S}$ that uses $\mathcal{A}$ to solve the GAIP problem. We assume that $\mathcal{S}$ receives E_0 and E' from GAIP. The interactions between $\mathcal{S}$ and $\mathcal{A}$ use a hybrid argument with the following series of games:

$\mathsf{SDVS.SKGen}(\mathsf{pp})$

$a_0 \leftarrow\!\!\$\ \mathbb{Z}_N$
$A_0^0 \leftarrow E_0$
$A_0^1 \leftarrow [\mathfrak{g}^{a_0}] \star E_0$
$\mathbf{return}\ (\mathsf{ssk} = a_0, \mathsf{spk} = (A_0^1, A_0^0))$

$\mathsf{SDVS.VKGen}(\mathsf{pp})$

$a_1 \leftarrow\!\!\$\ \mathbb{Z}_N$
$A_1^0 \leftarrow E_0$
$A_1^1 \leftarrow [\mathfrak{g}^{a_1}] \star E_0$
$\mathbf{return}\ (\mathsf{vsk} = a_1, \mathsf{vpk} = (A_1^1, A_1^0))$

$\mathsf{SDVS.Sign}(\mathsf{vpk}, \mathsf{ssk}, \mathsf{spk}, \mathsf{m})$

$\mathbf{parse}\ a_0 \leftarrow \mathsf{ssk}$
$\mathbf{parse}\ (A_0^1, A_0^0) \leftarrow \mathsf{spk}$
$\mathbf{parse}\ (A_1^1, A_1^0) \leftarrow \mathsf{vpk}$
$\mathbf{y}_0 \leftarrow\!\!\$\ \mathbb{Z}_N^n$
$\mathbf{Y}_0 \leftarrow [\mathfrak{g}^{\mathbf{y}_0}] \star E_0$
$\mathbf{c}_1 \leftarrow\!\!\$\ \{0,1\}^n$
$\mathbf{r}_1 \leftarrow\!\!\$\ \mathbb{Z}_N^n$
$\mathbf{Y}_1 \leftarrow [\mathfrak{g}^{\mathbf{r}_1}] \star A_1^{\mathbf{c}_1}$
$\mathsf{K} \leftarrow \mathsf{H}'([\mathfrak{g}^{a_0}] \star A_1^1)$
$\mathbf{c} \leftarrow \mathsf{H}(\mathbf{Y}_0 \| \mathbf{Y}_1 \| \mathsf{K} \| \mathsf{m})$
$\mathbf{c}_0 \leftarrow \mathbf{c} \oplus \mathbf{c}_1 \in \{0,1\}^n$
$\mathbf{r}_0 \leftarrow \mathbf{y}_0 - a_0 \cdot \mathbf{c}_0$
$\mathbf{return}\ \sigma = (\mathbf{c}_0, \mathbf{c}_1, \mathbf{r}_0, \mathbf{r}_1)$

$\mathsf{SDVS.Sim}(\mathsf{vpk}, \mathsf{vsk}, \mathsf{spk}, \mathsf{m})$

$\mathbf{parse}\ a_1 \leftarrow \mathsf{vsk}$
$\mathbf{parse}\ (A_1^1, A_1^0) \leftarrow \mathsf{vpk}$
$\mathbf{parse}\ (A_0^1, A_0^0) \leftarrow \mathsf{spk}$
$\mathbf{y}_1 \leftarrow\!\!\$\ \mathbb{Z}_N^n$
$\mathbf{Y}_1 \leftarrow [\mathfrak{g}^{\mathbf{y}_1}] \star E_0$
$\mathbf{c}_0 \leftarrow\!\!\$\ \{0,1\}^n$
$\mathbf{r}_0 \leftarrow\!\!\$\ \mathbb{Z}_N^n$
$\mathbf{Y}_0 \leftarrow [\mathfrak{g}^{\mathbf{r}_0}] \star A_0^{\mathbf{c}_0}$
$\mathsf{K} \leftarrow \mathsf{H}'([\mathfrak{g}^{a_1}] \star A_0^1)$
$\mathbf{c} \leftarrow \mathsf{H}(\mathbf{Y}_0 \| \mathbf{Y}_1 \| \mathsf{K} \| \mathsf{m})$
$\mathbf{c}_1 \leftarrow \mathbf{c} \oplus \mathbf{c}_0 \in \{0,1\}^n$
$\mathbf{r}_1 \leftarrow \mathbf{y}_1 - a_1 \cdot \mathbf{c}_1$
$\mathbf{return}\ \sigma = (\mathbf{c}_0, \mathbf{c}_1, \mathbf{r}_0, \mathbf{r}_1)$

$\mathsf{Verify}(\mathsf{vsk}, \mathsf{vpk}, \mathsf{spk}, \sigma, \mathsf{m})$

$\mathbf{parse}\ a_1 \leftarrow \mathsf{vsk}$
$\mathbf{parse}\ (A_0^1, A_0^0) \leftarrow \mathsf{spk}$
$\mathbf{parse}\ (A_1^1, A_1^0) \leftarrow \mathsf{vpk}$
$\mathbf{parse}\ (\mathbf{c}_0, \mathbf{c}_1, \mathbf{r}_0, \mathbf{r}_1) \leftarrow \sigma$
$\mathbf{Y}_0' \leftarrow [\mathfrak{g}^{\mathbf{r}_0}] \star A_0^{\mathbf{c}_0}$
$\mathbf{Y}_1' \leftarrow [\mathfrak{g}^{\mathbf{r}_1}] \star A_1^{\mathbf{c}_1}$
$\mathsf{K}' \leftarrow \mathsf{H}'([\mathfrak{g}^{a_1}] \star A_0^1)$
$\mathbf{c}' \leftarrow \mathsf{H}(\mathbf{Y}_0' \| \mathbf{Y}_1' \| \mathsf{K}' \| \mathsf{m})$
$\mathbf{if}\ \mathbf{c}_0 \oplus \mathbf{c}_1 = \mathbf{c}'\ \mathbf{then}$
$\quad \mathbf{return}\ 1$
$\mathbf{else\ return}\ 0$

Fig. 1. Strong Designated Verifier Signatures from Isogeny Assumptions

Game_1 : This is the original SU-CMA experiment defined in Definition 5. Specifically, the simulator $\mathcal{S}$ sets $\mathsf{pp} = (p, N, E_0)$, then $\mathcal{S}$ chooses $a_0, a_1 \leftarrow \mathbb{Z}_N$, computes $A_0^1 = [\mathfrak{g}^{a_0}] \star E_0$, sets $A_0^0 = A_1^0 = E_0$, keeps $(\mathsf{ssk}, \mathsf{vsk}) = (a_0, a_1)$ and publishes $\mathsf{spk} = (A_0^1, A_0^0)$, $\mathsf{vpk} = (A_1^1, A_1^0)$. The simulator $\mathcal{S}$ exactly follows $\mathsf{Exp}_{\mathsf{SDVS}}^{\mathsf{SU\text{-}CMA}}$ to answer hash queries, signing, and simulation oracle.

Game_2 : This is the same as Game_1 except for some modifications as follows:

- **Hash Query** $\mathsf{H}(\cdot)$**:** $\mathcal{S}$ maintains a hash list to record queries to H and their responses. When $\mathcal{A}$ queries $\mathsf{H}(\cdot)$, $\mathcal{S}$ responds as follows: If the query input has been queried before, return the same hash value. Otherwise, pick a random hash value from $\{0,1\}^n$ and return it. Additionally, $\mathcal{S}$ can program the hash oracle at specific points to facilitate the use of the Forking Lemma.

- **KeyGen:** The simulator $\mathcal{S}$ flips a coin b. If $b = 0$, it sets $\mathsf{vsk} = \perp$ and $\mathsf{vpk} = (A_1^1, A_1^0) = (E', E_0)$ instead of using $\mathsf{vsk} = a_1$ and $\mathsf{vpk} = (A_1^1, A_1^0) = ([\mathfrak{g}^{a_1}] \star E_0, E_0)$. If $b = 1$, it sets $\mathsf{ssk} = \perp$ and $\mathsf{spk} = (A_0^1, A_0^0) = (E', E_0)$ instead of using $\mathsf{ssk} = a_0$ and $\mathsf{spk} = (A_0^1, A_0^0) = ([\mathfrak{g}^{a_0}] \star E_0, E_0)$.
- **Signing and Simulation Oracles:** For whichever secret key the simulator does not know, it answers signing and simulation queries by programming the random oracle. Without loss of generality, we assume $b = 0$ for the following descriptions of the signing and simulation oracles.
  - $\mathcal{O}_{\mathsf{Sign}}(\mathsf{vpk}, \mathsf{spk}, \mathsf{m})$: $\mathcal{S}$ runs $\mathsf{SDVS.Sign}(\mathsf{vpk}, \mathsf{ssk}, \mathsf{spk}, \mathsf{m})$ using $\mathsf{ssk} = a_0$ and provides the signature σ to $\mathcal{A}$.
  - $\mathcal{O}_{\mathsf{Sim}}(\mathsf{vpk}, \mathsf{spk}, \mathsf{m})$: Since $\mathcal{S}$ does not know vsk, it cannot compute response $\mathbf{r}_1$ normally. However, in the ROM, $\mathcal{S}$ can simulate signatures by programming the hash oracle and selecting appropriate values. Specifically, $\mathcal{S}$ operates as follows:
    * Choose random $\mathbf{c}_0 \leftarrow_\$ \{0,1\}^n$ and $\mathbf{r}_0 \leftarrow_\$ \mathbb{Z}_N^n$.
    * Compute $\mathbf{Y}_0 = [\mathfrak{g}^{\mathbf{r}_0}] \star A_0^{\mathbf{c}_0}$.
    * Choose random $\mathbf{c}_1 \leftarrow_\$ \{0,1\}^n$ and $\mathbf{r}_1 \leftarrow_\$ \mathbb{Z}_N^n$.
    * Compute $\mathbf{Y}_1 = [\mathfrak{g}^{\mathbf{r}_1}] \star A_1^{\mathbf{c}_1}$.
    * Compute $\mathsf{K} = \mathsf{H}'([\mathfrak{g}^{a_0}] \star A_1^1)$
    * Set $\mathbf{c} = \mathbf{c}_0 \oplus \mathbf{c}_1$.
    * Program the hash oracle such that $\mathsf{H}(\mathbf{Y}_0 \| \mathbf{Y}_1 \| \mathsf{K} \| \mathsf{m}) = \mathbf{c}$.
    * Output $\sigma = (\mathbf{c}_0, \mathbf{c}_1, \mathbf{r}_0, \mathbf{r}_1)$
- Verification Oracle $\mathcal{O}_{\mathsf{Verify}}(\mathsf{vpk}, \mathsf{spk}, \mathsf{m}, \sigma)$: Since $\mathcal{S}$ does not know vsk, $\mathcal{S}$ computes $\mathsf{K} = \mathsf{H}'([\mathfrak{g}^{a_0}] \star A_1^1)$. Then, $\mathcal{S}$ runs $\mathsf{Verify}(\mathsf{vsk}, \mathsf{vpk}, \mathsf{spk}, \sigma, \mathsf{m})$ normally.

We see that the probability that the adversary can distinguish between Game_1 and Game_2 is negligible. With a probability ϵ, $\mathcal{A}$ outputs a forgery $(M', \sigma' = (\mathbf{c}_0', \mathbf{c}_1', \mathbf{r}_0', \mathbf{r}_1'))$ such that:

- $\mathsf{SDVS.Verify}(\mathsf{vsk}, \mathsf{vpk}, \mathsf{spk}, \sigma', \mathsf{m}') = 1$.
- (m', σ') was not obtained from $\mathcal{S}$'s oracles.

Notice that if the random oracle H was not queried or programmed on some input, then $\mathcal{A}$ only has a $1/2^n$ chance of producing $\mathbf{c}' = \mathbf{c}_0' \oplus \mathbf{c}_1'$ such that $\mathsf{H}(\mathbf{Y}_0' \| \mathbf{Y}_1' \| \mathsf{K} \| \mathsf{m}') = \mathbf{c}'$. Thus, the probability that $\mathcal{A}$ succeeds in a forgery and $\mathbf{c}'$ is one of the output the H is at least $\epsilon - 1/2^n$. We have two possibilities: $\mathbf{c}'$ equals programmed response during simulating, or it was a response to a hash query and signing query made by $\mathcal{A}$.

Suppose that $\mathcal{S}$ programmed the random oracle $\mathsf{H}(\mathbf{Y}_0 \| \mathbf{Y}_1 \| \mathsf{K} \| \mathsf{m}) = \mathbf{c}'$ when simulating a message m. If $\mathcal{A}$ outputs a valid forgery $\sigma' = (\mathbf{c_0}', \mathbf{c}_1', \mathbf{r}_1', \mathbf{r}_2')$ for some message m', then we have $\mathsf{H}(\mathbf{Y}_0 \| \mathbf{Y}_1 \| \mathsf{K} \| \mathsf{m}) = \mathsf{H}(\mathbf{Y}_0' \| \mathbf{Y}_1' \| \mathsf{K} \| \mathsf{m}')$. If $\mathsf{m} \neq \mathsf{m}'$ or $\mathbf{Y}_0 \neq \mathbf{Y}_0'$ or $\mathbf{Y}_1 \neq \mathbf{Y}_1'$, it mean that $\mathcal{S}$ found a collision of H. If $\mathsf{m} = \mathsf{m}'$ and $\mathbf{Y}_0 = \mathbf{Y}_0'$ and $\mathbf{Y}_1 = \mathbf{Y}_1'$, then we have

$$\mathbf{Y}_0 = [\mathfrak{g}^{\mathbf{r}_0}] \star A_0^{\mathbf{c}_0} = [\mathfrak{g}^{\mathbf{r}'_0}] \star A_0^{\mathbf{c}'_0} = \mathbf{Y}'_0 \tag{1}$$

$$\mathbf{Y}_1 = [\mathfrak{g}^{\mathbf{r}_1}] \star A_1^{\mathbf{c}_1} = [\mathfrak{g}^{\mathbf{r}'_1}] \star A_1^{\mathbf{c}'_1} = \mathbf{Y}'_1 \tag{2}$$

Since $\mathbf{c}_0 \oplus \mathbf{c}_1 = \mathbf{c}'_0 \oplus \mathbf{c}'_1$, then we have $\mathbf{c}_0 \neq \mathbf{c}'_0$ and $\mathbf{c}_1 \neq \mathbf{c}'_1$. Note that, if $\mathbf{c}_0 = \mathbf{c}'_0$ and $\mathbf{c}_1 = \mathbf{c}'_1$ then $\mathbf{r}_0 = \mathbf{r}'_0$ and $\mathbf{r}_1 = \mathbf{r}'_0$. It means that $\mathcal{A}$ just output an old signature on m. Let $i, j \in [n]$ be the index such that $\mathbf{c}_{0,i} \neq \mathbf{c}'_{0,i}$ and $\mathbf{c}_{1,j} \neq \mathbf{c}'_{1,j}$, where $\mathbf{c}_{0,i}, \mathbf{c}_{0,i}, \mathbf{c}'_{1,j}, \mathbf{c}'_{1,j} \in \{0,1\}$. Assume without loss of generality that $(\mathbf{c}_{0,i}, \mathbf{c}_{0,i}) = (1,0)$ and $(\mathbf{c}'_{1,j}, \mathbf{c}'_{1,j}) = (0,1)$. From (1) and (2), we have

$$[\mathfrak{g}^{\mathbf{r}_{0,i}}] \star A_0^1 = [\mathfrak{g}^{\mathbf{r}'_{0,i}}] \star A_0^0 = [\mathfrak{g}^{\mathbf{r}'_{0,i}}] \star E_0$$

$$[\mathfrak{g}^{\mathbf{r}_{1,j}}] \star A_1^0 = [\mathfrak{g}^{\mathbf{r}_{1,j}}] \star E_0 = [\mathfrak{g}^{\mathbf{r}'_{1,j}}] \star A_1^1$$

This implies $a_0 = (\mathbf{r}'_{0,i} - \mathbf{r}_{0,i})$ and $\mathsf{vsk} = a_1 = (\mathbf{r}_{1,j} - \mathbf{r}'_{1,j})$.

Now, we turn to the case that $\mathbf{c}'$ was a response to a random oracle query or signing query made by $\mathcal{A}$. By applying the Forking Lemma, $\mathcal{S}$ runs $\mathcal{A}$ again with the same random tape but programs the hash oracle differently at the point corresponding to the forgery. Assume that $\mathcal{A}$ outputs a signature $(\mathbf{c}'', \sigma'' = (\mathbf{c}''_0, \mathbf{c}''_1, \mathbf{r}''_0, \mathbf{r}''_1))$ of the message m', where $\mathbf{c}'' \neq \mathbf{c}'$, and

$$\mathbf{Y}''_0 = [\mathfrak{g}^{\mathbf{r}''_0}] \star A_0^{\mathbf{c}''_0} = [\mathfrak{g}^{\mathbf{r}'_0}] \star A_0^{\mathbf{c}'_0} = \mathbf{Y}'_0$$

$$\mathbf{Y}''_1 = [\mathfrak{g}^{\mathbf{r}''_1}] \star A_1^{\mathbf{c}''_1} = [\mathfrak{g}^{\mathbf{r}'_1}] \star A_1^{\mathbf{c}'_1} = \mathbf{Y}'_1$$

Since $\mathbf{c}''_0 \oplus \mathbf{c}''_1 = \mathbf{c}'' \neq \mathbf{c}' = \mathbf{c}''_0 \oplus \mathbf{c}''_1$, either $\mathbf{c}''_0 \neq \mathbf{c}'_0$ or $\mathbf{c}''_1 \neq \mathbf{c}'_1$. If $\mathbf{c}''_0 \neq \mathbf{c}'_0$, $\mathcal{S}$ can extract a_0. However, this does not have meaning. Hence, in this case the $\mathcal{S}$ runs again reduction algorithm. If $\mathbf{c}''_1 \neq \mathbf{c}'_1$, without loss of generality, assume $(\mathbf{c}''_{1,i}, \mathbf{c}'_{1,i}) = (0,1)$ for some $i \in [n]$. Then, we have $[\mathfrak{g}^{\mathbf{r}''_{1,i}}] \star A_1^0 = [\mathfrak{g}^{\mathbf{r}''_{1,i}}] \star E_0 = [\mathfrak{g}^{\mathbf{r}'_{1,i}}] \star A_1^1 = [\mathfrak{g}^{\mathbf{r}'_{1,i}}] \star E'$. This implies $[\mathfrak{g}^{\mathbf{r}''_{1,i} - \mathbf{r}'_{1,i}}] = E'$. Therefore, $\mathcal{S}$ can solve GAIP problem.

Remark 1. In 2005, Lipmaa et al. [30] introduced the non-delegatability (ND) property and pointed out that almost all previous security models did not capture this realistic threat. They were the first to realize an SDVS scheme achieving this property. The ND security for an SDVS scheme states that if someone generates a valid designated verifier signature, they must know a corresponding secret key. It is important to note that this secret key does not necessarily have to be that of the signer or the designated verifier; it may be derived from their respective secret keys.

Our scheme also achieves the ND property. We observe that this property is inherently covered by the unforgeability guarantee in our security proof. Consider a scenario where the signer chooses a random value $a'_0 \leftarrow_{\$} \mathbb{Z}_n$ and uses their secret key $\mathsf{ssk} = a_0$ to compute $\mathsf{ssk}' = a_0 + a'_0$. The signer then provides $\mathsf{spk}' = ([\mathfrak{g}^{a_0 + a'_0}] \star E_0, A_0^0 = E_0)$ to an external party. We observe that if anyone uses spk' to generate a valid signature, they must know the corresponding secret key ssk'. Notably, the resulting signature is valid for the new public key spk', not for the original spk. Indeed, we can employ a simulator S in Game 2 with input spk'. Through this simulation, we can extract the corresponding secret key ssk'.

Theorem 3 (Strong Off-the-Record). *Our isogeny-based* SDVS *scheme is* SOTR *secure in the random oracle model.*

Proof. We can observe that both the signer S and the verifier V generate proofs that are identically distributed by utilizing their respective secret keys. This symmetry in the signature generation process ensures that, from the adversary's perspective, the distributions of the signatures are indistinguishable. This holds true even if the adversary gains knowledge of both the signer's secret key and the designated verifier's secret key.

Now, let us consider the $\mathsf{Exp}^{\mathsf{SOTR}}_{\mathsf{SDVS}}(\mathcal{A})$ experiment in Definition 3.

- The challenger $\mathcal{C}$ sets $\mathsf{pp} = (p, N, E_0)$, then chooses $a_0, a_1 \leftarrow_{\$} \mathbb{Z}_N$, computes $A_0^1 = [\mathfrak{g}^{a_0}] \star E_0$, sets $A_0^0 = A_1^0 = E_0$, keeps $(\mathsf{ssk}, \mathsf{vsk}) = (a_0, a_1)$, and publishes $\mathsf{spk} = (A_0^1, A_0^0)$ and $\mathsf{vpk} = (A_1^1, A_1^0)$.
- The adversary $\mathcal{A}$ chooses a message $\mathsf{m}^* \in \mathcal{M}$ and sends it to $\mathcal{C}$.
- The challenger $\mathcal{C}$ samples $b \leftarrow_{\$} \{0, 1\}$:
  - If $b = 0$, the challenger $\mathcal{C}$ runs $\mathsf{SDVS.Sign}(\mathsf{vpk}, \mathsf{ssk}, \mathsf{spk}, \mathsf{m}^*)$ to compute a signature $\sigma = (\mathbf{c}_0, \mathbf{c}_1, \mathbf{r}_0, \mathbf{r}_1)$ and sends it to the adversary $\mathcal{A}$.
  - If $b = 1$, the challenger $\mathcal{C}$ runs $\mathsf{SDVS.Sim}(\mathsf{vpk}, \mathsf{vsk}, \mathsf{spk}, \mathsf{m}^*)$ to compute a signature $\sigma = (\mathbf{c}_0, \mathbf{c}_1, \mathbf{r}_0, \mathbf{r}_1)$ and sends it to the adversary $\mathcal{A}$.
- The challenger $\mathcal{C}$ provides both the secret key of the signer ssk and the secret key of the designated verifier vsk to the adversary $\mathcal{A}$.
- The adversary $\mathcal{A}$ guesses the bit b chosen by the challenger $\mathcal{C}$.

In the above operational process, for all $b \in \{0, 1\}$, we see that the signature σ contains $(\mathbf{c}_0, \mathbf{c}_1, \mathbf{r}_0, \mathbf{r}_1)$, where $\mathbf{c}_0, \mathbf{c}_1 \in \{0, 1\}^n$ and $\mathbf{r}_0, \mathbf{r}_1 \in \mathbb{Z}_N^n$. Hence, the signatures from the signer and the designated verifier are identical.

By using the secret key of the signer ssk or the designated verifier vsk, the adversary can verify the signature. Specifically, the adversary can check as follows:

- Compute $\mathbf{Y}_0 = [\mathfrak{g}^{\mathbf{r}_0}] \cdot A_0^{\mathbf{c}_0}$ and $\mathbf{Y}_1 = [\mathfrak{g}^{\mathbf{r}_1}] \cdot A_1^{\mathbf{c}_1}$.
- Compute $\mathsf{K} = \mathsf{H}'([\mathfrak{g}^{a_1}] \star A_0^1) = \mathsf{H}'([\mathfrak{g}^{a_0}] \star A_1^1)$.
- Check $\mathbf{c}_0 \oplus \mathbf{c}_1 = \mathsf{H}(\mathbf{Y}_0 \| \mathbf{Y}_1 \| \mathsf{K} \| \mathsf{m})$.

However, for any $b \in \{0, 1\}$, the signature σ is always valid. Therefore, the adversary cannot determine whether the signature originated from the signer or the designated verifier.

Theorem 4 (PSI). *Our isogeny-based* SDVS *scheme is* PSI *secure in the random oracle model.*

Proof. We prove PSI using a hybrid argument with the following series of games.

Game_1 : This is the original PSI experiment defined in Definition 7. Specifically, the challenger sets $\mathsf{pp} = (p, N, E_0)$, then $\mathcal{S}$ chooses $a_{0,0}, a_{0,1}, a_1 \leftarrow_{\$} \mathbb{Z}_N$, computes $A_{0,0}^1 = [\mathfrak{g}^{a_{0,0}}] \star E_0$, $A_{0,1}^1 = [\mathfrak{g}^{a_{0,1}}] \star E_0$, $A_1^1 = [\mathfrak{g}^{a_1}] \star E_0$, sets $A_{0,0}^0 = A_{0,1}^0 = A_1^0 = E_0$. The challenger set $(\mathsf{ssk}_0, \mathsf{spk}_0) = (a_{0,0}, (A_{0,0}^1, A_{0,0}^0))$, $(\mathsf{ssk}_1, \mathsf{spk}_1) = (a_{0,1}, (A_{0,1}^1, A_{0,1}^0))$ and $(\mathsf{vsk}, \mathsf{vpk}) = (a_1, (A_1^1, A_1^0))$. The simulator $\mathcal{S}$ exactly follows $\mathsf{Exp}^{\mathsf{PSI}}_{\mathsf{SDVS}}$ to answer hash query $\mathsf{H}(\cdot)$, signing $\mathcal{O}_{\mathsf{Sign}}(\cdot)$, and simulation $\mathcal{O}_{\mathsf{Sim}}(\cdot)$ oracles.

Game_2 : This is the same as Game_1 except for some modifications as follows:

- KeyGen: The challenger $\mathcal{C}$ samples $A^1_{0,0}$ from the uniform distribution over $\mathcal{E}\ell\ell$, then sets $\mathsf{ssk}_0 = \perp$ and $\mathsf{spk}_0 = (A^1_{0,0}, A^0_{0,0} = E_0)$ instead of using $a_{0,0} \leftarrow\!\!\$\, \mathbb{Z}_N$, then sets $\mathsf{ssk}_0 = a_{0,0}$ and $\mathsf{spk}_0 = (A^1_{0,0}, A^0_{0,0}) = ([\mathfrak{g}^{a_{0,0}}] \star E_0, E_0)$. We see that the probability that the adversary can distinguish between KeyGen algorithm in Game_1 and Game_2 is negligible.
- Signing Oracle $\mathcal{O}_{\mathsf{Sign}}(\mathsf{vpk}, \mathsf{spk}_i, \mathsf{m}), \forall i \in \{0,1\}$: If $i = 0$, the challanger $\mathcal{C}$ runs $\mathsf{SDVS.Sim}(\mathsf{vpk}, \mathsf{vsk}, \mathsf{spk}_0, \mathsf{m})$ using $\mathsf{vsk} = a_1$ and provides the signature σ to $\mathcal{A}$. If $i = 1$, $\mathcal{C}$ runs $\mathsf{SDVS.Sign}(\mathsf{vpk}, \mathsf{ssk}_1, \mathsf{spk}_1, \mathsf{m})$ using $\mathsf{ssk}_1 = a_{0,1}$ and provides the signature σ to $\mathcal{A}$. Since the probability that the adversary can distinguish between signatures generated by signing and simulation algorithms is negligible, the difference in Signing Oracle between Game_1 and Game_2 is also negligible.

Game_3 : This is the same as Game_2 except for some modifications as follows:

- KeyGen: The challenger $\mathcal{C}$ samples $A^1_{0,1}$ from the uniform distribution over $\mathcal{E}\ell\ell$, then sets $\mathsf{ssk}_1 = \perp$ and $\mathsf{spk}_1 = (A^1_{0,1}, A^0_{0,1} = E_0)$ instead of using $a_{0,1} \leftarrow\!\!\$\, \mathbb{Z}_N$, then sets $\mathsf{ssk}_1 = a_{0,1}$ and $\mathsf{spk}_1 = (A^1_{0,1}, A^0_{0,1}) = ([\mathfrak{g}^{a_{0,1}}] \star E_0, E_0)$. We see that the probability that the adversary can distinguish between KeyGen algorithm in Game_2 and Game_3 is negligible.
- Signing Oracle $\mathcal{O}_{\mathsf{Sign}}(\mathsf{vpk}, \mathsf{spk}_i, \mathsf{m}), \forall i \in \{0,1\}$: For all $i \in \{0,1\}$, the challanger $\mathcal{C}$ runs $\mathsf{SDVS.Sim}(\mathsf{vpk}, \mathsf{vsk}, \mathsf{spk}_i, \mathsf{m})$ using $\mathsf{vsk} = a_1$ and provides the signature σ to $\mathcal{A}$. Since the probability that the adversary can distinguish between signatures generated by signing and simulation algorithms is negligible, the difference in Signing Oracle between Game_3 and Game_2 is also negligible.

Finally, observe that in Game_3, the challenger does not use any secret key of the signer to generate a signature. Thus, it does not leak any information about the secret key. Moreover, since the adversary does not know K, it cannot verify any signatures. Therefore, the probability that the adversary can distinguish between signatures generated by the signers S_0 and S_1 is negligible.

6 Optimisation and Evaluation

6.1 Optimisation

We present an optimized SDVS construction with an enlarged challenge space $[-S, S]$. Let $\mathsf{H} : \{0,1\}^* \to \{-S, \dots, S\}^n$ and $\mathsf{H}' : \{0,1\}^* \to \{0,1\}^{2\lambda}$ be secure hash functions, modeled as random oracles in our security analysis. In this section, whenever we write $\mathbf{x} \oplus \mathbf{y}$ for challenges, we mean component-wise addition modulo $2S + 1$. Our optimized algorithms are summarized in Fig. 2.

$\mathsf{SDVS.SKGen}(\mathsf{pp})$**:** On input the public parameters pp, this algorithm samples $a^i_0 \leftarrow\!\!\$\, \mathbb{Z}_N$ for each $i \in [1, S]$, sets $A^0_0 = E_0$, and computes $A^i_0 = [\mathfrak{g}^{a^i_0}] \star E_0$. It outputs the secret key $\mathsf{ssk} = (a^1_0, \dots, a^S_0)$ and the public key $\mathsf{spk} = (A^0_0, A^1_0, \dots, A^S_0)$.

$\mathsf{SDVS.VKGen(pp)}$: On input the public parameters pp, this algorithm samples $a_1^i \leftarrow_{\$} \mathbb{Z}_N$ for each $i \in [1, S]$, sets $A_1^0 = E_0$, and computes $A_1^i = [\mathfrak{g}^{a_1^i}] \star E_0$. It outputs the secret key $\mathsf{vsk} = (a_1^1, \ldots, a_1^S)$ and the public key $\mathsf{vpk} = (A_1^0, A_1^1, \ldots, A_1^S)$.

$\mathsf{SDVS.Sign(vpk, ssk, spk, m)}$: To sign a message m, the signer parses the keys $(a_0^1, \ldots, a_0^S) \leftarrow \mathsf{ssk}$, $(A_0^0, A_0^1, \ldots, A_0^S) \leftarrow \mathsf{spk}$, and $(A_1^0, A_1^1, \ldots, A_1^S) \leftarrow \mathsf{vpk}$. It samples $\mathbf{y}_0 \leftarrow_{\$} \mathbb{Z}_N^n$ and computes $\mathbf{Y}_0 = [\mathfrak{g}^{\mathbf{y}_0}] \star E_0$. Then it samples $\mathbf{c}_1 \leftarrow_{\$} \{-S, \ldots, S\}^n$ and $\mathbf{r}_1 \leftarrow_{\$} \mathbb{Z}_N^n$, and computes $\mathbf{Y}_1 = [\mathfrak{g}^{\mathbf{r}_1}] \star A_1^{\mathbf{c}_1}$. The shared value is computed as $\mathsf{K} = \mathsf{H}'([\mathfrak{g}^{a_0^1}] \star A_1^1 \| \ldots \| [\mathfrak{g}^{a_0^S}] \star A_1^S)$. The challenge $\mathbf{c}$ is set to $\mathsf{H}(\mathbf{Y}_0 \| \mathbf{Y}_1 \| \mathsf{K} \| \mathsf{m})$, and the signer computes $\mathbf{c}_0 = \mathbf{c} \oplus \mathbf{c}_1$ and $\mathbf{r}_0 = \mathbf{y}_0 - \mathsf{sgn}(\mathbf{c}_0) \cdot a_0^{|\mathbf{c}_0|}$, where $a_0^0 := 0$. The signature is $\sigma = (\mathbf{c}_0, \mathbf{c}_1, \mathbf{r}_0, \mathbf{r}_1)$.

$\mathsf{SDVS.Sim(vpk, vsk, spk, m)}$: To simulate a signature, the designated verifier parses $(a_1^1, \ldots, a_1^S) \leftarrow \mathsf{vsk}$, $(A_1^0, A_1^1, \ldots, A_1^S) \leftarrow \mathsf{vpk}$, and $(A_0^0, A_0^1, \ldots, A_0^S) \leftarrow \mathsf{spk}$. It samples $\mathbf{y}_1 \leftarrow_{\$} \mathbb{Z}_N^n$ and computes $\mathbf{Y}_1 = [\mathfrak{g}^{\mathbf{y}_1}] \star E_0$. Then it samples $\mathbf{c}_0 \leftarrow_{\$} \{-S, \ldots, S\}^n$ and $\mathbf{r}_0 \leftarrow_{\$} \mathbb{Z}_N^n$, and computes $\mathbf{Y}_0 = [\mathfrak{g}^{\mathbf{r}_0}] \star A_0^{\mathbf{c}_0}$. The shared value is computed as $\mathsf{K} = \mathsf{H}'([\mathfrak{g}^{a_1^1}] \star A_0^1 \| \ldots \| [\mathfrak{g}^{a_1^S}] \star A_0^S)$. The challenge is $\mathbf{c} = \mathsf{H}(\mathbf{Y}_0 \| \mathbf{Y}_1 \| \mathsf{K} \| \mathsf{m})$, from which it computes $\mathbf{c}_1 = \mathbf{c} \oplus \mathbf{c}_0$ and $\mathbf{r}_1 = \mathbf{y}_1 - \mathsf{sgn}(\mathbf{c}_1) \cdot a_1^{|\mathbf{c}_1|}$, where $a_1^0 := 0$. The simulated signature is $\sigma = (\mathbf{c}_0, \mathbf{c}_1, \mathbf{r}_0, \mathbf{r}_1)$.

$\mathsf{SDVS.Verify(vsk, vpk, spk}, \sigma, \mathsf{m)}$: To verify a signature $\sigma = (\mathbf{c}_0, \mathbf{c}_1, \mathbf{r}_0, \mathbf{r}_1)$ on message m, the verifier parses $(a_1^1, \ldots, a_1^S) \leftarrow \mathsf{vsk}$, and extracts $(A_0^0, A_0^1, \ldots, A_0^S)$ and $(A_1^0, A_1^1, \ldots, A_1^S)$ from spk and vpk respectively. It computes $\mathbf{Y}'_0 = [\mathfrak{g}^{\mathbf{r}_0}] \star A_0^{\mathbf{c}_0}$, $\mathbf{Y}'_1 = [\mathfrak{g}^{\mathbf{r}_1}] \star A_1^{\mathbf{c}_1}$, and $\mathsf{K}' = \mathsf{H}'([\mathfrak{g}^{a_1^1}] \star A_0^1 \| \ldots \| [\mathfrak{g}^{a_1^S}] \star A_0^S)$. Then, it computes $\mathbf{c}' = \mathsf{H}(\mathbf{Y}'_0 \| \mathbf{Y}'_1 \| \mathsf{K}' \| \mathsf{m})$. The verifier accepts the signature if $\mathbf{c}_0 \oplus \mathbf{c}_1 = \mathbf{c}'$, and rejects otherwise.

The correctness and the security proofs for the SU-CMA, SOTR, and PSI properties remain identical to those in Theorems 1, 2, 3, and 4, respectively. The only change is that the assumption is switched from the GAIP problem to the MT-GAIP problem.

6.2 Evaluation

Our SDVS requires knowledge of the class-group structure, specifically the group order $|\mathcal{C}\ell(\mathcal{O})|$ and a short relation lattice, in order to sample and update secret values modulo $|\mathcal{C}\ell(\mathcal{O})|$ and to represent exponents in a compact form. PEGASIS [16] offers a practical effective class-group action in the CSIDH setting without computing the class group, but does not reveal this structural information. Consequently, the algebraic steps required by our SDVS cannot be performed under PEGASIS, even though it supports arbitrary ideal-class actions at higher security levels (e.g., CSIDH-2048 or CSIDH-4096).

Therefore, in our evaluation we adopt the CSIDH-512 setting proposed by Beullens et al. [7], which offers a 128-bit classical security level and over 63 bits of quantum security [12]. This setting has also been used in (linkable) ring signatures [6], group signatures [5], blind signatures [27], and adaptor signatures [25].

$\mathsf{SDVS.SKGen}(\mathsf{pp})$

$\quad$ **for** $i \in [1, S]$ **do**
$\quad\quad a_0^i \leftarrow\!\!\$\ \mathbb{Z}_N$
$\quad\quad A_0^0 \leftarrow E_0$
$\quad\quad A_0^i \leftarrow [\mathfrak{g}^{a_0^i}] \star E_0$
$\quad \mathsf{ssk} = (a_0^1, \dots, a_0^S)$
$\quad \mathsf{spk} = (A_0^0, A_0^1, \dots, A_0^S)$
$\quad$ **return** $(\mathsf{ssk}, \mathsf{spk})$

$\mathsf{SDVS.VKGen}(\mathsf{pp})$

$\quad$ **for** $i \in [1, S]$ **do**
$\quad\quad a_{1,i} \leftarrow\!\!\$\ \mathbb{Z}_N$
$\quad\quad A_1^0 \leftarrow E_0$
$\quad\quad A_1^{1,i} \leftarrow [\mathfrak{g}^{a_{1,i}}] \star E_0$
$\quad \mathsf{vsk} = (a_1^1, \dots, a_1^S)$
$\quad \mathsf{vpk} = (A_1^0, A_1^1, \dots, A_1^S)$
$\quad$ **return** $(\mathsf{vsk}, \mathsf{vpk})$

$\mathsf{SDVS.Sign}(\mathsf{vpk}, \mathsf{ssk}, \mathsf{spk}, \mathsf{m})$

$\quad$ **parse** $(a_0^1, \dots, a_0^S) \leftarrow \mathsf{ssk}$
$\quad$ **parse** $(A_0^0, A_0^1, \dots, A_0^S) \leftarrow \mathsf{spk}$
$\quad$ **parse** $(A_1^0, A_1^1, \dots, A_1^S) \leftarrow \mathsf{vpk}$
$\quad \mathbf{y}_0 \leftarrow\!\!\$\ \mathbb{Z}_N^n$
$\quad \mathbf{Y}_0 \leftarrow [\mathfrak{g}^{\mathbf{y}_0}] \star E_0$
$\quad \mathbf{c}_1 \leftarrow\!\!\$\ \{-S, \dots, S\}^n$
$\quad \mathbf{r}_1 \leftarrow\!\!\$\ \mathbb{Z}_N^n$
$\quad \mathbf{Y}_1 \leftarrow [\mathfrak{g}^{\mathbf{r}_1}] \star A_1^{\mathbf{c}_1}$
$\quad \mathsf{K} \leftarrow \mathsf{H}'([\mathfrak{g}^{a_0^1}] \star A_1^1 \| \dots \| [\mathfrak{g}^{a_0^S}] \star A_1^S)$
$\quad \mathbf{c} \leftarrow \mathsf{H}(\mathbf{Y}_0 \| \mathbf{Y}_1 \| \mathsf{K} \| \mathsf{m})$
$\quad \mathbf{c}_0 \leftarrow \mathbf{c} \oplus \mathbf{c}_1 \in \{-S, \dots, S\}^n$
$\quad a_0^0 \leftarrow 0$
$\quad \mathbf{r}_0 \leftarrow \mathbf{y}_0 - \mathsf{sgn}(\mathbf{c}_0) \cdot a_0^{|\mathbf{c}_0|}$
$\quad$ **return** $\sigma = (\mathbf{c}_0, \mathbf{c}_1, \mathbf{r}_0, \mathbf{r}_1)$

$\mathsf{SDVS.Sim}(\mathsf{vpk}, \mathsf{vsk}, \mathsf{spk}, \mathsf{m})$

$\quad$ **parse** $(a_1^1, \dots, a_1^S) \leftarrow \mathsf{vsk}$
$\quad$ **parse** $(A_1^0, A_1^1, \dots, A_1^S) \leftarrow \mathsf{vpk}$
$\quad$ **parse** $(A_0^0, A_0^1, \dots, A_0^S) \leftarrow \mathsf{spk}$
$\quad \mathbf{y}_1 \leftarrow\!\!\$\ \mathbb{Z}_N^n$
$\quad \mathbf{Y}_1 \leftarrow [\mathfrak{g}^{\mathbf{y}_1}] \star E_0$
$\quad \mathbf{c}_0 \leftarrow\!\!\$\ \{-S, \dots, S\}^n$
$\quad \mathbf{r}_0 \leftarrow\!\!\$\ \mathbb{Z}_N^n$
$\quad \mathbf{Y}_0 \leftarrow [\mathfrak{g}^{\mathbf{r}_0}] \star A_0^{\mathbf{c}_0}$
$\quad \mathsf{K} \leftarrow \mathsf{H}'([\mathfrak{g}^{a_1^1}] \star A_0^1 \| \dots \| [\mathfrak{g}^{a_1^S}] \star A_0^S)$
$\quad \mathbf{c} \leftarrow \mathsf{H}(\mathbf{Y}_0 \| \mathbf{Y}_1 \| \mathsf{K} \| \mathsf{m})$
$\quad \mathbf{c}_1 \leftarrow \mathbf{c} \oplus \mathbf{c}_0 \in \{-S, \dots, S\}^n$
$\quad a_1^0 \leftarrow 0$
$\quad \mathbf{r}_1 \leftarrow \mathbf{y}_1 - \mathsf{sgn}(\mathbf{c}_1) \cdot a_1^{|\mathbf{c}_1|}$
$\quad$ **return** $\sigma = (\mathbf{c}_0, \mathbf{c}_1, \mathbf{r}_0, \mathbf{r}_1)$

$\mathsf{Verify}(\mathsf{vsk}, \mathsf{vpk}, \mathsf{spk}, \sigma, \mathsf{m})$

$\quad$ **parse** $(a_1^1, \dots, a_1^S) \leftarrow \mathsf{vsk}$
$\quad$ **parse** $(A_0^0, A_0^1, \dots, A_0^S) \leftarrow \mathsf{spk}$
$\quad$ **parse** $(A_1^0, A_1^1, \dots, A_1^S) \leftarrow \mathsf{vpk}$
$\quad$ **parse** $(\mathbf{c}_0, \mathbf{c}_1, \mathbf{r}_0, \mathbf{r}_1) \leftarrow \sigma$
$\quad \mathbf{Y}'_0 \leftarrow [\mathfrak{g}^{\mathbf{r}_0}] \star A_0^{\mathbf{c}_0}$
$\quad \mathbf{Y}'_1 \leftarrow [\mathfrak{g}^{\mathbf{r}_1}] \star A_1^{\mathbf{c}_1}$
$\quad \mathsf{K}' \leftarrow \mathsf{H}'([\mathfrak{g}^{a_1^1}] \star A_0^1 \| \dots \| [\mathfrak{g}^{a_1^S}] \star A_0^S)$
$\quad \mathbf{c}' \leftarrow \mathsf{H}(\mathbf{Y}'_0 \| \mathbf{Y}'_1 \| \mathsf{K}' \| \mathsf{m})$
$\quad$ **if** $\mathbf{c}_0 \oplus \mathbf{c}_1 = \mathbf{c}'$ **then**
$\quad\quad$ **return** 1
$\quad$ **else return** 0

Fig. 2. Optimized Strong Designated Verifier Signatures from Isogeny Assumptions

The soundness error of the scheme is $\frac{1}{2S+1}$. To achieve a security level of λ bits, it suffices to choose $n \geq \frac{\lambda}{\log_2(2S+1)}$. Our SDVS signature takes the form $\sigma = (\mathbf{c}_0, \mathbf{c}_1, \mathbf{r}_0, \mathbf{r}_1)$, where $\mathbf{c}_0, \mathbf{c}_1 \in [-S, S]^n$ and $\mathbf{r}_0, \mathbf{r}_1 \in \mathbb{Z}_N^n$. Therefore, the total signature size is $2n \cdot (\log_2(2S+1) + \log_2 N)$ bits. The secret key of the signer is $\mathbf{a}_0 = (a_0^1, \ldots, a_0^S) \in \mathbb{Z}_N^S$. Although this key conceptually consists of S group elements, each approximately 256 bits, we can instead store only a 16-byte seed. This seed is deterministically expanded into the full key using a pseudorandom generator or hash-based key derivation function. The public key of the signer is $\mathbf{A}_0 = (A_0^1, \ldots, A_0^S)$ (note that the base point A_0^0 is part of the public parameters and need not be included in the public key). Each element A_0^i is a supersingular elliptic curve represented by its j-invariant, which fits in 64 bytes. Thus, the public key size is $64S$ bytes.

To further optimize the signature size, we adopt a technique inspired by CSI-FiSh [7], which introduces a slowdown factor k into the Fiat–Shamir transform. This factor models the use of a deliberately slower hash function (e.g., via repeated hashing or memory-hard constructions) that is 2^k times more expensive to evaluate than a standard hash function. As a result, the soundness requirement can be relaxed from $(2S+1)^{-n} \leq 2^{-\lambda}$ to $(2S+1)^{-n} \leq 2^{-\lambda+k}$, allowing for a smaller number of repetitions n. This reduction in n directly translates into shorter signature sizes. In Table 2, we present optimized parameter sets for various values of S, each paired with a corresponding slowdown factor k, demonstrating the trade-off between hash computation cost and signature compactness.

Table 2. Parameter sets, signature sizes, and key sizes of our SDVS scheme.

S	k	n	Signer Key Size		Designated Verifier Key Size		Signature Size
			Secret Key	Public Key	Secret Key	Public Key	
2^1	16	49	128 bits	128 B	128 bits	128 B	3.09 kB
2^2	14	36	128 bits	256 B	128 bits	256 B	2.28 kB
2^3	16	28	128 bits	0.5 kB	128 bits	0.5 kB	1.78 kB
2^4	13	23	128 bits	1.0 kB	128 bits	1.0 kB	1.47 kB
2^6	16	16	128 bits	4.0 kB	128 bits	4.0 kB	1.03 kB
2^8	11	13	128 bits	16.0 kB	128 bits	16 kB	862 B
2^{10}	7	11	128 bits	64.0 kB	128 bits	64 kB	735 B
2^{12}	11	9	128 bits	256.0 kB	128 bits	256 kB	606 B
2^{15}	16	7	128 bits	2.0 MB	128 bits	2.0 MB	477 B

7 Conclusion

We have proposed a strong designated verifier signature (SDVS) scheme based on isogeny assumptions, achieving smaller keys and signatures than existing post-quantum SDVS constructions. Our results highlight the efficiency and practicality of isogeny-based approaches for this primitive. Future work includes strengthening security against emerging threats and extending functionality to support broader application scenarios with more complex requirements.

References

1. Assidi, H., Souidi, E.M.: Strong designated verifier signature based on the rank metric. In: Laurent, M., Giannetsos, T. (eds.) WISTP 2019. LNCS, vol. 12024, pp. 85–102. Springer, Cham (2020). https://doi.org/10.1007/978-3-030-41702-4_6
2. Basso, A., et al.: Supersingular curves you can trust. In: Annual International Conference on the Theory and Applications of Cryptographic Techniques, pp. 405–437. Springer, Heidelberg (2023). https://doi.org/10.1007/978-3-031-30617-4_14
3. Basso, A., Codogni, G., Connolly, D., De Feo, L., Fouotsa, T.B., Lido, G.M., Morrison, T., Panny, L., Patranabis, S., Wesolowski, B.: Supersingular curves you can trust. In: Annual International Conference on the Theory and Applications of Cryptographic Techniques. pp. 405–437. Springer (2023)
4. Bernstein, D.J., Lange, T., Martindale, C., Panny, L.: Quantum circuits for the CSIDH: optimizing quantum evaluation of isogenies. In: Ishai, Y., Rijmen, V. (eds.) EUROCRYPT 2019. LNCS, vol. 11477, pp. 409–441. Springer, Cham (2019). https://doi.org/10.1007/978-3-030-17656-3_15
5. Beullens, W., Dobson, S., Katsumata, S., Lai, Y.F., Pintore, F.: Group signatures and more from isogenies and lattices: generic, simple, and efficient. In: Annual International Conference on the Theory and Applications of Cryptographic Techniques, pp. 95–126. Springer, Heidelberg (2022). https://doi.org/10.1007/978-3-031-07085-3_4
6. Beullens, W., Katsumata, S., Pintore, F.: Calamari and falafl: logarithmic (linkable) ring signatures from isogenies and lattices. In: Moriai, S., Wang, H. (eds.) ASIACRYPT 2020. LNCS, vol. 12492, pp. 464–492. Springer, Cham (2020). https://doi.org/10.1007/978-3-030-64834-3_16
7. Beullens, W., Kleinjung, T., Vercauteren, F.: CSI-FiSh: efficient isogeny based signatures through class group computations. In: Galbraith, S.D., Moriai, S. (eds.) ASIACRYPT 2019. LNCS, vol. 11921, pp. 227–247. Springer, Cham (2019). https://doi.org/10.1007/978-3-030-34578-5_9
8. Bonnetain, X., Schrottenloher, A.: Quantum security analysis of CSIDH. In: Canteaut, A., Ishai, Y. (eds.) EUROCRYPT 2020. LNCS, vol. 12106, pp. 493–522. Springer, Cham (2020). https://doi.org/10.1007/978-3-030-45724-2_17
9. Cai, J., Jiang, H., Zhang, P., Zheng, Z., Lyu, G., Xu, Q.: An efficient strong designated verifier signature based on r sis assumption. IEEE Access **7**, 3938–3947 (2019)
10. Castryck, W., Decru, T.: An efficient key recovery attack on SIDH. In: Hazay, C., Stam, M. (eds.) EUROCRYPT 2023, vol. 14008, pp. 423–447. Springer, Heidelberg (2023). https://doi.org/10.1007/978-3-031-30589-4_15
11. Castryck, W., Lange, T., Martindale, C., Panny, L., Renes, J.: CSIDH: an efficient post-quantum commutative group action. In: Peyrin, T., Galbraith, S. (eds.) ASIACRYPT 2018. LNCS, vol. 11274, pp. 395–427. Springer, Cham (2018). https://doi.org/10.1007/978-3-030-03332-3_15
12. Chávez-Saab, J., Chi-Domínguez, J.J., Jaques, S., Rodríguez-Henríquez, F.: The sqale of csidh: sublinear vélu quantum-resistant isogeny action with low exponents. J. Cryptogr. Eng. **12**(3), 349–368 (2022)
13. Chen, M., Leroux, A., Panny, L.: Scallop-hd: group action from 2-dimensional isogenies. In: IACR International Conference on Public-Key Cryptography, pp. 190–216. Springer, Heidelberg (2024). https://doi.org/10.1007/978-3-031-57725-3_7

14. Childs, A., Jao, D., Soukharev, V.: Constructing elliptic curve isogenies in quantum subexponential time. J. Math. Cryptol. **8**(1), 1–29 (2014)
15. Damgård, I., Haagh, H., Mercer, R., Nitulescu, A., Orlandi, C., Yakoubov, S.: Stronger security and constructions of multi-designated verifier signatures. In: Pass, R., Pietrzak, K. (eds.) TCC 2020. LNCS, vol. 12551, pp. 229–260. Springer, Cham (2020). https://doi.org/10.1007/978-3-030-64378-2_9
16. Dartois, P., et al.: Pegasis: practical effective class group action using 4-dimensional isogenies (2025)
17. De Feo, L., Kohel, D., Leroux, A., Petit, C., Wesolowski, B.: SQISign: compact post-quantum signatures from Quaternions and Isogenies. In: Moriai, S., Wang, H. (eds.) ASIACRYPT 2020. LNCS, vol. 12491, pp. 64–93. Springer, Cham (2020). https://doi.org/10.1007/978-3-030-64837-4_3
18. De Feo, L., Meyer, M.: Threshold schemes from isogeny assumptions. In: Kiayias, A., Kohlweiss, M., Wallden, P., Zikas, V. (eds.) PKC 2020. LNCS, vol. 12111, pp. 187–212. Springer, Cham (2020). https://doi.org/10.1007/978-3-030-45388-6_7
19. De Feo, L., et al.: Séta: supersingular encryption from torsion attacks. In: Tibouchi, M., Wang, H. (eds.) ASIACRYPT 2021. LNCS, vol. 13093, pp. 249–278. Springer, Cham (2021). https://doi.org/10.1007/978-3-030-92068-5_9
20. El Kaafarani, A., Katsumata, S., Pintore, F.: Lossy CSI-FiSh: efficient signature scheme with tight reduction to decisional CSIDH-512. In: Kiayias, A., Kohlweiss, M., Wallden, P., Zikas, V. (eds.) PKC 2020. LNCS, vol. 12111, pp. 157–186. Springer, Cham (2020). https://doi.org/10.1007/978-3-030-45388-6_6
21. Feo, L.D., et al.: Scallop: scaling the csi-fish. In: IACR International Conference on Public-Key Cryptography, pp. 345–375. Springer, Heidelberg (2023). https://doi.org/10.1007/978-3-031-31368-4_13
22. Huang, Q., Yang, G., Wong, D.S., Susilo, W.: Efficient strong designated verifier signature schemes without random oracle or with non-delegatability. Int. J. Inf. Secur. **10**, 373–385 (2011)
23. Huang, X., Susilo, W., Mu, Y., Zhang, F.: Short designated verifier signature scheme and its identity-based variant. Int. J. Netw. Secur. **6**(1), 82–93 (2008). http://ijns.jalaxy.com.tw/contents/ijns-v6-n1/ijns-2008-v6-n1-p82-93.pdf
24. Jakobsson, M., Sako, K., Impagliazzo, R.: Designated verifier proofs and their applications. In: Maurer, U. (ed.) EUROCRYPT 1996. LNCS, vol. 1070, pp. 143–154. Springer, Heidelberg (1996). https://doi.org/10.1007/3-540-68339-9_13
25. Jana, P., Shaw, S., Dutta, R.: Compact adaptor signature from isogenies with enhanced security. In: International Conference on Cryptology and Network Security, pp. 77–100. Springer, Heidelberg (2024). https://doi.org/10.1007/978-981-97-8013-6_4
26. Jao, D., De Feo, L.: Towards quantum-resistant cryptosystems from supersingular elliptic curve isogenies. In: Yang, B.-Y. (ed.) PQCrypto 2011. LNCS, vol. 7071, pp. 19–34. Springer, Heidelberg (2011). https://doi.org/10.1007/978-3-642-25405-5_2
27. Katsumata, S., Lai, Y.F., LeGrow, J.T., Qin, L.: Csi-otter: isogeny-based (partially) blind signatures from the class group action with a twist. Des. Codes Crypt. **92**(11), 3587–3643 (2024)
28. Kuperberg, G.: A subexponential-time quantum algorithm for the dihedral hidden subgroup problem. SIAM J. Comput. **35**(1), 170–188 (2005)
29. Kuperberg, G.: Another subexponential-time quantum algorithm for the dihedral hidden subgroup problem. arXiv preprint arXiv:1112.3333 (2011)

30. Laguillaumie, F., Vergnaud, D.: Designated verifier signatures: anonymity and efficient construction from *any* bilinear map. In: Blundo, C., Cimato, S. (eds.) SCN 2004. LNCS, vol. 3352, pp. 105–119. Springer, Heidelberg (2005). https://doi.org/10.1007/978-3-540-30598-9_8
31. Maino, L., Martindale, C., Panny, L., Pope, G., Wesolowski, B.: A direct key recovery attack on SIDH. In: EUROCRYPT 2023, pp. 448–471. Springer, Heidelberg (2023). https://doi.org/10.1007/978-3-031-30589-4_16
32. Noh, G., Jeong, I.R.: Strong designated verifier signature scheme from lattices in the standard model. Secur. Commun. Netw. **9**(18), 6202–6214 (2016)
33. Peikert, C.: He gives C-sieves on the CSIDH. In: Canteaut, A., Ishai, Y. (eds.) EUROCRYPT 2020. LNCS, vol. 12106, pp. 463–492. Springer, Cham (2020). https://doi.org/10.1007/978-3-030-45724-2_16
34. Robert, D.: Breaking sidh in polynomial time. In: Annual International Conference on the Theory and Applications of Cryptographic Techniques, pp. 472–503. Springer, Heidelberg (2023). DOI: https://doi.org/10.1007/978-3-031-30589-4_17
35. Sahu, R.A., Gini, A., Pal, A.: Supersingular isogeny-based designated verifier blind signature (2019)
36. Schoof, R.: Counting points on elliptic curves over finite fields. J. de théorie des nombres de Bordeaux **7**(1), 219–254 (1995)
37. Shooshtari, M.K., Ahmadian-Attari, M., Aref, M.R.: Provably secure strong designated verifier signature scheme based on coding theory. Int. J. Commun. Syst. **30**(7), e3162 (2017)
38. Shor, P.: Algorithms for quantum computation: discrete logarithms and factoring. In: Proceedings 35th Annual Symposium on Foundations of Computer Science, pp. 124–134 (1994). https://doi.org/10.1109/SFCS.1994.365700
39. Sun, X., Tian, H., Wang, Y.: Toward quantum-resistant strong designated verifier signature from isogenies. In: 2012 Fourth International Conference on Intelligent Networking and Collaborative Systems, pp. 292–296. IEEE (2012)
40. Wang, F.H., Hu, Y.P., Wang, C.X.: Identity-based strong designate verifier signature over lattices. J. China Univ. Posts Telecommun. **21**(6), 52–60 (2014)
41. Wang, F., Hu, Y., Wang, B.: Lattice-based strong designate verifier signature and its applications. Malays. J. Comput. Sci. **25**(1), 11–22 (2012)
42. Yoo, Y., Azarderakhsh, R., Jalali, A., Jao, D., Soukharev, V.: A post-quantum digital signature scheme based on supersingular isogenies. In: Kiayias, A. (ed.) FC 2017. LNCS, vol. 10322, pp. 163–181. Springer, Cham (2017). https://doi.org/10.1007/978-3-319-70972-7_9
43. Zhang, Y., Susilo, W., Guo, F.: Lattice-based strong designated verifier signature with non-delegatability. Comput. Stand. Interfaces **92**, 103904 (2025)

To Extend or Not to Extend: Agile Masking Instructions for PQC

Markus Krausz[1], Georg Land[2], Florian Stolz[3(✉)], Jan Richter-Brockmann[3], and Tim Güneysu[3,4]

[1] TÜV Informationstechnik GmbH, Essen, Germany
m.krausz@tuvit.de
[2] Intel Labs, Portland, OR, USA
georg.land@intel.com
[3] Ruhr-University, Bochum, Germany
{florian.stolz,jan.richter-brockmann,tim.guneysu}@rub.de
[4] DFKI GmbH, Bremen, Germany

Abstract. Splitting up sensitive data into multiple shares – termed *masking* – has proven an effective countermeasure against various types of Side-Channel Analysis (SCA) on cryptographic implementations. However, in software this approach leads to dramatic performance overheads for non-linear operations. This problem can be addressed with hardware accelerators particularly designed to process masked data securely. In this context, Gao et *al.* [24] presented a RISC-V Instruction Set Extension (ISE) with masked Boolean and arithmetic instructions to accelerate masked software implementations of block ciphers. In this work, we demonstrate how this ISE can be applied to and extended for Post-Quantum Cryptography (PQC) components, forming a crypto-agile solution. We provide masked implementations based on three different ISE constellations for multiple highly relevant components, including Cumulative Distribution Table (CDT) sampling and polynomial rotation. With the masked instructions, we measure speedups of up to a factor 4.2 compared to sophisticated bitsliced implementations and even up to more than two orders of magnitude for non-bitsliced implementations. We assert the first-order security of our new instructions with a practical evaluation.

Keywords: PQC · Masking · HQC · Kyber · RISC-V

1 Introduction

Nowadays, embedded devices are interconnected via a broad variety of communication channels. In case sensitive data is transmitted via these channels, the communication should be protected. Although the chosen algorithms are considered secure, *implementations* of cryptographic algorithms are generally vulnerable to side-channel attacks on any platform. For example, an adversary can exploit

G. Land—The author has contributed to this work solely during his time at Ruhr-University.

Y. Kim et al. (Eds.): CANS 2025, LNCS 16351, pp. 70–92, 2026.
https://doi.org/10.1007/978-981-95-4434-9_4

secret-dependent runtime differences of the algorithms caused by instructions with data-dependent runtime. Moreover, having physical access to the target device allows the adversary to measure the device's power consumption directly or indirectly via its electromagnetic emission, thereby gaining information about secret key material. Especially power Side-Channel Analysis (SCA) has recently become more and more accessible due to simple and inexpensive measurement setups [28].

Researchers from academia and industry proposed many approaches to counteract these attack vectors. In order to prevent timing attacks, the *constant-time* programming paradigm [36] emerged as a generic defense mechanism. The most promising countermeasure against power SCA is *masking* [37], splitting sensitive data into secret shares. Consequently, underlying operations have to be transformed to be able to perform these operations on shares.

Applying masking techniques to implementations of novel cryptographic schemes raises new challenges. This includes novel schemes designed to be secure against attacks mounted on quantum computers. The NIST already selected five different Post-Quantum Cryptography (PQC) schemes for standardization and 40 new schemes have been submitted to the call for additional signature schemes, out of which 14 recently advanced to a second round. On top of that, agencies from other countries with a strong economic infrastructure (e.g. the French ANSSI or German BSI) partially recommend other PQC schemes, South Korea even started a similar competition process as NIST, and has announced a final selection recently [39]. On the other hand, the cryptographic foundations of many schemes require more scrutiny, which can lead to drop-outs of promising candidates [8]. The set of relevant PQC schemes is therefore extensive and dynamic, and brings new issues regarding efficient and secure implementations.

For example, as shown by Krausz et *al.* [31], protecting fixed-weight polynomial samplers of common PQC schemes like BIKE, HQC, NTRU and many others with masking introduces a huge overhead with respect to the runtime and randomness requirements of the design. One reason for this overhead lies in the simultaneous protection against timing and power side channels.

Besides performance degradation, masked software implementations also have to tackle the issue of microarchitectural power leakage [33], where a masked implementation can be secure from a source code perspective, but still exhibits side-channel leakage due to unforeseeable combinations of shares induced by microarchitectural behavior.

A powerful solution to tackle performance degradation and microarchitectural leakage, is to extend cores with dedicated accelerators for masking. In this context, Gao et *al.* [24] presented a RISC-V Instruction Set Extension (ISE) with masked Boolean and arithmetic instructions. With *masked instructions* we refer to instructions that operate on both shares (for first-order masking) of their masked operands simultaneously. The simultaneous computation on both shares leads can lead to significant speedups. Additionally, controlling the hardware allows for mitigation of any unintended microarchitectural behavior. However, their evaluation is limited to block ciphers.

In this work, we explore the application of masked instructions for PQC components that are used in multiple schemes. Besides the already mentioned

Table 1. Masked implementations presented and evaluated in this work. A green check mark indicates an implementation that completely originates from this work. The orange check marks (with brackets) indicate implementations that are based on the public code by Krausz et *al.* [31]. Dashes indicate combinations that are not applicable.

Application	Scheme	Algorithm	Representation	
			standard	bitsliced
Fixed-Weight Polynomial Sampling	each applicable to BIKE, HQC, NTRU, and many on-ramp signatures	Fisher-Yates	✔	(✔)
		Sorting	✔	(✔)
		Rejection	✔	(✔)
		Comparison	✔	(✔)
		I2C Conversion	✔	(✔)
Gaussian Sampling	FrodoKEM	CDT Sampling	✔	✔
	Haetae	CDT Sampling	✔	✔
	Hawk	CDT Sampling	—	✔
Polynomial Rotation	BIKE	Barrel Shifter	✔	—
Hashing	all PQC	Keccak	✔	—

fixed-weight sampling, this includes discrete Gaussian sampling based on Cumulative Distribution Tables (CDTs), and polynomial rotation by a secret amount. Furthermore, we implement a masked Keccak, which is used within SHA-3 and SHAKE, both of which are deployed in the majority of relevant PQC schemes. Eventually, we also show that our work is applicable to a crucial part of Kyber (which is standardized under the name ML-KEM), achieving a significant speed-up. We identify a small set of performance-critical core operations, relevant for most of the previously mentioned use cases. These operations are the conditional move (cmov) and integer comparisons (cmp) with Boolean shared operands.

The general-purpose nature of the masked instructions evaluated in this work makes them useful for any cryptographic primitive or scheme and leads to great crypto-agility: Instead of accelerating only one or a small subset of the relevant PQC schemes, they are able to significantly improve the performance of a large quantity of quantum-secure, asymmetric cryptography on top of symmetric cryptography.

Contribution. To summarize the contributions of this work, we provide masked software implementations for a wide set (see Table 1) of algorithms used in PQC in multiple variants, to evaluate the impact of masked instructions as proposed by Gao et *al.* [24]. To allow a fair and in-depth comparison, we develop or adapt existing bitsliced implementations, besides our non-bitsliced variants. The latter profit significantly more from masked instructions. Nevertheless, we are able to reach speed-up factors more than an order of magnitude.

Moreover, we identify core operations (cmov, cmp) required in multiple critical PQC components and extend the RISC-V core presented in [24] with masked instructions for these operations. Furthermore, we improve upon the work by Uhle et *al.* [40] and eliminate leakage within the core. We validate the side-channel security of our implementations by performing t-test evaluations on our additional instructions. Finally, we perform extensive benchmarks with multiple parameter sets and Instruction Set Architecture (ISA) constellations to evaluate the performance impact of masked instructions on PQC. To facilitate adaption and future research, our source code for software and hardware is publicly available at https://github.com/Chair-for-Security-Engineering/agile-maskingise-pqc.

Related Work. Gao et *al.* [24] present an ISE for RISC-V featuring power side-channel secure (first masking order) instructions operating on shared values. The ISE consists of instructions for Boolean operations, arithmetic operations, domain conversations and finite field operations. They implement the ISE in the SCARV CPU, a 5-stage pipelined microprocessor, and evaluate it with common block ciphers. Uhle et *al.* [40] identify several vulnerabilities in this core, and we incorporate their improvements into our work. Marshall and Page [32] investigate how higher masking orders can be realized, utilizing RISC-V's vector ISE. Cheng et *al.* [10] also work with an ISE to address power side-channel leakage, but focus on the aspect of microarchitectural leakage.

Accelerators for masked Kyber and Saber implementations have been presented by Fritzmann et *al.* [23]. In contrast to our work, they provide masked accelerators for higher-level functionalities. Nevertheless, they include, e.g., a masked adder for Boolean shared values.

2 Preliminaries

This work focuses on three PQC components: fixed-weight polynomial sampling, CDT sampling, and syndrome rotation, all prone to SCA in unprotected implementations and costly in masked software. These components, along with Keccak (common in PQC) and the ML-KEM decompression function, can be accelerated with a small set of core operations.

2.1 Fixed-Weight Polynomial Sampling

A wide range of PQC schemes requires fixed-weight polynomial samplers to randomly generate a binary or ternary polynomial with a fixed length N and a fixed number of non-zero coefficients (weight) W from a uniform distribution.

Fixed-weight polynomial sampling algorithms produce polynomials in either index or coefficient representation. The index representation, which stores non-zero coefficient indices, is more compact for low W/N ratios, while the coefficient representation stores the plain coefficients. The choice of representation depends on the polynomial operations following sampling, with most requiring the coefficient representation. Converting between these representations is computationally expensive when masked.

Fixed-weight polynomial sampling is used in BIKE, HQC, McEliece, NTRU, Streamlined NTRU Prime, and NTRU LPRrime, well-known from NIST's standardization process, and also SMAUG [12] and Haetae [11], which are selected for standardization by KpqC [39]. Moreover, several schemes for NIST's signature on-ramp feature related procedures (CROSS, EagleSign, Raccoon, ALTEQ, FuLeeca, LESS). A recent paper [7] about sampling random permutations in PQC presents further applications.

While requirements and parameters slightly differ between the schemes, the sampling problem at its heart is the same. Timing side-channel attacks on the samplers of BIKE and HQC have already been demonstrated [25,30,38] and it is probable that similar attacks based on power leakage exist.

Krausz et *al.* [31] compare the performance of fixed-weight polynomial sampling algorithms as masked software implementations. The benchmarks show that the performance of the algorithms clearly varies depending on the parameters N and W, and the preference for different algorithms depends on the individual use case. However, all reported runtimes remain unsatisfactory, often impractical. The situation is worst for BIKE and HQC, where the *decapsulation* requires sampling, and side-channel secure implementations cannot use the most efficient algorithms due to timing leakage of the secret seed (cf. [25]). While a previous masked implementation approach [15] exists, it is likely insecure in practice [1,31].

The most critical operation for most sampling algorithms is a masked conditional move or integer comparison, sometimes required in nested loops. Accelerating these operations with dedicated hardware instructions therefore can greatly improve the sampling performance and lead to practical runtimes. Section 3.2 details about why exactly these operations are so crucial.

2.2 Sampling from a Discrete Gaussian Distribution

Discrete Gaussian sampling is essential for many lattice-based cryptographic schemes [4,19]. We denote the discrete Gaussian distribution with variance σ^2 as $\mathcal{N}_{\mathbb{Z}}(\sigma^2)$. Then, $\mathcal{N}_{\mathbb{Z}}^{+}(\sigma^2)$ is the equivalent to $\mathcal{N}_{\mathbb{Z}}(\sigma^2)$ which only produces non-negative samples. There are multiple well-studied algorithms to perform sampling from discrete Gaussian distribution [6,19,20]. The most common approach is CDT sampling [35], where a uniform random bit string is compared with the entries in a pre-computed Cumulative Distribution Table. This CDT approximates $\mathcal{N}_{\mathbb{Z}}^{+}(\sigma^2)$ for a given precision and σ^2. For a random bit string r, the output sample is the index i in the table T, for which $T_i < r \leq T_{i+1}$. To avoid branches and secret-depending memory accesses, the random bit string must be compared against each entry in the table. Then, the comparison result bits are accumulated to obtain the sample, which is mapped to $\mathcal{N}_{\mathbb{Z}}(\sigma^2)$ by conditional negation with another random bit.

The most notable application of CDT sampling is FrodoKEM, where it is used for sampling error terms during key generation, encapsulation and decapsulation. In particular, the procedure is performed deterministically during decapsulation in the re-encryption step, because of the Fujisaki-Okamoto transform. Notably, a practical attack on FrodoKEM was already shown [34].

Algorithm 1. Word-unit rotation used in BIKE's decapsulation.

Data: Vector $v = \{s, s, s\}$ holding three consecutive copies of s, secret index δ
Result: Rotated syndrome s
function WORD_UNIT_ROTATION(v, δ)
    $i \leftarrow \lceil \log_2(r/32/2) \rceil$
    while $i \geq 1$ **do**
        $m \leftarrow$ 0xFFFFFFFF **if** $\delta > i$ **else** 0x00000000
        $\delta \leftarrow \delta - (i \,\&\, m)$
        for $j = 0$ **to** $r/32 + i$ **do**
            $v[j] \leftarrow (v[j] \,\&\, \sim m) \mid (v[j+i] \,\&\, m)$
        $i \leftarrow i >> 1$
    return Lower r bits of v

Another important example is Hawk [21], whose authors claim that the only missing part to enable a fully masked implementation is sampling discrete Gaussian variates from a CDT.

Finally, there is Haetae [11]. Haetae is similar to Dilithium, but sampling the signature nonce $\mathbf{y}$ involves CDT sampling. For a high-assurance version of its deterministic variant, this sampler must be protected accordingly using masking countermeasures.

The basic operation within the sampler is the comparison of a *secret bit string* with a *public constant*. A standard software approach to achieve this is bitslicing the inputs and then using the optimized comparison as described in [31]. For a masked comparison, masked subtraction and shift operations as provided by [24] are sufficient. However, a dedicated masked greater-than comparison instruction could further improve the performance while inducing only a miniscule area overhead in the core.

2.3 BIKE Syndrome Rotation

For our third example, we investigate the side-channel resistance of BIKE. In contrast to the numerous lattice-based schemes, BIKE's security foundation relies on linear error-correcting codes. Cheriere et *al.* [13] presented a power side-channel attack on the optimized Cortex-M4 microcontroller implementation presented at CHES 2021 by Chen et *al.* [9]. Independently of the work by Cheriere et *al.*, we developed a similar attack, which we briefly describe in this section. We show that the conditional move operations in BIKE's portable C implementation [16] allow to perform a Simple Power Analysis (SPA) leading to a partial secret key recovery even for ephemeral keys.

In the decapsulation of BIKE, the error polynomials, which are intentionally added to the encrypted message in the encapsulation are iteratively decoded by the Black-Grey-Flip (BGF) decoder [17]. In this decoding step, the syndrome s is rotated by the secret indices of the private key (similar to the multiplication presented in [14]). More precisely, these indices are represented by $\lceil \log r \rceil$ bits where r denotes the size of the polynomials used in BIKE. On a 32-bit architecture, the vector storing the syndrome s is divided into $\lceil r/32 \rceil$ chunks. Hence, applying a rotation by k bits (i.e., a secret index of the private key), can be accomplished by performing a *word-unit rotation* by the upper $\lceil \log r \rceil - 5$ bits of k (denoted by δ in the following) and a subsequent *bit-unit rotation* by the lower five bits of k. In the presented attack, we only measure the power consumption of the word-unit rotation (i.e., rotation by δ) as differences in the power consumption depending on the applied private key can already be distinguished by using just one single trace.

To this end, we show the constant-time implementation of the word-unit rotation in Algorithm 1. For each bit δ_i in δ, the algorithm computes a mask m which is set to 0xFFFFFFFF in case the bit is one or to 0x00000000 in case the bit is zero. Afterwards, the implementation loops over the whole syndrome, loads the shifted and the unshifted value and selects one of them based on m. This procedure ensures that both – the rotated and unrotated – values are loaded from the memory and no timing differences with respect to the secret index (i.e., δ) can be observed.

As mentioned above, the aforementioned procedure is required to achieve a constant-time implementation, and masking all relevant parts is straightforward but incurs a huge implementation overhead. More precisely, the crucial operation that generates the leakage is the *conditional move* controlled by the mask m. To this end, first-order masking of the syndrome would double the implementation's memory footprint. A masked implementation should therefore focus on improving the performance of a conditional move instruction.

2.4 Hashing

Hashing, or related tasks like deterministic randomness expansion as a Pseudo-Random Function (PRF) or an Extendable-output Function (XOF), are part of nearly all PQC schemes. For the NIST standardization efforts, it is required to use NIST-standardized algorithms such as SHA-3 or SHAKE. Often, these tasks process or generate secret data that needs to be protected against power SCA. The basic permutation function behind this is Keccak-f. Apart from that, hashing, PRFs, and XOFs have a major influence on the overall performance of the execution of PQC schemes. This is especially the case for embedded devices, where hashing takes up to 75 % of the clock cycles for relevant procedures [29]. For masked implementations, it is to be expected that this percentage even increases for some schemes (e.g., Haetae), as Keccak involves many non-linear operations.

Keccak-f consists of 24 permutation rounds, each of which performs five steps on the 1 600-bit state. The first three steps of each permutation round are linear in the Boolean sharing domain, and the fourth step is constant addition. Thus, these steps can be masked trivially. The main challenge of masking Keccak is the χ step, which is a quadratic mapping.

2.5 Kyber Decompression

Kyber is standardized by NIST under the name ML-KEM, and has been subject to extensive side-channel analyses. In this context, a particular focus has been set on the Fujisaki-Okamoto transform, that turns a CPA-secure encryption scheme into a CCA-secure Key Encapsulation Mechanism (KEM). For this, the ciphertext is first CPA-decrypted during CCA-decapsulation, and the resulting plaintext m is CPA-reencrypted given deterministic randomness. Here, even a small (side-channel-)adversarial knowledge about m before reencryption can result in key recovery attacks[1].

One crucial step during reencryption is the conversion of the message bit string to a polynomial, which is termed $\mathsf{Decompress}_q$ in the specification. For this, a one bit is converted to $\lfloor q/2 \rfloor$ (with $q = 3229$), and a zero bit is converted to a 0 coefficient. In their masked Kyber implementation, Heinz et *al.* [26] have chosen a trivial way to mask this, which turned out to be insecure practically, as shown by Dubrova et *al.* [18]. We observe that this procedure essentially is a *conditional move* of $\lfloor q/2 \rfloor$ into a zero-initialized vector.

3 Software Implementation

We develop efficient C code for all applications to evaluate the hardware accelerators. Table 1 provides an overview of the algorithms implemented in this work. Our code works for arbitrary masking orders, however, the masked instructions on the core only support first-order masking.

Bitslicing. For highspeed symmetric cryptographic software implementations, bitslicing [3] has been an important technique for many years. The general idea is to reach better resource utilization by using the full register width although operating on values bounded by fewer bits – in particular when operating on single bits. Therefore, data has to be transformed to the bitsliced representation. Operations can then be done on 32 values in parallel, always using the full register width. In theory, a speedup of a factor equal to the register width can be achieved for operations on single-digit values, whenever parallelization is possible. However, transformations from and to the bitsliced representation and sometimes padding introduce overhead. Bitslicing is also a very efficient technique to optimize *masked* software implementations because it can reduce the number of costly non-linear operations significantly [5,31]. To allow a fair comparison, we provide standard (non-bitsliced) and bitsliced implementations for all algorithms if applicable.

Masked Instructions. We implement wrapper functions with inline assembly utilizing the masked instructions. Via preprocessor directives, we are able to compile versions with standard instructions, with masked instruction and with

[1] Hermelink et *al.* [27] state that as little as 60 % of the message bits must be recovered correctly for a successful attack.

our extension. From the masked instructions by Gao et *al.*, only a subset is used in our code, all of them operate on Boolean shares: mask, unmask, not, and, or, xor, slli, srli, add and sub. The rest of the instructions – e.g., instructions to switch from Boolean to arithmetic masking domain and vice versa – do not apply. Without masked instructions, all masked operations are realized by secure gadgets presented by [5,31], which rely on unmasked instructions.

3.1 Additional Masked Instructions

During our work we identified a small set of repeatedly occurring operations. For a branch-less, secret-dependent selection of different values, timing side-channel secure implementations rely on dedicated select or conditional move instructions, if available on the architecture. A corresponding *masked* cmov can be applied at performance critical locations for multiple fixed-weight polynomial sampling algorithms, all CDT samplers and is the most relevant operation for a polynomial rotation. Two other common general purpose instructions are integer comparisons. Many sampling algorithms repeatedly check if a random value exceeds a threshold (cmpgt), or if two values collide (cmpeq). We therefore investigate if dedicated masked instructions for these operations are worthwhile. They clearly do not provide an advantage for the block ciphers implemented by Gao et *al.*, but are potentially useful for asymmetric cryptography beyond the applications presented in this paper.

To allow a fair evaluation of the benefit of the additional instructions, we examine in detail how the operations can alternatively be computed with only the masked instructions by Gao et *al.* and without any masked instructions.

cmov. Given a mask c of zeros if the condition is false, or a mask of ones if the condition is true, we can implement a conditional move of b to a with only three Boolean operations: $tmp := b \oplus a$, followed by $tmp := tmp \wedge c$ and $a := a \oplus tmp$. All of these sub-operations are realized with their respective masked instructions by Gao et *al.* if available. All of these sub-operations must be side-channel secure and can be realized with their respective masked instructions by Gao et *al.* if available.

cmpeq. For the base ISA, we xor the two operands and use a sequence of shifting and oring to compress xor into a single bit. If the inputs are equal, the xor returns 0 and compression also results in 0. The operation sequence depicted in Algorithm 2. Its performance is dominated by five secure or operations. In contrast to this, we use a faster, dedicated operation sequence whenever masked, Boolean instructions are available. In this case, we compute the first operand minus the second one and vice versa, combining the two results with a or, which is shown in Algorithm 3. Then, the most significant bit is set if the operands are *not* equal.

Algorithm 2. cmpeq with base ISA. All Boolean operations are performed with secure gadgets.

Input: Boolean-shared values a, b
Output: Boolean-shared res, 1 if a and b are equal
res $:= a \oplus b$
res $:=$ res $\vee$ $(res \gg 16)$
res $:=$ res $\vee$ $(res \gg 8)$
res $:=$ res $\vee$ $(res \gg 4)$
res $:=$ res $\vee$ $(res \gg 2)$
return (res $\vee$ $(res \gg 1)) \oplus 1$

Algorithm 3. cmpeq with ISE by Gao et *al.* All arithmetic operations are performed with the Boolean-masked instructions.

Input: Boolean-shared values a, b
Output: Boolean-shared res, 1 if a and b are equal
$\text{tmp}_0 := a - b$
$\text{tmp}_1 := b - a$
res $:= \text{tmp}_0 \vee \text{tmp}_1$
return (res $\gg 31) \oplus 1$

cmpgt. We apply a similar handling for the cmpgt operation. For the base ISA, we adapt the optimized comparison from [31] to the standard representation. However, in a non-bitsliced fashion this is still costly, which is why a bitsliced implementation is preferable when no ISE is available. If masked masked subtraction and shift instructions are available, we can express the comparison efficiently with a subtraction followed by a shift to the right to get the most significant bit. This only works when both operands can be represented with at most 31 bit, or in other words, when the most significant bit of both operands is zero. Due to the possible parameter ranges for N and W, this is always the case in our applications.

3.2 Masked Fixed-Weight Polynomial Sampling

For fixed-weight polynomial sampling we implemented non-bitsliced variants for four different approaches: Fisher-Yates, sorting, rejection, and comparison. Additionally we implemented the I2C conversion. We also adapted the bitsliced code from Krausz et *al.* [31] so that it can be compiled with masked instructions to enable a fair comparison.

In the following, we briefly summarize the algorithms presented in [31] and discuss their key instructions.

Fisher-Yates. In the inner loop of the side-channel secure Fisher-Yates method, a masked cmov based on the result of a masked cmpeq is executed. Nevertheless, for the standard implementation, we use bitslicing for another single loop, because it requires a 48-bit transformation from the Boolean to the arithmetic domain and vice versa. Although the core by Gao et *al.* has dedicated instructions for these conversions, they only work for 32-bit operands. In contrast, the gadget implemented by Bronchain and Cassiers [5] allows (with minor modifications) efficient bitsliced conversions for this size, and thus the costs are amortized.

Sorting. Constant-time sorting can be done with sorting networks. The bitsliced sorting algorithm in [31] is based on Batchers's Bitonic mergesort, which is easy to parallelize. This algorithm is narrowly outperformed by djb-sort [2] for the non-bitsliced implementation. The fundamental operation in a sorting network is a cmpgt followed by a conditional swap (i.e., two cmov). We can use an optimized instruction sequence based on subtraction by exploiting the fact that only the upper 30 bits consist of the random values that are compared.

Rejection Sampling. Rejection sampling requires a cmpgt to verify whether a sampled bitstring represents a valid index below N. Additionally, a loop over the already sampled indices checks for collisions using cmpeq. We did not implement and evaluate the bounded rejection sampling method, because the Fisher-Yates approach is strictly superior as already pointed out by Krausz et *al.* [31].

Comparison Sampling. Comparison sampling sets each coefficient bit individually with probability $p = W/N$. This is implemented by comparing a random l-bit string with the constant $\lfloor 2^l p \rceil$ and setting the coefficient to one if the random value is below the threshold. Naturally, this heavily relies on a cmpgt operation.

I2C Conversion. Both the Fisher-Yates shuffle and rejection sampling generate polynomials in the index representations. In most cases, however, the coefficient representation is required. The conversion is straightforward: we start from a polynomial in coefficient representation where all coefficients are set to zero. Then, a public counter i runs from 0 to $N-1$ and in each iteration, we check whether i is equal to each coefficient in the list of indices. Depending on this cmpeq result, we cmov a one into the position i in the result polynomial. Thus, the conversion performs exactly $N \cdot W$ cmpeq and cmov.

3.3 Masked CDT Sampler

The most important masked operations are integer greater-than comparison and bit accumulation. For our bitsliced variant, we implement the optimized comparison with a public constant from [31], which only uses $\lceil \log_2 t \rceil$ secure and operations. Bit accumulation can be performed with half adders, adapting the masked implementation from Bronchain and Cassiers [5].

Our non-bitsliced implementation varies depending on the masked instructions available. Again, the operands for the greater-than comparison are bounded (e.g., 15 bits in the case of FrodoKEM), which allows us to use different optimal operation sequences. Note that for the case of Hawk, the CDT entries have a size of 80 bit, which renders a non-bitsliced implementation infeasible as our comparison instruction can only handle 32 bit values. An overview of our CDT Sampler is provided in Algorithm 4.

Algorithm 4. Bitsliced CDT Sampler

```
System parameters: the CDT T, a tuple of ascending-sorted comparison values;
    L = ⌈log_2(max(T))⌉, l = ⌈log_2(|T|)⌉
Input: Boolean-shared uniform randomness bitslices r_0, ..., r_{L-1}
Output: Boolean-shared, bitsliced resulting discrete Gaussians x_0, ..., x_{l-1}
x_0, ..., x_{l-1} := 0                       ▷ initialize masked result bitslices
for j := 0 until |T| - 1 do
    k := 0
    c := 0                                   ▷ initialize masked comparison result
    while (T_j ≫ k) > 0 do                   ▷ perform bitsliced comparison with entry T_j
        t := SecNot(r_k)
        if (T_j ≫ k)&1 = 1 then              ▷ comparison method from [31]
            c := SecOr(c, t)
        else
            c := SecAnd(c, t)
        k := k + 1
    if j = 0 then                            ▷ c carries inverted comparison result
        x_j := SecNot(c)
    else                                     ▷ add inverted comparison result
        c := SecNot(c)
        t := SecAnd(x_0, c)
        x_0 := SecXor(x_0, c)
        for k := 1 until ⌈log_2(j + 1)⌉ do   ▷ ripple-carry over significant bits
            u := SecXor(x_k, t)
            t := SecAnd(x_k, t)
            x_k := u
```

3.4 Masked BIKE Rotation

A naïve implementation of the polynomial rotation with word granularity in BIKE could be structured very similarly to Algorithm 1. However, this would lead to many unnecessary loads and stores. Instead, we follow the optimized but unmasked implementation for the Cortex-M4 [9] and optimize the memory accesses by operating on chains of values. Thus, we keep an entry in the registers during the cmov to the next entry and the cmov from the previous entry. Consequently, the rotation obviously relies heavily on the masked cmov.

Our implementation expects a pointer to three consecutive instances of the masked polynomial. Three instances are required because the number of registers for one polynomial, which is the maximum secret rotation amount r, is not a power of two. As the side-channel secure rotation works bitwise, it covers rotation amounts up to $2^{\lceil \log_2 r \rceil} - 1 > r$, and thus, extends over the second copy. Apart from $\lceil \log_2 r \rceil$ masked shift operations that are required to select the desired bit for each round, the rotation mainly consists of $\lceil \log_2 r \rceil r$ masked cmov operations. Bitslicing is not applicable here, because the conditional move already operates on the full register width.

3.5 Masked Keccak

To the best of our knowledge, we are the first to report numbers for a masked Keccak implementation for the RISC-V ISA. Previous work implemented a masked Keccak by employing a HW/SW codesign with hardware acceleration for specific substeps [22]. As already explained before, Keccak consists of three linear steps, one affine step, and a quadratic step. For the linear and affine steps, the masked xor instructions are expected to yield a moderate speed-up, while the biggest contribution to an overall acceleration will come from the masked and instructions that speed up the quadratic χ step. However, in contrast to the other use cases, Keccak does not profit from the additional cmov and cmp instructions.

3.6 Masked Kyber Decompression

As pointed out in Sect. 2.5, we can deploy the masked cmov instruction to improve security and efficiency here. The procedure then is straightforward: First, we initialize a masked vector of 256 zero values. Then, we iterate over the 256 message bits m_i, using each as select bit for the cmov instruction, and a freshly masked $\lfloor q/2 \rfloor$ as first input and a freshly masked zero as second input. The output will use new randomness by design from the instructions and a side-channel adversary cannot distinguish between a zero and one message bit.

4 Hardware Implementation

Our hardware implementation is based on the SCARV[2], an embedded class 32-bit RISC-V processor. The masking ISE by Gao et *al.* stores shares in the adjacent general-purpose registers. A *masked* Arithmetic Logic Unit (ALU) module implements all necessary primitives. We employ the ALU by Uhle et *al.* [40], which fixes several flaws in the original design, but still showed measurable leakage. For our implementation we thus had to first eliminate leakage sources and secondly, add the three new instructions which implement the additional frequent core operations. This requires us to modify the masked ALU, the data paths inside the processor as well as the instruction scheduling in software.

Improvements to SCARV. As mentioned by Uhle et *al.*, even with the improved masked ALU, SCARV still leaks information via power side-channels. The authors suggest that other functional units, which also receive parts of the input and perform computations in parallel, may cause accidental share combination. We decided to eliminate this potential leakage source by implementing *operand isolation.* A multiplexer in front of every functional unit suppresses the inputs if they are not required. So instead of running all operations in parallel and choosing the correct output afterwards, only one computation runs at a time. We added the same principle inside the masked ALU. Furthermore, we wanted to align our implementation with their simulations, which always assume a clean

[2] https://github.com/scarv.

Table 2. Encoding for the additional, masked instructions.

31 - 25	24 - 20	19 - 15	14 - 12	11 - 7	6 - 0	Instruction
0x7c	rs2 (condition)	rs1	0x0	rd	0x5b	mask.b.cmov
0x7c	rs2	rs1	0x1	rd	0x5b	mask.b.cmpeq
0x7c	rs2	rs1	0x2	rd	0x5b	mask.b.cmpgt

state, which is not true for the SCARV core. Therefore, we added circuitry which issues a reset signal to the masked ALU after each operation at the cost of one additional clock cycle for masked instructions.

Improvements to Instruction Scheduling. Further analysis showed that the loading and storing of shares in memory creates significant leakage, because of internal registers which hold data from previous accesses. Therefore, if two shares of the same operand are loaded consecutively, both shares are accidentally combined. Because our implementation is organizing shares in 2D arrays, this happens relatively often. Fixing the memory subsystem is out-of-scope for this paper, however, we remedied this situation by carefully scheduling our load and store instructions. If no useful value can be interleaved during a load, we load a dummy value. A dummy store is always required when storing the resulting shares back in memory. This technique overcomes the weaknesses of SCARV's microarchitecture and eliminates leakage on the algorithm level as shown in Sect. 5.3.

General Architecture. RISC-V instructions support up to two source operands and one destination operand. However, we require three operands to implement the cmov instruction. More specifically, we have to use the value of the destination register as a third input. We thus modify the register file, forwarding and hazard unit to account for a third operand and extend the data path of the CPU. The encoding of the new instructions is shown in Table 2.

Masked ALU. Our new instructions cmov and cmpeq are implemented as additional units, whereas cmpgt is an extension to an existing unit inside the masked ALU. The cmov module receives three input operands in their shared representation: the destination register's contents, a value and a 1-bit condition. Algorithm 5 describes how the cmov module works using already provided secure primitives. As the secure and requires two cycles the overall instructions takes three cycles when taking the previously mentioned ALU reset into account. The cmpeq module generates a 1-bit condition by first xoring both operands and propagating the result through an or-tree, which checks if the xor output is not 0. We require five stages to compress the 32-bit result to just a single bit, resulting in a 11 cycle overhead. A simplified example is shown in Fig. 1, which compares a 4-bit number and generates the result bit using three stages. Lastly, the cmpgt operation generates a 1-bit condition based on the result of a subtraction. We modified the masked adder to output the borrow bit in its shared representation, which is

Algorithm 5. cmov Implementation

Data: masked 32-bit values dest, new, cond
Result: new is moved into dest if the least significant bit in cond is 1

function CMOV(dest,new,cond)
  $a \leftarrow \text{dest} \oplus \text{new}$ ▷ share-wise
  $b \leftarrow a \wedge \text{cond}$ ▷ using secure and
  return $b \oplus \text{dest}$ ▷ share-wise

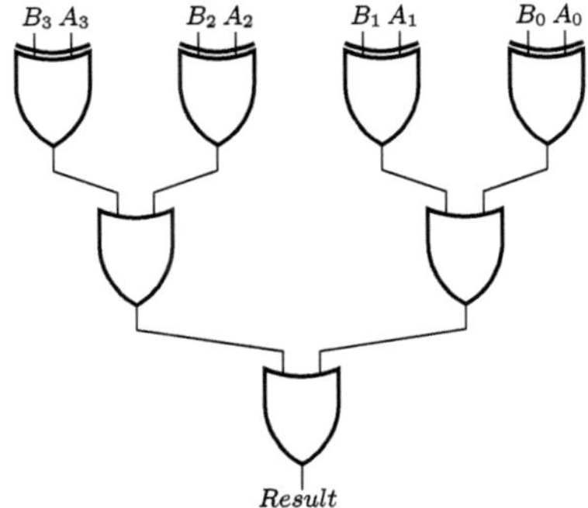

Fig. 1. Simplified diagram for a 4-bit cmpeq as included in the extended core.

only set if a larger value is subtracted from a smaller value. The adder computes the result of a 32-bit subtraction within 14 cycles, thus cmpgt exhibits the same performance overhead.

5 Evaluation

We evaluate the modified SCARV Core on the ChipWhisperer CW305 FPGA board. Using the SCARV SoC project, the Central Processing Unit (CPU) is connected to 256 kB of memory and runs at 25 MHz. We present results on hardware overhead, software performance, and side-channel measurements.

5.1 Hardware

Table 3a shows a moderate hardware overhead compared to Uhle et *al.*. Overall, there is an increase of approximately 21 % in combinatorial logic and 14 % in registers. The area costs in Table 3a classified as *other* mainly stem from the extended data path for a third operand, as well as the additional protections mentioned earlier. We note that we did not perform iterative synthesizing to optimize the frequency, instead basing it on the worst negative slack. Thus, when adding our extension and improvements by Uhle et *al.*, the overhead is overall moderate.

Table 3. Hardware performance results. Note that for the Field-Programmable Gate Array (FPGA) results cover the whole core, whereas the Application-Specific Integrated Circuit (ASIC) numbers only feature the ALU.

(a) FPGA performance results.

	Area			Freq.
	[LUTs]	[FFs]	[Slices]	[MHz]
Bool.,arith.	9245	4905	3063	30.02
cmov	555	258	201	
cmpeq	581	260	231	
cmpgt	51	12	2	
other	1455	598	402	
combined	11223	5634	3430	28.73
Overhead	21.4 %	14.9 %	12.0 %	4.3 %

(b) Hardware overhead in gate equivalents (GE) of our modified ALU using 45 nm technology compared to Uhle et *al.*.

	Bool.,arith.	all
cmpeq	—	2875.00 GE
cmov	—	2972.33 GE
Add/Sub	4819.66 GE	4889.98 GE
Other	9610.67 GE	11167.34 GE
Total Area	14430.33 GE	21904.65 GE

Furthermore, we determined the area overhead created by our modified masked ALU for an ASIC implementation by synthesizing it using Synopsys Design Compiler and Silvaco's Open-Cell 45nm FreePDK. The results are shown in Table 3b. In general, the extended ALU features 21904.65 additional gates, which are mainly comprised of the cmpeq and cmov modules. The cmpgt instruction only requires minimal modifications to the subtraction circuit, as we only extract the borrow bit.

5.2 Software

Note that for each use case, the generation of input randomness is not benchmarked, and may take another significant part of the cycle counts.

Fix-Weight Sampling. Table 4 shows our benchmark results for all fix-weight sampling algorithms applied to a representative selection of parameter sets such that our results can be generalized to other parameter sets easily. For our selection, we choose polynomial sizes (N) from each relevant order of magnitude, and consider different W/N ratios. Moreover, we include use cases from key generation, encapsulation, and decapsulation, which all have different requirements, as pointed out in more details in [31]. Particularly, for the BIKE decapsulation, the last parameter set, only Fisher-Yates and sorting are secure algorithms [25], because their runtime is independent of the randomness, which is extended from a secret value in this case.

Fisher-Yates and rejection sampling generate polynomials in index representation, sorting and the comparison method generate polynomials in coefficient representation. In most applications, subsequent operations on the polynomials require the coefficient representation. For these applications, comparison sampling is superior, when implementing for the base ISA, confirming the results

Table 4. Masked fixed-weight polynomial sampling performance with different parameters and ISEs in kilo cycles. For each parameter set, we state the cycle count for: (1) the base RISC-V ISA, (2) the improved core by Uhle et *al.* ("Bool., arith.") and (3) the core by Uhle et *al.* with our extension ("all"). Furthermore, we underline the cycle count of the fastest algorithm with output in coefficient representation. For Fisher-Yates and Rejection sampling, we also take the index-to-coefficient (I2C) conversion into account.

Parameter set	Algorithm	Poly. Format	Bitsliced		Standard		
			Base ISA	Masked ISE	Base ISA	Masked ISE	
				Bool., arith.		Bool., arith.	all
NTRU key gen. $N = 677$ $W = 254$	Fisher-Yates	index	7013	6979	47 852	6695	2484
	Sorting	coeff.	13 818	5588	25 541	3891	927
	Rejection	index	1288	1144	53 561	222	174
	Comparison	coeff.	2307	1707	78 059	2780	1863
	I2C Conv.	coeff.	5839	5387	252 757	32 731	8293
sNTRU Prime key gen. $N = 953$ $W = 396$	Fisher-Yates	index	12 479	12 346	129 323	15 767	5517
	Sorting	coeff.	19 882	7982	39 081	5947	1406
	Rejection	index	2930	2493	150 885	362	282
	Comparison	coeff.	4647	3254	146 814	5233	3751
	I2C Conv.	coeff.	12 029	10 691	619 128	71 787	18 170
McEliece encaps. $N = 6688$ $W = 128$	Fisher-Yates	index	3286	3265	12 266	1855	789
	Sorting	coeff.	218 829	82 435	456 032	68 890	15 823
	Rejection	index	418	383	11 830	111	87
	Comparison	coeff.	22 982	14 676	656 167	23 547	16 981
	I2C Conv.	coeff.	28 224	25 233	1 259 048	163 238	41 484
BIKE key gen. $N = 12323$ $W = 71$	Fisher-Yates	index	1878	1867	3894	712	386
	Sorting	coeff.	464 691	172 037	960 845	144 944	33 053
	Rejection	index	193	180	3687	83	65
	Comparison	coeff.	34 911	21 534	958 053	34 378	32 014
	I2C Conv.	coeff.	30 883	27 610	1 288 023	167 316	42 720
BIKE decaps. $N = 49318$ $W = 199$	Fisher-Yates	index	6101	6064	29 510	4276	1693
	Sorting	coeff.	—	—	—	—	—
	I2C Conv.	coeff.	377 254	332 361	14 428 175	1 869 227	473 935

from Krausz et *al.* [31]. When index representation is required, rejection sampling is clearly faster. Because sorting requires more than the available 256 kB of RAM, for the BIKE decapsulation use case only Fisher-Yates remains as a suitable algorithm. To get the required coefficient representation, the costs of the index-to-coefficient conversion lead to unpractical cycle counts of over 300 million cycles.

The picture changes distinctly when we utilize masked instructions. With the ISE, the non-bitsliced implementations are faster by a factor of at least 5, but often 10 and more. Consequently, sorting comes close to comparison, but still not fastest for small N. For the index representation, rejection sampling remains the preferable method. The advantage of the additional masked instructions compared to the plain Boolean and arithmetic instructions is in the range of about 6 percent to a factor 4.2 speed-up, resulting in sorting being the fastest algorithm for small N in coefficient representation, even outperforming all bitsliced implementations.

Table 5. Masked CDT sampler performance in kilo cycles. N is contained in the parameter set name. For Haetae, all parameter sets have $N = 256$.

Algorithm	Bitsliced		Standard		
	Base ISA	Masked ISE	Base ISA	Masked ISE	
		Bool., arith.		Bool., arith.	all
FrodoKEM-640	1263	291	28 743	692	505
FrodoKEM-976	1665	381	37 411	858	665
FrodoKEM-1344	1451	328	33 831	824	652
Haetae	2326	559	53 418	1198	1050
Hawk-256	2935	744	—	—	—
Hawk-512	7640	1938	—	—	—
Hawk-1024	16 032	3876	—	—	—

Table 6. Masked BIKE rotation performance in kilo cycles.

(a) Masked BIKE rotation performance in kilo cycles.

Parameter set	N	Base ISA	Masked ISE	
			Bool., arith.	all
BIKE-1	12323	368	365	202
BIKE-3	24659	789	777	429

(b) Masked SHA/Keccak performance in kilo cycles. Note that one Keccak permutation consists of 24 rounds.

# Keccak Permutations	Base SA	Masked ISE
		Bool., arith.
1	471	241
2	942	481
3	1413	721
4	1884	962
5	2355	1202
6	2825	1442

CDT Sampling. Our results for the CDT sampler of FrodoKEM, Haetae, and Hawk can be found in Table 5. Most importantly, the base ISA numbers for the bitsliced representation indicate that side-channel resistant sampling from a CDT is generally feasible but costly for all use cases. The bitsliced variants, moreover, are constantly faster than the implementations on standard representation for FrodoKEM, albeit the featured numbers do not include transformation into and from bitsliced representation. We note that for Hawk only a bitsliced implementation is reasonable, because of the large CDT values, and we achieve a speed-up of factor five to six, similar to FrodoKEM

Polynomial Rotation. Table 6a shows the speed-ups that can be achieved for rotation of BIKE polynomials. Again, the base ISA numbers indicate that this operation is generally feasible with a masked implementation. However, with the masked cmov instruction the masked rotation cycle count is reduced by about 45 %. Moreover, the ISE gives side-channel security guarantees that the pure software implementation does not.

Keccak. As shown in Table 6b, the masked instructions achieve cycle count reduction of nearly 50 %. This translates to a significant overall speed-up for various PQC schemes. As mentioned before, it is reported for Haetae that more than 60 % of the signing cycles account for randomness generation of the hyperball sample. Then, a fully masked deterministic Haetae implementation requires at least 102 masked Keccak permutations for generating a hyperball sample, which

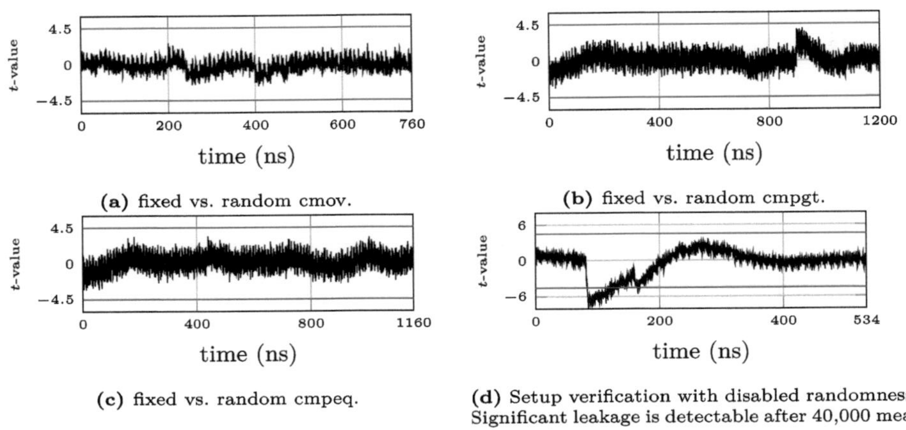

(a) fixed vs. random cmov.

(b) fixed vs. random cmpgt.

(c) fixed vs. random cmpeq.

(d) Setup verification with disabled randomness. Significant leakage is detectable after 40,000 measurements.

Fig. 2. Side-channel evaluation of our instruction set extension using a fixed vs. random t-test with 100,000 measurements.

translates to an approximated cycle count of nearly 50 million cycles without ISE, but only 25 million with masked ISE. Another example, Kyber-768 decapsulation, requires eight masked Keccak permutations where the masked ISE would yield an acceleration from approximately 3.7 million cycles down to 1.9 million cycles for the Keccak part alone.

Kyber Decompression. As the polynomial size does not vary for the single Kyber parameter sets, we only do one benchmark here, comparing the base ISA to the Uhle et *al.* masked ISE, compared to our instructions. While the purely software-based masking takes 31 kcycles, the masked ISE reduces this only slightly to 30 kcycles. In contrast, our cmov instruction reduces the cycle count to 21 kcycles. In addition to the performance improvements, the *security* gain is considerably more important, keeping in mind that the implementation of Heinz et *al.* [26] was broken at exactly this part, whereas our instructions guarantee fresh randomization and are practically verified.

5.3 Side-Channel Security

We verify the first-order power side channel resistance by measuring the individual power consumption of our newly added instruction as well as measuring whole algorithms. For both test cases we perform *fixed vs. random* t-tests with 100 000 measurements. For individual instructions, we run an assembly microbenchmark, which loads the masks, sets a trigger to start the oscilloscope, executes a single instruction and then resets the trigger. The results in Table 2, captured at 2.5 GS/s, exhibit no leakage in the first order (Subfigures (a)-(c)). We verified our results by disabling the internal randomness generator for the masked ALU, as seen in Subfigure (d), causing leakage as expected.

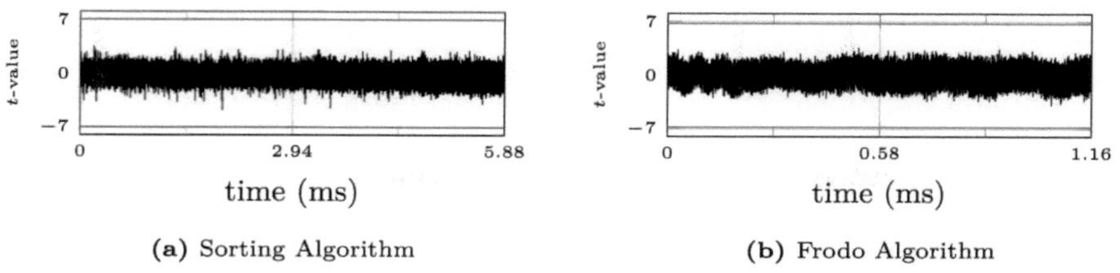

(a) Sorting Algorithm

(b) Frodo Algorithm

Fig. 3. Side-channel evaluation of two masked algorithms using a fixed vs. random t-test with 100,000 measurements.

Additionally, we measured whole algorithms using our new instructions. For demonstration purposes we limit our selection to two algorithms that utilize all the new instructions: the sorting based sampling and CDT sampling for FrodoKEM. Both measurements where carried out using a sample rate of 625 MS/s. The results can be seen in Fig. 3. We note that because of the amount of sample points (3,678,750 for Sorting; 723,125 for Frodo), we adjusted the t-test threshold in accordance with the results by Ding et *al.* [41] to 6.99 for sorting and 6.76 for CDT sampling. Both algorithms stay clearly below the threshold.

6 Conclusion

In our work, we demonstrate how an ISE featuring masked instructions for Boolean and arithmetic operations, developed in previous work for symmetric cryptography can be applied to widespread PQC components. We identify common critical operations, for which we develop efficient instruction sequences based on the masked Boolean and arithmetic instructions. Furthermore, we evaluate the introduction of dedicated masked instructions for these critical operations. For fixed-weight sampling, this leads to speed-ups of more than two orders of magnitude, and to significant speed-ups for masked CDT sampling, masked bit polynomial rotation, Keccak, and Kyber decompression.

Acknowledgements. We would like to thank all our reviewers for their constructive feedback. The work described in this paper has been supported by the Deutsche Forschungsgemeinschaft (DFG, German Research Foundation) through the projects RAINCOAT II (440059533) and EMBOSOM (535695900), by the DFG through Germany's Excellence Strategy - EXC 2092 CASA - 390781972, and by the German Federal Ministry of Research, Technology and Space (BMFTR) through the projects FlexKI (01IS22086I) and 6GEM (16KISK038).

References

1. Battistello, A., Coron, J.-S., Prouff, E., Zeitoun, R.: Horizontal side-channel attacks and countermeasures on the ISW masking scheme. In: Gierlichs, B., Poschmann, A.Y. (eds.) CHES 2016. LNCS, vol. 9813, pp. 23–39. Springer, Heidelberg (2016). https://doi.org/10.1007/978-3-662-53140-2_2

2. Bernstein, D.J., Chuengsatiansup, C., Lange, T., van Vredendaal, C.: NTRU prime: reducing attack surface at low cost. In: Adams, C., Camenisch, J. (eds.) SAC 2017. LNCS, vol. 10719, pp. 235–260. Springer, Cham (2018). https://doi.org/10.1007/978-3-319-72565-9_12
3. Biham, E.: A fast new DES implementation in software. In: Biham, E. (ed.) FSE 1997. LNCS, vol. 1267, pp. 260–272. Springer, Heidelberg (1997). https://doi.org/10.1007/BFb0052352
4. Bos, J.W., et al.: Frodo: take off the ring! practical, quantum-secure key exchange from LWE. In: Weippl, E.R., Katzenbeisser, S., Kruegel, C., Myers, A.C., Halevi, S. (eds.) ACM CCS 2016, pp. 1006–1018. ACM Press (2016)
5. Bronchain, O., Cassiers, G.: Bitslicing arithmetic/boolean masking conversions for fun and profit with application to lattice-based KEMs. IACR TCHES **2022**(4), 553–588 (2022)
6. Buchmann, J., Cabarcas, D., Göpfert, F., Hülsing, A., Weiden, P.: Discrete ziggurat: a time-memory trade-off for sampling from a Gaussian distribution over the integers. In: Lange, T., Lauter, K., Lisonek, P. (eds.) SAC 2013. LNCS, vol. 8282, pp. 402–417. Springer, Berlin, Heidelberg (2014)
7. Budroni, A., Canales-Martínez, I.A., Perin, L.P.: SoK: methods for sampling random permutations in post-quantum cryptography. Cryptology ePrint Archive, Report 2024/008 (2024)
8. Castryck, W., Decru, T.: An efficient key recovery attack on SIDH. In: Hazay, C., Stam, M. (eds.) EUROCRYPT 2023. Part V, volume 14008 of LNCS, pp. 423–447. Springer, Cham (2023). https://doi.org/10.1007/978-3-031-30589-4_15
9. Chen, M.-S., Chou, T., Krausz, M.: Optimizing BIKE for the intel haswell and ARM Cortex-M4. IACR TCHES **2021**(3), 97–124 (2021)
10. Cheng, H., Page, D., Wang, W.: eLIMInate: a leakage-focused ISE for masked implementation. IACR TCHES **2024**(2), 329–358 (2024)
11. Cheon, J.H., et al.: HAETAE: shorter lattice-based fiat-shamir signatures. IACR Trans. Cryptogr. Hardw. Embed. Syst. **2024**(3), 25–75 (2024)
12. Cheon, J.H., Choe, H., Hong, D., Yi, M.J.: SMAUG: pushing lattice-based key encapsulation mechanisms to the limits. In: Carlet, C., Mandal, K., Rijmen, V. (eds.) Selected Areas in Cryptography - SAC 2023 - 30th International Conference, Fredericton, Canada, 14–18 August 2023, Revised Selected Papers, vol. 14201 of Lecture Notes in Computer Science, pp. 127–146. Springer, Heidelberg (2023). https://doi.org/10.1007/978-3-031-53368-6_7
13. Cheriere, A., Aragon, N., Richmond, T., Gérard, B.: BIKE key-recovery: combining power consumption analysis and information-set decoding. In: Tibouchi, M., Wang, X. (eds.) ACNS 23International Conference on Applied Cryptography and Network Security. Part I, volume 13905 of LNCS, pp. 725–748. Springer, Cham (2023). https://doi.org/10.1007/978-3-031-33488-7_27
14. Chou, T.: QcBits: constant-time small-key code-based cryptography. In: Gierlichs, B., Poschmann, A.Y. (eds.) CHES 2016. LNCS, vol. 9813, pp. 280–300. Springer, Berlin, Heidelberg (2016). https://doi.org/10.1007/978-3-662-53140-2_14
15. Coron, J.-S., Gérard, F., Trannoy, M., Zeitoun, R.: High-order masking of NTRU. IACR TCHES **2023**(2), 180–211 (2023)
16. Drucker, G., Kostic.: Additional Implementation of BIKE (Bit Flipping Key Encapsulation). https://github.com/awslabs/bike-kem. Accessed 20 May 2023
17. Drucker, N., Gueron, S., Kostic, D.: QC-MDPC decoders with several shades of gray. In: Ding, J., Tillich, J.-P. (eds.) PQCrypto 2020. LNCS, vol. 12100, pp. 35–50. Springer, Cham (2020). https://doi.org/10.1007/978-3-030-44223-1_3

18. Dubrova, E., Ngo, K., Gärtner, J., Wang, R.: Breaking a fifth-order masked implementation of crystals-kyber by copy-paste. In: Fukumitsu, M., Hasegawa, S. (eds.) Proceedings of the 10th ACM Asia Public-Key Cryptography Workshop, APKC 2023, Melbourne, VIC, Australia, 10–14 July 2023, pp. 10–20. ACM (2023)
19. Ducas, L., Durmus, A., Lepoint, T., Lyubashevsky, V.: Lattice signatures and bimodal Gaussians. In: Canetti, R., Garay, J.A. (eds.) CRYPTO 2013. LNCS, vol. 8042, pp. 40–56. Springer, Heidelberg (2013). https://doi.org/10.1007/978-3-642-40041-4_3
20. Ducas, L., Nguyen, P.Q.: Faster gaussian lattice sampling using lazy floating-point arithmetic. In: Wang, X., Sako, K. (eds.) ASIACRYPT 2012. LNCS, vol. 7658, pp. 415–432. Springer, Heidelberg (2012). https://doi.org/10.1007/978-3-642-34961-4_26
21. Ducas, L., Postlethwaite, E.W., Pulles, L.N., van Woerden, W.P.J.: Hawk: module LIP makes lattice signatures fast, compact and simple. In: Agrawal, S., Lin, D. (eds.) ASIACRYPT 2022. Part IV. LNCS, vol. 13794, pp. 65–94. Springer, Cham (2022). https://doi.org/10.1007/978-3-031-22972-5_3
22. Fritzmann, T., et al.: Masked accelerators and instruction set extensions for post-quantum cryptography. In: TCHES 2022 (2021)
23. Fritzmann, T., et al.: Masked accelerators and instruction set extensions for post-quantum cryptography. IACR TCHES **2022**(1), 414–460 (2022)
24. Gao, S., Großschädl, J., Marshall, B., Page, D., Pham, T., Regazzoni, F.: An instruction set extension to support software-based masking. IACR TCHES **2021**(4), 283–325 (2021)
25. Guo, Q., Hlauschek, C., Johansson, T., Lahr, N., Nilsson, A., Schröder, R.L.: Don't reject this: key-recovery timing attacks due to rejection-sampling in HQC and BIKE. IACR TCHES **2022**(3), 223–263 (2022)
26. Heinz, D., Kannwischer, M.J., Land, G., Pöppelmann, T., Schwabe, P., Sprenkels, A.: First-order masked Kyber on ARM Cortex-M4. Cryptology ePrint Archive, Report 2022/058 (2022)
27. Hermelink, J., Ning, K.C., Petri, R., Strieder, E.: The insecurity of masked comparisons: SCAs on ML-KEM's FO-transform. In: Luo, B., Liao, X., Xu, J., Kirda, E., Lie, D. (eds.) ACM CCS 2024, pp. 2430–2444. ACM Press (2024)
28. NewAE Technology Inc. ChipWhisperer. https://www.newae.com/chipwhisperer. Accessed 25 June 2023
29. Kannwischer, M.J., Rijneveld, J., Schwabe, P., Stoffelen, K.: pqm4: testing and benchmarking nist PQC on ARM Cortex-M4. Cryptology ePrint Archive, Report 2019/844 (2019)
30. Karabulut, E., Alkim, E., Aysu, A.: Single-trace side-channel attacks on ω-small polynomial sampling: With applications to ntru, NTRU prime, and CRYSTALS-DILITHIUM. In: IEEE International Symposium on Hardware Oriented Security and Trust, HOST 2021, Tysons Corner, VA, USA, 12–15 December 2021, pp. 35–45. IEEE (2021)
31. Krausz, M., Land, G., Richter-Brockmann, J., Güneysu, T.: A holistic approach towards side-channel secure fixed-weight polynomial sampling. In: Boldyreva, A., Kolesnikov, V. (eds.) PKC 2023. Part II, volume 13941 of LNCS, pp. 94–124. Springer, Cham (2023). https://doi.org/10.1007/978-3-031-31371-4_4
32. Marshall, B., Page, D.: SME: Scalable masking extensions. Cryptology ePrint Archive, Report 2021/1416 (2021)
33. Marshall, B., Page, D., Webb, J.: MIRACLE: MIcRo-ArChitectural leakage evaluation a study of micro-architectural power leakage across many devices. IACR TCHES **2022**(1), 175–220 (2022)

34. Marzougui, S., Kabin, I., Krämer, J., Aulbach, T., Seifert, J.P.: On the feasibility of single-trace attacks on the gaussian sampler using a CDT. In: Kavun, E.B., Pehl, M. (eds.) Constructive Side-Channel Analysis and Secure Design - 14th International Workshop, COSADE 2023, Munich, Germany, 3–4 April 2023, Proceedings. LNCS, vol. 13979, pp. 149–169. Springer, Heidelberg (2023). https://doi.org/10.1007/978-3-031-29497-6_8
35. Peikert, C.: An efficient and parallel Gaussian sampler for lattices. In: Rabin, T. (ed.) CRYPTO 2010. LNCS, vol. 6223, pp. 80–97. Springer, Berlin, Heidelberg (2010). https://doi.org/10.1007/978-3-642-14623-7_5
36. Thomas Pornin. Why Constant-Time Crypto? https://www.bearssl.org/constanttime.html. Accessed 30 June 2023
37. Prouff, E., Rivain, M.: Masking against side-channel attacks: a formal security proof. In: Johansson, T., Nguyen, P.Q. (eds.) EUROCRYPT 2013. LNCS, vol. 7881, pp. 142–159. Springer, Heidelberg (2013). https://doi.org/10.1007/978-3-642-38348-9_9
38. Sendrier, N.: Secure sampling of constant-weight words – application to BIKE. Cryptology ePrint Archive, Report 2021/1631 (2021)
39. KpqC team. Final algorithms from the kpqc competition. Google Groups: KpqC-bulletin. Message posted to Google Groups. Accessed 22 Jan 2025
40. Uhle, F., Stolz, F., Moradi, A.: Another evidence to not employ customized masked hardware identifying and fixing flaws in SCARV. IACR Trans. Cryptogr. Hardw. Embed. Syst. **2024**(4), 133–155 (2024)
41. Zhang, L., Ding, A.A., Durvaux, F., Standaert, F.X., Fei, Y.: Towards sound and optimal leakage detection procedure. Cryptology ePrint Archive, Report 2017/287 (2017)

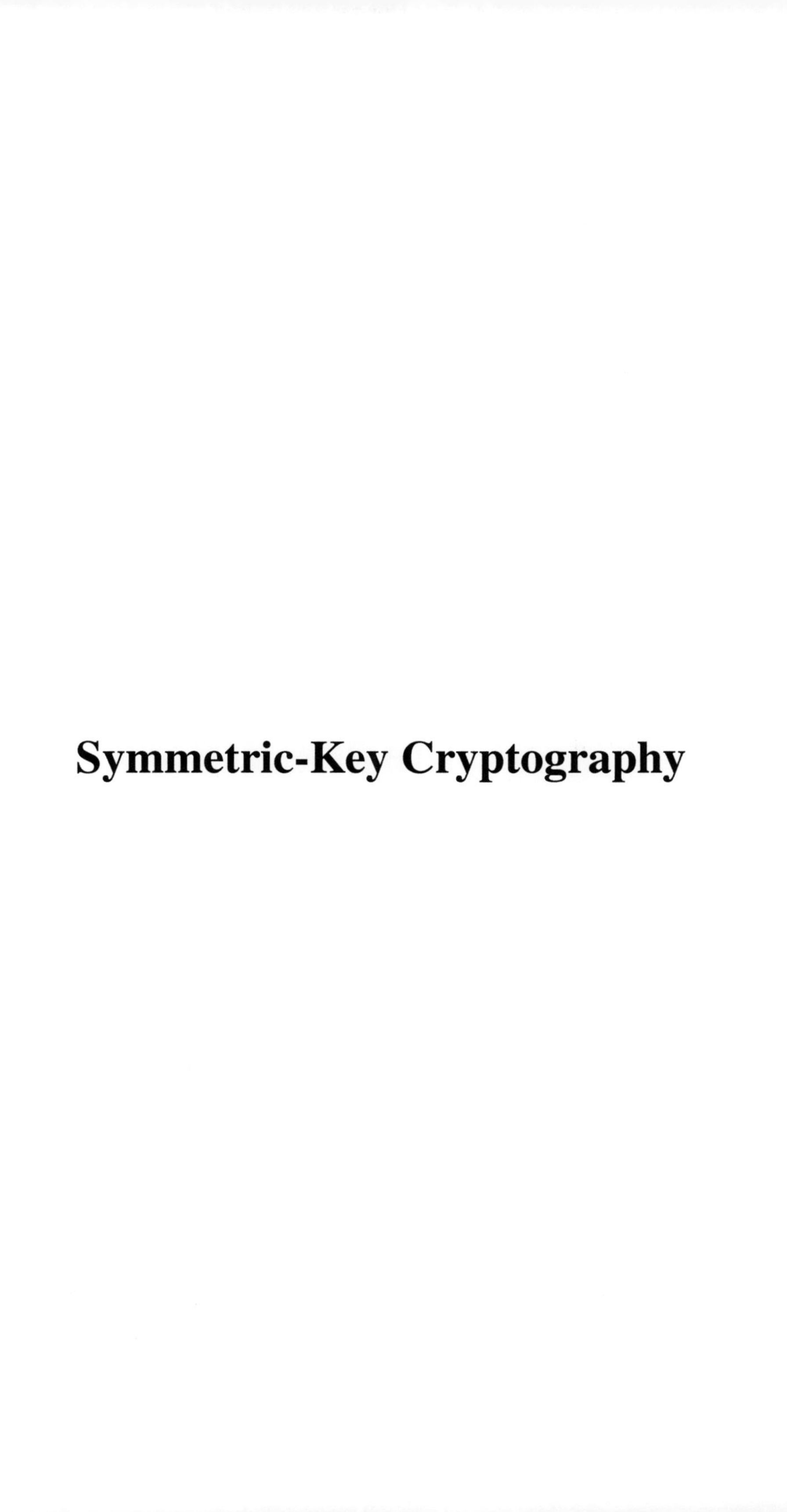

Symmetric-Key Cryptography

Comparing Gaston with Ascon-p: Side-Channel Analysis and Hardware Evaluation

Parisa Amiri Eliasi(✉), Lejla Batina, and Silvia Mella

Radboud University, Nijmegen, The Netherlands
{parisa.amirieliasi,silvia.mella}@ru.nl, lejla@cs.ru.nl

Abstract. Gaston is a cryptographic permutation introduced by El Hirch et al. at Crypto 2023. It uses the same number of bitwise operations as Ascon-p, the core permutation of the NIST-selected standard for lightweight authenticated encryption Ascon. Despite this similarity in complexity, Gaston provides stronger resistance to differential and linear cryptanalysis, making it a promising option for lightweight cryptographic applications. In this work, we evaluate the hardware performance of Gaston and Ascon-p, and conduct power side-channel analysis on the initialization phase of Ascon when instantiated with each permutation on an FPGA. We propose a majority voting technique that leverages the structure of Ascon-p, where the diffusion layer follows the non-linear layer. This method improves the key recovery success rate for Ascon instantiated with Ascon-p, even with fewer traces than in previous studies. To explore the role of layer ordering, we also consider a modified version of Gaston, named Gaston-R, in which the non-linear and diffusion layers are swapped. While this modification does not affect theoretical security, it may influence both the hardware cost and the effectiveness of the specific side-channel attack applied in this study. Our hardware analysis shows a small overhead for Gaston-R, and the side-channel results indicate noticeably reduced key recovery success compared to the original Gaston. To our knowledge, this is the first work to investigate how layer ordering impacts the complexity of side-channel attacks of this kind. Our findings suggest that this aspect may deserve further exploration in the design of side-channel-aware cryptographic permutations.

Keywords: Side-channel Analysis · Correlation Power Analysis · Ascon-p · Gaston · Permutation · Diffusion Layer · Hardware

1 Introduction

NIST recently published the draft standard for Ascon, formally specifying Ascon-AEAD128, which is based on Ascon-128a [21], as the lightweight cryptography (LWC) standard for authenticated encryption with associated data (AEAD). It was selected for its strong security properties and efficient performance in both software and hardware. The Ascon family [8] had already

Y. Kim et al. (Eds.): CANS 2025, LNCS 16351, pp. 95–119, 2026.
https://doi.org/10.1007/978-981-95-4434-9_5

received attention earlier during the CAESAR competition, which was launched in 2013 to evaluate authenticated encryption schemes [2]. Both Ascon-128 and Ascon-128a were included in its final portfolio in 2019 and were recommended for lightweight applications. In parallel, the LWC competition was initiated by NIST in 2018 to identify AEAD schemes suited for resource-constrained environments, where conventional cryptographic algorithms may not perform well [16].

In 2023, El Hirch et al. [12] introduced a new type of mixing layer called the twin column parity mixer (TCPM), which generalizes the column parity mixer (CPM) used in Keccak-f permutations [6]. They also presented a new cryptographic permutation called Gaston, built using TCPM. Gaston uses the same state layout and requires the same number of bitwise operations per round as the Ascon permutation Ascon-p, with each round performing 3.2 XORs and 1 AND per bit. However, it offers better resistance to differential and linear cryptanalysis [12]. This means Gaston might reach the same level of security with fewer rounds, making it potentially more efficient for lightweight use cases.

Related Works. While the original paper on Gaston [12] did not report any hardware results or comparisons with Ascon-p, a more recent study evaluated its ASIC performance alongside Ascon-p [14].

Most existing research on side-channel analysis (SCA) for Ascon has focused on software implementations. This work shifts the focus to hardware implementation, evaluating both Ascon-p and Gaston through SCA and hardware performance comparison. A brief summary of previous key works is provided below.

Gross et al. [11] present several hardware implementations of Ascon, including Ascon-fast, Ascon-64-bit, and Ascon-x-low-area, along with differential power analysis (DPA) on unprotected versions of Ascon-fast and Ascon-x-low-area. In the attack on Ascon-fast, changes in a single output bit of the state were monitored, with 64 separate attacks performed on each of two state registers. For Ascon-x-low-area, a Hamming distance (HD) leakage model between consecutive S-box outputs was used to recover four key bits at a time. These attacks target the initialization phase of the AEAD scheme, and were performed using *simulated* power traces derived from post-synthesis ASIC toggle counts.

Using real measurements, Samwel and Daemen [20] analyzed a hardware implementation of Ascon. They conducted a DPA on an unprotected implementation, executing one round of Ascon-p per clock cycle, running on a Spartan-6 XC6SLX75 FPGA, part of the Sakura-G evaluation board.

Ramezanpour et al. [19] introduced a novel SCA technique called SCARL, which leverages reinforcement learning to recover secret data from cryptographic hardware without the need for a predefined leakage model or a training set. They applied both classical DPA and SCARL to recover the key of Ascon during its initialization phase [18]. In their implementation, S-box operations on state columns are performed across 64 cycles, with one S-box calculation per column in each clock cycle. Power traces were collected using a PicoScope 5 000 during the execution of Ascon on an Artix-7 FPGA. While their classical DPA failed to recover the correct key after analyzing 40 000 traces, SCARL, successfully recovered the secret key using just 24 000 traces.

More recently, in a separate study [3], we investigated the side-channel resistance of the ASCON mode when instantiated with the GASTON permutation instead of ASCON-p. In that work, we performed both correlation power analysis (CPA) and template attacks (TA) on a hardware implementation running on an FPGA platform. The CPA in [3] followed a divide-and-conquer strategy, inspired by the CPA on KEYAK presented in [20], analyzing the activity of the state register bit by bit. In the present work, we propose an alternative CPA attack on GASTON, inspired by the approach in [9,10], which targets an entire column of the key state in each attack and achieves higher key-recovery success rates. In [3], the reported success rate remained below 75% even with 100 000 traces, while a stable success rate above 70% required at least 44 000 traces. For a fair comparison, we use the same hardware implementation and evaluation board, with identical clock and sampling frequencies. Furthermore, this work extends our previous analysis by also evaluating the hardware cost of GASTON when the order of its layers is modified.

Our Contribution. This paper makes the following contributions:

- We integrate GASTON into the ASCON-128 AEAD mode and refer to the resulting scheme as GASTON-AEAD. We then evaluate the resistance of GASTON-AEAD and ASCON-128 to power SCA. In particular, we propose two separate approaches for CPA: in ASCON-128, the attack targets individual bits in the state registers to recover one key bit per attack, while in GASTON-AEAD, the attack targets entire columns of the key state, recovering one column at a time. The analysis focuses on the initialization phase, which is identical across ASCON-128, ASCON-128a, and ASCON-AEAD128 [13], allowing the same attack strategy to be applied in all cases.
- We introduce a simple majority voting method that leverages the structure of ASCON-p, where the diffusion layer follows the non-linear layer. This technique improves the success rate of key recovery in our attack on ASCON-128 and reduces the number of traces required. Using this method, we are able to fully recover the key with only 31k traces. As far as we know, this is the first time such a method has been applied in this context, and no prior work has demonstrated full key recovery with so few traces in an implementation where all S-boxes of one round are evaluated in a single clock cycle.
- To study how the order of layers affects our attack, we consider a modified version of GASTON in which the orders of the non-linear and diffusion layers are switched. We call this variant GASTON-R, and the AEAD scheme built from it GASTON-R-AEAD. While this change does not affect the theoretical security of the permutation, it may affect both the hardware cost and its resistance to the type of SCA examined in this work. We evaluate the hardware performance of GASTON-R and apply the same power SCA approach as used for ASCON-p, since they now share the same layer structure. To our knowledge, this is the first study that explores how the order of these layers

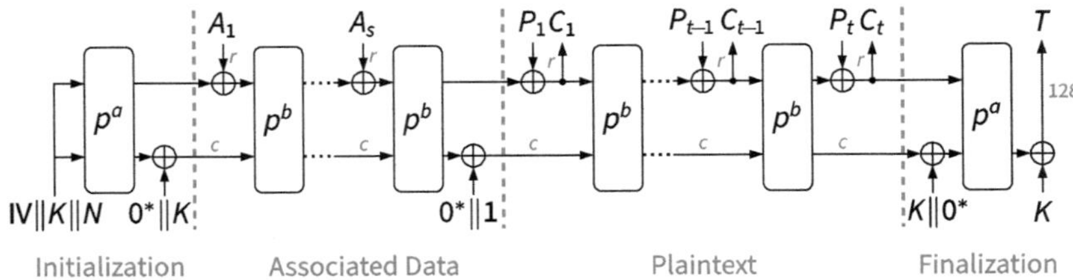

Fig. 1. ASCON-128 AEAD scheme taken from [8].

may influence the difficulty of such attacks. Our results suggest that studying the effect of layer ordering more systematically could provide useful insights for designing permutations with better side-channel resistance.
- We compare GASTON-R with GASTON and ASCON-p in terms of resource usage on both ASIC and FPGA platforms.

Paper Organization. In Sect. 2, we review the ASCON-128 scheme, as well as the ASCON-p and GASTON permutations. In Sect. 3, we discuss the CPA on ASCON-128 as introduced in [20] and describe the majority voting method. In Sect. 4, we propose the column-based CPA designed for GASTON-AEAD, while in Sect. 5, we extend a similar approach that we used to attack ASCON-p to recover the key in GASTON-R-AEAD. We present hardware performance metrics and detailed attack results in Sect. 6. Finally, we conclude by summarizing our findings and highlighting potential directions for future work in Sect. 8.

2 Background

2.1 ASCON

ASCON [8] is a family of algorithms for authenticated encryption (AE) and hashing. It is built using the duplex construction [4] and relies on the ASCON-p permutation as its core component. The family includes two AEAD schemes, ASCON-128 and ASCON-128a. In this work, we focus on ASCON-128.

As shown in Fig. 1, the AEAD process in ASCON-128 consists of several phases. It starts with the initialization phase, where the key K, nonce N, and an initialization vector IV are combined and processed using the permutation p^a. Next, each associated data AD block A_i is absorbed into the state using the permutation p^b. This step authenticates the AD but does not produce any ciphertext. Then, the plaintext P is encrypted one block at a time. Each 64-bit block P_i is XORed with part of the internal state, producing the ciphertext block C_i. After each encryption step, the state is updated using p^b. Finally, the algorithm enters the finalization phase, where the authentication tag T is generated. Decryption works similarly, but includes an additional step to verify the tag. p^r refers to applying the ASCON-p permutation p with r rounds, and in ASCON-128, a is 12 and b is 6.

The internal state of Ascon-p, denoted S, has 320 bits and is organized as five 64-bit words. Each round of the permutation consists of three layers applied in sequence,

$$p[\mathsf{S}] = p_L \circ p_S \circ p_C\,[\mathsf{S}].$$

The first layer, p_C, adds a round constant c_i to the middle word of the state in round i. The list of round constants used is given in [8, Table 6]. The second layer, p_S, is the only non-linear part of the round function. It applies 64 identical S-boxes in parallel, each operating on a group of 5 bits—one bit from the same position in each of the five state words, i.e., a single column. The S-box performs a simple linear step, applies the χ operation from Keccak-f permutation [5], and finishes with an affine transformation. A detailed diagram of the S-box is shown in Fig. 6, in Sect. A. The final layer, p_L, is a linear diffusion layer that mixes bits within each word: to update a bit at a given position, p_L mixes that bit with two other bits from the same word. The mixing offsets differ across the five words.

2.2 Gaston

Like Ascon-p, the Gaston permutation operates on a 320-bit state, which is arranged as 5 words or rows and 64 columns. The round function of Gaston, denoted as p, consists of several layers applied to the state S, as shown below,

$$p[\mathsf{S}] = \chi \circ \iota \circ \rho_{\text{west}} \circ \theta \circ \rho_{\text{east}}[\mathsf{S}]\,. \tag{1}$$

The round function includes a combination of linear and non-linear operations. The linear part is formed by a central diffusion layer θ, which is placed between two row shifting layers, ρ_{east} and ρ_{west}. A round constant is added through the ι layer. The only non-linear operation is the χ function, applied in parallel to each 5-bit column of the state. Further details on the permutation layers, parameters, and constants can be found in [12, Algorithm 1 and Table 6].

Each round of Gaston requires the same number of binary operations per bit as Ascon-p, specifically 3.2 XORs and 1 AND. However, these operations are used differently in the two designs. In Ascon-p, 2 XORs per bit are spent on the mixing layer, and the remaining 1.2 XORs and 1 AND come from the non-linear layer. In contrast, Gaston spends all 3.2 XORs on building a stronger diffusion layer while keeping the non-linear part minimal. This design choice gives Gaston better diffusion. Its diffusion layer achieves a differential branch number of 12, compared to 4 in Ascon-p. As a result, the best known 3-round differential and linear trails in Gaston have higher weights: 106 and 40 compared to 40 and 28 for Ascon-p. This means that Gaston achieves stronger resistance to differential and linear cryptanalysis, while keeping the round-wise computational cost similar to that of Ascon-p.

3 Attacks on Ascon-128

In Ascon-128, both the initialization and finalization phases involve application of the secret key. This design ensures that the key remains protected even if an attacker manages to recover the internal state after the initialization phase or just before finalization. Recovering the key through DPA during finalization is difficult, as the attacker must deal with both the key and many unknown parts of the state that do not directly affect the tag.

In contrast, the initialization phase is easier to attack and has been the main target in earlier DPA studies. The internal state of ASCON-p consists of five 64-bit words, labeled x_0 through x_4. At the start of initialization, a fixed IV is loaded into x_0, the secret key is stored in x_1 and x_2, and the changing nonce is loaded into x_3 and x_4. As a result, each 5-bit column entering the first S-box contains three known bits, from the IV and nonce, and two unknown bits from the secret key.

3.1 CPA

The reference VHDL implementation used for our analysis [17] executes each round of ASCON-p in a single clock cycle. The CPA method used in this work follows the approach outlined in [20].

In ASCON-p, the non-linear properties of the p_S layer allow the attacker to choose the nonce and exploit the underlying non-linearity of the permutation. To recover the key, we aim to extract each key bit stored in the x_1 and x_2 registers through separate attacks. For this, we need to define a selection function for each targeted key bit. As the first step, we express the output of the ASCON-p round in algebraic normal form (ANF), which helps us model how each output bit depends on the input bits, including the secret key. The five state words after the p_S layer, denoted $z_0, z_1, \ldots, z_4$, can be written in ANF as follows,

$$z_0 = x_0 + x_1 + x_2 + x_3 + x_0x_1 + x_1x_2 + x_1x_4 \tag{2}$$
$$z_1 = x_0 + x_1 + x_2 + x_3 + x_4 + x_1x_2 + x_1x_3 + x_2x_3 \tag{3}$$
$$z_2 = x_1 + x_2 + x_4 + x_3x_4 + 1$$
$$z_3 = x_0 + x_1 + x_2 + x_3 + x_4 + x_0x_3 + x_0x_4$$
$$z_4 = x_1 + x_3 + x_4 + x_0x_1 + x_1x_4. \tag{4}$$

Then the linear diffusion layer, p_L, applies a linear function to each 64-bit words, z_0 to z_4, as follows,

$$y_0 \leftarrow \Sigma_0(z_0) = z_0 + (z_0 \ggg 19) + (z_0 \ggg 28) \tag{5}$$
$$y_1 \leftarrow \Sigma_1(z_1) = z_1 + (z_1 \ggg 61) + (z_1 \ggg 39) \tag{6}$$
$$y_2 \leftarrow \Sigma_2(z_2) = z_2 + (z_2 \ggg 1) + (z_2 \ggg 6)$$
$$y_3 \leftarrow \Sigma_3(z_3) = z_3 + (z_3 \ggg 10) + (z_3 \ggg 17)$$
$$y_4 \leftarrow \Sigma_4(z_4) = z_4 + (z_4 \ggg 7) + (z_4 \ggg 41).$$

To recover a key bit from x_1 or x_2, we look for a quadratic term in the ANF after the non-linear layer that includes both a nonce bit and a key bit from the corresponding part of the key. For key bits in the first part, suitable terms can be found in z_0, z_1, or z_4, see Eqs. (2) to (4), so any of these can be used as the sensitive variable in the attack. For key bits in the second part, the only available option is to use a bit from z_1, see Eq. (3).

In our attack on the first part of the key, we choose a bit from z_0 as the sensitive variable. The ANF for z_0 is given in Eq. (2), and can be rearranged as,

$$z_0 = \underbrace{x_1x_4 + x_3}_{\mathtt{a}} + \underbrace{x_1 + x_2 + x_0 + x_0x_1 + x_1x_2}_{\mathtt{b}}. \tag{7}$$

In this equation, the part labeled "a" depends on the changing nonce registers and is used for the attack. The part labeled "b" remains constant since the IV and key bits are fixed during the attack, so it can be ignored as it contributes a constant amount to the register's activity. Thus, the intermediate value depends on one bit of the key stored in x_1 and two bits of the nonce stored in x_3 and x_4. In the remainder of this paper, we represent the key bits in registers x_1 and x_2 as k and k', respectively, and the nonce bits in x_3 and x_4 as n and n'. Therefore, Eq. (7) simplifies to,

$$z_0 = kn' + n.$$

To build the selection function $S_{z_0,i}(N, k)$, where the subscript i refers to the position of the bit under attack, we apply the linear layer p_L to the intermediate value z_0, as shown in Eq. (5). After this step, each output bit becomes a linear combination of three bits from the S-box output. As a result, there are 2^3 possible key guesses for each target bit. This process is illustrated for the bit at position with index zero in the y_0 register in Fig. 2, with the selection function $S_{z_0,0}(N, k)$ represented mathematically in Eq. (8). In this equation $k_0^\star, k_{36}^\star, k_{45}^\star$ are the key bits to be guessed, while n_0, n_{36}, n_{45} and n_0', n_{36}', n_{45}' represent the contributing nonce bits from x_3 and x_4.

$$S_{z_0,0}(N, k) = k_0^\star n_0' + n_0 + k_{36}^\star n_{36}' + n_{36} + k_{45}^\star n_{45}' + n_{45}. \tag{8}$$

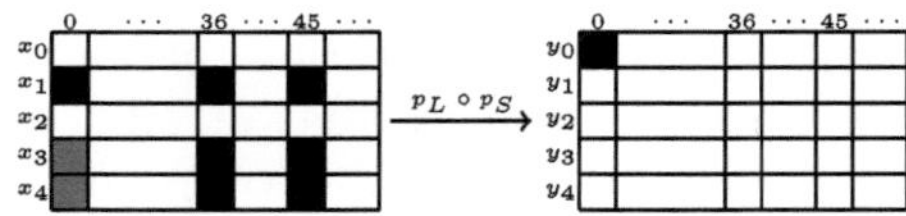

Fig. 2. p_S and p_L are applied to obtain one bit in the resulting register y_0.

The selection function can be generalized for other bits in the register z_0 as follows,

$$S_{z_0,i}(N, k) = k_i^\star n_i' + n_i + k_{i+36}^\star n_{i+36}' + n_{i+36} + k_{i+45}^\star n_{i+45}' + n_{i+45}. \tag{9}$$

Index additions are modulo 64, as the bits are stored in a 64-bit words.

Choosing z_0 as the sensitive variable allows recovery of only half of the key stored in x_1. To recover key bits from the second part of the key stored in x_2, we use bits from z_1 as sensitive variables. To construct the selection function, we start from the corresponding ANF expression shown in Eq. (3),

$$y_1 = x_3(x_1 + x_2 + 1) + x_4 . \quad (10)$$

This allows us to infer information about the value of $x_1 + x_2$ from the leakage. Combining this information with the recovered x_1 allows full recovery of the second part of the key stored in x_2. Denoting x_1+x_2 as $\tilde{k}$, we can rewrite Eq. (10) as,

$$y_1 = n(\tilde{k} + 1) + n' \quad (11)$$

After applying p_L in Eq. (6), this leads to the following selection function,

$$S_{z_1,i}(N, k) = n_i(k_i^\star+1)+n'_i+n_{i+3}(k_{i+3}^\star+1)+n'_{i+3}+n_{i+25}(k_{i+25}^\star+1)+n'_{i+25}. \quad (12)$$

3.2 Majority Voting

Since p_L is a linear combination of three S-boxes, recovering a single bit requires guessing key bits from three different positions within the key registers. Consequently, each key bit is recovered three times during the attack. For instance, the key bit at index 0 of word x_1 is involved in three selection functions: $S_{z_0,0}(N, k)$, $S_{z_0,39}(N, k)$, and $S_{z_0,61}(N, k)$. Once all three bits are attacked, the value of bit 0 is determined through majority voting: if it is recovered as 1 in two or more cases, we conclude it is 1; if it is recovered as 0 in two or more cases, we conclude it is 0. This majority voting approach increases the likelihood of accurately recovering key bits with fewer traces.

4 Attacks on Gaston-AEAD

A permutation must be part of a larger construction to serve a cryptographic purpose. Since there is no dedicated construction specifically designed for Gaston, and its state layout closely matches that of Ascon-p, we use it within the Ascon-128 AEAD scheme in place of Ascon-p. We refer to the resulting scheme as Gaston-AEAD. In our implementation, we keep the same number of rounds as defined for Ascon-p. However, based on current bounds on differential and linear trails, Gaston may reach a similar security level with fewer rounds, potentially offering better performance. A formal analysis to confirm this is outside the scope of this paper.

4.1 CPA

As illustrated in Fig. 3, the initial state of the Gaston permutation can be written as the XOR of two states: $\mathsf{S} = \mathsf{K} + \mathsf{N}$. The first state, K, holds the secret key: rows $\mathtt{k}_1$ and $\mathtt{k}_2$ contain the two halves of the key, while $\mathtt{k}_0$, $\mathtt{k}_3$, and $\mathtt{k}_4$ are set to zero. The second state, N, contains public inputs: the IV is placed in row $\mathtt{n}_0$, and the nonce is split between rows $\mathtt{n}_3$ and $\mathtt{n}_4$, with rows $\mathtt{n}_1$ and $\mathtt{n}_2$ set to zero. Given this structure, the round function in Eq. (1) can be rewritten as,

$$\chi(\lambda(\mathsf{K}+\mathsf{N})) = \chi(\lambda(\mathsf{K}) + \lambda(\mathsf{N})) = \chi(\mathsf{K}^\lambda + \mathsf{N}^\lambda), \tag{13}$$

where λ represents the full sequence of linear layers, defined as $\lambda = \iota \circ \rho_{\text{west}} \circ \theta \circ \rho_{\text{east}}$, and $\mathsf{S}^\lambda = \lambda(\mathsf{S})$ denotes the state after applying these layers. For Eq. (13) to hold, the round constant addition ι must be applied to only one of the two state. We apply ι to N only and, for simplicity, use the same notation λ for both cases.

In our target implementation, the 320-bit state register is updated with the round output at each clock cycle. We take advantage of the switching activity in the state register after the first round to perform our CPA. Our approach is inspired by [9,10] and follows a divide-and-conquer strategy, where each attack focuses on a single column of the state. Our leakage model assumes HD leakage between the five bits of each column before and after the round.

For clarity, we refer to Fig. 3 to illustrate how we recover two specific bits of the secret key, those in column 0 of the state S. The same approach is used to recover all other bits. We denote the five bits of column 0 in the state N^λ as $(n_0^\lambda, n_1^\lambda, n_2^\lambda, n_3^\lambda, n_4^\lambda)$. Similarly, the five bits of the same column in the state K^λ are denoted as $(k_0^\lambda, k_1^\lambda, k_2^\lambda, k_3^\lambda, k_4^\lambda)$. We refer to the bit at column 0, row 1 in S as k_1, and the bit at column 0, row 2 as k_2.

In our CPA, we calculate the values of $(n_0^\lambda, n_1^\lambda, n_2^\lambda, n_3^\lambda, n_4^\lambda)$ for each experiment. Next, we guess the corresponding five bits, $(k_0^\lambda, k_1^\lambda, k_2^\lambda, k_3^\lambda, k_4^\lambda)$, resulting in 32 possible guesses. We then compute $\chi(n_0^\lambda+k_0^\lambda, n_1^\lambda+k_1^\lambda, n_2^\lambda+k_2^\lambda, n_3^\lambda+k_3^\lambda, n_4^\lambda+k_4^\lambda)$. Our focus is on the HD between these five bits and the same bits in the state S at the input of the round. Since two of these key bits in the initial state, S, are unknown, we must also guess them. This leads to a total of 2^7 hypotheses for the values of $(k_0^\lambda, k_1^\lambda, k_2^\lambda, k_3^\lambda, k_4^\lambda, k_1, k_2)$. For each hypothesis, we compute the correlation between the power traces and the calculated HD. The maximum correlation result is selected, and we rank the hypotheses from 0 to 127 based on the corresponding maximum correlation values.

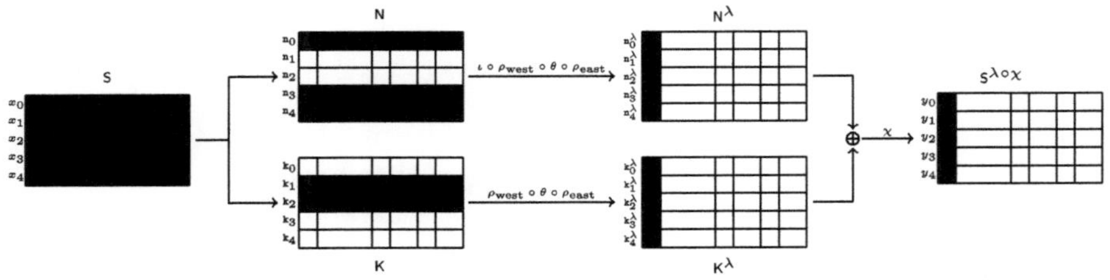

Fig. 3. Leakage model used in correlation power analysis on GASTON-AEAD.

5 Changing the Order of the Layers

To examine how the order of the diffusion and non-linear layers affects our attacks, we modified the round function of the GASTON permutation by switching the positions of the θ and χ layers. The reordered round function is defined as,

$$p[\mathsf{S}] = \iota \circ \rho_{\text{west}} \circ \theta \circ \rho_{\text{east}} \circ \chi[\mathsf{S}] .$$

We refer to this modified permutation as GASTON-R, and the AEAD scheme obtained by replacing ASCON-p with GASTON-R in ASCON-128 as GASTON-R-AEAD. This change in layer order does not affect the known bounds on differential and linear trails. In fact, reordering layers in a round function is a common technique used to study how different components influence the diffusion of input differences [7].

In our experiments, combining majority voting with the CPA on ASCON-128 significantly improved key recovery, allowing us to achieve a higher success rate with fewer traces, as shown in Sect. 6. However, this technique cannot be applied to GASTON-AEAD. The reason is structural: in ASCON-p, the diffusion layer follows the non-linear layer, so each output bit depends on multiple S-box outputs, which makes majority voting possible. In contrast, GASTON applies the diffusion layer before the non-linear layer, so such mixing does not occur at the point where CPA is applied. Since GASTON-R uses the same order of layers as ASCON-p, we can apply the same CPA and majority voting strategy used for ASCON-128 to GASTON-R-AEAD. We explore this approach in the remainder of this section.

5.1 CPA Attack

We start by deriving the ANF of the non-linear layer, which is now the first layer applied in the GASTON-R round function,

$$\begin{aligned} z_0 &= x_0 + x_2 + x_1 x_2, \\ z_1 &= x_1 + x_3 + x_2 x_3, \\ z_2 &= x_2 + x_4 + x_3 x_4, \\ z_3 &= x_3 + x_0 + x_0 x_4, \\ z_4 &= x_4 + x_1 + x_0 x_1. \end{aligned} \tag{14}$$

To recover each part of the secret, we need to identify a quadratic term in the ANF where one term is the key and the other is the changing nonce. The only equation that satisfies this condition is Eq. (14) that we can use to recover the second part of the key, x_2. Similar to the CPA on ASCON-128, we need to realize the ANF through the diffusion layer λ. The selection function used to recover the i-th bit of the second part of the key, denoted as $S_{z_1,i}(N, k)$, is given by,

$$\begin{aligned} S_{z_1,i}(N,k) =& n'_{i+18} + n'_{i+19} + n'_{i+20} + n'_{i+25} + n'_{i+36} + n'_{i+37} + n'_{i+38} + n'_{i+43} \\ &+ n_{i+37}n'_{i+37} + n_{i+38}n'_{i+38} + n_{i+25}n'_{i+25} + n_{i+43}n'_{i+43} \\ &+ IV_{i+42}n'_{i+42} + IV_{i+43}n'_{i+43} + IV_{i+38}n'_{i+38} + IV_{i+56}n'_{i+56} \\ &+ k^\star_{i+11}n_{i+11} + k^\star_{i+12}n_{i+12} + k^\star_{i+43}n_{i+43} + k^\star_{i+52}n_{i+52} + k^\star_{i+61}n_{i+61}. \end{aligned} \tag{15}$$

The detailed steps for deriving $S_{z_1,i}(N,k)$ are provided in Appendix B. To recover the 64-bit key stored in the third row, we repeat the attack 64 times, with 2^5 key hypotheses for each attempt.

The first half of the key, stored in x_1, still needs to be recovered. However, there are no quadratic terms involving x_1 and a varying nonce in the first round. We consider two approaches to recover the first part of the key: either perform an exhaustive key search or extend the ANF to the second round of GASTON-R, where quadratic terms involving x_1 and a varying term appear. For a 64-bit key space, an exhaustive key search requires testing 2^{64} possible keys. In the second approach, we compute the ANF up to the end of the second round to evaluate the number of key hypotheses and the computational cost of determining the selection function for each key bit. Since every row contains a relevant quadratic term, we calculate the ANF for all rows. Each of the five ANFs contains approximately 49 000 terms with at least one part of the varying nonce. About 17 500 of these terms involve the first part of the key. We analyze the indexes within each ANF to determine how many key bits from the first part contribute to the selection function. Our findings show that all selection functions depend on all 64 bits from the first part of the key, effectively turning this approach into an exhaustive key search.

5.2 Majority Voting

The majority voting technique used to improve the success rate of the CPA on ASCON-p can also be applied to GASTON-R, as the diffusion layer θ follows the non-linear layer χ. Recovering a single bit within the key registers requires guessing key bits at five different positions. As before, when attacking all the bits in the second half of the key, each bit is recovered five times. For instance, the first bit of the second half, bit 64, is recovered during attacks targeting bits 75, 76, 107, 116, and 125. In fact this bit is involved in five selection functions: $S_{z_1,11}(N,k)$, $S_{z_1,12}(N,k)$, $S_{z_1,43}(N,k)$, $S_{z_1,52}(N,k)$, and $S_{z_1,61}(N,k)$. Once these five bits are attacked, we determine the value of bit 64 using majority voting: if it is recovered as 1 in three or more cases, we conclude it is 1; otherwise, we conclude it is 0.

6 Experimental Results

6.1 Hardware Implementation Results

In this section, we present the resource usage for the GASTON and GASTON-R permutations and compare them with the ASCON-p permutation. We implemented all three permutations in VHDL using a round-based approach, where each round of the permutation is executed per clock cycle. A combinational logic block generates round constants on-the-fly.

For ASIC, we synthesized the designs using Cadence Genus v21.15 and various open-source libraries to facilitate the replication of our results. Specifically, we used the NanGate OpenCell 45 nm [23], NanGate OpenCell 15 nm [15], and Google/SkyWater 130 nm libraries [1]. The results are summarized in Table 1. For FPGA, we synthesized the designs using Vivado v.2022.1 and the Artix-7 (xc7a12tcsg325-3), that is the platform recommended by George Mason University for benchmarking during the NIST LWC competition [24]. The results are summarized in Table 2. To ensure a fair comparison of resource usage, we fixed the operating frequency for synthesis across each platform and technology library.

Even if the cost in terms of operations per bit is the same for the three permutations, we observe that GASTON and GASTON-R in general require more resources than ASCON-p in practice. For ASIC, this difference reduces as the technology becomes smaller, at the point that the difference becomes negligible for the NanGate OpenCell 15 nm library. Additionally, these figures suggest that rephasing GASTON does not cause any overhead, on the contrary for some libraries it is slightly beneficial. On Artix-7 we notice a significant difference between GASTON-R and GASTON, where the former takes 7.1% more resources than ASCON-p while the latter even 30.7%.

Table 1. ASIC synthesis figures for the permutations. *Here, GE refers to *Gate Equivalent*

Technology library	Freq.	Permutation	Area (μm^2)	GE*	Ratio
NanGate 15 nm	4 GHz	GASTON	1302.68	6626	102.5%
		GASTON-R	1305.97	6643	102.7%
		ASCON-p	1271.22	6466	100.0%
NanGate 45 nm	1 GHz	GASTON	5244.72	6572	105.8%
		GASTON-R	5028.73	6302	101.5%
		ASCON-p	4956.38	6211	100.0%
SkyWater 130 nm	400 MHz	GASTON	33858.72	9020	129.9%
		GASTON-R	31941.89	8510	122.6%
		ASCON-p	26049.98	6940	100.0%

Table 2. FPGA synthesis figures for the permutations on Artix-7

Permutation	LUT	FF	Ratio
GASTON	1108	330	130.7%
GASTON-R	908	330	107.1%
ASCON-p	848	330	100.0%

6.2 Setup for Side-Channel Evaluation

Our target platform for SCA is the Sakura-G evaluation board, which is specifically designed for SCA and equipped with a Xilinx Spartan-6 XC6SLX75 FPGA. The hardware designs are implemented in VHDL and synthesized using Xilinx ISE 14.7. We used the hardware implementation of ASCON-128 provided by the ASCON team [17]. For the GASTON and GASTON-R permutations, we adopted the same construction as ASCON-128, with an identical number of rounds as the ASCON-p permutation. Power traces were collected from the Sakura-G board's power sink, operating at 24 MHz, using a Lecroy WaveRunner 610Zi oscilloscope with a 500 MHz sampling rate. These traces were aligned across all permutations during the initialization phase of the AEAD mode. To accelerate computation and trace acquisition, we used 4 bytes each for the plaintext and associated data.

6.3 Evaluation Metrics

Following the approach outlined in [22], we compare different SCAs using two key metrics: success rate (SR) and guessing entropy (GE). These metrics assess how effectively an attacker can exploit side-channel information to recover a cryptographic key. An SR of order 1 refers to the likelihood that the correct key is ranked first by the attacker. An SR of order 2 means the correct key is within the top two guesses, and so on. This metric evaluates the effectiveness of an attack strategy, assuming the attacker has fixed computational resources after analyzing the physical leaks. On the other hand, GE measures the average number of key candidates an attacker would need to test after performing a side-channel attack. This average is calculated across multiple attack attempts or simulations.

6.4 Attack Results

We report the SR of order 1 and the GE for both the bits that were successfully recovered and those that could not be recovered using the available traces. We also analyze the attack's performance based on the number of traces used. For each part of the secret key, we assign a rank of 0 to the hypothesis with the highest correlation value, and the lowest rank (based on the number of key hypotheses) to the hypothesis with the lowest correlation. Since calculating the GE for the entire secret state is impractical, we focus on using the SR to measure the effectiveness of our attacks. Specifically, we used between 1 000 and 50 000 traces, increasing in increments of 1 000, and from 50 000 to 100 000 traces, increasing by 10 000 per step, to calculate these metrics.

For the CPA on ASCON-p, the SR is determined based on 128 independent attacks, each targeting the recovery of a single key bit. For GASTON, the key is recovered through 64 separate attacks, with each attack focusing on a specific column of the state. For CPA on GASTON-R, each individual attack attempts to recover a single key bit. Recovering the first 64 bits of the key requires an exhaustive key search. As a result, the reported SR for GASTON-R is based solely on the recovery of the second half of the key. In our experiments to compute the GE, we measured the rank of the correct key hypothesis across ten different CPA, each using a different set of traces.

CPA on ASCON-p. As discussed earlier, recovering one bit of the key requires guessing key bits at three different positions within the key registers. The SR is calculated based on the number of correctly recovered 3-tuples: $(k_i, k_{i+36}, k_{i+45})$ for the first part of the key, and (k_i, k_{i+3}, k_{i+25}) for the second part, as shown in Eq. (9), Eq. (12).

Figure 4a illustrates the SR for our CPA on ASCON-p across all 128 key bits. The graph shows that to achieve a stable SR above 90%, more than 34 000 traces are required. It is important to note that we first recover the key bits stored in the x_1 register by selecting z_0 as the sensitive variable and using the selection function from Eq. (9). Next, we use the selection function defined in Eq. (12), this time with z_1 chosen as the sensitive variable. In this step, we recover $\tilde{k}$, which represents $x_1 + x_2$, as shown in Eq. (10), Eq. (11). If a bit in x_1 is not recovered correctly, it affects the accuracy of the corresponding bit in x_2. However, to ensure a fair comparison, we report the overall SR.

Figure 4a also presents the results of combining CPA with the majority voting technique. With 18 000 traces, we fully recover the first part of the key, achieving a 100% SR. The majority voting technique can also be applied to recover x_1+x_2, where we achieve a 100% SR using just 12 000 traces. However, with fewer traces, the SR is not always stable. When attempting to recover both the first and second parts of the key using the same set of traces, we first reach a 100% SR with 27 000 traces. Afterward, the SR temporarily drops by 1%, but with 31 000 traces, we regain a stable 100% SR using the majority voting technique. Without majority voting, the SRs are lower, with 87.5%, 91.41%, and 91.41% SRs achieved using 18 000, 27 000, and 31 000 traces, respectively. It is worth noting that without majority voting, the key cannot be fully recovered even when using 100 000 traces.

Figure 5a illustrates the GE for the correct key hypothesis of bit 14. While this bit can be recovered, it takes approximately 90 000 traces for the GE to reach zero. At 60 000 traces, the GE is around 0.7. When the trace count increases to 70 000, the GE drops to 0.1, as only one experiment shows a non-zero rank. The GE remains unchanged at 80 000 traces, with a rank of 1 for the correct hypothesis in one experiment. Figure 5b shows the GE for the correct hypothesis of key bit 87. This bit cannot be recovered, even with 100 000 traces. However,

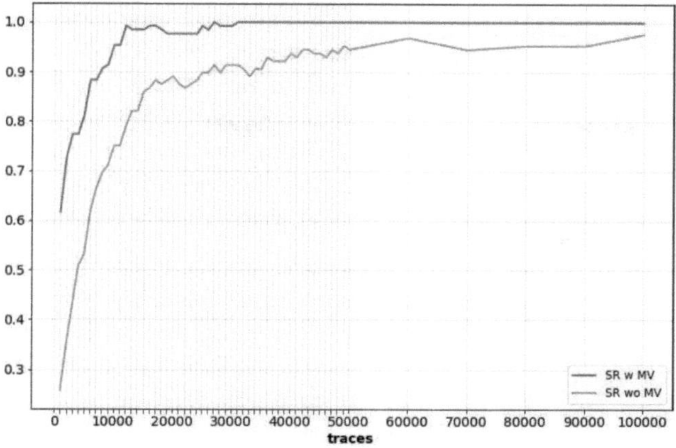

(a) SR for attack on ASCON-p, calculated for 128 bits of the key

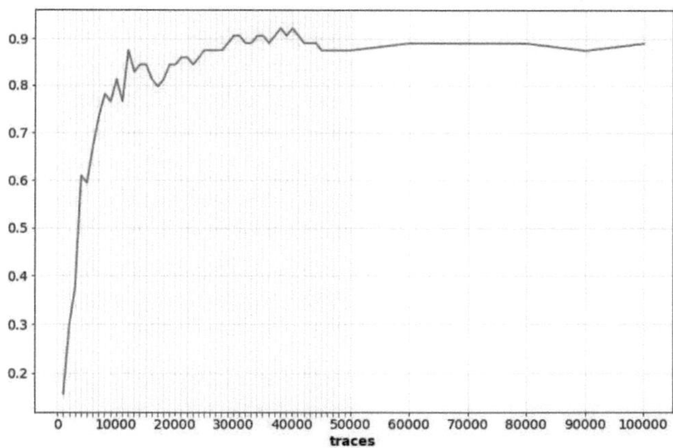

(b) SR for the attack on GASTON, calculated for 64 columns

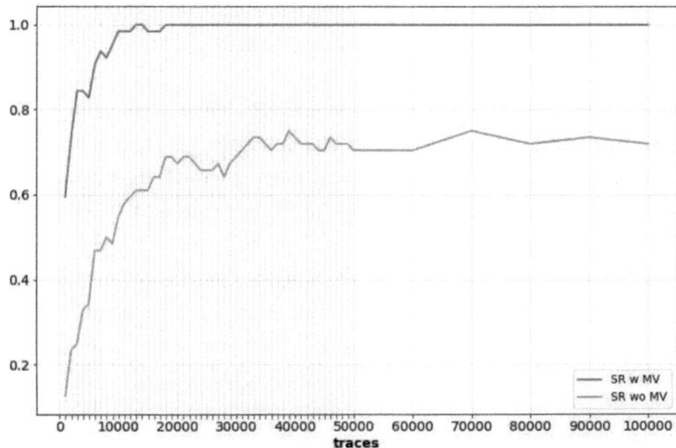

(c) SR for attack on GASTON-R, calculated for 64 bits of the key

Fig. 4. SR on ASCON-128, GASTON-AEAD, and GASTON-R-AEAD.

it is interesting to observe how the GE changes as more traces are used for the attack. While the GE decreases, it never reaches zero. At 60 000 traces, the GE stands at 2.5. With 70 000 traces, the GE drops to 1.8. At 80 000 traces, the GE further decreases to 1.4, but the bit is still not recovered in any of the ten experiments. With 90 000 traces, the GE improves to 1, but in all experiments, the correct hypothesis consistently remains the second guess. Even at 100 000 traces, no further improvement is observed, and the GE remains unchanged.

CPA on Gaston. In our second approach, we focus on recovering an entire column of the state. This involves guessing 5 bits from the target column before the non-linear layer, along with 2 bits from the register rows where the key bits are stored at the start of the round. The SR is calculated as the number of times the 7-tuple $(k_0^\lambda, k_1^\lambda, k_2^\lambda, k_3^\lambda, k_4^\lambda, k_1, k_2)$ is correctly recovered across all targeted columns. Figure 4b shows the SR based on the correctly recovered 7-tuples for all 64 columns in the state. The graph indicates that at least 25 000 traces are required to achieve a stable SR above 87.5%. It also demonstrates that the SR reaches its peak value of 92.19% with 38 000 traces.

Figure 5c illustrates the GE for the correct key hypothesis of column 45. While the 7-tuple can be correctly recovered, it takes approximately 60 000 traces for the GE to reach zero. The GE drops below 0.5 after just 15 000 traces, and when using more than 15 000 traces, the correct hypothesis consistently ranks either first or second. In contrast, column 21 cannot be fully recovered, even with 100 000 traces. Figure 5d shows the GE for the correct hypothesis of this column. Although the GE never reaches zero, at least 48 000 traces are required to bring it below 2. Moreover, with more than 60 000 traces, the correct hypothesis never ranks worse than fourth.

CPA on Gaston-R. We calculate the SR for Gaston-R when recovering the second part of the key (64 bits) using the selection function defined in Eq. (15). The SR is determined by how many 5-tuples $(k_{i+11}, k_{i+12}, k_{i+43}, k_{i+52}, k_{i+61})$ are correctly guessed during the attacks targeting the second part of the key stored in x_2. Figure 4c presents the SR results. The SR peaks at 75% with 39 000 traces but slightly decreases and stabilizes around 72% as the number of traces increases.

The majority voting technique significantly improves the SR. As shown in Fig. 4c, without majority voting, it was impossible to recover all the key bits in x_2, with the SR stabilizing around 72%. However, with majority voting, a 100% SR is achieved with just 13 000 traces, and it remains at 100% with more than 18 000 traces.

Figure 5e illustrates the GE for bit 3, which can be correctly recovered. The GE drops below 0.5 with just 4 000 traces, and in the worst case, the correct hypothesis ranks second in the experiments. After 60 000 traces, the GE reaches zero and remains stable. Figure 5f shows the GE for bit 39, which cannot be recovered, as the GE never reaches zero, even with up to 100 000 traces. However, the GE exhibits a clear downward trend, falling below 1 after 29 000 traces. As the number of traces increases, the correct hypothesis is never ranked worse than second. The lowest GE of 0.3 is achieved with 40 000 and 41 000 traces.

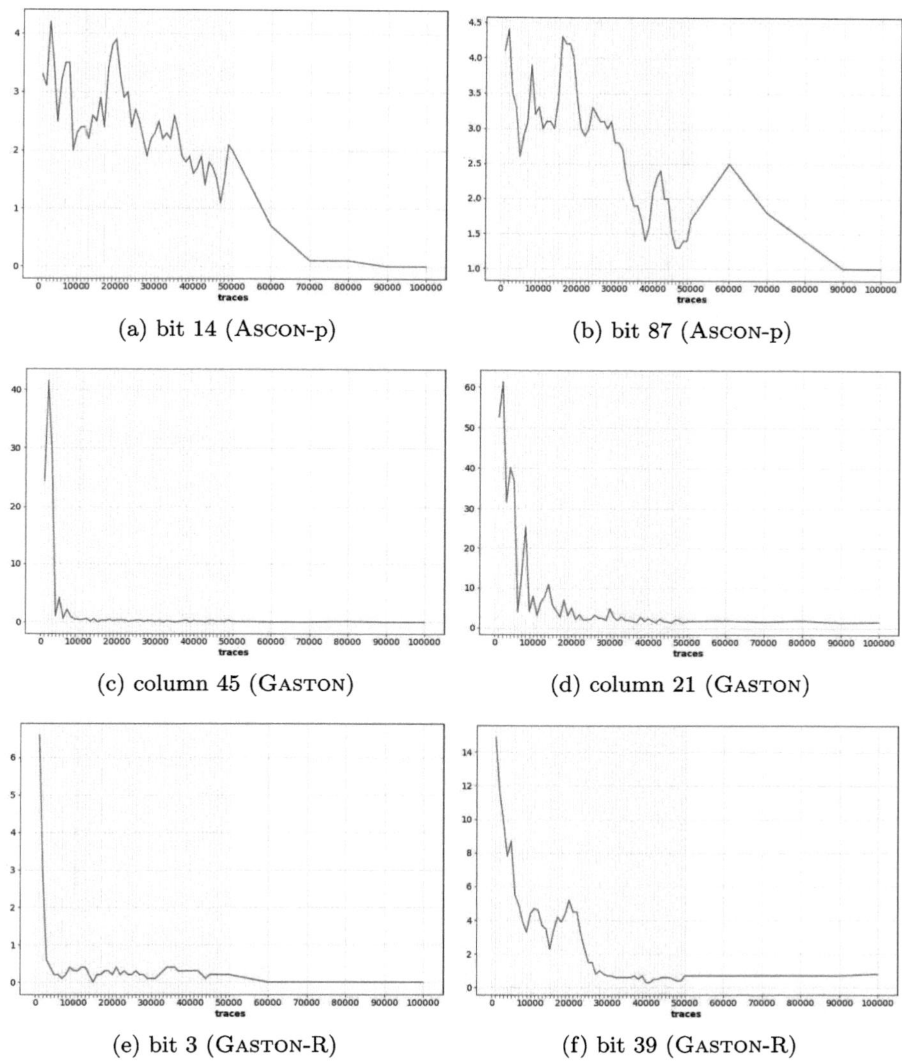

Fig. 5. GE for attacks on Ascon128, Gaston-AEAD, and Gaston-R-AEAD.

Table 3. Overview of results for CPA on the evaluated AEAD schemes

scheme	CPA on # attacks recovered	# hypo	SR	SR with MV
ASCON-128	bit 128 all key bits	2^3	>90 % w 34k tr	1st: 100% w 18k tr 2nd: 100% w 12k tr overall: 100% w 31k tr 1st 100% SR hit: 27k tr
GASTON-AEAD	column 64 all key bits	2^7	>87.5% w 25k tr peak: 92.19 w 38k tr	MV not possible
GASTON-R-AEAD	bit 64 2nd half of key bits	2^5	>72 % w 40k tr peak: 75 % w 39k tr	2nd: 100% w 18k tr 1st 100% SR hit: 13k tr no overall

7 Discussion

None of the CPA (without majority voting) on the evaluated schemes reach a 100% SR with 100k traces. The highest SR, 92.19%, is achieved for GASTON-AEAD using 38k traces. ASCON-128 comes close, reaching 90% SR with 34k traces. The lowest SR is observed in the attack on GASTON-R-AEAD, where the first half of the key (64 bits) is not directly recovered and instead requires an exhaustive key search. For the second half, the attack achieves a success rate of 72% using 40k traces, which is the lowest among all results. However, for both ASCON-128 and the second half of GASTON-R-AEAD, majority voting allows the CPA to reach 100% SR with fewer traces, 31k for ASCON-128 and 18k for GASTON-R-AEAD. This is possible because in these schemes the diffusion layer follows the non-linear layer, which enables independent targeting of each key bit and supports majority voting. In contrast, for GASTON-AEAD, the diffusion layer comes before the non-linear layer. This design makes it impossible to apply majority voting and changes the attack approach: the CPA must recover one column of the key state per attack, requiring a total of 64 separate attacks. A summary of these results is provided in Table 3.

Overall, the GASTON permutation leads to higher hardware cost compared to ASCON-p, while the AEAD scheme built from it, GASTON-AEAD, does not demonstrate better resistance to CPA in our experiments. By reordering the layers in GASTON, placing the non-linear layer before the diffusion layer, we obtain GASTON-R, which has a slightly lower hardware cost compared to the original GASTON permutation. Its AEAD variant, GASTON-R-AEAD, shows significantly better resistance to CPA performed in this study.

These findings suggest that although the order of layers in a permutation does not affect its theoretical security, it can make a clear difference in how vulnerable the design is to certain side-channel attacks. To the best of our knowledge, this is the first study to explore the impact of layer ordering on side-channel resistance. Further systematic analysis could help designers create permutations that are better protected against specific classes of physical attacks.

8 Conclusion and Future Works

This paper presents a comparison of the GASTON and ASCON-p permutations with respect to hardware resource usage and vulnerability to side-channel attacks. Our analysis focused on the initialization phase of the ASCON AEAD mode. We introduced a simple technique called *majority voting*, which can be applied when the non-linear layer in the permutation comes before the diffusion layer, as is the case in ASCON-p. This method significantly improved the results of our CPA. While standard CPA did not reach full key recovery even with 100k traces, using majority voting we were able to recover the entire key with just 31k traces. We also proposed a variant of the GASTON permutation, called GASTON-R, which has a slightly lower hardware cost while maintaining the same theoretical security bounds compared to the original GASTON permutation. However, our CPA on the AEAD scheme built from GASTON-R was only able to recover half of the key. The remaining half of the key requires exhaustive search, making the overall attack more demanding in both time and hardware resources. To the best of our knowledge, this is the first study that specifically investigates how the ordering of layers in a permutation may influence its resistance to certain side-channel attacks. This work is an early step toward understanding this aspect, and more in-depth analysis is needed to better characterize its effects. A possible next direction is to examine this question in the context of other permutation designs, as well as to study how layer ordering impacts the leakage and efficiency of masked implementations. Such studies could provide valuable guidance for designing lightweight permutations with improved resistance to specific classes of physical attacks.

Acknowledgments. This work was in part supported by the Dutch Research Council (NWO) through the PROACT project (NWA.1215.18.014), the TTW PREDATOR project 19782, and the CiCS project of the research programme Gravitation under the grant 024.006.037.

A Ascon-p and Gaston permutations

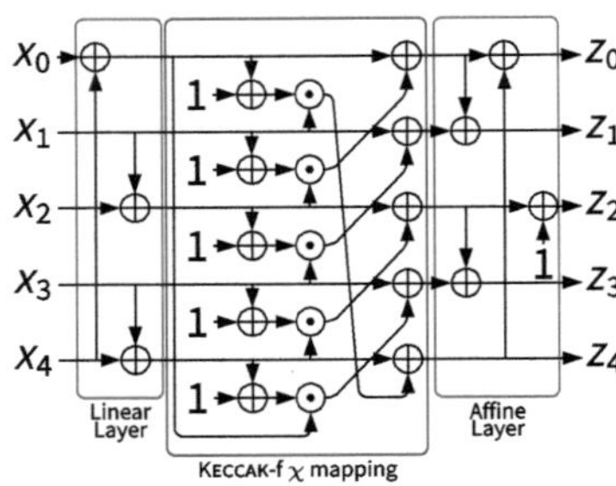

Fig. 6. 5-bit S-box of Ascon-p, original figure without highlights is taken from [8]

B Realizing the ANF of z_1 Through Linear Layers

Our goal is to recover the second part of the key stored in the x_2 register (or row). To achieve this, we select a bit from z_1 as the sensitive variable. Thus, we need to express y_1 in terms of the linear layers that follow the non-linear χ layer. The ANF for z_1 is given by $z_1 = x_1 + x_3 + x_2x_3$.

However, in the Gaston-R permutation, the diffusion layer θ mixes bits across all rows (see the calculation of row E in [12, Algorithm 1]). Due to this, expressing z_1 through the linear layers also requires the ANF for the other registers,

$$z_0 = x_0 + x_2 + x_1x_2, \qquad z_2 = x_2 + x_4 + x_3x_4,$$

$$z_3 = x_3 + x_0 + x_0x_4, \qquad z_4 = x_4 + x_1 + x_0x_1.$$

We follow the same notation as outlined in Sect. 3.1. The register x_0 holds the IV, which we denote as IV. The first 64 bits of the key are stored in register x_1, represented as k, while x_2 contains the second part of the key, denoted as k'. The 128-bit nonce is stored across registers x_3 and x_4, referred to as n and n', respectively. We denote the j-th bit in row a as a_j. Additionally, we use a superscript to indicate the output after specific layers have been applied to z_i. For example, $z_i^{\theta \circ \rho_{\text{east}}}$ represents the output register after applying the ρ_{east} layer followed by the θ layer to z_i.

To simplify the notation, instead of directly computing the selection function $S_{z_1,i}(N,k)$, we first calculate the selection function for recovering the first bit of the second part of the key, $S_{z_1,0}(N,k)$. This can then be generalized to obtain $S_{z_1,i}(N,k)$, where i represents the bit index in the second part of the key.

After applying the ρ_{east} layer to the output registers of the χ function, we obtain the following,

$$\begin{aligned}
z_0^{\rho_{\text{east}}} &= IV_0 + k_0' + k_0 k_0', \\
z_1^{\rho_{\text{east}}} &= k_{60} + n_{60} + k_{60}' n_{60}, \\
z_2^{\rho_{\text{east}}} &= k_{22}' + n_{22}' + n_{22} n_{22}', \\
z_3^{\rho_{\text{east}}} &= n_{27} + IV_{27} + IV_{27} n_{27}', \\
z_4^{\rho_{\text{east}}} &= n_4' + k_4 + IV_4 k_4.
\end{aligned}$$

To apply the θ layer, we first compute the values for the E row,

$$\begin{aligned}
E =&(IV_0 + k_0 k_0' + k_0') + (k_{60} + k_{60}' n_{60} + n_{60}) + (k_{22}' + n_{22} n_{22}' + n_{22}') \\
&+(n_{27} + IV_{27} n_{27}' + IV_{27}) + (n_4' + IV_4 k_4 + k_4) + (IV_1 + k_1 k_1' + k_1') \\
&+(k_{61} + k_{61}' n_{61} + n_{61}) + (k_{23}' + n_{23} n_{23}' + n_{23}') + (n_{28} + IV_{28} n_{28}' + IV_{28}) \\
&+(n_5' + IV_5 k_5 + k_5) + (IV_{25} + k_{25} k_{25}' + k_{25}') + (k_{28} + k_{28}' n_{28} + n_{28}) \\
&+(k_{10}' + n_{10} n_{10}' + n_{10}') + (n_{23} + IV_{23} n_{23}' + IV_{23}) + (n_3' + IV_3 k_3 + k_3) \\
&+(IV_{43} + k_{43} k_{43}' + k_{43}') + (k_{46} + k_{46}' n_{46} + n_{46}) + (k_{28}' + n_{28} n_{28}' + n_{28}') \\
&+(n_{41} + IV_{41} n_{41}' + IV_{41}) + (n_{21}' + IV_{21} k_{21} + k_{21}).
\end{aligned}$$

As a result, we have,

$$\begin{aligned}
z_0^{\theta \circ \rho_{\text{east}}} &= IV_0 + k_0' + k_0 k_0' + (E \lll 23), \\
z_1^{\theta \circ \rho_{\text{east}}} &= k_{60} + n_{60} + k_{60}' n_{60} + (E \lll 23), \\
z_2^{\theta \circ \rho_{\text{east}}} &= k_{22}' + n_{22}' + n_{22} n_{22}' + (E \lll 23), \\
z_3^{\theta \circ \rho_{\text{east}}} &= n_{27} + IV_{27} + IV_{27} n_{27}' + (E \lll 23), \\
z_4^{\theta \circ \rho_{\text{east}}} &= n_4' + k_4 + IV_4 k_4 + (E \lll 23).
\end{aligned}$$

The only remaining layers that we need to apply are $\iota \circ \rho_{\text{west}}$,

$$\begin{aligned}
z_0^{\iota \circ \rho_{\text{west}} \circ \theta \circ \rho_{\text{east}}} &= IV_0 + k_0' + k_0 k_0' + (E \lll 23) + C_{-11}, \\
z_1^{\iota \circ \rho_{\text{west}} \circ \theta \circ \rho_{\text{east}}} &= k_{60} + n_{60} + k_{60}' n_{60} + ((E \lll 23) \lll 56), \\
z_2^{\iota \circ \rho_{\text{west}} \circ \theta \circ \rho_{\text{east}}} &= k_{22}' + n_{22}' + n_{22} n_{22}' + ((E \lll 23) \lll 31), \\
z_3^{\iota \circ \rho_{\text{west}} \circ \theta \circ \rho_{\text{east}}} &= n_{27} + IV_{27} + IV_{27} n_{27}' + ((E \lll 23) \lll 46), \\
z_4^{\iota \circ \rho_{\text{west}} \circ \theta \circ \rho_{\text{east}}} &= n_4' + k_4 + IV_4 k_4 + ((E \lll 23) \lll 43).
\end{aligned}$$

If we simplify further, we obtain,

$$
\begin{aligned}
z_0^{\iota\circ\rho_{\text{west}}\circ\theta\circ\rho_{\text{east}}} =& IV_0 + k_0k'_0 + k'_0 + IV_{23} + k_{23}k'_{23} + k'_{23} + k_{19} + k'_{19}n_{19} + n_{19} \\
&+k'_{45} + n_{45}n'_{45} + n'_{45} + n_{50} + IV_{50}n'_{50} + IV_{50} + n'_{27} + IV_{27}k_{27} + k_{27} \\
&+IV_{24} + k_{24}k'_{24} + k'_{24} + k_{20} + k'_{20}n_{20} + n_{20} + k'_{46} + n_{46}n'_{46} + n'_{46} \\
&+n_{51} + IV_{51}n'_{51} + IV_{51} + n'_{28} + IV_{28}k_{28} + k_{28} + IV_{48} + k_{48}k'_{48} + k'_{48} \\
&+k_{51} + k'_{51}n_{51} + n_{51} + k'_{33} + n_{33}n'_{33} + n'_{33} + n_{46} + IV_{46}n'_{46} + IV_{46} \\
&+n'_{26} + IV_{26}k_{26} + k_{26} + IV_2 + k_2k'_2 + k'_2 + k_5 + k'_5n_5 + n_5 \\
&+k'_{51} + n_{51}n'_{51} + n'_{51} + n_0 + IV_0n'_0 + IV_0 + n'_{44} + IV_{44}k_{44} + k_{44} \\
&+C_{-11}.
\end{aligned}
$$

$$
\begin{aligned}
z_1^{\iota\circ\rho_{\text{west}}\circ\theta\circ\rho_{\text{east}}} =& k_{52} + k'_{52}n_{52} + n_{52} + IV_{15} + k_{15}k'_{15} + k'_{15} + k_{11} + k'_{11}n_{11} + n_{11} \\
&+k'_{37} + n_{37}n'_{37} + n'_{37} + n_{42} + IV_{42}n'_{42} + IV_{42} + n'_{19} + IV_{19}k_{19} + k_{19} \\
&+IV_{16} + k_{16}k'_{16} + k'_{16} + k_{12} + k'_{12}n_{12} + n_{12} + k'_{38} + n_{38}n'_{38} + n'_{38} \\
&+n_{43} + IV_{43}n'_{43} + IV_{43} + n'_{20} + IV_{20}k_{20} + k_{20} + IV_{40} + k_{40}k'_{40} + k'_{40} \\
&+k_{43} + k'_{43}n_{43} + n_{43} + k'_{25} + n_{25}n'_{25} + n'_{25} + n_{38} + IV_{38}n'_{38} + IV_{38} \\
&+n'_{18} + IV_{18}k_{18} + k_{18} + IV_{58} + k_{58}k'_{58} + k'_{58} + k_{61} + k'_{61}n_{61} + n_{61} \\
&+k'_{43} + n_{43}n'_{43} + n'_{43} + n_{56} + IV_{56}n'_{56} + IV_{56} + n'_{36} + IV_{36}k_{36} + k_{36}.
\end{aligned} \tag{16}
$$

$$
\begin{aligned}
z_2^{\iota\circ\rho_{\text{west}}\circ\theta\circ\rho_{\text{east}}} =& k'_{53} + n_{53}n'_{53} + n'_{53} + IV_{54} + k_{54}k'_{54} + k'_{54} + k_{50} + k'_{50}n_{50} + n_{50} \\
&+k'_{12} + n_{12}n'_{12} + n'_{12} + n_{17} + IV_{17}n'_{17} + IV_{17} + n'_{58} + IV_{58}k_{58} + k_{58} \\
&+IV_{55} + k_{55}k'_{55} + k'_{55} + k_{51} + k'_{51}n_{51} + n_{51} + k'_{13} + n_{13}n'_{13} + n'_{13} \\
&+n_{18} + IV_{18}n'_{18} + IV_{18} + n'_{59} + IV_{59}k_{59} + k_{59} + IV_{15} + k_{15}k'_{15} + k'_{15} \\
&+k_{18} + k'_{18}n_{18} + n_{18} + k'_0 + n_0n'_0 + n'_0 + n_{13} + IV_{13}n'_{13} + IV_{13} \\
&+n'_{57} + IV_{57}k_{57} + k_{57} + IV_{33} + k_{33}k'_{33} + k'_{33} + k_{36} + k'_{36}n_{36} + n_{36} \\
&+k'_{18} + n_{18}n'_{18} + n'_{18} + n_{31} + IV_{31}n'_{31} + IV_{31} + n'_{11} + IV_{11}k_{11} + k_{11}.
\end{aligned}
$$

$$
\begin{aligned}
z_3^{\iota\circ\rho_{\text{west}}\circ\theta\circ\rho_{\text{east}}} =& n_9 + IV_9n'_9 + IV_9 + IV_5 + k_5k'_5 + k'_5 + k_1 + k'_1n_1 + n_1 \\
&+k'_{27} + n_{27}n'_{27} + n'_{27} + n_{32} + IV_{32}n'_{32} + IV_{32} + n'_9 + IV_9k_9 + k_9 \\
&+IV_6 + k_6k'_6 + k'_6 + k_2 + k'_2n_2 + n_2 + k'_{28} + n_{28}n'_{28} + n'_{28} \\
&+n_{33} + IV_{33}n'_{33} + IV_{33} + n'_{10} + IV_{10}k_{10} + k_{10} + IV_{30} + k_{30}k'_{30} + k'_{30} \\
&+k_{33} + k'_{33}n_{33} + n_{33} + k'_{15} + n_{15}n'_{15} + n'_{15} + n_{28} + IV_{28}n'_{28} + IV_{28} \\
&+n'_8 + IV_8k_8 + k_8 + IV_{48} + k_{48}k'_{48} + k'_{48} + k_{51} + k'_{51}n_{51} + n_{51} \\
&+k'_{33} + n_{33}n'_{33} + n'_{33} + n_{46} + IV_{46}n'_{46} + IV_{46} + n'_{26} + IV_{26}k_{26} + k_{26}.
\end{aligned}
$$

$$
\begin{aligned}
z_4^{\iota\circ\rho_{\text{west}}\circ\theta\circ\rho_{\text{east}}} =& n'_{47} + IV_{47}k_{47} + k_{47} + IV_2 + k_2k'_2 + k'_2 + k_{62} + k'_{62}n_{62} + n_{62} \\
&+k'_{24} + n_{24}n'_{24} + n'_{24} + n_{29} + IV_{29}n'_{29} + IV_{29} + n'_6 + IV_6k_6 + k_6 \\
&+IV_3 + k_3k'_3 + k'_3 + k_{63} + k'_{63}n_{63} + n_{63} + k'_{25} + n_{25}n'_{25} + n'_{25} \\
&+n_{30} + IV_{30}n'_{30} + IV_{30} + n'_7 + IV_7k_7 + k_7 + IV_{27} + k_{27}k'_{27} + k'_{27} \\
&+k_{30} + k'_{30}n_{30} + n_{30} + k'_{12} + n_{12}n'_{12} + n'_{12} + n_{25} + IV_{25}n'_{25} + IV_{25} \\
&+n'_5 + IV_5k_5 + k_5 + IV_{45} + k_{45}k'_{45} + k'_{45} + k_{48} + k'_{48}n_{48} + n_{48} \\
&+k'_{30} + n_{30}n'_{30} + n'_{30} + n_{43} + IV_{43}n'_{43} + IV_{43} + n'_{23} + IV_{23}k_{23} + k_{23}.
\end{aligned}
$$

We retain only the terms in each ANF that depend on the changing nonce registers and eliminate those involving the key and IV bits. The relevant terms in Eq. (16) are as follows,

$$
\begin{aligned}
&n'_{18} + n'_{19} + n'_{20} + n'_{25} + n'_{36} + n'_{37} + n'_{38} + n'_{43} + n_{37}n'_{37} + n_{38}n'_{38} + \\
&n_{25}n'_{25} + n_{43}n'_{43} + IV_{42}n'_{42} + IV_{43}n'_{43} + IV_{38}n'_{38} + IV_{56}n'_{56} + \\
&k'_{11}n_{11} + k'_{12}n_{12} + k'_{43}n_{43} + k'_{52}n_{52} + k'_{61}n_{61}.
\end{aligned}
$$

Finally we derive and generalize the selection for any target bit i in the second part of the key,

$$
\begin{aligned}
S_{z_1,i}(N,k) =& n'_{i+18} + n'_{i+19} + n'_{i+20} + n'_{i+25} + n'_{i+36} + n'_{i+37} + n'_{i+38} + n'_{i+43} \\
&+n_{i+37}n'_{i+37} + n_{i+38}n'_{i+38} + n_{i+25}n'_{i+25} + n_{i+43}n'_{i+43} \\
&+IV_{i+42}n'_{i+42} + IV_{i+43}n'_{i+43} + IV_{i+38}n'_{i+38} + IV_{i+56}n'_{i+56} \\
&+k^\star_{i+11}n_{i+11} + k^\star_{i+12}n_{i+12} + k^\star_{i+43}n_{i+43} + k^\star_{i+52}n_{i+52} + k^\star_{i+61}n_{i+61}.
\end{aligned}
$$

References

1. Skywater open source pdk. https://github.com/google/skywater-pdk
2. CAESAR: Competition for Authenticated Encryption: Security, Applicability, and Robustness (2019). https://competitions.cr.yp.to/caesar-submissions.html
3. Amiri Eliasi, P., Mella, S., Batina, L.: Assessing gaston: side-channel security and hardware cost comparison with ascon-p. In: 2025 IEEE Computer Society Annual Symposium on VLSI (ISVLSI). IEEE (2025)
4. Bertoni, G., Daemen, J., Peeters, M., Van Assche, G.: Duplexing the sponge: single-pass authenticated encryption and other applications. In: Miri, A., Vaudenay, S. (eds.) SAC 2011. LNCS, vol. 7118, pp. 320–337. Springer, Heidelberg (2012). https://doi.org/10.1007/978-3-642-28496-0_19
5. Bertoni, G., Daemen, J., Peeters, M., Van Assche, G.: Keccak. In: Johansson, T., Nguyen, P.Q. (eds.) EUROCRYPT 2013. LNCS, vol. 7881, pp. 313–314. Springer, Heidelberg (2013). https://doi.org/10.1007/978-3-642-38348-9_19
6. Bertoni, G., Daemen, J., Peeters, M., Van Assche, G., Ronny, V.K.: Fips pub 202—sha-3 standard: permutation-based hash and extendable-output functions (2015)
7. Daemen, J., Hoffert, S., Assche, G.V., Keer, R.V.: The design of Xoodoo and Xoofff. IACR Trans. Symm. Cryptol. **2018**(4), 1–38 (2018). https://doi.org/10.13154/tosc.v2018.i4.1-38

8. Dobraunig, C., Eichlseder, M., Mendel, F., Schläffer, M.: Ascon v1.2: lightweight authenticated encryption and hashing. J. Cryptol. **34**(3), 33 (2021). https://doi.org/10.1007/s00145-021-09398-9
9. Eliasi, P.A., Mella, S., Weissbart, L., Batina, L., Picek, S.: Xoodyak under SCA siege. In: 27th International Symposium on Design & Diagnostics of Electronic Circuits & Systems, DDECS 2024, Kielce, Poland, 3–5 April 2024, pp. 61–66. IEEE (2024). https://doi.org/10.1109/DDECS60919.2024.10508930
10. Eliasi, P.A., Mella, S., Weissbart, L., Batina, L., Picek, S.: A comprehensive evaluation of side-channel resistance of xoodyak hardware implementations. J. Circ. Syst. Comput. (2025). https://www.worldscientific.com/doi/full/10.1142/S0218126625430042
11. Groß, H., Wenger, E., Dobraunig, C., Ehrenhöfer, C.: Ascon hardware implementations and side-channel evaluation. Microprocess. Microsyst. **52**, 470–479 (2017). https://doi.org/10.1016/j.micpro.2016.10.006
12. Hirch, S.E., Daemen, J., Rohit, R., Makarim, R.H.: Twin column parity mixers and gaston - a new mixing layer and permutation. In: Handschuh, H., Lysyanskaya, A. (eds.) Advances in Cryptology - CRYPTO 2023 - 43rd Annual International Cryptology Conference, CRYPTO 2023, Santa Barbara, CA, USA, 20–24 August 2023, Proceedings, Part III. LNCS, vol. 14083, pp. 475–506. Springer, Heidelberg (2023). https://doi.org/10.1007/978-3-031-38548-3_16
13. Lefevre, C., Mennink, B.: SoK: security of the Ascon modes. IACR Trans. Symm. Cryptol. **2025**(1), 138–210 (2025). https://doi.org/10.46586/tosc.v2025.i1.138-210
14. Lei, H., et al.: Symmetric twin column parity mixers and their applications. IACR Trans. Symm. Cryptol. **2024**(4), 1–37 (2024). https://doi.org/10.46586/tosc.v2024.i4.1-37
15. Martins, M.G.A., et al.: Open cell library in 15 nm FreePDK technology. In: Davoodi, A., Young, E.F.Y. (eds.) Proceedings of the 2015 Symposium on International Symposium on Physical Design, ISPD 2015, Monterey, CA, USA, 29 March–1 April 2015, pp. 171–178. ACM (2015). https://doi.org/10.1145/2717764.2717783
16. NIST: Lightweight cryptography standardization process (2015). https://csrc.nist.gov/projects/lightweight-cryptography
17. Primas, R.: NIST LWC Hardware Reference Design of Ascon v1.2. https://github.com/ascon/ascon-hardware
18. Ramezanpour, K., Abdulgadir, A., Diehl, W., Kaps, J.P., Ampadu, P.: Active and passive side-channel key recovery attacks on ascon. In: Proceedings of NIST Lightweight Cryptography Workshop, pp. 1–27 (2020)
19. Ramezanpour, K., Ampadu, P., Diehl, W.: SCARL: side-channel analysis with reinforcement learning on the ascon authenticated cipher. CoRR (2020). https://arxiv.org/abs/2006.03995
20. Samwel, N., Daemen, J.: DPA on hardware implementations of Ascon and Keyak. In: Proceedings of the Computing Frontiers Conference, CF'17, Siena, Italy, 15–17 May 2017, pp. 415–424. ACM (2017). https://doi.org/10.1145/3075564.3079067
21. Sönmez Turan, M., McKay, K., Chang, D., Kang, J., Kelsey, J.: Ascon-based lightweight cryptography standards for constrained devices: authenticated encryption, hash, and extendable output functions. Technical report, NIST (2024)
22. Standaert, F.-X., Malkin, T.G., Yung, M.: A unified framework for the analysis of side-channel key recovery attacks. In: Joux, A. (ed.) EUROCRYPT 2009. LNCS, vol. 5479, pp. 443–461. Springer, Heidelberg (2009). https://doi.org/10.1007/978-3-642-01001-9_26

23. Stine, J.E., et al.: FreePDK: an open-source variation-aware design kit. In: IEEE International Conference on Microelectronic Systems Education, MSE '07, San Diego, CA, USA, 3–4 June 2007, pp. 173–174. IEEE Computer Society (2007). https://doi.org/10.1109/MSE.2007.44
24. University, G.M.: FPGA platforms and tools (2020). https://cryptography.gmu.edu/athena/LWC/LWC_FPGA_Platforms_and_Tools.pdf

Sonikku: Gotta Speed, Keed! A Family of Fast and Secure MACs

Amit Singh Bhati[1,2(✉)], Elena Andreeva[3], Simon Müller[3], and Damian Vizár[4]

[1] COSIC, KU Leuven, Leuven, Belgium
[2] 3MI Labs, Leuven, Belgium
amitsingh.bhati@3milabs.tech
[3] TU Wien, Vienna, Austria
{elena.andreeva,simon.mueller}@tuwien.ac.at
[4] CSEM, Neuchâtel, Switzerland
damian.vizar@csem.ch

Abstract. Message authentication codes (MACs) are fundamental symmetric key cryptographic functions used to generate a short, secret-key-dependent tag for a given message. This tag ensures both message authenticity and integrity, as computing a valid tag without the secret key is computationally infeasible, thereby revealing any unauthorized modification. Existing MACs often rely on block ciphers (BCs) and tweakable block ciphers (TBCs). The design of these MACs involves various trade-offs regarding properties such as data processing rate, the number of secret keys, achievable security definitions and concrete margins, the necessity for pre- or post-processing, parallelization capabilities, internal state size, and performance optimization for diverse message lengths. This work introduces Sonikku, a new family of MACs based on expanding primitives, comprising three distinct instances: BabySonic, DarkSonic, and SuperSonic. The Sonikku MACs offer a compelling combination of advantages: 1) superior speed compared to state-of-the-art TBC-based MACs; 2) security beyond the birthday bound related to the input block size; 3) a smaller internal state than comparable contemporary MACs; and 4) design flexibility considering diverse trade-offs, including pre/post-processing-free operation, parallel processing, a small resource footprint, and suitability for both short and long messages. These characteristics make them highly attractive for widespread applications, including resource-constrained environments like IoT and embedded devices. Performance evaluations on a Cortex-M4 32-bit microcontroller demonstrate that BabySonic instantiated with ForkSkinny achieves a significant speed-up of at least 2.11x (and up to 4.36x) compared to the state-of-the-art ZMAC instantiated with SKINNY for 128-bit block sizes and messages up to 95 bytes. Similarly, DarkSonic and SuperSonic instantiated with ForkSkinny exhibit speed improvements of at least 1.93x for short messages (up to 95 bytes) and 1.48x for larger messages (up to 64KB), respectively, when benchmarked against ZMAC instantiated with SKINNY for both 64- and 128-bit block sizes. Building upon the approach of ZMAC and PMAC2x, we further illustrate the

Y. Kim et al. (Eds.): CANS 2025, LNCS 16351, pp. 120–141, 2026.
https://doi.org/10.1007/978-981-95-4434-9_6

potential of the Sonikku family by employing SuperSonic to construct SonicAE, a highly efficient, beyond-birthday secure, stateless, and deterministic authenticated encryption scheme.

Keywords: Authentication · MAC · forkcipher · lightweight cryptography · provable security · related-tweakey · parallel · sequential · length independent security · short queries

1 Introduction

Message Authentication Codes (MACs) are fundamental cryptographic tools ensuring authenticity and integrity in two-party secret key communication. The sender computes a tag over the message using a MAC algorithm and a shared secret key K. Upon receiving the message-tag pair, the receiver verifies the message's authenticity and integrity using the same MAC algorithm and key K.

In recent years, numerous MACs based on block ciphers (BCs) and tweakable block ciphers (TBCs) have been proposed. Notable examples include PMAC [16], the NIST standard CMAC [24], the ISO/IEC standard LightMAC [32], and their optimized successors such as PMAC1 [37], PMAC_Plus [43], 1k-PMAC_Plus [20], PMAC_TBC1k [33], and the state-of-the-art (SotA) MACs PMAC2x [30] and ZMAC [25].

Many of these MACs offer birthday-bound (BB) security guarantees relative to the block size n. Specifically, they achieve $n/2$-bit security. While (T)BCs with small block sizes ($n = 64$) have a smaller footprint and are better suited for constrained environments compared to those with larger blocks ($n = 128$), using BB-secure MACs with $n = 64$ is often deemed impractical due to feasible attacks [10]. This makes MACs offering security beyond the birthday bound (BBB) particularly desirable for lightweight platforms.

(T)BC-based MACs can be broadly categorized into sequential and parallel processing types. Sequential MACs typically have a smaller footprint and can avoid post-processing/finalization call overheads, making them suitable for memory-constrained applications processing primarily short messages. Parallel MACs enable full parallelization, offering significant speedups with hardware acceleration on multi-core platforms. They can also benefit from incremental processing [7], where modifying a few message bits/blocks does not necessitate recomputing the entire tag for long messages, reducing update costs. This property is valuable when the tag is frequently generated and updated.

Furthermore, (T)BC-based MACs can be nonce-based [17], serving as crucial components not only for authentication but also within authenticated encryption (AE) schemes.

Designing MACs suitable for low-cost, low-power IoT or embedded devices often requires balancing conflicting constraints, especially when dedicated cryptographic hardware is not available. Factors such as block size (larger for security, smaller for area), state size, the number of primitive calls, and the need for pre/post-processing must be carefully considered to optimize performance for varying message lengths while maintaining adequate security.

For example, in industrial heavy machinery remote control, authentication data is typically a few bytes (e.g., button states, joystick position) transmitted via optimized protocols. The communication round-trip demands stringent low latency (often < 100 ms [39,40,44]). Minimizing tag computation time is critical in such scenarios.

Another similar example is Automotive V2X (Vehicle-to-Everything) Communication that requires authentication for safety-critical messages such as collision warnings or traffic updates. These messages are often short, require low-latency processing, and must be highly secure against forgery.

Conversely, longer messages requiring authentication might include large binary files like multimedia content for embedded devices (KB for pictures, MB for videos). On low-end microcontrollers, content processing can consume significant resources, leaving limited time for MAC computation, particularly without hardware acceleration.

While using an expanding primitive for authentication might initially seem counterintuitive, this work demonstrates that MACs based on tweakable expanding primitives like forkciphers [4], such as ForkSkinny [35], can overcome traditional limitations in lightweight MAC design. A forward forkcipher evaluation is computationally less expensive than two parallel (T)BC calls with independent keys, yet yields two outputs. ForkSkinny, for instance, achieves favorable performance-security trade-offs by forking its internal SKINNY state partway through execution.

Expanding primitives have previously been shown useful in constructing cryptographic schemes with optimized performance and/or security for various applications, including authenticated encryption with associated data (AEAD) for short messages [4] and with leakage resilience [9,18]; robust online AEAD [2,3,12]; transciphering-friendly AEAD schemes [14]; efficient and beyond BB-secure confidentiality-only encryption [1]; length-preserving encryption [15]; pseudo random number generators [5]; and key derivation functions [13].

Our Contribution. In this work, we introduce the Sonikku MAC family, based on expanding primitives. This family comprises two sequential MACs, BabySonic and DarkSonic, and one fully parallelizable MAC, SuperSonic. Sonikku MACs achieve strong variable-input-length (VIL) pseudorandom function (PRF) security, ranging from beyond birthday bound (BBB) up to full n-bit levels. DarkSonic and SuperSonic achieve PRF security when the forkcipher with a random and secret key is modeled as a pair of two tweakable random permutations, corresponding to the standard *pseudorandom tweakable forked permutation* (prtfp) definition [4]. Furthermore, all Sonikku members achieve PRF security under our extended prtfp definition for an XOR-related-tweakey setting, termed xrtk-prtfp. All Sonikku instances provide security *strictly* beyond the birthday bound in n, the forkcipher input block size, assuming its tweak size $t \geq n$. More precisely, DarkSonic and SuperSonic achieve close to full n-bit security, while BabySonic achieves $3n/4$-bit security.

In addition, our MACs significantly improve upon State-of-the-Art (SotA) TBC-based MACs in terms of performance and flexibility. Compared to ZMAC, the Sonikku members offer the following advantages:

1. Require significantly lower number of primitive calls (at least 33% fewer calls).
2. More concretely, on a 32-bit Cortex-M4 processor with $n = 64$ (or 128), they save at least 40% (or 34%) in clock cycles for any message size. For short messages ($\leq$ 48B), BabySonic with $n = 128$ can save up to 77% in clock cycles.
3. Include pre- and/or post-processing free options, optimizing them for both short and long queries.
4. SuperSonic requires comparable state size, whereas the other two Sonics require strictly smaller state sizes for any given security level.

For a detailed comparison of Sonikku MACs with relevant existing (T)BC-based MACs, we refer the reader to Table 1. Performance comparisons of Sonikku MACs instantiated with ForkSkinny against SotA ZMAC and PMAC2x instantiated with SKINNY are shown in Fig. 5 and Table 2. For simplicity, in the remainder of this work, $\Pi[\mathsf{E}]$ denotes the MAC function Π instantiated with the primitive E.

BabySonic[ForkSkinny] achieves a speed-up of at least **2.11x** (and up to **4.36x**) over ZMAC[SKINNY] for $n = t = k = 128$ (where k is the key size) for messages up to 95B. DarkSonic[ForkSkinny] and SuperSonic[ForkSkinny] achieve speed-ups of at least **1.93x** and **1.48x** over ZMAC[SKINNY] for $k = 128$ and $t = n \in \{64, 128\}$ for short messages up to 95B and large messages up to 64 KB, respectively.

Finally, we propose an AEAD scheme called SonicAE based on the SIV-type composition of SuperSonic and the GCTR_2-3 [1] encryption scheme (Sect. 5). Our SonicAE mode provides the strong MRAE security guarantee [38]. Performance comparisons of SonicAE with other SotA AEAD schemes are provided in Fig. 7 and Table 3. SonicAE[ForkSkinny] achieves a speed-up of at least **1.41x** and **1.32x** over existing MRAE schemes ZAE[SKINNY] and Deoxys-II[SKINNY] under $k = 128$, $t = n \in \{64, 128\}$ for short messages up to 95B and large messages up to 64 KB, respectively.

Related Work. Datta et al. in [19] proposed LightFORK, a forkcipher variant of LightMAC that achieves beyond birthday security. However, in contrast to our parallel MAC SuperSonic, which can process at least $n + k$ bits in the standard single-key setting (and up to $n + t + k - e$ bits in the XRTK setting) per "*one-legged*" forkcipher call, LightFORK processes only n bits per "*two-legged*" forkcipher call. This makes LightFORK significantly costlier than SuperSonic, specifically at least **3x** costlier for $k \geq n$.

Paper Organization. Section 2 introduces necessary notations and security notions. Section 3 formally describes the Sonikku family and its security results, with proofs deferred to App. A in the full version [11]. Section 4 discusses our Sonikku results and software performance. Section 5 presents SonicAE as

Table 1. Comparison of Sonikku modes with state-of-the-art MACs with comparable instances. Each entry referring to a binary string size or security parameter of a MAC is in bits. n, t, and k are the block, tweak, and key sizes of the underlying primitive, respectively, whereas $e = \log_2\left(\left\lceil \frac{\max_i m_i}{n+t+k-e} \right\rceil\right)$ and $s = \log_2\left(\left\lfloor \frac{\max_i m_i}{n-s} \right\rfloor\right)$ are reserved tweak bits for the counter in the corresponding MAC. BC, TBC, FC, BM, Par., L.I.Sec., and IT are short for block cipher, tweakable block cipher, forkcipher, binary field multiplications, parallelization support, message length independent security, and information-theoretic security, respectively. $|\mathcal{K}|$ and $|Tag|$ represent the key length and the maximum possible tag length of the MAC, respectively. For DarkSonic and SuperSonic, the table rows remain correct even if the parts in blue are removed, i.e., the security improves to single-key setting, potentially with some reduced performance. The cells in red highlight the key points of comparison against Sonikku modes.

MAC	Primitive	PRF Security (IT)	$\|\mathcal{K}\|$	Minimal State	Cost[a] (to process an m-bit message)	$\|Tag\|$	L.I.Sec.	Par.
CMAC [24]	BC as prp [29]	$n/2$	k	$3n+k$	$(\lceil m/n \rceil + 1)$BC + 2BM	$\leq n$	✗	✗
PMAC [16]	BC as prp	$n/2$	k	$3n+k$	$(\lceil m/n \rceil + 1)$BC + $\lceil m/n \rceil$BM	$\leq n$	✗	✓
PMAC1 [37]	TBC as tprp [29]	$n/2$	k	$2n+t+k$	$\lceil m/n \rceil$TBC	$\leq n$	✗	✓
lightMAC [32]	BC as prp	$n/2$	$2k$	$3n+2k$	$\lceil m/(n-s) \rceil$BC	$\leq n$	✓	✓
SUM-ECBC [42]	BC as prp	$2n/3$	$4k$	$2n+4k$	$2(\lceil m/n \rceil + 1)$BC	$\leq n$	✗	✗
PMAC_Plus [43]	BC as prp	$2n/3$	$3k$	$5n+3k$	$(\lceil m/n \rceil + 4)$BC + $(3\lceil m/n \rceil$-1)BM	$\leq n$	✗	✓
1k-PMAC_Plus [20]	BC as prp	$2n/3$	k	$5n+k$	$(\lceil m/n \rceil + 4)$BC + $3\lceil m/n \rceil$BM	$\leq n$	✗	✓
ZMAC [25]	TBC as tprp	$\min\{n, (n+t)/2\}$	k	$4n+2t+k$	$\left(\left\lceil \frac{m}{n+t-4} \right\rceil + 6\right)$TBC + $\left(2\left\lceil \frac{m}{n+t-4} \right\rceil - 1\right)$BM	$\leq 2n$	✗	✓
PMAC_TBC1k [33]	TBC as tprp	n (if $t \geq n/2$)	k	$3n+t+k$	$(\lceil m/n \rceil + 2)$TBC + $(\lceil m/n \rceil - 1)$BM	$\leq n$	✓	✓
PMACx/PMAC2x [30]	TBC as tprp	n	k	$3n+t+k$	$(\lceil m/n \rceil + 2)$TBC + $\lceil m/n \rceil$BM	$\leq 2n$	✓	✓
BabySonic [Our Work]	FC as xrtk-prtfp	$3n/4$	k	$2n+t+k$	$\left\lceil \frac{m}{n+t+k-2} \right\rceil$FC	$\leq 1.5n$	✗	✗
DarkSonic [Our Work]	FC as xrtk-prtfp	$\min\{n, t\} - \log_2 \mu$	k	$2n+t+2k$	$\left(\left\lceil \frac{m-2(t+k-2)}{n+t+k-2} \right\rceil\right)$TBC + 2FC	$\leq 2n$	✗	✗
SuperSonic [Our Work]	FC as xrtk-prtfp	$\min\{n, (n+t)/2\}$	k	$2n+2t+3k$	$\left(\left\lceil \frac{m}{n+t+k-e} \right\rceil\right)$(TBC + BM) + 1FC	$\leq 2n$	✓	✓

[a] Actual performance cost of an FC, BC, and TBC depends on their instantiations. To exemplify, when instantiated using SKINNY's round function with the same key, block, and/or tweak size, 1 FC costs approximately 1.6(T)BC. For concrete performance comparison, see Sect. 4.

an application of SuperSonic for misuse-resistant authenticated encryption. Section 6 concludes the paper.

2 Preliminaries

2.1 Notation

Strings and Operations. All strings are considered binary strings. The set of all strings of all possible lengths is denoted by $\{0,1\}^*$, and the set of all strings of length n (a positive integer) is denoted by $\{0,1\}^n$. For a string X of ℓ bits, $X[i]$ denotes the i-th bit of X for $i = 1, \ldots, \ell$ (counting from left to right), and $X[i \ldots j] = X[i] \| X[i+1] \| \ldots \| X[j]$ for $1 \leq i < j \leq \ell$. For two strings $X, Y \in \{0,1\}^*$ with $|X| \leq |Y|$ without loss of generality, $X \oplus Y$ denotes the bitwise XOR of $X \| 0^{|Y|-|X|}$ and Y. For the same strings, $X \oplus_a Y = (X \oplus Y)[1 \ldots a]$.

For an arbitrary integer n, which we fix as the block size for this work, we define the partitioning of a string X into n-bit blocks as $X = X_1 \| \ldots \| X_x \| X_*$, where $|X_i| = n$ for $i = 1, \ldots, x$ and $0 < |X_*| \leq n$. Here, $x = \lceil |X|/n \rceil - 1$ represents the number of full n-bit blocks before the last block. For two distinct strings $X, Y \in \{0,1\}^*$, we define $\mathsf{llcp}_n(X, Y)$ as the number of common full n-bit blocks at the beginning of X and Y. Formally, $\mathsf{llcp}_n(X,Y) = i$ if $X_j = Y_j$ for all $1 \le j \le i$ and either $X_{i+1} \ne Y_{i+1}$ or X or Y ends after block i. If $X_1 \ne Y_1$, then $\mathsf{llcp}_n(X,Y) = 0$.

Adversary Interaction. An adversary, denoted by $\mathcal{A}$, is a probabilistic algorithm. Its function involves interacting with oracles, which are indicated by superscripts. The adversary's ultimate output is either 0 or 1. The notation $\mathcal{A}^{\mathcal{O}} \Rightarrow 1$ specifically describes the scenario where the adversary $\mathcal{A}$ makes queries to the oracle $\mathcal{O}$ during its process and subsequently produces an output of 1.

Miscellaneous. $X \leftarrow_{\$} \mathcal{X}$ denotes the sampling of an element X from a finite set $\mathcal{X}$ according to the uniform distribution. $(p)_q$ denotes the falling factorial $p(p-1)\dots(p-q+1)$, with $(p)_0 = 1$. A predicate $\mathsf{P}(x)$ is defined as $\mathsf{P}(x) = 1$ if it is true and $\mathsf{P}(x) = 0$ if it is false. Integer tuples (i', j') are compared lexicographically, i.e., $(i', j') < (i, j)$ if and only if $i' < i$ or ($i' = i$ and $j' < j$).

2.2 MAC Syntax and Security Definition

Let $\mathcal{X}$ and $\mathcal{Y}$ be non-empty finite sets. Let $\mathrm{Func}(\mathcal{X}, \mathcal{Y})$ be the set of all functions from $\mathcal{X}$ to $\mathcal{Y}$. A uniform random function (URF) with domain $\mathcal{X}$ and range $\mathcal{Y}$, denoted $R : \mathcal{X} \to \mathcal{Y}$, is a random function sampled uniformly from $\mathrm{Func}(\mathcal{X}, \mathcal{Y})$.

A MAC is defined by a tuple: $(\mathcal{K}, \mathsf{MAC}, \mathsf{Verify})$, where $\mathcal{K}$ is the non-empty key space, $\mathsf{MAC} : \mathcal{K} \times \mathcal{X} \to \mathcal{Y}$ is the tag generation function, and $\mathsf{Verify} : \mathcal{K} \times \mathcal{X} \times \mathcal{Y} \to \{1, \perp\}$ is the tag verification function. For any key $K \in \mathcal{K}$ and message $X \in \mathcal{X}$, $\mathsf{Verify}_K(X, Y)$ returns 1 if and only if $\mathsf{MAC}_K(X) = Y$, and $\perp$ otherwise. The verification function is typically defined as recomputing the tag and checking for equality; thus, for brevity, we refer to a MAC scheme by the tuple $(\mathcal{K}, \mathsf{MAC})$ in the remainder of this paper. A secure pseudorandom function (PRF) is known to imply a secure MAC; however, the converse is not necessarily true. We recall the standard definition of PRF security for a MAC.

Definition 1 (PRF Advantage). *For* $\mathsf{MAC} : \mathcal{K} \times \mathcal{X} \to \mathcal{Y}$*, let* $\mathcal{A}$ *be an adversary whose goal is to distinguish* $\mathsf{MAC}(K, \cdot)$ *from a URF* $R(\cdot) : \mathcal{X} \to \mathcal{Y}$ *via oracle access. The PRF advantage of* $\mathcal{A}$ *against* MAC *is defined as:*

$$\mathbf{Adv}^{\mathsf{PRF}}_{\mathsf{MAC}}(\mathcal{A}) = \left| \Pr[K \xleftarrow{\$} \mathcal{K} : \mathcal{A}^{\mathsf{MAC}(K,\cdot)} \Rightarrow 1] - \Pr[R \xleftarrow{\$} \mathrm{Func}(\mathcal{X}, \mathcal{Y}) : \mathcal{A}^{R(\cdot)} \Rightarrow 1] \right|.$$

2.3 Tweakable Expanding Primitives

A tweakable expanding primitive $\mathsf{F} : \{0,1\}^k \times \{0,1\}^t \times \{0,1\}^n \to \{0,1\}^{\alpha n}$ for $\alpha \ge 2$ maps a k-bit key K, a t-bit tweak T, and an n-bit input M to α output blocks $Y_1, \dots, Y_\alpha$, each of n bits. When all α outputs are permutations of the input for any fixed key and tweak, F_α is called a multiforkcipher (MFC) [1]. In this work, we focus on $\alpha = 2$, referring to such a primitive as forkcipher (FC) [4]. We denote a forkcipher as F. The parameters k, n, and t are its key size, block size, and tweak size, respectively. We use the notations $\mathsf{F}(K, T, M)$, $\mathsf{F}_K(T, M)$, or $\mathsf{F}^T_K(M)$ interchangeably. The output $Y_1 \| Y_2 \in \{0,1\}^{2n}$.

We use an additional parameter $s \in \{0, 1, b\}$ to specify which output(s) are returned from an F call: $\mathsf{F}_K^{T,s}(M) := \mathsf{F}_K^T(M)[1 \dots n]$ when $s = 0$ (left output), $\mathsf{F}_K^T(M)[n+1 \dots 2n]$ when $s = 1$ (right output), and $\mathsf{F}_K^T(M)$ when $s = b$ (both outputs). For the rest of the paper, we use $\mathcal{K} := \{0,1\}^k$ and $\mathcal{T} := \{0,1\}^t$.

2.4 XOR-Related-Tweakey (XRTK) Security

Security of cryptographic constructions is typically analyzed in the Standard Model, where primitives are treated as fixed algorithms with secret random keys. More idealized models, like the Ideal Cipher Model (ICM), simplify analysis by treating primitives as truly random permutations for *any* adversarially chosen key.

We introduce the XOR-Related-Tweakey (XRTK) model, positioned between the Standard Model and the ICM. In this model, the adversary does not know the secret random base key $K_{base} \leftarrow_\$ \{0,1\}^k$ and tweak $T_{base} \leftarrow_\$ \{0,1\}^t$. However, the adversary can query the primitive F with inputs $(T_{base} \oplus \varDelta T, K_{base} \oplus \varDelta K, M)$, where $\varDelta T \in \{0,1\}^t$ and $\varDelta K \in \{0,1\}^k$ are chosen by the adversary. This model captures scenarios where keys or tweaks might be updated via XOR operations with secret state, which is especially relevant for feedback-based MAC designs. It grants the adversary more power than the Standard Model (where only queries under a single secret key are allowed) but is weaker than the ICM, which assumes ideal behavior for arbitrary, potentially unrelated, adversarially chosen keys.

Formally, the XRTK *pseudorandom tweakable forked permutation* (xrtk-prtfp) security of a forkcipher F is defined as the indistinguishability between the real ($\mathbf{xrtk\text{-}prtfp}_{\mathsf{F}}^{\mathrm{real}}$) and ideal ($\mathbf{xrtk\text{-}prtfp}_{\mathsf{F}}^{\mathrm{ideal}}$) worlds by an adversary making chosen-plaintext queries.

In the real world ($\mathbf{xrtk\text{-}prtfp}_{\mathsf{F}}^{\mathrm{real}}$), depicted in Fig. 1 (left), the oracle uses secret random bases $K_1 \leftarrow_\$ \{0,1\}^t$ and $K_2 \leftarrow_\$ \{0,1\}^k$. For an adversary query $(\mathsf{T}_1, \mathsf{T}_2, M, s)$, the oracle computes $T = K_1 \oplus \mathsf{T}_1$ and $K' = K_2 \oplus \mathsf{T}_2$, evaluates $\mathsf{F}_{K'}(T, M)$, and returns the specified output(s) according to $s \in \{0, 1, b\}$. Note that the adversary's input $(\mathsf{T}_1, \mathsf{T}_2)$ directly corresponds to the XOR differences $(\varDelta T, \varDelta K)$ applied to the secret bases.

In the ideal world ($\mathbf{xrtk\text{-}prtfp}_{\mathsf{F}}^{\mathrm{ideal}}$), depicted in Fig. 1 (right), the oracle is a collection of independent random permutations $\pi_{V,0}, \pi_{V,1} \leftarrow_\$ \mathrm{Perm}(n)$ for each $V \in \{0,1\}^{t+k}$. For an adversary query $(\mathsf{T}_1, \mathsf{T}_2, M, s)$, the oracle sets $V = \mathsf{T}_1 \| \mathsf{T}_2$, evaluates $(\pi_{V,0}(M), \pi_{V,1}(M))$, and returns the specified output(s) according to s. The xrtk-prtfp advantage of an adversary $\mathcal{A}$ is defined as

$$\mathbf{Adv}_{\mathsf{F}}^{\mathsf{xrtk\text{-}prtfp}}(\mathcal{A}) := \left|\Pr[\mathcal{A}^{\mathbf{xrtk\text{-}prtfp}_{\mathsf{F}}^{\mathrm{real}}} \Rightarrow 1] - \Pr[\mathcal{A}^{\mathbf{xrtk\text{-}prtfp}_{\mathsf{F}}^{\mathrm{ideal}}} \Rightarrow 1]\right|.$$

This notion provides a strong security guarantee for primitives used in constructions where the effective key/tweak can be modeled as a secret base XORed with public or state-dependent values. xrtk-prtfp reduces to its single-key counterpart; the standard prtfp [4] when $\varDelta K = 0$.

Game **xrtk-prtfp-real**$_{\mathsf{F}}$	Game **xrtk-prtfp-ideal**$_{\mathsf{F}}$
$f_1 \leftarrow^{\$} \text{Func}(k,t), f_2 \leftarrow^{\$} \text{Func}(k,k)$	**for** $\mathsf{T}_1 \| \mathsf{T}_2 \in \{0,1\}^{t+k}$ **do**
$K \leftarrow^{\$} \mathcal{K}, K_1 \leftarrow f_1(K), K_2 \leftarrow f_2(K)$	$\pi_{\mathsf{T}_1\|\mathsf{T}_2,0}, \pi_{\mathsf{T}_1\|\mathsf{T}_2,1} \leftarrow^{\$} \text{Perm}(n)$
$b \leftarrow \mathcal{A}^{\mathcal{E}}$	$b \leftarrow \mathcal{A}^{\mathcal{E}}$
return b	**return** b
Oracle $\mathcal{E}(\mathsf{T}_1, \mathsf{T}_2, X)$	**Oracle** $\mathcal{E}(T_1, T_2, X)$
return $\mathsf{F}_{K_2 \oplus \mathsf{T}_2}(K_1 \oplus \mathsf{T}_1, X)$	**return** $\pi_{T_1\|T_2,0}(X), \pi_{T_1\|T_2,1}(X)$

Fig. 1. xrtk-prtfp security games for a forkcipher F. The adversary queries $(\mathsf{T}_1, \mathsf{T}_2, M, s)$, representing chosen XOR differences $\Delta T = \mathsf{T}_1$ and $\Delta K = \mathsf{T}_2$. The real oracle uses secret random bases $K_1 \leftarrow\$ \{0,1\}^t, K_2 \leftarrow\$ \{0,1\}^k$ as base tweak $T_{base} = K_1$ and base key $K_{base} = K_2$. The ideal oracle uses random permutations indexed by $\mathsf{T}_1\|\mathsf{T}_2$.

Justification for the XRTK Model. The xrtk-prtfp notion is a powerful yet realistic assumption for modern primitives like ForkSkinny. While weaker than the ideal cipher assumption (which implies ideal behavior for *any* key/tweak choice), it significantly strengthens the Standard Model assumption by allowing adversarial control over XOR differences relative to secret bases. Unlike the ICM, xrtk-prtfp security can potentially be argued based on the specific design of the primitive and its key/tweak schedule. The feasibility of this assumption for ForkSkinny is supported by the extensive cryptanalysis of SKINNY and the general tweakey framework under related-key and related-tweakey models [6, 21, 31, 36, 45]. These analyses provide evidence that ForkSkinny's design resists attacks that exploit XOR relations in keys and tweaks, making the xrtk-prtfp assumption a well-justified basis for the security of our MAC constructions in this work.

Further, the generic attack results of [8, Lemma 5.3, 5.4, Theorem 6.3 and 8.8] against an ideal primitive suggest security for a forkcipher in XOR-related setting up to the birthday bound in the effective key length, i.e., up to $\mathcal{O}(2^{\frac{t+k}{2}})$ queries. For ForkSkinny, where $t + k \geq 2n$, this translates to n bits of security against generic attacks, aligning with our beyond-birthday security claims for FC-based MACs.

3 Sonikku Family of Fast and Secure MACs

The Sonikku family comprises three fast and secure MACs based on tweakable expanding primitives: BabySonic, SuperSonic, and DarkSonic. All Sonikku instances provably achieve Beyond Birthday Bound (BBB) PRF-security and demonstrate significant speed improvements compared to state-of-the-art (SotA) MACs in various application settings (see Sect. 4). To achieve this speed-up,

Sonikku MACs effectively utilize the input space, tweak space, and, importantly, the key space of the underlying primitive to securely combine message blocks with available key material.

Design Choices. The Sonikku MACs offer distinct trade-offs in their design. SuperSonic is designed for hardware parallelization and fast performance on long messages. It employs parallel primitive calls for message processing and maintains an extra internal state to accumulate chained values for a final primitive evaluation (the finalization call), as detailed in Fig. 3.

In contrast, DarkSonic and BabySonic are sequential MACs. They sacrifice hardware parallelization support to reduce the minimal state size (the amount of required RAM), making them more suitable for platforms without parallel processing capabilities or with stringent resource constraints.

BabySonic minimizes state by using the key only during an initial setup phase, eliminating the need to store the full key in the main processing loop's state. This results in an optimal minimal state size, equivalent to the state size of the underlying expanding primitive. BabySonic utilizes both outputs of the expanding primitive (F) to generate an internal pseudorandom state, which helps eliminate dedicated pre- or post-processing calls (such as the initial call in DarkSonic or the final call in SuperSonic). This design optimizes BabySonic for short message queries, particularly those up to 95 bytes.

DarkSonic, on the other hand, is a nonce-based construction. It achieves improved performance with increasing message length (approaching SuperSonic's speed for various message sizes when there is no parallel processing) by utilizing only one output branch in most F calls. However, this comes at the cost of requiring a nonce input for security (see Table 1).

Our Recommendation. Based on their performance characteristics across message lengths (illustrated in Fig. 5(b)), we recommend BabySonic for short messages (up to approximately 136 bytes) and SuperSonic for longer messages (above approximately 96 bytes). DarkSonic serves as a valuable option with intermediate trade-offs, particularly where a nonce is available and efficient processing of longer sequential messages is needed.

The following subsections formally define each Sonikku instance and state their PRF security results. Detailed proofs are provided in App. A in the full version [11].

3.1 BabySonic and Its PRF Security

$\mathsf{BabySonic}_{n/a}$ is a sequential MAC utilizing a tweakable expanding primitive F with tweak space $\mathcal{T} = \{0,1\}^t$ for $t > 0$. $\mathsf{BabySonic}_{n/a}[\mathsf{F}] := (\mathcal{K}, \mathsf{MAC})$ has key space $\mathcal{K} = \{0,1\}^k$ and message space $\mathcal{M} = \{0,1\}^*$. It offers an "*optimal*" internal state size, meaning the memory required for the internal state during processing is equal to the minimal state size of the underlying expanding primitive itself, incurring no state overhead from the MAC construction. The MAC algorithm for $\mathsf{BabySonic}_{n/a}$ is depicted in Fig. 2 and its pseudocode is given in Fig. 8. Its PRF security is formally stated in Theorem 1, with its proof deferred to App. A.1 in the full version [11].

Theorem 1. *Let* F *be a forkcipher with* $\mathcal{T} = \{0,1\}^t$ *and* $k \leq n + a \leq k + t - 2$ *for some integer* $1 \leq a \leq n$. *Then for any adversary* $\mathcal{A}$ *who makes at most* q *queries to* $\mathsf{BabySonic}_{n/a}$, *with maximum query length* ℓ *(in blocks), such that the total number of* F *calls induced is at most* σ *and* $10 \leq a \leq \min\{n - 10, 11n/12\}$, *we have*

$$\mathbf{Adv}^{\mathsf{PRF}}_{\mathsf{BabySonic}_{n/a}[\mathsf{F}]}(\mathcal{A}) \leq \ell \cdot \mathbf{Adv}^{\mathsf{xrtk\text{-}prtfp}}_{\mathsf{F}}(\mathcal{A}') + \frac{(\sigma - q)^2}{2^{n+a+1}} + \frac{6\sigma}{2^{n-a/2}}$$

for some adversary $\mathcal{A}'$ *making at most* q F *queries (under fixed but secret and random bases as per the* $\mathsf{xrtk\text{-}prtfp}$ *model), running in time bounded by the running time of* $\mathcal{A}$ *plus* $\gamma \cdot \sigma$, *where* γ *is the runtime of an* F *call.*

From this bound, $\mathsf{BabySonic}_{n/a}$ achieves a maximum information-theoretic PRF security of approximately $3n/4$ bits (with respect to primitive queries) when $a = n/2$. Thus, $\mathsf{BabySonic}_2$ emerges as the optimal variant of $\mathsf{BabySonic}_{n/a}$. For simplicity, this variant is referred to as $\mathsf{BabySonic}$ throughout the paper.

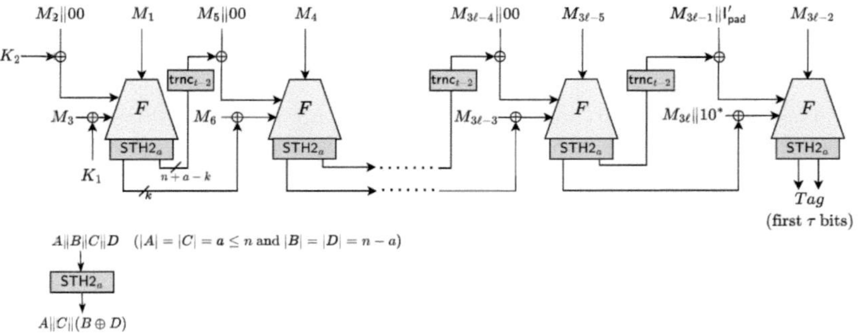

Fig. 2. The $\mathsf{BabySonic}_{n/a}$ MAC mode. Processing of a message M is illustrated. Padding of 10^* is applied to make the message size a multiple of $(n + t + k - 2)$ for the smallest possible positive integer x' blocks (see Fig. 8). The padding indicator $\mathsf{l}'_{\mathsf{pad}}$ is 01 if the original message size was a multiple of the block size $(n + t + k - 2)$, and 11 otherwise. The $\mathsf{STH2}$ function (Summation-Truncation Hybrid-2 [23], shown below) processes the $2n$-bit F output to produce the $(n + a)$-bit internal chaining value (or tag), where $k + t - 2 \geq n + a \geq k$. The k-bit key K is used to derive sub-keys $K_1 \in \{0,1\}^k$ and $K_2 \in \{0,1\}^{t-2}$ using a key derivation function.

3.2 SuperSonic and Its PRF Security

$\mathsf{SuperSonic}$ is a parallel MAC based on a tweakable expanding primitive F with tweak space $\mathcal{T} = \{0,1\}^t$. $\mathsf{SuperSonic}[\mathsf{F}] := (\mathcal{K}, \mathsf{MAC})$ has key space $\mathcal{K} = \{0,1\}^k$ and message space $\mathcal{M} = \{0,1\}^*$. The $\mathsf{SuperSonic}$ algorithm is illustrated in Fig. 3

and its pseudocode is in Fig. 8. The formal claim regarding the PRF security of SuperSonic is presented in Theorem 2, with its proof deferred to App. A.2 in the full version [11].

Theorem 2. *Let* F *be a forkcipher with* $\mathcal{T} = \{0,1\}^t$*. Then for any adversary* $\mathcal{A}$ *who makes at most* q *queries to* SuperSonic *such that the total number of induced* F *calls is at most* σ*, we have*

$$\mathbf{Adv}^{\mathsf{PRF}}_{\mathsf{SuperSonic[F]}}(\mathcal{A}) \leq \mathbf{Adv}^{\mathsf{xrtk\text{-}prtfp}}_{\mathsf{F}}(\mathcal{A}') + \frac{4q^2}{2^{n+\min\{n,t-2\}}}$$

for some adversary $\mathcal{A}'$ *making at most* σ F *queries (under fixed but secret and random bases as per the* xrtk-prtfp *model), running in time bounded by the running time of* $\mathcal{A}$ *plus* $\gamma \cdot \sigma$*, where* γ *is the runtime of an* F *call.*

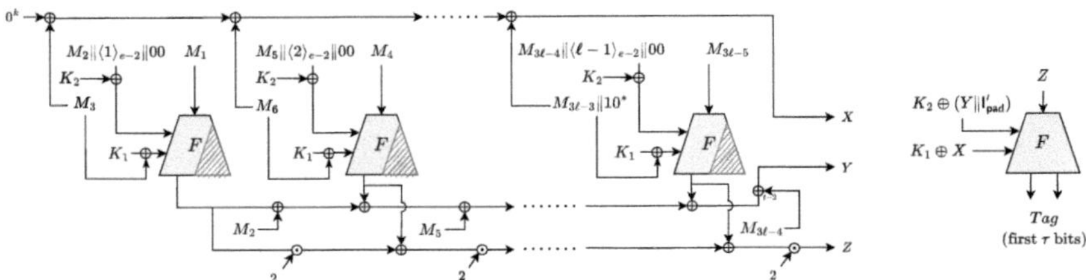

Fig. 3. The SuperSonic MAC mode. Processing of a message M is illustrated. Padding of 10^* is applied to make the message size the smallest possible multiple of $(n+t+k-e)$ blocks (see Fig. 8). The padding indicator $\mathsf{I}'_{\mathsf{pad}}$ is 01 if the original message size was a multiple of the block size $(n+t+k-e)$, and 11 otherwise. The k-bit key K is used to derive sub-keys $K_1 \in \{0,1\}^k$ and $K_2 \in \{0,1\}^{t-2}$ using a key derivation function. Note that e is a constant depending on the maximum message length (defined in Table 1).

3.3 DarkSonic and Its PRF Security

DarkSonic is a nonce-based sequential MAC employing a tweakable expanding primitive F with tweak space $\mathcal{T} = \{0,1\}^t$. DarkSonic[F] := $(\mathcal{K}, \mathcal{N}, \mathsf{MAC})$ has key space $\mathcal{K} = \{0,1\}^k$, nonce space $\mathcal{N} = \{0,1\}^n$, and message space $\mathcal{M} = \{0,1\}^*$. The DarkSonic algorithm is depicted in Fig. 4 and its pseudocode is in Fig. 8. Its PRF security (under nonce misuse setting) is formally stated in Theorem 3 with its proof deferred to App. A.3 in the full version [11].

Theorem 3. *Let* F *be a forkcipher with* $\mathcal{K} = \{0,1\}^k$ *and* $\mathcal{T} = \{0,1\}^t$*. Then for any nonce-misusing adversary* $\mathcal{A}$ *who makes at most* q *queries to the* DarkSonic *nonce-based MAC, such that the total number of* F *calls induced is at most* σ *and the maximum number of times a nonce is repeated is* μ*, we have*

$$\mathbf{Adv}^{\mathsf{PRF}}_{\mathsf{DarkSonic[F]}}(\mathcal{A}) \leq \mathbf{Adv}^{\mathsf{xrtk\text{-}prtfp}}_{\mathsf{F}}(\mathcal{A}') + \frac{6(\sigma-q)^2}{2^{n+\min\{n,t-2\}}} + \frac{2q(\mu-1)}{2^{\min\{n,t-2\}}}$$

for some adversary $\mathcal{A}'$ making at most σ F queries (under fixed but secret and random bases as per the xrtk-prtfp *model), running in time bounded by the running time of $\mathcal{A}$ plus $\gamma \cdot \sigma$, where γ is the runtime of an* F *call.*

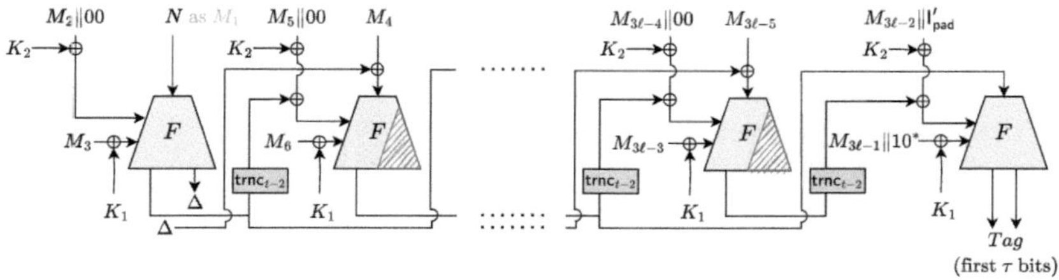

Fig. 4. The DarkSonic MAC mode. Processing of a full message M (including the n-bit nonce N) is illustrated. Padding of 10^* is applied to make the message size the smallest possible multiple of $(n + t + k - 2) - n$ for some positive integer x' blocks, resulting in total length $(x'(n + t + k - 2) - n) + n$ after appending the nonce (see Fig. 8). The padding indicator $\mathsf{I}'_{\mathsf{pad}}$ is 01 if the original message size was a multiple of the message block size $(n+t+k-2)-n$, and 11 otherwise. $\mathsf{trnc}_{t-2}(X)$ returns the first $t-2$ bits of $X\|0^{t-2}$. The k-bit key K is used to derive sub-keys $K_1 \in \{0,1\}^k$ and $K_2 \in \{0,1\}^{t-2}$ using a key derivation function.

Novelty. The Sonikku MACs introduce several novel aspects:

- BabySonic: This design is unique in utilizing key feedback to avoid storing the full key during the main processing loop, achieving an optimal minimal state size equal to that of the underlying primitive. It processes message blocks at a rate of 1 primitive call per block and achieves beyond birthday security. Unlike Nested-MAC (NMAC) [22]; a popular key feedback mode, which achieves a rate of $(n + t)/(n + t + k)$ but requires a FIL-PRF and offers security below the birthday bound in the key size k, BabySonic provides BBB security in the block size n. The key feedback structure necessitates a dedicated security proof technique involving iterative replacement of primitive calls with ideal components.
- DarkSonic: This is the first efficient nonce-based MAC (with nonce-misuse security) designed specifically around forkciphers or tweakable block ciphers. It uniquely achieves full n-bit security with only an n-bit chaining state (compared to the standard $2n$ bits in similar schemes) by securely re-using randomness from the previous state. The security analysis using the H-coefficient technique captures the complexities introduced by this novel state management.
- SuperSonic: While following the general structure of parallel BBB-secure MACs like PMAC_Plus, PMACx/2x, and ZMAC, SuperSonic introduces several innovations:

1. It efficiently incorporates message blocks into the key argument of the internal primitive calls by maintaining a checksum of these blocks processed in a refined finalization step. Existing designs and their proofs do not directly support passing message blocks into the key argument in this manner.
2. It features a novel, efficient finalization call compared to SotA ZMAC. Specifically, it replaces four final TBC calls with a single FC call, which is particularly beneficial for short message processing.
3. It employs strategies such as "*counter-in-tweak*" and tweak domain separation to yield a simpler, less error-prone design with smaller long-term secret material, potentially reducing the cost of threshold implementations. The resulting security proof for SuperSonic is notably compact and simple, providing a length-independent bound.

TBC Variants. DarkSonic and SuperSonic can be instantiated with TBCs instead of FCs (replacing each branch of an FC with a tweak-domain separated TBC). These variants achieve security based on the related-key properties of the underlying TBC (by incorporating message blocks into the TBC's key input) and the security results transfer from the xrtk-prtfp model for FCs to related-key TBC models.

Switching to Single-Key Setting. DarkSonic's and SuperSonic's security results can also be transferred from related-key to single-key setting without any changes to the MAC designs, except by fixing all the message blocks in the key arguments to 0 s.

Even when instantiated with TBCs and analyzed in a single-key setting (which typically reduces performance compared to utilizing related keys), DarkSonic and SuperSonic still demonstrate significant speed advantages over ZMAC. As shown in Table 2, for $n = 128$, these TBC variants in a single-key setting still achieve speed-ups of up to 1.6x and 1.77x for messages $\leq$ 95B, respectively. The speed-up converges towards 1x for very long messages ($\geq$ 64KB).

4 Performance and Discussion

We evaluated the performance of Sonikku MACs on a 32-bit Cortex-M4 processor (with no parallelization). Our fully parallelizable MAC, SuperSonic, offers length-independent security up to full n bits. When instantiated with ForkSkinny (and comparing against ZMAC instantiated with SKINNY) with $k = 128$ bits and $t = n \in \{64, 128\}$, SuperSonic significantly reduces the computation cost for tag generation. Specifically, it provides speed-ups of 2.76x (for $n = 64$) and 2.66x (for $n = 128$) for messages up to 16B (relevant for IoT/embedded devices), 1.93x (for $n = 64$) and 2.15x (for $n = 128$) for messages up to 95B (relevant for Noise framework [34] based protocols), and 1.58x (for $n = 64$) and 1.48x (for $n = 128$) for messages up to 64KB. Beyond performance, SuperSonic requires a minimal state up to $2n$ bits smaller than ZMAC in single-key setting (see Table 1).

Compared to PMAC_TBC1k and PMACx/PMAC2x, SuperSonic processes approximately $n+t+k$ bits of input per F call, whereas the mentioned schemes are limited to processing n bits per TBC call, regardless of tweak/key size. Table 1 provides a detailed comparison of Sonikku modes with existing state-of-the-art MACs.

The sequential MACs, DarkSonic and BabySonic, are well-suited for applications lacking parallel processing support or facing severe resource constraints like small, fixed state size. BabySonic excels by using the key only during initialization, thus eliminating the need for dedicated key storage state and achieving an optimal minimal state equal to the primitive's state size. DarkSonic, a nonce-based MAC, utilizes only one output leg of the F calls, achieving significantly better performance than BabySonic for longer messages while offering comparable security (albeit nonce-based).

ZMAC was originally recognized as achieving optimal efficiency/rate among TBC-based MACs by processing $n+t$ bits of data per TBC call [25], assuming a TBC could handle n-bit input and t-bit tweak per call. Our work pushes this boundary by exploiting the k-bit key argument space of a tweakable primitive (particularly FCs) in each of the Sonikku MACs to incorporate an additional k-bit of public input per call, thereby resetting the margin for achievable optimality towards $n+t+k$ bits per call.

It is worth noting that introducing public inputs into the key argument of a traditional (tweakable) cipher is generally discouraged due to potential security vulnerabilities (e.g., related-key attacks) and efficiency concerns (e.g., key schedule recomputation). However, this approach is viable for Sonikku because: 1) Our security analysis relies on the well-defined xrtk-prtfp model (Sect. 2), which specifically accounts for XOR-related keys and tweaks; and 2) Modern lightweight primitives like SKINNY and ForkSkinny feature lightweight key schedules where recomputation cost is minimal, or benefit from hardware parallelism where key schedule updates are for free.

The feasibility of using primitives in an XOR-related-tweakey manner is supported by concrete security analyses and results on the tweakey framework [26] and the related-tweakey security of SKINNY [6] and ForkSkinny [4] as discussed in Sect. 2.

Figure 5 provides an efficiency comparison of Sonikku MACs (instantiated with ForkSkinny) against SotA TBC-based MACs (instantiated with SKINNY) for $n=k=128$. The plots show that Sonikku MACs require significantly fewer clock cycles than ZMAC and PMAC2x. Among the Sonikku family, DarkSonic and SuperSonic perform similarly for longer messages and outperform BabySonic due to their use of one-legged F calls in the main loop. For short messages, BabySonic is faster as it avoids pre/post-processing calls. Table 2 provides a detailed speed-up comparison against ZMAC for both $n=64$ and $n=128$ settings, confirming these observations.

Our data also indicates that increasing the tweak size t can improve a Sonic MAC's performance, but this benefit is most pronounced for messages exceeding a certain length threshold (approximately 2KB for Cortex-M4).

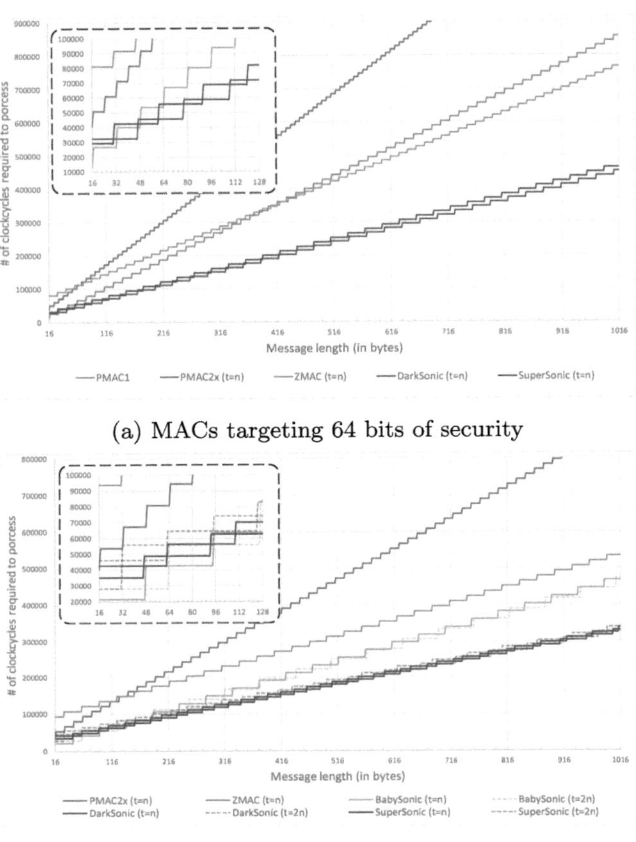

(a) MACs targeting 64 bits of security

(b) MACs targeting 96 to 128 bits of security

Fig. 5. Efficiency comparison of Sonikku with other (tweakable) primitive based SotA MACs, using $k = 128$ and $n = 64$ or 128 bits depending on the targeted security. All TBCs and FCs are instantiated with SKINNY and ForkSkinny, respectively. The plots show the number of clock cycles required to process messages of corresponding lengths.

5 SonicAE: SuperSonic Based Deterministic AE

Following the design paradigms of SIVx [30] (based on PMAC2x) and ZAE [25] (based on ZMAC), we construct SonicAE, a stateless or deterministic authenticated encryption (DAE) scheme. A DAE scheme provides security that does not rely on inputs such as random IVs or unique nonces for its core security guarantees [38]. The security notion for DAE is known as dae. Importantly, a scheme proven dae-secure can accept a nonce as part of the associated data (AD) and inherently provides security against nonce misuse. Such schemes and their achieved security are referred to as misuse-resistant AEs (MRAEs) and the mrae notion, respectively. SonicAE is dae-secure and thus provides mrae security.

Table 2. Efficiency comparison of Sonikku (instantiated with ForkSkinny) against ZMAC (instantiated with SKINNY) with $k = 128$ bits and $t = n \in \{64, 128\}$ bits. Entries show the ratio of clock cycles for ZMAC relative to the corresponding Sonikku MAC for a given maximum message length. Green cells indicate where Sonikku is faster than ZMAC, while red indicates it is slower.

MAC →	BabySonic	DarkSonic		SuperSonic	
Block size n (bits) →	128	64	128	64	128
IT PRF Security (bits) →	96	64	128	64	128
Max. message length ↓	Speed-up (factor) against ZMAC				
16B	4.36x	2.49x	2.19x	2.76x	2.66x
95B	2.11x	2.26x	2.39x	1.93x	2.15x
4KB	1.02x	1.66x	1.56x	1.60x	1.51x
64KB	0.98x	1.64x	1.52x	1.58x	1.48x

SonicAE is an SIV [38]-like composition utilizing the SuperSonic MAC (from Sect. 3.2) and a modified GCTR_2-3 [1] encryption mode, denoted GCTR'_2-3. The composition is illustrated in Fig. 6. GCTR'_2-3 is based on GCTR_2-3 but incorporates two key modifications:

1. Tweak domain separation is achieved by fixing the last two tweak bits to 10.
2. The nonce input used in GCTR_2-3 is replaced by the second n-bit half of the $2n$-bit tag generated by SuperSonic.

SonicAE is a dae-secure scheme, achieving beyond birthday security of $\min\{n, (n+t)/2\}$ bits (as stated in Theorem 4). It processes, on average, $2n(n+t+k)/(3n+t+k)$ bits per primitive call of the underlying expanding primitive F. For minimal settings of $t = 0$ and $k = n$, this processing rate is n bits per F call, comparable to existing FC-based AE schemes like PAEF, SAEF, and RPAEF [4]. However, unlike these schemes, SonicAE offers the stronger dae security guarantee. For larger values of t and/or k, SonicAE's processing rate approaches $2n$ bits per F call, which is significantly higher and better than the rates of SotA AE schemes such as ZAE and Deoxys-II [27].

We provide a concrete performance comparison of SonicAE with other SotA AE schemes (ZAE, Deoxys-I [27], Deoxys-II, OCB3 [28], SIV [38], and CCM [41]) in Fig. 7 and Table 3. For this comparison, all FCs are instantiated with ForkSkinny and all TBCs/BCs with SKINNY. We set the associated data length to 0 to provide a conservative estimate of speedup, as increasing AD length would further improve SonicAE's relative performance.

As evidenced by Fig. 7 and Table 3, SonicAE offers significantly better performance than SotA AE schemes providing comparable nonce-misuse (mrae) security. Notably, SonicAE[ForkSkinny] achieves speed-ups of at least 1.41x (for 95B messages) and 1.32x (for 64 KB messages) compared to ZAE[SKINNY] and Deoxys-II[SKINNY] under the setting $k = 128$, $t = n \in \{64, 128\}$.

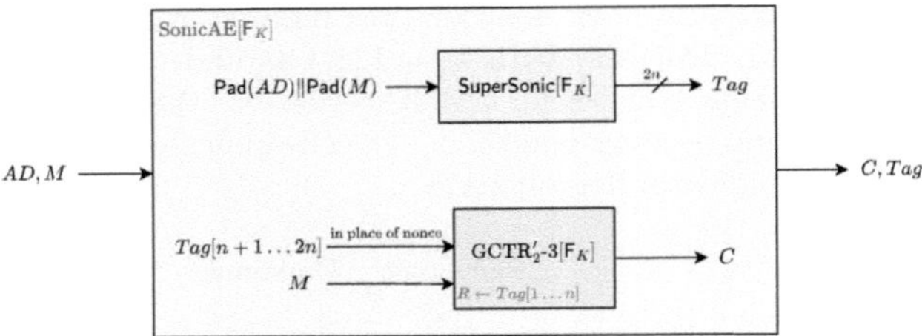

Fig. 6. The SonicAE AEAD mode. This figure illustrates the SIV-like composition processing injectively padded associated data AD and message M using the SuperSonic MAC mode and the GCTR$'_2$-3 encryption mode with key K. The second half of the $2n$-bit tag from SuperSonic is used as the effective nonce for GCTR$'_2$-3.

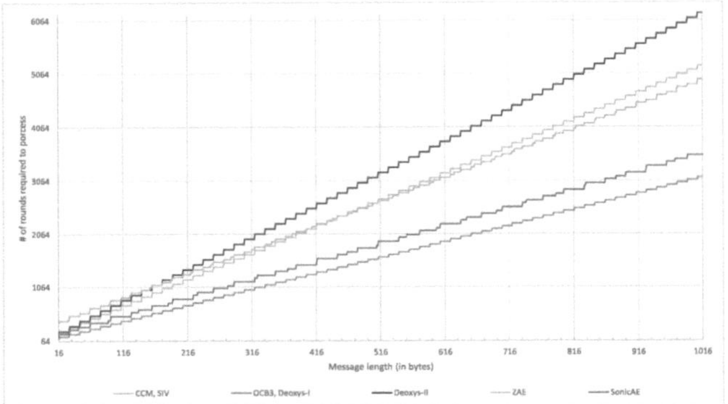

Fig. 7. Efficiency comparison of SonicAE (SIV composition of SuperSonic and GCTR$'_2$-3 instantiated with ForkSkinny) with other SotA AE modes (instantiated with SKINNY) for $n = k = 128$ bits. The plot shows the total number of primitive calls required to process a message of corresponding length (assuming 0 AD length).

Security of SonicAE. We formally state the claim regarding the dae security of SonicAE in Theorem 4. The detailed proof is deferred to App. C in the full version [11].

Theorem 4. *Let* F *be a forkcipher with* $\mathcal{T} = \{0,1\}^t$. *Then for any adversary* $\mathcal{A}$ *who makes at most* q *queries to* SonicAE *such that the total number of induced* F *calls is at most* σ, *we have*

$$\mathbf{Adv}^{\mathsf{dae}}_{\mathrm{SonicAE}[\mathsf{F}]}(\mathcal{A}) \leq \mathbf{Adv}^{\mathsf{xrtk\text{-}prtfp}}_{\mathsf{F}}(\mathcal{A}') + \frac{3q(\sigma+q)}{2^{n+\min\{n,t-2\}}} + \frac{q}{2^{2n}}$$

for some adversary $\mathcal{A}'$ *making at most* σ F *queries (under fixed but secret and random bases as per the* xrtk-prtfp *model), running in time bounded by the running time of* $\mathcal{A}$ *plus* $\gamma \cdot \sigma$, *where* γ *is the runtime of an* F *call.*

Table 3. Efficiency comparison of SonicAE (instantiated with ForkSkinny) against SotA AE modes (instantiated with SKINNY) with $k = 128$ bits, $n \in \{64, 128\}$ bits and $t \in \{0, n\}$ depending on the need of the compared AE mode. Entries show the ratio of the number of primitive calls required by the corresponding SotA AE mode relative to SonicAE for a given maximum message length (assuming 0 AD length). Green cells indicate where SonicAE is faster/better than the compared mode, while red indicates it is slower.

AE →	ZAE		Deoxys-II		OCB3, Deoxys-I		CCM, SIV	
Block size n (bits) →	64	128	64	128	64	128	64	128
IT nAE Security (bits) →	64	128	64	128	32, 64	64, 128	32	64
IT MRAE Security (bits) →	64	128	<64	<128	NIL	NIL	NIL, 32	NIL, 64
Max. message length	SonicAE speed-up/slow-down (multiplicative factor) against the mode							
16B	2.41x	1.94x	1.20x	0.73x	0.72x	0.48x	1.30x	0.81x
95B	1.56x	1.73x	1.56x	1.41x	0.81x	0.76x	1.46x	1.26x
4KB	1.33x	1.35x	1.74x	1.77x	0.87x	0.88x	1.57x	1.47x
64KB	1.32x	1.34x	1.75x	1.78x	0.87x	0.89x	1.57x	1.48x

6 Conclusion

In this work, we introduced Sonikku, a novel family of fast and secure MACs based on tweakable expanding primitives, comprising the sequential BabySonic and DarkSonic, and the parallel SuperSonic. The Sonikku family provides significant advantages over state-of-the-art (T)BC-based MACs: substantially higher performance, beyond birthday to full n-bit security, smaller state, and design flexibility for diverse applications including resource-constrained IoTs.

BabySonic is particularly effective for short queries, offering strong security ($3n/4$ bits) and efficiency due to its lack of pre/post-processing and optimal state size, achieving at least **2.11x** (and up to **4.36x**) speed-up over ZMAC ($n = t = k = 128$) for messages $\leq$ 95B.

DarkSonic improves upon BabySonic for longer messages, enhancing security (near n bits) and performance by using primarily one primitive output branch, providing nonce-misuse resistance with logarithmically degrading security upon nonce repetition.

SuperSonic offers message-length-independent security (near n bits) without a nonce, is fully parallelizable, and provides performance comparable to DarkSonic in sequential execution. DarkSonic and SuperSonic achieve speed-ups of at least **1.93x** and **1.48x**, respectively, against ZMAC ($k = 128, t = n \in \{64, 128\}$) for messages up to 95B and 64KB.

We also demonstrated the family's versatility by constructing SonicAE, an efficient, beyond-birthday secure, stateless, and deterministic authenticated encryption scheme based on SuperSonic.

Overall, Sonikku represents a significant advancement in designing fast, secure, and efficient MACs and AEADs leveraging expanding primitives, offering strong guarantees across various applications and environments.

Acknowledgments. This work was supported by CyberSecurity Research Flanders with reference number VR20192203. This work was supported in part by the Research Council KU Leuven C1 on Security and Privacy for Cyber-Physical Systems and the Internet of Things with contract number C16/15/058, and by the Flemish Government through FWO Project G.0835.16 A security Architecture for IoT. Elena Andreeva was supported by the Austrian Science Fund (FWF) SpyCoDe grant with number 10.55776/F8507-N.

A Sonikku: Pseudocodes

```
function Pad(x, y, M)    // y ≤ x
    l'_pad ← 01; res ← |M|%x
    if res ≠ y then
        l'_pad ← 11
        if res < y then
            M ← M || 10^{y-1-res}
        else
            M ← M || 10^{x+y-1-res}
        end if
    end if
    return M, l'_pad
end function

function BabySonic(K, a, τ, M)    // k ≤ n + a
    K_1, K_2 ← Derive(K)
    M, l'_pad ← Pad(n + t + k − 2, 0, M)
    P_1, ..., P_{ℓ-1}, P_* ←^{n+t+k-2} M
    (Δ_1, Δ_2) ← (K_1, K_2)
    for i ← 1 to ℓ − 1 do
        M_{3i-2} ← P_i[1 ... n]
        M_{3i-1} ← P_i[n + 1 ... n + t − 2]
        M_{3i} ← P_i[n+t−1 ... n+t+k−2]
        T ← M_{3i-1} || 00
        (Δ'_1, Δ'_2) ← F^{Δ_2⊕T,b}_{Δ_1⊕M_{3i}}(M_{3i-2})
        Δ ← Δ'_1[1 ... a] || Δ'_2[1 ... a] || ((Δ'_1 ⊕ Δ'_2)[a + 1 ... n])
        (Δ_1, Δ_2) ← (Δ[1 ... k], Δ[k + 1 ... n + a])
    end for
    T ← (P_*[n + 1 ... n + t − 2]) || l'_pad
    X, Y ← F^{Δ_2⊕T,b}_{Δ_1⊕P_*[n+t−1 ... n+t+k−2]}(P_*[1 ... n])
    Z ← X[1 ... a] || Y[1 ... a] ||
    ((X ⊕ Y)[a + 1 ... n])
    Tag ← Z[1 ... τ]
    return Tag
end function

function SuperSonic(K, e, τ, M)
    K_1, K_2 ← Derive(K)
    M, l'_pad ← Pad(n + t + k − e, 0, M)
    P_1, ..., P_{ℓ-1} ←^{n+t+k-e} M
    Δ_1, Δ_2, Δ_3 ← 0^n
    for i ← 1 to ℓ − 1 do
        M_{3i-2} ← P_i[1 ... n]
        M_{3i-1} ← P_i[n + 1 ... n + t − e]
        M_{3i} ← P_i[n+t−e+1 ... n+t+k−e]
        T ← M_{3i-1} || ⟨i⟩_{e-2} || 00
        Δ_1 ← (F^{K_2⊕T,0}_{K_1⊕M_{3i}}(M_{3i-2}) ⊕ Δ_1) ⊕_{t-2} M_{3i-1}
        Δ_2 ← 2 · (F^{K_2⊕T,0}_{K_1⊕M_{3i}}(M_{3i-2}) ⊕ Δ_2)
        Δ_3 ← M_{3i} ⊕ Δ_3
    end for
    T ← Δ_1 || l'_pad
    X, Y ← F^{K_2⊕T,b}_{K_1⊕Δ_3}(Δ_2)
    Tag ← (X || Y)[1 ... τ]
    return Tag
end function

function DarkSonic(K, τ, N, M)
    K_1, K_2 ← Derive(K)
    M ← N || M
    M, l'_pad ← Pad(n+t+k−2, t+k−2, M)
    P_1, ..., P_{ℓ-1}, P_* ←^{n+t+k-2} M
    (Δ_1, Δ_2) ← (0^n, 0^n)
    for i ← 1 to ℓ − 1 do
        M_{3i-2} ← P_i[1 ... n]
        M_{3i-1} ← P_i[n + 1 ... n + t − 2]
        M_{3i} ← P_i[n+t−1 ... n+t+k−2]
        T ← (M_{3i-1} ⊕_{t-2} Δ_2) || 00
        if i = 1 then
            (Δ_2, Δ_1) ← F^{K_2⊕T,b}_{K_1⊕M_{3i}}(M_{3i-2})
        else
            Δ ← Δ_2
            Δ_2 ← F^{K_2⊕T,0}_{K_1⊕M_{3i}}(M_{3i-2} ⊕ Δ_1)
            Δ_1 ← Δ
        end if
    end for
    T ← (P_*[1 ... t − 2] ⊕_{t-2} Δ_2) || l'_pad
    X, Y ← F^{K_2⊕T,b}_{K_1⊕P_*[t−1 ... t+k−2]}(Δ_1)
    Tag ← (X || Y)[1 ... τ]
    return Tag
end function
```

Fig. 8. MAC algorithm/pseudocode of $\mathsf{BabySonic}_{n/a}$ (top), SuperSonic (center) and DarkSonic (bottom) mode. Here Derive is some secure key derivation function that is used to generate k-bit and $(t-2)$-bit keys K_1 and K_2, respectively.

References

1. Andreeva, E., Bhati, A.S., Preneel, B., Vizár, D.: 1, 2, 3, fork: counter mode variants based on a generalized forkcipher. IACR Trans. Symmetric Cryptol. **2021**(3), 1–35 (2021)
2. Andreeva, E., Bhati, A.S., Vizár, D.: Nonce-misuse security of the SAEF authenticated encryption mode. In: Dunkelman, O., Jacobson, Jr., M.J., O'Flynn, C. (eds.) SAC 2020. LNCS, vol. 12804, pp. 512–534. Springer, Cham (2021). https://doi.org/10.1007/978-3-030-81652-0_20
3. Andreeva, E., Deprez, A., Pittevils, J., Roy, A., Bhati, A.S., Vizár, D.: New results and insighs on forkae. In: NIST LWC Workshop (2020)
4. Andreeva, E., Lallemand, V., Purnal, A., Reyhanitabar, R., Roy, A., Vizár, D.: Forkcipher: a new primitive for authenticated encryption of very short messages. In: Galbraith, S.D., Moriai, S. (eds.) ASIACRYPT 2019. LNCS, vol. 11922, pp. 153–182. Springer, Cham (2019). https://doi.org/10.1007/978-3-030-34621-8_6
5. Andreeva, E., Weninger, A.: A forkcipher-based pseudo-random number generator. In: Tibouchi, M., Wang, X. (eds.) ACNS 2023. LNCS, vol. 13906, pp. 3–31. Springer, Cham (2023). https://doi.org/10.1007/978-3-031-33491-7_1
6. Beierle, C., et al.: The SKINNY family of block ciphers and its low-latency variant MANTIS. In: Robshaw, M., Katz, J. (eds.) CRYPTO 2016. LNCS, vol. 9815, pp. 123–153. Springer, Heidelberg (2016). https://doi.org/10.1007/978-3-662-53008-5_5
7. Bellare, M., Goldreich, O., Goldwasser, S.: Incremental cryptography: the case of hashing and signing. In: Desmedt, Y.G. (ed.) CRYPTO 1994. LNCS, vol. 839, pp. 216–233. Springer, Heidelberg (1994). https://doi.org/10.1007/3-540-48658-5_22
8. Bellare, M., Kohno, T.: A theoretical treatment of related-key attacks: RKA-PRPs, RKA-PRFs, and applications. In: Biham, E. (ed.) EUROCRYPT 2003. LNCS, vol. 2656, pp. 491–506. Springer, Heidelberg (2003). https://doi.org/10.1007/3-540-39200-9_31
9. Berti, F., Standaert, F.X., Levi, I.: Authenticity in the presence of leakage using a forkcipher. Cryptology ePrint Archive, Paper 2024/1325 (2024)
10. Bhargavan, K., Leurent, G.: On the practical (in-)security of 64-bit block ciphers: collision attacks on HTTP over TLS and OpenVPN. In: ACM SIGSAC Conference on Computer and Communications Security, pp. 456–467 (2016)
11. Bhati, A.S., Andreeva, E., Müller, S., Vizar, D.: Sonikku: gotta speed, keed! A family of fast and secure MACs. Cryptology ePrint Archive, Paper 2024/1980 (2024). https://eprint.iacr.org/2024/1980
12. Bhati, A.S., Andreeva, E., Vizár, D.: OAE-RUP: a strong online AEAD security notion and its application to SAEF. In: Galdi, C., Phan, D.H. (eds.) SCN 2024. LNCS, vol. 14974, pp. 117–139. Springer, Cham (2024). https://doi.org/10.1007/978-3-031-71073-5_6
13. Bhati, A.S., Dufka, A., Andreeva, E., Roy, A., Preneel, B.: Skye: an expanding PRF based Fast KDF and its applications. In: Proceedings of the 19th ACM Asia Conference on Computer and Communications Security, pp. 1082–1098 (2024)
14. Bhati, A.S., Pohle, E., Abidin, A., Andreeva, E., Preneel, B.: Let's go Eevee! A friendly and suitable family of AEAD modes for IoT-to-cloud secure computation. In: Proceedings of the 2023 ACM SIGSAC Conference on Computer and Communications Security, pp. 2546–2560 (2023)
15. Bhati, A.S., Verbauwhede, M., Andreeva, E.: Breaking, repairing and enhancing XCBv2 into the tweakable enciphering mode GEM. Cryptology ePrint Archive, Paper 2024/1554 (2024)

16. Black, J., Rogaway, P.: A block-cipher mode of operation for parallelizable message authentication. In: Knudsen, L.R. (ed.) EUROCRYPT 2002. LNCS, vol. 2332, pp. 384–397. Springer, Heidelberg (2002). https://doi.org/10.1007/3-540-46035-7_25
17. Cogliati, B., Lee, J., Seurin, Y.: New constructions of MACs from (tweakable) block ciphers. IACR Trans. Symmetric Cryptol. **2017**(2), 27–58 (2017)
18. Datta, N., Dutta, A., List, E., Mandal, S.: FEDT: forkcipher-based leakage-resilient beyond-birthday-secure AE. IACR Commun. Cryptol. (2024)
19. Datta, N., Dutta, A., Mancillas-López, C.: LightMAC: Fork it and make it faster. Adv. Math. Commun. **18**(5), 1406–1441 (2024)
20. Datta, N., Dutta, A., Nandi, M., Paul, G., Zhang, L.: Single key variant of PMAC_Plus. IACR Trans. Symmetric Cryptol. 268–305 (2017)
21. Dong, X., Qin, L., Sun, S., Wang, X.: Key guessing strategies for linear key-schedule algorithms in rectangle attacks. In: Dunkelman, O., Dziembowski, S. (eds.) EUROCRYPT 2022. LNCS, vol. 13277, pp. 3–33. Springer, Cham (2022). https://doi.org/10.1007/978-3-031-07082-2_1
22. Gaži, P., Pietrzak, K., Rybár, M.: The exact PRF-security of NMAC and HMAC. Cryptology ePrint Archive, Paper 2014/578 (2014)
23. Gunsing, A., Mennink, B.: The summation-truncation hybrid: reusing discarded bits for free. In: Micciancio, D., Ristenpart, T. (eds.) CRYPTO 2020. LNCS, vol. 12170, pp. 187–217. Springer, Cham (2020). https://doi.org/10.1007/978-3-030-56784-2_7
24. Iwata, T., Kurosawa, K.: OMAC: one-key CBC MAC. In: Johansson, T. (ed.) FSE 2003. LNCS, vol. 2887, pp. 129–153. Springer, Heidelberg (2003). https://doi.org/10.1007/978-3-540-39887-5_11
25. Iwata, T., Minematsu, K., Peyrin, T., Seurin, Y.: ZMAC: a fast tweakable block cipher mode for highly secure message authentication. In: Katz, J., Shacham, H. (eds.) CRYPTO 2017. LNCS, vol. 10403, pp. 34–65. Springer, Cham (2017). https://doi.org/10.1007/978-3-319-63697-9_2
26. Jean, J., Nikolić, I., Peyrin, T.: Tweaks and keys for block ciphers: the TWEAKEY framework. In: Sarkar, P., Iwata, T. (eds.) ASIACRYPT 2014. LNCS, vol. 8874, pp. 274–288. Springer, Heidelberg (2014). https://doi.org/10.1007/978-3-662-45608-8_15
27. Jean, J., Nikolić, I., Peyrin, T., Seurin, Y.: Deoxys v1.41 (2016). https://competitions.cr.yp.to/round3/deoxysv141.pdf
28. Krovetz, T., Rogaway, P.: The software performance of authenticated-encryption modes. In: Joux, A. (ed.) FSE 2011. LNCS, vol. 6733, pp. 306–327. Springer, Heidelberg (2011). https://doi.org/10.1007/978-3-642-21702-9_18
29. Liskov, M., Rivest, R.L., Wagner, D.: Tweakable block ciphers. In: Yung, M. (ed.) CRYPTO 2002. LNCS, vol. 2442, pp. 31–46. Springer, Heidelberg (2002). https://doi.org/10.1007/3-540-45708-9_3
30. List, E., Nandi, M.: Revisiting full-PRF-secure PMAC and using it for beyond-birthday authenticated encryption. In: Handschuh, H. (ed.) CT-RSA 2017. LNCS, vol. 10159, pp. 258–274. Springer, Cham (2017). https://doi.org/10.1007/978-3-319-52153-4_15
31. Liu, G., Ghosh, M., Song, L.: Security analysis of SKINNY under related-tweakey settings. Cryptology ePrint Archive (2016)
32. Luykx, A., Preneel, B., Tischhauser, E., Yasuda, K.: A MAC mode for lightweight block ciphers. In: Peyrin, T. (ed.) FSE 2016. LNCS, vol. 9783, pp. 43–59. Springer, Heidelberg (2016). https://doi.org/10.1007/978-3-662-52993-5_3

33. Naito, Y.: Full PRF-secure message authentication code based on tweakable block cipher. In: Au, M.-H., Miyaji, A. (eds.) ProvSec 2015. LNCS, vol. 9451, pp. 167–182. Springer, Cham (2015). https://doi.org/10.1007/978-3-319-26059-4_9
34. Perrin, T.: The Noise protocol framework (2016). noiseprotocol.org
35. Purnal, A., Andreeva, E., Roy, A., Vizár, D.: What the fork: implementation aspects of a forkcipher. In: NIST Lightweight Cryptography Workshop 2019 (2019)
36. Qin, L., Dong, X., Wang, X., Jia, K., Liu, Y.: Automated search oriented to key recovery on ciphers with linear key schedule. In: IACR ToSC, pp. 249–291 (2021)
37. Rogaway, P.: Efficient instantiations of tweakable blockciphers and refinements to modes OCB and PMAC. In: Lee, P.J. (ed.) ASIACRYPT 2004. LNCS, vol. 3329, pp. 16–31. Springer, Heidelberg (2004). https://doi.org/10.1007/978-3-540-30539-2_2
38. Rogaway, P., Shrimpton, T.: A provable-security treatment of the key-wrap problem. In: Vaudenay, S. (ed.) EUROCRYPT 2006. LNCS, vol. 4004, pp. 373–390. Springer, Heidelberg (2006). https://doi.org/10.1007/11761679_23
39. Soliton: Teleoperation of Remote Machinery. https://www.solitonsystems.com/low-latency-video/remote-operation/remote-operation-of-machinery
40. TER: BRICK Radio Remote Control (2018). https://www.controldevices.group/PDFS/TER/TER%20Brick%20Radio%20Remote%20Control%20Data%20Sheet.pdf
41. Whiting, D., Housley, R., Ferguson, N.: Counter with CBC-MAC (CCM). IETF RFC 3610 (Informational) (2003). http://www.ietf.org/rfc/rfc3610.txt
42. Yasuda, K.: The sum of CBC MACs is a secure PRF. In: Pieprzyk, J. (ed.) CT-RSA 2010. LNCS, vol. 5985, pp. 366–381. Springer, Heidelberg (2010). https://doi.org/10.1007/978-3-642-11925-5_25
43. Yasuda, K.: A new variant of PMAC: beyond the birthday bound. In: Rogaway, P. (ed.) CRYPTO 2011. LNCS, vol. 6841, pp. 596–609. Springer, Heidelberg (2011). https://doi.org/10.1007/978-3-642-22792-9_34
44. YOURCONTROL: The Proxo Wireless Remote Control System. https://your-control.com/proxo/
45. Zhao, B., Dong, X., Meier, W., Jia, K., Wang, G.: Generalized related-key rectangle attacks on block ciphers with linear key schedule: applications to SKINNY and GIFT. Des. Codes Crypt. **88**(6), 1103–1126 (2020). https://doi.org/10.1007/s10623-020-00730-1

Computing the Restricted Algebraic Immunity, and Application to Weightwise Perfectly Balanced Functions

Luca Bonamino[1(✉)] and Pierrick Méaux[2(✉)]

[1] DCS – Department of Computer Science, Luxembourg university, Esch-sur-Alzette, Luxembourg
luca.bonamino.001@uni.student.lu

[2] SnT – Interdisciplinary Centre for Security, Reliability and Trust, Luxembourg university, Esch-sur-Alzette, Luxembourg
pierrick.meaux@uni.lu

Abstract. Algebraic Immunity (AI) is a fundamental property in the security analysis of stream ciphers and Boolean functions, measuring the resistance of a function against algebraic attacks. In this work, we focus on the computation of AI and, more specifically, on its generalization to restricted algebraic immunity, which considers annihilators constrained to specific subsets of $\mathbb{F}_2^n$. While the computation of AI has been studied using methods based on Reed-Muller codes and iterative rank-based algorithms, these approaches have not been formally adapted to the restricted setting. We address this gap by establishing the theoretical foundations required for the adaptation of these techniques and providing explicit algorithms for computing restricted algebraic immunity.

To assess the efficiency of our algorithms, we conduct practical experiments comparing the computational cost of the Reed-Muller and iterative approaches in terms of time and memory. As a case study, we analyze the algebraic immunity restricted to the slices of $\mathbb{F}_2^n$, *i.e.* the sets of binary vectors of fixed Hamming weight, denoted AI_k. The slices are of particular interest in areas of cryptography, such as side-channel analysis and stream cipher design, where the input weight may be partially predictable. We further investigate restricted algebraic immunity for Weightwise (Almost) Perfectly Balanced (W(A)PB) functions, which have been extensively studied since 2017. Our results include an empirical analysis of AI_k distributions for WPB functions with 4, 8, and 16 variables, as well as an evaluation of AI_k for various known function families.

Keywords: Boolean functions · Algebraic immunity · Restricted algebraic immunity · Weightwise (almost) perfectly balanced functions

1 Introduction

Since the introduction of algebraic attacks on filtered LFSRs [15] in 2003, Algebraic Immunity (AI) has become a crucial property to consider in the security of stream ciphers. As defined in [50], algebraic immunity refers to the minimum degree of a nontrivial annihilator of a Boolean function f or its complement $1 + f$. In the context of filtered LFSRs, AI directly corresponds to the degree of the algebraic system

Y. Kim et al. (Eds.): CANS 2025, LNCS 16351, pp. 142–169, 2026.
https://doi.org/10.1007/978-981-95-4434-9_7

an adversary can derive from the keystream, since only affine mappings occur before the application of the nonlinear filter f. Consequently, AI plays a key role in settings where affine updates are followed by a filtering function, as demonstrated in [1] for Goldreich's pseudorandom generator [28] and for (improved) filtered permutators [46,47]. Studying algebraic immunity (*e.g.* [8,20,43]) or constructing Boolean functions that optimize this parameter (*e.g.* [4,6,12,16,17,33,35–37,39,40,53,55–59,61]) has been an important line of research in the area of Boolean functions used in cryptography since the 2000s. With the recent resurgence of filtered LFSRs [10,11]—now operating on Boolean functions in over 100 variables—or other stream ciphers over $\mathbb{Z}_{2^t}$ that use filtering functions in many variables [13,31] for efficient hybrid homomorphic encryption [32], determining the algebraic immunity (or its variants) has become increasingly relevant for assessing the practical security of these schemes. Following this trend, algebraic immunity has been of of the primary criteria studied for the newly proposed functions in [9,44,48]. Concerning recent attacks on AI variants, the attack on Elisabeth-4 in [22] exploits the existence of low-degree annihilators whose monomials are restricted to a specific subspace. Similarly, the attack framework of [49] investigates AI variants that depend on the updating process of the stream cipher.

We first recall methods for computing of this parameter, specifically on a generalization of it. The complexity of computing the algebraic immunity of a Boolean function has been investigated in various works (*e.g.* [3,15,21,30]). One approach, which to our knowledge has rarely been formally articulated and is often considered folklore, relies on submatrices of generator matrices of the Reed-Muller codes. We briefly recall its theoretical foundation here. The truth table of an n-variable Boolean function of degree at most r can be identified with a codeword of the Reed-Muller code $RM(r, n)$, where each codeword's element corresponds to the evaluation of a function at an element of $\mathbb{F}_2^n$. Thus, by puncturing the Reed-Muller code of order r, keeping only the elements x such that $f(x) = 1$, one obtains the code of the products of f with functions of degree at most r. The dimension of this code equals that of the Reed-Muller code of order r if and only if f does not admit a nonzero annihilator of degree at most d. The most efficient algorithm for computing the AI is the iterative method introduced in [3]. Rather than constructing submatrices of the generator matrix of a Reed-Muller code for successive values of d, this algorithm builds them incrementally by adding one row and one column at a time. Using the same theoretical foundation as the initial approach, a rank drop in the constructed matrices indicates the existence of an annihilator. This iterative process improves computational efficiency, and specific operations designed to reduce the cost of updating successive matrices improve the initial time complexity from $\mathcal{O}(\binom{n}{\mathsf{AI}(f)}^{\omega})$ (where $\mathsf{AI}(f)$ denotes the AI of f) with $\omega = 3$ to a value closer to 2 [3,30]. In this work, we focus on a generalization of algebraic immunity, namely the restricted algebraic immunity, introduced in [7]. This property considers a subset $S \subseteq \mathbb{F}_2^n$ and corresponds to the minimal degree of an annihilator g that annihilates f or $f+1$ over the entire set S but is not identically zero on S. More formally, it is defined as: $\mathsf{AI}_S(f) = \min_g (\mathsf{deg}(g) \mid fg = 0 \text{ or } g(f+1) = 0, \text{ and } \exists x \in S \text{ such that } g(x) = 1)$. In this setting, classical algebraic immunity corresponds to the special case where $S = \mathbb{F}_2^n$. Since the Reed-Muller approach has not been formalized for this generalization[1], and the iterative method has not been studied for this generalization, we address this gap by establishing the key properties that ensure the correctness of the adapted algorithms for restricted algebraic immunity, for any subset of $\mathbb{F}_2^n$. Additionally, we provide corresponding algorithms and code implementations.

Our contributions start in Sect. 3, where we formalize the Reed-Muller approach, and in Sect. 4, we analyze the iterative method, emphasizing the theoretical and practical challenges that arise when applying this technique to restricted sets. Variants of the algebraic attack, such as fast algebraic attacks [2, 14] and attacks leveraging monomials of extreme degrees [49], require computing parameters in a manner similar to restricted algebraic immunity. Accordingly, we hope that this work will be useful for further research in these directions, and that the new algorithms can be a basis for determinations of variants of the AI.

Next, we perform various experiments with our algorithms. First, we compare the practical efficiency of the two main approaches in terms of both runtime and memory usage. For this comparison, we consider algebraic immunity restricted to a slice of $\mathbb{F}_2^n$, specifically a set $\mathsf{E}_{k,n}$ consisting of all binary vectors of length n with Hamming weight k. These sets, as well as functions that are balanced on all such sets, known as Weightwise (Almost) Perfectly Balanced (W(A)PB) functions, have attracted considerable attention since the introduction of restricted criteria in [7]. Slices of $\mathbb{F}_2^n$ frequently appear in cryptographic research, notably in contexts such as the Hamming weight model in side-channel analysis (where the Hamming weight of an intermediate variable, or a noisy version of it, can be learned by the adversary) and the fixed input weight setting in FLIP [47] (where by design the Hamming weight in input of the filtering function is known by the adversary). In particular, WAPB functions have been extensively studied, with research focusing primarily on two aspects. The first is the construction of such functions, which has been explored in various works [7, 18, 19, 24, 27, 29, 34, 38, 41, 42, 45, 51, 52, 57, 60, 62–65]. The second is the study of their cryptographic properties, including nonlinearity restricted to slices [23], overall nonlinearity [26], and algebraic immunity [25].

In this work, we further investigate algebraic immunity restricted to slices, denoted as AI_k, particularly in the context of WAPB functions, which are relevant when the Hamming weight of a function's input can be inferred. In Sect. 5.1, we analyze the distribution of AI_k for WPB functions with 4, 8, and even 16 variables. Then, in Sect. 5.2, we determine the values of AI_k for several families of functions introduced in previous works.

2 Preliminaries

For readability, we use the notation $+$ instead of $\oplus$ to denote the addition in $\mathbb{F}_2$, and $\sum$ instead of $\bigoplus$. In addition to classic notations, we denote by $[a, b]$ the subset of all integers between a and b: $\{a, a+1, \ldots, b\}$. For a vector $v \in \mathbb{F}_2^n$ we use $\mathsf{w_H}(v)$ to denote its Hamming weight $\mathsf{w_H}(v) = |\{i \in [1, n] \mid v_i = 1\}|$. For two vectors v

[1] in [7] some techniques to derive bounds on the restricted algebraic immunity are based on properties of the corresponding punctured Reed-Muller code, but no algorithm is given to determine the restricted algebraic immunity.

and w in $\mathbb{F}_2^n$ we denote by $\mathsf{d_H}(v, w)$ the Hamming distance between v and w, that is, $\mathsf{d_H}(v, w) = \mathsf{w_H}(v+w)$. For two functions f and g we denote by $\mathsf{d_H}(f, g)$ the Hamming distance between their vectors of values.

2.1 Boolean Functions, Cryptographic Criteria, and Weightwise Properties

In this section, we recall fundamental concepts concerning Boolean functions and their weightwise properties, which are utilized throughout this article. For a more comprehensive introduction to Boolean functions and their cryptographic parameters, we recommend consulting the book by Carlet [5], and for insights into weightwise properties—also known as properties on the slices—the article [7]. We denote by $\mathsf{E}_{k,n}$ the set $\{x \in \mathbb{F}_2^n \mid \mathsf{w_H}(x) = k\}$ for $k \in [0, n]$, referring to it as a slice of the Boolean hypercube (of dimension n). Consequently, the Boolean hypercube is divided into $n+1$ slices, where the elements share the same Hamming weight.

Definition 1 (Boolean Function). *A Boolean function f in n variables is a function from $\mathbb{F}_2^n$ to $\mathbb{F}_2$. The set of all Boolean functions in n variables is denoted by $\mathcal{B}_n$.*

When a property or a definition is restricted to a slice, we denote it by using the subscript k. For example, for an n-variable Boolean function f we denote its support $\mathsf{supp}(f) = \{x \in \mathbb{F}_2^n \mid f(x) = 1\}$. Furthermore, we denote by $\mathsf{supp}_k(f)$ the support of f restricted to a slice, which is defined as $\mathsf{supp}(f) \cap \mathsf{E}_{k,n}$.

Definition 2 (Balancedness). *A Boolean function $f \in \mathcal{B}_n$ is called balanced if $|\mathsf{supp}(f)| = 2^{n-1} = |\mathsf{supp}(f+1)|$.*

For $k \in [0, n]$ the function is said balanced on the slice k if $||\mathsf{supp}_k(f)| - |\mathsf{supp}_k(f+1)|| \leq 1$. In particular when $|\mathsf{E}_{k,n}|$ is even $|\mathsf{supp}_k(f)| = |\mathsf{supp}_k(f+1)| = |\mathsf{E}_{k,n}|/2$.

Using the notion of restricted balancedness we can define the weightwise (almost) perfectly balanced functions, the focus of our work.

Definition 3 (Weightwise (Almost) Perfectly Balanced Function (WPB and WAPB)). *Let $m \in \mathbb{N}^*$ and f be a Boolean function in $n = 2^m$ variables. It will be called weightwise perfectly balanced (WPB) if, for every $k \in [1, n-1]$, f is balanced on the slice k, that is $\forall k \in [1, n-1]$, $|\mathsf{supp}_k(f)| = \binom{n}{k}/2$, and:*

$$f(0, \cdots, 0) = 0, \quad \text{and } f(1, \cdots, 1) = 1.$$

The set of WPB functions in 2^m variables is denoted $\mathcal{WPB}_m$.

When n is not a power of 2, other weights than $k = 0$ and n can lead to slices of odd cardinality, we call $f \in \mathcal{B}_n$ weightwise almost perfectly balanced (WAPB) if:

$$|\mathsf{supp}_k(f)| = \begin{cases} |\mathsf{E}_{k,n}|/2 & \text{if } |\mathsf{E}_{k,n}| \text{ is even,} \\ (|\mathsf{E}_{k,n}| \pm 1)/2 & \text{if } |\mathsf{E}_{k,n}| \text{ is odd.} \end{cases}$$

The set of WAPB functions in n variables is denoted $\mathcal{WAPB}_n$.

We define additional crucial concepts for studying Boolean functions, namely the algebraic normal form and the Walsh transform. Subsequently, we introduce key cryptographic criteria for these functions, including algebraic immunity (both general and weightwise) and nonlinearity (both general and weightwise).

Definition 4 (Algebraic Normal Form (ANF) and degree). *We call Algebraic Normal Form of a Boolean function f its n-variable polynomial representation over $\mathbb{F}_2$ (i.e. belonging to $\mathbb{F}_2[x_1, \ldots, x_n]/(x_1^2 + x_1, \ldots, x_n^2 + x_n)$):*

$$f(x_1, \ldots, x_n) = \sum_{I \subseteq [1,n]} a_I \left(\prod_{i \in I} x_i \right),$$

where $a_I \in \mathbb{F}_2$. The (algebraic) degree of f, denoted $\mathsf{deg}(f)$ is:

$$\mathsf{deg}(f) = \max_{I \subseteq [1,n]} \{|I| \mid a_I = 1\} \textit{ if } f \textit{ is not null}, 0 \textit{ otherwise}.$$

We also recall the concept of order on $\mathbb{F}_2^n$, as it will be utilized in the algorithms involving Boolean functions.

Definition 5 (Order). *A binary relation $\preceq$ on a set X is called partial order if $\preceq$ is reflexive, transitive and antisymmetric. Moreover, $\preceq$ is a total order if for all $a, b \in X$ it holds $a \preceq b$ or $b \preceq a$.*

We give two examples of orders on n-length binary strings, more examples can be found in *e.g.* [54]:

- Lexicographic, given $a, b \in \mathbb{F}_2^n$ as $a = a_1, \ldots, a_n$ and $b = b_1, \ldots, b_n$, $a \preceq_{lex} b$ if and only if $a_i < b_i$ on the first index $i \in [1, n]$ such that $a_i \neq b_i$, or $a = b$.
- Graded lexicographic, given $a, b \in \mathbb{F}_2^n$ as $a = a_1, \ldots, a_n$ and $b = b_1, \ldots, b_n$, $a \preceq_{glex} b$ if $w_H(a) < w_H(b)$ or $w_H(a) = w_H(b)$ and $a \preceq_{lex} b$

Definition 6 (Truth table). *Let $f \in \mathcal{B}_n$ be a Boolean function, its truth table is the Boolean vector defined as:*

$$TT(f) \in \mathbb{F}_2^{2^n},\ TT(f) = (f(0_n), \ldots, f(1_n)).$$

Denoting by f_S the restriction of f to a subset $S \subseteq \mathbb{F}_2^n$ written as $S = \{a_1, a_2, \cdots, a_{|S|}\}$, the truth table of f_S refers to the vector $\big(f(a_1), f(a_2), \ldots, f(a_{|S|})\big)$.

If not specified otherwise, the (restricted) truth table follows the lexicographic order.

Definition 7 (Algebraic immunity and restricted algebraic immunity). *The algebraic immunity of a Boolean function $f \in \mathcal{B}_n$, denoted as $\mathsf{AI}(f)$, is defined as:*

$$\mathsf{AI}(f) = \min_{g \neq 0} \{\mathsf{deg}(g) \mid fg = 0 \textit{ or } (f+1)g = 0\},$$

where $\mathsf{deg}(g)$ is the algebraic degree of g. The function g is called an annihilator of f (or $f + 1$).

The restricted algebraic immunity of a Boolean function $f \in \mathcal{B}_n$ on the set $S \subseteq \mathbb{F}_2^n$, denoted as $\mathsf{AI}_S(f)$, is defined as:

$$\mathsf{AI}_S(f) = \min_{g \neq 0 \text{ over } S} \{\deg(g) \mid fg = 0 \text{ or } (f+1)g = 0\}.$$

For $S = \mathsf{E}_{k,n}$ we denote $\mathsf{AI}_{\mathsf{E}_{k,n}}(f)$ by $\mathsf{AI}_k(f)$ and call it weightwise algebraic immunity.

Remark 1. Let $f \in \mathcal{B}_n$. We use the notation $f^{(o)}$ referring to either f or $f+1$ when the same process or result applies to any of them. In particular, $f^{(o)} \in \{f, f+1\}$.

2.2 Reed-Muller Codes

Definition 8 (Monomials and set of monomials). *Let $u, x \in \mathbb{F}_2^n$ denoted as $x = (x_1, \cdots, x_n)$ and $u = (u_1, \cdots, u_n)$, the monomial x^u is calculated as:*

$$x^u = \prod_{i=1}^{n} x_i^{u_i}.$$

Let $E = \{\alpha_1, \alpha_2, \cdots, \alpha_k\} \subseteq \mathbb{F}_2^n$, we denote by $x^E = \{x^{\alpha_1}, x^{\alpha_2}, \cdots, x^{\alpha_k}\}$ the set of all monomials associated to E.

Definition 9 (Reed-Muller code - RM). *Let $n \in \mathbb{N}^*$ and $r \in \mathbb{N}$ with $r \leq n$, the Reed-Muller code $RM(r,n)$ is the set of all 2^n-bit length binary vectors where each code word is the evaluation of one distinct Boolean function of degree at most r in n variables.*

Definition 10 (RM generator matrix). *Let X be the set of the 2^n elements in $\mathbb{F}_2^n$ in lexicographical order and $P_{r,n} = \{\, u \in \mathbb{F}_2^n \mid w_H(u) \leq r\}$ the set of all the elements of $\mathbb{F}_2^n$ with Hamming weight smaller than or equal to r. Let $D_r^n = \sum_{i=0}^{r} \binom{n}{r}$, the generator matrix $G_{r,n} \in Mat_{D_r^n, 2^n}$ is defined as*

$$(G_{r,n})_{i,j} = x_j^{u_i},\ x_j \in X,\ u_i \in P_{r,n}.$$

We denote by $G_{r,n}^Y \in Mat_{D_r^n, |Y|}$, the Reed-Muller generator matrix restricted on the set $Y \subseteq X$:

$$(G_{r,n})_{i,j}^Y = x_j^{u_i},\ x_j \in Y,\ u_i \in P_{r,n}.$$

Remark 2. Let $\hat{a}$ be the vector corresponding to the coefficients in the ANF of a Boolean function f of n variables and degree r, then: $\hat{a} \cdot G_{r,n} = TT(f)$.

3 Computing the Restricted AI from (punctured) Generator Matrices of Reed-Muller Codes

In this section we provide an algorithm to compute the algebraic immunity of a Boolean function restricted on a general subset $S \subseteq \mathbb{F}_2^n$.

The algorithm aims to determine whether the systems of equations $S_1^r \hat{=} g_1^r * f_S(x) = \hat{0}$ or $S_2^r \hat{=} g_2^r (f+1)_S(x) = \hat{0}$ admit a non-zero solution for $x \in \mathbb{F}_2^n$, where g_1^r and g_2^r are Boolean functions of algebraic degree at most r. This is achieved by examining whether the rank of one of the punctured Reed-Muller (RM) matrices is smaller than one with the columns corresponding to the entire S. If f is non-constant on S, the algorithm searches for the existence of either g_1^r solving S_1^r or g_2^r solving S_2^r, where neither function vanishes over the entire set S. If such solutions g_1^r or g_2^r do not exist, new systems S_1^{r+1} and S_2^{r+1} are considered (through bigger matrices), and the search for solutions g_1^{r+1} and g_2^{r+1} continues. This iterative process is repeated until either an annihilator of f or $f+1$ is found or an upper bound $r+\delta$ is reached. The procedure for f_S and $(f+1)_S$ is carried out in parallel. Conversely, if f is constant on S, the algorithm terminates and returns 0, as justified by Proposition 1.

Proposition 1. *A Boolean function f has an AI_S of 0 if and only if the restriction f_S on S is constant.*

Proof. First, we show the reverse implication. We suppose that $f \in \mathcal{B}_n$ is constant on S, either $f(x) = 0$ for all $x \in S$, or $f(x) = 1$ for all $x \in S$. If f is not null everywhere but $f(x) = 0 \; \forall x \in S$, then the constant function $g(x) = 1$ is not zero on all S, and is it such that $g(x)f(x) = 0$ for all $x \in S$. Similarly, if for all $x \in S$ $f(x) = 1$, the same argument can be used for the function $f+1$ on S.

Then, we show the direct implication. We suppose that a function $g \in \mathcal{B}_n$ is a non-zero-annihilator of f restricted to S of degree 0. Then, $g \neq 0$ and $\deg(g) = 0 \Rightarrow g = 1$, therefore since g annihilates f in S, $g(x)f(x) = 0$ for all $x \in S$, resulting in $f(x)g(x) = f(x) = 0$. Similarly, if g annihilates $f+1$ on S instead of f, we have that $g(x)(f(x)+1) = 0$ implying that $f+1 = 0 \Rightarrow f(x) = 1$ for all $x \in S$. □

The matrices corresponding to the systems of equations S_1^r and S_2^r are obtained by extracting the punctured Reed-Muller generator matrices, as defined in Definition 11, from the Reed-Muller generator matrix, considering only the columns corresponding to elements in S.

Definition 11. *Let $r, n \in \mathbb{N}^*$ with $r \leq n$. Let $G_{r,n}$ be the generator matrix of the Reed-Muller code $RM(r,n)$, we define the object $G_{r,n}^{f_S^{(o)},S}$ by setting to zero all the columns of $G_{r,n}^S$ which do not correspond to elements of $supp(f^{(o)}) \cap S$. For the remaining columns, we calculate $G_{r,n}^{f_S^{(o)},S}$ as*

$$\left(G_{r,n}^{f_S^{(o)},S}\right)_{i,j} = f_S^{(o)}(u_j) \cdot \left(G_{r,n}^S\right)_{i,j}, \; u_j \in S$$

Moreover, we define the object $G_{r,n}^{f^{(o)}_{supp(f^{(o)})\cap S},S}$*, by taking all the columns of* $G_{r,n}$ *which corresponds to element of* $\mathbb{F}_2^n$ *which are in supp* $\left(f^{(o)}\right) \cap S$*.*

$$\left(G_{r,n}^{f^{(o)}_{supp(f^{(o)})\cap S},S}\right)_{:,j} = (G_{r,n}^S)_{:,j} \text{ if } f_S^{(o)}(u_j) = 1 \tag{1}$$

Proposition 2. *Let* $Z = \mathsf{supp}\left(f^{(o)}\right) \cap S$*. If rank* $\left(G_{r,n}^{f_Z^{(o)},S}\right) <$ *rank*$(G_{r,n}^S)$*, then* $f^{(o)}$ *admits a non-zero-annihilator restricted to* S *of degree at most* r*.*

Proof. Let $D_r^n = \sum_{i=0}^r \binom{n}{i}$. Since $D_r^n = \text{rank}(G_{r,n}^{f_S^{(o)},S}) + |\text{Ker}(G_{r,n}^{f_S^{(o)},S})| = \text{rank}(G_{r,n}^S) + |\text{Ker}(G_{r,n}^S)|$, we have that $\text{rank}(G_{r,n}^{f_S^{(o)},S}) < \text{rank}(G_{r,n}^S) \iff |\text{Ker}(G_{r,n}^{f_S^{(o)},S})| > |\text{Ker}(G_{r,n}^S)|$. Therefore $\exists v \in \text{Ker}(G_{r,n}^{f_S^{(o)},S})$ such that $v \notin \text{Ker}(G_{r,n}^S)$. Hence, it exists a Boolean function g of degree r, whose truth table is given by $v \cdot G_{r,n}$, which is such that $v \cdot G_{r,n} \neq 0$ and $v \cdot G_{r,n}^S \neq 0$, but $(g \cdot f_S^{(o)})_S = v \cdot G_{r,n}^{f_S^{(o)},S} = 0$. Since $\text{rank}\left(G_{r,n}^{f_S^{(o)},S}\right) = \text{rank}\left(G_{r,n}^{f^{(o)},S}\right)$, $\text{rank}(G_{r,n}^{f^{(o)},S}) < \text{rank}(G_{r,n}^S) \Rightarrow \text{rank}(G_{r,n}^{f_Z^{(o)},S}) < \text{rank}(G_{r,n}^S)$ and hence the condition $\text{rank}(G_{r,n}^{f_Z^{(o)},S}) < \text{rank}(G_{r,n}^S)$ is enough to justify the existence of such v giving the non-zero-annihilator g of f^o restricted to S. □

Algorithm 3, provided in Appendix B, details the full procedure to determine the restricted algebraic immunity of a function f of n variables on the subset S. We give additional details:

Remark 3.

1. [7] established that the upper bound of $\mathsf{AI}_S(f)$ for any Boolean function f and any set $S \subseteq \mathbb{F}_2^n$, is the smallest integer r such that $\left(G_{r,n}^n\right) > |S|/2$. As a consequence, the search of the annihilator for f and $f+1$ in our algorithm terminates once rank $\left(G_{r,n}^S\right) > \lfloor |S|/2 \rfloor$.
2. The generator matrix of a Reed-Muller code does not depend on the Boolean function. It is therefore possible to pre-compute and store the generator matrices of all Reed-Muller codes with r and n smaller than some maximum values r_{max} and n_{max}. In particular, when computing AI_S of a function with nn variables using Algorithm 3, the pre-computation of $G_{n,n}$ is required. However, to facilitate the use of the algorithm for functions with fewer than n variables, we also pre-compute matrices for smaller values of n. We therefore fix an n_{max} and pre-compute the hash table

$$G^{\leq n_{max}} = \{(n, G_{n,n})\}_{1\leq n\leq n_{max}} \tag{2}$$

and store it in a file.
Similarly, we can also pre-compute and store a second hash table, containing all the D^ns such that $n \leq n_{max}$. Such hash table is

$$D^{\leq n_{max}} = \{(n, D^n)\}_{0\leq n\leq n_{max}} = \{(n, \{(n, D_i^n)\}_{0\leq i\leq n})\}_{0\leq n\leq n_{max}} \tag{3}$$

In Algorithm 3, we therefore use the function READ_VALUES_FROM_FILE, to read to two pre-computed hash tables from the files where they have been pre-stored before the execution of the algorithm.

3. The procedure FIND_DEG_SMALLEST_S_ANNIHILATOR in Algorithm 3 is performed in parallel for f and $f+1$ with the additional condition that if one of the two branches returns the value 1, the other branch is stopped, without having to wait for it to finish.

4 Computing the Restricted AI Iteratively

In this section, we present an algorithm (Algorithm 1) to determine the algebraic immunity restricted to a set $S \subseteq \mathbb{F}_2^n$ with improved time and space complexity compared to the method presented in Sect. 3.

The core idea is to iteratively construct the objects $G_{r,n}^{f_{supp(f)\cap S},S}$ and $G_{r,n}^{(f+1)_{supp(f+1)\cap S},S}$ for varying r, increasing the size of the matrix by one row per iteration while minimizing computations. This approach checks for the existence of annihilators dynamically, rather than extracting them from a large, pre-computed Reed-Muller generator matrix restricted to S. The method extends the approach of [3] for determining the standard algebraic immunity. As with Algorithm 3, this procedure returns 0 if the function f is constant on S. Hence, we focus on explaining the case of determining $\mathsf{AI}_S(f)$ for functions such that $\mathsf{AI}_S(f) \geq 1$. (The full algorithm, however, also addresses functions with null AI_S.)

We begin with definitions and remarks necessary to introduce the general idea of the algorithm.

Definition 12 (T-Vandermonde matrix). *Let $Z = \{z_1, \cdots, z_{k_Z}\} \subseteq \mathbb{F}_2^n$ and $E = \{\alpha_1, \cdots, \alpha_{k_E}\} \subseteq \mathbb{F}_2^n$, we define the matrix $V_{E,Z}$ whose entries are*

$$(V_{E,Z})_{i,j} = z_j^{\alpha_i} \quad \forall i \in [1, k_E] \text{ and } j \in [1, k_Z].$$

We refer to this matrix as the T-Vandermonde matrix, as it is the transpose of a Vandermonde matrix. Denoting by $Z_j = \{z_1, z_2, \cdots, z_j\}$ and $E_i = \{\alpha_1, \ldots, \alpha_i\}$ for $j \in [1, z_{k_Z}]$ and $i \in [1, \alpha_{k_E}]$, the sub-matrix V_{E_i,Z_j} of $V_{E,Z}$, is given by the elements:

$$\left(V_{E_i,Z_j}\right)_{m,l} = z_l^{\alpha_m} \quad \forall m \in [1, i] \text{ and } l \in [1, j].$$

Similarly, we define the matrices $S_{E,S}$ and S_{E_i,S_j} as the T-Vandermonde sub-matrices corresponding to the elements of the set $S \subseteq \mathbb{F}_2^n$.

Remark 4. Let $Z = supp(f) \cap S$ and $E = \{\alpha_2, \alpha_2, \cdots, \alpha_{D_d^n}\}$ be such that x^E is the set of all monomials with degree at most d ordered by the graded lex order. We remark the following:

- $V_{E,Z} = G_{d,n}^{f_Z,S}$.
- Let $E^* \subset E$, ordered by graded lex order. V_{Z,E^*} is a sub-matrix of $G_{d,n}^{f_Z,S}$.

Remark 5. Let $i \geq 1$. If $1 < i+1 \leq \min\left(|Z|, |E_{D_n^n}|\right)$, then $V_{E_{i+1},Z_{i+1}}$ can be computed as

$$V_{E_{i+1},Z_{i+1}} = \begin{pmatrix} & & & z_{i+1}^{\alpha_1} \\ & V_{E_i,Z_i} & & z_{i+1}^{\alpha_2} \\ & & & \vdots \\ & & & z_{i+1}^{\alpha_i} \\ z_1^{\alpha_{i+1}} & z_2^{\alpha_{i+1}} & \cdots\ z_i^{\alpha_{i+1}} & z_{i+1}^{\alpha_{i+1}} \end{pmatrix}.$$

This can be seen by combining Definition 12 and the fact that for all i such that $1 < i+1 \leq \min(|Z|, |E|-1)$, the matrix $V_{E_{i+1},Z_{i+1}}$ is square.

Definition 13 (Sequence of V_k matrices). *As a consequence of Remark 5, we define the sequence of sub-matrices* $(V_k)_{k \in [1, D^n_{\lceil n/2 \rceil - 1}]}$ *by*

$$V_k = \begin{cases} \begin{pmatrix} & & & z_k^{\alpha_1} \\ & V_{k-1} & & z_k^{\alpha_2} \\ & & & \vdots \\ & & & z_k^{\alpha_{k-1}} \\ z_1^{\alpha_k} & z_2^{\alpha_k} & \cdots\ z_{k-1}^{\alpha_k} & z_k^{\alpha_k} \end{pmatrix} & \text{if } 2 \leq k \leq \min\left(|Z|, |E_{D_n^n}|\right), \\ \begin{pmatrix} & V_{k-1} & \\ z_1^{\alpha_k} & z_2^{\alpha_k} & \cdots\ z_k^{\alpha_k} \end{pmatrix} & \text{if } |Z| < k \leq |E_{D_n^n}|, \end{cases}$$

with $V_1 = \left(z_1^{\alpha_1}\right) = z_1^{0_n} = (1)\,.$

With Definition 12 and Remark 4 in mind, we describe the algorithm's procedure as follows. Let $Z = \text{supp}\left(f^{(o)}\right) \cap S$, and let $1 \leq i \leq |Z|$. If the function f is not constant on S, the algorithm begins by constructing the matrix V_{E_i,Z_i} and searches for functions vanishing on the set Z_i by identifying vectors corresponding to the elements of the kernel of V_{E_i,Z_i}. If such functions exist, the procedure checks whether any of them are also annihilators restricted to S for the full function $f^{(o)}$. This is done by verifying that they vanish on all elements of Z but not on all elements of S. If such an annihilator is found, the algorithm returns the degree of the last monomial added, x^{α_i}. Otherwise, it increments the index i, constructs the next matrix following Definition 13, and continues until a solution is found or all square matrices up to $V_{E_i,|Z|}$ have been constructed and tested. If no annihilator is found after all the elements of Z have been added, the algorithm iteratively adds new monomials and generates the matrices $V_{E_i,Z}$ and S_{E_i,S_i}. It then returns the degree of the monomial x^{α_i} if $\text{rank}\left(V_{E_i,Z}\right) < \text{rank}\left(S_{E_i,S_i}\right)$. Following point 1 in Remark 3, if this condition is not satisfied at step i, the iteration continues until $\text{rank}\left(S_{E_i,S_i}\right) > |S|/2$. Indeed, if for some i, $\text{rank}\left(V_{E_i,Z}\right) < \text{rank}\left(S_{E_i,S_i}\right)$, then there exists a non-null annihilator over S of degree at most $\deg(\alpha_i)$. Conversely, if the condition is not met before $\text{rank}\left(S_{E_i,S_i}\right) > |S|/2$, Remark 3 guarantees that either f or $f+1$ admits a non-trivial annihilator on S of this degree.

4.1 Keeping the Cardinality of the Kernel of V_k Upper-Bounded by 1

In the procedure described, we aim to identify at least one element from a vector space that satisfies certain required conditions (corresponding to an annihilator, not trivial on S), while maintaining the algorithm's desired efficiency. Since this vector space can potentially be too large, we address this issue as follows: if we find an element $\hat{g}_k$ in the kernel of V_k that does not vanish on Z, we re-order the vector Z by swapping the element z_{k+1} with the element that does not vanish in $\hat{g}_k$. This ensures that such elements of the kernel of V_k do not propagate into the kernel of subsequent matrices.

Furthermore, if an element of the kernel of V_k is found that vanishes on all of Z and S, the monomial α_k is dropped. The matrix V_{k+1} is then constructed by replacing the row corresponding to the monomial α_k with one corresponding to the monomial α_{k+1}. This procedure guarantees that the cardinality of the kernel of V_k is upper-bounded by 1 for all $k \leq |Z|$. Propositions 3, 4, and 5 provide formal justifications for these claims.

Proposition 3. *Let $k < \min\{(|Z|, |E_{D_n^n}|\}$ and let V_k constructed following Definition 13. Suppose ker$(V_k) = \langle \hat{g}_k \rangle = \langle (\epsilon_1, \epsilon_2, \ldots, \epsilon_k) \rangle$ and let $g_k \in \mathcal{B}_n$ be the Boolean function having $\hat{g}_k$ as ANF. Furthermore, assume there exists a z_{k+j}, for $j \geq 1$ such that $g_k(z_{k+j}) = 1$. Then, the matrix V'_{k+1} constructed as:*

$$V'_{k+1} = \begin{pmatrix} & & & & z_{k+j}^{\alpha_1} \\ & & & & z_{k+j}^{\alpha_2} \\ & & V_k & & \vdots \\ & & & & z_{k+j}^{\alpha_k} \\ z_1^{\alpha_{k+1}} & z_2^{\alpha_{k+1}} & \cdots & z_k^{\alpha_{k+1}} & z_{k+j}^{\alpha_{k+1}} \end{pmatrix}$$

is such that $(\epsilon_1, \epsilon_2, \ldots, \epsilon_k, 0) \notin$ ker(V'_{k+1}).

Proof. Suppose $\ker(V_k) = \langle \hat{g}_k \rangle = \langle (\epsilon_1, \epsilon_2, \ldots, \epsilon_k) \rangle$, and that there exists $j \geq 1$ such that $g_k(z_{k+j}) = 1$, but it is also such that $(\epsilon_1, \epsilon_2, \ldots, \epsilon_k, 0) \in \ker(V'_{k+1})$.

If $(\epsilon_1, \epsilon_2, \ldots, \epsilon_k, 0) \in \ker(V'_{k+1})$, then $(\epsilon_1, \epsilon_2, \ldots, \epsilon_k, 0) \cdot V'_{k+1} = \hat{0}$. Specifically, the last equation in the system of equations described by $(\epsilon_1, \epsilon_2, \ldots, \epsilon_k, 0) \cdot V'_{k+1} = \hat{0}$ is:

$$\epsilon_1 z_{k+j}^{\alpha_1} + \cdots + \epsilon_k z_{k+j}^{\alpha_k} + 0 \cdot z_{k+j}^{\alpha_{k+1}} = \epsilon_1 z_{k+j}^{\alpha_1} + \cdots + \epsilon_k z_{k+j}^{\alpha_k} = 0.$$

However, from our hypothesis, we have:

$$g_k(z_{k+j}) = 1 \iff g_k(z_{k+j}) = (\epsilon_1, \epsilon_2, \ldots, \epsilon_k) \begin{pmatrix} z_{k+j}^{\alpha_1} \\ z_{k+j}^{\alpha_2} \\ \vdots \\ z_{k+j}^{\alpha_k} \end{pmatrix} = \epsilon_1 z_{k+j}^{\alpha_1} + \cdots + \epsilon_k z_{k+j}^{\alpha_k} = 1.$$

This contradiction shows that it cannot be the case that $(\epsilon_1, \ldots, \epsilon_k, 0)$ is in the kernel of V'_{k+1}. □

Proposition 4. *The sequence of matrices $(V_k)_k$, constructed as described in Proposition 3, ensures that:*

$$dim\,(ker\,(V_k)) \leq 1, \quad \forall k \in [1, |Z|].$$

Proof. We prove the result by induction:

- Base case. The initial matrix $V_1 = (1)$ has full rank, so $\dim(\ker(V_1)) = 0 \leq 1$.
- Induction step. We suppose that $\dim(\ker(V_k)) \leq 1$. We show that $\dim(\ker(V_{k+1})) \leq 1$.
  - If $\dim(\ker(V_k)) = 0$, adding a new row and column to form V_{k+1} can increase the kernel by at most 1. Hence, $\dim(\ker(V_{k+1})) \leq 1$.
  - If $\dim(\ker(V_k)) = 1$, let $\hat{z}$ be an element of $\ker(V_{k+1})$. Then either:
    * $\hat{z} = (\hat{\epsilon}, 0)$:

$$\hat{z} \cdot V_{k+1} = 0 \implies \hat{\epsilon} \cdot V_k = 0 \implies \hat{\epsilon} \in \ker(V_k).$$

By Proposition 3, $\hat{\epsilon}$ can only be a trivial solution.
    * $\hat{z} = (\hat{y}, 1)$, where $\hat{y} \in \mathbb{F}_2^k$: In this case $\hat{z} \cdot V_{k+1} = 0$ implies:

$$\hat{y} \cdot V_k + (z_1^{\alpha_{k+1}}, \cdots, z_k^{\alpha_{k+1}}) = 0 \iff \hat{y} \cdot V_k = (z_1^{\alpha_{k+1}}, \cdots, z_k^{\alpha_{k+1}}), \quad (4)$$

and

$$\hat{y} \cdot (z_{k+1}^{\alpha_1}, \cdots, z_{k+1}^{\alpha_k})^T + z_{k+1}^{\alpha_{k+1}} = 0 \iff \hat{y} \cdot (z_{k+1}^{\alpha_1}, \cdots, z_{k+1}^{\alpha_k})^T = z_{k+1}^{\alpha_{k+1}}. \quad (5)$$

Since $\dim(\ker(V_k)) = 1$, $\text{rank}(V_k) = k - 1$. Hence, there exists at most one particular solution $\hat{y}_p$ for Eq. 4. If $\hat{y}_p$ also solves Eq. 5, then $\hat{y}_p$ is in $\ker(V_{k+1})$.

Since $(\hat{\epsilon}, 0)$ cannot be in $\ker(V_{k+1})$, the only possible element in $\ker(V_{k+1})$ is $\hat{y}_p$, if it exists. Therefore, $\dim(\ker(V_{k+1})) \leq 1$. □

Remark 6. Notice that the definition of $V_{k+1}^{'}$ in Proposition 3, does not conflict with Definition 13, as constructing the sequence $(V_k)_k$ does not require a specific order of the elements in the support Z.

Proposition 5. *Let* $\ker(V_{E_k,Z_k}) = \langle \hat{g}_k \rangle = \langle (\epsilon_1, \ldots, \epsilon_k) \rangle$, *where the corresponding Boolean function* $g_k \in \mathcal{B}_n$ *satisfies* $g_k(x) = 0,\ \forall x \in Z$.

Define $E^* = (\alpha_1, \alpha_2, \ldots, \alpha_{k-1}, \alpha_{k+1})$, *a vector constructed from* E_k *by replacing the last element* α_k *with* α_{k+1}. *Let* $V_{k+1} = V_{E_{k+1}^*, Z_k}$ *be the matrix defined by replacing the monomial* α_k *in* V_{E_k,Z_k}, *with the monomial* α_{k+1}:

$$V_{E_{k+1}^*, Z_k} = \begin{pmatrix} & & & & z_k^{\alpha_1} \\ & E_{k-1}, V_{Z_{k-1}} & & & z_k^{\alpha_2} \\ & & & & \vdots \\ & & & & z_k^{\alpha_{k-1}} \\ z_1^{\alpha_{k+1}} & z_2^{\alpha_{k+1}} & \cdots & z_{k-1}^{\alpha_{k+1}} & z_k^{\alpha_{k+1}} \end{pmatrix}.$$

Then, either $\hat{g}_k \notin \ker(V_{E_{k+1}^*, Z_k})$, *or* $\hat{g}_k$ *is the only element (aside from* $\hat{0}$*) in the kernel of* $V_{E_{k+1}^*, Z_k}$. *Hence:*

$$\dim\left(\ker(V_{E_{k+1}^*, Z_k})\right) \leq 1.$$

Proof. Proposition 3 ensures that the kernel of $V_{E_{k+1}^*, Z_k}$ does not contain elements derived from the kernel of $V_{E_{k-1},Z_{k-1}}$. Therefore, $V_{E_{k-1},Z_{k-1}}$ can be treated as a full-rank matrix. Modifying the last row of a matrix that contains a full-rank sub-matrix does not increase the size of the kernel. This is because the first k entries of the elements in the kernel of V_{E_k,Z_k} and $V_{E^*_{k+1},Z_k}$ are the same, with the only difference arising from the last row. Since this row is the only one that can introduce linear dependence, the dimension of the kernel of $V_{E^*_{k+1},Z_k}$ is bounded by 1. □

4.2 Using Column Echelon Form Matrices of the Previous Steps

At the iteration k, the matrix V_k already contains all the columns of the matrix from the previous step, V_{k-1}. This means the column echelon form of V_{k-1} is already embedded within V_k. Therefore, instead of recalculating the column echelon form for the entire matrix V_k, we only need to update it for the newly added column. This approach saves computation because we are focusing only on the last column rather than reprocessing the whole matrix.

Definition 14 (Column Echelon form). *Let $k_r, k_c \in \mathbb{N}^*$ and $M \in Mat_{k_r,k_c}$. We denote by $EF : Mat_{k_r,k_c} \to Mat_{k_r,k_c}$, the function transforming a matrix to its column echelon form.*

For each iteration k of the algorithm, the matrix V_k already includes the sub-matrix V_{k-1}. Thus, it is possible to compute the column echelon form of V_{k-1} and use it to derive the column echelon form of V_k. This approach allows V_k to inherently contain $EF(V_{k-1})$, which is already in column echelon form, thereby reducing the computational steps required to determine the rank of V_k. However, to apply this method effectively, careful attention must be paid during the construction of the matrix. Since rows are appended to the matrix at each step, computing $EF(V_k)$ requires keeping track of all column operations performed while computing $EF(V_j)$ for all $j < k$. These operations must be applied before computing $EF(V_k)$. Remark 7 and Proposition 6 provide further justification for this claim.

Definition 15 (Equality up to row permutation). *Two matrices M_1 and M_2 are equal up-to-permutation if there exists a column permutation ρ such that*

$$M_1 = \rho M_2.$$

We denote it as $M_1 =_p M_2$

Remark 7. Let $k_r, k_c \in \mathbb{N}$ and $M \in Mat_{k_r,k_c}(\mathbb{F}_2^n)$. Let $M = L \cdot U$ where L a lower triangular matrix and U is an upper triangular matrix, then: $EF(M) =_p L$.

Proposition 6. *Let k be such that $1 < k < \min\left(|Z|, |E_{D_n^n}|\right)$ it holds that*

$$EF(V_k) =_p EF\left(\left(\begin{array}{cc} & z_k^{\alpha_1} \\ & z_k^{\alpha_2} \\ EF(V_{k-1}) & \vdots \\ & z_k^{\alpha_{k-1}} \\ (z_1^{\alpha_k}\ z_2^{\alpha_k}\ \cdots\ z_{k-1}^{\alpha_k})P_{k-1} & z_k^{\alpha_k} \end{array}\right)\right).$$

where P_{k-1} is such that $U_{k-1}^{-1} = P_{k-1}$, where $V_{k-1} = L_{k-1}U_{k-1}$ with $EF(V_{k-1}) =_p L_{k-1}$

Proof. Let k be such that $1 < k < \min\left(|Z|, |E_{D_n^n}|\right)$. The LU-decomposition of V_{k-1} is $V_{k-1} = L_{k-1}U_{k-1}$, where U_{k-1} is an upper triangular matrix and $L_{k-1} = EF\left(V_{k-1}\right)$ is the lower triangular matrix.

$$V_k = \begin{pmatrix} & & & z_k^{\alpha_1} \\ & L_{k-1}U_{k-1} & & z_k^{\alpha_2} \\ & & & \vdots \\ & & & z_k^{\alpha_{k-1}} \\ z_1^{\alpha_k} & z_2^{\alpha_k} & \cdots \; z_{k-1}^{\alpha_k} & z_k^{\alpha_k} \end{pmatrix} = \begin{pmatrix} & & z_k^{\alpha_1} \\ & L_{k-1} & z_k^{\alpha_2} \\ & & \vdots \\ & & z_k^{\alpha_{k-1}} \\ (z_1^{\alpha_k} \; z_2^{\alpha_k} & \cdots \; z_{k-1}^{\alpha_k})U_{k-1}^{-1} & z_k^{\alpha_k} \end{pmatrix} \begin{pmatrix} & 0 \\ U_{k-1} & 0 \\ & \vdots \\ & 0 \\ 0\,0 \cdots 0 & 1 \end{pmatrix}.$$

Since U_{k-1} is an upper triangular matrix, $\begin{pmatrix} & 0 \\ U_{k-1} & 0 \\ & \vdots \\ & 0 \\ 0\,0 \cdots 0 & 1 \end{pmatrix}$ is also an upper triangular matrix, and therefore

$$EF\left(V_k\right) =_p EF\left(\begin{pmatrix} & & z_k^{\alpha_1} \\ & L_{k-1} & z_k^{\alpha_2} \\ & & \vdots \\ & & z_k^{\alpha_{k-1}} \\ (z_1^{\alpha_k} \; z_2^{\alpha_k} & \cdots \; z_{k-1}^{\alpha_k})U_{k-1}^{-1} & z_k^{\alpha_k} \end{pmatrix}\right).$$

Taking $L_{k-1} =_p EF\left(V_{k-1}\right)$ and $P_{k-1} = U_{k-1}^{-1}$:

$$EF\left(V_k\right) =_p EF\left(\begin{pmatrix} & & z_k^{\alpha_1} \\ & EF\left(V_{k-1}\right) & z_k^{\alpha_2} \\ & & \vdots \\ & & z_k^{\alpha_{k-1}} \\ (z_1^{\alpha_k} \; z_2^{\alpha_k} & \cdots \; z_{k-1}^{\alpha_k})P_{k-1} & z_k^{\alpha_k} \end{pmatrix}\right).$$

□

Remark 8. P_{k-1} is the matrix corresponding to the history of operations applied to the columns of V_{k-1} to be able to obtain $EF\left(V_{k-1}\right)$.

As a consequence of Remark 8, it can be seen that when calculating the column echelon form of the matrix V_k using P_{k-1}, we construct the application P_k which can be used to compute the column echelon form of V_{k+1} in the next iteration. Remark 9 shows this more formally.

Remark 9.

$$EF(V_k) = EF\left(\left(\begin{matrix} & z_k^{\alpha_1} \\ EF(V_{k-1}) & z_k^{\alpha_2} \\ & \vdots \\ & z_k^{\alpha_{k-1}} \\ (z_1^{\alpha_k}\ z_2^{\alpha_k}\ \cdots\ z_{k-1}^{\alpha_k})P_{k-1} & z_k^{\alpha_k} \end{matrix}\right)\right) =_p \left(\begin{matrix} & 0 \\ EF(V_{k-1}) & 0 \\ & \vdots \\ & 0 \\ (z_1^{\alpha_k}\ z_2^{\alpha_k}\ \cdots\ z_{k-1}^{\alpha_k}\ z_k^{\alpha_k})P_k & \end{matrix}\right).$$

Algorithm 1 shows the procedure to calculate the degree of the minimal degree non-zero-annihilator restricted to $S \subseteq \mathbb{F}_2^n$ of a function $f^{(o)} \in \{f, f+1\}$, while Algorithm 2, provided in Appendix B, shows the full procedure to determine the restricted algebraic immunity of f in S, calling Algorithm 1 for f and $f+1$ in parallel.

Algorithm 2 includes the additional function FIND_DEG_SMALLEST_S_ANNIHILATOR_SEQ which triggers the same process as Algorithm 1, but applies it sequentially to f and $f+1$, to avoid waiting for both processes to complete simultaneously. This function is triggered only when $\mathsf{supp}(f) \cap S$ and $\mathsf{supp}(f+1) \cap S$ differ significantly in cardinality, as in such cases, the probability of one of the two processes terminating quickly is high.

Remark 10. To keep the pseudocode in line with the theory, the elements in the vector or sets are often parsed by name instead of by index, namely let $Z = (z_1, z_2, \cdots, z_k)$ we consider that $Z[i-1] = z_i$.
Therefore, we have to clarify our notation in the case in which two vector elements get swapped. In the case of Algorithm 1, we consider that the swap generates a new vector with the name of the variables adapted with their index position in the vector to keep satisfying the condition $Z[i-1] = z_i$. Meaning that

$$\text{SWAP}(z_i, z_j) \rightarrow (z_{\sigma(1)}, \cdots, z_{\sigma(i)}, \cdots, z_{\sigma(j)}, \cdots, z_{\sigma(k)}) = Z' = (z_1', \cdots, z_i', \cdots, z_j', \cdots, z_k')$$

where σ is a permutation describing the swap:

$$\sigma = \begin{pmatrix} 1 \cdots i \cdots j \cdots k \\ 1 \cdots j \cdots i \cdots k \end{pmatrix}.$$

Algorithm 1. Algorithm to find the degree of the minimum-degree non-zero-annihilator restricted on S of a function $f^{(o)}$.

Input: restricted set $S \subseteq \mathbb{F}_2^n$, $Z = supp\left(f^{(o)}\right) \cap S$ and $E = \{\alpha_1, \cdots, \alpha_{D_n^n}\}$

Output: Degree of minimal degree non-zero-annihilator restricted on S of $f^{(o)}$.

```
V ← (1);
ops ← [];
k ← 2;
while k ≤ |Z| do
    V_previous ← V;
    (v_1, ··· , v_{k-1}) ← APPLY_OPERATIONS(((z_1^{α_k}, ··· , z_{k-1}^{α_k}), ops))^a;
    M ← ( V                               z_k^{α_1}
                                          z_k^{α_2}
                                          ⋮
                                          z_k^{α_{k-1}}
          v_1  v_1  ···  v_{k-1}          z_k^{α_k} );
    V, ops_k ← EF_LAST_COL(M)^b;
    if rank(V) < k then
        k ← kernel(V).base();
        ĝ ← k[0];
        nonVanishingPointIndex, vanishingFlag ← Null, True;
        for all z_idx ∈ (Z\Z_k) do
            vanishCheck ← VANISHES_ON(ĝ, z_idx)^c;
            if vanishCheck = False then
                vanishingFlag ← False;
                nonVanishingPointIndex ← idx
                break;
            end if
        end for
        if vanishingFlag = True then
            for all z_c ∈ S\Z do
                vanishCheckOnS ← VANISHES_ON(ĝ, z_c);
                if vanishCheckOnS = False then
                    return w_H(α_i);
                end if
            end for
            V ← V_previous;
            REMOVE(α_i, E); // Remove α_i from the array E.
            continue; // Go to the next iteration.
        else
            zIndex ← k + nonVanishingPointIndex;
            Z ← SWAP(z_{k+1}, z_{zIndex})^d;
        end if
        ops ← ops || ops_k;
        k ← k + 1;
    end if
end while
S, ops_S ← EF( ( s_1^{α_1}  s_2^{α_1}  ···  s_{|S|}^{α_1}
                 ⋮          ⋮          ⋱    ⋮
                 s_1^{α_k}  s_2^{α_k}  ···  s_{|S|}^{α_k} ) );
r ← rank(S);
r_V ← rank(V);
if r_V < r then
    return w_H(α_k);
end if
// The algorithm continues in the next page.
```

while $r \leq \lfloor |S|/2 \rfloor$ **do**
  if $r_V < k$ **then**
    $(v_1, \cdots, v_{k-1}) \leftarrow$ APPLY_OPERATIONS $\left(\left(z_1^{\alpha_k}, \cdots, z_{k-1}^{\alpha_k}\right), ops\right)$
    $V \leftarrow \begin{pmatrix} & V & \\ v_1\ v_2 & \cdots\ v_{k-1} & z_k^{\alpha_k} \end{pmatrix}$;
    $r_V \leftarrow rank(V)$;
  end if
  $(v_1, \cdots, v_{k-1}) \leftarrow$ APPLY_OPERATIONS $\left(\left(s_1^{\alpha_k}, \cdots, s_{k-1}^{\alpha_k}\right), ops_S\right)$;
  $S \leftarrow \begin{pmatrix} & S & \\ s_1\ s_2 & \cdots\ s_{k-1} & s_k^{\alpha_k} \end{pmatrix}$;
  $r \leftarrow rank(S)$;
  if $r_V < r$ **then**
    return $w_H(\alpha_k)$;
  end if
end while

[a] APPLY_OPERATIONS: applies column ops from P_{k-1} (Remark 8) to a vector.
[b] EF_LAST_COL: variant of EF, echelonizing only last added row/col, not full matrix.
[c] VANISHED_ON: given ANF coeffs of $g \in \mathcal{B}_n$ and point z, returns $True$ if $g(z) = 0$, else $False$.
[d] See Remark 10.

Algorithm 2. Algorithm to compute the algebraic immunity of a function $f \in \mathcal{B}_n$ restricted to S

Input: $x \in \mathbb{F}_2^{2^n}$ evaluation of the truth table of $f \in \mathcal{B}_n$ and the restricted set $S \subseteq \mathbb{F}_2^n$.
Output: $\mathsf{AI}_S(f)$
$Z, Z_c \leftarrow supp(x) \cap S, supp(x+1) \cap S$;
if $Z = \emptyset$ or $Z_c = \emptyset$ **then return** 0;
end if
$E_{D_n^n} \leftarrow$ CONSTRUCT_MONOMIALS$(n = n, d = n)$[a];
$r \leftarrow \frac{|Z|}{|Z_c|}$ **if** $|Z| < |Z_c|$ **else** $\frac{|Z_c|}{|Z|}$;
if $r \geq \frac{1}{4}$ **then**
  $immunity_f, immunity_{f+1} \leftarrow ($
FIND_DEG_SMALLEST_S_ANNIHILATOR$(Z = Z, E = E_{D_n^n}, S = S)$
| FIND_DEG_SMALLEST_S_ANNIHILATOR$(Z = Z_c, E = E_{D_n^n}, S = S)$);
  return MIN$(immunity_f, immunity_{f+1})$;
else
  return FIND_DEG_SMALLEST_S_ANNIHILATOR_SEQ(Z=Z, $Z_c, E = E_{D_n^n}, S = S)$)[b];
end if

[a] CONSTRUCT_MONOMIALS: generates all monomials up to degree d in n vars. $E_{D_n^n}$ can be pre-computed to skip this step.
[b] FIND_DEG_SMALLEST_S_ANNIHILATOR_SEQ: like Algorithm 1 but finds degree sequentially, not in parallel.

5 Experiments and Applications to W(A)PB Functions

In this section, we apply the algorithms to the weightwise perfectly balanced (WPB) Boolean functions with the intent to study their algebraic immunity restricted to subsets of constant Hamming weight. In particular, we determine the probability distributions of the AI_k of WPB functions and we compute the AI_k of some WPB Boolean functions already studied. In addition, in Appendix A, we compare the execution time of Algorithm 3 and Algorithm 2. The source code implementing Algorithm 3 and Algorithm 2, along with the probability distributions and the values of AI_k for the published functions, is available in the public repository.

5.1 Determination of AI_k Distribution of WPB Functions

Similar to the approach in [25] for analyzing the weightwise nonlinearity NL_k, we determine the discrete probability distribution of AI_k for weightwise perfectly balanced Boolean functions. This distribution describes the probability that a function $f \in \mathcal{WPB}_m$ has a specific algebraic immunity restricted to the slice $\mathsf{E}_{k,n}$. A formal definition is provided in Definition 16:

Definition 16. *Let $m \in \mathbb{N}^*$, $n = 2^m$ and $k \in [1, n-1]$, we define the discrete probability distribution of AI_k as:*

$$p_{\mathsf{AI}_k}(x) = \left|\{f \in \mathcal{WPB}_m \mid \mathsf{AI}_k(f) = x\}\right| \cdot |\mathcal{WPB}_m|^{-1}$$

We aim to determine this distribution for $m = 2, 3$, and 4. However, the number of WPB functions increases fast with the growth of m, making this computation infeasible for $m > 2$. In fact, as stated in [25], $|\mathcal{WPB}_2| = 720$, while $|\mathcal{WPB}_3| > 2^{243}$ and $|\mathcal{WPB}_4| > 2^{65452}$. Therefore, we have to take a different approach for $m > 2$ by generating a certain number of samples from the set $\mathcal{WPB}_m$ and calculating the probability over it. The larger the sample size we select, the better we approximate the distribution. Table 1 presents the estimated probability distribution obtained.

Definition 17. *We define the AI_k distribution over a sample Ω as:*

$$p_{\Omega,\mathsf{AI}_k}(x) = \left|\{f \in \Omega \mid \mathsf{AI}_k(f) = x\}\right| \cdot |\Omega|^{-1}.$$

Determination of the Full Distribution for M = 2. For $m = 2 \Rightarrow n = 4$, it is possible to determine the full probability distribution from Definition 16 without using the random sampling strategy. The resulting probability distribution table is presented in Table 1a.

Random Sampling. In practice, random sampling is performed by generating a set $\Omega_k = \{\omega_1^{(k)}, \cdots, \omega_{|\Omega|}^{(k)}\}$ consisting of $|\Omega|$ random balanced sub-truth tables for each slice $\mathsf{E}_{k,n}$. Then, for each slice $\mathsf{E}_{k,n}$, the AI_k is computed for each restricted set in Ω_k the frequency of each particular AI_k value is recorded. The following procedure is done for each slice $\mathsf{E}_{k,n}$:

1. Initialize a hash table of all possible values of AI_k.
2. For each sub-truth table in $\omega_i^{(k)} \in \Omega_k$ (note that $\omega_i^{(k)}$ may be generated on the fly by an iterator).[2]:
   (a) Run Algorithm 2 with $S = \omega_i^{(k)}$.
   (b) Increment the value in the hash table from the output of the previous step.
3. Divide each value in the hash table by $|\Omega|$.

Results for $n = 8$ and Sample Size = 2^{15}. Table 1b represents the AI_k distribution. We observe that for $n = 4$ all WPB functions have the same values of AI_k, for every k. However, for $n = 8$, there are WPB functions with different restricted AI_k, for example with $k = 4$ we observe functions reaching the lowest value (2, such as families exhibited in [25]) and some reaching 3 which is optimal for this size.

Results for $n = 16$ and Sample Size = 2^{10}. Table 1c represents the AI_k distribution. We observe that there are WPB functions with different restricted AI_k for this value of n, and that for the central values of k, all functions we sampled reach the optimal value of AI_k.

Table 1. AI_k probability distribution of $\mathcal{WPB}_2$, $\mathcal{WPB}_3$ and $\mathcal{WPB}_4$.

(a) Probability distribution p_{AI_k} for $n = 4$, $m = 2$.

$p(x), k$	0	1	2	3	4
0	1.00	0.00	0.00	0.00	1.00
1	0.00	1.00	0.00	1.00	0.00
2	0.00	0.00	1.00	0.00	0.00

(b) Probability distribution p_{Ω,AI_k} for $n = 8$, $m = 3$, $\Omega = 2^{15}$.

$p(x), k$	0	1	2	3	4	5	6	7	8
0	1.00	0.00	0.00	0.00	0.00	0.00	0.00	0.00	1.00
1	0.00	1.00	0.00	0.00	0.00	0.00	0.05	1.00	0.00
2	0.00	0.00	1.00	0.98	0.00	0.98	0.95	0.00	0.00
3	0.00	0.00	0.00	0.02	0.13	0.02	0.00	0.00	0.00
4	0.00	0.00	0.00	0.00	0.87	0.00	0.00	0.00	0.00

(c) Probability distribution p_{Ω,AI_k} for $n = 16$, $m = 4$, $\Omega = 2^{10}$.

$p(x), k$	0	1	2	3	4	5	6	7	8	9	10	11	12	13	14	15	16
0	1.00	0.00	0.00	0.00	0.00	0.00	0.00	0.00	0.00	0.00	0.00	0.00	0.00	0.00	0.00	0.00	1.00
1	0.00	1.00	0.00	0.00	0.00	0.00	0.00	0.00	0.00	0.00	0.00	0.00	0.00	0.00	0.00	1.00	0.00
2	0.00	0.00	1.00	0.02	0.00	0.00	0.00	0.00	0.00	0.00	0.00	0.00	0.00	0.01	1.00	0.00	0.00
3	0.00	0.00	0.00	0.98	0.13	0.00	0.00	0.00	0.00	0.00	0.00	0.00	0.13	0.99	0.00	0.00	0.00
4	0.00	0.00	0.00	0.00	0.87	0.63	0.00	0.00	0.00	0.00	0.00	0.60	0.87	0.00	0.00	0.00	0.00
5	0.00	0.00	0.00	0.00	0.00	0.37	1.00	0.00	0.00	0.00	1.00	0.40	0.00	0.00	0.00	0.00	0.00
6	0.00	0.00	0.00	0.00	0.00	0.00	0.00	1.00	1.00	1.00	0.00	0.00	0.00	0.00	0.00	0.00	0.00

[2] Step 2 may be executed in parallel on the $\omega_i^{(k)}$s if memory is not a constraint. In fact, depending on the value of m and the chosen sample size, the number of sub-truth tables generated may be too large to fit in memory simultaneously.

5.2 Determination of AI_k of Known WPB Families

In this part, we determine the AI_ks of functions introduced in [18,57,63] and in [7] for $n = 8$ and 16 variables.

The results are summarized in Table 2. Of the four WPB calculations we performed, the one in [57] is the one that would resist the best to algebraic attacks (with constant Hamming weight inputs), as it achieves higher AI_k values for both $n = 8$ and $n = 16$. In contrast, the one in [63], would be the least resistant, as it has the overall lower AI_k for both $n = 8$ and $n = 16$. Specifically:

- $n = 8$. The function in [63] has a constant AI_k of 2 for $k \in [2, 6]$ and the functions in [7] a constant AI_k of 2 for $k \in [3, 6]$, whereas the functions in [18] and in [57] achieve an AI_4 of 3.
- $n = 16$. The function in [63] again has a constant AI_k of 2 for $k \in [2, 14]$. In contrast, the function in [57] achieves an AI_k of 3 for $k = 4, 5, 11$ and 12, an AI_k of 4 for $k = 6, 7, 9$ and 10 and an AI_k of 5 for $k = 8$. The functions [18] and in [7], both reach an AI_k of 3 but for $k \in [4, 12]$ and $k \in [5, 13]$ respectively.

The maximum execution times for [18,57,63] and [7] with $n = 8$ occur with $k = 4$ and are around 0.014, 0.029, 0.011 and 0.012 s, respectively. For $n = 16$, the maximum execution times for [57,63] and [7] occur with $k = 8$ and are 5.898671, 126.627561 and 12.048051 s respectively. In contrast, for [18], the maximum execution time occurs for $k = 9$ and is 7.935819 s.

Table 2. AI_k of the construction from [18], from [63], from [57] and from [7] with $m = 3$ ($n = 8$) and $m = 4$ ($n = 16$).

[18]																	
n, k	0	1	2	3	4	5	6	7	8	9	10	11	12	13	14	15	16
8	0	1	1	2	3	2	2	1	0								
16	0	1	1	2	3	3	3	3	3	3	3	3	3	2	2	1	0
[63]																	
n, k	0	1	2	3	4	5	6	7	8	9	10	11	12	13	14	15	16
8	0	1	2	2	2	2	2	1	0								
16	0	1	2	2	2	2	2	2	2	2	2	2	2	2	2	1	0
[57]																	
n, k	0	1	2	3	4	5	6	7	8	9	10	11	12	13	14	15	16
8	0	1	2	2	3	2	2	1	0								
16	0	1	2	2	3	3	4	4	5	4	4	3	3	2	2	1	0
[7]																	
n, k	0	1	2	3	4	5	6	7	8	9	10	11	12	13	14	15	16
8	0	1	1	2	2	2	2	1	0								
16	0	1	1	2	2	3	3	3	3	3	3	3	3	3	2	1	0

In Table 3, we summarize the results on AI_k for WPB functions with 8 variables, including both our findings and those from the state of the art. Similarly, Table 4 presents the corresponding results for functions with 16 variables. We observe that most of the studied families exhibit lower weightwise algebraic immunity than a randomly chosen WPB function, with the exception of the field order construction [45] (usually a function is considered good if its parameters are the same or better than the ones of a random function).

Table 3. AI_k of WPB functions in 8 variables.

Function	AI_2	AI_3	AI_4	AI_5	AI_6
[18]	1	2	3	2	2
[63]	2	2	2	2	2
[57]	2	2	3	2	2
[7]	1	2	2	2	2
Estimated average	1.95	2.02	2.88	2.02	1.95
Field order [45]	1	2	3	2	2
Upper bound	2	3	3	3	2

Table 4. AI_k of WPB functions in 16 variables.

Function	AI_2	AI_3	AI_4	AI_5	AI_6	AI_7	AI_8	AI_9	AI_{10}	AI_{11}	AI_{12}	AI_{13}	AI_{14}
[18]	1	2	3	3	3	3	3	3	3	3	3	2	2
[63]	2	2	2	2	2	2	2	2	2	2	2	2	2
[57]	2	2	3	3	4	4	5	4	4	3	3	2	2
[7]	1	2	2	3	3	3	3	3	3	3	3	3	2
Estimated average	2.00	2.99	3.89	4.37	5.00	6.00	6.00	6.00	5.00	4.40	3.87	2.99	2.00
Field order [45]	2	3	4	4	5	6	6	6	5	4	3	2	2
Upper bound	2	3	4	5	5	6	6	6	5	5	4	3	2

6 Conclusion

In this article, we formalized the main theoretical foundations and provided algorithms for computing restricted algebraic immunity over any set $S \subseteq \mathbb{F}_2^n$, using both the Reed-Muller and iterative approaches. We compared the practical complexity of these algorithms and showed that the iterative approach is more efficient. Additionally, we applied our methods to compute or estimate, for the first time, the distribution of AI_k for WPB functions with 4, 8, and 16 variables. Furthermore, we determined the values of AI_k for various families of WPB functions introduced in previous works and showed that, in most cases, these functions exhibit lower weightwise algebraic immunity than a randomly chosen WPB function.

By formalizing the theoretical background and providing both algorithms and implementations for computing restricted algebraic immunity, we hope this work will contribute to further research and the practical implementation of algebraic attack variants.

Acknowledgments. Pierrick Méaux was supported by the ERC Advanced Grant no. 787390. This work was conducted in the context of Luca Bonaminos M.Sc. thesis in the Master of Information and Computer Science (MICS) programme run by the Department of Computer Science (DCS) of the University of Luxembourg.

A Comparison Between Algorithm 3 and Algorithm 2 on WAPB Functions

In this part, we compare the execution times of Algorithm 3 and Algorithm 2 by running both algorithms on multiple WAPB functions restricted to the largest set $\mathsf{E}_{\lceil n/2 \rceil, n}$, with different numbers of variables. Specifically, the experiment is done by running the algorithms with the number of variables n going from 1 to 12. For both algorithms, if $n \leq 4$, we calculate the average over the $\mathsf{AI}_{\lceil n/2 \rceil}$ of all functions in $\mathcal{WAPB}_n$, whereas for $n > 4$, we calculate the average over the $\mathsf{AI}_{\lceil n/2 \rceil}$ of a random sample of 10^4 $\mathcal{WAPB}_n$ functions.

Figure 1 shows the mean execution time per value of n of the two algorithms. We denote by $T\left(G^{\leq n_{max}}\right) = T\left(G^{\leq 12}\right)$ the necessary time to pre-compute all the necessary Reed-Muller codes's generator matrices following Eq. (2): we recall that it is the necessary time to compute the sequence $(G_{n,n})_{n \in [1, 12 = n_{max}]}$, not only the generator matrix $G_{n,n}$ for the current iteration n. In fact, $T\left(G^{\leq 12}\right)$ is constant, that is because the computation occurs before beginning the experiment since it is expected that Algorithm 3 is able to run for any number of variable n up to an upper bound n_{max}, without having to compute the Reed-Muller code for it.

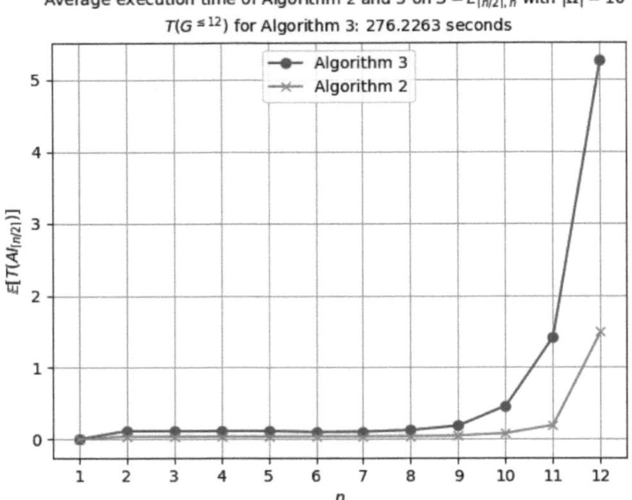

Fig. 1. Average time execution per number of variables of Algorithms 3 and 2 over 10^4 random $\mathcal{WAPB}_n$ functions on the set $E_{\lceil n/2 \rceil,n}$. $T\left(G^{\leq 12}\right)$ gives the time of the pre-computation of the sequence of all Reed-Muller matrices up to $G_{12,12}$.

The pre-computation times of $G^{\leq n_{max}}$ for Algorithm 3 are given in the Table 5. From Fig. 1, we observe that Algorithm 2 outperforms Algorithm 3 for $n \leq 12$, even without considering the pre-computation time required for $G^{\leq n_{max}}$ and $D^{\leq n_{max}}$ in Algorithm 3. Furthermore, Algorithm 3 becomes impractical for $n > 12$ due to the excessive complexity of pre-computation. In contrast, Algorithm 2 remains feasible for larger values of n.

Table 5. Pre-computation time (in seconds) for $G^{\leq n_{max}}$ for n_{max} from 1 to 12.

$G^{\leq 1}$	$G^{\leq 2}$	$G^{\leq 3}$	$G^{\leq 4}$	$G^{\leq 5}$	$G^{\leq 6}$	$G^{\leq 7}$	$G^{\leq 8}$	$G^{\leq 9}$	$G^{\leq 10}$	$G^{\leq 11}$	$G^{\leq 12}$
0.0126	0.0042	0.0017	0.004	0.0149	0.0470	0.1938	0.806	3.5456	14.9168	65.5014	276.2263

Both implementations of the algorithms used to generate the plot in Fig. 1 have been developed in *Python*, with the following enhancements:

- The linear algebra operations in Algorithm 3 are performed using the *SageMath* library, while those in Algorithm 2 are executed using an ad-hoc custom *Python* package implemented in *Rust*. This setup ensures comparability between the two implementations, as the *SageMath* library is highly optimized for linear algebra operations.
- The computation of $G^{\leq n_{max}}$ for Algorithm 3 is performed using the *generator_matrix* method of the *SageMath* object *BinaryReedMullerCodes*. While this computation could be more efficient if implemented in *Rust*, the current overall implementation still faces scalability issues. Specifically, for $n \geq 16$, the algorithm becomes impractical because $G_{16,16}$ cannot be stored in a native *Python* list or a

SageMath matrix object. However, if the entire algorithm were implemented in *Rust*, it could potentially be feasible. Consequently, for larger values of n, Algorithm 3 is not usable, while Algorithm 2 remains viable.

B Algorithms

Algorithm 3. Algebraic immunity of f restricted to the set S, Reed-Muller method.

Input: $x \in \mathbb{F}_2^{2^n}$ evaluation of the truth table of $f \in \mathcal{B}_n$ and the restricted set $S \subseteq \mathbb{F}_2^n$.
Output: $\mathsf{AI}_S(f)$

function FIND_DEG_SMALLEST_S_ANNIHILATOR($G_{n,n}^{f_Z^{(o)},S}, G_{d,n}^S, D^n$)
    $r, i, previousIndex \leftarrow 0, 0, 0$;
    $ef_f, ef_S \leftarrow null, null$;
    while $r \leq |S|/2$ **do**
        $D_i^n \leftarrow D^n[i]$;
        $ef_f \leftarrow$ ECHELON_FORM_LAST_D_i^n_ROWS $\left(ef_f \,||\, G_{n,n}^{f_Z^{(o)},S}[previousIndex : D_i^n]\right)$[a];
        $ef_S \leftarrow$ ECHELON_FORM_LAST_D_i^n_ROWS $(ef_S \,||\, G_{n,n}^S[previousIndex : D_i^n])$;
        $r \leftarrow rank\,(ef_S)$;
        if $rank\,(ef_f) < r$ **then**
            return i;
        end if
        $previousIndex \leftarrow D_i^n$;
        $i \leftarrow i + 1$;
    end while
end function

$Z, Z_c \leftarrow supp(x) \cap S, supp(x+1) \cap S$;
if $Z = \emptyset$ of $Z_c = \emptyset$ **then return** 0;
end if
$m_{max}, D^{\leq n_{max}} \leftarrow$ READ_VALUES_FROM_FILE();
$G_{n,n} \leftarrow m_{max}[n]$;
$D^n \leftarrow D^{\leq n_{max}}[n]$;
$G_{n,n}^{f_Z,S}, G_{n,n}^{(f+1)_Z,S}, G_{n,n}^S \leftarrow$ CONSTRUCT_RESTRICTED_GENERATOR_MATRICES($G_{n,n}, x, S$)[b]
$immunity_f, immunity_{f+1} \leftarrow$ (
 FIND_DEG_SMALLEST_S_ANNIHILATOR($G_{n,n}^{f_Z,S}, G_{n,n}^S, D^n$)
 | FIND_DEG_SMALLEST_S_ANNIHILATOR($G_{n,n}^{(f+1)_Z,S}, G_{n,n}^S, D^n$)
);
return MIN($immunity_f, immunity_{f+1}$)[c];

[a] The symbol $||$ is used as row-concatenation of matrices, meaning that $C = A||B$ is the matrix constructed by appending all the row of the matrix B to the matrix A.

[b] CONSTRUCT_RESTRICTED_GENERATOR_MATRICES is a function extracting $G_{n,n}^{f_{supp(f)\cap S},S}$, $G_{n,n}^{f_{supp(f+1)\cap S},S}$ and $G_{n,n}^S$ from the full Reed-Muller code generator matrix $G_{n,n}$ following Definition 11.

[c] The function MIN takes care of $null$ values: MIN($immunity_f, null$) $=$ $immunity_f$ and MIN($null, immunity_{f+1}$) $= immunity_{f+1}$.

References

1. Applebaum, B., Lovett, S.: Algebraic attacks against random local functions and their countermeasures. SIAM J. Comput. 52–79 (2018)
2. Armknecht, F.: Improving fast algebraic attacks. In: Roy, B., Meier, W. (eds.) FSE 2004. LNCS, vol. 3017, pp. 65–82. Springer, Heidelberg (2004). https://doi.org/10.1007/978-3-540-25937-4_5
3. Armknecht, F., Carlet, C., Gaborit, P., Künzli, S., Meier, W., Ruatta, O.: Efficient computation of algebraic immunity for algebraic and fast algebraic attacks. In: Vaudenay, S. (ed.) EUROCRYPT 2006. LNCS, vol. 4004, pp. 147–164. Springer, Heidelberg (2006). https://doi.org/10.1007/11761679_10
4. Carlet, C.: Constructing balanced functions with optimum algebraic immunity. In: IEEE International Symposium on Information Theory, ISIT 2007, Nice, France, 24–29 June 2007, pp. 451–455. IEEE (2007). https://doi.org/10.1109/ISIT.2007.4557094
5. Carlet, C.: Boolean Functions for Cryptography and Coding Theory. Cambridge University Press (2021). https://doi.org/10.1017/9781108606806
6. Carlet, C., Feng, K.: An infinite class of balanced functions with optimal algebraic immunity, good immunity to fast algebraic attacks and good nonlinearity. In: Pieprzyk, J. (ed.) ASIACRYPT 2008. LNCS, vol. 5350, pp. 425–440. Springer, Heidelberg (2008). https://doi.org/10.1007/978-3-540-89255-7_26
7. Carlet, C., Méaux, P., Rotella, Y.: Boolean functions with restricted input and their robustness; application to the FLIP cipher. IACR Trans. Symmetric Cryptol. **2017**(3) (2017)
8. Carlet, C., Merabet, B.: Asymptotic lower bound on the algebraic immunity of random balanced multi-output boolean functions. Adv. Math. Commun. **7**(2), 197–217 (2013). https://doi.org/10.3934/AMC.2013.7.197
9. Carlet, C., Sarkar, P.: Constructions of efficiently implementable boolean functions possessing high nonlinearity and good resistance to algebraic attacks. IACR Cryptol. ePrint Arch. p. 1305 (2024). https://eprint.iacr.org/archive/2024/1305/20240821:123900.5
10. Carlet, C., Sarkar, P.: The nonlinear filter model of stream cipher redivivus. Cryptology ePrint Archive, Paper 2025/160 (2025). https://eprint.iacr.org/2025/160
11. Chacal, N., Méaux, P., AnonymousBeforeAcceptance: Nostalgia cipher: can filtered LFSRS be secure again? ORBilu Archive (2025). https://hdl.handle.net/10993/64454
12. Chen, Y., Lu, P.: Two classes of symmetric boolean functions with optimum algebraic immunity: construction and analysis. IEEE Trans. Inf. Theory **57**(4), 2522–2538 (2011). https://doi.org/10.1109/TIT.2011.2111810
13. Cosseron, O., Hoffmann, C., Méaux, P., Standaert, F.: Towards case-optimized hybrid homomorphic encryption - featuring the Elisabeth stream cipher. In: Agrawal, S., Lin, D. (eds.) ASIACRYPT 2022, Part III. LNCS, vol. 13793, pp. 32–67. Springer, Cham (2022). https://doi.org/10.1007/978-3-031-22969-5_2
14. Courtois, N.T.: Fast algebraic attacks on stream ciphers with linear feedback. In: Boneh, D. (ed.) CRYPTO 2003. LNCS, vol. 2729, pp. 176–194. Springer, Heidelberg (2003). https://doi.org/10.1007/978-3-540-45146-4_11
15. Courtois, N.T., Meier, W.: Algebraic attacks on stream ciphers with linear feedback. In: Biham, E. (ed.) EUROCRYPT 2003. LNCS, vol. 2656, pp. 345–359. Springer, Heidelberg (2003). https://doi.org/10.1007/3-540-39200-9_21
16. Dalai, D.K., Gupta, K.C., Maitra, S.: Results on algebraic immunity for cryptographically significant boolean functions. In: Canteaut, A., Viswanathan, K. (eds.) INDOCRYPT 2004. LNCS, vol. 3348, pp. 92–106. Springer, Heidelberg (2004). https://doi.org/10.1007/978-3-540-30556-9_9

17. Dalai, D.K., Maitra, S., Sarkar, S.: Basic theory in construction of boolean functions with maximum possible annihilator immunity. Designs, Codes and Cryptography (2006)
18. Dalai, D.K., Mallick, K.: A class of weightwise almost perfectly balanced boolean functions. Adv. Math. Commun. **18**(2), 480–504 (2024)
19. Dalai, D.K., Mallick, K., Méaux, P.: Weightwise almost perfectly balanced functions, construction from A permutation group action view. IACR Cryptol. ePrint Arch. p. 2068 (2024). https://eprint.iacr.org/2024/2068
20. Didier, F.: A new upper bound on the block error probability after decoding over the erasure channel. IEEE Trans. Inf. Theory **52**(10), 4496–4503 (2006)
21. Didier, F., Tillich, J.-P.: Computing the algebraic immunity efficiently. In: Robshaw, M. (ed.) FSE 2006. LNCS, vol. 4047, pp. 359–374. Springer, Heidelberg (2006). https://doi.org/10.1007/11799313_23
22. Gilbert, H., Boissier, R.H., Jean, J., Reinhard, J.: Cryptanalysis of elisabeth-4. In: Guo, J., Steinfeld, R. (eds.) Advances in Cryptology - ASIACRYPT 2023 - 29th International Conference on the Theory and Application of Cryptology and Information Security, Guangzhou, China, 4–8 December 2023, Proceedings, Part III. LNCS, vol. 14440, pp. 256–284. Springer, Cham (2023). https://doi.org/10.1007/978-981-99-8727-6_9
23. Gini, A., Méaux, P.: On the weightwise nonlinearity of weightwise perfectly balanced functions. Discret. Appl. Math. **322**, 320–341 (2022). https://doi.org/10.1016/j.dam.2022.08.017
24. Gini, A., Méaux, P.: Weightwise almost perfectly balanced functions: secondary constructions for all n and better weightwise nonlinearities. In: Isobe, T., Sarkar, S. (eds.) Progress in Cryptology - INDOCRYPT 2022. LNCS, vol. 13774, pp. 492–514. Springer, Cham (2022)
25. Gini, A., Méaux, P.: On the algebraic immunity of weightwise perfectly balanced functions. In: Aly, A., Tibouchi, M. (eds.) Progress in Cryptology - LATINCRYPT 2023. LNCS, vol. 14168, pp. 3–23. Springer, Cham (2023). https://doi.org/10.1007/978-3-031-44469-2_1
26. Gini, A., Méaux, P.: Weightwise perfectly balanced functions and nonlinearity. In: Hajji, S.E., Mesnager, S., Souidi, E.M. (eds.) Codes, Cryptology and Information Security 2023. LNCS, vol. 13874, pp. 338–359. Springer, Cham (2023). https://doi.org/10.1007/978-3-031-33017-9_21
27. Gini, A., Méaux, P.: S_0-equivalence classes, a new direction to find better weightwise perfectly balanced functions, and more. Cryptogr. Commun. **16**(6), 1211–1234 (2024). https://doi.org/10.1007/S12095-024-00719-W
28. Goldreich, O.: Candidate one-way functions based on expander graphs. Electronic Colloquium on Computational Complexity (ECCC) **7**(90) (2000)
29. Guo, X., Su, S.: Construction of weightwise almost perfectly balanced boolean functions on an arbitrary number of variables. Discret. Appl. Math. **307**, 102–114 (2022)
30. Hawkes, P., Rose, G.G.: Rewriting variables: the complexity of fast algebraic attacks on stream ciphers. In: Franklin, M. (ed.) CRYPTO 2004. LNCS, vol. 3152, pp. 390–406. Springer, Heidelberg (2004). https://doi.org/10.1007/978-3-540-28628-8_24
31. Hoffmann, C., Méaux, P., Standaert, F.: The patching landscape of elisabeth-4 and the mixed filter permutator paradigm. In: Chattopadhyay, A., Bhasin, S., Picek, S., Rebeiro, C. (eds.) INDOCRYPT 2023, Part I. LNCS, vol. 14459, pp. 134–156. Springer, Cham (2023). https://doi.org/10.1007/978-3-031-56232-7_7
32. Lauter, K., Naehrig, M., Vaikuntanathan, V.: Can homomorphic encryption be practical? Cryptology ePrint Archive, Report 2011/405 (2011)
33. Li, J., Carlet, C., Zeng, X., Li, C., Hu, L., Shan, J.: Two constructions of balanced boolean functions with optimal algebraic immunity, high nonlinearity and good behavior against fast algebraic attacks. Des. Codes Cryptogr. **76** (2014)
34. Li, J., Su, S.: Construction of weightwise perfectly balanced boolean functions with high weightwise nonlinearity. Discret. Appl. Math. **279**, 218–227 (2020)

35. Li, N., Qi, W.: Boolean functions of an odd number of variables with maximum algebraic immunity. Sci. China Ser. F: Inf. Sci. 307–317 (2007). https://doi.org/10.1007/s11432-007-0027-4
36. Limniotis, K., Kolokotronis, N.: Boolean functions with maximum algebraic immunity: further extensions of the Carlet–Feng construction. DCC **86**, 1685–1706 (2018)
37. Limniotis, K., Kolokotronis, N., Kalouptsidis, N.: Secondary constructions of boolean functions with maximum algebraic immunity. Cryptogr. Commun. **5** (2013)
38. Liu, J., Mesnager, S.: Weightwise perfectly balanced functions with high weightwise nonlinearity profile. Des. Codes Cryptogr. **87**(8), 1797–1813 (2019)
39. Liu, M., Lin, D.: Almost perfect algebraic immune functions with good nonlinearity. In: 2014 IEEE International Symposium on Information Theory, pp. 1837–1841 (2014). https://doi.org/10.1109/ISIT.2014.6875151
40. Liu, M., Zhang, Y., Lin, D.: Perfect algebraic immune functions. In: Wang, X., Sako, K. (eds.) ASIACRYPT 2012. LNCS, vol. 7658, pp. 172–189. Springer, Heidelberg (2012). https://doi.org/10.1007/978-3-642-34961-4_12
41. Mandujano, S., Ku Cauich, J.C., Lara, A.: Studying special operators for the application of evolutionary algorithms in the seek of optimal boolean functions for cryptography. In: Advances in Computational Intelligence, pp. 383–396. Springer, Cham (2022)
42. Mariot, L., Picek, S., Jakobovic, D., Djurasevic, M., Leporati, A.: Evolutionary construction of perfectly balanced boolean functions. In: 2022 IEEE Congress on Evolutionary Computation (CEC), pp. 1–8. IEEE Press (2022)
43. Méaux, P.: On the algebraic immunity of direct sum constructions. Discret. Appl. Math. **320**, 223–234 (2022). https://doi.org/10.1016/j.dam.2022.05.021
44. Méaux, P.: From at least n/3 to at most $3\sqrt{n}$: correcting the algebraic immunity of the hidden weight bit function. IACR Cryptol. ePrint Arch. p. 615 (2025). https://eprint.iacr.org/2025/615, to appear at Latincrypt 2025
45. Méaux, P.: Weightwise (almost) perfectly balanced functions based on total orders. In: Eichlseder, M., Gambs, S. (eds.) Selected Areas in Cryptography - SAC 2024, pp. 112–138. Springer, Cham (2025)
46. Méaux, P., Carlet, C., Journault, A., Standaert, F.-X.: Improved filter permutators for efficient FHE: better instances and implementations. In: Hao, F., Ruj, S., Sen Gupta, S. (eds.) INDOCRYPT 2019. LNCS, vol. 11898, pp. 68–91. Springer, Cham (2019). https://doi.org/10.1007/978-3-030-35423-7_4
47. Méaux, P., Journault, A., Standaert, F.-X., Carlet, C.: Towards stream ciphers for efficient FHE with low-noise ciphertexts. In: Fischlin, M., Coron, J.-S. (eds.) EUROCRYPT 2016. LNCS, vol. 9665, pp. 311–343. Springer, Heidelberg (2016). https://doi.org/10.1007/978-3-662-49890-3_13
48. Méaux, P., Seuré, T., Tang, D.: The revisited hidden weight bit function. IACR Cryptol. ePrint Arch. p. 2022 (2024). https://eprint.iacr.org/2024/2022, to appear at Selected Areas in Cryptography – SAC 2025
49. Méaux, P., Wang, Q.: Towards a generalization of the algebraic attack on stream ciphers: a study of the case with only extremal-degree monomials. IACR Commun. Cryptol. **2**(1), 29 (2025). https://doi.org/10.62056/ABY7QJP10
50. Meier, W., Pasalic, E., Carlet, C.: Algebraic attacks and decomposition of boolean functions. In: Cachin, C., Camenisch, J.L. (eds.) EUROCRYPT 2004. LNCS, vol. 3027, pp. 474–491. Springer, Heidelberg (2004). https://doi.org/10.1007/978-3-540-24676-3_28
51. Mesnager, S., Su, S.: On constructions of weightwise perfectly balanced boolean functions. Cryptogr. Commun. (2021)
52. Mesnager, S., Su, S., Li, J., Zhu, L.: Concrete constructions of weightwise perfectly balanced (2-rotation symmetric) functions with optimal algebraic immunity and high weightwise nonlinearity. Cryptogr. Commun. **14**(6), 1371–1389 (2022)

53. Qu, L., Feng, K., Liu, F., Wang, L.: Constructing symmetric boolean functions with maximum algebraic immunity. IEEE Trans. Inf. Theory **55**, 2406–2412 (2009). https://doi.org/10.1109/TIT.2009.2015999
54. Stevens, B., Williams, A.: The coolest order of binary strings. In: Kranakis, E., Krizanc, D., Luccio, F. (eds.) FUN 2012. LNCS, vol. 7288, pp. 322–333. Springer, Heidelberg (2012). https://doi.org/10.1007/978-3-642-30347-0_32
55. Tang, D., Carlet, C., Tang, X., Zhou, Z.: Construction of highly nonlinear 1-resilient boolean functions with optimal algebraic immunity and provably high fast algebraic immunity. IEEE Trans. Inf. Theory 6113–6125 (2017). https://doi.org/10.1109/TIT.2017.2725918
56. Tang, D., Carlet, C., Tang, X.: Highly nonlinear boolean functions with optimal algebraic immunity and good behavior against fast algebraic attacks. IEEE Trans. Inf. Theory 653–664 (2013). https://doi.org/10.1109/TIT.2012.2217476
57. Tang, D., Liu, J.: A family of weightwise (almost) perfectly balanced boolean functions with optimal algebraic immunity. Cryptogr. Commun. **11**(6), 1185–1197 (2019). https://doi.org/10.1007/s12095-019-00374-6
58. Tang, D., Luo, R., Du, X.: The exact fast algebraic immunity of two subclasses of the majority function. IEICE Trans. 2084–2088 (2016)
59. Tu, Z., Deng, Y.: A conjecture about binary strings and its applications on constructing boolean functions with optimal algebraic immunity. DCC **60**, 1–14 (2011)
60. Yan, L., et al.: IGA: an improved genetic algorithm to construct weightwise (almost) perfectly balanced boolean functions with high weightwise nonlinearity. In: ASIA CCS 2023, pp. 638–648 (2023)
61. Zeng, X., Carlet, C., Shan, J., Hu, L.: More balanced boolean functions with optimal algebraic immunity and good nonlinearity and resistance to fast algebraic attacks. IEEE Trans. Inf. Theory **57**(9), 6310–6320 (2011)
62. Zhang, R., Su, S.: A new construction of weightwise perfectly balanced boolean functions. Adv. Math. Commun. **17**(4), 757–770 (2023). https://doi.org/10.3934/AMC.2021020
63. Zhao, Q., Jia, Y., Zheng, D., Qin, B.: A new construction of weightwise perfectly balanced functions with high weightwise nonlinearity. Mathematics **11**(5) (2023)
64. Zhao, Q., Li, M., Chen, Z., Qin, B., Zheng, D.: A unified construction of weightwise perfectly balanced boolean functions. Discret. Appl. Math. **337**, 190–201 (2023)
65. Zhu, L., Su, S.: A systematic method of constructing weightwise almost perfectly balanced boolean functions on an arbitrary number of variables. Discret. Appl. Math. **314**, 181–190 (2022)

Multi-Party Computation

Efficient Fuzzy Labeled PSI from Vector Ring-OLE

Dung Bui[1(✉)] and Kelong Cong[2]

[1] EPITA, LIP6, Université Sorbonne, Paris, France
dung.bui@lip6.fr
[2] Zama, Paris, France
kelong.cong@zama.ai

Abstract. Fuzzy-labeled private set intersection (PSI) outputs the corresponding label if there is a "fuzzy" match between two items, for example when the Hamming distance is low between the two items. Such protocols can be applied in privacy-preserving biometric authentication, proximity testing, and so on. The only fuzzy-labeled PSI protocol designed for practical purposes is by Uzun *et al.* (USENIX'21), which is based on homomorphic encryption. This design puts constraints on the item size, label size, and communication cost since it is difficult for homomorphic encryption to support large plaintext space and it is well-known that the ciphertext-expansion factor is large.

Our construction begins with a new primitive which we call vector ring-oblivious linear evaluation (vector ring-OLE). This primitive does not rely on existing instantiations of ring-OLE over the quotient ring, but leverages the more efficient vector-OLE. It is ideal for building unbalanced threshold-labeled PSI and is also of independent interest.

Our main contribution, fuzzy-labeled PSI, is bootstrapped from our threshold-labeled PSI protocol. Through a prototype implementation, we demonstrate our communication cost is up to 4.6× better than the prior state-of-the-art with comparable end-to-end latency while supporting a significantly higher label size.

1 Introduction

Private set intersection is a secure computation task where two parties compute the intersection of their private sets without revealing anything beyond the result. It has many real-world uses, such as advertising [26], contact discovery [27], and password breach detection [13,16]. Over the years, significant progress has been made [17,25,29–31], especially following the introduction of pseudorandom correlation generators [7,8], which enabled more efficient protocols [11,14,31,32]. Variants of PSI exist, such as PSI with labels, where a label is revealed when two items match. In this work, we are interested in a variant of labeled PSI that is *fuzzy-labeled PSI* based on PCG.

Specifically, we consider an unbalanced setting, i.e., the receiver has one item and the sender has many items (possibly millions). This problem is also known

Y. Kim et al. (Eds.): CANS 2025, LNCS 16351, pp. 173–198, 2026.
https://doi.org/10.1007/978-981-95-4434-9_8

as private membership testing. Two items are matched if they are close in some distance metric, e.g., Hamming distance. Labeled means a label is returned if two items "fuzzily" match, instead of a binary flag that indicates that a match is found. This functionality is especially useful in applications such as biometric authentication, where the only thing we may want to check is if a specific fingerprint (or face) matches a fingerprint (or face) from a database [33]. Another application is privacy-preserving proximity-testing [24], to compute the output whether two parties are close enough without revealing their relative distances or positions. The only labeled fuzzy PSI protocol in Hamming distance for high dimensions (e.g., $d = 128$) is by Uzun *et al.* [33], using sub-sampling and a t-out-of-T threshold PSI over leveled homomorphic encryption (HE). It achieves communication independent of the sender's set size, but suffers from large ciphertext expansion [15] and limited label size support. Chaudhuri *et al.* [12] proposed fuzzy PSI (without label) using additive homomorphic encryption (AHE), which is slower asymptotically but outperforms [33] concretely for databases up to 1M items.

Another line of work by Garimella, Rosulek, and Singh [21,22] initiated a structure-aware PSI (without labels) where the receiver holds N balls of radius σ and dimension d and the sender holds a set of M points. In the end, the receiver learns which of the sender's points are inside one of their balls. These constructions use Function Secret Sharing (FSS) [9] and Oblivious Transfer (OT) for L_∞ and L_1 distances, with recent work [20] improving computation via incremental FSS. Van Baarsen and Pu [5] constructed a fuzzy PSI based on the decisional Diffie-Hellman assumption (DDH) for general L_p distances, but with high cost for large d. Recently, [19] introduced Fuzzy mapping, a new primitive supporting Hamming distance with linear complexity based on AHE and DDH. The details of related works can be found in the full version [10].

1.1 Our Contribution

Vector Ring-OLE. We propose a new primitive called vector ring-oblivious linear function evaluation (vector ring-OLE) in Sect. 4 where we achieve a batch of m instances of ring-OLE of degree d ($m \gg d$). This primitive is used to construct our fuzzy-labeled PSI protocols and it may be of independent interest. Using the chosen ring-OLE in previous works [14,23], it is possible to obtain vector ring-OLE correlations of length m of degree d over a field $\mathbb{F}$ from $O(md)$ random OLEs. But the communication cost is at least $6md \log |\mathbb{F}|$ (online and offline cost) [14]. We compare with [14,23] in the same setting and present the results in Table 1. Compared to the state-of-art of chosen ring-OLE [14,23], our vector ring-OLE enjoys two main advantages:

1. Our protocol achieves the same functionality, for the same parameters with a communication cost that is over 50% smaller compared to prior work [14,23].
2. Our protocol has a faster setup phase using vector-OLE (VOLE) while prior work needs OLE [14,23]. When we cast their constructions to follow our functionality, [23] needs $4md$ OLEs and it is instantiated from homomorphic

encryption. Chongchitmate *et al.* [14] need $2md$ OLEs, which is instantiated from ring-OLE. The setup cost of VOLE setup is much faster (less than a second [34]) when compared to ring OLE or OLE (10–20 s [8]).

Fuzzy-Labeled PSI. Our primary contribution is a fuzzy-labeled PSI protocol (Sect. 5) that is built on top of our threshold-labeled PSI protocol (Sect. 5.1). Our fuzzy-labeled PSI improves over the state of the art and other related works [5, 12, 14, 20, 21, 33] in the following aspects:

- Our fuzzy-labeled PSI focuses on the Hamming distance and supports a high dimension (up to κ bits) efficiently as opposed to [5, 20, 21], which only support less than 10 dimensions efficiently.
- The asymptotic online communication complexity does not depend on the computational security parameter κ.
- We support a label space that is not fixed in bit-length size and can go up to κ bits, which was not possible in prior works [12, 14, 19–21]. The works of [5, 19] also support labels as an extension of their constructions; however, labeled PSI in [5] relies on ElGamal encryption, whereas [19] uses both ElGamal and AHE, resulting in poor performance.
- We implemented our protocol and it outperforms the state-of-the-art [33] for database sizes of up to 1 million in both computation and communication. For smaller database sizes, we achieve 4.6× improvement in communication.

2 Technical Overview

2.1 Vector Ring-OLE from VOLE

Construction. Our goal is to build correlations of the form $(z_i = u_0 \cdot u_i + v_i)_{i \in [m]}$ where $\deg(u_0) = \deg(u_i) = d$ for $d \ll m$, and $\deg(z_i) = \deg(v_i) = 2d$ for all $i \in [m]$. The receiver inputs u_0 and gets $(z_i)_{i \in [m]}$ while sender inputs $(v_i)_{i \in [m]}$ and gets $(u_i)_{i \in [m]}$. The correlation is available from VOLE.

Given two polynomials of degree d, their product can be computed by evaluating on $2d+1$ fixed evaluation points $\{x_1, \ldots, x_{2d+1}\}$, perform point-wise multiplication and then interpolate the $2d+1$ points to obtain a degree $2d$ polynomial. In other words, $(z_i(x_1), z_i(x_2), \ldots, z_i(x_{2d+1}))$ and $(v_i(x_1), v_i(x_2), \ldots, v_i(x_{2d+1}))$ are additive shares of

$$(u_0(x_1), u_0(x_2), \ldots, u_0(x_{2d+1})) \odot (u_i(x_1), u_i(x_2), \ldots, u_i(x_{2d+1})),\ i \in [m]$$

where $\odot$ denotes element-wise multiplication. Since z_i and v_i are degree-$2d$ polynomials, if parties hold these shares then z_i and v_i can be constructed. If we view the problem from another angle by fixing the evaluation point x_j, we have $(z_1(x_j), z_2(x_j), \ldots, z_m(x_j))$ and $(v_1(x_j), v_2(x_j), \ldots, v_m(x_j))$ are shares of $u_0(x_j) \cdot (u_1(x_j), u_2(x_j), \ldots, u_m(x_j))$ for $j \in [2d+1]$. Therefore if we define $\mathbf{u_0} := (u_0(x_j))_{j \in [2d+1]}$, matrices $\mathbf{U}, \mathbf{V}, \mathbf{Z} \in \mathbb{F}^{m \times (2d+1)}$ as the column $\mathbf{U}_j := \{u_1(x_j), u_2(x_j), \ldots, u_m(x_j)\}$, and $\mathbf{V}_i, \mathbf{Z}_i$ are defined the same way as $\mathbf{U}_i$ from the polynomials v_i and z_i, then the goal is to securely distributed the share $\mathbf{V}$ and $\mathbf{Z}$ of $\mathbf{u_0} \odot \mathbf{U}$ to parties, where $\mathbf{u_0}$ and $\mathbf{V}$ are chosen in advance by receiver and sender. This kind of functionality can be achieved using VOLE correlations as the masking for the parties' input. The outline is given below.

Step 1. First of all, we use VOLE of length m and execute it $2d+1$ times to give sender $\mathbf{U}', \mathbf{V}' \leftarrow_\$ \mathbb{F}^{m\times(2d+1)}$, and give receiver vector $\mathbf{u_0}' \leftarrow_\$ \mathbb{F}^{2d+1}, \mathbf{Z}' \in \mathbb{F}^{m\times(2d+1)}$ such that $\mathbf{Z}' := \mathbf{u_0}' \odot \mathbf{U}' + \mathbf{V}'$.

Step 2. We now de-randomize this correlation to get $\mathbf{Z} = \mathbf{u_0} \odot \mathbf{U} + \mathbf{V}$, the naive method to do de-randomize is:

1. Receiver sends $\Delta\mathbf{u_0} = \mathbf{u_0} - \mathbf{u_0}' \in \mathbb{F}^{2d+1}$ to sender.
2. Sender then sends $\Delta\mathbf{U} = \mathbf{U} - \mathbf{U}' \in \mathbb{F}^{m\times(2d+1)}$ and $\Delta\mathbf{V} = \Delta\mathbf{u_0} \odot \mathbf{U}' + \mathbf{V} - \mathbf{V}' \in \mathbb{F}^{m\times(2d+1)}$ to receiver.
3. Now receiver can locally compute $\mathbf{Z} := \mathbf{u_0} \odot \Delta\mathbf{U} + \Delta\mathbf{V} + \mathbf{Z}'$, by a simple calculation.

Step 3. Viewing this relation from each row i of matrix $\mathbf{Z}$, parties now can get a share of $(u_0 \cdot u_i)$ in the form of evaluation values for $i \in [m]$. In other words, row i^{th} of $\mathbf{Z}$ defines a polynomial z_i of degree $2d$ such that $z_i = u_0 \cdot u_i + v_i$.

2.2 Fuzzy-Labeled PSI

Our fuzzy-labeled PSI (FLPSI) construction is based on two main building blocks (1) an efficient threshold-labeled PSI (TLPSI) for small threshold parameters and (2) a masked OPRF to transform any TLPSI into a fuzzy-labeled PSI while keeping a low false negative rate (FNR) and false positive rate (FPR).

Threshold-Labeled PSI. The threshold labeled PSI (TLPSI) functionality takes input X from the receiver and Y and ℓ from the sender, and then outputs ℓ and $|X \cap Y|$ to the receiver if $|X \cap Y| \geq t$ where t is some threshold. This functionality can be instantiated using Shamir secret sharing and our vector ring-OLE functionality. Our construction is only efficient for small threshold parameter t however we show that small t and d values are enough for us to construct an efficient fuzzy-labeled PSI. The details are given in Sect. 5.1.

Fuzzy-Labeled PSI. In our setting, receiver has an input $x \in \{0,1\}^d$ while sender has a set of inputs $Y = \{(y_i, l_i)\}$. If x and y_i are close enough in the Hamming distance $\mathsf{HW}(x \oplus y) \leq d_k$ for a threshold $d_k \ll d$ then receiver learns the corresponding label l_i. We now show how to transform from our threshold-labeled PSI to fuzzy-labeled PSI. Our transformation is inspired by [33] which uses sub-sampling to gain efficiency and masked OPRF to protect privacy.

In particular, the sub-sampling allows us to map receiver and sender's input x and y_i into sets $\bar{X}$ and $\bar{Y_i}$ of size T, respectively, such that if $\mathsf{HW}(x \oplus y) \leq d_k$

then $|\bar{X} \cap \bar{Y}_i| \geq t$ for a small t. The sets $\bar{X}$ and $\bar{Y}_i$ are constructed by applying x and y_i with T different masks $\{m_i\}_{i\in[T]}$, such that $\mathsf{HW}(m_i) = d_s \leq d$. Namely, $\bar{X} \leftarrow \{x \wedge m_1, \ldots, x \wedge m_T\}$ and $\bar{Y}_i \leftarrow \{y \wedge m_1, \ldots, y \wedge m_T\}$. For $d_k \ll d$ and an appropriate parameters choice for d_s, T we only need a very small t ($t = 2$ in our instantiation) with low false negative rate and false positive rate (FNR and FPR), details of the parameter choices are in Sect. 6.2.

Observe that fuzzy-labeled PSI is instantiated using a threshold PSI with a small threshold parameter. Receiver and sender now can join the threshold-labeled PSI for a threshold parameter t with input $\bar{X}$ and $\{\bar{Y}_i\}_{i\in[m]}$, after that receiver learns label l_i and $\bar{X} \cap \bar{Y}_i$ if $|\bar{X} \cap \bar{Y}_i| \geq t$. Since our threshold-labeled PSI is instantiated from our vector ring-OLE, to instantiate m TLPSI of input size T it requires only one $\mathcal{F}^{m,T}_{\mathsf{vrOLE}}$.

If sub-sampling masks $\{m_i\}_{i\in[T]}$ are public, this protocol leaks the d_s sub-sampled plaintext bits of sender's input $y_i \in \{0,1\}^d$ if there is an intersection above the threshold t. This leakage allows receiver to learn information about sender's input, for example, when in case of a false-positive match, receiver will now learn with confidence the positions in the bit vector of sender's input. To resolve this concern, a masked OPRF protocol is used where receiver inputs her item x and sender inputs a PRF key k and T masks. At the end of the protocol, receiver obtains $\{\mathsf{PRF}_k(x \wedge m_1), \mathsf{PRF}_k(x \wedge m_2), \ldots, \mathsf{PRF}_k(x \wedge m_T)\}$. This functionality is very similar to the OPRF functionality except that a mask is applied to input of receiver prior to the OPRF, it is instantiated using garbled circuits [35] where the cost is minor and only dependent on T, and not m. Finally, the two parties execute the threshold-labeled PSI functionality using the masked OPRF output as the input to obtain the label. For security, our fuzzy-labeled PSI is secure against semi-honest setting and follows from the security of TLPSI and masked OPRF.

3 Preliminaries

Below we describe the notation and some important ideal functionalities.

3.1 Notation

The notation $x \leftarrow_{\$} \mathcal{D}$ denotes sampling from a probability distribution $\mathcal{D}$, with uniform sampling if $\mathcal{D}$ is a set. A sequence from a to b (inclusive) is written as $[a, b]$, and $[b]$ implies the sequence starts at 1. We use κ and λ for computational and statistical security parameters, and denote an adversary as $\mathcal{A}$.

For a matrix $\mathbf{M} \in \mathbb{F}^{n\times m}$, $\mathbf{M}_{i,j}$ refers to the entry in the ith row and j^{th} column; $\mathbf{M_j}$ and $\mathbf{M^i}$ refer to the jth column and i^{th} row, respectively. $\mathbf{M}[i,j]$ is the submatrix from the ith to j^{th} column. The symbol $\odot$ represents the point-wise product between a vector and a matrix: for $\mathbf{u} = (u_1, \ldots, u_m) \in \mathbb{F}^m$, $\mathbf{u}\odot\mathbf{M} = (u_1 \cdot \mathbf{M_1}, \ldots, u_m \cdot \mathbf{M_m}) \in \mathbb{F}^{n\times m}$. $0^d\|\mathbf{M} \in \mathbb{F}^{n\times(d+m)}$ denotes a matrix with the first d columns as zeros followed by $\mathbf{M}$. For a polynomial $f(x) \in \mathcal{R}$, $\deg(f)$ is the degree of $f(x)$.

3.2 Secure Two-Party Computation

In our work, all proofs are given in simulation-based proof and we give the formal definition of security under the semi-honest setting below.

Semi-Honest Security. Given a security parameter κ and a pair of inputs $(X, Y) \in \{0,1\}^*$, let $\mathsf{view}_1^{\Pi}(X, Y, \kappa)$ and $\mathsf{view}_2^{\Pi}(X, Y, \kappa)$ be the views of P_1 and P_2 respectively in the protocol Π, $\mathsf{out}^{\Pi}(X, Y, \kappa)$ be the output of the protocol, and $f_i(X, Y)$ be the output of P_i from the ideal functionality $f := (f_1, f_2)$. The protocol Π securely computes f in the presence of static semi-honest adversaries if there exist PPT simulators Sim_1 and Sim_2 such that for all valid inputs X, Y of f,

$$\left(\mathsf{view}_1^{\Pi}(X, Y, \kappa), \mathsf{out}^{\Pi}(X, Y, \kappa)\right) \approx \left(\mathsf{Sim}_1(1^{\kappa}, X, f_1(X, Y)), f(X, Y)\right);$$
$$\left(\mathsf{view}_2^{\Pi}(X, Y, \kappa), \mathsf{out}^{\Pi}(X, Y, \kappa)\right) \approx \left(\mathsf{Sim}_2(1^{\kappa}, Y, f_2(X, Y)), f(X, Y)\right).$$

3.3 Threshold Shamir's Secret Sharing

Shamir's secret sharing allows each of d parties to get a share of the secret input such that this secret can only be revealed by at least t honest parties. The functionality is given in Fig. 1.

Fig. 1: $\mathcal{F}_{\mathsf{TSSS}}^{d,t}$ over $\mathbb{F}$.

PARAMETERS: Given a field $\mathbb{F}$, a threshold value t, and d distinct points $t_i \in \mathbb{F}$ such that $t_i \neq 0$.

FUNCTIONALITY:

- **Share.** For a secret input $s \in \mathbb{F}$, pick a random polynomial f of degree $(t-1)$ over $\mathbb{F}[x]$ such that $f(0) = s$. Output the set $S := \{f(t_i)\}_{i \in [d]}$.
- **Reconstruct.** Given a vector $\mathbf{c} := \{c_i\}_{i \in [d]}$, if there are at least t value c_i such that $c_i = f(t_i)$ for $i \in [d]$, reconstruct f and output $s := f(0)$. Otherwise, output $\perp$.

3.4 Ideal Functionality of Fuzzy-Labeled PSI

The ideal functionality of fuzzy-labeled PSI in the semi-honest setting is shown in Fig. 2. Our fuzzy-labeled PSI is constructed from a threshold-labeled PSI, we present its ideal functionality on Fig. 3. Since fuzzy matching is not exact and may have false positives or false negatives due to techniques such as locality-sensitive hashing and the sub-sampling method used in [33], and the permute and partition method used in [12], which we define the context as below.

Definition 1 (Closeness Domain [12]). *We say that $\delta := (\mathcal{D}, \mathsf{Cl})$ is a closeness function that takes any $x, y \in \mathcal{D}$ and outputs a member of $\{\mathsf{close}, \mathsf{far}\}$, so that Cl is symmetric (i.e., $\mathsf{Cl}(x, y) = \mathsf{Cl}(y, x)$).*

Definition 2 (Correctness of Fuzzy-Labeled PSI (FLPSI) [12]). *Π_{FLPSI} protocol is defined for a closeness domain $(\mathcal{D}, \mathsf{Cl})$ and a label space $\mathcal{LS}$ and for two parties: a sender and a receiver. The receiver inputs a query $x \in \mathcal{D}$, and the sender inputs a database $Y := \{(y_i, \ell_i)\}_{i \le m}$ where items $y_i \in \mathcal{D}$ and labels $\ell_i \in \mathcal{LS}$. At the end, the receiver receives a set R, and the sender receives $\perp$. The set R is defined in the following correctness.*

Correctness. *We denote by* TPR *the true positive rate and by* TNR *the true negative rate. For x and Y, the output set R consists of labels $\ell \in \mathcal{LS}$ such that for each $i \in [m]$:*

1. *If $\mathsf{Cl}(x, y_i) = \mathsf{far}$, then $\Pr[\ell_i \notin R] \ge \mathsf{TNR}$,*
2. *If $\mathsf{Cl}(x, y_i) = \mathsf{close}$, then $\Pr[\ell_i \in R] \ge \mathsf{TPR}$.*

In our work, we define Cl as the Hamming distance with a threshold rate t, i.e., with overwhelming probability, $\mathsf{Cl}(x, y_i) = \mathsf{close} \iff \mathsf{HW}(x \oplus y_i) \le t$, otherwise, Cl outputs far, where HW denotes the Hamming weight. Additionally, the false positive rate FPR is $1 - \mathsf{TPR}$ and the false negative rate FNR is $1 - \mathsf{TNR}$.

We note that in our construction, the leakage profile of the ideal FLPSI functionality depends on the real Π_{FLPSI} protocol, the challenge we are facing is that ideal functionality must align precisely with the behavior of the real-world protocol. Our approach is defining an ideal functionality $\mathcal{F}_{\mathsf{FLPSI}}$ that outputs whatever Π_{FLPSI} protocol formally outputs. In particular, we formalize in functionality: giving a trusted party to run Π_{FLPSI} and giving to both parties what Π_{FLPSI} outputs. A similar issue regarding ideal functionalities is addressed in [12].

Definition 3 (Security of a FLPSI protocol [12]). *We say that a protocol $\Pi^{\delta,\mathcal{L}}_{\mathsf{FLPSI}}$ defined w.r.t. the closeness domain $\delta = (\mathcal{D}, \mathsf{Cl})$ having the true positive rate* TPR *and the true negative rate* TNR *is a secure* FLPSI *protocol with leakage profile $\mathcal{L} = \{\mathcal{L}_{\mathsf{S}}, \mathcal{L}_{\mathsf{R}}\}$, if Π_{FLPSI} securely realizes the functionality $\mathcal{F}_{\mathsf{FLPSI}}$.*

Fig. 2: $\mathcal{F}_{\mathsf{FLPSI}}$ in semi-honest setting.

PARAMETERS:

- There are two parties, a receiver has input $x \in \mathcal{D}$ while a sender has a set of inputs $Y = \{(y_i, \ell_i)\}_{i \in [m]}$ where $y_i \in \mathcal{D}$ and $\ell_i \in \mathcal{LS}$.
- The protocol Π_{FLPSI} with closeness domain $\delta = (\mathcal{D}, \mathsf{Cl})$ having the true positive rate TPR and the true negative rate TNR.
- The leakage profile $\mathcal{L} = \{\mathcal{L}_{\mathsf{S}}, \mathcal{L}_{\mathsf{R}}\}$.

FUNCTIONALITY:

- The trusted party runs an honest execution of the protocol Π_{FLPSI} on the players' inputs and obtains the output result set R;
- Return $(\mathsf{OutputR}, R, \mathcal{L}_{\mathsf{R}})$ to receiver and $(\mathsf{OutputS}, \mathcal{L}_{\mathsf{S}})$ to sender.

Given a leakage profile $\mathcal{L}$ that is allowed beforehand depending on the use context, the above security notion guarantees that no additional information beyond the output of the protocol Π and the leakage profile $\mathcal{L}$ is revealed. As discussed in [33], this security notion, which is a combination between simulation-based security and game-based security, helps to avoid the need to specify exactly the probability that CI outputs close or far for each pair of inputs in the ideal functionality. A protocol Π_{FLPSI} is said to be correct and secure if it satisfies both the above correctness and security notions.

Ideal Functionality of TLPSI. A key building block to construct FLPSI is the threshold-labeled PSI (TLPSI). We give the ideal functionality of TLPSI against semi-honest adversaries in Fig. 3.

Masked Oblivious Pseudorandom Function. From our threshold-labeled PSI, we use a masked oblivious pseudorandom function (masked OPRF) to get an efficient fuzzy-labeled PSI.

Fig. 3: $\mathcal{F}^{d,t}_{\mathsf{TLPSI}}$ in semi-honest setting.

PARAMETERS:

- An arbitrary field $\mathbb{F}$, threshold value t.
- There are two parties, a receiver with a input set $X \subseteq \mathbb{F}$ and a sender with a input set $Y \subseteq \mathbb{F}$ with a secret label $l \in \mathbb{F}$.

FUNCTIONALITY:

- Wait for receiver to send the input set (InputR, X).
- Wait for sender to send the input set (InputS, Y, l).
- If $|X \cap Y| \geq t$, gives receiver $(\mathsf{OutputR}, X \cap Y, \ell)$, otherwise outputs $\perp$.

The masked OPRF is a two-party protocol that is similar to OPRF except the receiver's input is masked by some masks given by the sender before it is used as the input to the PRF. Specifically, we consider a batch of T different masks applied to one input. The exact functionality is given in Fig. 4. The same functionality appears in [33] and the authors refer to it as "oblivious sub-sampling". This functionality is straightforward to instantiate using a garbled circuit which we describe in Sect. 6.2.

Fig. 4: $\mathcal{F}_{\mathsf{mOPRF}}^{T}$ in the semi-honest setting.

PARAMETERS:

- Given a PRF function $F : \mathcal{K} \times \mathcal{M} \rightarrow \mathcal{D}$, a number T of instances, two parties a sender and a receiver.
- The receiver has an input $x \in \mathcal{M}$, the sender has a key $k \in \mathcal{K}$ and T masking values $\{m_1, m_2, \ldots, m_T\} \in \mathcal{M}^T$.

FUNCTIONALITY:

- Wait for receiver and sender to input their inputs (InputR, x) and $(\mathsf{InputS}, k, (m_i)_{i\in[T]})$ respectively.
- Output $(\mathsf{OutputR}, (F(k, x \wedge m_i))_{i\in[T]})$ to receiver.

3.5 Vector-OLE from PCG

We represent on Fig. 5 the ideal functionality $\mathcal{F}_{\mathsf{VOLE}}^{n,\mathbb{F}}$ of vector-OLE[1]. In our concrete instantiations, we instantiate this functionality using the general template in [6,7,34], which can be instantiated under various flavors of the learning parity with noise (LPN) assumption. Using the protocol of [6] to distribute the seeds[2], the theoretical communication cost to have $\mathcal{F}_{\mathsf{VOLE}}^{n,\mathbb{F}}$ is $(\log(cn/t)|\mathsf{OT}| + 10|\mathbb{F}|) \cdot t$, where t is Hamming weight of noises for the underlying LPN assumption, $|\mathsf{OT}| = O(\kappa)$ is the size of chosen OT [28] and c is the ratio between number of samples and the length of VOLE. We also provide an analysis of the cost of generating other correlations from PCG, specifically, ring-OLE and OLE in [8], to demonstrate the concrete efficiency of VOLE.

[1] Since the role of sender and receiver are equal, for simplicity, we assume receiver holds global Δ.

[2] This protocol uses a length-t reverse VOLE protocol as a black box, which we instantiate with the construction of [2].

Fig. 5: $\mathcal{F}_{\mathsf{VOLE}}^{n,\mathbb{F}}$ ideal functionality.

PARAMETERS: Two parties, a sender and a receiver, an integer n, the size of the output vector, a finite field $\mathbb{F}$.
FUNCTIONALITY:

- **Initialize:** Upon receiving $(\mathsf{init}, \mathsf{InputS})$ and $(\mathsf{init}, \mathsf{InputR})$ from sender and receiver, sample $\Delta \leftarrow\$ \mathbb{F}$ if receiver is honest or receive $\Delta \in \mathbb{F}$ from the adversary otherwise. It stores global key Δ and send Δ to receiver, and ignores all subsequent init commands.
- **Extend:** This procedure can be run multiple times. Upon receiving $(\mathsf{extend}, \mathsf{n})$ from sender and receiver, do:
  1. If receiver is corrupted then wait for $\mathcal{A}$ to send $\mathbf{w} \in \mathbb{F}^n$; samples $\mathbf{u} \leftarrow\$ \mathbb{F}^n$ and computes $\mathbf{v} := \mathbf{w} - \Delta \cdot \mathbf{u}$.
  2. If sender is corrupted then wait for $\mathcal{A}$ to send vectors $\mathbf{u} \in \mathbb{F}^n, \mathbf{v} \in \mathbb{F}^n$ and computes $\mathbf{w} := \Delta \cdot \mathbf{u} + \mathbf{v}$.
  3. Otherwise, samples $\mathbf{u} \leftarrow\$ \mathbb{F}^n, \mathbf{v} \leftarrow\$ \mathbb{F}^n$ and computes $\mathbf{w} := \Delta \cdot \mathbf{u} + \mathbf{v}$.
- **Return:** Functionality sends $(\mathsf{OutputS}, \mathbf{u}, \mathbf{v})$ to sender and $(\mathsf{OutputR}, \Delta, \mathbf{w})$ to receiver.

4 Vector Ring-OLE and its Applications

We propose a new primitive called vector ring-OLE that allows receiver and sender to execute the batch of chosen polynomial OLE where receiver's input in each instance is the same, its ideal functionality $\mathcal{F}_{\mathsf{vrOLE}}^{m,d}$ and its construction $\Pi_{\mathsf{vrOLE}}^{m,d}$ are described in Fig. 6, Fig. 7, respectively. Our construction offers *two advantages*: (1) the de-randomization communication cost is cheaper compared to prior works, (2) faster setup phase compared to ring-OLE protocols. We leverage the efficiency of our construction to develop our main contribution—fuzzy labeled PSI.

4.1 Ideal Functionality of Vector Ring-OLE

Compared with the standard ring-OLE [8], the sender and the receiver in our construction can choose components of the OLE relation ahead of time and the operation is computed without reduction, i.e., we do not work in a quotient ring. Particularly, receiver will choose an input $u_0 \in \mathbb{F}[x]$ of degree d and sender will choose an input $\{v_i\}_{i\in[m]} \in \mathbb{F}[x]$ of degree $2d$, then receiver obtains $\{z_i\}_{i\in[m]} \in \mathbb{F}[x]$ such that $z_i = u_0 \cdot u_i + v_i \in \mathbb{F}[x]$ (degree $2d$) while sender gets $\{u_i\}_{i\in[m]} \in \mathbb{F}[x]$ that are set of random degree-d polynomials. The ideal functionality $\mathcal{F}_{\mathsf{vrOLE}}^{m,d}$ is shown in Fig. 6.

Fig. 6: $\mathcal{F}_{\mathsf{vrOLE}}^{m,d}$ in semi-honest setting.

PARAMETERS: Given a finite field $\mathbb{F}$, a polynomial ring $\mathcal{R} = \mathbb{F}[x]$, length d and instance count m, a set of $(2d+1)$ random elements $(x_j)_{j\in[2d+1]}$ over $\mathbb{F}$; the protocol is executed between two parties, a sender and a receiver.

- Receiver has an input polynomial $u_0 \neq 0$ of degree less than $d+1$ over $\mathcal{R}$.
- Sender has an input of m polynomials $(v_i)_{\in[m]} \neq 0$ of degree less than $2d+1$ over $\mathcal{R}$.

FUNCTIONALITY:

1. Waiting for inputs (InputR, u_0) and $(\mathsf{InputS}, (v_i)_{i\in[m]})$ from receiver and sender, respectively:
   - If receiver is corrupted then verify that $u_0 \in \mathcal{R}$, $u_0 \neq 0$. else abort the protocol.
   - If sender is honest, sample $(u_i)_{i\in[m]} \leftarrow\$ \mathcal{R}$ of degree d. Otherwise, sender is corrupted, wait for sender to send $(\mathsf{InputS}, (u_i)_{i\in[m]})$.
2. Compute z_i is a polynomial of degree $2d$ such that $z_i(x_j) := u_0(x_j)\cdot u_i(x_j) + v_i(x_j)$ for $i \in [m]$, $j \in [2d+1]$.
3. Output $(\mathsf{OutputS}, (u_i)_{i\in[m]})$ to sender and $(\mathsf{OutputR}, (z_i)_{i\in[m]})$ to receiver.

4.2 Vector Ring-OLE

We assume that before executing the protocol, there is a trusted third-party[3] samples randomly $2d+1$ distinct evaluation points $(x_j)_{j\in[2d+1]} \leftarrow\$ \mathbb{F}^{2d+1}$. The concept of the setup phase is widely recognized and utilized in many other related PSI works [1,3,4,23]. We then instantiate our semi-honest $\mathcal{F}_{\mathsf{vrOLE}}^{m,d}$ using $\mathcal{F}_{\mathsf{VOLE}}^{m,\mathbb{F}}$, resulting in a total communication cost of just $m(3d+1)\log|\mathbb{F}|$. The technical overview for distributing correlation is shown in the Sect. 2.1. We show how to build a simulator to interact with semi-honest adversaries by a hybrid proof. The detailed protocol and theorem for correctness and security are given in Fig. 7 and Theorem 1. See the full version [10] for the complete proof.

Theorem 1. *The protocol $\Pi_{\mathsf{vrOLE}}^{m,d}$ in Fig. 7 securely realizes the ideal functionality $\mathcal{F}_{\mathsf{vrOLE}}^{m,d}$ for the semi-honest setting and in the $\mathcal{F}_{\mathsf{VOLE}}^{m,\mathbb{F}}$-hybrid model.*

Fig. 7: $\Pi_{\mathsf{vrOLE}}^{m,d}$ from $\mathcal{F}_{\mathsf{VOLE}}^{m,\mathbb{F}}$ in semi-honest setting.

PARAMETERS AND INPUTS:

- Defines polynomial ring $\mathcal{R} = \mathbb{F}[X]$, and $2d+1$ distinct evaluation points $(x_i)_{i\in[2d+1]} \in \mathbb{F}^{2d+1}$.

[3] The setup can be reused multiple times by any number of senders and receivers.

- Receiver has a polynomial input $u_0 \in \mathcal{R}$ of degree d, sender has a set input of m polynomials $(v_i)_{i\in[m]} \in \mathcal{R}^m$ of degree $2d$.
- An instantiation of vector-OLE $\mathcal{F}_{\mathsf{VOLE}}^{m,\mathbb{F}}$.

PROTOCOL:

- **Preprocessing phase:**
  1. Sender with input (init, InputS) and receiver with input (init, InputR) invoke $\mathcal{F}_{\mathsf{VOLE}}^{m,\mathbb{F}}$ $2d+1$ times, for each time $i \in [1, 2d+1]$:
     - Sender gets $\mathbf{U}'_i \in \mathbb{F}^m$, $\mathbf{V}'_i \in \mathbb{F}^m$.
     - Receiver gets $u'_{0,i} \in \mathbb{F}$, $\mathbf{Z}'_i := u'_{0,i} \cdot \mathbf{U}'_i + \mathbf{V}'_i \in \mathbb{F}^m$.
  2. Receiver defines $\mathbf{u}'_0 := \{u'_{0,1}, \ldots, u'_{0,2d+1}\} \in \mathbb{F}^{2d+1}$, $\mathbf{Z}' \in \mathbb{F}^{m\times(2d+1)}$, sender defines $\mathbf{U}' \in \mathbb{F}^{m\times(2d+1)}$, $\mathbf{V}' \in \mathbb{F}^{m\times(2d+1)}$ such that $\mathbf{U}'_i, \mathbf{V}'_i$ and $\mathbf{Z}'_i$ are respectively columns of $\mathbf{U}', \mathbf{V}'$ and $\mathbf{Z}'$. Note that $\mathbf{Z}' := \mathbf{u}'_0 \odot \mathbf{U}' + \mathbf{V}'$ where $\odot$ is the point-wise product.
  3. From matrix $\mathbf{U}'[1, d+1] \in \mathbb{F}^{m\times(d+1)}$, sender defines the set of m degree-d polynomials $(u_i)_{i\in[m]} \in \mathcal{R}^m$ as below:
     - For each row $i \in [1, m]$ of $\mathbf{U}'[1, d+1]$, defines a degree-d polynomial u_i such that $(u_i(x_1), \ldots, u_i(x_{d+1})) = \mathbf{U}'^i[1, d+1]$.
       // $(u_i)_{i\in[m]}$ is unique and is defined by interpolation of first $(d+1)$ columns of $\mathbf{U}'$.
  4. Sender defines two new matrices $\Delta\mathbf{U}$, $\mathbf{U}$:
     - Defines a matrix $\mathbf{U} \in \mathbb{F}^{m\times d}$, such that the column $\mathbf{U}_i := \{u_1(x_{i+d+1}), \ldots, u_m(x_{i+d+1})\} \in \mathbb{F}^m$ for $i \in [1, d]$.
     - Compute a matrix $\Delta\mathbf{U} := \mathbf{U} - \mathbf{U}'[d+2, 2d+1] \in \mathbb{F}^{m\times d}$.

- **Online phase:**
  1. Sender defines a matrix $\mathbf{V} \in \mathbb{F}^{m\times(2d+1)}$ such that its columns are defined as $\mathbf{V}_i := \{v_1(x_i), \ldots, v_m(x_i)\} \in \mathbb{F}^m$ for $i \in [1, 2d+1]$.
  2. Receiver computes $2d+1$ evaluations $\mathbf{u}_0 := \{u_0(x_1), \ldots, u_0(x_{2d+1})\} \in \mathbb{F}^{2d+1}$, and defines $\Delta\mathbf{u}_0 := \mathbf{u}_0 - \mathbf{u}'_0 \in \mathbb{F}^{2d+1}$ then sends $\Delta\mathbf{u}_0$ to sender.
  3. Sender defines $\Delta\mathbf{V} := \Delta\mathbf{u}_0 \odot \mathbf{U}' + \mathbf{V} - \mathbf{V}' \in \mathbb{F}^{m\times(2d+1)}$ and sends $\Delta\mathbf{U}, \Delta\mathbf{V}$ to receiver.
     // $\Delta\mathbf{U}$ is defined in the preprocessing phase, $\mathbf{V} - \mathbf{V}'$ can be computed in preprocessing phase.
  4. Receiver defines $\mathbf{Z} \in \mathbb{F}^{m\times(2d+1)}$ as follows:
     - $\mathbf{Z}[1, d+1] = \Delta\mathbf{V}[1, d+1] + \mathbf{Z}'[1, d+1] \in \mathbb{F}^{m\times(d+1)}$.
     - $\mathbf{Z}[d+2, 2d+1] := \mathbf{u}_0[d+1, 2d+1] \odot \Delta\mathbf{U} + \Delta\mathbf{V}[d+1, 2d+1] + \mathbf{Z}'[d+1, 2d+1] \in \mathbb{F}^{m\times d}$.

     Finally, receiver defines the polynomials $z_i(x)$ of degree $2d$ by polynomial interpolation of $2d+1$ points $\{(x_j, \mathbf{Z}_{i,j})\}_{j\in[1,2d+1]}$. Note here $z_i(x) = u_0(x) \cdot u_i(x) + v_i(x)$ for $i \in [1, m]$.

4.3 Proof for Vector Ring OLE in Semi-Honest Setting

Proof (Proof of Theorem 1*).* Our proof consists of two parts, correctness and security.

Correctness. Firstly, we show that our protocol in Fig. 7 realizes the correctness of the ideal functionality $\mathcal{F}^{m,d}_{\mathsf{vrOLE}}$. In particular, we obtain $\mathcal{F}^{m,d}_{\mathsf{vrOLE}}$ with the input of receiver u_0 of degree d is the same in m instances while the sender has a set input of m polynomials $(u_i)_{i\in[m]} \in \mathcal{R}^m$ of degree d and m polynomials $(v_i)_{i\in[m]} \in \mathcal{R}^m$ of degree $2d$; in the end of protocol receiver gets $(z_i := u_0 \cdot u_i + v_i)_{i\in[m]}$, where the degree of $(z_i)_{i\in[m]}$ is $2d$.

Indeed, observe that $(u_i)_{i\in[m]}$ is defined from the first $(d+1)$ columns of matrix $\mathbf{U}'$, therefore, we do not need to de-randomize these columns and can reuse them; the matrix $\mathbf{Z} \in \mathbb{F}^{m\times(2d+1)}$ is computed in two parts, first $(d+1)$ columns and last d columns, we can formalize as:

$$
\begin{aligned}
\mathbf{Z} &= 0^{d+1}\|(\mathbf{u}_0[d+2, 2d+1] \odot \Delta\mathbf{U}) + \Delta\mathbf{V} + \mathbf{Z}' \\
&= 0^{d+1}\|(\mathbf{u}_0[d+2, 2d+1] \odot (\mathbf{U} - \mathbf{U}'[d+2, 2d+1])) \\
&\quad + (\Delta\mathbf{u}_0 \odot \mathbf{U}' + \mathbf{V} - \mathbf{V}') + (\mathbf{u}_0' \odot \mathbf{U}' + \mathbf{V}') \\
&= 0^{d+1}\|(\mathbf{u}_0[d+2, 2d+1] \odot (\mathbf{U} - \mathbf{U}'[d+2, 2d+1])) \\
&\quad + ((\mathbf{u}_0 - \mathbf{u}_0') \odot \mathbf{U}' + \mathbf{V} - \mathbf{V}') + (\mathbf{u}_0' \odot \mathbf{U}' + \mathbf{V}') \\
&= 0^{d+1}\|(\mathbf{u}_0[d+2, 2d+1] \odot (\mathbf{U} - \mathbf{U}'[d+2, 2d+1])) + \mathbf{u}_0 \odot \mathbf{U}' + \mathbf{V} \\
&= 0^{d+1}\|(\mathbf{u}_0[d+2, 2d+1] \odot \mathbf{U}) + (\mathbf{u}_0[1, d+1] \odot \mathbf{U}'[1, d+1]\|0^d) + \mathbf{V} \\
&= \mathbf{u}_0 \odot (\mathbf{U}'[1, d+1]\|\mathbf{U}) + \mathbf{V}.
\end{aligned}
$$

We recall, $\mathbf{u}_0 := \{u_0(x_1), \ldots, u_0(x_{2d+1})\} \in \mathbb{F}^{2d+1}$, and if we define $\mathbf{M} = (\mathbf{U}'[1, d+1]\|\mathbf{U}) \in \mathbb{F}^{m\times(2d+1)}$ then matrices $\mathbf{M}, \mathbf{V}, \mathbf{Z} \in \mathbb{F}^{m\times(2d+1)}$ as the column $\mathbf{M}_j$ defined by $\{u_1(x_j), u_2(x_j), \ldots, u_m(x_j)\}$, and $\mathbf{V}_j, \mathbf{Z}_j$ are defined the same way as $\mathbf{M}_j$ from the polynomials $(v_i)_{i\in[m]}$ and $(z_i)_{i\in[m]}$, we then argue that $\mathbf{Z} = \mathbf{u}_0 \odot \mathbf{U} + \mathbf{V}$. It means for row $\mathbf{Z}^i$ of matrix $\mathbf{Z}$, we have $\mathbf{Z}^i = \mathbf{u}_0 \odot \mathbf{U}^i + \mathbf{V}^i \implies \mathbf{Z}^i = (u_0(x_1)\cdot u_i(x_1) + v_i(x_1), u_0(x_2)\cdot u_i(x_2) + v_i(x_2), \ldots, u_0(x_{2d+1})\cdot u_i(x_{2d+1}) + v_i(x_{2d+1})) \in \mathbb{F}^{2d+1}$. So the polynomial z_i of degree $2d$ is well-defined by polynomial interpolation of $2d+1$ points $\{(x_j, \mathbf{Z}_{i,j})\}_{j\in[1,2d+1]}$.

Security. We prove our security in the simulation-based model by showing there exists a simulator Sim who can simulate the view of $\mathcal{A}$ in two cases.

Corrupted receiver.
- Sim emulates the $\mathcal{F}^{m,\mathbb{F}}_{\mathsf{VOLE}}$ and gets the input $\mathbf{u}_0'$ from $\mathcal{A}$. Sim samples randomly matrices $\mathbf{U}', \mathbf{V}' \leftarrow\$ \mathbb{F}^{m\times(2d+1)}$ then sends $\mathbf{Z}' := \mathbf{u}_0' \odot \mathbf{U}' + \mathbf{V}' \in \mathbb{F}^{m\times(2d+1)}$ to $\mathcal{A}$.
- Sim acts as an honest sender and receives $\Delta\mathbf{u}_0 = \mathbf{u}_0 - \mathbf{u}_0'$, Sim defines $\mathbf{u}_0 := \Delta\mathbf{u}_0 + \mathbf{u}_0'$.
- Sim defines a polynomial u_0 as the interpolation of $2d+1$ points $(x_i, \mathbf{u}_{0,i})$.
  - Sim acts as an honest sender in the real protocol.
    - Sim joins $\mathcal{F}^{m,d}_{\mathsf{vrOLE}}$ as a receiver with input u_0 then Sim gets a set of polynomials $\{z_i\}_{i\in[m]}$. Sim defines a matrix $\mathbf{Z}$ such that each row

$$\mathbf{Z}^i := (z_i(x_1), z_i(x_2), \ldots, z_i(x_{2d+1})) \in \mathbb{F}^{2d+1}.$$

* Sim defines set of degree-d polynomials $(u_i)_{i\in[m]}$ over $\mathcal{R}^m$ from $\mathbf{U}'[1, d+1]$ by interpolation using $(d+1)$ points $(x_1, \ldots, x_{d+1})$ and then defines a matrix $\mathbf{U}$ such that the column

$$\mathbf{U}_i := \{u_1(x_{d+1+i}), u_2(x_{d+1+i}), \ldots, u_m(x_{d+1+i})\} \in \mathbb{F}^m$$

for $i \in [1, d]$.
then sends a matrix $\Delta\mathbf{U} := \mathbf{U} - \mathbf{U}'[d+2, 2d+1] \in \mathbb{F}^{m\times d}$ to $\mathcal{A}$.
* Sim computes $\Delta\mathbf{V} := \mathbf{Z} - \mathbf{u}_0 \odot (0^{d+1} \| \Delta\mathbf{U}) - \mathbf{Z}' \in \mathbb{F}^{m\times(2d+1)}$. On behalf of sender, Sim sends $\Delta\mathbf{V}$ to $\mathcal{A}$.

The simulation against corrupted receiver is indistinguishable from the real protocol as following hybrids:

- Hyb 0. The same as the real protocol with an honest sender and $\mathbb{F}^{m,\mathbb{F}}_{\mathsf{VOLE}}$ is executed honestly.
- Hyb 1. Sim emulates the $\mathcal{F}^{m,\mathbb{F}}_{\mathsf{VOLE}}$ and gets the input $\mathbf{u}'_0$ from $\mathcal{A}$. Sim samples randomly matrices $\mathbf{U}', \mathbf{V}' \leftarrow\$ \mathbb{F}^{m\times(2d+1)}$ then sends $\mathbf{Z}' := \mathbf{u}'_0 \odot \mathbf{U}' + \mathbf{V}' \in \mathbb{F}^{m\times(2d+1)}$ to $\mathcal{A}$. Sim simulates the sender and receives $\Delta\mathbf{u}_0 = \mathbf{u}_0 - \mathbf{u}'_0$, Sim defines $\mathbf{u}_0 := \Delta\mathbf{u}_0 + \mathbf{u}'_0$. Sim defines a polynomial u_0 as the interpolation of $2d+1$ points $(x_i, \mathbf{u}_{0,i})$.
This hybrid is indistinguishable from the previous hybrid since the output of $\mathcal{F}^{m,\mathbb{F}}_{\mathsf{VOLE}}$ are pseudorandom in the view of $\mathcal{A}$.
- Hyb 3. Sim simulate as a sender in real protocol.
  * Sim joins $\mathcal{F}^{m,d}_{\mathsf{vrOLE}}$ as a receiver with input u_0 then Sim gets a set of polynomials $\{z_i\}_{i\in[m]}$. Sim defines a matrix $\mathbf{Z}$ such that each row

$$\mathbf{Z}^i := (z_i(x_1), z_i(x_2), \ldots, z_i(x_{2d+1})) \in \mathbb{F}^{2d+1}.$$

  * Sim defines set of degree-d polynomials $(u_i)_{i\in[m]}$ over $\mathcal{R}^m$ from $\mathbf{U}'[1, d+1]$ by interpolation using $(d+1)$ points $(x_1, \ldots, x_{d+1})$ and then defines a matrix $\mathbf{U}$ such that the column

$$\mathbf{U}_i := \{u_1(x_{d+1+i}), u_2(x_{d+1+i}), \ldots, u_m(x_{d+1+i})\} \in \mathbb{F}^m$$

  for $i \in [1, d]$.
  then sends a matrix $\Delta\mathbf{U} := \mathbf{U} - \mathbf{U}'[d+2, 2d+1] \in \mathbb{F}^{m\times d}$ to $\mathcal{A}$.
  This hybrid is indistinguishable from the previous hybrid since in real execution $\Delta\mathbf{U}$ is randomized by $\mathbf{U}'$ and $\mathbf{U}' \leftarrow\$ \mathbb{F}^{m\times(2d+1)}$ so in the view of $\mathcal{A}$, $\Delta\mathbf{U}$ is random vector.

- Hyb 4. Sim computes $\Delta\mathbf{V} := \mathbf{Z} - \mathbf{u}_0 \odot (0^{d+1} \| \Delta\mathbf{U}) - \mathbf{Z}' \in \mathbb{F}^{m\times(2d+1)}$. On behalf of sender, Sim sends $\Delta\mathbf{V}$ to $\mathcal{A}$.
This hybrid is indistinguishable from the previous hybrid. Indeed, the output of $\mathcal{A}$ is identical to the output of ideal functionality by the correctness of protocol. Moreover, $\Delta\mathbf{V}$ is randomized by $\mathbf{V}'$ which is sampled uniformly random so $\Delta\mathbf{V}$ looks random in the view of $\mathcal{A}$.
Corrupted sender.

- Sim emulates the $\mathcal{F}_{\mathsf{VOLE}}^{m,\mathbb{F}}$ and gets the input $\mathbf{U}', \mathbf{V}'$ from $\mathcal{A}$, samples $\mathbf{u}'_0 \leftarrow\$ \mathbb{F}^{2d+1}$ and defines $\mathbf{Z}' := \mathbf{u}'_0 \odot \mathbf{U}' + \mathbf{V}'$.
- Sim samples randomly a polynomial u_0 being different zero of degree d and defines $\Delta\mathbf{u}_0 = \mathbf{u}_0 + \mathbf{u}'_0$, then sends it to $\mathcal{A}$.
- Sim plays the role of receiver, and learns $\Delta\mathbf{U}, \Delta\mathbf{V}$ from $\mathcal{A}$.
  From $\Delta\mathbf{U}$, Sim defines $\mathbf{U} := \Delta\mathbf{U} + \mathbf{U}'[d+2, 2d+1] \in \mathbb{F}^{m\times d}$.
  From $\Delta\mathbf{V}$, Sim defines $\mathbf{V} := \Delta\mathbf{V} + \mathbf{V}' - \Delta\mathbf{u}_0 \odot \mathbf{U}' \in \mathbb{F}^{m\times(2d+1)}$.
- Define a matrix $\mathbf{M} := (\mathbf{U}'[1, d+1] \| \mathbf{U})$, for each row $\mathbf{M}^i, \mathbf{V}^i$ of $\mathbf{M}, \mathbf{V}$, Sim defines a polynomial u_i, v_i as the interpolation polynomial of a set of points $\{(x_j, \mathbf{M}^i[j])\}_{j\in[2d+1]}$ and $\{(x_j, \mathbf{V}^i[j])\}_{j\in[2d+1]}$ respectively.
- Sim joins $\mathcal{F}_{\mathsf{vrOLE}}^{m,d}$ as a sender with input $\{u_i, v_i\}_{i\in[m]}$ and outputs whatever $\mathcal{F}_{\mathsf{vrOLE}}^{m,d}$ outputs.

The simulation against corrupted sender is indistinguishable from the real protocol as following hybrids:

- Hyb 0. The same as the real protocol with an honest sender and $\mathbb{F}_{\mathsf{VOLE}}^{m,\mathbb{F}}$ is executed honestly.
- Hyb 1.Sim emulates the $\mathcal{F}_{\mathsf{VOLE}}^{m,\mathbb{F}}$ and gets the input $\mathbf{U}', \mathbf{V}'$ from $\mathcal{A}$, samples $\mathbf{u}'_0 \leftarrow\$ \mathbb{F}^{2d+1}$ and defines $\mathbf{Z}' := \mathbf{u}'_0 \odot \mathbf{U}' + \mathbf{V}'$.
  This hybrid is indistinguishable from the previous hybrid since the output of $\mathcal{F}_{\mathsf{VOLE}}^{m,\mathbb{F}}$ are pseudorandom in the view of $\mathcal{A}$.
- Hyb 3. Sim samples randomly a degree-d polynomial u_0 being different zero and defines $\Delta\mathbf{u}_0 = \mathbf{u}_0 - \mathbf{u}'_0$, then sends it to $\mathcal{A}$. This hybrid is indistinguishable from the previous hybrid since in real execution $\mathbf{u}_0$ is randomized by $\mathbf{u}'_0$ and $\mathbf{u}'_0 \leftarrow\$ \mathbb{F}^{2d+1}$ so in the view of $\mathcal{A}$, $\Delta\mathbf{u}_0$ is random vector.
- Hyb 4. Sim plays the role of sender, and learns $\Delta\mathbf{U}, \Delta\mathbf{V}$ from $\mathcal{A}$.
  From $\Delta\mathbf{U}$, Sim defines $\mathbf{U} := \Delta\mathbf{U} + \mathbf{U}'[d+2, 2d+1] \in \mathbb{F}^{m\times d}$.
  From $\Delta\mathbf{V}$, Sim defines $\mathbf{V} := \Delta\mathbf{V} + \mathbf{V}' - \Delta\mathbf{u}_0 \odot \mathbf{U}' \in \mathbb{F}^{m\times(2d+1)}$.
  Define a matrix $\mathbf{M} := (\mathbf{U}'[1, d+1] \| \mathbf{U})$, for each row $\mathbf{M}^i, \mathbf{V}^i$ of $\mathbf{M}, \mathbf{V}$, Sim defines a polynomial u_i, v_i as the interpolation polynomial of a set of points $\{(x_j, \mathbf{M}^i_j)\}_{j\in[2d+1]}$ and $\{(x_j, \mathbf{V}^i_i)\}_{j\in[2d+1]}$ respectively. Sim joins $\mathcal{F}_{\mathsf{vrOLE}}^{m,d}$ as a sender with input $\{u_i, v_i\}_{i\in[m]}$ and outputs whatever $\mathcal{F}_{\mathsf{vrOLE}}^{m,d}$ outputs.
  This hybrid is indistinguishable from the previous hybrid. □

4.4 Efficiency of Vector Ring-OLE

Communication. The communication complexity of our vector ring-OLE consists of the offline cost for setting up $\mathcal{F}_{\mathsf{VOLE}}^{m,\mathbb{F}}$ $(2d+1)$ times and the online cost which is primarily the de-randomizing step (sending $\Delta\mathbf{u}_0, \Delta\mathbf{U}, \Delta\mathbf{V}$). In our setting, m is significantly larger than d so the dominant communication cost is $m(3d-1)\log|\mathbb{F}|$ bits, the exact total number of online bits communicated is

$$\underbrace{(2d+1)\log|\mathbb{F}|}_{\Delta\mathbf{u}_0} + \underbrace{md\log|\mathbb{F}|}_{\Delta\mathbf{U}} + \underbrace{m(2d+1)\log|\mathbb{F}|}_{\Delta\mathbf{V}}$$

Computation. In the preprocessing phase, we consider the computation cost of the sender and the receiver (when invoking $2d+1$ instances of $\mathcal{F}_{\mathsf{VOLE}}^{m,\mathbb{F}}$) is minor since the instantiation of $\mathcal{F}_{\mathsf{VOLE}}^{m,\mathbb{F}}$ is efficient [34]. Therefore, the dominant computation cost in this phase comes from the polynomial interpolation to obtain m polynomials of degree d over $\mathbb{F}$.

In the online phase, the sender's computation is dominated by polynomial evaluation of m polynomials on $(2d+1)$ points over $\mathbb{F}$ and linear operations on vector and matrix over $\mathbb{F}^{m\times(2d+1)}$. The receiver's computation is dominated by interpolating m polynomials of degree $2d$ on $(2d+1)$ points. As long as our vector ring-OLE is not used in applications that require a large d, this is a reasonable cost as shown in our fuzzy-labeled PSI construction Sect. 5.

Comparison. In our setting, we require only $(2d+1)$ $\mathcal{F}_{\mathsf{VOLE}}^{m,\mathbb{F}}$ set up, where m is large (possibly millions) and d is small (e.g., 64). We compare with related work [14,23], and the results are given in Table 1. Specifically, we use the same mechanism as in [14] to build a batch of m chosen ring-OLE of degree-d and then compute its theoretical performance in our setting. To instantiate this construction in our setting, it requires m PCG-based ring-OLE of degree-$(2d+1)$ which can be instantiated from $2md$ $\mathcal{F}_{\mathsf{OLE}}$ by using interpolation polynomial, where $\mathcal{F}_{\mathsf{OLE}}$ can be obtained from $\mathcal{F}_{\mathsf{rOLE}}$.

Table 1. The communication of online and offline phase for several chosen ring-OLE protocol over field $\mathbb{F}$ [14,23]. All protocols have m instantiations, and we omit minor communication costs that are independent of m. We denote d as the degree of polynomial in ring-OLE correlation.

Protocol	Online	Offline	Assumption
Our vrOLE	$m(3d+1)\log\lvert\mathbb{F}\rvert$	$(2d+1)\mathcal{F}_{\mathsf{VOLE}}^{m,\mathbb{F}}$	LPN
GN19 [23]	$9md\log\lvert\mathbb{F}\rvert$	$4md\mathcal{F}_{\mathsf{OLE}}^{\mathbb{F}}$	FHE
CILO22 [14]	$m(4d+3)\log\lvert\mathbb{F}\rvert$	$2md\mathcal{F}_{\mathsf{OLE}}^{\mathbb{F}}$ $+2md\log\lvert\mathbb{F}\rvert$	Ring-LPN

5 Unbalanced Fuzzy-Labeled PSI

The primary building block of our fuzzy-labeled PSI is a threshold-labeled PSI which we describe in Sect. 5.1. Specifically, receiver and sender each have an input set, and sender additionally has a label ℓ. At the end of the protocol execution receiver receives ℓ if the intersection of their sets is greater than some threshold t. Our construction is efficient when the threshold parameter t is small ($t=O(1)$) and we show in Sect. 5.2 that it is sufficient for us to build an effective model of fuzzy PSI using masked OPRF.

5.1 Threshold-Labeled PSI from Vector Ring-OLE

Instantiation. In this section, we present a new, efficient threshold-labeled PSI which is built from our vector ring-OLE and a threshold secret sharing scheme. Receiver has an input set X and sender has an input set Y where $0 \notin Y$ and a secret label l where $|X| = |Y| = d$. At the end of the protocol, receiver learns $X \cap Y$ and l if $|X \cap Y| \geq t$ otherwise receiver learns nothing. The main idea of our protocol is that receiver and sender join the $\mathcal{F}^{1,d}_{\mathsf{vrOLE}}$ with input u_0 and (u_1, v_1), respectively, where $u_0(x) = \prod_{i=1}^{d}(x - x_i)$, u_1 is uniformly random of degree d and v_1 is a polynomial of degree $2d$ such that $v_1(y) = f(y)$ for all $y \in Y$ where f is polynomial degree of t defined by the secret label $\ell'_B = \mathsf{PRF}_k(\ell)$ from $\mathcal{F}^{d,t}_{\mathsf{TSSS}}$ $(f(0) = \ell'_B)$. By the definition of v_1, we have $v_1(x) = f(x) + \prod_{i=1}^{d}(x - y_i) \cdot R(x)$ where R is uniformly random polynomial of degree d. At the end of protocol, receiver gets a polynomial $v_0 := u_0 \cdot u_1 + v_1 = u_0 \cdot u_1 + \prod_{i=1}^{d}(x - y_i) \cdot R(x) + f(x)$ if the receiver's polynomial input being different to 0 has the degree less than d, otherwise receiver learns nothing.

To reconstruct ℓ, receiver sends $h_\ell = \mathcal{H}_1(\ell'_B)$ and $\Delta\ell = \mathcal{H}_2(\ell'_B) + \ell$ to sender. Receiver computes $V_0 := \{v_0(x_i)\}_{i \in [d]}$ and tries each combination of t elements in V_0 to recover ℓ'_A from $\mathcal{F}^{d,t}_{\mathsf{TSSS}}$. Receiver checks if $h_\ell = \mathcal{H}_1(\ell'_A)$, then recomputes $\ell = \Delta\ell - \mathcal{H}_2(\ell'_A)$ and ℓ is the correct label of sender. Since ℓ'_B is random in the view of sender (output of a PRF), the receiver learns no information about ℓ from h_ℓ and $\Delta\ell$. We show our protocol in Fig. 8, the correctness and security in Theorem 2, and the details of proof can be found in the full version [10].

Notably, it is not enough if the sender sends a digest of the label $h_\ell := \mathcal{H}(\ell)$ and then the receiver determines whether it obtained the correct label but check $h_\ell = \mathcal{H}(\ell')$, where ℓ' is the output of the reconstruction. The label domain may be small and a corrupted receiver is able to brute force the pre-image. Our construction does not have the aforementioned issue.

An alternative TLPSI instantiation that avoids expensive trial-reconstruction for a concrete parameter $t = 2$ (parameter we used for fuzzy construction) can be found in the full version [10].

Fig. 8: $\Pi^{d,t}_{\mathsf{TLPSI}}$ from $\mathcal{F}^{m,d}_{\mathsf{vrOLE}}$ and $\mathcal{F}^{d,t}_{\mathsf{TSSS}}$.

PARAMETERS:

- Receiver has input set $X \in \mathbb{F}^d$, sender has input set $Y \in \mathbb{F}^d$ and a secret label $\ell \in \mathbb{F}$ and $0 \notin Y$. The cardinality of two sets is $|X| = |Y| = d$. The threshold value is $t \leq d$.
- A vector ring-OLE $\mathcal{F}^{1,d}_{\mathsf{vrOLE}}$ followed ideal functionality of $\mathcal{F}_{\mathsf{vrOLE}}$ over $\mathbb{F}[x]$ (Fig. 6).
- A threshold Shamir's secret sharing $\mathcal{F}^{d,t}_{\mathsf{TSSS}}$ over $\mathbb{F}$.
- Collision-resistant hash functions $\mathcal{H}_1, \mathcal{H}_2 : \{0,1\}^* \to \{0,1\}^\kappa$.

PROTOCOL:

- **Preprocessing phase:**
  1. For $X = \{x_i\}_{i \in [d]}$, receiver computes $u_0(x) = \prod_{i=1}^{d}(x - x_i)$.

2. Sender samples a $\mathsf{PRF}_k : \{0,1\}^* \to \{0,1\}^\kappa$ and compute $\ell'_B = \mathsf{PRF}_k(\ell)$. For $Y = \{y_i\}_{i\in[d]}$, sender chooses a random degree -t polynomial f such that $f(0) = \ell'_B$ (f is defined by the secret label ℓ'_B from $\mathcal{F}^{d,t}_{\mathsf{TSSS}}$) then sender samples at random a degree-$2d$ polynomial $v_1(x) \in \mathbb{F}[x]$ such that $v_1(y_i) = f(y_i)$ for all $y_i \in Y$. Note that $\{v_1(y_i)\}_{i\in[d]}$ are then secret shares of ℓ'_B.

- **Online phase:**
  1. Receiver and sender invoke to $\mathcal{F}^{1,d}_{\mathsf{vrOLE}}$ with inputs (InputR, u_0) and (InputS, v_1). If $\mathcal{F}^{1,d}_{\mathsf{vrOLE}}$ aborts then aborts, otherwise sender gets $(\mathsf{OutputS}, u_1)$ and receiver gets $(\mathsf{OutputR}, v_0)$ such that $v_0 = u_0 \cdot u_1 + v_1$.
  2. Sender sends $h_\ell = \mathcal{H}_1(\ell'_B)$ and $\Delta\ell = \mathcal{H}_2(\ell'_B) + \ell$ to receiver.
  3. Receiver computes $V_0 := \{v_0(x_i)\}_{i\in[d]}$ and tries each combination of t elements in V_0 to recover ℓ'_A from $\mathcal{F}^{d,t}_{\mathsf{TSSS}}$.
  4. Receiver checks if $h_\ell = \mathcal{H}_1(\ell'_A)$, then
     - recompute $\ell = \Delta\ell - \mathcal{H}_2(\ell'_A)$ and ℓ is the correct label of sender.
     - define the set $I = \{x_i | v_0(x_i) \text{ is a correct share of } \ell\}$ is $X \cap Y$.

     Otherwise, the output is $\perp$.

Theorem 2. *Figure 8 securely realizes the ideal functionality $\mathcal{F}^{d,t}_{\mathsf{TLPSI}}$ against semi-honest adversaries in the $\mathcal{F}^{m,d}_{\mathsf{vrOLE}}$-hybrid model where $|\mathbb{F}| \geq 2^{\lambda+2\log d}$.*

5.2 Fuzzy-Labeled PSI

With the masked OPRF $\mathcal{F}_{\mathsf{mOPRF}}$ functionality, which enables oblivious subsampling and the threshold-labeled PSI $\mathcal{F}_{\mathsf{TLPSI}}$, we are ready to describe our fuzzy-labeled PSI protocol. In our setting, receiver has input $x \in \{0,1\}^d$ while sender has a set of inputs $Y := \{(y_i, \ell_i)\}_{i\in[m]}$ where $y_i \in \{0,1\}^d, \ell_i \in \mathbb{F}$ and the threshold parameter for Hamming distance is $d_k \ll d$ with TPR and TNR.

Sub-Sampling. The sub-sampling method from [33] is adapted to our work to construct fuzzy PSI from threshold-labeled PSI that works as follows. Suppose receiver has input $x \in \{0,1\}^d$ and sender has input $y_i \in \{0,1\}^d$ for $i \in [m]$ (ignoring the label for now). For every binary vector of length d the parties map it to T vectors of length d_s, where $d_s < d$. That is, $x \mapsto \{x_1, \dots, x_T\}$, $y_i \mapsto \{y_{i,1}, \dots, y_{i,T}\}$ and $|y_{i,j}| = d_s$. If x and y_i are close in Hamming distance d_k, then $|\bar{X} \cap \bar{Y}_i| \geq t$. where $\bar{X} := \{x_1, \dots, x_T\}$ and $\bar{Y}_i := \{y_{i,1}, \dots, y_{i,T}\}$

In practice, elements in $\bar{X}$ and $\bar{Y}_i$ are computed by applying x and y_i with T different masks $\{m_i\}_{i\in[T]}$, such that $\mathsf{HW}(m_i) = d_s$. Namely, $\bar{X} \leftarrow \{x \wedge m_1, \dots, x \wedge m_T\}$ and $\bar{Y}_i \leftarrow \{y \wedge m_1, \dots, y \wedge m_T\}$. Just like the work of [33], this approach inherently introduces false negative and false positives we analyze the probabilities in detail in the full version [10]. We select parameters t, T and d_s such that if $\mathsf{HW}(x \oplus y) \leq d_k$, then $(\bar{X} \cap \bar{Y}_i) \geq t$ with a low false positive rate FPR and a low false negative rate FNR (discussed in Sect. 6.2).

Masked OPRF. The sub-sampling procedure above does not discuss a concrete protocol for obtaining the masks and performing the sub-sampling. Consider the naive case where receiver and sender agree on the masks, perform OPRF on the masked inputs (to protect sender's privacy), and then use TLPSI to compute the final label. Since the sub-sampling is public, this protocol leaks the d_s sub-sampled plaintext bits of sender's input $y_i \in \{0,1\}^d$ if there is an intersection above the threshold t.

To avoid the leakage issue above, receiver and sender need to run a modified OPRF protocol, which we call masked OPRF. In masked-OPRF, the input of receiver is her original input $x \in \{0,1\}^d$ instead of the sub-sampled input. sender additionally inputs masks $\{m_j : j \in [T]\}$, where every mask has Hamming weight d_s. The output of receiver becomes $X' := \{\mathsf{PRF}_k(x \wedge m_1), \ldots, \mathsf{PRF}_k(x \wedge m_T)\}$ (without knowing the PRF key k). sender performs the same except his input is also masked: $Y_i' := \{\mathsf{PRF}_k(y_i \wedge m_1), \ldots, \mathsf{PRF}_k(y_i \wedge m_T)\}$ for $i \in [m]$. The functionality can be found in Fig. 4.

We note that the communication cost of masked OPRF is only dependent on d ($d \ll m$) since sender holds both PRF key and the set of masks, hence sender can *local* compute the masked PRF output. In addition, the instantiation of masked OPRF is straightforward if a garbled circuit based OPRF is given. Creating the masks are trivial in this setting since, if the mask is 0, the receiver (receiver) can simply set both of the evaluator's input labels to the zero-label as input to the oblivious transfer. If the mask is 1, the input labels are unchanged.

Instantiation. Our fuzzy-labeled PSI protocol consists of two steps (1) the parties run sub-sampling using masked OPRF $\mathcal{F}_{\mathsf{mOPRF}}$ to obtain X' and $\{Y_i'\}_{i\in[m]}$ and (2) using X' and $\{Y_i'\}_{i\in[m]}$ as input to the threshold-labeled PSI functionality $\mathcal{F}_{\mathsf{TLPSI}}$ to obtain labels for the corresponding matching elements, if any. Since X' and $\{Y_i'\}_{i\in[m]}$ are obtained from subsampling, if x and y_i are close then the size of intersection of X' and Y_i' are always larger than a small t, which enables us to use our TLPSI construction. We note that $\{Y_i'\}_{i\in[m]}$ is output of masked OPRF then with high probability $0 \notin Y_i'$. The protocol is described in Fig. 9, and the security proof in a semi-honest setting is given Theorem 3. The detail of proof can be found in the full version [10].

Fig. 9: Π_{FLPSI} from $\mathcal{F}^{T,t}_{\mathsf{TLPSI}}$ and $\mathcal{F}^{T}_{\mathsf{mOPRF}}$.

PARAMETERS AND INPUTS:

- Receiver has input $x \in \{0,1\}^d$ while sender has a set of inputs $Y := \{(y_i, \ell_i)\}_{i\in[m]}$ where $y_i \in \{0,1\}^d, \ell_i \in \mathbb{F}$.
- A Hamming distance with a threshold parameter $d_k \ll d$ having TPR and TNR.
- A t-out-of-T threshold-labeled PSI protocol $\mathcal{F}^{T,t}_{\mathsf{TLPSI}}$ in Fig. 8 over $\mathcal{R}$ where T is the number of sub-samples.

- A masked-OPRF $\mathcal{F}_{\mathsf{mOPRF}}$ instantiated using a pseudorandom function $\mathsf{PRF}_k(m) : \{0,1\}^\kappa \times \{0,1\}^\kappa \rightarrow \{0,1\}^\kappa$ that takes input a key $k \in \{0,1\}^\kappa$ and message $m \in \{0,1\}^\kappa$.

PROTOCOL:

1. Sender samples uniformly a PRF key k and masks $\{m_1, \ldots, m_T\}$, each mask has Hamming weight d_s where $d_s < d_k$ (see Sect. 6.2 for concrete choice of d_s).
2. Receiver and sender invoke to $\mathcal{F}_{\mathsf{mOPRF}}$ with input (InputR, x) and $(\mathsf{InputS}, k, \{m_1, \ldots, m_T\})$. At the end of the protocol, receiver obtains
$$X' := \{\mathsf{PRF}_k(x \wedge m_1), \ldots, \mathsf{PRF}_k(x \wedge m_T)\}.$$
3. Sender executes PRF on his input to obtain
$$\{Y_i' := \{\mathsf{PRF}_k(y_i \wedge m_1), \ldots, \mathsf{PRF}_k(y_i \wedge m_T)\} : i \in [m]\}.$$
4. Add a tweak where receiver's input to $\mathcal{F}_{\mathsf{TLPSI}}^{T,t}$ becomes $X' := \{X_1' \oplus 1, X_2' \oplus 2, \ldots, X_T' \oplus T\}$ and sender's input $(Y_i')_{i \in [m]}$ is tweaked in the same way.
5. For $i \in [m]$, receiver inputs (InputR, X') and sender inputs $(\mathsf{InputS}, Y_i', \ell_i)$ to $\mathcal{F}_{\mathsf{TLPSI}}^{T,t}$ then:
   - Receiver obtains ℓ_i if $|X' \cap Y_i'| \geq t$,
   - Otherwise receiver learns $\perp$.

   // need only one instance of $\mathcal{F}_{\mathsf{vrOLE}}^{m,T}$ to instantiate m times of $\mathcal{F}_{\mathsf{TLPSI}}^{T,t}$.
6. The leakage profile is $\mathcal{L} := \{\mathcal{L}_{\mathbf{R}}, \mathcal{L}_{\mathbf{S}}\}$ such that $\mathcal{L}_{\mathbf{R}} = \{X' \cap Y_i' : |X' \cap Y_i'| \geq t\}_{i \in [m]}$ and $\mathcal{L}_{\mathbf{S}} = \perp$.

A subtle issue may occur depending on the sub-sampling parameters. Specifically, there might be duplicates in X', or one or more Y_i', especially when T is large or d_s is small. In the extreme case, if $d_s = 1$, then the probability that two sub-samples will match is 1/2. This can be resolved by adding a tweak to every output of the PRF, which we specify in step 4. of Fig. 9. For more details about leakage profile $\mathcal{L}$, in our construction, sender learns nothing $\mathcal{L}_{\mathsf{S}} = \perp$ and receiver learns the label ℓ_i (actually output) with overwhelming probability (at least TPR) if $\mathsf{HW}(x \oplus y_i) < t$, receiver also learns extra information $\mathcal{L}_{\mathsf{R}}$, which is the set of (obviously) encrypted sub-samplings that matched. However, we emphasize that this leakage to the receiver is strictly less than the receiver learning the matching entries of the sender's database, because of the masked OPRF, which helps to obfuscate the actual sender's database.

Theorem 3. *The protocol with the leakage profile $\mathcal{L}$ in Fig. 9 is correct and securely realizes the ideal functionality $\mathcal{F}_{\mathsf{FLPSI}}$ against a semi-honest setting in the $\{\mathcal{F}_{\mathsf{TLPSI}}^{T,t}, \mathcal{F}_{\mathsf{mOPRF}}^{T}\}$-hybrid models.*

6 Evaluation

6.1 Theoretical Comparison

We compare our fuzzy-labeled PSI with the state-of-the-art protocol [33] which builds an efficient threshold set-matching protocol from leveled homomorphic encryption, garbled circuits (GC), and t-out-of-T secret sharing. However, we found that the parameter selection of [33] somewhat fails to meet the functionality requirement, which we discuss in detail in the full version [10]. Since our scheme is based on vector OLE, we also compare our work in terms of performance with the work of Chakraborti et al. [12] that uses OLE as well, even though their work does not support labels. In particular, [12] presents a fuzzy PSI protocol for Hamming distance based on additively homomorphic encryption and vector oblivious linear evaluation (VOLE).

Additionally, we give an asymptotic comparison with PCG-based ring OLE PSI [14] and fuzzy PSIs [5,19,21] that support different distance metrics than us. The protocols described in [14,21] do not support labels and [5,19] supports labels but it performs well due to its reliance on ElGamal encryption and additive homomorphic encryption (AHE). While [14] uses ring-OLE instead of VOLE and then obtains efficient PSI protocol variants; Garimella, Rosulek and Singh [21] supports distance L_∞ and L_1 with a large receiver's computation, later [5] overcomes this limit by proposing fuzzy PSI based on DDH that can support L_∞ and L_p for $p \in [1, \infty)$, however the receiver's computation and communication cost is still $O(2^d \cdot N)$ leaving a poor performance when dimension d is large.

The asymptotic communication comparison is shown in Table 2. We ignore the cost of setting up masked OPRF since all protocols uses the same masked OPRF and the cost for this is independent to the dataset size. The dominant term $O(T\lambda M)$ in our online cost comes from de-randomizing VOLE to obtain vector ring-OLE over the field $\mathbb{F}$ where $|\mathbb{F}| \geq 2^{\lambda + 2\log d}$. Our offline communication cost is $O(\kappa)$ as the cost for generating VOLE (omitted the minor logarithmic on length of VOLE term). Compared to [12,33], our online communication cost does not depend on the computational security parameter κ. We support an arbitrarily large label size which equals the bit-length of field $\mathbb{F}$ and in the same setting, our FPR and FNR are both negligible.

6.2 Concrete Comparison

Implementation. We provide an open source implementation[4] of our fuzzy PSI protocol using the swanky [18] framework in the Rust programming language.

Our masked OPRF is based on evaluating fixed-key AES-128 using garbled circuits. The specific instantiation of the masked OPRF does not affect the communication or computation cost significantly since the cost does not depend on the size of sender's database m. For sub-sampling, the specific parameters we use are $d = 128$, $T = 64$, $d_s = 14$ and $t = 2$ which achieves a FPR of less than 7×10^{-6} and a FNR of less than 2×10^{-16} for $d_k \leq 20$.

[4] https://github.com/kc1212/flash-psi.

Next, we perform semi-honest threshold labeled PSI (Fig. 8), which we implement using VOLE in $\mathbb{F}_p$ where $p = 2^{61} - 1$. This is possible since we can simply truncate the mOPRF output to 61 bits. Note that this field size is much higher than what is used in Uzun et al. [33], which is only 23 bits due to their FHE parameterization[5]. The effect of truncation on the FPR in our scheme is negligible and the statement above remains true. Together, our parameters guarantee $\kappa = 128$ and $\lambda = 40$.

Table 2. We use M and N to denote the input sizes of the sender and the receiver, respectively, where $M \gg N$. T is number of sub-sampling vectors, λ, κ are statistical and computational parameters. For HE-based protocols [12,33] We use our existing notation except c and B are HE parameters for the number of slots and the number of partitions, respectively. Logarithmic terms are hidden in $\tilde{O}$. For [5,19,21], sender and receiver's input are hyperballs of radius δ with dimension $d \ll \kappa$, we cast their setting in L_1 distance while others are in Hamming distance.

Protocol	Communication	Technique	Distance	Label
[33] online [33] offline	$\tilde{O}(\kappa \cdot \frac{MT}{cB})$ $\tilde{O}(\kappa)$	HE	Hamming (dim. κ)	not support
[14] online [14] offline	$O(\lambda M)$ $O(\lambda M)$	ring-OLE	✗	✗
[21]	$O(\delta 4^d N + (2^d/d)M)$ [a]	OT	L_1 (dim. d)	✗
[12] online [12] offline	$O(T\kappa M)$ $O(\kappa)$	AHE, OLE	Hamming (dim. κ)	✗
[5]	$O(\delta 2^d dN + \delta M)^b$	DDH	L_1 (dim. d)	yes
[19]	$O(d^2 M + \delta dN)$	AHE DDH	Hamming (dim. d)	yes
ours online ours offline	$O(T\lambda M)$ $O(\kappa)$	VOLE	Hamming (dim. κ)	yes with size $\log_2 \lvert\mathbb{F}\rvert$

[a] The overhead over L_1 is $2^d/d$ larger than over L_∞ so we take the cost over L_∞ for setting when the receiver's points are distance $> 4\delta$ apart and factor $2^d/d$ times.
[b] The receiver's points are distance $> 2\delta(d+1)$ apart.

Performance. All the experiments are performed on GNU/Linux machines running on Intel(R) Core(TM) i9-9900 CPU @ 3.10GHz. The end-to-end latency (on LAN) and communication costs can be found in Table 3. Similar to Uzun

[5] From our understanding, the parameters used in Uzun et al. [33] cannot support labels. See the full version [10] for details.

et al. [33], we consider the steps that do not depend on the receiver input to be in the preprocessing step. This includes generating the VOLE correlations, garbling the AES-128 circuit, and so on. Our protocol has slightly better end-to-end latency while using less than 30% of their communication and supporting a much higher label size at the same time. We remark that the protocol from [12] has similar performance characteristics as our protocol but it does not support labels. Note that since neither work has an open source implementation, we only compare with values reported in the papers.

Table 3. End-to-end latency and communication cost of our fuzzy PSI protocol on a single thread (Fig. 9), where m is the set size of sender.

m	end-to-end latency (s)			communication (MB)		
	ours	[33]	[12]	ours	[33]	[12]
10, 000	1.69	2.12	2.00	15.5	72	25.8
100, 000	16.5	17.8	11.0	153	528	220
1, 000, 000	167	189	130	1533	2124	1504

Acknowledgment. Dung Bui is supported by the funding from the European Union's Horizon Europe research and innovation programme under the project "Quantum Security Networks Partnership" (QSNP, grant agreement No 101114043). This work was done partially when both authors were at COSIC, KU Leuven (Belgium).

References

1. Alamati, N., Branco, P., Döttling, N., Garg, S., Hajiabadi, M., Pu, S.: Laconic private set intersection and applications. In: Nissim, K., Waters, B. (eds.) TCC 2021. LNCS, vol. 13044, pp. 94–125. Springer, Cham (2021). https://doi.org/10.1007/978-3-030-90456-2_4
2. Applebaum, B., Damgård, I., Ishai, Y., Nielsen, M., Zichron, L.: Secure arithmetic computation with constant computational overhead. In: Katz, J., Shacham, H. (eds.) CRYPTO 2017. LNCS, vol. 10401, pp. 223–254. Springer, Cham (2017). https://doi.org/10.1007/978-3-319-63688-7_8
3. Aranha, D.F., Lin, C., Orlandi, C., Simkin, M.: Laconic private set-intersection from pairings. In: Yin et al. [36], pp. 111–124. https://doi.org/10.1145/3548606.3560642
4. Ateniese, G., De Cristofaro, E., Tsudik, G.: (If) size matters: size-hiding private set intersection. In: Catalano, D., Fazio, N., Gennaro, R., Nicolosi, A. (eds.) PKC 2011. LNCS, vol. 6571, pp. 156–173. Springer, Heidelberg (2011). https://doi.org/10.1007/978-3-642-19379-8_10
5. van Baarsen, A., Pu, S.: Fuzzy private set intersection with large hyperballs. Cryptology ePrint Archive, Paper 2024/330 (2024). https://eprint.iacr.org/2024/330

6. Boyle, E., et al.: Efficient two-round OT extension and silent non-interactive secure computation. In: Cavallaro, L., Kinder, J., Wang, X., Katz, J. (eds.) ACM CCS 2019, pp. 291–308. ACM Press (2019).https://doi.org/10.1145/3319535.3354255
7. Boyle, E., Couteau, G., Gilboa, N., Ishai, Y., Kohl, L., Scholl, P.: Efficient pseudorandom correlation generators: silent OT extension and more. In: Boldyreva, A., Micciancio, D. (eds.) CRYPTO 2019. LNCS, vol. 11694, pp. 489–518. Springer, Cham (2019). https://doi.org/10.1007/978-3-030-26954-8_16
8. Boyle, E., Couteau, G., Gilboa, N., Ishai, Y., Kohl, L., Scholl, P.: Efficient pseudorandom correlation generators from ring-LPN. In: Micciancio, D., Ristenpart, T. (eds.) CRYPTO 2020. LNCS, vol. 12171, pp. 387–416. Springer, Cham (2020). https://doi.org/10.1007/978-3-030-56880-1_14
9. Boyle, E., Gilboa, N., Ishai, Y.: Function secret sharing. In: Oswald, E., Fischlin, M. (eds.) EUROCRYPT 2015. LNCS, vol. 9057, pp. 337–367. Springer, Heidelberg (2015). https://doi.org/10.1007/978-3-662-46803-6_12
10. Bui, D., Cong, K.: Efficient fuzzy labeled PSI from vector ring-OLE. Cryptology ePrint Archive, Paper 2025/1470 (2025). https://eprint.iacr.org/2025/1470
11. Bui, D., Couteau, G.: Improved private set intersection for sets with small entries. In: Boldyreva, A., Kolesnikov, V. (eds.) PKC 2023, Part II. LNCS, vol. 13941, pp. 190–220. Springer, Heidelberg (2023). https://doi.org/10.1007/978-3-031-31371-4_7
12. Chakraborti, A., Fanti, G., Reiter, M.K.: Distance-aware private set intersection. In: 32nd USENIX Security Symposium (USENIX Security 2023), pp. 319–336. USENIX Association, Anaheim, CA (2023)
13. Chen, H., Huang, Z., Laine, K., Rindal, P.: Labeled PSI from fully homomorphic encryption with malicious security. In: Lie, D., Mannan, M., Backes, M., Wang, X. (eds.) ACM CCS 2018, pp. 1223–1237. ACM Press (2018). https://doi.org/10.1145/3243734.3243836
14. Chongchitmate, W., Ishai, Y., Lu, S., Ostrovsky, R.: PSI from ring-OLE. In: Yin et al. [36], pp. 531–545. https://doi.org/10.1145/3548606.3559378
15. Cong, K., Das, D., Park, J., Pereira, H.V.L.: SortingHat: efficient private decision tree evaluation via homomorphic encryption and transciphering. In: Yin et al. [36], pp. 563–577. https://doi.org/10.1145/3548606.3560702
16. Cong, K., et al.: Labeled PSI from homomorphic encryption with reduced computation and communication. In: Vigna, G., Shi, E. (eds.) ACM CCS 2021, pp. 1135–1150. ACM Press (2021). https://doi.org/10.1145/3460120.3484760
17. Freedman, M.J., Nissim, K., Pinkas, B.: Efficient private matching and set intersection. In: Cachin, C., Camenisch, J.L. (eds.) EUROCRYPT 2004. LNCS, vol. 3027, pp. 1–19. Springer, Heidelberg (2004). https://doi.org/10.1007/978-3-540-24676-3_1
18. Galois, Inc.: swanky: A suite of rust libraries for secure computation (2019). https://github.com/GaloisInc/swanky
19. Gao, Y., Qi, L., Liu, X., Luo, Y., Wang, L.: Efficient fuzzy private set intersection from fuzzy mapping. In: Advances in Cryptology – ASIACRYPT 2024: 30th International Conference on the Theory and Application of Cryptology and Information Security, Kolkata, India, 9–13 December 2024, Proceedings, Part VI, pp. 36–68. Springer, Heidelberg (2024). https://doi.org/10.1007/978-981-96-0938-3_2
20. Garimella, G., Goff, B., Miao, P.: Computation efficient structure aware PSI from incremental function secret sharing. Cryptology ePrint Archive, Paper 2024/842 (2024). https://eprint.iacr.org/2024/842

21. Garimella, G., Rosulek, M., Singh, J.: Structure-aware private set intersection, with applications to fuzzy matching. In: Dodis, Y., Shrimpton, T. (eds.) CRYPTO 2022, Part I. LNCS, vol. 13507, pp. 323–352. Springer, Heidelberg (2022). https://doi.org/10.1007/978-3-031-15802-5_12
22. Garimella, G., Rosulek, M., Singh, J.: Malicious secure, structure-aware private set intersection. In: Handschuh, H., Lysyanskaya, A. (eds.) CRYPTO 2023, Part I. LNCS, vol. 14081, pp. 577–610. Springer, Heidelberg (2023). https://doi.org/10.1007/978-3-031-38557-5_19
23. Ghosh, S., Nilges, T.: An algebraic approach to maliciously secure private set intersection. In: Ishai, Y., Rijmen, V. (eds.) EUROCRYPT 2019. LNCS, vol. 11478, pp. 154–185. Springer, Cham (2019). https://doi.org/10.1007/978-3-030-17659-4_6
24. Hallgren, P.A., Orlandi, C., Sabelfeld, A.: PrivatePool: privacy-preserving ridesharing. In: Köpf, B., Chong, S. (eds.) CSF 2017 Computer Security Foundations Symposium, pp. 276–291. IEEE Computer Society Press (2017). https://doi.org/10.1109/CSF.2017.24
25. Huberman, B.A., Franklin, M., Hogg, T.: Enhancing privacy and trust in electronic communities. In: Proceedings of the 1st ACM Conference on Electronic Commerce, EC 1999, pp. 78–86. Association for Computing Machinery, New York (1999). https://doi.org/10.1145/336992.337012
26. Ion, M., et al.: On deploying secure computing commercially: private intersection-sum protocols and their business applications. Cryptology ePrint Archive, Report 2019/723 (2019). https://eprint.iacr.org/2019/723
27. Kales, D., Rechberger, C., Schneider, T., Senker, M., Weinert, C.: Mobile private contact discovery at scale. In: Heninger, N., Traynor, P. (eds.) USENIX Security 2019, pp. 1447–1464. USENIX Association (2019)
28. Liu, H., Wang, X., Yang, K., Yu, Y.: The hardness of LPN over any integer ring and field for PCG applications. Cryptology ePrint Archive, Report 2022/712 (2022). https://eprint.iacr.org/2022/712
29. Pinkas, B., Rosulek, M., Trieu, N., Yanai, A.: PSI from PaXoS: fast, malicious private set intersection. In: Canteaut, A., Ishai, Y. (eds.) EUROCRYPT 2020. LNCS, vol. 12106, pp. 739–767. Springer, Cham (2020). https://doi.org/10.1007/978-3-030-45724-2_25
30. Pinkas, B., Schneider, T., Smart, N.P., Williams, S.C.: Secure two-party computation is practical. In: Matsui, M. (ed.) ASIACRYPT 2009. LNCS, vol. 5912, pp. 250–267. Springer, Heidelberg (2009). https://doi.org/10.1007/978-3-642-10366-7_15
31. Raghuraman, S., Rindal, P.: Blazing fast PSI from improved OKVS and subfield VOLE. In: Yin et al. [36], pp. 2505–2517. https://doi.org/10.1145/3548606.3560658
32. Rindal, P., Schoppmann, P.: VOLE-PSI: fast OPRF and circuit-PSI from vector-OLE. In: Canteaut, A., Standaert, F.-X. (eds.) EUROCRYPT 2021. LNCS, vol. 12697, pp. 901–930. Springer, Cham (2021). https://doi.org/10.1007/978-3-030-77886-6_31
33. Uzun, E., Chung, S.P., Kolesnikov, V., Boldyreva, A., Lee, W.: Fuzzy labeled private set intersection with applications to private real-time biometric search. In: Bailey, M., Greenstadt, R. (eds.) USENIX Security 2021, pp. 911–928. USENIX Association (2021)
34. Weng, C., Yang, K., Katz, J., Wang, X.: Wolverine: fast, scalable, and communication-efficient zero-knowledge proofs for boolean and arithmetic circuits. In: 2021 IEEE Symposium on Security and Privacy, pp. 1074–1091. IEEE Computer Society Press (2021). https://doi.org/10.1109/SP40001.2021.00056

35. Yao, A.C.C.: How to generate and exchange secrets (extended abstract). In: 27th FOCS, pp. 162–167. IEEE Computer Society Press (1986). https://doi.org/10.1109/SFCS.1986.25
36. Yin, H., Stavrou, A., Cremers, C., Shi, E. (eds.): ACM CCS 2022. ACM Press (2022)

Efficient Three-Input and Four-Input AND Protocols Using Playing Cards with Partial-Open Actions

Yoshiaki Honda[1] and Kazumasa Shinagawa[2,3](✉)

[1] Ibaraki University, Hitachi, Japan
[2] University of Tsukuba, Tsukuba, Japan
shinagawa@cs.tsukuba.ac.jp
[3] National Institute of Advanced Industrial Science and Technology, Tokyo, Japan

Abstract. Card-based protocols are cryptographic protocols that perform secure computations using a physical deck of playing cards. In this paper, we focus on card-based protocols that operate with standard commercially available playing cards. A partial-open action is an operation that reveals only a specific portion of a face-down playing card. In 2022, Miyahara and Mizuki proposed a four-card two-input AND protocol using partial-open actions, which requires only a single random cut. In this paper, we extend this line of research by presenting a six-card three-input AND protocol requiring two random cuts and an eight-card four-input AND protocol requiring three random cuts using partial-open actions.

Keywords: Card-based cryptography · Secure computation · Partial-open action · AND protocol

1 Introduction

Secure computation is a cryptographic technique that allows parties to compute a function over private inputs while revealing only the output. Card-based cryptography [2,3,14] is a research field that realizes secure computation using a deck of physical cards. In card-based cryptography, a pair of face-down cards following an encoding rule is called a *commitment*. Given a sequence of commitments to $x_1, x_2, \ldots, x_n \in \{0, 1\}$, a card-based protocol publicly reveals the output value $f(x_1, x_2, \ldots, x_n)$ at the end of the protocol.

Among various functions, the AND function $x_1 \wedge x_2 \wedge \cdots \wedge x_n$ is considered to be the most basic Boolean function. Indeed, since an AND protocol is an important component for constructing a protocol for general functions [18], improving the efficiency of AND protocols will also improve the efficiency of protocols for general functions.

In 1989, den Boer [2] designed a two-input AND protocol using five cards of a *two-colored deck*, which consists of cards with two different face colors [♣] and [♡], and identical backs [?]. This protocol is considered to be extremely efficient in terms of shuffling operations since it uses only one *random cut*, which is a shuffle of a random cyclic shift. In 2012, Mizuki, Kumamoto, and Sone [13] designed a two-input AND

Y. Kim et al. (Eds.): CANS 2025, LNCS 16351, pp. 199–212, 2026.
https://doi.org/10.1007/978-981-95-4434-9_9

protocol using four cards of a two-colored deck, which reduces the number of cards from five to four. These protocols use two-colored decks, but since two-colored decks are custom-made, there is also active research into constructing protocols using the standard deck of playing cards, which is commercially available.

In 2022, Miyahara and Mizuki [10] introduced a *half-open action*, which reveals only the suit of a face-down card of the standard deck. Using the half-open actions, they designed a two-input AND protocol using four cards of the standard deck. Their protocol achieves exceptional efficiency because it requires no additional cards beyond the input commitments, and uses only a *random cut* as its shuffle operation.

Can we construct a $2n$-card n-input AND protocol using only random cuts for $n \geq 3$? Note that their two-input AND protocol reveals the output value, so it cannot be used directly to construct an AND protocol with three or more inputs.

1.1 Our Contribution

In this paper, we construct three- and four-input AND protocols using a *partial-open action*, which is introduced by the authors [4] as a generalization of the half-open action. Our three-input AND protocol uses six cards of the standard deck with two random cuts. Our four-input AND protocol uses eight cards of the standard deck with three random cuts. By combining the Miyahara–Mizuki's AND protocol, we have obtained a $2n$-card n-input AND protocol with $n-1$ random cuts for $2 \leq n \leq 4$. In this sense, our protocols can be seen as a natural generalization of the Miyahara–Mizuki's AND protocol.

1.2 Related Work

Niemi and Renvall [17] pioneered protocols using the standard deck. Mizuki [12] later developed various protocols using the standard deck.

A card-based protocol is said to be *non-committed-format* if it publicly reveals the output value at the end of the protocol. Conversely, a protocol is said to be *committed-format* if it outputs a commitment to the result value. In this paper, we study non-committed-format AND protocols. Generally, non-committed-format protocols are more efficient than committed-format protocols.

Many previous papers have addressed AND protocols [1–3, 5–9, 11, 13, 15–17, 19–21]. However, most of these papers study two-input AND protocols. In 2016, Mizuki [11] designed a $2n$-card n-input AND protocol. In 2021, Isuzugawa et al. [5] designed a $2n$-card n-input AND protocol using two shuffles. Unlike our protocols, these protocols use shuffling operations that are different from random cuts.

2 Preliminaries

In this section, we introduce the terminology and operations in our protocols.

2.1 Commitments

Let $\boxed{i}$ and $\boxed{j}$ be two cards such that $i < j$. A bit $x \in \{0, 1\}$ can be encoded by the pair $\boxed{i}\,\boxed{j} = 0$ and $\boxed{j}\,\boxed{i} = 1$. A pair of face-down cards that encode x in this way is called a *commitment to* x, denoted by $[x]^{\{i,j\}}$.

Table 1. Relationship between disclosure positions and results

The position	A	2	3	4	5	6	7	8	9	10
(a)	♡	♡	♡	♡	♡	♡	♡	♡	♡	♡
(b)						♡	♡	♡		
(c)		♡	♡							
(d)	♡		♡		♡				♡	

2.2 Random Cut

A *random cut* is a shuffling operation that performs a uniformly random cyclic permutation on a sequence of cards. For a sequence of n cards, a random cut draws a permutation σ from the cyclic group $\langle(1, 2, \ldots, n)\rangle$ uniformly at random and then applies σ to the sequence of cards. A random cut can be seen as a probabilistic function that takes a sequence of cards and outputs a new sequence of cards. We denoted the application of a random cut to a sequence of cards Γ by $\langle\Gamma\rangle$. For example, a random cut for a sequence of four face-down cards is shown as follows:

$$\left\langle \overset{1}{\boxed{?}}\,\overset{2}{\boxed{?}}\,\overset{3}{\boxed{?}}\,\overset{4}{\boxed{?}} \right\rangle \rightarrow \begin{cases} \overset{1}{\boxed{?}}\,\overset{2}{\boxed{?}}\,\overset{3}{\boxed{?}}\,\overset{4}{\boxed{?}} & \text{with probability } 1/4; \\ \overset{2}{\boxed{?}}\,\overset{3}{\boxed{?}}\,\overset{4}{\boxed{?}}\,\overset{1}{\boxed{?}} & \text{with probability } 1/4; \\ \overset{3}{\boxed{?}}\,\overset{4}{\boxed{?}}\,\overset{1}{\boxed{?}}\,\overset{2}{\boxed{?}} & \text{with probability } 1/4; \\ \overset{4}{\boxed{?}}\,\overset{1}{\boxed{?}}\,\overset{2}{\boxed{?}}\,\overset{3}{\boxed{?}} & \text{with probability } 1/4. \end{cases}$$

2.3 Partial-Open Action

A *partial-open action* reveals only a part of the card's face instead of its entire face. Miyahara and Mizuki [10] introduced a *half-open action*, which is a suit-only partial-open action, which was generalized to arbitrary positions by the authors [4].

Figure 1 illustrates several positions for partial-open actions. Table 1 summarizes the results. Position (a) reveals only the suit, i.e., a half-open action. Positions (b), (c), and (d) reveal the suit in the left, upper-middle, and center, respectively.

The result of a partial-open action is denoted as ♡ if the suit is revealed, and as $\perp$ otherwise. For example, applying partial-open actions to the first three of five cards and observing a heart on the third card is denoted by:

$$\boxed{?}\,\boxed{?}\,\boxed{?}\,\boxed{?}\,\boxed{?} \rightarrow \boxed{\perp}\,\boxed{\perp}\,\boxed{\heartsuit}\,\boxed{?}\,\boxed{?}.$$

A partial-open action can be easily implemented using a physical cover. The cover is a sheet of paper with a hole at the desired position. For a face-down card, we first place the cover beneath the card and then flip them together. This allows us to see whether

Fig. 1. The positions revealed by the partial-open action.

the suit appears at the position of the hole. The procedure reveals no information other than whether the suit exists at that position.

2.4 Base Conversion Protocol

Honda and Shinagawa [4] proposed a four-card base conversion protocol using a random cut and a partial-open action. Let $\boxed{1}\boxed{2}\boxed{3}\boxed{4}$ be cards for executing the protocol. Then these cards must satisfy the following condition for partial-open actions:

– A partial-open action determines whether a given face-down card is whether $\boxed{1}\boxed{2}$ or $\boxed{3}\boxed{4}$. Alternatively, it is also sufficient to distinguish whether a face-down card is $\boxed{1}$ or $\boxed{2}$ or $\boxed{3}\boxed{4}$.

The protocol proceeds as follows:

1. Arrange the cards as:

$$\underbrace{\boxed{?}\boxed{?}}_{[a]^{\{1,2\}}}\boxed{3}\boxed{4}.$$

2. Turn the face-up cards face-down and swap the middle two cards as follows:

$$\boxed{?}\boxed{?}\boxed{?}\boxed{?}$$
$$\boxed{?}\boxed{?}\boxed{?}\boxed{?}$$

3. Apply a random cut:

$$\left\langle \boxed{?}\boxed{?}\boxed{?}\boxed{?} \right\rangle.$$

4. Apply the partial-open to determine whether the first card is $\boxed{1}\boxed{2}$ or otherwise:

$$\boxed{?}\boxed{?}\boxed{?}\boxed{?} \rightarrow \begin{cases} \boxed{1}\boxed{?}\boxed{?}\boxed{?}; \\ \boxed{2}\boxed{?}\boxed{?}\boxed{?}; \\ \boxed{\perp}\boxed{?}\boxed{?}\boxed{?}. \end{cases}$$

5. If it is $\boxed{1}$ or $\boxed{2}$, open the first and third cards as follows:

$$\boxed{1}\boxed{?}\boxed{2}\boxed{?} \text{ or } \boxed{2}\boxed{?}\boxed{1}\boxed{?}.$$

   Otherwise, open the second and fourth as follows:

$$\boxed{?}\boxed{1}\boxed{?}\boxed{2} \text{ or } \boxed{?}\boxed{2}\boxed{?}\boxed{1}.$$

6. Shift the sequence cyclically so that $\boxed{1}$ appears at the leftmost position as follows:

$$\boxed{1}\boxed{?}\boxed{2}\boxed{?}.$$

7. Swap the center cards and output the right two cards as the result:

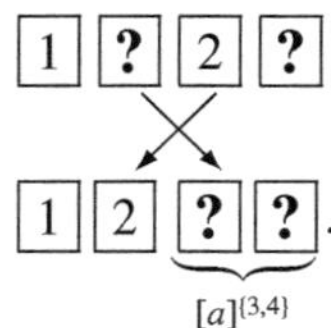

In general, protocols with partial-open actions require cards that are suitable for the conditions of partial-open actions used in the protocol. In the base conversion protocol, examples of cards for the protocol are shown as follows:

$$\boxed{1}\boxed{2}\boxed{3}\boxed{4} = \begin{cases} \boxed{A^{\clubsuit}}\boxed{2^{\clubsuit}}\boxed{3^{\heartsuit}}\boxed{4^{\heartsuit}}; \\ \boxed{A^{\clubsuit}}\boxed{2^{\spadesuit}}\boxed{3^{\heartsuit}}\boxed{4^{\heartsuit}}; \\ \boxed{7^{\clubsuit}}\boxed{9^{\diamondsuit}}\boxed{5^{\spadesuit}}\boxed{6^{\spadesuit}}. \end{cases}$$

The protocol works as long as the suits of $\boxed{3}$ and $\boxed{4}$ are the same and different from the suits of $\boxed{1}$ and $\boxed{2}$, which can be determined by half-open actions.

3 Existing Two-Input AND Protocol

We present the two-input AND protocol proposed by Miyahara–Mizuki [10], which uses one random cut and the half-open action. This protocol uses four cards $\boxed{3^{\clubsuit}}\boxed{9^{\heartsuit}}\boxed{3^{\heartsuit}}\boxed{9^{\clubsuit}}$ and takes $[a]^{\{\clubsuit 3, \heartsuit 9\}}$ and $[b]^{\{\heartsuit 3, \clubsuit 9\}}$ as the input commitments.

The protocol proceeds as follows:

1. Input two commitments as follows:

$$\underbrace{\boxed{?}\,\boxed{?}}_{[a]^{\{\clubsuit 3,\heartsuit 9\}}}\ \underbrace{\boxed{?}\,\boxed{?}}_{[b]^{\{\heartsuit 3,\clubsuit 9\}}}.$$

2. Apply a random cut:

$$\left\langle \boxed{?}\,\boxed{?}\,\boxed{?}\,\boxed{?} \right\rangle.$$

3. Open the first card:

$$\boxed{?}\,\boxed{?}\,\boxed{?}\,\boxed{?} \rightarrow \begin{cases} \boxed{3^{\clubsuit}}\,\boxed{?}\,\boxed{?}\,\boxed{?}\,; \\ \boxed{9^{\heartsuit}}\,\boxed{?}\,\boxed{?}\,\boxed{?}\,; \\ \boxed{3^{\heartsuit}}\,\boxed{?}\,\boxed{?}\,\boxed{?}\,; \\ \boxed{9^{\clubsuit}}\,\boxed{?}\,\boxed{?}\,\boxed{?}\,. \end{cases}$$

   (a) If it is either $\boxed{3^{\clubsuit}}$ or $\boxed{3^{\heartsuit}}$, apply the half-open action to the second card:

$$\begin{cases} \boxed{3^{\clubsuit}}\,\boxed{\clubsuit}\,\boxed{?}\,\boxed{?}\,; \\ \boxed{3^{\clubsuit}}\,\boxed{\heartsuit}\,\boxed{?}\,\boxed{?}\,; \\ \boxed{3^{\heartsuit}}\,\boxed{\clubsuit}\,\boxed{?}\,\boxed{?}\,; \\ \boxed{3^{\heartsuit}}\,\boxed{\heartsuit}\,\boxed{?}\,\boxed{?}\,. \end{cases}$$

   (b) If it is either $\boxed{9^{\clubsuit}}$ or $\boxed{9^{\heartsuit}}$, apply the half-open action to the fourth card:

$$\begin{cases} \boxed{9^{\clubsuit}}\,\boxed{?}\,\boxed{?}\,\boxed{\clubsuit}\,; \\ \boxed{9^{\clubsuit}}\,\boxed{?}\,\boxed{?}\,\boxed{\heartsuit}\,; \\ \boxed{9^{\heartsuit}}\,\boxed{?}\,\boxed{?}\,\boxed{\clubsuit}\,; \\ \boxed{9^{\heartsuit}}\,\boxed{?}\,\boxed{?}\,\boxed{\heartsuit}\,. \end{cases}$$

4. If the suits of the opened cards are the same, output 1; otherwise, output 0:

$$\begin{cases} \boxed{3^{\clubsuit}}\,\boxed{\clubsuit}\,\boxed{?}\,\boxed{?} \\ \boxed{3^{\heartsuit}}\,\boxed{\heartsuit}\,\boxed{?}\,\boxed{?} \\ \boxed{9^{\clubsuit}}\,\boxed{?}\,\boxed{?}\,\boxed{\clubsuit} \\ \boxed{9^{\heartsuit}}\,\boxed{?}\,\boxed{?}\,\boxed{\heartsuit} \end{cases} \rightarrow 1, \qquad \begin{cases} \boxed{3^{\clubsuit}}\,\boxed{\heartsuit}\,\boxed{?}\,\boxed{?} \\ \boxed{3^{\heartsuit}}\,\boxed{\clubsuit}\,\boxed{?}\,\boxed{?} \\ \boxed{9^{\clubsuit}}\,\boxed{?}\,\boxed{?}\,\boxed{\heartsuit} \\ \boxed{9^{\heartsuit}}\,\boxed{?}\,\boxed{?}\,\boxed{\clubsuit} \end{cases} \rightarrow 0.$$

4 Our Three-Input AND Protocol

In this section, we propose a three-input AND protocol with partial-open actions using six cards of the standard deck and two random cuts.

4.1 Protocol Description

Let $\boxed{1}\boxed{2}\boxed{3}\boxed{4}\boxed{5}\boxed{6}$ be cards for executing the protocol. Then these cards must satisfy the following condition for partial-open actions:

(i) A partial-open action determines whether a face-down card is $\boxed{4}$ or one of $\boxed{1}\boxed{2}\boxed{3}\boxed{5}$.

(ii) A partial-open action determines whether a face-down card is $\boxed{1}$ or one of $\boxed{2}\boxed{3}\boxed{5}$.

(iii) A partial-open action determines whether a face-down card is one of $\boxed{5}\boxed{6}$ or one of $\boxed{1}\boxed{2}\boxed{3}\boxed{4}$.

The protocol proceeds as follows:

1. Arrange the cards as follows:

$$\underbrace{\overset{\alpha_0}{\boxed{?}}\overset{\alpha_1}{\boxed{?}}}_{[x_1]^{\{1,2\}}}\ \underbrace{\overset{\beta_0}{\boxed{?}}\overset{\beta_1}{\boxed{?}}}_{[x_2]^{\{3,4\}}}\ \underbrace{\overset{\gamma_0}{\boxed{?}}\overset{\gamma_1}{\boxed{?}}}_{[x_3]^{\{5,6\}}}.$$

Name these cards $\alpha_0, \alpha_1, \beta_0, \beta_1, \gamma_0, \gamma_1$ from the left so that they can be referenced.

2. Using the partial-open action for the condition (iii), apply the base conversion protocol in Sect. 2.4, which uses one random cut and one partial-open action, to the commitment to x_3 and the pair (α_1, β_0) so that $\boxed{5}\boxed{6}$ are opened at the end of the base conversion protocol as follows:

$$\underbrace{\overset{\gamma_0}{\boxed{?}}\overset{\gamma_1}{\boxed{?}}}_{[x_3]^{\{5,6\}}}\overset{\alpha_1}{\boxed{?}}\overset{\beta_0}{\boxed{?}} \rightarrow \boxed{5}\boxed{6}\overset{\delta_0}{\boxed{?}}\overset{\delta_1}{\boxed{?}}.$$

Note that the rightmost pair (δ_0, δ_1) is $\boxed{4}\boxed{1}$ if and only if $x_1 = x_2 = x_3 = 1$.

3. Arrange the cards as follows:

$$\boxed{5}\overset{\delta_0}{\boxed{?}}\overset{\delta_1}{\boxed{?}}\overset{\beta_1}{\boxed{?}}.$$

4. Turn all cards face-down and apply a random cut to the sequence as follows:

$$\big\langle \boxed{?}\boxed{?}\boxed{?}\boxed{?} \big\rangle.$$

5. Apply the partial-open action for the condition (i) from the leftmost card to the right until we can determine the position of $\boxed{4}$ as follows:

$$\boxed{?}\boxed{?}\boxed{?}\boxed{?} \rightarrow \begin{cases} \boxed{4}\boxed{?}\boxed{?}\boxed{?}; \\ \boxed{\perp}\boxed{4}\boxed{?}\boxed{?}; \\ \boxed{\perp}\boxed{\perp}\boxed{4}\boxed{?}; \\ \boxed{\perp}\boxed{\perp}\boxed{\perp}\boxed{?}. \end{cases}$$

Note that the number of partial-open actions is at most three because we can determine the position of $\boxed{4}$ if we partially open the leftmost three cards.

6. Shift the sequence cyclically so that $\boxed{4}$ appears at the leftmost position as follows:

$$\boxed{?}\boxed{?}\boxed{?}\boxed{?} \rightarrow \begin{cases} \boxed{4}\boxed{?}\boxed{?}\boxed{?}; \\ \boxed{\bot}\boxed{4}\boxed{?}\boxed{?}; \\ \boxed{\bot}\boxed{\bot}\boxed{4}\boxed{?}; \\ \boxed{\bot}\boxed{\bot}\boxed{\bot}\boxed{?}. \end{cases}$$

7. Apply the partial-open action for the condition (ii) to the second card as follows:

$$\boxed{4}\boxed{?}\boxed{?}\boxed{?} \rightarrow \begin{cases} \boxed{4}\boxed{1}\boxed{?}\boxed{?}; \\ \boxed{4}\boxed{\bot}\boxed{?}\boxed{?}. \end{cases}$$

If the second card is $\boxed{1}$, the output is 1. If it is not $\boxed{1}$, the output is 0.

Table 2. Correctness of our three-input AND protocol

	After Step 1	(δ_0, δ_1)	After Step 3	Step 6
(0,0,0)	1 2 3 4 5 6	2 3	5 2 3 4	4 5 2 3
(0,0,1)	1 2 3 4 6 5	3 2	5 3 2 4	4 5 3 2
(0,1,0)	1 2 4 3 5 6	2 4	5 2 4 3	4 3 5 2
(0,1,1)	1 2 4 3 6 5	4 2	5 4 2 3	4 2 3 5
(1,0,0)	2 1 3 4 5 6	1 3	5 1 3 4	4 5 1 3
(1,0,1)	2 1 3 4 6 5	3 1	5 3 1 4	4 5 3 1
(1,1,0)	2 1 4 3 5 6	1 4	5 1 4 3	4 3 5 1
(1,1,1)	2 1 4 3 6 5	4 1	5 4 1 3	4 1 3 5

In this protocol, the number of cards is six, the number of random cuts is two, and the number of partial-open actions is five.

Correctness According to Table 2, the card to the right of $\boxed{4}$ in Step 6 is $\boxed{1}$ if and only if the input is $(1, 1, 1)$, and thus correctness holds.

Security In our protocol, cards are (partially) opened in the base conversion protocol in Step 2 and the partial-open actions in Steps 5 and 7. The opened values in Step 2 are independent of the input information due to the security of the base conversion protocol. The partial-open action in Step 5 reveals only the position of $\boxed{4}$, which is chosen uniformly at random by the random cut in Step 4. The partial-open action in Step 6 reveals only whether the second card is $\boxed{1}$ or not, which is determined from the output value $x_1 \wedge x_2 \wedge x_3$. Therefore, our protocol is secure.

4.2 Example of Cards

Since our protocol uses partial-open actions, we need to use cards [1][2][3][4][5][6] that are suitable for the conditions (i), (ii), and (iii). An example of cards satisfying the conditions is as follows:

$$\boxed{1}\boxed{2}\boxed{3}\boxed{4}\boxed{5}\boxed{6} = \boxed{2^\clubsuit}\boxed{4^\clubsuit}\boxed{5^\clubsuit}\boxed{6^\clubsuit}\boxed{4^\heartsuit}\boxed{5^\heartsuit}.$$

(i) The partial-open action to the position (b) in Fig. 1 determines whether a face-down card is $\boxed{6^\clubsuit}$ or $\boxed{2^\clubsuit}\boxed{4^\clubsuit}\boxed{5^\clubsuit}\boxed{4^\heartsuit}$.
(ii) The partial-open action to the position (c) in Fig. 1 determines whether a face-down card is $\boxed{2^\clubsuit}$ or $\boxed{4^\clubsuit}\boxed{5^\clubsuit}\boxed{4^\heartsuit}$.
(iii) The half-open action determines whether a face-down card is $\boxed{4^\heartsuit}\boxed{5^\heartsuit}$ or $\boxed{2^\clubsuit}\boxed{4^\clubsuit}\boxed{5^\clubsuit}\boxed{6^\clubsuit}$.

5 Our Four-Input AND Protocol

In this section, we propose a four-input AND protocol with partial-open actions using eight cards of the standard deck and three random cuts.

5.1 Protocol Description

Let $\boxed{1}\boxed{2}\boxed{3}\boxed{4}\boxed{5}\boxed{6}\boxed{7}\boxed{8}$ be cards for executing the protocol. Then these cards must satisfy the following condition for partial-open actions:

(i) A partial-open action determines whether a face-down card is $\boxed{1}$ or $\boxed{2}\boxed{3}\boxed{4}\boxed{5}\boxed{6}\boxed{7}$.
(ii) A partial-open action determines whether a face-down card is $\boxed{3}$ or $\boxed{2}\boxed{4}\boxed{5}\boxed{6}\boxed{7}$.
(iii) A partial-open action determines whether a face-down card is $\boxed{5}\boxed{6}$ or $\boxed{1}\boxed{2}\boxed{3}\boxed{4}$.
(iv) A partial-open action determines whether a face-down card is $\boxed{7}\boxed{8}$ or $\boxed{1}\boxed{2}\boxed{3}\boxed{4}$.

The protocol proceeds as follows:

1. Arrange the cards as follows:

$$\underbrace{\overset{\alpha_0}{\boxed{?}}\overset{\alpha_1}{\boxed{?}}}_{[x_1]^{\{1,2\}}}\underbrace{\overset{\beta_0}{\boxed{?}}\overset{\beta_1}{\boxed{?}}}_{[x_2]^{\{3,4\}}}\underbrace{\overset{\gamma_0}{\boxed{?}}\overset{\gamma_1}{\boxed{?}}}_{[x_3]^{\{5,6\}}}\underbrace{\overset{\delta_0}{\boxed{?}}\overset{\delta_1}{\boxed{?}}}_{[x_4]^{\{7,8\}}}.$$

Name these cards $\alpha_0, \alpha_1, \beta_0, \beta_1, \gamma_0, \gamma_1, \delta_0, \delta_1$ from the left for reference.

2. Using the partial-open action for the condition (iii), apply the base conversion protocol in Sect. 2.4, which uses one random cut and one partial-open action, to the commitment to x_3 and the pair (α_1, β_0) so that $\boxed{5}\boxed{6}$ are opened at the end of the base conversion protocol as follows:

$$\underbrace{\overset{\gamma_0}{\boxed{?}}\overset{\gamma_1}{\boxed{?}}}_{[x_3]^{\{5,6\}}}\overset{\alpha_1}{\boxed{?}}\overset{\beta_0}{\boxed{?}} \rightarrow \boxed{5}\boxed{6}\overset{\epsilon_0}{\boxed{?}}\overset{\epsilon_1}{\boxed{?}}.$$

   Let the rightmost pair be (ϵ_0, ϵ_1).

3. Using the partial-open action for the condition (iv), apply the base conversion protocol in Sect. 2.4, which uses one random cut and one partial-open action, to the commitment to x_4 and the pair (α_0, β_1) so that $\boxed{7}\boxed{8}$ are opened at the end of the base conversion protocol as follows:

$$\underbrace{\overset{\delta_0}{\boxed{?}}\overset{\delta_1}{\boxed{?}}}_{[x_4]^{\{7,8\}}}\overset{\alpha_0}{\boxed{?}}\overset{\beta_1}{\boxed{?}} \rightarrow \boxed{7}\boxed{8}\overset{\zeta_0}{\boxed{?}}\overset{\zeta_1}{\boxed{?}}.$$

   Let the rightmost pair be (ζ_0, ζ_1). Note that the pair (ϵ_1, ζ_0) is equal to $\boxed{1}\boxed{3}$ if and only if $x_1 = x_2 = x_3 = x_4 = 1$.

4. Arrange the cards as:

$$\overset{\epsilon_0}{\boxed{?}}\boxed{5}\overset{\epsilon_1}{\boxed{?}}\overset{\zeta_0}{\boxed{?}}\boxed{6}\overset{\zeta_1}{\boxed{?}}\boxed{7}.$$

   Note that $\boxed{1}$ appears cyclically to the left of $\boxed{3}$ only when $x_1 = x_2 = x_3 = x_4 = 1$.

5. Turn all cards face down and apply a random cut:

$$\left\langle \boxed{?}\boxed{?}\boxed{?}\boxed{?}\boxed{?}\boxed{?}\boxed{?} \right\rangle.$$

6. Apply the partial-open action for the condition (i) from the leftmost card to the right until we can determine the position of $\boxed{1}$ as follows:

$$\boxed{?}\boxed{?}\boxed{?}\boxed{?}\boxed{?}\boxed{?}\boxed{?} \rightarrow \begin{cases} \boxed{1}\boxed{?}\boxed{?}\boxed{?}\boxed{?}\boxed{?}\boxed{?}; \\ \boxed{\bot}\boxed{1}\boxed{?}\boxed{?}\boxed{?}\boxed{?}\boxed{?}; \\ \boxed{\bot}\boxed{\bot}\boxed{1}\boxed{?}\boxed{?}\boxed{?}\boxed{?}; \\ \boxed{\bot}\boxed{\bot}\boxed{\bot}\boxed{1}\boxed{?}\boxed{?}\boxed{?}; \\ \boxed{\bot}\boxed{\bot}\boxed{\bot}\boxed{\bot}\boxed{1}\boxed{?}\boxed{?}; \\ \boxed{\bot}\boxed{\bot}\boxed{\bot}\boxed{\bot}\boxed{\bot}\boxed{1}\boxed{?}; \\ \boxed{\bot}\boxed{\bot}\boxed{\bot}\boxed{\bot}\boxed{\bot}\boxed{\bot}\boxed{?}. \end{cases}$$

   Note that the number of partial-open actions is at most six because we can determine the position of $\boxed{1}$ if we partially open the leftmost six cards.

7. Shift the sequence cyclically so that $\boxed{1}$ appears at the leftmost position as follows:

$$\boxed{1}\boxed{?}\boxed{?}\boxed{?}\boxed{?}\boxed{?}\boxed{?}.$$

Table 3. Correctness of our four-input AND protocol

	Input	(ϵ_1, ζ_0)	After Step 4	Opened card in Step 7
(0,0,0,0)	1 2 3 4 5 6 7 8	3 1	2 5 3 1 6 4 7	1 6 4 7 2 5 3
(0,0,0,1)	1 2 3 4 5 6 8 7	3 4	2 5 3 4 6 1 7	1 7 2 5 3 4 6
(0,0,1,0)	1 2 3 4 6 5 7 8	2 1	3 5 2 1 6 4 7	1 6 4 7 3 5 2
(0,0,1,1)	1 2 3 4 6 5 8 7	2 4	3 5 2 4 6 1 7	1 7 3 5 2 4 6
(0,1,0,0)	1 2 4 3 5 6 7 8	4 1	2 5 4 1 6 3 7	1 6 3 7 2 5 4
(0,1,0,1)	1 2 4 3 5 6 8 7	4 3	2 5 4 3 6 1 7	1 7 2 5 4 3 6
(0,1,1,0)	1 2 4 3 6 5 7 8	2 1	4 5 2 1 6 3 7	1 6 3 7 4 5 2
(0,1,1,1)	1 2 4 3 6 5 8 7	2 3	4 5 2 3 6 1 7	1 7 4 5 2 3 6
(1,0,0,0)	2 1 3 4 5 6 7 8	3 2	1 5 3 2 6 4 7	1 5 3 2 6 4 7
(1,0,0,1)	2 1 3 4 5 6 8 7	3 4	1 5 3 4 6 2 7	1 5 3 4 6 2 7
(1,0,1,0)	2 1 3 4 6 5 7 8	1 2	3 5 1 2 6 4 7	1 2 6 4 7 3 5
(1,0,1,1)	2 1 3 4 6 5 8 7	1 4	3 5 1 4 6 2 7	1 4 6 2 7 3 5
(1,1,0,0)	2 1 4 3 5 6 7 8	4 2	1 5 4 2 6 3 7	1 5 4 2 6 3 7
(1,1,0,1)	2 1 4 3 5 6 8 7	4 3	1 5 4 3 6 2 7	1 5 4 3 6 2 7
(1,1,1,0)	2 1 4 3 6 5 7 8	1 2	4 5 1 2 6 3 7	1 2 6 3 7 4 5
(1,1,1,1)	2 1 4 3 6 5 8 7	1 3	4 5 1 3 6 2 7	1 3 6 2 7 4 5

8. Apply the partial-open action for the condition (ii) to the second card as follows:

$$\boxed{1}\boxed{?}\boxed{?}\boxed{?}\boxed{?}\boxed{?}\boxed{?} \rightarrow \begin{cases} \boxed{1}\boxed{3}\boxed{?}\boxed{?}\boxed{?}\boxed{?} \\ \boxed{1}\boxed{\perp}\boxed{?}\boxed{?}\boxed{?}\boxed{?} \end{cases}$$

If the second card is $\boxed{3}$, output 1; otherwise, output 0.

In this protocol, the number of cards is eight, the number of random cuts is three, and the number of partial-open actions is nine.

Correctness According to Table 3, the card to the right of $\boxed{1}$ in Step 8 is $\boxed{3}$ if and only if the input is (1, 1, 1, 1), and thus correctness holds.

Security In our protocol, cards are (partially) opened in the base conversion protocol in Steps 2 and 3, and the partial-open actions in Steps 6 and 8. The opened values in Step 2 and 3 are independent of the input information due to the security of the base conversion protocol. The partial-open action in Step 6 reveals only the position of

$\boxed{1}$, which is chosen uniformly at random by the random cut in Step 5. The partial-open action in Step 8 reveals only whether the second card is $\boxed{3}$ or not, which is determined from the output value $x_1 \wedge x_2 \wedge x_3 \wedge x_4$. Therefore, our protocol is secure.

5.2 Examples of Cards

Since our protocol uses partial-open actions, we need to use cards $\boxed{1}\boxed{2}\boxed{3}\boxed{4}\boxed{5}\boxed{6}\boxed{7}\boxed{8}$ that are suitable for the conditions (i), (ii), (iii), and (iv). An example of cards satisfying the conditions is as follows:

$$\boxed{1}\boxed{2}\boxed{3}\boxed{4}\boxed{5}\boxed{6}\boxed{7}\boxed{8} = \boxed{2^{\clubsuit}}\boxed{4^{\clubsuit}}\boxed{5^{\clubsuit}}\boxed{6^{\clubsuit}}\boxed{4^{\heartsuit}}\boxed{6^{\heartsuit}}\boxed{4^{\diamondsuit}}\boxed{6^{\diamondsuit}}.$$

(i) The partial-open action to the position (c) in Fig. 1 determines whether a face-down card is $\boxed{2^{\clubsuit}}$ or $\boxed{4^{\clubsuit}}\boxed{5^{\clubsuit}}\boxed{6^{\clubsuit}}\boxed{4^{\heartsuit}}\boxed{6^{\heartsuit}}\boxed{4^{\diamondsuit}}$.

(ii) The partial-open action to the position (d) in Fig. 1 determines whether a face-down card is $\boxed{5^{\clubsuit}}$ or $\boxed{4^{\clubsuit}}\boxed{6^{\clubsuit}}\boxed{4^{\heartsuit}}\boxed{6^{\heartsuit}}\boxed{4^{\diamondsuit}}$.

(iii) The half-open action determines whether a face-down card is $\boxed{4^{\heartsuit}}\boxed{6^{\heartsuit}}$ or $\boxed{2^{\clubsuit}}\boxed{4^{\clubsuit}}\boxed{5^{\clubsuit}}\boxed{6^{\clubsuit}}$.

(iv) The half-open action determines whether a face-down card is $\boxed{4^{\diamondsuit}}\boxed{6^{\diamondsuit}}$ or $\boxed{2^{\clubsuit}}\boxed{4^{\clubsuit}}\boxed{5^{\clubsuit}}\boxed{6^{\clubsuit}}$.

6 Efficiency of Our Protocols

Table 4 shows a summary of AND protocols using only random cuts with the standard deck. The Miyahara-Mizuki two-input AND protocol uses four cards and one random cut. Our three-input AND protocol uses six cards and two random cuts. Our four-input AND protocol uses eight cards and three random cuts. Regarding the number of partial-open actions, the MiyaharaMizuki's two-input AND protocol uses one, our three-input AND protocol uses five, and our four-input AND protocol uses nine. In summary, within the range $2 \leq n \leq 4$, a $2n$-card n-input AND protocol using $n-1$ random cuts and $4n-7$ partial disclosure operations has been obtained.

Table 4. Summary of AND protocols using only random cuts with the standard deck

	function	# of cards	# of random cuts	# of partial-open
Miyahara–Mizuki [10]	$x_1 \wedge x_2$	4	1	1
Ours (Sect. 4)	$x_1 \wedge x_2 \wedge x_3$	6	2	5
Ours (Sect. 5)	$x_1 \wedge x_2 \wedge x_3 \wedge x_4$	8	3	9

7 Conclusion

In this paper, we constructed three-input and four-input AND protocols using partial-open actions with standard playing cards. The proposed three-input AND protocol uses six cards and two random cuts, while the proposed four-input AND protocol uses eight cards and three random cuts.

In the setting where only partial-open actions and random cuts are allowed, designing efficient n-input AND protocols for $n \geq 5$ remains an open problem. Furthermore, in this setting, it is also open whether one can construct more efficient three-input or four-input AND protocols in terms of the number of random cuts or the number of partial-open actions.

Acknowledgments. This work was supported by JSPS KAKENHI Grant Numbers JP21K17702 and JP23H00479, and JST CREST Grant Number JPMJCR22M1, Japan.

References

1. Abe, Y., Hayashi, Y., Mizuki, T., Sone, H.: Five-card AND protocol in committed format using only practical shuffles. In: 5th ACM on ASIA Public-Key Cryptography Workshop, pp. 3–8. ACM, New York (2018)
2. Boer, B.: More efficient match-making and satisfiability *the five card trick*. In: Quisquater, J.-J., Vandewalle, J. (eds.) EUROCRYPT 1989. LNCS, vol. 434, pp. 208–217. Springer, Heidelberg (1990). https://doi.org/10.1007/3-540-46885-4_23
3. Crépeau, C., Kilian, J.: Discreet solitary games. In: Stinson, D.R. (ed.) CRYPTO 1993. LNCS, vol. 773, pp. 319–330. Springer, Heidelberg (1994). https://doi.org/10.1007/3-540-48329-2_27
4. Honda, Y., Shinagawa, K.: Efficient card-based protocols with a standard deck of playing cards using partial opening. In: Minematsu, K., Mimura, M. (eds.) IWSEC 2024. LNCS, vol. 14977, pp. 85–100. Springer, Singapore (2024). https://doi.org/10.1007/978-981-97-7737-2_5
5. Isuzugawa, R., Toyoda, K., Sasaki, Y., Miyahara, D., Mizuki, T.: A card-minimal three-input AND protocol using two shuffles. In: Chen, C.-Y., Hon, W.-K., Hung, L.-J., Lee, C.-W. (eds.) COCOON 2021. LNCS, vol. 13025, pp. 668–679. Springer, Cham (2021). https://doi.org/10.1007/978-3-030-89543-3_55
6. Kastner, J., et al.: The minimum number of cards in practical card-based protocols. In: Takagi, T., Peyrin, T. (eds.) ASIACRYPT 2017. LNCS, vol. 10626, pp. 126–155. Springer, Cham (2017). https://doi.org/10.1007/978-3-319-70700-6_5

7. Koch, A.: The landscape of optimal card-based protocols. Math. Cryptol. **1**(2), 115–131 (2022)
8. Koch, A., Schrempp, M., Kirsten, M.: Card-based cryptography meets formal verification. In: Galbraith, S.D., Moriai, S. (eds.) ASIACRYPT 2019. LNCS, vol. 11921, pp. 488–517. Springer, Cham (2019). https://doi.org/10.1007/978-3-030-34578-5_18
9. Koch, A., Walzer, S., Härtel, K.: Card-based cryptographic protocols using a minimal number of cards. In: Iwata, T., Cheon, J.H. (eds.) ASIACRYPT 2015. LNCS, vol. 9452, pp. 783–807. Springer, Heidelberg (2015). https://doi.org/10.1007/978-3-662-48797-6_32
10. Miyahara, D., Mizuki, T.: Secure computations through checking suits of playing cards. In: Li, M., Sun, X. (eds.) IJTCS-FAW 2022. LNCS, vol. 13461, pp. 110–128. Springer, Cham (2023). https://doi.org/10.1007/978-3-031-20796-9_9
11. Mizuki, T.: Card-based protocols for securely computing the conjunction of multiple variables. Theor. Comput. Sci. **622**(C), 34–44 (2016)
12. Mizuki, T.: Efficient and secure multiparty computations using a standard deck of playing cards. In: Foresti, S., Persiano, G. (eds.) CANS 2016. LNCS, vol. 10052, pp. 484–499. Springer, Cham (2016). https://doi.org/10.1007/978-3-319-48965-0_29
13. Mizuki, T., Kumamoto, M., Sone, H.: The five-card trick can be done with four cards. In: Wang, X., Sako, K. (eds.) ASIACRYPT 2012. LNCS, vol. 7658, pp. 598–606. Springer, Heidelberg (2012). https://doi.org/10.1007/978-3-642-34961-4_36
14. Mizuki, T., Shizuya, H.: A formalization of card-based cryptographic protocols via abstract machine. Int. J. Inf. Secur. **13**(1), 15–23 (2014)
15. Mizuki, T., Sone, H.: Six-card secure and and four-card secure XOR. In: Deng, X., Hopcroft, J.E., Xue, J. (eds.) FAW 2009. LNCS, vol. 5598, pp. 358–369. Springer, Heidelberg (2009). https://doi.org/10.1007/978-3-642-02270-8_36
16. Niemi, V., Renvall, A.: Secure multiparty computations without computers. Theor. Comput. Sci. **191**(1–2), 173–183 (1998)
17. Niemi, V., Renvall, A.: Solitaire zero-knowledge. Fundam. Inf. **38**(1,2), 181–188 (1999)
18. Nishida, T., Hayashi, Y., Mizuki, T., Sone, H.: Card-based protocols for any Boolean function. In: Jain, R., Jain, S., Stephan, F. (eds.) TAMC 2015. LNCS, vol. 9076, pp. 110–121. Springer, Cham (2015). https://doi.org/10.1007/978-3-319-17142-5_11
19. Ruangwises, S., Itoh, T.: AND protocols using only uniform shuffles. In: van Bevern, R., Kucherov, G. (eds.) CSR 2019. LNCS, vol. 11532, pp. 349–358. Springer, Cham (2019). https://doi.org/10.1007/978-3-030-19955-5_30
20. Stiglic, A.: Computations with a deck of cards. Theor. Comput. Sci. **259**(1–2), 671–678 (2001)
21. Yoshida, T., Tanaka, K., Nakabayashi, K., Chida, E., Mizuki, T.: Upper bounds on the number of shuffles for two-helping-card multi-input AND protocols. In: Deng, J., Kolesnikov, V., Schwarzmann, A.A. (eds.) CANS 2023. LNCS, vol. 14342, pp. 211–231. Springer, Singapore (2023). https://doi.org/10.1007/978-981-99-7563-1_10

Impossibility of Four-Card AND Protocols with a Single Closed Shuffle

Shizuru Iino[1(✉)], Shota Ikeda[2], Kazumasa Shinagawa[3,4], Yang Li[1], Kazuo Sakiyama[1], and Daiki Miyahara[1,4(✉)]

[1] The University of Electro-Communications, Tokyo, Japan
{s.iino,miyahara}@uec.ac.jp
[2] Ibaraki University, Ibaraki, Japan
[3] University of Tsukuba, Ibaraki, Japan
[4] National Institute of Advanced Industrial Science and Technology, Tokyo, Japan

Abstract. Card-based cryptography performs a secure computation using a deck of playing cards through a series of physical actions, such as shuffling a sequence of cards. In 1989, the first card-based protocol called the five-card trick was proposed to compute the two-input AND function. The five-card trick needs a practical shuffling action called a random cut only once, which shifts a sequence of cards by a random offset. Subsequent research aimed to extend the five-card trick to compute any Boolean function and to reduce the number of cards required to compute it, but Mizuki, Kumamoto, and Sone in 2012 showed that the five-card trick itself can be done with four cards. This Mizuki–Kumamoto–Sone protocol uses the minimal number of cards required for computing two-input Boolean functions (as long as we encode an input bit with two cards); however, it needs a practical step of shuffling action twice, and the question of minimizing the number of steps, particularly the number of shuffling, remains an open problem. In this study, we negatively answer this problem; we prove that any four-card AND protocol cannot be realized using only a single practical shuffle. This implies that the Mizuki–Kumamoto–Sone protocol utilizes the minimal number of practical shuffles. For this, we enumerate all possible practical shuffles and prove that applying any one of them only once either cannot compute the AND function or leak information about the input.

Keywords: Card-based cryptography · Secure computation · Logical AND function · Impossibility proof

1 Introduction

Card-based cryptography enables a secure computation using a deck of physical cards. The most well-known card-based protocol is the five-card trick, proposed by Den Boer in 1989 [3]. Given $a, b \in \{0, 1\}$, this protocol computes $a \wedge b$ without leaking any information about a, b. In this setting, we use a deck consisting of two colors: black $\boxed{\clubsuit}$ and red $\boxed{\heartsuit}$, with identical backs $\boxed{?}$. Boolean values are encoded based on the arrangement of one black and one red card, as follows:

$$\boxed{\clubsuit}\boxed{\heartsuit} = 0, \quad \boxed{\heartsuit}\boxed{\clubsuit} = 1. \tag{1}$$

Y. Kim et al. (Eds.): CANS 2025, LNCS 16351, pp. 213–229, 2026.
https://doi.org/10.1007/978-981-95-4434-9_10

This pair is called a *commitment* to x if it represents the value of a bit $x \in \{0, 1\}$. The five-card trick requires two input commitments to a, b along with one helping card $\boxed{\heartsuit}$:

$$\underbrace{\boxed{?}\boxed{?}}_{a}\ \underbrace{\boxed{?}\boxed{?}}_{b}\ \boxed{\heartsuit} \rightarrow \cdots \rightarrow a \wedge b.$$

Here, the first four cards denote the commitments to a, b. The five-card trick is called a *non-committed format* protocol, because the output in the five-card trick is not in the form of a commitment. A protocol is in *committed format* if it outputs a commitment to a desired value.

1.1 Mizuki–Kumamoto–Sone AND Protocol

In 2012, Mizuki, Kumamoto, and Sone [10] showed that the five-card trick [3] can be done with four cards, i.e., they proposed a four-card non-committed format AND protocol, which needs no helping card. We call this protocol the *MKS protocol* in short.

$$\underbrace{\boxed{?}\boxed{?}}_{a}\ \underbrace{\boxed{?}\boxed{?}}_{b} \rightarrow \cdots \rightarrow a \wedge b.$$

Clearly, this protocol uses the minimal number of cards as long as we follow the encoding rule in Eq. 1, because it only uses two input commitments. The MKS protocol proceeds as follows.

1. Apply a *random bisection cut*, which bisects the sequence and randomly swaps the two halves and is denoted by $[\cdots|\cdots]$ as follows:

$$\left[\boxed{?}\boxed{?}\,\middle|\,\boxed{?}\boxed{?}\right] \rightarrow \boxed{?}\boxed{?}\boxed{?}\boxed{?}.$$

2. Apply a *random cut* to the middle two cards, which applies a random cyclic shift to the sequence and is denoted by $\langle\cdots\rangle$ as follows:

$$\boxed{?}\left\langle\boxed{?}\boxed{?}\right\rangle\boxed{?} \rightarrow \boxed{?}\boxed{?}\boxed{?}\boxed{?}.$$

3. Reveal the second card;
   (a) if it is $\boxed{\clubsuit}$, then reveal the forth to obtain the value of $a \wedge b$ as follows:

$$\boxed{?}\boxed{?}\boxed{?}\boxed{?} \rightarrow \begin{cases} \boxed{?}\boxed{\clubsuit}\boxed{?}\boxed{\heartsuit} & \text{if } a \wedge b = 0, \\ \boxed{\clubsuit}\boxed{?}\boxed{\clubsuit} & \text{if } a \wedge b = 1. \end{cases}$$

   (b) if it is $\boxed{\heartsuit}$, reveal the first:

$$\boxed{?}\boxed{?}\boxed{?}\boxed{?} \rightarrow \begin{cases} \boxed{\clubsuit}\boxed{\heartsuit}\boxed{?}\boxed{?} & \text{if } a \wedge b = 0, \\ \boxed{\heartsuit}\boxed{?}\boxed{?} & \text{if } a \wedge b = 1. \end{cases}$$

See Table 1 to show the correctness and the security: The initial sequence has four possibilities, which have a one-to-one correspondence with the four input values. Through

Table 1. Sequences of cards in the MKS protocol [10]

(a, b)	Initial sequence	After step 2	After step 3
$(1, 1)$	♡ ♣ ♡ ♣	♡ ♣ ♡ ♣ or ♡ ♡ ♣ ♣	? ♣ ? ♣ or ♡ ♡ ? ?
$(0, 0)$	♣ ♡ ♣ ♡	♣ ♣ ♡ ♡ or ♣ ♡ ♣ ♡	? ♣ ? ♡ or ♣ ♡ ? ?
$(0, 1)$	♣ ♡ ♡ ♣	♡ ♣ ♣ ♡ or ♣ ♡ ♡ ♣	? ♣ ? ♡ or ♣ ♡ ? ?
$(1, 0)$	♡ ♣ ♣ ♡	♡ ♣ ♣ ♡ or ♣ ♡ ♡ ♣	? ♣ ? ♡ or ♣ ♡ ? ?

the application of a random bisection cut and a random cut in steps 1 and 2 respectively, each of the four possible sequences is randomized as shown in the third column. For example, the initial sequence ♡ ♣ ♡ ♣ when $(a, b) = (1, 1)$ is randomized into the two sequences of ♡ ♣ ♡ ♣ and ♡ ♡ ♣ ♣ with equal probability, because the two middle cards are swapped randomly. Note that for each input, the initial sequence is randomized into exactly two sequences with equal probability. Note furthermore that these actions are performed with all the cards facing down, and hence, no information about the input value is leaked. After step 3, observe that only the case of $(a, b) = (1, 1)$ differs from the other three input cases, regardless of whether the color of the second card revealed is red or black. Moreover, the other three input cases are indistinguishable from the colors that appeared. For these reasons, the MKS protocol can determine $a \wedge b$ and leaks no further information.

1.2 Motivation

The number of cards in the MKS protocol [10] is optimal with respect to the encoding scheme because four cards are needed to input two bits. To discuss the number of shuffles in the MKS protocol, we need to give a formal definition of shuffles.

Let S_n denote the symmetric group on degree $n \in \mathbb{N}$. A *shuffle* acted on a sequence of n cards is defined as a pair of a permutation set $\Pi \subseteq S_n$ and a probability distribution $\mathcal{F}$ on Π, and is denoted by $(\mathsf{shuf}, \Pi, \mathcal{F})$ [11]. By applying a shuffle $(\mathsf{shuf}, \Pi, \mathcal{F})$ to a sequence of n cards, a permutation π is drawn from Π according to $\mathcal{F}$ and the sequence is rearranged by the chosen permutation π. Here, the chosen permutation π is hidden from all parties, and only Π and $\mathcal{F}$ are public information in the shuffle. A shuffle $(\mathsf{shuf}, \Pi, \mathcal{F})$ is called *uniform* if $\mathcal{F}$ is a uniform distribution over Π, *closed* if Π forms a group under composition of permutations, and *uniform closed* if it is uniform and closed. When $(\mathsf{shuf}, \Pi, \mathcal{F})$ is uniform (or uniform closed), we omit $\mathcal{F}$ and denote it as (shuf, Π). Since all easy-to-implement shuffles (e.g., random cuts, random bisection cuts, pile-shifting shuffles, and pile-scramble shuffles) in the literature are uniform closed, it is considered to be the necessary condition for shuffles to be *practical*. Indeed, there are various methods [4,7,8,14] to implement uniform closed shuffles physically[1].

[1] Koch et al. [8] showed that any uniform closed shuffle can be implemented by the use of private permutations, which apply a permutation covertly. Koch [7] showed that any uniform closed shuffle can be implemented from pile-shifting shuffles. Shinagawa et al. [14] showed that (possibly any) uniform closed shuffle can be implemented by cyclic shuffles, based on group-theoretic factorization [4].

Following this formalization, the shuffling actions in steps 1 and 2 in the MKS protocol are denoted by $(\mathsf{shuf}, \{\mathsf{id}, (1\,3)(2\,4)\})$ and $(\mathsf{shuf}, \{\mathsf{id}, (2\,3)\})$, respectively, where id denotes the identity permutation and a probability distribution is omitted when it is uniform. In this formalization, one can observe that the two shuffling actions above can be described as a single action [11], as follows:

$$(\mathsf{shuf}, \{\mathsf{id}, (1\,3)(2\,4), (2\,3), (1\,3\,2\,4)\}), \tag{2}$$

because they are acted sequentially. However, this action is not considered practical because the permutation set $\{\mathsf{id}, (1\,3)(2\,4), (2\,3), (1\,3\,2\,4)\}$ does not form a group. In summary, the MKS protocol uses two practical shuffles, and it can be viewed as a protocol with a single non-closed shuffle.

A natural question is stated as: *Is it possible to construct a four-card AND protocol with a single practical (i.e., uniform closed) shuffle* (shuf, Π)*?*

1.3 Contributions

In this study, we present a negative answer to the above problem, which is summarized in the following theorem.

Theorem 1. *Any four-card non-committed format AND protocol cannot be realized using only one practical shuffle.*

This result implies that the two practical shuffles used in the MKS protocol [10] constitute the minimal requirement to perform a secure computation. To establish this, we enumerate all practical shuffles and show that any single shuffle either fails to compute the logical AND function correctly or leaks information about the inputs (and thus needs an additional shuffle as in the MKS protocol).

Our approach leverages a state tree proposed by Koch et al. [8], which formalizes the transition of the "actual" sequence of cards during the execution of a protocol, similar to the transition shown in Table 1. We enumerate all closed shuffles for a sequence of four cards and show that there are 30 subgroups in S_4, say $G_i \subseteq S_4$ for $1 \leq i \leq 30$, as shown later. Our impossibility proof using a state tree shows that any "output state" cannot be derived if we apply any uniform closed shuffle (shuf, G_i) to the "start state" only once. In the proof, we do not depict a state tree for every case of applying (shuf, G_i), but employ the subset and conjugacy relation among G_i to reduce the number of cases, allowing us to simplify the proof. Then we extend the impossibility proof to the case of $(\mathsf{shuf}, G_i, \mathcal{F}_i)$ for any probability distribution $\mathcal{F}_i$ on G_i, i.e., non-uniform closed shuffles.

1.4 Related Work

Both committed- and non-committed-format AND protocols have a long history of improvements. We summarize the history for committed format ones in Table 2. As introduced above, Koch et al. [8] classified shuffles based on two elements: uniform and closed. They then proved that no four-card AND protocol exists that terminates within a finite runtime regardless of shuffles used, meaning that a finite runtime AND

Table 2. The minimum number of cards required for committed format AND protocols

	Cards	Finite Runtime	Uniform	Closed
Mizuki–Sone [12]	6	✓	✓	✓
Koch et al. [8]	4			✓
Koch et al. [8]	5	✓		
Abe et al. [1]	5		✓	✓
Koch [6] & Ruangwises—Itoh [13]	4		✓	
Koch [6] & Ruangwises—Itoh [13]	5	✓	✓	

protocol requires at least five cards. They also proposed two protocols: one is a four-card Las Vegas protocol using a closed shuffle, and the other is a five-card finite-runtime protocol using a non-uniform non-closed shuffle. Building on this perspective, Kastner et al. [5] focused on the shuffle classification and proved the following two results:

- No five-card finite-runtime AND protocol exists using only closed shuffles. This result implies that a six-card finite-runtime AND protocol proposed by Mizuki and Sone [12] with the use of a random bisection cut uses the minimal number of cards. This also implies that Koch et al.'s five-card finite-runtime protocol uses the minimal number of cards. However, the case of using only uniform shuffles remains unknown.
- No four-card AND protocol exists using only uniform and closed shuffles. This result implies that Koch et al.'s four-card Las Vegas protocol uses the minimal number of cards. However, the construction of a five-card AND protocol using only uniform closed shuffles remains unknown.

These open problems were soon positively resolved; In 2018, Abe et al. [1] proposed a five-card Las Vegas protocol using uniform closed shuffles. Regarding the other open problem concerning uniform shuffles, Koch [6] and Ruangwises and Itoh [13] independently devised both a four-card Las Vegas protocol and a five-card finite-runtime protocol using only uniform shuffles. These existing studies have clarified the trade-off between the type of shuffling actions and the number of cards required in commitment format AND protocols. More recently, protocols have been developed by restricting shuffle actions to only random cuts (cf. [2,9,16]). However, the minimal number of shuffles in (non-)committed format AND protocols remains unsolved.

2 Preliminaries

In this section, we introduce a computational model for card-based cryptographic protocols. We use this model to prove our result in a rigorous way.

2.1 Model of Card-Based Protocols

In this paper, we deal with the Mizuki–Shizuya model [11] as a model for card-based protocols. Let $\mathcal{D}$ be a non-empty finite multiset not containing the back symbol ?, and call it a *deck*. The number of elements in $\mathcal{D}$, $d = |\mathcal{D}|$, is called the number of cards.

For $c \in \mathcal{D}$, $\frac{c}{?}$ denotes a *face-up card* and $\frac{?}{c}$ denotes a *face-down card*. A face-up or face-down card is also called a *lying card*. We define $\mathsf{atom}(\frac{c}{?}) := c$ and $\mathsf{atom}(\frac{?}{c}) := c$ to denote an *atomic card*. The surface of the lying card is defined as $\mathsf{top}\left(\frac{c}{?}\right) := c$ and $\mathsf{top}\left(\frac{?}{c}\right) := ?$. A sequence of lying cards $\Gamma = (\alpha_1, \alpha_2, \cdots, \alpha_d)$ is called a *sequence* of the deck $\mathcal{D}$, if it satisfies $[\mathsf{atom}(\alpha_1), \mathsf{atom}(\alpha_2), \ldots, \mathsf{atom}(\alpha_d)] = \mathcal{D}$. Denote the set of all sequences in a deck $\mathcal{D}$ as $\mathsf{Seq}^{\mathcal{D}}$. We define the visible sequence $\mathsf{vis}(\Gamma)$ of the card sequence $\Gamma = (\alpha_1, \alpha_2, \ldots, \alpha_d)$ as follow:

$$\mathsf{vis}\left((\alpha_1, \alpha_2, \ldots, \alpha_d)\right) := \left(\mathsf{top}\left(\alpha_1\right), \mathsf{top}\left(\alpha_2\right), \ldots, \mathsf{top}\left(\alpha_d\right)\right).$$

Denote the set of all visible sequences in a deck $\mathcal{D}$ as $\mathsf{Vis}^{\mathcal{D}} := \{\mathsf{vis}(\Gamma) | \ \Gamma \in \mathsf{Seq}^{\mathcal{D}}\}$.

Let us define an action swap to be $\mathsf{swap}\left(\frac{c}{?}\right) := \frac{?}{c}$ and $\mathsf{swap}\left(\frac{?}{c}\right) := \frac{c}{?}$. For $\Gamma = (\alpha_1, \alpha_2, \ldots, \alpha_d)$, the action of turning over the lying cards at the position specified by the set $T \subseteq \{1, 2, \ldots, d\}$ is called a *turn* action. The turn action $\mathsf{turn}_T(\cdot)$ is defined as follows:

$$\mathsf{turn}_T((\alpha_1, \alpha_2, \ldots, \alpha_d)) := (\beta_1, \beta_2, \ldots, \beta_d)$$

such that

$$\beta_i = \begin{cases} \mathsf{swap}(\alpha_i) & \text{if } i \in T; \\ \alpha_i & \text{otherwise.} \end{cases}$$

For $\Gamma = (\alpha_1, \alpha_2, \ldots, \alpha_d)$, the action of rearranging the lying cards based on the permutation $\pi \in S_d$ is called the *permutation* action. The permutation action $\mathsf{perm}_\pi(\cdot)$ is defined as follows:

$$\mathsf{perm}_\pi((\alpha_1, \alpha_2, \ldots, \alpha_d)) := (\alpha_{\pi^{-1}(1)}, \alpha_{\pi^{-1}(2)}, \ldots, \alpha_{\pi^{-1}(d)}).$$

For $\Gamma = (\alpha_1, \alpha_2, \ldots, \alpha_d)$, based on the the pair $(\Pi, \mathcal{F})$ (*permutation set* $\Pi \subseteq S_d$ and the probability distribution $\mathcal{F}$ on Π), the action of applying the permutation $\Pi \subseteq S_d$ chosen with probability distribution $\mathcal{F}$ for the lying cards is called *shuffle* action. The shuffle action $\mathsf{shuf}_{\Pi,\mathcal{F}}(\cdot)$ is defined as follows:

$$\mathsf{shuf}_{\Pi,\mathcal{F}}((\alpha_1, \alpha_2, \ldots, \alpha_d)) := \mathsf{perm}_\pi((\alpha_1, \alpha_2, \ldots, \alpha_d)).$$

Here, $\pi \in \Pi$ is a permutation chosen randomly following $\mathcal{F}$. Then, we define SP^d as the entire set $(\Pi, \mathcal{F})$ of permutation sets Π and probability distributions $\mathcal{F}$ on Π.

A card-based protocol is defined by the quadruple $\mathcal{P} = (\mathcal{D}, U, Q, A)$:

- $\mathcal{D}$ is a deck;
- $U \subseteq \mathsf{Seq}^{\mathcal{D}}$ is an input set;
- Q is a state set containing initial state q_0 and final state q_f;
- $A \colon (Q \setminus \{q_f\}) \times \mathsf{Vis}^{\mathcal{D}} \to Q \times (2^{\{1,2,\ldots,d\}} \cup S_d \cup \mathsf{SP}^d)$ is an action function.

In the Mizuki–Kumamoto–Sone AND protocol [10], $\mathcal{D} = [\clubsuit, \clubsuit, \heartsuit, \heartsuit]$, and $d = 4$, $U = \left\{(\frac{?}{\clubsuit}, \frac{?}{\heartsuit}, \frac{?}{\clubsuit}, \frac{?}{\heartsuit}), (\frac{?}{\clubsuit}, \frac{?}{\heartsuit}, \frac{?}{\heartsuit}, \frac{?}{\clubsuit}), (\frac{?}{\heartsuit}, \frac{?}{\clubsuit}, \frac{?}{\clubsuit}, \frac{?}{\heartsuit}), (\frac{?}{\heartsuit}, \frac{?}{\clubsuit}, \frac{?}{\heartsuit}, \frac{?}{\clubsuit})\right\}$. The action function takes as input the current state q of the protocol and the visible sequence $\mathsf{vis}(\Gamma)$ and returns the next state q' and the next action. The next actions are the turn action turn, the permutation action perm, and the shuffle action shuf, each of which outputs as follows.

- $A(q, \mathsf{vis}(\Gamma)) = (q', T \in 2^{\{1,2,\ldots,d\}}) : \mathsf{turn}_T(\Gamma)$;
- $A(q, \mathsf{vis}(\Gamma)) = (q', \pi \in S_d) : \mathsf{perm}_\pi(\Gamma)$;
- $A(q, \mathsf{vis}(\Gamma)) = (q', (\Pi, \mathcal{F}) \in \mathsf{SP}^d) : \mathsf{shuf}_{\Pi,\mathcal{F}}(\Gamma)$.

For instance, the action function of the first step of the Mizuki–Kumamoto–Sone AND protocol is $A(q_0, (?, ?, ?, ?)) = (q_1, (\{\mathsf{id}, (1\,3)(2\,4)\}, \mathcal{F}))$ (but $\mathcal{F}$ is the uniform distribution) and $(\mathsf{shuf}, \{\mathsf{id}, (1\,3)(2\,4)\})$ is to be applied. Thus, the card-based protocol is to perform one of the following actions on lying cards from the initial state: turn action turn, permutation action perm, or shuffle action shuf, until the final state. In addition to the card-based protocol in this sense, for non-committed format protocols, there is a defined function that determines the output value from the entire history of the visible sequence from the initial state to the final state.

2.2 KWH-Tree

A state tree proposed by Koch, Walzer, and Härtel [8] is called the *KWH-tree* and is useful to show a card-based protocol visually. Figure 1 depicts the KWH-tree for the MKS protocol [10].

Let us introduce how the KWH-tree works using Fig. 1. Each "box" from the top to the bottom is called a *state*, in which every possible sequence of symbols[2] (left) is mapped to a probability (right), where X_{ab} denotes a random variable for the input value being $(a, b) \in \{0, 1\}^2$, and each probability associated with a sequence of symbols represents a probability that the atomic sequence of the current sequence placed on the table is exactly that sequence. Note that $X_{11} + X_{10} + X_{01} + X_{00} = 1$. For example, the topmost state means that a probability of the initial sequence being ♡♣♡♣ is X_{11}, ♡♣♣♡ is X_{10}, ♣♡♡♣ is X_{01}, and ♣♡♣♡ is X_{00}. The transition of a state corresponds to the visible sequence trace in the protocol, and each state is transformed into its subsequent state(s) according to directed edge(s) annotated with a unique action that is specified in the protocol for that situation. Thus, permutation and shuffle actions always lead to a single state, but any turn action results in multiple states depending on the symbol appeared, i.e., ♡ or ♣.

More formally, a state for a four-card protocol is a map $\mu \colon S \to P$ where S is a set of all possible sequences of four symbols

$$S := \{♡♣♡♣, ♣♡♣♡, ♡♡♣♣, ♣♣♡♡, ♡♣♣♡, ♣♡♡♣\},$$

and P is a set of homogeneous polynomials of degree 1 with non-negative coefficients

$$P := \{p_{11}X_{11} + p_{10}X_{10} + p_{01}X_{01} + p_{00}X_{00} \mid p_{xy} \geq 0\}.$$

For example, the *start* state μ_s shown in Fig. 1 is a unique state and is described as follows:

$$\begin{aligned} \mu_s(♡♣♡♣) &= X_{11}, \\ \mu_s(♡♣♣♡) &= X_{10}, \\ \mu_s(♣♡♡♣) &= X_{01}, \\ \mu_s(♣♡♣♡) &= X_{00}. \end{aligned} \tag{3}$$

[2] Here, a sequence of symbols rather than cards is employed for simplicity.

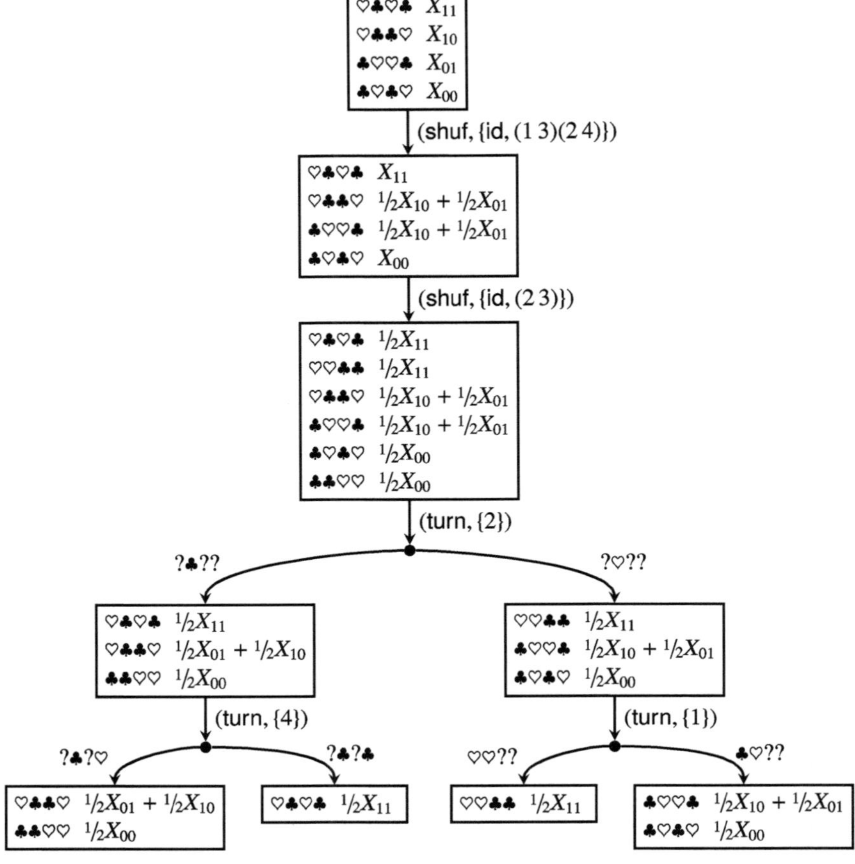

Fig. 1. The KWH-tree [8] for the Mizuki–Kumamoto–Sone AND protocol [10].

Note that $\mu_s(♣♣♡♡) = \mu_s(♡♡♣♣) = 0$. In particular, for a non-committed format AND protocol, the security of the protocol means that *when the output value is 0, it must be indistinguishable whether the input value is (0,0), (0,1), or (1,0)*. This implies that some non-negative real numbers $0 \leq p_0, p_1 \leq 1$ with either $p_0 \neq 0$ or $p_1 \neq 0$ exist for the state μ such that

$$\sum_{s \in S} \mu(s) = p_1 X_{11} + p_0(X_{00} + X_{10} + X_{01}). \tag{4}$$

Here, the part of the equation $p_0(X_{00} + X_{10} + X_{01})$ implies that each coefficient of X_{00}, X_{01}, and X_{10} is the same, i.e., the protocol leaks no information about whether the input value is $(0,0)$, $(0,1)$, or $(1,0)$. Note that Eq. 4 is the necessary and sufficient condition of the security; thus, every secure non-committed format protocol satisfies it in all states.[3]

[3] For a committed format AND protocol, Eq. 4 along with $p_0 = p_1$ is the necessary and sufficient condition of the security, i.e., the coefficient of X_{ab} is the same for all $(a, b) \in \{0, 1\}^2$.

2.3 Turnability for a State

Kastner et al. [5] introduced the *turnability* for a state μ, which defines the condition for not leaking information when applying a turn action to a state. Formally, for a non-committed format AND protocol $([\clubsuit, \clubsuit, \heartsuit, \heartsuit], U, Q, A)$, we say that μ is *turnable for* $i \in \{1,2,3,4\}$ if for any $c \in \{\heartsuit, \clubsuit\}$, there exists non-negative real numbers $0 \leq p_0, p_1 \leq 1$ with either $p_0 \neq 0$ or $p_1 \neq 0$ such that:

$$\sum_{s \in S, s[i]=c} \mu(s) = p_1 X_{11} + p_0(X_{00} + X_{10} + X_{01}), \tag{5}$$

where i denotes the position of a sequence s and $s[i]$ denotes the i-th symbol of s. In other words, a state μ is turnable for i if both of its subsequent states satisfy Eq. 4 when (turn, i) is applied to μ; a state μ is not turnable for i if (turn, i) leaks information about the input.

2.4 ⊥-Sequence

As seen in Fig. 1, any non-committed format AND protocol finally reaches a state μ such that either $\sum_{s \in S} \mu(s) = p_1 X_{11}$ or $\sum_{s \in S} \mu(s) = p_0(X_{00} + X_{10} + X_{01})$ for some real numbers $0 < p_0, p_1 \leq 1$. Such a state is called a *final* state, and if a protocol reaches the former (resp. latter) state, it means that the output value is 1 (resp. 0). From this viewpoint, a non-committed format AND protocol can be regarded as a mechanism to split a variable X_{11} with X_{00}, X_{10}, and X_{01}. If a protocol violates this, i.e., there is a state μ and a sequence $s \in S$ such that

$$\mu(s) = \sum_{i,j} p_{ij} X_{ij} \quad (p_{11} > 0, p_{00} + p_{10} + p_{01} > 0), \tag{6}$$

then the protocol can no longer split the variable X_{11} with X_{00}, X_{10}, and X_{01}, making it impossible to terminate correctly. Such a sequence $s \in S$ satisfying Eq. 6 is called a $\perp$-*sequence* (for a state μ). Note that a correct protocol never has a $\perp$-sequence.

3 Impossibility Proof

In this section, we prove Theorem 1, i.e., it is impossible to construct a four-card AND protocol using only one practical (i.e., uniform closed) shuffle.

First, constructing an AND protocol without the use of any shuffle (i.e., the number of shuffles is zero) is impossible. This is because the start state is not turnable for any $i \in \{1,2,3,4\}$ according to Eq. 5, and a state μ obtained by just applying (perm, π) (for any $\pi \in S_4$) to the start state is also not turnable for any $i \in \{1,2,3,4\}$ because π is a bijective function. Thus, any AND protocol must have at least one shuffle.

Now we consider whether an AND protocol can be constructed by using one practical shuffle. We first claim that any protocol having permutation actions can be converted into another protocol (computing the same function) without permutation actions as follows. If (perm, π) is applied *before* the shuffle action (shuf, G), this is equivalent to applying a uniform closed shuffle (shuf, G') such that $G' := \pi^{-1}G\pi$, i.e., G' is conjugate to G, and then applying (perm, π). If (perm, π) is applied *before* the turn action $(\mathsf{turn}, \{t_1, \ldots, t_k\})$, this is equivalent to applying just a turn action $(\mathsf{turn}, \{\pi^{-1}(t_1), \ldots, \pi^{-1}(t_k)\})$. Therefore, it suffices to consider the following protocol for an arbitrary group G and an arbitrary set $T \subseteq \{1, 2, 3, 4\}$:

1. Apply a uniform closed shuffle (shuf, G).
2. Apply a turn action (turn, T).

As described in Sect. 1, we examine all 30 subgroups of the symmetric group S_4, say G_i for $1 \le i \le 30$ as listed in Table 3, and show that every state after (shuf, G_i) is applied to the start state either does not satisfy the turnability in Eq. 5 or produces a $\bot$-sequence in Eq. 6. Let μ'_i be a state after (shuf, G_i) is applied to the start state for $1 \le i \le 30$. Among these, μ'_1 can be immediately rejected, as it leads to a protocol equivalent to the case with no shuffling. In the next two subsections, we examine the remaining 29 groups as follows.

- Sect. 3.1 deals with the five groups of G_3, G_4, G_5, G_6, and G_9, where any $\bot$-sequence does not arise. Our approach shows that, for such groups, none of the five resulting states is turnable for any $i \in \{1, 2, 3, 4\}$.
- Sect. 3.2 deals with the remaining groups, in which we show that a $\bot$-sequence appears in every resulting state.

3.1 Shuffles Not Producing $\bot$-Sequences

Let us consider the five shuffles using G_3, G_4, G_5, G_6, and G_9 listed in Table 3. First, note that G_5 and G_6 are symmetric to G_4 and G_3 with respect to the order of the two inputs, respectively, and hence, G_5 and G_6 yield the same results; the output of applying (shuf, G_3) to the two input commitments to a, b, is identical to that of applying (shuf, G_6) to the case when the two commitments are swapped beforehand, i.e., b, a, for instance. Therefore, we omit the cases for G_5 and G_6 and prove only the cases for G_3, G_4, and G_9.

Figure 2 depicts the KWH-trees when each of (shuf, G_3), (shuf, G_4), (shuf, G_9) is applied to the start state. Here, no $\bot$-sequence is produced, since there exists no $s \in S$ satisfying Eq. 6. However, according to Eq. 5, none of the three resulting states is turnable for any $i \in \{1, 2, 3, 4\}$. More precisely, when (shuf, G_3) is applied to the start state, the resulting state μ'_3 is not turnable for any i as shown below.

$$\sum_{s \in S, s[i]=\heartsuit} \mu'_3(s) = \begin{cases} X_{11} + 1/2(X_{01} + X_{10}) + 0(X_{00}) & \text{for } i = 1, \\ 0(X_{11}) + 1/2(X_{01} + X_{10}) + X_{00} & \text{for } i = 2, \\ X_{11} + 1/2(X_{01} + X_{10}) + 0(X_{00}) & \text{for } i = 3, \\ 0(X_{11}) + 1/2(X_{01} + X_{10}) + X_{00} & \text{for } i = 4. \end{cases}$$

Observe that in each equation, the coefficient of X_{00} differs from those of X_{01} and X_{10}; thus, it does not satisfy Eq. 5, indicating that μ'_3 is not turnable. Similarly, in both μ'_4 and μ'_9, we observe that the coefficient of X_{00} differ to those of X_{10} and X_{01} as shown in Fig. 2, i.e., they are not turnable. Therefore, we have proved the impossibility of constructing an AND protocol using G_3, G_4, G_5, G_6, and G_9.

Table 3. List of all the 30 subgroups of the symmetric group S_4

Group	Elements of group	Group	Elements of group
G_1	{id}	G_{11}	{id, (1 2 3), (1 3 2)}
G_2	{id, (1 2)}	G_{12}	{id, (1 2 4), (1 4 2)}
G_3	{id, (1 3)}	G_{13}	{id, (1 3 4), (1 4 3)}
G_4	{id, (1 4)}	G_{14}	{id, (2 3 4), (2 4 3)}
G_5	{id, (2 3)}	G_{15}	{id, (1 2)(3 4), (1 3 2 4), (1 4 2 3)}
G_6	{id, (2 4)}	G_{16}	{id, (1 3)(2 4), (1 2 3 4), (1 4 3 2)}
G_7	{id, (3 4)}	G_{17}	{id, (1 4)(2 3), (1 2 4 3), (1 3 4 2)}
G_8	{id, (1 2)(3 4)}	G_{18}	{id, (1 2), (3 4), (1 2 3 4)}
G_9	{id, (1 3)(2 4)}	G_{19}	{id, (1 3), (2 4), (1 3 2 4)}
G_{10}	{id, (1 4)(2 3)}	G_{20}	{id, (1 4), (2 3), (1 4 2 3)}

Group	Elements of group
G_{21}	{id, (1 2)(3 4), (1 3)(2 4), (1 4)(2 3)}
G_{22}	{id, (1 2 3), (1 3 2), (1 2), (1 3), (2 3)}
G_{23}	{id, (1 2 4), (1 4 2), (1 2), (1 4), (2 4)}
G_{24}	{id, (1 3 4), (1 4 3), (1 3), (1 4), (3 4)}
G_{25}	{id, (2 3 4), (2 4 3), (2 3), (2 4), (3 4)}
G_{26}	{id, (3 4), (1 2), (1 2)(3 4), (1 3)(2 4), (1 4)(2 3), (1 3 2 4), (1 4 2 3)}
G_{27}	{id, (2 3), (1 4), (1 2)(3 4), (1 3)(2 4), (1 4)(2 3), (1 2 3 4), (1 4 3 2)}
G_{28}	{id, (2 4), (1 3), (1 2)(3 4), (1 3)(2 4), (1 4)(2 3), (1 2 3 4), (1 4 3 2)}
G_{29}	All even permutations (i.e., G_{29} is the alternating group A_4)
G_{30}	All permutations (i.e., G_{30} is the symmetric group S_4)

3.2 Shuffles Producing ⊥-Sequences

We now verify the remaining cases, i.e., the shuffles other than the five shuffles discussed in the previous section, which produce a ⊥-sequence. First, we examine G_2 and G_7. Figure 3 depicts the KWH-tree for the case where (shuf, G_2) is applied to the start state. Here, we can observe that the sequence ♡♣♡♣ is a ⊥-sequence because it satisfies Eq. 6:

$$\mu'_2(\heartsuit\clubsuit\heartsuit\clubsuit) = {}^1\!/_2 X_{11} + {}^1\!/_2 X_{01}.$$

That is, $\mu'_2(\heartsuit\clubsuit\heartsuit\clubsuit)$ contains both X_{11} and X_{01}, i.e., both the sum of coefficients of X_{10}, X_{01}, and X_{00} and that of X_{11} are greater than 0. The same holds for G_7 since G_2 and G_7 are symmetric with respect to the order of the two inputs, as discussed in Sect. 3.1.

From Table 3, it can be seen that G_2 is a subgroup of G_{18}:

$$G_2 = \{\mathsf{id}, (1\,2)\} \subseteq G_{18} = \{\mathsf{id}, (1\,2), (3\,4), (1\,2\,3\,4)\}.$$

More generally, G_2 and G_7 are subgroups of the following groups:

$$G_2 = G_{18} \cap G_{22} \cap G_{23} \cap G_{26} \cap G_{30},$$
$$G_7 = G_{18} \cap G_{24} \cap G_{25} \cap G_{26} \cap G_{30}.$$

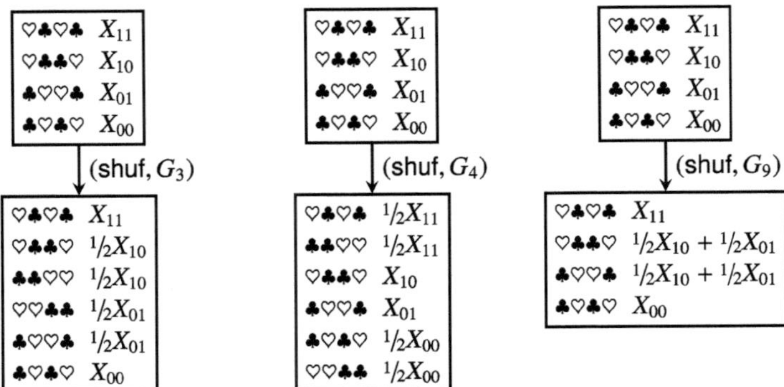

Fig. 2. The KWH-trees when each of (shuf, G_3), (shuf, G_4), and (shuf, G_9) is applied to the start state

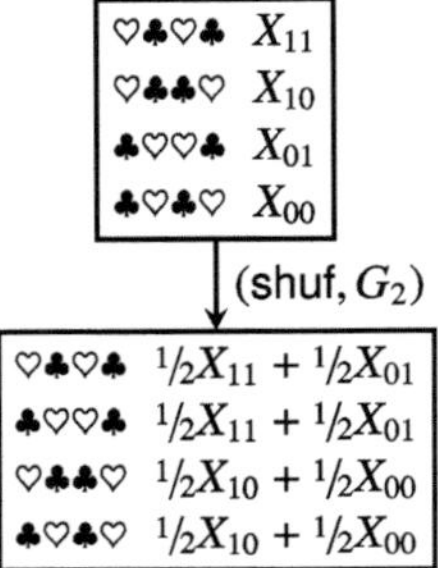

Fig. 3. The KWH-tree constructed with G_2.

Since both G_2 and G_7 produce a $\perp$-sequence, as shown above, any group that contains them, i.e., G_{18}, G_{22}, G_{23}, G_{24}, G_{25}, G_{26}, and G_{30}, must also produce a $\perp$-sequence.

Let us move on to G_{11}, G_{12}, G_{13}, and G_{14}. Since G_{11} and G_{12} are symmetric to G_{14} and G_{13}, respectively, we consider G_{11} and G_{12}, as depicted in Fig. 4. Here, $\heartsuit\clubsuit\heartsuit\clubsuit$ is a $\perp$-sequence, i.e.,

$$\mu'_{11}(\heartsuit\clubsuit\heartsuit\clubsuit) = {}^1\!/\!_3 X_{11} + {}^1\!/\!_3 X_{01},$$
$$\mu'_{12}(\heartsuit\clubsuit\heartsuit\clubsuit) = {}^1\!/\!_3 X_{11} + {}^1\!/\!_3 X_{01}.$$

Therefore, this demonstrates the impossibility for G_{11} and G_{12}, and likewise for G_{13} and G_{14}.

Regarding G_8 and G_{10} shown in Fig. 5, both produce a $\perp$-sequence, as can be seen from the following equations:

$$\mu'_{8}(\heartsuit\clubsuit\heartsuit\clubsuit) = {}^1\!/\!_2 X_{11} + {}^1\!/\!_2 X_{00},$$
$$\mu'_{10}(\heartsuit\clubsuit\heartsuit\clubsuit) = {}^1\!/\!_2 X_{11} + {}^1\!/\!_2 X_{00}.$$

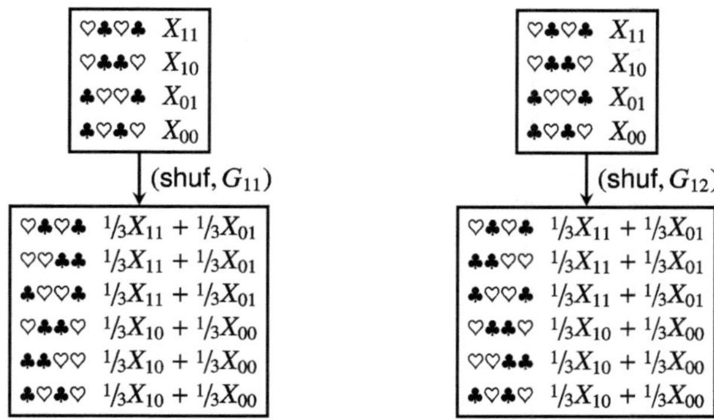

Fig. 4. The KWH-trees when each of (shuf, G_{11}) and (shuf, G_{12}) is applied to the start state

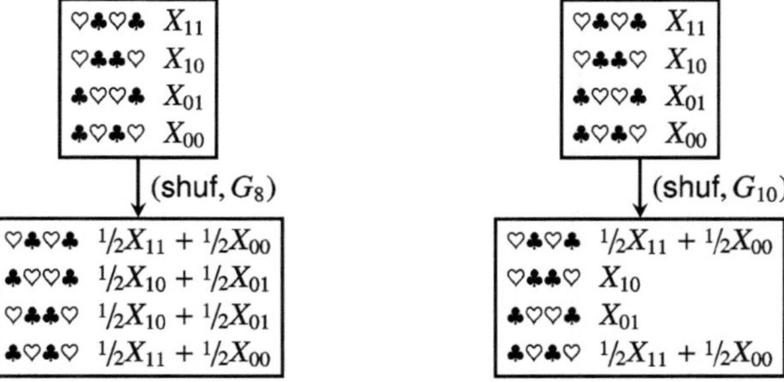

Fig. 5. The KWH-trees when each of (shuf, G_8) and (shuf, G_{10}) is applied to the start state.

Moreover, G_8 and G_{10} are subgroups of the following groups:

$$G_8 = G_{15} \cap G_{21} \cap G_{27} \cap G_{28} \cap G_{29},$$
$$G_{10} = G_{17} \cap G_{21} \cap G_{27} \cap G_{28} \cap G_{29}.$$

Since both G_8 and G_{10} produce a $\perp$-sequence, it follows that these six groups, i.e., G_{15}, G_{17}, G_{21}, G_{27}, G_{28}, and G_{29}, also produce a $\perp$-sequence. Therefore, we have confirmed the impossibility for all of these eight groups.

Lastly, as shown in Fig. 6, the cases of G_{16}, G_{19}, and G_{20} also produce a $\perp$-sequence:

$$\mu'_{16}(\heartsuit\clubsuit\heartsuit\clubsuit) = {}^1\!/\!_2X_{11} + {}^1\!/\!_4X_{01} + {}^1\!/\!_4X_{00},$$
$$\mu'_{19}(\heartsuit\clubsuit\heartsuit\clubsuit) = {}^3\!/\!_4X_{11} + {}^1\!/\!_4X_{10},$$
$$\mu'_{20}(\heartsuit\clubsuit\heartsuit\clubsuit) = {}^1\!/\!_4X_{11} + {}^1\!/\!_4X_{00}.$$

Thus, we have confirmed the case of (shuf, G_i) for all i, which proves Theorem 1.

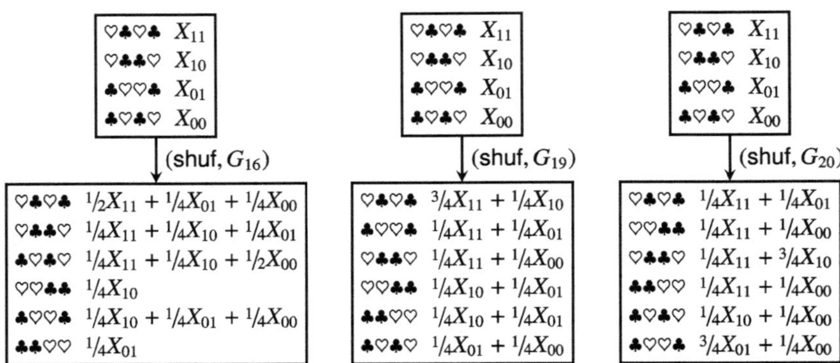

Fig. 6. The KWH-trees when each of (shuf, G_{16}), (shuf, G_{19}), and (shuf, G_{20}) is applied to the start state.

3.3 Extension to Closed Shuffles

The impossibility proof presented in the previous sections can be extended to the case of using a single *closed* shuffle instead of a single uniform closed shuffle. This result is formalized in the following theorem.

Theorem 2. *Any four-card non-committed format AND protocol cannot be realized using only a single non-uniform closed shuffle.*

Proof. The proof for non-uniform closed shuffles is similar to that for uniform closed shuffles, i.e., we show that after applying $(\mathsf{shuf}, G_i, \mathcal{F}_i)$ for each $1 \leq i \leq 30$ and any probability distribution $\mathcal{F}_i$ on G_i, the resulting state is either not turnable or contains a $\perp$-sequence. Here, a $\perp$-sequence arises independently of the distribution of $\mathcal{F}_i$ as shown in Sect. 3.2, and hence, we focus on the five groups of G_3, G_4, G_5, G_6, and G_9, as listed in Sect. 3.1. For any real number $p \in \mathbb{R}$ such that $0 < p < 1$, let $\mathcal{F}_3$ denote a probability distribution on G_3 such that:

$$\mathcal{F}_3 : \mathsf{id} \mapsto p,\ (1\,3) \mapsto 1 - p,$$

and $\mathcal{F}_4$ and $\mathcal{F}_9$ are defined analogously. Figure 7 depicts the KWH-tree when each of $(\mathsf{shuf}, G_3, \mathcal{F}_3)$, $(\mathsf{shuf}, G_4, \mathcal{F}_4)$, and $(\mathsf{shuf}, G_9, \mathcal{F}_9)$ is applied. Here, all of the three states are not clearly turnable according to Eq. 5, because the coefficient of X_{00} differs from those of X_{10} and X_{01} in every state. Since we can omit the cases for G_5 and G_6 due to the symmetry of the order of two inputs as discussed in Sect. 3.1, this proves the impossibility for the case of closed shuffles. □

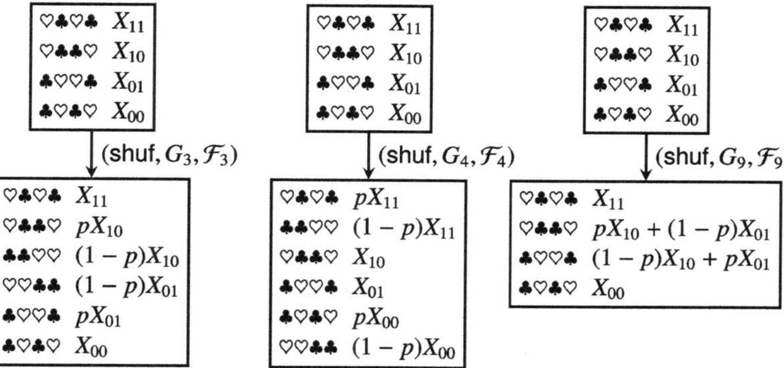

Fig. 7. The KWH-trees when each of non-uniform closed shuffles corresponding to G_3, G_4, and G_9 is applied to the start state, where p is a real number such that $0 < p < 1$.

4 Concluding Remarks

In this study, we proved the impossibility of constructing any four-card non-committed format AND protocol when only a single application of a uniform closed shuffle, i.e., practical shuffle, is allowed. The proof classifies all possible shuffle actions into two categories: those that generate a $\perp$-sequence and those that result in a state which is not turnable. Additionally, our proof employs the KWH-tree [8] to verify each case rigorously. Our result implies that the two-shuffle AND protocol proposed by Mizuki–Kumamoto–Sone [10] achieves the minimum number of shuffles.

Several problems regarding the minimal number of shuffles remain unsolved. We leave them as open problems, as follows.

- Six-card committed-format AND/XOR protocols using a random cut twice are known [2, 16]. Whether there exists such a protocol using only a single random cut remains open. Recall that there is no five-card finite-runtime AND protocol using only closed shuffles [5], though a protocol for computing XOR might be possible.
- There is a six-card non-committed-format protocol for computing the three-input majority function using each of a random cut and a random bisection cut (i.e., twice in total) [15]. Note that these two shuffles are acted sequentially, and hence, they can be described as a single action, as in the MKS protocol [10]. Whether there exists such a protocol using only a single uniform closed shuffle remains open.

Acknowledgments. We thank the anonymous referees, whose comments have helped us to improve the presentation of the paper. This work was supported in part by JSPS KAKENHI Grant Number JP23H00479 and by Institute of Mathematics for Industry, Joint Usage/Research Center in Kyushu University. (FY2023 Short-term Joint Research "Organizing open problems in card-based cryptography through industry-academia collaboration" (2023a020) and FY2024 Short-term Joint Research "Deepening and new frontiers in card-based cryptography through industry-academia collaboration and cooperation in the fields of mathematics and cryptography" (2024a035)).

Disclosure of Interests. The authors have no competing interests to declare that are relevant to the content of this article.

References

1. Abe, Y., Hayashi, Y., Mizuki, T., Sone, H.: Five-card AND protocol in committed format using only practical shuffles. In: ACM ASIA Public-Key Cryptography Workshop, pp. 3–8, New York. ACM (2018). https://doi.org/10.1145/3197507.3197510
2. Abe, Y., Mizuki, T., Sone, H.: Committed-format AND protocol using only random cuts. Nat. Comput. **20**(4), 639–645 (2021). https://doi.org/10.1007/s11047-021-09862-2
3. Boer, B.D.: More efficient match-making and satisfiability the five card trick. In: Quisquater, J.J., Vandewalle, J. (eds.) EUROCRYPT 1989. LNCS, vol. 434, pp. 208–217. Springer, Heidelberg (1990). https://doi.org/10.1007/3-540-46885-4_23
4. Kanai, K., Miyamoto, K., Nuida, K., Shinagawa, K.: Uniform cyclic group factorizations of finite groups. Comm. Algebra **52**(5), 2174–2184 (2024). https://doi.org/10.1080/00927872.2023.2285908
5. Kastner, J., Koch, A., Walzer, S., Miyahara, D., Hayashi, Y., Mizuki, T., Sone, H.: The minimum number of cards in practical card-based protocols. In: Takagi, T., Peyrin, T. (eds.) Advances in Cryptology—ASIACRYPT 2017. LNCS, vol. 10626, pp. 126–155. Springer, Cham (2017). https://doi.org/10.1007/978-3-319-70700-6_5
6. Koch, A.: The landscape of optimal card-based protocols. Math. Cryptol. **1**(2), 115–131 (2022). https://journals.flvc.org/mathcryptology/article/view/130529
7. Koch, A., Walzer, S.: Foundations for actively secure card-based cryptography. In: Farach-Colton, M., Prencipe, G., Uehara, R. (eds.) Fun with Algorithms. LIPIcs, vol. 157, pp. 17:1–17:23. Schloss Dagstuhl, Dagstuhl, Germany (2020). https://doi.org/10.4230/LIPIcs.FUN.2021.17
8. Koch, A., Walzer, S., Härtel, K.: Card-based cryptographic protocols using a minimal number of cards. In: Iwata, T., Cheon, J.H. (eds.) Advances in Cryptology—ASIACRYPT 2015. LNCS, vol. 9452, pp. 783–807. Springer, Berlin, Heidelberg (2015). https://doi.org/10.1007/978-3-662-48797-6_32
9. Koyama, H., Toyoda, K., Miyahara, D., Mizuki, T.: New card-based copy protocols using only random cuts. In: ACM ASIA Public-Key Cryptography Workshop, pp. 13–22. ACM, NY (2021). https://doi.org/10.1145/3457338.3458297
10. Mizuki, T., Kumamoto, M., Sone, H.: The five-card trick can be done with four cards. In: Wang, X., Sako, K. (eds.) Advances in Cryptology—ASIACRYPT 2012. LNCS, vol. 7658, pp. 598–606. Springer, Berlin, Heidelberg (2012). https://doi.org/10.1007/978-3-642-34961-4_36
11. Mizuki, T., Shizuya, H.: A formalization of card-based cryptographic protocols via abstract machine. Int. J. Inf. Secur. **13**(1), 15–23 (2013). https://doi.org/10.1007/s10207-013-0219-4
12. Mizuki, T., Sone, H.: Six-card secure AND and four-card secure XOR. In: Deng, X., Hopcroft, J.E., Xue, J. (eds.) Frontiers in Algorithmics. LNCS, vol. 5598, pp. 358–369. Springer, Berlin, Heidelberg (2009). https://doi.org/10.1007/978-3-642-02270-8_36
13. Ruangwises, S., Itoh, T.: AND protocols using only uniform shuffles. In: van Bevern, R., Kucherov, G. (eds.) Computer Science–Theory and Applications. LNCS, vol. 11532, pp. 349–358. Springer, Cham (2019). https://doi.org/10.1007/978-3-030-19955-5_30
14. Shinagawa, K., Kanai, K., Miyamoto, K., Nuida, K.: How to covertly and uniformly scramble the 15 puzzle and rubik's cube. In: Broder, A.Z., Tamir, T. (eds.) Fun with Algorithms. LIPIcs, vol. 291, pp. 30:1–30:15. Schloss Dagstuhl, Dagstuhl, Germany (2024). https://doi.org/10.4230/LIPIcs.FUN.2024.30

15. Toyoda, K., Miyahara, D., Mizuki, T.: Another use of the five-card trick: Card-minimal secure three-input majority function evaluation. In: Adhikari, A., Küsters, R., Preneel, B. (eds.) Progress in Cryptology—INDOCRYPT 2021. LNCS, vol. 13143, pp. 536–555. Springer, Cham (2021). https://doi.org/10.1007/978-3-030-92518-5_24
16. Toyoda, K., Miyahara, D., Mizuki, T., Sone, H.: Six-card finite-runtime XOR protocol with only random cut. In: ACM ASIA Public-Key Cryptography Workshop, pp. 2–8. ACM, New York (2020). https://doi.org/10.1145/3384940.3388961

webSPDZ: Versatile MPC on the Web

Thomas Buchsteiner[1], Karl W. Koch[1,2](✉), Dragos Rotaru[3](✉), and Christian Rechberger[1]

[1] Graz University of Technology, Graz, Austria
karl.koch@tugraz.at, christian.rechberger@tugraz.at
[2] Secure Information Technology Center Austria (A-SIT), Graz, Austria
[3] Circle Internet Financial, New York, USA
dragos.rotaru@circle.com

Abstract. Multi-party computation (MPC) has become increasingly practical in the last two decades, solving privacy and security issues in various domains, such as healthcare, finance, and machine learning. One big caveat is that MPC sometimes lacks usability since the knowledge barrier for *regular* users can be high. Users have to deal with, e.g., various CLI tools, private networks, and sometimes even must install many dependencies, which can be hardware-dependent.

A solution to improve the usability of MPC is to build browser-based MPC engines where each party runs within a browser window. Two examples of such an MPC web engine are JIFF and the web variant of MPyC. Both support an honest majority with passive corruptions.

`webSPDZ`: Our work brings one of the most performant and versatile general-purpose MPC engines, MP-SPDZ, to the web. MP-SPDZ supports ≥40 MPC protocols with different security models, enabling many security models on the web. To port MP-SPDZ to the web, we use Emscripten to compile MP-SPDZ's C++ BackEnd to WebAssembly and upgrade the party communication for the browser (WebRTC or WebSockets). We call the new MPC web engine webSPDZ. As with the native versions of the mentioned MPC web engines, MPyC-Web and JIFF, webSPDZ outperforms them in our end-to-end experiments.

We believe that webSPDZ brings forth many interesting and practically relevant use cases. Thus, webSPDZ pushes the boundaries of MPC: enabling MPC for a broader audience by making it more usable.

Keywords: Privacy-Enhancing Technology · Private Computations · Multi-Party Computation · MP-SPDZ · MPC Web Engine · webSPDZ

1 Introduction

With the ever-increasing gathering and availability of data, the amount of use cases to learn from data has increased virtually in all areas of our lives. E.g., in the areas of (i) health care, (ii) smart driving, or (iii) smart energy management.

Authors in alphabetical order and expressed views are those of the authors and should not be interpreted as reflecting views of Circle or any other organization.

Y. Kim et al. (Eds.): CANS 2025, LNCS 16351, pp. 230–248, 2026.
https://doi.org/10.1007/978-981-95-4434-9_11

Multi-party computation (MPC) has proven to be an *increasingly* practical cryptographic building block for realizing such computations in a privacy-preserving way. For instance, MPC has been used to protect privacy in (i) detection of early brain tumors through inference of MRI images [25], (ii) reducing fuel consumption through speed advisory systems for vehicles [24], or (iii) saving energy through smart-meter systems in buildings [33]. The *popular* Danish sugar-beet trading [8] was the first-known large-scale real-life use case of MPC in 2008. In 2024, MPC was used to perform *real-life* cross-hospital analytics [4].

One primary aspect to practically enable MPC are ready-to-use MPC engines. Especially general-purpose engines are of interest as they virtually allow arbitrary computations with a dynamic range of participating parties.

Motivation. Imagine a meeting where everyone should participate in a spontaneous privacy-preserving survey. One must set up the respective MPC engine to actively join an MPC computation. E.g., installing all requirements and configuring the engine for each party. Although many MPC engines provide Docker containers with tutorial programs, getting everything running is still an initial hurdle, especially for *regular users* (no technical experts).

Bogdanov et al. [7] conducted an end-user survey regarding the potential use of MPC in various areas and use cases. Their survey results underline the relevance of MPC for regular users. Further, in the area of biomedical data, Wirth et al. [37] explained the relevance of learning from shared data while ensuring the privacy of thereof. As such, Wirth et al. chose MPC as their privacy-preserving computational building block. However, they also noted its practical limitations:

> "SMPC is still rarely used in real-world biomedical data sharing activities due to several barriers, including its technical complexity and lack of usability" [37].

Barak et al. [5] reported the same relevance of *commoditizing MPC* in 2018, explaining the web browser's importance and advantage for end users:

> "A far more compelling way of carrying out the above study would be to have each company run its own copy of the MPC. However, ..., none of these companies would install software and would only use a browser interface" [5].
> ...
> "As the browser is becoming the new OS for end users, additional features and capabilities are constantly added ... open the possibility of achieving high performance MPC directly in the browser" [5].

Ballhausen et al. [4] reported the use of a native general-purpose MPC engine to analyze real-world cancer-related data across hospitals. However, they mentioned practical hurdles of using MPC in this project: "*...included a complex tech stack, demanding implementation, complicated technology management...*". Hence, it is a relevant issue to make MPC more accessible and usable for a broader audience.

One of the most promising cross-platform solutions is to bring MPC engines to the web browser. Users *just* need a compatible browser. Moreover, the portable nature of web-based solutions enables MPC on many end-user devices. E.g., PCs, smartphones, tablets, or even "wearables" like smartwatches [31]. The smooth setup of web-based solutions, with the cross-platform aspect, enables the advantages of MPC for nearly everyone.

Related Work. Already in 2018, Barak et al. [5] have performed MPC in the web browser. They built upon `Emscripten` but reported issues of not having "Single Instruction, Multiple Data" (SIMD) [36] in the browser. However, while the web app's source code is available on GitHub [11], we did not find the source code of their MPC engine for the browser.

The "JavaScript library for building web apps that employ MPC" (`JIFF`) [17] and the "Web Variant of Multiparty Computation in Python" (`MPyC-Web`) [27] are two recent popular general-purpose frameworks for performing MPC on the web. However, both engines only support one security model (passive security using Shamir's secret sharing with honest majority) and `JIFF` needs a central server for party communication. Although messages sent between parties are end-to-end encrypted, the central server presents a single point of failure, could be a communication bottleneck, and could infer certain computation-related metadata, like the amount of communication rounds.

Hence, while running MPC on the web is possible, one cannot choose from various security models for general-purpose computations with p2pH party communication and a dynamic amount of participating parties.

For an additional overview of general MPC frameworks, please refer to, e.g., Rotaru's "Awesome MPC" list [2], Hastings et al.'s SoK paper [18], or Keller's MPC framework overview in the "Multi-Protocol SPDZ - A Versatile Framework for MPC" (`MP-SPDZ`) paper [21].

Our Contributions. For the first time, this work enables general-purpose MPC computations on the web that support different security models by utilizing virtually >40 MPC protocols (e.g., active or passive corruptions and an honest or dishonest majority).

We achieve this variety by bringing the native general-purpose MPC engine `MP-SPDZ` [21] to the web browser, dubbed `webSPDZ`. We built upon `MP-SPDZ` due to its variety of protocols, active development (frequent bug fixes and updates), regular stable releases (every few months), and "popularity" (>1000 stars on GitHub with >250 forks).

Inspired by the pioneering work of Barak et al. [5], we use `Emscripten` to compile `MP-SPDZ`'s C++ backend to WebAssembly (Wasm), which is *usually* faster than JavaScript in the web browser [28,34]. For p2pH-based party communication in the browser, we build upon "Web Real-Time Communication" (`WebRTC`).

Moreover, `webSPDZ` achieves the fastest MPC runtimes in our end-to-end benchmarks compared to the related general-purpose MPC web engines. For benchmarking, we choose the dot·product between two secret vectors since MPC programs often use it as a building block. As MPC protocols' secret-sharing scheme, we use (i) Shamir (to compare `webSPDZ` with the related MPC web engines) and (ii) Replicated. To show a real-life case, we answer "Who pays for dinner?" via MPC on three smartphone browsers in ~0.1 s.

Outline. Section 3 describes the developed MPC web engine, `webSPDZ`. Section 4 evaluates and discusses the runtime performance of `webSPDZ`, `MPyC-Web`, and `JIFF`, as well as `webSPDZ`'s native variant (`MP-SPDZ`, which is dubbed `natSPDZ` in this section). Additionally, Sect. 2 presents supporting preliminaries, and Sect. 5 concludes this work.

2 Preliminaries for WebSPDZ

In this section, we first briefly describe MPC with the related security models and protocols, and define the term "general-purpose MPC (web) engine". For further information, the interested reader can check, e.g., Smart [30] and Lindell [23]. Then, we show the main tools that bring `MP-SPDZ` to the web browser: Wasm, `Emscripten`, and `WebRTC`.

2.1 MPC-Related Building Blocks

MPC enables various parties to jointly compute a function over secret inputs. While no party learns the input of other parties or intermediate results, all or a subset of dedicated parties receive the function outputs.MPC computations use a dedicated MPC protocol under a specific security model. To practically enable computations using generic MPC protocols/programs, parties use so-called "MPC engines".

MPC Security Models. One usually decides how many parties an adversary can corrupt and the type of corruption. Depending on the number of parties that can be (statically) corrupt, protocols are classified primarily into two categories:

1. **Honest majority**, where at most half of the parties are corrupt.
2. **Dishonest majority**, which allows up to all but one corrupted parties.

For corruption types, the MPC literature states primarily two:

1. **Passive or semi-honest security**, where corrupted parties try to learn as much as possible from the protocol transcript while following the protocol's instructions.
2. **Active or malicious security**, where corrupted parties, additionally, can arbitrarily deviate from the protocol (e.g., sending malformed data).

MPC Protocols. To perform MPC computations, various protocols provide different levels of security. In this paper, we focus on protocols that work with arithmetic circuits. We build upon five major MPC protocols: semi-honest and malicious Shamir [1,10,29], semi-honest Replicated [3] for 3 parties, and malicious Replicated for 4 parties by Dalskov et al. [12].

Moreover, we also provide an implementation in webSPDZ for the passive version of the SPDZ protocol for dishonest majority MPC, based on oblivious transfer (OT) preprocessing working for $\mathbb{Z}_{2^{128}}$ [9,13,14] (dubbed Semi2k).

In MP-SPDZ, the program is described using a high-level language similar to Python. Then, the high-level code gets compiled down to a series of basic instructions such as openings, additions, and multiplications [22]. The resulted instructions are generic enough so that when instantiated using the correct virtual machine (VM), implemented by MP-SPDZ, these yield into a secure MPC protocol [21]. Depending on the VM, the protocol can offer security against various type of corrupted parties and adversary models.

Due to MP-SPDZ's modularity, one *only* needs to implement the few basic operations described above. Then, the protocol can be *fairly easily* integrated in MP-SPDZ's protocol suite.

General-Purpose MPC Web Engines. With MPC engines, we denote a framework which enables parties to *actively participate* in MPC computations. If an MPC engine can be run in a web browser, we denote it as MPC web engine. With general-purpose, we denote an MPC engine which *virtually* supports arbitrary computations and a dynamic number of participating parties.

2.2 Web-Browser-Related Building Blocks

To bring MP-SPDZ to the web browser, we primarily built upon three pillars: (1) Wasm to run code in the browser, (2) Emscripten to compile MP-SPDZ's C++ BackEnd to Wasm, and (3) WebRTC for P2P communication in the browser.

Wasm [16]. WebAssembly (Wasm) has been developed to run code in the web browser safe, fast, portable, and compact [28].As such, Wasm is a low-level binary instruction format, which uses only integers and floats, and is supported by most popular browsers [35]. An essential browser feature for our work is native 64-bit memory, which, e.g., Chrome and Firefox recently enabled by default. Since Wasm's pure runtime is close to native, it usually runs alongside JavaScript to speed up certain code parts.

Emscripten [15]. Is the most-popular (open-source) tool that compiles native C/C++ code to Wasm. Emscripten builds upon an LLVM frontend and uses a backend that generates JavaScript code [39]. The toolchain is well-documented and provides many features. Some important features for our work are a set of already ported libraries to Wasm and many APIs that allow easy integration of, e.g., file systems, Wasm workers (threads), or C++ support for JavaScript objects.

The Emscripten compiler emcc replaces the native compiler and provides a variety of flags to, e.g., optimize performance and code size. emcc outputs a Wasm and JavaScript file. The JavaScript file loads the Wasm file and provides an API to interact with the compiled Wasm modules. For testing purposes, emcc also auto-generates an HTML file.

WebRTC [16]. Google released the "Web Real-Time Communication" (WebRTC) project as an open-source framework in 2011. Since then, WebRTC has been further developed and standardized by the World Wide Web Consortium (W3C). and the World Wide Web Consortium (W3C) further developed and standardized it. By now, most popular browsers support the technology.

WebRTC is a collection of APIs that enables encrypted peer-to-peer (P2P) communication between web browsers without additional plugins. Every WebRTC connection is encrypted using the protocols Datagram Transport Layer Security (DTLS) for key exchange and Secure Real Time (SRT) for encrypted data transmission. For further details on WebRTC's security architecture, the interested reader can check, e.g., the Internet Engineering Task Force (IETF) [19].

The connection-building process is called Interactive Connectivity Establishment (ICE). First, each peer uses a STUN (Session Traversal Utilities for NAT) server to dissolve the public IP address and create an ICE candidate; while a TURN (Traversal Using Relays around NAT) server acts as a fallback. Then, these ICE candidates are exchanged between any two peers via a signaling server. When parties establish a WebRTC connection, the STUN/TURN/signaling servers are not needed anymore and the whole communication is p2p. Please note that the signaling process is not part of the WebRTC standard as it relies on other protocols like SIP (Session Initiation Protocol) over WebSockets. E.g., Blum et al. [6] and Sredojev et al. [32] give further details on WebRTC.

3 webSPDZ

This section describes the "Web Variant of Multi-Protocol-SPDZ" (webSPDZ). Initially, we describe webSPDZ's source-code approach. Then, we describe how to transform MP-SPDZ into an MPC web engine.

Section 3.1 describes how to cross-compile MP-SPDZ's C++ backend to Wasm using Emscripten. Section 3.2 describes the changes to enable P2P communication in the browser using WebRTC. Besides WebRTC, Appendix B describes an alternative communication approach using WebSockets. Then, Sect. 3.3 gives an example of performing MPC in the web browser using webSPDZ. Finally, Sect. 3.4 describes security and privacy considerations for practical instantiations of webSPDZ.

Source Code. We open-sourced webSPDZ[1] Since we base webSPDZ on MP-SPDZ, most of the source code is identical to MP-SPDZ's C++ backend. For further information on practical use of webSPDZ, please refer to the repository. For instance, we show webSPDZ's tech stack, provide ready-to-use test files, and highlight some additional information on transforming MP-SPDZ to webSPDZ.

3.1 Compiling MP-SPDZ's C++ Backend to WebAssembly

We show how to compile MP-SPDZ's C++ backend to Wasm by first compiling the library dependencies. Then we describe the relevant code changes in MP-SPDZ

[1] https://github.com/HEMPZeed/webSPDZ.

to make it compatible with Wasm. Finally we show some features we had to bring in, such as compiler settings, thread management, and various APIs. For more details on compiling C++ to Wasm using `Emscripten`, please refer to, e.g., Emscripten's documentation.

Porting Library Dependencies. To support the >40 protocols, `MP-SPDZ` mainly relies on four (open-source) libraries: Boost, Libsodium, OpenSSL, and GMP. We have added pre-compiled ".a archives" of the libraries so we can link them to the Wasm version.

Boost. Includes a set of libraries that `MP-SPDZ` uses, e.g., for network communication and multithreading. We replace the original library by linking a ported version of Boost from the open-source project Ports, using the flag `-sUSE_BOOST_HEADERS=1`.

Libsodium. `Emscripten` provides the command `emconfigure`, which can replace all default environment variables with `Emscripten`-specific ones. Libsodium provides a build script for `Emscripten`, which provides the necessary commands to build it from source.

OpenSSL. We must build OpenSSL manually using several flags. Then, we must adapt the compiler path in the resulting Makefile. The resulting ".a archive" is then linked in the framework.

GMP. `MP-SPDZ` uses GMP for arithmetic operations. We can use the original GMP library without any patches since the datatype `long` has the correct size of 8 bytes in 64-bit Wasm. We focus on 64-bit Wasm since most web browsers, such as Firefox and Chrome, support it now. For our experiments with 32-bit Wasm, please refer to Appendix A *(GMP Library for 32-bit webSPDZ)*.

Modifying MP-SPDZ Implementation. Since some commands and functions are unavailable in a Wasm-based environment, we must adapt the respective code parts in `MP-SPDZ`'s C++ backend. For instance, some optimization approaches or network parts have to be revised. The following paragraphs show the most relevant code modifications to enable `webSPDZ`.

Architecture-Specific Inline Assembly. `MP-SPDZ` optimizes runtime in many different ways. One is using inline assembly to enable high-speed operations via the CPU. However, since Wasm does not support inline assembly, we need to replace it with equivalent C++ code. Fortunately, `MP-SPDZ` provides architecture-specific implementations in many cases.

SIMD Instructions. "Single Instruction, Multiple Data" (SIMD) instructions are another optimization technique in `MP-SPDZ`. For instance, MP-SPDZ uses AVX 256-bit instructions and the AES-NI and PCLMUL instruction sets to speed up AES and certain multiplications. However, e.g., these AES-related instructions are not available. AVX 256-bit instructions as well as the instruction sets of AES-NI and PCLMUL to speed up AES and certain multiplications respectively, are not available. Moreover, SIMD instructions in

Wasm are usually less performant than the original instruction sets. As such, we emulate many SIMD via software-specific code.

Networking. MP-SPDZ bases its networking on C++ (POSIX) sockets, either SSL sockets of the Boost library or default BSD sockets. Since web browsers do not support POSIX socket functions, such as `listen()` or `accept()`, Emscripten bridges WebSockets and POSIX sockets via proxy servers. Further, we also want P2P communication for the MPC computations on the web to enhance privacy. Therefore, we introduce a new networking layer for p2p party communication in a web browser environment. Section 3.2 *(Peer-to-Peer Party Communication in the Web Browser)* describes this new networking layer.

Makefile. In MP-SPDZ's Makefile, we must change the compiler and linker flags for the used Emscripten APIs and the unsupported flags in a web browser environment. The remaining MP-SPDZ's Makefile is mostly unchanged. Finally, the Emscripten compiler `emcc` replaces the original `gcc` compiler.

Compiler Settings, Threads, and APIs. The large variety of implemented features in Emscripten simplifies the cross-compilation process. We use several APIs from Emscripten and various compiler settings. For instance, we use the compiler flags `-sMEMORY64=1`, which generates 64-bit Wasm code and `-sASYNCIFY`, which enables synchronous C++ code and asynchronous JavaScript code. We require this interplay of C++ and JavaScript code when waiting for a network response, such as input from other parties. However, such Emscripten compiler flags *can* lead to decreased performance and a larger code size.

Dealing with the UI Thread. The web browser uses the main thread to execute code and perform tasks in the UI. When we have a synchronous operation, such as waiting for another party's input, the UI will freeze until the operation has finished. We have implemented a solution that avoids this UI freezing by carefully implementing a thread-management solution. webSPDZ's web application runs in a separate thread, using the `-sPROXY_TO_PTHREAD` compiler flag. The UI thread spawns a new thread within the application and only becomes active if needed. Within the application thread, multithreading is still possible.

However, in some cases, the application thread needs the support of the UI thread. For instance, the WebRTC API must access the web browser's Window component, which the UI thread handles. Therefore, some networking parts can only run in the UI thread. Emscripten provides the `proxying.h` API to proxy between the threads. However, this proxying *can* lead to a performance decrease.

File System in the Web Browser. Emscripten's file system API provides a POSIX-like file system in a web browser environment. We use WasmFS, a Wasm-based file system. WasmFS is faster than, e.g., the JavaScript-based filesystem.

3.2 Peer-to-Peer Party Communication in the Web Browser

Due to security and privacy considerations, We do not want to rely on an external (proxy) server for party communication within MPC computations. Thus, as a second preparation step, we enable **P2P** communication between MPC parties in the web browser.

To enable **P2P** communication, we adapt MP-SPDZ's networking layer. We built upon WebRTC to be portable across various browsers while retaining security & privacy. To support WebRTC in MP-SPDZ's C++ backend, we use the C++ library libdatachannel. The library's developer provides a ported Wasm version with a limited feature set called libdatachannel-wasm14. Since the library does not yet support Wasm64, we had to change the library's code for webSPDZ in some places. We benefited from MP-SPDZ's modular C++ design when integrating the new networking layer. MP-SPDZ implements most communication in the Player class. We create a subclass called WebPlayer for the new WebRTC communication.

Further, we implement WebRTC's signaling process for connection establishment. To establish a connection to a signaling web-socket server, which exchanges necessary *meta* connection information between parties, we use Emscripten's WebSocket API. We implemented a JavaScript-based signaling server that accepts incoming web-socket connections from parties and forwards sent data to the other parties. When the signaling process finishes, the web-socket connection is closed and parties *purely* communicate via **P2P** for, e.g., MPC computations. Figure 1 shows webSPDZ's networking communication with three parties. Please refer to, e.g., Sect. 2.2 for details on WebRTC's connection establishment.

Moreover, we can introduce another networking approach for other cases with different networking requirements. As for the WebPlayer's subclass, we can add another Player's subclass with *relatively few* lines of code.

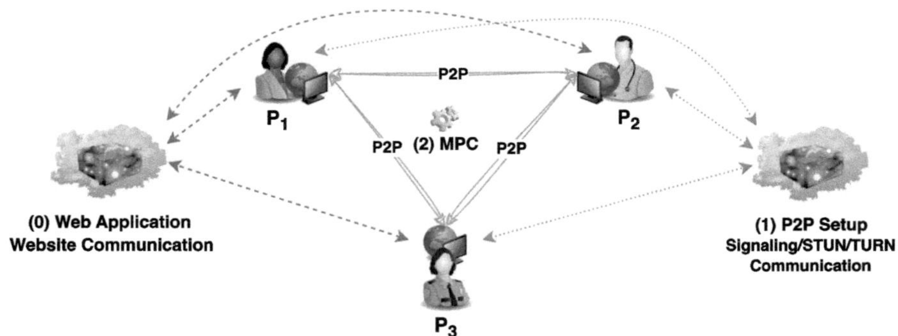

Fig. 1. wsz's networking communication with three parties. First (0) each party communicates with a web-app server that provides the MPC program. Next (1), each party sets up p2p channels using WebRTC's signaling server. Finally (2), parties communicate via p2p for the actual MPC computation.

3.3 Running MP-SPDZ in the Web Browser Using WebSPDZ

This section describes the final assembly of transforming MP-SPDZ into webSPDZ. First, we describe a complete flow of performing an MPC computation in the web browser. While the execution steps are similar to the native variant of MP-SPDZ, we highlight the differences. The complete flow is the following:

1. **Compile webSPDZ.** After compilation, `Emscripten` outputs a `.wasm`, `.js` , and test `.html` file. We use the auto-generated `.html` file. The `.js` file serves as a bridge between the web browser's JavaScript engine and Wasm. Further, we can call the C++-backend's functions via the `.js` file.
2. **Write and compile the MPC program.** As for native `MP-SPDZ`, we write an MPC program in `MP-SPDZ`'s Python-based front-end language and compile it. Then, `MP-SPDZ`'s compiler outputs a schedule file containing the computation's meta information and a bytecode file containing low-level instructions for the C++ virtual machine.
3. **Provide webSPDZ's web application.** Now, we can host `webSPDZ` using the web-application server, which provides the `.wasm`, `.js`, and `.html` files.
4. **Parties join the MPC computation.** To start the MPC computation, each party opens `webSPDZ`'s web application via a web browser tab. Parties provide `webSPDZ`'s execution parameters as query parameters via the browser's address bar.
5. **Parties set up P2P communication.** When all required parties have joined, each party performs the P2P setup via `WebRTC`. When each party has finished the P2P setup, parties can communicate in a P2P way for the MPC computation.
6. **Parties perform the MPC computation in the web browser.** As for native `MP-SPDZ`, parties might provide input, depending on the respective MPC program, and jointly perform the MPC computation. After a successful MPC computation, pre-defined parties can read the computation results in their browser interface.

3.4 Security and Privacy Considerations of webSPDZ

This section discusses security- and privacy-related considerations of `webSPDZ`. First, we discuss (networking) communication-related aspects. Then, we discuss (MPC) computation-related aspects.

Communication-Related Security and Privacy. For the MPC computations, parties communicate in a P2P way via `WebRTC`. `WebRTC` encrypts these communications using the Secure Real-time Transport Protocol (SRTP). We only need the signaling server for the communication setup. However, the default communication setup does not authenticate parties' messages.

We use the signaling server due to usability. With the signaling server, parties can establish a P2P communication without *manually* exchanging connection information (the ICE candidates). In sensitive cases, we could use other channels to exchange connection information. For instance, one could use a *trusted* group channel in the Signal messaging app.

Regarding external entities, we can host both the signaling and `webSPDZ`'s web application, which provides the MPC program and engine, on the same server. Since both applications run on the same server, they fall into the same trust domain. This unification of trust increases the overall trust in the system, as one already needs to trust webSPDZ's web application, which is the same as trusting the content of other web applications, such as https://google.com or https://eprint.iacr.org.

We use a Google STUN server (https://stun.1.google.com) to translate a party's IP address and create the ICE candidates. While the respective server learns when an IP address starts communicating, we must also trust the STUN server's answers. Hence, we balance a trade-off between privacy, usability, and trust. One can change the STUN server according to their needs. For instance, many publicly available STUN servers exist. Ideally, each application/organization self-hosts its STUN/TURN servers in sensitive cases.

Computation-Related Security and Privacy. In general, webSPDZ provides the same computational security & privacy as the native variant of MP-SPDZ [21]. Virtually, webSPDZ can support the same protocols. Hence, we can select the same protocols based on the desired level of security. For instance, we can equally select the corruption mode (passive vs. active security) and trust in the parties' majority (honest vs. dishonest majority). MP-SPDZ gives a detailed overview of supported security models and protocols, e.g., in its GitHub repository.

4 Performance Evaluation of webSPDZ

In this section, we practically evaluate the performance of webSPDZ. Initially, we describe the MPC program for our lab-environment benchmarks, the dot·product, and our benchmarking approach. Then, we show our results for the lab- environment benchmarks and the exemplary real-life case on three Android smartphones, "Dining MPC Phones", which answers who pays for dinner. Finally, we show our results.

Since both the native and web variants of MP-SPDZ are built upon the same BackEnd and use the same FrontEnd, in this section, we dub the native variant of MP-SPDZ MP-SPDZ "natSPDZ".

4.1 Evaluation Strategy

Programs and Protocols. For the lab-environment benchmarks, we build upon the strategy from Keller [21] and compute the **dot·product** of two vectors (multiplication is one of the most expensive operations in MPC).

Figure 2 shows the source code for webSPDZ and natSPDZ, respectively (both use the same FrontEnd code). We select the most comparable MPC web engines, JIFF and MPyC-Web, and run them for one setting (they only support one protocol).

As MPC protocol, we first use Shamir as all engines support it, with 3 parties for 100,000 vector elements. Additionally, we use Replicated with 3 and 4 parties, respectively, using webSPDZ and natSPDZ for 100 up to 1,000,000 vector elements. Shamir and Replicated for 3 parties provide passive security for an honest majority (threshold $t = \left\lceil \frac{\#parties}{2} \right\rceil - 1$; e.g., $t = 1$ for 3 parties). Replicated with 4 parties provides active security. We set a field size of 128 bits. Except for JIFF, which we set to 48 bits as it could only handle up to 53 bits in our experiments.

Inspired by Yao's millionaire problem [38], as an **exemplary real-life case** ("Dining MPC Phones"), we answer "Who pays for dinner?". The program only reveals the party with the highest salary while keeping the parties' salaries private. Three Android smartphones (= 3 parties) use webSPDZ via the Chrome browser, using the MPC protocol Replicated.

```
start_timer(1) # Full Program
n = int(program.args[1])
start_timer(2) # Input Phase
a = sint.Array(n)
b = sint.Array(n)
a.input_from(0) # Party 0
b.input_from(1) # Party 1
stop_timer(2)
start_timer(3) # Pure Dot·Product Computation
res = sint.dot_product(a,b)
stop_timer(3)
stop_timer(1)
```

Fig. 2. Source code of the **dot·product** for the two MPC engines webSPDZ and natSPDZ. Inspired by Keller's benchmarking code [20]. # denotes a comment.

Input and Measurements. In our benchmarks, Party 0 and 1 each input a secret vector and share it among all parties. We measure the runtime for (1) the whole program (Full), from startup until the final result, (2) the input phase (creating or reading in the vectors and sharing them among all parties), and (3) the pure dot·product computation. We do not measure compile times since we can compile an MPC program in advance. Moreover, we can reuse such compilations given the same parameters. We measured each setting three times and took the average.

Selected MPC Engines and Run Environment. We benchmarked the following MPC web engines:

- JIFF: "JavaScript library for building web apps that employ MPC" [17]
  - *Version:* from June 6th 2024 (GitHub Commit ID: *f5a22d8*).
    To improve performance, we reduced the server's log output.
  - *Browser:* we use node.js to run JIFF. Since both node.js and the web-browser Chrome run on the V8 engine, using node.js should be comparable to a pure browser environment. Further, as JIFF's runtimes are far beyond the other engines (as seen in the results below), we did not investigate runtimes within a browser.

- MPyC-Web: "Web Variant of Multiparty Computation in Python" [27]
  - *Version:* from February 16th 2024 (GitHub Commit ID: *5b72f19*).
  - *Browser:* Firefox 137.0. (compiles the (Python) backend source to Wasm)
- webSPDZ: "Web Variant of Multi-Protocol-SPDZ" (this work)
  - *Version:* based on MP-SPDZ's source code from June 20th 2024 (GitHub Commit ID: *18e934f*; webSPDZ repository's GitHub Commit ID *bfffc9d*).
  - *Browser:* Firefox 137.0. (compiles the (C++) backend source to Wasm)

Additionally, we compare webSPDZ with the native variant of MP-SPDZ (natSPDZ). For an as-fair-as-possible comparison, natSPDZ uses the same version of MP-SPDZ as webSPDZ. Dot·product implementations are based on Keller's benchmarking code [20] and Hastings et al.'s example code [26].

We crafted Docker containers for each engine. Each party ran in its own Docker container with a limit of 4GB RAM and 4 CPUs of an *x86_64 AMD EPYC 7502 32-Core Processor* using Linux. webSPDZ's and MPyC-Web's Docker containers simulated the Firefox browser using Selenium's Python module.

Reproducibility. We have open-sourced webSPDZ and our benchmarking data[2]. For instance, we provide the source code and Docker files for all benchmarked MPC engines. Based on the benchmarking machine, the results may vary. However, the relative runtimes of the various engines should be similar.

4.2 Evaluation Results

Table 1 shows the results of our lab-environment benchmarks. Additionally, Fig. 3 shows Replicated runtimes with 3 parties for 100 up to 1,000,000 (1 million) vector elements for the program phases Input and Pure Computation. Figure 4 shows the "Dining MPC Phones" case evaluation on three smartphones. webSPDZ nominated the party that pays for dinner (highest salary) in ~0.1 s.

For readability, the following paragraphs abbreviate the "Pure Computation" runtime measure with Pure Comp.

Shamir Protocol for 3 Parties. Computing the dot·product for 100,000 vector elements using Shamir for 3 parties takes JIFF overall ~**4.5min** (50 s Input; 3.5min Pure Comp). MPyC-Web takes overall ~**10 s** (2.39 s Input; 0.002 s (2ms) Pure Comp). Thus, MPyC-Web seems to have a heavier initialization phase.

webSPDZ takes overall ~**0.5 s** (0.45 s Input; 0.05 s Pure Comp). natSPDZ takes overall ~**0.1 s** and aligns with Keller's results [21] (0.08 s using 64 bits).

Replicated Protocol for 3 and 4 Parties. Computing the dot·product for 100,000 vector elements using Replicated takes webSPDZ overall ~**0.12 s** for 3 parties (100ms Input; 10ms Pure Comp) and ~**0.67 s** for 4 parties (0.63 s Input; 0.031 s (31ms) Pure Comp).

natSPDZ takes overall ~**0.072 s** for 3 parties (68ms Input; 4ms Pure Comp) and ~**0.12 s** for 4 parties (113ms Input; 6ms Pure Comp). As for the Shamir

[2] https://github.com/HEMPZeed/webSPDZ.

protocol, `natSPDZ`'s runtime aligns with Keller's results [21] (0.03 s using 64 bits for the 3-party variant).

For the extended evaluation of Replicated with 3 parties using 100 up to 1,000,000 (1 million) vector elements, the **overall runtime** of `webSPDZ` is first similar to `natSPDZ` and then increases faster when inputting more data. The **Pure Computation runtime** of `webSPDZ` is similar to `natSPDZ` up to 100,000 vector elements. However, interestingly, for 1,000,000 vector elements, `webSPDZ` was even slightly faster than `natSPDZ`.

Table 1. Time in seconds to compute the dot-product for 100,000 vector elements, using the MPC protocols Shamir and Replicated with 3 parties in an unrestricted (LAN-like) environment. In an honest-majority setting with passive security, where 2 parties provide input. Averaged over 3 runs. and party with max. Full runtime shown. Since only `webSPDZ` supports protocols beyond Shamir, we do not show Replicated timings for the other MPC web engines.

MPC Engines	**Shamir (3P)**			**Replicated (3P)**		
	Full	Input	Pure Comp	Full	Input	Pure Comp
Web						
JIFF (48-bit)	265.11	49.76	215.34	$\perp$	$\perp$	$\perp$
MPyCweb (128-bit)	10.19	2.39	**0.002**	$\perp$	$\perp$	$\perp$
webSPDZ (128-bit)	**0.5**	**0.45**	0.05	0.117	0.102	0.013
Native						
natSPDZ (128-bit)	0.12	0.11	0.007	0.072	0.068	0.004

Σ **Evaluation Summary.** One of the main runtime bottlenecks is the input phase. In the web browser, 3in a native environment, probably because of higher networking costs.

Further, for `JIFF`, the Pure Computation runtime, and `MPyC-Web`, the initialization phase, took relatively long too. Although `JIFF` uses only a field size of 48 bits, it is the slowest engine in our experiments. We assume that `JIFF`'s slow runtime originates from (i) JavaScript and (ii) routing each party message via a coordination server. On the other hand, `MPyC-Web` has the fastest Pure Computation runtime.

Overall, `webSPDZ` is the **fastest and most versatile MPC web engine** (in our end-to-end benchmarks). Virtually, `webSPDZ` can support each of `MP-SPDZ`'s MPC protocols (>40).

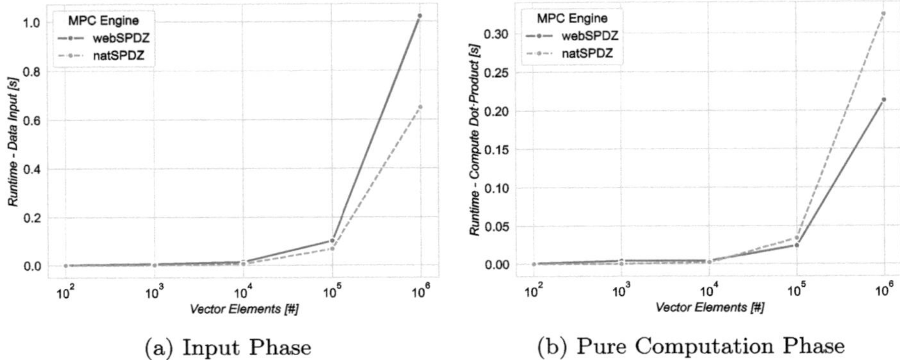

(a) Input Phase (b) Pure Computation Phase

Fig. 3. Runtime in seconds of the dot·product for various vector elements in an unrestricted (LAN-like) network. Using the MPC protocol Replicated for 3 parties with the MPC engines `webSPDZ` and `MP-SPDZ` (dotted line).

Fig. 4. "Dining MPC phones". Three Android smartphones evaluated who pays for dinner in ~0.1 s, using `webSPDZ` (Replicated protocol) in the Chrome browser.

5 Conclusions and Future Work

Our vision is to enable MPC for everyone by making it simple to use. One promising solution is to use web-based MPC engines, which enable a party to actively join an MPC computation by *simply* opening a Web browser tab.

The state-of-the-art's main limitation is the versatility of MPC protocols and security models. Besides, some engines use a central server for communication (e.g., `JIFF`), which adds privacy concerns and potential bottlenecks.

That is why we created `webSPDZ`, the web variant of `MP-SPDZ`, one of the most performant and flexible general-purpose MPC engines, which supports >40 protocols with different security models. Hence, `webSPDZ` enables many security models on the web. To transform `MP-SPDZ` into an MPC web engine, we use (i) `Emscripten` to compile `MP-SPDZ`'s C++ BackEnd to WebAssembly and (ii) `WebRTC` to enable peer-to-peer (P2P) party communication in the browser.

As with the native variants of the two recent MPC web engines, `MPyC-Web` and `JIFF`, `webSPDZ` outperforms them in our end-to-end experiments. Compared to native engines, one of the main bottlenecks in the browser seems to be the phase of inputting data. For pure computation, `webSPDZ` performed almost identically to its native variant and even outperformed it for one setting. The slower input phase in the browser could originate from, e.g., a slower file system or less efficient p2p party communication. Closing the gap between MPC native and web engines would be one of the interesting future works. As such, we must further evaluate `webSPDZ` with related work by performing more exhaustive benchmarks; e.g., running each experiment more often and considering standard deviation. Further, investigating a broader range of MPC protocols, like dishonest-majority protocols such as Semi2k, which `webSPDZ` already supports.

While our primary evaluation goal was checking the performance overhead of `webSPDZ`, we must further evaluate secure (`WebRTC`-based) p2p channels in web environments for real-life deployments. As one usability-enhancing aspect, `webSPDZ` could add a GUI for, e.g., inputting data.

We believe that `webSPDZ` brings forth many interesting and practically relevant use cases. Thus, `webSPDZ` pushes the boundaries of practical MPC: enabling MPC for a broader audience by making it more usable.

Acknowledgments. This work received funding from PREPARED, an Austrian KIRAS project of the Federal Ministry of Finance and LICORICE, an EU Horizon project (no. 101168311). And we thank Marcel Keller for feedback on MP-SPDZ.

A GMP Library for 32-Bit WebSPDZ

In earlier versions of `webSPDZ`, we experimented with 32-bit Wasm. However, since, e.g., the web browsers Firefox and Chrome now support 64-bit Wasm, we focus on 64-bit Wasm in this paper. For the interested reader, in this section, we describe one of our main challenges of 32-bit `webSPDZ`, porting the C++ library GMP to 32-bit Wasm.

As GMP relies on C89, where the datatype `long long` is unavailable, porting GMP to Wasm requires manual effort. Since the datatypes `long` and `size_t` have only 4 bytes in 32-bit architectures like Wasm32, we need the datatype `long long` as it has 8 bytes in any architecture.

Luckily, one of the developers of GMP has been very helpful and provided a patched version of GMP. After adding the patch to the library, we can define the GMP datatype `mp_limb_t` as 8 bytes, equal to a `long long`. Then, we can compile GMP to Wasm using `Emscripten`. We configure cross-compilation to Wasm using the following command: `emconfigure ./configure -disable-assembly -host none -enable-cxx ABI=longlong CFLAGS=-fPIC CXXFLAGS=-fPIC`. The patch helped a lot in porting the library, though it was not officially available in the GMP repository when we experimented with 32-bit `webSPDZ`.

B Alternative Party Communication Using WebSockets

Besides the described (P2P) party communication using `WebRTC`, we experimented with WebSockets to increase performance. Each (communication) thread can open a `WebSocket` connection. Thus, `WebSockets` enable multi-threading for sending and receiving data, while WebRTC can only send and receive data via the browser's main thread.. However, we did not see a significant performance increase in our experiments. Moreover, `WebSocket` communication needs a server, while `WebRTC` communication is p2p (for the MPC computation).

For further details, e.g., Emscripten's documentation shows various ways to use `WebSockets` with `Emscripten`.

References

1. Abspoel, M., Dalskov, A., Escudero, D., Nof, A.: An efficient passive-to-active compiler for honest-majority MPC over rings. In: Sako, K., Tippenhauer, N.O. (eds.) ACNS 2021. LNCS, vol. 12727, pp. 122–152. Springer, Cham (2021). https://doi.org/10.1007/978-3-030-78375-4_6
2. awesome-MPC: a curated list of multi party computation resources and links (2024). https://github.com/rdragos/awesome-mpc. Accessed 25 Nov 2024
3. Araki, T., Furukawa, J., Lindell, Y., Nof, A., Ohara, K.: High-throughput semi-honest secure three-party computation with an honest majority. In: Weippl, E.R., Katzenbeisser, S., Kruegel, C., Myers, A.C., Halevi, S. (eds.) Proceedings of the 2016 ACM SIGSAC Conference on Computer and Communications Security, Vienna, Austria, 24–28 October 2016, pp. 805–817. ACM (2016). https://doi.org/10.1145/2976749.2978331
4. Ballhausen, H., et al.: Privacy-friendly evaluation of patient data with secure multiparty computation in a European pilot study. NPJ Digit. Med. **7**(1) (2024). https://doi.org/10.1038/s41746-024-01293-4
5. Barak, A., Hirt, M., Koskas, L., Lindell, Y.: An end-to-end system for large scale P2P MPC-as-a-service and low-bandwidth MPC for weak participants. In: Proceedings of the 2018 ACM SIGSAC Conference on Computer and Communications Security, CCS 2018, Toronto, ON, Canada, 15–19 October 2018, pp. 695–712. ACM (2018). https://doi.org/10.1145/3243734.3243801
6. Blum, N., Lachapelle, S., Alvestrand, H.: Webrtc: real-time communication for the open web platform. Commun. ACM **64**(8), 50–54 (2021). https://doi.org/10.1145/3453182

7. Bogdanov, D., Kamm, L., Laur, S., Pruulmann-Vengerfeldt, P.: Secure multi-party data analysis: end user validation and practical experiments. IACR Cryptol. ePrint Arch. p. 826 (2013)
8. Bogetoft, P., et al.: Secure multiparty computation goes live. In: Dingledine, R., Golle, P. (eds.) FC 2009. LNCS, vol. 5628, pp. 325–343. Springer, Heidelberg (2009). https://doi.org/10.1007/978-3-642-03549-4_20
9. Cramer, R., Damgård, I., Escudero, D., Scholl, P., Xing, C.: Spdz2k: efficient MPC mod 2k for dishonest majority (2018)
10. Cramer, R., Damgård, I., Maurer, U.: General secure multi-party computation from any linear secret-sharing scheme. In: Preneel, B. (ed.) EUROCRYPT 2000. LNCS, vol. 1807, pp. 316–334. Springer, Heidelberg (2000). https://doi.org/10.1007/3-540-45539-6_22
11. cryptobiu: MPC simulation framework (github) (2018). https://github.com/cryptobiu/MATRIX. Accessed 13 Nov 2024
12. Dalskov, A.P.K., Escudero, D., Keller, M.: Fantastic four: honest-majority four-party secure computation with malicious security. In: Bailey, M.D., Greenstadt, R. (eds.) 30th USENIX Security Symposium, USENIX Security 2021, 11–13 August 2021, pp. 2183–2200. USENIX Association (2021). https://usenix.org/conference/usenixsecurity21/presentation/dalskov
13. Damgård, I., Escudero, D., Frederiksen, T.K., Keller, M., Scholl, P., Volgushev, N.: New primitives for actively-secure MPC over rings with applications to private machine learning. In: 2019 IEEE Symposium on Security and Privacy, pp. 1102–1120. IEEE Computer Society Press (2019). https://doi.org/10.1109/SP.2019.00078
14. Damgård, I., Pastro, V., Smart, N., Zakarias, S.: Multiparty computation from somewhat homomorphic encryption. In: Safavi-Naini, R., Canetti, R. (eds.) CRYPTO 2012. LNCS, vol. 7417, pp. 643–662. Springer, Heidelberg (2012). https://doi.org/10.1007/978-3-642-32009-5_38
15. Emscripten: Emscripten is a complete compiler toolchain to webassembly, using llvm, with a special focus on speed, size, and the web platform (2024). https://emscripten.org. Accessed 28 Nov 2024
16. Google: Real-time communication for the web (2024). https://webrtc.org. Accessed 28 November 2024
17. multiparty group, B.U.: Jiff: Javascript library for building applications that rely on secure multi-party computation (landing page) (2024). https://multiparty.org/jiff. Accessed 13 Nov
18. Hastings, M., Hemenway, B., Noble, D., Zdancewic, S.: SoK: general purpose compilers for secure multi-party computation. In: 2019 IEEE Symposium on Security and Privacy, SP 2019, San Francisco, CA, USA, 19–23 May 2019, pp. 1220–1237. IEEE (2019). https://doi.org/10.1109/SP.2019.00028
19. (IETF), I.E.T.F.: Webrtc security architecture (2021). https://datatracker.ietf.org/doc/html/rfc8827. Accessed 28 Nov 2024
20. Keller, M.: Benchmarks for various multi-party computation frameworks (2020). https://github.com/mkskeller/mpc-benchmarks. Accessed 13 Nov
21. Keller, M.: MP-SPDZ: a versatile framework for multi-party computation. In: Proceedings of the 2020 ACM SIGSAC Conference on Computer and Communications Security (2020). https://doi.org/10.1145/3372297.3417872
22. Keller, M., Scholl, P., Smart, N.P.: An architecture for practical actively secure MPC with dishonest majority. In: Sadeghi, A.R., Gligor, V.D., Yung, M. (eds.) ACM CCS 2013, pp. 549–560. ACM Press (2013). https://doi.org/10.1145/2508859.2516744

23. Lindell, Y.: Secure multiparty computation. Commun. ACM **64**(1), 86–96 (2021). https://doi.org/10.1145/3387108
24. Liu, M., Cheng, L., Gu, Y., Wang, Y., Liu, Q., O'Connor, N.E.: MPC-CSAS: multi-party computation for real-time privacy-preserving speed advisory systems. IEEE Trans. Intell. Transp. Syst. **23**(6), 5887–5893 (2022)
25. Lytvyn, O., Nguyen, G.T.: Secure multi-party computation for magnetic resonance imaging classification. In: ANT/EDI40. Procedia Computer Science, vol. 220, pp. 24–31. Elsevier (2023)
26. Hastings, M., et al.: Sample code and build environments for MPC frameworks (2024). https://github.com/MPC-SoK/frameworks. Accessed 13 Nov 2024
27. Nikolov, E., Schoenmakers, B.: Mpyc web (github) (2024). https://github.com/e-nikolov/mpyc-web. Accessed 13 Nov 2024
28. Rossberg, A., et al.: Bringing the web up to speed with webassembly. Commun. ACM **61**(12), 107–115 (2018)
29. Shamir, A.: How to share a secret. Commun. ACM **22**(11), 612–613 (1979). https://doi.org/10.1145/359168.359176
30. Smart, N.P.: Computing on encrypted data. IEEE Secur. Priv. **21**(4), 94–98 (2023). https://doi.org/10.1109/MSEC.2023.3279517
31. Song, J., Jin, M., Woo, H.: A fast browsing model for web contents on wearable devices. In: ICCE, pp. 376–377. IEEE (2017)
32. Sredojev, B., Samardzija, D., Posarac, D.: Webrtc technology overview and signaling solution design and implementation. In: Biljanovic, P., et al. (eds.) 38th International Convention on Information and Communication Technology, Electronics and Microelectronics, MIPRO 2015, Opatija, Croatia, 25–29 May 2015, pp. 1006–1009. IEEE (2015). https://doi.org/10.1109/MIPRO.2015.7160422
33. Thoma, C., Cui, T., Franchetti, F.: Secure multiparty computation based privacy preserving smart metering system. In: 2012 North American Power Symposium (NAPS), pp. 1–6 (2012). https://doi.org/10.1109/NAPS.2012.6336415
34. Wang, W.: Empowering web applications with webassembly: are we there yet? In: ASE, pp. 1301–1305. IEEE (2021)
35. WebAssembly: Webassembly: Feature extensions (2024). https://webassembly.org/features. Accessed 28 Nov 2024
36. Wikipedia: Single instruction, multiple data (simd) (2024). https://en.wikipedia.org/wiki/Single_instruction,_multiple_data. Accessed 29 Apr 2024
37. Wirth, F.N., Kussel, T., Müller, A., Hamacher, K., Prasser, F.: EasySMPC: a simple but powerful no-code tool for practical secure multiparty computation. BMC Bioinform. **23**(1), 531 (2022)
38. Yao, A.C.: Protocols for secure computations (extended abstract). In: 23rd Annual Symposium on Foundations of Computer Science, Chicago, Illinois, USA, 3–5 November 1982, pp. 160–164. IEEE Computer Society (1982). https://doi.org/10.1109/SFCS.1982.38
39. Zakai, A.: Emscripten: an LLVM-to-Javascript compiler. In: Lopes, C.V., Fisher, K. (eds.) Companion to the 26th Annual ACM SIGPLAN Conference on Object-Oriented Programming, Systems, Languages, and Applications, OOPSLA 2011, part of SPLASH 2011, Portland, OR, USA, 22–27 October 2011, pp. 301–312. ACM (2011). https://doi.org/10.1145/2048147.2048224

Advanced Encryption

Group Signatures with Message-Dependent Opening Directly Imply Timed-Release Encryption

Yuto Imura[1] and Keita Emura[1,2(✉)]

[1] Kanazawa University, Kanazawa, Japan
imuimu@stu.kanazawa-u.ac.jp, k-emura@se.kanazawa-u.ac.jp
[2] National Institute of Advanced Industrial Science and Technology, Tokyo, Japan

Abstract. Group signatures (GS, Chaum and van Heyst, EUROCRYPT 1991) are digital signatures that allow a signer to anonymously prove the membership and also allow the special authority called the opener can identify the signer. Group signatures with message-dependent opening (GS-MDO, Sakai et al., Pairing 2012) weakened the power of the opener by introducing another authority called the admitter who issues a message-dependent token. It would be a natural research topic to clarify whether cryptographic primitives that are required to construct GS-MDO are stronger than those of GS or not, according to the enhanced functionality of GS-MDO. In this paper, we propose a generic construction of timed-release encryption (TRE) from GS-MDO. Note that Sakai et al. have shown that GS-MDO implies identity-based encryption (IBE), and Nakai et al. (IWSEC 2009) and Matsuda et al. (Pairing 2010) demonstrated generic constructions of TRE from IBE. Thus, we do not show any new result from the viewpoint of feasibility. We show that (1) GS-MDO *directly* implies TRE without employing the generic constructions of TRE from IBE, and (2) the proposed TRE construction provides public verifiability, that is not usually supported by TRE, because a TRE ciphertext is a group signature in our construction. Our result implies that GS-MDO is a very strong cryptographic primitive.

Keywords: Group signatures with message-dependent opening · Timed-release encryption · Implication result

1 Introduction

Group signatures (GSs) [17] are digital signatures that allow a signer to anonymously prove the membership and also allow the special authority called the opener can identify the signer.

Feasibility of Group Signatures. Bellare, Micciancio, and Warinschi (BMW) introduced a formal definition of Group signatures in [8] which we call the BMW model. The model contains full anonymity and full traceability as fundamental

Y. Kim et al. (Eds.): CANS 2025, LNCS 16351, pp. 251–271, 2026.
https://doi.org/10.1007/978-981-95-4434-9_12

security definitions of GS. They also showed that GS secure in the BMW model can be generically constructed from public key encryption (PKE), signatures, and non-interactive zero-knowledge proof (NIZK). Security models providing enhanced security/functionality (Bellare-Shi-Zhang (BSZ) [9] and fully dynamic GS [14]) also can be generically constructed from the same building blocks.

As the opposite direction, it has been shown that fully anonymous GS implies PKE [1,8]. Moreover, the GS-based PKE provides public verifiability, that is not usually supported by PKE, because a PKE ciphertext is a group signature in the GS-based PKE construction. Concretely, Ohtake et al. [45] mentioned that "*It remarks that the PKE scheme, which is constructed with the above method, has public verifiability. Namely, anyone can verify validity of a ciphertext by using* gpk" (Here, the above method means the GS-based PKE [1] construction explained in Sect. 4). As a similar result, in [28], it has been shown that dynamic GS [9,48] implies public key encryption with non-interactive opening (PKENO) [22,30]. These results suggest that GSs with additional functionalities may imply cryptographic primitives with enhanced functionalities, and claim that GS is a strong cryptographic primitive.

GS-MDO. Since the opener can freely open signatures in GS, group signatures with message-dependent opening (GS-MDO) [47] have been proposed to weakened the power of the opener by introducing the other authority called the admitter. The signer of a group signature on the message M is identified by using both the token t_{M} (associated to M) issued by the admitter and the opener's secret key ok. There are two anonymity notions, opener anonymity and admitter anonymity that guarantee anonymity from the viewpoint of the opener and the admitter, respectively. As concrete constructions, pairing-based GS-MDO schemes [5,36,44,47] and lattice-based GS-MDO schemes [18,37] have been proposed so far.

The following example explains well the functionality of GS-MDO. A bidder of an auction signs the bidding price using a GS-MDO and sends the group signature and the bidding price to the admitter. The admitter checks whether a bidder is a legitimate user of the auction or not via the verification algorithm. Due to admitter anonymity, the admitter cannot identify users. Here, we simply assume that the user who bids the highest price is the winner. The admitter generates a token associated to the highest price, and sends the token to the opener. The opener identifies who the winner of the auction is. Due to opener anonymity, the opener cannot identify losers.

GS-MDO examines the functionality that allows user anonymity to be revealed based on the content. As a related approach, set pre-constrained (SPC) group signatures [7,43] have been proposed in an End-to-End (E2EE) secure messaging context. The key difference between GS-MDO and SPC-GS lies in the timing of when constrained messages are determined. GS-MDO primarily assumes that the admitter selects a message after a user generates a group signature (of course, the admitter can generate a token for a message before a user generates a group signature on the message). Consequently, GS-MDO is well-suited for indicating messages in an ad-hoc manner, such as in anonymous auctions since the winning bid will be determined after generating group signatures. In contrast, SPC-GS defines content in a pre-constrained manner.

Our Motivation. As a natural question,

Are cryptographic primitives that are required to construct GS-MDO stronger than those of GS or not, according to the enhanced functionality of GS-MDO?

Sakai et al. [47] gave an answer to this question where GS-MDO implies identity-based encryption (IBE). Here, Boneh et al. [13] showed that there is no blackbox construction from PKE to IBE, and the construction of fully anonymous GS requires PKE as its building block. These results suggest that GS-MDO is stronger than GS.[1]

We pay attention to the fact that Sakai et al. [47] employed only opener anonymity to construct IBE from GS-MDO, and did not employ admitter anonymity which is one of the fundamental security properties in GS-MDO. This suggests that we directly construct an advanced cryptographic primitive from GS-MDO by employing admitter anonymity. Clarifying a security property or functionality, that GS-MDO originally achieved implicitly, strengthens the previous result where GS-MDO implies IBE.

Our Contribution. In this paper, we propose a generic construction of timed-release encryption (TRE) (e.g., [20,23,34,40,42,46]) from GS-MDO. In TRE, a time server broadcasts a time-dependent token. In our construction, we regard the admitter as the time server and the opener as the user (decryptor). Due to *both* admitter anonymity and opener anonymity, a group signature whose signed message is the time T can be identified by using *both* the corresponding time-dependent token and the opening key ok. Our result well explains that the GS-MDO functionality is strongly related to those of TRE.

We note that Nakai et al. [42] and Matsuda et al. [40] have demonstrated generic constructions of TRE from IBE. Since GS-MDO implies IBE as mentioned above, we do not show any new result from the viewpoint of feasibility. Our result implies that GS-MDO is a very strong cryptographic primitive because:

1. We show that GS-MDO *directly* implies TRE without employing the generic constructions of TRE from IBE [40,42].
2. Because a TRE ciphertext is a group signature in the proposed TRE construction, it provides public verifiability, that is not usually supported by TRE.

[1] To simplify the discussion, we ignore the NIZK part. Actually, it is non-trivial to construct NIZKs proving a NP-relation induced by IBE. For example, Libert and Joye [36] proposed a partially structure-preserving IBE scheme to employ the Groth-Sahai proofs [33] for constructing a GS-MDO scheme in the standard model. This is caused by the non-triviality of the construction of IBE-friendly NIZKs. Moreover, some non-blackbox IBE constructions from PKE-related tools have been proposed [25,26,32]. Thus, GS-MDO might be constructed from GS in a non-blackbox manner. For these reasons, we chose to use the word "suggest" in the above explanations.

On Generic Constructions of TRE from IBE. Note that in the Nakai et al.'s TRE construction [42], the randomness (used for generating an IBE ciphertext) is contained in a TRE ciphertext. Thus, the construction does not provide public verifiability even if the building blocks (IBE and PKE) are publicly verifiable. Matsuda et al.'s TRE construction [40] employed the KEM/DEM framework (where KEM stands for key encapsulation mechanism and DEM stands for data encapsulation mechanism) and employed IBE-KEM, tag-KEM, and DEM as building blocks. Though CCA-secure tag-KEM can be constructed from CCA-secure KEM and one-time secure message authentication codes (MACs) as mentioned in [2], the MAC part does not provide public verifiability. Thus, due to the above observation, we conclude that these TRE constructions are not publicly verifiable even when the PKE part and the IBE part are publicly verifiable, e.g., they are constructed from GS(-MDO). Note that their constructions consider pre-open capability. Thus, there is a room for providing public verifiability by removing components for providing pre-oepn capability.

2 GS-MDO: Group Signatures with Message-Dependent Opening

2.1 Syntax of GS-MDO

In this section, we define GS-MDO. Note that the opening key ok and the admitter's key ask are generated by the same algorithm, GKg, in the original definition given by Sakai et al. [47]. In this paper, we divide these key generation processes since it is assumed that two authorities (the opener and the admitter) do not collude with each other. Moreover, we introduce the setup algorithm $\mathsf{GS\text{-}MDO.Setup}$ to support multiple users in the proposed TRE construction. That is, we can capture the case that the GKg algorithm is run multiple times (i.e., there are multiple openers), whereas the GKg algorithm is usually run only once in the GS-MDO context. We also remove the group public key gpk from the input of the token generation algorithm Td. Then, we can capture the situation that a token does not depend on gpk (user in the TRE context) and is commonly used for all users. For example, the Ohara et al.'s pairing-based GS-MDO scheme [44] and the Libert et al.'s lattice-based GS-MDO scheme [37] can be modified to match the syntax (See the Appendices A and B). That is, our syntax modification is a natural requirement and is not a restriction. We also note that the security of an opener must be preserved even if other openers are compromised. Since the number of openers is bounded by a polynomial in the security parameter, GS-MDO in the single-opener setting and in the multi-opener setting are essentially equivalent, provided that a polynomial reduction loss is acceptable. Therefore, we define GS-MDO in the single-opener setting here and explain the definition for the multi-opener setting in the Appendix C.1.

A GS-MDO scheme $\mathsf{GS\text{-}MDO}$ consists of seven algorithms ($\mathsf{GS\text{-}MDO.Setup}$, $\mathsf{GKg}, \mathsf{AKg}, \mathsf{GSig}, \mathsf{Td}, \mathsf{GVf}, \mathsf{Open}$) defined as follows.

Definition 1 (Syntax of GS-MDO).

- GS-MDO.Setup*: The setup algorithm takes a security parameter λ as input, and outputs a common parameter* $\mathsf{pp}_{\mathsf{GS\text{-}MDO}}$*. We implicitly assume that all algorithms take* $\mathsf{pp}_{\mathsf{GS\text{-}MDO}}$ *as input, even if it is not explicitly mentioned.*
- GKg*: The group key generation algorithm takes* $\mathsf{pp}_{\mathsf{GS\text{-}MDO}}$ *and the number of group members* $n \in \mathbb{N}$ *as input, and outputs a group public key* gpk*, an opening key* ok*, and* n *group signing keys* $\{\mathsf{gsk}_i\}_{i\in[n]}$.
- AKg*: The admitter key generation algorithm takes* $\mathsf{pp}_{\mathsf{GS\text{-}MDO}}$ *as input, and outputs an admitter's public key* apk *and an admitter's secret key* ask.
- GSig*: The signing algorithm takes* gpk, apk, gsk_i, *and a message* M *as input, and outputs a group signature* σ.
- Td*: The message-dependent token generation algorithm takes* ask *and* M *as input, and outputs a token* $\mathsf{t_M}$.
- GVf*: The verification algorithm takes* gpk, apk, M, *and* σ *as input, and outputs 1 (accept) or 0 (reject).*
- Open*: The opening algorithm takes* gpk, apk, ok, M, σ, *and* $\mathsf{t_M}$ *as input, and outputs a user index* $i \in [n]$ *or* $\perp$.

Correctness is defined as follows. For any $\mathsf{pp}_{\mathsf{GS\text{-}MDO}} \leftarrow \mathsf{GS\text{-}MDO.Setup}(1^\lambda)$, $(\mathsf{gpk}, \mathsf{ok}, \{\mathsf{gsk}_i\}_{i\in[n]}) \leftarrow \mathsf{GKg}(\mathsf{pp}_{\mathsf{GS\text{-}MDO}}, 1^n)$, $(\mathsf{apk}, \mathsf{ask}) \leftarrow \mathsf{AKg}(\mathsf{pp}_{\mathsf{GS\text{-}MDO}})$, $\mathsf{M} \in \{0,1\}^*$, and $i \in [n]$, we say that GS-MDO is correct if

$$\mathsf{GVf}(\mathsf{gpk}, \mathsf{apk}, \mathsf{M}, \mathsf{GSig}(\mathsf{gpk}, \mathsf{apk}, \mathsf{gsk}_i, \mathsf{M})) = 1$$

and

$$\mathsf{Open}(\mathsf{gpk}, \mathsf{apk}, \mathsf{ok}, \mathsf{M}, \mathsf{GSig}(\mathsf{gpk}, \mathsf{apk}, \mathsf{gsk}_i, \mathsf{M}), \mathsf{Td}(\mathsf{ask}, \mathsf{M})) = i$$

hold.

2.2 Security Definitions

Next, we define two anonymity notions, admitter anonymity and opener anonymity. Admitter anonymity guarantees that anonymity holds against an adversary who has the admitter's secret key ask and all signing keys $\{\mathsf{gsk}_i\}_{i\in[\ n]}$ unless the adversary has the opener's secret key ok, and is defined as follows.

Definition 2 (Admitter Anonymity). *Let $\mathcal{A}$ be an adversary and $\mathcal{C}$ be the challenger.*

- **Setup:** $\mathcal{C}$ *computes* $\mathsf{pp}_{\mathsf{GS\text{-}MDO}} \leftarrow \mathsf{GS\text{-}MDO.Setup}(1^\lambda)$, $(\mathsf{gpk}, \mathsf{ok}, \{\mathsf{gsk}_i\}_{i\in[n]}) \leftarrow \mathsf{GKg}(\mathsf{pp}_{\mathsf{GS\text{-}MDO}}, 1^n)$, *and* $(\mathsf{apk}, \mathsf{ask}) \leftarrow \mathsf{AKg}(\mathsf{pp}_{\mathsf{GS\text{-}MDO}})$, *and gives* $(\mathsf{gpk}, \mathsf{apk}, \mathsf{ask}, \{\mathsf{gsk}_i\}_{i\in[n]})$ *to* $\mathcal{A}$.
- **Open Query (Phase I):** $\mathcal{A}$ *sends* (σ, M) *to* $\mathcal{C}$. *If* M *is not previously queried, then* $\mathcal{C}$ *computes* $\mathsf{t_M} \leftarrow \mathsf{Td}(\mathsf{ask}, \mathsf{M})$, *and stores* $(\mathsf{M}, \mathsf{t_M})$. *Otherwise,* $\mathcal{C}$ *retrieves* $\mathsf{t_M}$. $\mathcal{C}$ *gives the result of* $\mathsf{Open}(\mathsf{gpk}, \mathsf{apk}, \mathsf{ok}, \mathsf{M}, \sigma, \mathsf{t_M})$ *to* $\mathcal{A}$.
- **Challenge:** $\mathcal{A}$ *declares* $i_0, i_1 \in [n]$ *and* M^*. $\mathcal{C}$ *chooses* $b \xleftarrow{\$} \{0,1\}$, *computes the challenge group signature* $\sigma^* \leftarrow \mathsf{GSig}(\mathsf{gpk}, \mathsf{apk}, \mathsf{gsk}_{i_b}, \mathsf{M}^*)$, *and gives* σ^* *to* $\mathcal{A}$.

Open Query (Phase II): *$\mathcal{A}$ sends $(\sigma, \mathsf{M}) \neq (\sigma^*, \mathsf{M}^*)$ to $\mathcal{C}$. If M is not previously queried, then $\mathcal{C}$ computes $\mathsf{t_M} \leftarrow \mathsf{Td}(\mathsf{ask}, \mathsf{M})$, and stores $(\mathsf{M}, \mathsf{t_M})$. Otherwise, $\mathcal{C}$ retrieves $\mathsf{t_M}$. $\mathcal{C}$ gives the result of $\mathsf{Open}(\mathsf{gpk}, \mathsf{apk}, \mathsf{ok}, \mathsf{M}, \sigma, \mathsf{t_M})$ to $\mathcal{A}$.*
Guess: *A outputs $b' \in \{0, 1\}$.*

We say that GS-MDO *provides admitter anonymity if, for all PPT (Probabilistic Polynomial-Time) adversaries $\mathcal{A}$, the advantage*

$$\mathsf{Adv}^{\mathsf{admitter\text{-}anon}}_{\mathsf{GS\text{-}MDO},\mathcal{A}}(\lambda, n) = \left| \Pr[b' = b] - \frac{1}{2} \right|$$

is negligible in the security parameter.

Opener anonymity guarantees that anonymity holds against an adversary who has the opener's secret key ok and all signing keys $\{\mathsf{gsk}_i\}_{i \in [n]}$ unless the adversary has the corresponding token, and is defined as follows.

Definition 3 (Opener Anonymity). *Let $\mathcal{A}$ be an adversary and $\mathcal{C}$ be the challenger.*

Setup: *$\mathcal{C}$ computes $\mathsf{pp}_{\mathsf{GS\text{-}MDO}} \leftarrow \mathsf{GS\text{-}MDO.Setup}(1^\lambda)$, $(\mathsf{gpk}, \mathsf{ok}, \{\mathsf{gsk}_i\}_{i \in [n]}) \leftarrow \mathsf{GKg}(\mathsf{pp}_{\mathsf{GS\text{-}MDO}}, 1^n)$, and $(\mathsf{apk}, \mathsf{ask}) \leftarrow \mathsf{AKg}(\mathsf{pp}_{\mathsf{GS\text{-}MDO}})$, and gives $(\mathsf{gpk}, \mathsf{ok}, \mathsf{apk}, \{\mathsf{gsk}_i\}_{i \in [n]})$ to $\mathcal{A}$.*
Token Query (Phase I): *$\mathcal{A}$ sends M to $\mathcal{C}$. If M is not previously queried, then $\mathcal{C}$ computes $\mathsf{t_M} \leftarrow \mathsf{Td}(\mathsf{ask}, \mathsf{M})$, and stores $(\mathsf{M}, \mathsf{t_M})$. Otherwise, $\mathcal{C}$ retrieves $\mathsf{t_M}$. $\mathcal{C}$ gives $\mathsf{t_M}$ to $\mathcal{A}$.*
Challenge: *$\mathcal{A}$ declares $i_0, i_1 \in [n]$ and M^*. Note that $\mathcal{A}$ is not allowed to send messages as M^* if $\mathcal{A}$ has sent these messages as token queries. $\mathcal{C}$ chooses $b \xleftarrow{\$} \{0, 1\}$, computes the challenge group signature $\sigma^* \leftarrow \mathsf{GSig}(\mathsf{gpk}, \mathsf{apk}, \mathsf{gsk}_{i_b}, \mathsf{M}^*)$, and gives σ^* to $\mathcal{A}$.*
Token Query (Phase II): *$\mathcal{A}$ sends $\mathsf{M} \neq \mathsf{M}^*$ to $\mathcal{C}$. If M is not previously queried, then $\mathcal{C}$ computes $\mathsf{t_M} \leftarrow \mathsf{Td}(\mathsf{ask}, \mathsf{M})$, and stores $(\mathsf{M}, \mathsf{t_M})$. Otherwise, $\mathcal{C}$ retrieves $\mathsf{t_M}$. $\mathcal{C}$ gives $\mathsf{t_M}$ to $\mathcal{A}$.*
Guess: *$\mathcal{A}$ outputs $b' \in \{0, 1\}$.*

We say that GS-MDO *provides opener anonymity if, for all PPT adversaries $\mathcal{A}$, the advantage*

$$\mathsf{Adv}^{\mathsf{opener\text{-}anon}}_{\mathsf{GS\text{-}MDO},\mathcal{A}}(\lambda, n) = \left| \Pr[b' = b] - \frac{1}{2} \right|$$

is negligible in the security parameter.

From these two anonymity notions, GS-MDO guarantees that anonymity holds unless both the opener's secret key and the corresponding token are used.

3 TRE: Timed-Release Encryption

3.1 Syntax of TRE

In this section, we define TRE. We adopt the model from [40,42]. Though they considered additional functionality of TRE which they called pre-open capability, we do not consider it in this paper. We also note that TRE must take into account a multi-user setting. That is, the security of each user must remain intact even if other users are compromised. Given that the number of users is bounded by a polynomial in the security parameter, the single-user and multi-user settings for TRE are essentially equivalent, provided a polynomial reduction loss is acceptable. Therefore, we define TRE in the single-user setting here, and explain the definition for the multi-user setting in the Appendix C.2.

A TRE scheme TRE consists of five algorithms $(\mathsf{TRE.Setup}, \mathsf{TRE.Ext}, \mathsf{TRE.UKg}, \mathsf{TRE.Enc}, \mathsf{TRE.Dec})$ defined as follows. We denote m as a plaintext to distinguish a signed message M of GS-MDO.

Definition 4 (Syntax of TRE).

$\mathsf{TRE.Setup}$: *The setup algorithm takes a security parameter* λ *as input, and outputs a common parameter* $\mathsf{pp_{TRE}}$. *Assume that all algorithms implicitly take* $\mathsf{pp_{TRE}}$ *as input, even if it is not explicitly mentioned.*

$\mathsf{TRE.TKg}$: *The time server key generation algorithm takes* $\mathsf{pp_{TRE}}$ *as input, and outputs a time-server's public key* tpk *and a time-server's secret key* tsk.

$\mathsf{TRE.UKg}$: *The user key generation algorithm takes* $\mathsf{pp_{TRE}}$ *as input, and outputs a user's public key* $\mathsf{pk_u}$ *and a user's secret key* $\mathsf{sk_u}$. *Assume that* $\mathsf{pk_u}$ *implicitly contains a plaintext space* $\mathsf{MS_{TRE}}$.

$\mathsf{TRE.Ext}$: *The token generation algorithm takes* tsk *and a time* $\mathsf{T} \in \{0,1\}^*$ *as input, and outputs a token* $\mathsf{s_T}$.

$\mathsf{TRE.Enc}$: *The encryption algorithm takes* $\mathsf{pk_u}$, tpk, T, *and a plaintext* $\mathsf{m} \in \mathsf{MS_{TRE}}$ *as input, and outputs a ciphertext* C.

$\mathsf{TRE.Dec}$: *The decryption algorithm* tpk, $\mathsf{sk_u}$, $\mathsf{s_T}$, *and* C *as input, and outputs* m *or a failure symbol* $\perp$.

Correctness is defined as follows. For any $\mathsf{pp_{TRE}} \leftarrow \mathsf{TRE.Setup}(1^\lambda)$, $(\mathsf{tpk}, \mathsf{tsk}) \leftarrow \mathsf{TRE.TKg}(\mathsf{pp_{TRE}})$, $(\mathsf{pk_u}, \mathsf{sk_u}) \leftarrow \mathsf{TRE.UKg}(\mathsf{pp_{TRE}})$, $\mathsf{m} \in \mathsf{MS_{TRE}}$, and $\mathsf{T} \in \{0,1\}^*$, we say that TRE is correct if

$$\mathsf{TRE.Dec}(\mathsf{tpk}, \mathsf{sk_u}, \mathsf{TRE.Ext}(\mathsf{tsk}, \mathsf{T}), \mathsf{TRE.Enc}(\mathsf{pk_u}, \mathsf{tpk}, \mathsf{T}, \mathsf{m})) = \mathsf{m}$$

holds.

3.2 Security Definitions

Next, we define two security properties, time server security and insider security. The time server security, which is denoted as $\mathsf{IND\text{-}TR\text{-}CCA_{TS}}$, guarantees that even an adversary who has the time server's secret key tsk cannot obtain any information about the plaintext from the ciphertext without having the user's secret key $\mathsf{sk_u}$. Formally, the $\mathsf{IND\text{-}TR\text{-}CCA_{TS}}$ security is defined as follows.

Definition 5. (Time Server Security $\mathsf{IND\text{-}TR\text{-}CCA_{TS}}$). *Let $\mathcal{A}$ be an adversary and $\mathcal{C}$ be the challenger.*

Setup: *$\mathcal{C}$ computes* $\mathsf{pp_{TRE}} \leftarrow \mathsf{TRE.Setup}(1^\lambda)$, $(\mathsf{tpk}, \mathsf{tsk}) \leftarrow \mathsf{TRE.TKg}(\mathsf{pp_{TRE}})$, *and* $(\mathsf{pk_u}, \mathsf{sk_u}) \leftarrow \mathsf{TRE.UKg}(\mathsf{pp_{TRE}})$, *and gives* $(\mathsf{tpk}, \mathsf{tsk}, \mathsf{pk_u})$ *to* $\mathcal{A}$.

Decryption Query (Phase I): *$\mathcal{A}$ sends* (C, T) *to* $\mathcal{C}$. *If* T *is not previously queried,* $\mathcal{C}$ *computes* $\mathsf{s_T} \leftarrow \mathsf{TRE.Ext}(\mathsf{tsk}, \mathsf{T})$ *and stores* $(\mathsf{T}, \mathsf{s_T})$. *Otherwise,* $\mathcal{C}$ *retrieves* $\mathsf{s_T}$. $\mathcal{C}$ *gives the result of* $\mathsf{TRE.Dec}(\mathsf{tpk}, \mathsf{sk_u}, \mathsf{s_T}, \mathsf{C})$ *to* $\mathcal{A}$.

Challenge: *$\mathcal{A}$ declares two distinct challenge plaintexts* $\mathsf{m}_0^*, \mathsf{m}_1^* \in \mathsf{MS_{TRE}}$ *and the challenge time* T^*. $\mathcal{C}$ *chooses* $b \xleftarrow{\$} \{0,1\}$, *computes the challenge cipher text* $C^* \leftarrow \mathsf{TRE.Enc}(\mathsf{tpk}, \mathsf{pk_u}, \mathsf{T}^*, \mathsf{m}_b^*)$ *and gives* C^* *to* $\mathcal{A}$.

Decryption Query (Phase II): *$\mathcal{A}$ sends* $(\mathsf{C}, \mathsf{T}) \neq (\mathsf{C}^*, \mathsf{T}^*)$. *If* T *is not previously queried, then* $\mathcal{C}$ *computes* $\mathsf{s_T} \leftarrow \mathsf{TRE.Ext}(\mathsf{tsk}, \mathsf{T})$ *and stores* $(\mathsf{T}, \mathsf{s_T})$. *Otherwise,* $\mathcal{C}$ *retrieves* $\mathsf{s_T}$. $\mathcal{C}$ *gives the result of* $\mathsf{TRE.Dec}(\mathsf{tpk}, \mathsf{sk_u}, \mathsf{s_T}, \mathsf{C})$ *to* $\mathcal{A}$.

Guess: *$\mathcal{A}$ outputs* $b' \in \{0,1\}$.

We say that TRE *provides the* $\mathsf{IND\text{-}TR\text{-}CCA_{TS}}$ *security if, for all PPT adversaries* $\mathcal{A}$, *the advantage*

$$\mathsf{Adv}_{\mathsf{TRE},\mathcal{A}}^{\mathsf{IND\text{-}TR\text{-}CCA_{TS}}}(\lambda) = \left|\Pr[b' = b] - \frac{1}{2}\right|$$

is negligible in the security parameter.

The insider security, which is denoted as $\mathsf{IND\text{-}TR\text{-}CPA_{IS}}$, guarantees that even an adversary who has the user's secret key $\mathsf{sk_u}$ cannot obtain any information about the plaintext from the (challenge) ciphertext without having the corresponding token s_T^* for the ciphertext decryption time T^*. Formally, the $\mathsf{IND\text{-}TR\text{-}CPA_{IS}}$ security is defined as follows.

Definition 6. (Insider Security $\mathsf{IND\text{-}TR\text{-}CPA_{IS}}$) *Let $\mathcal{A}$ be an attacker and $\mathcal{C}$ be the challenger.*

Setup: *$\mathcal{C}$ computes* $\mathsf{pp_{TRE}} \leftarrow \mathsf{TRE.Setup}(1^\lambda)$, $(\mathsf{tpk}, \mathsf{tsk}) \leftarrow \mathsf{TRE.TKg}(\mathsf{pp_{TRE}})$, *and* $(\mathsf{pk_u}, \mathsf{sk_u}) \leftarrow \mathsf{TRE.UKg}(\mathsf{pp_{TRE}})$, *and gives* $(\mathsf{tpk}, \mathsf{pk_u}, \mathsf{sk_u})$ *to* $\mathcal{A}$.

Extract Query (Phase I): *$\mathcal{A}$ sends* T *to* $\mathcal{C}$. *If* T *is not previously queried, then* $\mathcal{C}$ *computes* $\mathsf{s_T} \leftarrow \mathsf{TRE.Ext}(\mathsf{tsk}, \mathsf{T})$ *and stores* $(\mathsf{T}, \mathsf{s_T})$. *Otherwise,* $\mathcal{C}$ *retrieves* $\mathsf{s_T}$. $\mathcal{C}$ *gives* $\mathsf{s_T}$ *to* $\mathcal{A}$.

Challenge: *$\mathcal{A}$ declares two distinct challenge plaintexts* $\mathsf{m}_0^*, \mathsf{m}_1^* \in \mathsf{MS_{TRE}}$ *and the challenge time* T^* *where* T^* *has not been sent as an extract query.* $\mathcal{C}$ *chooses* $b \xleftarrow{\$} \{0,1\}$, *computes* $\mathsf{C}^* \leftarrow \mathsf{TRE.Enc}(\mathsf{tpk}, \mathsf{pk_u}, \mathsf{T}^*, \mathsf{m}_b^*)$, *and gives* C^* *to* $\mathcal{A}$.

Extract Query (Phase II): *$\mathcal{A}$ sends* $\mathsf{T} \neq \mathsf{T}^*$. *If* T *is not previously queried, then* $\mathcal{C}$ *computes* $\mathsf{s_T} \leftarrow \mathsf{TRE.Ext}(\mathsf{tsk}, \mathsf{T})$ *and stores* $(\mathsf{T}, \mathsf{s_T})$. *Otherwise,* $\mathcal{C}$ *retrieves* $\mathsf{s_T}$. $\mathcal{C}$ *gives* $\mathsf{s_T}$ *to* $\mathcal{A}$.

Guess: *$\mathcal{A}$ outputs* $b' \in \{0,1\}$.

We say that TRE *provides the* $\mathsf{IND\text{-}TR\text{-}CPA_{IS}}$ *security if, for any PPT adversaries* $\mathcal{A}$*, the advantage*

$$\mathsf{Adv}^{\mathsf{IND\text{-}TR\text{-}CPA_{IS}}}_{\mathsf{TRE},\mathcal{A}}(\lambda) = \left|\Pr[b' = b] - \frac{1}{2}\right|$$

is negligible in the security parameter.

4 Proposed Construction

In this section, we give our proposed generic construction of TRE from GS-MDO. Before giving the proposed construction, we revisited Abdalla et al.'s PKE construction from GS [1] and Sakai et al.'s IBE construction from GS-MDO [47] because we combine these techniques.

GS-based PKE [1]**:** For a plaintext $\mathsf{m} \in \{0,1\}$, two signing keys $(\mathsf{gsk}_1, \mathsf{gsk}_2)$ are set as the public key of PKE. A ciphertext is a group signature σ generated by $\mathsf{gsk}_{\mathsf{m}+1}$ (here, a message to be signed is not specifically indicated). Due to full anonymity of GS, information of which signing key is used for generating a group signature is not revealed even all signing keys are made public. The opening key ok is regarded as the decryption key of PKE.

GS-MDO-based IBE [47]**:** As in the above PKE construction, two signing keys $(\mathsf{gsk}_1, \mathsf{gsk}_2)$ are set as the public parameter. In addition to these signing keys, the opening key ok is also included to the parameter. A ciphertext is a group signature σ generated by $\mathsf{gsk}_{\mathsf{m}+1}$ where ID is regarded as the message to be signed, i.e., $\sigma \leftarrow \mathsf{GSig}(\mathsf{gpk}, \mathsf{apk}, \mathsf{gsk}_{\mathsf{m}+1}, \mathsf{ID})$. The key generation center has the admitter's secret key ask as the master secret key, and for an identity ID, the center generates a token $\mathsf{t_{ID}}$ which is regarded as the decryption key. A ciphertext is decrypted by using the opening algorithm that takes $\mathsf{t_{ID}}$ (and ok that is contained in the public parameter). Due to opener anonymity of GS-MDO, information of which signing key is used for generating a group signature is not revealed even all signing keys and ok are made public. We emphasize that admitter anonymity is not employed in the construction.

High-Level Description: Our construction is a combination of the above constructions. We set $(\mathsf{gpk}, \mathsf{gsk}_1, \mathsf{gsk}_2)$ as a user's public key $\mathsf{pk_u}$ and ok as a user's secret key $\mathsf{sk_u}$. As in the GS-based PKE construction, $(\mathsf{gsk}_1, \mathsf{gsk}_2)$ is contained in the public key. To encrypt a plaintext $\mathsf{m} \in \{0,1\}$, a ciphertext C is a group signature σ generated by $\mathsf{gsk}_{\mathsf{m}+1}$ where the time T is regarded as the message to be signed, i.e.,

$$\mathsf{C} := \sigma \leftarrow \mathsf{GSig}(\mathsf{gpk}, \mathsf{apk}, \mathsf{gsk}_{\mathsf{m}+1}, \mathsf{T})$$

Since a TRE ciphertext is a group signature on T, C can be publicly verified whether $\mathsf{GVf}(\mathsf{gpk}, \mathsf{apk}, \mathsf{T}, \mathsf{C}) = 1$ holds or not. We note that ok is not contained to a public value unlike the GS-MDO-based IBE construction. The time server has the admitter's secret key ask as the time server's secret key tsk, and generates a token $\mathsf{t_T}$ for T. Then, by using both $\mathsf{ok} = \mathsf{sk_u}$ and $\mathsf{t_T}$, a group signature on T can be opened, i.e., the opening algorithm (the decryption algorithm in the TRE context) identifies which signing key is used. Intuitively, due to admitter anonymity, the time server that has ask does not obtain information of which signing key is used. Due to opener anonymity, a user that has ok does not obtain information of which signing key is used unless the user obtains the corresponding time token.

The proposed generic construction of $\mathsf{TRE} = (\mathsf{TRE.Setup}, \mathsf{TRE.TKg}, \mathsf{TRE.UKg}, \mathsf{TRE.Ext}, \mathsf{TRE.Enc}, \mathsf{TRE.Dec})$ from $\mathsf{GS\text{-}MDO} = (\mathsf{GS\text{-}MDO.Setup}, \mathsf{GKg}, \mathsf{AKg}, \mathsf{GSig}, \mathsf{Td}, \mathsf{GVf}, \mathsf{Open})$ is as follows.

$\mathsf{TRE.Setup}(1^\lambda)$: Run $\mathsf{pp_{GS\text{-}MDO}} \leftarrow \mathsf{GS\text{-}MDO.Setup}(1^\lambda)$ and output $\mathsf{pp_{TRE}} = \mathsf{pp_{GS\text{-}MDO}}$.

$\mathsf{TRE.TKg}(\mathsf{pp_{TRE}})$: Parse $\mathsf{pp_{TRE}} = \mathsf{pp_{GS\text{-}MDO}}$. Run $(\mathsf{apk}, \mathsf{ask}) \leftarrow \mathsf{AKg}(\mathsf{pp_{GS\text{-}MDO}})$ and output $(\mathsf{tpk}, \mathsf{tsk}) = (\mathsf{apk}, \mathsf{ask})$.

$\mathsf{TRE.UKg}(\mathsf{pp_{TRE}})$: Run $(\mathsf{gpk}, \mathsf{ok}, \mathsf{gsk}_1, \mathsf{gsk}_2) \leftarrow \mathsf{GKg}(\mathsf{pp_{GS\text{-}MDO}}, 1^2)$ and output $\mathsf{pk_u} = ((\mathsf{gpk}, (\mathsf{gsk}_1, \mathsf{gsk}_2))$ and $\mathsf{sk_u} = (\mathsf{pk_u}, \mathsf{ok})$.

$\mathsf{TRE.Ext}(\mathsf{tsk}, \mathsf{T})$: Parse $\mathsf{tsk} = \mathsf{ask}$. Run $\mathsf{t_T} \leftarrow \mathsf{Td}(\mathsf{ask}, \mathsf{T})$ and output $\mathsf{s_T} = \mathsf{t_T}$.

$\mathsf{TRE.Enc}(\mathsf{tpk}, \mathsf{pk_u}, \mathsf{T}, \mathsf{m})$: Parse $\mathsf{tpk} = \mathsf{apk}$ and $\mathsf{pk_u} = (\mathsf{gpk}, (\mathsf{gsk}_1, \mathsf{gsk}_2))$, and let $\mathsf{m} \in \{0, 1\}$. Run $\sigma \leftarrow \mathsf{GSig}(\mathsf{gpk}, \mathsf{apk}, \mathsf{gsk_{m+1}}, \mathsf{T})$ and output $\mathsf{C} = \sigma$.

$\mathsf{TRE.Dec}(\mathsf{tpk}, \mathsf{sk_u}, \mathsf{s_T}, \mathsf{T}, \mathsf{C})$: Parse $\mathsf{tpk} = \mathsf{apk}$, $\mathsf{sk_u} = (\mathsf{pk_u}, \mathsf{ok})$, $\mathsf{pk_u} = ((\mathsf{gpk}, (\mathsf{gsk}_1, \mathsf{gsk}_2))$, $\mathsf{s_T} = \mathsf{t_T}$, and $\mathsf{C} = \sigma$. Run $i \leftarrow \mathsf{Open}(\mathsf{gpk}, \mathsf{apk}, \mathsf{ok}, \mathsf{T}, \mathsf{t_T}, \sigma)$. Output $\perp$ if $i = \perp$. Otherwise, output $\mathsf{m} = i - 1$

Obviously, the proposed construction is correct if the underlying GS-MDO scheme is correct.

On Multi-bit Encryption: Our TRE construction provides the 1-bit plaintext space. If no CCA security is required, then the plaintext space can be amplified by simply arranging ciphertexts of 1-bit plaintext. To preserve the CCA security, the GS-based PKENO construction [28] uses a message to be signed as a tag, and a verification key $\mathsf{vk_{OTS}}$ of the one-time signature scheme is set as the tag to employ the CHK transformation [16]. That is, a ciphertext of the i-th bit m_i is a group signature generated by $\mathsf{gsk}_{\mathsf{m}_i+1}$ on $\mathsf{vk_{OTS}}$, and all group signatures are signed by the OTS scheme. Unfortunately, this technique cannot be applied directly in GS-MDO-based IBE/TRE since the signed message is ID or T and $\mathsf{vk_{OTS}}$ is chosen on the fly (i.e., in the encryption algorithm). Note that Sakai et al. did not mention how to amplify the message space in their GS-MDO-based IBE construction. How to amplify the plaintext space in GS-MDO-based IBE/TRE is an interesting open problem, e.g., the Myers-Shelat technique [41] might be employed.

5 Security Analysis

In the following proofs, due to the one-bit plaintext space, we set the challenge plaintexts $(\mathsf{m}_0^*, \mathsf{m}_1^*) = (0, 1)$ without loss of generality. Similarly, we set the challenge users $(i_0^*, i_1^*) = (1, 2)$.

Theorem 1. *The proposed construction provides the time server security if the underlying GS-MDO provides admitter anonymity.*

Intuitively, due to admitter anonymity, the admitter that has ask does not obtain information of which signing key is used from group signatures. Since the admitter is set as the time server in our TRE construction, the $\mathsf{IND\text{-}TR\text{-}CCA_{TS}}$ adversary $\mathcal{A}$ that has $\mathsf{tsk} = \mathsf{ask}$ does not obtain information of plaintext from ciphertexts. Let $\mathcal{C}$ be the challenger of admitter anonymity. We construct an algorithm $\mathcal{B}$ that breaks admitter anonymity using $\mathcal{A}$ as follows. Here, $\mathcal{B}$ simulates the decryption oracle using the opening oracle. Note that $\mathcal{A}$ sends a decryption query $(\mathsf{C}, \mathsf{T}) \neq (\mathsf{C}^*, T^*)$, $\mathcal{B}$ can simulate the decryption oracle using the opening oracle where the adversary is not allows to send (σ^*, M^*).

Proof. We give the security proof as follows.

Setup: $\mathcal{C}$ computes $\mathsf{pp_{GS\text{-}MDO}} \leftarrow \mathsf{GS\text{-}MDO.Setup}(1^\lambda)$, $(\mathsf{gpk}, \mathsf{ok}, \mathsf{gsk}_1, \mathsf{gsk}_2) \leftarrow \mathsf{GKg}(\mathsf{pp_{GS\text{-}MDO}}, 1^2)$, and $(\mathsf{apk}, \mathsf{ask}) \leftarrow \mathsf{AKg}(\mathsf{pp_{GS\text{-}MDO}})$, and gives $(\mathsf{gpk}, \mathsf{apk}, \mathsf{ask}, \mathsf{gsk}_1, \mathsf{gsk}_2)$ to $\mathcal{B}$. $\mathcal{B}$ sets $\mathsf{tpk} = \mathsf{apk}$, $\mathsf{tsk} = \mathsf{ask}$, $\mathsf{pk_u} = (\mathsf{gpk}, \mathsf{gsk}_1, \mathsf{gsk}_2)$ and gives $(\mathsf{tpk}, \mathsf{tsk}, \mathsf{pk_u})$ to $\mathcal{A}$.

Decryption Query (Phase I): $\mathcal{A}$ sends (C, T) to $\mathcal{B}$. $\mathcal{B}$ parses $\sigma = \mathsf{C}$ and sends the opening query (σ, T) to $\mathcal{C}$. $\mathcal{C}$ returns $i \leftarrow \mathsf{Open}(\mathsf{gpk}, \mathsf{apk}, \mathsf{ok}, \mathsf{T}, \sigma, \mathsf{t_T})$ to $\mathcal{B}$. $\mathcal{B}$ answers $\perp$ $i = \perp$, and $\mathsf{m} = i - 1$, otherwise.

Challenge: $\mathcal{A}$ sends $(\mathsf{m}_0^*, \mathsf{m}_1^*) = (0, 1)$ and T^* to $\mathcal{B}$. $\mathcal{B}$ sends $(1, 2, T^*)$ to $\mathcal{C}$. $\mathcal{C}$ chooses $b \xleftarrow{\$} \{0, 1\}$, computes $\sigma^* \leftarrow \mathsf{GSig}(\mathsf{gpk}, \mathsf{apk}, \mathsf{gsk}_{b+1}, \mathsf{T}^*)$, and sends σ^* to $\mathcal{B}$. $\mathcal{B}$ sets $\mathsf{C}^* = \sigma^*$ and sends C^* to $\mathcal{A}$.

Decryption Query (Phase II): $\mathcal{A}$ sends $(\mathsf{C}, \mathsf{T}) \neq (\mathsf{C}^*, T^*)$ to $\mathcal{B}$. $\mathcal{B}$ parses $\sigma = \mathsf{C}$ and sends the opening query (σ, T) to $\mathcal{C}$. $\mathcal{C}$ returns $i \leftarrow \mathsf{Open}(\mathsf{gpk}, \mathsf{apk}, \mathsf{ok}, \mathsf{T}, \sigma, \mathsf{t_T})$ to $\mathcal{B}$. $\mathcal{B}$ answers $\perp$ $i = \perp$, and $\mathsf{m} = i - 1$, otherwise.

Guess: $\mathcal{A}$ outputs $b' \in \{0, 1\}$. $\mathcal{B}$ outputs b' and breaks the $\mathsf{IND\text{-}TR\text{-}CCA_{TS}}$ security with the same advantage of $\mathcal{A}$.

□

Theorem 2. *The proposed construction provides the insider security if the underlying GS-MDO provides opener anonymity.*

Intuitively, due to opener anonymity, an opener with ok cannot obtain information of which signing key is used from group signatures unless they have a token corresponding to the message. Since the opener is set as the user in our TRE construction, the $\mathsf{IND\text{-}TR\text{-}CPA_{IS}}$ adversary $\mathcal{A}$ that has $\mathsf{sk_u} = \mathsf{ok}$ cannot obtain information of plaintext from ciphertexts. Let $\mathcal{C}$ be the challenger of opener anonymity. We construct an algorithm $\mathcal{B}$ that breaks opener anonymity using $\mathcal{A}$ as follows. Here, $\mathcal{B}$ simulates the extract oracle using token generation oracle. When $\mathcal{A}$ sends an extract query $\mathsf{T} \neq \mathsf{T}^*$, $\mathcal{B}$ can simulate the extract oracle using the token generation oracle where the adversary is not allowed to send T^*.

Proof. We give the security proof as follows.

Setup: $\mathcal{C}$ computes $\mathsf{pp}_{\mathsf{GS\text{-}MDO}} \leftarrow \mathsf{GS\text{-}MDO.Setup}(1^\lambda)$, $(\mathsf{gpk}, \mathsf{ok}, \mathsf{gsk}_1, \mathsf{gsk}_2) \leftarrow \mathsf{GKg}(\mathsf{pp}_{\mathsf{GS\text{-}MDO}}, 1^2)$, and $(\mathsf{apk}, \mathsf{ask}) \leftarrow \mathsf{AKg}(\mathsf{pp}_{\mathsf{GS\text{-}MDO}})$, and gives $(\mathsf{gpk}, \mathsf{apk}, \mathsf{ask}, \mathsf{gsk}_1, \mathsf{gsk}_2)$ to $\mathcal{B}$. $\mathcal{B}$ sets $\mathsf{tpk} = \mathsf{apk}$, $\mathsf{tsk} = \mathsf{ask}$, $\mathsf{pk}_\mathsf{u} = (\mathsf{gpk}, \mathsf{gsk}_1, \mathsf{gsk}_2)$ and gives $(\mathsf{tpk}, \mathsf{tsk}, \mathsf{pk}_\mathsf{u})$ to $\mathcal{A}$.

Decryption Query (Phase I): $\mathcal{A}$ sends (C, T) to $\mathcal{B}$. $\mathcal{B}$ parses $\sigma = \mathsf{C}$ and sends the opening query (σ, T) to $\mathcal{C}$. $\mathcal{C}$ returns $i \leftarrow \mathsf{Open}(\mathsf{gpk}, \mathsf{apk}, \mathsf{ok}, \mathsf{T}, \sigma, \mathsf{t_T})$ to $\mathcal{B}$. $\mathcal{B}$ answers $\perp$ $i = \perp$, and $\mathsf{m} = i - 1$, otherwise.

Challenge: $\mathcal{A}$ sends $(\mathsf{m}_0^*, \mathsf{m}_1^*) = (0, 1)$ and T^* to $\mathcal{B}$. $\mathcal{B}$ sends $(1, 2, T^*)$ to $\mathcal{C}$. $\mathcal{C}$ chooses $b \xleftarrow{\$} \{0, 1\}$, computes $\sigma^* \leftarrow \mathsf{GSig}(\mathsf{gpk}, \mathsf{apk}, \mathsf{gsk}_{b+1}, \mathsf{T}^*)$, and sends σ^* to $\mathcal{B}$. $\mathcal{B}$ sets $\mathsf{C}^* = \sigma^*$ and sends C^* to $\mathcal{A}$.

Decryption Query (Phase II): $\mathcal{A}$ sends $(\mathsf{C}, \mathsf{T}) \neq (\mathsf{C}^*, T^*)$ to $\mathcal{B}$. $\mathcal{B}$ parses $\sigma = \mathsf{C}$ and sends the opening query (σ, T) to $\mathcal{C}$. $\mathcal{C}$ returns $i \leftarrow \mathsf{Open}(\mathsf{gpk}, \mathsf{apk}, \mathsf{ok}, \mathsf{T}, \sigma, \mathsf{t_T})$ to $\mathcal{B}$. $\mathcal{B}$ answers $\perp$ $i = \perp$, and $\mathsf{m} = i - 1$, otherwise.

Guess: $\mathcal{A}$ outputs $b' \in \{0, 1\}$. $\mathcal{B}$ outputs b' and breaks the $\mathsf{IND\text{-}TR\text{-}CCA_{TS}}$ security with the same advantage of $\mathcal{A}$.

□

6 Conclusion and Open Problems

In this paper, we show that GS-MDO directly implies TRE. We also mentioned that the TRE scheme provides public verifiability. We argue that our result is evidence that GS-MDO is a strong cryptographic primitive. Our TRE construction is a combination of GS-based PKE [1] and GS-MDO-based IBE [47].

Our work introduces some open problems that may further strengthen the evidence that GS-MDO is a strong cryptographic primitive that we claimed in this paper.

On Token Unforgeability. As mentioned in [35], a token $\mathsf{t_M}$ can be regarded as a signature since GS-MDO implies IBE and a decryption key of IBE can be regarded as a signature due to the Naor transformation [11]. For example, a token in the Ohara et al.'s pairing-based GS-MDO scheme [44] is a Boneh-Lynn-Shacham (BLS) signature [12], and a token in the Libert et al.'s lattice-based GS-MDO scheme [37] is a Gentry-Peikert-Vaikuntanathan (GPV) signature [31]. Thus, we expect that GS-MDO provides a kind of unforgeability of tokens by nature.

On Traceability. We did not employ traceability which is also a fundamental security notion in GS-MDO. That is, there is a room for enhancing our result by providing traceability to construct a cryptographic primitive from GS-MDO. It is expected that the public verifiability guarantees that a valid TRE ciphertext is always decryptable if the underlying GS-MDO provides traceability. Providing a formal security definition of the public verifiability of GS-MDO-based TRE is left as future work, e.g., by extending the result in [27] that explores the public verifiability of GS-based PKE.

On Opening Soundness. We consider a static group setting as in the original GS-MDO definition [47]. In GS, Bellare, Shi, and Zhang (BSZ) [9] introduced a dynamic group setting and introduced the Judge algorithm that verifies a proof of ownership of a group signature. Later, Sakai et al. [48] introduced opening soundness as a security of the proof of ownership. Emura et al. [28] showed that dynamic GS implies PKENO and they employed opening soundness in their security proof. Due to these results and our result, we may be able to construct a TRE-variant of PKENO scheme from GS-MDO, e.g., by employing the Chen et al.'s dynamic GS-MDO scheme [18] that considers the Judge algorithm.

On Strongly Key-Insulated Public Key Encryption. Our result connects GS-MDO with other cryptographic primitive. Cheon et al. [19] demonstrated that TRE is equivalent to strongly key-insulated public key encryption (SKIE) (with optimal threshold and random access key updates). In their TRE-to-SKIE construction, a SKIE ciphertext is a TRE ciphertext. Thus, if the underlying TRE scheme is publicly verifiable, then the SKIE scheme is also publicly verifiable. Note that a multiple-encryption technique [24] is employed in their SKIE-to-TRE construction. Thus, although SKIE might be constructed from GS-MDO, the TRE scheme constructed via the SKIE-to-TRE construction seems not publicly verifiable. Exploring the public verifiability of SKIE is also left as future work.

On Certificateless Encryption. In certificateless encryption (CLE) [4], the key generation center (KGC) issues a secret key for each user (as in IBE) and each user also manages own public and secret keys. As mentioned by Chow et al. [21], TRE is implicitly supported by a CLE mechanism. They also introduce a generalized model for CLE that fulfills the requirements of TRE. They mentioned that, the security of a user is preserved even if other users are compromised in a secure multi-user system, and a difference in the definitions of security between CLE and TRE where the public keys in TRE are certified while there is no certification in CLE, so public keys can be chosen adversarially. To support such adversarially chosen keys, their TRE model is somewhat different from ours, e.g., they introduced a partial decryption algorithm, a security-mediator, and a strong decryption oracle that works even if the public key is adversarially chosen but the secret key is not supplied. Thus, our result does not show that GS-MDO implies CLE (in the Chow et al.'s model). As another related work, Zhang et al. [49] proposed structure-preserving CLE and introduced Group Signatures with Certified Limited Opening (GS-CLO) as its application. GS-CLO can be seen as a generalization of GS-MDO. In GS-CLO, an entity called a master certifier is introduced, who certifies openers case by case depending on the context. These results suggest that there is a relation between GS-MDO and CLE. Exploring the implication between GS-MDO and CLE is also left as future work.

Acknowledgment. The authors thank Prof. Yohei Watanabe for his invaluable comments on the equivalence between SKIE and TRE. The authors also thank Scott Griffy for his insightful feedback and support. This work was supported by the Telecommunications Advancement Foundation and JSPS KAKENHI Grant Number JP21K11897.

Appendix

A Modified Ohara et al.'s GS-MDO Scheme

Here, we give the modified Ohara et al.'s GS-MDO scheme. The original Ohara et al.'s GS-MDO scheme [44] can be seen as a combination of the Boneh-Boyen-Shacham (BBS) group signature scheme [10] and the Boneh-Franklin (BF) IBE scheme [11]. A token is a decryption key of the BF IBE scheme and thus it can be regarded as a Boneh-Lynn-Shacham (BLS) signature [12]. The original Ohara et al.'s GS-MDO scheme is constructed on symmetric pairings. However, asymmetric pairings are suitable for providing an efficient implementation [29]. Arai et al. [6] employed the Abe-Hoshino-Ohkubo transformation [3], that transforms a scheme constructed using a symmetric pairing to a scheme constructed using an asymmetric pairing, to the Ohara et al. GS-MDO scheme. Since the Arai et al.'s variant of the Ohara et al.'s GS-MDO scheme follows the original syntax defined in [47], we modify it to match the syntax defined in Def. 1 as follows. Let p is a λ-bit prime, $\mathbb{G}_1, \mathbb{G}_2$ and $\mathbb{G}_T$ are groups of order p, $e : \mathbb{G}_1 \times \mathbb{G}_2 \to \mathbb{G}_T$ is a bilinear map, and g_1 and g_2 are generators of $\mathbb{G}_1$ and $\mathbb{G}_2$, respectively. We require bilinearlity: for all $h_1 \in \mathbb{G}_1$, $h_2 \in \mathbb{G}_2$, and $a, b \in \mathbb{Z}_p$, $e(h_1^a, h_2^b) = e(h_1, h_2)^{ab}$ holds, and non-degeneracy: $e(g_1, g_2) \neq 1$ holds.

$\mathsf{GS\text{-}MDO.Setup}(1^\lambda)$: Let $(p, \mathbb{G}_1, \mathbb{G}_2, \mathbb{G}_T, e, g_1, g_2)$ be an asymmetric bilinear group where $\langle g_1 \rangle = \mathbb{G}_1$ and $\langle g_2 \rangle = \mathbb{G}_2$. Let $H_1 : \{0,1\}^* \to \mathbb{G}_2$ and $H_2 : \{0,1\}^* \to \mathbb{Z}_p$ be hash functions (modeled as random oracles). Output $\mathsf{pp}_{\mathsf{GS\text{-}MDO}} = (p, \mathbb{G}_1, \mathbb{G}_2, \mathbb{G}_T, e, g_1, g_2, H_1, H_2)$.

$\mathsf{GKg}(\mathsf{pp}_{\mathsf{GS\text{-}MDO}}, 1^n)$: Parse $\mathsf{pp}_{\mathsf{GS\text{-}MDO}} = (p, \mathbb{G}_1, \mathbb{G}_2, \mathbb{G}_T, e, g_1, g_2, H_1, H_2)$.

1. Choose $u, v, h \xleftarrow{\$} \mathbb{G}_1$ and $\xi_1, \xi_2, \xi_3, \gamma \xleftarrow{\$} \mathbb{Z}_p$.
2. Compute $\bar{g}_1 = u^{\xi_1} v^{\xi_3}$, $\bar{g}_2 = v^{\xi_2} h^{\xi_3}$, and $\omega = g_2^\gamma$.
3. For $i \in [1, n]$, choose $x_i \xleftarrow{\$} \mathbb{Z}_p$, compute $A_i = g_1^{1/(\gamma + x_i)}$, and set $\mathsf{gsk}_i = (A_i, x_i)$.

Output $\mathsf{gpk} = ((p, \mathbb{G}_1, \mathbb{G}_2, \mathbb{G}_T, e, g_1, g_2), u, v, h, \bar{g}_1, \bar{g}_2, \omega, H_1, H_2)$, $\{\mathsf{gsk}_i\}_{i \in [n]}$, and $\mathsf{ok} = (\xi_1, \xi_2, \xi_3, \{e(A_i, g_2)\}_{i \in [1,n]})$.

$\mathsf{AKg}(\mathsf{pp}_{\mathsf{GS\text{-}MDO}})$: Parse $\mathsf{pp}_{\mathsf{GS\text{-}MDO}} = (p, \mathbb{G}_1, \mathbb{G}_2, \mathbb{G}_T, e, g_1, g_2, H_1, H_2)$.

1. Choose $\xi \xleftarrow{\$} \mathbb{Z}_p$.
2. Compute $y = g_1^\xi$.

Output $\mathsf{apk} = y$ and $\mathsf{ask} = \xi$.

$\mathsf{GSig}(\mathsf{gpk}, \mathsf{apk}, \mathsf{gsk}_i, \mathsf{M})$: Parse $\mathsf{gpk} = ((p, \mathbb{G}_1, \mathbb{G}_2, \mathbb{G}_T, e, g_1, g_2), u, v, h, \bar{g}_1, \bar{g}_2, \omega, H_1, H_2)$, $\mathsf{apk} = y$, and $\mathsf{gsk}_i = (A_i, x_i)$.

1. Choose $\alpha, \beta, \rho, \eta \xleftarrow{\$} \mathbb{Z}_p$.

2. Compute

$$T_1 = u^{\alpha}, T_2 = v^{\beta}, T_3 = h^{\alpha+\beta}, T_4 = \bar{g}_1^{\alpha}\bar{g}_2^{\beta}A_i g_1^{\eta}$$
$$T_5 = g_1^{\rho}, T_6 = e(y, H_1(\mathsf{M}))^{\rho}e(g_1, g_2)^{-\eta}$$

3. Choose $r_\alpha, r_\beta, r_\rho, r_\eta, r_x, r_{\alpha x}, r_{\beta x}, r_{\rho x}, r_{\eta x} \xleftarrow{\$} \mathbb{Z}_p$.
4. Compute

$$\begin{aligned}
R_1 &= u^{r_\alpha}, R_2 = v^{r_\beta}, R_3 = h^{r_\alpha + r_\beta},\\
R_4 &= e(T_4, g_2)^{r_x} e(g_1, \omega)^{-r_\alpha} e(\bar{g}_1, g_2)^{-r_{\alpha x}} e(\bar{g}_2, \omega)^{-r_\beta} e(\bar{g}_2, g_2)^{-r_{\beta x}}\\
&\quad \times e(g_1, \omega)^{-r_\eta} e(g_1, g_2)^{-r_{\eta x}},\\
R_5 &= g_1^{r_\rho}, R_6 = e(y, H_1(\mathsf{M}))^{r_\rho} e(g_1, g_2)^{-r_\eta},\\
R_7 &= T_1^{r_x} u^{-r_{\alpha x}}, R_8 = T_2^{r_x} v^{-r_\beta}, R_9 = T_5^{r_x} g_1^{-r_\rho}\\
R_{10} &= T_6^{r_x} e(y, H_1(\mathsf{M}))^{-r_\rho} e(g_1, g_2)^{r_{\eta x}}.
\end{aligned}$$

5. Compute $c = H_2(M, T_1, \ldots, T_6, R_1, \ldots, R_{10})$, $s_\alpha = r_\alpha + c\alpha$, $s_\beta = r_\beta + c\beta$, $s_\rho = r_\rho + c\rho$, $s_\eta = r_\eta + c\eta$, $s_x = r_x + cx_i$, $s_{\alpha x} = r_{\alpha x} + c\alpha x_i$, $s_{\beta x} = r_{\beta x} + c\beta x_i$, $s_{\rho x} = r_{\rho x} + c\rho x_i$, and $s_{\eta x} = r_{\eta x} + c\eta x_i$.

Output $\sigma = (T_1, \ldots, T_6, c, s_\alpha, s_\beta, s_\rho, s_\eta, s_x, s_{\alpha x}, s_{\beta x}, s_{\rho x}, s_{\eta x})$.

$\mathsf{Td}(\mathsf{pp}_{\mathsf{GS\text{-}MDO}}, \mathsf{ask}, \mathsf{M})$: Parse $\mathsf{pp}_{\mathsf{GS\text{-}MDO}} = (p, \mathbb{G}_1, \mathbb{G}_2, \mathbb{G}_T, e, g_1, g_2, H_1, H_2)$ and $\mathsf{ask} = \xi$. Output $\mathsf{t_M} = H_1(\mathsf{M})^{\xi}$.

$\mathsf{GVf}(\mathsf{gpk}, \mathsf{apk}, \mathsf{M}, \sigma)$: Parse $\mathsf{gpk} = ((p, \mathbb{G}_1, \mathbb{G}_2, \mathbb{G}_T, e, g_1, g_2), u, v, h, \bar{g}_1, \bar{g}_2, \omega, H_1, H_2)$, $\mathsf{apk} = y$, and $\sigma = (T_1, \ldots, T_6, c, s_\alpha, s_\beta, s_\rho, s_\eta, s_x, s_{\alpha x}, s_{\beta x}, s_{\rho x}, s_{\eta x})$. Compute

$$\begin{aligned}
R'_1 &= u^{s_\alpha} T_1^{-c}, R'_2 = v^{s_\beta} T_2^{-c}, R'_3 = h^{s_\alpha + s_\beta} T_3^{-c},\\
R'_4 &= e(T_4, g_2)^{s_x} e(\bar{g}_1, \omega)^{-s_\alpha} e(\bar{g}_1, g_2)^{-s_{\alpha x}} e(\bar{g}_2, \omega)^{-s_\beta} e(\bar{g}_2, g_2)^{-s_{\beta x}} e(g_1, \omega)^{-s_\eta}\\
&\quad \times e(g_1, g_2)^{-s_{\eta x}} (e(g_1, g_2)/e(T_4, \omega))^{-c},\\
R'_5 &= g_1^{s_\rho} T_5^{-c}, R'_6 = e(y, H_1(\mathsf{M}))^{s_\rho} e(g_1, g_2)^{-s_\eta} T_6^{-c},\\
R'_7 &= T_1^{s_x} u^{-s_{\alpha x}}, R'_8 = T_2^{s_x} v^{-s_{\beta x}}, R'_9 = T_5^{s_x} g_1^{-s_{\rho x}},\\
R'_{10} &= T_6^{s_x} e(y, H_1(\mathsf{M}))^{-s_{\rho x}} e(g_1, g_2)^{s_{\eta x}}
\end{aligned}$$

If $c = H_2(M, T_1, \ldots, T_6, R'_1, \ldots, R'_{10})$, then return 1, and 0 otherwise.

$\mathsf{Open}(\mathsf{gpk}, \mathsf{apk}, \mathsf{ok}, M, \sigma, \mathsf{t_M})$: Parse $\mathsf{gpk} = ((p, \mathbb{G}_1, \mathbb{G}_2, \mathbb{G}_T, e, g_1, g_2), u, v, h, \bar{g}_1, \bar{g}_2, \omega, H_1, H_2)$, $\mathsf{apk} = y$, $\mathsf{ok} = (\xi_1, \xi_2, \xi_3, \{e(A_i, g_2)\}_{i \in [1,n]})$, and $\sigma = (T_1, \ldots, T_6, c, s_\alpha, s_\beta, s_\rho, s_\eta, s_x, s_{\alpha x}, s_{\beta x}, s_{\rho x}, s_{\eta x})$. If $\mathsf{GVf}(\mathsf{gpk}, \mathsf{apk}, M, \sigma) = 0$, then output $\perp$. Otherwise, If $\exists i \in [1, n]$ s.t.

$$e(T_4/T_1^{\xi_1}T_2^{\xi_2}T_3^{\xi_3}, g_2) \cdot T_6/e(T_5, \mathsf{t_M}) = e(A_i, g_2)$$

then output i. Otherwise, output $\perp$.

B Modified Libert et al.'s GS-MDO Scheme

The Libert et al.'s GS-MDO scheme can be seen as a combination of the Lin-Nguyen-Wang (LNW) group signature scheme [38] and the GPV IBE scheme [31]. A group signing key is a Boyen's signature [15]. A token is a decryption key of the GPV IBE scheme and thus it can be regarded as a GPV signature. In the Libert et al.'s GS-MDO scheme, some lattice-related parameters depend on the number of group members $2^\ell = \mathsf{poly}(\lambda)$. That is, $\mathsf{GKg}(\mathsf{pp}_{\mathsf{GS\text{-}MDO}}, 1^n)$ needs to indicate these parameters since the algorithm takes the number of group members n as input. Moreover, the AKg algorithm takes these parameters as input. This fact prevents to directly modify the syntax. One simple solution is that the maximum number of group members N_{max} is set in the $\mathsf{GS\text{-}MDO.Setup}$ algorithm. Then, we can modify the syntax. The maximum number of group users N_{max} is often set to specify the lattice-related parameters, e.g., the Lin et al.'s lattice-based fully dynamic group signature scheme [39]. For consistency, we denote $n \leq N_{\mathsf{max}}$ as the number of group members, though n is often employed to indicate a lattice parameter such as $\mathbf{A} \in \mathbb{Z}_q^{n\times m}$. We denote N as the lattice parameter.

$\mathsf{GS\text{-}MDO.Setup}(1^\lambda)$: Choose the lattice parameter $N = O(\lambda)$. Set the maximum number of group members $N_{\mathsf{max}} = 2^\ell = \mathsf{poly}(\lambda)$, a prime modulus $q = O(\ell \cdot N^2)$, the infinity norm bound for signatures (generated by the Boyen's signature scheme) $\beta = \tilde{O})(\sqrt{\ell N})$, $m \leq \mathsf{poly}(N)$, and the infinity norm bound for LWE noises sampled from error distribution χ. Assume that $\mathsf{pp}_{\mathsf{GS\text{-}MDO}}$ contains these lattice parameters, N_{max}, two hash functions $H_1 : \{0,1\} \to \mathbb{Z}_q^{N\times\ell}$ and $H_2 : \{0,1\} \to \mathbb{Z}_q^{N\times\ell\lceil\log q\rceil}$ and a strongly unforgeable one-time signature scheme $\Pi_{\mathsf{OTS}} = (\mathsf{OTS.KeyGen}, \mathsf{OTS.Sign}, \mathsf{OTS.Verify})$. We denote $(\mathsf{vk}, \mathsf{sigk})$ be a key pair of Π_{OTS}.

$\mathsf{GKg}(\mathsf{pp}_{\mathsf{GS\text{-}MDO}}, 1^n)$: Assume that $n \leq N_{\mathsf{max}}$. Generate a key pair of the Boyen's signature scheme: a verification key $(\mathbf{A}, \mathbf{A}_0, \ldots, \mathbf{A}_\ell, \mathbf{u}) \in (\mathbb{Z}_q^{N\times m})^{\ell+2}$ and a signing key $\mathbf{T_A} \in \mathbb{Z}^{m\times m}$. For each $d \in \{0, \ldots, 2^{\ell-1}\}$, generate the Boyen's signature for the message $\mathsf{bin}(d) = (d_1, \ldots, d_\ell) \in \{0,1\}^\ell$ using the trapdoor $\mathbf{T_A}$ such that $\mathsf{gsk}_d = (\mathbf{v}_{d,1}^T \mid \mathbf{v}_{d,2}^T) \in \mathbb{Z}^{2m}$. Generate an encryption key $\mathbf{B} \in \mathbb{Z}_q^{N\times m}$ and a decryption key $\mathbf{T_B} \in \mathbb{Z}^{m\times m}$ of the GPV-IBE scheme. Output $\mathsf{gpk} = (\mathsf{pp}_{\mathsf{GS\text{-}MDO}}, \mathbf{A}, \{\mathbf{A}_i\}_{i=0}^\ell, \mathbf{u}, \mathbf{B})$, $\{\mathsf{gsk}_i\}_{i\in[n]}$, and $\mathsf{ok} = \mathbf{T_B}$.

$\mathsf{AKg}(\mathsf{pp}_{\mathsf{GS\text{-}MDO}})$: Generate an encryption key $\mathbf{C} \in \mathbb{Z}_q^{N\times m}$ and a decryption key $\mathbf{T_C} \in \mathbb{Z}^{m\times m}$ of the GPV-IBE scheme. Output $\mathsf{apk} = \mathbf{C}$ and $\mathsf{ask} = \mathbf{T_C}$.

$\mathsf{GSig}(\mathsf{gpk}, \mathsf{apk}, \mathsf{gsk}_i, \mathsf{M})$: Generate $(\mathsf{vk}, \mathsf{sigk}) \leftarrow \mathsf{OTS.KeyGen}(1^\lambda)$. Compute $\mathbf{G} = H_1(\mathsf{vk})$ and a GPV ciphertext (with vk as the identity for the message i) $(\mathbf{c}_1 = \mathbf{B}^T\mathbf{s} + \mathbf{e}_1, \mathbf{c}_2 = \mathbf{G}^T\mathbf{s} + \mathbf{e}_2 + \lfloor q/2\rfloor \cdot \mathsf{bin}(i)) \in \mathbb{Z}_q^m \times \mathbb{Z}_q^\ell$ where $\mathbf{s}$, $\mathbf{e}_1$, and $\mathbf{e}_2$ are appropriately sampled. Compute $\hat{\mathbf{G}} = H_2(\mathsf{M})$ and a GPV ciphertext (with M as the identity for the message $\mathbf{c}_2$) $(\hat{\mathbf{c}}_1 = \mathbf{C}^T\hat{\mathbf{s}} + \hat{\mathbf{e}}_1, \hat{\mathbf{c}}_2 = \hat{\mathbf{G}}^T\hat{\mathbf{s}} + \hat{\mathbf{e}}_2 + \lfloor q/2\rfloor \cdot \mathsf{bin}(\mathbf{c}_2)) \in \mathbb{Z}_q^m \times \mathbb{Z}_q^{\ell\lceil\log q\rceil}$ where $\hat{\mathbf{s}}$, $\hat{\mathbf{e}}_1$, and $\hat{\mathbf{e}}_2$ are appropriately sampled. Generate a NIZKAoK (zero-knowledge arguments of knowledge) π for the relation R_{gsmdo} and convert via the Fiat-Shamir transformation

(See [37] for detail). Compute a OTS Σ for $(\mathbf{c}_1, \hat{\mathbf{c}}_1, \hat{\mathbf{c}}_2)$ and π. Output $\sigma = (\mathsf{vk}, \Sigma, \mathbf{c}_1, \hat{\mathbf{c}}_1, \hat{\mathbf{c}}_2, \pi)$.

$\mathsf{Td}(\mathsf{pp}_{\mathsf{GS\text{-}MDO}}, \mathsf{ask}, \mathsf{M})$: Compute $\hat{\mathbf{G}} = H_2(\mathsf{M})$. Using $\mathbf{T}_{\mathbf{C}}$, compute a small-norm matrix $\mathbf{E}_{\mathsf{M}}$ satisfying $\mathbf{C} \cdot \mathbf{E}_M = \hat{\mathbf{G}}$ which is a decryption key of the GPV-IBE scheme for the identity M. Output $\mathsf{t}_{\mathsf{M}} = \mathbf{E}_{\mathsf{M}}$.

$\mathsf{GVf}(\mathsf{gpk}, \mathsf{apk}, \mathsf{M}, \sigma)$: Output 1 of the OTS Σ and the proof π are correct. Otherwise, output 0.

$\mathsf{Open}(\mathsf{gpk}, \mathsf{apk}, \mathsf{ok}, M, \sigma, \mathsf{t}_{\mathsf{M}})$: Decrypt $(\hat{\mathbf{c}}_1, \hat{\mathbf{c}}_2)$ using $\mathsf{t}_{\mathsf{M}} = \mathbf{E}_{\mathsf{M}}$ and obtain $\mathbf{c}_2$. Decrypt $(\mathbf{c}_1, \mathbf{c}_2)$ using $\mathsf{ok} = \mathbf{T}_{\mathbf{B}}$ and obtain i. Output i if $i \in [n]$ and $\perp$ otherwise.

C On Multiple Openers and Users

C.1 GS-MDO in a Multi-opener Setting

Let $\{\mathsf{gpk}_i, \mathsf{ok}_i\}_{i \in [\ell]}$ be the set of openers' keys where $\ell \in \mathbb{N}$ denotes the number of openers. First of all, an adversary must obtain $\{\mathsf{gpk}_i\}_{i \in [\ell]}$. The situations we need to capture in a multi-opener setting are (1) an adversary of opener anonymity obtains all openers' secret keys that can be easily handled, and (2) an adversary of admitter anonymity obtains all openers' secret keys except the challenge opener. In an adaptive security manner, the adversary may corrupt up to $\ell - 1$ openers and obtain the corresponding ok. With the reduction loss $1/\ell$, the final (i.e., challenge) opener can be guessed. This implies that we can follow a selective security manner, where an adversary declares who will be the challenge opener, with the reduction loss $1/\ell$. We assume that the adversary issues open queries for the challenge opener since the adversary can run the Open algorithm using other openers' secret keys. The remaining procedure follows that of admitter anonymity in the single-opener setting as defined in Def. 2.

We also remark that an adversary of traceability, that is not required to construct TRE, receives ok in the security model. As with opener anonymity, traceability in the multi-opener setting can be handled by providing all openers' secret keys to the adversary.

C.2 TRE in a Multi-user Setting

Let $\{(\mathsf{pk}_{\mathsf{u},i}, \mathsf{sk}_{\mathsf{u},i})\}_{i \in [\ell]}$ be the set of users' keys where $\ell \in \mathbb{N}$ denotes the number of users. First of all, an adversary must obtain $\{\mathsf{pk}_{\mathsf{u},i}\}_{i \in [\ell]}$. The situations we need to capture in a multi-user setting are (1) an adversary of insider security obtains all users' secret keys $\{\mathsf{sk}_{\mathsf{u},i}\}_{i \in [\ell]}$ that can be easily handled, and (2) an adversary of time server security obtains all users' secret keys except the challenge user. In an adaptive security manner, the adversary may corrupt up to $\ell - 1$ users and obtain the corresponding sk_{u}. With the reduction loss $1/\ell$, the final (i.e., challenge) user can be guessed. This implies that we can follow a selective security manner, where an adversary declares who will be the challenge user, with the reduction loss $1/\ell$. We assume that the adversary issues decryption queries for the challenge user since the adversary can run the TRE.Dec algorithm using other users' secret keys. The remaining procedure follows that of time server security in the single-user setting as defined in Def. 6.

C.3 Remark on Security Proofs

Security proofs of Theorem 1 and Theorem 2 are essentially the same even in a multi-user setting. To reduce admitter anonymity to time server security, the reduction algorithm obtains all openers' secret keys from the challenger of admitter anonymity in the multi-opener setting. Thus, the reduction algorithm simply forwards these keys to the adversary of time server security. To reduce opener anonymity to insider security, the reduction algorithm obtains all openers' secret keys, except the challenge opener's secret key, from the challenger of opener anonymity in the multi-opener setting. Since the adversary of time server security declares who the challenge user is, the reduction algorithm assigns the challenge opener as the challenge user.

References

1. Abdalla, M., Warinschi, B.: On the minimal assumptions of group signature schemes. In: ICICS, pp. 1–13 (2004)
2. Abe, M., Gennaro, R., Kurosawa, K.: Tag-KEM/DEM: a new framework for hybrid encryption. J. Cryptol. **21**(1), 97–130 (2008)
3. Abe, M., Hoshino, F., Ohkubo, M.: Design in type-I, run in type-III: fast and scalable bilinear-type conversion using integer programming. In: Robshaw, M., Katz, J. (eds.) CRYPTO 2016. LNCS, vol. 9816, pp. 387–415. Springer, Heidelberg (2016). https://doi.org/10.1007/978-3-662-53015-3_14
4. Al-Riyami, S.S., Paterson, K.G.: Certificateless public key cryptography. In: Laih, C.-S. (ed.) ASIACRYPT 2003. LNCS, vol. 2894, pp. 452–473. Springer, Heidelberg (2003). https://doi.org/10.1007/978-3-540-40061-5_29
5. Anada, H., Fukumitsu, M., Hasegawa, S.: Dynamic group signatures with message dependent opening and non-interactive signing. In: CANDAR, pp. 76–82. IEEE (2022)
6. Arai, H., Emura, K., Hayashi, T.: Privacy-preserving data analysis: providing traceability without big brother. IEICE Trans. Fundam. Electron. Commun. Comput. Sci. **104-A**(1), 2–19 (2021)
7. Bartusek, J., Garg, S., Jain, A., Policharla, G.: End-to-end secure messaging with traceability only for illegal content. In: Hazay, C., Stam, M. (eds.) EUROCRYPT 2023, Part V. LNCS, vol. 14008, pp. 35–66. Springer, Cham (2023). https://doi.org/10.1007/978-3-031-30589-4_2
8. Bellare, M., Micciancio, D., Warinschi, B.: Foundations of group signatures: formal definitions, simplified requirements, and a construction based on general assumptions. In: Biham, E. (ed.) EUROCRYPT 2003. LNCS, vol. 2656, pp. 614–629. Springer, Heidelberg (2003). https://doi.org/10.1007/3-540-39200-9_38
9. Bellare, M., Shi, H., Zhang, C.: Foundations of group signatures: the case of dynamic groups. In: Menezes, A. (ed.) CT-RSA 2005. LNCS, vol. 3376, pp. 136–153. Springer, Heidelberg (2005). https://doi.org/10.1007/978-3-540-30574-3_11

10. Boneh, D., Boyen, X., Shacham, H.: Short group signatures. In: Franklin, M. (ed.) CRYPTO 2004. LNCS, vol. 3152, pp. 41–55. Springer, Heidelberg (2004). https://doi.org/10.1007/978-3-540-28628-8_3
11. Boneh, D., Franklin, M.: Identity-based encryption from the weil pairing. In: Kilian, J. (ed.) CRYPTO 2001. LNCS, vol. 2139, pp. 213–229. Springer, Heidelberg (2001). https://doi.org/10.1007/3-540-44647-8_13
12. Boneh, D., Lynn, B., Shacham, H.: Short signatures from the weil pairing. In: Boyd, C. (ed.) ASIACRYPT 2001. LNCS, vol. 2248, pp. 514–532. Springer, Heidelberg (2001). https://doi.org/10.1007/3-540-45682-1_30
13. Boneh, D., Papakonstantinou, P.A., Rackoff, C., Vahlis, Y., Waters, B.: On the impossibility of basing identity based encryption on trapdoor permutations. In: FOCS, pp. 283–292. IEEE Computer Society (2008)
14. Bootle, J., Cerulli, A., Chaidos, P., Ghadafi, E., Groth, J.: Foundations of fully dynamic group signatures. In: Manulis, M., Sadeghi, A.-R., Schneider, S. (eds.) ACNS 2016. LNCS, vol. 9696, pp. 117–136. Springer, Cham (2016). https://doi.org/10.1007/978-3-319-39555-5_7
15. Boyen, X.: Lattice mixing and vanishing trapdoors: a framework for fully secure short signatures and more. In: Nguyen, P.Q., Pointcheval, D. (eds.) PKC 2010. LNCS, vol. 6056, pp. 499–517. Springer, Heidelberg (2010). https://doi.org/10.1007/978-3-642-13013-7_29
16. Canetti, R., Halevi, S., Katz, J.: Chosen-ciphertext security from identity-based encryption. In: Cachin, C., Camenisch, J.L. (eds.) EUROCRYPT 2004. LNCS, vol. 3027, pp. 207–222. Springer, Heidelberg (2004). https://doi.org/10.1007/978-3-540-24676-3_13
17. Chaum, D., van Heyst, E.: Group signatures. In: Davies, D.W. (ed.) EUROCRYPT 1991. LNCS, vol. 547, pp. 257–265. Springer, Heidelberg (1991). https://doi.org/10.1007/3-540-46416-6_22
18. Chen, S., Chen, J., Miyaji, A., Chen, K.: Constant-size group signatures with message-dependent opening from lattices. In: ProvSec, pp. 166–185 (2023)
19. Cheon, J.H., Hopper, N., Kim, Y., Osipkov, I.: Timed-release and key-insulated public key encryption. In: Di Crescenzo, G., Rubin, A. (eds.) FC 2006. LNCS, vol. 4107, pp. 191–205. Springer, Heidelberg (2006). https://doi.org/10.1007/11889663_17
20. Cheon, J.H., Hopper, N., Kim, Y., Osipkov, I.: Provably secure timed-release public key encryption. ACM Trans. Inf. Syst. Secur. **11**(2), 4:1–4:44 (2008)
21. Chow, S.S.M., Roth, V., Rieffel, E.G.: General certificateless encryption and timed-release encryption. In: Ostrovsky, R., De Prisco, R., Visconti, I. (eds.) SCN 2008. LNCS, vol. 5229, pp. 126–143. Springer, Heidelberg (2008). https://doi.org/10.1007/978-3-540-85855-3_9
22. Damgård, I., Hofheinz, D., Kiltz, E., Thorbek, R.: Public-key encryption with non-interactive opening. In: Malkin, T. (ed.) CT-RSA 2008. LNCS, vol. 4964, pp. 239–255. Springer, Heidelberg (2008). https://doi.org/10.1007/978-3-540-79263-5_15
23. Dent, A.W., Tang, Q.: Revisiting the security model for timed-release encryption with pre-open capability. In: Garay, J.A., Lenstra, A.K., Mambo, M., Peralta, R. (eds.) ISC 2007. LNCS, vol. 4779, pp. 158–174. Springer, Heidelberg (2007). https://doi.org/10.1007/978-3-540-75496-1_11
24. Dodis, Y., Katz, J.: Chosen-ciphertext security of multiple encryption. In: Kilian, J. (ed.) TCC 2005. LNCS, vol. 3378, pp. 188–209. Springer, Heidelberg (2005). https://doi.org/10.1007/978-3-540-30576-7_11

25. Döttling, N., Garg, S.: From selective IBE to full IBE and selective HIBE. In: Kalai, Y., Reyzin, L. (eds.) TCC 2017, Part I. LNCS, vol. 10677, pp. 372–408. Springer, Cham (2017). https://doi.org/10.1007/978-3-319-70500-2_13
26. Döttling, N., Garg, S.: Identity-based encryption from the Diffie-Hellman assumption. In: Katz, J., Shacham, H. (eds.) CRYPTO 2017, Part I. LNCS, vol. 10401, pp. 537–569. Springer, Cham (2017). https://doi.org/10.1007/978-3-319-63688-7_18
27. Emura, K.: On the traceability of group signatures: uncorrupted user must exist. IACR Cryptol. ePrint Arch. 2014 (2024). https://eprint.iacr.org/2024/2014
28. Emura, K., Hanaoka, G., Sakai, Y., Schuldt, J.C.N.: Group signature implies public-key encryption with non-interactive opening. Int. J. Inf. Secur. **13**(1), 51–62 (2014)
29. Galbraith, S.D., Paterson, K.G., Smart, N.P.: Pairings for cryptographers. Discret. Appl. Math. **156**(16), 3113–3121 (2008)
30. Galindo, D., et al.: Public-key encryption with non-interactive opening: new constructions and stronger definitions. In: Bernstein, D.J., Lange, T. (eds.) AFRICACRYPT 2010. LNCS, vol. 6055, pp. 333–350. Springer, Heidelberg (2010). https://doi.org/10.1007/978-3-642-12678-9_20
31. Gentry, C., Peikert, C., Vaikuntanathan, V.: Trapdoors for hard lattices and new cryptographic constructions. In: ACM STOC, pp. 197–206 (2008)
32. Goyal, R., Koppula, V., Rajasree, M.S.: A note on adaptive security in hierarchical identity-based encryption. In: CRYPTO (2025, to appear)
33. Groth, J., Sahai, A.: Efficient non-interactive proof systems for bilinear groups. In: Smart, N. (ed.) EUROCRYPT 2008. LNCS, vol. 4965, pp. 415–432. Springer, Heidelberg (2008). https://doi.org/10.1007/978-3-540-78967-3_24
34. Hwang, Y.H., Yum, D.H., Lee, P.J.: Timed-release encryption with pre-open capability and its application to certified E-mail system. In: Zhou, J., Lopez, J., Deng, R.H., Bao, F. (eds.) ISC 2005. LNCS, vol. 3650, pp. 344–358. Springer, Heidelberg (2005). https://doi.org/10.1007/11556992_25
35. Imura, Y., Emura, K.: An identity management system using group signatures with message-dependent opening. In: AsiaJCIS, pp. 40–47. IEEE (2024)
36. Libert, B., Joye, M.: Group signatures with message-dependent opening in the standard model. In: Benaloh, J. (ed.) CT-RSA 2014. LNCS, vol. 8366, pp. 286–306. Springer, Cham (2014). https://doi.org/10.1007/978-3-319-04852-9_15
37. Libert, B., Mouhartem, F., Nguyen, K.: A lattice-based group signature scheme with message-dependent opening. In: Manulis, M., Sadeghi, A.-R., Schneider, S. (eds.) ACNS 2016. LNCS, vol. 9696, pp. 137–155. Springer, Cham (2016). https://doi.org/10.1007/978-3-319-39555-5_8
38. Ling, S., Nguyen, K., Wang, H.: Group signatures from lattices: simpler, tighter, shorter, ring-based. In: Public-Key Cryptography, pp. 427–449 (2015)
39. Ling, S., Nguyen, K., Wang, H., Xu, Y.: Lattice-based group signatures: achieving full dynamicity with ease. In: Gollmann, D., Miyaji, A., Kikuchi, H. (eds.) ACNS 2017. LNCS, vol. 10355, pp. 293–312. Springer, Cham (2017). https://doi.org/10.1007/978-3-319-61204-1_15
40. Matsuda, T., Nakai, Y., Matsuura, K.: Efficient generic constructions of timed-release encryption with pre-open capability. In: Joye, M., Miyaji, A., Otsuka, A. (eds.) Pairing 2010. LNCS, vol. 6487, pp. 225–245. Springer, Heidelberg (2010). https://doi.org/10.1007/978-3-642-17455-1_15
41. Myers, S.A., Shelat, A.: Bit encryption is complete. In: FOCS, pp. 607–616. IEEE (2009)

42. Nakai, Y., Matsuda, T., Kitada, W., Matsuura, K.: A generic construction of timed-release encryption with pre-open capability. In: Takagi, T., Mambo, M. (eds.) IWSEC 2009. LNCS, vol. 5824, pp. 53–70. Springer, Heidelberg (2009). https://doi.org/10.1007/978-3-642-04846-3_5
43. Nguyen, T.N., Susilo, W., Duong, D.H., Guo, F., Fukushima, K., Kiyomoto, S.: A fault-tolerant content moderation mechanism for secure messaging systems. In: Zhu, T., Li, Y. (eds.) ACISP 2024, Part II. Lecture Notes in Computer Science, vol. 14896, pp. 269–289. Springer, Singapore (2024)
44. Ohara, K., Sakai, Y., Emura, K., Hanaoka, G.: A group signature scheme with unbounded message-dependent opening. In: ACM ASIACCS, pp. 517–522 (2013)
45. Ohtake, G., Fujii, A., Hanaoka, G., Ogawa, K.: On the theoretical gap between group signatures with and without unlinkability. In: Preneel, B. (ed.) AFRICACRYPT 2009. LNCS, vol. 5580, pp. 149–166. Springer, Heidelberg (2009). https://doi.org/10.1007/978-3-642-02384-2_10
46. Rivest, R.L., Shamir, A., Wagner, D.A.: Time-lock puzzles and timed-release crypto. In: Technical report MITLCSTR-684, MIT (1996)
47. Sakai, Y., Emura, K., Hanaoka, G., Kawai, Y., Matsuda, T., Omote, K.: Group signatures with message-dependent opening. In: Abdalla, M., Lange, T. (eds.) Pairing 2012. LNCS, vol. 7708, pp. 270–294. Springer, Heidelberg (2013). https://doi.org/10.1007/978-3-642-36334-4_18
48. Sakai, Y., Schuldt, J.C.N., Emura, K., Hanaoka, G., Ohta, K.: On the security of dynamic group signatures: preventing signature hijacking. In: Fischlin, M., Buchmann, J., Manulis, M. (eds.) PKC 2012. LNCS, vol. 7293, pp. 715–732. Springer, Heidelberg (2012). https://doi.org/10.1007/978-3-642-30057-8_42
49. Zhang, T., Wu, H., Chow, S.S.M.: Structure-preserving certificateless encryption and its application. In: Matsui, M. (ed.) CT-RSA 2019. LNCS, vol. 11405, pp. 1–22. Springer, Cham (2019). https://doi.org/10.1007/978-3-030-12612-4_1

On the Relations Between Matchmaking Public Key Encryption and Public Key Authenticated Encryption with Keyword Search

Takeshi Yoshida[1] and Keita Emura[1,2](✉)

[1] Kanazawa University, Kanazawa, Japan
y0xxss1@stu.kanazawa-u.ac.jp, k-emura@se.kanazawa-u.ac.jp
[2] National Institute of Advanced Industrial Science and Technology, Tokyo, Japan

Abstract. Ateniese et al. (CRYPTO 2019/JoC 2021) introduced a cryptographic primitive which they call matchmaking encryption (ME), and Identity-based ME (IB-ME) is its identity-based variant. IB-ME supports an equality matching where a sender (encryptor) indicates a receiver's (decryptor's) identity (rcv) in addition to their own ID (σ), and a receiver indicates a sender's identity (snd) in addition to the own identity (ρ). A ciphertext is decrypted if $(\sigma, \rho) = (\mathsf{snd}, \mathsf{rcv})$. In this paper, we pay attention to the search condition of public key authenticated encryption with keyword search (PAEKS) (Huang-Li, Information Sciences 2017) is reminiscent of the equality matching. We introduce a public key variant of ME which we call PK-ME, and propose a generic construction of PK-ME from PAEKS. As a conceptual contribution, our work lies in revealing a connection between ME and public key searchable encryption, which were independently researched so far. Due to the generic construction of PAEKS (Li-Boyen, IACR CiC 2024), we can instantiate the proposed generic construction from pairings or lattices. Finally, we discuss the advantage/disadvantage of PK-ME compared to IB-ME.

Keywords: Matchmaking Encryption · Public Key Authenticated Encryption with Keyword Search

1 Introduction

1.1 Background

Matchmaking Encryption. In 2019, Ateniese et al. [3,4] introduced a cryptographic primitive which they call matchmaking encryption (ME) as a non-interactive variant of secret handshake or affiliation-Hiding group key exchange protocols. A sender (encryptor) indicates a policy of a receiver (decryptor), and simultaneously, a receiver also indicates a policy of a sender. A ciphertext is decrypted if both sender attributes satisfy the sender policy and receiver attributes satisfy the receiver policy.

Y. Kim et al. (Eds.): CANS 2025, LNCS 16351, pp. 272–291, 2026.
https://doi.org/10.1007/978-981-95-4434-9_13

IB-ME, an identity-based variant of ME, is also introduced where the policy is restricted as a equality matching: a sender (encryptor) indicates a receiver's (decryptor's) identity (rcv) in addition to the own ID (σ), and a receiver indicates a sender's identity (snd) in addition to the own identity (ρ). A ciphertext is decrypted if

$$(\sigma, \rho) = (\mathsf{snd}, \mathsf{rcv})$$

As a special requirement, when the decryption fails, then no information beyond the decryption failure is revealed, i.e., a receiver does not know whether $\mathsf{rcv} \neq \rho$ or $\mathsf{snd} \neq \sigma$. Ateniese et al. proposed an IB-ME scheme which is secure in the random oracle model. As subsequent works, Francati et al. [23] and Chen et al. [11] proposed IB-ME schemes secure in the standard model. Francati et al. [23] introduced a stronger flavor of privacy which they call enhanced privacy. It captures privacy according to every possible mismatch condition for the receiver where an adversary holds a decryption key but does not know the sender's identities. Chiku et al. [14] proposed an efficient IB-ME scheme in the random oracle model. Wang et al. [40] proposed a generic construction of IB-ME from 2-level anonymous hierarchical identity-based encryption (HIBE) and identity-based signature (IBS) and gave a lattice-based instantiation. Boyen and Li [7] also proposed a generic construction of IB-ME from IBE, an average-case randomness extractor, and a reusable computational extractor, and gave several instantiations. Lin et al. [32] considers a chosen-ciphertext security. Chiku et al. [13] proposed a key-escrow free IB-ME scheme by considering IBE with security against the key generation center (KGC) [15,21,22]. As another attempt to solve the key-escrow problem, Chen et al. [10] and Yang et al. [41] proposed certificateless ME, and Francati et al. [24] proposed registered ME. Chu et al. [16] proposed inner-product ME that supports more expressive policy than that of IB-ME. Jiang et al. [29] proposed revocable IB-ME. As mentioned above, ME has been widely researched from the viewpoint of several aspects.

Public Key Authenticated Encryption with Keyword Search. As a searchable encryption in a public key setting, public key encryption with keyword search (PEKS) [5] has been proposed. A keyword kw is encrypted using the receiver's public key and a trapdoor associated to a keyword kw' is generated using the receiver's secret key. The test algorithm that takes a ciphertext and a trapdoor outputs 1 if $kw = kw'$ and 0, otherwise. Abdalla et al. [1] proposed a generic construction of PEKS from anonymous IBE.

It is well-known that the following keyword guessing attack works in PEKS where an adversary, who has a trapdoor, arbitrarily chooses a keyword kw, generates its ciphertext, and checks whether the trapdoor is associated to kw or not by running the test algorithm. The keyword guessing attack is inevitable in PEKS since anyone can freely produce a ciphertext of a keyword using the receiver's public key. To prevent the keyword guessing attack, Huang and Li [28] introduced public key authenticated encryption with keyword search (PAEKS) that provides TI (trapdoor indistinguishability) where no information of keyword is revealed from trapdoors. In PAEKS, a keyword kw is encrypted by using a secret key of a sender S and a public key of a receiver R. To generate a trapdoor for a keyword kw', a public key of a sender S' and a secret key of a receiver R' are used. The test algorithm outputs 1 when

$$(\mathsf{S}, \mathsf{R}, kw) = (\mathsf{S}', \mathsf{R}', kw')$$

Moreover, consistency for multi users was introduced in [20] where the test algorithm outputs 0 when $(\mathsf{S}, \mathsf{R}, kw) \neq (\mathsf{S}', \mathsf{R}', kw')$. Note that it is not required to reveal information whether $\mathsf{S} \neq \mathsf{S}'$, $\mathsf{R} \neq \mathsf{R}'$, or $kw \neq kw'$ when the test algorithm outputs 0.

Li and Boyen [31] proposed a generic construction of PAEKS from symmetric-key equality-predicate encryption (EPE) (which they introduced) and non-interactive key exchange (NIKE) [25]. They instantiated EPE by pseudo-random function (PRF), pairings, or lattices. The generic construction can be instantiated by several complexity assumptions such as pairing-free computational/decisional Diffie-Hellman, pairings, integer factorizations, lattices, and isogenies based on several NIKEs [8,9,17,26]. Later, Shinoki et al. [38] pointed out a flaw of Li-Boyen's pairing-based EPE construction, and proposed another pairing-based EPE construction.[1]

For TI, there are two security notions: no information of keyword is revealed from trapdoors when an adversary is (resp. is not) allowed to send challenge keywords to the trapdoor oracle. The former is called full TI and the latter is called TI. Full TI is stronger that TI, and the Li-Boyen construction [31] instantiates PAEKS schemes with the full TI security from pairings or lattices.

Our Motivation. We pay attention to the search condition of PAEKS, $(\mathsf{S}, \mathsf{R}, kw) \stackrel{?}{=} (\mathsf{S}', \mathsf{R}', kw')$ as above, is reminiscent of the equality matching of IB-ME, $(\sigma, \rho) \stackrel{?}{=} (\mathsf{snd}, \mathsf{rcv})$ as above. As a natural observation, there is a relation between ME and PAEKS. However, no explicit implication result has been mentioned between them so far, to the best of our knowledge. Thus, as a natural question:

Is there any relation between ME and searchable encryption?

1.2 Our Contribution

In this paper, we explicitly show the relation between ME and searchable encryption. Concretely,

1. We introduce a public key variant of ME which we call PK-ME.[2]
   - We define security notions of PK-ME, privacy and authenticity, by considering the security notions of IB-ME.

[1] Shinoki et al. [38] called EPE SSE (searchable symmetric encryption).

[2] MPKE or MMPKE might be straightforward when we directly abbreviate matchmaking public key encryption. However, Alwen et al. [2] have introduced them as abbreviations for multi-recipient public-key encryption (mPKE) and multi-message multi-recipient PKE (mmPKE), respectively. By considering IB-ME, we named PK-ME as the abbreviation of matchmaking public key encryption.

- We also discuss the merit/demerit of PK-ME compared to IB-ME. Especially, we explore whether PK-ME can be used for realizing applications of IB-ME considered by Ateniese et al. [3,4].

2. We propose a generic construction of PK-ME from PAEKS.
   - As a conceptual contribution, our work lies in revealing a connection between ME and public key searchable encryption, which were basically researched independently.

Technical Overview. Basically, we follow the generic construction of IBE from PEKS given by Boneh et al. [5]. Briefly, a plaintext $M \in \{0,1\}$ is regarded as a keyword and is encrypted by the underlying PAEKS scheme. The decryption key consists of two trapdoors for two keywords 0 and 1. The PK-ME decryption algorithm outputs M if the test algorithm with the trapdoor of M outputs 1 where $M \in \{0,1\}$.

Here, we point out that the Boneh et al.'s generic construction did not consider the case where the test algorithm with the trapdoor of 0 outputs 1, and with the trapdoor of 1 also outputs 1. Then, the decryption result is not uniquely determined and correctness does not hold. To provide correctness, (1) we additionally introduce $\mathsf{Uncertain}$ as an output of the decryption algorithm, and (2) prove that the decryption algorithm does not output $\mathsf{Uncertain}$ if the underlying PAEKS scheme provides consistency. In addition to this, we introduce key privacy of PAEKS, that is not usually required as a security of PAEKS, to hide information of sender and receiver from ciphertexts. Later, we explain the Li-Boyen generic construction of PAEKS provides key privacy.

Since (PK-)ME does not consider information leakage from decryption keys, intuitively, the TI security of PAEKS is not necessary to construct PK-ME. Counterintuitively, our security proof (of authenticity) is reduced to full TI which seems to be the most non-trivial part of our security proof. Thus, our construction requires that the underlying PAEKS is to be fully TI secure, which can be instantiated from pairings or lattices via the Li-Boyen generic construction.

Remark. If PAEKS can be constructed from PK-ME, then two cryptographic primitives are equivalent. However, we expect that PK-ME does not imply PAEKS because PK-ME does not consider information leakage from decryption keys whereas PAEKS requires that no information of keyword is leaked from trapdoors. Moreover, key privacy is not always required in PAEKS. Exploring this expectation is an interesting open problem.

1.3 Related Work

Inspired by ME, Mongardin et al. [34] introduced identity-based matchmaking signatures (IB-MSS) and proposed a (semi-)generic construction[3] of IB-MSS

[3] Mongardin et al. assumed that the form of a public key is represented as g^{sk}, and sk is generated via IB-KD in their IB-MSS construction.

from identity-based non-interactive key distribution (IB-NIKD) [36] and signatures. IB-NIKD can be seen as an identity-based variant of NIKE, and NIKE is a building block of the Li-Boyen generic construction of PAEKS as mentioned above. We observe that these relations between non-interactive KD/KE and ME variants may suggest that our PK-ME construction from PAEKS is reasonable and natural.

Chiku et al. [14] mentioned the difference/similarity between IB-ME and identity-based signcryption [33] because both primitives consider privacy and authenticity simultaneously. They claimed that IB-ME provides better security properties than identity-based signcryption because IB-ME ensures anonymity of users and the confidentiality of messages when ciphertexts are tried to be decrypted with mismatched sender identities. Chiku et al. also proposed a generic construction of IB-ME from IBE, identity-based signatures, and reusable extractors.

Wang et al. [39] proposed a searchable asymmetric encryption (SAE) with bilateral access control. They mentioned that their security model is inspired by ME. Though this attempt connects ME and searchable encryption, they did not mention a similarity of the decryption condition of IB-ME and the search condition of PAEKS, and no explicit implication result was given. To sum up, no explicit implication result has been mentioned between ME and searchable encryption so far, to the best of our knowledge.

Hovd and Stam proposed vetted encryption (VE) [27], and discussed differences/similarities between VE and IB-ME. Especially, they mentioned that VE does not require the KGC unlike IB-ME. Since one difference between PK-ME and IB-ME is whether the KGC is required or not, we discuss differences between PK-ME and VE here, for the sake of clarity. VE introduces an outside filter that a recipient restricts who can send a message to the recipient. There are three variants by whether a sender is identified or not. In anonymous vetted encryption (AVE), both the filter and the recipient do not identify a sender. The authors mentioned that AVE is reminiscent of group signatures in this perspective. In identifiable vetted encryption (IVE), both the filter and the recipient identify a sender. The authors mentioned that AVE is reminiscent of signcryption in this perspective. In opaque vetted encryption (OVE), the filter does not identify a sender whereas the recipient identifies the sender. The authors mentioned that AVE is reminiscent of group signatures and its opening functionality in this perspective. A difference between OVE and IB-ME besides the KGC is how to indicate a sender. The decryption algorithm takes a sender identity snd in IB-ME whereas the decryption result contains a sender identity in OVE. Moreover, a sender indicates a receiver identity and a receiver indicates a sender identity, respectively, in IB-ME. That is, a sender and a receiver indicate the partner with each other. In VE, only a recipient specifies a sender. This difference is the same as that of between PK-ME and VE.

2 Preliminaries: Definitions of PAEKS

Let $\mathsf{PAEKS} = (\mathsf{PAEKS.SetUp}, \mathsf{PAEKS.KGen_S}, \mathsf{PAEKS.KGen_R}, \mathsf{PAEKS.Enc}, \mathsf{Trapdoor}, \mathsf{Test})$ be a PAEKS scheme defined as follows.

Definition 1 (Syntax of PAEKS).

$\mathsf{PAEKS.SetUp}(1^\lambda)$: *The setup algorithm takes a security parameter* $\lambda \in \mathbb{N}$ *as input, and outputs a common parameter* $\mathsf{pp_{PAEKS}}$. *Assume that* $\mathsf{pp_{PAEKS}}$ *contains a keyword space* $\mathcal{KW}$.

$\mathsf{PAEKS.KGen_S}(\mathsf{pp_{PAEKS}})$: *The sender key generation algorithm takes* $\mathsf{pp_{PAEKS}}$ *as input, and outputs a sender's public key* $\mathsf{PAEKS.pk_S}$ *and a sender's secret key* $\mathsf{PAEKS.sk_S}$.

$\mathsf{PAEKS.KGen_R}(\mathsf{pp_{PAEKS}})$: *The receiver key generation algorithm takes* $\mathsf{pp_{PAEKS}}$ *as input, and outputs a receiver's public key* $\mathsf{PAEKS.pk_R}$ *and a receiver's secret key* $\mathsf{PAEKS.sk_R}$.

$\mathsf{PAEKS.Enc}(\mathsf{PAEKS.pk_S}, \mathsf{PAEKS.pk_R}, \mathsf{PAEKS.sk_S}, kw)$: *The keyword encryption algorithm takes* $\mathsf{PAEKS.pk_S}$, $\mathsf{PAEKS.pk_R}$, $\mathsf{PAEKS.sk_S}$, *and a keyword* $kw \in \mathcal{KW}$ *as input, and outputs a ciphertext* $\mathsf{PAEKS.ct}_{\mathsf{S},\mathsf{R},kw}$.

$\mathsf{Trapdoor}(\mathsf{PAEKS.pk_S}, \mathsf{PAEKS.pk_R}, \mathsf{PAEKS.sk_R}, kw)$: *The trapdoor generation algorithm takes* $\mathsf{PAEKS.pk_S}$, $\mathsf{PAEKS.pk_R}$, $\mathsf{PAEKS.sk_R}$, *and* $kw \in \mathcal{KW}$ *as input, and outputs a trapdoor* $\mathsf{td}_{\mathsf{S},\mathsf{R},kw}$.

$\mathsf{Test}(\mathsf{PAEKS.ct}_{\mathsf{S},\mathsf{R},kw}, \mathsf{td}_{\mathsf{S}',\mathsf{R}',kw'})$: *The test algorithm takes* $\mathsf{PAEKS.ct}_{\mathsf{S},\mathsf{R},kw}$ *and* $\mathsf{td}_{\mathsf{S}',\mathsf{R}',kwv}$ *as input, and outputs 1 or 0.*

Next, we define correctness. It guarantees that for an honestly generated ciphertext $\mathsf{PAEKS.ct}_{\mathsf{S},\mathsf{R},kw}$ and honestly generated trapdoor $\mathsf{td}_{\mathsf{S}',\mathsf{R}',kw'}$, the Test algorithm outputs 1 if $(\mathsf{S}, \mathsf{R}, kw) = (\mathsf{S}', \mathsf{R}', kw')$.

Definition 2 (Correctness). *For all* $\lambda \in \mathbb{N}$, $\mathsf{pp_{PAEKS}} \leftarrow \mathsf{PAEKS.SetUp}(1^\lambda)$, $(\mathsf{PAEKS.pk_S}, \mathsf{PAEKS.sk_S}) \leftarrow \mathsf{PAEKS.KGen_S}(\mathsf{pp_{PAEKS}})$, $(\mathsf{PAEKS.pk_R}, \mathsf{PAEKS.sk_R}) \leftarrow \mathsf{PAEKS.KGen_R}(\mathsf{pp_{PAEKS}})$, *and* $kw \in \mathcal{KW}$, *we say that* PAEKS *is correct if* $\mathsf{Test}(\mathsf{PAEKS.Enc}(\mathsf{PAEKS.pk_S}, \mathsf{PAEKS.pk_R}, \mathsf{PAEKS.sk_S}, kw), \mathsf{Trapdoor}(\mathsf{PAEKS.pk_S}, \mathsf{PAEKS.pk_R}, \mathsf{PAEKS.sk_R}, kw)) = 1$.

Next, we define consistency. It guarantees that for an honestly generated ciphertext $\mathsf{PAEKS.ct}_{\mathsf{S},\mathsf{R},kw}$ and honestly generated trapdoor $\mathsf{td}_{\mathsf{S}',\mathsf{R}',kw'}$, the Test algorithm outputs 0 if $(\mathsf{S}, \mathsf{R}, kw) \neq (\mathsf{S}', \mathsf{R}', kw')$. Let $\mathcal{A}$ be a probabilistic polynomial-time (PPT) adversary and $\mathcal{C}$ be the challenger.

Definition 3 (Consistency). $\mathcal{C}$ *runs* $\mathsf{pp_{PAEKS}} \leftarrow \mathsf{PAEKS.SetUp}(1^\lambda)$, $(\mathsf{PAEKS.pk_{S_0}}, \mathsf{PAEKS.sk_{S_0}}) \leftarrow \mathsf{PAEKS.KGen_S}(\mathsf{pp_{PAEKS}})$, $(\mathsf{PAEKS.pk_{S_1}}, \mathsf{PAEKS.sk_{S_1}}) \leftarrow \mathsf{PAEKS.KGen_S}(\mathsf{pp_{PAEKS}})$, $(\mathsf{PAEKS.pk_{R_0}}, \mathsf{PAEKS.sk_{R_0}}) \leftarrow \mathsf{PAEKS.KGen_R}(\mathsf{pp_{PAEKS}})$, *and* $(\mathsf{PAEKS.pk_{R_1}}, \mathsf{PAEKS.sk_{R_1}}) \leftarrow \mathsf{PAEKS.KGen_R}(\mathsf{pp_{PAEKS}})$, *and gives* $(\mathsf{pp_{PAEKS}}, \mathsf{PAEKS.pk_{S_0}}, \mathsf{PAEKS.pk_{S_1}}, \mathsf{PAEKS.pk_{R_0}}, \mathsf{PAEKS.pk_{R_1}})$ *to* $\mathcal{A}$. $\mathcal{A}$ *outputs* $(i, j, kw, i',$

$j', kw') \in (\{0,1\}^2 \times \mathcal{KW})^2$. $\mathcal{C}$ computes $\mathsf{PAEKS.ct}_{\mathsf{S}_i,\mathsf{R}_j,kw} \leftarrow \mathsf{PAEKS.Enc}(\mathsf{PAEKS.pk}_{\mathsf{S}_i}, \mathsf{PAEKS.pk}_{\mathsf{R}_j}, \mathsf{PAEKS.sk}_{\mathsf{S}_i}, kw)$ *and* $\mathsf{td}_{\mathsf{S}_{i'},\mathsf{R}_{j'},kw'} \leftarrow \mathsf{Trapdoor}(\mathsf{PAEKS.pk}_{\mathsf{S}_{i'}}, \mathsf{PAEKS.pk}_{\mathsf{R}_{j'}}, \mathsf{PAEKS.sk}_{\mathsf{R}_{j'}}, kw')$. *$\mathcal{A}$ wins if* $\mathsf{Test}(\mathsf{PAEKS.ct}_{\mathsf{S}_i,\mathsf{R}_j,kw}, \mathsf{td}_{\mathsf{S}_{i'},\mathsf{R}_{j'},kw'}) = 1$ *and $(\mathsf{S}_i, \mathsf{R}_j, kw) \neq (\mathsf{S}_{i'}, \mathsf{R}_{j'}, kw')$ holds. We say that* PAEKS *is consistent if for any PPT adversaries $\mathcal{A}$, the advantage*

$$\mathsf{Adv}^{\mathsf{consist}}_{\mathsf{PAEKS},\mathcal{A}}(\lambda) = \Pr[\mathcal{A} \textit{ wins}]$$

is negligible in λ.

Next, we define full ciphertext-keyword indistinguishability (full CI).[4] It guarantees that no information of keyword is revealed from ciphertexts. Here, full means that an adversary is allowed to obtain ciphertexts of the challenge keywords. We also consider key privacy where a ciphertext does not leak information of the sender $(\mathsf{PAEKS.pk}_\mathsf{S}, \mathsf{PAEKS.sk}_\mathsf{S})$ and the receiver $(\mathsf{PAEKS.pk}_\mathsf{R})$. Let $\mathcal{C}$ be the challenger and $\mathcal{A}$ be an adversary.

Definition 4 ***(Full CI with Key Privacy)*** *$\mathcal{C}$ runs* $\mathsf{pp}_{\mathsf{PAEKS}} \leftarrow \mathsf{PAEKS.SetUp}(1^\lambda)$, $(\mathsf{PAEKS.pk}_{\mathsf{S}_0}, \mathsf{PAEKS.sk}_{\mathsf{S}_0}) \leftarrow \mathsf{PAEKS.KGen}_\mathsf{S}(\mathsf{pp}_{\mathsf{PAEKS}})$, $(\mathsf{PAEKS.pk}_{\mathsf{S}_1}, \mathsf{PAEKS.sk}_{\mathsf{S}_1}) \leftarrow \mathsf{PAEKS.KGen}_\mathsf{S}(\mathsf{pp}_{\mathsf{PAEKS}})$, $(\mathsf{PAEKS.pk}_{\mathsf{R}_0}, \mathsf{PAEKS.sk}_{\mathsf{R}_0}) \leftarrow \mathsf{PAEKS.KGen}_\mathsf{R}(\mathsf{pp}_{\mathsf{PAEKS}})$, *and* $(\mathsf{PAEKS.pk}_{\mathsf{R}_1}, \mathsf{PAEKS.sk}_{\mathsf{R}_1}) \leftarrow \mathsf{PAEKS.KGen}_\mathsf{R}(\mathsf{pp}_{\mathsf{PAEKS}})$, *and gives* $(\mathsf{pp}_{\mathsf{PAEKS}}, \mathsf{pk}_{\mathsf{S}_0}, \mathsf{pk}_{\mathsf{S}_1}, \mathsf{pk}_{\mathsf{R}_0}, \mathsf{pk}_{\mathsf{R}_1})$ *to $\mathcal{A}$.*

$\mathcal{A}$ declares the challenge keywords $(kw_0^*, kw_1^*) \in \mathcal{KW}^2$. $\mathcal{C}$ chooses $b \xleftarrow{\$} \{0,1\}$, computes the challenge ciphertext $\mathsf{PAEKS.ct}^*_{\mathsf{S}_b,\mathsf{R}_b,kw_b^*} \leftarrow \mathsf{PAEKS.Enc}(\mathsf{PAEKS.pk}_{\mathsf{S}_b}, \mathsf{PAEKS.pk}_{\mathsf{R}_b}, \mathsf{PAEKS.sk}_{\mathsf{S}_b}, kw_b^*)$, *and returns* $\mathsf{PAEKS.ct}^*_{\mathsf{S}_b,\mathsf{R}_b,kw_b^*}$ *to $\mathcal{A}$.*

During the game, $\mathcal{A}$ is allowed to issue the following queries.

Encryption query: *$\mathcal{A}$ sends $(i, j, kw) \in \{0,1\}^2 \times \mathcal{KW}$ to $\mathcal{C}$. $\mathcal{C}$ computes* $\mathsf{PAEKS.ct}_{\mathsf{S}_i,\mathsf{R}_j,kw} \leftarrow \mathsf{PAEKS.Enc}(\mathsf{PAEKS.pk}_{\mathsf{S}_i}, \mathsf{PAEKS.pk}_{\mathsf{R}_j}, \mathsf{PAEKS.sk}_{\mathsf{S}_i}, kw)$, *and returns* $\mathsf{PAEKS.ct}_{\mathsf{S}_i,\mathsf{R}_j,kw}$ *to $\mathcal{A}$. There is no restriction here.*

Trapdoor query: *$\mathcal{A}$ sends $(i, j, kw) \in \{0,1\}^2 \times \mathcal{KW}$ to $\mathcal{C}$. Here, $\mathcal{A}$ is not allowed to send $(0, 0, kw_0^*)$ or $(1, 1, kw_1^*)$. $\mathcal{C}$ computes* $\mathsf{td}_{\mathsf{S}_i,\mathsf{R}_j,kw} \leftarrow \mathsf{Trapdoor}(\mathsf{PAEKS.pk}_{\mathsf{S}_i}, \mathsf{PAEKS.pk}_{\mathsf{R}_j}, \mathsf{PAEKS.sk}_{\mathsf{R}_j}, kw)$, *and returns* $\mathsf{td}_{\mathsf{S}_i,\mathsf{R}_j,kw}$ *to $\mathcal{A}$.*

Finally, $\mathcal{A}$ outputs $b' \in \{0,1\}$. We say that PAEKS *provides the full CI security if for all PPT adversaries $\mathcal{A}$, the advantage*

$$\mathsf{Adv}^{\mathsf{Full\text{-}KP\text{-}CI}}_{\mathsf{PAEKS},\mathcal{A}}(\lambda) = |\Pr[b = b'] - 1/2|$$

is negligible in λ.

[4] In the definition by Li-Boyen, an adversary is allowed to issue encryption/trapdoor queries by using a public key that is chosen by the adversary. In this paper, our main aim is to provide a minimum functionality as matchmaking encryption, and thus we do not consider such an adversarial public key.

Note that key privacy does not always hold. For example, the Chen et al.'s pairing-based full CI secure PAEKS scheme [12] does not provide key privacy because for $\mathsf{pk_R} = g^x$, a ciphertext contains g^{xr} and g^r that reveal information of $\mathsf{pk_R}$ (via $e(\mathsf{pk_R}, g^r) = e(g^{xr}, g)$ holds or not). We emphasize that this is not an attack against the Chen et al.'s PAEKS scheme. On the other hand, the generic construction of Li-Boyen [31] provides key privacy. In the generic construction, a NIKE key, defined by public keys of a sender S and a receiver R, is used as an encryption key of EPE. Due to the security of NIKE, the NIKE key is indistinguishable from random. Thus, a PAEKS ciphertext does not leak information of S and R. We employed PAEKS schemes instantiated by the Li-Boyen's generic construction later.

Next, we define full trapdoor indistinguishability (full TI). It guarantees that no information of keyword is revealed from trapdoors. Here, full means that an adversary is allowed to obtain trapdoors of the challenge keywords.

Definition 5 (Full TI). *$\mathcal{C}$ runs* $\mathsf{pp_{PAEKS}} \leftarrow \mathsf{PAEKS.SetUp}(1^\lambda)$, $(\mathsf{PAEKS.pk_S}, \mathsf{PAEKS.sk_S}) \leftarrow \mathsf{PAEKS.KGen_S}(\mathsf{pp_{PAEKS}})$, *and* $(\mathsf{PAEKS.pk_R}, \mathsf{PAEKS.sk_R}) \leftarrow \mathsf{PAEKS.KGen_R}(\mathsf{pp_{PAEKS}})$, *and gives* $(\mathsf{pp_{PAEKS}}, \mathsf{PAEKS.pk_S}, \mathsf{PAEKS.pk_R})$ *to* $\mathcal{A}$.

$\mathcal{A}$ declares the challenge keywords $(kw_0^*, kw_1^*) \in \mathcal{KW}^2$. *$\mathcal{C}$ chooses* $b \xleftarrow{\$} \{0,1\}$, *computes the challenge trapdoor* $\mathsf{td}_{\mathsf{S},\mathsf{R},kw_b^*} \leftarrow \mathsf{Trapdoor}(\mathsf{PAEKS.pk_S}, \mathsf{PAEKS.pk_R}, \mathsf{PAEKS.sk_R}, kw_b^*)$, *and returns* $\mathsf{td}_{\mathsf{S},\mathsf{R},kw_b^*}$ *to* $\mathcal{A}$.

During the game, $\mathcal{A}$ is allowed to issue the following queries.

- **Encryption query:** *$\mathcal{A}$ sends kw to $\mathcal{C}$. Here, $\mathcal{A}$ is not allowed to send kw_0^* or kw_1^*. $\mathcal{C}$ computes* $\mathsf{PAEKS.ct}_{\mathsf{S},\mathsf{R},kw} \leftarrow \mathsf{Enc}(\mathsf{PAEKS.pk_S}, \mathsf{PAEKS.pk_R}, \mathsf{PAEKS.sk_S}, kw)$ *and returns* $\mathsf{PAEKS.ct}_{\mathsf{S},\mathsf{R},kw}$ *to* $\mathcal{A}$.
- **Trapdoor query:** *$\mathcal{A}$ sends kw to $\mathcal{C}$. $\mathcal{C}$ computes* $\mathsf{td}_{\mathsf{S},\mathsf{R},kw} \leftarrow \mathsf{Trapdoor}(\mathsf{PAEKS.pk_S}, \mathsf{PAEKS.pk_R}, \mathsf{PAEKS.sk_R}, kw)$ *and returns* $\mathsf{td}_{\mathsf{S},\mathsf{R},kw}$ *to $\mathcal{A}$. There is no restriction here.*

Finally, $\mathcal{A}$ outputs $b' \in \{0,1\}$. We say that PAEKS *provides the full TI security if for all PPT adversaries $\mathcal{A}$, the advantage*

$$\mathsf{Adv}^{\mathsf{Full\text{-}TI}}_{\mathsf{PAEKS},\mathcal{A}}(\lambda) = |\Pr[b = b'] - 1/2|$$

is negligible in λ.

If the adversary is not allowed to send the challenge keywords kw_0^* and kw_1^* as a trapdoor query, then the security definition is said to be TI.

3 Definitions of PK-ME

3.1 Syntax of PK-ME

In this section, we newly define PK-ME PK-ME $= (\mathsf{SetUp}, \mathsf{SKGen}, \mathsf{RKGen}, \mathsf{Enc}, \mathsf{Dec})$ as follows. To clarify the relations between PK-ME and IB-ME, we introduce an index space $\mathcal{IDX}$ (which is not an identity space) and $\sigma, \rho \in \mathcal{IDX}$

are just indexes unlike IB-ME. Then, similar to IB-ME, we can describe the decryption condition of PK-ME: a ciphertext generated by $(\mathsf{ek}_\sigma, \mathsf{pk}_{\mathsf{rcv}})$ can be decrypted by $(\mathsf{dk}_\rho, \mathsf{pk}_{\mathsf{snd}})$ if $(\sigma, \rho) = (\mathsf{snd}, \mathsf{rcv})$. We note that, in addition to a plaintext M and a failure symbol $\perp$, the decryption algorithm Dec may output $\mathsf{Uncertain}$ which means that the decryption result is not uniquely determined. We will explain the reason behind later.

Definition 6 ***(Syntax of PK-ME)***

$\mathsf{SetUp}(1^\lambda)$: *The setup algorithm takes a security parameter* $\lambda \in \mathbb{N}$ *as input, and outputs a common parameter* pp. *Assume that* pp *contains a plaintext space* $\mathcal{MSG}$ *and an index space* $\mathcal{IDX}$.

$\mathsf{SKGen}(\mathsf{pp}, \sigma)$: *The sender key generation algorithm takes* pp *and index* $\sigma \in \mathcal{IDX}$ *as input, and outputs a sender's public key* pk_σ *and sender's encryption key* ek_σ.

$\mathsf{RKGen}(\mathsf{pp}, \rho)$: *The receiver key generation algorithm takes* pp *and index* $\rho \in \mathcal{IDX}$ *as input, and outputs a receiver's public key* pk_ρ *and receiver's decryption key* dk_ρ.

$\mathsf{Enc}(\mathsf{pp}, \mathsf{ek}_\sigma, \mathsf{pk}_{\mathsf{rcv}}, M)$: *The encryption algorithm takes* pp, ek_σ, *an intended receiver's public key* $\mathsf{pk}_{\mathsf{rcv}}$, *where* $\mathsf{rcv} \in \mathcal{IDX}$, *and a plaintext* M *as input, and outputs a ciphertext* ct.

$\mathsf{Dec}(\mathsf{pp}, \mathsf{dk}_\rho, \mathsf{pk}_{\mathsf{snd}}, \mathsf{ct})$: *The decryption algorithm takes* pp, dk_ρ, *an intended sender's public key* $\mathsf{pk}_{\mathsf{snd}}$, *where* $\mathsf{rcv} \in \mathcal{IDX}$, *and* ct *as input, and outputs* M *or* $\perp$ *or* $\mathsf{Uncertain}$.

3.2 Security Definition

Next, we define correctness. Intuitively, it guarantees that ciphertext generated by $(\mathsf{ek}_\sigma, \mathsf{pk}_{\mathsf{rcv}})$ can be decrypted by $(\mathsf{dk}_\rho, \mathsf{pk}_{\mathsf{snd}})$ if $(\sigma, \rho) = (\mathsf{snd}, \mathsf{rcv})$. Here, we define it in two steps because the output of the decryption algorithm contains $\mathsf{Uncertain}$. First (correctness 1), we define the case that the decryption algorithm with honestly generated keys and an honestly generated ciphertext outputs either a plaintext or $\mathsf{Uncertain}$ with overwhelming probability. Second (correctness 2), we define the case that no PPT adversary can produce a plaintext where the decryption result of the corresponding ciphertext is $\mathsf{Uncertain}$. We say that PK-ME is correct if PK-ME provides both correctness 1 and 2.

Definition 7 (Correctness 1). *For any* $\lambda \in \mathbb{N}$, $\mathsf{pp} \leftarrow \mathsf{SetUp}(1^\lambda)$, $\sigma, \rho \in \mathcal{IDX}$, $(\mathsf{pk}_\sigma, \mathsf{ek}_\sigma) \leftarrow \mathsf{SKGen}(\mathsf{pp}, \sigma)$, $(\mathsf{pk}_\rho, \mathsf{sk}_\rho) \leftarrow \mathsf{RKGen}(\mathsf{pp}, \rho)$, *and* $M \in \mathcal{MSG}$, *we say that* PK-ME *provides correctness 1 if* $\mathsf{Dec}(\mathsf{pp}, \mathsf{dk}_\rho, \mathsf{pk}_\sigma, \mathsf{Enc}(\mathsf{pp}, \mathsf{ek}_\sigma, \mathsf{pk}_\rho, M)) = M/\mathsf{Uncertain}$ *holds with overwhelming probability.*

Definition 8 (Correctness 2). *Let* $\mathcal{C}$ *be the challenger and* $\mathcal{A}$ *be an adversary.* $\mathcal{C}$ *chooses distinct indexes* $\sigma, \rho \in \mathcal{IDX}$, *computes* $\mathsf{pp} \leftarrow \mathsf{SetUp}(1^\lambda)$, $(\mathsf{pk}_\sigma, \mathsf{ek}_\sigma) \leftarrow \mathsf{SKGen}(\mathsf{pp}, \sigma)$, *and* $(\mathsf{pk}_\rho, \mathsf{sk}_\rho) \leftarrow \mathsf{RKGen}(\mathsf{pp}, \rho)$, *and gives* $(\mathsf{pp}, \mathsf{pk}_\sigma, \mathsf{pk}_\rho)$ *to* $\mathcal{A}$. $\mathcal{A}$ *outputs* $M \in \mathcal{MSG}$. $\mathcal{C}$ *computes* $\mathsf{ct} \leftarrow \mathsf{Enc}(\mathsf{pp}, \mathsf{ek}_\sigma, \mathsf{pk}_\rho, M)$. $\mathcal{A}$ *wins if*

$\mathsf{Dec}(\mathsf{pp}, \mathsf{dk}_\rho, \mathsf{pk}_\sigma, \mathsf{ct}) = \mathsf{Uncertain}$. *We say that* PK-ME *provides correctness 2 if the advantage*

$$\mathsf{Adv}^{\mathsf{correct2}}_{\mathsf{PK\text{-}ME},\mathcal{A}}(\lambda) = \Pr[\mathcal{A} \ wins]$$

is negligible in the security parameter for all PPT adversaries $\mathcal{A}$.

Ateniese et al. [3,4] defined privacy and authenticity as security notions of IB-ME. We define privacy and authenticity of PK-ME by considering Ateniese et al.'s definitions. For privacy, Ateniese et al. defined that no information of plaintext and key is revealed from ciphertexts for a malicious decryptor who does not have dk_ρ. Here, an adversary is allowed to obtain encryption keys without any restriction. That is, privacy guarantees that no information of which encryption key was used for generating a ciphertext even if the adversary has the encryption key. In the following, we weaken the security level by defining the encryption oracle that reflects the situation where an adversary is allowed to access the encryption oracle but is not allowed to obtain sender's secret keys in the full CI security model. Let $\mathcal{C}$ be the challenger and $\mathcal{A}$ be an adversary.

Definition 9 (Privacy). *$\mathcal{C}$ computes* $\mathsf{pp} \leftarrow \mathsf{SetUp}(1^\lambda)$, $(\mathsf{pk}_{\sigma_0}, \mathsf{ek}_{\sigma_0}) \leftarrow \mathsf{SKGen}(\mathsf{pp}, \sigma_0)$, $(\mathsf{pk}_{\sigma_1}, \mathsf{ek}_{\sigma_1}) \leftarrow \mathsf{SKGen}(\mathsf{pp}, \sigma_1)$, $(\mathsf{pk}_{\rho_0}, \mathsf{dk}_{\rho_0}) \leftarrow \mathsf{RKGen}(\mathsf{pp}, \rho_0)$, *and* $(\mathsf{pk}_{\rho_1}, \mathsf{dk}_{\rho_1}) \leftarrow \mathsf{RKGen}(\mathsf{pp}, \rho_1)$, *and gives* $(\mathsf{pp}, \mathsf{pk}_{\sigma_0}, \mathsf{pk}_{\sigma_1}, \mathsf{pk}_{\rho_0}, \mathsf{pk}_{\rho_1})$ *to $\mathcal{A}$. $\mathcal{A}$ declares (M_0^*, M_1^*). $\mathcal{C}$ chooses $b \xleftarrow{\$} \{0,1\}$, computes the challenge ciphertext $ct^* \leftarrow$* $\mathsf{Enc}(\mathsf{pp}, \mathsf{ek}_{\sigma_b}, \mathsf{pk}_{\rho_b}, M_b^*)$, *and gives* ct^* *to $\mathcal{A}$. During the game, $\mathcal{A}$ is allowed to issue the following queries.*

Encryption query: *$\mathcal{A}$ sends (i,j,M) $(i,j \in \{0,1\})$ to $\mathcal{C}$. $\mathcal{C}$ computes* $\mathsf{ct} \leftarrow \mathsf{Enc}(\mathsf{pp}, \mathsf{ek}_{\sigma_i}, \mathsf{pk}_{\rho_j}, M)$, *and gives* ct *to $\mathcal{A}$.*

$\mathcal{A}$ outputs $b' \in \{0,1\}$. We say that PK-ME *provides privacy if for all PPT adversaries $\mathcal{A}$, the advantage*

$$\mathsf{Adv}^{\mathsf{priv}}_{\mathsf{PK\text{-}ME},\mathcal{A}}(\lambda) = |\Pr[b = b'] - 1/2|$$

is negligible in the security parameter λ.

For authenticity, Ateniese et al. defined that no adversary who does not have $\mathsf{ek}_{\mathsf{snd}}$ can produce a ciphertext where the ciphertext is decryptable (i.e., the decryption algorithm does not output $\perp$) when snd is indicated as the sender. We also consider the case that the decryption result is not Uncertain as a winning condition. Let $\mathcal{C}$ be the challenger and A be an adversary.

Definition 10 (Authenticity). *$\mathcal{C}$ computes* $\mathsf{pp} \leftarrow \mathsf{SetUp}(1^\lambda)$, $(\mathsf{pk}_\sigma, \mathsf{ek}_\sigma) \leftarrow \mathsf{SKGen}(\mathsf{pp}, \sigma)$, *and* $(\mathsf{pk}_\rho, \mathsf{dk}_\rho) \leftarrow \mathsf{RKGen}(\mathsf{pp}, \rho)$, *and gives $(pp, \mathsf{pk}_\sigma, \mathsf{pk}_\rho)$ to $\mathcal{A}$. $\mathcal{A}$ outputs* ct^*. *$\mathcal{C}$ computes $M^* \leftarrow$* $\mathsf{Dec}(\mathsf{pp}, \mathsf{dk}_\rho, \mathsf{pk}_\sigma, \mathsf{ct}^*)$. *We say that* PK-ME *provides authenticity if for all PPT adversaries $\mathcal{A}$, the advantage*

$$\mathsf{Adv}^{\mathsf{Auth}}_{\mathsf{PK\text{-}ME},\mathcal{A}}(\lambda) = \Pr[(M^* \neq \perp) \cap (M^* \neq \mathsf{Uncertain})]$$

is negligible in the security parameter λ.

4 Proposed Generic Construction

In this section, we give the proposed generic construction of PK-ME from PAEKS. Before giving our construction, we revisited a generic construction of IBE from PEKS given by Boneh et al. [5] because our construction can be seen as an extension of the generic construction.

Generic Construction of IBE from PEKS [5]**.** For an identity ID and a plaintext $M \in \{0,1\}$, $ID||M$ is regarded as a keyword and is encrypted by the underlying PEKS scheme. The decryption key consists of two trapdoors for two keywords $ID||0$ and $ID||1$. The IBE decryption algorithm outputs M if the test algorithm with the trapdoor of $ID||M$ outputs 1 where $M \in \{0,1\}$. Due to the security of PEKS, no information of keyword (here $ID||M$) is revealed from PEKS ciphertext. Thus, no information of plaintext is revealed from IBE ciphertext. To simulate a decryption key query in (the IND-CPA security of) IBE, the reduction algorithm can employ the trapdoor oracle of the underlying PEKS scheme.

Why Uncertain **is Introduced in Our Construction?** To decrypt a ciphertext via the search functionality of the underlying searchable encryption, we need to consider the following "uncertain" case where the test algorithm outputs 1 in both cases. Concretely, assume that the test algorithm outputs 1 with the trapdoor of $ID||0$, and also outputs 1 with the trapdoor of $ID||1$. Then, the decryption result is not uniquely determined. This uncertain case can be excluded if the underlying PEKS scheme provides consistency (though Boneh et al. did not explicitly mention it). This is the reason why we introduced "Uncertain" in the syntax. Since consistency is defined as a computational security manner in many cases,[5] we define correctness of PK-ME (correctness 2) as a computational security manner.

Rhee and Lee [37] presented a generic construction of anonymous identity-based encryption (IBE) based on public-key encryption with keyword search (PEKS). They defined correctness in computational terms and asserted that the proposed anonymous IBE construction is correct if the underlying PEKS scheme is computationally consistent. However, the correctness of an IBE constructed from PEKS using Rhee and Lee's generic construction cannot be guaranteed solely by consistency. This is because a consistent PEKS scheme lacking correctness can be easily devised-specifically, a scheme in which the test algorithm always outputs 0. Therefore, in this paper, we define the correctness of PK-ME separately, distinguishing between the portion ensured by the correctness of PAEKS and the portion ensured by the consistency of PAEKS.

Proposed Generic Construction. In our construction, a plaintext $M \in \{0,1\}$ is regarded as a keyword, and is encrypted by the underlying PAEKS scheme. The decryption algorithm runs the test algorithm using trapdoors of keywords 0 and 1. Though we consider the case that the decryption result is Uncertain, this case can be excluded due to consistency of the underlying PAEKS

[5] Some P(A)EKS schemes with statistical consistency have been proposed, e.g., [1,35].

scheme, and does not happen. Unlike the Boneh et al.'s construction [5], the proposed construction is not identity-based because the encryption algorithm takes a public key $\mathsf{pk}_{\mathsf{rcv}}$. We construct $\mathsf{PK\text{-}ME} = (\mathsf{SetUp}, \mathsf{SKGen}, \mathsf{RKGen}, \mathsf{Enc}, \mathsf{Dec})$ from $\mathsf{PAEKS} = (\mathsf{PAEKS.SetUp}, \mathsf{PAEKS.KGen_S}, \mathsf{PAEKS.KGen_R}, \mathsf{PAEKS.Enc}, \mathsf{Trapdoor}, \mathsf{Test})$ as follows.

$\mathsf{SetUp}(1^\lambda)$: Run $\mathsf{pp_{PAEKS}} \leftarrow \mathsf{PAEKS.SetUp}(1^\lambda)$ and output $\mathsf{pp} = \mathsf{pp_{PAEKS}}$. Here, set $\mathcal{MSG} = \mathcal{KW} = \{0,1\}$ and $\mathcal{IDX} = \{0,1\}^\lambda$.

$\mathsf{SKGen}(\mathsf{pp}, \sigma)$: Parse $\mathsf{pp} = \mathsf{pp_{PAEKS}}$. Run $(\mathsf{PAEKS.pk}_\sigma, \mathsf{PAEKS.sk}_\sigma) \leftarrow \mathsf{PAEKS.KGen_S}(\mathsf{pp_{PAEKS}})$ and output $(\mathsf{pk}_\sigma, \mathsf{ek}_\sigma) = (\mathsf{PAEKS.pk}_\sigma, \mathsf{PAEKS.sk}_\sigma)$.

$\mathsf{RKGen}(\mathsf{pp}, \rho)$: Parse $\mathsf{pp} = \mathsf{pp_{PAEKS}}$. Run $(\mathsf{PAEKS.pk}_\rho, \mathsf{PAEKS.sk}_\rho) \leftarrow \mathsf{PAEKS.KGen_R}(\mathsf{pp_{PAEKS}})$ and output $(\mathsf{pk}_\rho, \mathsf{sk}_\rho) = (\mathsf{PAEKS.pk}_\rho, \mathsf{PAEKS.sk}_\rho)$.

$\mathsf{Enc}(\mathsf{pp}, \mathsf{ek}_\sigma, \mathsf{pk}_{\mathsf{rcv}}, M)$: Parse $\mathsf{pp} = \mathsf{pp_{PAEKS}}$, $\mathsf{ek}_\sigma = \mathsf{PAEKS.sk}_\sigma$, and $\mathsf{pk}_{\mathsf{rcv}} = \mathsf{PAEKS.pk}_{\mathsf{rcv}}$. Compute $\mathsf{PAEKS.ct}_{\sigma,\mathsf{rcv},M} \leftarrow \mathsf{PAEKS.Enc}(\mathsf{PAEKS.pk}_\sigma, \mathsf{PAEKS.pk}_{\mathsf{rcv}}, \mathsf{PAEKS.sk}_\sigma, M)$ and output $\mathsf{ct} = \mathsf{PAEKS.ct}_{\sigma,\mathsf{rcv},M}$.

$\mathsf{Dec}(\mathsf{pp}, \mathsf{dk}_\rho, \mathsf{pk}_{\mathsf{snd}}, \mathsf{ct})$: Parse $\mathsf{pp} = \mathsf{pp_{PAEKS}}$, $\mathsf{dk}_\rho = \mathsf{PAEKS.sk}_\rho$, $\mathsf{pk}_{\mathsf{snd}} = \mathsf{PAEKS.pk}_{\mathsf{snd}}$, and $\mathsf{ct} = \mathsf{PAEKS.ct}_{\sigma,\mathsf{rcv},M}$. Compute $\mathsf{td}_{\mathsf{snd},\rho,0} \leftarrow \mathsf{Trapdoor}(\mathsf{PAEKS.pk}_{\mathsf{snd}}, \mathsf{PAEKS.pk}_\rho, \mathsf{PAEKS.sk}_\rho, 0)$ and $\mathsf{td}_{\mathsf{snd},\rho,1} \leftarrow \mathsf{Trapdoor}(\mathsf{PAEKS.pk}_{\mathsf{snd}}, \mathsf{PAEKS.pk}_\rho, \mathsf{PAEKS.sk}_\rho, 1)$.

- Output $M = 0$ if $\mathsf{Test}(\mathsf{PAEKS.ct}_{\sigma,\mathsf{rcv},M}, \mathsf{td}_{\mathsf{snd},\rho,0}) = 1 \wedge \mathsf{Test}(\mathsf{PAEKS.ct}_{\sigma,\mathsf{rcv},M}, \mathsf{td}_{\mathsf{snd},\rho,1}) = 0$.
- Output $M = 1$ if $\mathsf{Test}(\mathsf{PAEKS.ct}_{\sigma,\mathsf{rcv},M}, \mathsf{td}_{\mathsf{snd},\rho,0}) = 0 \wedge \mathsf{Test}(\mathsf{PAEKS.ct}_{\sigma,\mathsf{rcv},M}, \mathsf{td}_{\mathsf{snd},\rho,1}) = 1$.
- Output $\mathsf{Uncertain}$ if $\mathsf{Test}(\mathsf{PAEKS.ct}_{\sigma,\mathsf{rcv},M}, \mathsf{td}_{\mathsf{snd},\rho,0}) = 1 \wedge \mathsf{Test}(\mathsf{PAEKS.ct}_{\sigma,\mathsf{rcv},M}, \mathsf{td}_{\mathsf{snd},\rho,1}) = 1$.
- Output $\perp$ if $\mathsf{Test}(\mathsf{PAEKS.ct}_{\sigma,\mathsf{rcv},M}, \mathsf{td}_{\mathsf{snd},\rho,0}) = 0 \wedge \mathsf{Test}(\mathsf{PAEKS.ct}_{\sigma,\mathsf{rcv},M}, \mathsf{td}_{\mathsf{snd},\rho,1}) = 0$.

Instantiations. Here, we summarize the underlying PAEKS schemes that can be employed for instantiating the proposed generic construction in Table 1. We describe EPE and NIKE for instantiating the Li-Boyen generic construction of PAEKS [31]. Here, the lattice-based EPE is given by Li-Boyen [31]. Shinoki et al. [38] pointed out a flaw of the Li-Boyne pairing EPE and proposed a MDDH (Matrix Decisional Diffie-Hellman) based EPE. Thus, we employ the Shinoki et al.'s EPE in the table. Here, DBDH stands for Decisional Bilinear Diffie-Hellman and MLWE stands for Module Learning with Errors. Via the proposed construction with these PAEKS schemes, we can obtain pairing-based and lattice-based PK-ME schemes.

Table 1. PAEKS for Instantiating the Proposed Construction

PAEKS	Complexity Assumption	Standard Model
EPE [38]+NIKE [17]	MDDH	Yes
EPE [31]+NIKE [19,26]	MLWE NTRU	No
EPE [31] +NIKE [19,30]	MLWE NTRU	Yes

5 Security Analysis

Correctness. If the underlying PAEKS scheme is correct, then the proposed construction obviously provides correctness 1. We prove that the proposed construction provides correctness 2 if the underlying PAEKS is consistent. Intuitively, if the decryption result is $\mathsf{Uncertain}$, then the test algorithm outputs 1 regardless of the keyword to be searched. This violates consistency.

Theorem 1. *If the underlying PAEKS scheme is consistent, then the proposed construction provides correctness 2.*

Proof. Let $\mathcal{C}$ be the challenger $\mathcal{A}$ be the adversary to correctness 2. We construct a reduction algorithm $\mathcal{B}$ that breaks consistency of PAEKS as follows. First, $\mathcal{C}$ computes $\mathsf{pp}_{\mathsf{PAEKS}} \leftarrow \mathsf{PAEKS.SetUp}(1^\lambda)$, $(\mathsf{PAEKS.pk}_\mathsf{S}, \mathsf{PAEKS.sk}_\mathsf{S}) \leftarrow \mathsf{PAEKS.KGen}_\mathsf{S}(\mathsf{pp}_{\mathsf{PAEKS}})$, $(\mathsf{PAEKS.pk}_\mathsf{R}$, and $\mathsf{PAEKS.sk}_\mathsf{R}) \leftarrow \mathsf{PAEKS.KGen}_\mathsf{R}(\mathsf{pp}_{\mathsf{PAEKS}})$, and gives $(\mathsf{pp}_{\mathsf{PAEKS}}, \mathsf{PAEKS.pk}_\mathsf{S}$ and $\mathsf{PAEKS.pk}_\mathsf{R})$ to $\mathcal{B}$. $\mathcal{B}$ sets $\mathsf{pp} = \mathsf{pp}_{\mathsf{PAEKS}}$ and $(\mathsf{pk}_\sigma, \mathsf{pk}_\rho) = (\mathsf{PAEKS.pk}_\mathsf{S}, \mathsf{PAEKS.pk}_\mathsf{R})$, and gives $(\mathsf{pp}, \mathsf{pk}_\sigma, \mathsf{pk}_\rho)$ to $\mathcal{A}$. $\mathcal{A}$ outputs M. Since $\mathsf{Dec}(\mathsf{pp}, \mathsf{dk}_\rho, \mathsf{pk}_\sigma, \mathsf{ct}) = \mathsf{Uncertain}$ where $\mathsf{ct} = \mathsf{PAEKS.ct}_{\sigma,\mathsf{rcv},M}$, $\mathsf{Test}(\mathsf{PAEKS.ct}_{\sigma,\mathsf{rcv},M}, \mathsf{td}_{\mathsf{snd},\rho,0}) = 1 \wedge \mathsf{Test}(\mathsf{PAEKS.ct}_{\sigma,\mathsf{rcv},M}, \mathsf{td}_{\mathsf{snd},\rho,1}) = 1$ hold. $\mathcal{B}$ outputs M and breaks correctness 2. □

Privacy. Next, we prove that the proposed construction provides privacy. The proof is relatively straightforward because no information of keyword is leaked from ciphertext if the underlying PAEKS scheme provides the full CI security. The underlying PAEKS scheme is also required to be key private because privacy guarantees that no information of (σ, rcv) is leaked from ciphertext.

Theorem 2. *If the underlying PAEKS scheme provides the full CI security with key privacy, then the proposed construction provides privacy.*

Proof. Let $\mathcal{C}$ be the challenger $\mathcal{A}$ be the adversary of privacy. We construct a reduction algorithm $\mathcal{B}$ that breaks the full CI security of PAEKS as follows. First, $\mathcal{C}$ computes $\mathsf{pp}_{\mathsf{PAEKS}} \leftarrow \mathsf{PAEKS.SetUp}(1^\lambda)$, $(\mathsf{PAEKS.pk}_{\mathsf{S}_0}, \mathsf{PAEKS.sk}_{\mathsf{S}_0}) \leftarrow \mathsf{PAEKS.KGen}_\mathsf{S}(\mathsf{pp}_{\mathsf{PAEKS}})$, $(\mathsf{PAEKS.pk}_{\mathsf{S}_1}, \mathsf{PAEKS.sk}_{\mathsf{S}_1}) \leftarrow \mathsf{PAEKS.KGen}_\mathsf{S}(\mathsf{pp}_{\mathsf{PAEKS}})$, $(\mathsf{PAEKS.pk}_{\mathsf{R}_0}, \mathsf{PAEKS.sk}_{\mathsf{R}_0}) \leftarrow \mathsf{PAEKS.KGen}_\mathsf{R}(\mathsf{pp}_{\mathsf{PAEKS}})$, $(\mathsf{PAEKS.pk}_{\mathsf{S}_1}, \mathsf{PAEKS.sk}_{\mathsf{S}_1}) \leftarrow \mathsf{PAEKS.KGen}_\mathsf{S}(\mathsf{pp}_{\mathsf{PAEKS}})$, and gives $(\mathsf{PAEKS.pk}_{\mathsf{S}_0}, \mathsf{PAEKS.pk}_{\mathsf{S}_1}, \mathsf{PAEKS.pk}_{\mathsf{R}_0}, \mathsf{PAEKS.pk}_{\mathsf{R}_1})$ to $\mathcal{B}$. $\mathcal{B}$ sets $\mathsf{pk}_{\sigma_0} = \mathsf{PAEKS.pk}_{\mathsf{S}_0}$, $\mathsf{pk}_{\sigma_1} = \mathsf{PAEKS.pk}_{\mathsf{S}_1}$, $\mathsf{pk}_{\rho_0} = \mathsf{PAEKS.pk}_{\mathsf{R}_0}$, $\mathsf{pk}_{\rho_1} = \mathsf{PAEKS.pk}_{\mathsf{R}_1}$, and gives $(\mathsf{pk}_{\sigma_0}, \mathsf{pk}_{\sigma_1}, \mathsf{pk}_{\rho_0}, \mathsf{pk}_{\rho_1})$ to $\mathcal{A}$.

When $\mathcal{B}$ receives an encryption query (i, j, M) from $\mathcal{A}$, $\mathcal{B}$ sends (i, j, M) to $\mathcal{C}$ as an encryption query where M is regarded as a keyword. $\mathcal{C}$ computes $\mathsf{PAEKS.ct}_{\mathsf{S}_i,\mathsf{R}_j,M} \leftarrow \mathsf{PAEKS.Enc}(\mathsf{PAEKS.pk}_{\mathsf{S}_i}, \mathsf{PAEKS.pk}_{\mathsf{R}_j}, \mathsf{PAEKS.sk}_{\mathsf{S}_i}, M)$ and returns $\mathsf{PAEKS.ct}_{\mathsf{S}_i,\mathsf{R}_j,M}$ to $\mathcal{B}$. $\mathcal{B}$ sets $\mathsf{ct} = \mathsf{PAEKS.ct}_{\mathsf{S}_i,\mathsf{R}_j,M}$, and returns ct to $\mathcal{A}$.

In the challenge phase, $\mathcal{A}$ declares (M_0^*, M_1^*). We set $(M_0^*, M_1^*) = (0, 1)$ without loss of generality. $\mathcal{B}$ sends (M_0^*, M_1^*) to $\mathcal{C}$ as the challenge keywords. $\mathcal{C}$ chooses $b \xleftarrow{\$} \{0,1\}$, computes the challenge ciphertext $\mathsf{PAEKS.ct}^*_{\mathsf{S}_b,\mathsf{R}_b,M_b^*} \leftarrow \mathsf{PAEKS.Enc}$ $(\mathsf{PAEKS.pk}_{\mathsf{S}_b}, \mathsf{PAEKS.pk}_{\mathsf{R}_b}, \mathsf{PAEKS.sk}_{\mathsf{S}_b}, M_b^*)$, and returns $\mathsf{PAEKS.ct}^*_{\mathsf{S}_b,\mathsf{R}_b,M_b^*}$ to $\mathcal{B}$. $\mathcal{B}$ sets $\mathsf{ct}^* = \mathsf{PAEKS.ct}^*_{\mathsf{S}_b,\mathsf{R}_b,M_b^*}$ and sends ct^* to $\mathcal{A}$.

Finally, $\mathcal{A}$ outputs $b' \in \{0,1\}$ to $\mathcal{B}$ and $\mathcal{B}$ outputs b'. Therefore, $\mathcal{A}$ breaks the full CI security with key privacy with the same advantage of $\mathcal{A}$. □

Authenticity. Next, we prove that the proposed construction provides authenticity. Intuitively, the (full) TI security is not required to prove the following theorem since PK-ME does not consider information leakage from decryption keys. Counterintuitively, we reduce authenticity to the full TI security in our security proof. The intuition of the proof is explained as follows. According to the security definition, an adversary of authenticity outputs a decryptable ciphertext ct^* without possessing the corresponding encryption key. The reduction algorithm $\mathcal{B}$ tries to distinguish the challenge bit $b \in \{0,1\}$ from the challenge trapdoor $\mathsf{td}_{\mathsf{S},\mathsf{R},kw_b^*}$, where kw_b^* is either 0 or 1 in our construction. We focus on the fact that the challenge keywords are not allowed to be sent to the encryption oracle in the security definition of the (full) TI security, whereas ct^* is a ciphertext of a challenge keyword. Thus, it is expected that the test result of ct^* using $\mathsf{td}_{\mathsf{S},\mathsf{R},kw_b^*}$ reveals information of b. However, the test result does not help to break the TI security unless the decryption result of ct^* is explicitly known. That is, since ct^* is just required to be a decryptable ciphertext, the decryption result is not obvious (it is only guaranteed to be 0 or 1). If $\mathcal{B}$ knows that the decryption result of ct^* is 0 or 1, then $\mathcal{B}$ can recover b from the test result of ct^* using $\mathsf{td}_{\mathsf{S},\mathsf{R},kw_b^*}$. To decrypt ct^*, $\mathcal{B}$ sends the challenge keywords to $\mathcal{C}$ as trapdoor queries, and decrypts ct^* using the trapdoors. This is the reason why the underlying PAEKS scheme needs to be full TI secure.

Theorem 3. *If the underlying PAEKS scheme provides the full TI security, then the proposed construction provides authenticity.*

Proof. Let $\mathcal{C}$ be the challenger $\mathcal{A}$ be the adversary of authenticity. We construct a reduction algorithm $\mathcal{B}$ that breaks the full TI security of PAEKS as follows. First, $\mathcal{C}$ computes $\mathsf{pp}_{\mathsf{PAEKS}} \leftarrow \mathsf{PAEKS.SetUp}(1^\lambda)$, $(\mathsf{PAEKS.pk}_\mathsf{S}, \mathsf{PAEKS.sk}_\mathsf{S})$ $\leftarrow \mathsf{PAEKS.KGen}_\mathsf{S}(\mathsf{pp}_{\mathsf{PAEKS}})$, and $(\mathsf{PAEKS.pk}_\mathsf{R}, \mathsf{PAEKS.sk}_\mathsf{R}) \leftarrow \mathsf{PAEKS.KGen}_\mathsf{R}$ $(\mathsf{pp}_{\mathsf{PAEKS}})$, and sends $(\mathsf{pp}_{\mathsf{PAEKS}}, \mathsf{PAEKS.pk}_\mathsf{S}, \mathsf{PAEKS.pk}_\mathsf{R})$ to $\mathcal{B}$. $\mathcal{B}$ declares the challenge keywords $(kw_0^*, kw_1^*) = (0, 1)$, and sends it to $\mathcal{C}$. $\mathcal{C}$ chooses $b \xleftarrow{\$} \{0,1\}$, computes the challenge trapdoor $\mathsf{td}_{\mathsf{S},\mathsf{R},kw_b^*} \leftarrow \mathsf{Trapdoor}(\mathsf{PAEKS.pk}_\mathsf{S},$ $\mathsf{PAEKS.pk}_\mathsf{R}, \mathsf{PAEKS.sk}_\mathsf{R}, kw_b^*)$, and sends $\mathsf{td}_{\mathsf{S},\mathsf{R},kw_b^*}$ to $\mathcal{B}$.

$\mathcal{B}$ sends $kw_0^* = 0$ to $\mathcal{C}$ as a trapdoor query. $\mathcal{C}$ computes $\mathsf{td}_{\mathsf{S},\mathsf{R},kw_0^*} \leftarrow \mathsf{Trapdoor}$ $(\mathsf{PAEKS.pk}_\mathsf{S}, \mathsf{PAEKS.pk}_\mathsf{R}, \mathsf{PAEKS.sk}_\mathsf{R}, kw_0^*)$, and sends $\mathsf{td}_{\mathsf{S},\mathsf{R},kw_0^*}$ to $\mathcal{B}$. $\mathcal{B}$ also sends

$kw_1^* = 1$ to $\mathcal{C}$ as a trapdoor query. $\mathcal{C}$ computes $\mathsf{td}_{\mathsf{S},\mathsf{R},kw_0^*} \leftarrow \mathsf{Trapdoor}(\mathsf{PAEKS.pk_S}, \mathsf{PAEKS.pk_R}, \mathsf{PAEKS.sk_R}, kw_1^*)$, and sends $\mathsf{td}_{\mathsf{S},\mathsf{R},kw_1^*}$ to $\mathcal{B}$.

$\mathcal{B}$ sets $\mathsf{pk}_\sigma = \mathsf{PAEKS.pk_S}$, $\mathsf{pk}_\rho = \mathsf{PAEKS.pk_R}$, and $\mathsf{pp} = \mathsf{pp_{PAEKS}}$, and sends $(\mathsf{pp}, \mathsf{pk}_\sigma, \mathsf{pk}_\rho)$ to $\mathcal{A}$. $\mathcal{A}$ outputs ct^*. Let M^* be the decryption result of ct^*. Since ct^* is a decryptable ciphertext and thus $M^* \in \{0,1\}$ and $M^* \notin \{\mathsf{Uncertain}, \perp\}$ hold, we do not have to consider the cases $\mathsf{Test}(\mathsf{ct}^*, \mathsf{td}_{\mathsf{S},\mathsf{R},kw_0^*}) = 1 \wedge \mathsf{Test}(\mathsf{ct}^*, \mathsf{td}_{\mathsf{S},\mathsf{R},kw_1^*}) = 1$ and $\mathsf{Test}(\mathsf{ct}^*, \mathsf{td}_{\mathsf{S},\mathsf{R},kw_0^*}) = 0 \wedge \mathsf{Test}(\mathsf{ct}^*, \mathsf{td}_{\mathsf{S},\mathsf{R},kw_1^*}) = 0$. $\mathcal{B}$ recovers b as follows.

- If $\mathsf{Test}(\mathsf{ct}^*, \mathsf{td}_{\mathsf{S},\mathsf{R},kw_0^*}) = 1 \wedge \mathsf{Test}(\mathsf{ct}^*, \mathsf{td}_{\mathsf{S},\mathsf{R},kw_1^*}) = 0$, then $M^* = 0$. If $\mathsf{Test}(\mathsf{ct}^*, \mathsf{td}_{\mathsf{S},\mathsf{R},kw_b^*}) = 0$, then $b = 1$. If $\mathsf{Test}(\mathsf{ct}^*, \mathsf{td}_{\mathsf{S},\mathsf{R},kw_b^*}) = 1$, then $b = 0$.
- If $\mathsf{Test}(\mathsf{ct}^*, \mathsf{td}_{\mathsf{S},\mathsf{R},kw_0^*}) = 0 \wedge \mathsf{Test}(\mathsf{ct}^*, \mathsf{td}_{\mathsf{S},\mathsf{R},kw_1^*}) = 1$, then $M^* = 1$. If $\mathsf{Test}(\mathsf{ct}^*, \mathsf{td}_{\mathsf{S},\mathsf{R},kw_b^*}) = 0$, then $b = 0$. If $\mathsf{Test}(\mathsf{ct}^*, \mathsf{td}_{\mathsf{S},\mathsf{R},kw_b^*}) = 1$, then $b = 1$.

$\mathcal{B}$ outputs b, and breaks the full TI security with the same advantage of $\mathcal{A}$. □

6 Discussion

In this section, we compare PK-ME with IB-ME and explore its advantages and disadvantages.

6.1 Advantages of PK-ME

Security against the KGC: In IBE including IB-ME, the KGC generates secret keys for each identity. Thus, the KGC potentially can decrypt all ciphertexts. Though IB-ME secure against the KGC has been proposed in [13], the scheme requires additional authority. This key escrow problem does not happen in the public key encryption setting including PK-ME at the expense of introducing public key infrastructure (PKI) (see below).

(Towards) Efficient Instantiation: Boneh et al. demonstrated that no black-box construction of IBE exists from PKE [6]. Thus, basically, PKE is efficiently instantiated compared to IBE. Though an IBE construction from the computational Diffie-Hellman assumption has been proposed by Döttling and Garg [18], it requires garbled circuits and is much less efficient compared to those of pairing–based IBE schemes. Since PK-ME is a public key encryption variant, PK-ME is not affected by the impossibility result. We note that the current security proof requires full TI security, and current PAEKS schemes with full TI security were realized by IBE-related techniques. Potentially, PK-ME can be instantiated without employing IBE-related techniques.

6.2 Disadvantages of PK-ME

PKI: In exchange for the absence of the key escrow problem, it is necessary to assume a PKI system. In this paper, it is implicitly assumed that the PKI issues a certificate for each public key. Issuance of public key certificates by PKI is a cost and is a disadvantage of PK-ME.

Impossibility of Enhanced Privacy: Francati et al. [23] introduced a stronger flavor of privacy which they call enhanced privacy. It captures privacy in IB-ME according to every possible mismatch condition for the receiver where an adversary holds a decryption key but does not know the sender's identities. Enhanced privacy implicitly requires an exponentially large number of identities (public keys). In the security model, two challenge sender's identities σ_0 and σ_1 are chosen from the identity space by the challenger. Here, the space is required to have a non-trivial amount of min-entropy. Obviously, the adversary wins if the size of the identity space is polynomially bounded. Due to this observation, PK-ME has no way to provide enhanced privacy since the number of public keys is bounded by a polynomial of the security parameter. Nonetheless, we would like to claim that our definitions, privacy and authenticity, capture fundamental security notions of PK-ME similar to those of IB-ME defined by Ateniese et al. [3,4]. Simultaneously, we do not deny any possibility to strengthen the privacy or authenticity of PK-ME. Considering such an enhanced security of PK-ME is left as a future work.

6.3 Applications

Next, we explore whether PK-ME can be used for realizing applications of IB-ME. Ateniese et al. [3,4] considered an application of IB-ME where "*an FBI agent may want to communicate only with CIA agents, and if this is not the case, the communication should drop without revealing membership information and why the communication failed.*". The sender can specify that the message is intended for an FBI agent during encryption, and the receiver can also specify that he/she wants to read messages only if they come from CIA agents during decryption. In this example, the KGC issues keys after confirming the attributes. Ateniese et al. explicitly mentioned that "*The sender's attributes are certified by the authority, so that no malicious sender can forge a valid ciphertext which embeds fake attributes.*". The receiver's attributes are also certified by the KGC. That is, we can employ PK-ME for this application if we assume that PKI confirms the sender's and receiver's attributes and issues certificates for their public keys.

Ateniese et al. constructed an anonymous bulletin board using IB-ME and Tor. Senders post encrypted messages to a bulletin board, hosted by a Tor hidden service. As well as the encryption key corresponding to their own identity, senders specify a target identity string that acts as the receiver's access policy. Receivers also specify the expected identity of the sender. Regarding the key generation by the KGC, Ateniese et al. mentioned that the key generation service could be implemented as another Tor hidden service that automatically converts email addresses or phone numbers into keys. Ateniese et al. also mentioned the key escrow problem where "*We stress that ME is susceptible to key escrow attacks. For this reason, the key generation service must be trusted. Promising approaches to mitigate (or solve) key escrow attacks in ME (not considered in this paper) are the ones that have been developed for identity-based and attribute-based cryptosystems, e.g., multi-authorities or the registration-based setting.*". Let assume that PKI issues a certificate on, e.g., a public key||identity, where the identity (e.g., email addresses or phone numbers as mentioned above) has the same role of those in the IB-ME based anonymous bulletin board system. Then, we can construct a key escrow free anonymous bulletin board system using PK-ME and Tor at the expense of the cost of the PKI system. To sum up, the public key setting does not affect the above applications of IB-ME.

7 Conclusion

In this paper, we focus on a similarity of matchmaking encryption and PAEKS. We formalize PK-ME and propose a generic construction of PK-ME from PAEKS. Our security proof of authenticity requires that the underlying PAEKS scheme is to be full TI secure. Thus, we can instantiate the proposed generic construction from pairing or lattice as mentioned before. The proposed construction considers 1-bit plaintext. It is expected that the plaintext space can be amplified by simply arranging ciphertexts of 1-bit plaintext. Exploring more an efficient way for plaintext amplification is left as a future work of this paper.

Our work indicates some interesting open problems in both PK-ME and PAEKS contexts. The Li-Boyen's generic construction can be instantiated from (pairing-free) computational Diffie-Hellman, integer factorization, or isogenies via NIKEs [8,9,17,26], if it requires only the TI security. Thus, proving authenticity of the proposed generic construction by the TI security is desirable from the efficiency point of view. For privacy, we weaken the security level by defining the encryption oracle. If an adversary is allowed to obtain sender's secret keys in the full CI security model, then we can enhance the security level of privacy by giving the challenge encryption key to the adversary. However, the Li-Boyen's generic construction of PAEKS seems insecure when an adversary has the sender's secret key because the adversary can produce NIKE keys (we emphasize that this is not an attack against the Li-Boyen's construction). Considering a secret key exposure attack in PAEKS itself seems interesting topic to enhance the security level of full CI in PAEKS, and it also enhances the security level of privacy in PK-ME via the proposed generic construction.

Acknowledgment. This work was supported by JSPS KAKENHI Grant Number JP21K11897.

References

1. Abdalla, M., et al.: Searchable encryption revisited: Consistency properties, relation to anonymous IBE, and extensions. J. Cryptol. **21**(3), 350–391 (2008)
2. Alwen, J., Hartmann, D., Kiltz, E., Mularczyk, M., Schwabe, P.: Post-quantum multi-recipient public key encryption. In: ACM CCS, pp. 1108–1122 (2023)

3. Ateniese, G., Francati, D., Nuñez, D., Venturi, D.: Match me if you can: matchmaking encryption and its applications. In: Boldyreva, A., Micciancio, D. (eds.) CRYPTO 2019. LNCS, vol. 11693, pp. 701–731. Springer, Cham (2019). https://doi.org/10.1007/978-3-030-26951-7_24
4. Ateniese, G., Francati, D., Nuñez, D., Venturi, D.: Match me if you can: matchmaking encryption and its applications. J. Cryptol. **34**(3), 16 (2021)
5. Boneh, D., Di Crescenzo, G., Ostrovsky, R., Persiano, G.: Public key encryption with keyword search. In: Cachin, C., Camenisch, J.L. (eds.) EUROCRYPT 2004. LNCS, vol. 3027, pp. 506–522. Springer, Heidelberg (2004). https://doi.org/10.1007/978-3-540-24676-3_30
6. Boneh, D., Papakonstantinou, P.A., Rackoff, C., Vahlis, Y., Waters, B.: On the impossibility of basing identity based encryption on trapdoor permutations. In: IEEE FOCS, pp. 283–292 (2008)
7. Boyen, X., Li, Q.: Identity-based matchmaking encryption with enhanced privacy - a generic construction with practical instantiations. In: Tsudik, G., Conti, M., Liang, K., Smaragdakis, G. (eds.) ESORICS 2023. LNCS, vol. 14345, pp. 425–445. Springer, Cham (2023)
8. Cash, D., Kiltz, E., Shoup, V.: The twin Diffie-Hellman problem and applications. In: Smart, N. (ed.) EUROCRYPT 2008. LNCS, vol. 4965, pp. 127–145. Springer, Heidelberg (2008). https://doi.org/10.1007/978-3-540-78967-3_8
9. Castryck, W., Lange, T., Martindale, C., Panny, L., Renes, J.: CSIDH: an efficient post-quantum commutative group action. In: Peyrin, T., Galbraith, S. (eds.) ASIACRYPT 2018. LNCS, vol. 11274, pp. 395–427. Springer, Cham (2018). https://doi.org/10.1007/978-3-030-03332-3_15
10. Chen, B., Xiang, T., Ma, M., He, D., Liao, X.: CL-ME: efficient certificateless matchmaking encryption for internet of things. IEEE Internet Things J. **8**(19), 15010–15023 (2021)
11. Chen, J., Li, Y., Wen, J., Weng, J.: Identity-based matchmaking encryption from standard assumptions. In: Agrawal, S., Lin, D. (eds.) ASIACRYPT 2022. LNCS, vol. 13793, pp. 394–422. Springer, Cham (2022). https://doi.org/10.1007/978-3-031-22969-5_14
12. Cheng, L., Qin, J., Feng, F., Meng, F.: Security-enhanced public-key authenticated searchable encryption. Inf. Sci. **647**, 119454 (2023)
13. Chiku, S., Hara, K., Shikata, J.: Identity-based matchmaking encryption secure against key generation center. In: Zhang, M., Au, M.H., Zhang, Y. (eds.) ProvSec 2023. LNCS, vol. 14217, pp. 251–273. Springer, Cham (2023). https://doi.org/10.1007/978-3-031-45513-1_14
14. Chiku, S., Hashimoto, K., Hara, K., Shikata, J.: Identity-based matchmaking encryption, revisited: Strong security and practical constructions from standard classical and post-quantum assumptions. IACR Cryptol. ePrint Arch. 1435 (2023)
15. Chow, S.S.M.: Removing escrow from identity-based encryption. In: Jarecki, S., Tsudik, G. (eds.) PKC 2009. LNCS, vol. 5443, pp. 256–276. Springer, Heidelberg (2009). https://doi.org/10.1007/978-3-642-00468-1_15
16. Chu, Q., Fu, A., Qian, H., Chen, J.: Inner-product matchmaking encryption: bilateral access control and beyond equality. IET Inf. Secur. **2023**, 1–17 (2023)
17. Diffie, W., Hellman, M.E.: New directions in cryptography. IEEE Trans. Inf. Theory **22**(6), 644–654 (1976)
18. Döttling, N., Garg, S.: Identity-based encryption from the Diffie-Hellman assumption. In: Katz, J., Shacham, H. (eds.) CRYPTO 2017. LNCS, vol. 10401, pp. 537–569. Springer, Cham (2017). https://doi.org/10.1007/978-3-319-63688-7_18

19. Ducas, L., Lyubashevsky, V., Prest, T.: Efficient identity-based encryption over NTRU lattices. In: Sarkar, P., Iwata, T. (eds.) ASIACRYPT 2014. LNCS, vol. 8874, pp. 22–41. Springer, Heidelberg (2014). https://doi.org/10.1007/978-3-662-45608-8_2
20. Emura, K.: Generic construction of public-key authenticated encryption with keyword search revisited: stronger security and efficient construction. In: ACM APKC, pp. 39–49 (2022)
21. Emura, K., Katsumata, S., Watanabe, Y.: Identity-based encryption with security against the KGC: a formal model and its instantiation from lattices. In: Sako, K., Schneider, S., Ryan, P.Y.A. (eds.) ESORICS 2019. LNCS, vol. 11736, pp. 113–133. Springer, Cham (2019). https://doi.org/10.1007/978-3-030-29962-0_6
22. Emura, K., Katsumata, S., Watanabe, Y.: Identity-based encryption with security against the KGC: a formal model and its instantiations. Theoret. Comput. Sci. **900**, 97–119 (2022)
23. Francati, D., Guidi, A., Russo, L., Venturi, D.: Identity-based matchmaking encryption without random oracles. In: Adhikari, A., Küsters, R., Preneel, B. (eds.) INDOCRYPT 2021. LNCS, vol. 13143, pp. 415–435. Springer, Cham (2021). https://doi.org/10.1007/978-3-030-92518-5_19
24. Francati, D., Huang, V., Venturi, D.: Registered matchmaking encryption. In: Applied Cryptography and Network Security (2025, to appear)
25. Freire, E.S.V., Hofheinz, D., Kiltz, E., Paterson, K.G.: Non-interactive key exchange. In: Kurosawa, K., Hanaoka, G. (eds.) PKC 2013. LNCS, vol. 7778, pp. 254–271. Springer, Heidelberg (2013). https://doi.org/10.1007/978-3-642-36362-7_17
26. Gajland, P., de Kock, B., Quaresma, M., Malavolta, G., Schwabe, P.: SWOOSH: efficient lattice-based non-interactive key exchange. In: USENIX Security (2024)
27. Hovd, M.N., Stam, M.: Vetted encryption. In: Bhargavan, K., Oswald, E., Prabhakaran, M. (eds.) INDOCRYPT 2020. LNCS, vol. 12578, pp. 488–507. Springer, Cham (2020). https://doi.org/10.1007/978-3-030-65277-7_22
28. Huang, Q., Li, H.: An efficient public-key searchable encryption scheme secure against inside keyword guessing attacks. Inf. Sci. **403**, 1–14 (2017)
29. Jiang, Z., Wang, X., Zhang, K., Gong, J., Chen, J., Qian, H.: Revocable identity-based matchmaking encryption in the standard model. IET Inf. Secur. **17**(4), 567–581 (2023)
30. de Kock, B.: A non-interactive key exchange based on ring-learning with errors. phD thesis, Master's thesis. Master's thesis, Eindhoven University of Technology (2018)
31. Li, Q., Boyen, X.: Public-key authenticated encryption with keyword search made easy. IACR Commun. Cryptol. **1**(2), 16 (2024)
32. Lin, S., Li, Y., Chen, J.: CCA-secure identity-based matchmaking encryption from standard assumptions. In: Ge, C., Yung, M. (eds.) Inscrypt 2023. Lecture Notes in Computer Science, vol. 14526, pp. 253–273. Springer, Cham (2023). https://doi.org/10.1007/978-981-97-0942-7_13
33. Malone-Lee, J.: Identity-based signcryption. IACR Cryptol. ePrint Arch. 98 (2002)
34. Mongardini, A.M., Friolo, D., Ateniese, G.: Stealth and beyond: attribute-driven accountability in Bitcoin transactions. IACR Cryptology ePrint Archive, Paper 2024/1789 (2024). https://eprint.iacr.org/2024/1789
35. Mukherjee, S.: Statistically consistent broadcast authenticated encryption with keyword search - adaptive security from standard assumptions. In: Simpson, L., Rezazadeh Baee, M.A. (eds.) ACISP 2023. LNCS, vol. 13915, pp. 523–552. Springer, Cham (2023). https://doi.org/10.1007/978-3-031-35486-1_23

36. Paterson, K.G., Srinivasan, S.: On the relations between non-interactive key distribution, identity-based encryption and trapdoor discrete log groups. Des. Codes Crypt. **52**(2), 219–241 (2009)
37. Rhee, H.S., Lee, D.H.: Anonymous IBE from PEKS: a generic construction. In: Kim, H. (ed.) WISA 2021. LNCS, vol. 13009, pp. 105–118. Springer, Cham (2021). https://doi.org/10.1007/978-3-030-89432-0_9
38. Shinoki, H., Sato, H., Yoshino, M.: Fully secure searchable encryption from PRFs, pairings, and lattices. In: Fischlin, M., Moonsamy, V. (eds.) ACNS 2025, Part I. LNCS, vol. 15825, pp. 62–88. Springer, Cham (2025). https://doi.org/10.1007/978-3-031-95761-1_3
39. Wang, X., Zhang, K., Li, J., Wen, M., Xu, S., Ning, J.: Non-interactive Boolean searchable asymmetric encryption with bilateral access control. Comput. J. **67**(1), 179–194 (2024)
40. Wang, Y., Wang, B., Lai, Q., Zhan, Y.: Identity-based matchmaking encryption with stronger security and instantiation on lattices. Theoret. Comput. Sci. **1029**, 115048 (2025)
41. Yang, N., Tang, C., He, D.: A lightweight certificateless multi-user matchmaking encryption for mobile devices: enhancing security and performance. IEEE Trans. Inf. Forensics Secur. **19**, 251–264 (2024)

Faster FHEW Bootstrapping with Adaptive Key Update

Qi Zhang[1,2], Mingqiang Wang[1](✉), and Xiaopeng Cheng[1]

[1] School of Mathematics, Shandong University, Jinan 250100, China
{zhang_qi,chengxiaopeng}@mail.sdu.edu.cn, wangmingqiang@sdu.edu.cn
[2] Zhongtai Securities Institute for Financial Studies, Shandong University, Jinan 250100, China

Abstract. Lee et al. proposed a new bootstrapping algorithm based on homomorphic automorphism, which merges the empty sets of ciphertexts by adjusting the window size. This algorithm supports arbitrary secret key distributions with no additional runtime costs while using small evaluation keys. However, our implementation reveals that once the window size exceeds a certain threshold, the time required for bootstrapping remains relatively constant. This observation prompts the question of how to further reduce the running time. To address this challenge, we introduce a new trick called Adaptive Key Update (AKU). With AKU and automorphism techniques, we propose a new bootstrapping algorithm for Gaussian secret keys that requires only n external products and no switching for blind rotation. Building on this, we employ window size optimization and key switching techniques to further improve the algorithm. The improved algorithm provides a useful trade-off between key storage and computational efficiency, depending on the choice of the window size. Compared to the current fastest FHEW bootstrapping method for Gaussian secret keys (the LLWW+ method proposed by Li et al.), our AKU-based algorithm reduces the number of key switching by 76% and decreases the running time of bootstrapping by 20.7%. At this point, the practical runtime for bootstrapping is approximately equal to that of performing only n external products.

Keywords: Automorphism · Key Switching · Blind Rotation · Bootstrapping · Fully Homomorphic Encryption (FHE)

1 Introduction

Homomorphic encryption (HE) allows computations to be performed on encrypted data without revealing the underlying plaintext, ensuring data confidentiality throughout the process. This unique capability makes HE an attractive tool for a wide range of privacy-preserving applications, allowing data to be processed without ever exposing sensitive information. Most HE schemes rely on the difficulty of computational problems such as Learning With Errors (LWE) [25] or Ring Learning With Errors (RLWE) [22], where ciphertexts contain small noise

Y. Kim et al. (Eds.): CANS 2025, LNCS 16351, pp. 292–312, 2026.
https://doi.org/10.1007/978-981-95-4434-9_14

to guarantee security. However, as computations on ciphertexts accumulate, the noise also increases, which can increase the probability of decryption failure, and limit the number of operations that can be performed on the encrypted data. Since Craig Gentry's pioneering introduction of the first fully homomorphic encryption (FHE) scheme [15], HE has seen significant advancements. These advancements include the development of several novel schemes that significantly improve Gentry's original construction [7,9,10,12,13]. Additionally, HE has found practical applications in various domains, such as private information retrieval [4], privacy-preserving genome-wide association studies [5], and logistic regression learning [17,28] and others. A major community initiative has also been established to standardize homomorphic encryption [2].

Most existing FHE constructions adhere to the paradigm initially proposed by Gentry [15], which consists of two main components: 1) the construction of a somewhat homomorphic encryption (SHE) scheme, typically supporting only a limited number of homomorphic operations due to the accumulation of noise during computation; and 2) the design of a bootstrapping algorithm that homomorphically evaluates the decryption function, thereby refreshing the ciphertext and mitigating the noise buildup. Early research efforts [8,13,16,22,26] primarily focused on developing SHE schemes capable of evaluating their own (augmented) decryption circuits. These schemes were later transformed into FHE schemes through Gentry's bootstrapping theorem [15], which remains foundational in the field. However, since bootstrapping is a critical and computationally intensive process in nearly all FHE constructions, it has become a significant bottleneck in achieving practical performance for real-world applications. As a result, the development of efficient bootstrapping techniques has become one of the central challenges in FHE research, with ongoing efforts to optimize this procedure being essential for enhancing the overall efficiency and scalability of FHE systems.

The FHEW FHE scheme [3,12] and its TFHE variant [11] are among the most well-known methods for performing bit-level homomorphic computations on encrypted data. These schemes enable efficient processing of encrypted binary data and have been the foundation for subsequent innovations in homomorphic encryption. Three classic approaches have been developed for FHEW-like bootstrapping: 1) AP bootstrapping method: Originally proposed by Alperin-Sheriff and Peikert [3], this method was efficiently instantiated in the ring setting by the FHEW cryptosystem [12]. It is particularly effective for LWE secret keys that follow Gaussian or uniform distributions, but it requires relatively large evaluation keys. 2) GINX bootstrapping method: Introduced by Gama et al. [14], the GINX method has been further optimized for ternary secret keys, reducing the computational overhead by approximately half. We refer to this optimized version as GINX* [6,18]. The GINX method, especially its TFHE variant, excels in scenarios with binary LWE secret keys. 3) LMKC+ bootstrapping method: Proposed by Lee et al. [20], LMKC+ method leverages the homomorphic automorphism technique and introduced a window size optimization strategy to effectively merge ciphertexts. This method supports arbitrary secret key distributions without additional runtime costs, while using small evaluation keys.

Recently, Wang et al. [27] and Li et al. [21] proposed the WWLL+ and LLWW+ methods, respectively, both of which build upon the LMKC+ method [20]. The WWLL+ method further reduces the number of homomorphic automorphisms by employing a naive sparse approach. While this approach is effective in minimizing the number of homomorphic automorphisms, it can lead to a rapid increase in noise, potentially degrading the performance of homomorphic computations. On the other hand, the LLWW+ method achieves similar reductions in the number of homomorphic automorphisms by merging symmetric sets, and mitigating some of the noise issues associated with the naive sparse approach. However, one notable limitation of LLWW+ is that the size of the blind rotation keys is approximately twice that of the original LMKC+ method.

Efficiency aside, the use of secret keys with large entries remains interesting for both theoretical and practical reasons. Theoretically, lattice cryptography supports Gaussian-distributed secret keys with a standard deviation of $O(\sqrt{n})$, where n is the dimension of the secret vector and serves as a security parameter [22,25]. Research [23] shows that LWE with binary secrets can be as hard as standard LWE with uniform or Gaussian secrets, but at the cost of increasing the secret dimension by a factor of $O(\log q)$ and the error magnitude by a factor of $O(\sqrt{n})$. For practical reasons, such as limiting error growth during homomorphic computation and efficiently implementing GINX bootstrapping, these theoretical results supporting binary secrets are often overlooked. Instead, practical parameters are set based on the best-known attacks to balance security and efficiency. For Gaussian secret keys, almost all bootstrapping algorithms can achieve the same level of security with a smaller value of n. In this paper, we adopt a similar approach when comparing our work to previous schemes.

Although both the WWLL+ and LLWW+ methods reduce the number of homomorphic automorphisms compared to the LMKC+ method, it is observed that, when the window size is small, the number of homomorphic automorphisms in both the LMKC+ and LLWW+ methods decreases significantly as the window size increases. However, once the window size exceeds a certain threshold (approximately 10), the number of homomorphic automorphisms required for bootstrapping stabilizes and shows little change. This observation raises an important question: Is it possible to achieve bootstrapping for keys with a Gaussian distribution that provides faster performance and lower noise both theoretically and practically, or even matches the theoretical complexity of binary GINX?

1.1 Our Results

We have answered the above questions in the affirmative, and have the following three main contributions to the algorithmic-level and implementation-level of bootstrapping schemes.

- **Algorithmic-Level Contributions**
  We introduce a new trick, called Adaptive Key Update (AKU), to reduce the number of key switching during blind rotation. With AKU and automorphism

techniques, we design a new bootstrapping procedure that supports the use of arbitrary secret key distributions without any performance penalty (similar to AP/LMKC+ bootstrapping) while requiring only n external products and no switching for blind rotation. One consideration is that the key size can be relatively large.

We combine AKU, automorphism, window size and key switching techniques to propose an improved bootstrapping algorithm. This algorithm provides a useful trade-off between the storage requirements for evaluation keys and computational efficiency based on the choice of the window size. By significantly reducing the number of key switching during blind rotation, our method also reduces running time compared to LLWW+ method. This method can be naturally extended to bootstrapping algorithms based on NTRU.

- **Implementation-Level Verification**

  We verify our theoretical results of the proposed method through experiments based on the OpenFHE open-source homomorphic encryption library [1]. Concretely, in the case of a gate bootstrapping operation at a 128-bit security level, our scheme outperforms the current fastest FHEW bootstrapping algorithm [21] by reducing the number of key-switching operations by 76% (from 301 to 77). This results in a 20.7% reduction in gate bootstrapping time. At this point, the practical runtime for bootstrapping is approximately equal to that of performing only n external products(See Sect. 5 for details). Since the key size increases by a factor of 2, this trade-off makes the scheme more suitable for scenarios where there is ample key storage capacity.

1.2 Techniques

The main operation in FHEW bootstrapping is the evaluation of a so-called "blind rotation". This operation takes some polynomial f_0 as an input and "rotates" it by some value encrypted within a given LWE ciphertext $(\mathbf{a} = (a_0, ..., a_{n-1}), b)$ under secret key $\mathbf{s} = (s_0, ..., s_{n-1})$ (See Sect. 2 for more details). Starting with the ciphertext RLWE(f_0) of a polynomial f_0 under $\mathbf{z}(X)$, previous blind rotation algorithms work as follows: at step i, given a ciphertext RLWE(f_{i-1}) of a polynomial $f_{i-1}(X) = f_0 \cdot X^{\sum_{j \leq i-1} a_j s_j}$, homomorphically compute RLWE(f_i) of an updated polynomial $f_i = f_{i-1} \cdot X^{a_i \cdot s_i} = f_0 \cdot X^{\sum_{j \leq i} a_j s_j}$, using a publicly known constant a_i part of the input LWE ciphertext and an encryption $E(s_i)$ of a secret key coordinate s_i. After repeating this step n times, we obtain the encryption of RLWE$(f_0 \cdot X^{\langle \mathbf{a}, \mathbf{s} \rangle})$, which is a negacyclic rotation of f_0 by $\langle \mathbf{a}, \mathbf{s} \rangle$ positions.

In this paper, We first propose Adaptive Key Update(AKU) to optimize the blind rotation algorithm by automorphism technique. For homomorphic automorphism, consider a ciphertext $c(X) \in R_Q$ that encrypts X^{s_i} under the secret key $z(X)$, we can easily obtain a new ciphertext $c(X^{a_i})$ that encrypts $X^{a_i s_i}$ by applying the automorphism $X \to X^{a_i}$ to $c(X)$ if $a_i \in \mathbb{Z}_{2N}^*$. The challenge, however, is that $c(X^{a_i})$ is encrypted under a different secret key $z(X^{a_i})$, not the original secret key $z(X)$. To allow further homomorphic computations, methods like LMKC+ and LLWW+ require key switching to convert $c(X^{a_i})$ back to the ciphertext under $z(X)$ that encrypts $X^{a_i s_i}$. We observe that the time required for automorphism is almost negligible compared to the time required for key switching. Abstractly, AKU involves adaptively "rotating" the secret key in RLWE ciphertexts during blind rotation, with the number of bits per rotation determined by a specific value in the given LWE ciphertext. The purpose is to perform no key switching after applying an automorphism, or perform one key switching after several automorphisms, so as to reduce the total time required for blind rotation and improve the efficiency of bootstrapping.

Recall that the goal of blind rotation is to homomorphically compute $f_0(X) \cdot X^{\langle \mathbf{a},\mathbf{s} \rangle} = f_0(X) \cdot X^{\sum_{i=0}^{n-1} a_i s_i}$. Suppose each $a_i \in \mathbb{Z}_{2N}^*$ and $a_i' \cdot a_i \equiv 1 \mod 2N$. Starting with the ciphertext $\text{RLWE}(f_0(X^{a_0'}))$ of a polynomial $f_0(X^{a_0'})$ under $\mathbf{z}(X^{a_0'})$, our blind rotation algorithm works as follows: at step i, given a ciphertext $\text{RLWE}(f_{i-1})$ of a polynomial $f_{i-1} = f_0(X^{a_i'}) \cdot X^{a_i' \sum_{j=0}^{j=i-2} a_j s_j}$ under secret key $\mathbf{z}(X^{a_i'})$, homomorphically compute $\text{RLWE}(f_i)$ of an updated polynomial $f_i = f_{i-1} \cdot X^{a_i' \cdot a_{i-1} s_{i-1}}$. Then we apply the automorphism $\psi_{a_i a_{i+1}'}(\cdot)$ to get an encryption of $f_0(X^{a_{i+1}'}) \cdot X^{a_{i+1}' \sum_{j=0}^{j=i-1} a_j s_j}$ under secret key $\mathbf{z}(X^{a_{i+1}'})$. Repeating the above process and completing the loop with respect to i, we can get $f_0(X^{a_n'}) \cdot X^{a_n' \sum_{j=0}^{j=n-1} a_j s_j}$ under secret key $\mathbf{z}(X^{a_n'})$, where $a_n' = 1$. We obtain the fastest bootstrapping theoretically and practically, which has the same theoretical complexity as binary GINX. It only takes n external products and no key switching! Two considerations are that the key size can be relatively large, and naive sparse approach may lead to a notable increase in noise, similar to what has been observed in WWLL+ method. Building on this, we employ window size optimization and key switching techniques to further improve the algorithm, which performs a key switching only when the secret key of RLWE ciphertexts rotates at least w bits during blind rotation. Finally, the algorithm provides a useful trade-off between storage requirements for evaluation keys and computational complexity, depending on the choice of the window size.

2 Preliminaries

Let N be a power of two. We denote the $2N$-th cyclotomic ring by $\mathcal{R} := \mathbb{Z}[X]/(X^N + 1)$ and its quotient ring by $\mathcal{R}_Q := \mathcal{R}/Q\mathcal{R}$. We use regular letters to represent (modular) integers, such as $a \in \mathbb{Z}_q$, while bold letters represent polynomials $\mathbf{a} \in \mathcal{R}$ or vectors $\mathbf{a} \in \mathbb{Z}^n$. For two vectors $\mathbf{a}$ and $\mathbf{b}$, we denote their inner product by $\langle \mathbf{a}, \mathbf{b} \rangle$. We write the floor, ceiling and round functions as $\lfloor \cdot \rfloor$, $\lceil \cdot \rceil$ and $\lfloor \cdot \rceil$, respectively. For $q \in \mathbb{Z}$ and $q > 1$, we identify the ring $\mathbb{Z}_q$ with the representative interval $(-q/2, q/2]$. These notations are extended to elements of $\mathcal{R}$ by applying them coefficient-wise. We use $a \leftarrow S$ to denote uniform sampling from the set S. Sampling according to a distribution χ is denoted by $a \leftarrow \chi$. We denote χ_{err} as a subgaussian distribution with parameter σ.

2.1 Basic Lattice-Based Encryption

For positive integers q and n, the basic LWE encryption of $m \in \mathbb{Z}$ under the secret key $\mathbf{s} \leftarrow \chi_{\mathsf{key}}$ is defined as

$$\mathrm{LWE}_{q,\mathbf{s}}(m) = (\mathbf{a}, b) = (\mathbf{a}, -\langle \mathbf{a}, \mathbf{s} \rangle + m + e) \in \mathbb{Z}_q^{n+1},$$

where $\mathbf{a} \leftarrow \mathbb{Z}_q^n$ and the error term $e \leftarrow \chi_{\mathsf{err}}$. In some cases, we may omit the subscripts q and $\mathbf{s}$ when they are understood from the context.

For an integer Q and a power of two N, the basic RLWE encryption of $\mathbf{m} \in \mathcal{R}$ under the secret key $\mathbf{z} \leftarrow \chi_{\mathsf{key}}$ is defined as

$$\mathrm{RLWE}_{Q,\mathbf{z}}(\mathbf{m}) := (\mathbf{a}, -\mathbf{a} \cdot \mathbf{z} + \mathbf{e} + \mathbf{m}) \in \mathcal{R}_Q^2,$$

where $\mathbf{a} \leftarrow \mathcal{R}_Q$, and for each coefficient e_i of $\mathbf{e}$ is sampled from χ_{err}, with $i \in [0, N-1]$.

As in the case of LWE, we will often omit the subscripts Q and $\mathbf{z}$ when they are clear from the context. Gadget decomposition plays a crucial role in maintaining error control within Fully Homomorphic Encryption (FHE) schemes. There are two distinct types of gadget decomposition, which differ in the choice of the gadget vectors.

Canonical Gadget Decomposition: The gadget vector of the canonical gadget decomposition is consisted with the power of B, where $\mathbf{g} = (1, B, B^2, ..., B^{d-1})$. Here, $d = \lceil \log_B Q \rceil$ is referred to as the gadget length, and B is the gadget base. Using this gadget vector, any ring polynomial $\mathbf{t}$ can be decomposed into a sequence of polynomials $(\mathbf{t}_0, ..., \mathbf{t}_{d-1})$ such that the absolute values of the coefficients of each polynomial $\mathbf{t_i}$ are bounded by $B/2$. This decomposition satisfies the equation $\sum_i g_i \mathbf{t_i} = \mathbf{t}$.

Approximate Gadget Decomposition: Approximate gadget decomposition generalizes the canonical gadget decomposition. When $B^d < Q$, the decomposition of a ring element is no longer exact. In this case, the decomposition error is defined as $\varepsilon_{\text{gadget}}(\mathbf{t}) = \sum_i g_i \mathbf{t_i} - \mathbf{t}$, with ϵ denoting its infinite norm, i.e., $\epsilon = \| \sum_i g_i \mathbf{t_i} - \mathbf{t} \|_\infty$. In the approximate decomposition, the gadget vector is typically chosen as $\mathbf{g} = (\lceil Q/B^d \rceil, \lceil Q/B^d \rceil B, ..., \lceil Q/B^d \rceil B^{d-1})$. Each ring polynomial $\mathbf{t}$ is then decomposed into a set of polynomials $(\mathbf{t}_0, ..., \mathbf{t}_{d-1})$ where the absolute values of the coefficients of each $\mathbf{t}_i$ are still bounded by $B/2$, and the infinite norm of decomposition error ϵ satisfies $\epsilon \leq \frac{1}{2} \lceil Q/B^d \rceil$.

We adapt the definitions of RLWE$'$ and RGSW from [24]. Given a gadget vector $\mathbf{g}$, we define $\mathrm{RLWE}'_\mathbf{z}(\mathbf{m})$ and $\mathrm{RGSW}_\mathbf{z}(\mathbf{m})$ as follows

$$\mathrm{RLWE}'_\mathbf{z}(\mathbf{m}) := (\mathrm{RLWE}_\mathbf{z}(g_0 \cdot \mathbf{m}), \mathrm{RLWE}_\mathbf{z}(g_1 \cdot \mathbf{m}), \cdots, \mathrm{RLWE}_\mathbf{z}(g_{d_g-1} \cdot \mathbf{m})) \in \mathcal{R}_Q^{2d},$$
$$\mathrm{RGSW}_\mathbf{z}(\mathbf{m}) := (\mathrm{RLWE}'_\mathbf{z}(\mathbf{z} \cdot \mathbf{m}), \mathrm{RLWE}'_\mathbf{z}(\mathbf{m})) \in \mathcal{R}_Q^{2\times 2d}.$$

Gadget Product: The scalar multiplication between an element in $\mathcal{R}_Q$ and RLWE$'$ ciphertext

$$\odot : \mathcal{R}_Q \times \mathrm{RLWE}' \to \mathrm{RLWE}$$

is defined as

$$\begin{aligned} t \odot \mathrm{RLWE}'_{\mathbf{z}}(\mathbf{m}) &= \langle (\mathbf{t}_0, \cdots, \mathbf{t}_{d_g-1}), (\mathrm{RLWE}_{\mathbf{z}}(g_0 \cdot \mathbf{m}), \cdots, \mathrm{RLWE}_{\mathbf{z}}(g_{d_g-1} \cdot \mathbf{m})) \rangle \\ &= \sum_{i=0}^{d_g-1} \mathbf{t}_i \cdot \mathrm{RLWE}_{\mathbf{z}}(g_i \cdot \mathbf{m}) \\ &= \mathrm{RLWE}_{\mathbf{z}}(\mathbf{t} \cdot \mathbf{m}) \in \mathcal{R}_Q^2. \end{aligned}$$

Let $\mathbf{e}_i$ be the error in $\mathrm{RLWE}_{\mathbf{z}}(g_i \cdot \mathbf{m})$. Then, the error after multiplication is given by $\sum_{i=0}^{d_g-1} \mathbf{t}_i \cdot \mathbf{e}_i + \epsilon_{\mathsf{gadget}}(t)$, where the total error remains small if both $\mathbf{t}_i$ and $\mathbf{e}_i$ are small.

Lemma 1 (Kim et al. [19]). *Let B and d denote the base and the length of the gadget decomposition, respectively, then the error variance of the result of the gadget product is bounded by*

$$\sigma^2_{\odot,input} \le dN\frac{B^2}{12}\sigma^2_{input} + \frac{1}{3}\|\mathbf{m}\|_2^2\epsilon^2,$$

where σ^2_{input} is the error variance of the input RLWE$'$ *ciphertext.*

Lemma 1 is derived from [19] proposition 1 using the fact that $\epsilon \le \frac{1}{2}\lceil \frac{q}{B^\ell} \rceil$. When applying canonical gadget decomposition, the error term $\frac{1}{3}\|\mathbf{m}\|_2^2\epsilon^2$ is absent.

External Product: The multiplication between RLWE and RGSW ciphertexts

$$\circledast : \mathrm{RLWE} \times \mathrm{RGSW} \to \mathrm{RLWE}$$

is defined as

$$\begin{aligned} \mathrm{RLWE}_{\mathbf{z}}(\mathbf{m}_1) \circledast \mathrm{RGSW}_{\mathbf{z}}(\mathbf{m}_2) &= (\mathbf{a}, \mathbf{b}) \circledast \left(\mathrm{RLWE}'_z(\mathbf{z} \cdot \mathbf{m}_2), \mathrm{RLWE}'_z(\mathbf{m}_2)\right) \\ &= \mathbf{a} \odot \mathrm{RLWE}'_{\mathbf{z}}(\mathbf{z} \cdot \mathbf{m}_2) + \mathbf{b} \odot \mathrm{RLWE}'_{\mathbf{z}}(\mathbf{m}_2) \\ &= \mathrm{RLWE}_{\mathbf{z}}(\mathbf{m}_1 \cdot \mathbf{m}_2 + \mathbf{e}_1 \cdot \mathbf{m}_2) \in \mathcal{R}_Q^2. \end{aligned}$$

This result represents an encryption of the product $\mathbf{m}_1 \cdot \mathbf{m}_2$ with an additional error term $\mathbf{e}_1 \cdot \mathbf{m}_2$ under the RLWE scheme. To ensure that $\mathrm{RLWE}_{\mathbf{z}}(\mathbf{m}_1) \circledast \mathrm{RGSW}_{\mathbf{z}}(\mathbf{m}_2) \approx \mathrm{RLWE}_{\mathbf{z}}(\mathbf{m}_1 \cdot \mathbf{m}_2)$, it is crucial to keep the error term $\mathbf{e}_1 \cdot \mathbf{m}_2$ small. This can be achieved by using monomials $\mathbf{m}_2 = \pm X^v$ as messages.

Key Switching in RLWE: Given an key switching key $\mathsf{SWK} = \mathrm{RLWE}'_{\mathbf{z_2}}(\mathbf{z_1})$, then the key switching algorithm $\mathsf{KS}_{\mathbf{z_1} \to \mathbf{z_2}} : \mathrm{RLWE}_{\mathbf{z_1}}(\mathbf{m}) \to \mathrm{RLWE}_{\mathbf{z_2}}(\mathbf{m})$ is defined by

$$\begin{aligned} \mathsf{KS}_{\mathbf{z_1} \to \mathbf{z_2},}(\mathrm{RLWE}_{\mathbf{z_1}}(\mathbf{m}), \mathsf{SWK}) &= \mathbf{a} \odot \mathrm{RLWE}'_{\mathbf{z_2}}(\mathbf{z_1}) + (0, \mathbf{b}) \\ &= \mathrm{RLWE}_{\mathbf{z_2}}(\mathbf{a} \cdot \mathbf{z_1} + \mathbf{b}) \\ &= \mathrm{RLWE}_{\mathbf{z_2}}(\mathbf{m}), \end{aligned}$$

where $(\mathbf{a}, \mathbf{b}) = \mathrm{RLWE}_{\mathbf{z_1}}(\mathbf{m})$.

Homomorphic Automorphism: For $t \in \mathbb{Z}_{2N}^*$, an automorphism $\psi_t\colon \mathcal{R} \to \mathcal{R}$ is defined as $\mathbf{a}(X) \to \mathbf{a}(X^t)$, where $\mathcal{R}$ is the ring of polynomials. The associated automorphism key is given by $\mathsf{ATK}_t = \mathrm{RLWE}'_{\mathbf{z}}(\mathbf{z}(X^t))$, the homomorphic automorphism $\mathsf{HomAuto}_t : \mathrm{RLWE}_{\mathbf{z}}(\mathbf{m}) \to \mathrm{RLWE}_{\mathbf{z}}(\mathbf{m}(X^t))$ is defined by

$$\begin{aligned}\mathsf{HomAuto}_t(\mathrm{RLWE}_{\mathbf{z}}(\mathbf{m}), \mathsf{ATK}_t) &= \mathbf{a}(X^t) \odot \mathrm{RLWE}'_{\mathbf{z}}(\mathbf{z}(X^t)) + (0, \mathbf{b}(X^t)) \\ &= \mathrm{RLWE}_{\mathbf{z}}\left(\mathbf{a}(X^t) \cdot \mathbf{z}(X^t) + \mathbf{b}(X^t)\right) \\ &= \mathrm{RLWE}_{\mathbf{z}}\left(\mathbf{m}(X^t)\right),\end{aligned}$$

where $(\mathbf{a}, \mathbf{b}) = \mathrm{RLWE}_{\mathbf{z}}(\mathbf{m})$.

2.2 FHEW-Like Bootstrapping

We briefly explain FHEW-like bootstrapping for NAND gates [12,24]. FHEW like NAND gate bootstrapping starts with two $\mathrm{LWE}_{q,\mathbf{s}}$ ciphertexts with a small modulus q and adds them together. After performing blind rotation and extraction procedures, we obtain an LWE encryption of the NAND gate operation on the plaintexts, now with a higher ciphertext modulus Q. As described in [24], the core bootstrapping procedure based on an accumulator is first followed by modulus switching, which changes the parameters from (Q, N) to (Q_{ks}, N). Then, key switching is performed, changing the parameters from (Q_{ks}, N) to (Q_{ks}, n). Finally, another modulus switching step reduces the parameters from (Q_{ks}, n) to (q, n). The full bootstrapping procedure is illustrated in Fig. 1. We focus on the blind rotation part and refer to [24] for further details on the other steps of the FHEW-like bootstrapping process.

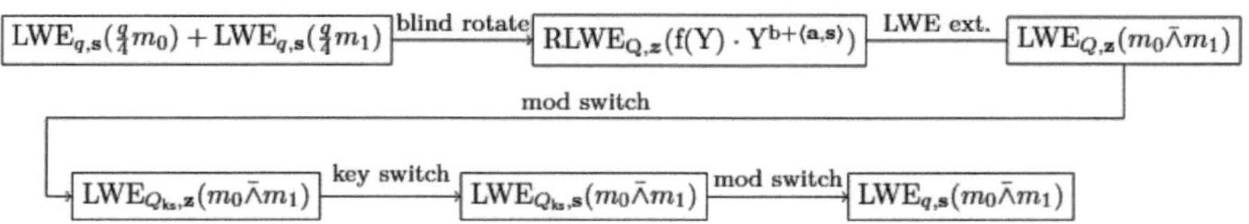

Fig. 1. NAND gate bootstrapping procedure of FHEW scheme

The core of bootstrapping algorithm can be divided into two steps:

Blind Rotation. For $q|2N$, let $Y = X^{\frac{2N}{q}}$. Blind rotation is an algorithm which takes as input a ring element $f(Y) \in \mathcal{R}_Q$, an $\mathrm{LWE}_{q,\mathbf{s}}$ ciphertext $(\mathbf{a}, b) \in \mathbb{Z}_q^{n+1}$, and blind rotation keys $\mathsf{BRK}_{\mathbf{z},\mathbf{s}}$ corresponding to secrets $\mathbf{z}$ and $\mathbf{s}$ and outputs an RLWE ciphertext:

$$\mathrm{RLWE}_{\mathbf{z}}\left(f(Y) \cdot Y^{b+\langle \mathbf{a},\mathbf{s}\rangle}\right) \in \mathcal{R}_Q^2.$$

Three different blind rotation algorithms are introduced in [11,12,20]. These methods are referred to as "AP blind rotation", 'GINX blind rotation", and

"LMKC+ blind rotation", respectively. All of these algorithms make use of the properties of RGSW ciphertexts as described earlier. In this section, we describe the blind rotation algorithm for LMKC+.

LMKC+ Automorphism-Based Blind Rotation. Under the observation that $\mathbb{Z}_{2N}^* \cong \mathbb{Z}_{N/2} \otimes \mathbb{Z}_2$, if $a_i \in \mathbb{Z}_{2N}^*$ for all $i \in [0, n-1]$, then each a_i can be expressed in terms of the generators $\{g, -1\}$. In the case of modulus $2N$, consider the decomposition of the sum $\sum_i a_i s_i$ as follows

$$\sum_i a_i s_i = \sum_{j \in I_0^+} s_j + \cdots + g\left(\sum_{j \in I_{N/2-1}^+} s_j - g\left(\sum_{j \in I_0^-} s_j + \cdots + g\left(\sum_{j \in I_{N/2-1}^-} s_j\right)\right)\right) \mod 2N,$$

where $I_\ell^+ = \{i : a_i = g^\ell\}$ and $I_\ell^- = \{i : a_i = -g^\ell\}$, for $\ell \in [0, N/2-1]$. The blind rotation keys are generated as

$$\mathsf{BSK} = \{\mathsf{BSK}_i = \mathrm{RGSW}_{\mathbf{z}}(X^{s_i})\}_i,$$

Algorithm 1. Blind Rotation: LMKC+ [20] for $q = N$

Input: $(\mathbf{a}, b)$, acc, $\{\mathsf{BSK}_i\}_{i\in[0,n-1]}$, $\mathsf{BRK_{sum}}$, $\{\mathsf{ATK}_{g^u}\}_{u\in[1,w]}$, ATK_{-g}
Output: $\mathbf{c}$

```
a ← 2a + 1 mod 2N
v ← 0
for (ℓ = N/2 − 1; ℓ > 0; ℓ = ℓ − 1) do
    for j ∈ I_ℓ^− do
        acc = acc ⊛ BSK_j
    v ← v + 1
    if (I_{ℓ−1}^− ≠ ∅ or v = w or ℓ = 1) then
        acc = HomAuto_{g^v}(acc, ATK_{g^v})
        v ← 0
for j ∈ I_0^− do
    acc = acc ⊛ BSK_j
acc = HomAuto_{−g}(acc, ATK_{−g});
for (ℓ = N/2 − 1; ℓ > 0; ℓ = ℓ − 1) do
    for j ∈ I_ℓ^+ do
        acc = acc ⊛ BSK_j
    v ← v + 1
    if (I_{ℓ−1}^+ ≠ ∅ or v = w or ℓ = 1) then
        acc = HomAuto_{g^v}(acc, ATK_{g^v})
        v ← 0
for j ∈ I_0^+ do
    acc = acc ⊛ BSK_j
acc = acc ⊛ BRK_sum
return c = acc
```

where $i \in [0, n-1]$, and homomorphic automorphism keys are generated as $\{\mathsf{ATK}_{g^u} = \mathrm{RLWE}'_{\mathbf{z}}(\mathbf{z}(X^{g^u}))\}_{u \in [1,w]}$, $\mathsf{ATK}_{-g} = \mathrm{RLWE}'_{\mathbf{z}}(\mathbf{z}(X^{-g}))$. In the algorithm, the accumulator acc is initiated as

$$\mathsf{acc} = \mathrm{RLWE}_{\mathbf{z}}(f(Y) \cdot Y^b) = (0, f(X^{-g}) \cdot X^{-gb}).$$

The blind rotation algorithm proceeds by first multiplying (via the external product) the accumulator by BSK_j for all $j \in I^-_{N/2-1}$, then applying $\mathsf{HomeAuto}_g$ and repeating the process for each index set I. However, after multiplying with I^-_0, the algorithm applies $\mathsf{HomAuto}_{-g}$ instead. The final results is $\mathrm{RLWE}_{\mathbf{z}}(f(Y) \cdot Y^{b+\sum_i a_i s_i})$. By utilizing $w+1$ pre-stored automorphism keys, the number of automorphisms is reduced from n to $\frac{w-1}{w}\kappa + \frac{N}{w}\ \kappa \approx N(1-e^{-n/N})$. Since the round-to-odd operation may lead to a significant increase in noise, we focus on the Algorithm 6 in LMKC+ [20], which introduces an additional key $\mathsf{BRK}_{\mathsf{sum}} = \mathrm{RGSW}_{\mathbf{z}}(X^{-\sum_i s_i})$. The full procedure for LMKC+ blind rotation is described in Algorithm 1.

Additionally, LLWW+ method further reduces the number of automorphisms by merging the symmetric sets. For a detailed description of the specific algorithm, refer to [21].

Sample Extraction. The algorithm $\mathsf{SampleExtract}$ takes as input an RLWE ciphertext $\mathbf{c} = (\mathbf{a}, \mathbf{b}) \in \mathrm{RLWE}_{Q,\mathbf{z}}(\mathbf{m})$, and outputs an $\mathrm{LWE}_{Q,\mathbf{z}}(m_0)$, where m_0 denotes the constant term of $\mathbf{m}$.

3 New Blind Rotation Algorithms

3.1 Description

In this paper, we first define a set $S = \{k \cdot 2^\theta + 1 \in \mathbb{Z}_{2N} | k = 0, ..., 2N/2^\theta - 1\}$ for $\theta \geq 1$. It is known that the elements of S form a multiplicative group. Next, consider an LWE ciphertext $(\mathbf{a}, b) \in S^{n+1}$. Define the set $A = \{w_0, w_1, ..., w_L\}$, where w_i represents the distinct elements of the vector $\mathbf{a}$, ordered such that $w_0 < w_1 < ... < w_L$. We define $w_{L+1} = 1$, $I_l = \{i : a_i = w_l\}$ and $w'_l w_l \equiv 1 \mod 2N$ for $l \in [0, L]$.

The blind rotation keys are generated as

$$\mathsf{BSK} = \{\mathsf{BSK}_{i,t} = \mathrm{RGSW}_{\mathbf{z}}(X^{s_i \cdot t})\}_{i,t},$$

where $i \in [0, n-1]$, $t \in S$. The accumulator acc is initialized to the trivial ciphertext

$$\mathsf{acc} = \mathrm{RLWE}_{\mathbf{z}(X^{w'_1})}(f(X^{w'_1}) \cdot X^{bw'_1}) = (0, f(X^{w'_1}) \cdot X^{bw'_1}).$$

By the above definition, we have the decomposition

$$\sum_i a_i s_i = w_0 \left(\sum_{j \in I_0} s_j \right) + w_1 \left(\sum_{j \in I_1} s_j \right) + ... + w_L \left(\sum_{j \in I_L} s_j \right) \mod 2N.$$

For w_0, $j \in I_0$, we apply the automorphism $X \to X^{w'_1}$ to BSK_{j,w_0}, the corresponding ciphertext is given by

Algorithm 2. Blind Rotation for $a_i = k \cdot 2^\theta + 1(\mathsf{BR}_2)$

Input: $(\mathbf{a}, b)$, acc, $\{\mathsf{BSK}_{i,t}\}_{i\in[0,n-1],t\in S}$
Output: $\mathbf{c}$

for $(l = 0; l \leq L; l = l + 1)$ **do**
  for $j \in I_l$ **do**
    $\mathsf{BSK}'_j = \psi_{w'_{l+1}}(\mathsf{BSK}_{j,w_l})$
    $\mathsf{acc} \leftarrow \mathsf{acc} \circledast \mathsf{BSK}'_j$.
  if $l < L$ **then**
    $\mathsf{acc} = \psi_{w_{l+1}w'_{l+2}}(\mathsf{acc})$
return $\mathbf{c} = \mathsf{acc}$

$$\mathsf{BSK}'_j = \mathrm{RGSW}_{\mathbf{z}(X^{w'_1})}(X^{w_0 w'_1 s_j}).$$

The accumulator acc is updated sequentially as

$$\mathsf{acc} \leftarrow \mathsf{acc} \circledast \mathsf{BSK}'_j,$$

for all $j \in I_0$. This process results in the ciphertext

$$\mathsf{acc} = \mathrm{RLWE}_{\mathbf{z}(X^{w'_1})}\left(f(X^{w'_1}) \cdot X^{bw'_1 + w_0 w'_1(\sum_{j\in I_0} s_j)}\right).$$

Finally, we apply the automorphism $X \to X^{w_1 w'_2}$ to acc, yielding the updated ciphertext

$$\mathsf{acc} = \mathrm{RLWE}_{\mathbf{z}(X^{w'_2})}\left(f(X^{w'_2}) \cdot X^{bw'_2 + w_0 w'_2(\sum_{j\in I_0} s_j)}\right).$$

This process continues in a similar fashion, performing continuous updates on subsequent values of w_l, where $l \in [0, L]$. Throughout the process, the exponent r in the key $\mathbf{z}(X^r)$ of RLWE ciphertext adaptively updates with w'_i. A detailed description of the full procedure for blind rotation can be found in Algorithm 2.

Algorithm 2 represents the most efficient FHEW bootstrapping scheme both theoretically and practically, exhibiting the same time complexity as the binary GINX method. It requires only n external products and no key switching for its execution. Two considerations to note are that the key size can become relatively large, and the naive sparse approach may lead to a significant increase in noise, as similarly observed in the WWLL+ method. To mitigate the key size expansion and prevent the noise growth induced by the naive sparse approach [27], we propose two optimized algorithms based on the specific decomposition of the sum $\sum_i a_i s_i$.

Memory Efficient Algorithm. As discussed in LMKC+ method, consider the decomposition of the sum $\sum_i a_i s_i$ as follows

$$\sum_i a_i s_i = \sum_{j \in I_0^+} s_j + \cdots + g\left(\sum_{j \in I_{N/2-1}^+} s_j - g\left(\sum_{j \in I_0^-} s_j + \cdots + g\left(\sum_{j \in I_{N/2-1}^-} s_j\right)\right)\right) \mod 2N.$$

Recall that the objective of blind rotation is to homomorphically compute

$$f(Y) \cdot Y^{b+\sum_i a_i s_i} = f(X^{\frac{2N}{q}}) \cdot X^{\frac{2N}{q}b+\sum_i (\frac{2N}{q}a_i+1)s_i - \sum_i s_i}.$$

When $\frac{2N}{q} = 2^\theta$, $\theta \geq 1$, it follows that each term $\frac{2N}{q}a_i+1$ is odd. The accumulator acc is initialized to the trivial ciphertext

$$\mathsf{acc} = \mathrm{RLWE}_{\mathbf{z}}(f(Y^{-g}) \cdot Y^{-bg}) = (0, f(Y^{-g}) \cdot Y^{-bg}) = (0, f(X^{-2^\theta g}) \cdot X^{-2^\theta g}).$$

Building on the window size optimization method, we introduce a threshold for performing key switching. Specifically, a key switching operation is triggered when the accumulator exponent r in the key $\mathbf{z}(X^r)$ reaches or exceeds a threshold w. The exponent r is adaptively updated throughout the process. Accordingly, the keys required for blind rotation include automorphism keys ATK_{-g}, key switching keys

$$\mathsf{SWK} = \{\mathsf{SWK}_v = \mathrm{RLWE}'_{\mathbf{z}}(z(X^{g^v}))\}_v,$$

where $v \in [1, 2w-1]$, and blind rotation keys

$$\mathsf{BRK_{sum}} = \mathrm{RGSW}_{\mathbf{z}}(X^{-\sum_i s_i}),\ \mathsf{BSK} = \{\mathsf{BSK}_{i,t} = \mathrm{RGSW}_{\mathbf{z}(X^{g^t})}(X^{s_i})\}_{i,t},$$

where $i \in [0, n-1]$, $t \in [0, w-1]$. The full procedure of blind rotation is described in Algorithm 3.

Computation Efficient Algorithm. Similar to the approach used in the WWLL+ method, by merging the symmetric sets, we have the following decomposition under the condition that $a_i \in \mathbb{Z}_{2N}^*$ for all $i \in [0, n-1]$

$$\sum_i a_i s_i = \sum_{j \in I_0^+} s_j - \sum_{k \in I_0^-} s_j + \cdots + g\left(\sum_{j \in I_{N/2-1}^+} s_j - \sum_{k \in I_{N/2-1}^-} s_j\right) \mod 2N.$$

Algorithm 3. Memory Efficient Blind Rotation for $\frac{2N}{q} = 2^\theta, \theta \geq 1$

Input: $(\mathbf{a}, b)$, acc, $\{\mathsf{BSK}_{i,t}\}_{i\in[0,n-1],t\in[0,w-1]}$, $\{\mathsf{SWK}_v\}_{v\in[1,2w-1]}$, $\mathsf{BRK}_{\mathsf{sum}}$
Output: $\mathbf{c}$
$\mathbf{a} \leftarrow 2^\theta \mathbf{a} + 1 \mod 2N$
$v \leftarrow 0,\ r \leftarrow 0$
for $(\ell = \frac{N}{2} - 1;\ \ell > 0;\ \ell = \ell - 1)$ **do**
  for $j \in I_\ell^-$ **do**
    $\mathsf{acc} = \mathsf{acc} \circledast \mathsf{BSK}_{j,r}$
  $v \leftarrow v + 1$
  if $(v = w \text{ or } \ell = 1)$ **then**
    $\mathsf{acc} = \psi_{g^v}(\mathsf{acc}),\ \mathsf{acc} = \mathsf{KS}_{\mathbf{z}(X^{g^{r+v}})\to\mathbf{z}(X)}(\mathsf{acc}, \mathsf{SWK}_{r+v}),\ v \leftarrow 0,\ r \leftarrow 0$
  else if $I_{\ell-1}^- \neq \emptyset$ **then**
    $\mathsf{acc} = \psi_{g^v}(\mathsf{acc}),\ r \leftarrow r + v,\ v \leftarrow 0$
    if $r \geq w$ **then**
      $\mathsf{acc} = \mathsf{KS}_{\mathbf{z}(X^{g^r})\to\mathbf{z}(X)}(\mathsf{acc}, \mathsf{SWK}_r),\ r \leftarrow 0$
for $j \in I_0^-$ **do**
  $\mathsf{acc} = \mathsf{acc} \circledast \mathsf{BSK}_{j,0}$
$\mathsf{acc} = \mathsf{HomAuto}_{-g}(\mathsf{acc}, \mathsf{ATK}_{-g})$
for $(\ell = \frac{N}{2} - 1;\ \ell > 0;\ \ell = \ell - 1)$ **do**
  for $j \in I_\ell^+$ **do**
    $\mathsf{acc} = \mathsf{acc} \circledast \mathsf{BSK}_{j,r}$
  $v \leftarrow v + 1$
  if $(v = w \text{ or } \ell = 1)$ **then**
    $\mathsf{acc} = \psi_{g^v}(\mathsf{acc}),\ \mathsf{acc} = \mathsf{KS}_{\mathbf{z}(X^{g^{r+v}})\to\mathbf{z}(X)}(\mathsf{acc}, \mathsf{SWK}_{r+v}),\ v \leftarrow 0,\ r \leftarrow 0$
  else if $I_{\ell-1}^+ \neq \emptyset$ **then**
    $\mathsf{acc} = \psi_{g^v}(\mathsf{acc}),\ r \leftarrow r + v,\ v \leftarrow 0$
    if $r \geq w$ **then**
      $\mathsf{acc} = \mathsf{KS}_{\mathbf{z}(X^{g^r})\to\mathbf{z}(X)}(\mathsf{acc}, \mathsf{SWK}_r),\ r \leftarrow 0$
for $j \in I_0^+$ **do**
  $\mathsf{acc} = \mathsf{acc} \circledast \mathsf{BSK}_{j,0}$
$\mathsf{acc} = \mathsf{acc} \circledast \mathsf{BRK}_{\mathsf{sum}}$
return $\mathbf{c} = \mathsf{acc}$

The accumulator acc is initialized to the trivial ciphertext

$$\mathsf{acc} = \mathrm{RLWE}_{\mathbf{z}}(f(Y^g) \cdot Y^{bg}) = (0, f(Y^g) \cdot Y^{bg}) = (0, f(X^{2^\theta g}) \cdot X^{2^\theta g}).$$

As with Memory Efficient Algorithm, we introduce the same threshold for performing key switching. The key switching keys are generated as

$$\mathsf{SWK} = \{\mathsf{SWK}_v = \mathrm{RLWE}'_{\mathbf{z}}(\mathbf{z}(X^{g^u}))\}_v,$$

where $v \in [1, 2w-1]$. The blind rotation keys are generated as

$$\mathsf{BRK}_{\mathsf{sum}} = \mathrm{RGSW}\mathbf{z}(X^{-\sum_i s_i}),\ \mathsf{BSK}^{\pm} = \{\mathsf{BSK}_{i,t}^{\pm} = \mathrm{RGSW}_{\mathbf{z}(X^{g^t})}(X^{\pm s_i})\}_{i,t},$$

where $i \in [0, n-1]$, $t \in [0, w-1]$. The full procedure is described in Algorithm 4.

Algorithm 4. Computation Efficient Blind Rotation for $\frac{2N}{q} = 2^\theta, \theta \geq 1$

Input: $(\mathbf{a}, b)$, acc, $\{\mathsf{BSK}^{\pm}{}_{i,t}\}_{i\in[0,n-1],t\in[0,w-1]}$, $\mathsf{BRK}_{\mathsf{sum}}$, $\{\mathsf{SWK}_v\}_{v\in[1,2w-1]}$
Output: $\mathbf{c}$

$\mathbf{a} \leftarrow 2^\theta \mathbf{a} + 1 \mod 2N$
$v \leftarrow 0,\ r \leftarrow 0$
for $(\ell = \frac{N}{2} - 1;\ \ell > 0;\ \ell = \ell - 1)$ **do**
  for $j \in I_\ell^+$ or $k \in I_\ell^-$ **do**
    if $j \in I_\ell^+$ **then**
      $\mathsf{acc} = \mathsf{acc} \circledast \mathsf{BSK}^+_{j,r}$
    if $k \in I_\ell^-$ **then**
      $\mathsf{acc} = \mathsf{acc} \circledast \mathsf{BSK}^-_{k,r}$
  $v \leftarrow v + 1$
  if $v = w$ or $\ell = 1$ **then**
    $\mathsf{acc} = \psi_{g^v}(\mathsf{acc}),\ \mathsf{acc} = \mathsf{KS}_{\mathbf{z}(X^{g^{r+v}})\to\mathbf{z}(X)}(\mathsf{acc}, \mathsf{SWK}_{r+v}),\ v \leftarrow 0,\ r \leftarrow 0$
  else if $I_{\ell-1}^+ \neq \emptyset$ or $I_{\ell-1}^- \neq \emptyset$ **then**
    $\mathsf{acc} = \psi_{g^v}(\mathsf{acc}),\ r \leftarrow r + v,\ v \leftarrow 0$
    if $r \geq w$ **then**
      $\mathsf{acc} = \mathsf{KS}_{\mathbf{z}(X^{g^r})\to\mathbf{z}(X)}(\mathsf{acc}, \mathsf{SWK}_r),\ r \leftarrow 0$
for $j \in I_0^+$ or $k \in I_0^-$ **do**
  if $j \in I_0^+$ **then**
    $\mathsf{acc} = \mathsf{acc} \circledast \mathsf{BSK}^+_{j,0}$
  if $k \in I_0^-$ **then**
    $\mathsf{acc} = \mathsf{acc} \circledast \mathsf{BSK}^-_{k,0}$
$\mathsf{acc} = \mathsf{acc} \circledast \mathsf{BRK}_{\mathsf{sum}}$
return $\mathbf{c} = \mathsf{acc}$

3.2 Correctness

In this subsection, we present the correctness theorems for Algorithm 2, 3 and 4. Formal proofs of these theorems are provided in the full version of the paper [29].

Theorem 1. *Let* $S = \{k \cdot 2^\theta + 1 \in \mathbb{Z}_{2N} | k = 0, ..., 2N/2^\theta - 1\}$, *where* $\theta \geq 1$. *For the procedure described in Algorithm 2, given an* LWE *ciphertext* $(\mathbf{a}, b) \in S^{n+1}$, *an initial accumulator* $\mathsf{acc} = (0, f(X^{w_1'}) \cdot X^{bw_1'})$, *and the blind rotation keys* $\mathsf{BSK} = \{\mathrm{RGSW}_{\mathbf{z}}(X^{s_i \cdot t})\}_{i\in[0,n-1],t\in S}$, *the resulting ciphertext* $\mathbf{c}$ *will belong to the set* $\mathrm{RLWE}_{\mathbf{z}}\left(f(X) \cdot X^{b+\langle \mathbf{a},\mathbf{s}\rangle}\right)$.

Theorem 2. *Given Algorithm 3, on input a ciphertext* $(\mathbf{a}, b) \in \mathrm{LWE}_{q,\mathbf{s}}(m)$, *an accumulator* $\mathsf{acc} = (0, f(Y^{-g}) \cdot Y^{-bg})$, *keys* $\mathsf{SWK} = \{\mathrm{RLWE}'_{\mathbf{z}}(\mathbf{z}(X^{g^v}))\}_{v\in[1,2w-1]}$, $\mathsf{BSK} = \{\mathrm{RGSW}_{\mathbf{z}(X^{g^t})}(X^{s_i})\}_{i\in[0,n-1],t\in[0,w-1]}$ *and* $\mathsf{BRK}_{\mathsf{sum}} = \mathrm{RGSW}_{\mathbf{z}}(X^{-\sum_i s_i})$, *outputs a ciphertext* $\mathbf{c} \in \mathrm{RLWE}_{\mathbf{z}}\left(f(Y) \cdot Y^{b+\langle \mathbf{a},\mathbf{s}\rangle}\right)$.

Theorem 3. *Given Algorithm 4, on input a ciphertext* $(\mathbf{a}, b) \in \mathrm{LWE}_{q,\mathbf{s}}(m)$, *an accumulator* $\mathsf{acc} = (0, f(Y^g) \cdot Y^{bg})$, *keys* $\mathsf{SWK} = \{\mathrm{RLWE}'_{\mathbf{z}}\ (\mathbf{z}(X^{g^v}))\}_{v \in [1,2w-1]}$, $\mathsf{BSK}^{\pm} = \{\mathrm{RGSW}_{\mathbf{z}(X^{g^t})}(X^{\pm s_i})\}_{i \in [0,n-1], t \in [0,w-1]}$ *and* $\mathsf{BRK}_{\mathsf{sum}} = \mathrm{RGSW}_{\mathbf{z}}$ $(X^{-\sum_i s_i})$, *outputs a ciphertext* $\mathbf{c} \in \mathrm{RLWE}_{\mathbf{z}}(f(Y) \cdot Y^{b + \langle \mathbf{a}, \mathbf{s} \rangle})$.

4 Analysis and Comparisons

To compare the computational complexity and bootstrapping key size of several blind rotation schemes, we use the following parameters:

- q, LWE modulus;
- n, lattice parameter for the LWE scheme;
- Q, RLWE/RGSW modulus used in the core bootstrapping procedure based on an accumulator;
- N, ring dimension for RLWE/RGSW;
- B_{ep}, gadget base for $\circledast$, which breaks integers mod Q into d_{ep} digits;
- B_{ks}, gadget base, which breaks integers mod Q_{ks} into d_{ks} digits;
- B_r, gadget base in AP, which breaks integers mod q into d_r digits;
- w, window size of automorphisms;
- σ^2, error variance of a fresh RLWE ciphertext.

The comparison of computational complexity, key size, and error is summarized in Table 1. For the purpose of evaluating the performance of the blind rotation algorithms, we quantify their time complexity based on the number of $\mathcal{R} \odot \mathrm{RLWE}'$ products executed. A single RLWE$\circledast$RGSW operation requires two $\odot$ multiplications, whereas key switching only involves one $\odot$ multiplication. Consequently, both the $\circledast$ product and key switching can be effectively expressed in terms of the $\odot$ operation. The $\odot$ operation itself serves as a fundamental abstraction in FHEW, as well as in its torus variant TFHE [11]. In prior studies of FHEW-like homomorphic encryption schemes, an alternative complexity measure often used is the number of NTT/FFT operations performed by the algorithm. Since each $\odot$ operation requires $(d+1)$ NTT operations (with d being the dimension of a gadget vector), it is straightforward to convert the count of $\odot$ products to the number of required NTT operations.

In a similar fashion, we assess the memory consumption of the various blind rotation algorithms by evaluating the total number of RLWE' ciphertexts. The blind rotation keys in all algorithms consist of a series of RGSW and RLWE' ciphertexts, with each RGSW ciphertext encompassing two RLWE' ciphertexts.

To estimate the variance σ^2_{acc} introduced by the blind rotation procedure, we follow an approach described in [12,24]. The overall error for algorithms utilizing blind rotation, such as FHEW/TFHE bootstrapping [11,12,24] can be conveniently estimated using this variance. According to Lemma 1, the error variance induced by a single $\odot$ operation under canonical gadget decomposition is expressed as $\sigma^2_{\odot} = d_{\mathsf{ep}} N \frac{B^2_{\mathsf{ep}}}{12} \sigma^2$. For approximate gadget decomposition, the error variance introduced by the $\odot$ and $\circledast$ operations are, respectively, given as $\sigma'^2_{\odot} = d_{\mathsf{ep}} N \frac{B^2_{\mathsf{ep}}}{12} \sigma^2 + \frac{1}{3}\epsilon^2_{\mathsf{ep}}$ and $\sigma'^2_{\circledast} = d_{\mathsf{ep}} N \frac{B^2_{\mathsf{ep}}}{6} \sigma^2 + \frac{N\sigma^2+1}{3}\epsilon^2_{\mathsf{ep}}$ for Gaussian secrets.

In AP, the operation $\circledast$ is executed by encrypting the monomial with RGSW, which results in an additive error characterized by a variance of $2 \cdot \sigma_{\odot}^2$. In LMKC+ and LLWW+ methods, the homomorphic automorphism operation due to key switching introduces an additive error with variance $\sigma_{\odot}^2$. Thus the variance σ_{acc}^2 can be estimated as $\sigma_{\odot}^2$ multiplied by the number of $\odot$ operations. In GINX, due to the preprocessing of RGSW ciphertexts before $\circledast$ multiplications, each $\circledast$ introduces an additive error with variance $4 \cdot \sigma_{\odot}^2$.

Table 1. Complexity, key size, and error variance of each blind rotation technique. Key size (# keys) is the number of RLWE$'$ ciphertexts, and computational complexity (# mult) is the number of $\mathcal{R}_Q \odot$ RLWE$'$. $\kappa \approx N(1 - e^{-n/N})$.

Method	# keys	# mult	σ_{acc}^2
AP	$2d_r(B_r - 1)n$	$2d_r\left(1 - \frac{1}{B_r}\right)n$	$2d_r\left(1 - \frac{1}{B_r}\right)n\sigma_{\odot}^2$
GINX*	$4n$	$2n$	$8n\sigma_{\odot}^2$
LMKC+	$2n + w + 3$	$2n + \frac{w-1}{w}\kappa + \frac{N}{w} + 2$	$(n+1)\sigma'_{\circledast} + (\frac{w-1}{w}\kappa + \frac{N}{w})\sigma'^2_{\odot}$
LLWW+	$4n + w + 2$	$2n + \frac{w-1}{w}\kappa + \frac{N}{2w} + 2$	$(n+1)\sigma'^2_{\circledast} + (\frac{w-1}{w}\kappa + \frac{N}{2w})\sigma'^2_{\odot}$
Algorithm 3	$2nw + 2w + 1$	$2n + \frac{N}{w} + 2$	$(n+1)\sigma'^2_{\circledast} + \frac{N}{w}\sigma'^2_{\odot}$
Algorithm 4	$4nw + 2w + 1$	$2n + \frac{N}{2w} + 2$	$(n+1)\sigma'^2_{\circledast} + \frac{N}{2w}\sigma'^2_{\odot}$

As shown in Table 1, the total key size required by our algorithm for blind rotation and key switching is approximately w times larger than the original size prior to the improvement. However, the value of w required to achieve the optimal runtime for each algorithm may vary. Furthermore, the LWE key switching operation introduces an additional overhead. On the whole, the overall increase in bootstrapping key size remains modest.

Regarding time complexity, we observe that the theoretical complexity of blind rotation in Algorithm 3 and Algorithm 4 is higher than that of GINX*. However, this theoretical analysis should not be taken to mean that the algorithm with the smaller complexity expression will necessarily exhibit better runtime performance in practice. This discrepancy arises because different sets of parameters are used to achieve the same security level. For instance, while ternary GINX* exhibits the smallest theoretical expressions for computational complexity in this analysis, our proposed blind rotation algorithm outperforms GINX* in practice for two main reasons. First, our algorithm experiences less noise growth compared to GINX*, allowing it to operate with a smaller parameter set. Second, by leveraging Gaussian secrets, our algorithm can achieve the same level of security with a smaller value of n, without incurring any performance penalties.

5 Implementation

In this section, we present the implementation results of our new blind rotation algorithms. In our implementation, we optimize performance by selecting the appropriate window size to reduce the number of key switching operations. We compare our approach with the AP, GINX, LMKC+, and LLWW+ blind rotation techniques.

5.1 Parameter Sets

Similar to [10,12,24], the parameters are set to ensure a decryption failure upper bound of less than 2^{-32} while achieving the highest possible efficiency under each respective algorithm to ensure a fair comparison. Table 2 presents optimized parameter sets from the OpenFHE library for FHEW schemes. Based on these criteria, we propose the following 128-bit secure parameter sets: STD_128 for AP/GINX with ternary secrets, STD128_LMKC+ for LMKC+/Algorithm 3 with Gaussian secrets, and 128_OURS for Algorithm 4 with Gaussian secrets.

Table 2. Optimized paramater sets for FHEW schems [20]

Parameter set	key	n	q	N	Q	Q_{ks}	B_{ep}	B_{ks}	B_{r}	w
STD_128	ternary	503	1024	1024	2^{27}	2^{14}	512	32	32	×
STD128_LMKC+	$\sigma = 3.19$	447	1024	1024	2^{28}	2^{14}	1024	32	×	10
128_OURS	$\sigma = 3.19$	447	1024	1024	2^{28}	2^{14}	1024	32	×	5

Theoretical Estimates . We use the approach from [12] to write the error of a refreshed ciphertext as a Gaussian of standard deviation

$$\beta = \sqrt{\frac{q^2}{Q_{\mathsf{ks}^2}}\left(\frac{Q_{\mathsf{ks}}^2}{Q^2}\sigma_{\mathsf{acc}}^2 + \sigma_{\mathsf{ms1}}^2 + \sigma_{\mathsf{ks}}^2\right) + \sigma_{\mathsf{ms2}}^2},$$

where σ_{ms1}^2, σ_{ks}^2, and σ_{ms2}^2 denote the error variances introduced by modulus switching from Q to $Q_{\mathbf{ks}}$, key switching from $\boldsymbol{z}$ to $\boldsymbol{s}$, and modulus switching from $Q_{\mathbf{ks}}$ to q, respectively. We have

$$\sigma_{\mathrm{ms1}}^2 = \frac{\|\boldsymbol{z}\|^2 + 1}{12},\ \sigma_{\mathrm{ks}}^2 = \sigma^2\, N d_{\mathrm{ks}},\ \sigma_{\mathrm{ms2}}^2 = \frac{\|\boldsymbol{s}\|^2 + 1}{12}.$$

We assume $\|\boldsymbol{z}\| \leq \sqrt{2N/3}$ and $\|\boldsymbol{s}\| \leq \sqrt{2n/3}$ for ternary secrets [12], and $\|\boldsymbol{z}\| = \sqrt{N\sigma^2}$ and $\|\boldsymbol{s}\| = \sqrt{n\sigma^2}$ for Gaussian secrets. The ciphertext $\mathrm{LWE}_{q,\mathbf{s}}(q/4 \cdot m)$ exhibits the largest noise, characterized by a standard deviation of $\sqrt{2}\beta$. Decryption fails when the noise in $\mathrm{LWE}_{q,\mathbf{s}}(q/4 \cdot m)$ exceeds $q/8$. As a result, the decryption failure probability per NAND operation is given by 1-erf$(\frac{q/8}{2\beta})$.

5.2 Runtime Results

To ensure a fair comparison of the bootstrapping algorithms, we implemented all of them using identical libraries and computing environments. The evaluation was conducted on a system with an 11th Gen Intel(R) Core(TM) i5-1135G7 processor running at 2.40 GHz, under Ubuntu 24.04.1 LTS. The code was compiled using Clang 12, with the following CMake flags: NATIVE SIZE = 32, WITH_OPENMP = OFF, WITH_ NATIVEOPT = ON.

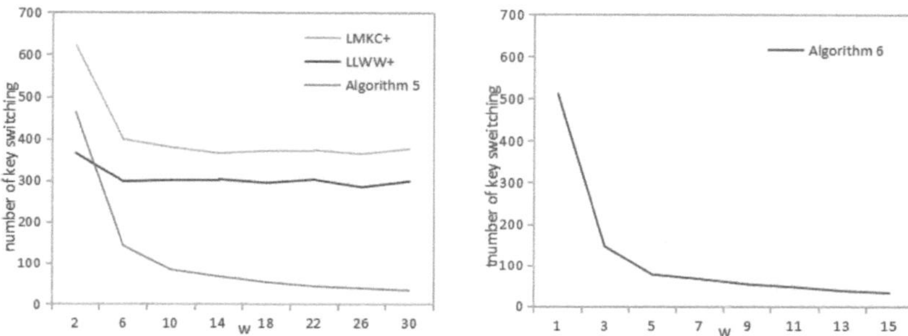

Fig. 2. The window size and corresponding number of key switching for different of bootstrapping algorithms

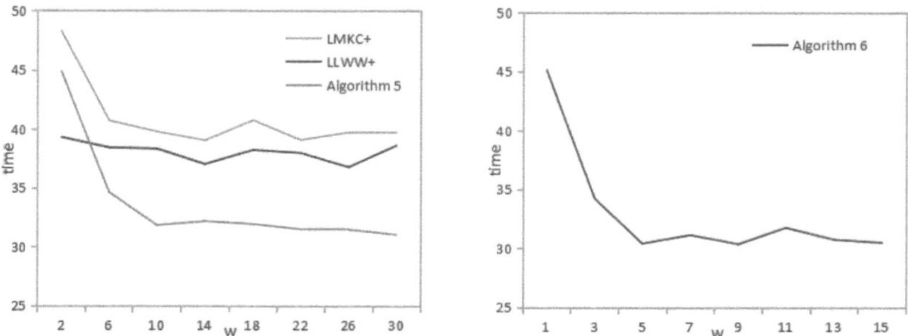

Fig. 3. The window size and corresponding time for different of bootstrapping algorithms

As shown in the figures, Fig. 2 illustrates the relationship between window size and the number of key switching, while Fig. 3 shows the correlation between window size and bootstrapping time for NAND gate evaluation in FHEW. Additionally, since the window size w in Algorithm 6 is configured to be half of that in Algorithm 5, its results are illustrated in a separate figure for clarity. For LMKC+ and LLWW+ methods, we observe that the number of key switching decreases as the window size w increases when w is small. However, once all empty sets are merged, the window size no longer influences the number of key switching. In contrast, for Algorithm 3, the number of key switching consistently decreases with increasing window size w. The bootstrapping time stabilizes once w exceeds 10, which can be attributed to the fact that, for $w \geq 10$, the number of key switching operations becomes very small, meaning the runtime is primarily determined by the inherent randomness of the algorithm. At this point, the practical runtime required for bootstrapping is approximately equal to that for performing only n external products. Specifically, for Algorithm 4, the bootstrapping time remains relatively constant once the window size exceeds 5.

Table 3. Timing results (average of 400), the number of key switching, bootstrapping key size, and failure probability for FHEW bootstrapping (NAND gate)

Method	Number	Time[ms]	Key size[MB]	Fail.prob
AP [3,12]	×	55.49	1316.12	2^{-84}
GINX* [6,18]	×	36.33	153.41	2^{-66}
LMKC+ [20]	380	39.79	92.1	2^{-34}
LLWW+ [21]	301	38.38	110.41	2^{-35}
Ours(Algorithm 3)	84	31.81	257.27	2^{-37}
Ours(Algorithm 4)	**77**	**30.41**	257.07	2^{-36}

We set the window size $w = 10$ for LMKC+, LLWW+, and Algorithm 3, and $w = 5$ for Algorithm 4. It is important to note that the entire bootstrapping key consists of both the evaluation keys for blind rotation and key switching keys. The size of the LWE key switching key is given by $(n+1)NB_{\mathsf{sk}}d_{\mathsf{ks}} \log Q_{\mathsf{ks}}$ bits. The resulting values for the number of key switching, bootstrapping time, key size, and the probability of decryption failure are summarized in Table 3. The results indicate that Algorithm 4 performs only 77 key switching, representing a reduction of 80% and 74% compared to LMKC+ and LLWW+, respectively. Moreover, the running time of bootstrapping is 30.41 ms, which corresponds to a 20.7% reduction in bootstrapping time compared to LLWW+.

Acknowledgments. This work was supported by the National Key Research and Development Program of China (No. 2021YFA1000600) and the National Natural Science Foundation of China (No. 12441104).

References

1. Al Badawi, A., et al.: Openfhe: open-source fully homomorphic encryption library. In: WAHC 2022 – 10th Workshop on Encrypted Computing & Applied Homomorphic Cryptography, pp. 53–63 (2022)
2. Albrecht, M., et al.: Homomorphic encryption standard. In: Protecting Privacy through Homomorphic Encryption, pp. 31–62 (2021)

3. Alperin-Sheriff, J., Peikert, C.: Faster bootstrapping with polynomial error. In: Garay, J.A., Gennaro, R. (eds.) CRYPTO 2014. LNCS, vol. 8616, pp. 297–314. Springer, Heidelberg (2014). https://doi.org/10.1007/978-3-662-44371-2_17
4. Angel, S., Chen, H., Laine, K., Setty, S.: PIR with compressed queries and amortized query processing. In: SP 2018 - 2018 IEEE Symposium on Security and Privacy, pp. 962–979. IEEE (2018)
5. Blatt, M., Gusev, A., Polyakov, Y., Goldwasser, S.: Secure large-scale genome-wide association studies using homomorphic encryption. Proc. Natl. Acad. Sci. **117**(21), 11608–11613 (2020)
6. Bonte, C., Iliashenko, I., Park, J., Pereira, H.V.L., Smart, N.P.: FINAL: faster FHE instantiated with NTRU and LWE. In: ASIACRYPT 2022 - 28th International Conference on the Theory and Application of Cryptology and Information Security, pp. 188–215. Springer, Cham (2022). https://doi.org/10.1007/978-3-031-22966-4_7
7. Brakerski, Z., Gentry, C., Vaikuntanathan, V.: (Leveled) fully homomorphic encryption without bootstrapping. ACM Trans. Comput. Theory **6**(3), 1–36 (2014)
8. Brakerski, Z., Vaikuntanathan, V.: Fully homomorphic encryption from ring-LWE and security for key dependent messages. In: Rogaway, P. (ed.) CRYPTO 2011. LNCS, vol. 6841, pp. 505–524. Springer, Heidelberg (2011). https://doi.org/10.1007/978-3-642-22792-9_29
9. Cheon, J.H., Kim, A., Kim, M., Song, Y.: Homomorphic encryption for arithmetic of approximate numbers. In: Takagi, T., Peyrin, T. (eds.) ASIACRYPT 2017. LNCS, vol. 10624, pp. 409–437. Springer, Cham (2017). https://doi.org/10.1007/978-3-319-70694-8_15
10. Chillotti, I., Gama, N., Georgieva, M., Izabachène, M.: Faster fully homomorphic encryption: bootstrapping in less than 0.1 s. In: Cheon, J.H., Takagi, T. (eds.) ASIACRYPT 2016. LNCS, vol. 10031, pp. 3–33. Springer, Heidelberg (2016). https://doi.org/10.1007/978-3-662-53887-6_1
11. Chillotti, I., Gama, N., Georgieva, M., Izabachène, M.: TFHE: fast fully homomorphic encryption over the torus. J. Cryptol. **33**(1), 34–91 (2020)
12. Ducas, L., Micciancio, D.: FHEW: bootstrapping homomorphic encryption in less than a second. In: Oswald, E., Fischlin, M. (eds.) EUROCRYPT 2015. LNCS, vol. 9056, pp. 617–640. Springer, Heidelberg (2015). https://doi.org/10.1007/978-3-662-46800-5_24
13. Fan, J., Vercauteren, F.: Somewhat practical fully homomorphic encryption. In: Cryptology ePrint Archive, p. 144 (2012)
14. Gama, N., Izabachène, M., Nguyen, P.Q., Xie, X.: Structural lattice reduction: generalized worst-case to average-case reductions and homomorphic cryptosystems. In: Fischlin, M., Coron, J.-S. (eds.) EUROCRYPT 2016. LNCS, vol. 9666, pp. 528–558. Springer, Heidelberg (2016). https://doi.org/10.1007/978-3-662-49896-5_19
15. Gentry, C.: Fully homomorphic encryption using ideal lattices. In: STOC 2009 - 41st Annual ACM Symposium on Theory of Computing, pp. 169–178. ACM (2009)
16. Gentry, C., Sahai, A., Waters, B.: Homomorphic encryption from learning with errors: conceptually-simpler, asymptotically-faster, attribute-based. In: Canetti, R., Garay, J.A. (eds.) CRYPTO 2013. LNCS, vol. 8042, pp. 75–92. Springer, Heidelberg (2013). https://doi.org/10.1007/978-3-642-40041-4_5
17. Han, K., Hong, S., Cheon, J.H., Park, D.: Logistic regression on homomorphic encrypted data at scale. In: AAAI 2019 - The Thirty-Third AAAI Conference on Artificial Intelligence, pp. 9466–9471. AAAI Press (2019)
18. Kim, A., et al.: General bootstrapping approach for RLWE-based homomorphic encryption. IEEE Trans. Comput. **73**(1), 86–96 (2024)

19. Kim, A., Lee, Y., Deryabin, M., Eom, J., Choi, R.: LFHE: fully homomorphic encryption with bootstrapping key size less than a megabyte. In: Cryptology ePrint Archive, p. 767 (2023)
20. Lee, Y., et al.: Efficient FHEW bootstrapping with small evaluation keys, and applications to threshold homomorphic encryption. In: EUROCRYPT 2023 - 42nd Annual International Conference on the Theory and Applications of Cryptographic Techniques, pp. 227–256. Springer, Heidelberg (2023). https://doi.org/10.1007/978-3-031-30620-4_8
21. Li, Z., et al.: Faster NTRU-based bootstrapping in less than 4 MS. IACR Trans. Cryptogr. Hardw. Embed. Syst. **2024**(3), 418–451 (2024)
22. Lyubashevsky, V., Peikert, C., Regev, O.: On ideal lattices and learning with errors over rings. J. ACM **60**(6), 1–35 (2013)
23. Micciancio, D.: On the hardness of learning with errors with binary secrets. Theory Comput. **14**(1), 1–17 (2018)
24. Micciancio, D., Polyakov, Y.: Bootstrapping in FHEW-like cryptosystems. In: WAHC 2021 - 9th on Workshop on Encrypted Computing & Applied Homomorphic Cryptography, pp. 17–28. Association for Computing Machinery (2021)
25. Regev, O.: On lattices, learning with errors, random linear codes, and cryptography. J. ACM **56**(6), 1–40 (2009)
26. Stehlé, D., Steinfeld, R.: Faster fully homomorphic encryption. In: Abe, M. (ed.) ASIACRYPT 2010. LNCS, vol. 6477, pp. 377–394. Springer, Heidelberg (2010). https://doi.org/10.1007/978-3-642-17373-8_22
27. Wang, R., et al.: Circuit bootstrapping: faster and smaller. In: EUROCRYPT 2024 - 43rd Annual International Conference on the Theory and Applications of Cryptographic Techniques, pp. 342–372. Springer, Heidelberg (2024). https://doi.org/10.1007/978-3-031-58723-8_12
28. Xiang, B., Zhang, J., Deng, Y., Dai, Y., Feng, D.: Fast blind rotation for bootstrapping FHEs. In: CRYPTO 2023 - 43rd Annual International Cryptology Conference, pp. 3–36. Springer, Heidelberg (2023). https://doi.org/10.1007/978-3-031-38551-3_1
29. Zhang, Q., Wang, M., Cheng, X.: Faster FHEW bootstrapping with adaptive key update. In: Cryptology ePrint Archive, p. 381 (2025)

Cryptographic Protocols and Blockchain

Attribute-Based Key Exchange with Optimal Efficiency

Liqun Chen[1], Long Meng[1], Mark Manulis[2], Yangguang Tian[1(✉)], and Yinghui Zhang[3]

[1] School of Computer Science and Electronic Engineering, University of Surrey, Guildford, UK
yangguang.tian@surrey.ac.uk

[2] Department of Computer Science, Universität der Bundeswehr München, Neubiberg, Germany

[3] Xi'an University of Posts and Telecommunications, Xi'an, China

Abstract. Attribute-based key exchange (ABKE) is a useful cryptographic primitive that allows authorized users to establish a session key for data transport based on whether their attributes satisfy a policy. In this paper, we reconstruct ABKE from *fast* attribute-based encryptions (ABE) and *efficient* authenticated key exchanges (AKE). Fast ABE supports adaptive security and fast decryption. Efficient AKE allows authorized users to establish session keys with minimal communication overhead and perfect forward secrecy (PFS). Our main contribution is a generic construction of ABKE with enhanced security and optimal efficiency. For enhanced security, our construction offers adaptive security, PFS and impersonation-resistance. For optimal efficiency, our construction ensures that the session key establishment runs fast and the communication between users incurs minimal overhead. We present concrete ABKE instantiation and confirm that its performance outperforms the existing ABKE schemes through implementation and evaluation. Briefly, our ABKE scheme requires a constant number of pairings for session key establishment, which is not offered by existing ones. More concretely, a user requires 0.15 s to establish a session key for a policy with 100 attributes.

Keywords: Attribute-based Key Exchange · Enhanced Security · Optimal Efficiency

1 Introduction

Attribute-based encryption (ABE) is an asymmetric encryption scheme that allows users to fine-tune access control to encrypted data based on attributes or policies. ABE has key-policy (KP) and ciphertext-policy (CP) categories. In KP-ABE, the decryption key is associated with a policy and the ciphertext involves a set of attributes. The decryption succeeds if the ciphertext attributes satisfy the key's policy. While in CP-ABE, the decryption key is associated with a set

Y. Kim et al. (Eds.): CANS 2025, LNCS 16351, pp. 315–334, 2026.
https://doi.org/10.1007/978-981-95-4434-9_15

of attributes and the ciphertext involves a policy, where again the attribute set satisfies the policy.

Since the first KP-ABE scheme [22] and CP-ABE scheme [6] were proposed almost two decades ago, ABE has been studied in various application scenarios considering different features like expressiveness, large universe and adaptive security; properties like revocability [16], traceability [26], multi-authority [15] and anonymity (e.g., attribute privacy) [38]; schemes are based on key encapsulation mechanism (KEM) [21]; even post-quantum ones [10]. This work aims at applying ABE to key-exchange, namely attribute-based key exchange (ABKE). The purpose of ABKE is to enable a set of authorized users holding different decryption keys to establish a shared session key based on their attributes. As a result, by using the shared session key, those users can use symmetric encryption such as AES.

ABKE is suitable for secure communications. For a centralized client-server scenario, a client that has a set of attributes wishes to establish secure channels with an authentication server that holds a policy. For a decentralized scenario, mutually distrusted users try to establish secure channels based on their roles or responsibilities. In these scenarios, the success of establishing secure communications requires implicit (but also fine-grained) authentication, meaning that a user holding an attribute-based key can decrypt a policy-based ciphertext encrypting a session key for confidential data transport.

Motivations. The state-of-the-art ABKE schemes include [21,24,37]. For example, the generic ABKE scheme in [21] is designed for attribute-based one-round group key exchange. Each user broadcasts an attribute-based KEM ciphertext of a secret key, and computes a shared session key from the received secret keys by decrypting each other's ciphertext. The recent scheme in [24] is designed for client-server setting. Their scheme relies on ABE, ABC (attribute-based credential [12]) and garbled circuit to realize boolean circuits. The common limitation is that their instantiations are based on selective-secure ABE schemes like Bethencourt et al. [6] and Waters [36].

Fast ABE was treading in recent years [1,29,30,34]. The fast ABE is constructed from type-3 pairings, supports expressive policies, adaptive security and fast decryption. Fast decryption means that the number of pairings in the decryption process is constant, compared to the traditional ABE schemes [6,36] that require varied pairings for decryption depending on the number of attributes. This feature is related to computational complexity. The first question is to ask, can we build a new generic construction of ABKE that leverages fast ABE schemes to achieve optimal computational complexity? The new construction will benefit fast key establishment among authorized users.

Optimal communication complexity is another desired feature for key exchange protocols [17,31]. In TOPAS [31], a one-round (i.e., two-pass) key exchange protocol requires each transmitted message to consist of 160 bits (for 80-bit security) in a prime-order elliptic curve (ECC) setting, which equals to the unauthenticated Diffie-Hellman (DH) protocol and the implicitly-authenticated

HMQV protocol [25]. The Protoss [17] follows the design of TOPAS. The message transmitted from a user is a single group element in the ECC setting. The mutual authentication relies on (identity-based) secret keys in TOPAS and (high-entropy) password in Protoss. The second question is to ask, can we optimize our ABKE scheme to support optimal communication complexity?

There is no existing ABKE scheme with optimal efficiency. For example, if we follow the generic ABKE construction [21] by replacing attribute-based KEM with any fast ABE, the communication overhead of the resulting scheme is too high. In particular, the message transmitted from a user contains a group element of $\mathbb{G}_T$ consisting of ≈ 480 bits (for 80-bit security) in the ECC setting. This is undesired in a large-scale multi-party setting as the communication overhead grows significantly. Large communication overhead might delay even cancel session key establishment and subsequent data transport. Our motivation is to reconstruct ABKE with optimal efficiency and enhanced security, which will be described in detail below.

Our Contributions. We provide a step-to-step guidance to explain our design rationales and the relevant security claims.

First, we propose a generic construction of ABKE by making fast ABE schemes and two-pass key exchange protocols work together with optimal computational and communication complexity. We clarify our designs using a fast KP-ABE scheme [30] and the classical HMQV protocol [25]. We consider a communication channel between users Alice and Bob. A natural solution is to let Alice and Bob exchange their ABE ciphertext on DH ephemeral public keys $(g_1^{s_a}, g_1^{s_b})$ for implicit authentication, where $(s_a, s_b) \in \mathbb{Z}_p^2$ are DH ephemeral secret keys. The basic idea of ABKE is that if Alice/Bob's attribute set satisfies each other's ciphertext policy, they can decrypt ciphertext, retrieve ephemeral public keys and derive a session key. The resulting ABKE protocol can easily achieve optimal computational complexity due to the underlying fast ABE scheme, but the communication overhead is not optimal as the exchanged ABE ciphertext involves group elements from $\mathbb{G}_T$, which is we try to avoid in our efficient ABKE construction.

In fast KP-ABE [30], a ciphertext includes a set of attributes $\mathcal{S}$ denoted as $(\mathsf{ct}_1, \mathsf{ct}_2) = (\{H(attr)^s\}_{attr \in \mathcal{S}}, g_2^s)$, and an encrypted message denoted as $\mathsf{ct}_3 = e(g_1, g_2)^{\alpha \cdot s} \oplus msg$, where $e : \mathbb{G}_1 \times \mathbb{G}_2 \rightarrow \mathbb{G}_T$ is a type-3 pairing, α is master secret key, s is ciphertext randomness, $\oplus$ is the bitwise XOR operation and $H : \{0,1\} \rightarrow \mathbb{G}_1$ is a cryptographic hash function. The ciphertext element ct_3 belongs to $\mathbb{G}_T$, and its size is *three times* that of $\mathbb{G}_1$. If we apply $H[e(g_1, g_2)^{\alpha \cdot s}]$ to eliminate group element in $\mathbb{G}_T$ and ensure optimal communication overhead, the ct_3 becomes

$$\mathsf{ct}_3 = H(d) \oplus g_1^s$$

where g_1^s is the encrypted DH ephemeral public key and $d = e(g_1, g_2)^{\alpha \cdot s}$. The construction of DH-based ABKE is sketched in Fig. 1. In our construction, Alice derives $d_b = e(g_1, g_2)^{\alpha \cdot s_b}$ from Bob's ABE ciphertext elements $(\mathsf{ct}_1, \mathsf{ct}_2)$ using her decryption key; then she retrieves $g_1^{s_b}$ from ABE ciphertext element

$Alice: (dk_a, sk_a, pk_a)$		$Bob: (dk_b, sk_b, pk_b)$
$s_a \in \mathbb{Z}_p$ $\mathsf{ct}_a : (\mathsf{ct}_{a1}, \mathsf{ct}_{a2}, \mathsf{ct}_{a3}) \leftarrow ABE.Enc(g_1^{s_a})$ $where\ \mathsf{ct}_{a3} = H(d_a) \oplus g_1^{s_a}$		$s_b \in \mathbb{Z}_p$ $\mathsf{ct}_b : (\mathsf{ct}_{b1}, \mathsf{ct}_{b2}, \mathsf{ct}_{b3}) \leftarrow ABE.Enc(g_1^{s_b})$ $where\ \mathsf{ct}_{b3} = H(d_b) \oplus g_1^{s_b}$
	$\xrightarrow{\mathsf{ct}_a}$ $\xleftarrow{\mathsf{ct}_b}$	
$g_1^{s_b} \leftarrow ABE.Dec(dk_a, \mathsf{ct}_b)$ $sk = AKE.Kex(s_a, g_1^{s_b}, sk_a, pk_b)$ $\mathsf{sk} = H'(sk\|\|sid)$		$g_1^{s_a} \leftarrow ABE.Dec(dk_b, \mathsf{ct}_a)$ $sk = AKE.Kex(g_1^{s_a}, s_b, sk_b, pk_a)$ $\mathsf{sk} = H'(sk\|\|sid)$

Fig. 1. DH-based ABKE. For pairing-based ABE, $d_a = e(g_1, g_2)^{\alpha \cdot s_a}, d_b = e(g_1, g_2)^{\alpha \cdot s_b}$. For two-pass HMQV protocol, $sk = (g_1^{s_b} \cdot pk_b^{e_b})^{(s_a + e_a \cdot sk_a)} = (g_1^{s_a} \cdot pk_a^{e_a})^{(s_b + e_b \cdot sk_b)}$, (e_a, e_b) are hash outputs of session's states, and sid is a session's identifier.

ct_3 and computes a shared key using the HMQV protocol. One may consider a more communication-efficient approach by allowing Alice/Bob to derive a shared key *without* transmitting ct_3 such as $sk = e(g_1, g_2)^{\alpha s_b s_b}$. This approach is not suitable for the two-pass AKE protocol (see Sect. 5).

Second, our ABKE secures against impersonations and prevents anyone from tampering DH ephemeral public keys. There are two types of authentication for key exchanges: implicit and explicit. The explicit authentication means digital signatures of ephemeral public keys have been exchanged to prevent tampering by active adversaries [23]. This is effective but increases communication overhead. Implicit authentication means that digital signatures are not exchanged. For example, the classical HMQV protocol requires Alice and Bob to establish a shared key based on a combination of ephemeral and long-term (or static) keys. Specifically, Alice and Bob exchange two ephemeral public keys $(g_1^{s_a}, g_1^{s_b})$ and derive a shared key $sk = (g_1^{s_b} \cdot pk_b^{e_b})^{(s_a + e_a \cdot sk_a)}$, where sk_a/pk_b denotes Alice/Bob's secret-key/public-key. The impersonation prevention is achieved due to a Schnorr-like digital signature [32] is used in the key derivation. Moreover, if ephemeral public keys are exchanged in the form of $\mathsf{sk} \oplus g_1^s$, where sk denotes some secrets (e.g., id-based key in mOT and TOPAS, pre-shared password in Protoss), it achieves *full* perfect forward secrecy (PFS) which implicitly-authenticated HMQV protocol only supports *weak* PFS[1]. We stress that our ABKE incorporates all implicitly-authenticated and secret-based key exchange protocols, except those based on explicit authentication. To this end, our ABKE achieves enhanced security due to: 1) implicit authentication, users decrypt (fast and adaptive-secure) ABE ciphertext using their keys; and 2) secret-based authentication, users derive session keys using their secrets to ensure impersonation resistance and weak/full PFS.

[1] PFS ensures that even if user's long-term keys are compromised, the session key security is still guaranteed based on the security of ephemeral keys.

Third, we introduce a modified CK model in the attribute-based setting to encompass adaptive security (i.e., adversary can adaptively choose challenge attributes in a test session), impersonation-resistance, and weak/full PFS (i.e., passive/active adversary in the test session). Finally, we present a practical instantiation based on a fast ABE scheme called FABEO, and a modified PKI-based TOPAS. The construction outperforms all existing ABKE schemes in the two-party setting, which is confirmed by our detailed performance analysis and experiments. Our contributions can be summarized as follows:

- *Generic Construction.* We reconstruct the construction of ABKE from fast attribute-based encryptions and two-pass key exchange protocols. The new generic construction ensures enhanced security (i.e., adaptive security, weak/full PFS and impersonation-resistance) and optimal efficiency (i.e., fast decryption and minimal communication overhead).
- *Practical & Flexible Instantiations.* We present a concrete ABKE scheme based on the state-of-the-art schemes FABEO [30] and PKI-based TOPAS [31]. Our implementation and evaluation show the practicality of our instantiation compared to the existing ABKE schemes [21,37]. We also clarify the construction of ABKE schemes from other fast ABE schemes and identity/password-based AKE protocols.

2 Related Work

Attribute-based authenticated key exchange (ABKE) was firstly proposed by Gorantla et al. [21]. The scheme is to let a set of users establish a session key via attribute-based KEM. The design idea is to let each user choose a symmetric key and broadcast a policy-based ciphertext encrypting the symmetric key [6]. Eventually, a set of users with attribute-based decryption keys can decrypt the received ciphertext and derive a session key from multiple symmetric keys. The scheme involves one-round communication and achieves implicit authentication, meaning that users with valid decryption keys can compute the final session key. However, the underlying attribute-based KEM scheme is impractical (e.g., no fast decryption is supported) and subject to impersonations (e.g., a user holding a valid decryption key may impersonate others). Recently, Boyd et al. [8] introduced a KEM-based authenticated key exchange (AKE) with post-quantum security in the Canetti-Krawczyk (CK) model [14]. The generic scheme in [8] focused on KEM-based post-quantum AKE protocols, and they left real-world implementation for future work. Our ABKE scheme is based on pairings and we provide real implementations. Since ABE is our main building block, we can consider post-quantum ABE [2,10]. However, due to concerns about its maturity, it is unlikely to replace fast ABE with post-quantum ones in the near future [35].

Yoneyama [37] introduced a two-pass ABKE scheme based on Waters ABE [36] and standard DH key exchange. The scheme applied a NAXOS trick to achieve eCK security [27], which is a variant of CK security [14]. Both CK and eCK security models have been widely used in analyzing AKE protocols. The

NAXOS trick is to let a user compute a secret value from an ephemeral key and a static key, then the user performs a DH key exchange and derives a session key based on the secret value. The adversary is disallowed to compromise the user's ephemeral key and static key simultaneously in the eCK model. However, the limitations remain the same as [21].

Kolesnikov et al. [24] proposed a new ABKE scheme using CP-ABE [6] and attribute-based credential (ABC), which is different from KEM/DH-based ABKE. A client with certified attributes authenticates to a server based on a policy. The server will share a session key when the client's attributes satisfy the server's policy. One of key features is called attribute privacy, client attributes are never disclosed. In this sense, their ABKE scheme is close to anonymous credential [11]. We stress that ABC (or anonymous credential) with attribute privacy is beyond the scope of this work, although fast and anonymous ABE is available [29]. Similar to [24], Ateniese et al. introduced match-making encryption (ME) that allows two users to specify policies the other party must satisfy in order for the message to be revealed [4]. ME offers privacy-preserving policy matching, which is close to secret handshakes [5]. We leave the construction of privacy-preserving ABKE with optimal efficiency for future work.

3 Preliminary

In this section, we present the state-of-the-art KP-ABE scheme called FABEO [30] and a two-pass AKE protocol called TOPAS [31], which will be used in our instantiation.

3.1 Fast Attribute-Based Encryption

Access Structures. If $\mathcal{U}$ denotes an attribute universe, an access structure $\mathcal{P}$ is a collection of non-empty subsets of $\mathcal{U}$, i.e., $\mathcal{P} \subseteq 2^{\mathcal{U}} \backslash \{0\}$. It is called monotone if for every $B,\ C \subseteq \mathcal{U}$ such that $B \subseteq C,\ B \in \mathcal{P} \Rightarrow C \in \mathcal{P}$. Typically, a Boolean formula consists of AND and OR gates, where each input is associated with an attribute in $\mathcal{U}$. A set of attributes $\mathcal{S} \subseteq \mathcal{U}$ satisfies a Boolean formula if we set all inputs of the formula that map to an attribute in $\mathcal{S}$ to true and the others to false and the formula evaluates to true.

Monotone span programs (MSP) is a more general class of functions and include Boolean formulas. We encode an access structure by a policy $\mathcal{P} = (M, \pi)$ where M of size $\ell \times n$ over $\mathbb{Z}_p$ and a mapping function $\pi : \{1, \ldots, \ell\} \to \mathcal{U}$. Lewko and Waters [28] described a simple and efficient method to convert any Boolean formula F into an MSP$(M,\ \pi)$ such that every row of M corresponds to input in F and the number of columns is same as the number of AND gates in F. Let $\mathcal{S} = \{u_i\}_{i \in [m]} \subseteq \mathcal{U}$ be a set of m attributes and $\mathcal{I} = \{i \mid i \in \{1, \ldots, \ell\},\ \pi(i) \in \mathcal{S}\}$ be the set of rows in M that belong to $\mathcal{S}$. We say that $\mathcal{P} = (M, \pi)$ accepts $\mathcal{S}$ if there exists a linear combination of rows in $\mathcal{I}$ that gives $(1, 0, \cdots, 0)$. We denote it as $\mathcal{P}(\mathcal{S}) = 1$. This means, there exist constants $\gamma_i \in \mathbb{Z}_p$ for $i \in \mathcal{I}$ such that $\sum_{i \in \mathcal{I}} \gamma_i M_i = (1,\ 0,\ \ldots,\ 0)$. These constants can be computed in polynomial time in the size of M.

Bilinear Maps. Let GroupGen be a probabilistic polynomial time (PPT) algorithm that takes a security parameter λ as input, outputs a set of group parameters $\mathsf{par} = (p, \mathbb{G}_1, \mathbb{G}_2, \mathbb{G}_T, e, g_1, g_2)$, where p is a prime number, $\mathbb{G}_1, \mathbb{G}_2$ and $\mathbb{G}_T$ are cyclic groups of order p, g_1 and g_2 are the generators of $\mathbb{G}_1$ and $\mathbb{G}_2$ respectively. $e : \mathbb{G}_1 \times \mathbb{G}_2 \rightarrow \mathbb{G}_T$ is a Type-3 pairing where there exists no efficiently computable homomorphism between $\mathbb{G}_1$ and $\mathbb{G}_2$.

KP-ABE. A KP-ABE scheme consists of four algorithms $\mathsf{ABE} = (\mathsf{Setup}, \mathsf{KeyGen}, \mathsf{Enc}, \mathsf{Dec})$. The KP-ABE scheme called FABEO [30] is presented below.

- Setup (λ): Key Generation Center (KGC) runs $\mathsf{GroupGen}(1^\lambda)$ to obtain the group parameters $\mathsf{par} := (p, e, \mathbb{G}_1, \mathbb{G}_2, \mathbb{G}_T, g_1, g_2)$. Picks $\alpha \xleftarrow{\$} \mathbb{Z}_p$ and a hash function $H : \{0,\ 1\}^* \rightarrow \mathbb{G}_1$. Computes the master key pair as follows

$$\mathsf{mpk} = (\mathsf{par}, H, e(g_1, g_2)^\alpha), \mathsf{msk} = \alpha.$$

- KeyGen $(\mathtt{msk}, \mathcal{P})$: KGC picks $r \xleftarrow{\$} \mathbb{Z}_p$, $\mathbf{v} \xleftarrow{\$} \mathbb{Z}_p^{n-1}$. Computes

$$\mathsf{sk}_1 = g_2^r,\ \mathsf{sk}_{2,i} = g_1^{\mathrm{M}_i(\alpha\|\mathbf{v})^\top} \cdot H(\pi(i))^r.$$

  Outputs $\mathsf{sk} = (\mathsf{sk}_1, \{\mathsf{sk}_{2,i}\}_{i\in[\ell]})$.
- Enc $(\mathtt{mpk}, \mathcal{S}, \mathsf{msg})$: Pick $s \xleftarrow{\$} \mathbb{Z}_p$. Compute

$$\mathsf{ct}_{1,i} = H(u_i)^s, \mathsf{ct}_2 = g_2^s, \mathsf{ct}_3 = e(g_1, g_2)^{\alpha s} \cdot \mathsf{msg}.$$

  Output $\mathsf{ct} = (\{\mathsf{ct}_{1,i}\}_{i\in[m]}, \mathsf{ct}_2, \mathsf{ct}_3)$.
- Dec $(\mathsf{ct}, \mathsf{sk})$: If $\mathcal{S}$ satisfies $\mathcal{P}$, there exists constants $\{\gamma_i\}_{i\in\mathcal{I}}$ s.t. $\sum_{i\in\mathcal{I}} \gamma_i \mathrm{M}_i = (1,\ 0,\ \ldots,\ 0)$ and reconstruct the message msg by computing:

$$\mathsf{msg} = \frac{e(\prod_{i\in\mathcal{I}}(\mathsf{ct}_{1,\pi(i)})^{\gamma_i},\ \mathsf{sk}_1) \cdot \mathsf{ct}_3}{e(\prod_{i\in\mathcal{I}}(\mathsf{sk}_{2,i})^{\gamma_i},\ \mathsf{ct}_2)}.$$

We consider an adaptive chosen plaintext attack (CPA) security for the underlying KP-ABE scheme, where adaptive means that the adversary can decide attribute set during the challenge phase. We do not consider chosen ciphertext attack (CCA) security in this work, and CPA security can be extended to CCA security via generic transformations like [20]. The adaptive CPA security game is executed between an adversary $\mathcal{A}$ and a challenger $\mathcal{C}$:

- $\mathsf{Setup}(\lambda)$: $\mathcal{C}$ runs $\mathsf{Setup}(1^\lambda)$ to obtain a master public key mpk and a master secret key msk. It sends mpk to $\mathcal{A}$.
- $\mathsf{Training}(\mathcal{P})$: $\mathcal{A}$ issues queries to a key generation oracle for polynomial many times:
  - Key generation oracle: Given an access policy $\mathcal{P}$, the oracle returns $\mathsf{sk} \leftarrow \mathsf{KeyGen}(\mathsf{msk}, \mathcal{P})$ to $\mathcal{A}$.

- $\mathsf{Challenge}(\mathcal{S}^*, \mathsf{m}_0, \mathsf{m}_1)$. $\mathcal{A}$ outputs a challenge attribute set $\mathcal{S}^*$ and two equal-size messages $\mathsf{m}_0, \mathsf{m}_1$ with the restriction that $\mathcal{P}(\mathcal{S}^*) = 0$ for any $\mathcal{P}$ that has been queried in the training phase. Then $\mathcal{C}$ selects a random bit $b \in \{0, 1\}$, and returns $\mathsf{ct}_b^* \leftarrow \mathsf{Enc}(\mathsf{mpk}, \mathcal{S}^*, \mathsf{m}_b)$ to $\mathcal{A}$. $\mathcal{A}$ can continue to issue key generation queries on any access policy $\mathcal{P}$ with the restriction that $\mathcal{P}(\mathcal{S}^*) = 0$.
- Guess (b'): $\mathcal{A}$ outputs $b' \in \{0, 1\}$ and wins the game if $b' = b$. We define the advantage of $\mathcal{A}$ in the this game as

$$\mathsf{Adv}_{\mathcal{A}}(\lambda) = \left| \Pr[b' = b] - \frac{1}{2} \right|.$$

Definition 1. *An KP-ABE scheme is adaptively CPA secure if for any PPT* $\mathcal{A}$, $\mathsf{Adv}_{\mathcal{A}}(\lambda)$ *is negligible.*

3.2 Two-Pass Key Exchange with Optimal Communication

Optimal communication requires the number of bits exchanged between communicated users to be optimal. Below, we sketch an AKE protocol with optimal communication called TOPAS [31]. TOPAS includes identity-based and PKI-based versions, and we focus on the latter one.

In the PKI-based TOPAS, assume that two communicated users Alice and Bob exchange two messages $(\overline{a}, \overline{b})$ and establish a shared key using pairing-based DH key exchange, and assume that KGC setups the system parameters containing $(p, e, g_1, g_2, g_1^z, g_2^z)$, where z denotes master secret key. We denote Alice's certified key pair as $(sk_a, pk_a) = (g_1^{x_a}, (g_1^z)^{x_a})$, where $x_a \xleftarrow{\$} \mathbb{Z}_p$. Alice computes her transmitted message $\overline{a} = g_1^{s_a} \cdot sk_a$ and derives a shared key sk as follows

$$sk = [\frac{e(\overline{b}, g_2^z)}{e(pk_b, g_2)}]^{s_a} = e(g_1, g_2)^{z s_a s_b}$$

where s_a/s_b denotes Alice/Bob's ephemeral DH secret key.

The design of $\overline{a}$ has two benefits. One is optimal message size. Each user transmits a single group element in $\mathbb{G}_1$ for key establishment. Another is full PFS. Alice and Bob exchange "blinded" versions of their long-term DH secret keys. That is, Alice "authenticates" her ephemeral DH public key $g_1^{s_a}$ using sk_a. This design is also applied to a pairing-free password-based AKE protocol called Protoss [17]. In Protoss, the ephemeral DH public keys are blinded by the hashed high-entropy password, in which the password is pre-shared by Alice and Bob.

4 Our ABKE Model and Constructions

In this section, we first present the ABKE syntax along with the definitions of its security requirements. Then, we present our generic ABKE construction and analyze its security.

4.1 ABKE Syntax and Security Definitions

In the literature, we can find two approaches to formally analyze authenticated (attribute-based) key exchange protocols, including universal composability (UC) [13] and game-based framework. In this work, we rely on a game-based security model called CK [14]. We extend the original CK security model to an attribute-based setting, and we revise the oracle freshness to capture active adversary in the test session. Briefly, we consider adaptive security (i.e., the challenge attributes/policies are not predefined), single-challenge (i.e., a single test session), and single-bit security (i.e., a single global b).

Syntax. An attribute-based key exchange (ABKE) protocol consists of the following algorithms. We present a KP version below, and the CP version can be defined similarly.

- Setup (λ): It takes a security parameter λ as input, outputs a master key pair ($\mathtt{msk}, \mathtt{mpk}$) for a key generation center (KGC).
- KeyGen ($\mathtt{msk}$, $\mathcal{P}$, id): KGC takes $\mathtt{msk}$ as input, outputs a decryption key dk based on a policy $\mathcal{P}$ for a user id with secret information sk.
- KeyExchange (Kex): This is an interactive protocol between users (id, id'). Each user takes $\mathtt{mpk}$, its decryption key dk, its secret information sk, and an attribute set $\mathcal{S} \in \mathcal{U}$ as input, outputs a session key sk if $\mathcal{P}_{id'}(\mathcal{S}_{id}) = 1$ and $\mathcal{P}_{id}(\mathcal{S}_{id'}) = 1$.

Remark on Secret sk. Our ABKE syntax requires a user to have secret information sk and apply it to the session key derivation, which is not required by existing ABKE schemes [21,37]. Alternatively, one can add sk to dk to align with standard syntax of ABKE. We consider three types of sk to cover PKI/identity/password-based settings: 1) a user creates a key pair (sk, pk), where pk is authenticated via a certificate from KGC; 2) KGC issues an identity-based key sk for a user; 3) a pre-shared password between communicated users. From security's perspective, sk has two benefits. First, sk ensures impersonation resistance. Implicit authentication in the ABKE setting cannot prevent impersonations. For example, Alice may impersonate (uncorrupted) Bob and establish a conversation with Charlie, but Bob was not involved in the conversation with Charlie. This impersonation is possible when Alice & Bob's attribute-based keys satisfy Charlie's policy [33]. We assume that KGC is an honest party and will not impersonate users, regardless of whether KGC knows sk or not. Second, sk can be used to "authenticate" the exchanged ephemeral DH keys to ensure full PFS. The full PFS considers active attackers toward the test session. The importance of full PFS has been discussed in [31], and the importance of secret-based authentication refers to Appendix A.

States. We consider a system with n users and a key generation center (KGC). We define an instance oracle Π_{id}^{i}, i.e., a session i of user id. The oracle is considered as unused if it has never been initialized. Each unused oracle Π_{id}^{i} can be initialized with an attribute-based key dk issued by KGC via a secure channel along with a secret information sk. After the initialization the oracle is marked as used and turns into the stand-by state where it waits for an invocation to execute a protocol operation. Upon receiving such invocation the oracle Π_{id}^{i} learns its partner pid_{id}^{i} (as defined below) and turns into a processing state where it sends, receives and processes messages according to the protocol description. During that stage, the internal state information $state_{id}^{i}$ is maintained by the oracle. The oracle Π_{id}^{i} remains in the processing state until it collects enough information to compute a session key sk. If sk is computed, Π_{id}^{i} accepts and terminates the protocol execution. If the protocol execution fails, Π_{id}^{i} terminates without having accepted.

Partnering. We denote a partner identifier as pid_{id}^{i}, which includes the identities (including id) in the i-th session of a user id with the condition that $\forall id' \in \mathsf{pid}_{id}^{i}$ and $\mathcal{S}_{id'} \in \mathcal{P}_{id}$. In other words, pid_{id}^{i} is a collection of identities by the instance oracle Π_{id}^{i}. We also define sid_{id}^{i} as a unique session identifier belonging to user id of session i. Specifically, $\mathsf{sid}_{id}^{i} = \{m\}$, where $m \in \{0,1\}^*$ is the message transcript by users in pid_{id}^{i}. We say two instance oracles Π_{id}^{i} and $\Pi_{id'}^{j}$ are partners if $\mathsf{sid}_{id}^{i} = \mathsf{sid}_{id'}^{j}$ and $\mathsf{pid}_{id}^{i} = \mathsf{pid}_{id'}^{j}$.

Passive and Active Attacker. We say that an attacker is passive with respect to Π_{id}^{i} if the messages m send to/from id in the i-th session is produced by the instance oracle, or the users (id, id') are not corrupted prior to the i-th session. We say that the attacker is active if any of these conditions is violated.

Session Key Security. Informally, an adversary $\mathcal{A}$ cannot distinguish a session key from random in a test session. We define a game between a PPT $\mathcal{A}$ and a challenger $\mathcal{C}$ as follows.

- Setup: $\mathcal{C}$ generates a master key pair $(\mathtt{mpk}, \mathtt{msk})$ for KGC and key pairs $\{sk, pk\}$ for n users. $\mathcal{C}$ returns all users' public keys (or identities) to $\mathcal{A}$. $\mathcal{C}$ also tosses a random coin b which is used later in the game.
- Training: $\mathcal{A}$ can make the following queries in arbitrary sequence to $\mathcal{C}$.
  - Send: If $\mathcal{A}$ issues a send query in the form of (id, i, m) to simulate a network message for the i-th session of user id, $\mathcal{C}$ will simulate the reaction of instance oracle Π_{id}^{i} upon receiving message m, and return to $\mathcal{A}$ the response that Π_{id}^{i} would generate. If $\mathcal{A}$ issues a send query in the form of $(id, \text{`}start\text{'})$, $\mathcal{C}$ creates a new instance oracle Π_{id}^{i} and returns to $\mathcal{A}$ the first protocol message.
  - Key reveal: If $\mathcal{A}$ issues a key reveal query to an instance oracle Π_{id}^{i} and the session is accepted, $\mathcal{C}$ returns the session key to $\mathcal{A}$; Otherwise, a special symbol '$\perp$' is returned to $\mathcal{A}$.
  - State reveal: If $\mathcal{A}$ issues a state reveal query to (possibly unaccepted) instance oracle Π_{id}^{i}, $\mathcal{C}$ returns all state-related values (e.g., ephemeral keys) contained in Π_{id}^{i} when the query is asked.

- Corrupt: If $\mathcal{A}$ issues a corrupt query to a user id, $\mathcal{C}$ returns the user's static keys to $\mathcal{A}$.
- Test: This query can only be made to an accepted and *fresh* (as defined below) session i of a user id. $\mathcal{C}$ returns the real key to $\mathcal{A}$ if $b = 1$; Otherwise, $\mathcal{C}$ returns a random key to $\mathcal{A}$. $\mathcal{A}$ can continue to issue other queries after Test query. However, the test session must maintain fresh throughout the entire game.

Finally, $\mathcal{A}$ outputs b' as its guess for b. If $b' = b$, $\mathcal{C}$ outputs 1; Otherwise, $\mathcal{C}$ outputs 0.

Oracle Freshness (with full PFS). We say an *accepted* instance oracle Π^i_{id} is fresh if $\mathcal{A}$ does not perform any of the following actions during the game:

- $\mathcal{A}$ issues a Key reveal query to Π^i_{id} or its accepted partnered instance oracle $\Pi^j_{id'}$ (if $\Pi^j_{id'}$ exists);
- $\mathcal{A}$ issues a Corrupt query to id or id' s.t. $id' \in \mathsf{pid}^i_{id}$ (and $\mathcal{A}$ has been *active* with respect to Π^i_{id}).
- $\mathcal{A}$ has made Test query to $\Pi^j_{id'}$.

Full PFS requires that when an active attacker sends any message m to Π^i_{id}, the user id must not be corrupted. If the message m is produced by other instance oracle, the user id can be corrupted. We require that $\mathcal{A}$ never issue State reveal queries to Π^i_{id} in the test session, and $\mathcal{A}$ never issue Corrupt query to KGC. We define the advantage of $\mathcal{A}$ in the above game as

$$\mathtt{Adv}_{\mathcal{A}}(\lambda) = \left| \Pr[b' = b] - \frac{1}{2} \right| .$$

Definition 2. *An ABKE protocol is session key secure if for any PPT $\mathcal{A}$, $\mathtt{Adv}_{\mathcal{A}}(\lambda)$ is negligible in λ.*

4.2 Generic ABKE Construction

Our proposed generic ABKE construction consists of the following two building blocks:

- A fast, expressiveness and adaptive CPA-secure ABE scheme ABE=(Setup, KeyGen, Enc, Dec). For example, FAME, FABEO, FABSEA, etc.
- A two-pass AKE protocol AKE=(KeyGen, Kex). For example, PKI-based HMQV, identity-based mOT, TOPAS and TOPAS+, password-based Protoss, etc.

Our generic ABKE construction is specified as follows:

- Setup (λ): KGC picks two hash functions $H : \{0,1\} \rightarrow \mathbb{G}_1$ and $H' : \{0,1\} \rightarrow \mathbb{Z}_p$, runs $(\mathtt{msk}, \mathtt{mpk}) \leftarrow \mathsf{ABE.Setup}(1^\lambda)$, and publishes public parameters $\mathtt{mpk}$.

- KeyGen ($\mathtt{msk}$, $\mathcal{P}$, id): KGC takes $\mathtt{msk}$ and a policy $\mathcal{P}$ as input, outputs a decryption key $dk \leftarrow \mathsf{ABE.KeyGen}(\mathtt{msk}, \mathcal{P})$ for a user id. Each user owns a secret key sk, and its key generation depends on the underlying AKE protocol.
- $\mathsf{KeyExchange}$: This is an interactive protocol between users Alice and Bob. The interaction is as follows.
  1. Alice with (dk_a, sk_a) picks an ephemeral key pair (esk_a, epk_a); She picks an attribute set $\mathcal{S}_a$, runs $\mathsf{ct}_a \leftarrow \mathsf{ABE.Enc}(\mathtt{mpk}, \mathcal{S}_a, epk_a)$. During the ciphertext generation, Alice computes $H(d_a) \oplus epk_a$ to encrypt message epk_a. Eventually, Alice sends ct_a to Bob.
  2. Upon receiving ct_b from Bob, Alice performs the following steps to derive a session key. She decrypts $epk_b \leftarrow \mathsf{ABE.Dec}(dk_a, \mathsf{ct}_b)$ if Bob's attribute set $\mathcal{S}_b$ satisfies her policy $\mathcal{P}_a$. Specifically, she recovers d_b using her dk_a and computes $epk_b = H(d_b) \oplus (H(d_b) \oplus epk_b)$; She computes a shared key $sk \leftarrow \mathsf{AKE.Kex}(esk_a, epk_b, sk_a, pk_b)$ and derives a session key as $\mathsf{sk} = H'(sk||sid)$.
  3. Bob will perform the same procedure to derive sk.

Design Rationale. We present certain insights to our designs. First, we consider a two-party setting where Alice and Bob know each other's public-key (i.e., identity), so ABE ciphertext will not encrypt user's public-key. We stress that we do not consider (user or attribute) privacy in this work. Second, we consider three cases in generating secret key sk. One case is to let user create a key pair using public parameters, and KGC issues a certificate on user's public key. This case captures PKI-based key exchange protocols. Another case is to let KGC create a secret key using master secret key. This case considers identity-based key exchanges. For password-based key exchanges, we set $sk = H(pwd)$, where pwd indicates the pre-shared password between users. Third, our ABKE construction supports full PFS by changing the encrypted message as $H(d) \oplus sk \oplus epk$. Last, our construction supports both KP and CP versions. We choose KP-based construction due to presentation convenience.

Deniability. Our ABKE construction offers plausible deniability as our considered two-pass AKE protocols require no digital signatures for authentications. Deniable ABKE is suitable for the "off-the-record" communications over an insecure channel. Deniable key exchange says that Bob cannot convince a Judge that Alice talked to him previously [18]. To realize deniability, all protocol transcript and the session key presented by Bob to the Judge can be produced by a public simulation algorithm which runs by a simulator. The definition of deniability is various, one can refer to [33]. Our ABKE construction ensures strong deniability that allows the simulator to access Alice/Bob's secret key sk. Specifically, the ABE ciphertext is uniformly distributed as ephemeral secret key esk_a (or ciphertext randomness) is uniform, the simulator (or adversary Bob) can simulate Alice's ciphertext by choosing a random group element from $\mathbb{G}_1$ to simulate epk_a and produce the ABE ciphertext according to protocol description. The simulator can also compute a session key using Bob's secret key.

Theorem 1. *Our generic construction ensures session key security in the modified CK model if H' has collision-resistance, ABE is adaptive CPA secure and AKE is (passively and actively) session key secure.*

Proof. The proof sketch is given by sequence of games. We allow $\mathcal{A}$ to issue at most q key reveal queries. We define the following games.

- $\mathbb{G}_0$: This is original session key security game.
- $\mathbb{G}_1$: This game aims to prevent replay attacks. Since the hash function H' offers collision-resistance, the probability of replay attack is bounded by $1/2^{\lambda}$.
- $\mathbb{G}_2$: This game aims to prevent impersonations, it is usually called a forge event. We consider an adversary $\mathcal{C}$ against the underlying AKE protocol with either weak or full PFS. If forge event occurs in the test session, $\mathcal{C}$ should find a solution (usually from random oracles) and use it to break the session key security of AKE. $\mathcal{C}$ needs to answer all queries of the adversary by invoking the oracles from his challenger during the training phase, and $\mathcal{C}$ needs to consider two types of test session: passive (i.e., weak PFS) and active (i.e., full PFS).
  - Passive Test Session: We also consider two types of AKE protocols. One is HMQV that achieves weak PFS, another is TOPAS that achieves full PFS but assuming the adversary is passive against test session. In the first simulation, the simulator $\mathcal{C}$ is actually a forger against an exponential challenge-response (XCR) signature. Obviously, $\mathcal{C}$ can answer all queries (except corrupting the target signer) from $\mathcal{A}$ by interacting with his challenger. In the test session, if $\mathcal{A}$ queried a valid XCR forgery to random oracle, $\mathcal{C}$ will extract it from random oracle and use it as the solution to Computational Diffie-Hellman Assumption. Similarly, when it comes to TOPAS protocol and assume that the test session is passive, $\mathcal{C}$ can easily embed Computational Bilinear Diffie-Hellman instances into the exchanged DH messages. Overall, in the test session, the exchanged messages such as $H(d) \oplus epk$ or $H(d) \oplus epk \oplus sk$ will not be produced or modified by passive adversary. $\mathcal{C}$ can find a solution from H' to break computational assumption. This reduction incurs security loss, such as guessing the challenge session or users, etc.
  - Active Test Session: We start with a pairing-based TOPAS with full PFS. Here, $\mathcal{A}$ can modify the message send and received by the test session. In the full PFS security proof, adversary $\mathcal{A}_{[1-6]}$ interacts with a challenger via a sequence of games. The challenger provides knowledge of pairing pre-image assumption (KPA) and modified knowledge of Co-CDH assumption (MKCoCDH) instances to respective adversaries in the consecutive games. In these games, $\mathcal{A}_{1-5}$ is required to output additional values (or the forged values which were not returned by its simulator) so that its challenger can use them to break KPA and MKCoCDH assumptions. In the last game, adversary $\mathcal{A}_6$ will embed computational bilinear Diffie-Hellman inversion (CBDHI) instances into the exchanges messages for adversary $\mathcal{A}_5$ and complete the proof. The proof in TOPAS relies on

non-interactive knowledge-type assumptions to capture adversary's forging capabilities and a computational assumption in the last game, all these assumption can be covered by Uber-assumption [9]. When it comes to pairing-free password-based Protoss, the reduction relies a variant of Strong Diffie-Hellman assumption and an interactive Decisional Diffie-Hellman (DDH) oracle to achieve a tight security proof. Our security reduction depends on the underlying AKE protocols and follows their proof strategies respectively.

- $\mathbb{G}_3$: This game is the same as previous one, except the encrypted ephemeral public keys will be replaced with random values. In this game, $\mathcal{A}$ is passive (i.e., no replay and impersonations), and she can adaptively select attribute set involved in the test session. The difference between these two games is bounded by the underlying ABE's adaptive CPA security. If $\mathcal{A}$ could distinguish these consequence games, $\mathcal{C}$ can break the CPA security of ABE. Finally, $\mathcal{A}$ has no non-negligible advantage to break session key security.

$$\mathtt{Adv}_{\mathcal{A}}(\lambda) \leq q \cdot [\mathtt{Adv}_{\mathcal{A}}^{\mathrm{AKE}}(\lambda) + \mathtt{Adv}_{\mathcal{A}}^{\mathrm{ABE}}(\lambda) + 1/2^{\lambda}].$$

□

5 ABKE Instantiations

The PKI-based ABKE with optimal efficiency and weak PFS can be easily constructed from fast KP-ABE scheme FABEO [30] and implicitly-authenticated HMQV protocol [25]. We select FABEO because its construction offers adaptive security, supports fast decryption and involves less group elements in $\mathbb{G}_2$ than other fast ABE schemes such as FAME [1] and FABESA [29]. Now, we consider ABKE with optimal efficiency and full PFS. We select TOPAS [31] because its construction achieves full PFS and the communication overhead is just one group element in $\mathbb{G}_1$. Also, TOPAS provides both identity-based and PKI-based constructions. We discover that the concrete PKI-based ABKE construction that supports optimal efficiency and full PFS is an open problem.

In the PKI-based TOPAS, the protocol requires KGC to publish (g_1^z, g_2^z) and a user's key pair to be $(sk, pk) = (g_1^x, (g_1^z)^x)$, where x indicates user's (static) secret key. We replace z with α (i.e., master secret key) to match FABEO's setup. The problem is that g_1^α is a secret value used to generate user's decryption keys, which contradicts to PKI-based TOPAS that publishes (g_1^α, g_2^α). Our novel solution is that, KGC only publishes a master public key $g_2^\alpha \in \mathbb{G}_2$ and user's key pair to be $(sk, \text{ pk}) = (g_1^x, (g_2^\alpha)^x)$, where $g_1^x \in \mathbb{G}_1$ indicates user's secret key. KGC can verify user's public key *pk* via a technique called "proof of possession" [19] (see key generation process below). The concrete PKI-based ABKE scheme is the following.

- Setup: KGC runs $\mathsf{GroupGen}(1^\lambda)$ to obtain the group parameters $\mathsf{par} = (p, e, \mathbb{G}_1, \mathbb{G}_2, \mathbb{G}_T, g_1, g_2)$. Picks $\alpha \xleftarrow{\$} \mathbb{Z}_p$, hash functions $H : \{0,1\}^* \rightarrow \mathbb{G}_1$ and $H' : \{0,1\}^* \rightarrow \mathbb{Z}_p$. Computes

$$\mathsf{mpk} = (H, H', \mathsf{par}, g_2^\alpha, e(g_1, g_2)^\alpha), \mathsf{msk} = \alpha.$$

- KeyGen: This is an interactive protocol between a user Alice and KGC. The interaction is as follows.
  1. Alice picks $x_a \xleftarrow{\$} \mathbb{Z}_p$, computes $(sk_a, pk_a, pk_a') = (g_1^{x_a}, (g_2^\alpha)^{x_a}, g_2^{x_a})$ and a proof $\pi \leftarrow H(PoP, pk_a')$, where PoP is a fixed string used as a prefix for domain separation. For example, $\pi = H(PoP, pk_a')^{x_a}$ which is based on BLS signatures [7].
  2. KGC verifies (pk_a, pk_a') via pairings $e(\pi, g_2) = e(H(PoP, pk_a'), pk_a')$ and $e(g_1, pk_a) = e(g_1^\alpha, pk_a')$. If verification passes, KGC picks $r_a \xleftarrow{\$} \mathbb{Z}_p$, $\mathbf{v} \xleftarrow{\$} \mathbb{Z}_p^{n-1}$, computes $\mathsf{sk}_1 = g_2^{r_a}$ and $\mathsf{sk}_{2,i} = g_1^{\mathrm{M}_i(\alpha \| \mathbf{v})} \cdot H(\pi(i))^{r_a}$ and sends $dk_a = (\mathsf{sk}_1, \mathsf{sk}_{2,i})$ to Alice.
  3. Alice outputs $\mathsf{sk}_a = (dk_a, sk_a)$ and publishes pk_a.
- KeyExchange: This is an interactive protocol between users Alice and Bob. The interaction is as follows.
  1. Alice chooses an ephemeral key pair (esk_a, epk_a), where $esk_a = s_a \xleftarrow{\$} \mathbb{Z}_p$ and $epk_a = g_1^{s_a}$; She picks an attribute set $\mathcal{S}_a$ and computes $\mathsf{ct}_{1,i} = H(u_i)^{s_a}, \mathsf{ct}_2 = g_2^{s_a}, \mathsf{ct}_3 = H(d_a) \cdot epk_a \cdot sk_a$, where $d_a = e(g_1, g_2)^{\alpha s_a}$. Eventually, Alice sends a ciphertext $\mathsf{ct}_a = (\mathsf{ct}_{1,i}, \mathsf{ct}_2, \mathsf{ct}_3)$ to Bob.
  2. Upon receiving a ciphertext ct_b from Bob generated using his secret key $g_1^{x_b}$ and ephemeral secret key s_b, Alice performs the following steps to derive a session key. She tests if there is any subset $\mathcal{I}$ that matches $\mathcal{S}_b$ in the ciphertext with $\mathcal{P}_a$ in sk_a. If not, return $\perp$. Otherwise, it finds constants $\{\gamma_i\}_{i \in \mathcal{I}}$ s.t. $\sum_{i \in \mathcal{I}} \gamma_i \mathrm{M}_i = (1,\ 0,\ \ldots,\ 0)$ and reconstructs d_b by computing:

$$d_b = e(g_1, g_2)^{\alpha s_b} = \frac{e\Big(\prod_{i \in \mathcal{I}} (\mathsf{sk}_{2,i})^{\gamma_i},\ \mathsf{ct}_2\Big)}{e\Big(\prod_{i \in \mathcal{I}} (\mathsf{ct}_{1,\pi(i)})^{\gamma_i},\ \mathsf{sk}_1\Big)}.$$

  Then, she recovers $epk_b \cdot sk_b$ from ct_3, and derives a shared key by computing

$$sk = e(g_1, g_2)^{\alpha s_a s_b} = [\frac{e(epk_b \cdot sk_b, g_2^\alpha)}{e(g_1, pk_b)}]^{s_a} = [\frac{e(g_1^{s_b} \cdot g_1^{x_b}, g_2^\alpha)}{e(g_1, (g_2^\alpha)^{x_b})}]^{s_a}$$

  Eventually, Alice computes a session key as $\mathsf{sk} = H'(sk \| sid)$, where sid includes all transmitted messages between Alice and Bob. Bob performs the same procedure to compute sk.

Remarks. We provide further explanations towards our ABKE construction. First, the ephemeral public key is not publicly available. Only the authorized users (e.g., Bob's attributes satisfy Alice's policy) can access ephemeral public keys and compute sessions keys, which reflects implicit authentication. Moreover, one may notice that Alice can compute the shared key $sk = d_b^{s_a} = e(g_1^{s_b}, g_2^{\alpha})^{s_a}$ after decrypting ciphertext ct_b. We stress that the value $\frac{e(epk_b \cdot sk_b, g_2^{\alpha})}{e(g_1, pk_b)}$ prevents impersonations. In other words, Alice can confirm that Bob has generated ciphertext ct_b. This is one of key differences between our generic/concrete construction and the existing ABKE schemes [21,37]. Second, for identity-based AKE protocol like TOPAS [31], we set $sk_a = H(id_a)^{1/\alpha}$. For password-based AKE protocol such as Protoss [17], we set $sk_{a/b} = H(pwd)$, where Alice and Bob share the same high-entropy password pwd. The shared key derivation follows TOPAS and Protoss protocols respectively, and the key generation process is non-interactive (i.e., no interaction between user and KGC). Third, we explain the use of ephemeral public key epk. In case of AKE with weak PFS, Alice can recover epk_b from $\mathsf{ct}_{3b} = H(d_b) \cdot epk_b$ where $d_b = e(g_1, g_2)^{\alpha s_b}$, while in case of AKE with full PFS, Alice can recover $epk_b \cdot sk_b$ from $\mathsf{ct}_{3b} = H(d_b) \cdot epk_b \cdot sk_b$. One may optimize the ABKE scheme by computing $sk = (g_1, g_2)^{\alpha s_a s_b}$ and *without* exchanging ciphertext elements $(\mathsf{ct}_{3a}, \mathsf{ct}_{3b}) = (H(d_a) \cdot g_1^{s_a}, H(d_b) \cdot g_1^{s_b})$. However, this approach will enforce the shared key derivation to be executed on $\mathbb{G}_T$. Especially, when it comes to AKE with full PFS, the "authenticated" ephemeral DH public keys $(epk_a \cdot sk_a, epk_b \cdot sk_b)$ must be exchanged between Alice and Bob. Therefore, we let Alice and Bob exchange the ciphertext elements $(\mathsf{ct}_{3a}, \mathsf{ct}_{3b})$.

5.1 Performance Analysis

We evaluate the computational cost of a user and the communication overhead sent from the user. Our implementation runs in Python and uses the Charm 0.5 framework [3]. We use BN254 curve for type-3 pairings. The execution time below is measured on a PC with a 3.59 GHz AMD Ryzen 5 3600 6-Core Processor and 16GB RAM. We implement two ABKE schemes based on our modified PKI-based TOPAS and two state-of-the-art fast ABE schemes called FABEO [30] and FABESA [29] to show the computational efficiency in Fig. 2. For (KP-based) decryption, FABEO requires 2 pairings and FABESA requires 4 pairings regradless of the size of the attributes. We do not implement non-fast ABE schemes such as [6,22], as the pairing operations for decryption are not constant. Based on our implementation, a user spends 0.15 s to derive a session key when applying 100 attributes to FABEO KP-ABE, where the session key derivation includes ciphertext generation, ciphertext decryption and shared key generation.

For communication overhead, a user will broadcast a (e.g., FABEO) ciphertext in the form of $\mathsf{ct} = (\mathsf{ct}_{1,i}, \mathsf{ct}_2, \mathsf{ct}_3)$, where $|\mathsf{ct}_{1,i}| = i\mathbb{G}_1$, $|\mathsf{ct}_2| = \mathbb{G}_2 \approx 3\mathbb{G}_1$ (note that the size of an element in $\mathbb{G}_2$ is 3 times of $\mathbb{G}_1$), $|\mathsf{ct}_3| = \mathbb{G}_1$, and $i \in [1, m]$ indicates the number of attributes in attribute set $\mathcal{S}$. The overhead is $(i+4)\mathbb{G}_1$. When using type-3 pairing, we assume that $\log_2(p) \approx 160$ and the elements of $\mathbb{G}_1$ can be implemented with 160 bits for a security level of 80 bits [7]. Compared

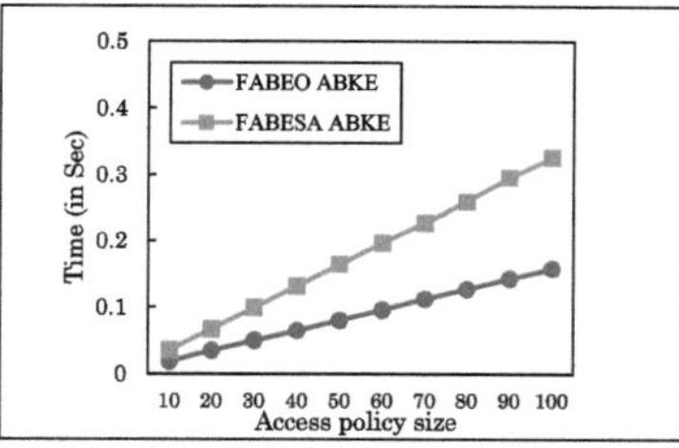

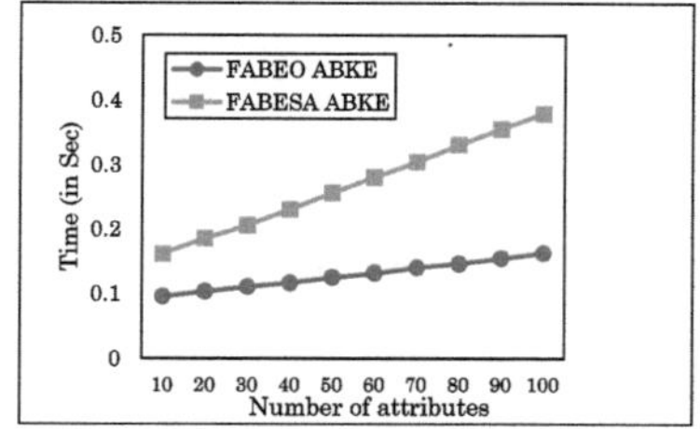

Fig. 2. Execution time of two ABKE schemes. Left-subfigure refers to **Key Generation** for FABEO KP-ABE + PKI-TOPAS; Right-subfigure refers to **Key Exchange** for FABESA KP-ABE + PKI-TOPAS.

to an ABKE scheme [37] which used Waters' CP-ABE, the size of ciphertext depends on the row and column of the matrix M. The size of the ciphertext in our ABKE scheme depends only on the row M. Compared to another ABKE scheme [21], the message send from a user includes a CP-ABE ciphertext [6] (involves group elements in $\mathbb{G}_T$), a one-time signature along with a verification key (due to CCA security). Our ABKE scheme avoids group elements in $\mathbb{G}_T$ and explicit digital signatures.

6 Conclusion

In this paper, we introduced a new generic construction of attribute-based key exchange (ABKE) with enhanced security and optimal efficiency. Our generic construction leverages two research domains: fast attribute-based encryptions and two-pass authenticated key exchanges. Our generic/concrete construction outperforms all existing ABKE schemes in terms of security and efficiency. Specifically, the enhanced security considers several desired features including adaptive security, weak/full PFS and impersonation-resistance. The optimal efficiency ensures a user's session key derivation runs fast and the communication between users requires a minimal overhead. As for future works, we can redesign ABKE schemes to support other features like attribute privacy and multi-authority.

Acknowledgments. This work is supported by the EU's research and innovation program: 952697 (ASSURED), 101069688 (CONNECT), 101095634 (ENTRUST), 101070627 (REWIRE) and 101167904 (CASTOR). These projects are funded by the UK government Horizon Europe guarantee and administered by UKRI. Yinghui Zhang is supported by the National Cryptologic Science Fund of China: 2025NCSF02037. Mark Manulis is supported by project LIONS (part of dtec.bw) funded under NextGenerationEU programme.

A Importance of Secret-Based Authentication

Assume an ABKE protocol is executed between users Alice and Bob, and assume that after establishing a secure session key, Alice sends encrypted sensitive data using the established session key to Bob. In case of whistleblowing, Bob acts as an obliged authority, and Alice who wishes to "leak a secret" to Bob privately must verify his public-key (or identity) during session key establishment. Another use case is that a payer Alice sends encrypted Bitcoin (to hide transaction amount) to explicit beneficiary (or payee) Bob in privacy-preserving payment channels.

Moreover, secret-based authentication can work with (plausible) deniability. To establish secure communications between Alice and Bob for sensitive data transport, Alice verifies Bob's public-key to avoid potential impersonations caused by implicit authentication. Later on, Alice (e.g., whisterblower, payer) can deny the previous secure communications after leaking the secret or sending the Bitcoin to Bob, as Bob cannot convince others that Alice once send some sensitive information to him.

On the other hand, implicit authentication is designed for fine-grained data storage and generic data transport. For data storage, multiple authorized users should be able to access the encrypted data if their key policies satisfy the data's attributes. For generic data transport, original ABKE schemes are sufficient to handle it, as Alice will not need to verify Bob's public-key before sending generic data to him via secure communications.

References

1. Agrawal, S., Chase, M.: FAME: fast attribute-based message encryption. In: CCS, pp. 665–682 (2017)
2. Agrawal, S., Biswas, R., Nishimaki, R., Xagawa, K., Xie, X., Yamada, S.: Cryptanalysis of boyen's attribute-based encryption scheme in tcc 2013. Des. Codes Crypt. **90**(10), 2301–2318 (2022)
3. Akinyele, J.A., et al.: Charm: a framework for rapidly prototyping cryptosystems. J. Cryptogr. Eng. **3**(2), 111–128 (2013)
4. Ateniese, G., Francati, D., Nuñez, D., Venturi, D.: Match me if you can: matchmaking encryption and its applications. In: Boldyreva, A., Micciancio, D. (eds.) CRYPTO 2019. LNCS, vol. 11693, pp. 701–731. Springer, Cham (2019). https://doi.org/10.1007/978-3-030-26951-7_24
5. Balfanz, D., Durfee, G., Shankar, N., Smetters, D., Staddon, J., Wong, H.C.: Secret handshakes from pairing-based key agreements. In: S&P, pp. 180–196 (2003)
6. Bethencourt, J., Sahai, A., Waters, B.: Ciphertext-policy attribute-based encryption. In: S&P, pp. 321–334 (2007)
7. Boneh, D., Lynn, B., Shacham, H.: Short signatures from the weil pairing. In: Boyd, C. (ed.) ASIACRYPT 2001. LNCS, vol. 2248, pp. 514–532. Springer, Heidelberg (2001). https://doi.org/10.1007/3-540-45682-1_30
8. Boyd, C., de Kock, B., Millerjord, L.: Modular design of kem-based authenticated key exchange. In: ACISP, pp. 553–579 (2023)
9. Boyen, X.: The uber-assumption family: a unified complexity framework for bilinear groups. In: Galbraith, S.D., Paterson, K.G. (eds.) Pairing 2008. LNCS, vol. 5209, pp. 39–56. Springer, Heidelberg (2008). https://doi.org/10.1007/978-3-540-85538-5_3
10. Boyen, X.: Attribute-based functional encryption on lattices. In: Sahai, A. (ed.) TCC 2013. LNCS, vol. 7785, pp. 122–142. Springer, Heidelberg (2013). https://doi.org/10.1007/978-3-642-36594-2_8

11. Camenisch, J., Lysyanskaya, A.: An efficient system for non-transferable anonymous credentials with optional anonymity revocation. In: Pfitzmann, B. (ed.) EUROCRYPT 2001. LNCS, vol. 2045, pp. 93–118. Springer, Heidelberg (2001). https://doi.org/10.1007/3-540-44987-6_7
12. Camenisch, J., Lysyanskaya, A.: Signature schemes and anonymous credentials from bilinear maps. In: Franklin, M. (ed.) CRYPTO 2004. LNCS, vol. 3152, pp. 56–72. Springer, Heidelberg (2004). https://doi.org/10.1007/978-3-540-28628-8_4
13. Canetti, R.: Universally composable security: a new paradigm for cryptographic protocols. In: S&P, pp. 136–145 (2001)
14. Canetti, R., Krawczyk, H.: Analysis of key-exchange protocols and their use for building secure channels. In: Pfitzmann, B. (ed.) EUROCRYPT 2001. LNCS, vol. 2045, pp. 453–474. Springer, Heidelberg (2001). https://doi.org/10.1007/3-540-44987-6_28
15. Chase, M.: Multi-authority attribute based encryption. In: Vadhan, S.P. (ed.) TCC 2007. LNCS, vol. 4392, pp. 515–534. Springer, Heidelberg (2007). https://doi.org/10.1007/978-3-540-70936-7_28
16. Cui, H., Deng, R.H., Li, Y., Qin, B.: Server-aided revocable attribute-based encryption. In: Askoxylakis, I., Ioannidis, S., Katsikas, S., Meadows, C. (eds.) ESORICS 2016. LNCS, vol. 9879, pp. 570–587. Springer, Cham (2016). https://doi.org/10.1007/978-3-319-45741-3_29
17. Di Giandomenico, E., Li, Y., Schäge, S.: Protoss: protocol for tight optimal symmetric security. In: CCS, pp. 4718–4731 (2024)
18. Di Raimondo, M., Gennaro, R., Krawczyk, H.: Deniable authentication and key exchange. In: CCS, pp. 400–409 (2006)
19. Drijvers, M., Gorbunov, S., Neven, G., Wee, H.: Pixel: multi-signatures for consensus. In: USENIX, pp. 2093–2110 (2020)
20. Fujisaki, E., Okamoto, T.: Secure integration of asymmetric and symmetric encryption schemes. In: Wiener, M. (ed.) CRYPTO 1999. LNCS, vol. 1666, pp. 537–554. Springer, Heidelberg (1999). https://doi.org/10.1007/3-540-48405-1_34
21. Gorantla, M.C., Boyd, C., González Nieto, J.M.: Attribute-based authenticated key exchange. In: Steinfeld, R., Hawkes, P. (eds.) ACISP 2010. LNCS, vol. 6168, pp. 300–317. Springer, Heidelberg (2010). https://doi.org/10.1007/978-3-642-14081-5_19
22. Goyal, V., Pandey, O., Sahai, A., Waters, B.: Attribute-based encryption for fine-grained access control of encrypted data. In: CCS, pp. 89–98 (2006)
23. Katz, J., Yung, M.: Scalable protocols for authenticated group key exchange. In: Boneh, D. (ed.) CRYPTO 2003. LNCS, vol. 2729, pp. 110–125. Springer, Heidelberg (2003). https://doi.org/10.1007/978-3-540-45146-4_7
24. Kolesnikov, V., Krawczyk, H., Lindell, Y., Malozemoff, A., Rabin, T.: Attribute-based key exchange with general policies. In: CCS, pp. 1451–1463 (2016)
25. Krawczyk, H.: HMQV: a high-performance secure Diffie-Hellman protocol. In: Shoup, V. (ed.) CRYPTO 2005. LNCS, vol. 3621, pp. 546–566. Springer, Heidelberg (2005). https://doi.org/10.1007/11535218_33
26. Lai, J., Tang, Q.: Making *Any* attribute-based encryption accountable, efficiently. In: Lopez, J., Zhou, J., Soriano, M. (eds.) ESORICS 2018. LNCS, vol. 11099, pp. 527–547. Springer, Cham (2018). https://doi.org/10.1007/978-3-319-98989-1_26
27. LaMacchia, B., Lauter, K., Mityagin, A.: Stronger security of authenticated key exchange. In: Susilo, W., Liu, J.K., Mu, Y. (eds.) ProvSec 2007. LNCS, vol. 4784, pp. 1–16. Springer, Heidelberg (2007). https://doi.org/10.1007/978-3-540-75670-5_1

28. Lewko, A., Waters, B.: Unbounded HIBE and attribute-based encryption. In: Paterson, K.G. (ed.) EUROCRYPT 2011. LNCS, vol. 6632, pp. 547–567. Springer, Heidelberg (2011). https://doi.org/10.1007/978-3-642-20465-4_30
29. Meng, L., Chen, L., Tian, Y., Manulis, M.: FABESA: fast (and anonymous) attribute-based encryption under standard assumption. In: CCS, pp. 4688–4702 (2024)
30. Riepel, D., Wee, H.: FABEO: fast attribute-based encryption with optimal security. In: CCS, pp. 2491–2504 (2022)
31. Schäge, S.: TOPAS: 2-pass key exchange with full perfect forward secrecy and optimal communication complexity. In: CCS, pp. 1224–1235 (2015)
32. Schnorr, C.P.: Efficient signature generation by smart cards. J. Cryptol. **4**(3), 161–174 (1991). https://doi.org/10.1007/BF00196725
33. Tian, Y., et al.: DABKE: secure deniable attribute-based key exchange framework. J. Comput. Secur. **27**(2), 259–275 (2019)
34. Tomida, J., Kawahara, Y., Nishimaki, R.: Fast, compact, and expressive attribute-based encryption. Des. Codes Crypt. **89**(11), 2577–2626 (2021). https://doi.org/10.1007/s10623-021-00939-8
35. Venema, M., Alpár, G., Hoepman, J.H.: Systematizing core properties of pairing-based attribute-based encryption to uncover remaining challenges in enforcing access control in practice. Des. Codes Crypt. **91**(1), 165–220 (2023)
36. Waters, B.: Ciphertext-policy attribute-based encryption: an expressive, efficient, and provably secure realization. In: Catalano, D., Fazio, N., Gennaro, R., Nicolosi, A. (eds.) PKC 2011. LNCS, vol. 6571, pp. 53–70. Springer, Heidelberg (2011). https://doi.org/10.1007/978-3-642-19379-8_4
37. Yoneyama, K.: Strongly secure two-pass attribute-based authenticated key exchange. In: Joye, M., Miyaji, A., Otsuka, A. (eds.) Pairing 2010. LNCS, vol. 6487, pp. 147–166. Springer, Heidelberg (2010). https://doi.org/10.1007/978-3-642-17455-1_10
38. Zhang, Y., Chen, X., Li, J., Wong, D.S., Li, H.: Anonymous attribute-based encryption supporting efficient decryption test. In: AsiaCCS, pp. 511–516 (2013)

Codes on Any Cayley Graph Have an Interactive Oracle Proof of Proximity

Hugo Delavenne[1,2](✉) and Louise Lallemand[1,2]

[1] LIX, École Polytechnique, Institut Polytechnique de Paris, Palaiseau, France
[2] INRIA, Palaiseau, France
hugo.delavenne@inria.fr

Abstract. Interactive Oracle Proofs of Proximity (IOPP) are at the heart of code-based SNARKs, a family of zeroknowledge protocols. The first and most famous one is the FRI protocol [3], that efficiently tests proximity to Reed-Solomon codes. This paper generalizes the flowering IOPP introduced in [13] for some specific $(2, n)$-regular Tanner codes to a much broader variety of codes: any code with symbols indexed on the edges of a Cayley graph. The flowering protocol of [13] had a soundness parameter much lower than the FRI protocol [5], and complexity parameters that could compete with the FRI [3]. The lower soundness and the absence of restriction on the base field may lead to other practical speedups, however the codes considered in [13] have an $o(1)$ minimum distance. The generalization proposed in this paper preserves the soundness parameter with a slight decrease of the complexity parameters, while allowing being applied on codes with constant rate and constant minimum distance thanks to the good expansion properties of some families of Cayley graphs.

Keywords: SNARK · IOP · Error-correcting codes · Proximity test · Tanner codes · Cayley graphs

1 Introduction

1.1 Code-Based SNARKs

Succinct Non-interactive ARguments of Knowledge (SNARK) allow a computationally powerful entity, called the Prover, to convince a weaker entity, called the Verifier, that it has correctly performed a long computation. The computation is stated for instance as a program and an input. The Prover provides the output of the execution as well as a proof that the output was actually obtained from the given program on the given input. The goal is for that proof to be much shorter than the length of the computation, and efficiently verifiable, that is verifying the proof should be much faster than running the program again.

The main practical application of SNARKs is for blockchains. It allows to perform huge computations out of chain and only add the SNARK proof to the chain. SNARKs can be applied on very general computations and other

Y. Kim et al. (Eds.): CANS 2025, LNCS 16351, pp. 335–357, 2026.
https://doi.org/10.1007/978-981-95-4434-9_16

applications emerge. It can preserve authenticity signature [12], for instance when one has a camera authenticating pictures as being from the real world and wants to crop or compress a picture to JPEG while preserving the authentication. The SNARK would be a proof of the correct use of the image editing program. It can also be used to create AI regulation [15] by turning the training process into a SNARK. Other properties can then be proved on the training, for instance that the training data was free of use, or was unbiased.

One of the main approaches to build SNARKs relies on efficient proximity tests to error-correcting codes. The program is first written in an arithmetic form in the *arithmetization* phase. It can be an arithmetic circuit for the R1CS [6] or PlonK [17] arithmetizations, or directly as a system of polynomial constraints for the AIR [4] arithmetization. Verifying the computation is then reduced to testing proximity of words built from the arithmetized computation to a Reed-Solomon code. These words satisfy the property that if the computation is correct then they belong to a Reed-Solomon code, but if the computation is not correct then at least some of them are very far from the Reed-Solomon code. This last gap obtained for non-correct computations explains why one can rely on proximity testing rather than code membership.

An important issue about SNARKs is that they often imply intrinsic arithmetic constraints on the field used. For instance the existence of pairing friendly curves [1] or a prime characteristic p with $p - 1$ being very smooth [2,3]. This hinders applications when the field is imposed and cannot be changed by the SNARK designer. This is the case for example when trying to compose or interoperate SNARKs, or when dealing with signatures using the "Bitcoin curve" `secp256k1` [11] that require the field to be $\mathbb{F}_p$ with $p = 2^{256} - 2^{32} - 977$.

1.2 Interactive Oracle Proofs of Proximity

Given a finite field $\mathbb{F}$ and $n \in \mathbb{N}$, a (linear) error-correcting code is a linear subspace of $\mathbb{F}^n$. Two important parameters of a code are its dimension and its minimum distance for a given distance over $\mathbb{F}^n$, often the Hamming distance $\Delta_H(u, u') := \frac{1}{n}|\{j \in [n] \mid u_j \neq u'_j\}|$. The minimum distance of the code is the minimum distance between two distinct codewords.

Codes with efficient (non-interactive) proximity testing are a recent breakthrough [14] but those codes are not easily suitable for arithmetization. The idea introduced in [7] is to allow the proximity test to be made interactively between the Verifier and the Prover. There can be several rounds of interaction. At each round, the Verifier sends randomness to the Prover, and the Prover gives the Verifier an *oracle access* to a word. That means that the Prover commits to a word $u = (u_1, ..., u_n)$, and the Verifier can later ask to get a coordinate u_j for some j and be assured that it gets u_j and not $\tilde{u}_j \neq u_j$. Such a proof is thus called an Interactive Oracle Proof of Proximity (IOPP).

Since the protocol involves randomness from the Verifier and that it does not read words entirely, the probability of failure is nonzero. More precisely, there are two ways for the protocol to fail. There could be false negatives, if the word tested u is indeed a codeword of C but that the Verifier rejects after the execution of the protocol. This property is called the *completeness* and is the probability for the Verifier to accept a valid codeword. One can usually obtain a perfect completeness, that is a completeness of 1. There could also be false positives, if the word tested u is very far from C but that the Verifier accepts after the execution of the protocol. This property is called the *soundness* and is the probability for the Verifier to accept a word u too far from C. One tries to built IOPP with a soundness as small as possible. It is important to notice that completeness gives the probability for the Verifier to accept if $u \in C$ whereas the soundness gives the probability for the Verifier to accept given that $\Delta_H(u, C) \geq \delta$ with δ a fixed gap parameter.

There are several complexity aspects have to be considered for such interactive protocols. First, we count the number of rounds of the protocol, called the *round complexity.* Then we must consider the computational complexity of the Prover and the Verifier executing honestly the protocol, called the *prover complexity* and the *verifier complexity.* We count the total length of commited messages to the Verifier as oracles, called the *proof length.* We also count the number of queries to the oracles that the Verifier asks, called the *query complexity,* and the amount of randomness it is using, called the *randomness complexity.*

When the Verifier can have public coin randomness, the IOPP is actually turned into a non-interactive proof using a Fiat-Shamir-like heuristic [7,16], and it is succinct thanks to the oracles instantiated with Merkle trees [22]. These two primitives rely on cryptographic hash functions, hence the only security assumption that we assume is that the Prover cannot find collisions for that hash function, and that the output of that hash function can be considered random. Hence we only assume the random oracle model.

1.3 Fast Reed-Solomon IOPP

IOPPs allow proximity testing to arithmetization-friendly codes such as Reed-Solomon codes using the Fast Reed-Solomon IOPP (FRI) protocol [3]. Given n distinct values $x_1, ..., x_n \in \mathbb{F}$, the Reed-Solomon code of length n and dimension $k \leq n$, denoted $\mathrm{RS}[n, k]$, is the vector space of evaluation of polynomials of degree $\leq k-1$ on $x_1, ..., x_n$:

$$\mathrm{RS}[n, k] := \{(\hat{f}(x_1), ..., \hat{f}(x_n)) \mid \hat{f} \in \mathbb{F}[X]_{\leq k-1}\} \subseteq \mathbb{F}^n.$$

We can see Reed-Solomon codes as the words $f = (f_1, ..., f_n)$ whose least degree interpolating polynomial $\hat{f}$ on $x_1, ..., x_n$ has degree $\leq k-1$. The idea of the FRI protocol is to reduce testing the proximity to a word f of length n, to testing the proximity to a word of length $n/2$. For k even, we have that a polynomial $\hat{f}$ has degree $\leq k-1$ if, and only if, its even and odd parts, denoted $\hat{f}_{\text{even}}$ and $\hat{f}_{\text{odd}}$, have degree $\leq (k-2)/2$. But proving successively that $\hat{f}_{\text{even}}$ and $\hat{f}_{\text{odd}}$ have the right degree would not gain in complexity compared to proving that $\hat{f}$ has the right degree. Therefore the FRI protocol reduces testing the degree of $\hat{f}$ to testing the degree of $\hat{f}_{\text{even}} + \rho \hat{f}_{\text{odd}}$ using the randomness ρ given by the Verifier. This linear combination is called the *folding* of $\hat{f}$. It has two important properties. First, the folding at value $y = x^2$ can be computed using only two values of f since we have that

$$\hat{f}_{\text{even}}(y) = \frac{\hat{f}(x) + \hat{f}(-x)}{2} \qquad \hat{f}_{\text{odd}}(y) = \frac{\hat{f}(x) - \hat{f}(-x)}{2x}. \tag{1}$$

Second, it can be can proven [9, Theorem 10] that if f is far from $\text{RS}[n, k]$, then the folding will be far from $\text{RS}[n/2, k/2]$ with high probability over the randomness of the Verifier. This property is called the *commit soundness.* Hence applying successively the folding operator on a word far from the original Reed-Solomon code will preserve a gap of distance to the successive codes. However the issue of that folding is that it requires the field used to have 2^m roots of the unity with $2^m \approx n$ in order to be able to apply Eq. (1) on successive domain of evaluation being the squares of the previous ones.

The FRI protocol on the input f_0 runs as follows. During the commit phase, the Verifier sends randomness to the Prover which then gives oracle access to a word f_1, and they repeat for R rounds, the Prover giving oracle to f_r at each round $r \in [R]$. Since the words commited by the Prover have a priori no link between each other, the Verifier checks during the query phase that each f_r is indeed built as the folding of f_{r-1} by testing on some random values. Finally, the Verifier checks that f_R has the right degree. The FRI protocol has perfect completeness. The soundness parameter has a component giving the probability that the commit phase goes wrong, the commit soundness, computed here in Proposition 4, and a component giving the probability that the query phase goes wrong, called the query soundness, computed here in Proposition 5.

The STIR IOPP [2] allows the Verifier to query less coordinates. It works by folding and expanding the resulting domain, leading to a much faster decrease in the rate of the codes. However, both FRI and STIR protocol require the field $\mathbb{F}$ to be very smooth: the FRI requires $|\mathbb{F}| - 1$ to have a lot of small factors and the STIR requires $|\mathbb{F}| - 1$ to be divisible by a large power of 2.

1.4 Codes on Graphs

We work here on the flowering protocol [13], which it an IOPP for some codes built on graphs, that mimics the FRI protocol by defining a different folding operator. We consider codes on graphs similar to the ones used by Sipser and Spielman [25] where the graph is n-regular and the symbols of the words are values on the edges between the vertices. Given a base code that will be here a Reed-Solomon code $\text{RS}[n, k]$, the code is defined as the set of words such that the "local view" around each vertex, composed of the vector of values of edges around that vertex, is a Reed-Solomon codeword. These codes can also be seen as Tanner codes. A Tanner graph is a bipartite graph with the symbols on one side and the constraints on the other side, and the edges link symbols to constraints to be satisfied. With our graphs, the symbols (the values on the edges) would be linked to two constraints (the vertices that require their local view to be a Reed-Solomon codeword).

The graphs we consider are Cayley graphs [10]. Given a group G and a symmetric generating set $S \subseteq G$, the Cayley graph $\mathrm{Cay}(G, S)$ has vertices the elements of G and there is an edge between g and $g' \in G$ if there exists $s \in S$ such that $g' = g \cdot s$. We are interested in Cayley graphs for the symmetries they provide and that helps to create a folding operator, but also for the good *expansion* of some of these graphs [19,23]. These expansion properties imply both a lower bound on the minimum distance of graph codes built on them [18], and an upper bound on their diameter [14, Lemma 2.1].

1.5 Flowering Protocol

An IOPP, called *Flowering*, for codes on graphs was proposed in [13]. The authors create a folding operator to mimic the FRI protocol. They do not split the codeword in two halves, instead they take a coarser view and split the set of vertices of the graph in two halves, and create two words with the edges of the two resulting subgraphs, that will play the role of the even and odd parts of the FRI. This operation is called *cutting* the graph. When the two cut graphs are isomorphic, it is possible to define a folding operator by simply doing a linear combination of the codewords using that isomorphism. Then the protocol is the same as the FRI protocol.

Since the number of vertices is divided by two at each step, the graph must have a number of edges that is a power of two. To achieve this and having a lot of symmetries to create isomorphic cuts, the authors apply their protocol to Cayley graphs of the additive group over $(\mathbb{Z}/2\mathbb{Z})^r$. Using this, they achieve complexity parameters close to the FRI protocol, and soundness parameters that surpass the FRI protocol. However the codes built on these graphs have a relative minimal distance that goes to 0 as the length of the code increases.

1.6 Results

We generalize the Flowering protocol from [13] by allowing to separate the vertices in more than two sets, and most importantly to sets of vertices that may overlap and thus not form a partition of the vertices. While this reduces less the size of the folding compared to exactly dividing the size, and yields higher factors for the Prover complexity, it allows us to construct a folding operator for Cayley graphs on any group and any symmetric generating set. Using the expansion properties of Cayley graphs, we can then achieve an IOPP for codes on graphs with a constant rate and constant relative minimum distance.

We manage to keep the same soundness parameters as in [13, Theorem 2] by giving different weights to the vertices depending on the number of cuts they are part of. Therefore we achieve an IOPP with constant rate and minimum distance, and lower soundness than the FRI and STIR protocols, since our protocol require a smaller field and can be applied up to the covering radius whereas the FRI and the STIR protocols are only proven up to the Johnson radius [5, Theorem 7.2], while being conjectured up to the covering radius [8, Conjecture 2.3].

We compare in Tables 1 and 2 the complexity and soundness parameters of the FRI protocol [3,5] and the STIR protocol [2] with the original flowering protocol [13] and our generalization, stated more precisely in Theorems 1 and 2. All protocols are applied on a code of length N and dimension K. The codes used for the flowering protocol are those built in Sect. 5, where n and κ are constants. Note that the $\log N$ factors of the prover complexity and proof length are due to very rough estimations of the sizes of intermediate codes due to the overlap of the set of vertices, since they are considered all constant for the estimation.

Table 1. Comparison of the complexity parameters to reach λ bits of security when testing δ-proximity to a code of length N and dimension K. The constants for the STIR depend on δ. Here, κ and n are constant, $n := p+1$ and $\kappa := \kappa(p)$ with the notations of Sect. 5.2.

Protocol	FRI [3,5]	STIR [2]	Flowering [13]	Flowering (here)
Prover	$< 8N$	$O(N)$	$< 3N$	$< 5\kappa N \log N$
Verifier	$< \frac{2\lambda \log K}{\min(\delta, 1-\sqrt{K/N})}$	$O(\lambda^2 + \lambda \log\log K)$	$< \frac{4\lambda \log^2 N}{\delta + \log N/N}$	$< \frac{8\lambda n\kappa \log N}{\delta + \log N/N}$
Query	$\frac{2\lambda \log K}{\min(\delta, 1-\sqrt{K/N})}$	$O(\lambda \log\log K)$	$< \frac{2\lambda \log^2 N}{\delta + \log N/N}$	$< \frac{3\lambda n\kappa \log N}{\delta + \log N/N}$
Rounds	$\log K$	$O(\log K)$	$< \log N$	$< \kappa \log N$
Length	$< N$	$N + O(\log K)$	$< N$	$< \kappa N \log N$
Field size	$> \frac{2^\lambda 10^7 N^{3.5} \log K}{K^{1.5}}$	$\Omega\left(\frac{\lambda 2^\lambda K^2 N^{3.5}}{\log(N/K)}\right)$	$> 2^\lambda N \log N$	$> 2^{\lambda+1} \kappa N \log N$
Field structure	$\lvert\mathbb{F}\rvert - 1$ has lots of small factors	$2^{\lceil \log K \rceil} \mid \lvert\mathbb{F}\rvert - 1$	Any	

Table 2. Comparison of the soundness parameter when testing δ-proximity to a code of length N and dimension K, where $L \in \mathbb{N}$ is the repetition parameter, and κ and n are constant, $n := p + 1$ and $\kappa := \kappa(p)$ with the notations of Sect. 5.2. The total soundness is the sum of the commit and query soundness.

Protocol	FRI [3,5]	Flowering [13]	Flowering (here)
Commit soundness	$\frac{10^7 N^{3.5} \log K}{K^{1.5} \lvert\mathbb{F}\rvert}$	$\frac{N \log N}{\lvert\mathbb{F}\rvert}$	$\frac{2\kappa N \log N}{\lvert\mathbb{F}\rvert}$
Query soundness	$\left(1 - \min\left(\delta, 1 - 1.05\sqrt{\frac{K}{N}}\right)\right)^L$	$\left(1 - \delta - \frac{\log N}{N}\right)^L$	

The typical range of length and dimension when using the FRI or the STIR, as stated in the benchmark of [2] is $K \in [2^{18}, 2^{30}]$ and $N \in [2K, 16K]$. For $N = 2^{19}$, $K = 2^{18}$ and $\lambda = 128$ for instance, the STIR requires a field of size $> 2^{237}$ and the FRI a field of size $> 2^{194}$, while our protocol requires a generic field of size

$> 2^{160}$ with $\kappa \approx 2^7$. This means that our protocol could benefit in term of Prover and Verifier complexity from working on smaller fields.

2 Graphs and Codes on Graphs

In the paper, rounds of protocols will be indexed using the letter $r \in [R]$, edges outgoing from a vertex will be indexed using the letter $j \in [n]$, cuts will be indexed using the letter $i \in [m]$, and steps of repetitions of some phases using the letter $\ell \in [L]$.

2.1 Regular Indexed Multigraphs

Fix a finite field $\mathbb{F}$ and $n \leq |\mathbb{F}|$. We consider n-regular indexed multigraphs (n-RIM), which are graphs with multiple edges between vertices and loops around vertices, and whose edges around a vertex are indexed between 1 and n. We slightly extend the notion from [13] by allowing an edge between v and v' to be indexed differently in v and in v'.

Definition 1 (Regular Indexed Multigraph (RIM) [13, Definition 1]**).** *A n-RIM $\Gamma = (V, E)$ is given by a set of vertices V and a function $E : V \times [n] \to V$ such that for $(v, j) \in V \times [n]$, $E(v, j)$ is the neighbor of v through the edge indexed j, and such that E satisfies the* well-definedness property*: there is a permutation of $[n]$ denoted $j \mapsto \overline{j}$ such that*

$$\forall (v, j) \in V \times [n], \quad E\big(E(v, j), \overline{j}\big) = v.$$

We will consider that the permutation $j \mapsto \overline{j}$ is always fixed and clear from context. Given an n-RIM $\Gamma = (V, E)$, its set of edges, denoted edges(Γ), is defined as the quotient of $V \times [n]$ by the relation $\sim_E$ defined by $(v, j) \sim_E (v', j')$ iff either $(v, j) = (v', j')$, or $j = \overline{j'}$ and $E(v, j) = v'$:

$$\text{edges}(\Gamma) = (V \times [n]) / \sim_E .$$

Note that the equivalence classes of $\sim_E$ have either one element for loop edges, or two elements for edges between distinct vertices. We denote by petals$(\Gamma) \subseteq$ edges(Γ) the set of edges (v, j) that are loops, and that we call *petals*.

We study words on graphs whose symbols are indexed on the edges of the graphs. We see these words as functions edges$(\Gamma) \to \mathbb{F}$ and we denote by $W(\Gamma, \mathbb{F})$ the set of words on a graph Γ in $\mathbb{F}$. For $f \in W(\Gamma, \mathbb{F})$ and $v \in V$, denote by $f(v, \cdot) = (f(v, 1), ..., f(v, n))$ the vector of the values indexed by the edges around v. For clarity, we will actually use the words $f \in W(\Gamma, \mathbb{F})$ as functions $V \times [n] \to \mathbb{F}$, without proving explicitely that whenever $(v, j) \sim_E (v', j')$, then $f(v, j) = f(v', j')$.

Tanner codes [26] are codes built on (l, r)-regular bipartite graphs where the symbols are vertices of arity l on the left side and the constraints are vertices of arity r on the right side. The constraints are applied to the symbols connected to them. Since the symbols of our words are on the edges, hence connected to two constraints, we can see our codes as Tanner codes on $(2, n)$-regular bipartite graphs by adding vertices on the edges to put symbols on them. In the case studied in this paper, the constraints will be that the symbols connected to a vertex have to form a Reed-Solomon codeword.

Definition 2 (Code on graph). *Given an n-RIM $\Gamma = (V, E)$ and $k \leq n$, we define the code $\mathcal{C}[\Gamma, k] \subseteq W(\Gamma, \mathbb{F})$ by*

$$\mathcal{C}[\Gamma, k] := \{f \in W(\Gamma, \mathbb{F}) \mid \forall v \in V, f(v, \cdot) \in RS[n, k]\}.$$

We give a general lower bound on the dimension of these codes.

Proposition 1 (Lower bound on the dimension [13, Proposition 2]**).** *Let $\Gamma = (V, E)$ be an n-RIM and $k \leq n$. Then*

$$\dim \mathcal{C}[\Gamma, k] \geq (k - n/2)|V| + |\text{petals}(\Gamma)|/2.$$

We use the *relative Hamming distance*, denoted Δ_H between words of $W(\Gamma, \mathbb{F})$, and the relative vertex distance from [13].

Definition 3 (Vertex distance [13, Definition 8]**).** *Let $\Gamma = (V, E)$ be an n-RIM. Let $f, f' \in W(\Gamma, \mathbb{F})$. Define the relative* vertex distance *between f and f', denoted Δ_V, as*

$$\Delta_V(f, f') := \frac{1}{|V|}|\{v \in V \mid f(v, \cdot) \neq f'(v, \cdot)\}|.$$

The vertex distance can be thought as a coarser version of the Hamming distance.

Proposition 2 (Comparison between distances [13, Proposition 1]**).** *Let Γ be an n-RIM. Let $f, f' \in W(\Gamma, \mathbb{F})$. Then there exists $\mu(\Gamma) \in [0, 1]$ such that $\Delta_V(f, f') \geq \mu(\Gamma)\Delta_H(f, f')$. Furthermore, if all vertices of Γ have the same number of petals then $\mu(\Gamma) = 1$.*

In particular, if Γ has no petals then $\mu(\Gamma) = 1$. Moreover, the generalization in this paper requires weighted vertex distances.

Definition 4 (Weighted vertex distance). *Let $w : V \to \mathbb{R}^+$ be a weight function and $T \subseteq V$. Denote*

$$|T|_w := \sum_{v \in T} w(v).$$

If $f, f' \in W(\Gamma, \mathbb{F})$, denote $D_w(f, f') := |\{v \in V \mid f(v, \cdot) \neq f'(v, \cdot)\}|_w$, and define the relative w-weighted vertex distance *by*

$$\Delta_w(f, f') := \frac{D_w(f, f')}{|V|_w} \in [0, 1].$$

2.2 Cutting Graphs

In order to mimic the FRI protocol [3], we need to find a way to split the words of $W(\Gamma, \mathbb{F})$ into several pieces. To achieve this, we split the graph into several pieces according to some subsets of vertices, and cut the edges leaving these subsets.

Definition 5 (Cut-graph, cut-word [13, Definition 4]**).** *If $\Gamma = (V, E)$ is an n-RIM, for $V' \subseteq V$, define the* cut-graph $\mathrm{Cut}[\Gamma, V']$ *as the n-RIM (V', E') where*

$$E' : (v, j) \mapsto \begin{cases} E(v, j) & \text{if } E(v, j) \in V' \\ v & \text{otherwise.} \end{cases}$$

If $f \in W(\Gamma, \mathbb{F})$ and $V' \subseteq V$, define the cut-word $\mathrm{Cut}[f, V'] \in W(\mathrm{Cut}[\Gamma, V'], \mathbb{F})$ *as the restriction of f to $\mathrm{Cut}[\Gamma, V']$: for $(v, j) \in V' \times [n], \mathrm{Cut}[f, V'](v, j) = f(v, j)$.*

Figure 1 illustrates a graph cutting. Once we have several cuts $V_0, ..., V_{m-1} \subseteq V$, we also need a way to *fold* their cut-words together as a single word, like for the FRI protocol. We require to apply such a fold that the cuts are all *isomorphic.*

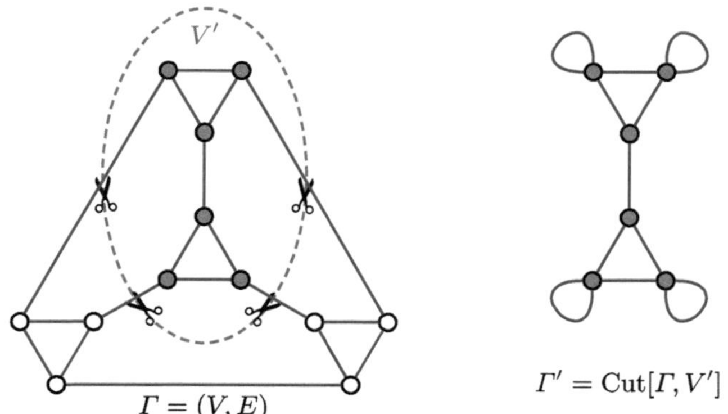

Fig. 1. Example of graph cutting. The cyan edges $V' \subseteq V$ are the ones kept for the cut. The edges leaving the subgraph are cut and become petals.

Definition 6 (RIM isomorphism [13, Definition 3]**).** *Let $\Gamma = (V, E)$ and $\Gamma' = (V', E')$ be n-RIM. An* isomorphism *from Γ to Γ' is a bijection $\varphi : V \to V'$ such that for any $(v, j) \in V \times [n]$ we have $\varphi(E(v, j)) = E'(\varphi(v), j)$.*

Definition 7 (Flowering cut collection [13, Definition 5]**).** *For $m \geq 2$, let $V_0, ..., V_{m-1} \subseteq V$ such that $\bigcup_{i=0}^{m-1} V_i = V$. If for all $i \in \{0, ..., m-1\}$, $\mathrm{Cut}[\Gamma, V_i]$ is isomorphic to $\mathrm{Cut}[\Gamma, V_0]$, then we say that $(V_0, ..., V_{m-1})$ is a* flowering cut collection *of order m from Γ to $\mathrm{Cut}[\Gamma, V_0]$.*

For $v \in V$*, denote* $\mathrm{mul}(v) := |\{i \in \{0, ..., m-1\} \mid v \in V_i\}| \geq 1$ *the number of cuts that overlap on* v*, that we call* multiplicity*. For the symmetries of the cuts, we furthermore require that a cut collection* $(V_0, ..., V_{m-1})$ *satisfies that the multiplicity is invariant under the isomorphisms, i.e. for any* $v \in V$ *and* $i \in \{0, ..., m-1\}$*,*

$$\mathrm{mul}(v) = \mathrm{mul}(\varphi_i(v)). \tag{2}$$

Figure 2 illustrates a flowering cut collection. The difference with [13] lies here: the flowering cuts collections were restricted to $m = 2$, and V_0 and V_1 being disjoint.

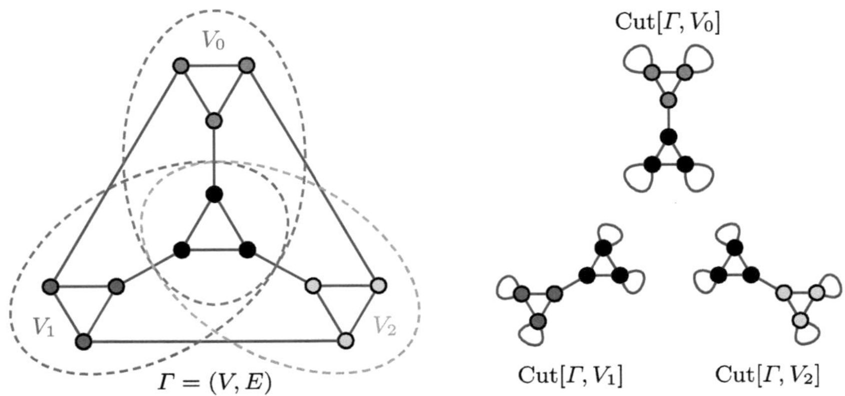

Fig. 2. Example of flowering cut collection. All cut-graphs are isomorphic. The black vertices have a multiplicity of 3 since they are contained in all cuts, while the other cyan, magenta and yellow vertices only have a multiplicity of 1. (Color figure online)

Definition 8 (Folding [13, Definition 6]**).** *Let* $\Gamma = (V, E)$ *be an* n*-RIM and let* $(V_0, ..., V_{m-1})$ *be a flowering cut of* V*, using* $\varphi_i : V_0 \to V_i$ *as RIM isomorphism for* $i \in \{0, ..., m-1\}$*. For* $f \in W(\Gamma, \mathbb{F})$ *and* $\rho \in \mathbb{F}$*, we define the* folding *of* f *over* ρ*, denoted* $\mathrm{Fold}[f, \rho]$*, as the word of* $W(\mathrm{Cut}[\Gamma, V_0], \mathbb{F})$ *such that*

$$\mathrm{Fold}[f, \rho] : (v, j) \mapsto \sum_{i=0}^{m-1} \rho^i \mathrm{Cut}[f, V_i](\varphi_i(v), j).$$

We will want to apply recursively such cuts and foldings, until we reach a graph composed of a single vertex with only petals, that we call the *flower*.

Definition 9 (Blossoming graph sequence). *Let* $\Gamma_0, ..., \Gamma_R$ *be a sequence of graphs such that* Γ_R *only has one vertex. If for every* $r \in [R]$ *there exists a flowering cut collections* $(V_{r,0}, ..., V_{r,m-1})$ *from* Γ_{r-1} *to* Γ_r*, then we say that* $(\Gamma_0, ..., \Gamma_R)$ *is a* blossoming graph sequence *of* Γ_0*.*

The blossoming graph sequences can also be defined for flowering cut collections of different order m_r at each step r. Figure 3 illustrates such a blossoming graph sequence, alternating cuts of order 3 and cuts of order 2.

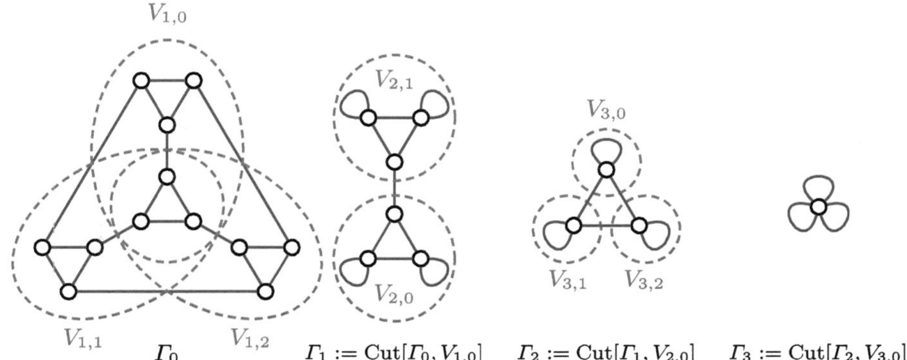

Fig. 3. Example of blossoming graph sequence. Γ_3 is a flower with only petals.

Along with the blossoming graph sequence, we define recursively a *sequence of weights* $w_0, ..., w_R$ such that, for $r \in [R]$, $w_r : V_r \to \mathbb{R}^+$. Start by the uniform weight, $w_0 : v \mapsto 1$. Therefore $\Delta_{w_0} = \Delta_V$. Then w_{r+1} is defined on V_{r+1} as

$$w_{r+1}(v) := \frac{w_r(v)}{\mathrm{mul}(v)}.$$

Using Eq. (2) we have by induction that these weights are invariant under the RIM isomorphisms, as stated in Proposition 3.

Proposition 3 (Symmetry of the weights). *Let $\Gamma_0, ..., \Gamma_R$ be a blossoming graph sequence and $w_0, ..., w_R$ be a sequence of weights defined as above. Then for $r \in \{0, ..., R\}$, $v \in V_r$ and $i \in \{0, ..., m-1\}$, we have*

$$w_r(v) = w_r(\varphi_i(v)). \tag{3}$$

3 Flowering Protocol

3.1 Distance Reduction Probability

By applying the folding operator, the Prover reduces testing proximity to $f \in W(\Gamma, \mathbb{F})$ to testing proximity to $f' \in W(\Gamma', \mathbb{F})$, and one must ensure that this reduction does not make f' too much closer to $\mathcal{C}[\Gamma', k]$ than f was to $\mathcal{C}[\Gamma, k]$. The commit soundness from [13, Proposition 3] do not apply exactly with the generalization of the cuts to m non-disjoint cuts. We generalize this result in Proposition 4 using the weighted distances.

Proposition 4 (Commit soundness). *Let $\epsilon > 0$ and $k < n$. Let $\Gamma = (V, E)$ be an n-RIM and $V_0, ..., V_{m-1} \subseteq V$ be a flowering cut from Γ to $\Gamma' = \mathrm{Cut}[\Gamma, V_0]$, with $\varphi_i : V_0 \to V_i$ as isomorphism. Let $w : V \to \mathbb{R}^+$ be a weight function invariant under the isomorphisms φ_i, i.e. satisfying Eq. (3). Denote $\tilde{w} : V \to \mathbb{R}^+$ the weight function such that $\tilde{w}(v) = \frac{w(v)}{\mathrm{mul}(v)}$. Denote $C := \mathcal{C}[\Gamma, k]$ and $C' := \mathcal{C}[\Gamma', k]$. Let $f \in W(\Gamma, \mathbb{F})$. Then*

$$\Pr_{\rho \in \mathbb{F}} [\Delta_{\tilde{w}}(\mathrm{Fold}[f, \rho], C') < \Delta_w(f, C) - \epsilon] \leq \frac{m-1}{\epsilon|\mathbb{F}|}.$$

Proof Denote $\delta := \Delta_w(f, C)$ and assume that $\delta > 0$ (otherwise $\delta - \epsilon < 0$ and the proof is trivial). We say that a vertex $v \in V$ is *valid* w.r.t. f if $f(v, \cdot) \in \mathrm{RS}[n, k]$. Let $T := \{v \in V \mid f(v, \cdot) \notin \mathrm{RS}[n, k]\}$ be the vertices of Γ that are not valid w.r.t. f, and $T' := \bigcup_{i=0}^{m-1} \varphi_i^{-1}(V_i \cap T) \subseteq V_0$ be the set of vertices $v_0 \in V_0$ for which $\mathrm{Fold}[f, \rho](v_0, \cdot)$ is built from at least a vertex $\varphi_i(v_0) \in V_i$ for $i \in \{0, ..., m\}$ that is not valid w.r.t. f.

We now prove Eq. (4).

$$|T'|_{\tilde{w}} \geq \frac{|T|_w}{m} = \frac{\delta |V|_w}{m} = \delta |V_0|_{\tilde{w}}. \tag{4}$$

By using Eqs. (2) and (3), we have

$$|V|_w = \sum_{v \in V} w(v) = \sum_{i=0}^{m-1} \sum_{v \in V_i} \frac{w(v)}{\mathrm{mul}(v)} = \sum_{i=0}^{m-1} \sum_{v \in V_0} \frac{w(\varphi_i(v))}{\mathrm{mul}(\varphi_i(v))} = m|V_0|_{\tilde{w}}. \tag{5}$$

Furthermore, since for any $i \in \{0, .., m-1\}$, $\varphi_i^{-1}(V_i \cap T) \subseteq T'$, we have by similar arguments that

$$|T|_w = \sum_{i=0}^{m-1} \sum_{v \in V_i \cap T} \tilde{w}(v) = \sum_{i=0}^{m-1} \sum_{v \in \varphi_i^{-1}(V_i \cap T)} \tilde{w}(\varphi_i(v)) \leq \sum_{i=0}^{m-1} \sum_{v \in T'} \tilde{w}(v) = m|T'|_{\tilde{w}}. \tag{6}$$

By definition of the distance, $|T|_w = \delta |V|_w$. Hence by Eqs. (5) and (6), we obtain Eq. (4) as expected.

For $\rho \in \mathbb{F}$, denote

$$S_\rho := \{v_0 \in T' \mid \mathrm{Fold}[f, \rho](v_0, \cdot) \in \mathrm{RS}[n, k]\}$$

the vertices of Γ' whose fold was built from non-valid vertices w.r.t. f, but are made valid w.r.t. $\mathrm{Fold}[f, \rho]$ because of ρ. Then

$$\begin{aligned}
&\Pr(\Delta_{\tilde{w}}(\mathrm{Fold}[f, \rho], \mathrm{RS}[n, k]) < \delta - \epsilon) \\
&= \Pr(|\{v_0 \in V_0 \mid \mathrm{Fold}[f, \rho](v_0, \cdot) \notin \mathrm{RS}[n, k]\}|_{\tilde{w}} < (\delta - \epsilon)|V_0|_{\tilde{w}}) \\
&= \Pr(|\{v_0 \in T' \mid \mathrm{Fold}[f, \rho](v_0, \cdot) \notin \mathrm{RS}[n, k]\}|_{\tilde{w}} < (\delta - \epsilon)|V_0|_{\tilde{w}}) \\
&= \Pr(|S_\rho|_{\tilde{w}} > |T'|_{\tilde{w}} - (\delta - \epsilon)|V_0|_{\tilde{w}}) \\
&\leq \Pr(|S_\rho|_{\tilde{w}} > \delta |V_0|_{\tilde{w}} - (\delta - \epsilon)|V_0|_{\tilde{w}}) \text{ by eq. (4)} \\
&= \Pr(|S_\rho|_{\tilde{w}} > \epsilon |V_0|_{\tilde{w}}),
\end{aligned}$$

i.e. with $A := \{\rho \in \mathbb{F} \mid |S_\rho|_{\tilde{w}} > \epsilon |V_0|_{\tilde{w}}\}$,

$$\Pr_{\rho \in \mathbb{F}}(\Delta_{\tilde{w}}(\mathrm{Fold}[f, \rho], C') < \delta - \epsilon) \le \frac{|A|}{|\mathbb{F}|}. \tag{7}$$

We now provide a bound on $|A|$.

Let $v_0 \in T'$ and denote $A_{v_0} := \{\rho \in \mathbb{F} \mid \mathrm{Fold}[f, \rho](v_0, \cdot) \in \mathrm{RS}[n, k]\}$. For $i = \{0, ..., m-1\}$, denote $\sum_{j=0}^{d_i} a_{i,j} X^j$ the least degree polynomial interpolating $\mathrm{Cut}[f, V_i]$. Let $d := \max_i d_i$. Since $v_0 \in T'$, there exists i such that $\mathrm{Cut}[f, V_i](\varphi_i(v_0), \cdot) \notin \mathrm{RS}[n, k]$ and hence $d \ge d_i \ge k$.

Moreover, $\mathrm{Fold}[f, \rho](v_0, \cdot) \in \mathrm{RS}[n, k]$ only if the polynomial interpolating $\mathrm{Fold}[f, \rho](v_0, \cdot)$ has degree $< d$. By construction, this polynomial is

$$\sum_{j=0}^{d} \left(\sum_{i=0}^{m-1} a_{i,j} \rho^i \right) X^j,$$

hence it has degree $< d$ only if ρ is a root of the polynomial $\sum_{i=0}^{m-1} a_{i,d} Y^i$, that has degree $\le m - 1$. Therefore $|A_{v_0}| \le m - 1$.

The bound on $|A|$ is the following. On the one hand, by definition of A,

$$\sum_{\rho \in A} \sum_{v_0 \in T'} \mathbb{1}_{A_{v_0}}(\rho) \tilde{w}(v_0) = \sum_{\rho \in A} \sum_{v_0 \in S_\rho} \tilde{w}(v_0) = \sum_{\rho \in A} |S_\rho|_{\tilde{w}} > \epsilon |V_0|_{\tilde{w}} |A|,$$

and on the other hand,

$$\sum_{v_0 \in T'} \sum_{\rho \in A} \mathbb{1}_{A_{v_0}}(\rho) \tilde{w}(v_0) = \sum_{v_0 \in T'} \tilde{w}(v_0) |A_{v_0}| \le (m-1)|T'|_{\tilde{w}} \le (m-1)|V_0|_{\tilde{w}}.$$

Thus $|A| \le \frac{m-1}{\epsilon}$ and by Eq. (7) we obtain the result. □

3.2 Flowering Protocol

Let $\Gamma_0 = (V_0, E_0), ..., \Gamma_R = (V_R, E_R)$ be a blossoming graph sequence. For $r \in [R]$, let $(V_{r,0}, ..., V_{r,m-1})$ be a flowering cut collection from Γ_{r-1} to Γ_r.

Definition 10 (Flowering protocol). *The flowering protocol is composed of two phases, the commit phase which is interactive, and the query phase, where the Verifier opens the commits. There are two complexity parameters that one can fix: the number L of repetitions of the query phase, and the proportion $\mu \in [0, 1]$ of edges of $[n]$ checked at each step. On input $f_0 \in W(\Gamma_0, \mathbb{F})$, the protocol runs as follows:*

COMMIT PHASE: *for r from 0 to $R - 1$, the Verifier picks and send $\rho_r \xleftarrow{\$} \mathbb{F}$ to the Prover, and the Prover provides to the Verifier an oracle access to a word $f_{r+1} \in W(\Gamma_{r+1}, \mathbb{F})$.*

Query phase: *for* $\ell \in [L]$, *the Verifier picks* $v_{0,\ell} \xleftarrow{\$} V_0$ *and a random set* $J_\ell \subseteq [n]$ *of size* μn. *For* $r \in [R]$, *the Verifier picks randomly* $i_{r,\ell} \xleftarrow{\$} \{i \mid v_{r,\ell} \in V_{r,i}\}$, *computes* $v_{r,\ell} := \varphi^{-1}_{r-1,i_{r,\ell}}(v_{r-1,\ell})$, *and checks that*

$$\forall j \in J_\ell, \mathrm{Fold}[f_{r-1}, \rho_{r-1}](v_{r,\ell}, j) = f_r(v_{r,\ell}, j)$$

by making μnm *queries if* $r = 1$, *or* $\mu n(m-1)$ *queries if* $r \geq 2$, *to* f_{r-1} *and* μn *queries to* f_r. *Finally with* v_R *the flower of* Γ_R, *the Verifier checks that*

$$f_R(v_R, \cdot) \in RS[n, k].$$

The Verifier accepts if and only if all checks pass.

The query phase is adapted from [13] to the cases where the cuts are not disjoint. When there are $m = 2$ disjoint cuts, the Verifier does not have a choice for the next vertex $v_{r+1,\ell}$: either $v_{r,\ell} \in V_{r,0}$ and $v_{r+1,\ell} := v_{r,\ell}$, either $v_{r,\ell} \notin V_{r,0}$ and $v_{r+1,\ell} := \varphi^{-1}_{r,1}(v_{r,\ell})$. Here, $v_{r,\ell}$ belongs to $\mathrm{mul}(v_r)$ different $V_{r,i}$'s, hence the Verifier has to pick one of these to pick $v_{r+1,\ell}$.

Since picking uniformly a subset $J_\ell \subseteq [n]$ of size μn is hard for $\mu \approx 1/2$, one can focus on the two extreme cases $\mu = 1/n$, to focus on the Verifier complexity, or $\mu = 1$, to focus on the soundness, as we do in Tables 1 and 2.

We give the complexity properties of the protocol in Theorem 1, and the soundness property in Theorem 2. The protocol easily has perfect completeness: the Prover just has to send $f_r = \mathrm{Fold}[f_{r-1}, \rho_{r-1}]$ at each step $r \in [R]$.

Theorem 1 (Complexity of the flowering protocol [13, Theorem 1]**).** *The flowering protocol defined in Definition 10 has the following complexities*

- *Prover complexity:* $(2m-1)\sum_{r=1}^{R} |\mathrm{edges}(\Gamma_r)| < (2m-1)R|\mathrm{edges}(\Gamma_0)|$ *field operations*
- *Verifier complexity:* $RL\mu n(m+2) + n\log n$ *field operations*
- *Query complexity:* $(mR + m - 1)\mu nL + n$
- *Round complexity:* R
- *Randomness complexity:* R *field elements and cuts,* L *vertices and subsets of* $[n]$
- *Proof length:* $\sum_{r=1}^{R} |\mathrm{edges}(\Gamma_r)| < R|\mathrm{edges}(\Gamma_0)|$ *field elements*

To obtain the soundness of the flowering protocol, stated in vertex distance in Proposition 5, we adapt the proof of [13, Proposition 4] using Proposition 4 instead of [13, Proposition 3] and the weighted vertex distances instead of the uniform vertex distance. The proof is done in Appendix A.

Proposition 5 (Query soundness). *Let* $\epsilon > 0$, $k < n$ *and* $f_0 \in W(\Gamma_0, \mathbb{F})$. *After running the Flowering protocol with* L *repetitions of the query phase by checking* μn *edges, the probability over its internal randomness that the Verifier accepts is at most*

$$\frac{R(m-1)}{\epsilon|\mathbb{F}|} + \left(1 - \mu \cdot \left(\Delta_V(f_0, \mathcal{C}[\Gamma_0, k]) - R\epsilon\right)\right)^L.$$

If the successive cut collections have a different order m_r, then the left term of the soundness becomes $\sum_{r=1}^{R} \frac{m_r-1}{\epsilon|\mathbb{F}|}$.

Combining Propositions 2 and 5, we obtain the soundness of the flowering protocol, stated in Theorem 2, stated here in Hamming distance.

Theorem 2 (Soundness of the flowering protocol). *Let $k < n$ and $f_0 \in W(\Gamma_0, \mathbb{F})$. After running the Flowering protocol with L repetitions of the query phase by checking μn edges, the probability over its internal randomness that the Verifier accepts is at most*

$$\min_{\epsilon>0} \left(\frac{R(m-1)}{\epsilon|\mathbb{F}|} + \left(1 - \mu \cdot \left(\Delta_H(f_0, \mathcal{C}[\Gamma_0, k]) - R\epsilon\right)\right)^L \right).$$

Here again, if the successive cut collections have a different order m_r, the left term of the soundness becomes $\sum_{r=1}^{R} \frac{m_r-1}{\epsilon|\mathbb{F}|}$.

4 Cutting Cayley Graphs

We describe how to apply the flowering protocol using any Cayley graph [10].

Definition 11 (Cayley graph). *Let G be a finite multiplicative group and $S = \{s_1, ..., s_n\}$ a symmetric generating set. We define the corresponding Cayley graph Cay(G, S) by $V = G$, and $E : (g, j) \mapsto g \cdot s_j$.*

We also allow ourselves to write the edges as a function $E : G \times S \to G$ where $E(g, s) := gs$.

Figure 4 illustrates the construction of a Cayley graph. Recall that in a graph $\Gamma = (V, E)$, a *path* of length ℓ is a sequence of vertices $v_0, ..., v_\ell$ such that for all $i \in [\ell]$, v_{i-1} and v_i are neighbors. The *distance* between two vertices $v, v' \in V$ is the length ℓ of the shortest path $v_0, ..., v_\ell$ such that $v_0 = v$ and $v_\ell = v'$. The *diameter* of a graph, denoted diam(Γ), is the maximum distance between two vertices of V.

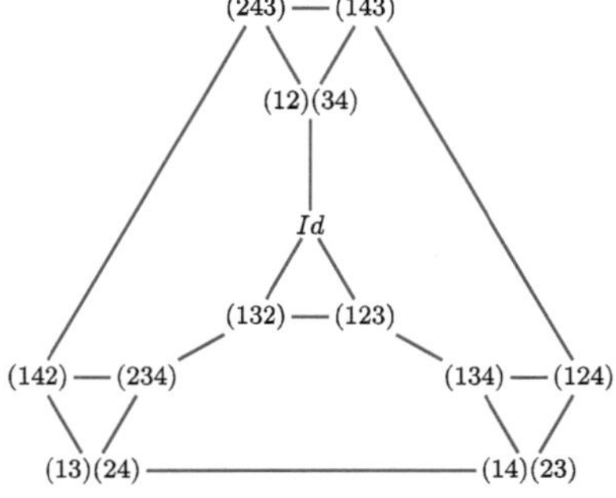

Fig. 4. Cayley graph on the alternating group $G = \mathcal{A}_4$ and $S = \{(123), (132), (12)(34)\}$.

Proposition 6 *Let G be a finite group. Fix $S_1 = \{s_0, ..., s_{\tilde{n}-1}\}$ a generative subset of G and consider $S = S_1 \cup S_{-1}$, where $S_{-1} = \{s_0^{-1}, ..., s_{\tilde{n}-1}^{-1}\}$, the induced symmetric generating set. Define $\tilde{s}_i := s_{i \bmod \tilde{n}}$. Let $\Gamma := Cay(G, S)$. Then with $R := \tilde{n}\, diam(\Gamma)$, we have*

$$G = \left\{\tilde{s}_0^{\alpha_0} \cdots \tilde{s}_{R-1}^{\alpha_{R-1}} \mid \alpha_0, ..., \alpha_{R-1} \in \{-1, 0, 1\}\right\}. \tag{8}$$

Proof Since S generates G, for any $g \in G$, there exists $\ell \in \mathbb{N}$ and a sequence $p = \left(s_{i_0}^{\beta_0}, ..., s_{i_{\ell-1}}^{\beta_{\ell-1}}\right) \in S^\ell$ where $\beta_j \in \{-1, 1\}$ such that $g = s_{i_0}^{\beta_0} \cdots s_{i_{\ell-1}}^{\beta_{\ell-1}}$. We can see p as a path from 1_G to g in Γ. By definition of the diameter, there exists such a path of length $\ell \leq d := \mathrm{diam}(\Gamma)$. Hence, any $g \in G$ can be written with a sequence of d elements $w := (s_{i_0}^{\gamma_0}, ..., s_{i_{d-1}}^{\gamma_{d-1}}) \in S^d$ with $\gamma_j \in \{-1, 0, 1\}$, such that $g = s_{i_0}^{\gamma_0} \cdots s_{i_{d-1}}^{\gamma_{d-1}}$. We obtain the following description of G:

$$G = \left\{ s_{i_0}^{\gamma_0} \cdots s_{i_{d-1}}^{\gamma_{d-1}} \mid \begin{cases} i_0, ..., i_{d-1} \in \{0, ..., \tilde{n}-1\} \\ \gamma_0, ..., \gamma_{d-1} \in \{-1, 0, 1\} \end{cases} \right\}. \tag{9}$$

Given $g \in G$ associated with a sequence $w = (s_{i_0}^{\gamma_0}, ..., s_{i_{d-1}}^{\gamma_{d-1}})$, let us construct a sequence $(\tilde{s}_0^{\alpha_0}, ..., \tilde{s}_{R-1}^{\alpha_{R-1}})$ such that $g = \tilde{s}_0^{\alpha_0} \cdots \tilde{s}_{R-1}^{\alpha_{R-1}}$. For s_j^γ in w, denote for $i \in \{0, ..., \tilde{n}-1\}$

$$\alpha_{j,i} := \begin{cases} \gamma & \text{if } i = j, \\ 0 & \text{otherwise.} \end{cases}$$

Then $s_0^{\alpha_{j,0}} ... s_{\tilde{n}-1}^{\alpha_{j,\tilde{n}-1}} = s_j^{\alpha_{j,j}} = s_j^\gamma$. Therefore with $\tilde{\alpha}_{j\tilde{n}+i} := \alpha_{j,i}$, g can be written

$$g = \prod_{j=0}^{d-1} \prod_{i=0}^{\tilde{n}-1} s_i^{\alpha_{j,i}} = \prod_{r=0}^{R-1} \tilde{s}_r^{\tilde{\alpha}_r}.$$

Thus, by Eq. (9) we obtain Eq. (8). □

Thanks to the writing of G as in Eq. (8) using Proposition 6, we can define a blossoming sequence of length R by taking shorter and shorter paths. For $i \in \{-1, 0, 1\}$ and $r \in [R]$, define

$$V_{r,i} := \left\{\tilde{s}_{r-1}^i \cdot \tilde{s}_r^{\alpha_r} \cdots \tilde{s}_{R-1}^{\alpha_{R-1}} \mid \alpha_r, ..., \alpha_{R-1} \in \{-1, 0, 1\}\right\}.$$

We have that $V_{R,0} = \{1_G\}$ is a singleton and we prove in Proposition 7 that for $r \in [R]$, the cuts $\mathrm{Cut}[\Gamma_{r-1}, V_{r,i}]$ for $i \in \{-1, 0, 1\}$ are isomorphic, and in Proposition 8 that they form a flowering cut collection, therefore the graphs form a blossoming graph sequence $\Gamma_0, ..., \Gamma_R$. For $r \in [R]$, we denote $\Gamma_r = (V_{r,0}, E_r) := \mathrm{Cut}[\Gamma_{r-1}, V_{r,0}]$, and for $i \in \{-1, 0, 1\}$, we denote $\Gamma_{r,i} := \mathrm{Cut}[\Gamma_{r-1}, V_{r,i}]$.

Proposition 7 *Let $r \in [R]$ and $i \in \{-1, 0, 1\}$. With the notations above, $\varphi_{r,i} : g \mapsto \tilde{s}_{r-1}^i \cdot g$ is an isomorphism from $\Gamma_{r,0}$ to $\Gamma_{r,i}$.*

Proof Let $g \in V_{r,0}$ and $s \in S$. Then $E_r(g,s) = gs$ if $gs \in V_{r,0}$ and g otherwise, and $E_r(\varphi_{r,i}(g), s) = \tilde{s}_r^i \cdot gs$ if $\tilde{s}_r^i \cdot gs \in V_{i,0}$ and $\tilde{s}_r^i \cdot g$ otherwise. Thus we only have to prove that $gs \in V_{r,0}$ iff $\tilde{s}_r^i \cdot gs \in V_{r,i}$. We have that $gs \in V_{r,0}$ iff there exists $\alpha_{r+1}, ...\alpha_R$ such that

$$gs = \tilde{s}_r^0 \prod_{k=r+1}^{R} \tilde{s}_k^{\alpha_k},$$

i.e.

$$\tilde{s}_r^i \cdot gs = \tilde{s}_r^i \prod_{k=r+1}^{R} \tilde{s}_k^{\alpha_k}.$$

The existence of such a decomposition is equivalent to $\tilde{s}_r^i \cdot gs \in V_{r,i}$. □

Proposition 8 *For $r \in [R]$, $i \in \{-1,0,1\}$ and $v \in V_{r,0}$, we have* $\mathrm{mul}(v) = \mathrm{mul}(\varphi_{r,i}(v))$.

Proof Let $g \in V_{r,0}$ and $i_0 \in \{-1,0,1\}$. For $i \in \{-1,0,1\}$, let $i_1 := i + i_0 \mod 2$. Since $g \in V_{r,i}$ iff $g = \tilde{s}_{r-1}^i \cdot \tilde{s}_r^{\alpha_r} \cdots \tilde{s}_{R-1}^{\alpha_{R-1}}$ for some $\alpha_r, ..., \alpha_{R-1} \in \{-1,0,1\}$, we have that $g \in V_{r,i}$ iff $\varphi_{r,i_0}(g) = \tilde{s}_{r-1}^{i_0} \cdot g \in V_{r,i_1}$. Hence $\mathrm{mul}(v) = \mathrm{mul}(\varphi_{r,i_0}(v))$. □

A blossoming graph sequence of the Cayley graph $\mathrm{Cay}(\mathcal{A}_4, S)$ defined in Fig. 4 is illustrated in Fig. 3. Proposition 6 was shown using $\{-1,0,1\}$ as decomposition set, but the result also holds for any superset of $\{-1,0,1\}$, or for different sets for each coefficient s_r. For instance if s_r has order m_r in G, then one could use the decomposition set $\{0, 1, ..., m_r - 1\}$.

5 Application to Expander Families of Cayley Graphs

5.1 Expansion in Graphs

In this section we recall spectral properties of expander graphs, and we establish bounds on parameters relevant to our setting.

Definition 12 (Relative spectral gap). *Let $\Gamma = (V,E)$ be a n-regular graph and $\{\lambda_1, ..., \lambda_{|V|}\}$ the eigenvalues of its adjency matrix, ordered by decreasing absolute value: $|\lambda_1| \geq ... \geq |\lambda_{|V|}|$. Then $\bar{\lambda} = \frac{\lambda_2}{\lambda_1} = \frac{\lambda_2}{n}$ is the* relative spectral gap *of Γ.*

A smaller $\bar{\lambda}$ corresponds to stronger expansion properties of the graph. For any $\tilde{\lambda} \geq \bar{\lambda}$, we say that $\Gamma(V,E)$ is a $\tilde{\lambda}$-expander graph. A family of graphs $(\Gamma_i = (V_i, E_i))_{i \in \mathbb{N}}$ is said to have **constant expansion** if there exist a $\tilde{\lambda}$ such that for all $i \in \mathbb{N}$, Γ_i is a $\tilde{\lambda}$-expander.

Definition 13 (Ramanujan Graph). *A n-regular graph with relative spectral expansion $\bar{\lambda}$ is a Ramanujan graph if and only if $\bar{\lambda} \leq 2\frac{\sqrt{n-1}}{n}$.*

Ramanujan graphs are those whose spectral expansion approaches the Alon-Boppana lower bound established in [24]. As such, they achieve the best possible spectral expansion.

We give the two properties that interest us when building codes on expander graphs in Propositions 9 and 10.

Proposition 9 (Bound on minimum distance). *Let a $\tilde{\lambda}$-expander n-regular graph $\Gamma(V,E)$ be given. Denote $\delta := 1 - \frac{k-1}{n}$ the relative minimum distance of RS$[n,k]$. Then:*

$$\Delta(\mathcal{C}[\Gamma,k]) \geq \delta(\delta - \tilde{\lambda}).$$

Proof Let $\Gamma = (V,E)$ be a $\tilde{\lambda}$-expander n-regular graph and let $c \in \mathcal{C}[\Gamma,k]$ be a nonzero word. Since $c \neq 0$, there exists $v_0 \in V$ such that at least one of its incident edges has nonzero value. For clarity, we will say that such a vertex is nonzero. Let $T \subset V$ be the smallest set such that $\forall v \in T$, $v \neq 0$.

If $c(v,\cdot) \in \mathrm{RS}[n,k] \neq 0$, then at least $n-k+1$ of its components are nonzero. Therefore, T's average arity is greater or equal to $n-k+1 = \delta n$. From [14, Lemma 2.1], we get that $|T| \geq (\delta - \tilde{\lambda})N$. □

Proposition 10 (Bound on the diameter). *Let $\Gamma = (V,E)$ be a n-regular $\tilde{\lambda}$-expander connected graph. Then we have:*

$$diam(\Gamma) \leq 2\frac{\log\left(\frac{|V|}{2}\right)}{\log\left(\frac{3-\tilde{\lambda}}{2}\right)} + 3$$

Proof A similar bound involving combinatorial expansion is established [18, Proposition 3.1.5]. We infer this spectral version of the bound using Cheeger inequality.

It naturally gives a bound on the round complexity of the protocol:

$$R \leq 2\tilde{n}\frac{\log\left(\frac{|V|}{2}\right)}{\log\left(\frac{3-\tilde{\lambda}}{2}\right)} + 3\tilde{n}.$$

5.2 Case Study: Ramanujan Cayley Graphs Family

In this part, we instanciate the protocol on codes built on a family of Cayley graphs with good expansion properties. The code and protocol parameters are explicitely computed for such graphs.

Several families of Cayley graphs have been proven to be expander families [19]. Among them, an explicit construction of Ramanujan expander graphs family was established independently by Margulis [21] and by Lubotzky, Phillips and Sanark [20]. A concise description of this construction can be found in [23, Section 11].

Proposition 11 (**[23]**) *Fix p prime such that $p \equiv 1[4]$. For any $q \neq p$ prime such that $q \equiv 1[4]$, denote:*

$$G_{p,q} = \begin{cases} \mathrm{PSL}_2(\mathbb{F}_q) & \text{if } p \text{ is a quadratic residue mod } q, \\ \mathrm{PGL}_2(\mathbb{F}_q) & \text{otherwise.} \end{cases}$$

A symmetric generating set $S_{p,q}$ of size $p+1$ can be explicitely built such that $Cay(G_{p,q}, S_{p,q})$ is a Ramanujan graph.

As a consequence, p being a fixed prime, one can construct a family of $(p+1)$-regular Ramanujan Cayley graphs whose size can grow arbitrarily with q. By definition of a Ramanujan graph, such a family has an upper bound $\tilde{\lambda} = 1/\sqrt{p}$ on its relative spectral expansion that only depends on p.

Fix p prime and select q such that $G_{p,q} = \mathrm{PGL}_2(\mathbb{F}_q)$. Denote $\Gamma_{p,q}(V, E)$ the associated Ramanujan graph. It has $|\mathrm{PGL}_2(\mathbb{F}_q)| = (q-1)q(q+1)$ vertices. Consider the graph code $\mathcal{C}[\Gamma_{p,q}, k]$ over the basecode $\mathrm{RS}[p+1, k]$, $(p+1)/2 < k < p+1$. The code has length

$$N = (p+1)(q-1)q(q+1)/2.$$

The code dimension is

$$\dim \mathcal{C}[\Gamma_{p,q}, k] \geq \left(k - \frac{p+1}{2}\right)(q-1)q(q+1).$$

From Proposition 9 we get $\mathcal{C}[\Gamma_{p,q}, k]$ minimum relative distance

$$\Delta\left(\mathcal{C}[\Gamma_{p,q}, k]\right) \geq \delta\,(\delta - \tilde{\lambda}),$$

where $\delta = \frac{p-k+2}{p+1}$ is the minimum relative distance of $\mathrm{RS}[p+1, k]$. Since $\tilde{\lambda}$ only depends on p, which does not depend on q, the minimum relative distance remains constant as the code length grows. The diameter of the graph is also bounded according to Proposition 10, which yields a bound on the number of round:

$$R \leq \kappa(p) \log(N),$$

where $\kappa(p)$ is constant with respect to q.

6 Conclusion

This paper generalized the IOPP for codes on $(2, n)$-regular Tanner graphs introduced in [13] that was only applied on codes with $o(1)$ minimum distance to any $(2, n)$-regular Tanner graph built as a Cayley graph. This generalization allows to use Cayley graphs with good expansion, yielding codes with constant rate and minimum distance. The great soundness parameter from [13] compared to the FRI protocol [5] is thus preserved, even if the complexity becomes slightly higher, while now allowing the use of codes with constant rate and constant minimum distance.

Acknowledgments. The authors deeply thank Tanguy Medevielle and Élina Roussel, with whom this work was initiated as the continuation of [13] that first defines the Flowering protocol. The authors also thank Daniel Augot for his proofreadings and guidance and Pierre Loisel for his help regarding group theory and Cayley graphs. The authors finally thank ChatGPT for its help to find relevant bibliography on expander graphs and to find spelling mistakes.

Disclosure of Interests. The authors have no competing interests to declare that are relevant to the content of this article.

A Proof of the Query Soundness

We first prove Lemmas 1 and 2 in order to prove Proposition 5.

Lemma 1 *([13, Lemma 1]) Using the notations of Definition 10, let* $\ell \in [L]$ *and* $i_{1,\ell}, ..., i_{R,\ell}$ *be fixed. There exists* $(f'_{0,\ell}, ..., f'_{R,\ell}) \in \prod_{r=0}^{R} W(\Gamma_r, \mathbb{F})$ *such that* $f'_{R,\ell} = f_R$*, and by denoting* $N_{r,\ell}$ *the event "*$\text{Fold}[f_{r-1}, \rho_{r-1}](v_{r,\ell}, \cdot) \neq f_r(v_{r,\ell}, \cdot)$*" and* $N'_{r,\ell}$ *the event "*$\text{Fold}[f'_{r-1,\ell}, \rho_{r-1}](v_{r,\ell}, \cdot) \neq f'_{r,\ell}(v_{r,\ell}, \cdot)$*", we have that* $N'_{1,\ell}, ..., N'_{R,\ell}$ *are disjoints and* $\bigsqcup_{r=1}^{R} N'_{r,\ell} \subseteq \bigcup_{r=1}^{R} N_{r,\ell}$*.*

Proof Define recursively for $r = 0, ..., R$ the "honest" function $\tilde{f}_r$ by $\tilde{f}_0 := f_0$ and for $r \geq 1$, $\tilde{f}_r := \text{Fold}[f_{r-1}, \rho_{r-1}]$. The $f'_{r,\ell}$ are also defined recursively as follows. First, $f'_{0,\ell} := f_0$. Then let $v_0 \in V_0$ and denote $(v_1, ..., v_R)$ the sequence such that for $r \in [R]$, $v_r = \varphi^{-1}_{r-1,i_{r,\ell}}(v_{r-1})$ is the vertex to be tested after v_{r-1} by the Verifier. Denote

$$\text{r}(v_0) := \max(\{r \in [R] \mid f_r(v_r, \cdot) \neq \text{Fold}[f_{r-1}, \rho_{r-1}]\} \cup \{0\}).$$

Let $j \in [n]$. For $r < \text{r}(v_0)$, define $f'_{r,\ell}(v_r, j) := \tilde{f}_r(v_r, j)$ and for $r \geq \text{r}(v_0)$, define $f'_{r,\ell}(v_r, j) := f_r(v_r, j)$.

We now prove that the $N'_{r,\ell}$ are disjoint. Denote $r_0 := \text{r}(v_{0,\ell})$. If $r_0 = 0$ then for any $r \in [R]$, $N'_{r,\ell}$ does not hold, and if $r_0 \geq 1$ then for $r \in [R]$, $N'_{r,\ell}$ holds iff $r = r_0$. Therefore there is at most one $r \in [R]$ such that $N'_{r,\ell}$ holds, hence they are disjoint.

Furthermore, if one $N'_{r,\ell}$ holds, i.e. if $\bigsqcup_{r=1}^{R} N'_{r,\ell}$ hords, then $r_0 > 0$ and hence $\bigcup_{r=1}^{R} N_{r,\ell}$ holds. Thus $\bigsqcup_{r=1}^{R} N'_{r,\ell} \subseteq \bigcup_{r=1}^{R} N_{r,\ell}$. □

We also use another lemma to adapt the proof of Proposition 5 to non-disjoint cuts.

Lemma 2 *Using the notations of the flowering protocol in Definition 10, for* $r \in \{0, ..., R\}$ *and* $v \in V_r$*, we have that* $\Pr(v_{r,1} = v) = \frac{w_r(v)}{|V_r|_{w_r}}$*.*

Proof We prove the result by induction on $r = 0, ..., R$. For $r = 0$, by definition for any $v \in V_0$ we have $\Pr(v_{i,0} = v) = \frac{1}{|V_0|} = \frac{w_0(v)}{|V_0|_{w_0}}$. Suppose that for any $v' \in V_r$

we have $\Pr(v_{r,1} = v') = \frac{w_r(v')}{|V_r|_{w_r}}$ and let $v \in V_{r+1}$. By the total probabilities, we have

$$\begin{aligned}\Pr(v_{r+1,1} = v) &= \sum_{i=0}^{m-1} \Pr(v_{r+1,1} = v \mid v_{r,1} = \varphi_i(v)) \Pr(v_{r,1} = \varphi_i(v)) \\ &= \sum_{i=0}^{m-1} \frac{1}{\#\varphi_i(v)} \cdot \frac{w_r(\varphi_i(v))}{|V_r|_{w_r}} \\ &= \frac{m w_{r+1}(v)}{|V_r|_{w_r}}.\end{aligned}$$

Furthermore, by Eq. (5), we have $|V_{r+1}|_{w_{r+1}} = |V_r|_{w_r}/m$, and thus the result.□

We can now prove Proposition 5.

Proof (of Proposition 5) If $f_R \notin C_R$ then the Verifier rejects with probability 1, therefore we assume in the following that

$$\Delta_{w_R}(f_R, C_R) = 0. \tag{10}$$

Let $f'_{0,\ell}, ..., f'_{R,\ell}$ be given by Lemma 1. For $(r,\ell) \in [R] \times [L]$, denote $B_{r,\ell}$ the event "$\exists j \in J_\ell, \text{Fold}[f'_{r-1,\ell}, \rho_{r-1}](v_{r,\ell}, j) \neq f'_{r,\ell}(v_{r,\ell}, j)$" meaning that the Verifier rejects that check. Then the probability of the event "the Verifier accepts" is at most $\Pr\left(\bigcap_{\ell=1}^{L} \bigcap_{r=1}^{R} \overline{B_{r,\ell}}\right)$. Denote A the event "$\forall r \in [R], \Delta_{w_r}(\text{Fold}[f_{r-1}, \rho_{r-1}], C_r) \geq \Delta_{w_{r-1}}(f_{r-1}, C_{r-1}) - \epsilon$" meaning that all R commits "passed" the commit soundness.

By the law of total probability, we have

$$\Pr(\text{the Verifier accepts}) \leq \Pr\left(\overline{A}\right) + \Pr\left(\bigcap_{\ell=1}^{L} \bigcap_{r=1}^{R} \overline{B_{r,\ell}} \mid A\right).$$

By Proposition 4, we have

$$\Pr\left(\overline{A}\right) \leq \frac{R(m-1)}{\epsilon|\mathbb{F}|},$$

and by independence and identical distribution of the repetitions of the query phase, we only consider the case $\ell = 1$ and we have

$$\Pr\left(\bigcap_{\ell=1}^{L} \bigcap_{r=1}^{R} \overline{B_{r,\ell}} \mid A\right) = \left(1 - \Pr\left(\bigcup_{r=1}^{R} B_{r,1} \mid A\right)\right)^L,$$

hence we only have to lower bound $\Pr\left(\bigcup_{r=1}^{R} B_{r,1} \mid A\right)$.

Take the notations $N_{r,1}$ and $N'_{r,1}$ from Lemma 1. Since $|J_1| = \mu n$, we have

$$\Pr\left(\bigcup_{r=1}^{R} B_{r,1} \mid A \cap \bigcup_{r=1}^{R} N_{r,1}\right) \geq \mu,$$

and thus by Lemma 1,

$$\Pr\left(\bigcup_{r=1}^{R} B_{r,1}\right) \geq \mu \Pr\left(\bigcup_{r=1}^{R} N_{r,1}\right) \geq \mu \Pr\left(\bigsqcup_{r=1}^{R} N'_{r,1}\right) = \mu \sum_{r=1}^{R} \Pr(N'_{r,1}).$$

Assuming that A holds and by denoting $\delta_r := \Delta_{w_r}(f'_{r,1}, C_r)$, we have by Lemma 2 and by triangle inequality that

$$\begin{aligned}\delta_r &\geq \Delta_{w_r}(\text{Fold}[f'_{r-1,1}, \rho_{r-1}], C_r) - \Delta_{w_r}(f'_{r,1}, \text{Fold}[f'_{r-1,1}, \rho_{r-1}]) \\ &\geq \delta_{r-1} - \epsilon - \Pr(N'_{r,1}).\end{aligned}$$

Thus $\Pr(N'_{r,1}) \geq \delta_0 - \delta_R - R\epsilon$ and by telescoping,

$$\sum_{r=1}^{R} \Pr(N'_{r,1}) \geq \delta_0 - \delta_R - R\epsilon. \tag{11}$$

Since $f'_{R,1} = f_R$, by Eqs. (10) and (11) and Appendix A we get the result. □

References

1. Aranha, D.F., El Housni, Y., Guillevic, A.: A survey of elliptic curves for proof systems. Des. Codes Crypt. **91**(11), 3333–3378 (2023)
2. Arnon, G., Chiesa, A., Fenzi, G., Yogev, E.: STIR: reed-solomon proximity testing with fewer queries. In: Reyzin, L., Stebila, D. (eds.) Advances in Cryptology – CRYPTO 2024. CRYPTO 2024. LNCS, vol. 14929, pp. 380–413. Springer, Cham (2024). https://doi.org/10.1007/978-3-031-68403-6_12
3. Ben-Sasson, E., Bentov, I., Horesh, Y., Riabzev, M.: Fast reed-solomon interactive oracle proofs of proximity. In: Chatzigiannakis, I., Kaklamanis, C., Marx, D., Sannella, D. (eds.) 45th International Colloquium on Automata, Languages, and Programming (ICALP 2018). Leibniz International Proceedings in Informatics (LIPIcs), vol. 107, pp. 14:1–14:17. Schloss Dagstuhl – Leibniz-Zentrum für Informatik, Dagstuhl, Germany (2018). https://doi.org/10.4230/LIPIcs.ICALP.2018.14, https://drops.dagstuhl.de/entities/document/10.4230/LIPIcs.ICALP.2018.14
4. Ben-Sasson, E., Bentov, I., Horesh, Y., Riabzev, M.: Scalable, transparent, and post-quantum secure computational integrity. Cryptology ePrint Archive (2018)
5. Ben-Sasson, E., Carmon, D., Ishai, Y., Kopparty, S., Saraf, S.: Proximity gaps for reed–solomon codes. J. ACM **70**(5) (2023). https://doi.org/10.1145/3614423
6. Ben-Sasson, E., Chiesa, A., Riabzev, M., Spooner, N., Virza, M., Ward, N.P.: Aurora: transparent succinct arguments for R1CS. In: Ishai, Y., Rijmen, V. (eds.) EUROCRYPT 2019. LNCS, vol. 11476, pp. 103–128. Springer, Cham (2019). https://doi.org/10.1007/978-3-030-17653-2_4
7. Ben-Sasson, E., Chiesa, A., Spooner, N.: Interactive oracle proofs. In: Hirt, M., Smith, A. (eds.) TCC 2016. LNCS, vol. 9986, pp. 31–60. Springer, Heidelberg (2016). https://doi.org/10.1007/978-3-662-53644-5_2
8. Ben-Sasson, E., Goldberg, L., Kopparty, S., Saraf, S.: DEEP-FRI: sampling outside the box improves soundness. In: Vidick, T. (ed.) 11th Innovations in Theoretical Computer Science Conference, ITCS 2020, 12–14 January 2020, Seattle, Washington, USA. LIPIcs, vol. 151, pp. 5:1–5:32. Schloss Dagstuhl - Leibniz-Zentrum für Informatik (2020). https://doi.org/10.4230/LIPICS.ITCS.2020.5

9. Ben-Sasson, E., Kopparty, S., Saraf, S.: Worst-case to average case reductions for the distance to a code. Electron. Colloq. Comput. Complex. **TR18-090** (2018). https://eccc.weizmann.ac.il/report/2018/090
10. Cayley, P.: Desiderata and suggestions: no. 2. The theory of groups: graphical representation. Am. J. Math. **1**(2), 174–176 (1878). http://www.jstor.org/stable/2369306
11. Certicom Research: Sec 2: Recommended elliptic curve domain parameters. Standards for Efficient Cryptography SEC 2, Certicom (2000)
12. Datta, T., Chen, B., Boneh, D.: VerITAS: verifying image transformations at scale. Cryptology ePrint Archive (2024)
13. Delavenne, H., Medevielle, T., Roussel, É.: Interactive Oracle Proofs of Proximity to Codes on Graphs. arXiv preprint arXiv:2501.14337 (2025). https://arxiv.org/abs/2501.14337
14. Dinur, I., Evra, S., Livne, R., Lubotzky, A., Mozes, S.: Locally Testable Codes with constant rate, distance, and locality. CoRR **abs/2111.04808** (2021). https://arxiv.org/abs/2111.04808
15. Fan, Y., Ma, K., Zhang, L., Liu, J., Xiong, N., Yu, S.: VeriCNN: integrity verification of large-scale CNN training process based on zk-SNARK. Expert Syst. Appl. **255**, 124531 (2024). https://doi.org/10.1016/j.eswa.2024.124531. https://www.sciencedirect.com/science/article/pii/S0957417424013988
16. Fiat, A., Shamir, A.: How to prove yourself: practical solutions to identification and signature problems. In: Odlyzko, A.M. (ed.) CRYPTO 1986. LNCS, vol. 263, pp. 186–194. Springer, Heidelberg (1987). https://doi.org/10.1007/3-540-47721-7_12
17. Gabizon, A., Williamson, Z.J., Ciobotaru, O.: Plonk: permutations over lagrange-bases for oecumenical noninteractive arguments of knowledge. Cryptology ePrint Archive (2019)
18. Kowalski, E.: An introduction to expander graphs. Société mathématique de France Paris (2019)
19. Lubotzky, A.: Expander graphs in pure and applied mathematics. Bull. Am. Math. Soc. **49**(1), 113–162 (2012)
20. Lubotzky, A., Phillips, R., Sarnak, P.: Ramanujan graphs. Combinatorica **8**(3), 261–277 (1988)
21. Margulis, G.A.: Explicit group-theoretical constructions of combinatorial schemes and their application to the design of expanders and concentrators. Problemy peredachi informatsii **24**(1), 51–60 (1988)
22. Merkle, R.C.: A digital signature based on a conventional encryption function. In: Pomerance, C. (ed.) CRYPTO 1987. LNCS, vol. 293, pp. 369–378. Springer, Heidelberg (1988). https://doi.org/10.1007/3-540-48184-2_32
23. Murty, M.R.: Ramanujan graphs: an introduction. Indian J. Discret. Math. **6**, 91–127 (2020)
24. Nilli, A.: On the second eigenvalue of a graph. Discret. Math. **91**(2), 207–210 (1991). https://doi.org/10.1016/0012-365X(91)90112-F. https://www.sciencedirect.com/science/article/pii/0012365X9190112F
25. Sipser, M., Spielman, D.A.: Expander codes. IEEE Trans. Inf. Theory **42**(6), 1710–1722 (1996)
26. Tanner, R.: A recursive approach to low complexity codes. IEEE Trans. Inf. Theory **27**(5), 533–547 (1981). https://doi.org/10.1109/TIT.1981.1056404

Decentralized Fair Exchange with Advertising

Pierpaolo Della Monica(✉), Ivan Visconti, Andrea Vitaletti, and Marco Zecchini

Sapienza University of Rome, Rome, Italy
{dellamonica,visconti,vitaletti,zecchini}@diag.uniroma1.it

Abstract. Before a fair exchange takes place, there is typically an advertisement phase with the goal of increasing the appeal of possessing a digital asset while keeping it sufficiently hidden. Advertisement phases are implicit in mainstream definitions, and therefore are not explicitly integrated within fair-exchange protocols.

In this work we give an explicit definition for such a fair exchange in a setting where parties communicate via broadcast messages only (i.e., no point-to-point connection between seller and buyer is needed). Next, we construct a fair-exchange protocol satisfying our new definition using zk-SNARKs and relying on mainstream decentralized platforms (i.e., a blockchain with smart contracts like Ethereum and a decentralized storage system like IPFS).

Experimental results confirm the practical relevance of our decentralized approach, paving the road towards building decentralized marketplaces where users can, even anonymously, and without direct off-chain communications, effectively advertise and exchange their digital assets as part of a system of enhanced NFTs.

1 Introduction

An exchange protocol involves two parties, Alice and Bob, each interested in exchanging her/his asset with that of the other party. A fair exchange protocol guarantees that, at the end, either the assets are exchanged or none of them is transferred. If Alice and Bob are interested in exchanging a *digital* asset through a

---

The full version of the paper is available in [14].

This work was partially supported by project SERICS (PE00000014) under the MUR National Recovery and Resilience Plan funded by the European Union - NextGenerationEU. Ivan Visconti is member of the Gruppo Nazionale Calcolo Scientifico-Istituto Nazionale di Alta Matematica (GNCS-INdAM) and his research contribution on his work was in part financially supported under the National Recovery and Resilience Plan (NRRP), Mission 4, Component 2, Investment 1.1, Call for tender No. 104 published on 2.2.2022 by the Italian Ministry of University and Research (MUR), funded by the European Union -NextGenerationEU - Project Title "PARTHENON" - CUP D53D23008610006 - Grant Assignment Decree No. 959 adopted on June 30, 2023 by the Italian Ministry of Ministry University and Research (MUR).

Y. Kim et al. (Eds.): CANS 2025, LNCS 16351, pp. 358–381, 2026.
https://doi.org/10.1007/978-981-95-4434-9_17

protocol run over a communication network, without the involvement of a trusted third party, a fair exchange is impossible. This is due to a general impossibility result proven by Cleve [11] on fairness in two-party protocols.

Advertising Before Exchanging: The Case of Physical Assets. In the physical world, advertising an asset typically consists of granting temporary access to it (e.g., before an auction, the bidders can watch a picture at a specific distance and can read documents proving possession of it). In general, such advertisement phases do not compromise the value of the asset because physical assets cannot be easily cloned or exploited (e.g., the bidders that have temporary access to the auctioned asset cannot easily reproduce an identical copy).

Fair Exchange in the NFT Era. Blockchains can realize a basic decentralized trusted party, and this suffices to bypass Cleve's impossibility. Indeed, smart contracts for Non-Fungible Token (NFT) allow to fairly exchange the ownership of an asset for tokens. However, digital assets can not be advertised by just showing their contents, since they can be trivially copied. Indeed, a general criticism about NFTs for artworks is that regulating the possession of publicly available digital assets is often considered of modest interest, since the asset can also be enjoyed without owning it. Systems for managing NFTs guarantee that there is one owner of an asset, but still anyone can download and enjoy to some extent the asset. In general, it is useful to provide mechanisms allowing a party, simply represented by a public key (i.e., there is no information about who is behind the public key and thus no idea about his reputation/reliability), to (appealingly and reliably) advertise her desire to exchange her asset giving some specific guarantees to buyers while, at the same time, keeping the asset sufficiently hidden (e.g., an artist producing high-value digital pictures shows only an appealing short preview of the picture, but then there is no guarantee that she has the full asset).

It is therefore essential when considering the fair exchange of digital assets, to model the possibility of keeping the original asset private while publicly advertising only a corresponding restricted preview (that is, a "low" quality version of the asset) that is appealing enough to stimulate the interest of others.

TTP-Based (or Reputation-Based) Approaches. An obvious way to realize the above goal of having advertisable fair exchange protocols, consists of introducing a Trusted Third Party (TTP) both in the advertisement phase and during the actual exchange. In this scenario, users and/or companies rely on a well-known and reputed TTP to advertise and trade their digital assets. Such a TTP manages the assets and implements access control policies that limit the exposed information about the assets to be traded. At the same time, the TTP advertises the assets through previews and performs the exchanges, commonly for money. There are two types of trust assumptions: (a) the TTP is trusted to correctly advertise the asset (e.g., the preview is correctly computed) and (b) the exchange will be fairly carried out (e.g., if the buyer transfers the amount specified by the seller, then the buyer will receive the asset and the seller will receive the money).

In the wild, nowadays, there exists a vast variety of marketplaces selling assets (i.e., services that offer Alice to advertise her asset and then to fairly sell Alice's asset for Bob's money) all sticking with the above centralized architecture. For the case of physical assets, notable examples can be found in the context of car dealerships, where the party willing to buy a car can get temporary access to it (e.g., performing a test drive before buying a car) or in real estate, where the party can get temporary access to a building. Also for the case of digital assets, there are renowned examples of marketplace allowing to advertise and fairly exchange: (a) high-resolution images (e.g., Getty Images, Shutter Stock) advertised by an image preview (e.g., blurring and/or watermarking are applied to the image), (b) streaming video (e.g., Netflix, Amazon Prime) advertised by a video trailer or (c) streaming audio (e.g., Spotify, Audible) where just a portion of the audio is made publicly available for the advertisement.

The above trust towards the TTP is not necessarily a leap of faith. Indeed, in real-world scenarios, if Alice or Bob detects a misbehavior from the TTP then some evidence can be provided damaging the reputation of the TTP, inducting other users to change service, or even pursue lawsuits. Essentially, the TTP is just a company that runs a business that, as usual, is economy driven and a good reputation is one of the key factors for its success.

Risks of Relying on Services Based on Reputation. While reliable servers (i.e., TTPs or companies with good reputations) are the main choice today to advertise and trade digital assets, there are several important limitations that make the state of affairs quite unsatisfying. Servers could be successfully attacked becoming unreliable against their will (e.g., images deposited on a server could be stolen in case of a data breach). Attacks are likely to happen when servers manage assets of great value. Moreover, in specific contexts server can be censored by a government, limiting in turn the free exchange of assets. A server (if any) that is considered resilient to the above vulnerabilities is likely to be expensive.

In turn, users might not be satisfied by the policies of the server (e.g., an artist selling her songs might be unhappy with the high fees of the service and the poor quality of the advertisement) or by the limited security and availability.

1.1 Fair Exchange in the Decentralization Era

For the reasons discussed above, it is natural to consider a setting in which a user wishes to deploy her own service and act as the server herself. However, establishing a trustworthy reputation in such a decentralized setting requires both time and effort. During the initial bootstrapping phase, buyers may be reluctant to engage in transactions with a seller who lacks any form of endorsement or reputation from a TTP. This motivates the need to design systems that avoid dependence on centralized or costly intermediaries, while still ensuring both a reliable advertisement phase and a fair exchange of digital assets.

To frame the discussion, consider an example where a buyer, Bob, wishes to purchase a digital asset (e.g., an image, video, or piece of music) from a seller, Alice. Bob wants to ensure that he receives the desired asset in exchange for his payment, while Alice wants to be confident that he will receive the correct payment in return. A fair exchange protocol should provide the following informal guarantees:

(I) The buyer (Bob) must be guaranteed that if he participates in the protocol but does not receive the agreed-upon digital asset, then he retains full control of his funds (i.e., no coins are lost or transferred).

(II) The seller (Alice) must be guaranteed that if she does not receive the correct payment, then the buyer learns nothing about the asset beyond what was intentionally made public during the advertisement phase (e.g., the preview). No sensitive or valuable information about the asset should be leaked.

(III) The advertising of the digital asset should occur in a public and unique manner. That is, the seller should be able to publish the preview once, after which it remains publicly accessible. This reflects the natural structure of real-world marketplaces, where advertisements are broadcast to all potential buyers rather than being shared privately on a per-request basis. This property has several implications: **(a)** it ensures that the seller is not vulnerable to DoS attacks from malicious buyers repeatedly requesting previews; **(b)** it avoids requiring the buyer to be constantly online to respond to preview requests; **(c)** it prevents malicious sellers from impersonating honest ones by copying their publicly available previews and falsely claiming ownership of the asset. Thus, to achieve transparency and resilience, the entire interaction, including both the advertisement and the exchange, should be conducted without a point-to-point communication between buyer and seller.

Other Works in the Literature. Starting with the popular solution based on Hashed TimeLock Contracts [7], fair exchange via blockchains has been widely explored in the scientific literature [2,3,8,16,17,21–23,25–27,29]. All such works essentially focus on an asymmetric setting considering a seller named Alice who would like to sell a digital asset for an amount of cryptocurrency provided by a buyer Bob, giving this type of fair exchange the name of *contingent payment.* Note that the impossibility result of [11] is circumvented since Alice and Bob are now equipped with a trusted (decentralized) infrastructure. Those results do not communicate the asset a upfront (thus protecting it) and guarantee to a specific buyer that the asset a is a witness of an NP relation that will be received when the payment is complete.

These protocols typically address a "witness-selling" problem, where a buyer offers an amount of coins for a witness value w of an NP relation (e.g., knowledge of the discrete logarithm), such that $\mathcal{R}(x, w) = 1$ for a shared instance x between the seller and the buyer. Therefore, it is natural to consider the NP relation as a formalism to capture interesting properties of the witness (i.e., the asset a) to be exchanged, thereby using such properties to "advertise" the asset a to the buyer.

For the sake of clarity, we sketch here the common pattern used in the above works. Let us suppose that Alice aims to sell a digital asset a. At first, Alice and

Bob somehow agree on the asset a to exchange (e.g., Alice publicly claims that she owns the asset a and Bob asks for it). Then (1) Alice, without disclosing the asset a to exchange, sends to Bob a preview $\mathsf{a_p}$ of the asset a also stating the price for it. Then (2), Bob, after having looked at the preview $\mathsf{a_p}$ and agreed on the price, asks Alice to begin a fair exchange protocol. After that, (3) Alice computes the encryption $\mathsf{a_{enc}}$ of a with a symmetric key $\mathsf{k_a}$ (i.e., $\mathsf{a_{enc}} = Enc(\mathsf{k_a}, \mathsf{a})$), the commitment $\mathsf{c_{k_a}}$ of the symmetric key (i.e., $\mathsf{c_{k_a}} = Com(\mathsf{k_a})$), and (4) privately sends $\mathsf{a_{enc}}$ and $\mathsf{c_{k_a}}$ along with a consistency proof for the following NP relation:

$$\mathcal{R}(x := (\mathsf{c_{k_a}}, \mathsf{a_{enc}}, f, \mathsf{a_p}), w := (\mathsf{k_a}, \mathsf{a})) = 1 \text{ if and only if}$$
$$(\mathsf{c_{k_a}} = Com(\mathsf{k_a}) \wedge \mathsf{a_{enc}} = Enc(\mathsf{k_a}, \mathsf{a}) \wedge \mathsf{a_p} = f(\mathsf{a}))$$

where w is the witness for the relation $\mathcal{R}$, given x as the instance. If Bob verified this consistency proof correctly, then (5) Bob deployed a smart contract that will transfer a certain amount of cryptocurrency to the user capable of opening the commitment (i.e., $\mathsf{c_{k_a}}$) received by Alice. Finally, (6) Alice opens $\mathsf{c_{k_a}}$ and redeems the cryptocurrency by publicly disclosing $\mathsf{k_a}$, thereby also allowing Bob to obtain it. Bob can now retrieve a (i.e., Bob can obtain $\mathsf{a} = Dec(\mathsf{k_a}, \mathsf{a_{enc}})$).

Security and Usability Issues of Standard Fair Exchanges. According to the above discussion on the blueprint that all fair exchanges share, the seller transmits $\mathsf{a_{enc}}$, $\mathsf{c_{k_a}}$ and a consistency proof over a point-to-point channel that would limit the usability of contingent payments, especially in the presence of large amounts of fair exchanges done by a party (e.g., requiring parties to be simultaneously online and/or to coordinate how they exchange messages directly and privately).

In the non-optimistic approach, as in [8] the seller, after having sent privately to a single buyer, in the above step (4), the commitment and the encryption, has also to compute and send an ad-hoc consistency proof to the buyer to provide guarantees on the witness (i.e., the asset). This can seriously affect the seller's performance, especially in the presence of high demand (i.e., many buyers' requests) and/or when the underlying NP statement being proved is complex (e.g., due to a large statement size or the inherent complexity of the NP relation).

In the optimistic approach such as the one described in [16], the consistency proof is missing and the unsatisfied buyer, after having verified that the received asset does not match the expected properties, must compute and send a proof-of-misbehavior. According to [17], this can be an expensive task for the buyer and the smart contract, therefore leading to high costs. Furthermore, in both approaches, the buyer may interact with *fake sellers* who do not possess the desired asset, thereby resulting in wasted effort and time. Such vulnerabilities have also been informally observed and discussed in [26].

A very recent work [32] also considers the setting of fair exchange in the context of advertising. Their approach employs adaptor signatures as the underlying cryptographic primitive to properly formalize the advertisements phase. In their protocol, the buyer creates a presignature on both the claim and the associated blockchain transaction. The seller can convert this presignature into a valid signature, and thereby obtain payment, only if she possesses a valid witness for the claim (i.e., the asset being sold). Although this approach provides a specific notion of fairness also with advertisements, it relies on the assumption of point-to-point communication between the parties. As in other prior works, also the work of [32] suffers from the "fake seller" problem, wherein multiple malicious sellers may initiate the protocol with no intention of completing it. Due to the private nature of the interaction, there is no public evidence of such aborts, preventing others from being aware or responding to this misbehavior.

In practice, existing fair exchange protocols are never executed exclusively through broadcast messages sent to decentralized platforms, and thus they require parties to communicate directly to each other (e.g., via point-to-point communication). As a result, property **(III)** is consistently violated: interactions often rely on private communication, and the advertisement phase is neither modeled as a separate component nor implemented in a one-time, publicly verifiable way. Moreover, current definitions typically omit an explicit treatment of the advertisement phase and fail to provide formal security guarantees for it. Consequently, property **(II)** is not explicitly addressed. Fully addressing these gaps remains an open problem.

1.2 Our Results

We show how to realize fair exchange protocols for a decentralized marketplace where parties publicly, efficiently and cheaply advertise and exchange their assets without off-chain interactions with other parties, hence securely working through decentralized platforms.

We give a definition that explicitly combines a fair-exchange protocol with a prior advertising phase, a direction that has been recently and independently explored also by [29]. In our definition, the malicious buyer that does not transfer the required tokens does not learn anything about an asset except what has been on purpose leaked by the seller through the desired advertised information. At the same time, the definition guarantees that malicious sellers will not obtain tokens from the honest buyer unless the buyer gets the entire asset that is legitimately corresponding to the advertised version.

In contrast to prior work, our definition explicitly models the advertisement phase as a distinct and one-time step, and mandates that all interactions through broadcast messages sent to decentralized platforms. This addresses directly the shortcomings discussed above.

Next, we present an optimistic construction that combines a zk-SNARK (off-chain, but still publicly verifiable as it is uploaded on IPFS) as a consistency proof for advertising the asset, along with an optimistic fair exchange over a blockchain, applied in the context of the NFT markets. As discussed above, the NFT market for digital artworks suffers from a fundamental limitation: the traded assets are publicly accessible, even to those who do not own the corresponding NFT. This significantly reduces the appeal of such applications. This is because the security of the smart contract relies on the transparency of the underlying blockchain, allowing any user to autonomously verify the system's status by accessing all its data. Improving the management of NFTs for confidential assets, potentially enables a new wave of interest in such an application context. Thanks to our construction, an NFT that manages confidential assets permits only the owner of the NFT to have access to the asset managed by such NFT, while interested buyers can access only a preview, with a guarantee that the preview is correctly computed and this limited access can encourage buyers to purchase the asset. If interested, buyers can then purchase the NFT and obtain access to the asset.

Our construction works as follows.

(a) As advertisement, the seller publishes on a decentralized storage platform the *preview of the asset*, an *encryption of the asset*, a *commitment on the encryption key* used to encrypt the asset and a *zk-SNARK* proving that she knows both the encryption key and the asset corresponding to the preview.

(b) The seller then generates a pair of DiffieâĂŞHellman (DH) *ephemeral keys* and deploys a *smart contract* to facilitate the fair exchange. In the contract, the seller publishes the *sale price* of the asset (i.e., the amount of cryptocurrency she wishes to receive), a commitment to the encryption key, and a DH message (i.e., her public contribution to the DH key exchange), while keeping the corresponding secret key private.

(c) Once the zk-SNARK is verified, and it is confirmed that the commitment to the encryption key stored in the smart contract's internal state matches the one used in the zk-SNARK, a user (acting as the buyer) proceeds as follows: she generates a DH message along with the corresponding secret key, initiates the fair exchange protocol by locking the sale price (i.e., the specified amount of cryptocurrency) in the smart contract, and publishes her DH message.

(d) The seller satisfied by the locked cryptocurrency, first computes a DH *session key* and computes a *cyphertext* (with this freshly computed session key) of a message that consists of the above encryption key (i.e., the committed one) concatenated with the randomness used to compute the commitment. Finally, she publishes the resulting ciphertext in the smart contract.

(e) The buyer, computing the DH session key, will decrypt the ciphertext uploaded by the seller obtaining the encryption key and the randomness used in the commitment.

If the encryption key matches the one committed in the decentralized storage, the buyer will correctly decrypt the asset and afterward the locked cryptocurrency will be automatically unlocked on the blockchain and the seller will receive the payment. Otherwise, the buyer can initiate a dispute by publishing in the smart contract his secret corresponding to his DH contribution.

The smart contract performs the following steps: **(1)** it verifies the correctness of the secret uploaded by the buyer by recomputing the buyer's DH message and checking that this corresponds to the one previously updated by the buyer; **(2)** it computes the DH session key combining the DH message of the seller with the secret of the buyer; **(3)** it uses the session key to get through decryption of the very same encryption key computed by the buyer along with the randomness for the commitment, and, finally, **(4)** it verifies whether this corresponds to the commitment stored in its internal state.

If the computed commitment does not correspond to the one that was previously updated by the seller, it means that the seller is trying to obtain the buyer's cryptocurrencies without disclosing the correct encryption key. In this case, the smart contract can penalize the seller (for example, by burning the NFT) to discourage bad behaviors. If the computed key corresponds to the committed key, then the buyer is cheating and the smart contract can discard the request or, similarly to the seller's case, penalize the buyer.

Note that by assigning a percentage of future revenues to previous owners, they can be economically incentivized not to disclose the encryption keys.

We have benchmarked our construction, focusing our experiments on the management of NFTs that represent images available in renowned collections (e.g., BAYC). The goal of our experiments is to evaluate the performance of the proposed construction for NFTs of confidential artworks, to show the viability of our solution and the advantages of the new definition. We have conducted two main experiments, that consist of a) proving the ability to compute the proofs to advertise the confidential images and b) evaluating the costs of the smart contract extending the ERC-721 standard and implementing the fair exchange. Both experiments confirm the viability of the proposed approach, and a comparison of layer-1 (Ethereum) and layer-2 (Optimism) deployment and operation costs for the smart contract is shown to allow the selection of the most appropriate technology according to the value given to the asset.

2 Preliminaries

We refer to the full version for standard notation of cyptographic primitives.

2.1 Tokens

Taking inspiration from [6], we define *tokens* with the following properties: (1) a token owner is the only user in possession of it, and it is ensured that no other entity can simultaneously own the same token; (2) tokens can be freely transferred from a sender to a receiver (i.e., the sender is no longer the token owner while the receiver becomes the new token owner) and the received token's validity can be immediately verified and confirmed; finally, we assume that each user should have access to a *wallet* $\mathfrak{U}$ to accumulate *tokens.*

More formally, we denote with $\mathcal{T}$ the set of all possible tokens with the same value. We denote with $\mathsf{tk}[n] := \{\mathsf{tk}_1, \mathsf{tk}_2, \ldots, \mathsf{tk}_n\}$ a set of n tokens such that $\mathsf{tk}_i \in \mathcal{T}$ for $1 \leq i \leq n$. We highlight that the comparison between two sets of tokens (e.g., $\mathsf{tk}[n] > \mathsf{tk}[m]$) is a comparison based on their total quantity. Specifically, $\mathsf{tk}[n] > \mathsf{tk}[m]$ holds if and only if $n > m$, with $n, m \in \mathbb{N}$.

We explicitly write $\mathsf{tk}[n] \triangleright \mathfrak{U}$ to indicate that the tokens $\{\mathsf{tk}_i\}_{1 \leq i \leq n}$ are owned by the user who controls the wallet $\mathfrak{U}$ (i.e., the user knows the secret key associated with $\mathfrak{U}$, enabling them to authorize transactions that spend these tokens). Following standard blockchain assumptions, ownership is defined by the ability to spend, which in turn requires knowledge of the corresponding secret key. As is common in prior work, we abstract away the cryptographic details of key management and refer to token ownership in terms of wallet access. We denote by owner a predicate that takes as input a set of tokens $\mathsf{tk}[n]$ and a wallet $\mathfrak{U}$, and outputs a bit in $\{0,1\}$. The output is 1 only if all tokens in $\mathsf{tk}[n]$ are contained in $\mathfrak{U}$ (i.e., $\forall i \in \{1,\ldots,n\},\ \mathsf{tk}_i \in \mathfrak{U}$); otherwise, it outputs 0.

2.2 Blockchain

Introduced in 2008, a blockchain is a distributed ledger with growing lists of records (i.e., blocks) securely linked together via cryptographic hashes [19].

The status of the system evolves through transactions. A transaction can transfer digital currency from a sender user to a receiver user. Every user that interacts with the system has a pair of keys of Π_{Sign} generated with the $\Pi_{\mathsf{Sign}}.\mathsf{KeyGen}$ algorithm. According to Sect. 2.1, we provide every user with a *wallet* containing tokens and the blockchain maintains a ledger of all wallets. A user U, that has $(\mathsf{pk}_{\mathsf{U}}, \mathsf{sk}_{\mathsf{U}})$, signs every transaction that she wants to add to the ledger, with sk_{U}. We denote the wallet of the user U as $\mathfrak{U}_{\mathsf{U}}$. A transaction is added to the ledger if the signature is correctly verified using the public key pk_{U} and if U has enough tokens in $\mathfrak{U}_{\mathsf{U}}$ to perform that operation.

Global Clock. In addition to managing transactions and maintaining a decentralized ledger, the blockchain can also serve as a global clock. Loosely speaking, we define time in the system as a value maintained by the blockchain in the form of a global clock, observable by all participants. This clock advances as time progresses (i.e., according to the creation of new blocks), ensuring that all parties share a consistent view of the current time, denoted by t. More formally, since we consider blockchains modeled as a synchronous model of communication, we implicitly assume that the blockchain acts also as a global clock [24], with protocols executed in rounds and every party aware of the current round. Thus, parties can expect messages to be received at a certain time. This assumption in the blockchain domain is indeed widely employed in other works in this area [20,28,30,31].

Smart Contracts. In 2015, Ethereum introduced the concept of smart contracts, i.e. it allows users to deploy arbitrary programs that not only define the conditions for spending money, but also enable the deployment of generic programs that use the blockchain to reach consensus on a program state. Therefore, user transactions can be viewed as inputs to these *smart contracts*. In summary, Ethereum has introduced and realized the concept of a virtual machine on top of a blockchain.

Taking inspiration from [1,30] and leveraging the capabilities of smart contracts, we equip the blockchain with two interfaces through which a (sender) user can interact to execute transactions: (1) $\mathsf{tx}(\mathsf{U}, \mathsf{tk}[n], t')$: given as input a (receiver) user U (where U represents the user identified by the public key pk_{U}), a set of n tokens $\mathsf{tk}[n]$, and (optionally) a future time instant t' such that $t' \geq t$

(where t denotes the current time), this transaction locks the tokens $\mathsf{tk}[n]$ until time t' on the blockchain (i.e., on a smart contract). After t', the tokens are transferred to the (receiver) user U. This transaction models the behavior of a simple *time-lock transaction*. Note that if $t' = \perp$ (i.e., t' is not specified), this denotes a simple transaction over the blockchain to transfer $\mathsf{tk}[n]$ tokens to the user U. (2) $\mathsf{store}(m)$: given a message $m \in \{0,1\}^*$ as input, the message m is made visible to all parties, similar to posting it on a public bulletin board.

3 Advertisement-Based Fair Exchange

Here, we define Advertisement-Based Fair Exchange. Following the approach of other works on fair exchange discussed in Sect. 1.1, we focus on the asymmetric case, where one party exchanges an asset for money. We consider this scenario as the most interesting case, while treating the symmetric case, in which both parties exchange assets, as an obvious extension.

In accordance with the definition of fair exchange (in the full version), the protocol involves three actors. The first two are Alice and Bob, who want to exchange their respective assets. In the protocol, Alice will be the seller who has advertised her asset, and Bob will be the buyer who wants to pay a certain amount of money to obtain this asset. Finally, the third actor is the TTP referred to as T[1].

For PPT algorithms A, B and C, we denote by $[x, y, z] \leftarrow [\mathsf{A}(a), \mathsf{B}(b), \mathsf{C}(c)](d)$ the random process obtained by having A,B and C interact on common input d and on (private) auxiliary inputs a, b and c, respectively, and with independent random coin tosses for A, B and C. The values x, y and z represent the outputs of A, B and C, respectively, after the interaction.

We define an asset and an asset preview as bit strings, namely $\mathsf{a}, \mathsf{a_p} \in \{0,1\}^*$, and a preview function $f : \{0,1\}^* \rightarrow \{0,1\}^*$ as an efficient deterministic function that, given in input an asset a, outputs $\mathsf{a_p}$.

Definition 1. *An Advertisement-Based Fair Exchange Π_{AFE} for a preview function f is a three-party protocol run by a* PPT *seller* A*, a* PPT *buyer* B *and a TTP* T *satisfying* Completeness, Seller Fairness, Buyer Fairness *and* Broadcast Communication only *and that works as follows:*

- $\mathsf{prm} \leftarrow \mathsf{Setup}(1^\lambda)$ *is a randomized algorithm that takes as input the security parameter λ, and outputs a string* $\mathsf{prm} \in \{0,1\}^*$ *that represents (possibly trusted) parameters.*
- $(\mathsf{a_{prv}}, \mathsf{a_{pub}}) \leftarrow \mathsf{Advertise}(\mathsf{prm}, \mathsf{a}, \mathsf{tk_{thr}})$ *is a randomized algorithm that takes as input* prm*, an asset* $\mathsf{a} \in \{0,1\}^*$ *and* $\mathsf{tk_{thr}} \in \mathbb{N}^+$ *and outputs a pair* $(\mathsf{a_{prv}}, \mathsf{a_{pub}})$*.*
- $[\alpha, \beta] \leftarrow [\mathsf{A}(\mathsf{a_{prv}}), \mathsf{B}(\mathsf{tk}[n]), \mathsf{T}](\mathsf{prm}, \mathsf{a_{pub}})$ *is a three-party protocol.* A *and* B *exchange* $\mathsf{a_{prv}}$ *and* $\mathsf{tk}[n]$*, respectively, where* $\mathsf{tk}[n]$ *are the buyer's tokens used to purchase* $\mathsf{a_{prv}}$*.* B *engages the protocol with* A *after evaluating* prm *and* $\mathsf{a_{pub}}$*. At the end of the protocol,* A *outputs α and* B *outputs β. The value $\perp$ as output indicates that the party has rejected the execution.*

---

[1] Jumping ahead, we adopt for our construction a restricted TTP T publicly maintaining all the information and assuming that T performs its operations correctly.

Completeness. *Given an honest seller* A*, with wallet* $\mathfrak{U}_\mathsf{A}$*, and an honest buyer* B*, with wallet* $\mathfrak{U}_\mathsf{B}$ *such that* $\mathsf{tk}[n] \rhd \mathfrak{U}_\mathsf{B}$[2]*, for any asset* $\mathsf{a} \in \{0,1\}^*$ *and any* $\mathsf{tk}_\mathsf{thr} \in \mathbb{N}^+$*, the following probability is equal to* 1*:*

$$\Pr\left[\begin{array}{c}[\mathsf{tk}[n], \mathsf{a}_\mathsf{prv}] \leftarrow [\mathsf{A}(\mathsf{a}_\mathsf{prv}), \mathsf{B}(\mathsf{tk}[n]), \mathsf{T}](\mathsf{prm}, \mathsf{a}_\mathsf{pub}) \\ \wedge \mathsf{owner}(\mathsf{tk}[n], \mathfrak{U}_\mathsf{A})\end{array} \middle| \begin{array}{c}\mathsf{prm} \leftarrow \mathsf{Setup}(1^\lambda) \\ (\mathsf{a}_\mathsf{prv}, \mathsf{a}_\mathsf{pub}) \leftarrow \mathsf{Advertise}(\mathsf{prm}, \mathsf{a}, \mathsf{tk}_\mathsf{thr})\end{array}\right]$$

We recall that, we denote with owner *a predicate that, taking as input any set of tokens* $\mathsf{tk}[n]$ *and any wallet* $\mathfrak{U}_\mathsf{U}$ *accessible by a user* U*, it outputs* 1 *if all the tokens are in the wallet* $\mathfrak{U}_\mathsf{U}$ *(i.e.,* $\forall i \in \{1, \ldots, n\}, \mathsf{tk}_i \in \mathfrak{U}_\mathsf{U}$*), otherwise* 0 .

Seller Fairness. *Given an honest seller* A*, for any asset* $\mathsf{a} \in \{0,1\}^*$ *and any* $\mathsf{tk}_\mathsf{thr} \in \mathbb{N}^+$*, for all* PPT *malicious buyer* B^* *with a wallet* $\mathfrak{U}_\mathsf{B}$ *and* $\mathsf{tk}[n] \rhd \mathfrak{U}_\mathsf{B}$ *(see footnote 2), there exists a PPT algorithm* $\mathtt{Sim}^\mathsf{T}_{\mathsf{B}^*}$ *with oracle access to* T *such that, for any* PPT *distinguisher* $\mathcal{D}$*, the following probability is at most* $\mathsf{negl}(\lambda)$*:*

$$\left|\Pr\left[\mathcal{D}(\mathsf{a}, \beta) = 1 \middle| \begin{array}{c}\mathsf{prm} \leftarrow \mathsf{Setup}(1^\lambda) \\ (\mathsf{a}_\mathsf{prv}, \mathsf{a}_\mathsf{pub}) \leftarrow \mathsf{Advertise}(\mathsf{prm}, \mathsf{a}, \mathsf{tk}_\mathsf{thr}) \\ [\bot, \beta] \leftarrow [\mathsf{A}(\mathsf{a}_\mathsf{prv}), \mathsf{B}^*(\mathsf{tk}[n]), \mathsf{T}](\mathsf{prm}, \mathsf{a}_\mathsf{pub})\end{array}\right] - \Pr\left[\mathcal{D}(\mathsf{a}, \beta) = 1 \,\middle|\, \beta \leftarrow \mathtt{Sim}^\mathsf{T}_{\mathsf{B}^*}(f(\mathsf{a}), \mathsf{tk}_\mathsf{thr})\right]\right|$$

Namely, this property requires that, at the end of the protocol, regardless of the output of B^* *(denoted generically as* β *in the above probability), if the output of* A *is* $\bot$ *(i.e.,* A *aborts the execution), the probability that* B^* *learns something more than* $f(\mathsf{a})$ *and* tk_thr *is negligible.*

Buyer Fairness. *Given an honest buyer* B*, with a wallet* $\mathfrak{U}_\mathsf{B}$ *such that* $\mathsf{tk}[n] \rhd \mathfrak{U}_\mathsf{B}$ *(see footnote 2), for all* PPT *malicious seller* A^* *the following probability is at most* $\mathsf{negl}(\lambda)$*:*

$$\Pr\left[\exists i \in \{1, \ldots, n\} \ s.t. \ \mathsf{tk}_i \notin \mathfrak{U}_\mathsf{B} \middle| \begin{array}{c}\mathsf{prm} \leftarrow \mathsf{Setup}(1^\lambda) \\ (\mathsf{a}_\mathsf{prv}, \mathsf{a}_\mathsf{pub}) \leftarrow \mathsf{A}^*(\mathsf{prm}) \\ [\alpha, \bot] \leftarrow [\mathsf{A}^*(\mathsf{a}_\mathsf{prv}), \mathsf{B}(\mathsf{tk}[n]), \mathsf{T}](\mathsf{prm}, \mathsf{a}_\mathsf{pub})\end{array}\right]$$

Namely, this property requires that, at the end of the protocol, regardless of the output of A^* *(denoted generically as* α *in the above probability), if the output of* B *is* $\bot$ *(i.e.,* B *aborts the execution), the probability that* B *has lost a token from* $\mathsf{tk}[n]$ *in* $\mathfrak{U}_\mathsf{B}$ *is negligible.*

Broadcast Communication Only. *All communication between the seller* A *and the buyer* B *is conducted exclusively via a broadcast messages towards decentralized platforms. That is, all messages exchanged between the parties must be forwarded via* T*, who ensures that every message is immediately made publicly visible.*

---

[2] We recall that, according to Sect. 2.1, the notation $\mathsf{tk}[n] \rhd \mathfrak{U}_\mathsf{B}$ indicates that the tokens $\mathsf{tk}[n] = \{\mathsf{tk}_i\}_{1 \leq i \leq n}$ are owned by the user who has access to the wallet $\mathfrak{U}_\mathsf{B}$ (i.e., the user who knows the secret key to transfer the token inside the wallet), in this case, B. Namely, that $\mathsf{tk}[n]$ are contained within B's wallet.

Note that the definition is parametrized for a preview function f. The description of this function is included in $\mathsf{a}_{\mathsf{pub}}$ during the execution of Advertise.

The fairness properties for both sellers and buyers are inspired by [29]. Specifically, in the context of *contingent payment* protocols, there is a natural asymmetry between the seller and the buyer in terms of guarantees provided by the fairness property, as highlighted in [29]. In general, the properties of Definition 1 grant the same level of security of the definition in [29] but our definition explicitly devises an advertisement operation for the seller, making it more suitable for a decentralized marketplace of confidential assets.

For seller fairness, the focus is on preserving the confidentiality of the seller's private information (denoted as $\mathsf{a}_{\mathsf{prv}}$ in our case) when the protocol between the seller and the buyer does not conclude successfully. If the honest seller aborts the protocol, no (non-trivial) information about $\mathsf{a}_{\mathsf{prv}}$ should be revealed. To formalize this, we adopt a simulation-based definition of fairness, where a malicious buyer cannot distinguish whether she is interacting with a simulator or the actual seller, and the simulator does not know the seller's secret (i.e., $\mathsf{a}_{\mathsf{prv}}$ in our case).

Following the definition provided in [29], we adopt a relaxed notion of security to ensure buyer fairness (i.e., protect the buyer's tokens). While a stronger definition would require the inclusion of a simulator even in this case, we align with the approach taken in previous works and opt for a more traditional game-based definition. Indeed, buyer fairness does not require confidentiality for the buyer's tokens, $\mathsf{tk}[n]$, and ensures that no token is transferred to the seller at the end of the protocol between the seller and the buyer, when the protocol does not conclude successfully; the entire amount of tokens for the exchange is still owned by the buyer.

Note that, this "asymmetry" between the seller and the buyer fairness (due to the *contingent payment* scenario) can also be observed in other cryptographic protocols such as the zero-knowledge and soundness properties of zero-knowledge proofs. W.r.t. the buyer fairness of [29], we do not focus on the tokens that the adversary holds at the end of the protocol, and, instead, we capture the property that the balance of the honest party (i.e., the buyer, B, in our definition) at the end of the protocol remains unchanged, when the buyer is honest and outputs $\perp$. This variation makes our definition meaningful also in those scenarios where a token can be destroyed. Due to space limitations, further considerations on how to easily extend Definition 1 to the "symmetric case" (i.e., both parties advertise and then exchange an asset) are deferred to the full version.

Finally, note that the three-party protocol in Definition 1 does not specify the number of messages exchanged between the parties. This generality allows for optimistic constructions, where parties can optionally raise complaints to T about misbehavior during protocol execution. Such an approach is valuable in practice, enabling efficient execution when all parties behave honestly, while still providing security guarantees through the complaint mechanism when needed.

More formally, our Advertisement-Based Fair Exchange definition accommodates a complaint mechanism within the protocol, allowing a party to provide cryptographic evidence to T demonstrating that the other party has deviated from the prescribed protocol. This mechanism can be instantiated by enabling a party to submit specific values (e.g., secret keys or intermediate protocol values) that allow T to verify the complaint's validity, and punish the (other) party that deviates from the protocol. The complaint mechanisms usually operate within a temporal framework defined by three critical time bounds. Let t_{init} denote the protocol initiation time (when assets are committed or tokens locked), t_{comp} denote the complaint deadline, and t_{final} denote the protocol conclusion time (when assets or tokens are irreversibly transferred). These time points must satisfy $t_{\mathsf{init}} < t_{\mathsf{comp}} < t_{\mathsf{final}}$ to ensure that: (1) parties have sufficient time to execute the protocol, (2) complaints can be filed before irreversible transfers occur, and (3) T has adequate time to evaluate complaints and take appropriate action.

We emphasize that Definition 1 naturally accommodates such complaint mechanisms without requiring explicit modification, as the fairness properties already capture the necessary security guarantees. The definition's flexibility allows various implementations of complaint mechanisms, e.g. including both single-round and multi-round complaint procedures.

4 Construction

We present a construction of an Advertisement-Based Fair Exchange, in which the TTP is implemented through a smart contract involving the fair exchange of confidential and authenticated Non-Fungible Tokens (NFTs). Fair exchanges in a public marketplace can involve a wide variety of digital items, ranging, for example, from videos and software vulnerabilities to trained neural networks and images. Our proposed construction specifically targets the fair exchange of NFTs managing confidential and authenticated assets on a blockchain. Enabling the trading of such tokens addresses a significant issue within the blockchain domain, as already deeply discussed in Sect. 1. In the following, we show how an Advertisement-Based Fair Exchange is perfectly suited to manage the advertisement and the trading of authenticated and confidential assets (i.e., realizing de facto a market of NFT managing confidential assets) by requiring only a blockchain equipped with smart contracts (e.g., Ethereum).

4.1 Advertisement-Based Fair Exchange for NFTs

W.l.o.g., we simplify the representation of an NFT omitting some values such as the association of an owner publicly visible on the blockchain or the unique ID assigned to every NFT (e.g., as in Ethereum ERC721 [4]). Instead, we primarily focus on the asset itself. The management of the other properties associated with the NFT can be easily integrated into the construction.

Parties and Asset Description. According to Definition 1, we consider an Advertisement-Based Fair Exchange where a seller A owns an NFT managing a (confidential) asset $\mathsf{a}^\star$ that she wants to publicly advertise and then trade with an interested buyer B for some tokens $\mathsf{tk}[n]$. The NFT and the Advertisement-Based

Fair Exchange involve a TTP T, which is a blockchain[3] (see Sect. 2.2). Note that, according to Sect. 2.2, T works correctly. We focus solely on the management of the asset $\mathsf{a}^\star$ and do not consider other boundary properties that characterize the NFT. This (1) simplifies the treatment and (2) enables us to embrace different types of NFT that can be defined and managed differently according to different blockchains (e.g., Ethereum ERC721 or Algorand ASA).

We consider the asset $\mathsf{a}^\star \in \{0,1\}^*$ composed of a set of bits, a public key and a signature that attest the authenticity of this asset. We adopt this type of representation because it seems very general and natural for a wide variety of assets in the NFT domain. That is, denoting the asset to exchange with $\mathsf{a}^\star = (\mathsf{a}, \mathsf{pk}, \sigma_\mathsf{a})$, we consider $\mathsf{a} \in \{0,1\}^*$ as a generic set of bits, pk as a public key of Π_{Sign} (see the full version) and σ_a as a digital signature of Π_{Sign}. A well-formed asset $\mathsf{a}^\star$ always has the following property: $\Pi_{\mathsf{Sign}}.\mathsf{Verify}(\mathsf{pk}, \mathsf{a}, \sigma_\mathsf{a}) = 1$. Note that, pk represents the public key of the creator (and sometimes also the current owner) of the asset a (e.g., a public key of the artist who created the image a, or the company that issued the ticket a).

Remarks on T When Represented by a Blockchain. The TTP, denoted as T, involved in the exchange between parties, is represented by a blockchain(See footnote 3). According to Sect. 2.2, all information held by T must be considered public. In other words, once T stores or uses a value for computation, that value is publicly available to everyone (i.e., it is equivalent to posting the value on a public bulletin board). Furthermore, as discussed in Sect. 2.2, we equip T with two interfaces with which each user can interact, namely tx_T and $\mathsf{store}_\mathsf{T}$.

Finally, according to the definition of an Advertisement-Based Fair Exchange (see Definition 1), oracle access to T is required. When T is represented by a blockchain, this requirement naturally follows, as it implies the ability to interact with T through the store and tx interfaces (according to Sect. 2.2), and to query the blockchain and retrieve all operations and information maintained within it. This aligns perfectly with the behavior of most real-world blockchains today.

Description of Algorithms. We recall that Π_{AFE} is parameterized by a preview function f. We denote our construction of Π_{AFE} as Ω_{AFE}. The construction Ω_{AFE} is parametrized by a function f that takes as input $\mathsf{a}^\star := (\mathsf{a}, \mathsf{pk}, \sigma_\mathsf{a})$ and outputs the tuple $(f_{\mathsf{sub}}(\mathsf{a}), \mathsf{pk})$ composed of the output of the transformation of a (leveraging f_{sub} that is described in f) and the pk, that is basically forwarded from the input.

Protocol Setup. In the Advertisement-Based Fair Exchange defined in Sect. 3, there is a setup algorithm namely $\Pi_{\mathsf{AFE}}.\mathsf{Setup}$, this algorithm outputs a string $\mathsf{prm} \in \{0,1\}^*$ representing the trusted parameters. $\Pi_{\mathsf{AFE}}.\mathsf{Setup}$ is run by an additional trusted party (not the blockchain T) that disappears after the execution of the algorithm. In our construction, prm is a pair composed of the common reference string crs generated with $\Pi_{\mathsf{ZK\text{-}snark}}.\mathsf{KeyGen}$, that is built starting from

[3] We generically refer to T as a blockchain rather than a smart contract. This mainly because, depending on the specific blockchain and how NFTs are managed, an NFT might be controlled by multiple smart contracts and/or with a different logic.

a relation $\mathcal{R}$ and the commitment key ck generated with $\Pi_{\mathsf{Com}}.\mathsf{KeyGen}(1^\lambda)$ (i.e., $\mathsf{prm} := (\mathsf{ck}, \mathsf{crs})$)[4]. The zk-SNARK, for which the crs is defined, is based on the following NP relation $\mathcal{R}$:

$$\mathcal{R}\,(x := (\mathsf{a_{enc}}, \mathsf{a_p}, \mathsf{c_{k_a}}, \mathsf{ck}), w := (\mathsf{k_a}, r)) = 1 \text{ if and only if}$$
$$\left(\begin{array}{c} (\mathsf{a}||\sigma_{\mathsf{a}}) = \Pi_{\mathsf{Enc}}.\mathsf{Dec}(\mathsf{k_a}, \mathsf{a_{enc}}) \wedge 1 = \Pi_{\mathsf{Sign}}.\mathsf{Verify}(\mathsf{pk}, \mathsf{a}, \sigma_{\mathsf{a}}) \\ \wedge \mathsf{a_p} = (f_{\mathsf{sub}}(\mathsf{a}), \mathsf{pk}) = f((\mathsf{a}, \mathsf{pk}, \sigma_{\mathsf{a}})) \wedge \mathsf{c_{k_a}} = \Pi_{\mathsf{Com}}.\mathsf{Commit}(\mathsf{ck}, \mathsf{k_a}; r) \end{array}\right)$$

Advertisement of the Asset. The definition of $\Pi_{\mathsf{AFE}}.\mathsf{Advertise}$ in Sect. 3 allows advertising the asset $\mathsf{a}^\star$ that the seller wants to trade for tokens. In particular, given a trusted parameter prm, an authenticated asset $\mathsf{a}^\star = (\mathsf{a}, \mathsf{pk}, \sigma_{\mathsf{a}})$ and an amount of tokens $\mathsf{tk_{thr}} \in \mathbb{N}^+$, the seller computes a pair of values $(\mathsf{a_{prv}}, \mathsf{a_{pub}})$ where $\mathsf{a_{pub}}$ is the information to advertise $\mathsf{a}^\star$ and $\mathsf{a_{prv}}$ is the information to trade $\mathsf{a}^\star$. That is, the seller: **1** provides guarantees about the asset $\mathsf{a}^\star$ through $\mathsf{a_{pub}}$, and **2** advertises $\mathsf{a}^\star$ by publishing $\mathsf{a_{pub}}$, that includes also the price, namely the amount of tokens that the seller wants to exchange for the asset.

In Algorithm 1, we formally describe how $\Pi_{\mathsf{AFE}}.\mathsf{Advertise}$ works in our construction, thus, how $(\mathsf{a_{pub}}, \mathsf{a_{prv}})$ are computed and how $\mathsf{a}^\star$ is advertised through $\mathsf{a_{pub}}$. Moreover, π is generated with a zk-SNARK, according to definition of zk-SNARK given in the full version. Algorithm 1 invokes at line 4 an internal sub-routine called $\mathsf{defineVerAlg_{A,B}}$ that, taking as input the amount of tokens that the seller wants to exchange for the asset (i.e., $\mathsf{tk_{thr}} \in \mathbb{N}^+$), outputs a verification algorithm V_{A} for the seller and a verification algorithm V_{B} for the buyer. The verification algorithm V_{A}, taking as input a set of tokens $\mathsf{tk}[k]$, outputs 1 if k is equal to $\mathsf{tk_{thr}}$; otherwise, it outputs 0. The verification algorithm V_{B} enables the buyer to verify that she has correctly received the asset $\mathsf{a}^\star$.

Algorithm 1: The algorithm $\Pi_{\mathsf{AFE}}.\mathsf{Advertise}$ for $\mathsf{a}^\star$.

Input: Trusted parameters prm such that $\mathsf{prm} := (\mathsf{ck}, \mathsf{crs})$, an asset $\mathsf{a}^\star := (\mathsf{a}, \mathsf{pk}, \sigma_{\mathsf{a}})$ and an amount of tokens $\mathsf{tk_{thr}} \in \mathbb{N}^+$ that the seller wants to exchange for the asset.

1 $\mathsf{a_p} \leftarrow f(\mathsf{a}^\star)$; $\mathsf{k_a} \leftarrow \Pi_{\mathsf{Enc}}.\mathsf{KeyGen}(1^\lambda)$; $\mathsf{a_{enc}} \leftarrow \Pi_{\mathsf{Enc}}.\mathsf{Enc}(\mathsf{k_a}, \mathsf{a}||\sigma_{\mathsf{a}})$; $r \leftarrow\$\ \mathbb{Z}_q$

2 $\mathsf{c_{k_a}} \leftarrow \Pi_{\mathsf{Com}}.\mathsf{Commit}(\mathsf{ck}, \mathsf{k_a}; r)$; $\pi \leftarrow \Pi_{\mathsf{ZK\text{-}snark}}.\mathsf{Prove}(\mathsf{crs}, (\mathsf{a_{enc}}, \mathsf{a_p}, \mathsf{c_{k_a}}, \mathsf{ck}), (\mathsf{k_a}, r))$

3 $V_{\mathsf{A}}, V_{\mathsf{B}} \leftarrow \mathsf{defineVerAlg_{A,B}}(\mathsf{tk_{thr}})$; $\mathsf{a_{pub}} := ((\mathsf{a_{enc}}, \mathsf{a_p}, \mathsf{c_{k_a}}, \mathsf{ck}), \pi, V_{\mathsf{A}}, V_{\mathsf{B}})$; $\mathsf{store_T}(\mathsf{a_{pub}})$

Output: $(\mathsf{a_{pub}}, \mathsf{a_{prv}} := \mathsf{k_a}||r)$

---

[4] We introduce this trusted party only for convenience, to generate the trusted parameters used by the protocol. In practice, one can instantiate the zk-SNARK in the RO model [5] and derive the commitment key via the RO as well (i.e., by standard hashing into the group technique). This eliminates the need for any trusted setup. Our use of a CRS-based setup is aligned with our experimental evaluation, but the same construction can be easily realized entirely in the RO model, avoiding this other party.

Exchange Protocol. In Fig. 1, we describe the protocol that the seller A and the buyer B engage to exchange their assets (i.e., the NFT $\mathsf{a}^\star$ and the set of tokens $\mathsf{tk}[n]$). According to the definition in Sect. 3, before engaging the protocol, the buyer B evaluates $\mathsf{a_{pub}} := ((\mathsf{a_{enc}}, \mathsf{a_p}, \mathsf{c_{k_a}}, \mathsf{ck}), \pi, V_\mathsf{A}, V_\mathsf{B})$. In our construction, this evaluation works as follows: first, the buyer B evaluates V_A from $\mathsf{a_{pub}}$ by simply looking at V_A and $\mathsf{a_p}$ and deciding whether it is worth purchasing the asset. Then, B evaluates the correctness of the algorithm V_B from $\mathsf{a_{pub}}$. Finally, regarding the remaining part of $\mathsf{a_{pub}}$ (i.e., $(\mathsf{a_{enc}}, \mathsf{a_p}, \mathsf{c_{k_a}}, \mathsf{ck})$ and the proof π), this involves B checking whether $\Pi_{\mathsf{ZK\text{-}snark}}.\mathsf{Verify}(\mathsf{crs}, (\mathsf{a_{enc}}, \mathsf{a_p}, \mathsf{c_{k_a}}, \mathsf{ck}), \pi) = 1$.

The protocol is detailed in Fig. 1. In a nutshell, the parties first execute an ephemeral Diffie-Hellman key exchange, obtaining the shared key k_AB. Next, the buyer B locks into T the tokens $\mathsf{tk}[n]$ for a time t'. Following this, the seller A, first checks if $\mathsf{tk}[n]$ (locked by B) fulfills her requirements (i.e., $V_\mathsf{A}(\mathsf{tk}[n]) = 1$), and then using the shared key k_AB, encrypts $\mathsf{a_{prv}}$ to securely complete the exchange of the asset $\mathsf{a}^\star$. We recall that $\mathsf{a_{prv}}$ is composed of two substrings that are: **1** the (symmetric) key $\mathsf{k_a}$ used to encrypt $\mathsf{a}^\star$ (i.e., $\Pi_\mathsf{Enc}.\mathsf{Enc}(\mathsf{k_a}, \mathsf{a}||\sigma_\mathsf{a})$), and **2** the randomness r used for the commitment of $\mathsf{k_a}$ (i.e., $\Pi_\mathsf{Com}.\mathsf{Commit}(\mathsf{ck}, \mathsf{k_a}; r)$).

Then, the seller publishes the encryption $\mathsf{e_{k_a}} := \Pi_\mathsf{Enc}.\mathsf{Enc}(k_\mathsf{AB}, \mathsf{k_a})$ in T by invoking $\mathsf{store_T}(\mathsf{e_{k_a}})$. Finally, B checks the correctness of $\mathsf{e_{k_a}}$ (i.e., the buyer runs an internal sub-routine V_B), and in case of failure she complains with T; otherwise, if B obtains the correct $\mathsf{k_a}$, she ends the protocol and A gets the locked tokens $\mathsf{tk}[n]$, after t'. To complain with T, we equip the blockchain with an additional interface $\mathsf{Complaint_T}(\mathsf{sk_B})$ that can be invoked by B executing Algorithm 2. Specifically, Algorithm 2 first verifies the complaint's timeline and the buyer's identity using the provided secret key. It then derive the shared key between buyer and seller, decrypt the encrypted asset key, and verify the commitment. If verification fails (indicating seller misbehavior), the arbiter returns tokens to the buyer. Note that this can be fairly done since we focus on blockchains where it is possible to run arbitrary smart contracts, according to Sect. 2.2.

On the Notation Used in Fig. 1. Here, we clarify some aspects related to the protocol described in Fig. 1. The function $\mathcal{H}_\ell$ is a *random oracle* where ℓ is the random oracle output size of the following dimension $\ell := |\mathcal{K}_e| + |\mathcal{M}_c|$. Within the protocol, $\mathsf{Gen}(1^\lambda)$ is used to generate a key pair $(\mathsf{sk}, \mathsf{pk})$. Specifically, the randomized algorithm Gen, when invoked, first selects $\mathsf{sk} \leftarrow\$\ \mathbb{Z}_q$ and then computes the public key as $\mathsf{pk} = (\mathsf{sk} \cdot G) \in \mathbb{G}$ with G a generator of $\mathbb{G}$ that is a group of prime order q. This naturally leads to the Diffie-Hellman key exchange.

According to the discussion in Sect. 2.2, we recall that we consider time as a value maintained by T in the form of a global clock, observable by all parties, which increases as time progresses and that we denote the current time with t.

Description of V_B. The internal subroutine V_B, executed by the buyer to verify the correctness of the received information $\mathsf{e_{k_a}}$, consists of the steps:

1. It checks whether T has received $\mathsf{e_{k_a}}$ (i.e., $\mathsf{e_{k_a}} = \perp$ in T). If T has received $\mathsf{e_{k_a}}$, the algorithm continues to the next step. If not, it checks whether the current

$\mathsf{A}(\mathsf{a}_{\mathsf{prv}} := (\mathsf{k}_\mathsf{a} \| r))$	$\mathsf{B}(\mathsf{tk}[n])$
	$(\mathsf{pk}_\mathsf{B}, \mathsf{sk}_\mathsf{B}) \leftarrow \mathsf{Gen}(1^\lambda); \mathsf{store}_\mathsf{T}(\mathsf{pk}_\mathsf{B})$
	$\mathsf{tx}_\mathsf{T}(\mathsf{A}, \mathsf{tk}[n], t')$
if $V_\mathsf{A}(\mathsf{tk}[n]) = 0$: **output** $\perp$	
$(\mathsf{pk}_\mathsf{A}, \mathsf{sk}_\mathsf{A}) \leftarrow \mathsf{Gen}(1^\lambda); \mathsf{store}_\mathsf{T}(\mathsf{pk}_\mathsf{A})$	
$k_{\mathsf{AB}} \leftarrow \mathcal{H}_\ell(\mathsf{sk}_\mathsf{A} \cdot \mathsf{pk}_\mathsf{B})$	
$\mathsf{e}_{\mathsf{k}_\mathsf{a}} \leftarrow \Pi_{\mathsf{Enc}}.\mathsf{Enc}(k_{\mathsf{AB}}, \mathsf{k}_\mathsf{a} \| r)$	
$\mathsf{store}_\mathsf{T}(\mathsf{e}_{\mathsf{k}_\mathsf{a}})$	
	$k_{\mathsf{AB}} \leftarrow \mathcal{H}_\ell(\mathsf{sk}_\mathsf{B} \cdot \mathsf{pk}_\mathsf{A})$
	if $V_\mathsf{B}(\mathsf{c}_{\mathsf{k}_\mathsf{a}}, \mathsf{e}_{\mathsf{k}_\mathsf{a}}, k_{\mathsf{AB}}) = 0$:
	output $\mathsf{Complaint}_\mathsf{T}(\mathsf{sk}_\mathsf{B})$

Fig. 1. The exchange protocol performed by A and B, namely a construction of the following protocol $[\mathsf{A}(\mathsf{a}_{\mathsf{prv}}), \mathsf{B}(\mathsf{tk}[n]), \mathsf{T}](\mathsf{prm}, \mathsf{a}_{\mathsf{pub}})$ in Definition 1.

time t (i.e., the time maintained by T) is greater than t_{comp}[5]. If $t \leq t_{\mathsf{comp}}$, the algorithm returns 1, indicating that A still has time to send the encryption $\mathsf{e}_{\mathsf{k}_\mathsf{a}}$. If $t > t_{\mathsf{comp}}$, it returns 0.

2. It decrypts $\mathsf{e}_{\mathsf{k}_\mathsf{a}}$ as $(\mathsf{k}'_\mathsf{a} \| r') \leftarrow \Pi_{\mathsf{Enc}}.\mathsf{Dec}(k_{\mathsf{AB}}, \mathsf{e}_{\mathsf{k}_\mathsf{a}})$, and returns the result of the committment opening, $\Pi_{\mathsf{Com}}.\mathsf{Open}(\mathsf{ck}, \mathsf{c}_{\mathsf{k}_\mathsf{a}}, \mathsf{k}'_\mathsf{a}, r')$.

Theorem 1. *Given a deterministic preview function f and* T *instantiated by a smart contract allowing general-purpose computations, consider the following 4 ingredients: (1)* $\Pi_{\mathsf{Enc}} = (\mathsf{KeyGen}, \mathsf{Enc}, \mathsf{Dec})$ *is a semantic secure encryption scheme, (2)* $\Pi_{\mathsf{Sign}} = (\mathsf{KeyGen}, \mathsf{Sign}, \mathsf{Verify})$ *is an EUF-CMA signature scheme, (3)* $\Pi_{\mathsf{Com}} = (\mathsf{KeyGen}, \mathsf{Commit}, \mathsf{Open})$ *is a commitment scheme and, (4)* $\Pi_{\mathsf{ZK\text{-}snark}} = (\mathsf{KeyGen}, \mathsf{Prove}, \mathsf{Verify})$ *is a zk-SNARK for the relation $\mathcal{R}$. Additionally, assume the Decisional DH assumption holds.*

Then, Ω_{AFE} is a secure Π_{AFE} protocol for f in the random oracle model.

Due to space limitations, the proof of Theorem 1 is in the full version.

For the same reasons, we defer to the full version for more details on Ω_{AFE}. Specifically, in the full version we look at the amount of information maintained by T, discuss the efficiency of Ω_{AFE}, and consider the implications for previous asset owners.

One Advertisement to Rule Them All. We observe that our construction, although simple, based on the definition in Definition 1 of Π_{AFE}, effectively overcomes the problems, described before in Sect. 1.1, that typically affect both the seller and buyer in state of the art fair exchange protocols when instantiated

[5] The value t_{comp} is an instant of time after the time lock transaction invoked by B (i.e., $\mathsf{tx}_\mathsf{T}(\mathsf{A}, \mathsf{tk}[n], t')$) but shorter than t'.

Algorithm 2: This is executed by T after calling $\mathsf{Complaint}_{\mathsf{T}}$. T can reuse all data that were previously stored in it. When invoked in the protocol described in Fig. 1, T knows $\mathsf{a}_{\mathsf{pub}}, \mathsf{pk}_{\mathsf{A}}, \mathsf{pk}_{\mathsf{B}}$ and $\mathsf{e}_{\mathsf{k_a}}$.

Input: The value sk_{B} representing the secret key of B.

if $t > t_{\mathsf{comp}}(See footnote 5)$ & $\mathsf{e}_{\mathsf{k_a}} = \bot$ **then**
  T gives the tokens $\mathsf{tk}[n]$ back to B; **return** $\bot$
end
$\mathsf{pk}'_{\mathsf{B}} \leftarrow (\mathsf{sk}_{\mathsf{B}} \cdot G) \in \mathbb{G}$
if $\mathsf{pk}'_{\mathsf{B}} \neq \mathsf{pk}_{\mathsf{B}}$ **then**
  return
end
$k_{\mathsf{AB}} \leftarrow \mathcal{H}_{\ell}(\mathsf{sk}_{\mathsf{B}} \cdot \mathsf{pk}_{\mathsf{A}})$; $(\mathsf{k_a} \| r) \leftarrow \Pi_{\mathsf{Enc}}.\mathsf{Dec}(k_{\mathsf{AB}}, \mathsf{e}_{\mathsf{k_a}})$
if $\Pi_{\mathsf{Com}}.\mathsf{Open}(\mathsf{ck}, \mathsf{c}_{\mathsf{k_a}}, \mathsf{k_a}, r) \neq 1$ **then**
  T gives the tokens $\mathsf{tk}[n]$ back to B; **return** $\bot$
end

in the wild. We quickly recall that these problems arise when an advertisement phase is required before the asset exchange and when the seller has to engage with multiple buyers.

More in details, regarding the issue of a DoS attack against the seller, we see that this problem does not arise in our construction Ω_{AFE}. This is because the seller generates the proof, which may be computationally heavy, only once for a given asset, rather than repeatedly for each buyer who wishes to engage in the exchange. Moreover, if the current seller is a previous buyer who has already purchased the asset and now wishes to resell it, she does not need to recompute the proof. Instead, she reuses the proof she received during their initial purchase and proceed directly with the exchange protocol, which remains lightweight. In fact, for an honest seller, the protocol involves only a Diffie-Hellman key exchange followed by an encryption of a secret key. In a nutshell, this greatly reduces the computational workload for the seller, as the potentially heavy proof generation is required only once. Additionally, if the seller is not the first owner of the asset, she can reuse the proof she obtained from the previous sale.

From the buyer's perspective, we address a potential replay attack scenario, where multiple smart contracts (thus sellers) attempt to trade the same asset, without actually known the asset itself but just by copy and paste $\mathsf{a}_{\mathsf{pub}}$ (in our construction the zk-SNARK proof). Since the buyer does not need to privately communicate with the seller and the proof is public, other buyers can inform them about the seller's reputation. Furthermore, additional protection measures can be easily put into place. It is possible to include in the relation $\mathcal{R}$, which generates the zk-SNARK proof, a reference to the specific smart contract address where the exchange will take place. In this way, the buyer can verify the address before engaging in the exchange, ensuring they interact with the correct smart contract and preventing them from wasting time on an incorrect/malicious one.

5 Experiments

In this section, we demonstrate the feasibility of our approach for advertising and selling NFTs that represent images. This choice is motivated by the natural alignment with the challenges affecting this technology, as discussed in Sect. 1, and the significant real-world importance of such assets.

We consider images from renowned NFT collections (https://ebutemetaverse.com/nft-image-size), confirming experimentally the viability of our Advertisement-Based Fair Exchange for NFTs (detailed in Sect. 4). We focus on two aspects: (a) the evaluation of the zk-SNARK setup and the zk-SNARK proof generation, in Algorithm 1 line 3, and (b) the costs of the smart contract that implements the fair exchange between the parties. In our experiment, we use different image sizes that correspond to the dimensions of the images in the NFT collections (e.g., Bored Ape Yacht Club (BAYC)), ranging from 128×128 to 631×631 pixels.

The bilinear resize function, that halves both the width and height of the original image, is used to generate the preview. According to [13] we focus solely on the resize as the preview function. That is, in [13] the authors, also focusing on images, demonstrate that during the computation of a zk-SNARK when additional operations, such as hashing the image (as in our case), are involved, changing the preview function introduces negligible overhead, namely using other preview functions (e.g., cropping or grayscale) would yield similar complexity.

A resize applied to an original small-size image might be considered of limited practical value. However, other transformations can be applied and we will discuss how to extend our framework to support larger images (up to $\sim$30 MP) considering the work in [12,13,15]. The ability to deal with large-size private images will open new opportunities for the NFT market. Current NFT standards, certify the ownership of a NFT, but the corresponding image can be easily accessed and copied. Keeping private the high-quality original image can incentivize the development of a "new" NFTs market, where not simply the ownership is guaranteed, but also the private access to the high-quality original image, thus overcoming a relevant issue in the current NFTs market.

In order to demonstrate the feasibility of our approach, in the following we consider the relatively small image sizes used in real-world NFT collections. We conducted our experiments on an Intel(R) Core(TM) i9-10900 CPU @ 2.80GHz processor with 20 cores and 32 GB of RAM[6]. Due to space limitations, we deferred the discussion about technical choices for the experiments to the full version.

Protocol Setup and Proof Generation. Figure 2a shows the time necessary to perform the setup, generation, and verification of the zk-SNARK. The memory usage is reported in Fig. 2b. The setup phase is largely the most time-consuming and memory-intensive, however, this operation is performed only once for a given image size and resize factor, its output does not contain any private information

[6] All the code is available on https://github.com/pierpaolodm/ContentPrivacyNFT.

and can be thus publicly shared. Therefore, the setup phase can also be computed on the cloud without violating the confidentiality of the private image. In Fig. 2b, we did not include setup memory because it constantly saturates all available RAM, relying on swap memory when necessary. The proof generation is the second most demanding operation. It is performed only once for a given preview, and it must be computed locally by the seller to preserve confidentiality. Remarkably, the verification of the proof that is performed by each potential buyer, is the most efficient.

Avoiding Demanding Setup. As described, the setup phase relies on the generation of a trusted CRS and commitment key, which in our experiments took approximately one day to compute on standard hardware. This cost is amortized by allowing the same setup to be reused for future exchanges of the same asset type. However, the setup time may still present a barrier for practical deployment, especially in applications requiring frequent updates or new asset types.

One way to mitigate this cost, as we said before, is to consider alternative zk-SNARK constructions that can be instantiated in the RO model. In such approaches, the CRS is replaced using cryptographic hash functions modeled as random oracles, removing the need for a trusted party and potentially reducing setup time. Recent works, such as [5,9,10], demonstrate practical efficient zk-SNARKs in the RO model, which could be adapted to our protocol. Another direction is to explore universal or updatable SNARKs, where a single setup supports many statements or can be efficiently updated for new relations [18]. These constructions can further reduce the setup overhead when protocol parameters or asset types change, if the RO is not an option. While for the commitment key one can rely on standard techniques such as "hashing into the curve" [33] in case of e.g. Pedersen commitment (and model the hash function as a RO) to avoid the presence of a trusted third party.

Dealing with Large Images. A valid criticism of our feasibility results concerns the size of the images used in our experiments, which may not reflect the high-resolution images typically exchanged in centralized services (e.g., on Getty Images, it is possible to buy and sell images with resolutions up to ∼20 MP). The main bottleneck preventing us from conducting experiments with high-resolution images was the need to generate the common reference string for Groth16 (the Setup in Fig. 2a) with only 32 GB of RAM, which required utilizing swap memory, significantly increasing execution time.

While our experiments are focused on smaller image sizes, it is important to consider that in the literature, there exists a rich line of work that addresses the problem of generating zk-SNARKs for high-resolution images, on statements comparable to those in our experiments. These works explore ad-hoc techniques (e.g., exploiting the internal structure of images, namely the RGB channels) for generating such proofs even with limited resources, enabling the computation of a zk-SNARK for images of almost any size. Specifically, recent works [12,15] demonstrate that it is possible to compute these proofs for images ∼10 MP within two hours, with a peak memory usage of approximately 10 GB.

Lastly, in [13], the authors demonstrated that by relaxing the confidentiality requirements of the image, it is possible to design an efficient proof system for images, requiring only 4 GB of RAM to compute a proof for images up to ~30 MP, in the order of minutes. That is, by directly leveraging [13], our approach becomes inherently scalable in large-scale markets: each user can independently generate proofs tailored to their specific requirements and computational resources, enabling the protocol to accommodate a broad class of users, including those with limited hardware. Users can flexibly produce proofs for images of practically any size, with computation time proportional to the resources available to them.

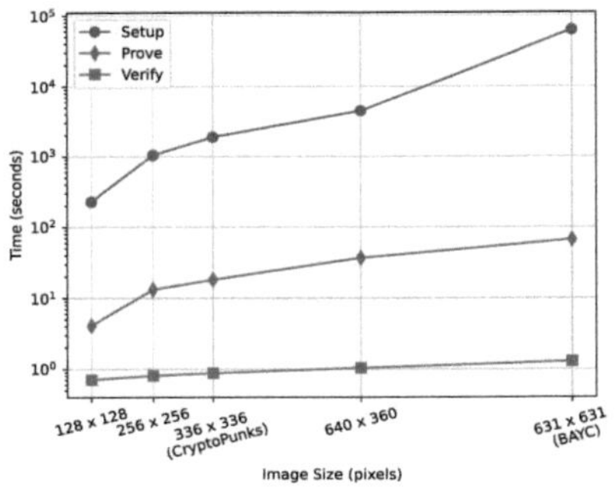

(a) Time consumption (in logarithmic scale) during the proving and verification phases of zk-SNARK generation in Alg. 1 line 3 using Groth16 and during the Setup phase (i.e., $\Pi_{\mathsf{ZK\text{-}snark}}.\mathsf{KeyGen}$ of Groth16), for images of varying sizes.

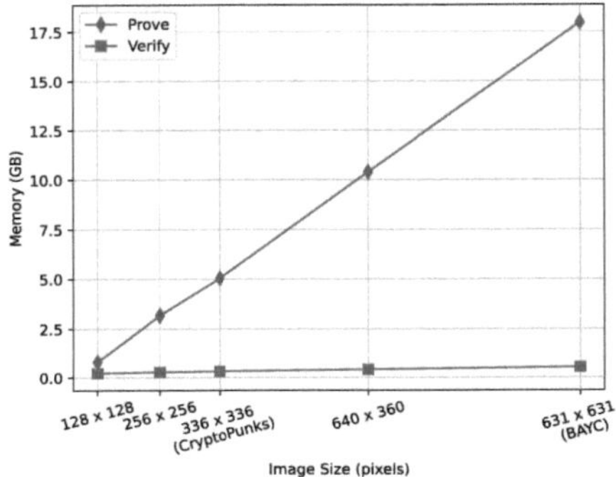

(b) Memory consumption (in logarithmic scale) during the proving and verification phases of zk-SNARK generation in Alg. 1 line 4 using Groth16, for images of varying sizes.

Fig. 2. Resource consumption during zk-SNARK generation and verification.

The Smart Contract. We developed a smart contract in Solidity that extends the ERC-721 standard and implements the logic of the fair exchange as described in Fig. 1 and Algorithm 2. The key exchange, along with key pair generation, has been implemented using the secp256k1 curve. We use SHA-3 as a heuristic for the random oracle. In our experiments, we evaluate the cost of running the main functions of the proposed smart contract that implements Ω_{AFE} as described in Sect. 4 both on Ethereum and on a layer 2 technology. The following functions correspond to the phases detailed in Sect. 4. Below, we briefly describe the purpose of each function. The `Deployment` function refers to the cost of deploying the smart contract. `Mint` creates a new NFT with a pointer (to an IPFS directory) to the corresponding zk-SNARK (along with its statement). Additionally, the smart contract stores in the state the commitment of the symmetric key needed to decrypt the asset (i.e., $\mathsf{c}_{\mathsf{k}_a}$), resembling the operation at line 4 of Algorithm 1. The `Bid` function is invoked by the buyer to make an offer, where the buyer also publishes their (ephemeral) public key on the smart contract. This operation resembles lines 1 to 3 of the fair exchange detailed in Fig. 1. The `Accept` function is invoked by the seller to accept the offer and deliver the encryption key, following the steps from lines 4 to 10 in Fig. 1. Finally, we developed two functions that allow the buyer to conclude the exchange by either accepting the value sent by the seller or raising a complaint to the smart contract. Both functions correspond to lines 11 to 13 of Fig. 1. The buyer can invoke the `Confirm` function to successfully conclude the exchange (this function allows both parties to conclude the exchange quickly, avoiding unnecessary delays) or the `Complain` function, which implements the logic described in Algorithm 2. The results in terms of fees are summarized in Fig. 3. Note that, as expected, if the fair exchange is successfully carried on, the costs are significantly lower than in the case of complaints. We highlight that, according to Fig. 3 the decision to deploy the contract on Ethereum mainnet or on a Layer 2 technology can be influenced by the value of the asset for which the NFT is created, in relation to the management costs. The deployment of high-value assets may justify the costs of Ethereum mainnet, while lower-value assets could benefit from the cost of Layer 2 solutions.

Function	**Gas**	**Ethereum fees (in $)**	**Layer 2 fees (in $)**
`Deployment`	2818661	117.54	0.00021
`Mint`	269247	11.23	0.00002
`Bid`	161394	6.73	0.000012
`Accept`	331532	13.83	0.000024
`Confirm`	69240	2.89	0.0000051
`Complain`	1633536	68.12	0.00012

Fig. 3. The costs associated with the main functions of the proposed smart contract extending the ERC-721 standard. The Layer 2 solution we selected for comparison is Optimism. The gas price was taken from October 10, 2024.

Broader Applicability Beyond NFT Images. While our experimental evaluation focuses on NFTs representing images, the underlying protocol is readily adaptable to a wide spectrum of digital assets. According to our experiments, what we effectively demonstrate and benchmark is the ability to generate privacy-preserving proofs for data represented as a multidimenional matrix, which is de facto the standard format for images and can be naturally extended to other asset types (e.g., audio, PDF files) or in general other multidimensional data, where the representation follows a similar structure.

References

1. Andrychowicz, M., Dziembowski, S., Malinowski, D., Mazurek, Ł: Fair two-party computations via bitcoin deposits. In: Böhme, R., Brenner, M., Moore, T., Smith, M. (eds.) FC 2014. LNCS, vol. 8438, pp. 105–121. Springer, Heidelberg (2014). https://doi.org/10.1007/978-3-662-44774-1_8

2. Baecker, R., Gerhart, P., Katz, J., Schröder, D.: Fair exchange for decentralized autonomous organizations via threshold adaptor signatures. Cryptology ePrint Archive, Paper 2025/388 (2025)
3. Banasik, W., Dziembowski, S., Malinowski, D.: Efficient zero-knowledge contingent payments in cryptocurrencies without scripts. In: Askoxylakis, I., Ioannidis, S., Katsikas, S., Meadows, C. (eds.) ESORICS 2016. LNCS, vol. 9879, pp. 261–280. Springer, Cham (2016). https://doi.org/10.1007/978-3-319-45741-3_14
4. Bauer, D.P.: ERC-721 nonfungible tokens. In: Getting Started with Ethereum: A Step-by-Step Guide to Becoming a Blockchain Developer, pp. 55–74. Apress, Berkeley (2022)
5. Ben-Sasson, E., Chiesa, A., Riabzev, M., Spooner, N., Virza, M., Ward, N.P.: Aurora: transparent succinct arguments for R1CS. In: Ishai, Y., Rijmen, V. (eds.) EUROCRYPT 2019. LNCS, vol. 11476, pp. 103–128. Springer, Cham (2019). https://doi.org/10.1007/978-3-030-17653-2_4
6. Bentov, I., Kumaresan, R.: How to use bitcoin to design fair protocols. In: Garay, J.A., Gennaro, R. (eds.) CRYPTO 2014. LNCS, vol. 8617, pp. 421–439. Springer, Heidelberg (2014). https://doi.org/10.1007/978-3-662-44381-1_24
7. Bitcoin, W.: Hash Time Locked Contracts (2024)
8. Campanelli, M., Gennaro, R., Goldfeder, S., Nizzardo, L.: Zero-knowledge contingent payments revisited: attacks and payments for services. In: Thuraisingham, B.M., Evans, D., Malkin, T., Xu, D. (eds.) ACM CCS 2017, pp. 229–243. ACM Press (2017)
9. Chiesa, A., Hu, Y., Maller, M., Mishra, P., Vesely, N., Ward, N.: Marlin: preprocessing zkSNARKs with universal and updatable SRS. In: Canteaut, A., Ishai, Y. (eds.) EUROCRYPT 2020. LNCS, vol. 12105, pp. 738–768. Springer, Cham (2020). https://doi.org/10.1007/978-3-030-45721-1_26
10. Chiesa, A., Ojha, D., Spooner, N.: Fractal: post-quantum and transparent recursive proofs from holography. In: Canteaut, A., Ishai, Y. (eds.) EUROCRYPT 2020. LNCS, vol. 12105, pp. 769–793. Springer, Cham (2020). https://doi.org/10.1007/978-3-030-45721-1_27
11. Cleve, R.: Limits on the security of coin flips when half the processors are faulty (extended abstract). In: 18th ACM STOC, pp. 364–369. ACM Press (1986)
12. Datta, T., Chen, B., Boneh, D.: VerITAS: verifying image transformations at scale. In: 2025 IEEE Symposium on Security and Privacy (SP), p. 97. IEEE Computer Society, Los Alamitos, CA, USA (2025)
13. Della Monica, P., Visconti, I., Vitaletti, A., Zecchini, M.: Trust nobody: privacy-preserving proofs for edited photos with your laptop. In: 2025 IEEE Symposium on Security and Privacy (SP), p. 14. IEEE Computer Society, Los Alamitos, CA, USA (2025)
14. Della Monica, P., Visconti, I., Vitaletti, A., Zecchini, M.: Public channel-based fair exchange protocols with advertising (2025). https://arxiv.org/abs/2503.10411
15. Dziembowski, S., Ebrahimi, S., Hassanizadeh, P.: VIMz: verifiable image manipulation using folding-based zkSNARKs. Cryptology ePrint Archive, Paper 2024/1063 (2024). Accepted at Privacy Enhancing Technologies Symposium (PETS) 2025
16. Dziembowski, S., Eckey, L., Faust, S.: FairSwap: how to fairly exchange digital goods. In: Lie, D., Mannan, M., Backes, M., Wang, X. (eds.) ACM CCS 2018, pp. 967–984. ACM Press (2018)
17. Eckey, L., Faust, S., Schlosser, B.: OptiSwap: fast optimistic fair exchange. In: Sun, H.M., Shieh, S.P., Gu, G., Ateniese, G. (eds.) ASIACCS 2020, pp. 543–557. ACM Press (2020)

18. Gabizon, A., Williamson, Z.J., Ciobotaru, O.: PLONK: permutations over Lagrange-bases for oecumenical noninteractive arguments of knowledge. Cryptology ePrint Archive, Report 2019/953 (2019)
19. Garay, J., Kiayias, A., Leonardos, N.: The bitcoin backbone protocol: analysis and applications. In: Oswald, E., Fischlin, M. (eds.) EUROCRYPT 2015. LNCS, vol. 9057, pp. 281–310. Springer, Heidelberg (2015). https://doi.org/10.1007/978-3-662-46803-6_10
20. Glaeser, N., Maffei, M., Malavolta, G., Moreno-Sanchez, P., Tairi, E., Thyagarajan, S.A.K.: Foundations of coin mixing services. In: Yin, H., Stavrou, A., Cremers, C., Shi, E. (eds.) ACM CCS 2022, pp. 1259–1273. ACM Press (2022)
21. Hafezi, H., Partap, A., Das, S., Bonneau, J.: Fair signature exchange. Cryptology ePrint Archive, Paper 2025/059 (2025)
22. He, S., Lu, Y., Tang, Q., Wang, G., Wu, C.Q.: Fair peer-to-peer content delivery via blockchain. In: Bertino, E., Shulman, H., Waidner, M. (eds.) ESORICS 2021. LNCS, vol. 12972, pp. 348–369. Springer, Cham (2021). https://doi.org/10.1007/978-3-030-88418-5_17
23. Janin, S., Qin, K., Mamageishvili, A., Gervais, A.: Filebounty: fair data exchange. In: 2020 IEEE European Symposium on Security and Privacy Workshops (EuroS&P W). IEEE (2020)
24. Katz, J., Maurer, U., Tackmann, B., Zikas, V.: Universally composable synchronous computation. In: Sahai, A. (ed.) TCC 2013. LNCS, vol. 7785, pp. 477–498. Springer, Heidelberg (2013). https://doi.org/10.1007/978-3-642-36594-2_27
25. Li, Y., et al.: ZKCPlus: optimized fair-exchange protocol supporting practical and flexible data exchange. In: Vigna, G., Shi, E. (eds.) ACM CCS 2021, pp. 3002–3021. ACM Press (2021)
26. Liu, X., Zhang, J., Wang, Y., Yang, X., Yang, X.: SmartZKCP: towards practical data exchange marketplace against active attacks. Cryptology ePrint Archive, Paper 2024/941 (2024). Accepted at International Conference on Blockchain Research and Applications (BCRA) 2024
27. Maxwell, G.: Zero knowledge contingent payment (2015)
28. Tairi, E., Moreno-Sanchez, P., Maffei, M.: A^2L: anonymous atomic locks for scalability in payment channel hubs. In: 2021 IEEE Symposium on Security and Privacy, pp. 1834–1851. IEEE Computer Society Press (2021)
29. Tas, E.N., et al.: Atomic and fair data exchange via blockchain. In: Luo, B., Liao, X., Xu, J., Kirda, E., Lie, D. (eds.) ACM CCS 2024, pp. 3227–3241. ACM Press (2024)
30. Thyagarajan, S.A.K., Malavolta, G.: Lockable signatures for blockchains: scriptless scripts for all signatures. In: 2021 IEEE Symposium on Security and Privacy, pp. 937–954. IEEE Computer Society Press (2021)
31. Thyagarajan, S.A.K., Malavolta, G., Moreno-Sanchez, P.: Universal atomic swaps: secure exchange of coins across all blockchains. In: 2022 IEEE Symposium on Security and Privacy, pp. 1299–1316. IEEE Computer Society Press (2022)
32. Vanjani, N., Soni, P., Thyagarajan, S.A.K.: Functional adaptor signatures: beyond all-or-nothing blockchain-based payments. In: Luo, B., Liao, X., Xu, J., Kirda, E., Lie, D. (eds.) ACM CCS 2024, pp. 1493–1507. ACM Press (2024)
33. Wahby, R.S., Boneh, D.: Fast and simple constant-time hashing to the BLS12-381 elliptic curve. IACR TCHES **2019**(4), 154–179 (2019)

Revisiting Rational Broadcast Protocols

Shunya Otomo and Kenji Yasunaga(✉)

Institute of Science Tokyo, Tokyo, Japan
otomo.s.461c@m.isct.ac.jp, yasunaga@comp.isct.ac.jp

Abstract. A recent study by Yamashita and Yasunaga (GameSec 2023) presented a constant-round deterministic broadcast protocol secure against *detection-averse* adversaries—those who prefer to attack without being detected. In this work, we revisit their protocol and observe that it remains secure even against a broader class of adversaries, not necessarily detection-averse. We formalize its detection mechanism as *local detectability* and construct broadcast protocols with local detectability that address two weaknesses of the original protocol: (1) it only guarantees weak validity, and (2) it may cause false detections. Our first protocol achieves round complexity four against rational adversaries and $t+4$ against malicious adversaries, where the adversary corrupts at most t parties. Our second protocol achieves the optimal round complexity of $t+1$ for malicious adversaries, while the round complexity is four against detection-averse adversaries.

1 Introduction

Byzantine broadcast is one of the most fundamental protocols in distributed computing and is used as a building block for various cryptographic protocols. In a broadcast protocol, a party called the *sender* wants to send its value m to all other parties. There are two requirements: (a) all honest parties output the same value (*agreement*), and (b) if the sender is honest, all honest (non-corrupted) parties output the sender's value (*validity*). The *round complexity* is one of the most significant measures of the efficiency of protocols. We focus on the synchronous communication model in which the public-key infrastructure (PKI) is available.

In the seminal work by Dolev and Strong [5], they gave a $(t+1)$-round deterministic broadcast protocol against malicious adversaries who corrupt t out of n parties for any $t < n$. They also showed that the round complexity $t+1$ is *optimal* among deterministic protocols. Since then, researchers have been focused on constructing *randomized* protocols for circumventing the lower bound of [5]. In the honest-majority setting ($t < n/2$), expected constant-round protocols have been proposed [6] [12] [1]. In the dishonest-majority setting ($t \geq n/2$), expected constant-round protocols have been presented for $t = n/2 + O(1)$ [9] and for $t = (1-\epsilon)n$ [16] with $\epsilon \in (0,1)$. However, it is known that constant-round randomized protocols cannot be constructed against malicious adversaries for $t = (1-o(1))n$ [9].

Y. Kim et al. (Eds.): CANS 2025, LNCS 16351, pp. 382–401, 2026.
https://doi.org/10.1007/978-981-95-4434-9_18

A recent study by Yamashita and Yasunaga [17] explored a *game-theoretic* approach to broadcast protocols. Specifically, they studied a class of *rational* adversaries who aim to violate security requirements while avoiding detection. These adversaries, which we refer to as *detection-averse* adversaries, attack the protocol while considering whether their actions can be detected. (In [17], these adversaries are termed *timid*, but we adopt the term *detection-averse* as it more accurately captures their behavior.) The authors of [17] proposed a constant-round deterministic broadcast protocol secure against detection-averse adversaries for any $t < n$. Their protocol circumvents a round-complexity lower bound of $t + 1$ [5] by considering rational adversaries, a weaker adversary model than traditional Byzantine/malicious models.

In this work, we revisit the problem of constructing broadcast protocols against rational adversaries by analyzing the protocol of [17] (referred to as the YY23 protocol) in more depth. We begin by observing that the YY23 protocol is secure against rational adversaries *without relying on any attack detection mechanism.* That is, their security proofs go through even when the protocol has no detection mechanism. We can show that their protocol is secure against a broader class of rational adversaries, who have an incentive to attack the protocol but do not necessarily have the detection-averse property. For instance, this broader class includes adversaries who can still obtain utility even if detected—for example, when detection does not lead to immediate exclusion from the protocol, or when anonymity prevents any effective punishment. Such adversaries are rational but not detection-averse, and we observe that the protocol remains secure against them as well.

The Mechanism for Securing the YY23 Protocol. We briefly explain why the YY23 protocol remains secure even against more general rational adversaries. The protocol has two possible termination points: round 4 and round $t + 4$.[1] It guarantees (weak) validity and agreement against malicious adversaries, in which case it terminates in round $t + 4$. For rational adversaries who honestly follow the protocol, it terminates early in round 4. Since rational adversaries cannot violate the security requirements and have no incentive to *delay protocol termination*, they achieve maximum utility by behaving honestly, which results in early termination in round 4.

Weaknesses of the YY23 Protocol. Besides the relaxed adversary model, there are two weaknesses in the protocol of [17] when $t \geq n/2$. First, the YY23 protocol only achieves *weak validity* because if the sender is honest, all honest parties output the sender's value *or* $\perp$, the failure symbol. Moreover, an adversary can easily cause this weaker validity condition: if $t \geq n/2$ corrupted parties do nothing in the protocol, all honest parties will output $\perp$ even if the sender

[1] The authors of [17] claimed that the round complexity of their protocol is 5 for rational adversaries and is $t + 5$ for malicious adversaries. However, we noticed that termination in round 5 can be incorporated into round 4. Thus, the actual termination rounds should be 4 and $t + 4$. We present a refined version of the YY23 protocol in Fig. 2.

Table 1. Comparison of Our Broadcast Protocols with the YY23 Protocol

Ref.	Resiliency	Local Detectability	Round Comp.	Adversary Model	Security Requirements
Π_{YY23} [17]	$t < n/2$	Yes	4	Rational	Agreement & Validity
	$t \geq n/2$	No	4	Rational	Agreement & Weak Validity
	$t < n$	No	$t+4$	Malicious	Agreement & Weak Validity
Π_{LD}	$t < n$	Yes	4	Rational	Agreement & Validity
			$t+4$	Malicious	
Π_{DA}	$t < n$	Yes	4	Detection Averse	Agreement & Validity
			$t+1$	Malicious	Weak Agreement & Validity

is honest. Second, the protocol may cause *false detections.* Namely, an honest party can be falsely detected as a cheater. Since the sender is the only party that can be detected as a cheater in the YY23 protocol, the adversary's strategy of doing nothing in the protocol for $t \geq n/2$ results in the situation that the honest sender is declared a cheater. These two weaknesses may limit the use of the YY23 protocol as a building block of cryptographic protocols. In addition, the work of [17] did not formalize the property of attack detection. Thus, it is unclear what type of detection mechanism is employed in the YY23 protocol.

1.1 This Work

In this work, we have three main contributions.

First, we formalize a detection mechanism achieved by the YY23 protocol for minority corruption ($t < n/2$). We term this mechanism *local detectability*, which consists of two properties. The first property, *detection correctness*, ensures that if some party i outputs a candidate list C_i of cheaters, then every party in C_i must be corrupted by the adversary. The second property, *detection soundness*, guarantees that any honest party that follows the protocol is never identified as a cheater.

The term *local* implies that each candidate list C_i is retained by party i. Thus, this detection mechanism does not guarantee global agreement on the cheater list among honest parties. Nevertheless, local detectability can still be useful in practice. For example, if multiple parties from the same organization participate in the protocol, their local candidate lists $\{C_i\}_i$ can be shared within the group, serving as a deterrent against misbehavior. An advantage of local detectability over *global* detectability is its feasibility: as discussed in [13], identifying cheaters globally is impossible when the adversary controls a majority ($t \geq n/2$). In contrast, our protocol ensures local detectability even when the adversary corrupts a majority of the parties.

Second, we construct a constant-round broadcast protocol with local detectability that is secure against rational adversaries corrupting $t < n$ parties. The round complexity is four against rational adversaries and is $t + 4$ against malicious ones. In contrast to the YY23 protocol, our protocol satisfies *standard validity* rather than *weak validity*. Moreover, since local detectability ensures no false detection, our protocol resolves both weaknesses of the YY23 protocol.

Third, we present a broadcast protocol with the optimal round complexity of $t+1$ against malicious adversaries while maintaining round complexity four against *detection-averse* adversaries. That is, the detection-averse property enables this optimal round complexity. The protocol also satisfies local detectability. Since, as discussed earlier, the YY23 protocol does not require the detection-averse property, our protocol is the first to explicitly leverage this property in broadcast protocols.

In Table 1, we compare our protocols with the YY23 protocol Π_{YY23} in Fig. 2, where our first and second protocols are referred to as Π_{LD} and Π_{DA}, respectively.

1.2 Technical Overviews

In [17], the authors define security against rational adversaries as follows. For an n-party broadcast protocol Π and adversary A, a broadcast game is defined such that Π is executed where A is a player controlling t out of n parties. The outcome of the game consists of three binary values: $\mathsf{validity}_{\mathsf{fail}}$, $\mathsf{agreement}_{\mathsf{fail}}$, and $\mathsf{undetected}$. The first two values represent whether A could violate validity and agreement of Π. The last one represents whether malicious actions of A were detected during the execution. They considered rational adversaries that have utilities such that the adversary prefers each of the three values to be satisfied. Then, Π is secure against rational adversaries if there is a harmless adversary B such that the expected utility of any rational adversary A is bounded above by that of B. This *best response* property ensures that every adversary has no incentive to deviate from the harmless strategy B.

Our observation on the YY23 protocol is that their security proof does not require the third value $\mathsf{undetected}$. In other words, the YY23 protocol is secure against any rational adversary that prefers the two values $\mathsf{validity}_{\mathsf{fail}}$ and $\mathsf{agreement}_{\mathsf{fail}}$ to be satisfied. Note that this rational adversary is different from *malicious* adversaries, which include one that wants to delay the termination of the protocol. For such an adversary, the YY23 protocol terminates in round $t+4$ and thus fails to achieve a constant-round execution.

We describe the construction ideas of our protocols. A key observation is that if the YY23 protocol is modified so that (standard) validity is satisfied for malicious adversaries, it satisfies local detectability, thus resolving false detection. Our goal is to modify the YY23 protocol to satisfy validity. To achieve this, we need a mechanism that allows the honest sender to send his message to all parties, even if $t \geq n/2$. Our idea is to perform the Dolev-Strong protocol [5] for sending the sender's message *in parallel with* the YY23 protocol. With this modification, each party may output a value in rounds 4, $t+1$, or $t+4$. One of the difficulties in designing our protocols is determining the termination rule. The termination rule of our first protocol Π_{LD} is that if each party fails to receive the message in round $t+4$, the party outputs the value received by the Dolev-Strong protocol in round $t+1$.

Our second protocol Π_{DA} achieves an optimal round complexity of $t+1$ for malicious adversaries, while the round complexity for *detection-averse* adversaries is 4. The construction idea is that we halt the main (YY23) part in Π_{LD} after round 4. With this modification, the resulting protocol guarantees only *weak agreement*, which requires that every honest party outputs either some value m or $\perp$. This modified protocol is sufficient to achieve a constant-round execution for detection-averse adversaries. Since Π_{DA} satisfies validity for malicious adversaries, it achieves local detectability, just as Π_{LD} does.

1.3 Related Work

This work builds on the work by Yamashita and Yasunaga [17], which presented a constant-round protocol against detection-averse adversaries. As described above, Dolev and Strong [5] provided a deterministic broadcast protocol with optimal round complexity for malicious adversaries. Since then, many studies have been on constructing *randomized* protocols that aim to circumvent the round-complexity lower bound [5]. In cryptography, relaxed notions of broadcast protocols have been proposed. *Detectable broadcast* [7] has a mechanism for detecting malicious behavior, but, to the best of our knowledge, no constant-round protocol achieving this notion has been proposed. The notion of *broadcast with abort* was introduced by Goldwasser and Lindell [10], where the security requirements are weak agreement and weak validity. They showed that this weaker security notion can be used to construct secure multiparty computation. The notion of *covert security*, introduced in [3], guarantees that any deviation from the protocol can be detected with a constant probability. Thus, covert security may be sufficient to protect against detection-averse adversaries. However, to our knowledge, no prior work has focused on constructing broadcast protocols with covert security. The work of [3] gave secure multiparty computation protocols with covert security by assuming the existence of broadcast channels. As discussed in [15], covert security is not necessarily weaker than malicious security. In contrast, our security against rational adversaries is weaker than the standard malicious security (see Sect. 2.1 for discussion). *Early-stopping* broadcast protocols [2,4,14] guarantee that the protocol terminates earlier when the number of corrupted parties is less than the assumed upper bound t. The actual round complexity depends on the number of faults that occur during execution rather than on t. Although the existence of multiple termination points is similar to rational broadcast protocols studied in [17] and this work, our protocols ensure that early termination results from the strategic behavior of rational adversaries.

A game-theoretic notion of detection-averse (timid) adversaries was introduced in [8] for constructing efficient secure-message transmission (SMT) protocols. The work of [17] applied this notion to the problem of constructing broadcast protocols.

1.4 Organization

Section 2 introduces the network model, setup assumptions, and formal definitions of broadcast protocols. Sections 2.2 and 3 provide overviews of the Dolev-Strong protocol [5] and the YY23 protocol [17], respectively. Our first and second protocols are presented in Sects. 4 and 5, respectively.

2 Preliminaries

We briefly describe the network model, setup assumptions, and the definition of Byzantine broadcast.

There are n parties in the network. We assume a synchronous communication model: the protocol proceeds in rounds, and in each round, every party can send messages to all other parties. Messages from non-corrupted (honest) parties are guaranteed to be delivered correctly before the next round begins.

We assume an authenticated setting where a public key infrastructure (PKI) and digital signature schemes are available. Each party can generate a signature using its secret key, and the validity of a signature can be verified using the corresponding public key.

A signature scheme consists of three algorithms $(\mathsf{Gen}, \mathsf{Sign}, \mathsf{Ver})$. The key generation algorithm Gen takes a security parameter n as input and outputs a pair of keys (pk, sk). The security parameter is usually represented by the string $1 \cdots 1$ of length n, denoted by 1^n. The signing algorithm Sign takes a secret key sk and a message m as input and outputs a signature σ. The verification algorithm Ver takes a public key pk and a pair (m, σ) as input and checks whether σ is a valid signature of m. As a correctness requirement, we require that $\mathsf{Ver}(pk, m, \mathsf{Sign}(sk, m)) = 1$ for any (pk, sk) generated by $\mathsf{Gen}(1^n)$ and message m. For simplicity, we assume an ideal signature scheme for which no one can generate a pair (m, σ) satisfying $\mathsf{Ver}(pk, m, \sigma) = 1$ without using sk, where the pair (pk, sk) is generated by $\mathsf{Gen}(1^n)$.

In the authenticated setting, for a set of parties $[n] = \{1, \ldots, n\}$, we assume that, for each $i \in [n]$, a key pair (pk_i, sk_i) is generated by $\mathsf{Gen}(1^n)$, the secret key sk_i is given to i, and the set $\{pk_i\}_{i \in [n]}$ of public keys is available to all parties.

We introduce a *broadcast game* to define the requirements of broadcast protocols. It is a single-player game played by an adversary.

Definition 1 (Broadcast Game). *Given an n-party protocol Π and adversary A, the broadcast game $\mathsf{G}^{\mathrm{BC}}_{\Pi,A}(n,t)$ of Π against A is defined as follows. Set the parameters $\mathsf{validity}_{\mathrm{fail}} = \mathsf{agreement}_{\mathrm{fail}} = 0$. The adversary A chooses a sender $s \in [n]$, a message m, and a set of corrupted parties $C \subseteq [n]$ satisfying $|C| \leq t$. Then, protocol Π is executed with $s \in [n]$ as a sender and m as the initial message of s. During the execution, the parties in C are controlled by A, while the others honestly follow the description of Π. After protocol execution, each party $i \in [n]$ outputs val_i, the output value of party i. Let $H = [n] \setminus C$.*

- *If $s \in H$ and there exists $i \in H$ such that $\mathsf{val}_i \neq m$, set $\mathsf{validity}_{\mathrm{fail}} = 1$.*

– *If there exist different* $i, j \in H$ *such that* $\mathsf{val}_i \neq \mathsf{val}_j$, *set* $\mathsf{agreement}_{\text{fail}} = 1$.

The outcome of the game is $\mathsf{out}_A = (\mathsf{validity}_{\text{fail}}, \mathsf{agreement}_{\text{fail}})$.

The traditional Byzantine broadcast is defined as follows. We refer to an adversary that controls at most t parties as a *t-adversary.*

Definition 2 (Byzantine Broadcast). *An n-party protocol Π is said to satisfy* validity *(respectively,* agreement*) against t-adversaries if for every t-adversary A, the outcome* $\mathsf{out}_A = (\mathsf{validity}_{\text{fail}}, \mathsf{agreement}_{\text{fail}})$ *of the broadcast game* $\mathsf{G}^{\mathrm{BC}}_{\Pi,A}(n,t)$ *satisfies* $\mathsf{validity}_{\text{fail}} = 0$ *(respectively,* $\mathsf{agreement}_{\text{fail}} = 0$*). We say Π is a t-*resilient broadcast protocol *if Π satisfies validity and agreement against t-adversaries.*

2.1 Rational Broadcast Protocols

In this section, we present our framework of the rational adversary model, which mainly follows that in [17]. We use the broadcast game of Definition 1 as a single-player game played by a rational adversary. Note that the information on whether the attack was detected, which was adopted in [17], is not included in the outcome of Definition 1.

We define the utility function of rational adversaries as follows.

Definition 3 (Utility Function). *A utility function is a function that maps outcome* $\mathsf{out} = (\mathsf{validity}_{\text{fail}}, \mathsf{agreement}_{\text{fail}})$ *of a broadcast game to a real value. A rational t-adversary has a utility function U satisfying*

1. $U(\mathsf{out}) > U(\mathsf{out}')$ *if* $\mathsf{validity}_{\text{fail}} > \mathsf{validity}'_{\text{fail}}$ *and* $\mathsf{agreement}_{\text{fail}} = \mathsf{agreement}'_{\text{fail}}$;
2. $U(\mathsf{out}) > U(\mathsf{out}')$ *if* $\mathsf{validity}_{\text{fail}} = \mathsf{validity}'_{\text{fail}}$ *and* $\mathsf{agreement}_{\text{fail}} > \mathsf{agreement}'_{\text{fail}}$,

where $\mathsf{out} = (\mathsf{validity}_{\text{fail}}, \mathsf{agreement}_{\text{fail}})$ *and* $\mathsf{out}' = (\mathsf{validity}'_{\text{fail}}, \mathsf{agreement}'_{\text{fail}})$ *are outcomes of the broadcast game.*

Namely, rational adversaries gain higher utility if they violate the security requirements of broadcast protocols. The following relation holds:

$$U(0,0) < \min\{U(0,1), U(1,0)\} \leq \max\{U(0,1), U(1,0)\} < U(1,1). \qquad (1)$$

The adversary's utility when following strategy A is the expected value of the utility when the adversary plays the broadcast game by following strategy A.

Definition 4 (Expected Utility). *The utility $u(A)$ of t-adversary A is the expected value* $\mathbb{E}[U(\mathsf{out}_A)]$, *where the expectation is taken over the randomness in the broadcast game* $\mathsf{G}^{\mathrm{BC}}_{\Pi,A}(n,t)$, *including random coins of adversary A.*

We define the security notion of broadcast protocols against a rational adversary based on the adversary's utility function. This formulation was also employed in [8,11] for other protocols.

Definition 5 (Security of Rational Broadcast). *A broadcast protocol Π is said to be* secure against rational t-adversaries *if there exists a t-adversary B such that*

1. *Security: The outcome of $\mathsf{G}^{\mathrm{BC}}_{\Pi,B}(n,t)$ satisfies $\mathsf{out}_B = (0,0)$.*
2. *Best Response: For any t-adversary A, the utility satisfies $u(A) \leq u(B)$.*

The round complexity against rational adversaries *is the number of rounds required to terminate the execution of Π in $\mathsf{G}^{\mathrm{BC}}_{\Pi,B}(n,t)$. The* round complexity against worst-case adversaries *is the number of rounds required to terminate the execution of Π in $\mathsf{G}^{\mathrm{BC}}_{\Pi,A}(n,t)$ for any t-adversary A.*

The first condition implies that adversary B does not violate the protocol's security requirements. The second ensures that B's strategy is optimal among all possible strategies of t-adversaries, meaning that no adversary A can gain a higher expected utility. Thus, if Π satisfies the two conditions, all rational adversaries have no incentive to deviate from the harmless strategy B.

We remark that the security against rational adversaries (Definition 5) is weaker than the traditional security against malicious adversaries (Definition 2). Suppose Π is a t-resilient broadcast protocol. Then, every t-adversary A satisfies $u(A) = U(0,0)$. Thus, by choosing any B in Definition 5, we can show that Π is secure against rational t-adversaries.

2.2 Dolev-Strong Protocol

Let us recall the Dolev-Strong authenticated broadcast protocol [5]. The protocol uses a *signature chain.* A signature chain for value v of length ℓ is defined as (1) $(v, \sigma_i(v))$ for some $i \in [n]$ if $\ell = 1$; (2) $(c, \sigma_i(c))$ for some $i \in [n]$ for $\ell > 1$, where c is a signature chain for v of length $\ell - 1$ that consists of signatures with $\ell - 1$ distinct signers other than i. A signature chain is valid if it satisfies the above conditions and all signatures are valid.

In the first round of the Dolev-Strong protocol, the sender with message m sends $(m, \sigma_s(m))$ to all parties. In round $r \geq 2$, each party i sends a signature chain of length r to all parties by appending his signature to a chain of length $r-1$ received in the previous round. After receiving chains in round $t+1$, if party i knows valid chains only for message m, i outputs m. Otherwise, i outputs $\perp$. This protocol has the property that once an honest party receives a valid signature chain for message m, every honest party will receive a valid chain for m in the later rounds. Hence, validity immediately follows. Since every valid signature chain sent in round r contains signatures of r different parties and the protocol continues until round $t+1$, there exists an honest party who sent a valid chain in round $r \in [t+1]$ (Otherwise, every honest party receives no valid chain and outputs $\perp$). Thus, after round $t+1$, every honest party receives valid chains for the same messages, implying agreement.

The protocol description is presented in Fig. 1. Protocol $\Pi_{\mathsf{DS}}(n,t,s)$ is a t-resilient broadcast protocol (Definition 2) for any $t < n$ [5].

Protocol $\Pi_{\mathsf{DS}}(n, t, s)$

This protocol is parameterized by the number of parties n, the threshold t with $t < n$, and the sender index $s \in [n]$. The protocol assumes a PKI, where each $i \in [n]$ can generate a signature $\sigma_i(m)$ for message m by $\mathsf{Sign}(sk_i, m)$ and can verify the validity of a signature σ of party j for message m' by $\mathsf{Ver}(pk_j, m', \sigma)$.

- Round 1: Each party $i \in [n]$ sets $V_i = \emptyset$. Sender s with input m sends $(m, \sigma_s(m))$ to all parties.
- Round $r = 2, \ldots, t+1$: Each party $i \in [n]$ do the following:
  - If party i receives a valid signature chain c for value v of length $r-1$ that does not contain i's signature, i adds v to V_i and sends $(c, \sigma_i(c))$ to all parties. (Party i performs this procedure once for each value v. Thus, once v is added to V_i, i does nothing for v thereafter.)
  - **Termination:** At the end of round $t+1$, if $|V_i| = 1$, i outputs $v \in V_i$. Otherwise, i outputs $\perp$.

Fig. 1. Dolev-Strong Protocol

3 YY23 Protocol

In this section, we review the YY23 protocol [17], which serves as the basis of our protocols. It satisfies agreement in Definition 2 and *weak validity*, meaning that if the sender is honest, all honest parties output the sender's value or $\perp$. The protocol uses several notions listed below:

- A *countersignature* is a signature for a signature: $(m, \sigma_i(m), \sigma_j(\sigma_i(m)))$, which is a signature chain of length 2 in the Dolev-Strong protocol, except that i and j are not necessarily distinct. A countersignature

$$\mathsf{CSig}_m^i = (m, \sigma_s(m), \sigma_i(\sigma_s(m))),$$

can serve as a certificate that the sender s sent message m to party i.
- A *Proof of Dissemination (PoD)* is a signed set of $t+1$ valid countersignatures:

$$\mathsf{PoD}_m^i = \left(\mathsf{PoD}_m = \{\mathsf{CSig}_m^j\}_j, \sigma_i(\mathsf{PoD}_m)\right).$$

In the protocol, it serves as a certificate that party i knows that every party obtained a countersignature for message m.
- A *Proof of Agreement (PoA)* is a signed set of $t+1$ valid PoDs:

$$\mathsf{PoA}_m^i = \left(\mathsf{PoA}_m = \{\mathsf{PoD}_m^j\}_j, \sigma_i(\mathsf{PoA}_m)\right).$$

It serves as a certificate that party i knows that every party knows that every party obtained a countersignature for message m.

In the first round of the YY23 protocol, the sender s sends a signed message $(m, \sigma_s(m))$ to all parties. In round 2, each party sends a countersignature to all parties. In round 3, each party generates a PoD from countersignatures sent in the previous round and sends a PoD to all parties. In round 4, each party generates a PoA from PoDs and sends a PoA to all parties via the Dolev-Strong protocol. At the end of round 4, if each party collected $t + 1$ valid PoAs for message m, it outputs m and halts. Otherwise, the party continues the DS protocol and outputs the value sent through the DS protocol after round $t+4$. If party i fails to obtain a PoA, i outputs $\perp$ and considers the sender s as cheating.

We briefly describe a reason why this protocol works. We can show the following two claims:

(1) PoAs can be generated only for a single message.
(2) If some honest party outputs $\perp$, then all honest parties output $\perp$.

To prove (1), suppose PoAs exist for different m and m'. Since a PoA contains $t+1$ PoDs, at least one PoD was sent by an honest party, who sent the PoD to all parties in round 3. Thus, all honest parties should have received PoDs for both m and m'. Since each valid PoD contains $t+1$ countersignatures, all honest parties should have received countersignatures for both m and m'. However, in that case, honest parties send nothing in round 3, a contradiction. (Note that PoDs can be generated for both m and m'.) To prove (2), note that an honest party outputs $\perp$ only when that party failed to receive a PoA via the DS protocol. Since the DS protocol satisfies validity, it implies that no honest party sent a PoA using the DS protocol. If some honest party received a PoA, then all honest parties receive the same PoA by the agreement property of the DS protocol. Thus, (2) follows.

To prove weak validity, suppose that an honest party outputs a message m' different from the original message m of the honest sender. However, this is impossible because the sender's signature cannot be generated by any party other than the sender. To prove agreement, suppose that two honest parties output different messages m and m'. If neither m nor m' is $\perp$, it implies that PoAs for different messages were generated, contradicting (1). If $m' = \perp$, (2) implies that a PoA for message m was never sent to honest parties, a contradiction.

We provide a protocol description of the YY23 protocol in Fig. 2 (Table 2).

By the same argument as in [17], we can show that $\Pi_{\mathsf{YY23}}(n, t, s)$ is secure against rational t-adversaries, where the security requirements of broadcast protocols are agreement and *weak validity* in the sense that an honest party may output $\perp$ even when a sender is honest. This security notion is formalized by modifying Definition 5 such that (a) Π satisfies weak validity and (standard) agreement against B, and (b) in the broadcast game of Definition 1, $\mathsf{validity}_{\mathsf{fail}}$ is set to be 1 when there exists $i \in H$ such that $\mathsf{val}_i \notin \{m, \perp\}$. If protocol Π satisfies the above, we say Π is *weak-validity secure* against rational t-adversaries.

Theorem 1. *For any $t < n$, protocol Π_{YY23} is weak-validity secure against rational t-adversaries. The round complexity is 4 against rational t-adversaries and is $t + 4$ against worst-case t-adversaries.*

The proof of Theorem 1 is almost the same as that of [17, Theorem 1].

Protocol $\Pi_{\mathsf{YY23}}(n, t, s)$

This protocol is parameterized by the number of parties n, the threshold t with $t < n$, and the sender index $s \in [n]$. The protocol assumes a PKI, where each $i \in [n]$ can generate a signature $\sigma_i(m)$ for message m by $\mathsf{Sign}(sk_i, m)$ and can verify the validity of a signature σ of party j for message m' by $\mathsf{Ver}(pk_j, m', \sigma)$. We denote by $\Pi^r_{\mathsf{DS}}(n, t, s)$ the protocol description of the rth round of $\Pi_{\mathsf{DS}}(n, t, s)$. The validity conditions of signature, countersignature, PoD, and PoA are summarized in Table 2.

- Round 1: Sender s with input m sends $(m, \sigma_s(m))$ to all parties.
- Round 2: Each party $i \in [n]$ checks whether it has received a valid signature $(m, \sigma_s(m))$ from s and no valid signature for any other value $m' \neq m$ in round 1. If so, i sends
$$\mathsf{CSig}^i_m = (m, \sigma_s(m), \sigma_i(\sigma_s(m)))$$
to all parties. Otherwise, i sends nothing.
- Round 3: Each party $i \in [n]$ checks whether it has received $t+1$ valid countersignatures CSig^j_m for the same value m, each from a distinct signer j, and no valid countersignature for any other value $m' \neq m$ in round 2. If so, i sends
$$\mathsf{PoD}^i_m = \left(\mathsf{PoD}_m = \{\mathsf{CSig}^j_m\}_j, \sigma_i(\mathsf{PoD}_m)\right)$$
to all parties, where PoD_m consists of $t+1$ valid countersignatures. Otherwise, i sends nothing.
- Round 4: Each party $i \in [n]$ checks whether it has received $t+1$ valid PoD^j_m for the same value m, each from a distinct signer j, in round 3. If so, i prepares
$$\mathsf{PoA}^i_m = \left(\mathsf{PoA}_m = \{\mathsf{PoD}^j_m\}_j, \sigma_i(\mathsf{PoA}_m)\right),$$
where PoA_m consists of $t+1$ valid PoDs, and performs $\Pi^1_{\mathsf{DS}}(n, t, i)$ where the input message of i is PoA^i_m. Otherwise, i sends nothing.
Termination: At the end of round 4, each party $i \in [n]$ checks whether it has received $t+1$ valid PoA^j_m for the same message, each from a distinct signer j. If so, i outputs m and halts. Otherwise, i continues with the later rounds.
- Round $r = 5, \ldots, t+4$: Each party $i \in [n]$ performs $\Pi^{r-3}_{\mathsf{DS}}(n, t, j)$ for every $j \in [n]$.
Termination: At the end of round $t+4$, for each $i \in [n]$, let V_i be the set of values output by party i via $\Pi_{\mathsf{DS}}(n, t, j)$ for $j \in [n]$. If V_i contains valid PoA^j_m for a single value m, then i outputs m. Otherwise, i outputs $\perp$.
Cheater Detection: For each $i \in [n]$, if party i outputs $\perp$ in termination, then i outputs $C_i = \{s\}$ as a candidate list of cheaters.

Fig. 2. YY23 Protocol

Table 2. Validity Conditions

Objects	Validity Conditions
Signature $\sigma_i(m)$	$\mathsf{Ver}(pk_i, m, \sigma_i(m)) = 1$
Countersignature $(m, \sigma_s(m), \sigma_i(\sigma_s(m)))$	$\sigma_s(m)$ and $\sigma_i(\sigma_s(m))$ are valid signatures
Proof of dissemination (PoD) $\mathsf{PoD}_m^i = (\mathsf{PoD}_m = \{\mathsf{CSig}_m^j\}_j, \sigma_i(\mathsf{PoD}_m))$	$\sigma_i(\mathsf{PoD}_m)$ is a valid signature $\wedge$ every CSig_m^j is a valid countersignature $\wedge$ each j of CSig_m^j is distinct $\wedge$ $\lvert\mathsf{PoD}_m\rvert = t + 1$
Proof of agreement (PoA) $\mathsf{PoA}_m^i = (\mathsf{PoA}_m = \{\mathsf{PoD}_m^j\}_j, \sigma_i(\mathsf{PoA}_m))$	$\sigma_i(\mathsf{PoA}_m)$ is a valid signature $\wedge$ every PoD_m^j is a valid PoD $\wedge$ each j of PoD_m^j is distinct $\wedge$ $\lvert\mathsf{PoA}_m\rvert = t + 1$

4 Protocols with Local Detectability

In this section, we define the property of local cheating detectability. To this end, we consider an extension of the broadcast game of Definition 1, where each party $i \in [n]$ can output a candidate list $C_i \subseteq [n]$, indicating the parties that party i suspects of cheating. We denote the game by $\mathsf{G}_{\Pi,A}^{\text{BC-LD}}(n, t)$.

Definition 6 (Local Detectability). *An n-party broadcast protocol Π is said to have* local detectability against t-adversaries *if for every t-adversary A, the broadcast game $\mathsf{G}_{\Pi,A}^{\text{BC-LD}}(n, t)$ satisfies that*

1. *Detection Correctness: If $i \in H$ outputs a candidate list C_i of cheaters, then $C_i \subseteq C$;*
2. *Detection Soundness: If $i \in H$, then no party $j \in H$ outputs C_j such that $i \in C_j$,*

where $C \subseteq [n]$ is a set of corrupted parties in the broadcast game and $H = [n] \backslash C$.

Detection Correctness means that whenever an honest party i outputs a list C_i, every party in C_i is indeed corrupted. Detection Soundness guarantees that honestly-behaving parties are never falsely detected as cheaters. Both properties prevent false cheating detections: the former ensures that any accusation made by an honest party is justified (from the accuser's perspective), while the latter protects honest parties from being wrongly accused (from the accused's perspective).

As discussed in [17], Π_{YY23} satisfies local detectability for $t < (n-1)/2$. However, it does not satisfy detection soundness for $t \geq (n-1)/2$.

In this section, we present a protocol that achieves local detectability for any $t < n$. As outlined in Sect. 1, the idea is to perform the Dolev-Strong protocol and the YY23 protocol in parallel. One difficulty in designing such protocols is defining an appropriate termination rule. The description of our protocol Π_{LD} is given in Fig. 3.

Protocol $\Pi_{\mathsf{LD}}(n, t, s)$

This protocol is parameterized by the number of parties n, the threshold t with $t < n$, and the sender index $s \in [n]$. The protocol assumes a PKI as in $\Pi_{\mathsf{YY23}}(n, t, s)$. We denote by $\Pi^r_{\mathsf{DS}}(n, t, s)$ the protocol description of the rth round of $\Pi_{\mathsf{DS}}(n, t, s)$. We use $\overline{\Pi^r_{\mathsf{DS}}}(n, t, s)$ as the description of the rth round of $\Pi_{\mathsf{DS}}(n, t, s)$ for performing the auxiliary part. The validity conditions are summarized in Table 2.

- Round 1: Sender s with input m sends $(m, \sigma_s(m))$ to all parties.
- Round 2: Henceforth, each party runs the auxiliary part (denoted by **[Aux]**) in parallel with the main part, described without an explicit label.
  Each party $i \in [n]$ checks whether it has received a valid signature $(m, \sigma_s(m))$ from s and no valid signature for any other value $m' \neq m$ in round 1. If so, i sends
  $$\mathsf{CSig}^i_m = (m, \sigma_s(m), \sigma_i(\sigma_s(m)))$$
  to all parties. Otherwise, i sends nothing.
  [Aux] Each party $i \in [n]$ regards the messages received in round 1 as those of $\overline{\Pi^1_{\mathsf{DS}}}(n, t, s)$ and then performs $\overline{\Pi^2_{\mathsf{DS}}}(n, t, s)$.
- Round 3: Each party $i \in [n]$ checks whether it has received $t + 1$ valid countersignatures CSig^j_m for the same value m, each from a distinct signer j, and no valid countersignature for any other value $m' \neq m$ in round 2. If so, i sends
  $$\mathsf{PoD}^i_m = \left(\mathsf{PoD}_m = \{\mathsf{CSig}^j_m\}_j, \sigma_i(\mathsf{PoD}_m)\right)$$
  to all parties. Otherwise, i sends nothing.
  [Aux] If $t \geq 2$, each party $i \in [n]$ performs $\overline{\Pi^3_{\mathsf{DS}}}(n, t, s)$.
- Round 4: Each party $i \in [n]$ checks whether it has received $t + 1$ valid PoD^j_m for the same value m, each from a distinct signer j, in round 3. If so, i prepares
  $$\mathsf{PoA}^i_m = \left(\mathsf{PoA}_m = \{\mathsf{PoD}^j_m\}_j, \sigma_i(\mathsf{PoA}_m)\right).$$
  and performs $\Pi^1_{\mathsf{DS}}(n, t, i)$ where the input message of i is PoA^i_m. Otherwise, i sends nothing.
  Termination: At the end of round 4, each party $i \in [n]$ checks whether it has received $t + 1$ valid PoA^j_m for the same value m, each from a distinct signer j. If so, i outputs m and halts both the main and the auxiliary parts. Otherwise, i continues with the auxiliary part.
  [Aux] If $t \geq 3$, each party $i \in [n]$ performs $\overline{\Pi^4_{\mathsf{DS}}}(n, t, s)$.
- Round $r = 5, \ldots, t + 4$: Each $i \in [n]$ performs $\Pi^{r-3}_{\mathsf{DS}}(n, t, j)$ for every $j \in [n]$.
  [Aux] In round $r \leq t + 1$, each party $i \in [n]$ performs $\overline{\Pi^r_{\mathsf{DS}}}(n, t, s)$. Let v^i_{aux} be the output of party i by performing the auxiliary part $\overline{\Pi_{\mathsf{DS}}}(n, t, s)$.
  Termination: At the end of round $t + 4$, for each $i \in [n]$, let V_i be the set of values output by party i via $\Pi_{\mathsf{DS}}(n, t, j)$ for $j \in [n]$. If V_i contains valid PoA^j_m for a single value m, then i outputs m. Otherwise, i outputs v^i_{aux}.
  Cheater Detection: For each $i \in [n]$, if party i outputs $\perp$ in termination, then i outputs $C_i = \{s\}$ as a candidate list of cheaters.

Fig. 3. Our Protocol with Local Detectability

4.1 Achieving Local Detectability

We present sufficient conditions for achieving local detectability.

Lemma 1. *Suppose that (a) a broadcast protocol Π satisfies validity against every t-adversary and that (b) every honest party i in Π outputs a candidate list C_i of cheaters with $|C_i| \geq 1$ only when i outputs $\perp$ and $C_i = \{s\}$. Then, Π achieves local detectability against t-adversaries.*

Proof. First, we prove detection correctness. Suppose $i \in H$ outputs a candidate list C_i with $|C_i| \geq 1$. Assumption (b) implies that i outputs $\perp$ and $C_i = \{s\}$. If $s \in H$, assumption (a) implies that every $i \in H$ outputs the message m of s. That means $i \in H$ outputs m, a contradiction. Hence, $s \in C$. Therefore, $C_i \subseteq C$.

Next, we prove detection soundness. By assumption (b), sender s is the only party that can be included in a candidate list C_i of honest party i. The above argument for proving correctness implies that if $s \in H$, each $i \in H$ outputs $m \neq \perp$, and thus $C_i = \emptyset$ by assumption (b). Hence, the soundness follows. □

We show that protocol Π_{LD} satisfies the conditions in Lemma 1, implying that Π_{LD} has local detectability.

Theorem 2. *For any $t < n$, the broadcast protocol Π_{LD} has local detectability against t-adversaries.*

Proof. It is sufficient to show that Π_{LD} satisfies (a) and (b) in Lemma 1.

First, we prove (a), validity of Π_{LD}. We need to show that when s is honest and has input m, every honest party outputs m in the protocol. By the validity of the DS protocol, it must be the case that $v^i_{\mathsf{aux}} = m$ for every honest party i. Then, if honest party i outputs $m' \neq m$, it must be either of the following two cases:

1. At the end of round 4, i collected $t+1$ valid $\mathsf{PoA}^j_{m'}$ for different j.
2. At the end of round $t+4$, it holds that $V_i = \{\mathsf{PoA}^j_{m'}\}$.

However, since s is honest, $\sigma_s(m')$ cannot be generated, and thus neither of the above two cases can occur. Hence, Π_{LD} satisfies validity.

Condition (b) immediately follows from the protocol description of Π_{LD}. □

4.2 Proving Security Against Rational Adversaries

We show that Π_{LD} is a secure broadcast protocol against rational adversaries.

The following is a useful lemma claiming that PoAs can be generated only for a single message in Π_{LD}.

Lemma 2. *In every broadcast game $\mathsf{G}^{\text{BC-LD}}_{\Pi_{\mathsf{LD}},A}(n,t)$ of protocol Π_{LD} against t-adversary A, if any party holds a valid proof of agreement PoA^i_m for some m, then no party can obtain a valid proof of agreement $\mathsf{PoA}^j_{m'}$ for any $m' \neq m$.*

Proof. Suppose some party obtained a valid PoA^i_m for m. Since it contains $t+1$ valid PoDs for m and at most t parties are corrupted, at least one PoD^j_m was generated by honest party j. Since PoD^j_m contains $t+1$ valid countersignatures for m, at least one countersignature CSig^k_m was generated by honest party k. Thus, all parties received this countersignature CSig^k_m sent from party k.

Suppose for contradiction that some party obtained a valid $\mathsf{PoA}^j_{m'}$ for $m' \neq m$. By the same argument, all parties received a valid countersignature for m'. However, in that case, every honest party ℓ should have sent nothing in round 3 since party ℓ saw valid countersignatures for different messages m and m'. It contradicts the fact that valid PoDs for m and m' exist. Therefore, the statement follows. □

We prove that Π_{LD} satisfies agreement.

Lemma 3. *For any $t < n$, Π_{LD} satisfies agreement for t-adversaries.*

Proof. We need to show that for any t-adversary A, the outcome $\mathsf{out}_A = (\mathsf{validity}_{\mathrm{fail}}, \mathsf{agreement}_{\mathrm{fail}})$ of the broadcast game $\mathsf{G}^{\mathrm{BC}}_{\Pi_{\mathsf{LD}},A}(n,t)$ satisfies $\mathsf{agreement}_{\mathrm{fail}} = 0$.

Suppose for contradiction that there exists a t-adversary A such that $\mathsf{agreement}_{\mathrm{fail}} = 1$ in $\mathsf{G}^{\mathrm{BC}}_{\Pi_{\mathsf{LD}},A}(n,t)$. It implies that there exist different $i, j \in H$ such that $\mathsf{val}_i \neq \mathsf{val}_j$. There are two cases: $(\mathsf{val}_i, \mathsf{val}_j) = (m, \perp)$ and $(\mathsf{val}_i, \mathsf{val}_j) = (m, m')$ for $m \neq m'$, $\perp \notin \{m, m'\}$. We show that the two cases cannot occur.

We observe that $\mathsf{val}_i = m$ occurs either in the following three cases:

(a) Party i outputs m in round 4 by collecting $t+1$ valid PoA^ℓ_m for different ℓ.
(b) Party i outputs m in round $t+4$ since V_i contains valid PoA^ℓ_m only for m.
(c) Party i outputs m in round $t{+}4$ since V_i contains no valid PoA and $v^i_{\mathsf{aux}} = m$.

Note that $\mathsf{val}_j = \perp$ occurs only in the following case:

(d) Party j outputs $\perp$ in round $t{+}4$ since V_j contains no valid PoA and $v^j_{\mathsf{aux}} = \perp$.

First, consider case (a). Since i has $t+1$ valid PoA^ℓ_m for different ℓ, one of them is a valid $\mathsf{PoA}^{\ell'}_m$ for $\ell' \in H$. Since ℓ' had sent $\mathsf{PoA}^{\ell'}_m$ to all parties in round 4, every honest party k added $\mathsf{PoA}^{\ell'}_m$ to V_k via $\Pi_{\mathsf{DS}}(n,t,\ell')$. Lemma 2 implies that no honest party could obtain valid $\mathsf{PoA}_{m'}$ for $m' \neq m$. Thus, V_j contains valid PoAs only for m, implying that $m' = m$, a contradiction.

Next, consider case (b). Since i receives a valid PoA^ℓ_m via $\Pi_{\mathsf{DS}}(n,t,\ell)$ for some ℓ, every honest party should receive PoA^ℓ_m by the agreement property of Π_{DS}. Since there is no PoAs for $m' \neq m$ by Lemma 2, V_j contains valid PoAs only for m, implying $m' = m$, a contradiction.

Finally, consider case (c). It is sufficient to consider the case that party j outputs m' in round $t+4$, in which case V_j contains no valid PoA and $v^j_{\mathsf{aux}} \in \{m', \perp\}$. However, since $i, j \in H$, the agreement property of $\overline{\Pi_{\mathsf{DS}}(n,t,s)}$ implies that $v^j_{\mathsf{aux}} = m$, which contradicts $v^j_{\mathsf{aux}} \in \{m', \perp\}$. □

Next, we show that Π_{LD} satisfies validity.

Lemma 4. *For any $t < n$, Π_{LD} satisfies validity for t-adversaries.*

Proof. To prove that Π_{LD} satisfies validity, we need to show that for any t-adversary A, the outcome $\mathsf{out}_A = (\mathsf{validity}_{\mathsf{fail}}, \mathsf{agreement}_{\mathsf{fail}})$ of the broadcast game $\mathsf{G}^{\mathrm{BC}}_{\Pi,A}(n,t)$ satisfies $\mathsf{validity}_{\mathsf{fail}} = 0$. Namely, if sender s with initial message m is not corrupted, every $i \in H$ outputs $\mathsf{val}_i = m$.

Suppose for contradiction that there exists $i \in H$ such that $\mathsf{val}_i = m' \neq m$. Since $s \in H$, the validity of the DS protocol $\overline{\Pi_{\mathsf{DS}}}(n,t,s)$ in the auxiliary part implies that $v^j_{\mathsf{aux}} = \{m\}$ for every $j \in H$. By the protocol description of Π_{LD}, it must be the case that i receives a valid $\mathsf{PoA}^{\ell}_{m'}$ in the execution. However, the existence of $\mathsf{PoA}^{\ell}_{m'}$ requires a valid signature of s for message m'. That is impossible as long as the signature scheme is secure. Hence, the statement follows. □

We show that Π_{LD} is a constant-round broadcast protocol against rational adversaries.

Theorem 3. *For any $t < n$, the broadcast protocol Π_{LD} is secure against rational t-adversaries. It has round complexity 4 against rational adversaries and $t+4$ against worst-case adversaries.*

Proof. Consider a t-adversary B that chooses a random sender $s \in [n]$, a random message m, and $C = \emptyset$. In this case, B does not perform any attacks on the protocol. Since each party i receives a valid PoA^{j}_{m} from all n parties in round 4 and outputs m in the same round, the outcome of the broadcast game $\mathsf{G}^{\mathrm{BC}}_{\Pi,B}(n,t)$ is $\mathsf{out}_B = (0,0)$.

Next, we show the best-response property. Since $u(B) = U(0,0)$, we need to show that $u(A) \leq U(0,0)$ for any t-adversary A. Lemmas 3 and 4 imply that Π_{LD} achieves validity and agreement for any t-adversary. It implies that every t-adversary A achieves $\mathsf{out}_A = (\mathsf{validity}_{\mathsf{fail}}, \mathsf{agreement}_{\mathsf{fail}}) = (0,0)$, meaning that $u(A) = U(0,0) \leq u(B)$.

The worst-case round complexity is $t+4$ by the protocol description. □

5 Protocols with Optimal Worst-Case Round Complexity

We show that if rational t-adversaries are *detection averse*, we can construct a broadcast protocol that achieves the optimal worst-case round complexity of $t+1$.

Before presenting the protocol, we formally define the security notion. First, we extend the broadcast game $\mathsf{G}^{\mathrm{BC\text{-}LD}}_{\Pi,A}(n,t)$ introduced in Sect. 4 to include an additional parameter, $\mathsf{undetected}$, which indicates whether the adversary's attack is locally detected by honest parties.

Definition 7 (Extended Broadcast Game with Local Detectability). *Given an n-party protocol Π and adversary A, the broadcast game $\mathsf{G}^{\mathrm{eBC\text{-}LD}}_{\Pi,A}(n,t)$ of Π against A is defined as follows. Set the parameters $\mathsf{validity}_{\mathsf{fail}} = \mathsf{agreement}_{\mathsf{fail}} = 0$ and $\mathsf{undetected} = 1$. The adversary A chooses a sender $s \in [n]$,* *a message m, and a set of corrupted parties $C \subseteq [n]$ satisfying $|C| \leq t$. Then, protocol Π is executed with $s \in [n]$ as a sender and m as the initial message. During the execution, the parties in C are controlled by A, while the others honestly follow the description of Π. After protocol execution, each party $i \in [n]$ outputs a value* val_i *and a candidate list $C_i \subseteq [n]$, Let $H = [n] \setminus C$.*

- *If $s \in H$ and there exists $i \in H$ such that* $\mathsf{val}_i \neq m$, *set* $\mathsf{validity}_{\mathrm{fail}} = 1$.
- *If there exist different $i, j \in H$ such that* $\mathsf{val}_i \neq \mathsf{val}_j$, *set* $\mathsf{agreement}_{\mathrm{fail}} = 1$.
- *If there exist $i \in C$ and $j \in H$ such that $i \in C_j$, set* $\mathsf{undetected} = 0$.

The outcome of the game is $\mathsf{out}_A = (\mathsf{validity}_{\mathrm{fail}}, \mathsf{agreement}_{\mathrm{fail}}, \mathsf{undetected})$.

The parameter $\mathsf{undetected}$ is initially set to 1, and is changed to 0 if there exists an honest party j that outputs a candidate list C_j containing a truly corrupted party i.

We define the utility function of detection-averse adversaries as follows.

Definition 8 (Utility of Detection-Averse Adversaries). *A* detection-averse *t-adversary has a utility function U_{DA} that maps an outcome* out_A *of* $\mathsf{G}_{\Pi,A}^{\mathrm{eBC\text{-}LD}}(n,t)$ *to a real value such that*

$$U_{\mathsf{DA}}(0,0,0) < u_1 \leq U_{\mathsf{DA}}(0,0,1) < u_2 < U_{\mathsf{DA}}(1,1,1) \tag{2}$$

for any $u_1 \in \{U_{\mathsf{DA}}(0,1,0), U_{\mathsf{DA}}(1,0,0), U_{\mathsf{DA}}(1,1,0)\}$ *and* $u_2 \in \{U_{\mathsf{DA}}(0,1,1), U_{\mathsf{DA}}(1,0,1)\}$

Intuitively, a detection-averse adversary gains higher utility when it violates the security requirements of broadcast protocols without having the attack detected.

The security notion is defined based on Definition 5 by replacing utility U with utility U_{DA} of detection-averse adversaries.

Definition 9 (Security of Broadcast against Detection-Averse Adversaries). *A broadcast protocol Π is said to be* secure against detection-averse t-adversaries *if there exists a t-adversary B such that*

1. *Security: The outcome of* $\mathsf{G}_{\Pi,B}^{\mathrm{eBC\text{-}LD}}(n,t)$ *satisfies* $\mathsf{out}_B = (0,0,1)$.
2. *Best response: For any t-adversary A, the utility satisfies $u_{\mathsf{DA}}(A) \leq u_{\mathsf{DA}}(B)$, where $u_{\mathsf{DA}}(A) = \mathbb{E}[U_{\mathsf{DA}}(\mathsf{out}_A)]$ and* out_A *is an outcome of the broadcast game* $\mathsf{G}_{\Pi,A}^{\mathrm{eBC\text{-}LD}}(n,t)$.

The best response property of Definition 9 guarantees that no adversary has an attack strategy A that violates either validity/agreement without its attack being locally detected.

Our Protocol

The construction idea for achieving the optimal worst-case round complexity is that we do not perform the main part of Π_{LD} after round 4. The protocol is presented in Fig. 4.

We show that Π_{DA} satisfies validity.

Protocol $\Pi_{\mathsf{DA}}(n,t,s)$

The protocol description up to round 4 is the same as $\Pi_{\mathsf{LD}}(n,t,s)$ and thus omitted.

- Round $r = 5, \ldots, t+1$:
  [Aux] Each $i \in [n]$ performs $\overline{\Pi^r_{\mathsf{DS}}}(n,t,s)$.
  Termination: At the end of round $t+1$, each party $i \in [n]$ outputs v^i_{aux}, which is the output of i by performing the auxiliary part $\overline{\Pi_{\mathsf{DS}}}(n,t,s)$.
  Cheater Detection: For each $i \in [n]$, if party i outputs $\perp$ in termination, then i outputs $C_i = \{s\}$ as a candidate list of cheaters.

Fig. 4. Our Protocol against Detection-Averse Adversaries

Lemma 5. *For any $t < n$, Π_{DA} satisfies validity for t-adversaries.*

Proof. To prove validity, suppose for contradiction that sender s with message m is not corrupted and some party $i \in H$ outputs $m' \neq m$ in the execution of Π_{DA}. Since s is honest, the validity of the DS protocol implies that $v^j_{\mathsf{aux}} = m$ for every $j \in H$. Thus, the output of party i should be $m' \neq \perp$. Honest party i outputs such m' by collecting $t+1$ valid PoAs in round 4. However, since s is honest, no party can generate a valid signature for message m', a contradiction. □

Combining the above lemma with Lemma 1, we have the following corollary.

Corollary 1. *For any $t < n$, Π_{DA} has local detectability against t-adversaries.*

To prove the security against detection-averse adversaries, we show that Π_{DA} satisfies *weak* agreement.

Lemma 6. *For any $t < n$ and t-adversary A, in the execution of $\mathsf{G}^{\text{eBC-LD}}_{\Pi_{\mathsf{DA}},A}(n,t)$, every output value val_i of party $i \in H$ satisfies $\mathsf{val}_i \in \{m, \perp\}$ for some m.*

Proof. Suppose for contradiction that there exists messages m and $m' \neq m$ and $i, j \in H$ such that $\mathsf{val}_i = m \neq \perp$ and $\mathsf{val}_j = m' \neq \perp$. Note that $\mathsf{val}_i = m$ occurs either in the following two cases:

(a) Party i outputs m in round 4 by collecting $t+1$ PoA^ℓ_m for different ℓ.
(b) Party i outputs m in round $t+1$ since $v^i_{\mathsf{aux}} = \{m\}$.

Similarly, we consider cases (a') and (b'), which describe the conditions under which j outputs m'.

Lemma 2 excludes cases (a) and (a') since $m \neq m'$.

Now consider cases (a) and (b'). Since there exist $t+1$ valid PoAs for m, some party $k \in H$ sent PoA^k_m to all parties in round 4. Since PoA^k_m contains $t+1$ valid PoD^ℓ_m for different ℓ, some party $k' \in H$ must have sent a valid $\mathsf{PoD}^{k'}_m$ to all parties in round 3. This implies that some party $k'' \in H$ received $(m, \sigma_s(m))$ in round 1, and hence k'' performs $\overline{\Pi^2_{\mathsf{DS}}}(n,t,k'')$ in the auxiliary part of round 2.

By the validity of the DS protocol, it follows that for every $\ell \in H$, we have $v^{\ell}_{\mathsf{aux}} \in \{m, \bot\}$. This contradicts the assumption (b') that j outputs m', since $v^{j}_{\mathsf{aux}} = \{m'\}$.

Finally, consider cases (b) and (b'). The assumption implies $v^{i}_{\mathsf{aux}} = \{m\}$ and $v^{j}_{\mathsf{aux}} = \{m'\}$. However, it contradicts the agreement property of the DS protocol.

Therefore, the statement follows. □

We prove the security against detection-averse adversaries.

Theorem 4. *For any $t < n$, Π_{DA} is secure against detection-averse t-adversaries. It has round complexity* 4 *against detection-averse adversaries and* $t+1$ *against worst-case adversaries.*

Proof. We consider the same adversary B as in the proof of Theorem 3. To prove the best response property, we need to show that $u_{\mathsf{DA}}(A) \leq U_{\mathsf{DA}}(0,0,1)$ for any t-adversary A. Inequality (2) implies that, to violate the best response, A needs to achieve either $U(0,1,1)$, $U(1,0,1)$, or $U(1,1,1)$. Since Π_{DA} satisfies validity by Lemma 5, A cannot achieve $\mathsf{validity}_{\mathrm{fail}} = 1$. Thus, A needs to achieve the case of $U(0,1,1)$.

To achieve $\mathsf{agreement}_{\mathrm{fail}} = 1$, adversary A needs to corrupt the sender s, because, otherwise, every honest party outputs the same value as the sender's input due to the validity of Π_{DA}. To achieve $\mathsf{undetected} = 1$, A needs the situation that

$$\begin{aligned} &\mathsf{agreement}_{\mathrm{fail}} = 1 \text{ and there is no honest party } k \text{ who outputs } C_k \neq \emptyset \\ \Leftrightarrow\ &\mathsf{agreement}_{\mathrm{fail}} = 1 \text{ and there is no honest party who outputs } \bot \\ \Leftrightarrow\ &\exists i, j \in H \text{ s.t. } \mathsf{val}_i \neq \mathsf{val}_j \ \text{ and } \ \forall k \in H,\ \mathsf{val}_k \neq \bot. \end{aligned}$$

However, Lemma 6 implies that such $(\mathsf{val}_i, \mathsf{val}_j)$ cannot occur. Thus, we have shown that Π_{DA} satisfies the best response property.

The round complexity analysis immediately follows. □

Acknowledgements. This work was supported in part by JSPS Grants-in-Aid for Scientific Research Number 23H00468 and 24H00071 and JST CRONOS Japan Grant Number JPMJCS24K2.

References

1. Abraham, I., Devadas, S., Dolev, D., Nayak, K., Ren, L.: Synchronous byzantine agreement with expected $O(1)$ rounds, expected $O(n^2)$ communication, and optimal resilience. In: Goldberg, I., Moore, T. (eds.) FC 2019. LNCS, vol. 11598, pp. 320–334. Springer, Cham (2019). https://doi.org/10.1007/978-3-030-32101-7_20
2. Abraham, I., Dolev, D.: Byzantine agreement with optimal early stopping, optimal resilience and polynomial complexity. CoRR **abs/1504.02547** (2015). http://arxiv.org/abs/1504.02547
3. Aumann, Y., Lindell, Y.: Security against covert adversaries: efficient protocols for realistic adversaries. J. Cryptol. **23**(2), 281–343 (2010)

4. Berman, P., Garay, J.A., Perry, K.J.: Optimal early stopping in distributed consensus. In: Segall, A., Zaks, S. (eds.) WDAG 1992. LNCS, vol. 647, pp. 221–237. Springer, Heidelberg (1992). https://doi.org/10.1007/3-540-56188-9_15
5. Dolev, D., Strong, H.R.: Authenticated algorithms for byzantine agreement. SIAM J. Comput. **12**(4), 656–666 (1983)
6. Feldman, P., Micali, S.: An optimal probabilistic protocol for synchronous byzantine agreement. SIAM J. Comput. **26**(4), 873–933 (1997)
7. Fitzi, M., Gottesman, D., Hirt, M., Holenstein, T., Smith, A.D.: Detectable byzantine agreement secure against faulty majorities. In: Ricciardi, A. (ed.) Proceedings of the Twenty-First Annual ACM Symposium on Principles of Distributed Computing, PODC 2002, pp. 118–126. ACM (2002)
8. Fujita, M., Koshiba, T., Yasunaga, K.: Perfectly secure message transmission against rational adversaries. IEEE J. Sel. Areas Inf. Theory **3**(2), 390–404 (2022)
9. Garay, J.A., Katz, J., Koo, C., Ostrovsky, R.: Round complexity of authenticated broadcast with a dishonest majority. In: 48th Annual IEEE Symposium on Foundations of Computer Science (FOCS 2007), pp. 658–668. IEEE Computer Society (2007)
10. Goldwasser, S., Lindell, Y.: Secure multi-party computation without agreement. J. Cryptol. **18**(3), 247–287 (2005)
11. Groce, A., Katz, J., Thiruvengadam, A., Zikas, V.: Byzantine agreement with a rational adversary. In: Czumaj, A., Mehlhorn, K., Pitts, A., Wattenhofer, R. (eds.) ICALP 2012. LNCS, vol. 7392, pp. 561–572. Springer, Heidelberg (2012). https://doi.org/10.1007/978-3-642-31585-5_50
12. Katz, J., Koo, C.: On expected constant-round protocols for byzantine agreement. J. Comput. Syst. Sci. **75**(2), 91–112 (2009)
13. Kondi, Y., Ravi, D.: Separating broadcast from cheater identification. IACR Cryptol. ePrint Arch. p. 52 (2025). https://eprint.iacr.org/2025/052
14. Loss, J., Nielsen, J.B.: Early stopping for any number of corruptions. In: Joye, M., Leander, G. (eds.) Advances in Cryptology – EUROCRYPT 2024. EUROCRYPT 2024. LNCS, vol. 14653, pp. 457–488. Springer, Cham (2024). https://doi.org/10.1007/978-3-031-58734-4_16
15. Scholl, P., Simkin, M., Siniscalchi, L.: Multiparty computation with covert security and public verifiability. In: Dachman-Soled, D. (ed.) 3rd Conference on Information-Theoretic Cryptography, ITC 2022. LIPIcs, vol. 230, pp. 8:1–8:13. Schloss Dagstuhl - Leibniz-Zentrum für Informatik (2022)
16. Wan, J., Xiao, H., Devadas, S., Shi, E.: Round-efficient byzantine broadcast under strongly adaptive and majority corruptions. In: Pass, R., Pietrzak, K. (eds.) TCC 2020. LNCS, vol. 12550, pp. 412–456. Springer, Cham (2020). https://doi.org/10.1007/978-3-030-64375-1_15
17. Yamashita, K., Yasunaga, K.: Rational broadcast protocols against timid adversaries. In: Fu, J., Kroupa, T., Hayel, Y. (eds.) Decision and Game Theory for Security. GameSec 2023. LNCS, vol. 14167, pp. 277–293. Springer, Cham (2023). https://doi.org/10.1007/978-3-031-50670-3_14

Vulnerability Detection

WiperSentinel: HPC Based Wiper Detection with Enhanced AutoEncoder

Shiva Agarwal(✉), Suvadeep Hajra, Ayantika Chatterjee, and Debdeep Mukhopadhyay

Indian Institute of Technology Kharagpur, Kharagpur, India
shivaagarwal793@gmail.com, ayantika@atdc.iitkgp.ac.in, debdeep@cse.iitkgp.ac.in

Abstract. Malware presents significant challenges to cybersecurity by exploiting system vulnerabilities, compromising sensitive data, disrupting operations, and rapidly evolving to evade traditional detection methods. Many types of malware, such as wipers, are challenging to detect due to their low computational footprint. This low activity level often causes existing detection methods, including those based on hardware performance counters (HPCs), to struggle. This paper investigates the impact of ransomware and wipers on various HPCs. Our study shows that wiper demands minimal computational activity due to its stealthy behaviour, which mostly affects only a small subset of HPCs, while most remain largely unaffected. Leveraging this insight, we propose improvements to supervised and unsupervised malware detection methods. For supervised detection, we introduce an ensemble-based algorithm to identify the most sensitive features (i.e., HPCs), leading to a 98% in-detection accuracy. For unsupervised detection, we propose replacing the commonly used Mean Squared Error (MSE) loss with Maximum Absolute Error (MAE) loss in an autoencoder-based framework, making the reconstruction loss more sensitive to the few HPCs heavily impacted by malware. Experimental results demonstrate that using MAE loss enables consistent detection of ransomware and wipers, whereas MSE loss often fails to detect wipers effectively.

Keywords: Ransomware · Wiper · Autoencoder · Machine Learning for Malware Analysis · Maximum Absolute Error

1 Introduction

In the ever-evolving landscape of cybersecurity, malicious software, commonly known as *malware*, has emerged as a pervasive and formidable threat. On average, an astonishing 560,000 new malware variants are detected each day [16], each crafted with the intent to harm, exploit, or compromise computer systems, networks, and users. Among the most dangerous and disruptive forms of malware are *ransomware* and *wiper malware*, both of which pose a critical threat to individuals and organizations by targeting one of their most valuable assets: data [20].

Y. Kim et al. (Eds.): CANS 2025, LNCS 16351, pp. 405–424, 2026.
https://doi.org/10.1007/978-981-95-4434-9_19

Ransomware has become the most financially damaging and widespread cyber threat in recent years. It operates by encrypting victims' data and demanding a ransom for its release, often paralyzing operations in the process [15]. Alarmingly, every minute, four organizations fall victim to ransomware, underscoring the scale and frequency of these attacks. In 2022 alone, over 236 million ransomware incidents were recorded globally, with the average cost of a single breach soaring to $4.54 million [13]. The threat has only intensified; in the first quarter of 2025, ransomware attacks surged by 126% worldwide, with North America accounting for 62% of these incidents. The Consumer Goods & Services sector was the most heavily targeted, though critical sectors like education, healthcare, government, and manufacturing [11] were also significantly impacted.

In parallel, a more insidious threat is gaining ground—**wiper malware**, sometimes referred to as *decoy ransomware* [18]. Wipers are increasingly used as tools of sabotage, particularly in the context of geopolitical conflicts and attacks on critical infrastructure such as energy grids, water systems, and telecommunications networks [1]. A prominent example of the use of wiper malware occurred during the recent Russia-Ukraine conflict [10], where several attacks were attributed to state-sponsored actors employing such tools to disable critical infrastructure and disrupt communication systems.

Despite the growing prevalence of wiper attacks, existing detection mechanisms remain limited, largely due to the malware's low computational footprint and lack of typical computational signatures like encryption or decryption routines [5]. Unlike ransomware, which performs noticeable operations on a system, wipers are stealthy, executing destructive actions with minimal trace. This stealth presents a significant challenge for cybersecurity defences [3], necessitating the development of advanced detection techniques tailored to the unique characteristics of wiper malware.

This paper explores the rising threat of wiper malware, its evolving tactics, and the urgent need for more effective detection methodologies to safeguard critical systems and organisational data in an increasingly hostile cyber environment.

Motivation: Detecting wiper malware presents a significant challenge due to its inherently stealthy behaviour. To address this critical limitation, our research explores the use of hardware performance counters (HPCs), low-level system indicators capable of capturing granular performance data of a running system.

During our analysis, we observed that HPC features associated with the Input-Output Memory Management Unit (IOMMU) were significantly influenced during wiper attacks. This unique behaviour offered an important clue: despite wiper malware's minimal system activity, its interaction with certain hardware-level components, such as memory management, can leave behind subtle but detectable traces. This discovery motivated us to pursue a more generalized detection strategy that could identify both ransomware and wiper malware through a common framework.

Our Contributions: In this research, we propose a novel, hybrid malware detection framework that efficiently leverages both supervised and unsupervised machine learning techniques to detect known and zero-day malware, including stealthy variants like wipers. The main contributions of this work are summarized as follows:

- **New HPC Features for Wiper Detection:** Traditional HPC-based detection methods often fall short when identifying low-footprint malware such as wipers. Through a detailed empirical analysis, we discovered that while wipers do not significantly alter conventional CPU-bound HPCs, they do trigger noticeable activity in the IOMMU—a key component of the kernel's Performance Monitoring Unit (PMU). This observation forms the foundation of our detection strategy, as it reveals subtle, yet detectable, traces left by wipers during their interaction with hardware-level memory management.
- **Ensemble Feature Selection for Optimized Supervised Learning:** To exploit the discovered HPC behavioural patterns of wipers, we design an ensemble feature selection algorithm that identifies the most discriminative HPCs affected by both wipers and ransomware. These selected features are then used to train a supervised machine learning (SML) framework. Our approach not only enhances the classification accuracy to 98% (which is more than an 60% improvement of previously proposed methods) but also reduces detection latency to <1 s for known malware (where previous approach requires around 5 s for the same), significantly outperforming prior models in both speed and precision.
- **Enhancing Autoencoder Sensitivity via Max Absolute Loss:** Supervised models often struggle with unknown or zero-day threats. To address this, we adopt an unsupervised approach using autoencoders, which are well-suited for anomaly detection. Since wipers impact a limited set of HPCs, the commonly used Mean Squared Error (MSE) reconstruction loss in autoencoders performs poorly in detecting wipers. We propose to use Max Absolute Error (MAE) loss in the autoencoder framework, making it more sensitive to the few impacted HPCs, which makes it possible to detect subtle anomalies such as wipers that MSE might overlook. This enhancement allows successful classification of both ransomware and wipers within 4 s (which is a 30% reduction compared to previously proposed methods).
- **Hybrid Supervised-Unsupervised Malware Detection Framework:** The proposed hybrid detection framework combines the advantages of supervised and unsupervised learning paradigms. Rapid and accurate classification of known malware by SML framework and zero-day malware classification by autoencoder. This combined Supervised-Unsupervised Machine Learning (SUML) framework delivers comprehensive protection with both speed and adaptability, addressing a critical gap in modern malware detection systems.

Organization: The rest of the paper is organized as follows: Sect. 2 contains the related work highlighting the limitation of prior works in detecting wiper malware. In Sect. 3, we introduce the workings of wiper malware and HPCs targeted by it. Section 4 proposes a hybrid framework for HPC-based malware detection. Our experimental results are presented in Sect. 5, underlining the effectiveness of our framework. Finally, Sect. 6 concludes our paper.

2 Related Works

Malware detection has traditionally relied on antivirus (AV) software, which, despite its widespread deployment, faces numerous limitations. AV systems typically operate based on static analysis—identifying known malicious patterns or instruction sequences within binaries [12]. However, this approach is increasingly ineffective against modern malware that employs polymorphism, metamorphism, and obfuscation techniques to evade detection. For example, the `AnserverBot` malware family demonstrated 187 functionally equivalent yet syntactically diverse variants, rendering static detection obsolete without continuous database updates.

Moreover, AV software itself is susceptible to exploitation. A prominent case is the **CVE-2022-27534** vulnerability in Kaspersky products [8], which allowed arbitrary code execution through a flaw in the data parsing module. Such weaknesses underscore the need for more robust and proactive detection techniques.

Hardware-based detection has emerged as a promising alternative. Demme et al. (2013) [7] introduced the use of Hardware Performance Counters (HPCs) special-purpose CPU registers monitoring low-level microarchitectural events—for malware detection. By collecting time-series HPC data from 503 malware and 210 benign programs across Linux and Android platforms, and applying machine learning classifiers such as Decision Trees, KNN, Random Forest, and FANN, they achieved up to 82.3% accuracy in identifying malware behaviors.

Building upon this foundation, Patel et al. (2017) [17] implemented HPC-based detection on FPGA boards. Their objective was to evaluate trade-offs in logic area, power consumption, and latency. Using models such as multilayer perceptrons and logistic regression, they attained nearly 90% accuracy. Their research emphasised that random forests offer superior accuracy-to-area trade-offs compared to more complex neural models. They concluded that four carefully selected HPC features suffice for real-time classification with minimal overhead.

Ransomware has gained prominence as a major cyber threat, prompting focused research into its detection. Alam et al. (2019) [2] proposed a novel framework employing Time and frequency-informed autoencoders. Using LSTM-based autoencoders, they collected HPC metrics such as instructions, cache-references, cache-misses, branches, and branch-misses at 10 ms intervals. They successfully detected several ransomware families within a reasonable span of time. Their dual-autoencoder framework—one for initial detection and another to distinguish ransomware from benign disk encryption—leveraged time-domain and frequency-domain analysis using a 3-sigma threshold. The method reduced false positives and demonstrated resilience to novel variants due to its unsupervised learning nature.

Despite its advantages, the key limitation of the method proposed in [2] was its significantly higher detection latency. To address this, Anand et al. (2023) [19]

improved detection speeds using 9th-generation Intel CPUs supporting up to 10 HPC features. Utilizing the Boruta feature selection algorithm, they selected nine critical counters such as `L1.dcache.loads`, `dTLB.loads`, `L1.dcache.stores`, and `cpu.migrations`. With data collected over a 5-s window in 100 ms intervals, their AdaBoost classifier achieved 92.68% accuracy. This model not only improved performance for ransomware detection but was also extended to wipers.

However, their approach remains significantly limited in wiper detection, achieving only 60% accuracy, with 10 out of 25 samples misclassified as benign. This is a significant concern as wipers often masquerade as ransomware by displaying misleading ransom notes while their true intent is to destroy data.

Wiper malware is particularly insidious due to its low computational footprint and destructive intent [21]. Unlike ransomware, which typically aims at financial gain, wipers target critical systems—e.g., government agencies and infrastructure—causing irreparable damage. Ukraine's critical systems have been prime targets, highlighting the need for faster, more accurate detection mechanisms.

Another notable approach by Hirano et al. (2022) [12] involved using live-forensic hypervisors to extract low-level memory access patterns, instead of high-level information like API calls or process IDs, which are inconsistent across real and virtual environments. Their dataset, however, was limited to just four malware (Three Ransomware and One Wiper) samples, and the differences between virtualized and real system behaviors limit generalizability.

These observations motivate a deeper exploration of HPC-based detection for wipers.

3 Preliminaries

3.1 Wiper

Wiper malware is a class of malicious software designed to permanently destroy data on a victim's system, making recovery extremely difficult or impossible [18].

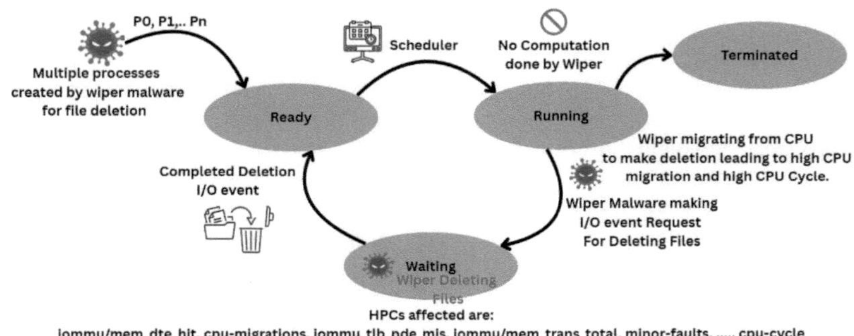

Fig. 1. Wiper Process flow Diagram

Our investigation revealed that wiper malware exhibits significant interaction with Input/Output Memory Management Unit (IOMMU), rather than typical processor-intensive metrics such as cache or instruction counters. This behavior aligns with the process state shown in Fig. 1, where wiper-invoked processes frequently transition between *running*, *waiting* (I/O wait), and *ready* (post-I/O completion) states [14]. These transitions occur during I/O operations, where the system awaits data-related operations [9].

3.2 The perf Tool: Performance Counter Interface

The Linux `perf` tool for acquiring HPC data [6]. `perf` offers a flexible command-line interface for collecting performance statistics from both user and kernel space. It enables monitoring of hardware events, software events, hardware cache events, and kernel Performance Monitoring Unit (PMU) events.

Table 1. HPC Features Monitored Using `perf`

Hardware Event	Software Event	Hardware Cache Event
1. branch-instructions	9. alignment-faults	21. L1-dcache-loads
2. branch-misses	10. bpf-output	22. L1-dcache-load-misses
3. cache-misses	11. duration_time	23.L1-dcache-prefetches
4. cache-references	12. context-switches	24. l1-icache-loads
5. cpu-cycles	13. cpu-clock	25. l1-icache-load-misses
6.instructions	14. cpu-migrations	26. branch-loads
7. stalled-cycles-backend	15. dummy	27. branch-load-misses
8. stalled-cycles-frontend	16. emulation-faults	28. dTLB-loads
	17. major-faults	29. dTLB-load-misses
	18. minor-faults	30. iTLB-load-misses
	19. task-clock	31. iTLB-loads
	20. page-faults	

Kernel PMU Event	
32. msr/tsc/	33. amd_iommu/cmd_processed/
34. amd_iommu/cmd_processed_inv/	35. amd_iommu/ign_rd_wr_mmio_1ff8h/
36. amd_iommu/int_dte_hit/	37. amd_iommu/int_dte_mis/
38. amd_iommu/mem_dte_hit/	39. amd_iommu/mem_dte_mis/
40. amd_iommu/mem_iommu_tlb_pde_hit/	41. amd_iommu/mem_iommu_tlb_pde_mis/
42. amd_iommu/mem_iommu_tlb_pte_hit/	43. amd_iommu/mem_iommu_tlb_pte_mis/
44. amd_iommu/mem_pass_excl/	45. amd_iommu/mem_pass_pretrans/
46. amd_iommu/mem_pass_untrans/	47. amd_iommu/mem_target_abort/
48. amd_iommu/mem_trans_total/	49. amd_iommu/page_tbl_read_gst/
50. amd_iommu/page_tbl_read_nst/	51. amd_iommu/page_tbl_read_tot/
52. amd_iommu/smi_blk/	53. amd_iommu/smi_recv/
54. amd_iommu/tlb_inv/	55. amd_iommu/vapic_int_guest/
56. amd_iommu/vapic_int_non_guest/	57. msr/aperf/
58. msr/irperf/	59. msr/mperf/

The complete list of HPC features monitored during profiling is shown in Table 1. The monitored events are classified into four categories: hardware events, software events, hardware cache events, and kernel PMU events. The `perf stat` command is used to collect the above performance statistics over periodic intervals:

```
perf stat -e branch-instructions,...,amd_iommu_0/ppr_requests/ -a
```

Here, the `-e` flag specifies the events to monitor, and the `-a` flag ensures system-wide (all-core) data acquisition. The ellipsis represents the inclusion of all previously listed events.

3.3 HPC-Based Malware Detection

HPC-based malware detection utilizes low-level hardware performance counter monitoring to identify abnormal system behavior at runtime. HPCs are specialized registers embedded within modern CPUs that record microarchitectural events such as cache misses, branch instructions, memory accesses, and CPU cycles [4]. These counters offer a high-resolution performance profile of executing applications with minimal overhead, making them particularly useful for real-time and stealth-aware security applications.

By collecting HPC traces from both benign and malicious executions, a dataset is constructed that reflects the distinct execution patterns of each class. Machine learning algorithms are then employed to model these patterns and identify deviations indicative of malware activity. Depending on the detection scenario, either supervised or unsupervised learning approaches may be adopted.

Supervised Machine Learning: In this approach, models are trained on labeled datasets consisting of known benign and malicious samples. These models learn to distinguish between classes based on prior examples and offer fast and highly accurate predictions on previously seen types of malware. However, their effectiveness diminishes against zero-day or unknown threats due to the lack of representative training data.

Unsupervised Machine Learning: To address the limitations of supervised methods, unsupervised techniques such as autoencoders are employed. These models are trained exclusively on benign samples to learn normal system behavior. During inference, they flag deviations from this learnt behaviour as anomalies—potentially indicating malware presence. Although autoencoders are effective in detecting zero-day threats, their reliance on time-series input introduces latency in classification. Nevertheless, their robustness in anomaly detection makes them an essential component of hybrid malware detection frameworks.

4 Proposed Framework for HPC-Based Wiper Detection

The supervised HPC-based wiper detection methods can perform early detection. However, it cannot perform zero-day detection of wiper. On the other hand,

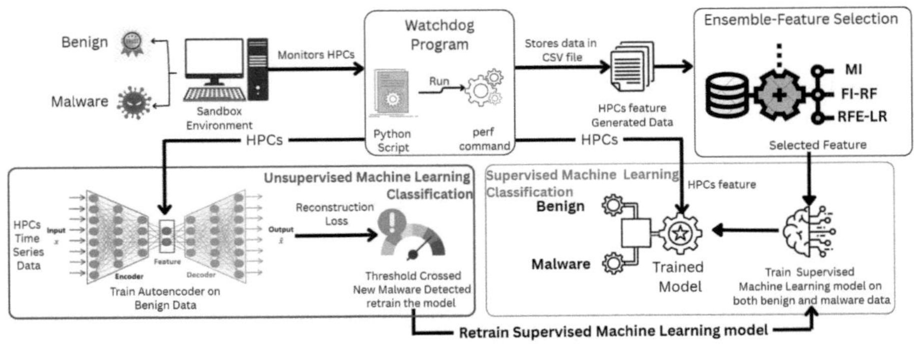

Fig. 2. Proposed Model Architecture

unsupervised methods are capable of performing zero-day detection though they take longer time to detect the presence of wipers.

To take the advantages of both supervised and unsupervised methods, we proposed a novel framework for HPC-based wiper detection shown in Fig. 2 that includes the following components:

- **Sandbox Environment:** The sandbox environment provides a secure, isolated space for testing and experimenting with software or applications. HPCs of the environment are continuously monitored by a watchdog program to detect the functioning of the running program.
- **Watch Dog Program:** It is a script to facilitate continuous profiling. This script repeatedly invokes appropriate commands to measure the values of HPCs of the sandbox environment. These values are then sent as the input to the downstream machine learning models for detection of the presence of malwares.
- **Ensemble Feature Selection (EFS):** The feature selection algorithm selects a small subset of HPCs (features) from all HPCs based on their improtance. The selected features are then sent to the supervised machine learning model for the detection of malware.
- **Supervised Machine Learning Model (SML):** The SML is used to classify the input features (i.e., the values of the HPCs selected by the EFS) into benign or malware. The SML provides a way to early detection of malware.
- **Unsupervised Machine Learning Model (UML):** Though the SML can detect the presence of malware faster, it often strugle at zero-day detection. An unsupervised machine learning model (autoencoder trained on benign data) is used for zero-day detection of the malware.

In the rest of the section, we provide the details of the three main components of the framework, namely EFS, SML and UML.

4.1 Ensemble Feature Selection (EFS)

The efficacy of any HPC-based malware detection technique heavily depends on the selection of relevant HPC features. Prior research primarily focused on detecting ransomware by leveraging a limited set of HPC features. These features were predominantly tied to computational activities such as instruction count, cache misses, and branch predictions metrics that are heavily influenced during encryption-based malicious activities typical of ransomware.

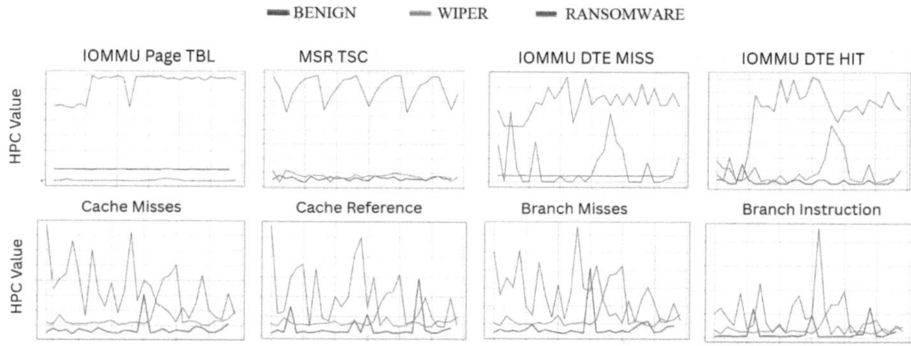

Fig. 3. HPC Feature Plot for Benign, Wiper and Ransomware

However, wiper malware operates with a fundamentally different behavioral footprint. Unlike ransomware, which imposes high computational overhead due to cryptographic operations, wipers are designed to execute file deletion operations with minimal CPU usage. Consequently, their behavior leaves a much subtler trace in traditional HPC metrics.

For instance, Fig. 3 plots values of several HPCs for the benign programs, wipers, and ransomware over a duration of time. The figure shows that the ransomware has impacted most of the plotted HPCs significantly, making those easily distinguishable from those of the benign program. However, except for some HPCs (i.e., MSR TSC), the HPC plots of wiper is not significantly distinguishable from the benign program. Therefore, HPCs sensitive to a wiper are largely different from those to ransomware.

Figures 1 and 3 demonstrate that wiper programs exhibit relatively low activity in computational counters. Instead, they significantly influence kernel-level Input/Output operations. This is evident through changes in specific Kernel PMU events, particularly those associated with the IOMMU. This nuanced understanding of wiper behavior forms the foundation of our classification approach. We introduce an expanded and more representative set of HPC features that account for both computational and I/O-related activities. This is crucial for detecting stealthy malware such as wipers, which tend to operate under the radar of conventional CPU-centric detection mechanisms.

The identification of highly discriminative HPCs is crucial for the reliable detection of stealthy malware like wipers. Unlike ransomware, which produces significant computational signatures, wipers often have minimal hardware-level footprints and interact more with the I/O memory subsystems.

To address this, we propose an ensemble-based feature selection strategy, formalized in Algorithm 1.

We begin with the full set of 59 HPC features shown in Table 1, denoted as $F = \{H_1, H_2, \ldots, H_{59}\}$.

Algorithm 1. Ensemble-Based HPC Feature Selection for Wiper Detection

Require: Set of HPC features $F = \{H_1, H_2, \ldots, H_{59}\}$
Ensure: Selected subset of informative features F^*
Initialize empty lists: $F_{MI} \leftarrow [\,]$, $F_{FI} \leftarrow [\,]$, $F_{RFE} \leftarrow [\,]$
Initialize an empty dictionary $Votes \leftarrow \{\}$
Step 1: Apply Individual Feature Selection Techniques
Apply Mutual Information (MI) on F to obtain top 10 features F_{MI}
Apply Feature Importance using Random Forest (FI-RF) to get top 10 features F_{FI}
Apply Recursive Feature Elimination with Logistic Regression to get top 10 features F_{RFE}
Step 2: Aggregate Features Using Voting
for each feature f in F **do**
    if f in $F_{MI} \cup F_{FI} \cup F_{RFE}$ **then**
        $Votes[f] \leftarrow 1$
    else
        $Votes[f] \leftarrow 0$
    end if
end for
Step 3: Return the Selected Features
$F^* \leftarrow \{f \in Votes \mid Votes[f]{=}1\}$
return F^*

To capture diverse views of feature relevance, we apply three distinct feature selection techniques: MI, FI-LR and RFE-LR.

Mutual Information (MI). As shown Eq. 1 measures the dependency between an HPC feature H_i and the target Y which contains benign and malware information:

$$I(H_i; Y) = \sum_{h_i \in X_i} \sum_{y \in Y} p(h_i, y) \log \left(\frac{p(h_i, y)}{p(h_i)p(y)} \right) \quad (1)$$

where:

- $p(h_i, y)$: Joint probability distribution of H_i and Y
- $p(h_i)$, $p(y)$: Marginal probability distributions

Our Goal: Select features H_i with the highest mutual information $I(H_i; Y)$.

Feature Importance with Random Forest (FI-RF). FI-RF is based on the average decrease in Gini impurity caused by a feature across all trees. The FI is calculated based on the formula described in Eq. 2:

$$FI(H_i) = \frac{1}{T}\sum_{t=1}^{T}\sum_{n\in N_i^{(t)}} \frac{w_n^{(t)}\Delta i_n^{(t)}}{\sum_{n'\in N^{(t)}} w_{n'}^{(t)}} \tag{2}$$

where:

- T: Number of trees in the forest
- $N_i^{(t)}$: Set of nodes in tree t where feature X_i is used
- $w_n^{(t)}$: Weighted number of samples at node n
- $\Delta i_n^{(t)}$: Decrease in impurity due to the split at node n

Our Goal: Rank and select features with the highest $FI(H_i)$.

Recursive Feature Elimination with Logistic Regression (RFE-LR). In logistic regression, the importance of the features H_i in Eq. 3 is based on the absolute value of the model coefficients:

$$\text{Importance}(H_i) = |w_i| \tag{3}$$

where w_i be the coefficient of feature H_i in the logistic regression model.

RFE Process: The RFE process consists of the following steps:

1. Train the model on the full set of features.
2. Compute $|w_i|$ for all features.
3. Remove the feature with the smallest $|w_i|$.
4. Repeat until the desired number of features is retained.

From each of the three methods, we select the top 10 ranked features and aggregate the results. To ensure robustness, we apply majority voting across the selections: any feature that appears in at least once in the three lists is considered highly informative and is included in the final subset F^*. This process is formalized in Algorithm 1.

This ensemble-based voting mechanism increases confidence in the selected features and minimizes method-specific biases. It is particularly effective for wiper detection because it captures both computational and Input/Output Memory Management Unit (IOMMU) related behaviors, which are otherwise overlooked in traditional techniques that emphasize CPU-intensive events.

4.2 Supervised Machine Learning Model (SML)

Having established a robust ensemble-based feature selection strategy in the previous Sect. 4.1, the next critical phase in our proposed framework is the classification of malware using a supervised machine learning classifier. The classifier takes the features selected by EFS module as input, and output whether the features are related to any benign program or a wiper. The classifier is trained using a labelled dataset comprising benign and wiper samples. The wiper samples are collected by executing the wipers from the existing database. As the supervised classifier, we employed the following widely used ensemble of the models: Random Forest (RF), Support Vector Machine (SVM), K-Nearest Neighbors (KNN), Classification and Regression Tree (CART), Gradient Boosting Machine (GBM), AdaBoost.

As stated earlier, the supervised classifier offers the advantage of rapid and accurate classification for known wiper samples, especially those belonging to previously encountered families. This makes it ideal for real-time monitoring in environments with well-characterized threat landscapes. However, they are poor at detecting previously unencountered wipers (zero-day detection). For such zero-day detection, we use a autoencoder-based unsupervised model, which is discussed in the next Subsect. 4.3.

4.3 Unsupervised Machine Learning Model (UML)

The RATAFIA framework proposed in [2] has utilized an autoencoder system for malware detection. The autoencoder-based unsupervised detection method works on the fact that autoencoders are good at anomaly detection. More precisely, an autoencoder is trained to reconstruct its input at its output using a set of benign samples. Therefore, if it encounters a benign sample at its input during test time, it can regenerate the sample at its output with very low reconstruction error. However, if it is tested with a malicious sample, it may lead to a high reconstruction error flagging the presence of the malware. Note that the UML takes all the features as input instead of the features selected by EFS. This is becuase, a novel wiper might be sensitive to an HPC feature that is undetected by the EFS module, which is trained on the labeled dataset.

Mean Squared Error (MSE) described in Eq. 4 is commonly used as the reconstruction loss in autoencoder-based anomaly detection. More specifically, let $\{x_1, x_2, \dots, x_n\}$ be the n input feature vectors (each of those are d-dimensional vector – one dimension for each HPC feature).

Let $\hat{x}_i$ be the output of the autoencoder for the i-th input feature vector x_i. Then for MSE loss, the recostruction loss for the i-th input feature vector is computed as $||\epsilon_i||_2^2 = ||x_i - \hat{x}_i||_2^2$, $\epsilon_i = x_i - \hat{x}_i$ is error vector for the i sample and $||\epsilon_i||_2^2$ denotes the squared l_2 norm or Eucleadian norm of the vector ϵ_i. The reconstruction loss over all samples is computed as

$$\text{MSE} = \frac{1}{nd}\sum_{i=1}^{n} ||\epsilon_i||_2^2 = \frac{1}{nd}\sum_{i=1}^{n} ||x_i - \hat{x}_i||_2^2 \tag{4}$$

As stated earlier, a wiper malware effects only a small subset of HPC features while leaving all others almost unperturbed. For instant, Fig. 3 shows that the HPC features *MSR TSC* and *IOMMU DTE MISS* are highly effected by the wiper, while its affect on the remaining HPC features is not much distinguishable from benign samples. However, while using MSE as the reconstruction loss, it takes the mean of squared error over all HPC features, resulting into lower reconstruction error (since only a few high value is averaged with a large number of small values). Therefore, we used Maximum Absolute Error (MAE) described in Eq. 5 as the reconstruction loss in our autoencoder model. More specifically, for MAE, the reconstruction loss over all samples is computed as

$$\text{MAE} = \frac{1}{n}\sum_{i=1}^{n} ||\epsilon_i||_\infty = \frac{1}{n}\sum_{i=1}^{n} ||x_i - \hat{x}_i||_\infty \tag{5}$$

where $||\epsilon_i||_\epsilon$ denotes the maximum norm of the vector ϵ_i[1].

In the next section, we present and analyse our experimental results.

5 Results and Discussion

In this section, we provide the performance analysis of our ESA, SML and UML modules. We also compare their performance with that of the previous approaches. In the next section, we provide the experimental setup.

Experimental Setup. All experiments were conducted on a system equipped with an AMD Ryzen 5 5600H processor, 8 GB of RAM, a 512 GB SSD, running on the Ubuntu 18.04 platform. We first collected a dataset consisting of 242 malware samples (containing wiper and ransomware) and 183 benign samples. A brief list of malware samples with SHA 256 Hash is shown in Table 2. All malware and benign programs are run in the Cuckoo sandbox environment. The HPCs of the executing program are monitored with the Python-based watchdog script, which calls the perf command repeatedly with a timeout every 100 ms.

Table 2. Brief List of Malware Programs with SHA 256 Hash

Name	SHA 256 Hash
WisperKill	191ca4833351e2e82cb080a42c4848cfbc4b1f3e97250f2700eff4e97cf72019
Wiper Gate	a196c6b8ffcb97ffb276d04f354696e2391311db3841ae16c8c9f56f36a38e92
Acid Rain	9b4dfaca873961174ba935fddaf696145afe7bbf5734509f95feb54f3584fd9a
Not Petya	027cc450ef5f8c5f653329641ec1fed91f694e0d229928963b30f6b0d7d3a745
Issac Wiper	13037b749aa4b1eda538fda26d6ac41c8f7b1d02d83f47b0d187dd645154e033
Hermetic	0385eeab00e946a302b24a91dea4187c1210597b8e17cd9e2230450f5ece21da
Double Zero	3b2e708eaa4744c76a633391cf2c983f4a098b46436525619e5ea44e105355fe
Candy Wip.	a294620543334a721a2ae8eaaf9680a0786f4b9a216d75b55cfd28f39e9430ea
Locky	afec2b2af3ace2c478382f9366f6cbc9b9579f2c9a4273150fc33a2ccd59284c
WannaCry	07c44729e2c570b37db695323249474831f5861d45318bf49ccf5d2f5c8ea1cd
petya	027cc450ef5f8c5f653329641ec1fed91f694e0d229928963b30f6b0d7d3a745

[1] $||\epsilon_i||_\infty$ is equivalent to taking the absolute value of each element of the vector ϵ_i and selecting the maximum among all.

5.1 Performance Analysis of FSA

As stated earlier, three feature selection techniques, namely MI, FI-RF, and RFE-LR, are used for identifying discriminative features. We show the features selected by MI and FI-RF in Figs. 4 and 5 respectively.

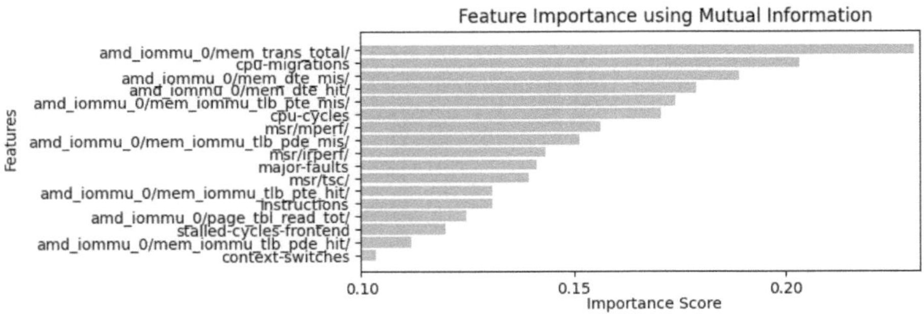

Fig. 4. Feature ranking using MI.

In Fig. 4, we observe that IOMMU events such as MEM Trans, DTE miss, and DTE hit have received high scores from the MI feature selector, underscoring their importance in wiper detection. These features also significantly overlap with those selected by FI-RF (as shown in Fig. 5) and by RFE-LR (as shown in Table 3).

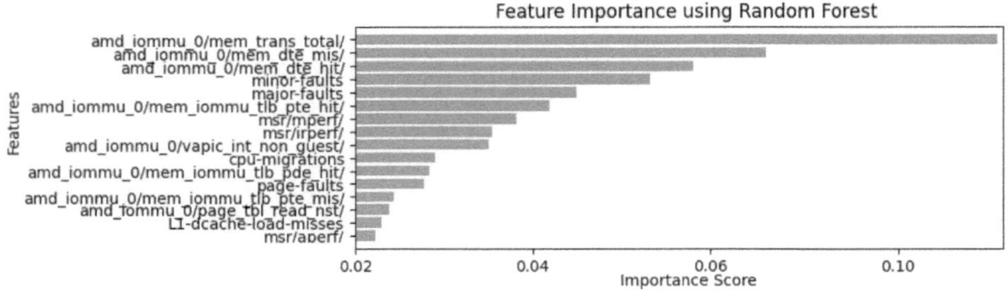

Fig. 5. Feature ranking using FI-RF.

The summary of the top 10 selected features by the three feature selectors is shown in Table 3. We consider only ten features for our analysis because after 10 features the importance score is reduced drastically. After selecting top 10 features using each of the three feature selector, we applied Algorithm 1 for generating the final set of features. The algorithm finally returned 16 most critical features, which are summarized in Table 3.

Table 3. Features Selected by Different Methods

MI		FI-RF		RFE-LR
Feature	**Score**	**Feature**	**Score**	**Feature**
amd_iommu/	0.232	amd_iommu/mem	0.111	major-faults
mem_trans_total/		_trans_total/		iTLB-load-misses
cpu-migrations	0.205	amd_iommu/mem	0.066	iTLB-loads
amd_iommu/	0.199	_dte_mis/		amd_iommu/
mem_dte_hit/		amd_iommu/mem	0.058	int_dte_mis/
amd_iommu/	0.189	_dte_hit/		amd_iommu/mem
mem_dte_mis/		minor-faults	0.053	_dte_hit/
major-faults	0.175	major-faults	0.045	amd_iommu/mem
amd_iommu/mem_	0.174	amd_iommu/mem_	0.042	_dte_mis/
iommu_tlb_pte_mis/		iommu_tlb_pte_hit/		amd_iommu/mem
cpu-cycles	0.171	msr/mperf/	0.038	_iommu_tlb_pde_
msr/mperf/	0.156	msr/irperf/	0.035	mis/amd_iommu/mem
amd_iommu/mem_	0.144	amd_iommu/vapic	0.035	_trans_total/
iommu_tlb_pde_mis/		_int_non_guest/		msr/irperf/
msr/irperf/	0.143	cpu-migrations	0.029	msr/mperf/

Final list of HPC Features by Algorithm 1	
amd_iommu/mem_dte_hit/	msr/mperf/
cpu-migrations	amd_iommu/mem_iommu_tlb_pde_mis/
amd_iommu/mem_trans_total/	iTLB-loads
minor-faults	amd_iommu/vapic_int_non_guest/
amd_iommu/mem_dte_mis/	amd_iommu/mem_iommu_tlb_pte_mis/
msr/irperf/	amd_iommu/int_dte_mis/
amd_iommu/mem_iommu_tlb_pte_hit/	cpu-cycles
major-faults	iTLB-load-misses

5.2 Performance Evaluation of SML

The performance of various machine learning models with individual feature selection techniques MI, FI-RF, RFE-LR are summarised in Table 4. Feature selection based on RFE-LR generally achieved the best performance across different SML classifiers, especially in terms of accuracy and reduced execution time. As seen from the above results in Table 4, we find that individual algorithms are not performing well, resulting accuracy between 80% to 92%. We find that RFE-LR with SVM classifier achieves the highest accuracy of 92%.

To improve the detection capability of SML-framework, we introduce ensemble feature selection Algorithm 1. The results in Table 5 show that the selected HPCs set shown in Table 3 outperform well against individual HPCs set of MI, FI-RF and RFE-LR. The ensemble and random forest models achieve the highest accuracy of 98% on malware classification.

The ensemble approach achieved superior performance, attaining an overall accuracy, precision, recall, and F1-score of 98%, demonstrating the effectiveness of the selected features in distinguishing between benign and malware samples with minimal false positives and false negatives.

Table 4. Model performance comparison with different feature selection methods.

Model	Accuracy (MI)	Accuracy (FI-RF)	Accuracy (RFE-LR)	Time (MI)	Time (FI-RF)	Time (RFE-LR)
Random Forest	0.91	0.92	0.92	0.1520	0.1624	0.1338
SVM	0.80	0.89	0.92	0.0249	0.0233	0.0202
KNN	0.81	0.82	0.90	0.0013	0.0011	0.0010
CART	0.80	0.89	0.91	0.0033	0.0041	0.0031
GBM	0.92	0.88	0.91	0.1281	0.1513	0.1388
AdaBoost	0.89	0.89	0.89	0.1551	0.1848	0.1543

Table 5. Performance comparison of models with final ensemble-selected features.

Model	Accuracy	Precision	Recall	F1-Score	Time (sec)
Ensemble Model	0.98	0.98	0.98	0.98	0.6283
Random Forest	0.98	0.98	0.98	0.98	0.1619
SVM	0.93	0.93	0.93	0.93	0.0310
KNN	0.86	0.87	0.86	0.86	0.0003
CART	0.89	0.89	0.89	0.89	0.0063
GBM	0.95	0.95	0.95	0.95	0.2383
AdaBoost	0.93	0.93	0.93	0.93	0.1740

5.3 Performance Evaluation of UML

The architecture of the autoencoder used in our experiment is detailed in Table 6. The architecture contains two LSTM layers, one working as an encoder and the other as a decoder. These encoders and decoders calculate the reconstruction loss of time series data to find anomalies.

Table 6. Model Architecture for Autoencoder

Working	Layer Type	Input Shape	Output Shape
Autoencoder 1			
Encoder	LSTM	(None, 100, 59)	(None, 100, 32)
Decoder	LSTM	(None, 100, 32)	(None, 100, 59)

In the RATAFIA [2] system, MSE is used as the reconstruction loss in the autoencoders to identify any anomaly in the HPC distribution caused by the malware. As discussed earlier, MSE reconstruction loss performs suboptimally

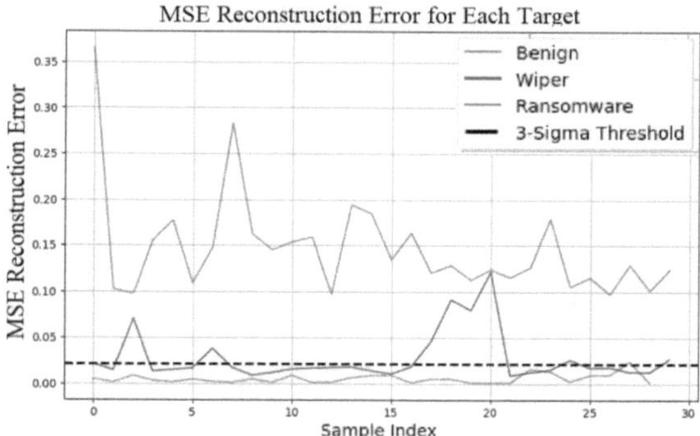

Fig. 6. Autoencoder reconstruction error using MSE loss for benign, ransomware, and wiper malware using the three-sigma threshold.

in scenarios where only a few performance counters are affected by the malware, which is typical for wipers. Further to illustrate the point, we trained the autoencoder used in [2] using MSE loss on a benign dataset. Then we utilized the trained autoencoder to plot the reconstruction error for the wiper and ransomware samples. From Fig. 6, it can be observed that while ransomware instances were successfully detected, the wiper malware remained undetected for most samples, which highlights the critical limitation for MSE.

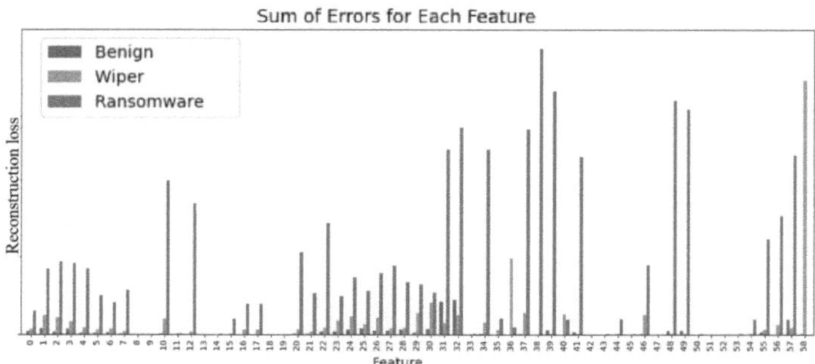

Fig. 7. Feature-wise reconstruction error comparison for benign, ransomware, and wiper malware samples.

For further investigation, the reconstruction error for each individual HPCs feature was plotted (Fig. 7). This analysis revealed that the wiper malware significantly alters only a few HPC features, leaving most HPCs almost unchanged. In particular, feature 58 is affected most. When using MSE, these few high reconstruction errors are averaged over lower errors, resulting to lower overall reconstruction error.

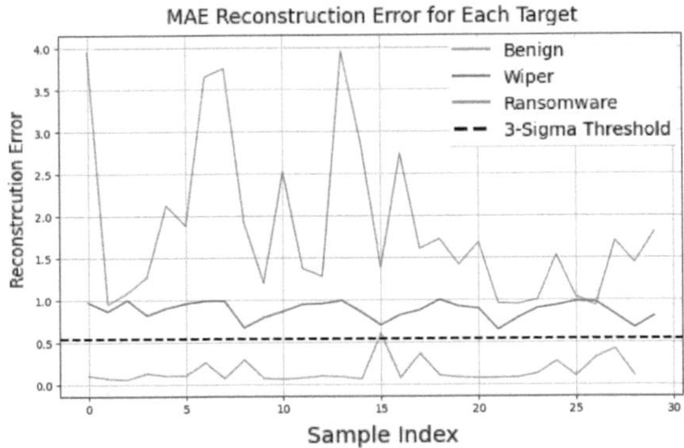

Fig. 8. Enhanced autoencoder performance after adopting Max Absolute Error, detecting both ransomware and wiper malware.

While using MAE as the reconstruction loss, it captures even if only a few features are significantly affected, while most of them remain almost unaffected. In Fig. 8, we plot the reconstruction error using MAE. The Figure shows that using the updated loss function, the autoencoder architecture successfully identified both ransomware and wiper malware in all the samples using 3σ threshold.

5.4 Performance Comparison

Table 7 presents a detailed comparison of our proposed methods and those proposed in [19] and [2]. The model proposed in [19] achieves fast detection times but struggles with accurately identifying wiper malware, reaching only 60% accuracy. Similarly, the model of [2] successfully detects ransomware but completely misses wiper detection, while taking approximately 5.313 s for classification. In contrast, our supervised model detects both ransomware and wiper with high

Table 7. Comparison of Malware Detection Techniques

Work	Ransomware Detection	Wiper Detection	Detection Time (sec)	Remarks
Mohan et al. [19]	Detected 92% Accuracy	Detected 60% Accuracy	<5 s	Faster, but limited for wiper detection
Alam et al. [2]	Detected	Not Detected	5.313 s	Good for ransomware, fails for wiper
Our Method (Supervised)	Detected 98% Accuracy	Detected 98% Accuracy	<1 s	High accuracy on known malware
Our Method (Unsupervised)	Detected	Detected	3.714 s	Robust against new/zero-day malware

accuracy, requiring less than one seconds for known malware detection. Furthermore, our unsupervised autoencoder-based model effectively identifies both ransomware and wiper in just 3.714 s, offering a significant improvement in speed and robustness for zero-day malware detection.

6 Conclusion

In this research, we leveraged the insight that malware activities typically do not affect all hardware performance counters uniformly. Based on this observation, we designed a robust ensemble-based feature selection algorithm to identify the most discriminative HPC features. Furthermore, we discovered that while wiper malware remains stealthy to conventional hardware events, it leaves detectable traces in the IOMMU, a component of the kernel's PMU events. This crucial finding enabled us to build a resilient supervised machine-learning model using the newly identified HPC features.

Additionally, we explored an unsupervised framework for wiper detection using autoencoders. Initially, we observed that the wiper malware's subtle changes resulted in low reconstruction errors, as the Mean Square Error (MSE) loss diluted the anomalies across features. To address this, we proposed using the Max Absolute Error (MAE), which effectively captures even minor deviations in specific HPCs. This approach significantly improves the detection accuracy, successfully identifying both wiper and ransomware. Finally, we propose a malware detection framework using a hybrid strategy of combining feature selection, supervised classification, and enhanced unsupervised detection providing a fast, accurate, and robust solution for zero-day malware detection.

References

1. Adamov, A.: Russian wipers in the cyberwar against Ukraine
2. Alam, M., Bhattacharya, S., Dutta, S., Sinha, S., Mukhopadhyay, D., Chattopadhyay, A.: Ratafia: ransomware analysis using time and frequency informed autoencoders. In: 2019 IEEE International Symposium on Hardware Oriented Security and Trust (HOST), pp. 218–227 (2019). https://doi.org/10.1109/HST.2019.8740837
3. Allegretta, M., Siracusano, G., Gonzalez, R., Gramaglia, M.: Are crowd-sourced cti datasets ready for supporting anti-cybercrime intelligence? Comput. Netw. **234**, 109920 (2023)
4. Ammons, G., Ball, T., Larus, J.R.: Exploiting hardware performance counters with flow and context sensitive profiling. ACM Sigplan Notices **32**(5), 85–96 (1997)
5. Biasini, N.: Ransomware or wiper? Lockergoga straddles the line (2019)
6. De Melo, A.C.: The new linux perf tools. In: Slides from Linux Kongress, vol. 18 (2010)
7. Demme, J., et al.: On the feasibility of online malware detection with performance counters. In: Proceedings of the 40th Annual International Symposium on Computer Architecture, pp. 559–570. ISCA '13, Association for Computing Machinery, New York, NY, USA (2013). https://doi.org/10.1145/2485922.2485970

8. Drovnikova, I., Popova, A.: Characteristics of security defects and analysis of the criticality of vulnerabilities in the software of automated systems of internal affairs agencies. Bulletin of the Dagestan State Technical University. Tech. Sci. **51**(1), 68–78 (2024)
9. Gilbert, S.: A programmable dynamic memory allocation system for input/output of digital data into standard computer memories at 40 megasamples/s. IEEE Trans. Comput. **100**(11), 1101–1109 (1976). Ballard, Hobrock, Wood
10. Guerrero-Saade, J.A.: Hermeticwiper—new destructive malware used in cyber attacks on Ukraine. Sentinel Labs (2022)
11. Guerrero-Saade, J.A., Van Amerongen, M.: Acidrain| a modem wiper rains down on Europe. Sentinel Labs **31** (2022)
12. Hirano, M., Kobayashi, R.: Machine learning-based ransomware detection using low-level memory access patterns obtained from live-forensic hypervisor. In: 2022 IEEE International Conference on Cyber Security and Resilience (CSR), pp. 323–330 (2022). https://doi.org/10.1109/CSR54599.2022.9850340
13. Imber, D.: The latest cyber crime statistics (updated april 2025) | aag it support (2025). https://aag-it.com/the-latest-cyber-crime-statistics/
14. Kornaros, G., Harteros, K., Christoforakis, I., Astrinaki, M.: I/O virtualization utilizing an efficient hardware system-level memory management unit. In: 2014 International Symposium on System-on-Chip (SoC), pp. 1–4. IEEE (2014)
15. Oz, H., Aris, A., Levi, A., Uluagac, A.S.: A survey on ransomware: evolution, taxonomy, and defense solutions. ACM Comput. Surv. (CSUR) **54**(11s), 1–37 (2022)
16. Palatty, N.J., Palatty, N.J.: 30+ malware statistics you need to know in 2025 (2025). https://www.getastra.com/blog/security-audit/malware-statistics
17. Patel, N., Sasan, A., Homayoun, H.: Analyzing hardware based malware detectors. In: Proceedings of the 54th Annual Design Automation Conference 2017. DAC '17, Association for Computing Machinery, New York, NY, USA (2017). https://doi.org/10.1145/3061639.3062202
18. Pitman, L., Crosier, W.: On the scale from ransomware to cyberterrorism: the cases of jbs USA, colonial pipeline and the wiperware attacks against Ukraine. J. Cyber Policy 1–21 (2024)
19. Putrevu, M.A., Putrevu, V.S.C., Shukla, S.K.: Early detection of ransomware activity based on hardware performance counters. In: Proceedings of the 2023 Australasian Computer Science Week, pp. 10–17. ACSW '23, Association for Computing Machinery, New York, NY, USA (2023). https://doi.org/10.1145/3579375.3579377
20. Ramsdell, K.A.W., Esbeck, K.E.: Evolution of ransomware. The Mitre Corporation (2021)
21. Ren, A., Liang, C., Hyug, I., Brohi, S., Jhanjhi, N.: A three-level ransomware detection and prevention mechanism. EAI Endorsed Trans. Energy Web 162691 (2020). https://doi.org/10.4108/eai.13-7-2018.162691

Attention-Based Code Summarization for Multi-label Vulnerability Detection

Maksuda Bilkis Baby[1], Md. Atabuzzaman[2], Md. Shajalal[3](✉), and Gunnar Stevens[3]

[1] University of Maryland Baltimore County, Maryland, USA
mstmakb1@umbc.edu
[2] Virginia Tech, Virginia, USA
atabuzzaman@vt.edu
[3] University of Siegen, Siegen, Germany
{md.shajalal,gunnar.stevens}@uni-siegen.de

Abstract. Vulnerabilities in source code can lead to a wide range of issues, such as privacy and security breaches, system crashes, data leaks, and unpredictable application behavior. These problems typically arise from improper handling of inputs, memory, or access control mechanisms. To address these challenges, we propose a novel Attention-based Code Summarization (ACS) approach for multi-label vulnerability detection in source code. Unlike traditional methods that are limited to binary or multi-class classification, our approach is designed to identify multiple types of vulnerabilities within a single code snippet—an essential capability, as real-world software often contains more than one vulnerability. Our method introduces a specialized, security-focused attention mechanism that utilizes vulnerability-specific queries to generate targeted representations for each vulnerability type. By extending pre-trained code models with a hierarchical summarization framework, we enable the creation of specialized representations tailored to different vulnerability categories. This design ensures a balance between general code understanding and precise vulnerability detection. Extensive evaluations on a multi-label vulnerability dataset show that our model outperforms existing baselines, especially for buffer-related vulnerabilities (e.g., CWE-119, CWE-120) and other complex security issues. Through comprehensive ablation studies, we validate the individual contributions of each architectural component, demonstrating the synergistic effects of our vulnerability-specific attention, security-focused summarization, and adaptive gating mechanisms. Furthermore, the attention visualization component of our model provides explainable outputs, helping security teams identify and understand the root causes of detected vulnerabilities. By enabling efficient and simultaneous detection of multiple vulnerability types, our approach significantly reduces the effort and time required to analyze and secure software systems.

Keywords: Multi-label Vulnerability Detection · Attention · Code Summarization · Security-focused Attention

Y. Kim et al. (Eds.): CANS 2025, LNCS 16351, pp. 425–447, 2026.
https://doi.org/10.1007/978-981-95-4434-9_20

1 Introduction

Software vulnerabilities refer to weaknesses or flaws in code that can be exploited to compromise the confidentiality, integrity, or availability of a system [11]. These vulnerabilities may arise from insecure coding practices, improper input validation, memory mismanagement, or incorrect access control configurations [27]. Common types include buffer overflows, SQL injection, cross-site scripting (XSS), and privilege escalation vulnerabilities [10]. The exploitation of such issues can lead to serious consequences, including data breaches, unauthorized access, service disruptions, and reputational damage. As software systems become increasingly complex and interconnected, the presence of such vulnerabilities poses an even greater threat, making timely and accurate detection critical for secure software development [11].

The National Vulnerability Database (NVD) reported 12,543 new vulnerabilities in early 2025 [20], highlighting the significant security risks posed by software vulnerabilities in modern applications. As a result, automated vulnerability detection has become a critical area of research to address the growing complexity and scale of contemporary codebases. Traditional approaches to vulnerability detection have relied on static analysis tools [3,16], dynamic analysis [21], and more recently, machine learning techniques [13,23].

Recent advancements in deep learning for vulnerability detection have followed two main directions. The first involves specialized architectures like VulBERTa [7], which achieved state-of-the-art results by pre-training a RoBERTa model with a custom tokenization pipeline. Similarly, GRACE [18] incorporated graph structural information to enhance LLM-based vulnerability detection, demonstrating significant improvements over baseline models. The second direction explores Large Language Models (LLMs) for vulnerability detection. Zhou et al. [30] investigated how state-of-the-art LLMs such as GPT-3.5 and GPT-4 perform with various prompts, while Zhang et al. [28] demonstrated improvements by enhancing prompts with structural and sequential auxiliary information.

Although these remarkable advancements have been made, current methods still encounter substantial challenges. Models including VulBERTa and CodeBERT require extensive fine-tuning for each vulnerability type [7], limiting their adaptability. Graph-based approaches (i.e. GRACE) improve performance but add computational complexity [18]. Meanwhile, LLM-based approaches struggle with prompt design limitations and lack the specialized attention mechanisms needed to focus on security-critical code segments. These limitations significantly reduce the effectiveness of these approaches in real-world secure software development environments, where rapid detection of vulnerabilities is crucial to minimize the window of exposure for critical systems.

Additionally, a significant gap in existing research is that most approaches focus on binary classification (vulnerable vs. non-vulnerable) or multi-class classification (single vulnerability type per sample), while in real-world scenarios, code often contains multiple distinct vulnerability types simultaneously.

Our analysis of the VDISC dataset [23] reveals that approximately 35% of functions contain two or more vulnerability types simultaneously (Table 2), with some functions exhibiting up to five different vulnerability patterns. This multi-label nature reflects the complex interdependencies in real-world C/C++ code, where memory management operations frequently involve multiple potential security flaws that manifest within the same function scope.

The co-occurrence patterns observed in our dataset demonstrate several common vulnerability combinations. Functions handling external data input often exhibit multiple vulnerability types when proper validation and error handling are absent. Consider the following example (Listing 1.1) from the VDISC dataset showing error handling for a data reading function that contains multiple concurrent vulnerabilities:

Listing 1.1. Example showing CWE-119 and CWE-120 vulnerabilities

```
// CWE-119: Improper restriction of buffer operations
// CWE-120: Buffer copy without size checking
if ((ident = MPC_read(ad->sptr, OID_IDENT, ASN_OCTET_STR)
    ) == NULL)
{
    LOG(PIL_CRIT, "%s: cannot read ident.", __FUNCTION__)
        ;
    return (S_ACCESS); // both vulnerabilities present
}
```

While this code snippet shows appropriate error handling by checking for NULL return values and logging failures, the comment indicates that the underlying **MPC_read** function contains multiple concurrent vulnerabilities. The function likely suffers from improper buffer bounds checking (CWE-119) and buffer copy operations without adequate size validation (CWE-120) within its implementation, though the calling code demonstrates proper defensive programming practices.

The statistical distribution of vulnerability co-occurrence in our dataset further emphasizes this complexity. While 6,954 samples (34.77%) contain exactly one vulnerability type, a substantial portion exhibits multiple concurrent vulnerabilities: 4,600 samples (23.00%) contain two vulnerabilities, 1,986 samples (9.93%) contain three vulnerabilities, 282 samples (1.41%) contain four vulnerabilities, and 8 samples (0.04%) contain all five vulnerability types. This distribution indicates that multi-label vulnerability detection is not merely an academic exercise but a practical necessity for comprehensive security analysis.

This co-occurrence pattern has significant implications for automated security analysis tools. Traditional binary classification approaches (vulnerable vs. non-vulnerable) would provide insufficient granularity for remediation planning, while multi-class classification approaches would miss 6,876 instances (34.38% of our dataset) that contain multiple vulnerability types simultaneously. Such missed detections could leave critical security flaws unaddressed in production systems, where the interaction between multiple vulnerability types often amplifies the overall security risk.

Furthermore, the interdependent nature of these vulnerabilities means that addressing only one type while ignoring co-occurring vulnerabilities may provide incomplete protection. This interdependency underscores the importance of multi-label approaches that can simultaneously identify and prioritize multiple vulnerability types within the same code segment, enabling more comprehensive and effective vulnerability remediation strategies.

To address these challenges, we propose a novel Attention-based Code Summarization (ACS) approach for multi-label vulnerability detection. Unlike previous binary or multi-class approaches, our method explicitly handles multiple vulnerability types within the same code sample, reflecting real-world security scenarios where various vulnerabilities can co-exist. Our approach extends pre-trained code models with vulnerability-specific attention mechanisms that create focused summaries of security-relevant code patterns. Instead of relying on a single representation of code for classification as in previous works, we generate targeted representations for each vulnerability type, enabling more nuanced detection capabilities. This approach strikes a balance between the representation power of pre-trained models and the specificity needed for vulnerability detection, making it particularly valuable for integration into secure software development life-cycle processes where early detection of subtle vulnerability patterns can prevent costly security breaches.

The experimental results show that the proposed security-focused attention model outperforms the standard CodeBERT classifier baseline, particularly for buffer-related vulnerabilities and other specialized security flaws. The attention visualization capabilities of our model also provide explainable outputs, highlighting the specific code patterns associated with different vulnerability types. Such explainability is crucial for security teams who need to understand and prioritize vulnerability remediation efforts. Furthermore, by simultaneously detecting multiple vulnerability types in a single pass, our approach significantly reduces the analysis time required to secure critical software systems, addressing an important operational security need. Overall, the key contributions of our work can be summarized as follows:

- A multi-label vulnerability detection approach that can simultaneously identify multiple vulnerability types within a single code sample, addressing a significant gap in existing research that primarily focuses on binary or multi-class classification.
- A novel security-focused attention mechanism with vulnerability-specific queries that explicitly models different vulnerability patterns in code, validated through systematic ablation studies.
- A hierarchical code summarization approach that generates specialized representations for different vulnerability types.
- Comprehensive evaluation on a multi-label vulnerability dataset, demonstrating improvements over standard approaches across multiple vulnerability types.

The remainder of this paper is organized as follows: Sect. 2 reviews related work in vulnerability detection and code representation learning. Section 3 details our proposed approach. Section 4 presents the experimental setup and evaluation results. Section 5 provides a comprehensive ablation study validating the contribution of each architectural component. Section 6 compares our approach with existing literature. Finally, Sect. 7 concludes the paper, and Sect. 8 discusses its limitations and directions for future work.

2 Related Work

2.1 Deep Learning Approaches to Vulnerability Detection

Deep learning has shown revolutionary capabilities across a wide range of applications in computer science, such as generating images from textual prompts, describing images through captions, enabling path planning, and discovering new materials. Recently, its application in software vulnerability detection has gained popularity, offering improvements in both detection efficiency and accuracy.

Li et al. [12] introduced one of the earliest deep learning-based vulnerability detection frameworks, named VulDeePecker. This approach extracts code gadgets by isolating and combining data streams from function calls, converting them into fixed-length vectors using `word2vec`, which are then fed into a Bi-LSTM network for classification. This model demonstrated improved vulnerability detection performance, notably by reducing false negatives. However, Chakraborty et al. [1] highlighted that many of these deep learning-based systems, though effective on synthetic datasets, struggle when applied to real-world scenarios. The reduced performance is often attributed to issues such as data redundancy, skewed sample distributions, or improper feature extraction.

To address some of these limitations, Zhou et al. [31] proposed Devign, a graph neural network (GNN)-based vulnerability detection model that operates on composite code representations. It uses abstract syntax trees and models control and data dependencies at multiple levels, forming a unified graph that enables GNNs to learn nuanced code patterns. Additionally, they released a C-language dataset used in the CodeXGLUE benchmark [19], a large-scale multi-task benchmark for code intelligence co-developed by Microsoft Research, Visual Studio, and Bing Search.

2.2 CodeBERT

CodeBERT, proposed by Feng et al. [5], is a bimodal pre-trained model leveraging multilayer bidirectional transformers, optimized for both programming and natural languages. It supports various programming-related tasks, including code similarity detection, vulnerability identification, natural language-based code retrieval, and generation. Based on BERT and RoBERTa architectures, CodeBERT was trained on the CodeSearchNet dataset [9], which encompasses over 21,000 bimodal and 64,000 unimodal code samples across six prominent programming languages. Further advancing the model, Zhou et al. [29] developed language-specific variants of CodeBERT tailored for Java, Python, C, C++, and JavaScript. These were trained on the CodeParrot dataset [24], which includes over 115 million code files.

2.3 LLM-Based Vulnerability Detection

A recent comprehensive survey [30] explored the rapid emergence of large language models (LLMs) in the context of vulnerability detection and repair. The survey revealed a surge in research interest, with 27.8% of the reviewed publications appearing within the first two months of 2024 alone. Most approaches (82%) employed fine-tuning, while zero-shot and few-shot methods constituted 11% and 7%, respectively. Among the models used, CodeBERT appeared most frequently (38.5%), followed by GPT-3.5 (10.3%) and GPT-4 (2.6%).

Despite the widespread success of GPT models in broader code-related tasks, their performance in vulnerability detection remains underwhelming without additional training. For example, Cheshkov et al. [2] found that ChatGPT and GPT-3 models, when used out-of-the-box, performed no better than random guessing on vulnerability classification tasks. Similarly, Fu et al. [6] found that these models significantly underperformed compared to domain-specific models like CodeBERT and GraphCodeBERT in vulnerability detection, classification, and repair.

To enhance GPT model performance, Liu et al. [15] applied retrieval-augmented generation (RAG), using BM-25 and TF-IDF to fetch relevant contextual information, which was then used for few-shot learning. Evaluated on the Devign dataset, their method yielded notable improvements in precision, recall, and F1 scores over traditional methods. Purba et al. [22] also investigated the potential of LLMs in detecting software vulnerabilities in C and C++ code, particularly targeting SQL injection and buffer overflow vulnerabilities. They tested both fine-tuned and zero-shot models using Code Gadgets and CVEfixes datasets. Although these models demonstrated strong recall, they exhibited high false positive rates, underscoring the continuing challenges in deploying LLMs for practical vulnerability detection tasks.

2.4 Research Gaps

While prior research has yielded substantial advancements in both classical and learning-based vulnerability detection, significant limitations persist in current methodologies—particularly regarding their adaptability and scalability in real-world secure development contexts. Most notably, existing systems tend to treat vulnerability detection as either a binary or multi-class classification problem, assuming a single vulnerability per code snippet. This assumption fails to capture the complexity of real-world software, where multiple distinct vulnerabilities may coexist within a single function or module. Furthermore, many deep learning models either require extensive fine-tuning for each vulnerability type (e.g., VulBERTa [7]) or introduce considerable computational overhead through complex graph structures (e.g., GRACE [18]). Large Language Models (LLMs) offer some flexibility, but their generalized nature, reliance on handcrafted prompts, and lack of task-specific attention mechanisms hinder their effectiveness in identifying subtle security-critical patterns.

To overcome these challenges, our work proposes a multi-label vulnerability detection framework driven by a novel attention-based code summarization technique. By extending pre-trained models with vulnerability-specific attention heads, our approach can focus on and extract features relevant to each type of vulnerability. This not only improves detection accuracy but also helps make it easier and faster to understand and prioritize each vulnerability. In doing so, our method bridges the gap between generic representation learning and the specialized demands of vulnerability detection, providing a practical and scalable solution for secure software development pipelines.

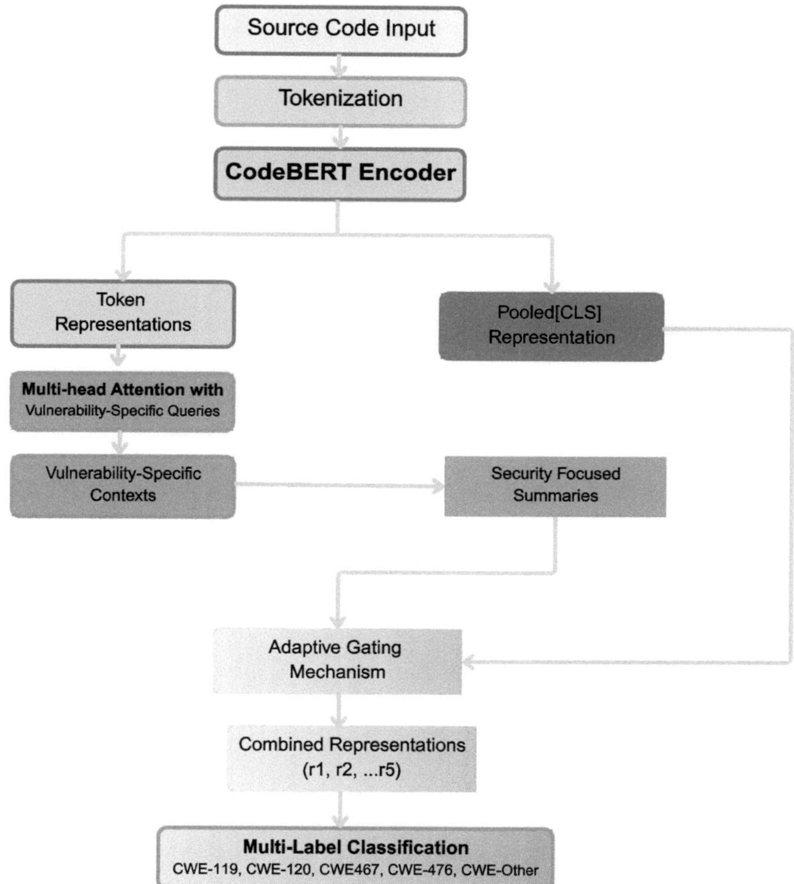

Fig. 1. Overall architecture of the proposed attention-based vulnerability detection model with security-focused summarization.

3 Proposed Method

3.1 Overview

Our approach addresses limitations in existing techniques that treat vulnerability detection as binary or multi-class classification. Instead, we frame it as a multi-label task where several vulnerability types can exist in the same code sample, better matching real security scenarios. Our key insight is that different vulnerabilities show up in specific code patterns and need targeted attention for effective detection. Figure 1 shows our proposed model architecture.

Our model combines four essential parts: a code encoder, multi-head attention with vulnerability-specific queries, a security-focused summarizer, and an adaptive gating mechanism. While CodeBERT provides general code understanding, it lacks security focus. Our innovation is in how these components work together: vulnerability-specific queries search for different vulnerability patterns simultaneously, the summarizer creates focused representations of these patterns, and the gating mechanism balances general code understanding with security-specific details. This design improves upon existing approaches by enabling detection of multiple vulnerabilities at once while providing more targeted attention to security-critical code elements.

3.2 Model Architecture

Our model architecture consists of four main components: (1) a code encoder based on a pre-trained transformer, (2) a multi-head attention mechanism with vulnerability-specific queries, (3) a security-focused summarizer, and (4) an adaptive gating mechanism. We detail each component below.

Code Encoder. We leverage CodeBERT [5], a bimodal pre-trained model for programming language and natural language, as our foundational encoder. Given an input code snippet $X = \{x_1, x_2, ..., x_n\}$ tokenized into n tokens, the encoder produces:

- A sequence of hidden representations $H = \{h_1, h_2, ..., h_n\}$ where each $h_i \in \mathbb{R}^d$ corresponds to token x_i
- A pooled representation $h_{pooled} \in \mathbb{R}^d$ derived from the [CLS] token, representing the entire code snippet

While these representations capture syntactic structure and semantic relationships within the code, they are not specifically optimized for vulnerability detection. Our subsequent components address this limitation.

Multi-head Attention with Vulnerability-Specific Queries. Unlike standard attention mechanisms in transformer models [25], we introduce a specialized attention component with vulnerability-specific query vectors. For each vulnerability type, we learn a dedicated query vector that attends to code patterns relevant to that vulnerability.

Let $Q_{vuln} = \{q_1, q_2, ..., q_m\} \in \mathbb{R}^{m \times d}$ be the set of m learnable vulnerability-specific query vectors. For each query vector q_j, we compute attention scores with the code token representations:

$$\alpha_{ij} = \frac{\exp(q_j \cdot h_i/\sqrt{d})}{\sum_{k=1}^{n} \exp(q_j \cdot h_k/\sqrt{d})} \tag{1}$$

where α_{ij} represents the attention weight of the j-th vulnerability query on the i-th code token. These attention weights are then used to compute vulnerability-specific context vectors:

$$c_j = \sum_{i=1}^{n} \alpha_{ij} h_i \tag{2}$$

The resulting context vectors $C = \{c_1, c_2, ..., c_m\}$ capture the most relevant code patterns for each vulnerability type, enabling the model to focus on security-critical aspects of the code.

Security-Focused Summarizer. To enhance the vulnerability-specific representations, we introduce a security-focused summarizer module. This module transforms each vulnerability context vector c_j into a more refined summary representation:

$$s_j = \text{Tanh}(W_2 \cdot \text{GELU}(W_1 \cdot c_j + b_1) + b_2) \tag{3}$$

where W_1, W_2, b_1, b_2 are learnable parameters, and GELU [8] is the Gaussian Error Linear Unit activation function. We further apply layer normalization and residual connections:

$$s_j = \text{LayerNorm}(s_j + c_j) \tag{4}$$

This summarization step distills the vulnerability-specific information into more compact and focused representations, which are better suited for the subsequent classification step.

Adaptive Gating Mechanism. One key challenge in vulnerability detection is balancing general code understanding with vulnerability-specific pattern recognition. To address this, we used an adaptive gating mechanism that dynamically combines the general code representation (from the pooled output) with the vulnerability-specific summaries.

For each vulnerability type j, we compute a gate value g_j that determines the contribution of the vulnerability-specific summary versus the general code representation:

$$g_j = \sigma(W_g \cdot [h_{pooled}; s_j]) \tag{5}$$

where σ is the sigmoid function, W_g is a learnable parameter matrix, and $[h_{pooled}; s_j]$ represents the concatenation of the pooled representation and the vulnerability-specific summary.

The final representation for each vulnerability type is then computed as:

$$r_j = g_j \cdot s_j + (1 - g_j) \cdot h_{pooled} \quad (6)$$

This adaptive combination allows the model to rely more on the general code understanding for common patterns while focusing on the specialized summaries for vulnerability-specific features.

3.3 Multi-label Classification.

For the final classification, we apply separate binary classifiers for each vulnerability type:

$$\hat{y}_j = \sigma(W_j \cdot r_j + b_j) \quad (7)$$

where W_j and b_j are the weights and bias for the classifier of vulnerability type j, and $\hat{y}_j$ is the predicted probability of the code containing vulnerability.

3.4 Training Methodology

Training our model involves addressing the inherent challenge of class imbalance in vulnerability datasets, where certain vulnerability types are significantly less common than others. We explore two different approaches to handle this imbalance:

Focal Loss Approach. In our first implementation, we use focal loss [14] to address class imbalance:

$$L_{focal}(y, \hat{y}) = -\alpha \cdot (1 - \hat{y})^{\gamma} \cdot y \cdot \log(\hat{y}) - (1 - \alpha) \cdot \hat{y}^{\gamma} \cdot (1 - y) \cdot \log(1 - \hat{y}) \quad (8)$$

where y is the ground truth label, $\hat{y}$ is the predicted probability, α is a balancing factor, and γ is the focusing parameter (set to 2.0 in our experiments). Focal loss gives more weight to hard-to-classify examples, making the model pay more attention to the minority vulnerability classes.

Weighted BCE Loss Approach. In our second implementation, we use a weighted binary cross-entropy loss:

$$L_{weighted}(y, \hat{y}) = -w_{pos} \cdot y \cdot \log(\hat{y}) - w_{neg} \cdot (1 - y) \cdot \log(1 - \hat{y}) \quad (9)$$

where w_{pos} and w_{neg} are the weights for positive and negative examples, respectively. We compute these weights based on the class distribution in the training set:

$$w_{pos} = \frac{N_{neg}}{N_{neg} + N_{pos}} \tag{10}$$

where N_{pos} and N_{neg} are the numbers of positive and negative examples for each vulnerability type.

3.5 Implementation Details

Our model is implemented using PyTorch and the Hugging Face Transformers library. We use the 'microsoft/codebert-base' model as our pre-trained code encoder[1]. The model is trained using the AdamW optimizer [17] with a linear learning rate schedule and warm up. To prevent overfitting, we employ early stopping based on the validation F1 score with a patience of 3 epochs.

We set the maximum sequence length to 512 tokens, batch size to 16, and train for up to 8 epochs. We use gradient accumulation with 2 steps to simulate larger batch sizes while staying within memory constraints. To further improve training efficiency, we employ mixed precision training where available.

The hidden size of the model is 768 (inherited from CodeBERT), and we use 8 attention heads in our multi-head attention mechanism. We apply a dropout probability of 0.2 to prevent overfitting.

4 Experimental Results

4.1 Dataset

For this study, we used a dataset of 20,000 samples, selected as a subset of the VDISC dataset [23] due to computational resource constraints. The original dataset comprises 1.27 million functions mined from open-source software, labeled using static analysis for potential vulnerabilities. These functions are written in C/C++ and are annotated with five vulnerability categories: CWE-119 (Improper Restriction of Memory Buffer Operations), CWE-120 (Buffer Copy without Size Checking), CWE-469 (Pointer Subtraction for Size Determination), CWE-476 (NULL Pointer Dereference), and CWE-other (miscellaneous vulnerabilities). Each function is labeled with a boolean value (True or False) for the presence of each vulnerability type.

Unlike standard binary or multi-class approaches, our dataset is structured for multi-label classification, where each function can contain multiple vulnerability types simultaneously. Table 1 shows the per-category vulnerability distribution, while Table 2 presents how many vulnerabilities appear per function. Approximately 35% of functions contain two or more vulnerability types, highlighting the importance of addressing the problem as a multi-label classification task. We divided the dataset into training (80%), validation (10%), and test (10%) splits using stratified sampling based on CWE-469 to maintain distribution consistency.

[1] The microsoft/codebert-base model is available at https://huggingface.co/microsoft/codebert-base.

Table 1. Vulnerability distribution in the dataset

Type	Count	Percentage
CWE-119	4940	24.70%
CWE-120	7893	39.46%
CWE-469	1853	9.27%
CWE-476	2972	14.86%
CWE-other	5622	28.11%

Table 2. Number of vulnerabilities per sample

Number of Vulnerabilities	Number of Samples	Percentage
0	6170	30.85%
1	6954	34.77%
2	4600	23.00%
3	1986	9.93%
4	282	1.41%
5	8	0.04%

4.2 Experimental Setup

We conducted a comprehensive evaluation of our proposed ACS approach for vulnerability detection. We compared our model against baseline approaches using identical training procedures for fair evaluation. We evaluated three different models to demonstrate the effectiveness of our approach:

- **Base CodeBERT**: A standard fine-tuned CodeBERT model with a simple classification head, serving as our primary baseline.
- **Base CodeBERT with Class Weights**: The same architecture as the base model, but incorporating class weights in the loss function to address class imbalance issues.
- **Attention-based Code Summarization(ACS) Model (Proposed)**: Our novel architecture incorporating vulnerability-specific attention queries, security-focused summarization, and adaptive gating. We implemented two variants:
  - **With Focal Loss**: Using focal loss ($\gamma = 2.0$) to address class imbalance.

Table 3. Overall performance comparison (macro-averaged metrics)

Model	Precision	Recall	F1	MCC
Base CodeBERT	0.7729	0.6852	0.7233	0.6577
Base + Class Weights	0.7976	0.6688	0.7230	0.6644
ACS + Focal Loss	**0.8030**	0.6795	**0.7324**	**0.6743**
ACS + Weighted BCE	0.7267	**0.7391**	0.7322	0.6559

Table 4. Performance in terms of F1 scores for different vulnerability types

Model	CWE-119	CWE-120	CWE-469	CWE-476	CWE-other
Base CodeBERT	0.8324	0.8220	0.5963	0.6763	0.6700
Base + Class Weights	**0.8484**	0.8028	0.6339	0.6742	0.6556
ACS + Focal Loss	0.8438	**0.8534**	0.6013	0.6802	**0.6805**
ACS + Weighted BCE	0.8353	0.8152	**0.6491**	**0.6843**	0.6772

- **With Weighted BCE Loss**: Using weighted binary cross-entropy with positive sample weights based on class distribution.

All models were trained using the AdamW optimizer with an initial learning rate of 2e-5 for our proposed models and 3e-5 for the baseline models, with a weight decay of 0.01 and a linear warmup schedule over 10% of total training steps.

4.3 Results and Analysis

Overall Performance. Table 3 presents the macro-averaged metrics across all vulnerability types. Our proposed ACS models showed improvements over the baseline approaches. The ACS model with focal loss achieved the highest F1 score (0.7324), precision (0.8030), and Matthews Correlation Coefficient (MCC) (0.6743), while the ACS with weighted binary cross-entropy (BCE) loss yields the best recall (0.7391). This demonstrated the effectiveness of different loss functions under multi-label settings. The ACS model with focal loss improved the MCC by 1.66% points over the base CodeBERT model, reflecting enhanced performance on imbalanced multi-label classification. Notably, the focal loss approach significantly improved precision compared to the base model (0.8030 vs 0.7729), indicating fewer false positives, while maintaining competitive recall. The attention model with weighted BCE showed a substantial improvement in recall (0.7391 vs 0.6852) compared to the base model, though with some reduction in precision.

Performance for Particular Vernerability Type. Table 4 details the F1 scores by vulnerability type. The results showed complementary strengths across models. The ACS model with weighted BCE performed better on CWE-469 and CWE-476, while the focal loss variant leads on CWE-120 and CWE-other.

Key observations from our results include:

- **Imbalanced Class Distribution**: As shown in Table 1, the dataset exhibited label imbalance, with CWE-120 representing nearly 40% of labels, while CWE-469 appears in less than 10%. This imbalance contributed to varying performance across classes and highlighted the need for tailored loss functions.

- **Multi-Label Complexity**: Table 2 showed that approximately 35% of samples contain two or more vulnerability types. This emphasizes the importance of multi-label classification, as traditional single-label methods would fail to capture co-occurring vulnerabilities.
- **Impact of Class Weights and Focal Loss**: Both weighted BCE and focal loss contributed to improved performance over the baseline. Despite the imbalanced distribution, these loss functions helped mitigate bias toward dominant classes, improving generalization, particularly for minority classes.
- **Loss Function Complementarity**: The weighted BCE loss excelled on structured, underrepresented vulnerabilities like CWE-469 and CWE-476. In contrast, focal loss provided better balance across common categories like CWE-120 and CWE-other. This suggests that hybrid or class-specific loss functions could further enhance model robustness.

Attention Visualization. To demonstrate the capability of our model, we present an analysis of CWE-120 (buffer overflow) vulnerabilities using attention visualization. The attention patterns reveal how the model processes source code to identify security flaws.

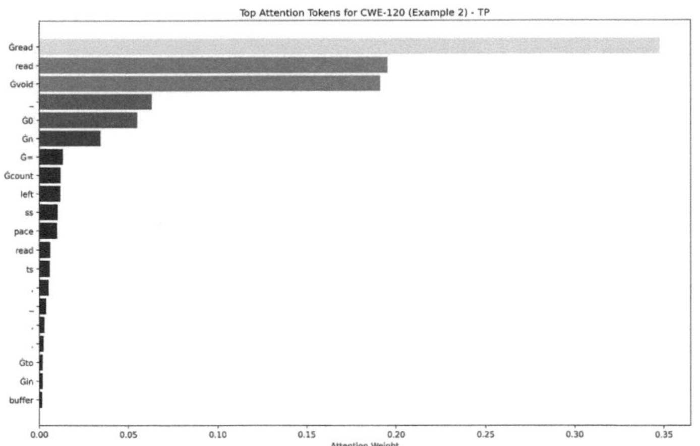

Fig. 2. True Positive case: Focused attention on semantically critical tokens

In the **True Positive** case (Fig. 2), the model exhibits a concentrated attention distribution, assigning significant weights to semantically meaningful tokens such as `"Gread"` (0.35) and `"read"` (0.20). This focused attention indicated the model's ability to correctly detect CWE-120 vulnerabilities by prioritizing memory-related operations that are critical for buffer overflow identification.

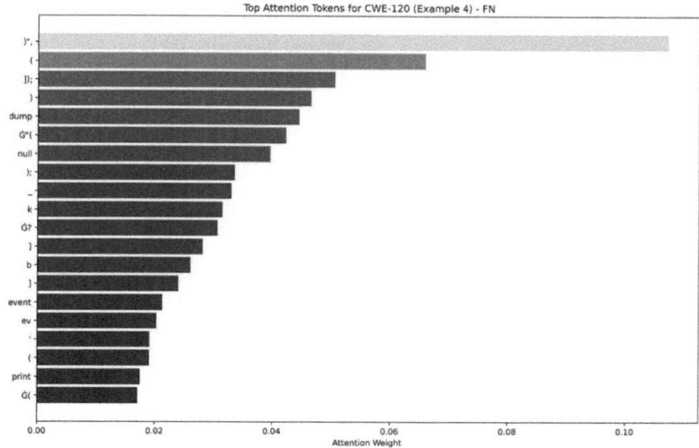

Fig. 3. False Negative case: Diffused attention across syntactic tokens

In contrast, the **False Negative** case (Fig. 3) displayed a more diffused attention distribution across numerous syntactic elements—such as “)”, “(”, and “]”—and less semantically relevant tokens. This scattered attention helped explain the model's occasional failure to detect vulnerabilities in certain contexts. In this case, the highest-weighted token received significantly less attention (~0.10) compared to critical tokens in successful detections, underscoring the challenge of recognizing vulnerability patterns in unfamiliar forms.

This comparative analysis not only validates the model's detection mechanisms but also highlights specific areas for improvement, particularly in handling syntactic variations of vulnerable code patterns.

5 Ablation Study

To validate the contribution of each component in our proposed ACS architecture, we conducted a comprehensive ablation study. We systematically removed individual components to assess their impact on overall performance. The ablation study evaluates five model variants:

1. **Baseline CodeBERT**: Standard fine-tuned CodeBERT with simple classification heads
2. **CodeBERT + Vulnerability Queries**: Adding only the vulnerability-specific attention queries
3. **CodeBERT + Summarizer**: Adding only the security-focused summarizer module
4. **CodeBERT + Gating**: Adding only the adaptive gating mechanism
5. **Full ACS Model**: Complete architecture with all components

5.1 Ablation Results and Component Analysis

Table 5. Ablation Study Results(Macro averaged metrics) - Focal Loss Variant

Model Variant	F1	Precision	Recall	MCC
Baseline CodeBERT	0.7233	0.7729	0.6852	0.6577
+ Vuln Queries	0.7306	0.7724	**0.6965**	0.6642
+ Summarizer	**0.7330**	0.7863	0.6911	0.6694
+ Gating	0.7236	0.7796	0.6831	0.6602
Full ACS Model	0.7324	**0.8030**	0.6795	**0.6743**

Table 6. Ablation Study Results(Macro averaged metrics - Weighted BCE Loss Variant

Model Variant	F1	Precision	Recall	MCC
Baseline CodeBERT	0.7233	**0.7729**	0.6852	**0.6577**
+ Vuln Queries	0.7017	0.6434	0.7788	0.6182
+ Summarizer	0.6821	0.6009	**0.7990**	0.5933
+ Gating	0.7195	0.6754	0.7723	0.6388
Full ACS Model	**0.7322**	0.7267	0.7391	0.6559

Table 7. Per-Class F1 Scores - Focal Loss Ablation Study

Model Variant	CWE-119	CWE-120	CWE-469	CWE-476	CWE-other
Baseline CodeBERT	0.8324	0.8220	0.5963	0.6763	0.6700
+ Vuln Queries	0.8604	0.8429	**0.6082**	0.6794	0.6620
+ Summarizer	**0.8620**	0.8367	0.6070	0.6679	0.6915
+ Gating	0.8488	0.8430	0.5753	0.6701	0.6802
Full ACS Model	0.8438	**0.8534**	0.6013	**0.6802**	**0.6805**

Tables 5 and 6 present the macro-averaged results for focal loss and weighted BCE loss variants, respectively. The summarizer component alone achieved the highest macro F1 score (0.7330) in the focal loss variant, while the full ACS model achieved competitive performance (0.7324) with the highest precision (0.8030) and MCC (0.6743). The weighted BCE loss variant showed similar trends, confirming consistent behavior across different loss functions.

Tables 7 and 8 present the per-class F1 scores for different model variants using focal loss and weighted BCE loss respectively, highlighting the impact of each component on specific vulnerability types. The results demonstrate that individual components contribute differently across vulnerability classes, with some showing particular strength for specific CWE types.

Table 8. Per-Class F1 Scores - Weighted BCE Loss Ablation Study

Model Variant	CWE-119	CWE-120	CWE-469	CWE-476	CWE-other
Baseline CodeBERT	0.8324	**0.8220**	0.5963	0.6763	0.6700
+ Vuln Queries	0.7904	0.8171	0.5660	0.6602	0.6749
+ Summarizer	0.7498	0.7986	0.5336	0.6574	0.6711
+ Gating	0.8260	0.8195	0.6037	0.6837	0.6644
Full ACS Model	**0.8353**	0.8152	**0.6491**	**0.6843**	**0.6772**

Vulnerability-Specific Queries Impact: The addition of vulnerability-specific queries consistently improved performance across both loss variants. In the focal loss setting, it contributed a 0.73% point improvement in macro F1 score (0.7233 → 0.7306), with notable gains in CWE-119 detection (0.8324 → 0.8604). However, in the weighted BCE variant, the queries alone showed decreased performance (0.7233 → 0.7017), indicating sensitivity to loss function choice. This demonstrates that while targeted attention mechanisms can identify vulnerability-specific patterns effectively, their impact varies depending on the training objective.

Security-Focused Summarizer Contribution: The summarizer module showed contrasting effects across loss variants. In the focal loss setting, it achieved the highest single-component improvement with macro F1 of 0.7330, particularly enhancing precision (0.7729 → 0.7863). However, in the weighted BCE variant, the summarizer alone decreased performance significantly (0.7233 → 0.6821), while achieving the highest recall (0.7990). This suggests the summarizer creates more refined vulnerability representations that work synergistically with focal loss but may require balancing mechanisms when used with weighted BCE loss.

Adaptive Gating Mechanism: The gating mechanism showed minimal individual impact in the focal loss variant (0.7233 → 0.7236) but demonstrated a slight decline in the weighted BCE variant (0.7233 → 0.7195). While the individual improvements appear modest or even negative, the gating mechanism's contribution becomes more apparent in the full model where it helps balance general code understanding with vulnerability-specific features. This suggests that the gating mechanism works synergistically with other components rather than providing standalone improvements, particularly when working with weighted loss functions.

Synergistic Effects: The full ACS model outperformed individual components across both loss variants, demonstrating that the combination of vulnerability-specific queries, security-focused summarization, and adaptive gating creates synergistic effects. The focal loss variant achieved the best balance with the highest precision (0.8030) while maintaining competitive recall, whereas the weighted BCE variant achieved superior recall (0.7391) in the full model configuration.

Loss Function Sensitivity: The ablation study reveals significant sensitivity to loss function choice. Individual components showed varying effectiveness between focal loss and weighted BCE variants. The focal loss variant maintained more consistent improvements across all individual components, while the weighted BCE variant showed higher volatility, with some components (summarizer, queries) performing worse than baseline when used alone, but contributing positively in the full model.

These findings validate our architectural design choices and confirm that each component contributes meaningfully to the overall vulnerability detection performance, with their combination yielding the best results for multi-label vulnerability detection tasks. The results also highlight the importance of considering loss function compatibility when designing attention-based architectures for imbalanced multi-label classification problems.

6 Comparison with Existing Literature

To evaluate the effectiveness of our proposed models, **ACS focal loss** and ACS weighted BCE loss **ACS(WBCE)**, we conducted comprehensive comparisons against several existing baselines, including *CODEBERT_LSTM* [26], *VDISC (CNN_RF)* [23] and *VulBERTa_CNN* [7] which have been previously adopted in similar vulnerability detection tasks. We adapted these approaches to the multi-label setting for comparison with our CodeBERT-based methods. Our adaptation extends their architecture to handle multiple vulnerability types simultaneously, modifying the architecture to output predictions for five vulnerability types. The comparison focuses on key macro-level metrics—**Precision**, **Recall**, **F1-score**, and **MCC**—as well as per-class F1 performance for five vulnerability types: *CWE-119*, *CWE-120*, *CWE-469*, *CWE-476*, and *CWE-other*.

The results, summarized in Fig. 4 and Fig. 5, demonstrated that both **ACS (Focal Loss)** and **ACS (WBCE)** achieved balanced and robust performance across all metrics. For macro metrics, ACS(focal loss) achieved a **Macro F1-score of 0.73** and **MCC of 0.67**, while ACS(WBCE) showed similar performance with a **Macro F1-score of 0.73** and **MCC of 0.65**. These results are comparable to *CODEBERT_LSTM* (Macro F1: 0.74, MCC: 0.67). However, our proposed models exhibited stronger consistency across all vulnerability classes.

In the per-class analysis, both **ACS(focal loss)** and **ACS(WBCE)** demonstrated strong performance on CWE-119 and CWE-120, with F1-scores above 0.80. On more challenging classes like CWE-469, **ACS(focal loss)** (0.60) and **ACS(WBCE)** (0.65) outperform VulBERTa_CNN (0.11) and VDISC (0.31) significantly. Similarly, for CWE-476, our models maintained F1-scores around 0.68, while VulBERTa_CNN struggles at 0.14.

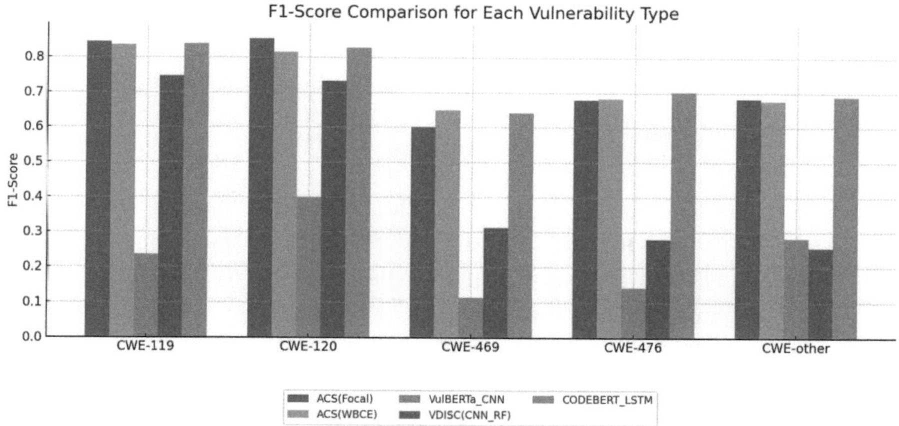

Fig. 4. F1-Score Comparison Across Models for different CWE vulnerability types. ACS (Focal Loss) and ACS (WBCE) demonstrate consistent performance across all vulnerability classes, while VulBERTa_CNN shows significantly lower F1-scores, especially for CWE-469 and CWE-476.

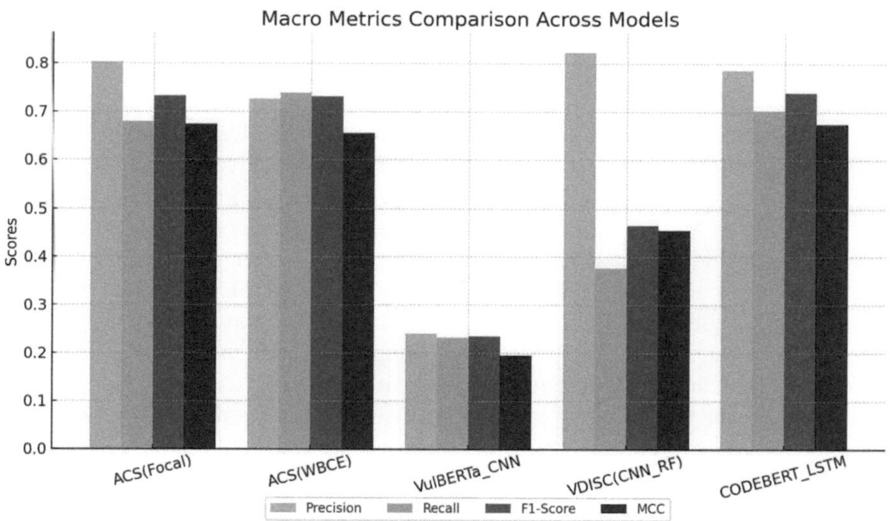

Fig. 5. Macro Metrics Comparison Across Models showing Precision, Recall, F1-Score, and Matthews Correlation Coefficient (MCC). ACS (Focal Loss), ACS (WBCE), and CODEBERT_LSTM achieve balanced performance across all metrics, while VulBERTa_CNN underperforms significantly.

CODEBERT_LSTM showed consistent performance across all classes. However, our method slightly outperformed it on certain vulnerability types. Meanwhile, *VulBERTa_CNN* demonstrated the weakest overall performance with particularly low F1-scores across most classes, achieving its best result only on CWE-120 (0.39).

Notably, **ACS with WBCE loss** achieved comparable or slightly better performance than **ACS with focal loss** on CWE-469, demonstrating its effectiveness for less represented vulnerability classes. ACS with focal loss maintains slightly higher F1-scores for CWE-119 and CWE-120.

Overall, these findings confirm that both **ACS(Focal loss and WBCE)** deliver competitive and reliable results while providing improved generalization over imbalanced class distributions—addressing a critical limitation observed in existing literature.

7 Conclusion

In this paper, we introduced an attention-based code summarization (ACS) approach for multi-label vulnerability detection in source code. Our method addresses critical limitations in existing vulnerability detection systems by explicitly modeling the presence of multiple concurrent vulnerabilities within the same code sample. By incorporating vulnerability-specific attention mechanisms and security-focused summarization techniques, our model can effectively identify subtle security patterns while maintaining the representation power of pre-trained code models. Experimental results demonstrate that our proposed approach achieves improved performance over baseline models across all vulnerability types, with particularly strong performance on buffer-related vulnerabilities (CWE-119, CWE-120) and meaningful improvements on challenging underrepresented classes like CWE-469. The attention-based model with weighted BCE loss showed superior performance in detecting underrepresented vulnerability classes, while the focal loss variant exhibited stronger precision and overall robustness. Our comprehensive ablation study validates the individual contributions of each architectural component, demonstrating that while some components show mixed individual performance, their combination creates complementary effects that achieve competitive performance. The attention visualization capabilities of our model provide valuable insights into its decision-making process, highlighting security-critical code segments that contribute to vulnerability detection. This explainability is essential for security practitioners who need to understand and prioritize remediation efforts in complex software systems.

8 Limitations and Future Work

While our attention-based code summarization approach demonstrates promising results for multi-label vulnerability detection, it shares fundamental limitations with other ML-based vulnerability detection methods. As highlighted by Ding et al. [4], current ML approaches, including our method, face significant challenges in capturing context-sensitive program behavior that is crucial for accurate vulnerability detection. Our function-level analysis inherently cannot access broader system context such as interprocedural data flows, input sanitization status, or system-wide invariants that human experts rely upon for vulnerability assessment. Additionally, our evaluation on 20,000 samples from the VDISC dataset, while computationally constrained, may limit generalizability to production environments where vulnerability patterns evolve rapidly. The focus on five vulnerability categories aggregates diverse security flaws under "CWE-other," and our C/C++ limitation restricts applicability in multilingual development environments.

Despite these challenges, our work makes significant contributions by addressing the multi-label nature of real-world vulnerabilities—a critical gap in existing research that typically treats vulnerability detection as binary or multi-class problems. Our vulnerability-specific attention mechanism and security-focused summarization provide interpretable outputs that help security practitioners understand detection rationale, addressing the "black box" problem common in deep learning approaches. Future work should integrate fine-grained program analysis techniques, such as control and data flow graphs, to better capture the contextual dependencies that current ML methods miss [4]. Developing hybrid approaches that combine our attention-based representations with traditional static analysis tools could bridge the gap between ML efficiency and the contextual reasoning required for robust vulnerability detection. Additionally, exploring cross-language transfer learning and conducting longitudinal studies on evolving codebases would strengthen the practical deployment potential of our approach.

References

1. Chakraborty, S., Krishna, R., Ding, Y., Ray, B.: Deep learning based vulnerability detection: are we there yet? IEEE Trans. Software Eng. **48**(9), 3280–3296 (2021)
2. Cheshkov, A., Zadorozhny, P., Levichev, R.: Evaluation of ChatGPT model for vulnerability detection. arXiv preprint arXiv:2304.07232 (2023)
3. Chess, B., McGraw, G.: Static analysis for security. IEEE Secur. Privacy **2**(6), 76–79 (2004)
4. Ding, Y., et al.: Vulnerability detection with code language models: how far are we? arXiv preprint arXiv:2403.18624 (2024)
5. Feng, Z., et al.: Codebert: A pre-trained model for programming and natural languages. In: Findings of the Association for Computational Linguistics: EMNLP 2020, pp. 1536–1547 (2020)
6. Fu, M., Tantithamthavorn, C.K., Nguyen, V., Le, T.: ChatGPT for vulnerability detection, classification, and repair: how far are we? In: 2023 30th Asia-Pacific Software Engineering Conference (APSEC), pp. 632–636. IEEE (2023)
7. Hanif, H., Maffeis, S.: Vulberta: Simplified source code pre-training for vulnerability detection. In: 2022 International Joint Conference on Neural Networks (IJCNN), pp. 1–8. IEEE (2022)
8. Hendrycks, D., Gimpel, K.: Gaussian error linear units (Gelus). arXiv preprint arXiv:1606.08415 (2016)
9. Husain, H., Wu, H.H., Gazit, T., Allamanis, M., Brockschmidt, M.: Codesearchnet challenge: evaluating the state of semantic code search. arXiv preprint arXiv:1909.09436 (2019)

10. Hydara, I., Sultan, A.B.M., Zulzalil, H., Admodisastro, N.: Current state of research on cross-site scripting (XSS)-a systematic literature review. Inf. Softw. Technol. **58**, 170–186 (2015)
11. Jang-Jaccard, J., Nepal, S.: A survey of emerging threats in cybersecurity. J. Comput. Syst. Sci. **80**(5), 973–993 (2014)
12. Li, Z., et al.: Vuldeepecker: a deep learning-based system for vulnerability detection. arXiv preprint arXiv:1801.01681 (2018)
13. Lin, G., Zhang, J., Luo, W., Pan, L., Xiang, Y.: Poster: Vulnerability discovery with function representation learning from unlabeled projects. In: Proceedings of the 2017 ACM SIGSAC Conference on Computer and Communications Security, pp. 2539–2541 (2017)
14. Lin, T.Y., Goyal, P., Girshick, R., He, K., Dollár, P.: Focal loss for dense object detection. In: Proceedings of the IEEE International Conference on Computer Vision, pp. 2980–2988 (2017)
15. Liu, Z., Liao, Q., Gu, W., Gao, C.: Software vulnerability detection with GPT and in-context learning. In: 2023 8th International Conference on Data Science in Cyberspace (DSC), pp. 229–236. IEEE (2023)
16. Livshits, V.B., Lam, M.S.: Finding security vulnerabilities in java applications with static analysis. In: Proceedings of the 14th USENIX Security Symposium, pp. 271–286. USENIX Association (2005)
17. Loshchilov, I., Hutter, F.: Decoupled weight decay regularization. arXiv preprint arXiv:1711.05101 (2017)
18. Lu, G., Ju, X., Chen, X., Pei, W., Cai, Z.: Grace: Empowering LLM-based software vulnerability detection with graph structure and in-context learning. J. Syst. Softw. **212**, 112031 (2024)
19. Microsoft Research: Codexglue: a benchmark dataset and open challenge for code intelligence (2021). https://github.com/microsoft/CodeXGLUE. Accessed: 2025-04-13
20. National Vulnerability Database: NVD dashboard (2025). https://nvd.nist.gov/general/nvd-dashboard
21. Newsome, J., Song, D.X.: Dynamic taint analysis for automatic detection, analysis, and signaturegeneration of exploits on commodity software. In: NDSS. vol. 5, pp. 3–4. Citeseer (2005)
22. Purba, M.D., Ghosh, A., Radford, B.J., Chu, B.: Software vulnerability detection using large language models. In: 2023 IEEE 34th International Symposium on Software Reliability Engineering Workshops (ISSREW), pp. 112–119. IEEE (2023)
23. Russell, R., et al.: Automated vulnerability detection in source code using deep representation learning. In: 2018 17th IEEE International Conference on Machine Learning and Applications (ICMLA), pp. 757–762. IEEE (2018)
24. Tunstall, L., Von Werra, L., Wolf, T.: Natural language processing with transformers. O'Reilly Media, Inc. (2022)
25. Vaswani, A., et al.: Attention is all you need. Adv. Neural Inf. Process. Syst. **30** (2017)
26. Yang, G.Y., Ko, Y.H., Wang, F., Yeh, K.H., Chang, H.S., Chen, H.Y.: Automated vulnerability detection using deep learning technique. arXiv preprint arXiv:2410.21968 (2024)
27. Younis, Y.A., Kifayat, K., Merabti, M.: An access control model for cloud computing. J. Inf. Secur. Appl. **19**(1), 45–60 (2014)
28. Zhang, C., Liu, H., Zeng, J., vdisc, K., Li, Y., Li, H.: Prompt-enhanced software vulnerability detection using ChatGPT (2024). arXiv preprint arXiv:2308.12697 (2024)

29. Zhou, S., Alon, U., Agarwal, S., Neubig, G.: Code-bertscore: evaluating code generation with pretrained models of code.(2023). arXiv preprint arXiv:2302.05527 (2023)
30. Zhou, X., Zhang, T., Lo, D.: Large language model for vulnerability detection: Emerging results and future directions. In: Proceedings of the 2024 ACM/IEEE 44th International Conference on Software Engineering: New Ideas and Emerging Results, pp. 47–51 (2024)
31. Zhou, Y., Liu, S., Siow, J., Du, X., Liu, Y.: Devign: effective vulnerability identification by learning comprehensive program semantics via graph neural networks. Adv. Neural Inf. Process. Syst. **32** (2019)

Lanstree: Cross-Architecture Binary Code Similarity Detection with a Bidirectional Tree-Structured Embedding Model

Congyu Cao, Xiaohan Wang, Shunda Pan, Guohang Shen, and Haipeng Qu(✉)

Faculty of Information Science and Engineering, Ocean University of China, Qingdao 266404, China
{caocongyu,wxh8066,panshunda,shenguohang}@stu.ouc.edu.cn, quhaipeng@ouc.edu.cn

Abstract. Binary code similarity detection (BCSD) is fundamental to various applications, including firmware vulnerability search, code clone detection, and malware code segment identification. Many deep learning models have been proposed to learn code semantics from graph structures. However, most existing methods struggle to capture long-range dependencies in binary code represented by tree structures. To address this issue, this paper proposes Lanstree, a cross-architecture binary code similarity detection framework based on a bidirectional Tree-Transformer. Lanstree performs bottom-up and top-down semantic learning on abstract syntax trees (ASTs), enabling each node to fully aggregate features from its parent and child nodes. It employs a global attention mechanism to obtain a comprehensive representation of the AST and adopts a Siamese architecture to enhance binary code similarity detection performance. We have implemented a prototype of Lanstree, and experimental results demonstrate that Lanstree outperforms previous state-of-the-art BCSD methods.

Keywords: Binary Analysis · Similarity Detection · Deep Learning · Representation Learning

1 Introduction

In the context of software security, vulnerabilities introduced by code reuse pose significant risks. The rapid growth of the open-source software community has led to a proliferation of publicly available implementations for common algorithms and protocols. Open-source contributors have developed and maintained a vast number of libraries, components, and applications, greatly facilitating software development. Particularly, permissive licenses such as MIT and Apache enable even enterprise developers to directly reuse open-source code. However, with the widespread adoption of such code, the security challenges associated with an untrusted software supply chain have become increasingly evident. The reuse of vulnerable components allows security flaws in one project to propagate across

The original version of the chapter has been revised. A correction to this chapter can be found at https://doi.org/10.1007/978-981-95-4434-9_34

Y. Kim et al. (Eds.): CANS 2025, LNCS 16351, pp. 448–466, 2025.
https://doi.org/10.1007/978-981-95-4434-9_21

the entire ecosystem, thereby elevating the overall risk. As a result, software developers, end-users, security administrators, regulators, and vendors are all are motivated to detect the potential propagation of newly disclosed vulnerabilities across the software they develop, use, or monitor. A primary technique employed for this purpose is code similarity detection.

For commercial software protected by intellectual property rights, end users, security personnel, regulatory authorities, and vendors typically do not have access to the source code and can only analyze the distributed binary executables. This necessitates binary code similarity detection across various processor architectures and operating systems. However, identical or similar source code compiled for different architectures may yield distinct binaries due to compiler behavior and architecture-specific optimizations. As a result, detecting function similarity in heterogeneous environments has become a critical and challenging problem in the field of software security.

Binary Code Similarity Detection (BCSD) refers to the process of determining whether two binary code segments originate from identical or similar source code. BCSD techniques have been widely applied in various security tasks, such as code clone detection, firmware vulnerability discovery, malware code identification, and software plagiarism detection [2,13,17,21]. Depending on specific application contexts and target requirements, different approaches such as static analysis, dynamic analysis, or testing can be employed. Code similarity can be assessed at varying granularities, including instructions, basic blocks, or functions [10,24,40]. In this work, considering that software reuse often occurs at the function level, our detection granularity is chosen accordingly. The objective is to identify function-level reuse, especially across software versions. Given this context, static analysis is particularly suitable as the primary methodology.

The main contributions of our work are as follows:

- We propose a general framework for binary code similarity detection, Lanstree, and analyze the design of each module, including AST encoding module, tree structure embedding generation module, and similarity calculation module.
- We design and implement a prototype of Lanstree. We have made Lanstree open-source to promote the future development of the BCSD field.
- We conducted extensive experiments to demonstrate the effectiveness of our proposed Lanstree method, which outperforms the baseline and demonstrates its transferability and practicality.

2 Background and Motivation

2.1 Binary Code Similarity Detection

Early research on binary code similarity detection primarily relied on statistical feature comparison, string matching, and graph matching techniques. However, with the significant advancements of deep learning in program analysis, an

```
mov     eax, offset _edata
cmp     eax, offset _edata
jz      short locret_804C998
mov     eax, 0
test    eax, eax
jz      short locret_804C998
push    ebp
mov     ebp, esp
sub     esp, 14h
push    offset _edata
call    eax
add     esp, 10h
leave
retn
```

(1) Assembly code under x86 architecture

```
mov     esi, offset _edata
push    rbp
sub     rsi, offset _edata
mov     rbp, rsp
sar     rsi, 3
mov     rax, rsi
shr     rax, 3Fh
add     rsi, rax
sar     rsi, 1
jz      short loc_405CB8
mov     eax, 0
test    rax, rax
jz      short loc_405CB8
pop     rbp
mov     edi, offset _edata
jmp     rax
```

(2) Assembly code under x64 architecture

```
lis     r3, ..load_data_sreg@ha
lis     r9, ..load_data_sreg@ha
addi    r3, r3, ..load_data_sreg@l
addi    r4, r9, ..load_data_sreg@l
subf    r4, r3, r4
srawi   r4, r4, 2
srawi   r4, r4, 1
addze.  r4, r4
beqlr
lis     r9, 0
addi    r9, r9, 0
cmpwi   cr7, r9, 0
beqlr   cr7
mtctr   r9
bctr
```

(3) Assembly code under PPC architecture

```
LDR     R0, =_edata
LDR     R3, =_edata
CMP     R3, R0
BXEQ    LR
LDR     R3, =0
CMP     R3, #0
BXEQ    LR
BX      R3
```

(4) Assembly code under ARM architecture

Fig. 1. Assembly comparison of the function deregister_tm_clones under different architectures

increasing number of studies have applied deep neural models to address various binary analysis tasks, such as binary code similarity detection [18], binary code search [38], malware classification [28], function boundary identification [31], function type inference [6], and reverse engineering [20]. Compared with traditional program analysis and conventional machine learning methods, deep learning exhibits superior capability in modeling complex patterns and semantics inherent in binary code, leading to substantial improvements in detection performance. A key enabler in deep learning-based binary analysis is the use of vectorized program representations. Figure 1 illustrates the assembly code of the deregister_tm_clones function across x86, x64, PPC, and ARM architectures. The example highlights the architecture-specific nature of binary code, which is typically closer to hardware, less interpretable, and contains limited semantic information. Therefore, in the context of binary code similarity detection, learning a robust intermediate representation and capturing latent semantic information are essential to accurately identifying function-level similarity. This forms the core objective of this study. Existing BCSD methods can be broadly classified into three categories based on how they represent binary code: methods based on binary code feature extraction, methods based on instruction embedding, and methods based on graph embedding.

Method Based on Binary Code Feature Extraction. Karta [12] is an IDA Pro plugin designed for identifying and matching binary code. It locates target functions by analyzing their order within binary files, compares numeric constants, strings, and other internal features, and uses function call relationships to match function clusters. This process enables accurate identification of statically linked open-source libraries and their specific versions, thereby supporting binary function similarity detection. GitZ [8] introduces a data stream slicing approach for fine-grained analysis of binary code. It decomposes binary files into basic block-level data stream slices and applies compiler optimization techniques to normalize these fragments. This method effectively mitigates discrepancies caused by compiler differences, optimization levels, and hardware architectures, significantly improving the accuracy of similar code fragment recognition. αDiff [23] presents an innovative solution for detecting cross-version binary code similarity. It leverages neural network models to automatically extract deep semantic features from binary code and incorporates function call graph in-degree and out-degree as auxiliary features. This approach demonstrates strong generalization in cross-version, cross-compiler, and cross-architecture scenarios. FOSSIL [3] is a system developed for identifying free and open-source software (FOSS) functions within malicious binaries. It disassembles and normalizes assembly code, extracts features from identified FOSS packages, and uses a Bayesian network to integrate multiple detection methods. FOSSIL enables accurate discovery of reused FOSS components in malware consistent with reverse engineering reports and threat intelligence.

Methods Based on Instruction Embedding. To generate fixed-length instruction vectors, PalmTree [22] designs three self-supervised pretraining tasks: masked language modeling, context window prediction, and data stream dependency prediction. By learning on large-scale unlabeled binary corpora, PalmTree produces high-quality instruction embeddings tailored for binary code understanding. BinShot [1] normalizes datasets through a preprocessing module and builds a database of normalized functions. It uses the BERT model [9] to learn function representations and constructs assembly code embeddings. During inference, candidate function vectors are preloaded, and a Siamese network is employed to retrieve similar functions. DeepDual-SD [14] integrates instruction and graph embeddings. It utilizes an enhanced BERT model to derive semantic features from assembly instructions and extracts control flow graphs (CFGs) for structural embedding. A gated attention mechanism fuses semantic and structural features with dynamic weighting, offering better semantic interpretation under diverse application scenarios. CLAP [34] addresses the challenge of few-shot or zero-shot training data in binary analysis. It uses a large language model (LLM) to generate a synthetic interpretation dataset comprising binary code and corresponding natural language descriptions. Fine-tuning is performed on the LLaMA model [32] to produce a shadow model trained on enhanced annotations. CLAP pretrains the binary dataset and aligns assembly and text encoders through contrastive learning. To reduce false positives caused by function inlining, OpTrans [29] integrates static program analysis with binary-level re-optimization. Rewritten binary functions are fed into a Transformer encoder for similarity learning. This process significantly enhances dataset usability through comprehensive code rewriting and analysis.

Methods Based on Graph Embedding. Gemini [36] is the first graph embedding-based deep learning framework for cross-platform binary code similarity detection. It converts binary functions into annotated control flow graphs (ACFGs) and uses Siamese networks to train Structure2Vec [7], computing similarity scores between ACFG representations. DEEPBINDIFF [11] combines instruction and graph embeddings by applying an improved Word2Vec [27] model to separately embed opcodes and operands. It merges call graphs and CFGs into an inter-procedural control flow graph and applies the TADW algorithm [37] to extract contextual embeddings, which are integrated with instruction-level features for basic block representation. Asteria [39] employs a deep learning-based AST encoder to assess functional semantic equivalence across architectures. It encodes abstract syntax trees using Tree-LSTM and calculates pairwise similarity via a Siamese network composed of dual Tree-LSTM encoders. JTrans [35] is the first approach to embed binary control flow information into a Transformer model. It pretrains using masked language modeling and jump-target prediction, and fine-tunes similarity detection via contrastive learning. XBA [19] reformulates binary similarity detection as a graph alignment task. It abstracts binaries into disassembly graphs and trains node correspondences via semi-supervised learning. A graph convolutional network (GCN) [5] is then used to generate node embeddings, offering a novel approach to cross-platform analysis. BMM [15] targets program- and process-level similarity tasks by constructing function call graphs, data flow graphs, and control flow graphs. It jointly embeds graph nodes and integrates semantic information from both graph structure and assembly instructions to capture both local and global features. HermesSim [16] proposes a semantic-oriented graph representation tailored for high-level semantic expression in binary code. It applies graph neural networks to aggregate node neighborhood information and uses a multi-head softmax module to generate graph-level embeddings optimized for similarity comparison.

3 Problem Definition

Given a pair of binary functions f_1 and f_2, compiled from potentially different processor architectures and operating systems, the goal of binary code similarity detection is to determine whether they originate from the same or similar source code. Let $\mathcal{F}_1 \in \mathcal{A}_1$ and $\mathcal{F}_2 \in \mathcal{A}_2$, where $\mathcal{A}_1$ and $\mathcal{A}_2$ denote different instruction set architectures (e.g., x64, x86, ARM, PPC). The challenge lies in learning robust function representations that are invariant to compilation differences, instruction-level transformations, and architecture-specific variations.

Formally, the problem can be defined as learning a similarity function $\mathcal{M}(f_1, f_2) \rightarrow [0, 1]$, where a value close to 1 indicates high semantic similarity between the two binary functions. An effective BCSD system should be able to generalize across architectures, optimize both precision and recall, and support large-scale analysis under realistic constraints.

4 Lanstree Design

4.1 Lanstree Overview

The overall architecture of Lanstree is illustrated in Fig. 2. Given a pair of binary functions, the workflow begins with disassembly and AST extraction, which serves as the structural representation of the code. The extracted ASTs are then standardized through digitization and formatting procedures. These standardized ASTs are subsequently fed into a Tree-LSTM network for bottom-up information propagation and a Tree-Transformer module for top-down semantic refinement, enabling comprehensive node encoding across the entire tree.

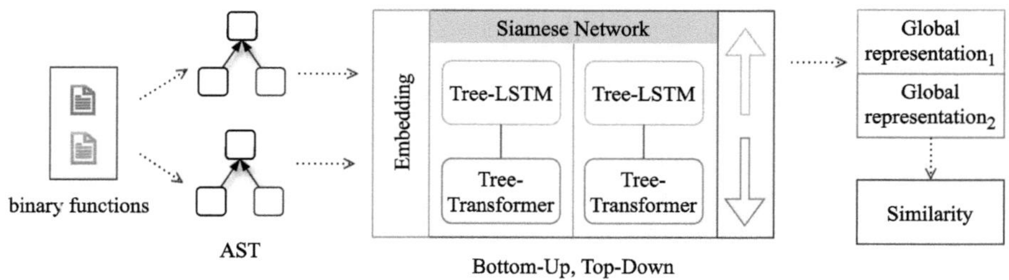

Fig. 2. System Overview

While LSTM excels at capturing local sequential dependencies in time series and natural language, the Transformer architecture offers strong capabilities in modeling long-range dependencies. By integrating the strengths of both, Lanstree leverages Tree-LSTM to encode AST nodes in a bottom-up manner, progressing from leaf nodes to the root. The resulting encoded AST is then processed by the self-attention layers of the Tree-Transformer, which model global dependencies and propagate semantic information from top to bottom. Through this mechanism, each node is enriched not only with its own features but also with the contextual features of its parent and child nodes. As a result, even leaf nodes are capable of representing complete semantic information about the AST. A global AST embedding is subsequently generated via the attention mechanism. Finally, the embeddings of the two ASTs are passed into a Siamese Network, where their similarity is computed to represent the similarity between the original binary functions.

4.2 Bottom-Up Semantic Learning: Abstract Syntax Trees Encoding Based on Tree-LSTM

LSTM is a widely adopted neural architecture in deep learning due to its proficiency in modeling sequential data and capturing temporal dependencies. The core innovation of LSTM lies in its gating mechanisms—namely, the forget gate, input gate, and output gate—which regulate information flow and help mitigate the vanishing and exploding gradient problems in long sequences. However, traditional LSTM models are inherently designed for linear sequences and do not generalize well to hierarchical or tree-structured data.

To address this limitation, Tree-LSTM is employed for processing inputs with hierarchical structures, such as ASTs. Tree-LSTM is specifically designed to model tree-structured data and is well-suited for capturing the hierarchical relationships found in syntactic trees. The central idea involves applying LSTM units to each node in the tree and propagating information upward along the tree topology. Each parent node aggregates and updates its representation by recursively combining features from its child nodes, thereby enabling the model to learn semantics within structured data. Unlike standard LSTMs, which process sequences over time, Tree-LSTM transmits information along structural rather than temporal dimensions, making it particularly effective at modeling the depth and complexity of tree hierarchies.

Tree-LSTM traverses the AST in post-order, starting from the leftmost leaf node. After standardization, each AST node is mapped to a high-dimensional embedding via an embedding layer. For a given node v_t, its input vector X_t, together with the memory cells C_{t-1} and hidden states H_{t-1} of its child nodes, are input into the Tree-LSTM unit. The input gate I_t, forget gate F_t, output gate O_t, and candidate memory cell $\tilde{C}_t$ are then computed:

$$I_t = \sigma(X_t W_{xi} + H_{t-1} W_{hi} + b_i) \tag{1}$$

$$F_t = \sigma(X_t W_{xf} + H_{t-1} W_{hf} + b_f) \tag{2}$$

$$O_t = \sigma(X_t W_{xo} + H_{t-1} W_{ho} + b_o) \tag{3}$$

$$\tilde{C} = tanh(X_t W_{xc} + H_{t-1} W_{hc} + b_c) \tag{4}$$

where W and b are parameters. Unlike conventional LSTM where inputs are derived from the previous time step, Tree-LSTM receives input from the left and right child nodes of the current node. Hence, the input is defined as $X_t = (Xl_t, Xr_t)$, $H_{t-1} = (Hl_{t-1}, Hr_{t-1})$, and $C_{t-1} = (Cl_{t-1}, Cr_{t-1})$.

The input gate controls how much of the candidate memory should be preserved, the forget gate determines how much memory from each child node should be retained, and the output gate generates the current node's hidden state. The Hadamard product $\odot$ is used in these operations.

$$C_t = F_t \odot C_{t-1} + I_t \odot \tilde{C}_t \tag{5}$$

$$H_t = O_t \odot tanh(C_t) \tag{6}$$

where $\odot$ represents Hadamard Product. Once v_t is encoded, its memory and hidden state are utilized to update the representation of its parent node. This process is repeated recursively from the bottom up, as illustrated in Fig. 3. After all AST nodes have been encoded, each node's hidden state serves as its semantic representation.

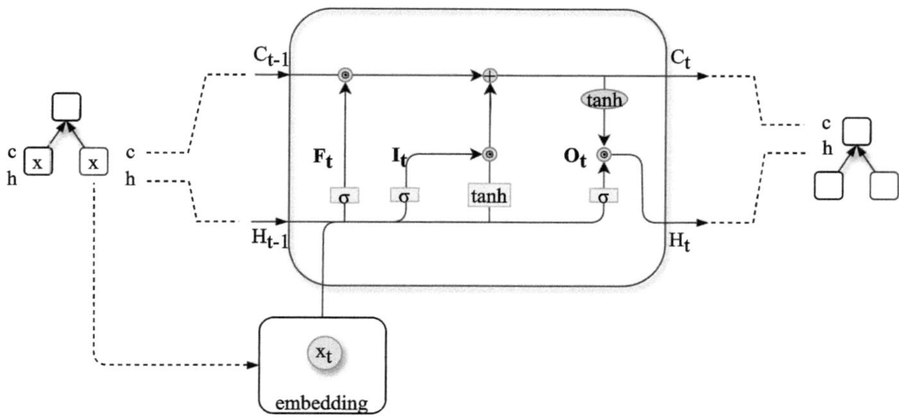

Fig. 3. AST encoding based on Tree-LSTM

In terms of code representation, Tree-LSTM based methods can better model the syntax structure of code compared to others. For example, expressions, statements, and control structures in program code can be naturally mapped to a tree structure. Through Tree-LSTM, the model can gradually extract the syntax and semantic features of the code in a bottom-up manner, and effectively learn semantics by combining the characteristics of the tree structure, providing rich contextual information for subsequent tasks.

Despite its effectiveness in bottom-up feature extraction, a major limitation of Tree-LSTM is that nodes are only informed by their descendants, not their ancestors. However, in real-world code semantics, contextual relationships are often bidirectional. Understanding code meaning often requires incorporating information from both child and parent nodes. While Tree-LSTM excels at modeling local and hierarchical dependencies, Transformer excels at capturing long-range, bidirectional interactions. Therefore, in our design, Tree-LSTM is first used to encode node-level semantics from bottom to top, after which the entire tree representation is refined through the Tree-Transformer's top-down attention mechanism to enable more comprehensive semantic learning.

4.3 Top-Down Feature Extraction: Attention Mechanism-Based Tree-Structured Embedding

The similarity between code and natural language lies in their semantic nature. For programmers who understand programming languages, code functions like a special form of language, enabling communication through syntax and logic. As with natural language, context plays a crucial role in understanding semantics. Therefore, in the previous section, we employed a bottom-up Tree-LSTM to encode each node, thereby capturing information from sibling nodes in the AST—referred to as the "context." In this section, we adopt an attention-based tree structure embedding method to extract the "context" of each node from a top-down perspective.

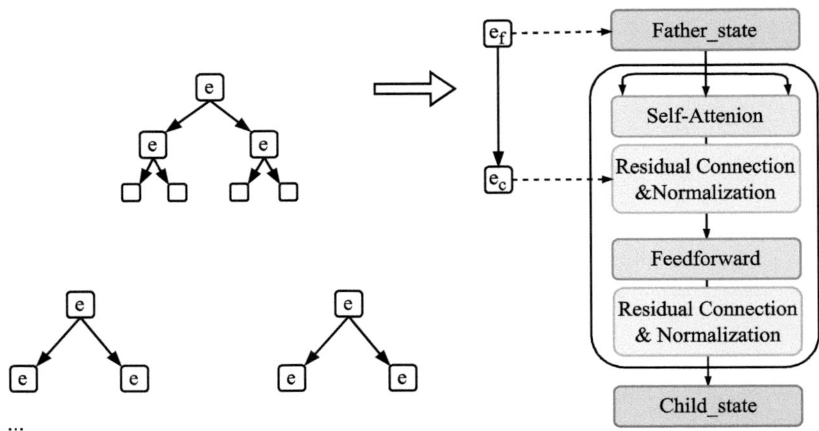

Fig. 4. Top down feature extraction: tree structure embedding based on attention mechanism

The architecture of the Tree-Transformer is illustrated in Fig. 4. It processes the encoded AST in a top-down, layer-by-layer manner starting from the root node. Each normalized AST node v_t first passes through a self-attention layer to update its features. At this stage, the node features consist of the memory cell C_t and the hidden state H_t, as obtained in the previous section. For the current node v_t, the memory cell C_t stores long-term dependency information in the sequence—specifically, data related to distant child nodes in the tree. Naturally, this memory component selectively retains information from distant nodes. The mechanism for learning which information to retain or discard was addressed in the previous section. Meanwhile, the hidden state H_t captures short-term memory, representing information from nearby child nodes.

To compute parent-child relationships, self-attention (MultiHead) is applied to the current node's hidden state H_t. In this top-down traversal, child nodes receive information from their parent nodes. Here, Q originates from the child node features, while K and V are derived from the parent node. These are then passed into a feedforward network (FFN) to update the child node representations. The multi-head attention and FFN layers are followed by residual connections and layer normalization. The computation is formulated as follows:

$$A_t = MultiHead(Q_t, K_t, V_t) \tag{7}$$
$$A'_t = LayerNorm(H_t + A_t) \tag{8}$$
$$H_t = LayerNorm(FFN(H_t) + A'_t) \tag{9}$$

where $MultiHead$ mechanism captures diverse subspace information via multiple parallel attention heads. Given input vectors Q, K, and V—representing child and parent node features respectively—each attention head maps the inputs to subspaces, allowing different heads to learn distinct representations.

$$MultiHead(Q_t, K_t, V_t) = Concat(head_1, ..., head_h)W \tag{10}$$
$$head_i = softmax(\frac{Q_t K_t^T}{\sqrt{d_k}})V_t \tag{11}$$

FFN denotes a feedforward neural network, primarily used to further refine the contextual information produced by multi-head attention. The FFN typically consists of linear transformations followed by nonlinear activation functions.

4.4 Global Embedding of ASTs

The preceding sections aim to extract node information from both directions of the AST, ensuring that each node has comprehensive access to both its parent and child contexts. This facilitates more holistic feature learning at the node level. As seen from the above, the proposed method does not aggregate all information into a single node (commonly the root). Instead, it emphasizes the contribution of every node within the tree structure. Consequently, we abandon the traditional approach of using the root node as a global tree representation. Instead, we apply a pooling function to the attention-enhanced features of all tree nodes (produced in the top-down embedding process) to obtain a global AST representation. We adopt a global attention pooling mechanism which aggregates node features via attention-based weighted summation. We calculate the global representation using the following equation:

$$H_{AST} = \sum_{i=1}^{N} softmax(W_h h_i) \odot h_i \tag{12}$$

where W is the weight matrix$H_{AST}$is the global embedding of AST.

4.5 Similarity Computation Using a Siamese Neural Network

Siamese neural networks are widely used in image similarity detection [30], code similarity analysis [33], and malware detection [4]. They consist of two identical subnetworks with shared weights—resembling a “twin” structure—and are primarily used for comparing the similarity between two input samples. The network projects both inputs into a shared feature space and determines similarity by calculating the distance between their feature vectors, often using cosine similarity. After obtaining the global AST embeddings of two binary functions, Lanstree employs a Siamese neural network [25] to compute their similarity, also using the Siamese neural network architecture. The formulation is as follows:

$$\mathcal{M}(H_{AST1}, H_{AST2}) = \text{softmax}\left(\sigma\left(\text{cat}\left(\left|H_{AST1} - H_{AST2}\right|, H_{AST1} \odot H_{AST2}\right) \times W\right)\right) \quad (13)$$

where W is the parameter matrix of $2n \times 2$.

The inputs to the Siamese network are the global embeddings of two ASTs. These embeddings are normalized into probability distributions via a softmax function. The output is a two-dimensional vector of size 2×1, representing [dissimilarity score, similarity score]. Ideally, homologous binary functions yield an output of $[0, 1]$, while non-homologous functions yield $[1, 0]$. By comparing the similarity score with a predefined threshold, we infer function homology: if the similarity score is greater than or equal to the threshold, the functions are deemed homologous; otherwise, they are considered non-homologous.

5 Evaluation

5.1 Experiment Settings

We developed Lanstree using PyTorch, one of the most widely adopted machine learning frameworks. At its core, Lanstree incorporates prototype implementations based on Tree-LSTM and Tree-Transformer architectures. To comprehensively capture the semantic similarities and differences between two binary functions, we employ a concatenation of the vector difference and Hadamard product, followed by fully connected layers and a softmax function. This design enables more accurate similarity measurement. We conducted extensive hyperparameter tuning and adopted the best-performing configuration: 30 training epochs, 2 attention heads, a node embedding dimension of 32, a binary classification threshold of 0.7, the binary cross-entropy loss function, and the Adam optimizer with a learning rate of 0.01. Experiments were carried out on a GPU virtual machine equipped with an AMD EPYC 7713 64-Core Processor @ 2.0 GHz, an NVIDIA A40 GPU with 40 GB VRAM, 755 GB of RAM, and 37 TB of storage. The implementation ran in a Python 3.7 environment.

5.2 Dataset

Buildroot Dataset used in this work originates from the paper published in DSN 2021 [39], and is utilized to train and evaluate Lanstree. Due to its considerable size, only 20% of the dataset is used for training, with an 8 : 2 split between the training and testing sets. Buildroot is a simple, efficient tool that supports multiple architectures and platforms, making it highly suitable for dataset construction. Specifically, the source code of 260 different software packages is first downloaded using Buildroot. These source codes are then compiled using the default settings for different architectures, yielding binary versions for four distinct architectures. Cross-architecture function pairs are then constructed from these binaries. As shown in Table 1, IDA Pro 7.3 and the Hex-Rays plugin were used to disassemble binary functions and construct their Abstract Syntax Trees (ASTs). During preprocessing, ASTs with fewer than five nodes were discarded. The number of function pairs varies across architectural combinations, making this dataset well-suited for cross-architecture binary code similarity detection.

Function names are preserved in the binaries during compilation. Therefore, the ground-truth labels for same-origin binary functions are determined based on whether the function pairs originate from the same source function—i.e., functions with the same name in the binary files are considered same-origin; otherwise, they are treated as different-origin.

Table 1. Number of Function Pairs for Architecture Combinations in the Buildroot Dataset

Architecture Combination	Number of Function Pairs	Architecture Combination	Number of Function Pairs
x86-ARM	174776	ARM-PPC	174916
x86-PPC	182596	ARM-x64	157976
x86-x64	167436	PPC-x64	164916

Vulnerability Dataset is constructed through static analysis of a series of ELF files. For each function, essential metadata—including the function name, address, ELF filename, and file path—is extracted and stored. This process is facilitated by IDA Pro, which parses symbol information and visualizes the structure and layout of functions.

Given that ASTs can reflect control flow, conditional statements, and loop structures, each function's AST is stored using a specialized encoding method for subsequent analysis. This encoding reflects the logical structure of the function. All extracted information—including function names, addresses, call graphs, optimization details, and AST encodings—is integrated into a database.

To construct the vulnerability dataset, we begin by identifying representative software vulnerability functions from the CVE database [26]. For each identified function, we apply the aforementioned information extraction process and aggregate the extracted data accordingly. Each vulnerability function contributes to the creation of a corresponding structured database. As illustrated in Table 2, we selected eight well-known vulnerability functions, extracted their AST hash codes, and constructed a database to store the relevant structural and semantic information. To ensure the dataset supports both similar and dissimilar function comparisons, we selected vulnerability functions across different architectures to

Table 2. Vulnerability Dataset

CVE	Software	Function Name	Vulnerability Type
CNVD-2011-4243	logsurfer	prepare_exec	Double Free Vulnerability
CNVD-2012-4977	Mcrypt	check_file_head	Stack Buffer Overflow Vulnerability
CVE-2017-14333	GNU Binutils	process_version_sections	Integer Overflow Vulnerability
CVE-2017-17122	GNU Binutils	dump_relocs_in_section	Denial of Service Vulnerability
CVE-2019-20795	iproute	get_netnsid_from_name	Resource Leak Vulnerability
CVE-2020-25412	gnuplot	com_line	Context-Dependent Arbitrary Code Execution Vulnerability
CVE-2021-44269	WavPack	WavpackPackSamples	Buffer Overflow Vulnerability
CVE-2022-28487	Appneta Tcpreplay	fix_ipv6_checksums	Memory Leak Vulnerability

form semantically similar function pairs, while pairing these with unrelated functions to construct dissimilar function pairs. This design facilitates robust training and evaluation in subsequent vulnerability detection experiments.

5.3 Evaluation Metrics

In binary similarity detection, each input consists of a function pair. The model predicts whether the pair is similar (output 1) or dissimilar (output 0). To assess the ability of Lanstree to accurately predict binary function similarity, we employ the following metrics: Area Under the Curve (AUC), Accuracy, Precision, and Recall.

AUC measures the area under the Receiver Operating Characteristic (ROC) curve and evaluates the model's discriminative capacity. Its value ranges from 0 to 1, with values closer to 1 indicating better performance. Accuracy represents the proportion of correctly predicted samples among all samples, serving as a general measure of classification performance. Precision indicates the ratio of correctly predicted positive samples to all predicted positives. Recall reflects the ratio of correctly predicted positive samples to all actual positives.

$$Acc = \frac{TP + TN}{TP + TN + FP + FN} \tag{14}$$

$$Precision = \frac{TP}{TP + FP} \tag{15}$$

$$Recall = \frac{TP}{TP + FN} \tag{16}$$

where true positive(TP) is a true counterexample, true negative(TN) is a true counterexample, false positive(FP) is a false positive example, and false negative(FN) is a false counterexample. TP represents the number of samples with similar predicted results when the real labels are similar; FP represents the number of similar samples predicted when the real labels are not similar; FN represents the number of dissimilar samples predicted when the real labels are similar; TN represents the number of dissimilar samples predicted when the real labels are dissimilar.

5.4 Effectiveness

This section evaluates the effectiveness of Lanstree across three critical aspects: cross-architecture similarity detection, the impact of different node information representations, and its performance in vulnerability detection tasks. Through comparative experiments and performance analysis, we demonstrate Lanstree's superiority in accuracy, recall, and generalization ability under various challenging scenarios.

Cross-Architecture. As shown in the Fig. 5, Lanstree consistently outperforms both Gemini and Asteria across the entire FPR range. Specifically, Lanstree achieves an AUC of 0.9855, compared to 0.9439 for Asteria and 0.9222 for Gemini, indicating significantly better discrimination ability between similar and dissimilar function pairs under cross-architecture settings. The superior performance of Lanstree can be attributed to two major advantages. First, it introduces a bidirectional Tree-Transformer that captures both bottom-up and top-down semantic dependencies within the abstract syntax tree (AST), enabling a more comprehensive representation of function semantics. Second, Lanstree explicitly models both parent-child and sibling relationships through multi-head attention mechanisms, which enhances structural understanding and cross-architecture generalization. These design choices allow Lanstree to achieve robust and architecture-agnostic similarity detection.

Node Information. Generally speaking, the update process of hidden units includes the information of memory elements, so hidden units are used as node information. However, since the focus of this article is to extract the global information of AST, compared to other tasks, the information of distant child nodes stored in memory elements is very important, and the information of nearby child nodes stored in hidden units cannot be used alone. The comparison of the effects of computing hidden unit information and computing memory elements as well as hidden units is shown in Fig. 6. After testing, it was found that computing only hidden unit information has poorer performance compared to computing memory elements and both hidden unit information.

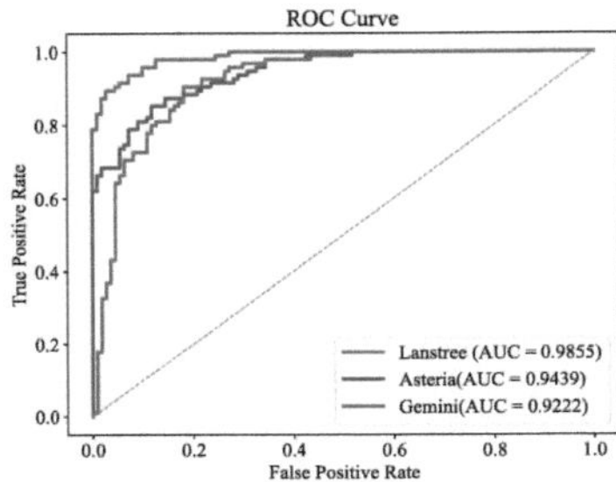

Fig. 5. The ROC curves for Lanstree, Asteria, Gemini in cross-architecture evaluation

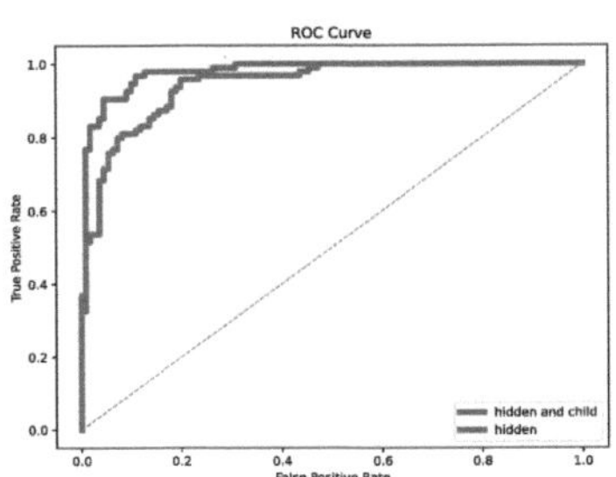

Fig. 6. Comparison of computing hidden unit information and computing memory element and hidden unit performance

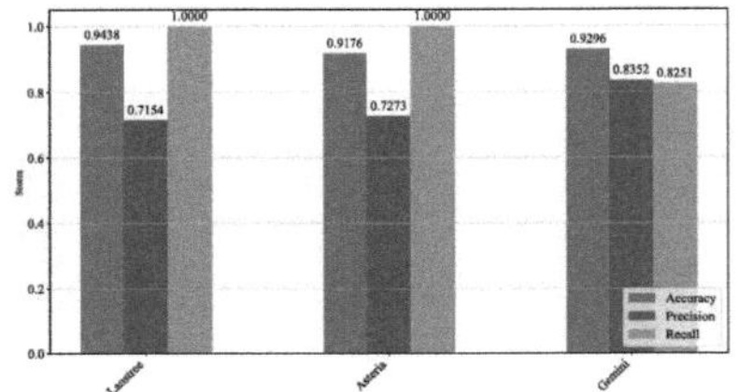

Fig. 7. Detecting same architecture and same source vulnerabilities using different models

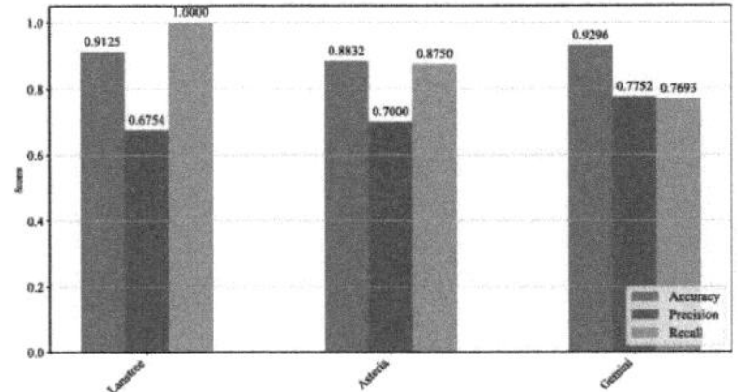

Fig. 8. Detecting cross architecture same origin vulnerabilities using different models

Vulnerability Detection. We use vulnerability datasets and evaluate the recognition performance of each model on vulnerability functions under similarity detection methods using same architecture and cross architecture same origin vulnerability datasets. In order to comprehensively evaluate the effectiveness of various models in identifying vulnerability functions based on similarity detection methods, a cross architecture and same origin vulnerability dataset and a same architecture and same origin vulnerability dataset were constructed on the basis of the vulnerability dataset. In a cross architecture same origin vulnerability dataset, two functions in a function pair come from different architectures; In the same architecture and same source vulnerability dataset, two functions in a function pair come from the same architecture. By comparing the detection results of these two datasets, the ability of different models to identify same origin vulnerabilities across architectures can be evaluated. As shown in Fig. 7 and Fig. 8, the performance of the four models in accuracy, precision, and recall is as follows: The Lanstree model performs well in all three indicators, especially in accuracy and recall. The accuracy, precision, and recall of the Asteria model are relatively stable, although they may not reach perfect values, they still have high recognition and coverage capabilities. The Gemini model performs slightly poorly, with high accuracy and precision, but relatively low recall, indicating that it still needs improvement in terms of coverage. Overall, Lanstree performs the best on multiple metrics and is suitable for high-precision tasks, while Asteria has a relatively balanced performance. Other models need to be optimized for the balance between accuracy and recall.

Table 3. Comparison of Time and Performance under Different Dataset Sizes

Model	Acc	Recall	Time
Lanstree	98.09%	0.9859	0.2584 s
Asteria	93.79%	0.9585	0.1963 s
Gemini	87.61%	0.9121	0.3947 s

Time Performance Comparison. Due to Lanstree's use of long short-term memory networks and self attention mechanisms to extract AST information, the dependency sequence relationship processing semantic information can effectively extract local order information and long-distance dependency information from time series and language. However, the drawback of Lanstree's dependency sequence relationship processing semantic information is that it cannot be processed in batches, resulting in only one AST being processed at a time. Table 3 presents a comparison of three models in terms of their performance and inference time under varying dataset sizes. As shown, Lanstree outperforms both Asteria and Gemini in accuracy (98.09%) and recall (0.9859), reflecting higher performance. Meanwhile, Lanstree encodes a pair of binary functions in 0.2584 s, slightly higher than Asteria (0.1963 s), but much lower than Gemini (0.3947 s), balancing accuracy and computational efficiency. Overall, Lanstree strikes a more favorable balance between detection performance and computational cost, validating the effectiveness and practicality of its design for cross-architecture binary code similarity detection.

6 Conclusion

In this paper, we analyzed and studied existing binary code similarity detection techniques, and proposed a binary code similarity detection Lanstree based on abstract syntax tree representation and bidirectional Tree Transformer to address the problems caused by cross architecture. We designed five modules for constructing and standardizing abstract syntax trees, encoding abstract syntax trees based on Tree LSTM, embedding tree structures based on attention mechanisms, global representation of AST, and computing similarity using Siamese neural networks. We have developed a prototype of Lanstree, and the results show that Lanstree is more robust in BCSD than existing state-of-the-art models. Our experimental results indicate that Lanstree's performance surpasses existing state-of-the-art methods, demonstrating its effectiveness and practicality.

References

1. Ahn, S., Ahn, S., Koo, H., Paek, Y.: Practical binary code similarity detection with bert-based transferable similarity learning. In: Proceedings of the 38th Annual Computer Security Applications Conference, pp. 361–374. ACM (2022)
2. Alrabaee, S., Debbabi, M., Wang, L.: A survey of binary code fingerprinting approaches: taxonomy, methodologies, and features. ACM Comput. Surv. **55**(1), 41 (2022)
3. Alrabaee, S., Shirani, P., Wang, L., Debbabi, M.: FOSSIL: a resilient and efficient system for identifying FOSS functions in malware binaries. ACM Trans. Privacy Secur. **21**(2), 1–34 (2018)
4. An, B., Yang, J., Kim, S., Kim, T.: Malware detection using dual Siamese network model. CMES-Comput. Model. Eng. Sci. **141**(1), 563–584 (2024)
5. Bhatti, U.A., Tang, H., Wu, G., Marjan, S., Hussain, A.: Deep learning with graph convolutional networks: an overview and latest applications in computational intelligence. Int. J. Intell. Syst. **2023**(1), 8342104 (2023)
6. Chua, Z.L., Shen, S., Saxena, P., Liang, Z.: Neural nets can learn function type signatures from binaries. In: Proceedings of the 26th USENIX Security Symposium, pp. 99–116. USENIX (2017)
7. Dai, H., Dai, B., Song, L.: Discriminative embeddings of latent variable models for structured data. In: International Conference on Machine Learning, pp. 2702–2711. ACM (2016)
8. David, Y., Partush, N., Yahav, E.: Similarity of binaries through re-optimization. In: Proceedings of the 38th ACM SIGPLAN Conference on Programming Language Design and Implementation, pp. 79–94. ACM (2017)
9. Devlin, J., Chang, M.W., Lee, K., Toutanova, K.: BERT: Pre-training of deep bidirectional transformers for language understanding. In: Proceedings of the 2019 Conference of the North American Chapter of the Association for Computational Linguistics, pp. 4171–4186. NAACL (2019)
10. Ding, S.H., Fung, B.C., Charland, P.: Asm2Vec: Boosting static representation robustness for binary clone search against code obfuscation and compiler optimization. In: 2019 IEEE Symposium on Security and Privacy, pp. 472–489. IEEE (2019)
11. Duan, Y., Li, X., Wang, J., Yin, H., et al.: Deepbindiff: Learning program-wide code representations for binary diffing. In: Proceedings of the 2020 Network and Distributed System Security Symposium, pp. 1–16. ISOC (2020)
12. Eyal Itkin: Karta - Source Code Assisted Fast Binary Matching Plugin for IDA. https://github.com/CheckPointSW/Karta.git
13. Feng, X., Zhu, X., Han, Q.L., Zhou, W., Wen, S., Xiang, Y.: Detecting vulnerability on IoT device firmware: a survey. IEEE/CAA J. Automatica Sinica **10**(1), 25–41 (2023)
14. Guo, J., Zhao, B., Liu, H., Leng, D., An, Y., Shu, G.: DeepDual-SD: deep dual attribute-aware embedding for binary code similarity detection. Int. J. Comput. Intell. Syst. **16**(1), 35 (2023)
15. Guo, Y., Li, P., Luo, Y., Wang, X., Wang, Z.: Exploring GNN based program embedding technologies for binary related tasks. In: Proceedings of the 30th IEEE/ACM International Conference on Program Comprehension, pp. 366–377. ACM (2022)
16. He, H., et al.: Code is not natural language: Unlock the power of semantics-oriented graph representation for binary code similarity detection. In: Proceedings of the 33rd USENIX Security Symposium, pp. 1759–1776. USENIX (2024)

17. Horváth, M., et al.: Code clones: a novel approach to detecting plagiarism in binary decomposition of c programs. Acta Electrotechnica et Informatica **24**(2), 13–18 (2024)
18. Jiang, L., et al.: BinaryAI: binary software composition analysis via intelligent binary source code matching. In: Proceedings of the IEEE/ACM 46th International Conference on Software Engineering, pp. 1–13. ACM (2024)
19. Kim, G., Hong, S., Franz, M., Song, D.: Improving cross-platform binary analysis using representation learning via graph alignment. In: Proceedings of the 31st ACM SIGSOFT International Symposium on Software Testing and Analysis, pp. 151–163. ACM (2022)
20. Lacomis, J., et al.: DIRE: A neural approach to decompiled identifier naming. In: Proceedings of the 34th IEEE/ACM International Conference on Automated Software Engineering, pp. 628–639. IEEE (2019)
21. Lei, M., Li, H., Li, J., Aundhkar, N., Kim, D.K.: Deep learning application on code clone detection: A review of current knowledge. J. Syst. Softw. **184**(C), 1–15 (2022)
22. Li, X., Qu, Y., Yin, H.: PalmTree: learning an assembly language model for instruction embedding. In: Proceedings of the 2021 ACM SIGSAC Conference on Computer and Communications Security, pp. 3236–3251. ACM (2021)
23. Liu, B., et al.: αDiff: cross-version binary code similarity detection with DNN. In: Proceedings of the 33rd ACM/IEEE International Conference on Automated Software Engineering, pp. 667–678. ACM (2018)
24. Luo, Z., et al.: VulHawk: Cross-architecture vulnerability detection with entropy-based binary code search. In: Proceedings of the 2023 Network and Distributed System Security Symposium, pp. 1–18. ISOC (2023)
25. Mehrotra, N., Agarwal, N., Gupta, P., Anand, S., Lo, D., Purandare, R.: Modeling functional similarity in source code with graph-based Siamese networks. IEEE Trans. Software Eng. **48**(10), 3771–3789 (2022)
26. Mitre: Common vulnerabilities and exposures. https://cve.mitre.org/
27. Naidu, P.A., Yadav, K.D.K., Meena, B., Meesala, Y.N.: Sentiment analysis by using modified RNN and a tree LSTM. In: 2022 International Conference on Computing, Communication and Power Technology, pp. 6–10. IEEE (2022)
28. Raff, E., Barker, J., Sylvester, J., Brandon, R., Catanzaro, B., Nicholas, C.K.: Malware detection by eating a whole EXE. In: Proceedings of the AAAI Conference on Artificial Intelligence, pp. 268–276. AAAI (2018)
29. Sha, Z., et al.: OpTrans: enhancing binary code similarity detection with function inlining re-optimization. Empir. Softw. Eng. **30**(2), 49 (2025)
30. Shen, C., et al.: Deep Siamese network with multi-level similarity perception for person re-identification. In: Proceedings of the 33rd ACM/IEEE International Conference on Automated Software Engineering, pp. 1942–1950. ACM (2017)
31. Shin, E.C.R., Song, D., Moazzezi, R.: Recognizing functions in binaries with neural networks. In: Proceedings of the 24th USENIX Security Symposium, pp. 611–626. USENIX (2015)
32. Touvron, H., et al.: LLaMA: Open and efficient foundation language models. https://doi.org/10.48550/arXiv.2302.13971
33. Wan, B., Dong, S., Zhou, J., Qian, Y.: SJBCD: a java code clone detection method based on bytecode using Siamese neural network. Appl. Sci. **13**(17), 9580 (2023)
34. Wang, H., et al.: CLAP: Learning transferable binary code representations with natural language supervision. In: Proceedings of the 33rd ACM SIGSOFT International Symposium on Software Testing and Analysis, pp. 503–515. ACM (2024)

35. Wang, H., et al.: jTrans: Jump-aware transformer for binary code similarity detection. In: Proceedings of the 31st ACM SIGSOFT International Symposium on Software Testing and Analysis, pp. 1–13. ACM (2022)
36. Xu, X., Liu, C., Feng, Q., Yin, H., Song, L., Song, D.: Neural network-based graph embedding for cross-platform binary code similarity detection. In: Proceedings of the 2017 ACM SIGSAC Conference on Computer and Communications Security, pp. 363–376. ACM (2017)
37. Yang, C., Liu, Z., Zhao, D., Sun, M., Chang, E.Y.: Network representation learning with rich text information. In: Proceedings of the Twenty-Fourth International Joint Conference on Artificial Intelligence, pp. 2111–2117. Morgan Kaufmann (2015)
38. Yang, J., Fu, C., Liu, X.Y., Yin, H., Zhou, P.: Codee: A tensor embedding scheme for binary code search. IEEE Trans. Software Eng. **48**(7), 2224–2244 (2021)
39. Yang, S., Cheng, L., Zeng, Y., Lang, Z., Zhu, H., Shi, Z.: Asteria: Deep learning-based AST-encoding for cross-platform binary code similarity detection. In: 2021 51st Annual IEEE/IFIP International Conference on Dependable Systems and Networks, pp. 224–236. IEEE (2021)
40. Yu, S., Qu, Y., Hu, X., Yin, H.: DeepDI: Learning a relational graph convolutional network model on instructions for fast and accurate disassembly. In: Proceedings of the 31st USENIX Security Symposium, pp. 2709–2725. USENIX (2022)

What Matters Most in Vulnerabilities? Key Term Extraction for CVE-to-CWE Mapping with LLMs

Stefano Simonetto(✉), Ronan Oosteven, Thijs Van Ede, Peter Bosch, and Willem Jonker

University of Twente, Enschede, The Netherlands
{s.simonetto,r.oostveen,t.s.vanede,p.bosch,w.jonker}@utwente.nl

Abstract. Mapping Common Vulnerabilities and Exposures (CVEs) to the related Common Weakness Enumerations (CWE) is crucial in cybersecurity because this link allows categorizing vulnerabilities, prioritizing remediation efforts, and improving mitigation strategies. However, this process often requires manual effort to understand and connect a CVE to its CWE, which is undesirable due to its time-consuming nature. Existing automated approaches typically rely on vectorizing CVE descriptions using embedding techniques followed by machine learning classifiers. However, little attention has been given to evaluating whether CVE descriptions are the most effective starting point for automated classification, as these descriptions often contain irrelevant details that do not contribute to CVE-to-CWE mapping. Our research investigates to what extent we can automatically extract key information from CVE descriptions required to perform such mapping and evaluates how this technique improves existing methods for identifying related weaknesses using this extracted information. To this end, we present an approach that automates extracting key terms of CVEs through Large Language Models and evaluate the effect of focusing on various parts of the CVE description. We show that our key term extraction technique improves the F1-score of transformer-based classification of CVEs into CWEs up to 8.88% while providing a modest increase for more traditional mapping approaches.

Keywords: CVE · CWE · mapping · key-term extraction

1 Introduction

In cybersecurity, mapping Common Vulnerabilities and Exposures (CVEs)[1] to their corresponding Common Weakness Enumerations (CWEs)[2] is a crucial yet challenging task. Knowing the CWE associated with a specific CVE is central to the threat analysis. The intricate nature of CVE descriptions, which often detail specific products and versions, makes mapping CVEs to CWEs a complex task.

[1] https://cve.mitre.org/.

[2] https://cwe.mitre.org/.

Y. Kim et al. (Eds.): CANS 2025, LNCS 16351, pp. 467–492, 2026.
https://doi.org/10.1007/978-981-95-4434-9_22

This process requires a higher level of abstraction, as CWEs focus on the root cause and type of vulnerability, which is not directly tied to specific components or vendors that are present in the CVE description.

From the beginning of 2025, an average of 130 new CVEs are added to the database each day [1], with every entry requiring manual processing by CVE Numbering Authorities (CNAs). This labor-intensive process is compounded by the complexity of the CWE taxonomy, which demands careful selection from a broad range of categories. As shown in Fig. 6 in the Appendix, experts struggle to assign appropriate CWE labels to new CVEs promptly. Accurately labeling CWEs is essential as it enables the clustering of related CVEs and provides valuable insights into the patterns exploited by threat actors.

The existing literature on CVE-to-CWE mapping typically begins with the CVE description, which is then transformed into a vector representation using various techniques such as TF-IDF [2], Text-CNN [24], Bag-of-Words [3], and transformer-based [18]. These vectors are subsequently classified using different machine-learning models. Our research question concerns a preprocessing step that extracts the key terms from a description to allow the creation of better embeddings that improve subsequent classification. We answer the following: "Which key terms from a CVE description are most useful for accurately mapping it to the corresponding CWE?". By understanding what type of information is essential for the mapping, we can improve the existing model's prediction performance and better understand how to write clear CVE descriptions that communicate what weaknesses are exposed by the vulnerability.

To tackle this challenge, the paper describes a novel methodology to automate the extraction of key terms for CVE representation and compare CVE sections to determine which parts classifiers should focus on. Existing tools focus on extracting the subject or general keywords of a text. However, for CVEs, this information often involves specific products and version numbers, which are insignificant when determining the corresponding CWE. Instead, we prioritize extracting only the key terms of the CVE useful for this mapping. We investigate the use of LLMs (Llama and GPT) for automatically extracting key terms (focusing on fundamental aspects, context, and impact) of the vulnerability description.

The contributions of this paper are as follows. First, we propose a structured approach for extracting key terms from CVE descriptions to enhance CVE-to-CWE mapping. Leveraging large language models and in-context learning, our method distills the essential semantic elements (namely, the core aspects, context, and impact) while omitting product-specific details that are generally irrelevant for CWE classification.

Second, we perform a detailed manual evaluation of the extracted key terms and conduct a thorough comparative analysis of various CVE representations. Our findings demonstrate that our method consistently improves mapping performance, achieving up to an 8.88% increment in the F1-score on transformer-based models. Notably, these performance gains hold consistently across both unsupervised and supervised learning frameworks, as well as when applied to more conventional mapping techniques.

To foster collaboration in this area, we have made our code and results publicly available[3].

2 Background

CVEs enable security professionals and organizations to communicate effectively about specific weaknesses, ensuring universal reference to vulnerabilities by a common name. CVEs are indispensable for facilitating knowledge-sharing and fostering collaboration among researchers and vendors to develop appropriate patches or mitigations, thus safeguarding systems from potential exploits.

Common Weakness Enumeration is a community-developed catalog of common software weaknesses and security flaws. Unlike CVEs, which pinpoint specific vulnerabilities, CWEs categorize broader classes of weaknesses, encompassing various instances of similar vulnerabilities.

Over the years, annual CVE reports have surged dramatically, from 1,579 in 1999 to over 38,000 in 2024. At the same time, a persistent and widening gap in mapping CVEs to CWEs highlights the urgent need for a rapid, reliable, and automated classification system that minimizes reliance on human intervention. This trend is illustrated in Fig. 6 in the Appendix.

2.1 Motivation

In real-world scenarios, threat actors sequentially exploit multiple vulnerabilities to breach systems [13]. To identify these attack sequences, extracting the root cause at each step is crucial, uncovering the specific weaknesses that enable progression through the exploit. These causes are systematically identified through the CWE framework, which provides a clear understanding of the underlying weaknesses. Accurately recognizing these root causes is crucial, as it directly informs where investments, policies, and practices should be focused to effectively eliminate vulnerabilities at their source [18].

Ideally, CVE descriptions use a specified template that allows us to extract the root cause easily and adhere to a structured format, such as the one proposed in [6] and highlighted in Fig. 1:

-[VULNTYPE] in [COMPONENT] of [VENDOR] [PRODUCT] [VERSION] allows [ATTACKER] to [IMPACT] via [VECTOR].
-[COMPONENT] in [VENDOR] [PRODUCT] [VERSION] has a [ROOT CAUSE], which enables [ATTACKER] to [IMPACT] via [VECTOR].

Fig. 1. Vulnerability Representation Templates

Unfortunately, as noted by [21], the use of templates in vulnerability descriptions has declined significantly, from 99.6% in 2010 to 58.5% in 2021. This suggests

[3] https://anonymous.4open.science/r/CVEtermsextraction/README.md.

the need for a more flexible yet informative format that maintains the essential elements while adapting to evolving semantic changes in CVE descriptions.

To address this issue in vulnerability descriptions, we focus on NLP methods to be flexible in mapping even where no template format is available. Our pre-processing method automatically extracts key terms from CVEs, capturing the core aspects, contextual details, and potential impact of each vulnerability.

2.2 CVE to CWE Linking Example

The CVE description is precise toward a specific product or version, providing detailed information on how it affects the system. As an example, consider the description of CVE-2013-2762 as follows:

> "The Schneider Electric Magelis XBT HMI controller has a default password for authentication of configuration uploads, which makes it easier for remote attackers to ... "

The CVE description focuses on the specific product (subject), and contrasts with the broader context required for fitting it into CWE classifications. However, when mapping to a CWE classification, the focus shifts toward the broader underlying weakness rather than the particular product details. While product names and versions are essential for describing a specific vulnerability, they offer little value in understanding the broader weakness category represented by a CWE.

2.3 Hierarchical CWE Structure

CWEs are structured in a parent-child relationship, where generic weaknesses (e.g., improper restriction of operation within the bounds of a Memory Buffer) have more specific child weaknesses (e.g., Out-of-bounds Read vs Out-of-bounds Write). This structure represents the generalization-specialization relationship as pointed out in [12]: the more elevated the position in the hierarchy, the greater the abstraction; in contrast, the lower the position, the more focused on specifics. To illustrate this concept and highlight the related challenge in the classification, consider the following hierarchy within the CWE framework:

- **Class:** Improper Restriction of Operations within the Bounds of a Memory Buffer
  - **Base:** Out-of-bounds Write
  - **Base:** Out-of-bounds Read
    - **Variant:** Buffer Under-read
    - **Variant:** Buffer Over-read

The challenge lies in extracting the differentiators between each classification option. Our method effectively identifies the nuances that differentiate one CWE from its parent or siblings, such as distinguishing between buffer overflow-read and buffer overflow-write. The CWE framework follows this hierarchical structure, as illustrated in the CWE-1003 view. The specification emphasizes that each CVE should be assigned the most specific, lowest-level label within the hierarchy whenever possible.

3 Related Work

Recent studies have explored two avenues to improve CVE-to-CWE mapping. One approach is to adopt better CVE description embedders, ranging from TF-IDF [4] to text-to-vec [16] and transformer-based methods [23]. The other approach focuses on mapping these embeddings to the correct CWE label through multi-stage processes.

In our work, we focus on the former, specifically on enhancing the embedding process by targeting only the keywords extracted from a CVE description rather than embedding the entire text. As demonstrated by [20], this keyword-focused embedding can significantly improve quality, since averaging embeddings over all words can dilute the meaning of the critical terms. To identify these significant keywords, key phrase extraction methods such as YAKE [5] and KeyBERT [11] have been applied. YAKE is an unsupervised and lightweight technique that determines term relevance based on statistical features within a document, whereas KeyBERT leverages BERT embeddings to extract keywords that best match the document's context, thereby providing a more context-aware extraction process.

Although these keyword extractors highlight the most important terms in the CVE text, they do not consider the specific application of those terms, such as CVE-to-CWE mapping. In this scenario, terms such as the CVE subject might be extracted as keywords by YAKE or KeyBERT but are not particularly helpful for accurately mapping CVEs to CWEs. Therefore, task-specific considerations are crucial to improving the usefulness of extracted keywords in specialized contexts such as CVE classification.

4 Dataset

Key term extraction can be applied to any CVE description, but evaluating its benefits requires a meticulously prepared dataset for both machine learning training and testing. To assess the extent to which key term extraction enhances the automated mapping of CVE descriptions to CWEs, we use NIST's National Vulnerability Database (NVD). The NVD provides a manually verified mapping of all vulnerabilities to the weaknesses listed in the default "CWE-1003 view".

The dataset was prepared through the following steps. First, we converted multi-label CVEs, comprising 1.5% of the dataset, into single-label instances by duplicating entries, increasing the total from 222,240 to 225,886. Next, we applied a minimum sample threshold to focus on prevalent CWEs to cover 95% of all CVEs, narrowing our focus to 57 classes. Finally, we split the data so that 10% of the original dataset forms the test set (12,845 samples) and the remaining data (comprising of the 57 classes) is divided into 90% for training and 10% for validation. For the training and validation sets, to mitigate bias from classes with excessively large sample sizes (e.g., CWE-79 with over 25,000 samples), we undersampled classes with more than 3,000 samples, resulting in a balanced set of 72,372 CVE descriptions with no overlap between the test and training-validation sets.

5 Preliminary Analysis

We conducted a comparison of two state-of-the-art key term extraction methods, YAKE and KeyBERT, to assess their effectiveness in extracting key terms that are useful for mapping CVEs to CWEs. The objective is to determine how well these tools could identify key terms relevant to this specific type of mapping while avoiding extracting terms that are simply the subject of the CVE, which are often not useful for this purpose.

To evaluate these tools, we selected two CVE descriptions for each CWE (114 examples in total) and extracted the top three key terms using both YAKE and KeyBERT. The results were manually analyzed to determine whether the retrieved terms provided useful information ('root cause' and 'vulnerability type') for CVE-to-CWE mapping and to what extent they included terms that merely represented the subject of the CVE.

YAKE identified the subject as a key term 74.56% of cases and provided useful information 47.37% of the time. On the other hand, KeyBERT detected the subject even more frequently (92.11%) and produced significantly fewer useful CWE-relevant terms (14.04%).

Overall, our comparison shows that YAKE offers a better balance in terms of avoiding overly specific subject-related terms and providing terms more directly related to the CWE. Both YAKE and KeyBERT exhibit significant limitations, which motivated us to experiment with our approach based on in-context learning leveraging LLMs to improve the accuracy and relevance of key term extraction for CVE-to-CWE mapping.

6 Term Extraction Methodology

This section details our approach for extracting key terms from CVE descriptions leveraging LLMs as illustrated in Fig. 2. In Subsect. 6.2, we explore the role of LLMs in key term extraction and conduct a case study to evaluate the impact of different models on our approach.

6.1 Term Extraction

In this section, we develop a pipeline for automatically extracting key terms from CVE descriptions, streamlining the process by avoiding the involvement of expert revision. The focus is on abstracting the CVE description from unrelated details to establish a direct mapping from CVE to CWE.

We define the following categories based on the standardized template that every vulnerability should adhere to, as shown in Fig. 1:

- **Core terms** represent fundamental concepts that define the primary aspects or components of a vulnerability. These terms are essential for understanding the central issue and correspond to the 'Vulnerability Type' and 'Root Cause'.
- **Consequences** refer to the outcomes or results of actions. Consequences often describe the 'Impact' of a vulnerability being exploited.

- **Contextual terms** provide additional details or conditions that help clarify the circumstances under which a vulnerability occurs. These terms correspond to the 'Vector' or 'Attacker' attributes.

As shown in Fig. 2, we leverage in-context learning (ICL) [10] to extract key terms. ICL operates on the principle of learning from analogy by using a few demonstration examples to build a prompt context. This context is then combined with a query to form the input for the language model, which generates the prediction. As shown in [9], the transformer block implicitly modifies the weights of the MLP layer according to the context.

Given the challenging nature of the CVE-to-CWE mapping, finding the right prompt design is crucial for capturing the essence of the CVE, as described in the following subsections.

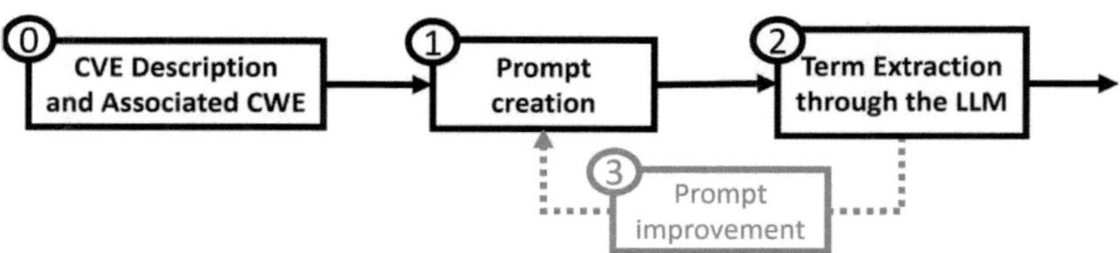

Fig. 2. Pipeline to extract key terms. **Note**: the blue dashed line represents a step used only during the prompt design phase. This step is omitted during inference, making the pipeline fully automated and constituted only by steps from 0 to 2.

1. Prompt Creation. Effective prompt design is essential for in-context learning, ensuring that the model fully understands the task requirements and produces meaningful outputs. We instructed the LLMs to extract three key elements from each CVE description (core terms, contextual terms, and consequences) while omitting extraneous details. Our final prompt includes an example illustrating these elements, derived from a typical CVE description that contains both relevant and irrelevant information. This example helps guide the LLM in prioritizing the most important aspects. The full prompt is provided in Appendix A.2.

2. Term Extraction Through the LLM. Our process summarizes CVE descriptions to their core components and outputs them in JSON format. For this task, we experimented with GPT-3.5 Turbo and LLaMA 2 (7B), which are referred to throughout the paper as **GPT** and **LLaMA**, respectively.

Notably, while GPT produced outputs that were immediately parsable as JSON, only 19% of Llama's outputs met this criterion. The remaining outputs required additional post-processing to achieve a valid JSON format, though regeneration was not necessary.

3. Prompt Improvement. In the design phase, we manually assessed the relevance of the extracted terms to ensure they accurately reflect the provided CVE descriptions. This manual review is crucial for validating the effectiveness of the automated term extraction, as discussed in Subsect. 6.2. After multiple iterations, we refined the prompt, achieving the association of each CVE description with the three sets of representative terms.

As an example, initially, we included 'technical details' as a fourth item in the key terms list to maintain the specificity of the CVE description towards items such as 'Vendor', as shown in Fig. 1. However, this approach led to the extraction of overly specific terms focused solely on vulnerability, such as the product name. Consequently, we decided not to include these technical details, resulting in the final core terms, contextual terms, and consequences. Once the prompt is finalized, this step is no longer performed, leaving the key term extraction pipeline fully automated from steps 0 to 2.

6.2 Extracted Terms Manual Evaluation

We manually validated 2 randomly selected CVE descriptions for each of the 57 CWE classes used in our evaluation, totaling 114 manually inspected samples.

Since there is no standardized benchmarking for evaluating LLM responses, as the assessment criteria vary based on the specific task and format, we evaluated the extracted terms from the CVE description based on three key attributes: hallucination, completeness, and consistency.

- Hallucination: This criterion checks whether the terms include any fabricated information not present in the original CVE description. Importantly, elaborations or clarifications of terms or concepts are not considered hallucinations. For example, in Table 5, if the short description mentions 'XSS' and the corresponding extracted core term is 'Cross-site scripting', this is *not* treated as a hallucination. This metric is analogous to *1-precision*, ensuring that the extracted terms are grounded in the source text.
- Completeness: We assess whether the extracted terms capture all the essential aspects of the CVE description, ensuring no critical information is omitted. Rather than emphasizing the categorization of terms (e.g., core terms, contextual terms, consequences), we focus on providing a global representation of the CVE description. This ensures that the extracted terms reflect the full scope of the vulnerability. This metric is analogous to recall.
- Consistency: To measure consistency, we extracted key terms three times with the temperature set to the default value and compared the results to see if the relevant terms were maintained in each category. If the key terms in each category were preserved, the extraction was considered consistent; otherwise, it was classified as inconsistent.

An example for each criterion is proposed in Appendix A.3.

Table 1. Llama and GPT comparison on hallucinations, completeness, and consistency. Consistency is measured across three extraction attempts, while hallucination and completeness are evaluated based on a single extraction.

Model	Subject present in core terms	Hallucination	Completeness	Consistency		
				Core	Contextual	Consequences
Llama	12.28%	15.78%	75.44%	82.46%	41.23%	64.06%
GPT	11.40%	6.14%	90.35%	97.37%	77.19%	87.72%

Table 1 clearly illustrates that the key terms extracted by GPT are more consistent, complete, and exhibit fewer hallucinations compared to those extracted by Llama. Consequently, we selected GPT as our primary key term extractor in subsequent experiments (see Sect. 7). While certain aspects of CVE descriptions can be challenging to capture for both language models (as evidenced by the trends in both models), GPT consistently outperforms Llama in all key metrics.

The results of in-context learning using LLMs show substantial improvement compared to YAKE and KeyBERT. Specifically, GPT and Llama show a reduction in irrelevant subjects within the extracted terms, as well as significant advancements in extracting useful information for effective mapping. GPT and Llama both achieve far greater completeness compared to YAKE and KeyBERT, reinforcing the effectiveness of LLMs in this domain.

Table 1 shows that GPT produces significantly fewer hallucinations. This reduced hallucination rate directly impacts the precision of the extracted terms, ensuring they remain faithful to the original CVE descriptions. Additionally, GPT's higher completeness score ensures a more comprehensive representation of CVE information, minimizing the risk of leaving out critical details. Consistency across multiple runs is crucial for the reproducibility of experiments and future work. Even if the correct terms were consistently identified, they were labeled as inconsistent if placed in incorrect categories (e.g., core terms classified as contextual terms). Despite this categorization challenge, GPT demonstrated greater stability, providing more consistent term classification compared to Llama.

7 Terms Comparison Methodology

We analyze different focus areas of the CVE text, such as using the complete description, a combination of the extracted terms, and descriptions without the subject. This analysis determines which modification most effectively captures the semantic essence needed for accurate CVE to CWE mapping, as shown in Fig. 3. As discussed in Sect. 3, two main approaches exist to improve CVE-to-CWE mapping: developing better CVE description embedders and mapping these embeddings to the correct CWE label via multi-stage processes (e.g., multi-stage neural networks). Our work focuses on enhancing the first approach, and for the second step, we implemented a basic neural network, as achieving the best possible classification is not the primary goal of this study. To understand which representation of a CVE should be embedded, we run different experiments, considering how a CVE can be summarized.

1. Different scenarios

To analyze and optimize how CVE descriptions are processed, we propose a systematic approach to test various configurations of the text. These configurations are designed to address common issues with CVE descriptions and evaluate the impact of different term selections. The rationale behind each step is as follows, and an example for each scenario is provided in Table 2:

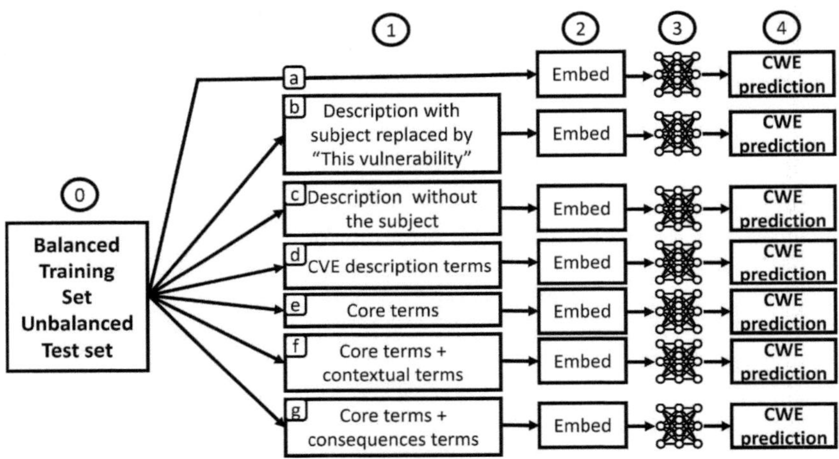

Fig. 3. Comparison of different CVE representations to select which is the best performing in the task of CVE to CWE mapping.

(a) Baseline Method

The simplest and widely adopted approach utilizes the entire CVE description. This method ensures that no information is omitted; however, CVE descriptions often include product-specific details that might limit generalization.

Replacing Subjects for Clarity

Many CVE descriptions start with product details, version numbers, and vendor information, making them less generalizable. To address this:

(b) Replace the subject (the portion of the sentence before the verb) with a generic term like "This vulnerability." This substitution aims to maintain sentence structure while removing product-specific identifiers.
(c) Replace the subject with a blank space to make the CVE description independent of any specific subject.

Term Extraction and Combination

Leveraging key terms extracted through a previously described pipeline, we conduct an ablation study to assess the best configuration:

(d) *Key terms*: Concatenate all extracted terms, including core, contextual, and consequence terms, to provide a comprehensive view of the CVE.
(e) Use only core terms.
(f) Combine core and contextual terms.
(g) Combine core and consequence terms.

Table 2. Description of CVE-2010-1459. In three scenarios, the subject (red) is a) left intact; b) replaced with "This vulnerability"; c) removed. Additionally, points d) to g) explore various combinations of core terms, contextual, and consequences: d) concatenate all of them, e) take only the core terms, f) combine core and contextual, and g) combine core and consequences.

CVE-2010-1459: The default configuration of ASP.NET in Mono before 2.6.4 has a value of FALSE for the EnableViewStateMac property, allowing remote attackers to conduct Cross-site Scripting (XSS) attacks via the __VIEWSTATE parameter to 2.0/menu/menu1.aspx. in the XSP sample project.

Core Terms	Contextual Terms	Consequences
Cross-site Scripting Vulnerability	Login form	Arbitrary HTML injection
Remote Attack	Remote attackers	Form parameter manipulation
Arbitrary Code Injection	Web script injection	Security compromise

NIST classification: CWE-79 (Cross-site Scripting)

2. Embed

As noted in Sect. 3, various embedding approaches have been proposed for mapping CVE text to CWE, with transformer-based embeddings emerging as the most promising. In our work, both the training and testing data are embedded using OpenAI's ada-embeddings, producing a 1536-dimensional dense vector that captures the semantic features of the text. Details on different transformer-based embedders can be found in Sect. 8.2.

3. Training

For the mapping step, we implemented a feed-forward neural network. This choice reflects our primary objective: to enhance the input representation for the downstream classifier (specifically, the embedding of CVE representation) rather than to replicate or benchmark state-of-the-art classification architectures. Notably, this design underpins the most recent and best-performing models in the literature [2,7,19], where only minor variations are introduced. Therefore, exploring these improvements was not within the scope of our study.

The network architecture consists of an input layer with 1,536 features, followed by a hidden layer of 128 neurons (ReLU activation), another hidden layer with 64 neurons (ReLU activation), and an output layer with 57 neurons (softmax activation) corresponding to the unique CWE classes. We trained the model using the Adam optimizer and sparse categorical cross-entropy loss over 40 epochs with a batch size of 32.

The validation phase was performed by using the weighted F1-score as metric. Based on that, the best checkpoint within the 40 epochs was identified and subsequently employed for inference tasks. This model was assessed on the validation data, revealing that, on average, there were no improvements beyond 23 epochs, with the latest improvement occurring at the 27th epoch. The training parameters were determined empirically through iterative experimentation and evaluation, as our aim was to test the methodology rather than achieve the optimal model.

4. Inference

After completing training and validation on a balanced dataset, we employed the finalized neural network model to predict the CWE associated with each entry in the unbalanced test set.

8 Evaluation

To evaluate the impact of key terms in predicting CWEs from CVEs, we first assess the effect of including different sections of the CVE descriptions as input to a generic embedding-based model (Sect. 8.1). This analysis enables us to identify which parts of the CVE have the most significant impact on the model's decision-making process. After identifying the terms that contribute most effectively to classification. In Sect. 8.2, we evaluate the improvement gained by using a transformer-based architecture over more traditional ones, highlighting the rapid pace of transformer improvements. Section 8.3 examines the influence of the specific information contained within CVE descriptions themselves. Finally, Sect. 8.4 further explores how these key terms enable stronger differentiation among closely related CWE subclasses.

8.1 Scenario Comparison

To evaluate the multiclass classification problem, we used precision, recall, and F1-score based on the weighted average and macro average. Unlike the weighted average, which considers the support (i.e., the number of true instances) for each class, the macro average treats each class equally, regardless of its size or frequency in the dataset.

The paper aims to compare and show which parts of a CVE description contain the most useful information to automate mapping CVEs to their corresponding CWEs. It does not aim to achieve state-of-the-art results in this complex classification but rather improve the performance for a given method as shown in Table 3. The table shows that the CVE representation based on key terms (concatenation of core, contextual, and consequences terms) outperforms all other approaches in both F1-score and accuracy. Specifically, this method outperforms utilizing the complete CVE description, exhibiting an improvement of 8.88% in the F1-score. Other combinations of core terms with contextual or consequence information perform similarly to each other and outperform the scenario using full CVE descriptions.

Subpar results are observed in scenarios where subjects are replaced or omitted. Specifically, substituting the subject with a fixed phrase: "This vulnerability", makes all CVE descriptions appear more similar to one another than they actually are, as they now share the same generic subject. Omitting the subject and substituting it with a blank space makes it more difficult for transformers to use in the embedding process, as it cannot properly relate the verb and the remaining sentence to an unspecified subject. This result highlights the need for

Table 3. Performance comparison of CWE classification using two distinct approaches: (1) **LLM Prompting**, where a language model is directly prompted with a CVE description, and (2) **Embedding-Based Classification**, where extracted components from the CVE text are embedded and classified using a downstream model. Bold indicates best performance.

Approach	Input format	Weighted Avg			Macro Avg		
		Prec	Rec	F1	Prec	Rec	F1
LLM Prompting	Chain-of-thought	69.06%	58.25%	60.52%	11.77%	9.80%	9.83%
	Zero-shot	71.96%	61.03%	62.27%	10.74%	8.76%	8.72%
Embedding Based	Full CVE description	71.18%	63.58%	64.62%	51.03%	62.89%	54.66%
	Without subject	66.01%	54.96%	56.16%	46.33%	52.93%	47.44%
	Replaced subject	67.65%	58.57%	60.28%	47.42%	53.54%	48.51%
	Key terms	**74.07%**	**69.84%**	**70.36%**	57.52%	**64.85%**	**59.66%**
	Core terms	72.61%	69.17%	69.48%	**57.97%**	63.62%	59.39%
	Core + context	73.71%	68.35%	69.40%	55.70%	64.25%	58.09%
	Core + consequences	72.75%	68.07%	68.27%	55.94%	64.33%	58.24%

a more flexible tool that doesn't rely on fixed text processing rules. In some CVE descriptions, the root cause and vulnerability type are mentioned at the beginning of the description, requiring a more adaptable approach.

By conducting a detailed analysis of CVE descriptions and key terms, we evaluate the effectiveness of our approach in improving performance across various CWE classes. On the macro average, there is a consistent improvement in the performance across all configurations compared to using only the CVE description. However, the low scores highlight the inherent difficulty of the task, regardless of the number of instances per class. For example, CWE-312 (Cleartext Storage of Sensitive Information) is frequently misclassified as CWE-200 (Exposure of Sensitive Information to an Unauthorized Actor) 33.33% of the time. Although CWE-312 has only 42 instances, these misclassifications significantly impact the model's performance on the macro average.

On the other hand, the enhancement observed in classes with higher frequencies within the original dataset was particularly notable. Specifically, CWE-79 (Cross-site Scripting) and CWE-89 (SQL Injection) together account for over 15% of the entire dataset, with observed improvements on the weighted F1-score of 10.43% and 10.95%, respectively.

To establish a strong baseline, we compared our method to LLM-only approaches by querying GPT via an API for CWE classification. Specifically, we reproduced the chain-of-thought prompting strategy proposed by Liu et al. [15], adopting their best-performing prompt configuration. In addition, we evaluated a zero-shot setting, where GPT was prompted with a CVE description and tasked with predicting the most appropriate CWE label without reasoning steps or examples. Both prompting strategies underperformed relative to our embedding-based methods. While the weighted-average scores of the LLM-based approaches are comparable, their macro-average performance is significantly lower. For a controlled comparison, we constrained GPT's output to the same set of 57 CWE classes used for training and evaluation in our method. Even under this restriction, LLM-only approaches failed to match the performance of the embedding-based classifiers.

8.2 Transformer-Based vs Traditional Architectures

Our evaluation leverages transformer-based embeddings because of their well-established ability to capture sentence-level semantics and contextual relationships, as demonstrated in [7,18]. In this work, we not only adopt these modern techniques but also extend our investigation to more traditional architectures, thereby demonstrating that our preprocessing method based on key term extraction is robust and generalizable across a range of models and learning paradigms.

Table 4. Comparison of CWE classification performance using the CVE full-description vs. term-extracted inputs across four scenarios: (1) Unsupervised Transformer-based model [18], (2) Supervised Transformer-based model (ours), (3) Supervised TextCNN [17], and (4) Supervised BiGRU-TextCNN [17]. Each model is evaluated on both the full CVE description ("Desc.") and extracted key terms ("Terms"). All results are reported as weighted averages. Bolded values indicate performance improvements from term-based input.

Method	Architecture	CVE	Prec.	Rec.	F1	Acc.
1) Unsupervised	Transformer-based	Desc.	53.53%	33.03%	31.94%	33.03%
		Terms	**54.39%**	**39.31%**	**37.84%**	**39.31%**
2) Supervised	Transformer-based	Desc.	71.18%	63.58 %	64.62%	63.58 %
		Terms	**74.07%**	**69.84%**	**70.36%**	**69.84%**
3) Supervised	TextCNN	Desc.	**75.32%**	68.96%	70.09%	68.96%
		Terms	75.20%	**70.39%**	**71.34%**	**70.39%**
4) Supervised	BiGRU-TextCNN	Desc.	**75.52%**	70.16%	70.59%	70.16%
		Terms	75.11%	**71.30%**	**71.64%**	**71.30%**

Table 4 summarizes the performance obtained with both unsupervised and supervised approaches. In the transformer-based setting, the use of key terms instead of the full CVE descriptions yields an improvement consistent with the supervised learning (e.g., a 5.9% point increase in the F1-score). Similar trends emerge with supervised models based on more traditional architectures, including TextCNN and BiGRU-TextCNN, although the improvements from key term representations are comparatively smaller. This observation reinforces the hypothesis that key terms provide a better representation for CVE-to-CWE mapping than the complete, and often noisy, descriptions.

The more modest improvements seen in the TextCNN and BiGRU-TextCNN architectures can be attributed to their dependence on capturing sequential and local context. When the CVE descriptions are reduced to only their essential key terms, some of the detailed sequential information is necessarily lost, which limits the performance gains in architectures optimized for such context. Nevertheless, the fact that key term extraction yields improvements across both unsupervised and supervised learning paradigms highlights its utility as a consistent enhancement, regardless of the underlying learning framework.

Furthermore, we investigated the generalizability of our approach across a range of transformer-based models representing an evolutionary timeline, from early bidirectional models like BERT [8] to more recent generative architectures such as Llama [22] and Phi [14], and finally the state-of-the-art, GPT. In our experiments, embeddings were obtained using different strategies for each model (e.g., averaging all token embeddings in BERT versus using the last token in Phi and LLama). Despite these extraction differences, as illustrated in Fig. 4 and reported in Appendix A.5, the rapid and consistent improvements associated with key term representations remain evident.

Importantly, given the rapid evolution of transformer-based models and the consistent gains observed with key term extraction, we anticipate that the combination of transformer architectures with key term extraction will soon outperform more traditional methods. This trend is evident across both unsupervised and supervised learning paradigms, reinforcing our central thesis: focusing on the core semantic elements within CVE descriptions not only enhances current mapping performance but also forecasts even greater improvements as transformer models continue to advance.

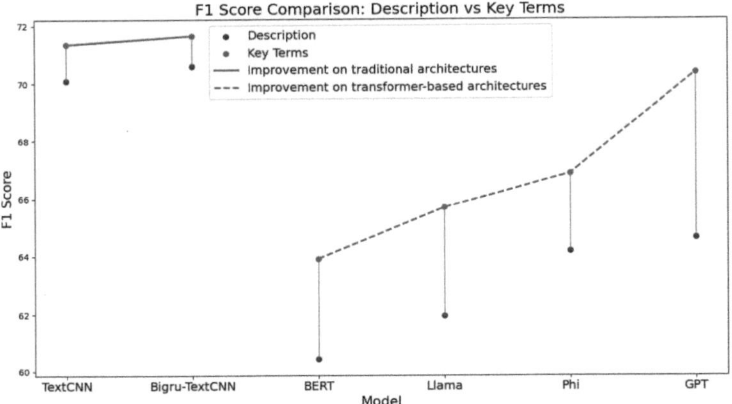

Fig. 4. Improved CVE-to-CWE classification by leveraging key terms instead of full-text descriptions across different architectures.

This consistent improvement, along with the broad generalizability of the approach, underscores the fundamental insight that isolating the key semantic information in CVE descriptions is a robust strategy for boosting CVE-to-CWE mapping performance across diverse modeling and learning frameworks.

8.3 Long vs Short CVE Descriptions

We explore whether the improvements achieved through key term extraction vary based on the length of CVE descriptions. By leveraging the extracted key terms, we observe an overall performance improvement across all data lengths, with particularly significant enhancements for both long and short CVE descriptions, as shown in Table 5.

The key terms extraction process effectively identifies and emphasizes the crucial elements of the description required for predicting the corresponding CWE. As shown in Table 5, the term extraction captures the essential information in lengthy CVE descriptions, while for shorter descriptions it reinforces the fundamental concepts. Essential terms such as ‘Cross-site Scripting’, ‘XSS’, and ‘Web Security’ are identified and appropriately replicated as required. Notably, in shorter descriptions, we observe the effective utilization of the inherent knowledge within the Language Model because it recognizes that XSS (Cross-Site Scripting) is related to web security and is a web vulnerability.

Table 5. Examples of Long and Short CVE Descriptions with Extracted Terms

Long CVE: A vulnerability was found in SourceCodester Class Scheduling System 1.0. It has been declared as critical. Affected by this vulnerability is an unknown functionality of the file `/admin/edit_subject.php` of the component GET Parameter Handler. The manipulation of the argument id leads to sql injection. The attack can be launched remotely. The exploit has been disclosed to the public and may be used. The identifier VDB-229597 was assigned to this vulnerability.

Core Terms	Contextual Terms	Consequences
SQL Injection	SourceCodester Class Scheduling System	Critical vulnerability
Remote Attack	GET Parameter Handler	Remote exploitation
Public Disclosure	File Manipulation	Public disclosure

Labels: Real: 89, Predicted using description: 94, Predicted using terms: 89

Short CVE: kkcms 1.3 has `jx.php?url=` XSS.

Core Terms	Contextual Terms	Consequences
Cross-site Scripting	kkcms 1.3	Data manipulation
XSS	jx.php?url=	Untrusted input
Web Security	URL parameter	Web vulnerability

Labels: Real: 79, Predicted using description: 611, Predicted using terms: 79

To generalize the improvements observed for both long and short CVE descriptions using our method and to ensure robust and reliable results, we restricted the CVE descriptions to those containing between 9 and 69 words. This range was chosen to minimize excessive variability in the analysis, as relying on descriptions with too few samples could skew the results and distort the graphical representation. The word count distribution is notably uneven, resembling a Gaussian curve with a pronounced right tail compared to the left one. The graphical representation in Fig. 5 depicts the misclassification percentage (left y-axis), indicating the frequency of misclassifications by the model, with lower values signifying better performance. The solid line denotes the average misclassification, with the green line corresponding to the performance of the key terms approach, exhibiting a lower misclassification than the comprehensive descriptions. The dashed lines represent the moving average of predictions related to the length of sentences. Especially, the green line consistently outperforms the descriptions' misclassification rate. The average misclassification demonstrates a consistent improvement of our approach across all CVE descriptions. Specifically, the key terms approach demonstrates an average misclassification rate of

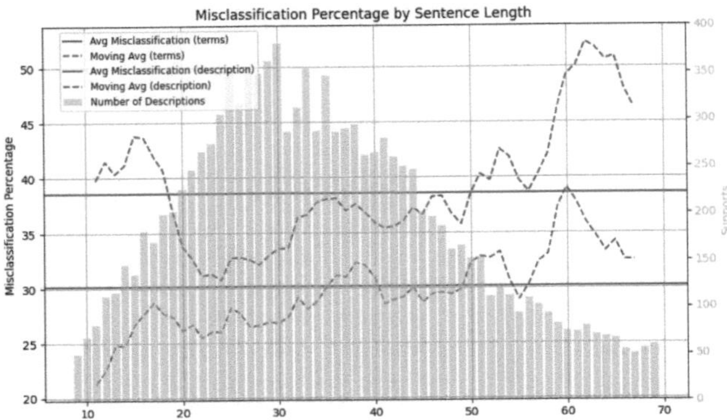

Fig. 5. Misclassification percentages by sentence length, showing consistent improvement of the key terms approach over comprehensive descriptions.

30.16%, compared to 38.58% for the CVE descriptions, reflecting a consistent improvement of over 8% points. By averaging the misclassification rates for CVE descriptions longer than 64 words (specifically the last five, ranging from 65 to 69 words), our method shows an improvement of 13.68% points. Similarly, for CVE descriptions shorter than 14 words (specifically the first five, ranging from 9 to 13 words), the improvement is 18.32% points. These results highlight a consistent enhancement across all data lengths, with particularly significant performance gains in handling extreme cases of very long and concise descriptions. To give more context, the blue bars represent the distribution of CVE descriptions by word count, with at least 50 elements to be included.

8.4 Subtle Differentiation of CWE Siblings

The primary advantage of term extraction is its capability to discern subtle distinctions among CWE siblings (children of the same parent). This can be seen when we compare the results of key terms vs. CVE descriptions to identify the CWE *classes* (CWE parent) related to all the CWE labels as shown in Table 6. The variation in this classification is less pronounced than that observed in the CWE base classification.

Table 6. Model performance of mapping CVE descriptions to CWEs classes (parent) on the weighted average. **Note**: This table differs from Table 3 because, instead of classifying CVE descriptions in CWE base (57 classes), in this case we classify CVE descriptions in CWE *classes* (28 classes).

CVE	Precision	Recall	F1-score	Accuracy
Description	79.10%	76.52%	76.87%	76.52%
Key terms	80.39%	79.56%	79.48%	79.56%

To showcase term extraction from closely related CWE siblings, consider the following example involving a buffer overflow vulnerability:

> "This vulnerability allows remote attackers to execute arbitrary code on affected installations of OpenText Brava! Desktop 16.6.3.84. User interaction is required ... which can result in a write past the end of an allocated buffer..."

The vulnerability involves a buffer overflow, and both the description and extracted terms can recognize it. However, the distinguishing factor lies in whether the buffer overflow occurs during the writing or reading process. While the classification based on the CVE description incorrectly labels the entry as a 'Buffer-Overflow read', the extracted terms accurately clarify that the vulnerability pertains to the writing process 'Buffer-Overflow write', as explicitly stated in the contextual term 'Write past end of buffer'.

9 Discussion and Future Work

Our study successfully distilled key information from CVE descriptions, highlighting the importance of focusing on essential elements while filtering out irrelevant details for effective CVE-to-CWE mapping. We observed that key term representations consistently outperform alternative methods, underscoring a critical challenge: CVE descriptions are often verbose and contain irrelevant information for CWE classification. While this additional information is valuable for other applications, automated CVE-to-CWE mapping methods must account for and possibly mitigate the impact of such noise.

A critical challenge in extracting key terms using LLMs is their tendency to generate hallucinations. In Sect. 6.2, we evaluated the models while considering these hallucinations as a key factor in the model selection process. Although GPT exhibits a relatively low rate of hallucinations, we further analyzed the seven extracted terms where hallucinations were detected during manual evaluation. Our findings indicate that four of these instances were correctly classified under the appropriate CWE, one was assigned to the correct CWE *class* (parent) but to the incorrect CWE base (child), and two were misclassified. Despite the small sample size, the overall CWE prediction accuracy for key terms with hallucinations was 57.14%, compared to the original model's accuracy of 69.84% (see Table 3). When the classification constraint is relaxed to CWE parent categories, the accuracy increases to 79.56% for the original model (see Table 6) and 71.43% for hallucination-affected cases. Although this represents a drop in performance, the impact of hallucinations is diluted, as each hallucination affects only a single term within a set of nine extracted terms (3 terms for each core, contextual, and consequences). Future research will explore to which extent we can reduce or correct hallucinations by using techniques such as self-verification [25].

We selected GPT for key term extraction over Llama due to its better performance. However, the proprietary nature of GPT imposes cost and accessibility constraints, particularly for newer models. An alternative is fine-tuning an open-source LLM, such as Phi or LLaMA, for key term extraction. This approach reduces costs and enhances data privacy, but, as discussed in Sect. 6.2, comes at the expense of performance, as GPT has demonstrated better extraction capabilities compared to LLaMA on the base models.

10 Limitations

The technique presented in this study does not encompass all possible CWEs, as it has not been exhaustively tested across the entire CWE spectrum. NIST recognizes a subset of 130 CWEs (CWE-1003 view), including classes, bases, and variants. Since we did not test our method across all possible CWEs, we cannot claim that our approach is generalizable to the entire CWE spectrum. However, our goal in this paper is not to classify CVEs into as many CWEs as possible but to demonstrate the effectiveness of key term extraction in this context.

A key limitation of using closed-source LLMs like GPT-3.5 Turbo lies in the cost per request. Appendix A.4 provides a detailed comparison of the per-request costs for various state-of-the-art LLMs, both open and proprietary. For open-source models, costs stem primarily from infrastructure usage. Among the models considered, GPT-4.1-nano emerged as the most cost-efficient, while Claude Sonnet 4 and Grok 4 were the most expensive. Notably, even under the most expensive configuration, replicating the experiments presented in this study would result in a total cost of approximately 200.

Although achieving state-of-the-art performance in this classification task was not our primary goal, we still enhanced all architectures, especially transformer-based ones. Instead, our focus is on determining which parts of a CVE description offer the most valuable information for automating CVE-to-CWE mapping.

11 Conclusions

This study introduces a methodology aimed at enhancing the automation of mapping CVEs to their corresponding CWEs. By leveraging in-context learning with LLMs, we extract key terms from CVEs that are highly relevant to CWE identification, enhancing the F1-score and accuracy of the mapping processes.

The comparative analysis of different CVE representation methods highlights the improvements brought by the term-based approaches in capturing the semantic essence of CVEs. Additionally, the study explains the impact of description length on key term extraction performance, showcasing the robustness of the methodology across various lengths of CVE descriptions.

Furthermore, this study demonstrates the embedding generalizability to multiple language models, showcasing its potential across language models of different sizes. The methodology also improves traditional CVE-to-CWE classification methods, although the gains are more modest compared to those observed with transformer architectures.

A Appendix

A.1 Mapping CVEs to CWEs over time

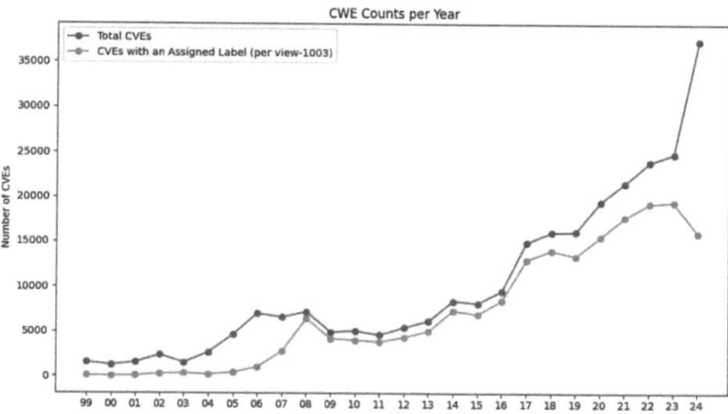

Fig. 6. The graph displays two trends: the total number of CVEs reported each year and the subset of CVEs that have an assigned a CWE label according to the 1003-view.

A.2 Prompt Design

To extract key terms from each CVE description, we designed a structured prompt for the language model. The CVE description was inserted dynamically in the prompt using the placeholder **cve_description**. The prompt aimed to guide the model in generating a well-organized and semantically relevant keyword list by providing task instructions, keyword generation tips, and a worked example:

> I want you to create a proper keyword list for a CVE, I will give you a list of tips for proper keyword list creation which are given below between triple backticks. Then I will give you and example CVE and the example keyword list in JSON, to help you understand the task better. Your result should also have 3 related keywords per item like the example result. Lastly I will give you a CVE and you have to give me the keyword list in JSON format.
> Tips:
> 1. Text Normalization: Standardize the text by converting it to lowercase, removing special characters, and expanding abbreviations. This helps in reducing variations in the text.
>
> 2. Abstraction: given the CVE description, create an abstraction of it by leaving aside the terms that are too specific (e.g. if a CVE is specifically targeting a cisco router, this detail is not important)

3. Keyword Extraction: Identify and extract key terms and concepts from both the CVE and CWE descriptions. For instance, phrases like "incorrectly handles a length field" or "buffer overflow" are critical.

CVE_example:
"CVE description": "Patient Information Center iX (PICiX) Versions B.02, PerformanceBridge Focal Point Version A.01, IntelliVue patient monitors MX100 IntelliVue X3 and X2 Versions N and prior. The software parses a formatted message or structure but does not handle or incorrectly handles a length field that is inconsistent with the actual length of the associated data, causing the application on the surveillance station to restart".
CVE_example result:
"core terms": ["Parsing Vulnerability", "Inconsistent Length Field Handling", "Application Restart"],
"contextual terms": ["Length field", "Inconsistency", "Improper handling"],
"consequences": ["Unexpected restart", "Data length mismatch", "Application instability"]

CVE: "**cve_description**"
Give the result like the example result in a JSON list, with proper representation of the keywords list applicable for this CVE.

A.3 Hallucination, Completeness, and Consistency: Illustrative Examples

In this section, we provide concrete examples of CVE descriptions that demonstrate the presence or absence of the three key attributes when using large language models for term extraction: **hallucination**, **incompleteness**, and **inconsistency**.

1. Hallucination Example: The LLM introduces concepts not grounded in the source text.

- **CVE Description:**
"IBM Security Directory Suite VA 8.0.1 through 8.0.1.19 stores user credentials in plain clear text which can be read by an authenticated user. IBM X-Force ID: 228567".
- **Extracted Core Terms:**
  - Credentials Exposure
  - Clear Text Storage
  - **Authentication Bypass** *(hallucinated)*
- **Explanation:** The CVE explicitly states that the credentials are accessible *by an authenticated user*, not that authentication can be bypassed. The inclusion of "Authentication Bypass" is a clear hallucination.

2. Incompleteness Example: Key information from the CVE is missing in extracted terms.

- **CVE Description:**
  "An improper neutralization of special elements used in an OS command vulnerability (CWE-78) in FortiADC 7.2.0, 7.1.0 through 7.1.1 may allow an authenticated attacker to execute unauthorized commands via specifically crafted arguments to existing commands".
- **Extracted Terms (GPT):**
  - **Core Terms:** Command Injection, OS Command Vulnerability, Authenticated Attack
  - **Contextual Terms:** Crafted Arguments, Unauthorized Commands, Specifically Crafted
  - **Consequences:** Unauthorized Code Execution, System Compromise, Authenticated Attack
- **Explanation:** The extraction fails to include "improper neutralization of special elements", which is a critical technical detail indicating the root cause (CWE-78). Instead, it focuses only on the effect and context.

3. Inconsistency Example: Repeated extractions from the same CVE yield differing concepts.

- **CVE Description:**
  "The Zoom Client for Meetings chat functionality was susceptible to Zip bombing attacks in the following product versions: Android before version 5.8.6, iOS before version 5.9.0, Linux before version 5.8.6, macOS before version 5.7.3, and Windows before version 5.6.3. This could lead to availability issues on the client host by exhausting system resources".
- **Extracted Core Terms (Three Runs):**
  1. Zip Bombing, Availability Issues, Resource Exhaustion
  2. Zip Bombing Vulnerability, Chat Functionality Vulnerability, Resource Exhaustion
  3. Zip Bomb Vulnerability, Chat Functionality Vulnerability, Resource Exhaustion
- **Explanation:** While runs 2 and 3 yield consistent outputs, run 1 omits "Chat Functionality Vulnerability" and instead includes a broader effect term ("Availability Issues"). This variability illustrates inconsistency in GPT's term extraction process.

A.4 Terms Extraction Cost

Key term extraction can be performed using either open-source or closed-source LLMs. This study explores both options by selecting the best-performing models publicly available at the time of writing. For the open-source implementation, we deployed **LLaMA 2 (7B)** on an A40 GPU, with the 7B parameter size chosen because of hardware limitations. For the closed-source implementation, we accessed **GPT-3.5 Turbo** via API.

To contextualize the cost of key term extraction, we compare the actual costs incurred in this study with estimated costs of executing the same task using a range of current state-of-the-art LLMs, both open and proprietary. Additionally, we provide an estimation of the total cost required to process the entire CVE dataset, which as of August 2025 includes 293,623 entries.

It is important to note that these costs are incurred only once during the extraction process and are not required for every subsequent training or evaluation of the downstream model. Table 7 summarizes the cost for both the experimental subset used in this study and the projected cost for the full dataset. While runtime pricing is reported for transparency, it is worth noting that most providers offer a discounted rate (approximately 50%) for batch processing via asynchronous APIs, which would be applicable in our case despite longer processing times.

Table 7. Cost of extracting key terms for this study and for the entire CVE dataset (293,623 CVEs as of August 2025) using different LLMs.

Scenario	GPT-4.1	GPT-4.1 Mini	GPT-4.1 Nano	GPT-3.5 Turbo	Claude Sonnet 4	DeepSeek	Grok4
This paper	\$123.74	\$24.75	\$6.19	\$28.40	\$200.84	\$33.98	\$200.84
Whole CVE dataset	\$426.37	\$85.27	\$21.32	\$97.85	\$692.04	\$117.08	\$692.04

A.5 Embedding comparison

(see Table 8).

Table 8. F1 performance and gain from using Key Terms instead of full CVE description as input, across different language models used as embedder for the downstream classification.

Model	Input Type	Prec.	Rec.	F1	Relative F1 Gain
BERT	Description	67.79%	59.10%	60.41%	**+5.78%**
	Key Terms	**69.23%**	**63.50%**	**63.90%**	
Phi	Description	71.37%	63.15%	64.17%	**+4.18%**
	Key Terms	**70.02%**	**66.55%**	**66.85%**	
LLaMA	Description	72.50%	60.58%	61.94%	**+6.57%**
	Key Terms	**73.29%**	**64.87%**	**66.01%**	
GPT	Description	71.18%	63.58%	64.62%	**+8.88%**
	Key Terms	**74.07%**	**69.84%**	**70.36%**	

References

1. NVD data feeds. https://nvd.nist.gov/vuln/data-feeds. Accessed 23 Jan 2024
2. Aghaei, E., Shadid, W., Al-Shaer, E.: ThreatZoom: hierarchical neural network for CVEs to CWEs classification. In: Park, N., Sun, K., Foresti, S., Butler, K., Saxena, N. (eds.) SecureComm 2020. LNICST, vol. 335, pp. 23–41. Springer, Cham (2020). https://doi.org/10.1007/978-3-030-63086-7_2
3. Aota, M., Kanehara, H., Kubo, M., Murata, N., Sun, B., Takahashi, T.: Automation of vulnerability classification from its description using machine learning. In: 2020 IEEE Symposium on Computers and Communications (ISCC), pp. 1–7 (2020). https://doi.org/10.1109/ISCC50000.2020.9219568
4. Bafna, P., Pramod, D., Vaidya, A.: Document clustering: TF-IDF approach. In: 2016 International Conference on Electrical, Electronics, and Optimization Techniques (ICEEOT), pp. 61–66. IEEE (2016)
5. Campos, R., Mangaravite, V., Pasquali, A., Jorge, A., Nunes, C., Jatowt, A.: Yake! keyword extraction from single documents using multiple local features. Inf. Sci. **509**, 257–289 (2020)
6. CVE Project: CVE project documentation (2023). https://cveproject.github.io/docs/. Accessed 04 Sept 2024
7. Das, et al.: V2W-BERT: a framework for effective hierarchical multiclass classification of software vulnerabilities. In: 2021 IEEE 8th International Conference on Data Science and Advanced Analytics (DSAA), pp. 1–12. IEEE (2021)
8. Devlin, J., Chang, M.W., Lee, K., Toutanova, K.: BERT: pre-training of deep bidirectional transformers for language understanding (2019)
9. Dherin, B., Munn, M., Mazzawi, H., Wunder, M., Gonzalvo, J.: Learning without training: the implicit dynamics of in-context learning. arXiv preprint arXiv:2507.16003 (2025)
10. Dong, Q., et al.: A survey on in-context learning. arXiv preprint arXiv:2301.00234 (2022)
11. Grootendorst, M.: Keybert: minimal keyword extraction with BERT (2020). https://doi.org/10.5281/zenodo.4461265
12. Han, Z., Li, X., Liu, H., Xing, Z., Feng, Z.: Deepweak: reasoning common software weaknesses via knowledge graph embedding. In: 2018 IEEE 25th International Conference on Software Analysis, Evolution and Reengineering (SANER), pp. 456–466. IEEE (2018)
13. Hutchins, E.M., Cloppert, M.J., Amin, R.M., et al.: Intelligence-driven computer network defense informed by analysis of adversary campaigns and intrusion kill chains. Leading Issues Inf. Warfare Secur. Res. **1**(1), 80 (2011)
14. Javaheripi, M., Bubeck, S.: Phi-2: the surprising power of small language models. In: Proceedings of the Annual Meeting of the Association for Computational Linguistics (ACL), vol. 2, no. 1 (2023), published version
15. Liu, X., Tan, Y., Xiao, Z., Zhuge, J., Zhou, R.: Not the end of story: an evaluation of chatgpt-driven vulnerability description mappings. In: Findings of the Association for Computational Linguistics: ACL 2023, pp. 3724–3731 (2023)
16. Mikolov, T., Chen, K., Corrado, G., Dean, J.: Efficient estimation of word representations in vector space. arXiv preprint arXiv:1301.3781 (2013)
17. Pan, M., Wu, P., Zou, Y., Ruan, C., Zhang, T.: An automatic vulnerability classification framework based on bigru-textcnn. Procedia Comput. Sci. **222**, 377–386 (2023)

18. Simonetto, S., van Ede, T.S., Bosch, P., Jonker, W.: Text2weak: mapping CVEs to CWEs using description embeddings analysis. In: 4th Workshop on Artificial Intelligence-Enabled Cybersecurity Analytics (2024)
19. Simonetto, S., Oostveen, R., van Ede, T.S., Bosch, P., Jonker, W.: Knowing your weaknesses is your greatest strength: mapping CVE to CWE by leveraging CWE hierarchy and LLMs (2025)
20. Sun, J., et al.: Aspect-level information discrepancies across heterogeneous vulnerability reports: severity, types and detection methods. ACM Trans. Softw. Eng. Methodol. **33**(2), 1–38 (2023)
21. Sun, X., et al.: Automatic software vulnerability assessment by extracting vulnerability elements. J. Syst. Softw. **204**, 111790 (2023)
22. Touvron, H., et al.: Llama: open and efficient foundation language models (2023). https://arxiv.org/abs/2302.13971
23. Vaswani, A., et al.: Attention is all you need. In: Advances in Neural Information Processing Systems, vol. 30 (2017)
24. Wang, Q., Gao, Y., Ren, J., Zhang, B.: An automatic classification algorithm for software vulnerability based on weighted word vector and fusion neural network. Comput. Secur. **126**, 103070 (2023)
25. Weng, Y., et al.: Large language models are better reasoners with self-verification. arXiv preprint arXiv:2212.09561 (2022)

Beyond CWEs: Mapping Weaknesses in Unstructured Threat Intelligence Text

Stefano Simonetto(✉), Ronan Oosteven, Thijs Van Ede, Peter Bosch, and Willem Jonker

University of Twente, Enschede, The Netherlands
{s.simonetto,r.oostveen,t.s.vanede,p.bosch,w.jonker}@utwente.nl

Abstract. In real-world cyberattacks, adversaries frequently exploit a combination of vulnerabilities, bugs, and misconfigurations to compromise systems. To systematically analyze the root causes behind these issues, the Common Weakness Enumeration (CWE) framework provides a standardized taxonomy of software weaknesses.

While vulnerability databases are central to cataloging known issues, many security-relevant descriptions first appear in informal sources such as blog posts, CTI reports, and social media. Although these sources predominantly offer broader cybersecurity insights, they occasionally yield details that may indicate underlying weaknesses not captured in formal databases.

We propose a two-step approach to extract these security-related descriptions from unstructured threat intelligence and automatically map them to their corresponding CWE categories. First, a binary classifier detects sentences resembling CVE descriptions, identifying information relevant to security teams. Then, we apply a self-supervised learning model to predict the most appropriate CWE, enabling structured analysis even in the absence of formal vulnerability tracking.

As no ground truth exists for this task, we conduct expert-driven validation. Our results show strong performance, with an F1-score of 98.17% for correctly assigning CWE labels, improving by at least 64% points over state-of-the-art reasoning LLMs. This demonstrates the feasibility of automating weakness classification in unstructured cybersecurity text.

Keywords: CVE-like extraction · CTI · security blog posts · CWE mapping · vulnerability analysis

1 Introduction

Accurately identifying the root causes that allow systems to be compromised is critical for effective cybersecurity. The Common Weakness Enumeration (CWE) framework provides a systematic taxonomy of software weaknesses, guiding investments, policies, and practices toward mitigating vulnerabilities at their source [28].

CWE labels are closely tied to the Common Vulnerabilities and Exposures (CVE) system, which standardizes the reference for publicly known security

Y. Kim et al. (Eds.): CANS 2025, LNCS 16351, pp. 493–517, 2026.
https://doi.org/10.1007/978-981-95-4434-9_23

issues [30]. Nevertheless, a significant number of security issues either do not appear in the National Vulnerability Database (NVD) or are cataloged with considerable delays. As noted by [10], over 75% of CVEs are disclosed online before their formal inclusion in the NVD. These disclosures emerge from a diverse range of sources, including mainstream outlets like news, blogs, and social media, as well as less conventional channels such as the dark web, paste sites, and criminal forums.

Extracting relevant security information from unstructured sources and linking it to the appropriate CWE categories presents a significant challenge. Without timely insight into emerging issues, organizations risk exposure to unknown and unmitigated vulnerabilities, complicating threat visibility for security teams. To address this gap, the CWE program[1] developed a framework that is valuable for analyzing vulnerabilities not tracked by the CVE Program.

In this work, we focus on identifying a specific type of security-related text, hereafter referred to as *CVE-like* text. We define CVE-like text as descriptions of software weaknesses extracted from unstructured sources that bear a resemblance to formal CVE entries. For example, consider the following fragment from a blog post, which can be mapped to CWE-22 (Path Traversal):

> Researcher Joel Langill of Luxembourg and founder of SCADAhacker.com discovered a directory traversal vulnerability in Experion PKS release 310.x and earlier.

Building on the need to bridge the gap between formal databases and informal threat intelligence, we propose a methodology for identifying CVE-like information from unstructured sources, such as CTI reports, and security blog posts. In addition, we introduce a self-supervised method to map the extracted security text to its corresponding CWE.
The question we are answering in this paper is:

> How accurately can CWEs be predicted from CVE-like text extracted from threat intelligence such as blog posts, CTIs, tweets, and misconfigurations?

2 Related Work

The extraction of cyber threat intelligence from unstructured textual data has obtained significant attention in recent years. Researchers have explored a variety of sources, including threat reports, forums, blogs, and social media platforms, to derive actionable insights for strengthening cybersecurity measures [22].

For instance, studies have focused on detecting threat events from natural language to gain early information on potential future attacks. Notable efforts in this area include work by [5,20,25], and [24], which leveraged platforms such as Twitter and other social media channels to identify emerging threats.

Cyber threat intelligence often includes detailed descriptions of hacker tools, techniques, exposures, and incidents. By classifying this information using

[1] https://cwe.mitre.org/documents/cwe_usage/guidance.html.

threat-related keywords, topics, and semantic relationships among CTI terms, researchers have successfully identified threat events within forums and online discussions as exemplified by [8,15], and [11]. Other research efforts, such as those by [12,16,18] and [26], have concentrated on extracting Indicators of Compromise (IoCs) and Tactics, Techniques, and Procedures (TTPs) from CTI reports. In addition, [23] has analyzed hacker assets, including tools, scripts, and other resources used within the attacker community.

Despite these extensive efforts in extracting IoCs and TTPs and mapping them to structured frameworks such as MITRE, they have not addressed the crucial task of directly mapping such text to CWE categories. This oversight limits security teams' ability to systematically assess and mitigate emerging threats based on informal sources, highlighting the need for dedicated approaches to map security issues to CWEs.

3 Methodology

We propose a two-step approach to map security-relevant text extracted from unstructured sources to their corresponding CWE categories. In the first step, used as a preprocessing phase, a binary classifier filters the input to identify text that describes exploited security issues. In the second step, a self-learning classifier assigns the appropriate CWE category to the filtered content.

The preprocessing is a critical step because it filters out non-relevant content, isolating text that bears a resemblance to formal vulnerability descriptions. However, while effective at detecting security-relevant text, the binary classifier does not capture the underlying root causes reflected in CWE categories. Since no ground truth directly maps such vulnerability-related text to specific CWEs, we adopt a self-learning (pseudo-labeling) approach.

Pseudo-labeling, as introduced by Lee [17], is a semi-supervised learning technique that begins by training an initial model on a small set of labeled data. This model is then used to predict labels for unlabeled data, and the most confident predictions are fed back into the training set. Through this iterative process, the model learns from its own predictions, effectively expanding the training dataset without requiring additional manual labeling.

To ensure reliability, the entire process is evaluated by domain experts on a smaller validation dataset (see Sect. 4). In the absence of a ground truth, expert validation remains the only viable method to assess accuracy and ensure that the approach aligns with domain-specific expectations. For transparency and collaboration, the code and results have been published in [1].

Figure 1 illustrates the complete pipeline. Steps A and B focus on training the binary classifier to distinguish between CVE-like and non-CVE-like text, while steps C to E describe the process for assigning CWE labels exclusively to the threat intelligence text that has been pre-filtered by the preprocessing step. Each step is detailed in the following subsections.

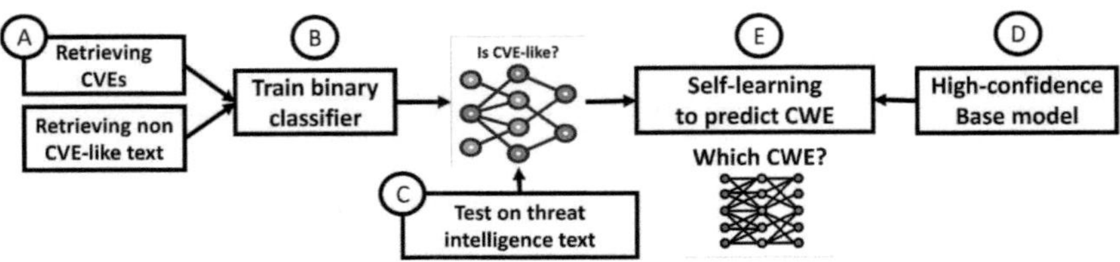

Fig. 1. Methodology: Steps A and B focus on training the binary classifier to distinguish between CVE-like and non-CVE-like text. Steps C to E aim to assign a CWE label exclusively to threat intelligence text that has been classified as CVE-like.

3.1 Dataset Preparation

To train our binary classifier, which distinguishes between vulnerability,related text and general cybersecurity content, we selected two sets of samples. Positive samples consist of CVE descriptions extracted from the National Vulnerability Database (NVD), while negative samples are drawn from a set of security-related texts that explicitly exclude any CVE content. By ensuring that the negative samples are semantically close to the expected decision boundary yet do not overlap with CVE-like text (CVE $\cap$ Security Text $= \emptyset$), we effectively train the classifier to distinguish CVE-like text from general content.

The security-related text included in the dataset ensures relevance to the cybersecurity domain while explicitly excluding any text containing CVE descriptions. Furthermore, each text is segmented into individual paragraphs rather than processing entire documents at once, ensuring a word distribution more similar to that of the CVE descriptions. The sources and rationale for the selected security text are as follows:

- **Abstracts from scientific papers in cybersecurity-related fields:** Abstracts provide an overview of research without delving into specific CVE details, ensuring that the content is relevant yet free of explicit vulnerability descriptions.
- **MITRE datasets:** We extracted descriptions from the Common Weakness Enumeration (CWE), Common Attack Pattern Enumeration and Classification (CAPEC), and the MITRE ATT&CK framework. These resources provide structured, security-relevant content without overlapping with CVE-specific text.
- **Black Hat conference transcripts:** Transcripts from Black Hat conferences capture discussions on tools, methodologies, and experiences without explicitly reading or detailing CVEs. Including these transcripts helps capture practical cybersecurity context.
- **General cybersecurity text:** To broaden the dataset, we included text from diverse cybersecurity resources, including textbooks, tool documentation (e.g., Wireshark), risk assessment frameworks, and whitepapers. These sources provide foundational and practical cybersecurity content that is distinct from CVE descriptions.

Table 1. Data distribution for positive (CVE) and negative (general cybersecurity text) classes. The security text category includes various subcategories.

Class	Subcategory	Count
CVE	-	241400
Security text	-	241400
	Abstracts	125779
	MITRE dataset	2043
	Black Hat	29634
	General cybersecurity	42545
	Masked CVE	41399

- **Masked CVE descriptions:** To further enhance the dataset, we apply masking to CVE descriptions to mask parts of the CVE description. This is achieved by selectively omitting entire sentences of the descriptions at random. The goal is to ensure the classifier focuses on recognizing complete CVEs rather than identifying partial fragments.

Table 1 presents the data distribution for the positive (CVE) and negative (general cybersecurity text) classes, along with their respective subcategories.

3.2 Preprocessing Step

To identify CVE-like text from non-CVE text, we implement a preprocessing step using a binary classifier. Our approach employs a feedforward neural network with a single hidden layer and leverages BERT for text embeddings, as described in Sect. 4.1. The network architecture and hyperparameters were empirically determined and comprise the following components:

- Input Layer: A fully connected layer with 768 input features, derived from BERT embeddings.
- Hidden Layer: One dense layer with 128 neurons and ReLU activation.
- Output Layer: A single neuron with a sigmoid activation function for binary classification.

The model is trained using the Adam optimizer and binary cross-entropy loss, with accuracy as the evaluation metric. We trained the model for 40 epochs using a batch size of 32, validating performance on a separate validation set.

The dataset (as shown in Table 1) is partitioned into training (70%), validation (15%), and test (15%) sets. The model achieves an accuracy of nearly 96%, indicating strong capability in differentiating between CVE descriptions and non-CVE text. This high accuracy suggests that the selected architecture effectively captures the distinguishing features between the two categories, as shown in Table 2.

Error Analysis. To further understand the classifier's performance, we manually analyzed the misclassified instances, with examples provided for each category in Appendix A.1. Out of a total of 72,420 samples in the test set, only

Table 2. Binary classification performance on the dataset from Table 1, demonstrating high accuracy in distinguishing CVE from non-CVE text.

Class	Precision	Recall	F1-Score	Accuracy
CVEs	93.68%	98.32%	95.94%	
General sec text	98.24%	93.36%	95.74%	
weighted avg	95.96%	95.84%	95.84%	95.84%

3,010 samples were misclassified. Among these misclassified samples, 20.17% of CVE descriptions were incorrectly classified as general security text.

In contrast, the misclassified general security texts labeled as CVE-like consisted of: **Masked CVEs** (76.98%), **general cybersecurity** (2.03%), **abstracts** (0.70%), **Black Hat transcripts** (0.10%), and **MITRE entries** (0.03%).

3.3 Test on Threat Intelligence Data

After training the binary classifier, we applied it to threat intelligence text to determine whether specific sentences resemble CVE descriptions. To ensure a reliable evaluation, threat intelligence sources (e.g., blogs and CTI reports) were excluded from the training data, thereby preventing data contamination and allowing these sources to serve as an independent test set. For testing, each threat intelligence text is segmented into individual paragraphs rather than processing entire documents at once, ensuring a word distribution more comparable to that of the training set.

The threat intelligence dataset is composed of four distinct text families, described in the following subsections. Example paragraphs from each category are provided in Appendix A.2.

Blog Posts. Blog posts serve as a platform for cybersecurity experts and enthusiasts to share information about recent attacks, vulnerabilities, and various other cybersecurity topics. To compile our dataset, we leveraged the list of cybersecurity blogs identified by [4], resulting in a collection of over 150,000 blog posts. This dataset encompasses a broad spectrum of cybersecurity discussions, making it a valuable resource for assessing the classifier's ability to identify CVE-related content within diverse and unstructured text.

CTI Reports. For CTI reports, we based our work on the resource provided in [31], where advanced natural language processing techniques were applied to extract structured threat intelligence from a corpus of more than 14,155 reports spanning diverse cybersecurity domains.

Tweets/LinkedIn Posts. The dataset for tweets and LinkedIn posts was compiled by searching for common cybersecurity indicators such as "CVE" and "vulnerability," along with hashtags like #infosec and #cybersecurity. To align with the classifier's focus on textual content, only text-based posts were included. Data refinement steps, which included filtering for English-language content, removing metadata (e.g., emoticons and hashtags), and manually excluding non-cybersecurity-related content, ensured that the dataset remained domain-specific.

Misconfigurations. Descriptions of various misconfigurations were collected from credible sources and grouped into the following categories:

- **General Misconfigurations:** A total of 23 misconfiguration descriptions were retrieved from the Cybersecurity and Infrastructure Security Agency (CISA) advisories.[2]
- **Cloud Misconfigurations:** Seven cloud misconfiguration examples were sourced from Sonrai Security's blog.[3]
- **Kubernetes Misconfigurations:** A total of 20 Kubernetes-specific misconfigurations were compiled from two sources: 10 examples from the Picus Security blog[4] and another 10 from Practical DevSecOps.[5]

3.4 Observation on the Test Set Binary Classification

Assuming that all misconfiguration descriptions qualify as CVE-like text by definition: "An incorrect or suboptimal configuration of an information system or system component that may lead to vulnerabilities" [14], we applied the binary classifier described in Sect. 3.2 to blogs, CTIs, and Tweets/LinkedIn posts. The goal is to determine whether a given piece of threat intelligence text is CVE-like or not, as presented in Table 3.

It is important to note that the total number of retrieved blog posts (over 150,000) and CTI reports (approximately 15,000) do not match the counts in Table 3. This discrepancy arises because each blog post and CTI report was segmented into multiple sentences using a paragraph-wise approach.

A key observation is that the more concise and direct a text is, the higher its likelihood of being classified as CVE-like. For example, only 1.39% of blog post paragraphs are categorized as CVE-like, likely due to the inherently verbose nature of blogs. In contrast, CTI reports tend to be more focused, offering direct descriptions of attacks, while tweets are even more concise and to the point, making them more prone to CVE-like classification. Moreover, these sources differ from vulnerability-sharing platforms like NVD, which exclusively focus on sharing vulnerabilities. In contrast, other sources, such as blogs, CTI reports, and tweets, tend to be more verbose, often including broader context, analysis, and discussions beyond just listing vulnerabilities.

---

[2] https://www.cisa.gov/news-events/cybersecurity-advisories.
[3] https://sonraisecurity.com/blog.
[4] https://www.picussecurity.com/resource/blog/.
[5] https://www.practical-devsecops.com/.

Table 3. Classification of threat intelligence texts using the binary classifier described in Sect. 3.2.

Type	Class	Count	Percentage
Blog Post	CVE-like Text	46,611	1.39%
	Other Text	3,300,620	98.61%
CTI report	CVE-like Text	4,329	3.23%
	Other Text	129,575	96.77%
Tweets and Linkedin post	CVE-like Text	7	7.00%
	Other Text	93	93.00%

3.5 High-Confidence Initial Model

The self-learning process involves training an initial model on a small set of labeled data and using this model to predict labels for the unlabeled data. Since no labeled data for the CVE-like to CWE mapping exists, we adopted the standard CVE to CWE labels which are available from NVD. Given that the primary objective of this paper is to map CVE-like text to CWE categories, we focused on 36 CWE parent classes. We excluded CWE subcategories because mapping to parent CWEs is sufficient to describe the root cause of a vulnerability, as defined in View-1003 [2].

The initial model is trained on the CVE-to-CWE relationships retrieved from the NVD, as it serves as the only available ground truth. To ensure class balance, we established a cut-off threshold based on the class with the fewest instances. Specifically, CWE-697 ("Incorrect Comparison"), which contains 96 samples, defines the upper limit for all other classes. For instance, CWE-74 ("Injection"), the most frequent CWE with 45,234 samples, was downsampled to match this threshold.

We employ a different embedding technique from the binary classifier because the task of CVE to CWE mapping is already being studied in the literature, and better embedding techniques have been provided. To map CVE-like sentences to CWE, we used a fine-tuned LLaMA 7B model specifically trained for CVE-to-CWE translation [27].

The embedded descriptions are then fed into a neural network designed for CWE classification (hereafter referred to as the *initial model*). Following the recommendations in [27], the neural network consists of two hidden layers with 128 and 64 neurons, respectively, and is trained for 40 epochs with a batch size of 64.

During the retraining phase described in Sect. 3.6, the updated model is trained on the augmented training set that includes additional pseudo-labeled instances, while evaluation is consistently conducted using the original test set to avoid bias. The initial model performances are presented in Table 7.

3.6 Self-learning

The final step of the methodology involves labeling CVE-like sentences with the most suitable CWE prediction. As described earlier, we adopted self-learning for this purpose. We create a high-confidence initial model (Sect. 3.5) and extract CVE-like candidate sentences using the preprocessing step to extract candidate CVE-like sentences from threat intelligence texts (Sect. 3.2).

To ensure high relevance, we applied a stricter selection threshold, raising the binary classifier's decision boundary from 0.5 to 0.9. This ensures that only the sentences most resembling CVE descriptions are included.

During the iterative retraining process, the model is updated using CWE labels predicted in the previous iteration, but only if the corresponding confidence score exceeds 0.9. This high-confidence filtering minimizes error propagation while progressively expanding the training dataset. A visual representation of the confidence distributions for the unlabeled dataset (predicted by the initial model) is provided in Appendix A.6.

The pseudo-labeling procedure concludes after 60 retraining cycles, which corresponds to the point when no new CWE predictions meet the confidence threshold of 0.9. Analysis of the validation F1 scores shows that, while the final F1-score remains roughly constant across iterations, the convergence speed improves as more training samples are incorporated. Specifically, models trained with an increasing number of samples reach their final F1 score more quickly. This relationship is evident in the validation plots, where the initial model and first retraining require more epochs to converge compared to the halfway (30th retraining) and final (60th retraining) cycles, as shown in Fig. 2.

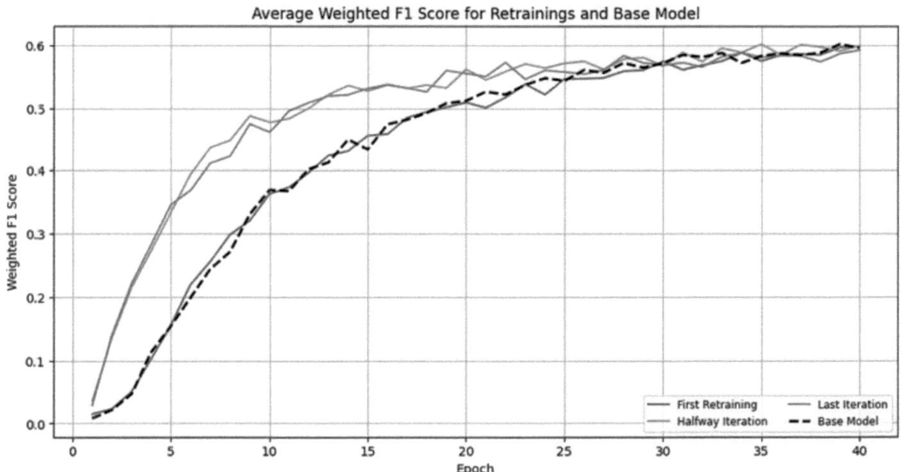

Fig. 2. F1-score progression over 40 epochs on the validation set, illustrating different stages of the pseudo-labeling process. The dashed line represents the initial model, while the solid lines depict different retraining phases. The initial model and first retraining exhibit a slower learning curve, likely due to a lower number of training samples.

4 Evaluation

In this section, we begin by evaluating the performance of the embedding strategy employed in the preprocessing step, which utilizes a binary classifier (Sect. 4.1). Next, we evaluate the individual performance of the classifiers as well as their combined effectiveness in predicting CVE-likeness and CWE categories (Sect. 4.2).

4.1 Embedder for the Preprocessing Step

A crucial design decision for the preprocessing step is selecting an appropriate embedding method for the binary classification task. We experimented with three different embedding models: BERT [9] which is the state-of-the-art embedder for general-purpose text. Roberta [19] which is an optimized Bert model and SecBert [3] which is a BERT model fine-tuned on security text.

We selected the embedder based on the binary classifier's performance during validation, aiming to identify the most effective model. Our primary objective was to maximize recall for CVE classification, as capturing all potential CVE-like text within cyber threat intelligence is critical. High recall ensures that emerging cybersecurity threats are not overlooked. Table 4 presents the results of our evaluation performed during validation. While all three models performed similarly, BERT achieved the highest recall, making it the preferred choice for embedding sentences in the binary classifier.

Table 4. Binary classifier (preprocessing) performance comparison of each embedding model in CVE classification on the validation set.

Embedder	Precision	Recall	F1-score
Bert	93.83%	**98.19%**	95.96 %
Roberta	96.12%	97.58%	96.84%
SecBert	96.88%	97.53%	97.20%

4.2 CVE-Likeness and CWE Prediction Evaluation

This subsection evaluates the core objective of our study: to assign the most appropriate CWE label to CVE-like sentences. To assess the effectiveness of our pipeline, we evaluated both the individual classifiers and their combined performance through expert evaluation, as no predefined ground truth exists. To establish a reliable evaluation benchmark, we consulted three domain experts. Each of them provides a view on the matter as further described in the following subsections. The questionnaires presented to each expert are summarized in Appendix A.3.

Among all the high-confidence CVE-like sentences extracted from threat intelligence text, 93.42% (21,458 out of 22,970) were confidently assigned a related CWE by the final retraining iteration of our pipeline.

Given the impracticality of manually reviewing all 21,458 sentences, we used a statistical sampling method [29] to assess classification performances. As detailed in Appendix A.8, Cochran's formula indicates that reviewing roughly 50 samples is sufficient to achieve a 96% confidence level with a 15% margin of error. The performance metrics (e.g., accuracy, F1-score) calculated from these 50 samples serve as estimates of the mean performance for the entire dataset, which is why we report only the mean values. Although these estimates are inherently subject to sampling error, the observed differences in CWE classification performance, as presented in Tables 5 and 6, are sufficiently large to remain valid despite this uncertainty.

Full Pipeline. As reported in Table 5, for CWE classification preceed by the preprocessing step, we randomly sampled 50 sentences from the predictions with high confidence, which are those with high confidence in both CWE classification and CVE-likeness, and asked the experts to evaluate them based on two criteria:

1. How likely is it that the given sentence represents a CVE?
2. Which CWE classification best describes the sentence?

CVE-Likeness Classifier. For the preprocessing step that identifies CVE-like sentences, we randomly sampled 50 sentences, evenly split between those classified as CVE-like and those not.

- 25 sentences classified as CVE-like
- 25 sentences not classified as CVE-like

The performance of the standalone binary classifier is reported in Appendix A.5. To determine the ground truth for CVE-likeness, three domain experts independently assigned each sentence a likelihood score from 1 (not a CVE) to 5 (very likely a CVE). The final score was obtained by averaging their ratings, and if the score exceeded 2.5, the sentence was labeled as CVE-like.

CWE Classifier. To independently assess the CWE classifier's performance, we randomly extracted 50 sentences that were not classified as CVE-like and predicted their CWE labels without applying the CVE-likeness filter. By testing on non-CVE-like data, we ensure that our classifier can still correctly map sentences to CWE categories even when they lack the typical structure or keywords associated with CVE descriptions. This broader evaluation demonstrates the model's versatility and practical applicability, as it accounts for various forms of threat intelligence that might otherwise go unrecognized.

For the CWE classification, we applied a majority voting approach among the three experts. If a majority consensus was reached, the assigned CWE label was considered valid; otherwise, the sentence was excluded from the evaluation, as no definitive expert agreement could be reached (only once when all the experts had different opinions).

The performance of the CWE classifier is reported in Table 5.

Table 5. Performance of the CWE classification with and without preprocessing

Preprocessing	Precision	Recall	F1-score	Accuracy
✓	98.33%	98.00%	98.17%	98.00%
✗	96.66%	93.88%	95.25%	93.88%

5 Results

Table 5 reveals that our CWE classification task achieves remarkably high performance. This success is largely attributed to the iterative classification of text segments for which the prediction confidence exceeds 0.9, thereby ensuring that only high-confidence predictions are considered.

We also observe a consistent improvement in the performances on the CWE classification due to the preprocessing step. The CWE classifier without preprocessing achieves an accuracy of 93.88% when applied to text that is not CVE-like. However, its performance improves when it has as input a CVE-like text. Specifically, once a text is identified as resembling a CVE, the CWE classifier's accuracy increases by more than 4%.

Analyzing the performance of the binary classifier individually (Appendix A.5), which distinguishes between CVE-like and non-CVE-like text, achieves high recall but low precision. This indicates that while it correctly classifies all CVE-like sentences, it also classifies some non-CVE-like text as CVE-like. The choice of favoring recall over precision was intentional (as discussed in Sect. 4.1). In security operations centers (SOCs), the early detection of potential threats is critical, and missing a true positive can have severe consequences. Although this approach results in a higher rate of false positives, these can typically be filtered out through subsequent analysis and verification steps. In contrast, overlooking a genuine threat might lead to significant security breaches. This trade-off underscores the rationale behind our approach: in SOCs and similar environments, it is preferable to err on the side of caution by accepting more false alarms rather than risking the omission of critical threat information.

5.1 Comparison with State-of-the-Art LLMs

To benchmark our approach, we compared it against three state-of-the-art reasoning-focused language models: GPT o3-mini, Grok-3, and Deepseek R1. As no prior work has directly addressed the combined task of CVE-likeness detection and CWE classification, we use these models as strong general-purpose baselines.

Each model was evaluated on the tasks described in Sect. 4.2. Following the same evaluation procedure applied to our proposed model (see Table 5), we tested the LLMs on their ability to predict the correct CWE label both with and without preprocessing. As a reminder, preprocessing involves filtering sentences based on their CVE-likeness classification.

The CWE classification results for all models are reported in Table 6. Performance metrics for the preprocessing step (i.e., CVE-likeness classification) are provided in Appendix A.5. All prompt templates used for the evaluations are listed in Appendix A.4.

Among the three LLMs, Grok-3 performs best on the CWE classification task when no preprocessing is applied, while Deepseek R1 and GPT excel at identifying CVE-like sentences, as shown in Appendix A.5. However, when considering CWE classification after applying preprocessing, GPT emerges as the top performer among the evaluated LLMs.

When comparing our approach to state-of-the-art LLMs on the CWE classification task, our model outperforms all baselines by at least 50% points across all evaluated metrics. When considering the CWE classifier preceded by the preprocessing step, our system achieves a significant improvement in CWE classification by at least 64% points on F1-score. These results suggest that LLMs struggle to maintain accurate predictions when faced with a large number of target classes and must choose from a predefined set of specific options.

A notable issue with the Deepseek R1 model is its significant bias toward predicting CWE-20 (Improper Input Validation). While the evaluation of the CWE classifier without preprocessing yields lower performance metrics for all models, Deepseek's bias becomes particularly prominent when preprocessing is applied, where a reduced number of CVE-like sentences associated with CWE-20 leads to a marked drop in its performance. This phenomenon is consistent with

Table 6. Comparing our approach to state-of-the-art LLMs on predicting the correct CWE label, with and without preprocessing.

Preprocessing	Model	Precision	Recall	F1-score	Accuracy
✓	Our Model	**98.33%**	**98.00%**	**98.17%**	**98.00%**
	Deepseek R1	4.00%	4.00%	4.00%	4.00%
	GPT o3-mini	38.57%	30.00%	33.75%	30.00%
	Grok-3	37.00%	12.00%	18.12%	12.00%
✗	Our Model	**96.66%**	**93.88%**	**95.25%**	**93.88%**
	Deepseek R1	21.89%	20.41%	21.12%	20.41%
	GPT o3-mini	24.17%	28.57%	26.19%	28.57%
	Grok-3	31.18%	40.82%	35.35%	40.82%

observations in other domains [13], where GPT and Grok-3 are noted for their balanced outputs, in contrast to Deepseek's high bias. One possible explanation for this discrepancy is that models like Deepseek, which are non-proprietary, may have limited access to high-quality training data. This scarcity can result in increased reasoning inconsistencies (i.e., hallucinations) and inherent biases [13].

We further compared the binary classification task (preprocessing) through an ablation-style analysis presented in Appendix A.5. The results show that although the LLMs achieve higher precision in addressing whether a sentence is CVE-like or not, our method achieves a higher recall, which is consistent with our design choice (see Sect. 5).

6 Discussion

In this section, we discuss our experimental results from multiple perspectives. First, we examine the performance of the pseudo-labeling process (Sect. 6.1). Next, we analyze the distribution of CWE classes (Sect. 6.2). We then investigate the utility and necessity of the binary classifier (Sect. 6.3). Finally, we assess the potential risk of data contamination in the CWE classifier (Sect. 6.4), where an unintended overlap between the test set and the training data of the embedder could lead to biased evaluation results.

6.1 Retraining Performances

During retraining, the F1 scores steadily increased compared to the initial model. Notably, the best-performing model, developed during the 12th retraining cycle, achieved an improvement of over 11% (from 51.98% to 58.08% Macro F1), while the worst-performing retraining (at the 47th cycle) still showed an improvement of more than 2% (see Table 7). Although pseudo-labeling alone does not fully automate CWE classification, it serves as a powerful augmentation technique, reducing reliance on manually labeled data and enhancing overall model performance.

Table 7. Macro and weighted F1-scores of the initial, best, and worst performing models. Improvements are reported as relative percentage increases over the initial model.

Model	Macro F1 (%)	Weighted F1 (%)	Macro F1 Improvement (%)	Weighted F1 Improvement (%)
Initial Model	51.98	52.05	–	–
Best Model	58.08	58.12	+11.74	+11.67
Worst Model	53.30	53.31	+2.54	+2.42

6.2 CWE Distribution

Understanding the distribution of CWE labels within threat intelligence text is essential for evaluating the effectiveness of our pseudo-labeling approach. By examining which CWE classes are most frequently predicted, we gain insights into the prevalent security issues that are publicly reported but not formally cataloged as CVEs in the NVD or similar databases. Our analysis of the 36 CWE classes reveals that the top three classes in our dataset are:

- CWE-610 (Externally Controlled Reference to a Resource in Another Sphere): 71.87%
- CWE-74 (Injection): 17.12%
- CWE-119 (Buffer overflow): 5.72%

In contrast, the CWE distribution derived from NVD data shows:

- CWE-74 (Injection): 29.60%
- CWE-119 (Buffer overflow): 19.03%
- CWE-20 (Improper Input Validation): 6.31%

Thus, while two of the top three CWE classes are consistent between our dataset and NVD, the most prevalent CWE in our threat intelligence corpus is CWE-610, a class that appears only marginally (2.23%) in the NVD dataset. This difference likely reflects the distinct characteristics of informal threat intelligence compared to formal vulnerability databases.

6.3 Why Do We Need the Preprocessing Step?

Without a preliminary filter, the CWE classifier assigns a CWE label to every sentence from threat intelligence texts. In some cases, the model assigns a high-confidence prediction, even for sentences classified as non-CVE-like. For example, consider the following case:

> Cross-site scripting is the most common security vulnerability that even the most trusted website can fall victim to. XSS occurs when hackers inject a malicious script into the input fields of web applications.

Although this sentence describes a general security issue (cross-site scripting), it lacks the detailed characteristics of a formal CVE description. Nevertheless, because it contains security-related terminology, the CWE classifier may confidently predict a CWE label. From a security assessment perspective, labeling such broad statements is not particularly useful, as it does not yield actionable insights about actual vulnerabilities.

The binary classifier, therefore, is essential. It filters out non-CVE-like text, ensuring that only those sentences that closely resemble formal CVE descriptions are passed on for CWE classification. This targeted approach helps maintain the relevance and utility of the CWE labels in practical security assessments.

6.4 Potential Data Contamination in the CWE Embedder

Since our initial model, described in Sect. 3.5, embeds CVEs using a fine-tuned version of LLaMA, an important concern is the risk of data contamination, where the model may have already encountered test set data either during fine-tuning or in the pretraining of the base model.

To avoid this risk for the fine-tuned model, we ensured that the test set used for evaluating the CWE classifier does not overlap with the fine-tuning training and validation sets of the fine-tuned LLaMA model.

For the LLaMA 7B base model, data contamination could arise from its pretraining on large-scale, publicly available datasets. If portions of the CVE dataset were included in the model's pretraining data, its performance could be artificially inflated, as it may have previously encountered instances from the test set. To assess this possibility, evaluation was restricted to CVEs published exclusively after the model's release, ensuring that no prior exposure to these instances could inflate performance.

Additionally, to determine whether observed performance variations result from the inherent differences in test set complexity, we compared results against alternative models that do not rely on LLaMA, such as BiGRU [7] and TextCNN [6]. As detailed in Appendix A.7, the performance drop observed in LLaMA was comparable to (or smaller than) that of the BiGRU-TextCNN and TextCNN baselines. Based on these findings, we conclude that there is no evidence of data contamination in the LLaMA base model.

7 Conclusions

This study presents a pseudo-labeling framework that effectively classifies vulnerability-related (CVE-like) sentences and maps them to their corresponding CWE labels within unstructured threat intelligence text. Our two-stage approach demonstrates that incorporating iterative self-supervised retraining leads to consistent improvements in classification performance. In particular, expert-driven evaluation shows that our methodology achieves a 98% F1-score on the CWE prediction task, outperforming state-of-the-art large language models by at least 64% points on F1-score. This framework marks an initial step toward associating CVE-like text from unstructured threat intelligence with the CWE framework.

A Appendix

A.1 Misclassified Examples

Examples of misclassified instances by the binary classifier. The'CVE' class represents a CVE description misclassified as general security text, while all other classes correspond to general security text misclassified as CVE descriptions.

Class	Example
CVE	Search queries in the default search engine could appear to have been the currently navigated URL if the search query itself was a well formed URL. This vulnerability affects Firefox < 117.
Abstract	Several instances of nonsensical word sequences were identified which triggered a target command in a voice-controlled digital assistant, but which were incomprehensible to humans, as shown in tests with human experimental subjects.
MITRE	An attacker leverages an adversary in the middle attack (CAPEC-94) in order to bypass the same origin policy protection in the victim's browser. This active adversary in the middle attack could be launched, for instance, when the victim is connected to a public WIFI hot spot. An attacker is able to intercept requests and responses between the victim's browser and some non-sensitive website that does not use TLS.
Black Hat	Values from the mailbox can be fully controlled from the acpu
General	This allows rules to only apply to clients or servers. This allows packets cybersecurity related to $HOME NET clients viewing web pages to be distinguished from servers running in the $HOME NET.
Masked CVE	(masked from CVE-2019-6158): This only affects LXCA when HTTP proxy credentials have been configured. This affects LXCA versions 2.0.0 to 2.3.x.

A.2 Examples of Test Set

The training examples for the binary classifier are sourced from well-established databases such as the NVD for CVEs, as well as from MITRE and academic paper abstracts. In contrast, the test set is designed to be more nuanced. Instead of relying on a clear-cut distinction between CVE and non-CVE texts, it includes sources where some sentences implicitly describe a security issue (CVE-like), while others do not. To illustrate this, we provide one example from each source category (blog post, CTI report, misconfiguration log, and tweet) in which a paragraph has been labeled as CVE-like.

category	Example
Blog post	In 2014, CMS platform Drupal experienced one of the most destructive code vulnerabilities ever seen by a CMS. Dubbed âĂŸDrupageddon' (the L was only added in more recent events) because of its magnitude, it was an SQL injection flaw that allowed remote code execution (RCE) attacks, backdoors, privilege escalation and more. Exploitation of the vulnerability was so widespread that, despite quick patching, site owners were told that if they had not updated within 7 h of the patch's release, they should all consider their websites compromised.
CTIs	Note: The domain meqashoppercom.com (77.78.240.233, 77.78.239.53) IS NOT blacklisted, so it has the potential to infect a very large number of visitors, specifically visitors with outdated AV signatures and definitions.
Misconfigurations	Overly Permissive Role-Based Access Control (RBAC): Granting excessive permissions to users, service accounts, or groups violates the principle of least privilege and increases security risks by allowing entities to perform unnecessary actions.
Tweets	CVSS 9.8 Alert Microsoft has issued a critical alert for a critical vulnerability CVE-2024-38063 that allows attackers to execute arbitrary code on Windows 10, 11, & Server systems. How the Vulnerability Works?

A.3 Expert Evaluation Questionnaire

To illustrate the type of input provided to the experts during the annotation process, we include two representative examples: one for CVE-likeness scoring (Table 8) and another for CWE classification (Table 9). These examples also demonstrate how ground truth labels were derived.

For CVE-likeness, each expert assigned a score from 1 (not CVE-like) to 5 (highly CVE-like). We calculated the average score across the three experts and used a threshold of 2.5 to determine whether the text was ultimately labeled as CVE-like. For CWE classification, experts selected one applicable CWE identifier, and we adopted a majority voting approach to assign the final label.

A.4 Prompts for LLM Classification Tasks

To assess the capabilities of large language models in classifying cybersecurity-related text, we designed three types of evaluation prompts targeting the three distinct tasks: detecting CVE-likeness, assigning CWE labels, and performing a combined classification of both.

Table 8. Example sentence annotated with CVE-likeness score

Text	Choices				
	5	4	3	2	1
	(CVE-like)				(Not CVE-like)
Are you looking for the best VPN to enhance your internet experience? Look no further than VeePN! With its impressive features, VeePN is here to provide you with speed and safety.					✓

Table 9. Example sentence annotated with the related CWE

Text	Answer									
	116	119	...	330	345	362	...	863	913	922
Namecheap issued a response on their website downplaying the significance of the bug, claiming that no customers had been impacted by the CSRF vulnerability. The registrar said that exploiting the vulnerability, which they monitored from the time it was reported until they fixed it, required very specific criteria.					✓					

CVE-Likeness Detection. This prompt determines whether a given sentence resembles a CVE entry:

> *Does the following text resemble a Common Vulnerabilities and Exposures (CVE) entry? Classify it as "CVE-like" if it describes a specific security vulnerability, or exploit typically found in CVE reports. Otherwise, classify it as "Not CVE-like":* ***"Sentence"***.

The evaluation set includes 50 manually selected"Sentence" examples: 25 labeled as CVE-like and 25 as Not CVE-like.

CWE Classification (Unfiltered). To test the model's ability to assign CWE labels without relying on CVE structure, we used the following prompt:

> *Given the following CWE-ID options (116, 119, 20, 200, 269, 287, 311, 327, 330, 345, 362, 400, 404, 407, 436, 610, 662, 665, 668, 669, 670, 672, 674, 682, 697, 704, 706, 732, 74, 754, 755, 834, 862, 863, 913, 922), which CWE best describes the vulnerability in the following sentence?:* ***"Sentence"***.

We randomly selected 50 sentences that had been previously classified as **Not CVE-like** and submitted them for CWE classification. This evaluation setup examines the model's robustness when encountering text that lacks typical CVE structure or terminology.

Joint CVE + CWE Classification. The final prompt combines both tasks. First, the model assesses whether the text is CVE-like, then selects the most appropriate CWE ID from a predefined list:

> *Does the following text resemble a Common Vulnerabilities and Exposures (CVE) entry? Classify it as "CVE-like" if it describes a specific security vulnerability or exploit typically found in CVE reports. Otherwise, classify it as "Not CVE-like". Then select the most appropriate CWE-ID from the following options (116, 119, 20, 200, 269, 287, 311, 327, 330, 345, 362, 400, 404, 407, 436, 610, 662, 665, 668, 669, 670, 672, 674, 682, 697, 704, 706, 732, 74, 754, 755, 834, 862, 863, 913, 922) that best describes the vulnerability:* ***"Sentence".***

For this task, we selected 50 high-confidence sentences where the model confidently predicted both CVE-likeness and CWE classification. This subset enables evaluation of the model's end-to-end reasoning across both dimensions.

A.5 Preprocessing Performance

While Sect. 5.1 presents CWE classification results with and without preprocessing, here we reverse the perspective. We evaluate the performance of the CVE-like classifier (preprocessing) both in isolation and when integrated into the full pipeline. This ablation-style analysis tests whether CVE-likeness detection improves when sentences are first filtered through the CWE classifier, simulating end-to-end usage.

The two scenarios in which we are testing the binary classifiers are:

1. **Not conditioned on CWE Label (✗)**: Classification on a balanced test set of 25 CVE-like and 25 non-CVE-like sentences. This measures the classifier's raw ability to detect CVE-like content without influence from any downstream components.
2. **Conditioned on CWE Label (✓)**: Evaluation restricted to sentences first identified as CVE-like and subsequently assigned a CWE label with high confidence. This simulates the classifier's behavior in an end-to-end setting where CWE-filtering has occurred.

The results reported in Table 10 show a consistent improvement in recall when the sentence has already been assigned a CWE label. This indicates a reduction in false negatives, suggesting that CWE-filtered sentences tend to resemble CVE descriptions more closely, making them easier for the classifier to identify.

Precision, on the other hand, decreases slightly for Deepseek R1 and GPT o3-mini, but improves for Grok-3 and our proposed model, stabilizing around 80%.

This suggests that while some LLMs may overgeneralize when CWE context is present. leading to more false positives, our model and Grok-3 benefit from the structural regularity introduced by the CWE-filtering step.

Table 10. CVE-likeness classification performance with and without prior CWE identification. This ablation setup evaluates whether CWE filtering improves the precision and robustness of CVE-likeness detection.

Conditioned on CWE Label	Model	Precision	Recall	F1-score	Accuracy
✗	Our Model	32.00%	**100.00%**	48.48%	66.00%
	Deepseek R1	**100.00%**	87.50%	**93.33%**	**98.00%**
	GPT o3-mini	**100.00%**	87.50%	**93.33%**	**98.00%**
	Grok-3	43.75%	87.50%	58.33%	80.00%
✓	Our Model	80.00%	**100.00%**	**88.89%**	80.00%
	Deepseek R1	80.00%	**100.00%**	**88.89%**	80.00%
	GPT o3-mini	**81.63%**	**100.00%**	**89.89%**	**82.00%**
	Grok-3	80.00%	**100.00%**	**88.89%**	80.00%

A.6 Heatmap of the Correlation Between Confidence Scores After the Initial Model's Initial Predictions

The heatmap shows the correlation between confidence scores after the initial model's predictions. Samples selected for retraining are located in the top-right corner, where the confidence of being a CVE is > 0.9 and the confidence in the predicted CWE is > 0.9. The heatmap uses a logarithmic scale to represent the concentration of items more effectively.

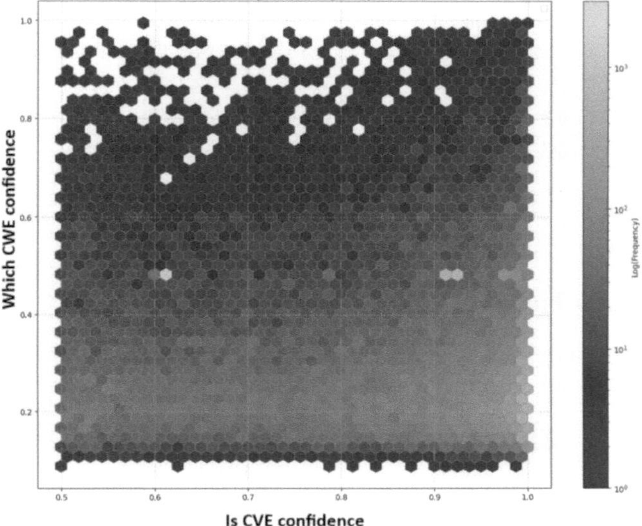

A.7 Data Contamination

An approach to address the data contamination issue involves testing the models exclusively on data published after the release of the base model, ensuring no overlap with the training dataset. We run the fine-tuned LLaMA model in inference mode to predict CWEs using only CVEs published after the model's release. This evaluation was restricted to CVEs with associated CWEs in the NIST database, following the guidelines of the CWE-1003 view, resulting in a test set of 3,094 CVEs with associated CWEs. Additionally, to discern whether the observed improvements or performance declines are attributable to the base models or reflect inherent complexity or simplicity in classifying the test set, we evaluated alternative approaches that operate independently of our base model. This comparative analysis shown in Table 11 helps identify whether the test set poses classification challenges independent of the model's architecture. The alternative approaches that operate independently of a base model are the ones proposed by [21], the authors classify CVE vulnerability into weaknesses based on the description using BiGRU-TextCNN. BiGRU captures the sequential information of text by processing words in order. Table 11 presents the results of this comparative evaluation. The analysis reveals that the performance decline for the LLaMA-based model is comparable to or even smaller than that of the BiGRU-TextCNN and TextCNN baselines. This suggests that the performance drop is not unique to LLaMA, but rather reflects the inherent difficulty of the newly introduced, unseen data. Therefore, there is no evidence of data contamination in the original test set from the base model's training data.

Table 11. Comparison of macro-average metrics across models on two distinct test sets: the Original test set (539 samples) and a New test set (3,094 samples) explicitly curated to exclude data from the Llama base model training set.

Model	Original test set (539 samples)			New test set (3,094 samples)			F1 Decrease (%)
	Precision	Recall	F1-score	Precision	Recall	F1-score	
TextCNN	53.47%	49.14%	49.45%	44.70%	48.12%	43.56%	11.91%
BiGRU-TextCNN	57.69%	53.78%	54.14%	45.22%	47.76%	43.41%	19.82%
Our approach	60.76%	58.04%	**58.08%**	56.54%	52.81%	**50.12%**	13.71%

A.8 Cochran's Formula

To determine the minimum sample size needed for reliable estimates of a population proportion, we employ Cochran's formula:

$$n = \frac{Z^2 \cdot p \cdot (1-p)}{E^2} = \frac{(1.96)^2 \cdot 0.5 \cdot (1-0.5)}{0.15^2} \approx 47$$

where:

- **Confidence Level**: Describes how often the sample reflects the true population. E.g. 96% ($Z = 1.96$)
- **Margin of Error**: Expresses how close the sample results are to the true population values. A smaller margin of error indicates more accuracy. E.g. 15% ($E = 0.15$)
- **Estimated Proportion** Represents the distribution of responses. 50% represents the worst-case variability to calculate the required sample size. E.g., p: 0.5 (no prior knowledge)

References

1. https://anonymous.4open.science/r/cveliketocwe/README.md, Accessed 07 Feb 2025
2. Common weakness enumeration. https://cwe.mitre.org/data/definitions/, Accessed 10 Oct 2025
3. Aghaei, E., Niu, X., Shadid, W., Al-Shaer, E.: Securebert: a domain-specific language model for cybersecurity. In: International Conference on Security and Privacy in Communication Systems, pp. 39–56. Springer (2022)
4. Bayer, M., Kuehn, P., Shanehsaz, R., Reuter, C.: Cysecbert: a domain-adapted language model for the cybersecurity domain (2022)
5. Bose, A., Behzadan, V., Aguirre, C., Hsu, W.H.: A novel approach for detection and ranking of trendy and emerging cyber threat events in twitter streams. In: Proceedings of the 2019 IEEE/ACM International Conference on Advances in Social Networks Analysis and Mining, pp. 871–878 (2019)
6. Chen, Y.: Convolutional neural network for sentence classification. Master's thesis, University of Waterloo (2015)
7. Chung, J., Gulcehre, C., Cho, K., Bengio, Y.: Empirical evaluation of gated recurrent neural networks on sequence modeling. arXiv preprint arXiv:1412.3555 (2014)
8. Deliu, I., Leichter, C., Franke, K.: Collecting cyber threat intelligence from hacker forums via a two-stage, hybrid process using support vector machines and latent dirichlet allocation. In: 2018 IEEE International Conference on Big Data (Big Data), pp. 5008–5013. IEEE (2018)
9. Devlin, J., Chang, M.W., Lee, K., Toutanova, K.: Bert: pre-training of deep bidirectional transformers for language understanding (2019). https://arxiv.org/abs/1810.04805
10. Future, R.: Press release: Understanding the timing of vulnerability disclosures (2017). https://www.recordedfuture.com/press-releases/20170607, Accessed 18 Dec 2025
11. Gautam, A.S., Gahlot, Y., Kamat, P.: Hacker forum exploit and classification for proactive cyber threat intelligence. In: Inventive Computation Technologies 4, pp. 279–285. Springer (2020)
12. Husari, G., Al-Shaer, E., Ahmed, M., Chu, B., Niu, X.: Ttpdrill: automatic and accurate extraction of threat actions from unstructured text of cti sources. In: Proceedings of the 33rd Annual Computer Security Applications Conference, pp. 103–115 (2017)

13. Jegham, N., Abdelatti, M., Hendawi, A.: Visual reasoning evaluation of grok, deepseek janus, gemini, qwen, mistral, and chatgpt. arXiv preprint arXiv:2502.16428 (2025)
14. Johnson, A., Johnson, A., Dempsey, K., Ross, R., Gupta, S., Bailey, D.: Guide for security-focused configuration management of information systems. US Department of Commerce, National Institute of Standards and Technology (2011)
15. Kadoguchi, M., Hayashi, S., Hashimoto, M., Otsuka, A.: Exploring the dark web for cyber threat intelligence using machine leaning. In: 2019 IEEE International Conference on Intelligence and Security Informatics (ISI), pp. 200–202. IEEE (2019)
16. Kim, D., Kim, H.K.: Automated dataset generation system for collaborative research of cyber threat analysis. Security Commun. Netw. **2019**(1), 6268476 (2019)
17. Lee, D.H., et al.: Pseudo-label: the simple and efficient semi-supervised learning method for deep neural networks. In: Workshop on Challenges in Representation Learning, ICML. vol. 3, p. 896. Atlanta (2013)
18. Li, Z., Zeng, J., Chen, Y., Liang, Z.: Attackg: constructing technique knowledge graph from cyber threat intelligence reports. In: European Symposium on Research in Computer Security, pp. 589–609. Springer (2022)
19. Liu, Y., et al.: Roberta: a robustly optimized bert pretraining approach (2019). https://arxiv.org/abs/1907.11692
20. Mittal, S., Das, P.K., Mulwad, V., Joshi, A., Finin, T.: Cybertwitter: using twitter to generate alerts for cybersecurity threats and vulnerabilities. In: 2016 IEEE/ACM International Conference on Advances in Social Networks Analysis and Mining (ASONAM), pp. 860–867. IEEE (2016)
21. Pan, M., Wu, P., Zou, Y., Ruan, C., Zhang, T.: An automatic vulnerability classification framework based on bigru-textcnn. Procedia Comput. Sci. **222**, 377–386 (2023)
22. Rahman, M.R., Mahdavi-Hezaveh, R., Williams, L.: A literature review on mining cyberthreat intelligence from unstructured texts. In: 2020 International Conference on Data Mining Workshops (ICDMW), pp. 516–525. IEEE (2020)
23. Samtani, S., Chinn, K., Larson, C., Chen, H.: Azsecure hacker assets portal: Cyber threat intelligence and malware analysis. In: 2016 IEEE Conference on Intelligence and Security Informatics (ISI), pp. 19–24. IEEE (2016)
24. Sapienza, A., Bessi, A., Damodaran, S., Shakarian, P., Lerman, K., Ferrara, E.: Early warnings of cyber threats in online discussions. In: 2017 IEEE International Conference on Data Mining Workshops (ICDMW), pp. 667–674. IEEE (2017)
25. Sapienza, A., Ernala, S.K., Bessi, A., Lerman, K., Ferrara, E.: Discover: mining online chatter for emerging cyber threats. In: Companion Proceedings of the The Web Conference 2018, pp. 983–990 (2018)
26. Satvat, K., Gjomemo, R., Venkatakrishnan, V.: Extractor: extracting attack behavior from threat reports. In: 2021 IEEE European Symposium on Security and Privacy (EuroS&P), pp. 598–615. IEEE (2021)
27. Simonetto, S.: Llama2_ft_for_cve_to_cwe (2025). https://huggingface.co/stefanosimonetto/Llama2_ft_for_CVE_to_CWE, Accessed 09 Feb 2025
28. Simonetto, S., van Ede, T.S., Bosch, P., Jonker, W.: Text2weak: mapping cves to cwes using description embeddings analysis. In: 4th Workshop on Artificial Intelligence-Enabled Cybersecurity Analytics (2024)
29. Singh, R., Mangat, N.S.: Elements of survey sampling, vol. 15. Springer Science & Business Media (2013)

30. Wu, X., Zheng, W., Chen, X., Wang, F., Mu, D.: Cve-assisted large-scale security bug report dataset construction method. J. Syst. Softw. **160**, 110456 (2020)
31. Zhu, Z., Dumitras, T.: Chainsmith: automatically learning the semantics of malicious campaigns by mining threat intelligence reports. In: 2018 IEEE European Symposium on Security and Privacy (EuroS&P), pp. 458–472. IEEE (2018)

Attacks

Unveiling the Critical Attack Path for Implanting Backdoors in Supply Chains: Practical Experience from XZ

Mario Lins(✉), René Mayrhofer, and Michael Roland

Johannes Kepler University Linz, Institute of Networks and Security, Linz, Austria
{lins,rm,roland}@ins.jku.at

Abstract. Recently, a previously unseen supply chain attack due to a backdoor in XZ Utils has been identified by A. Freund. This particular attack leverages highly sophisticated attack techniques, starting with social engineering attacks against the open source community up to implanting a backdoor in obfuscated binary blobs. This malware is designed to empower the attacker(s) to remotely run commands on vulnerable servers utilizing SSH evading authentication. A reverse dependency analysis revealed that the affected library is used by almost 30,000 packages in Debian and Ubuntu—the same order of magnitude as the GNU standard C library (`glibc`/`libc6`), a dependency for roughly 50,000 packages on these systems. This fact highlights the severity of such supply chain attacks and raises concerns about further backdoored packages still undetected in the wild. This paper identifies the critical attack path for successful implantation of such a backdoor and abstracts general key takeaways for future detection and mitigation of similar attacks. We also present *SketchyCrawler*, an open-source tool prototype designed to illustrate crawling repositories to reveal 'sketchy' signs of potential backdoor implantation attempts.

Keywords: Open source · Backdoor · Remote code execution · Supply chain attack

1 Introduction

We were extraordinarily lucky this time. On Friday, March 29th, 2024, Andres Freund ignited newspapers, social media channels, and security experts around the world when he revealed [13] a critical supply chain attack that introduces a backdoor in the widely used XZ Utils (CVE-2024-3094). He began investigating the XZ Utils package after noticing a slight 500 ms delay, an increase in CPU consumption, and some *valgrind* errors during test cases utilizing a remote SSH server. The affected package, XZ Utils, is a set of open source components, including `xz` and `lzma`, used for data compression. An attacker, using this backdoor, is able to execute arbitrary code remotely on vulnerable machines utilizing SSH without prior authentication. The seriousness of this security incident is underscored by the widespread usage of XZ Utils on a significant number of Linux

Y. Kim et al. (Eds.): CANS 2025, LNCS 16351, pp. 521–541, 2026.
https://doi.org/10.1007/978-981-95-4434-9_24

and other Unix-based systems, and the resulting CVSS rating of 10.0. Both the level of organizational attack complexity and the high code sophistication that were applied to compromise a widely distributed open source project with the aim of attacking a specific supply chain (and various other aspects) make this security incident particularly worthy of in-depth study. It highlights the need for careful consideration, both in addressing similar attacks in the future and in detecting potential active backdoors for which we were not yet as lucky to have become aware of. In this paper, we address relevant practical experiences with a focus on supply chain attacks by making the following theoretical and practical contributions:

- We analyze the malicious version of the XZ Utils package to identify and emphasize properties that could be relevant to other potential targets of interest for performing such a supply chain attack.
- We identify the essential stages of the critical attack path for implanting and activating a backdoor in an open source project.
- We generalize from this particular case to identify key takeaways as categories of important signals—both technical and social—to consider within the open source community in order to prevent similar attacks in the future.
- We implement *SketchyCrawler* as a first prototype to identify GitHub repositories with sketchy signs based on our evaluated takeaways.

2 Preliminaries

Both the infected package XZ Utils and the attack itself leverage various tools, functionalities, and well-established techniques. This section introduces them as essential preliminaries relevant to describe the critical attack path.

2.1 XZ Utils

XZ Utils is a widely distributed set of open source packages used for lossless data compression on Unix-like operating systems, including Linux. Beside supporting compression with the *xz file format*, XZ Utils also supports the legacy *lzma* format [41]. Because of its high compression ratio, in the last decade it has been included in many basic system components such as archival/compression tools, package installers like `dpkg` and `rpm`, the squashfs filesystem,[1] and even the Linux kernel itself for decompression of the kernel image and initramfs.[2]

2.2 Distribution Systems

Linux distributions, such as Debian, contain thousands of packages that work together to ensure seamless functionality. These packages are often developed by

[1] https://docs.kernel.org/filesystems/squashfs.html.
[2] https://docs.kernel.org/staging/xz.html.

multiple open source contributors and distributed either as already pre-existing components of the OS through package managers, like Advanced Package Tool (APT), or Dandified YUM (DNF). To include an open source package in their distribution system, it is a common practice to provide the related source code files. According to e.g., the "UpstreamGuide" of Debian [11], it is considered best practice to provide only source code files that make a rebuild possible. However, they also acknowledge that the rule "rebuild everything" is applied inconsistently, particularly for packages utilizing `autoconf` and `automake`. Thus, the current toolchain of Debian requires source code files to be submitted within a tarball. As a result, it is quite common to find a source tarball on the release pages of various open source projects available on VCS, like GitHub. Some open source projects also include pre-built binaries on these release pages. However, these are typically not used by package distribution systems, which build the final artifact from source instead. Another particularly relevant aspect of such package distribution systems is that the upstream sources are also expected to include test suites as part of the source tarball, which will be executed as part of the *Continuous Integration* (CI) pipeline to verify the intended behavior.

2.3 GNU M4

GNU `m4` [14] is used as an implementation of a macro processor standardized by POSIX including some additional built-in functions, such as running shell commands. Additionally, it is used by packages built with GNU `autoconf` for generating the `configure` scripts that customize the Makefile for compilation.

2.4 GNU Indirect Function Support (IFUNC)

Indirect function support (IFUNC) [30] is a feature of the GNU toolchain allowing developers to define multiple function implementations and to choose one of them at runtime. For selecting the proper implementation, the developer uses a resolver function. The dynamic loader calls the resolver function during startup and loads the corresponding implementation.

2.5 Google OSS-Fuzz

Google's OSS-Fuzz [16] is a continuous fuzzing tool for open source software to detect programming errors, like buffer overflows. According to the documentation [15] only projects with a significant user base and/or critical projects are included in the fuzzing process. To include a new project, it is necessary to open a pull request with information about the project (e.g., repository URL, primary contact).

3 Preliminary Considerations for Target Selection

First and foremost, XZ Utils is considered a well-known and widely distributed package used by various other packages and is shipped as an integral component of many operating systems, such as Debian. Due to its continuous development and long-standing presence, it has been highly trusted within the open source community for many years. We also believe that the attacker(s) may have chosen the XZ Utils project because they were looking for an open source project with a single maintainer who could become overwhelmed when increasing the workload. Another key observation relates to evasion, emphasizing that the actual target—servers utilizing OpenSSH—do not have a direct dependency on XZ Utils. Instead, some distributions utilize `systemd` in combination with `libsystemd` to manage services like OpenSSH. Notably, `libsystemd` depends on the library `liblzma`, which is part of the XZ Utils project. Considering further evasion and obfuscation signs with regards to the XZ project, the test files may play a crucial role as well. These files, being binary blobs, are not easily readable yet appear legitimate within the context of a data compression utility.

We outline the (supposed) key reasons for choosing an open source project like XZ Utils to strategically plan such a supply chain attack:

- Well-known package with sufficiently long history
- Trusted within the open source community
- Widely distributed package to increase attack surface
- Single maintainer, easily overwhelmed
- Actual target does not directly depend on infected package, making detection harder
- Using binary blobs that appear legitimate, but can be used to implant malicious code

Another important consideration when selecting the ideal target for such an attack is to determine how widely distributed the infected XZ Utils package actually is. To address this, we conduct a recursive reverse dependency analysis

Table 1. Results from a reverse dependency analysis* for a set of selected libraries on 2024-09-15

Library	reverse-depends count on	
	Ubuntu 24.04	Debian 12.7
libc6	51,209	45,344
libzstd1	32,249	27,548
liblzma5	**29,133**	**27,129**
libssl3(t64)	24,361	23,178
libbz2-1.0	24,871	21,246
liblz4-1	15,170	12,840
libsystemd0	14,579	12,040
libjpeg(62)-turbo(8)	11,102	11,124
libssh2-(4|1)	6,082	5,484
libcurl4(t64)	3,125	3,832

* Using: `apt-rdepends -r <library-package> | \`
`sed 's/^Reverse Depends: //;s/ (.*)//' | sort -u | wc -l`

of the affected `liblzma` and a set of other libraries for comparison. We chose that set as an exemplary representation of libraries (a) providing similar functionality (i.e., other compression libraries), (b) providing essential functionality that we expected to be widely used in general (i.e., GNU standard C library) and particularly in applications with network communication (e.g., OpenSSL's `libssl3`), (c) a randomly-picked image processing library (as an example for (in-)famous bugs leading to exploitable RCE on both consumer devices and server-side applications), and (d) libraries related to the exploitation target chosen in the XZ Utils incident. Table 1 summarizes the results of our analysis. As shown, `liblzma` is used by nearly 30,000 other packages. Compared to the ubiquitous glibc (`libc6`), we see the same order of magnitude. When compared to another popular, and potentially even more well-known tool, such as `curl`, `liblzma`, while supposedly more obscure to both users and administrators, shows a usage rate that is 10 times higher. These facts underscore the significant severity in having malicious code (e.g., a backdoor) hidden in a library with such widespread distribution.

4 Attack Analysis

This section describes relevant stages, including both human/social and technical aspects, that lead to the compromise of the XZ C library by incorporating a backdoor. We start with an analysis of the currently known facts [1,4,7,8,10,13] around the security incident and derive a critical attack path as shown in Fig. 1 by categorizing the available information (including the temporal sequence of the events) into individual stages.

4.1 Stage 1: Building Trust

The XZ security incident did not begin with fancy hacking tools or with sophisticated code; it all started with a hacking technique known as social engineering, which prays on humans' emotions, trust, and pressure. In case of XZ, especially pressure plays a crucial role in the social engineering attack targeting the open source community. This section summarizes insights into the social engineering tactics employed by the attacker(s) to gain necessary privileges on the repository.

In 2005 [42], a small group including Lasse Collin, started work on a project called LZMA Utils, which was later renamed XZ Utils. In 2021, "Jia Tan" (presumably a pseudonym) started to support the XZ Utils project by regularly contributing code improvements via the XZ developers mailing list. At the time of writing this paper, we are not aware of any malicious content in the first

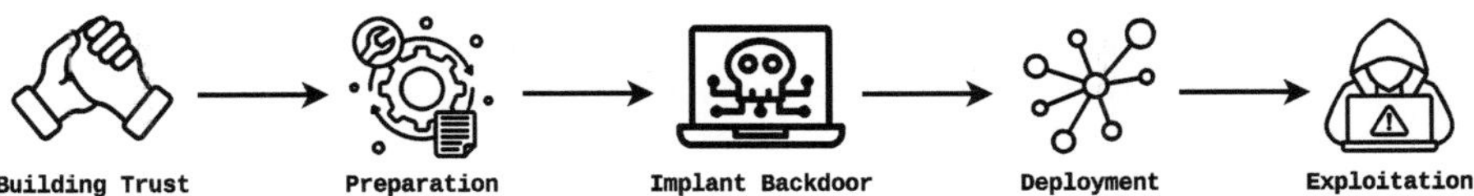

Fig. 1. Critical Attack Path

contributions of Jia Tan. Apparently, Jia Tan seems to be a friendly, interested, and supportive contributor of the open source project. However, some years later it became clear that Jia Tan had different intentions with the XZ Utils project. It appears that the initial intention of Jia Tan was to build up trust within the open source project, which plays a significant role with regards to the upcoming attack path. The first suspicious commit [22] involving Jia Tan under the username "JiaT75" dates back to November 2021. The commit was done within another project called "libarchive" and replaced the `safe_fprintf` function with `fprintf`, the less secure variant of this functionality. This commit has been approved and merged to the main branch of that project without noticing that this might be a suspicious change. At the time of writing this paper, it remains uncertain whether this commit is relevant to the XZ backdoor case.

A few months later, in April 2022, user JiaT75 tried to submit another patch via the XZ developers mailing list [37]. According to the conversation log, there was suddenly another pseudonym, called "Jigar Kumar" involved, who describes this patch as "*quality of life feature*" [27] and complains about the slow release schedule of the project maintainer. As one of the initial responses to this complaint, Jia Tan took on the role of a supportive, friendly, and loyal defender of the original maintainer, Lasse Collin, pointing out that the contributors are hobbyists and that can't dedicate 40+ hours a week. The conversation continued with putting more and more pressure on the original maintainer Lasse Collin. Meanwhile, in a separate project focused on XZ for Java, a new participant, Dennis Ens, enters the scene. This pseudonym also began in a similar manner, adding extra pressure on the original maintainer by, for example, inquiring whether the project was still maintained. In this particular conversation, Lasse Collin mentioned that the project is an unpaid hobby and that he is already in contact with Jia Tan who "will have a bigger role in the future". We detected the first commit [23] solely merged by Jia Tan from December 2022. Thus, we infer that Jia Tan obtained the required permissions for the repository and may have been promoted to co-maintainer of the project.

Based on these conversations and the similarities between these different types of individuals, we assume that the attacker(s) have set up these pseudonyms, commonly referred to as "sock puppet" accounts. More insights on the conversations can be found in Fig. 2. We explicitly note that attribution, i.e., trying to estimate the real source of these (supposedly coordinated) pseudonyms and tracing back to an attacking organization and/or geo-political region is outside the scope of this paper.

4.2 Stage 2: Preparation

In the second stage of the critical attack path we outline the various actions taken by the attacker(s) to prepare for the actual supply chain attack. A key aspect of this stage is that all their actions and steps remain deniable. Thus, if any malicious activity had been detected at this stage, the attacker would still have a valid reason to deny any malicious intent.

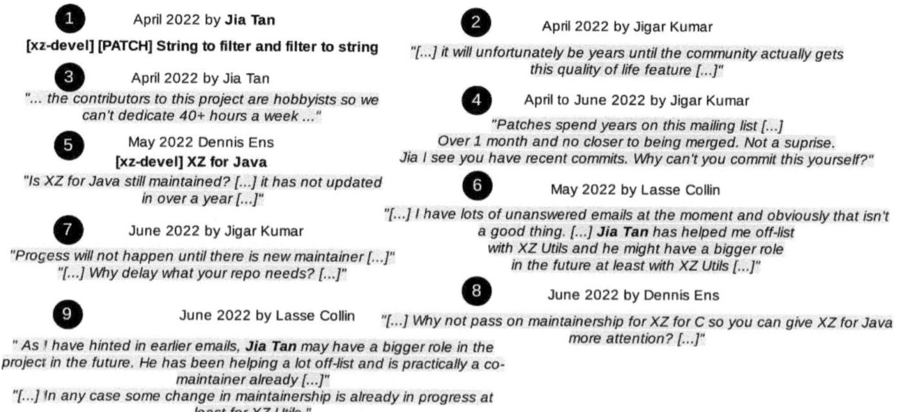

Fig. 2. Conversation highlights **(1)** Jia Tan wants to provide a patch via mailing list. **(2)** First signs of pressure by Jigar Kumar. **(3)** Support from Jia Tan. **(4)** Increasing pressure from Jigar Kumar. **(5)** Pressure from another pseudonym, Dennis Ens, on a different project. **(6)** First signs of being overwhelmed by Lasse Collin. **(7)** Attacker(s) want to become co-maintainer. **(8)** Again pressure to pass maintainership to attacker(s). **(9)** Finally, the attacker(s) were successful.

In March 2023, the primary contact mail for a component in the testing infrastructure, Google OSS-Fuzz, was changed from `lasse.collin@tukaani.org` to `jiat0218@gmail.com` by opening a merge request on OZZ-Fuzz. That change of contact was manually approved by Lasse Collin as the original maintainer, confirming that Jia Tan is an official co-maintainer of the XZ project [25]. After some months, a new contributor called "Hans Jansen" provided patches to the XZ Utils project that use the GNU indirect function (IFUNC) feature [19,20]. After some reworks and discussions, Jia Tan merged that functionality to the repository. Only later, it turned out that these patches are essential for the attack, because IFUNC is the function hooking mechanism eventually used by the backdoor code. However, the use of IFUNC cannot be fuzzed by OSS-Fuzz, due to compatibility issues. We assume that the adversary expected errors resulting from fuzzing with OSS-Fuzz after enabling IFUNC. Consequently, Jia Tan opened a pull request [24] within the OSS-Fuzz project, to disable IFUNC for the fuzzed XZ Utils build. In this request, Jia Tan mentioned that IFUNC is not compatible with "`-fsanitize=address`" that is also known as *Address-Sanitizer* (ASan) and used to detect memory errors. The OSS-Fuzz repository incorporates a GitHub action to automatically label pull requests as "ready to merge" if they originate from the maintainer of a fuzzed project by verifying that the committer has a contribution history for that project and is one of the responsible project contacts. As both applied to Jia Tan, the pull request was labeled as *ready to merge* by the bot, and then quickly approved and merged into OSS-Fuzz.

```
❶ gl_[$1]_config='sed \"r\n\" $gl_am_configmake |
  eval $gl_path_map |
  $gl_[$1]_prefix -d 2>/dev/null'

❷ gl_am_configmake=`grep - aErls "#{4}[[:alnum:]]{5}#{4}$"
  $srcdir/ 2>/dev/null`

❸ gl_path_map='tr "\t \-_" " \t_\-"'

❹ gl_[$1]_prefix=`echo $gl_am_configmake | sed "s/.*\.//g"`

❺ cat ./tests/files/bad-3-corrupt_lzma2.xz |
  tr "\t \-_" " \t_\-" | xz -d
```

Fig. 3. Obfuscated command hidden in `build-to-host.m4` file. **(1)** Obfuscated command including three variables: `gl_am_configmake`, `gl_path_map`, `gl_[$1]_prefix`. The `sed` command is actually a hidden `cat` command. **(2)** Extracts the relative path of the `bad-3-corrupt_lzma2.xz` test file. **(3)** `tr` command to uncorrupt the content of the test file. **(4)** Echoes the relative path of the test file and removes characters except the file ending: xz. **(5)** Unveiled command that fetches content of test file, pipes it into `tr` command to uncorrupt it, and afterwards extracts the hidden shell script by decompressing it with `xz`.

4.3 Stage 3: Implanting Backdoor

This stage consolidates the steps required for implanting the backdoor into an open source project, ensuring it stays hidden even in a public repository. Compared to the previous stage, the actions taken by the attacker(s) in this stage are no longer deniable.

On Sunday, February 23rd, 2024, Jia Tan added various lzma test files [38,39] to the project. Later, it turned out that the uploaded test files, called `bad-3-corrupt_lzma2.xz` and `good-large_compressed.lzma` contained the binary backdoor and some other obfuscated code necessary to inject the backdoor code. At this stage, the hidden backdoor is already part of the project, but is not yet deployed. Another essential preparation step was to add the file `build-to-host.m4` to the `.gitignore` file of the source code repository so that its source code does not get pushed to the repository. However, a modified version of the `build-to-host.m4` file was still part of the source tarball that gets fetched by the build system to build the final artifact. Comparing a previous version of the `build-to-host.m4` file with that one stored in the source tarball clearly yields some differences. We focus on one of these to show how the attacker(s) were able to obfuscate the malicious parts finally executed on the build machine. Figure 3 shows the obfuscated command hidden in the `build-to-host.m4` file.

4.4 Stage 4: Deployment

The following day (Monday, February 24th, 2024), Jia Tan released version 5.6.0 of XZ Utils via GitHub. In addition to the auto-generated source archives in `.zip` and `.tar.gz` form, XZ Utils releases include four additional, manually uploaded

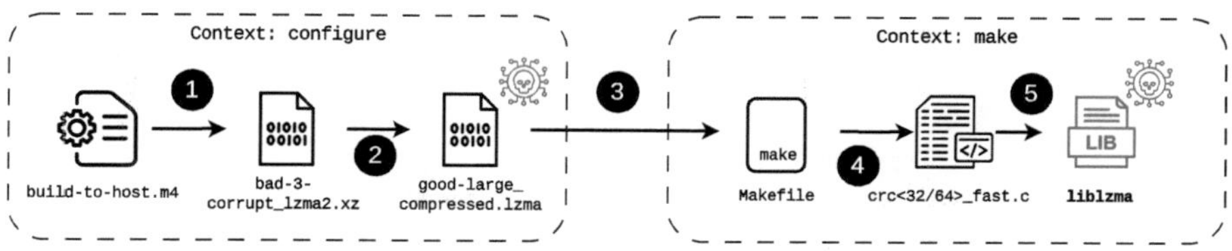

Fig. 4. Abstract overview of the remaining steps to implant the backdoor in the final artifact. The dashed lines are used to visualize the different build contexts. **(1)** The `build-to-host.m4` file initiates the implanting process by "repairing" the `bad-3-corrupt_lzma2.xz` file and executing a script hidden in there. **(2)** This script runs additional commands hidden in another test file called `good-large_compressed.lzma`. This test file is properly compressed with XZ, but contains junk data that gets removed by various operations, such as using the `head` command to get specific bytes. The final result is again piped into shell and gets executed. **(3)** Besides some checks on the environment, the actual binary backdoor also hidden in the `good-large_compressed.lzma` test file, but with another offset, gets extracted into `liblzma_la-crc64-fast.o`. Additionally, the `Makefile` is patched to incorporate the malicious backdoor in the compiled library. **(4)** After some preparation, verification, and cleanup steps, the patched `Makefile` modifies the code of the files `crc64_fast.c` and `crc32_fast.c`. This step is important for the exploitation stage, as the contained function `crc64_resolve` provides the actual ifunc resolver, which is used to call the `_get_cpuid` function that is provided by the backdoor. **(5)** Finally, the backdoor hidden in the `liblzma_la-crc64-fast.o` file including the ifunc resolver gets compiled in the liblzma library.

source archives with corresponding signature files. The manually uploaded source archives, which were uploaded to GitHub for this release, also include the modified `build-to-host.m4` file, which is not part of the repository itself to evade potential discovery through the repository change history. The malicious m4 file extracts the backdoor from the test files when building the deb or rpm packages.

The next step was to convince Linux distributions to include the latest, but malicious, release of XZ Utils in their package repositories. For that, the pseudonym Hans Jansen started to contact and pressure some Linux distributions (e.g. Debian [21]). Once the package maintainer upgraded to the new version by fetching the source code tarball, the malicious `build-to-host.m4` file gets integrated into the package build process. The malicious build script then initiates the steps required to extract the backdoor hidden in the test files. After several obfuscated modification, decompression, and execution steps on the malicious test files, as illustrated in Fig. 4, an object file named `liblzma_la-crc64_fast.o`, which contains the backdoor code, is linked into the `liblzma` library via setting the respective pointer which gets resolved by the IFUNC functionality. Additional information can also be found in [10].

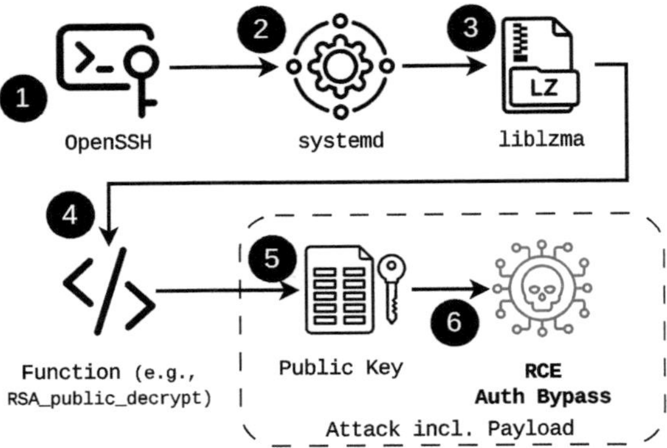

Fig. 5. Illustration of the actual exploitation of the backdoor hidden in XZ Utils. **(1)** The actual targets are vulnerable servers utilizing OpenSSH. The attack gets initiated by providing a specific OpenSSH certificate to these servers. **(2)** OpenSSH does not directly depend on the malicious liblzma library, but is managed on some systems via systemd. **(3)** systemd is used to load the malicious library liblzma. **(4)** The malicious library providing the ifunc resolver gets called before the GOT and PLT table are read-only. This allows the backdoor to rewrite the tables to hijack function calls, such as `RSA_public_decrypt`, which is used by SSH. **(5)** The SSH certificate provided by the attacker contains the payload. **(6)** The payload gets executed so the attacker is able to run commands remotely without prior authentication.

4.5 Stage 5: Exploitation

The final stage is the exploitation stage (Fig. 5) in which the backdoor gets triggered on the infected system. Current investigations show that a pointer of a function used by `RSA_public_decrypt` for OpenSSH (more specifically for any process of the executable located at `/usr/bin/sshd`) is changed to point on a function owned by the backdoor. The malicious function extracts a command from the certificate provided by the SSH client. This is only initiated for a specific private key which makes the backdoor only available to attackers who possess the corresponding key. Afterwards, the command is passed to the `system()` function, which executes it. Thus, an attacker who controls the private SSH key can send arbitrary commands to affected SSH servers which are executed remotely without ever completing the authentication to the SSH server.

5 Takeaways

We now try to generalize from the specific XZ incident and derive more abstract takeaways that we argue are applicable to different open source projects under the category of aspects described in Sect. 3.

5.1 Signs of Social Engineering

Lively discussions within an open source project are generally seen as positive and encouraged. However, if there are suddenly more and more messages of offensive or otherwise problematic nature such as increasing pressure on specific contributors, it might be a sign that should be taken seriously. Especially time pressure seems to be effective in this context and could be a sign for social manipulation as part of an attack. Other signs of social engineering are extending or transfer of maintainer status for a project or components, as has happened in this case, but also in many others with malicious intent (e.g., in the various NodeJS and Python cases [3,31,32]). The **first takeaway (T1)** for mitigating comparable future cases is therefore an increased focus on social engineering of project maintainer control.

5.2 Small Projects with Large Reverse Dependencies

The XZ Utils project was, in hindsight, an excellent target due to its relatively small code base and clear focus, but with a surprisingly large reverse dependency tree.

This **second takeaway (T2)** is potentially the lowest hanging fruit for future research by prioritizing independent analysis on and adding mitigations to exactly such projects matching this filter criterion—which are far fewer than the total number of packages in most Linux distributions or programming language package/module systems. Conversely, we can derive a **third takeaway (T3)** for critical software projects (such as OpenSSH) to particularly focus on their own dependency tree in terms of such small, potentially vulnerable projects they might depend on. This is not easy if the dependency tree is large or includes dynamic indirections,[3] potentially even crossing language/platform boundaries. Nonetheless, the same filter criterion can be applied to prioritize analysis efforts.

5.3 Potential for Bugdoors

Brittle code in the sense of source code or build system level meta code that, structurally or based on bad code quality, makes it easy to make "mistakes" with security-critical consequences, should be analyzed for its potential of introducing *bugdoors*.[4] Ideally, such brittle code should not be merged into projects,

[3] One of the changes after the XZ Utils incident is that `libsystemd` now loads compression libraries through `dlopen`, which makes this indirect dependency even harder to follow (cf. https://github.com/systemd/systemd/issues/32028 and https://github.com/systemd/systemd/pull/31550.

[4] The portmanteau "bugdoor" describes a backdoor—typically implanted in the source code—that can plausibly be argued to have been a genuine bug in the relevant code. It is unclear when and by whom this term was coined, but early sources include an analysis on embedded systems firmware from 2014 [40]. The concept itself is generic and not limited to pure memory safety issues, as formalized (but not explicitly named as potential bugdoor vectors) in the seminal "Weird Machines" work [12].

although that might happen in combination with social engineering as mentioned above. Additionally, unnecessary code or architectural complexity can be a sign of preparing for a future bugdoor. In the case of XZ, existing use of `autoconf` (with a high level of build system complexity with embedded arbitrary code execution on multiple layers) and the (presumably) maliciously introduced use of IFUNC indirection are, in hindsight, good signals for the potential of introducing bugdoors. Especially adding the whole IFUNC infrastructure was technically unnecessary for the existing code base, and should probably have been rejected without a clear architectural need that could not have been handled with simpler code. Unfortunately, the prevalence of both memory-unsafe languages such as C and (most of) C++ and build systems with arbitrary code execution instead of declarative and side-effect free (also called hermetic [36]) build statements makes this the hardest call for action. Detecting the actual bugdoor itself is, by definition, hard, as they are designed to look like benign human mistakes in another reasonable interpretation.

The **fourth takeaway (T4)** is therefore to avoid unnecessary complexity, both in structure/architecture and in actual source or build system meta code. That includes moving to strongly typed, memory safe languages (which do not make it impossible, but arguably harder to write bugdoors) and declarative build systems whenever possible (particularly for the filtered projects mentioned above), but at least avoiding complex indirections and layers of abstractions not strictly required in those legacy code bases that cannot (yet) be switched.

5.4 Signs of Obfuscation

The final, **fifth takeaway (T5)** is perhaps the clearest one: be alert to signs of obfuscation, including explicit ones (such as excerpted in Fig. 3) and implicit, unexplained binary blobs—which are much more common in many projects. While binary blobs acting as input for training or used for "error" test cases have their purpose, we should now start to demand reproducibility of all such binary blobs. That is, binary blobs should, e.g., be generated by explainable helper scripts checked into the repository. While there can be no guarantee that such helper scripts are not in themselves bugdoors in the sense of generating malicious, dual-purpose binary blobs, we argue that it lowers the probability of occurrence. Remaining input for (regression) test cases without reproducible generation processes that have, e.g., been submitted by users as part of bug reports, should only be used or executed within tight sandboxes during the build process.

6 SketchyCrawler

We implemented *SketchyCrawler*, an open-source tool prototype used to crawl GitHub repositories to detect sketchy signs for backdoor potential in open source projects. The main objective is to support software development teams in auditing and assessing such projects before they incorporate them in their own software project. Although there are established, well-known practices for mitigating certain risks in the supply chain, many challenges in this emerging threat landscape remain unresolved as demonstrated with the XZ incident. Established practices involve vulnerability scans, Software Composition Analysis (SCA), or manual auditing of the respective component and its source code. While auditing third party components before integrating them in a product is valuable, it is often impractical to (thoroughly) audit every component or update.

Our objective is to demonstrate how software development teams can leverage such a tool to prioritize their (ideally regular) audits and assess third party repositories, following the five key takeaways outlined in Sect. 5. First, we explain how *SketchyCrawler* addresses these takeaways. Then, we illustrate some of the information gathered by the first prototype. Finally, we discuss relevant deployment considerations including our assessment of the results.

6.1 Implementation

SketchyCrawler is a set of Python and Shell scripts used to crawl GitHub repositories. Currently, users of our tool simply need to provide their crawling targets and some additional information in a CSV file to collect relevant assessment information automatically. This includes the repository URL, owner, repository name, the time range for the analysis, currently trusted maintainers, potential sketchy files and types, and the package name. Below we describe the main features of *SketchyCrawler*:

Signs of Social Engineering (T1, cf. Sect. 5.1*).* Trust is essential not only within the open source community but also from a supply chain perspective when using third party components in software projects. In case of XZ, the primary objective of the adversary was, as outlined in Sect. 4.1, to build sufficient trust to gain commit permissions within the open source project. Based on this, one feature of *SketchyCrawler* is about detection of new maintainers that are not marked as trustworthy yet. Since auditing every update of the incorporated third party components requires significant effort, we believe that focusing on major changes (e.g., change of maintainers) offers a valuable advantage. Using a third party component requires some sort of trust in the maintainer anyway. However, when the previously trusted maintainers change, it may be a sign for a necessary re-audit of this component to ensure valid and conscious trust assumptions.

Reverse Dependency Analysis (T2, cf. Sect. 5.2*). SketchyCrawler* also includes a module for analyzing a package's reverse dependencies required at runtime. The main objective here is to highlight packages with a high number of reverse dependencies as these can increase the attack surface. In case of XZ, the adversaries planted a vulnerability into SSH servers not by compromising OpenSSH directly, but one of its (indirect) dependencies. The reverse dependency analysis is recursive so we also count the dependencies of the dependencies, and so on.

Forward Dependency Analysis (T3, cf. Sect. 5.2*).* The third feature is similar to the previous one, but addresses forward dependencies at runtime and build time. From an adversary point of view, forward dependencies may be interesting for critical software projects (such as OpenSSH) as the attack surface increases for every dependency that could be vulnerable too. We showcase the analysis of build dependencies by leveraging the *cargo tree* command to count the dependencies recursively. However, *SketchyCrawler* currently focuses on forward package dependencies and does not yet detect dependencies that are dynamically loaded during runtime, e.g. through `dlopen`.[5]

Identify Bugdoors (T4, cf. Sect. 5.3*).* Our fourth takeaway addresses the potential for bugdoors in open source projects. Thus, *SketchyCrawler* incorporates a module that allows defining a list of potential sketchy files and crawls the repository if those files exist. A good example is the `build.rs` file used in various Rust packages; legitimately, this can, e.g., be used to compile third-party C libraries before building the actual Rust package [35], but potentially for attacking the build process or host itself. Rust projects with a `build.rs` file cause Cargo to execute its content before building the Rust package. A report published by the Phylum Research team [33], dedicated to identifying software supply chain attacks, highlights an attack targeting Rust developers. They observed a case where an adversary initially tried to typosquat a package (e.g., name it postgress instead of postgres) containing almost no code. This was followed by a series of small, seemingly non-suspicious code changes. However, at some point the adversary included a `build.rs` file that was used to establish a communication channel to the adversary. This example illustrates why Rust projects using a `build.rs` file may require a closer look.

Additionally, we check whether sketchy files have been deliberately added to the `.gitignore` file. However, this specific crawling feature only highlights files that are not expected in the `.gitignore` file and adds a more critical sign when combined with the results of T5 (e.g., hidden file is part of the source tarball).

Signs of Obfuscation (T5, cf. Sect. 5.4*).* In this category we try to identify sketchy mime types that may reveal attempts to obfuscate code (e.g., by incorporating binary blobs). A possible example for a mime-type is *application* that is typically used for a binary file rather than a text file. Another indication of obfuscation is the presence of discrepancies between the actual source code repository and the published source tarball. In case of XZ, the adversaries tried to hide the malicious `build-to-host.m4` file by adding it to the `.gitignore` file. However, the source tarball, used to build the actual package, contained the malicious file.

[5] Work is independently underway to improve tooling for these dynamically loaded dependencies to be listed in the ELF header (cf. https://github.com/systemd/systemd/blob/main/docs/ELF_DLOPEN_METADATA.md). Future versions of *SketchyCrawler* should use this data when more broadly available.

6.2 Evaluation

We evaluate *SketchyCrawler* by crawling GitHub repositories of Debian packages to identify sketchy signs for a potential backdoor. To select our test examples, we use Debian PopCon,[6] a list of the most popular Debian packages. Currently, we support open-source projects hosted on GitHub only, but we believe that with some engineering effort, integrating additional version control systems would be straightforward. We select the top-three packages on Debian PopCon with the most installations that are also available on GitHub. This results in `libpam-modules`, `libblkid1`, and `zlib1g`. Although `liblzma5`, with 250,211 installations, ranked 95th out of 200,909 packages only, we included it in our evaluation to discuss the findings in case of XZ. Additionally, we also include two packages written in Rust in our evaluation as this ecosystem focuses on secure software development. We crawl 6,369 packages to find at least two Rust packages—`mdevctl` on rank 4,097 and `ripgrep` on rank 6,369. The final selection of packages can be found in Table 2. The crawler results are illustrated in Table 3. T3 includes the forward package- and build dependencies in the format x/y, where x represents the number of forward package dependencies and y represents the number of build dependencies. T5 includes the number sketchy file types and differences in the format x/y, where x represents the number of detected sketchy file types and y represents the number of differences between the source tarball and the repository for a given release tag. For simplicity, and to provide an initial indication of sketchy signals, we display only the number of differences that occur in either the source tarball or the repository. The specific list of differences can be printed to a log output. A full run, including fetching commits within the given time range, cloning the repository, performing the dependency-, file-, and file type analysis including the differences between the source tarball and the repository took 503.70 s on an Intel Core i7-1185G7 @ 3.00GHz CPU with 32GB of RAM.

Table 2. Selected Debian packages

Package	# Inst.	Since	Until	Trusted maintainer	Sketchy files	File types
liblzma5	250150	2022-01-01	2023-01-02	Larhzu, web-flow	configure.ac	application
libpam	251820	2022-01-01	2023-01-02	ldv-alt, thkukuk	configure.ac	application
libblkid1	251817	2022-01-01	2023-01-02	karelzak	configure.ac	application
zlib1g	251815	2022-01-01	2023-01-02	madler	configure.ac	application
mdevctl	14072	2024-01-01	2025-01-02	jonner	build.rs	application
ripgrep	6167	2024-01-01	2025-01-02	BurntSushi	build.rs	application

[6] https://popcon.debian.org/main/by_inst.

Table 3. SketchyCrawler results

Package	T1	T2	T3	T4	T5
liblzma	5	33436	4/80	1	99/38
libpam	8	5704	32/74	2	199/28
libblkid1	26	14448	4/85	3	422/45
zlib1g	0	41461	4/75	5	650/60
mdevctl	0	1	53/87	1	758/14
ripgrep	21	1	5/84	3	869/25

6.3 Discussion

We believe that tools such as *SketchyCrawler* can be utilized as part of a risk management process to gather metrics about sketchy findings and include them in further risk assessments. For example, a package maintained by many developers is likely more difficult to verify than one with a single maintainer (e.g., `zlib1g` or `mdevctl`), and can therefore be assigned to a higher risk category. In Table 3, `liblzma5`—relevant in case of XZ—is listed with 5 commits made by an untrusted maintainer, specifically Jia Tan, the adversary. Additionally, *SketchyCrawler* highlights packages with a high number of reverse dependencies (e.g., `liblzma5` and `zlib1g`), which may be a valuable target for an adversary, as demonstrated in the XZ case. Next, we identify packages with a high number of forward dependencies, which may increase the likelihood of a vulnerability. Currently, dynamically loaded dependencies during runtime are beyond the scope of the current implementation. However, there are already discussions [2,34] within the open source community going on concerning dependencies loaded dynamically by `dlopen()`. One potential risk mitigation—particularly on projects with a high number of dependencies—is that software developers may consider additional security controls before publicly exposing such components. As expected, the number of sketchy files represented in T4 is low, since we use only the `configure.ac` and `build.rs` files to showcase the functionality of our crawler. However, in projects like XZ, where sketchy files such as `build-to-host.m4` are included in the `.gitignore` file, we expect to see an increased number here. T5 illustrates sketchy types, especially binary files with regards to our sample set. This can certainly be legitimate; however, it is a sign that there is also a lot of potential to obfuscate malicious code such as a backdoor. Finally, T5 also highlights the number of differences between the source tarball and the actual repository for a specific tag. While the results show significant differences, most of the files, such as the `.gitignore` and the `.git` directory, are expected not to be part of the source tarball.

6.4 Deployment Consideration

Typically, Secure Software Development Life Cycles involve license clearing and component approval before third party libraries are integrated into a software product. As a result, software development teams may audit those third party components before adding them. However, since those components are often updated over time, it can be challenging for developers to audit every new version. We believe that integrating a tool such as *SketchyCrawler* into a *Continuous Integration/Continuous Deployment* (CI/CD) pipeline to identify sketchy signs allows development teams to focus first on critical parts in their supply chain. Particularly within the Rust ecosystem with its focus on secure software development, future integration with development team processes using the `cargo vet`[7] and/or `cargo geiger`[8] tools might be helpful to better manage audit resources.

7 Related Work

The challenge of describing different supply chain attacks to develop effective mitigation techniques has been explored in several academic papers. Naik et al. [29] compare a range of various attacker models on a more abstract level. Several works focus on generalizing security frameworks (e.g., MITRE ATT&CK [9] or the Diamond Model [6]). Additionally, there is also research [17,31] focusing on analyzing malicious software packages in general. Moreover, specific research efforts have investigated particular attacks, such as the SolarWinds attack presented by Martínez and Durán [28]. The variety of research tracks in the field of software supply chain security highlights the difficulty in mitigating such attacks properly and the XZ incident serves as a clear example that we still face open issues. Specifically concerning the XZ incident, there are existing attempts to counter such attacks, such as differential property monitoring [5] or a fuzzing approach to detect backdoor triggers at runtime [26]. However, our paper investigates emerging supply chain attacks such as the XZ incident, aiming to identify new methods in every stage by which adversaries can still successfully implant a backdoor in an open source project. In comparison with existing research, we outline a new critical attack path including corresponding mitigation techniques to support mitigation for similar attacks in the future. We abstract the critical attack path observed in the XZ incident, and believe this attack strategy could be applied to analogous supply chain attacks. During the course of our work, Hamer et al. [17] also conducted a study providing recommendations for preventing such supply chain attacks. However, their perspective focuses more on existing frameworks—suggesting the use of starter kits, improvements to current frameworks, and continued research into threat intelligence. In contrast, we analyze the critical attack path of a software supply chain attack based on new attacker strategies used in the XZ incident, highlight the main key takeaways, and provide a tool prototype to showcase how sketchy signs in open source projects can be identified.

---

[7] https://mozilla.github.io/cargo-vet/.

[8] https://github.com/geiger-rs/cargo-geiger.

8 Conclusion

The XZ Utils backdoor is another example of open source software that has become a central component of (too?) many foundational services, and therefore of critical Internet infrastructure components. Through the complexity and duration of the full attack path, we can speculate that the threat actor(s) are part of a highly sophisticated organization with stable funding. This example can be used as an excellent teaching opportunity for practical applications, both in terms of human/social/organizational and technical aspects. We have briefly summarized what we consider to be the critical components of the attack path, referencing many more detailed resources for specific parts of the attack analysis. We acknowledge that this is an empirical study for a single incident; however, as with social science, security incidents are rarely reproducible.

From this attack path, we derive five more generic takeaways for open source projects to mitigate future attacks on them or their (direct or indirect, forward or reverse) dependency tree. These should be seen as calls for action, but not as quick fixes. Particularly the complexity of old build toolchains around programming languages without strong type systems and memory safety will continue to leave open many different attack paths [18] that are hard to find, difficult to audit, and provide the cover of plausible deniability for attackers in the form of exploitable "bugdoor" attacks. Additionally, we illustrate how to support software development with a tool-based approach to identify new signs that may result from the continuous emerging threat landscape in the field of software supply chains. Our prototype tool, *SketchyCrawler*, demonstrate how such a solution can be built and utilized to support auditing of third party components by revealing sketchy signs.

One additional takeaway is a strengthened belief voiced by many of the experts involved with analyzing this case that similar attacks are possible on proprietary, closed source codebases, and that, as a security community, we have to assume other attacks with comparable complexity and sophistication to be actively deployed in multiple projects/products. It is now our shared task to find them, and we hope that this analysis and our prototype tool can help with a few steps on this difficult endeavor.

Availability

We provide an open-source repository of *SketchyCrawler* on https://github.com/linsm/sketchy-crawler.

Acknowledgments. This work has been carried out within the scope of Digidow, the Christian Doppler Laboratory for Private Digital Authentication in the Physical World and has partially been supported by the LIT Secure and Correct Systems Lab. We gratefully acknowledge financial support by the Austrian Federal Ministry of Economy, Energy and Tourism, the National Foundation for Research, Technology and

Development, the Christian Doppler Research Association, 3 Banken IT GmbH, ekey biometric systems GmbH, Kepler Universitätsklinikum GmbH, NXP Semiconductors Austria GmbH & Co KG, Österreichische Staatsdruckerei GmbH, and the State of Upper Austria.

References

1. Akamai Security Intelligence Group: XZ Utils Backdoor—Everything You Need to Know, and What You Can Do (2025). https://www.akamai.com/blog/security-research/critical-linux-backdoor-xz-utils-discovered-what-to-know. Accessed Apr 2025
2. Alden, D.: Identifying dependencies used via dlopen() (2024). https://lwn.net/Articles/969908/. Accessed July 2025
3. Birsan, A.: Dependency Confusion: How I Hacked Into Apple, Microsoft and Dozens of Other Companies. Medium (2021). https://medium.com/@alex.birsan/dependency-confusion-4a5d60fec610. Accessed Dec 2024
4. Boehs, E.: Everything I know about the XZ backdoor (2024). https://boehs.org/node/everything-i-know-about-the-xz-backdoor. Accessed Apr 2024
5. Brechelmacher, O., Ničković, D., Nießen, T., Sallinger, S., Weissenbacher, G.: Differential property monitoring for backdoor detection. In: Ogata, K., Mery, D., Sun, M., Liu, S. (eds.) Formal Methods and Software Engineering, pp. 216–236. Springer, Singapore (2024)
6. Caltagirone, S., Pendergast, A., Betz, C.: The diamond model of intrusion analysis. Threat Connect **298**(0704), 1–61 (2013)
7. Coldwind, G.: xz/liblzma: bash-stage Obfuscation Explained (2024). https://gynvael.coldwind.pl/?lang=en&id=782. Accessed Apr 2024
8. Collin, L.: XZ Utils backdoor (2024). https://tukaani.org/xz-backdoor/. Accessed Apr 2024
9. Corporation, T.M.: ATT&CK (2025). https://attack.mitre.org/. Accessed Apr 2025
10. Cox, R.: The XZ attack shell script (2024). https://research.swtch.com/xz-script. Accessed Apr 2024
11. Debian: UpstreamGuide (2025). https://wiki.debian.org/UpstreamGuide. Accessed Apr 2025
12. Dullien, T.: Weird machines, exploitability, and provable unexploitability. IEEE Trans. Emerg. Top. Comput. **8**(2), 391–403 (2020). https://doi.org/10.1109/TETC.2017.2785299
13. Freund, A.: Backdoor in upstream xz/liblzma leading to ssh server compromise. Post on mailing list oss-security@openwall (2024). https://openwall.com/lists/oss-security/2024/03/29/4. Accessed Apr 2024
14. GNU Project: GNU M4 1.4.19 macro processor (2024). https://www.gnu.org/software/m4/manual/m4.html. Accessed Dec 2024
15. Google: Accepting New Projects (2025). https://google.github.io/oss-fuzz/getting-started/accepting-new-projects/. Accessed Apr 2025
16. Google: OSS-Fuzz: Continuous Fuzzing for Open Source Software (2025). https://github.com/google/oss-fuzz. Accessed Feb 2025
17. Hamer, S., Bowen, J., Haque, M.N., Hines, R., Madden, C., Williams, L.: Closing the Chain: how to reduce your risk of being SolarWinds, Log4j, or XZ Utils. Computing Research Repository (CoRR), arXiv:2503.12192v1 [cs.SE] (2025). https://doi.org/10.48550/arXiv.2503.12192

18. Horn, J.: How a simple Linux kernel memory corruption bug can lead to complete system compromise. Project Zero (2021). https://googleprojectzero.blogspot.com/2021/10/how-simple-linux-kernel-memory.html. Accessed Apr 2024
19. Jansen, H.: Add ifunc check to CMakeLists.txt (2023). https://git.tukaani.org/?p=xz.git;a=commitdiff;h=b72d21202402a603db6d512fb9271cfa83249639. Accessed Apr 2024
20. Jansen, H.: Add ifunc check to configure.ac (2023). https://git.tukaani.org/?p=xz.git;a=commitdiff;h=23b5c36fb71904bfbe16bb20f976da38dadf6c3b. Accessed Apr 2024
21. Jansen, H.: xz-utils: New upstream version available. Debian Bug report #1067708 (2024). https://bugs.debian.org/cgi-bin/bugreport.cgi?bug=1067708. Accessed Apr 2024
22. JiaT75: Added error text to warning when untaring with bsdtar. Pull request #1609 (2021). https://github.com/libarchive/libarchive/pull/1609. Accessed Apr 2024
23. JiaT75: CMake: Update .gitignore for CMake artifacts from in source build (2022). https://github.com/tukaani-project/xz/commit/8ace358d65059152d9a1f43f4770170d29d35754. Accessed Apr 2024
24. JiaT75: xz: Disable ifunc to fix Issue 60259. Pull request #10667 (2023). https://github.com/google/oss-fuzz/pull/10667. Accessed Apr 2024
25. JiaT75: XZ updates. Pull request #9960 (2023). https://github.com/google/oss-fuzz/pull/9960. Accessed Apr 2024
26. Kokkonis, D., Marcozzi, M., Decoux, E., Zacchiroli, S.: ROSA: finding backdoors with fuzzing. In: 2025 IEEE/ACM 47th International Conference on Software Engineering (ICSE), pp. 720–720. IEEE (2025). https://doi.org/10.1109/ICSE55347.2025.00183
27. Kumar, J.: Re: [xz-devel] [PATCH] String to filter and filter to string. Reply on mailing list xz-devel (2022). https://www.mail-archive.com/xz-devel@tukaani.org/msg00555.html. Accessed Apr 2024
28. Martínez, J., Durán, J.M.: Software supply chain attacks, a threat to global cybersecurity: SolarWinds' case study. Int. J. Saf. Secur. Eng. **11**(5), 537–545 (2021)
29. Naik, N., Jenkins, P., Grace, P., Song, J.: Comparing attack models for IT systems: Lockheed Martin's cyber kill chain, MITRE ATT&CK framework and diamond model. In: 2022 IEEE International Symposium on Systems Engineering (ISSE), pp. 1–7 (2022). https://doi.org/10.1109/ISSE54508.2022.10005490
30. O'Donell, C.: GNU_IFUNC (2024). https://sourceware.org/glibc/wiki/GNU_IFUNC. Accessed Apr 2024
31. Ohm, M., Plate, H., Sykosch, A., Meier, M.: Backstabber's knife collection: a review of open source software supply chain attacks. In: Maurice, C., Bilge, L., Stringhini, G., Neves, N. (eds.) DIMVA 2020. LNCS, vol. 12223, pp. 23–43. Springer, Cham (2020). https://doi.org/10.1007/978-3-030-52683-2_2
32. Parilli, A., Maclachlan, J.: No Unaccompanied Miners: Supply Chain Compromises Through Node.js Packages. Google Cloud Blog (2021). https://cloud.google.com/blog/topics/threat-intelligence/supply-chain-node-js/. Accessed Dec 2024
33. Phylum Research: Rust Malware Staged on Crates.io (2023). https://blog.phylum.io/rust-malware-staged-on-crates-io/. Accessed Apr 2025
34. Poettering, L.: Expose dlopen() dependencies in an ELF section, and add spec for it (2024). https://github.com/systemd/systemd/pull/32234. Accessed July 2025
35. Rust: The Cargo Book (2025). https://doc.rust-lang.org/cargo/reference/build-scripts.html. Accessed Apr 2025

36. Schwaighofer, M., Roland, M., Mayrhofer, R.: Extending cloud build systems to eliminate transitive trust. In: Proceedings of the 2024 Workshop on Software Supply Chain Offensive Research and Ecosystem Defenses (SCORED 2024), pp. 45–55. ACM, Salt Lake City, UT, USA (2024). https://doi.org/10.1145/3689944.3696169
37. Tan, J.: [xz-devel] [PATCH] String to filter and filter to string. Post on mailing list xz-devel (2022). https://www.mail-archive.com/xz-devel@tukaani.org/msg00553.html. Accessed Apr 2024
38. Tan, J.: Tests: Add a few test files (2024). https://git.tukaani.org/?p=xz.git;a=commitdiff;h=cf44e4b7f5dfdbf8c78aef377c10f71e274f63c0. Accessed Apr 2024
39. Tan, J.: Tests: Update two test files (2024). https://git.tukaani.org/?p=xz.git;a=commitdiff;h=6e636819e8f070330d835fce46289a3ff72a7b89. Accessed Apr 2024
40. Tan, S.J., Bratus, S., Goodspeed, T.: Interrupt-oriented bugdoor programming: a minimalist approach to bugdooring embedded systems firmware. In: Proceedings of the 30th Annual Computer Security Applications Conference (ACSAC 2014), pp. 116–125. ACM, New Orleans, Louisiana, USA (2014). https://doi.org/10.1145/2664243.2664268
41. The Tukaani Project: LZMA Utils (2024). https://tukaani.org/lzma/. Accessed Apr 2024
42. Watson, R.: History of LZMA Utils and XZ Utils (2013). https://github.com/kobolabs/liblzma/blob/87b7682ce4b1c849504e2b3641cebaad62aaef87/doc/history.txt. Accessed Apr 2024

Synthetic Lateral Movement Data Generation for Azure Cloud: A Hopper-Based Approach

Mohammad Mamun[1(✉)], Hadeer Ahmed[2], Anas Mabrouk[3], and Sherif Saad[3]

[1] Digital Technologies Research Centre, National Research Council Canada, Ottawa, Canada
mohammad.mamun@nrc-cnrc.gc.ca

[2] Department of Computer Science, University of Victoria, Victoria, BC, Canada
hsahmed@uvic.ca

[3] School of Computer Science, University of Windsor, Windsor, ON, Canada
{mabrouk,shsaad}@uwindsor.ca

Abstract. The rapid evolution of enterprise network architectures from traditional monolithic systems to cloud-native platforms, such as Microsoft Azure, driven by its accessibility and cost-efficiency has introduced significant complexity and expanded the potential attack surface. As the boundaries of network perimeters blur within distributed cloud infrastructures, security solutions like lateral movement (LM) detection face significant challenges in keeping pace with evolving threats. Moreover, the scarcity of attack data hinders the development and testing of effective detection algorithms. To address this gap, we adapted the Hopper attack synthesis framework to model interactions among internal users, applications, and resources within cloud platforms. Our adaptation generates synthetic datasets that simulate various attack scenarios for Azure login data. These synthetic data serve as the foundation for our research, enabling the systematic evaluation of multiple detection approaches without the need for sensitive production data.

Keywords: Lateral Movement Detection · Cloud Security · Graph Learning · Azure Audit Logs

1 Introduction

LM attacks, where attackers move laterally through a network without authorization, pose a major threat in cloud environments. In Azure, these attacks often exploit weaknesses in authentication, allowing movement between resources and potential privilege escalation [5]. Azure's hybrid architecture, which links on-premises systems with cloud services, adds complexity, making LM attacks harder to detect and stop. The scale of the problem is clear: 98% of organizations store sensitive data in the cloud, and 89% run their most critical applications there. Nearly half of all cyberattacks in 2023 began in the cloud, emphasizing the urgent need for better detection and prevention strategies [14]. The increasing

Y. Kim et al. (Eds.): CANS 2025, LNCS 16351, pp. 542–561, 2026.
https://doi.org/10.1007/978-981-95-4434-9_25

adoption of identity-based access, coupled with remote and hybrid work models, has further amplified the attack surface in cloud platforms. Attackers often exploit legitimate credentials and session tokens, making LM attacks stealthy and harder to trace using traditional methods. As enterprises transition more workloads to the cloud, security strategies must evolve to detect subtle and context-driven movements indicative of compromise.

Traditional security tools often fall short in preventing LM attacks in cloud settings [1]. A major challenge is the lack of realistic attack datasets and publicly available cloud audit logs. Without these, it is difficult to develop and test detection techniques, especially those based on machine learning or graph analysis.

Existing enterprise network datasets, like the Los Alamos National Laboratory (LANL) authentication dataset [9], cover authentication events within LANL's internal systems, primarily Windows-based computers and Active Directory servers. While the LANL dataset has been widely used for studying LM pattern generation, it is rooted in a traditional, on-premise infrastructure and lacks explicit LM attack scenarios. More importantly, it fails to reflect the complexity and dynamics of modern, multitenant cloud environments.

Cloud platforms like Microsoft Azure record sign-in activities across distributed tenants, cloud-native applications, and hybrid resources. Azure introduces distinct authentication behaviours, identity models (e.g., OAuth), and federated access patterns that diverge from enterprise networks [26]. Its use of features like Conditional Access policies, device trust, just-in-time permissions, and multifactor authentication (MFA) adds layers of granularity and complexity, making LM behaviours more subtle and challenging to detect. Cloud-native platforms such as Microsoft Azure record sign-in activities across distributed tenants, cloud-native applications, and hybrid resources that diverge significantly from those in enterprise networks [26]. Furthermore, MS Azure's use of conditional access policies, device trust, just-in-time permissions, and distributed tenant architectures introduces additional layers of complexity that render LM behaviours more subtle and harder to detect.

To fill this gap, we present a comprehensive synthetic attack dataset designed for Azure environments. The dataset is meticulously crafted by integrating real-world Azure authentication logs with emulated LM attack patterns, simulating realistic malicious behaviours. By augmenting real-world Azure data with systematically engineered attack scenarios, it serves as a valuable benchmark for assessing and enhancing the resilience of Azure-based systems against advanced cyber threats.

We adapted the Hopper framework [12] to generate Azure-compatible data by transforming its original machine-to-machine graph model into heterogeneous graphs representing user, application, and resource interactions. Given the distinct features of Azure logs compared to conventional network telemetry, we re-engineered core components of the Hopper framework to support Azure-specific data hierarchies, event semantics, and metadata schemes. The redesigned framework effectively parses and models authentication workflows and LM paths inherent to Azure's cloud-native security model. Enhanced components enable the generation of realistic adversarial sequences based on observed authentication behaviour. Validation of the generated dataset involved applying three graph-based methodologies, each leveraging heterogeneous graph structures to capture authentication and access relationships. These methods were evaluated on a rich, nine-month dataset of sign-in activity collected from a real enterprise Azure environment. Our key contributions are detailed below.

1. A novel dataset combining real Azure authentication logs with synthetic LM attacks, enabling research into cloud-specific threat detection.
2. An adaptation of the Hopper framework for Azure, including changes to graph structures, attack simulations, and scenario generation.
3. Three graph-based methodologies for evaluating synthetic attack data quality using graph-based anomaly detection. These approaches leverage topological and behavioural features, including degree metrics, clustering coefficients, temporal patterns, and centrality measures, to assess anomalies in the generated LM attack dataset. By integrating graph-based anomaly detection, these methodologies ensure a robust and comprehensive evaluation of the effectiveness and fidelity of the generated LM attack dataset.

The rest of this paper is organized as follows: Sect. 2 reviews related work on data generation in cybersecurity. Section 3 describes the Hopper framework, our modifications, and the dataset. Section 4 explains our evaluation methods. Section 4.3 presents our results and discussion, and Sect. 5 concludes the paper.

2 Related Work

Several researchers have explored synthetic data generation approaches to address the challenges of limited attack data in cybersecurity.

Ring et al. [29] proposed a flow-based GAN architecture to generate high-quality synthetic network traffic flows, closely resembling actual network behaviour. Ammara et al. [3] generated synthetic network traffic using GAN due to the imbalanced classes in the NSL-KDD and CIC-IDS2017 datasets and achieved 96% accuracy on real data after training their model on the synthetic dataset.

Prior research has explored LM in both traditional and cloud-based environments, but key distinctions remain in terms of scope, data realism, and cloud specificity. Esteban's MIT thesis [8] presents CyberBattleSim, a platform for simulating post-compromise LM in generic enterprise networks using graph. It offers an interactive interface to model network topologies and vulnerabilities, focusing on educational simulations for traditional on-premise environments. This framework supports reinforcement learning agents and provides an interactive environment for simulating network topologies and attack paths. While this work includes Azure-relevant vulnerabilities in example scenarios, its primary focus remains on LAN-like, on-premise environments and does not generate synthetic telemetry nor simulate cloud-specific identity behaviours such as OAuth, Conditional Access, or multi-factor authentication (MFA), which are central to cloud-native attack surfaces.

Similarly, HetGLM [32] presents a graph neural network-based approach for detecting LM through anomalous link identification in heterogeneous graphs. Although effective as an LM detection framework, HetGLM relies heavily on high-quality representative cloud datasets that are especially scarce in Azure environments. Like other detection-focused studies, it assumes the availability of suitable data and does not address the challenge of synthetic data generation, which is the core contribution of our work.

Other efforts, such as CoZure [6], specifically targets Azure Active Directory (AAD) by employing context-free grammar learning to discover new LM paths based on real AAD command sequences. CoZure's discovery-driven approach offers valuable insights into Azure misconfiguration exploits, yet it remains confined to the AAD layer and does not support the generation of reusable datasets for systematic detection evaluation. The Synthetic Data and Graph Generation for Modeling Adversary Activity (MAA) project, led by the Pacific Northwest National Laboratory (PNNL), developed a comprehensive methodology along with scalable graph modelling and generation tools to produce synthetic, domain-agnostic, flexible, and realistic large-scale background activity graphs with embedded adversarial activity pathways. The publicly released datasets [27] include separate representations of background activities, adversarial activities of interest, merged graphs establishing ground truth, and filtered versions separated by individual data types. While these efforts address different aspects of adversary activity modelling, our work fills a gap by introducing a novel adversarial data generation framework designed for the Azure cloud environment. We simulate LM scenarios by modelling interactions among heterogeneous entities, users, applications, and resources, while incorporating Azure-specific semantics such as OAuth, Conditional Access, and MFA. By embedding these synthetic attack paths into real Azure authentication logs collected from an enterprise tenant, our framework generates realistic, labelled datasets that reflect actual usage patterns and adversarial behaviours.

Similarly to our approach, Jbeil in [17] proposes a threat sample augmentation mechanism that uses the Hopper framework on advanced LM attacks and evaluates their approach using authentication events from the LANL dataset. In contrast, our work focuses on Azure cloud data rather than typical enterprise network data such as LANL. Additionally, the Hopper framework was not readily applicable in our case.

Bai et al. [4] proposed an ML-based approach for detecting malicious Remote Desktop Protocol (RDP) sessions, which is particularly relevant to LM detection. To address the scarcity of attack data, they merged two datasets by incorporating red team activity from the LANL Comprehensive Events Dataset [16] into the Unified dataset. This was achieved by mapping source hosts, usernames, and destination hosts to randomly selected entries from the Unified Dataset.

Kaiafas et al. [15] did a survey examining LM detection algorithms across various settings. The study highlights the inherent complexities of cloud-native infrastructures and underscores the importance of synthetic data in replicating challenging attack scenarios, enabling robust system assessment.

Several studies have explored LM detection in the context of Advanced Persistent Threat (APT) models by analyzing behavioural patterns [20,23,24], while many others [18,35] have utilized provenance graphs to enhance host-based APT detection efforts.

3 Cloud LM Dataset Generation Framework

In this section, we present the Hopper framework and its adaptation for LM detection in cloud environments. We discuss our methodological approach to dataset generation that combines benign and malicious activities to create a labelled dataset for the LM detection system.

3.1 Overview of Hopper's LM Simulator

The Hopper framework [12] is an open-source tool designed to generate synthetic data that simulates LM within enterprise networks. It is tailored for homogeneous, on-premises environments, where nodes typically represent individual machines and edges denote direct login events. The framework operates under the assumption that authentication logs are complete and consistent, and that LM primarily occurs via credential reuse or direct host-to-host access.

Originally developed for Dropbox's internal infrastructure, Hopper builds a graph from user login activity by linking source and destination hosts based on authentication events. This graph structure enables the simulation of realistic attack scenarios in a controlled setting. However, Hopper's focus on straightforward credential-based traversal limits the scope of its simulated attacks. As a result, it captures only a narrow range of LM behaviours and does not reflect the full diversity or subtlety of real-world attack scenarios in cloud environment like Azure, where adversaries often exploit heterogeneous identities, service principals, and complex access patterns to evade detection.

Each simulation begins with a *foothold,* a compromised machine representing the attacker's initial entry point into the network. From this position, the simulated attack progresses until the attacker achieves their objectives or exhausts available options. The framework implements three principal attack strategies:

- **Exploration attacks**: The attacker selects each new hop based on the set of available neighbouring nodes and concludes the attack upon reaching a machine inaccessible to the initial victim
- **Spread attacks**: The attacker aims to maximize network compromise within a constrained number of hops by infecting all accessible neighbouring nodes
- **Targeted attacks**: The attacker focuses on specific high-value targets, such as domain controllers, by calculating and following the shortest path from the foothold to the target [12]

In its original implementation, the framework models login events as a directed homogeneous graph $G = (V, E)$, where V represents computers and

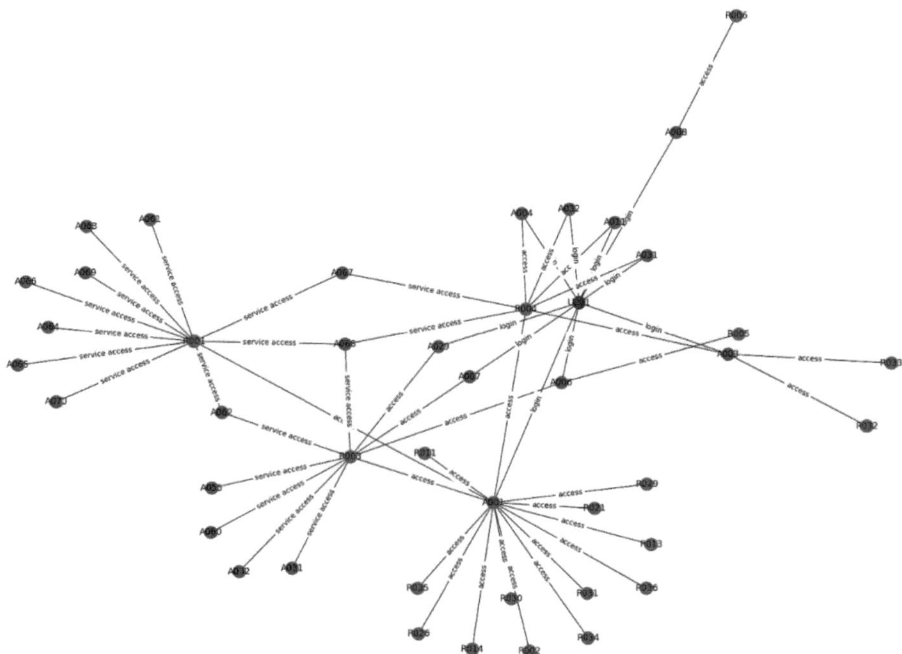

Fig. 1. A snapshot of normal Azure network interactions among Users (blue nodes), Applications (green nodes), and Resources (red nodes). (Color figure online)

$E \subseteq V \times V$ represents viable login paths. Each edge $(v_i, v_j) \in E$ signifies a login from the source machine v_i to the destination machine v_j, enabling the framework to inject synthetic login paths that accurately reflect LM attack patterns. A sequence of edges $(v_1 \rightarrow v_2 \rightarrow \cdots \rightarrow v_k)$ represents an attacker's LM trajectory across multiple machines.

3.2 Adaptation for Azure Environment

To accommodate Azure cloud logs, we extended the framework with a heterogeneous directed graph model incorporating diverse node types and relationship patterns. In our adapted model, V encompasses users, applications, and resources, while $E \subseteq V \times V$ represents the directed connections between these entities. Each authentication event consists of:

- A user accessing an application, formalized as edge $(u \rightarrow a)$
- An application accessing a resource, formalized as edge $(a \rightarrow r)$

These unidirectional relationships accurately capture the user-to-application-to-resource interaction pattern characteristic of modern cloud environments. Figure 2 illustrates the structural evolution from the original homogeneous model to our heterogeneous cloud-oriented adaptation.

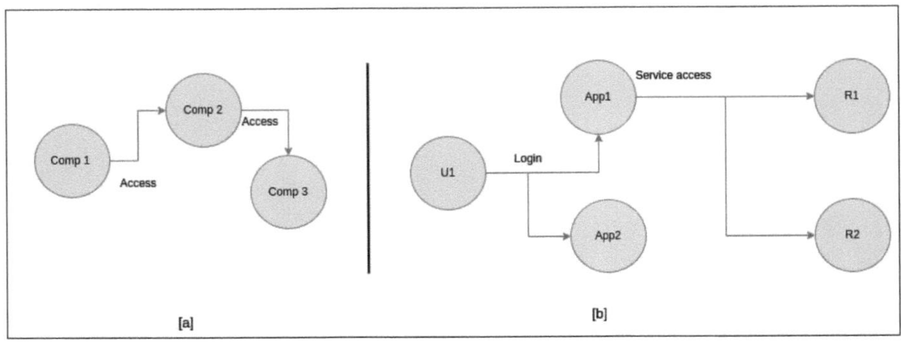

Fig. 2. Comparison of graph structures: (a) Original Hopper framework graph for Dropbox data, demonstrating homogeneous machine-to-machine connections; (b) Our adapted graph model for Azure cloud data, illustrating heterogeneous relationships between users, applications, and resources.

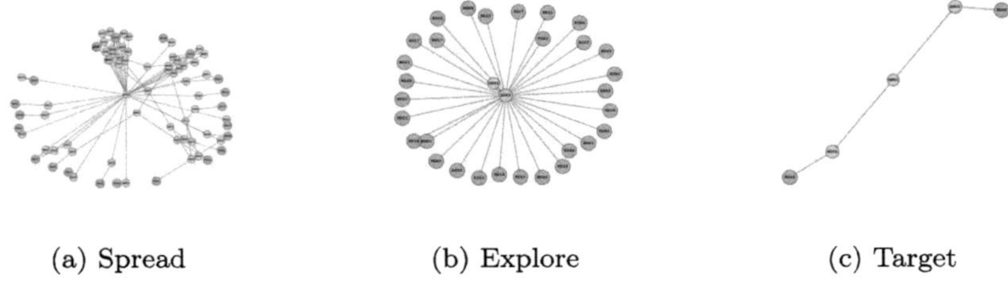

(a) Spread (b) Explore (c) Target

Fig. 3. Overview of different attack scenarios.

The attack strategies were refined to align with the structural characteristics of Azure logs, enabling their replication within the Hopper framework despite inherent mismatches between the log relationships and the simulator's data structures. Specifically, three attack scenarios were reimplemented as follows:

- **Exploration**: The attacker systematically accesses all applications connected to the initial compromised foothold.
- **Spread**: Focusing on accessing all available resources, the attacker thoroughly explores everything the compromised user's applications can reach and may move to another user if no more resources are found.
- **Targeted**: The attacker traverses laterally between users via shared application access points to reach predetermined high-value resources.

To enhance the realism of our simulations, we incorporate a configurable percentage of random edges between users and applications, generating variable LM patterns that better reflect the unpredictability and complexity of real-world attacks. These adaptations preserve the core principles of the original

Table 1. Overview of Attack Scenarios and Dataset Sizes

Goal	Description	#Events	#Scenario
Exploratory	Attacker accesses and explores a single machine	4,000	1,992
Aggressive	Attacker attempts to compromise many resources	19,000	380
Targeted	Attacker focuses on specific high-value resources	249	95

Hopper framework while optimizing it for cloud security analysis within Azure environments. Simulation code and anonymized dataset used in this study are available[1].

3.3 Cloud Authentication Logs and LM

Our benign dataset[2] consists of nine months of Microsoft Azure authentication records, offering a comprehensive foundation for our investigation. To our knowledge, the original dataset Fig. 1 does not contain any recorded incidents of APT assaults or LM. It encompasses three types of sign-in events: *interactive user sign-ins*, where users actively provide credentials or multi-factor authentication; *non-interactive sign-ins*, automatically triggered by client applications or browsers using stored tokens on behalf of users; and *service principal sign-ins*, where applications or service principals authenticate using certificates, client secrets, or managed identities without user interaction. The activity logs comprises Azure sign-in and audit events, encompassing interactions from 30 users, 68 applications, and 90 resources.

Malicious events were synthesized from real benign Azure sign-in logs, designed to align with three attack objectives: *exploration*, *aggressive spread*, and *targeted exploitation*. Each scenario generated synthetic malicious events by combining interactions among users, applications, and resources. We executed 380 exploration scenarios, 1433 spread scenarios, and 95 targeted attack scenarios. To emulate realistic attack patterns, malicious events were generated in sync with the timestamps and contextual patterns of the original benign dataset, ensuring temporal and behavioural fidelity. Table 1 details the volume of generated malicious data per attack type, while Fig. 3 visualizes each scenario, illustrating their mapping to a graph structure. This approach enables effective evaluation of the detection model's ability to identify each attack objective, offering clear insights into its strengths and areas for improvement.

3.4 Threat Model

Following prior work [12], we focus on generating interactive and credential-based LM attacks within enterprise cloud environments. In our setting, the underlying

[1] https://github.com/NRCsecLab/Azure-LM/.

[2] The dataset used in this study was provided in confidence by a Canadian government organization involved in the cyber defence of cloud infrastructure. To ensure compliance with privacy regulations and ethical standards, the data was thoroughly anonymized and sanitized prior to use.

infrastructure reflects heterogeneous authentication relationships between users, applications, and cloud-hosted resources—typical of Azure deployments.

Under this threat model, we assume that an attacker has gained an initial foothold in the cloud environment, such as through phishing, token theft, or exploitation of misconfigured access policies. From this position, the adversary:

1. seeks to acquire additional credentials or tokens to escalate privileges and access sensitive data or systems that are not directly reachable from the compromised entry point.
2. moves laterally across the environment by issuing authentication requests such as OAuth token exchanges, API calls, login events etc. involving new user–application–resource paths. These movements are observable through authentication logs and result in updates to the access graph.

We assume that lateral movement events generate loggable authentication artifacts within Azure e.g., sign-ins, app-role assignments, token uses. Although attackers may leverage techniques such as token replay, application impersonation, or privilege escalation, their actions ultimately manifest as changes in access relationships within the graph.

We assume human-driven attacks, where adversaries interactively explore the environment, impersonate users, and access applications or data using stolen credentials. We do not consider autonomous malware propagation that operates independently of authentication mechanisms. Instead, this threat model reflects the behaviour of real-world cloud-based lateral movement attacks, where attackers abuse legitimate identity infrastructure to pivot across services manually. Such attacks often begin with credential theft and exploit misconfigured identity and access management (IAM) policies to escalate privileges and access additional resources. This behaviour has been observed in both state-sponsored campaigns and modern ransomware operations, where tools like Azure Storage Explorer and long-lived authentication tokens are leveraged for stealthy data exfiltration and traversal. Our model thus captures a wide spectrum of adversarial behaviour—from targeted intrusions by advanced persistent threats to opportunistic, cloud-aware ransomware actors—who rely on interactive login operations to propagate across cloud environments [7,19,31].

4 Unsupervised Anomaly Detection Techniques for Evaluating Dataset

To rigorously assess the effectiveness of the synthetic dataset, we employ three distinct graph-based methodologies, each approach leverages a distinct type of graph construction and analysis, reflecting a range of evaluation perspectives from learned representations to statistical anomalies and rule-driven behaviours, thereby enabling a comprehensive assessment across four key objectives. Table 2 provides a comparative overview of these approaches.

Given the absence of real attack data, our evaluation framework uses real benign authentication logs as the reference baseline and is structured around four core criteria: *fidelity, utility, adversarial realism, and diversity*. Fidelity is evaluated by comparing the structural and statistical properties of the synthetic attack graphs against those of real benign graphs, ensuring both internal coherence and clear distinction from non-malicious behaviour. Utility is considered by assessing the potential of the synthetic dataset to support downstream tasks such as intrusion detection, with the goal of facilitating generalizable learning. Adversarial realism is examined through the lens of behavioural plausibility ensuring that the synthetic graphs manifest patterns indicative of realistic and distinguishable attack-like activity. Lastly, diversity is addressed by designing the synthetic dataset to reflect a broad spectrum of hypothetical attack scenarios, thereby reducing susceptibility to overfitting and enhancing its applicability across varied threat models.

For each detection method, we built custom graph representations to suit its needs while keeping the overall framework consistent. In all cases, nodes represent users, applications, and resources in Azure, and edges represent authentication or access events between them. Our detection-focused evaluation aims to:

- Detect a broad spectrum of lateral movement (LM) behaviours—including exploration, spread, and targeted access—across heterogeneous, role-aware Azure authentication graphs.
- Maintain a low false positive rate, emphasizing detection precision to reduce alert fatigue and improve operational relevance in enterprise environments.
- Enable meaningful prioritization through ranked suspicious paths, allowing for threshold-based triage similar to budget-aware alerting models.
- Assess model generalization by applying three fundamentally different detection methodologies (i) Using *Graph Attention Network (GAT)*, which learns structural embeddings in heterogeneous graphs using edge-level attention; (ii) *Isolation Forest*, which identifies statistical anomalies based on node and edge features in labelled graphs; and (iii) *Rule-based analysis*, which detects temporal anomalies by analyzing graph evolution patterns such as degree changes, clustering shifts, and access history.

A detection is considered successful if an anomalous path or node corresponds to an injected attacker login event. This setup enables rigorous, quantitative analysis of how well different approaches can identify lateral movement behaviours embedded in complex, multi-entity cloud access graphs.

4.1 Detection Methodologies

In the following sections, we provide a detailed explanation of each detection methodology, highlighting their underlying principles, graph construction specifics, feature engineering strategies, and the manner in which they capture distinct aspects of anomalous activity within heterogeneous authentication graphs.

Table 2. Graph-based Methodologies for Evaluating Synthetic Dataset

Graph Type	Features	Method
Hetero, directed, edge attention	GAT node embeddings	GNN (GAT)
Hetero, directed, labeled edges	Node/edge stats	Isolation Forest
Hetero, dynamic, temporal	Degree, clustering, history	Rule-based

GAT Analysis. GNNs, particularly GATs, have emerged as powerful tools for evaluating synthetic datasets, leveraging their ability to process complex graph-structured data. Synthetic datasets, often designed to emulate real-world networks such as social, biological, or transactional systems, require robust evaluation to ensure they capture realistic patterns and dependencies. GATs, introduced by Velickovic et al. [33], enhance traditional GNNs by incorporating an attention mechanism that dynamically assigns weights to neighbouring nodes based on their relevance. This enables GATs to prioritize informative connections, making them especially suited for heterogeneous and directed graphs where nodes and edges represent diverse entities and relationships.

In synthetic graph generation, especially when the target is to emulate real-world networks such as knowledge graphs, it is essential to verify whether structural properties such as degree distributions, clustering coefficients, and community structures are preserved. GATs provide a mechanism for stress-testing such synthetic graphs by learning context-aware node embeddings that reflect both local and global topology. These embeddings are valuable for downstream evaluation tasks such as node classification, link prediction, graph similarity measurement, or anomaly detection—each of which can serve as a proxy for dataset fidelity.

Edge-centric attention mechanisms in GATs also provide a granular tool for evaluating relational fidelity. In synthetic graphs, it's often crucial not just to replicate node connectivity but to mirror semantic coherence, whether the connections make sense in the context of the represented domain. This is particularly relevant in domains such as healthcare or finance, where artificial datasets must preserve not just structural but also functional realism.

In our implementation, we applied a GAT-based model to an authentication graph, where the layers generated node embeddings by attending to each node's neighbours with learned attention weights. These embeddings, combined with edge features, were passed through a fully connected network to classify interactions [10]. To maintain an unsupervised approach, we trained solely on benign interactions so the model could learn normal behaviour without exposure to attack data [30]. The trained model was then evaluated on both benign and malicious interactions to assess its anomaly detection capabilities.

Isolation Forest with Graph Statistics. Isolation Forest offers a lightweight, interpretable alternative that excels at identifying statistical and structural anomalies. This unsupervised method detects outliers by recursively partitioning a feature space constructed from node and edge statistics, such as degree distributions, edge weights, and centrality measures. The algorithm isolates anomalies based on the principle that such instances are few and distinct, requiring fewer splits to separate. This makes Isolation Forest effective for evaluating synthetic datasets where the goal is to ensure consistency with known statistical properties of real-world networks.

For synthetic graphs, this approach helps detect generation flaws—such as implausible node connectivity or inconsistently labelled edges—that may compromise data quality. Liu et al. [21] first established the algorithm's efficiency in high-dimensional settings, while more recent work by Wang et al. [34] demonstrated its utility in detecting structural and contextual anomalies in directed graphs using simple node and edge features.

In our implementation, the model constructs random decision trees that split the data using randomly chosen features and values [22]. It was trained solely on benign interactions to establish a baseline of normal behaviour, enabling it to identify potential anomalies during testing [11].

Rule-Based Approach with Temporal Graph Features. In addition to embedding-based and statistical techniques, rule-based methods offer a targeted approach for evaluating synthetic datasets particularly those with temporal dynamics. These methods operate by encoding domain specific heuristics or constraints, using them to assess whether a synthetic graph reflects expected structural and temporal behaviours. This is especially valuable in dynamic, heterogeneous graphs where node and edge properties evolve over time.

Rule-based evaluation typically draws on graph features like node degree, clustering coefficients, and historical connectivity patterns. For instance, a rule may enforce that highly connected nodes maintain stable clustering over successive time windows, reflecting the persistence of communities in real-world networks. These methods are intuitive and interpretable, translating domain knowledge directly into evaluative logic. Their use can expose unrealistic properties in the synthetic dataset, such as abrupt changes in centrality or implausible temporal spikes in connectivity.

In practice, rule-based approaches have been shown to be effective in applications requiring temporal fidelity and structural realism. Temporal Graph Benchmark (TGB) by Huang et al. [13] demonstrate the efficacy of rule-based methods in evaluating heterogeneous, dynamic graphs. By leveraging temporal features like node degree, clustering coefficients, and historical connectivity patterns, TGB's rule-based baselines provide a robust framework for assessing the structural and temporal fidelity of synthetic datasets. When applied to synthetic graph evaluation, rule-based methods help ensure that generated datasets adhere to known temporal patterns and application-specific constraints, making them invaluable for validating realistic graph structures.

In our work, we applied a snapshot-based rule-driven method to the authentication graph [2], generating ten snapshots at different time intervals to observe the evolution of patterns and relationships. Anomalies were detected using metrics such as edge weight and attack ratio, with interactions flagged when these metrics consistently exceeded predefined thresholds across multiple snapshots [28]. This focus on sustained suspicious activity, rather than isolated incidents, helps reduce false positives and better capture prolonged attack behaviours, ensuring that synthetic datasets reflect realistic temporal patterns and application-specific constraints.

4.2 Graph Attributes and Detection Techniques

Our graph construction process combined both topological and behavioural features to improve detection capabilities. Node attributes included basic structural metrics like in-degree, out-degree, and clustering coefficient, which are widely used for characterizing graph properties in anomaly detection [2]. In-degree and out-degree measure the number of incoming and outgoing connections for a node, revealing activity patterns and potential influence in the network. The clustering coefficient shows how nodes tend to form groups, helping identify community structures and deviations from normal connectivity patterns.

For edge attributes, we used features that capture both temporal dynamics and structural importance, including timestamp patterns, edge weights, and various centrality measures. These attributes are especially important for detecting anomalies in dynamic and heterogeneous graph environments, as they help identify irregular interaction patterns and unusual relationships. Table 3 provides a detailed overview of these graph attributes and their role in LM detection.

Table 3. Graph Attributes

Type	Feature	Description
Node	In/Out-Degree	Number of connections for each node
	Clustering	How connected a node's neighbours are
	Type	User, application, or resource
Edge	Time	When the interaction occurs
	Centrality	Importance as a network bridge
	Weight	Frequency of interactions
	Paths	Number/length of paths between nodes
	Auth Context	Login method, location, or device

4.3 Evaluation and Results

This section presents the results of the three graph-based models in detecting the simulated LM attack scenarios.

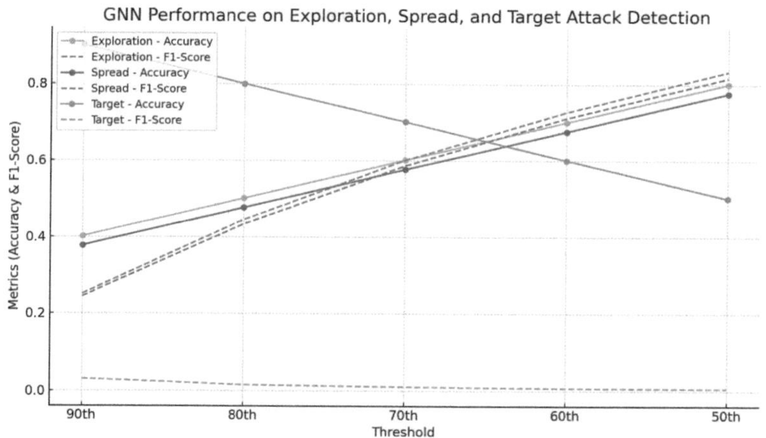

Fig. 4. GNN performance metrics for different attack detection scenarios.

Table 4 and Fig. 4 show how the GNN model performed at different detection thresholds for all three attack types. For exploration and spread attacks, the model achieved perfect precision (1.0) at every threshold, and both recall and F1-score improved as the threshold was lowered. For example, the recall for exploration attacks increased from 0.14 to 0.72 when the threshold was reduced from the 90th to the 50th percentile, raising the F1-score from 0.25 to 0.83. Spread attack detection showed a similar pattern, with the F1-score rising from 0.24 to 0.82. However, for targeted attacks, the model had perfect recall but very low precision at all thresholds, leading to poor F1-scores that dropped from 0.031 to 0.0064 as the threshold was lowered. This suggests that the model struggles to distinguish targeted attacks from normal activities, resulting in many false positives when trying to detect these more sophisticated threats.

Table 5 and Fig. 5 show how well the Isolation Forest model detects different types of attacks. The model performed strongly on exploration and spread attacks, reaching F1-scores of 0.92 for both, with high precision (over 0.96) and recall (over 0.87). This means it was able to accurately tell apart normal and abnormal patterns, with few false positives for these attack types. However, like the GNN model, Isolation Forest struggled with targeted attacks. Its F1-score dropped to 0.42, with precision at 0.58 and recall at 0.33. This decline highlights how difficult it is to detect targeted attacks, which usually involve fewer and more subtle actions that are harder to distinguish from normal activity.

Table 6 and Fig. 6 show how the rule-based model performed. The model achieved high F1-scores for exploratory (0.98) and spread (0.93) attacks, with perfect precision (1.0) and strong recall (0.97 and 0.86), indicating it can reliably

Table 4. GNN Performance On Different Attacks

Attack Type	Threshold	Accuracy	Precision	Recall	F1-Score
Exploration	90th	0.4013	1.0000	0.1433	0.2506
	80th	0.5014	1.0000	0.2865	0.4454
	70th	0.6015	1.0000	0.4298	0.6012
	60th	0.7012	1.0000	0.5723	0.7280
	50th	0.8013	1.0000	0.7156	0.8342
Spread	90th	0.3771	1.0000	0.1388	0.2437
	80th	0.4770	1.0000	0.2769	0.4337
	70th	0.5769	1.0000	0.4150	0.5866
	60th	0.6768	1.0000	0.5532	0.7123
	50th	0.7767	1.0000	0.6913	0.8175
Target	90th	0.9011	0.0159	1.0000	0.0312
	80th	0.8006	0.0079	1.0000	0.0157
	70th	0.7018	0.0053	1.0000	0.0106
	60th	0.6013	0.0040	1.0000	0.0079
	50th	0.5024	0.0032	1.0000	0.0064

Table 5. Isolation Forest Performance on Different Attacks

Attack Type	Accuracy	Precision	Recall	F1-Score
Exploration	0.8843	0.9660	0.8796	0.9208
Spread	0.8878	0.9695	0.8846	0.9251
Target	0.7295	0.5800	0.3283	0.4193

Table 6. Rule-Based Model Performance on Different Attacks

Attack Type	Accuracy	Precision	Recall	F1-Score
Exploration	0.9692	1.0000	0.9658	0.9826
Spread	0.8627	1.0000	0.8627	0.9263
Target	0.8517	0.9180	0.3889	0.5463

detect these attack types with very few false positives. However, as with the other models, its performance dropped sharply for targeted attacks, with an F1-score of 0.55, precision of 0.92, and recall of just 0.39. This result highlights that targeted attacks are much harder to detect and suggests that more specialized methods are needed to identify these subtle threats effectively.

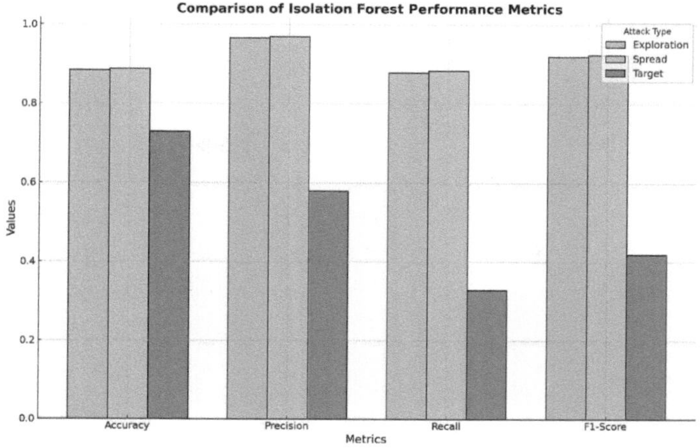

Fig. 5. Isolation Forest performance metrics for different attack detection scenarios.

4.4 Discussion

Figure 7 shows the differences in F1-scores across the three models for each attack type. All three models performed well in the exploration and spread scenarios, indicating that the synthetic dataset produces patterns realistic enough for the models to detect. Similar trends across methods also suggest that the generated attacks differ sufficiently from benign activity. These results are not surprising, as exploration and spread attacks are typically aggressive and produce a higher number of data points. In contrast, targeted attacks were much harder to detect. The GNN model had an F1-score below 0.04, the Isolation Forest reached 0.42, and the rule-based method scored 0.55, meaning even the best method still missed many of these attacks. This is largely due to the small volume of generated targeted events and the structure of our Azure log graphs, where almost all users communicate with each other. As a result, targeted attack paths often resembled legitimate workflows, unlike in the original Hopper dataset, making them difficult to distinguish from normal activity. These results highlight that strong performance on broad attack scenarios does not guarantee effectiveness against low-volume stealthy attacks. The rule-based method performed best for targeted attacks, likely because its snapshot-based analysis preserved temporal context and exposed minor but repeated changes in access patterns, whereas the other methods may have smoothed over these rare events during feature aggregation. Detection approaches that capture fine-grained behaviour shifts and integrate features from diverse log sources are better positioned to address such threats [25,36].

The weaker targeted attack performance can be addressed by enhancing both data generation and detection. In future framework versions, we plan to enrich targeted scenarios with multi-stage attack chains that include privilege escalation and cross-user credential pivots, increasing diversity and realism. We will

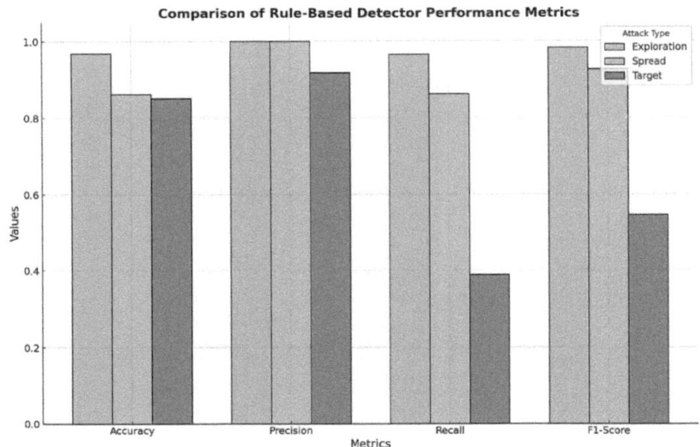

Fig. 6. Rule-based model performance metrics for different attack detection scenarios.

also embed subtle temporal cues, such as short bursts of rare application consent events, atypical resource sequences, and minor role changes, that are hard to detect in isolation but become apparent over time. On the detection side, we will evaluate rare event focused methods, including temporal subgraph matching and contrastive graph learning, which emphasize deviations from a user's historical activity rather than population-wide patterns. Due to current data availability, the framework focuses only on Azure sign-in logs, but we plan to extend it by correlating attack events with other sources, such as conditional access policy outcomes, resource activity logs, API usage traces, and lightweight network telemetry. Incorporating these modalities should improve separability for low-volume targeted movements that may otherwise appear benign in authentication-only views.

Overall, the adapted Hopper framework performed well after being re-engineered for Azure authentication logs. Replacing the original machine-to-machine graph with a heterogeneous model of users, applications, and resources enabled us to capture Azure-specific identity and access patterns, a valuable capability given the scarcity of publicly available Azure datasets. Our work demonstrates that Hopper can be extended to model cloud environments when tailored to their unique data structures. We also provide a publicly available Azure dataset containing attack patterns and a framework foundation that can be extended by the research community. However, the current adaptation is tied to Azure sign-in data and does not directly generalize to other cloud or on-premises logs without further modifications to the graph model and attack strategies. The framework is flexible but remains domain-dependent.

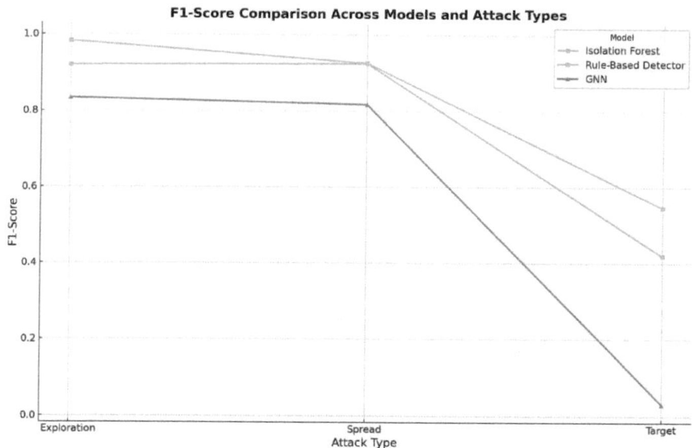

Fig. 7. This plot illustrates the F1-score results across all models for various attack detection scenarios.

5 Conclusion

Our approach addresses the shortage of data for studying cloud-based LM attacks by focusing specifically on Azure authentication logs, a setting where labelled attack data is virtually unavailable. We combine real benign Azure sign-in records with carefully designed synthetic attack patterns, producing a dataset that enables LM detection, attack simulation, and evaluation of detection methods. By adapting the Hopper framework and integrating simulated attack data into anonymized benign logs, we provide the research community with a realistic and reusable representation of LM activity in cloud environments, something that has not previously been accessible.

The F1-scores from the tested detection models demonstrate that the dataset can effectively support the identification of threats. These results underscore its utility in improving detection accuracy, refining algorithms, advancing APT detection research, and deepening understanding of Azure-specific attack behaviours that can inform better defence strategies. Our evaluation using standard graph-based anomaly detection models and machine learning classifiers confirms that the dataset performs consistently across different techniques. In addition to releasing the dataset, we make our adapted Hopper code publicly available, enabling other researchers to generate their own Azure-specific LM attacks, extend our scenarios, or adapt the framework to new contexts. This flexibility allows our approach to evolve with emerging attack techniques and changes in cloud services, ensuring continued relevance as threats and architectures develop. By sharing both our methodology and tools, we contribute a foundation for expanding the availability of cloud-specific security datasets and for advancing LM detection research in distributed systems.

References

1. Vectra AI: Using AI to detect and stop lateral movement in the cloud (2024). https://www.vectra.ai/resources/using-ai-to-detect-and-stop-lateral-movement-in-the-cloud
2. Akoglu, L., Tong, H., Koutra, D.: Graph based anomaly detection and description: a survey. Data Min. Knowl. Disc. **29**(3), 626–688 (2015)
3. Ammara, D.A., Ding, J., Tutschku, K.: Synthetic network traffic data generation: a comparative study (2025). https://arxiv.org/abs/2410.16326
4. Bai, T., Bian, H., Salahuddin, M.A., Abou Daya, A., Limam, N., Boutaba, R.: RDP-based lateral movement detection using machine learning. Comput. Commun. **165**, 9–19 (2021)
5. Chierici, S.: Sysdig cloud lateral movement: Breaking in through a vulnerable container (2021). https://sysdig.com/blog/lateral-movement-cloud-containers
6. Chowdhury, A., Nguyen, H.: Cozure: context free grammar co-pilot tool for finding new lateral movements in azure active directory. In: Proceedings of the 26th International Symposium on Research in Attacks, Intrusions and Defenses, pp. 426–439 (2023)
7. Cybersecurity and Infrastructure Security Agency (CISA): Joint cybersecurity advisory: Protecting against interlock ransomware (2025). https://www.cisa.gov/news-events/alerts/2025/07/22/joint-advisory-issued-protecting-against-interlock-ransomware. Accessed 22 July 2025
8. Esteban, J.: Simulating network lateral movements through the cyberbattlesim web platform. Ph.D. thesis, Massachusetts Institute of Technology (2022)
9. Hagberg, A., Kent, A., Lemons, N., Neil, J.: Credential hopping in authentication graphs. In: 2014 International Conference on Signal-Image Technology Internet-Based Systems (SITIS). IEEE Computer Society (2014)
10. Hamilton, W.L., Ying, R., Leskovec, J.: Inductive representation learning on large graphs. In: Advances in Neural Information Processing Systems, pp. 1024–1034 (2017)
11. Hariri, S., Kind, M.C., Brunner, R.J.: Extended isolation forest. In: 2021 IEEE 8th International Conference on Data Science and Advanced Analytics (DSAA), pp. 1–10. IEEE (2021)
12. Ho, G., et al.: Hopper: modeling and detecting lateral movement. In: 30th USENIX Security Symposium (USENIX Security 2021), pp. 3093–3110 (2021)
13. Huang, S., et al.: Temporal graph benchmark for machine learning on temporal graphs. Adv. Neural. Inf. Process. Syst. **36**, 2056–2073 (2023)
14. Illumio Editorial: Lateral movement: How to solve the cloud's biggest risk (2024). www.illumio.com/blog/lateral-movement-how-to-solve-the-clouds-biggest-risk. Accessed 13 Aug 2025
15. Kaiafas, P., Papadopoulos, G.K.: Detecting lateral movement: a systematic survey. Comput. Secur. J. (2024)
16. Kent, A.D.: Comprehensive, multi-source cyber-security events data set. Technical report, Los Alamos National Lab.(LANL), Los Alamos, NM (United States) (2015)
17. Khoury, J., Klisura, Đ., Zanddizari, H., Parra, G.D.L.T., Najafirad, P., Bou-Harb, E.: Jbeil: temporal graph-based inductive learning to infer lateral movement in evolving enterprise networks. In: 2024 IEEE Symposium on Security and Privacy (SP), pp. 3644–3660. IEEE (2024)
18. King, I.J., Huang, H.H.: Euler: detecting network lateral movement via scalable temporal link prediction. ACM Trans. Privacy Secur. **26**(3), 1–36 (2023)

19. Kroll: Q2 2024 threat landscape report (2024). https://www.kroll.com/en/reports/cyber/threat-intelligence-reports/q2-2024-threat-landscape-report-threat-actors-ransomware-cloud-risks-accelerate. Accessed 07 Nov 2024
20. Kushwaha, D., et al.: Lateral movement detection using user behavioral analysis. arXiv preprint arXiv:2208.13524 (2022)
21. Liu, F.T., Ting, K.M., Zhou, Z.H.: Isolation forest. In: 2008 Eighth IEEE International Conference on Data Mining, pp. 413–422. IEEE (2008)
22. Liu, F.T., Ting, K.M., Zhou, Z.H.: Isolation-based anomaly detection. ACM Trans. Knowl. Discov. Data (TKDD) **6**(1), 3 (2012)
23. Mamun, M., Buffett, S.: Taptree: process-tree based host behavior modeling and threat detection framework via sequential pattern mining. In: International Conference on Information and Communications Security, pp. 546–565. Springer, Cham (2022)
24. Mamun, M., Shi, K.: Deeptaskapt: insider apt detection using task-tree based deep learning. In: 2021 IEEE 20th International Conference on Trust, Security and Privacy in Computing and Communications (TrustCom), pp. 693–700. IEEE (2021)
25. Meijerink, T.: Anomaly-based detection of lateral movement in a Microsoft Windows environment. Master's thesis, University of Twente, Enschede, The Netherlands (2019). https://essay.utwente.nl/77122/1/Meijerink_MA_EWI.pdf
26. Morić, Z., Dakić, V., Kapulica, A., Regvart, D.: Forensic investigation capabilities of Microsoft azure: a comprehensive analysis and its significance in advancing cloud cyber forensics. Electronics **13**(22), 4546 (2024)
27. Purohit, S., Mackey, P.S., Cottam, J.A., Dunning, M.P., Chin, G.: Synthetic data and graph generation for modeling adversarial activity (final project report). Technical report, Pacific Northwest National Lab. (PNNL), Richland, WA (US) (2022)
28. Ranshous, S., Shen, S., Koutra, D., Harenberg, S., Faloutsos, C., Samatova, N.F.: Anomaly detection in dynamic networks: a survey. Wiley Interdisc. Rev.: Comput. Stat. **7**(3), 223–247 (2015)
29. Ring, M., Wunderlich, S., Scheuring, D., Landes, D.: Flow-based network traffic generation using generative adversarial networks. Comput. Secur. **82**, 156–172 (2019)
30. Ruff, L., et al.: A unifying review of deep and shallow anomaly detection. Proc. IEEE **109**(5), 756–795 (2021)
31. SentinelOne: The state of cloud ransomware in 2024 (2024). https://www.sentinelone.com/blog/the-state-of-cloud-ransomware-in-2024/. Accessed 02 Jan 2025
32. Sun, X., Yang, J.: Hetglm: lateral movement detection by discovering anomalous links with heterogeneous graph neural network. In: 2022 IEEE International Performance, Computing, and Communications Conference (IPCCC), p. 404 (2022). https://doi.org/10.1109/IPCCC55026.2022.9894347
33. Velickovic, P., Cucurull, G., Casanova, A., Romero, A., Liò, P., Bengio, Y.: Graph attention networks. In: 6th International Conference on Learning Representations, ICLR 2018, Vancouver, BC, Canada. OpenReview.net (2018)
34. Wang, R., et al.: Context correlation discrepancy analysis for graph anomaly detection. IEEE Trans. Knowl. Data Eng. (2024)
35. Wang, S., et al.: Threatrace: detecting and tracing host-based threats in node level through provenance graph learning. IEEE Trans. Inf. Forensics Secur. **17**, 3972–3987 (2022)
36. Xu, C., Li, D., Liu, Z., Yang, J., Shen, Q., Tong, N.: Few-shot network intrusion detection method based on multi-domain fusion and cross-attention. PLoS ONE **20**(7), e0327161 (2025). https://doi.org/10.1371/journal.pone.0327161

Acoustic Side Channel Attack on Keyboards Based on Typing Patterns

Alireza Tahiritajar(✉) and Reza Rahaeimehr

School of Computer and Cyber Sciences, Augusta University, Augusta, GA, USA
{ataheritajar,rrahaeimehr}@augusta.edu

Abstract. Acoustic side-channel attacks on keyboards can bypass security measures in many systems that use keyboards as one of the input devices. These attacks aim to reveal users' sensitive information by targeting the sounds made by their keyboards as they type. Most existing approaches in this field ignore the negative impacts of typing patterns and environmental noise in their results. This paper not only seeks to address these shortcomings by proposing an applicable method that takes into account the user's typing pattern in a realistic environment, but it also uses the differences in typing patterns to launch the attack. Our method achieves an average success rate of 43% in detecting average-length words across all our case studies, when considering typists in an individual office setting without any restrictions on their typing style. Achieving such a high success rate has not been reported without imposing significant restrictions on environmental noise, recording devices, and typing styles.

Keywords: Keyboard acoustic emanations · Signal processing · Side channel attacks · Acoustic analysis

1 Introduction

There has been a growing concern over personal data and information security in recent years. With the increasing use of digital devices and online communication, protecting sensitive data has become crucial to modern life. The process of acquiring knowledge about a system by analyzing its side effects is commonly referred to as a Side-Channel Attack [24]. Electronic device emissions have long been a concern within the security and privacy communities [6], as they are susceptible to side-channel attacks. Acoustic side-channel attacks [2,4] can pose significant threats to digital security by taking advantage of unintended sound emissions generated by electronic devices to extract sensitive information such as emails, passwords, or credit card details [5,17]. This type of attack can be hazardous, as they can bypass traditional security measures like passwords [20,26] and encryption.

One of the most concerning aspects of keyboard acoustic side-channel attacks is that they can be conducted remotely, without requiring physical access to

Y. Kim et al. (Eds.): CANS 2025, LNCS 16351, pp. 562–578, 2026.
https://doi.org/10.1007/978-981-95-4434-9_26

the victim's devices [8,24]. This makes them particularly appealing to cybercriminals, who can easily target numerous users. To prevent this type of attack, it is crucial to ensure that sounds cannot be captured in the environment, given the high sensitivity of modern microphones [27]. These attacks typically exploit the sound produced by each key in either the time or frequency domain.

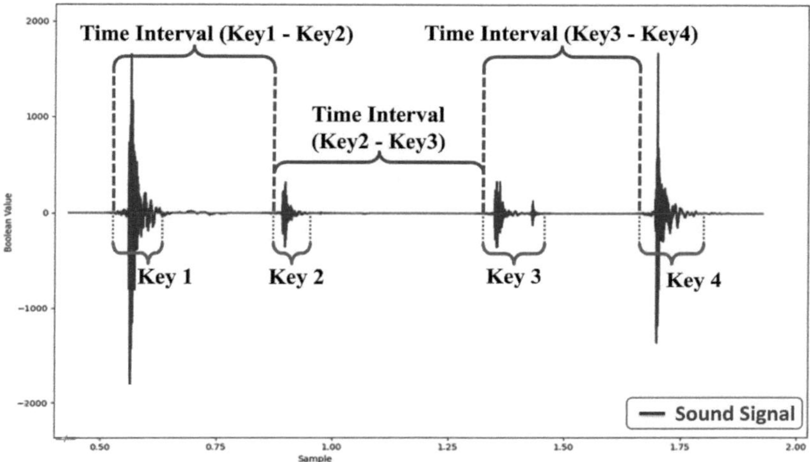

Fig. 1. Sample of acoustic waves produced by typing a four-letter word.

In the existing attacks, a major challenge is the precise capture of keystroke sounds. To address this challenge, researchers typically use high-quality microphones in a stereo-like setup and enforce predetermined typing patterns to isolate and detect keystroke sounds. Then, they apply various data analysis techniques, such as statistical analysis, machine learning algorithms, signal processing methods [24], acoustic triangulation [9], and Time Difference of Arrival (TDoA) [9], to the sound waveforms of keystrokes to decipher the typed text. By restricting the environmental conditions or neglecting the distinct features in their experiments, some past studies have demonstrated significant success with their methodologies [24].

Recognizing typing patterns is a complex task due to variations in how people use keys [12]. This variability adds to the challenge of achieving reliable and accurate recognition of keystroke waveforms, as highlighted in Asonov and Agrawal's study [2]. Furthermore, it is well-established that most attributes of emanations exhibit non-uniform patterns across different device models and are often affected by environmental factors. Another important factor that can disrupt existing methods is the keyboard model used by the user. Usually, when the keyboard model is changed, most algorithms can no longer maintain their previous predictive power due to the unique sound characteristics produced by each keyboard. In addition, recently proposed approaches, especially those that use deep learning networks, have added complexity to obtaining stable results during training, performance, or execution. So, it is interesting to propose a novel method that covers all of these disadvantages in this field of research.

This paper explores the concept of keyboard acoustic side-channel attacks and their potential to compromise digital security and proposes a method that covers the aforementioned problems and weaknesses. We keep our proposed method simple and applicable to a realistic scenario where the victim works in an individual office, and the attacker has a sample of the victim's typed text along with corresponding environmental audio recordings. To understand the realism and practicality of this scenario, consider a victim working in their office. An attacker enters the office under the guise of a client and makes a dummy request that requires the victim's response via email. The attacker leaves a small recorder in the victim's office. The attacker then receives the victim's response through email. A week later, the attacker returns to the office with an excuse and retrieves the recorder. Now, the attacker has a sample of the victim's typing (the email) and the environmental noises from the past week. By noting the time the email was received, and with minimal effort, the attacker can extract the corresponding environmental noise of the email.

Our method starts with capturing and analyzing audio recordings of keystrokes, extracting inter-keystroke time intervals, and keypress timings (Fig. 1). Then, we train a statistical model using this data to predict the user's keystrokes. The model is then tested on previously unknown recorded keystroke sounds from the same user to identify the typed text. The method generates several possible options for each keystroke sequence (phrase). Assuming typos are rare, we can narrow down the possible words by filtering the results through an English dictionary when processing noise associated with typing text, such as emails or chats.

Nowadays, it is pretty common for IT administrators in companies and organizations to secure their systems, such as email platforms, with security measures like two-factor authentication. However, our experimental results suggest that a user's typing patterns, when exploited through keyboard acoustic side-channel attacks, can be used to bypass these security measures and gain access to victims' email content. We collected confidential data from 20 users' typing samples to study the effect of letter count and typing patterns on success rate. On average, we were able to find approximately 43% of words across all of our test cases. The threat of keyboard acoustic side-channel attacks emphasizes the significance of having robust cybersecurity practices. By being well-informed about the risks of acoustic side-channel attacks and implementing appropriate measures to protect sensitive data, individuals and organizations can enhance their security against this threat.

The article is structured as follows: First, we provide a brief overview of previous research on keyboard emanation attacks in Sect. 2. Then, we present our proposed method in Sect. 3.3. In Sect. 4, we provide experimental results, while Sect. 5 covers the limitations and countermeasures. Finally, we conclude the paper and propose potential future research in Sect. 6.

2 Related Work

There is a significant body of research on using acoustic side channels to extract information from computing devices. Some of the authors of this paper have previously conducted a comprehensive literature review on acoustic side-channel attacks on keyboards, which is available [here][1], providing further background relevant to this study. Therefore, in this section, we highlight several key studies that have significantly contributed to the understanding of keyboard acoustic side-channel attacks. In 2004, Asonov and Agrawal [2] demonstrated the possibility of deducing the keystrokes made by an individual on a keyboard by using a simple microphone placed nearby. They achieved this by analyzing the acoustic emissions produced while typing using signal processing techniques. Furthermore, their study revealed the ability to extract sensitive information, such as passwords and credit card numbers, from the sound of keystrokes.

More recently, in 2011, Genkin et al. [11] presented a significant attack that used acoustic signals to extract cryptographic keys from a computer's processor. The authors demonstrated the ability to extract RSA keys from laptops, desktops, and even mobile phones using a smartphone placed near the target device. This work showed that even highly secure cryptographic systems can be vulnerable to acoustic side-channel attacks. In addition to attacks on computers, there have been studies on using acoustic side channels to extract information from other devices. For example, Quarta et al. [18] showed that it was possible to infer the content of printed documents by analyzing the acoustic signals generated by a printer. They showed that it was possible to reconstruct printed text with up to 90% accuracy from acoustic signals captured by a smartphone placed near a specific printer. Another example is the work by O'Leary et al. [16], who showed that we can use acoustic signals to infer the location of a smartphone in a room. By analyzing the acoustic signals generated by the smartphone's speaker and microphone, the authors were able to estimate the position of the device within a few centimeters. Also, there have been studies on using acoustic side channels to extract information from human-computer interfaces. For example, Backes et al. [3] showed that it was possible to infer PIN codes entered using a touchscreen by analyzing the sound of the user's finger tapping on the screen.

In the work by de Souza Faria and Kim [23], a low-cost side-channel attack, differential audio analysis(DAA), exploited the sound generated by physical[2] keypads. This attack, which was based on differential characteristics between sounds recorded by two microphones, achieved a 100% classification rate for two tested PIN pads of the same model. However, when applied to a different device, the success rate dropped to 63%; In this attack, the distances between the microphones and the PIN pad must be fixed and known to the attacker. In [25], Toreini et al. employed signal processing and machine learning techniques to explore the feasibility of discerning individual Enigma keys based on the acoustic emissions they produced. Their results demonstrated that identifying

[1] The reference will be added in the camera-ready version of this paper.

[2] We use the term physical versus virtual keypads or keyboards.

these keys could be consistently achieved with a success rate of 84%. In Anand and Saxena's work [1], they investigate remote keyboard acoustic side-channel attacks and propose a countermeasure. They demonstrate the adaptability of acoustic side-channel attacks to remote eavesdropper settings and introduce a software-based defense, using white noise and fake keystrokes to mitigate these threats effectively. In Harrison et al.'s recent work [13], a deep learning model was implemented to classify keystrokes using a smartphone microphone. They limited their experiments to a specific type of MacBook keyboard, assumed that the audio suppression level of Zoom was set to the lowest, and that no one else was in the meeting other than the victim. They reported a 95% accuracy in detecting a single key using nearby phone-recorded keystrokes and a 93% accuracy using Zoom-recorded keystrokes.

Many other approaches prove the feasibility of using acoustic side channel effects of keyboards to attack sensitive data; however, often, they overlook the effect of the user's typing style in their studies as a critical parameter that can reduce their success rates. In Song et al.'s study [22], they conducted a statistical analysis of typing patterns, revealing that such patterns can divulge key information. They utilized a Hidden Markov Model and a key sequence prediction algorithm to predict keystrokes from inter-keystroke timings. Furthermore, they devised an attacker system to monitor SSH sessions for password learning. In the work by Liu et al. [15], the authors introduce a novel approach to user-independent inter-keystroke timing attacks on PINs. Their attack methodology is based on constructing an inter-keystroke timing dictionary derived from a human cognitive model. Significantly, this model's parameters can be determined with minimal training data from any users, regardless of whether they are the intended target victims. This approach suggests the potential for large-scale deployment in real-world scenarios. The authors explore various online attack settings, evaluating their attack's performance across different levels of PIN strength. Their experimental results reveal that the proposed attack outperforms random guessing methods significantly.

3 Our Method

Typing patterns are often overlooked by other approaches and negatively affect their results. In our proposal, we turn this negative point into a positive one. We observed that the time interval between pressing keys on a keyboard varies for different key pairs. However, we noticed that an individual tends to type a particular key pair within a similar time interval in most cases, which is influenced by factors such as the arrangement of keys on the keyboard, the anatomy of their hands, and personal typing style, which we consider all these factors as typing patterns. For example, we observed that the selected users with their specific keyboards tended to type the "b" and "o" keys within a similar time in different words, such as "both" and "book", although these time intervals may vary from one user to another. On the other hand, there are variations in the time intervals between different key pairs. Using these two facts, we can model the victim's typing pattern. This model and a recording of the ambient noise captured in the victim's office can enable our keyboard acoustic side-channel attack. Our method shows that we can deduce sensitive information, such as emails and texts, by analyzing the acoustic emissions produced while typing.

Threat Model: We assume the victim uses a physical keyboard of their choice without any restrictions on the keyboard model or brand. We also assume the victim is identified. Moreover, we assume that the victim works in a private room like an individual office. Since the shape of audio waveforms is not important in our method, the environmental noises are well tolerated in such conditions. We presume that we can capture some typing samples of the victim in his working environment, including the text and the ambient noise, which we use to build and train our statistical models. We consider an oracle that can split the target audio file into separate files corresponding to each word. This is also a realistic assumption because usually, after typing a word, users press the Enter or Space keys, which generate distinguishable sounds even by human ears.

To illustrate the threat model, suppose a hacker (a malicious student) arranges a meeting with the dean of a faculty and then sends a fake request via email. During the meeting, the hacker places a small voice recorder in the dean's office. After a week, once the hacker receives a response to the email, they revisit the dean's office under a pretext and retrieve the recorder. The hacker can then extract the noise corresponding to the time when the email response was typed, based on the email's timestamp. Consequently, the hacker obtains a sample of noise related to the specific text, along with noise from other times, and can use our method to determine what other texts the dean typed during that period.

The previous example was a simple instance of our threat model. In more complex cases, the hacker may not even need to be physically present at the victim's workplace. For example, hacking the personal phone of a high-ranking military official is much easier than infiltrating the security computers they use, and by hacking such an individual's phone, one can easily obtain the ambient noise of their workplace without any physical presence.

In the rest of this section, we explain the steps that we took to test and prove the proposal.

3.1 Dataset Gathering

To test our proposal, we need to gather the typing patterns of some users. Hence, we developed a Windows-based application (Fig. 2) using *C#* programming language[3] that captures a user's typing pattern in three conditions. Firstly, the user types any desired text on their wish. Secondly, some common sentences in English are shown to the user, and the user needs to type them, and in the final step, he types a set of predetermined commonly used words to capture a diverse range of typing styles and patterns. We chose these sentences and words based on

[3] Python version of this program is available (link to both software available upon request).

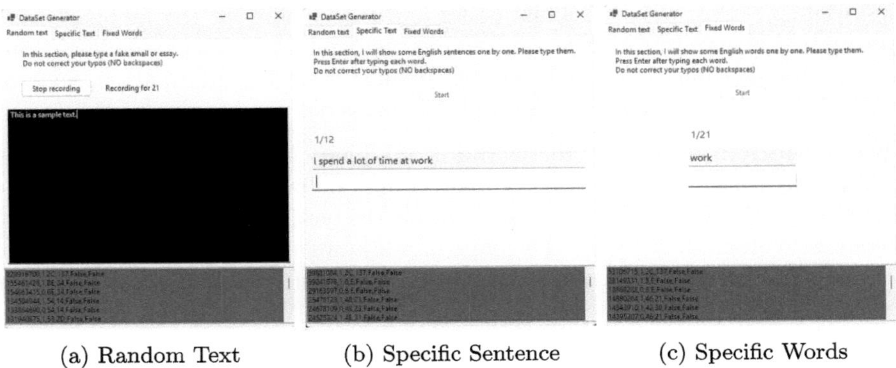

(a) Random Text (b) Specific Sentence (c) Specific Words

Fig. 2. The interface of the data gathering software.

the diversity needed to type letters and words in English. The developed software allows us to gather a comprehensive and confidential dataset to capture diverse typing styles and patterns, including the audio noises in the environment. We use the resulting dataset files to train models for our attack.

3.2 Training Statistical Model

As mentioned before, the main idea of this paper is to utilize a user's typing pattern to train a statistical model. In the first step, information from the dataset gathered by each user is used to calculate and store the time interval between two pressed keys in a table of a database. Next, we calculate the average and standard deviation of these time intervals for each sequence of similar keys and store them in another table, which serves as the trained model's data.

We utilize the information from both tables and compare the results. As the number of similar keystroke sequences increases, we can see that the user types those sequences with almost identical time intervals, with only minor differences. Hence, using the second table for larger user-generated datasets is preferable. Moreover, by examining the standard deviation values, we can infer the uniformity of the user's typing pattern. The higher the standard deviation values, the more inconsistent the user's typing pattern, resulting in a higher probability of mispredictions in our algorithm. To mitigate this problem, we propose a coefficient for time intervals to reduce such errors, which will be discussed in the subsequent sections.

3.3 Prediction

After determining the statistical model for each user, the next step is recognizing unknown keystrokes by analyzing the audio file recorded from their typing. First, we process the audio file to identify the segment corresponding to each keystroke, as explained below.

Segment Extraction for Each Keystroke. The process of extracting keystroke-related segments (e.g. Fig. 3) from the audio file is formulated in Algorithm 1. We observed that keystrokes, especially in the hunt-and-peck style, typically occur within a maximum duration of about 100 milliseconds, notably slower than alternative typing methods. This observation confirms the findings in the previous works. The segmentation process starts with employing a sliding window with a frame size of 100 milliseconds and a hop length of one, as illustrated in Fig. 4. Within this window, we calculate the sum of the absolute amplitude of the recorded audio signal.

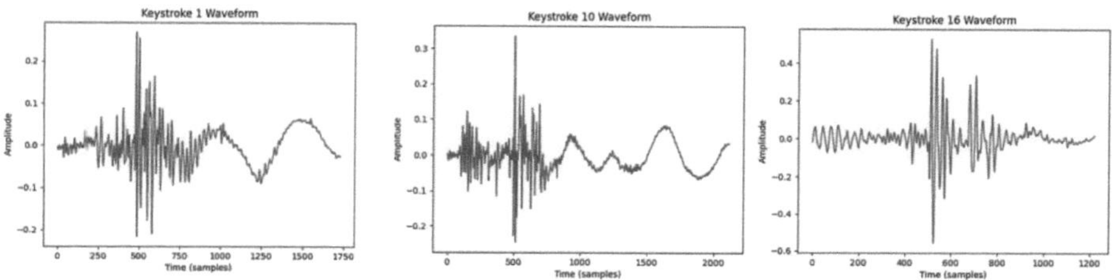

Fig. 3. Example of extracted segments related to keystrokes.

Algorithm 1 Segment extraction for each keystroke

Require: Recorded sound of typing S, Frame length l, Number of keystrokes to predict k, Minimum time between two keystrokes m, Tolerance factor t_f.
Ensure: List of timestamps corresponding to keystrokes B.
Set $F = \{f_i = 0 | 0 \leq i < |S|\}$.
while $i = 0$ to $|S| - l$ **do**
    Set $f_i = \sum_{t=i}^{i+l-1} |S[t]|$.
end while
while $n = 1$ to k **do**
    Set $b_n = Max(F)$.
    Update $F = \{f_i = 0 | b_n - m < i < b_n + l + m\}$.
end while
Set $B = (b_1, ..., b_k)$.
$Sort(B)$.
Return B.

Subsequently, we systematically search for the maximum point within these sliding windows and reset the values in the vicinity of this maximum to zero. This resetting operation extends over a range that spans from the index of the maximum point minus the frame length to the index of the maximum point plus the frame length. This range alteration allows us to pinpoint the keystroke signals, as we observe that the time intervals between keystrokes tend to be longer

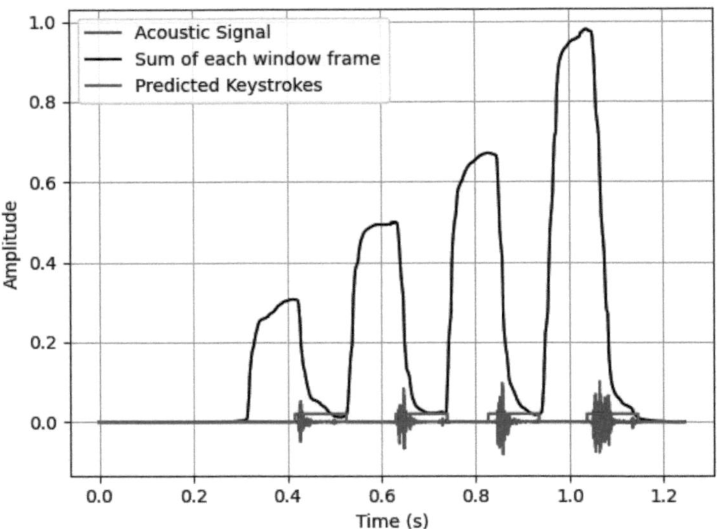

Fig. 4. Demonstrating keystroke segment extraction process.

than 100 milliseconds. By zeroing this range, we effectively eliminate the possibility of redundant keystroke predictions. We repeat this step iteratively until we've successfully identified the total number of keystrokes. This determination is made by listening to the recorded file and acting as an operator to ensure accuracy in our predictions.

Since the touch and press components of each keystroke generate the loudest sounds, the maximum amplitude often occurs within the initial ten percent of the keystroke segment. As our third step, after identifying all desired maximum indexes associated with each keystroke, we proceed to calculate segments corresponding to the keystrokes within a range extending from these indexes to indexes plus a frame length. These segments can represent the detected keystrokes. Additionally, we can save each segment in separate files, which can facilitate future analysis and enhance the comprehensibility of the extracted information for further study.

Finding Sequences of Possible Keystrokes. After extracting the keystroke segments, we need to determine the time intervals between each keystroke. Each keystroke involves three events: 1. Key touch, which occurs when the user touches a key; 2. Keypress, which happens when the key hits the keyboard plate; and 3. Key release, which occurs when the user lifts his hand from the key. Since we allowed some environmental noises, these events can't be identified clearly. We examined several options for calculating these intervals, including considering the time between the start or end of each segment, finding intervals based on the midpoint of each segment, and identifying the time intervals between the largest peaks within each segment. After some experiments, we opted to calculate the time intervals between the starting points of all keystroke segments. This approach yielded the best results as it maintained the highest consistency with the values recorded in the dataset and the statistical model we developed.

Algorithm 2 Finding sequences of possible keystrokes

Require: Trained model M, List of timestamps corresponding to keystrokes B, Number of keystrokes to predict k.
Ensure: List of predicted words W.

Set $root = \{'', \{\}\}$ // $node = \{value, children\}$
Set $L = \{'a', ..., 'z'\}$
while $i = 1$ to $k - 1$ **do**
  Set $\Delta T_i = b_{i+1} - b_i$.
  Set $C_i = \{(k_a, k_b, \Delta_{ab}) | k_a \in L \wedge \Delta_{ab} - t_f \leq \Delta T_i \leq \Delta_{ab} + t_f\}$
  Update $L = \{k_b | (k_a, k_b, \Delta_{ab}) \in C_i\}$
  $AddCandidatesToTree(root, C_i)$
end while
Set $W = GetAllPathesFromRootToLeaves(root)$
Return W

After calculating the time intervals between unidentified keystrokes, we look for the closest match within our statistical model for these intervals. However, as users may not consistently type the same key sequence at exact time intervals, we explore numbers within a range around the calculated interval. This range extends approximately five percent greater and five percent less than the calculated interval. We previously mentioned that a higher standard deviation in time values for similar keys can lead to a higher error rate in our algorithm. To address this, we calculate coefficients for the time intervals based on the average standard deviation (ASD) and adjust the mentioned five percent range accordingly.

Once we've identified all possible sequences of typed letters for each step, we construct a decision tree-like diagram for the subsequent steps. This diagram enables us to trace all branches connected from the root to the final branch. Any remaining unconnected branches are pruned. In the next step, we consolidate all connected branches, representing the potentially typed keystrokes we've identified. These serve as the raw prediction results. Algorithm 2 formulates the aforementioned process.

Enhancing the Results Using English Dictionary. The previous step generated a set of potential words typed by the user. Given our specific focus on text content, including emails and notes, we can augment our prediction accuracy by employing semantic correctness approaches, such as dictionary checks or AI-based methods like Large Language Models (LLMs) [7]. These methods enable us to refine our predictions and ascertain the accurate sentences and text corresponding to our predicted words. So, to enhance the accuracy of our predictions, we filter the predicted words by searching for them in an English dictionary and eliminating any invalid words. Given that a typical typist is likely to make fewer types compared to correctly typed words, checking the predicted words against a dictionary improves the prediction accuracy.

The procedure outlined in this section enables us to predict the letters the user has typed by utilizing a model trained on the user's typing pattern and employing a series of analytical procedures on the audio signal. In the following section, we will discuss the results and experiments conducted.

4 Experimental Analysis

This section provides a comprehensive analysis of the experimental results derived from our investigation. Our experiments were crafted to evaluate the effectiveness and implications of the proposed acoustic side-channel attack. Our evaluation encompasses various facets of the study, including accuracy, efficiency, and security implications.

4.1 User Study

We conducted an Institutional Review Board (IRB)-approved user study to collect typing patterns from participants. The data obtained are treated with confidentiality and anonymity. To achieve this, we carefully selected 20 adult users, each exhibiting their unique typing patterns, to train and test the accuracy of our approach using their respective samples. The test dataset was chosen for its prevalence in English texts and varied word lengths. This selection allowed us to measure the impact of word length on prediction accuracy. The effect of the number of letters in a word is visually represented in Fig. 5. The figure indicates that the success rate increases as the number of letters in words increases until we reach six letters. This is because having more letters creates a larger tree based on those letters. However, larger trees do not necessarily result in more meaningful words. Therefore, we have observed that in this situation, there are fewer words that result in bigger success rates. Interestingly, after number six, we reached the highest success rate.

4.2 Accuracy Assessment

We conducted a series of experiments and calculations to assess the accuracy of our proposed acoustic side-channel attack. The primary objective of these evaluations was to gauge the effectiveness of our approach in predicting user keystrokes based on their typing patterns. To assess the overall accuracy of the proposed method, we initially tallied the number of correctly detected words for each user's test dataset. Following this, we calculated the average number of correct detections for each user. Subsequently, we computed the average accuracy of our approach across all 20 users. Figure 6 illustrates both the collective accuracy of all users and the individual accuracy of each user. Our investigation

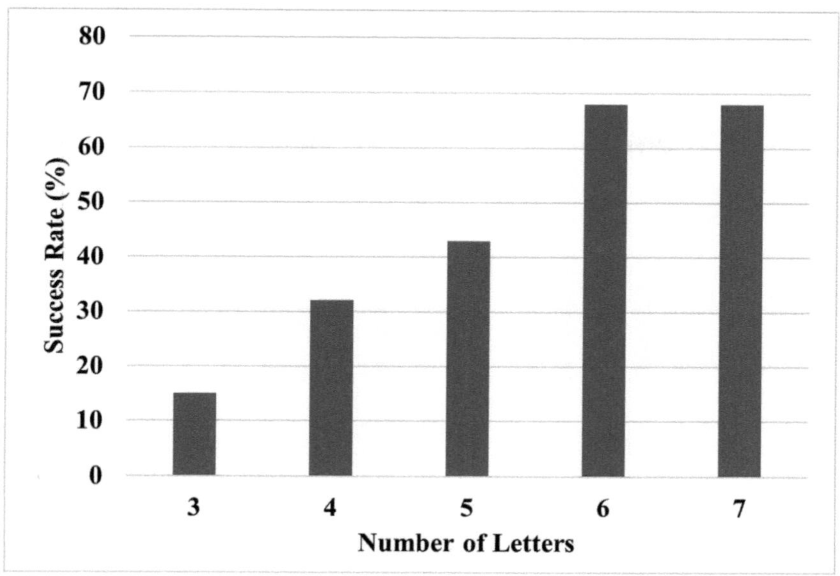

Fig. 5. The effect of the number of letters on the success rate.

reveals a linear relationship between the ASD of each user's typing sample and the success rate of prediction. This implies that users with a consistent typing pattern tend to have lower ASD, resulting in a higher prediction success rate. For instance, User 7 exhibits the lowest ASD and, consequently, the highest success rate. Our findings substantiate our initial hypothesis regarding the correlation between typing patterns and susceptibility to these types of attacks. Additionally, we computed the average success rate across all users as the final average success rate for our approach, which amounts to approximately 43%.

As mentioned earlier, our aim was to simulate a highly realistic environment and experiments. We deliberately chose:

- Not to eliminate acoustic noises during the data-gathering process
- Not to restrict the keyboard model
- Not compelled participants to adopt a specific typing style, such as hunt and peck, touch typing, two-fingered typing
- To keep our attack simulation more realistic,
- To use the laptop's microphone, which was not a high-quality microphone

Consequently, comparing our results with other approaches becomes challenging, as they often constrain various parameters in their experiments to showcase the success rate of their methods. However, our method outperforms other approaches that focus on detecting words. We compare some of our features and achievements to other similar methods in Table 1.

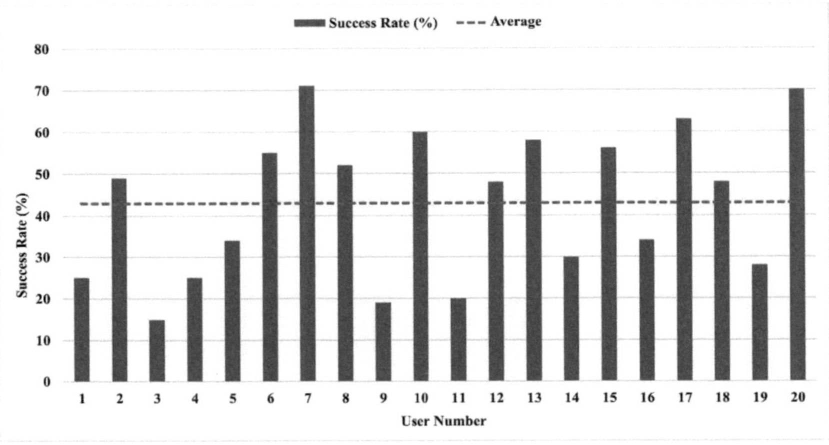

Fig. 6. The success rate per each user.

Table 1. Comparison of Key Characteristics Among Acoustic Side Channel Attack Approaches on Keyboards

Approach	Requires large dataset	Specific keyboard dependency	computational complexity	typing pattern limitation	Environment noise	Success Rate for words	Success Rate for Single Keys
cognitive modeling [15]	No	Yes	High	No	Ignored	%10	N/A
Deep learning [21]	Yes	Yes	High	Yes	Ignored	N/A	84.59%
Hidden Markov Model [10]	No	Yes	High	Yes	Ignored	N/A	80% *
triangulation [19]	Yes	Yes	High	Yes	Ignored	N/A	87.5%
timing dictionary [14]	No	Yes	High	Yes	Ignored	14.0%	N/A
Our Method	**No**	**No**	**Low**	**No**	**Considered**	**43%**	N/A

* The success rate was reported on a numeric PIN pad.

In comparing various acoustic side-channel attack approaches on keyboards, distinctive characteristics emerge. Cognitive modeling [15] stands out for not requiring a large dataset and considering both specific keyboard dependency and users' typing patterns; however, it does not account for environmental noise, resulting in a relatively low success rate of 10%. Deep learning [21] demands a large dataset, exhibits keyboard dependency, and involves complex model training. It achieves a success rate of 84.59% in detecting individual keys, but it neglects consideration of realistic environments. Note that the success rate for detecting a single key may decrease polynomially when detecting words, depending on the length of the words. Hidden Markov Model [10] is notable for its lack of dataset requirement; However, we could not find their final achievement accurately, and they overlook both users' typing patterns and environmental noise. Triangulation [19] requires a large dataset and is keyboard-dependent, yet it achieves a commendable success rate of 87.5%, neglecting considerations environmental noise. Timing dictionary [14] does not necessitate a large dataset but is keyboard-dependent, resulting in a modest success rate of 14%, with no consideration for users' typing patterns or environmental noise.

Our proposed method differs by not requiring a large dataset and minimizing keyboard dependency. It excels in considering users' typing patterns and environmental noise, achieving an outstanding success rate of 43% in detecting words. This highlights the trade-offs and strengths of each approach, emphasizing the importance of tailored considerations for real-world applicability. Our intention was to propose a practical approach aligned with real-world scenarios. Unlike approaches that limit destructive parameters for experimental convenience, we sought to mirror the conditions encountered in the actual world. Note that any success rate greater than a random guess in real-world scenarios is a significant achievement for an attacker. Furthermore, our proposed method can be combined with other approaches to get better results, addressing potential shortcomings they may have.

4.3 The Effect of Different Keyboards on Typing Patterns

In this section, we are examining the impact of using different keyboard models on the outcomes of our proposed approach. The goal of this analysis is to showcase the influence of various keyboards on users' typing patterns in a real-world setting. We used *Dell KB216-t* as the keyboard to gather our dataset in Sect. 3.1 and trained the model for each user based on their specific dataset. Now, we experimented using two different keyboard models: the *Dell KB212-B* and the *MSI Vigor GK30*. Our participants were asked to repeat the last step of Sect. 3.1, which involved typing predetermined words using the two mentioned keyboards. Upon analyzing the data, we observed that users exhibited almost identical typing patterns when using the *Dell KB212-B* and *Dell KB216-t*, as these two keyboards are similar and have the same brand. So, we could still use their specific trained model to predict their typed text with almost the same success rates as before. However, there were noticeable changes in their typing patterns when using the *MSI Vigor GK30*. This can be attributed to the mechanical style of this keyboard, featuring more rigid keys and greater spacing between them. Furthermore, We found that although users have different patterns, they still have their unique patterns with this new keyboard style, and we can find the coefficient factor and use that to predict typed text with the pretrained model.

5 Limitations

We have tried to minimize our approach's dependence on environmental conditions. However, it is a fundamental reality that if we cannot accurately capture the sound of the keyboard, we may not be able to precisely identify keystroke events, resulting in a reduction in overall accuracy. Another physical limitation to consider is that all acoustic keystroke detection methods rely on the strength of the sound generated by the keyboards. Therefore, keyboards with softer keys produce less sound power, which, in turn, can lead to reduced accuracy in the final detection.

The success rate of our attack can be adversely affected in the following groups:

- People who use computers rarely, because they do not maintain a consistent typing pattern.
- Professional typists, because they type very fast, and the *touch*, *key-press*, and *key-release* events of consecutive keystrokes usually have overlaps, and we can't detect the tying pattern accurately.

6 Conclusion

In this paper, we have explored the possibility of acoustic side-channel attacks on keyboards that are based on the user's typing pattern. This approach addresses some of the limitations of other methods and provides a more realistic method that can be used against criminal and terrorist groups.

Our proposed method uses the time differences between consecutive keystrokes to train a statistical model for extracting unknown keystrokes from a recorded acoustic sound. To test our method, we collected the ambient noise and typed text of 20 people based on an IRB-approved approach, and obtained approximately a 43% success rate through our experiments for detecting words. Our results were achieved in a realistic environment without any restrictions on users' keyboards, typing patterns, or environmental acoustic noises, which is a significant advantage over other approaches. However, we intend to explore the potential of AI-powered models like LLMs in future projects to improve our success rate.

Despite its high success rate, we acknowledge that our proposed method has inherent limitations, such as the quality of the acoustically recorded sound. Overall, we believe this approach underscores the need for more secure input methods and highlights potential vulnerabilities in digital security.

References

1. Anand, S.A., Saxena, N.: Keyboard emanations in remote voice calls: password leakage and noise (less) masking defenses. In: Proceedings of the Eighth ACM Conference on Data and Application Security and Privacy, pp. 103–110 (2018)
2. Asonov, D., Agrawal, R.: Keyboard acoustic emanations revisited. In: Proceedings of the 11th ACM Conference on Computer and Communications Security, pp. 373–382. ACM (2004)
3. Backes, M., Durmuth, M., Gerling, S., Pinkal, M.: Acoustic side-channel attacks on touchscreens. In: Proceedings of the 2013 ACM SIGSAC Conference on Computer and Communications Security, pp. 551–562. ACM (2013)
4. Backes, M., Dürmuth, M., Gerling, S., Pinkal, M., Sporleder, C., et al.: Acoustic side-channel attacks on printers. In: 19th USENIX Security Symposium (USENIX Security 2010) (2010)

5. Berger, Y., Wool, A., Yeredor, A.: Dictionary attacks using keyboard acoustic emanations. In: Proceedings of the 13th ACM Conference on Computer and Communications Security, pp. 245–254 (2006)
6. Briol, R.: Emanation: how to keep your data confidential. In: Proceedings of Symposium on Electromagnetic Security For Information Protection, pp. 225–234 (1991)
7. Brown, T., et al.: Language models are few-shot learners. Adv. Neural. Inf. Process. Syst. **33**, 1877–1901 (2020)
8. Compagno, A., Conti, M., Lain, D., Tsudik, G.: Don't skype & type! acoustic eavesdropping in voice-over-ip. In: Proceedings of the 2017 ACM on Asia Conference on Computer and Communications Security, pp. 703–715 (2017)
9. Fiona, A.H.Y.: Keyboard acoustic triangulation attack. The Chinese University of Hong Kong: bachelors thesis (2006)
10. Foo Kune, D., Kim, Y.: Timing attacks on pin input devices. In: Proceedings of the 17th ACM Conference on Computer and Communications Security, pp. 678–680 (2010)
11. Genkin, D., Shamir, A., Tromer, E.: RSA key extraction via low-bandwidth acoustic cryptanalysis. In: 23rd USENIX Security Symposium, pp. 575–590. USENIX Association (2014)
12. Halevi, T., Saxena, N.: A closer look at keyboard acoustic emanations: random passwords, typing styles and decoding techniques. In: Proceedings of the 7th ACM Symposium on Information, Computer and Communications Security, pp. 89–90 (2012)
13. Harrison, J., Toreini, E., Mehrnezhad, M.: A practical deep learning-based acoustic side channel attack on keyboards. In: 2023 IEEE European Symposium on Security and Privacy Workshops (EuroS&PW), pp. 270–280. IEEE (2023)
14. Liu, X.: When keystroke meets password: attacks and defenses. Dissertations and Theses Collection (2019)
15. Liu, X., Li, Y., Deng, R.H., Chang, B., Li, S.: When human cognitive modeling meets pins: user-independent inter-keystroke timing attacks. Comput. Secur. **80**, 90–107 (2019)
16. O'Leary, R., Rackliffe, L., Agbinya, J.: Acoustic location of smartphones. In: Proceedings of the 15th International Conference on Mobile and Ubiquitous Multimedia, pp. 307–311. ACM (2016)
17. Ponnam, S.: Keyboard acoustic emanations attack: an empirical study (2013)
18. Quarta, D., Milani Comparetti, P., Balzarotti, D., Zanero, S.: Acoustic side-channel attacks on printers. In: Proceedings of the 2018 ACM SIGSAC Conference on Computer and Communications Security, pp. 1938–1952. ACM (2018)
19. Ranade, V., Smith, J., Switala, B.: Acoustic side channel attack on ATM keypads (2009)
20. Ross, B., Jackson, C., Miyake, N., Boneh, D., Mitchell, J.C.: Stronger password authentication using browser extensions. In: USENIX Security Symposium, Baltimore, MD, USA, vol. 17, p. 32 (2005)
21. Slater, D., Novotney, S., Moore, J., Morgan, S., Tenaglia, S.: Robust keystroke transcription from the acoustic side-channel. In: Proceedings of the 35th Annual Computer Security Applications Conference, pp. 776–787 (2019)
22. Song, D.X., Wagner, D., Tian, X.: Timing analysis of keystrokes and timing attacks on {SSH}. In: 10th USENIX Security Symposium (USENIX Security 2001) (2001)
23. de Souza Faria, G., Kim, H.Y.: Differential audio analysis: a new side-channel attack on pin pads. Int. J. Inf. Secur. **18**, 73–84 (2019)

24. Taheritajar, A., Harris, Z.M., Rahaeimehr, R.: A survey on acoustic side channel attacks on keyboards. In: Information and Communications Security: 26th International Conference, ICICS 2024, Mytilene, Greece, August 26–28, 2024, Proceedings, Part I, (pp. 99–121). Springer-Verlag (2024). https://doi.org/10.1007/978-981-97-8798-2_6. ISBN: 978-981-97-8797-5
25. Toreini, E., Randell, B., Hao, F.: An acoustic side channel attack on enigma. School of Computing Science Technical Report Series (2015)
26. Yan, J., Blackwell, A., Anderson, R., Grant, A.: Password memorability and security: empirical results. IEEE Secur. Priv. **2**(5), 25–31 (2004)
27. Zhuang, L., Zhou, F., Tygar, J.D.: Keyboard acoustic emanations revisited. ACM Trans. Inf. Syst. Secur. (TISSEC) **13**(1), 1–26 (2009)

Short Papers

Enhancing Cold Boot Attacks with Probabilistic-Guided SAT-Solvers

Daniel Berend[1], Amit Cohen[1], Shahar Golan[2](✉), Boris Tsirkin[1], Yochai Twitto[3], and Itamar Zimerman[1]

[1] Ben-Gurion University, 84105 Beer Sheva, Israel
berend@bgu.ac.il
[2] Jerusalem College of Technology, 91160 Jerusalem, Israel
sgolan@jct.ac.il
[3] Shamoon College of Engineering, 84108 Beer Sheva, Israel
yochait@sce.ac.il

Abstract. A fundamental component of a Cold Boot Attack involves a reconstruction algorithm for recovering corrupted encryption keys. This paper introduces a novel heuristic designed to significantly augment the efficiency of such algorithms. Our work illustrates the heuristic's capacity to streamline key reconstruction across various encryption key types and integrates it into an AES Encryption key reconstruction algorithm. Subsequently, we perform an empirical assessment to gauge the performance of this algorithm compared to current state-of-the-art methods.

Keywords: Cold Boot Attack · Side-Channel Attack · AES

1 Introduction

A *Cold Boot Attack* (CBA) extracts sensitive data that persists in Dynamic Random-Access Memory (DRAM) for a short time after power loss [7,19]. By transplanting memory modules or briefly re-powering the machine, an adversary can obtain a noisy image that still reveals cryptographic material such as AES keys. Follow-up studies confirmed the practicality of CBAs against commodity PCs and servers [23,25,26], mobile devices [2,18], and even DDR3/DDR4 platforms [3,24]. Despite incremental physical mitigations in modern memory modules, DRAM retention times and physical access attacks indicate that sensitive systems will remain vulnerable for the foreseeable future.

Prerequisites. Two well-known facts underpin a successful CBA:

(i) Encryption software usually stores either the secret key or its full round-key schedule in DRAM to avoid repeated key expansion, as formalized in the AES specification [5].
(ii) The key-schedule algorithm is public, so relationships among round keys form deterministic constraints. These constraints allow the attacker to reconstruct flipped bits once an approximate image is available.

Y. Kim et al. (Eds.): CANS 2025, LNCS 16351, pp. 581–590, 2026.
https://doi.org/10.1007/978-981-95-4434-9_27

Decay Models. Early work modelled decay as a pure $1 \rightarrow 0$ leakage (erasure-only) process [7]. Later measurements showed asymmetric bit-flips in both directions, whose probabilities depend on temperature and refresh delay [8,21]. Key reconstruction thus becomes a noisy constraint-satisfaction (Max-SAT) problem.

Prior Reconstruction Algorithms. Kamal and Youssef applied maximum-likelihood decoding to the erasure-only model [9]. Liao *et al.* introduced a Max-SAT formulation for the realistic model and solved mid-sized instances with minisat-plus [11,12]. Subsequent work explored cardinality networks [6,13], core-guided search [17], parallel CDCL solvers [14–16], and domain-specific heuristics for cryptanalysis [4,10,25]. Nevertheless, modern DRAM capacities enlarge the search space, and advanced SAT solvers such as Glucose [1] and MiniSAT [20] are yet to be fully exploited in this context.

Our Approach. We propose a *cipher-agnostic Bayesian bit predictor* that assigns per-bit likelihoods based on measured decay bias, then embeds this information in a lightweight modification of a state-of-the-art SAT solver. The predictor steers branching decisions and clause activations, pruning infeasible assignments early. On both synthetic and real dumps, our technique shrinks solving time by up to two orders of magnitude compared with the best published results [27].

Our Primary Contributions Are as Follows:

1. **Bayesian decay heuristic:** a cipher-agnostic method that estimates per-bit error likelihoods from DRAM noise and steers key reconstruction.
2. **SAT integration:** custom modifications weave this heuristic into a modern CBA Max-SAT solver, significantly improving its performance.
3. **Empirical validation:** the resulting probabilistic-guided solver recovers AES keys under realistic decay faster and more accurately than prior methods.

Paper Organization. Section 2 details the heuristic, Sect. 3 the full algorithm, and Sect. 4 the empirical results.

2 A Heuristic for Identifying Corrupted Bits

In this section, we introduce a novel heuristic that leverages probabilistic reasoning to estimate the probability of each original bit having a certain value. In particular, the heuristic provides a means to identify the bits in the corrupted key that are most likely to have been reversely flipped.

2.1 Definitions and Intuition

We offer an intuitive problem definition. There are four main components involved in the problem:

1. An unknown *initial key*, denoted by $\vec{k}_{\texttt{init}} \in \{0,1\}^b$.
2. A known expansion function $f : \{0,1\}^b \to \{0,1\}^n$. The vector $f(\vec{k}_{\texttt{init}})$ is the *original key* $\vec{k} = (k_1, \ldots, k_n)$. We assume that the initial key is uniformly distributed in $\{0,1\}^b$ and, moreover, f has the property that each component of $\vec{k}$ is distributed uniformly in $\{0,1\}$, i.e., $k_i \sim \texttt{Ber}(\frac{1}{2})$. This assumption is common for cryptographic keys.
3. Corruption probabilities p_0 and p_1, indicating how often a 0-bit or a 1-bit, respectively, is flipped during the period that precedes the attack. We assume throughout that $p_1 \gg p_0$.
4. A *corrupted key* $\vec{m} = (m_1, m_2, \ldots, m_n)$, where $m_i = k_i \oplus X_i$ and $X_i \sim \texttt{Ber}(p_{k_i}), 1 \leq i \leq n$. The random variables X_i are independent.

The recovery challenge is to identify $\vec{k}$ from $\vec{m}$, despite these asymmetric errors. Our heuristic ranks each bit of $\vec{m}$ by its likelihood of having been corrupted, using known algebraic dependencies among the bits.

2.2 Illustrative Examples

To motivate the heuristic, it is instructive to examine two toy examples, in which $b = 1$ and $n = 2$.

Example 1. Assume that $f((x)) = (x, \neg x)$. Then $\vec{k} = (k_1, k_2) = (k_1, \neg k_1)$. Suppose that $\vec{m} = (m_1, m_2) = (1,1)$. Since $k_1 \neq k_2$, either m_1 or m_2 is corrupted, and the probability for each bit to be corrupted is $1/2$ due to the symmetry between the two bits.

Example 2. Assume that $f((x)) = (x, x)$. Then $\vec{k} = (k_1, k_2) = (k_1, k_1)$. Suppose that $\vec{m} = (m_1, m_2) = (1,0)$. Since $k_1 = k_2$, either m_1 or m_2 is corrupted. Since $p_1 \gg p_0$, the probability that $k_1 = 1$ is much higher than the probability that $k_1 = 0$.

The next example shows a slightly more elaborate computation, involving three bits:

Example 3. Let $f(x,y) = (x, y, x \oplus y)$, so $\vec{k} = (k_1, k_2, k_3) = (k_1, k_2, k_1 \oplus k_2)$. Assume the *corruption probabilities* $p_0 = 0.001$ and $p_1 = 0.4$. Suppose that $\vec{m} = (m_1, m_2, m_3) = (1,1,0)$. Given the definition of f, we know that $\vec{k} \in \{(0,0,0), (0,1,1), (1,0,1), (1,1,0)\}$, each option having the same *apriori* probability $\frac{1}{4}$.

For every candidate we multiply the bit-flip probabilities (p_0 for $0 \to 1$, $1 - p_0$ for $0 \to 0$, p_1 for $1 \to 0$, and $1 - p_1$ for $1 \to 1$):

Using Bayes' rule and the values above, we get

$$\Pr[k_3 = 0 \mid \vec{m}] = \frac{9.99 \times 10^{-7} + 3.5964 \times 10^{-1}}{9.99 \times 10^{-7} + 2.4 \times 10^{-4} + 2.4 \times 10^{-4} + 3.5964 \times 10^{-1}} \approx 0.9987.$$

$\vec{k}$	Bit transitions	$\Pr[\vec{m} \mid \vec{k}]$	Value
$(0,0,0)$	$0\to1,\ 0\to1,\ 0\to0$	$p_0^2(1-p_0)$	9.99×10^{-7}
$(0,1,1)$	$0\to1,\ 1\to1,\ 1\to0$	$p_0(1-p_1)p_1$	2.4×10^{-4}
$(1,0,1)$	$1\to1,\ 0\to1,\ 1\to0$	$(1-p_1)p_0p_1$	2.4×10^{-4}
$(1,1,0)$	$1\to1,\ 1\to1,\ 0\to0$	$(1-p_1)^2(1-p_0)$	3.5964×10^{-1}

This result is somewhat surprising, as one might expect that the corruption model allows us to make near-safe guesses only about bits whose value in the corrupted key is 1.

3 Improving the SoTA Reconstruction Algorithms

This chapter presents enhancements to improve the efficiency of certain State-of-the-Art reconstruction algorithms. To illustrate these improvements, we focus on AES-128. Nevertheless, our methods are applicable to any cipher. Our algorithm builds upon and improves the approach proposed in [12]. We begin by describing their algorithm and then detail our enhancements. In Sect. 4, we demonstrate that our algorithm outperforms the original algorithm.

3.1 Description of the Baseline Algorithm

In [9], it is demonstrated that a SAT solver is an effective tool for addressing the key reconstruction problem. Building on this, [12] shows that the approach can be successfully extended to scenarios where reverse flips are permitted, corresponding to the practical decay model. This extension builds on the observation that the probability p_0 is generally low, resulting in a small number of reverse flips, typically no more than two.

To demonstrate this point, let us consider AES-128. Recall that an AES-128 key comprises 1408 bits. As customary, we assume that each bit in the original key is equally likely to be 0 or 1. Moreover, the bits display "sufficient independence", making the number of 0-s in the original key close to 704 with high probability. Assuming for simplicity that it is exactly 704, the number of reverse flips is distributed $\texttt{Bin}(704, p_0)$. In particular, the probability that exactly k bits of the original key are reversely flipped in the corrupted key is $\binom{704}{k}{p_0}^k(1-p_0)^{704-k}$. As one can see, the probability of more than two reverse flips is negligible. Consequently, one can transition from the practical corruption model to the theoretical one by partitioning the search space based on the number of reverse flips that occurred. Translating a single problem from the practical model may produce up to $\binom{704}{0}+\binom{704}{1}+\binom{704}{2} = 248161$ instances of the problem under the theoretical model.

Algorithmically, we first attempt to solve the instance corresponding to the case where no reverse flips occurred. If successful, we halt and return the recovered key. If this attempt fails, we proceed to address cases where exactly one reverse flip occurred. This involves iterating through the 1-valued bits in the corrupted key one by one. For each such bit, we attempt to solve the problem under the assumption that it is the reversely flipped bit, while keeping all other 1-valued bits intact. This process may require up to approximately $704 \cdot (1 - p_1)$ solving attempts – one for each 1-valued bit in the corrupted key. If one of these attempts succeeds, we halt and return the recovered key. If all single-flip attempts fail, we proceed to the next stage, where we consider cases with two reverse flips. This stage may require up to approximately $\binom{704 \cdot (1-p_1)}{2}$ solving attempts – one for each pair of 1-valued bits in the corrupted key. If we are still unsuccessful, the method continues by assuming three reverse flips, then four, and so on, systematically increasing the number of assumed reverse flips and addressing each possible combination accordingly until the key is recovered or all combinations are exhausted.

3.2 Improved Algorithm via Probabilistic-Guided SAT-Solvers

We present two improvements to the algorithm described above. The first leverages the heuristic outlined in Sect. 2. Instead of iterating over the 1-valued bits or pairs of 1-valued bits in an arbitrary order and applying the SAT solver in each iteration, we order the executions based on the heuristic's estimations. This approach results in a shorter reconstruction process, as SAT instances that are more likely to identify the reversely flipped bits are prioritized. It is important to note that the runtime of computing this ordering is negligible compared to that of the SAT algorithm.

The second improvement involves grouping SAT instances and solving them together. At low corruption rates, the overall runtime of the baseline algorithm is primarily determined by the number of SAT solver runs and less by their hardness. This is because for feasible constraints, identifying a valid assignment is computationally simpler compared to exhaustively ruling out all possible assignments. Consequently, the overhead introduced by infeasible SAT solver runs becomes a dominant factor in the overall runtime, particularly at low corruption rates.

To reduce the number of SAT solver applications, we consolidate individual instances into new grouped instances by combining their constraints using an OR clause. This approach reduces the total number of instances to solve, albeit each grouped instance becomes incrementally harder to solve. One needs to find the right balance between reducing the number of instances and having as simple instances as possible. The optimal group size (and consequently the number of grouped instances) depends on various factors, such as hardware capabilities, solver efficiency, key size, and specific task requirements. Here, we present a simple version, that can be tuned for a specific task. The parameter that should be tuned is the size of the groups.

Interestingly, the inspiration for the latter improvement stemmed from an analysis of the findings of [11]. Counterintuitively, as the corruption rate increases, the running time of the algorithm decreases. This observation might seem surprising, as one would expect the problem to become more challenging with added noise. However, it was noted that an increase of the corruption rate actually reduces the number of 1-valued bits in the corrupted keys. Upon a closer examination of the baseline algorithms, this reduction translates into fewer iterations within the loops iterating over the 1-valued bits. It is crucial to emphasize that, despite the decrease in running time with higher corruption rates, each individual instance becomes more difficult to solve due to the increased noise.

The pseudocode improving the baseline algorithm is presented in Algorithm 1. For simplicity, we do not handle cases in which the number of reversely flipped bits exceeds two. In the algorithm, we denote by $\mathrm{SAT}(\Psi_{AES}, V)$ the result obtained from applying the solver to an instance of an AES key, where all bits corresponding to V must have the value 1, and Ψ_{AES} represents the constraints defined by the key expansion function.

It is important to highlight two aspects of our algorithm. Firstly, it can be efficiently parallelized without additional overhead because the $|V| + \binom{|V|}{2}$ SAT instances in steps 13 and 19 are independent in the sense that they may be solved simultaneously. This parallelization capability allows for concurrent execution of these steps, reducing overall computation time.

Secondly, the current implementation of the algorithm does not fully leverage the capabilities of our heuristic. Specifically, it focuses solely on the probabilities associated with bits that are set to 1 in the corrupted key. This approach addresses only a subset of the set of bits involved in the decryption process. Future enhancements could explore extending the heuristic to encompass a broader range of bits, thereby potentially improving overall performance and accuracy.

4 Evaluation of the Improved Algorithm

In this section we compare our algorithm with state-of-the-art SAT and MAX-SAT approaches for key reconstruction and show superior performance when our heuristics are incorporated into a SAT-based solver, significantly outperforming the MAX-SAT approach of [12].

We evaluated the algorithm with several SAT solvers [1,13,20] and several MAX-SAT solvers [14,16,17,22]. MiniSat emerged as the best SAT solver for this task and WBO as the best MAX-SAT solver. Both SAT and MAX-SAT baselines used a Java library[1] with default settings.

All measurements ran on the same laptop (Intel i5-6200, 2.3 GHz, 8 GB RAM). We executed 1000 instances per corruption rate and solver family, fixed $p_0 = 0.001$; the success rate was 100% for all methods and rates.

To analyze performance, we stratified by the number of reverse flips (0, 1, 2) and then formed weighted averages, ignoring > 2 flips as negligible. The consolidated results appear in Table 1. Each row corresponds to a corruption rate p_1; columns report our full method, our method without grouping, and the SAT and MAX-SAT baselines. The final three rows give the weighted averages across

[1] https://github.com/logic-ng/LogicNG.

Algorithm 1. Improved Reconstruction Algorithm via Probabilistic-Guided SAT-Solvers

Input:
SAT – Underlying SAT solver
Ψ_{AES} – Constraints for an AES key
CorruptedKey – the corrupted key $\vec{m} = (m_1, \ldots, m_n)$
`Size` – the number of instances in a joined instance
Output: The reconstructed key
procedure RECOVER(S)AT, Ψ_{AES}, CorruptedKey, `Size`
    Let V be the set of all positive literals in the CorruptedKey ($V = \{v_i | m_i = 1\}$)
    if SAT(Ψ_{AES}, V) **then** return SAT.key
    Apply the heuristic on V, and create the probability array P, which estimates for each bit its probability of being flipped.
    Sort V by P in decreasing order to get $O = (o_1, o_2, \ldots, o_{|V|})$
    Partition O to $\frac{|V|}{\texttt{Size}}$ sets, $G = (\{o_1, \ldots o_{\texttt{size}}\}, \ldots, \{o_{|V|-\texttt{size}+1}, \ldots, o_{|V|}\})$
    for i from 1 to $|G|$ **do**
        if SAT($\Psi_{AES}, V \setminus G_i$) **then** return SAT.key
    for i from 1 to $|G| - 1$ **do**
        for j from $i + 1$ to $|G|$ **do**
            if SAT($\Psi_{AES}, V \setminus \{G_i \cup G_j\}$) **then** return SAT.key
    return "Not found".

reverse-flip counts, using $(1 - p_0)^{704} = 0.494$ for 0 flips, $704 p_0 (1 - p_0)^{703} = 0.348$ for 1 flip, and $\binom{704}{2} p_0^2 (1 - p_0)^{702} = 0.123$ for 2 flips.

Our algorithm yields shorter reconstruction times than the best competitor, except for two reverse flips at $p_1 = 0.5$, where MAX-SAT is faster by 0.021 s. For each corruption rate, on average, we surpass the state of the art.

Unlike [12], our results show similar performance for the SAT and MAX-SAT baselines. This likely reflects implementation differences and our choice to avoid parallelization for a fair comparison.

Comparing the SAT baseline to our improved SAT without grouping: with no reverse flip the algorithms coincide, since the heuristic matters only when there is at least one reverse flip. When reverse flips occur, our method yields large gains; for two reverse flips at $p_1 = 0.7$ the time is $13\times$ shorter (1.429 vs. 18.6889). Grouping further helps at low corruption rates with at least one reverse flip, consistent with [12], and is evident in the runtime drop of the standard SAT baseline near $p_1 = 0.5$.

5 Conclusions and Future Work

We presented a bit-likelihood heuristic for Cold Boot Attack (CBA) key reconstruction. The heuristic estimates the probability of each bit in the corrupted key to have been 0 or 1 in the initial key. We showed, both theoretically for the general case and empirically for AES, that it enables more efficient algorithms.

We proposed two practical enhancements:

Table 1. Reconstruction times (sec.) by number of reverse flips and corruption rate.

Reverse flips	Corruption Rate	Algorithm			
		Ours	Ours without grouping	SAT	MAX-SAT
0	0.3	**0.018**	**0.018**	**0.018**	0.088
0	0.5	**0.021**	**0.021**	**0.021**	0.090
0	0.7	**0.391**	**0.391**	**0.391**	0.421
1	0.3	**0.022**	0.090	0.260	0.133
1	0.5	**0.052**	0.067	0.098	0.137
1	0.7	**2.861**	**2.853**	3.301	4.634
2	0.3	**0.060**	1.429	18.688	0.181
2	0.5	**0.235**	1.852	5.740	**0.214**
2	0.7	**15.711**	**15.814**	20.141	77.160
average	0.3	**0.025**	0.224	2.485	0.116
average	0.5	**0.060**	0.271	0.777	0.123
average	0.7	**3.236**	**3.245**	3.957	11.720

1. A SAT-based acceleration that uses the heuristic to prioritize the search space and prune unlikely assignments.
2. A grouping technique that reduces the number of solver invocations and therefore the overall running time.

Together, these improvements yield faster recovery of AES-128 keys across corruption rates.

We also clarified the relation between existing approaches. In [12], SAT and MAX-SAT are presented as distinct. In practice they are effectively similar when MAX-SAT follows the UNSAT strategy that repeatedly calls a SAT solver. This observation suggests that alternative MAX-SAT strategies may provide further gains and therefore merit systematic study.

Regarding neural CBA [27], we hypothesize that the network implicitly computes a form of our heuristic, refines it iteratively, and learns clause-aware weighting that favors bits appearing in more constraints. This interpretation is consistent with the architecture reported there.

Future work includes: evaluating Weighted MAX-SAT and MAX-SAT strategies that do not rely on UNSAT, identifying which is best for CBA-derived instances, and extending the algorithm in Sect. 3 to exploit the full per-bit probability estimates, including probabilities of flips to 0 as well as to 1.

References

1. Audemard, G., Simon, L.: Glucose: a solver that predicts learnt clauses quality. SAT Competition, pp. 7–8 (2009)

2. Bali, R.S.: Cold boot attack on cell phones, cryptographic attacks. ResearchGate (2018). https://www.researchgate.net/publication/326211565_Cold_Boot_Attack_On_Cell_Phones_Cryptographic_Attacks. Accessed 8 Aug 2025
3. Bauer, J., Gruhn, M., Freiling, F.C.: Lest we forget: cold-boot attacks on scrambled DDR3 memory. Digit. Investig. **16**, S65–S74 (2016)
4. BooleWorks GmbH: LogicNG: The Next Generation Logic Framework. https://logicng.org. Accessed 8 Aug 2025
5. Daemen, J., Rijmen, V.: The Rijndael encryption algorithm. In: AES Candidate Submission (1999), precursor to FIPS PUB 197
6. Fu, Z., Malik, S.: On solving the partial MAX-SAT problem. In: Biere, A., Gomes, C.P. (eds.) SAT 2006. LNCS, vol. 4121, pp. 252–265. Springer, Heidelberg (2006). https://doi.org/10.1007/11814948_25
7. Halderman, J.A., et al.: Lest we remember: cold-boot attacks on encryption keys. Commun. ACM **52**(5), 91–98 (2009)
8. Heninger, N.A.: Error Correction and the Cryptographic Key. Princeton University (2011)
9. Kamal, A.A., Youssef, A.M.: Applications of sat solvers to AES key recovery from decayed key schedule images. In: 2010 Fourth International Conference on Emerging Security Information Systems and Technologies (SECURWARE), pp. 216–220. IEEE (2010)
10. Lafitte, F., Nakahara, J., Jr., Van Heule, D.: Applications of sat solvers in cryptanalysis: finding weak keys and preimages. J. Satisfiability Boolean Model. Comput. **9**(1), 1–25 (2014)
11. Liao, X.: Maximum satisfiability approach to game theory and network security. Ph.D. thesis, Kyushu University (2013)
12. Liao, X., Zhang, H., Koshimura, M., Fujita, H., Hasegawa, R.: Using maxsat to correct errors in AES key schedule images. In: 2013 IEEE 25th International Conference on Tools with Artificial Intelligence, pp. 284–291. IEEE (2013)
13. Liffiton, M.H., Maglalang, J.C.: A cardinality solver: more expressive constraints for free. In: Cimatti, A., Sebastiani, R. (eds.) SAT 2012. LNCS, vol. 7317, pp. 485–486. Springer, Heidelberg (2012). https://doi.org/10.1007/978-3-642-31612-8_47
14. Martins, R., Joshi, S., Manquinho, V., Lynce, I.: Incremental cardinality constraints for MaxSAT. In: O'Sullivan, B. (ed.) CP 2014. LNCS, vol. 8656, pp. 531–548. Springer, Cham (2014). https://doi.org/10.1007/978-3-319-10428-7_39
15. Martins, R., Manquinho, V., Lynce, I.: Parallel search for maximum satisfiability. AI Commun. **25**(2), 75–95 (2012)
16. Martins, R., Manquinho, V., Lynce, I.: Open-WBO: a modular MaxSAT solver. In: Sinz, C., Egly, U. (eds.) SAT 2014. LNCS, vol. 8561, pp. 438–445. Springer, Cham (2014). https://doi.org/10.1007/978-3-319-09284-3_33
17. Morgado, A., Dodaro, C., Marques-Silva, J.: Core-guided MaxSAT with soft cardinality constraints. In: O'Sullivan, B. (ed.) CP 2014. LNCS, vol. 8656, pp. 564–573. Springer, Cham (2014). https://doi.org/10.1007/978-3-319-10428-7_41
18. Müller, T., Spreitzenbarth, M.: Frost - forensic recovery of scrambled telephones. In: International Conference on Applied Cryptography and Network Security (2013). https://api.semanticscholar.org/CorpusID:2637379. Accessed 8 Aug 2025
19. Skorobogatov, S.: Data remanence in flash memory devices. Cryptogr. Hardware Embed. Syst.-CHES **2005**, 339–353 (2005)
20. Sorensson, N., Een, N.: Minisat v1. 13-a sat solver with conflict-clause minimization. SAT **2005**(53), 1–2 (2005)

21. Tanigaki, T., Kunihiro, N.: Maximum likelihood-based key recovery algorithm from decayed key schedules. In: Kwon, S., Yun, A. (eds.) ICISC 2015. LNCS, vol. 9558, pp. 314–328. Springer, Cham (2016). https://doi.org/10.1007/978-3-319-30840-1_20
22. Terra-Neves, M., Lynce, I., Manquinho, V.: Non-portfolio approaches for distributed maximum satisfiability. In: 2016 IEEE 28th International Conference on Tools with Artificial Intelligence (ICTAI), pp. 436–443. IEEE (2016)
23. Threatpost: Researchers heat up cold boot attack that works on all laptops (2018). https://threatpost.com/researchers-heat-up-cold-boot-attack-that-works-on-all-laptops/137466/. Accessed 8 Aug 2025
24. Yitbarek, S.F., Aga, M.T., Das, R., Austin, T.: Cold boot attacks are still hot: security analysis of memory scramblers in modern processors. In: 2017 IEEE International Symposium on High Performance Computer Architecture (HPCA), pp. 313–324. IEEE (2017)
25. ZDNet: New cold boot attack affects nearly all modern computers (2018). https://www.zdnet.com/article/new-cold-boot-attack-affects-nearly-all-modern-computers/. Accessed 8 Aug 2025
26. ZDNet: New cold boot attack affects seven years of LG Android smartphones (2023). https://www.zdnet.com/article/new-cold-boot-attack-affects-seven-years-of-lg-android-smartphones/. Accessed 8 Aug 2025
27. Zimerman, I., Nachmani, E., Wolf, L.: Recovering AES keys with a deep cold boot attack. In: International Conference on Machine Learning, pp. 12955–12966. PMLR (2021)

DiSK - A Deniable Split KEM from Lattices

Brian Goncalves(✉) and Atefeh Mashatan

Cybersecurity Research Lab, Toronto Metropolitan University, Toronto, ON, Canada
{bgoncalves,amashatan}@torontomu.ca

Abstract. As the pending migration away from quantum-vulnerable cryptography becomes a reality, widely used key-exchange protocols like Signal need to be urgently replaced. One tool for finding replacements are deniable split Key Encapsulation Mechanisms (KEMs). Split KEMs are designed to mimic the message structure of Diffie-Hellman-based protocols such as X3DH used in Signal. In this work, we present a new deniable split KEM, which we call DiSK (Deniable Split KEM) based on the Module Learning With Error problem.

Keywords: Lattice Cryptography · Module Learning With Error · Quantum-Resistant Cryptography · Public-Key Cryptography · Key Encapsulation

1 Introduction

Shor's algorithm and quantum computers have threatened to render two of the most common public-key cryptosystems (RSA and ECC) completely insecure [21]. Countless hours of research have been spent globally to build new quantum-resistant cryptosystems. The biggest milestone of this effort so far has been the National Institute of Standards and Technology (NIST), which has announced their new standards for quantum-resistant algorithms [2,3,9,19]. Unfortunately, the efforts of NIST do not cover the full breadth of cryptographic algorithms that are susceptible to Shor's algorithm. An important example of the type of protocols not standardized by NIST is key-exchange protocols, which are fundamental for modern digital communication. In particular, Diffie-Hellman (DH) key exchange [10] is at the heart of one of the most famous and widely used end-to-end encrypted instant messaging protocols, the Signal Protocol [1], which is used by a number of encrypted messaging applications, including Signal and WhatsApp [14]. The Signal protocol is built on a variant of DH called the Extended Triple Diffie-Hellman (X3DH) [17]. Two important benefits of X3DH are that of asynchronicity and deniability; Alice does not need Bob online to derive the session key, and she can deny having contacted Bob.

In order to address the imminent need to migrate away from (X3)DH-based protocols, Brendel *et al.* defined a new type of Key Encapsulation Mechanism (KEM) that mirrored the message flow of DH, which they called a *split KEM*

Y. Kim et al. (Eds.): CANS 2025, LNCS 16351, pp. 591–601, 2026.
https://doi.org/10.1007/978-981-95-4434-9_28

[7]. Split KEMs function by encapsulation using Alice's private key and Bob's public key; while decapsulation requires Bob's private key and Alice's public key. A part of the motivation for this new primitive was the fact that attempting to replicate X3DH with standard KEMs required losing asynchronicity in order to replicate all X3DH key shares. However, this initial attempt to replace X3DH was incomplete because X3DH offered a form of (implicit) authentication and deniability that was not defined in Brendel *et al.* . Collins *et al.* completed the vision of split KEMs as a replacement for X3DH by formalizing what it means for a split KEM to be deniable [8].

1.1 Our Contribution

We present a new deniable split KEM is based on the Module Learning With Error (MLWE) problem [5,16]. The MLWE problem is the foundation of two of NIST's standardized quantum-resistant algorithms, namely ML-KEM (formerly CRYSTALS-Kyber) [3] and ML-DSA (formerly CRYSTALS-Dilithium) [19].

The construction itself is inspired by Gajland *et al.*'s Non-Interactive Key Exchange (NIKE) SWOOSH, itself based on MLWE [11]. In SWOOSH, Alice and Bob's public keys are, respectively, $\vec{s_1}^T A + \vec{e_1}^T$ and $A\vec{s_2} + \vec{e_2}$ for a public uniformly random matrix A. Their secret keys are the vectors $\vec{s_1}$ and $\vec{s_2}$, which are sampled from an appropriate error distribution. To compute the shared key, Alice computes $\vec{s_1}^T(A\vec{s_2} + \vec{e_2})$, while Bob computes $(\vec{s_1}^T A + \vec{e_1}^T)\vec{s_2}$, before both adding a random shift r, and using a reconciliation function to produce a random key. The random shift ensures that the resulting vector is uniformly distributed.

Our split KEM, which we call DiSK (<u>D</u>en<u>i</u>able <u>S</u>plit <u>K</u>EM), is constructed in the following manner: Alice and Bob have their own SWOOSH key pair on a shared public matrix A. To encapsulate, Alice generates an ephemeral secret, $\vec{s_c}$, and error $\vec{e_c}$ and creates a SWOOSH-style public key as above using $A, \vec{s_c}, \vec{e_c}$ to be sent as a ciphertext. She then computes two SWOOSH session keys using her secret key and the ephemeral secret to multiply on the left with Bob's public key. Finally, she XORs these two keys together to produce the final key. We note here that this method of constructing a split KEM from a NIKE can be generalized to apply to other NIKEs as well. However, whether or not the resulting split KEM is deniable is a separate question and requires a case-by-case investigation.

1.2 Related Work

In the original split KEM paper, Brendel *et al.* presented two constructions for split KEMs. The first is based on the Ring Learning with Errors problem, and the other is based on a classically hard but quantum-vulnerable problem Gap Hashed Diffie-Hellman introduced by Kiltz [7,15]. As previously stated, their work did not demonstrate any notion of deniability of their split KEM and so cannot directly be used to replace X3DH/Signal style protocols.

Goncalves and Mashatan approached the topic of split KEMs by developing a generic combiner that transforms a public-key encryption scheme, a signature algorithm, and a constrained PRF [12]. Although their approach leads to a method for building adaptively secure split KEMs, assuming the existence of sufficiently secure inputs, they do not address the topic of deniability either. Moreover, it is unlikely that their construction possesses any deniability due to the use of a traditional signature being a part of the ciphertext.

Finally, Collins *et al.* were the first to introduce the definition of deniability for split KEMs, along with the first such split KEM FrodoKEX+, based on LWE [20]. In addition to deniability, they introduced several other security notions for split KEMs, including UNF-1KCA and IND-1BatchCCA security. They present a QROM transform to give certain types of split KEMs these properties and build a secure DAKE as a potential replacement for the X3DH protocol. We present an alternative option to FrodoKEX+, based on MLWE. Given that NIST has standardized two MLWE-based algorithms, it is more likely that attention will be focused on optimizing and analyzing MLWE-based schemes as they become the default standard in the near future. Additionally, our work further diversifies the field of choices for deniable split KEMs, allowing for more plug-and-play options.

2 Preliminaries

We view a matrix as the a set of column vectors and denote the matrix by capital letters (e.g., A), and we denote (column) vectors with lowercase letters and arrows (e.g., $\vec{a}$). If $\vec{x}$ is a vector, then $\vec{x}_i$ denotes the i-th coordinate of $\vec{x}$. A function $f(n)$ is negligible (in n) if for every $c > 0$, there exists a N such that $f(n) < \frac{1}{n^c}$ for all $n > N$. By $y \leftarrow \mathcal{A}(x)$, we denote an algorithm, $\mathcal{A}$, that runs on input x, and output y. When $\mathcal{A}$ has access to an oracle, $\mathcal{B}$, which it can query, we write this as $\mathcal{A}(x)^{\mathcal{B}}$. We will refer to specific subroutines within $\mathcal{A}(\cdot)$ as $\mathcal{A}$.Subroutine. We write $x \leftarrow S$ to denote that x was outputted by S probabilistically according to an internal distribution. If S is some space, such as $\{0,1\}^l$, then we implicitly mean that x is sampled uniformly at random and denote uniform sampling with $\leftarrow\!\!\$$. We will consider all adversaries as algorithms (either classical or quantum) that are probabilistic polynomial-time (PPT) on their input length. We adopt the convention that QPT means that they are a quantum PPT algorithm.

2.1 Lattices

Let $\mathbb{Z}$ denote the ring of integers, q a prime number, and δ a power of 2. Then, $\mathbb{Z}_q$ is the ring of integers modulo q and $\mathcal{R} = \mathbb{Z}[X]/(X^\delta + 1)$ is the ring of polynomials modulo $X^\delta + 1$. Furthermore, $\mathcal{R}_q = \mathbb{Z}_q[X]/(X^\delta + 1)$ is the ring of polynomials modulo $X^\delta + 1$ whose coefficients are reduced modulo q.

The coefficient vector for a polynomial $f \in \mathcal{R}_q$ will be denoted as $\vec{f} \in \mathbb{Z}_q^\delta$, with the convention that f_0 is the constant term of f and f_i is the i-th term. Given an element $f_i \in \mathbb{Z}_q$, $\|f_i\|$ will represent $\|f_i \bmod q\|$. We define ℓ_∞ in $\mathcal{R}_q$ and $\mathcal{R}_q^k$ as follows, for $f = \sum_{i=0}^{\delta-1} c_i X^i \in \mathcal{R}_q$ and $\vec{f} \in \mathcal{R}_q^k$,

$$\|f\|_\infty = \max_{1 \le i \le k} \|c_i\|_\infty \text{ and } \left\|\vec{f}\right\|_\infty = \max_{1 \le i \le k} \|f_i\|_\infty .$$

The MLWE problem is parameterized by positive integers n, m, q a prime, δ a power of two, and an error distribution χ over $R_q = \mathbb{Z}_q[X]/(X^\delta + 1)$. Note that we implicitly assume these parameters are functions of some security parameter κ, which determines the hardness of the following problem in terms of bits.

Definition 1 (Decisional MLWE$_{n,m,q,\delta,\chi}$ Problem [5,16]**).** *Let $\mathcal{A}$ be a QPT deciding algorithm. Sample $A \leftarrow_\$ R_q^{n\times m}$ and $b \leftarrow_\$ \{0,1\}$ independently uniformly at random. If $b = 0$, then sample $\vec{s} \leftarrow \chi^m$ and $\vec{e} \leftarrow \chi^n$ and return $(A, \vec{t} = A\vec{s} + \vec{e})$ to $\mathcal{A}$. Else, $\mathcal{A}$ is given $\vec{u} \leftarrow R_q^n$ sampled uniformly at random. Eventually, $\mathcal{A}$ outputs a guess b' and wins if $b' = b$. We define the advantage of $\mathcal{A}$ winning for fixed $A \leftarrow_\$ R_q^{n\times m}$, $\vec{s} \leftarrow \chi^m$, and $\vec{e} \leftarrow \chi^n$ as,*

$$\mathsf{Adv}_{\mathcal{A}}^{MLWE}(\kappa) := \left|\Pr\left[b' \stackrel{?}{=} b : b \leftarrow_\$ \{0,1\}, \vec{t_0} = A\vec{s} + \vec{e}, \vec{t_1} = \vec{u} \leftarrow_\$ R_q^n, b' \leftarrow \mathcal{A}(A, t_b)\right] - \tfrac{1}{2}\right|.$$

Reconciliation Function. Reconciliation functions, such as Rec, take an element in $\mathcal{R}_q$ and map it to a bit string of length d, by rounding the coefficients in $\mathbb{Z}_q$ to 1 if it is in the interval $[\frac{q}{4}, \frac{3q}{4}]$, and 0 otherwise. Importantly, the probability of any $v \in \mathbb{Z}_q$ rounding to 0 or 1 is negligibly close to $\frac{1}{2}$ for a sufficient choice of q. Moreover, attempting to guess the output k of Rec would involve guessing 2^{d-1} keys even given the MLWE public keys, which becomes infeasible for large d [11].

2.2 Split KEMs

Definition 2 (Split KEM [7]**).** *A split KEM $\mathfrak{K}$ consists of four algorithms* DKeyGen, EKeyGen, sEncap, *and* sDecap.

- ***split KEM key generation:*** *for decapsulator and encapsulator, respectively: $(D, d) \leftarrow$ DKeyGen(1^κ) and $(E, e) \leftarrow$ EKeyGen(1^κ) are probabilistic algorithms that output a pair of keys, consisting of a public key (denoted with capital letters) and a secret key (denoted by lowercase letters).*
- ***split KEM encapsulation:*** *$(c, k) \leftarrow$ sEncap(e, D) is a probabilistic algorithm executed by the encapsulator. It takes as input e, the secret key of the encapsulator and D, the public key of the decapsulator. It outputs the shared secret k along with its encapsulation c.*
- ***split KEM decapsulation:*** *$k/\bot \leftarrow$ sDecap(d, E, c) is a deterministic algorithm executed by the decapsulator. On input a ciphertext c, the secret key of the decapsulator d, and the public key of the encapsulator E, it outputs the decapsulation k of c or $\bot$, if the operation fails.*

Definition 3. *(Split KEM* IND-CCA *[7]) Let $\mathfrak{K} =$* (EKeyGen, DKeyGen, sEncap, sDecap) *be a split KEM with key space $\mathcal{K_S}$. Let $l \in \{n, s, m\}$ (n means no queries, s means single, m means polynomial) and $r \in \{n, m\}$. We say $\mathfrak{K}$*

provides lr-indistinguishability under chosen-ciphertext attacks, or, $\mathfrak{K}$ *is lr-*IND-CCA*-secure*[1]*, if for all adversaries* $\mathcal{A}$ *the advantage for winning the experiment* $\mathrm{Expt}^{lr\text{-IND-CCA}}_{\mathfrak{K},\mathcal{A}}(\kappa)$ *is a negligible function in* κ*. Where* $\mathrm{Expt}^{lr\text{-IND-CCA}}_{\mathfrak{K},\mathcal{A}}(\kappa)$ *is depicted in Fig. 1, and the advantage* $\mathsf{Adv}^{lr\text{-IND-CCA}}_{\mathfrak{K},\mathcal{A}}(\kappa)$ *for winning is defined as,*

$$\mathsf{Adv}^{lr\text{-IND-CCA}}_{\mathfrak{K},\mathcal{A}}(\kappa) := \left|\Pr[\mathrm{Expt}^{lr\text{-IND-CCA}}_{\mathfrak{K},\mathcal{A}}(\kappa) \to 1] - \frac{1}{2}\right|.$$

$\mathrm{Expt}^{lr-\text{IND-CCA}}_{\mathfrak{K},\mathcal{A}}(\kappa)$:

1. $n_l, n_r \leftarrow 0$
2. $(D^*, d^*) \leftarrow \mathsf{DKeyGen}(1^\kappa)$
3. $(E^*, e^*) \leftarrow \mathsf{EKeyGen}(1^\kappa)$
4. $c^*, k_0^* \leftarrow \mathsf{sEncap}(e^*, D^*)$
5. $k_1^* \leftarrow_{\$} \mathcal{K_S}$
6. $b \leftarrow_{\$} \{0,1\}$
7. $b' \leftarrow \mathcal{A}^{\mathcal{O}_\mathcal{E}, \mathcal{O}_\mathcal{D}}(E^*, D^*, c^*, k_b^*)$
8. Return $b \stackrel{?}{=} b'$

$\mathcal{O}_D(E', c)$:

1. If $n_l \geq l$, return $\perp$
2. Else $n_l{+}{=}1$
3. If $(E', c) = (E^*, c^*)$, return $\perp$
4. Else $k \leftarrow \mathsf{sDecap}(d, E', c)$

$\mathcal{O}_E(D')$:

1. If $n_r \geq r$, return $\perp$
2. Else $n_r{+}{=}1$
3. $(c, k) \leftarrow \mathsf{sEncap}(e, D')$
4. If $(D', c) = (D^*, c^*)$, return $\perp$
5. Else return (c, k)

$\mathrm{Expt}^{\mathsf{REAL}}_{\mathfrak{K},\mathcal{S},\mathcal{A}}(\kappa)$:

1. $(D^*, d^*) \leftarrow \mathsf{DKeyGen}(1^\kappa)$
2. $(E^*, e^*) \leftarrow \mathsf{EKeyGen}(1^\kappa)$
3. $c^*, k^* \leftarrow \mathsf{sEncap}(e^*, D^*)$
4. $b \leftarrow \mathcal{A}(E^*, D^*, d^*, c^*, k^*)$
5. Return b

$\mathrm{Expt}^{\mathsf{SIM}}_{\mathfrak{K},\mathcal{S},\mathcal{A}}(\kappa)$:

1. $(D^*, d^*) \leftarrow \mathsf{DKeyGen}(1^\kappa)$
2. $(E^*, e^*) \leftarrow \mathsf{EKeyGen}(1^\kappa)$
3. $c^*, k^* \leftarrow \mathcal{S}(E^*, d^*)$
4. $b \leftarrow \mathcal{A}(E^*, D^*, d^*, c^*, k^*)$
5. Return b

Fig. 1. The lr-IND-CCA and Deniability experiment for Split KEMs.

Definition 4. *(Split KEM Deniability [8]) Let* $\mathfrak{K}$ *be a split KEM. We say that* $\mathfrak{K}$ *is* DENY *if there exists a simulator* $\mathcal{S}$ *such that for all adversaries* $\mathcal{A}$ *the advantage between winning in the experiments* $\mathrm{Expt}^{\mathsf{REAL}}_{\mathfrak{K},\mathcal{S},\mathcal{A}}(\kappa)$ *and* $\mathrm{Expt}^{\mathsf{SIM}}_{\mathfrak{K},\mathcal{S},\mathcal{A}}(\kappa)$ *is a negligible function in* κ*. Where* $\mathrm{Expt}^{\mathsf{REAL}}_{\mathfrak{K},\mathcal{S},\mathcal{A}}(\kappa)$ *and* $\mathrm{Expt}^{\mathsf{SIM}}_{\mathfrak{K},\mathcal{S},\mathcal{A}}(\kappa)$ *are depicted in Fig. 1, and the advantage* $\mathsf{Adv}^{\mathsf{DENY}}_{\mathfrak{K},\mathcal{A}}(\kappa)$ *is defined as*

$$\mathsf{Adv}^{\mathsf{DENY}}_{\mathfrak{K},\mathcal{A}}(\kappa) := \left|\Pr[\mathrm{Expt}^{\mathsf{REAL}}_{\mathfrak{K},\mathcal{S},\mathcal{A}}(\kappa) \to 1] - \Pr[\mathrm{Expt}^{\mathsf{SIM}}_{\mathfrak{K},\mathcal{S},\mathcal{A}}(\kappa) \to 1]\right|.$$

3 Split KEM Construction and Security

We present our split KEM, DiSK (Deniable Split KEM), $\mathfrak{D}$, and present it in Fig. 2. As mentioned above, the inspiration for the construction is the NIKE

[1] nn-IND-CCA-security is analogous to the IND-CPA-security for standard KEMs, as both attackers have no oracle access. We chose to use the default split KEM notation of nn-IND-CCA.

SWOOSH. In the nn-IND-CCA-security experiment, split KEMs behave like a passive NIKE. One potential issue with naively using NIKEs, such as SWOOSH, directly in key-exchange protocols is that in each session between two fixed parties the resulting key would be constant across all sessions. As a split KEM, DiSK overcomes this potential problem as sEncap is designed to run an ephemeral instance of SWOOSH. The random oracle is used to add a random shift to ensure that the intermediate keys, κ_i, are uniformly distributed in $\mathcal{R}_q$, resulting in unconditional correctness in any ring [11]. Importantly, the use of a random oracle has no bearing on the security of our construction as no secret values are used in computing the random shift.

$\mathfrak{D}.\mathsf{EKeyGen}(1^\kappa)$:

1. $\vec{s_E}, \vec{e_E} \leftarrow \chi^N$
2. $E = \vec{s_E}^T A + \vec{e_E}^T$
3. $e = \vec{s_E}$

$\mathfrak{D}.\mathsf{DKeyGen}(1^\kappa)$:

1. $\vec{s_D}, \vec{e_D} \leftarrow \chi^N$
2. $D = A\vec{s_D} + \vec{e_D}$
3. $d = \vec{s_D}$

$\mathfrak{D}.\mathsf{sEncap}(e, D)$:

1. $\vec{s_c}, \vec{e_c} \leftarrow \chi^N$
2. $c = \vec{s_c}^T A + \vec{e_c}^T$
3. $h = \mathsf{H}(E, D, c)$
4. $\kappa_0 = \vec{s_c}^T D + h$
5. $\kappa_1 = \vec{s_E}^T D + h$
6. $k = \mathsf{Rec}(\kappa_0) \oplus \mathsf{Rec}(\kappa_1)$
7. Output (c, k)

$\mathfrak{D}.\mathsf{sDecap}(E, d, c)$:

1. $h' = \mathsf{H}(E, D, c)$
2. $\kappa_0' = c \cdot d + h'$
3. $\kappa_1' = E \cdot d + h'$
4. $k' = \mathsf{Rec}(\kappa_0') \oplus \mathsf{Rec}(\kappa_1')$

Fig. 2. Our nn-IND-CCA-secure split KEM, $\mathfrak{D}$. Public parameters $A, q, \delta, N, \mathcal{R}_q = \mathbb{Z}_q[X]/(X^\delta + 1)$, and $\mathsf{H} : \mathcal{R}_q^N \times \mathcal{R}_q^N \times \mathcal{R}_q^N \rightarrow \mathcal{R}_q$.

Theorem 1. *Assume the quantum hardness of the $MLWE_{N,N,q,\delta,\chi}$ problem and that B is a bound on the maximum absolute value of the support of χ, then for any QPT adversary $\mathcal{A}$, making an arbitrary number of queries to the random oracle $|\mathsf{H}\rangle$ (that may be in superposition), then the split KEM defined in Fig. 2 is a nn-IND-CCA-secure, deniable split KEM that is $\frac{16B^2\delta^2N}{q}$-correct.*

More precisely, for any efficient QPT adversary $\mathcal{A}$, against the nn-IND-CCA-security of the Split KEM $\mathfrak{D}$, of arbitrary query depth and total query term, there exist efficient QPT adversaries $\mathcal{B}_1, \mathcal{B}_2, \mathcal{B}_3, \mathcal{B}_4$, and $\mathcal{B}_5$ such that

$$\mathsf{Adv}_{\mathfrak{D},\mathcal{A}}^{nn\text{-}\mathsf{IND\text{-}CCA}}(\kappa) \leq \mathsf{Adv}_{\mathcal{B}_1}^{MLWE}(\kappa) + \frac{8B\delta}{q} + \mathsf{Adv}_{\mathcal{B}_2}^{MLWE}(\kappa) + \mathsf{Adv}_{\mathcal{B}_3}^{MLWE},$$

$$\mathsf{Adv}_{\mathfrak{D},\mathcal{A}}^{\mathsf{DENY}}(\kappa) \leq \frac{4B\delta}{q} + \mathsf{Adv}_{\mathcal{B}_4}^{MLWE}(\kappa) + \mathsf{Adv}_{\mathcal{B}_5}^{MLWE}.$$

Proof. We begin with the proof of DiSK being $\frac{16B^2\delta^2N}{q}$-correct. To demonstrate the correctness of $\mathfrak{D}$, we must show that $k = k'$ except with negligible probability. Let $A \leftarrow\!\!\$\, GL_N(\mathcal{R}_q)$ be the shared public matrix, and $(E, e) \leftarrow\!\!\$\, \mathfrak{D}.\mathsf{EKeyGen}(1^\kappa)$

and $(D, d) \leftarrow_{\$} \mathfrak{D}.\mathsf{DKeyGen}(1^\kappa)$, and fix $\vec{s_c}, \vec{e_c} \leftarrow \chi^N$, $c = \vec{s_c}^T A + \vec{e_c}^T$, and let $h = \mathsf{H}(E, D, c)$. By the definition of k, $\mathfrak{D}.\mathsf{sEncap}$, k' and $\mathfrak{D}.\mathsf{sDecap}$,

$$k = \mathsf{Rec}(\vec{s_c}^T A \vec{s_D} + h + \vec{s_c}^T \vec{e_D}) \oplus \mathsf{Rec}(\vec{s_E}^T A \vec{s_D} + h + \vec{s_E}^T \vec{e_D}, \tag{3.1}$$

$$k' = \mathsf{Rec}(\vec{s_c}^T A \vec{s_D} + h + \vec{e_c}^T \vec{s_D}) \oplus \mathsf{Rec}(\vec{s_E}^T A \vec{s_D} + h + \vec{e_E}^T \vec{s_D}). \tag{3.2}$$

Thus, a disagreement on the final key occurs when there is a rounding error in any term between (3.1) and (3.1). We will bound the size of the largest coefficients of the terms within Rec, beginning with the error terms. Note here that all error terms can be bounded in a similar fashion, and so we only need to consider one. Thus, without loss of generality, consider $\vec{s_c}^T \vec{e_D}$. By definition, the largest coefficient of $\vec{s_c}^T \vec{e_D}$ is $\left\| \vec{s_c}^T \vec{e_D} \right\|_\infty$. By the assumption of χ being bounded by B and the triangle inequality we obtain the following bounds on the size of the error terms n Eqs. (3.1) and (3.2),

$$\left\| \vec{s_c}^T \vec{e_D} \right\|_\infty = \left\| \sum_{i=0}^{N} s_{c,i} e_{D,i} \right\|_\infty \leq \sum_{i=0}^{N} \| s_{c,i} e_{D,i} \|_\infty \leq B^2 \delta N.$$

Thus, a rounding error can occur if there is at least one coefficient in $\vec{s_c}^T A \vec{s_D} + h$ or $\vec{s_E}^T A \vec{s_D} + h$, that is in the interval $I = \left[\frac{q}{4} \pm B^2 \delta N\right] \cup \left[\frac{3q}{4} \pm B^2 \delta N\right]$.

Since both terms are uniformly distributed in $\mathcal{R}_q$, as H is a random oracle, both terms may have a coefficient in I with probability at most $\frac{\delta \cdot |I|}{|\mathbb{Z}_q|} = \frac{4B^2\delta^2 N}{q}$. Thus, we can apply a union bound across all δ coefficients of both terms for a probability of $\frac{4B^2\delta^2 N}{q}$. By the independence of the rounding error occurring in either Eq. (3.1) or Eq. (3.2), we obtain the final correctness error probability of $4 \cdot \frac{4B^2\delta^2 N}{q} = \frac{16B^2\delta^2 N}{q}$.

We now present a high-level description of the proof that $\mathfrak{D}$ is nn-IND-CCA-secure via a series of game hops, beginning with the Game G_0.

Game G_0***:*** The starting game is simply the nn-IND-CCA-security experiment. Thus, by definition $\Pr[G_0 \to 1] = \mathsf{Adv}^{nn\text{-}\mathsf{IND\text{-}CCA}}_{\mathfrak{D},\mathcal{A}}(\kappa)$.

Game G_1***:*** In the next game, we change the decapsulator's public-key D^* to $\vec{u_1} \leftarrow_{\$} \mathcal{R}_q^N$, which is sampled uniformly at random. Any non-negligible difference in the probability of $\mathcal{A}$ winning between G_0 and G_1 can be used by an attacker, $\mathcal{B}_1$, to solve the $\text{MLWE}_{N,N,q,\delta,\chi}$ problem. Thus, we obtain that $|\Pr[G_0 \to 1] - \Pr[G_1 \to 1]| \leq \mathsf{Adv}^{\text{MLWE}}_{\mathcal{B}_1}(\kappa)$.

Game G_2***:*** For G_2, k_0^* is computed as $\mathsf{Rec}(\kappa_0 + \vec{e_0}) \oplus \mathsf{Rec}(\kappa_1 + \vec{e_1})$, where $\vec{e_0}, \vec{e_1} \leftarrow \chi^N$. This change can only be noticed if it causes a rounding error, the probability of this can be bounded above by $\frac{4B\delta}{q}$. Thus, by independence, we have $|\Pr[G_1 \to 1] - \Pr[G_2 \to 1]| \leq \frac{8B\delta}{q}$.

Game G_3***:*** Next, we replace E^* with the uniformly sampled $\vec{u_2}$, and replace $\kappa_1 + \vec{e_1}$ with a uniformly random vector $\vec{u_3}$. As $\kappa_1 + \vec{e_1}$ is already uniformly distributed, its replacement cannot be noticed. If the change to E^* causes a non-negligible change in the adversary's probability of winning then there exists a $\mathcal{B}_2$ that can efficiently solve the $\text{MLWE}_{N,N,q,\delta,\chi}$ problem. Thus, we have $|\Pr[G_2 \rightarrow 1] - \Pr[G_3 \rightarrow 1]| \leq \mathsf{Adv}_{\mathcal{B}_2}^{\text{MLWE}}(\kappa)$.

Game G_4***:*** For this game, we replace the ciphertext c^* with a uniformly sampled vector $\vec{u_4}$. Once again, any non-negligible change in $\mathcal{A}$'s probability of winning results in an efficient decision algorithm for a $\mathcal{B}_3$ against the (transposed) $\text{MLWE}_{N,N,q,\delta,\chi}$ problem for the public matrix A^T and either $A^T\vec{s_c} + \vec{e_c}$ or $\vec{u_4}$. Consequently, $|\Pr[G_3 \rightarrow 1] - \Pr[G_4 \rightarrow 1]| \leq \mathsf{Adv}_{\mathcal{B}_3}^{\text{MLWE}}(\kappa)$.

Game G_5***:*** In the final game G_5, we once again modify how the key k_0^* is computed again. In this Game, $\kappa_0 + \vec{e_0}$ is replaced by a uniformly random $\vec{u_5}$ so that $k_0^* = \mathsf{Rec}(\vec{u_5}) \oplus \mathsf{Rec}(\vec{u_3})$. Since $\kappa_0 + \vec{e_0}$ and $\vec{u_5}$ have the same distribution, we have $\Pr[G_4 \rightarrow 1] = \Pr[G_5 \rightarrow 1]$.

Furthermore, with this change, we also see that k_0^* and k_1^* are identically distributed. At this point, all values given to $\mathcal{A}$ are in fact uniformly sampled, so $\mathcal{A}$'s best strategy is to guess b', and so $\Pr[G_5 \rightarrow 1] = \frac{1}{2}$. By combining the above probabilities we have that $\mathfrak{D}$ is nn-IND-CCA-secure under the quantum hardness of the $\text{MLWE}_{N,N,q,\delta,\chi}$ problem.

We now demonstrate the DENY property of $\mathfrak{D}$ through a separate series of game hops between the REAL and SIM as defined in Fig. 1. We assume that all secret keys contain copies of their corresponding public keys.

Game H_0***:*** The real deniability game and so, $\Pr[H_0 \rightarrow 1] = \text{Expt}_{\mathfrak{D},\mathcal{S},\mathcal{A}}^{\mathsf{REAL}}(\kappa)$.

Game H_1***:*** In this game, k^* is modified to be computed as $\mathsf{Rec}(\kappa_0) \oplus \mathsf{Rec}(\kappa_1 + \vec{e})$, where $\vec{e}$ is a freshly sampled error vector from χ^N. As above, this change is only noticed if a rounding error occurs, the probability of which can be bounded above by $\frac{4B\delta}{q}$. Thus, we have $|\Pr[H_0 \rightarrow 1] - \Pr[H_1 \rightarrow 1]| \leq \frac{4B\delta}{q}$.

Game H_2***:*** Next, w we replace the encapsulator's public key, E^*, and $\kappa_1 + \vec{e}$, with $\vec{u_1}$ and $\vec{u_2}$, both chosen independently and uniformly at random. As mentioned above, $\kappa_1 + \vec{e}$ and $\vec{u_2}$ are identically distributed, so this change cannot be detected. By the $\text{MLWE}_{N,N,q,\delta,\chi}$ assumption, the change to E^* cannot be noticed except within negligible probability. Thus, $|\Pr[H_1 \rightarrow 1] - \Pr[H_2 \rightarrow 1]| \leq \mathsf{Adv}_{\mathcal{B}_4}^{\text{MLWE}}(\kappa)$.

Game H_3***:*** For the final game hop we change E^* back from a uniformly random vector to being computed as $\vec{s_E}^T A + \vec{e_E}^T$, where $\vec{s_E}, \vec{e_E} \leftarrow \chi^N$. Under the $\text{MLWE}_{N,N,q,\delta,\chi}$ assumption, this change cannot meaningfully change the behavior of $\mathcal{A}$. Thus, $|\Pr[H_2 \rightarrow 1] - \Pr[H_3 \rightarrow 1]| \leq \mathsf{Adv}_{\mathcal{B}_5}^{\text{MLWE}}(\kappa)$.

We now observe that H_3 is in fact $\text{Expt}_{\mathfrak{D},\mathcal{S},\mathcal{A}}^{\mathsf{SIM}}(\kappa)$. We then conclude that $\Pr[H_3 \rightarrow 1] = \text{Expt}_{\mathfrak{D},\mathcal{S},\mathcal{A}}^{\mathsf{SIM}}(\kappa)$. Thus, $\mathfrak{D}$ has the property DENY. □

4 Parameters and Comparisons

In Table 1, the parameters used by Gajland *et al.* for the passive version of SWOOSH to achieve at least 120-bits of security are presented [11]. An important thing to note in these parameters is that the modulus q is a large prime number for two reasons. First, the correctness of both SWOOSH and consequentially DiSK depends on q being large enough to bring the probability of errors to tolerable levels. Secondly, q is a prime near enough to a power of two to allow for more efficient field arithmetic.

Currently, there is only one other deniable split KEM based on a quantum hard problem, namely the FrodoKEX+ by Collins *et al.* [8], based on the KEM Frodo [4]. Table 2 summarizes the key differences between DiSK and FrodoKEX+. We note that there are two potential benefits for DiSK over FrodoKEX+. As two of the NIST-selected algorithms for standardization are based on the MLWE problem, the hardness of the MLWE problem has been highly scrutinized over the last eight years, providing it with an additional degree of confidence in its security[9]. Secondly, NIST has also announced that quantum-vulnerable algorithms will be depreciated starting in 2030 and disallowed by 2035 [18]. This means that rapid adoption of MLWE-based schemes is likely, and any future optimizations or performance gains of MLWE schemes may be applicable to DiSK.

Table 1. Parameter set for passive NIKE-SWOOSH [11] for at least 120-bit security.

Parameter	Description	Value
B	Upper bound on $\|\vec{s}\|_\infty$ and $\|\vec{e}\|_\infty$	1
q	Prime modulus	$2^{214} - 255$
δ	Dimension of $\mathcal{R}_q = \mathbb{Z}_q[X]/(X^d + 1)$	256
l	Number of factor of $X^\delta + 1 \bmod q$	128
N	Number of rows in public matrices $A_{E/D}$	32
n	Lattice dimension	8192
χ	Error Distribution	$\Pr[-1] = 25\%$ $\Pr[0] = 50\%$ $\Pr[1] = 25\%$

Table 2. Summary of Comparison between deniable split KEM constructions [8].

Construction	Security	Deniability	Hardness	Size
FrodoKEX+ [8]	OW-CPA decaps-OW-CPA	✓	LWE+ELWE	pk: 21.3 KB c: 72B
This Work (DiSK)	nn-IND-CCA	✓	MLWE	pk:112 KB c: 112 KB

5 Conclusion and Future Work

In this paper, a new deniable split KEM named DiSK based on the MLWE problem and SWOOSH was presented. Moreover, the keys and ciphertext being computed from MLWE instances allowed for a direct and tight security reduction in the quantum random oracle model.

One direction of future research is to construct a full Deniable Asynchronous Key Exchange (DAKE) from DiSK and its performance against previous works studying DAKEs such as SPQR [6], SC-AKE [13], and K-Waay [8]. Another avenue is to determine whether DiSK possesses any of the other security notions for split KEM as defined by Collins *et al.*, such as UNF-1KCA and IND-1BatchCCA security. Finally, how to construct a fully deniable *mm*-IND-CCA-secure split KEM from a quantum hard problem remains an open problem. A split KEM being *mm*-IND-CCA-secure means that it is possible to reuse the same secret key multiple times. Thus, constructing such a split KEM remains a crucial problem.

References

1. Signal protocol. Technical documentation. https://whispersystems.org/docs/
2. Post-Quantum Cryptography (2017). https://csrc.nist.gov/projects/post-quantum-cryptography
3. Module-lattice-based key-encapsulation mechanism standard. Tech. rep., Gaithersburg, MD (2024)
4. Bos, J., et al.: Frodo: Take off the ring! practical, quantum-secure key exchange from LWE. In: Proceedings of the 2016 ACM SIGSAC Conference on Computer and Communications Security, CCS '16, pp. 1006–1018. Association for Computing Machinery, New York (2016)
5. Brakerski, Z., Gentry, C., Vaikuntanathan, V.: (leveled) fully homomorphic encryption without bootstrapping. In: Proceedings of the 3rd Innovations in Theoretical Computer Science Conference, ITCS '12, pp. 309–325. Association for Computing Machinery, New York (2012)
6. Brendel, J., Fiedler, R., Günther, F., Janson, C., Stebila, D.: Post-quantum asynchronous deniable key exchange and the signal handshake. In: IACR Cryptology ePrint Archive (2021)
7. Brendel, J., Fischlin, M., Günther, F., Janson, C., Stebila, D.: Towards post-quantum security for signal's X3DH handshake. In: Jr., M.J.J., Dunkelman, O., O'Flynn, C. (eds.) Proc. 27th Conference on Selected Areas in Cryptography (SAC) 2020. LNCS, Springer (2020), to appear. Cryptology ePrint Archive, Report 2019/1356. http://eprint.iacr.org/2019/1356
8. Collins, D., Huguenin-Dumittan, L., Nguyen, N.K., Rolin, N., Vaudenay, S.: K-waay: fast and deniable post-quantum x3dh without ring signatures. In: Proceedings of the 33rd USENIX Conference on Security Symposium, SEC '24. USENIX Association, USA (2025)
9. Computer Security Division, I.T.L.: Selected algorithms 2022 - post-quantum cryptography: CSRC. https://csrc.nist.gov/projects/post-quantum-cryptography/selected-algorithms-2022

10. Diffie, W., Hellman, M.: New directions in cryptography. IEEE Trans. Inf. Theor. **22**(6), 644–654 (2006)
11. Gajland, P., de Kock, B., Quaresma, M., Malavolta, G., Schwabe, P.: SWOOSH: efficient lattice-based non-interactive key exchange. In: Balzarotti, D., Xu, W. (eds.) 33rd USENIX Security Symposium, USENIX Security 2024, Philadelphia, PA, USA, 14–16 August 2024. USENIX Association (2024). https://www.usenix.org/conference/usenixsecurity24/presentation/gajland
12. Goncalves, B., Mashatan, A.: Towards generalized Diffie-Hellman-Esque key agreement via generic split KEM construction. In: Proceedings of the 10th International Conference on Information Systems Security and Privacy - ICISSP, pp. 594–608. INSTICC, SciTePress (2024)
13. Hashimoto, K., Katsumata, S., Kwiatkowski, K., Prest, T.: An efficient and generic construction for signal's handshake (X3DH): post-quantum, state leakage secure, and deniable. J. Cryptol. **35**(3) (2022)
14. Inc., W.: Whatsapp encryption overview technical white paper (2016). https://www.whatsapp.com/security/WhatsApp-Security-Whitepaper.pdf
15. Kiltz, E.: Chosen-ciphertext secure key-encapsulation based on gap hashed Diffie-Hellman. In: Okamoto, T., Wang, X. (eds.) Public Key Cryptography - PKC 2007, pp. 282–297. Springer, Berlin Heidelberg, Berlin, Heidelberg (2007)
16. Langlois, A., Stehlé, D.: Worst-case to average-case reductions for module lattices. Des. Codes Cryptography **75**(3), 565–599 (2015)
17. Marlinspike, M., Perrin, T.: The x3dh key agreement protocol. Open Whisper Syst. **283**, 10 (2016)
18. Moody, D., Perlner, R., Regenscheid, A., Robinson, A., Cooper, D.: Transition to post-quantum cryptography standards (2024). https://csrc.nist.gov/pubs/ir/8547/ipd
19. Nist, G.M.D.: Module-Lattice-Based digital signature standard. Tech. rep, Gaithersburg, MD (2024)
20. Regev, O.: On lattices, learning with errors, random linear codes, and cryptography. In: Proceedings of the Thirty-Seventh Annual ACM Symposium on Theory of Computing, STOC '05, pp. 84–93. Association for Computing Machinery, New York (2005)
21. Shor, P.: Algorithms for quantum computation: discrete logarithms and factoring. In: Proceedings 35th Annual Symposium on Foundations of Computer Science, pp. 124–134 (1994)

A Key-Update Mechanism for the Space Data Link Security Protocol

Andreas Hülsing[1(✉)], Tanja Lange[1,2(✉)], and Fiona Johanna Weber[1(✉)]

[1] Eindhoven University of Technology, Eindhoven, The Netherlands
andreas@huelsing.net, crypto@fionajw.de
[2] Academia Sinica, Taipei, Taiwan
tanja@hyperelliptic.org

Abstract. Communication between satellites and mission control centers is currently protected via the Space Data Link Security (SDLS) Protocol. This protocol uses exclusively symmetric cryptography, which makes it resilient against quantum computers, but prevents key updates from achieving post-compromise security and limits operational efficiency, especially in future federated environments.

To resolve these issues we designed a key-update/establishment protocol based on PQNoise that leverages KEMs to achieve confidentiality and authenticity. We prove the resulting scheme secure in a slightly modified version of the Bellare–Rogaway-model.

To keep the SDLS protocol untouched, the resulting protocol is not used as the handshake phase of a larger data-transmission protocol, but actually run independently, permitting to start from shared keys.

Keywords: Key establishment · Space Data Link Security · post-quantum cryptography · Bellare–Rogaway model

1 Introduction

The *Space Data Link Security* (SDLS) protocol is a security protocol to protect the communication of and with spacecraft, typically between a satellite and the mission-control center. It is a *Recommended Standard* published by the *Consultative Committee for Space Data Systems* (CCSDS), a standardization organization for space agencies. (As of 2025 the organizations of the European Union, France, Germany, Italy, Canada, Japan, Brazil, the United Kingdom, the People's Republic of China, the United States, and Russia are full members).

SDLS works on the data-link layer of the network stack and primarily standardizes headers and trailers for other packets. Given its highly international setting, SDLS does not itself standardize specific cryptographic algorithms, but an accompanying document provides recommendations.

One limitation of current versions of SDLS is that it only standardizes the use of symmetric cryptography[1]. This has the advantage of being largely immune to

[1] There are extensions to propose use of elliptic-curve cryptography.

Y. Kim et al. (Eds.): CANS 2025, LNCS 16351, pp. 602–611, 2026.
https://doi.org/10.1007/978-981-95-4434-9_29

adversaries with access to quantum computers, but it comes with the downside that no new communication can be established. While this is less of a concern for the current use of satellite-to-ground communication, CCSDS is working on plans to use SDLS for satellite-to-satellite communication, where such a feature is a critical requirement. A further downside is that it limits the methods to update keys, to those using symmetric primitives. This implies that any attacker who compromised a key, can decrypt any subsequent communication, including messages updating to a new key and hence any message under this key, i.e., a key update cannot recover security after a key compromise.

1.1 Requirements

The goal of this work is therefore to design a key-update/establishment protocol that relies on asymmetric algorithms for authenticity and confidentiality. This protocol should provide the key for SDLS, and key updates may use SDLS as secure channel for transport, but it should not touch SDLS itself. This means that the design is not just the handshake phase of a more complex protocol that is only ever run in conjunction with a data-transmission protocol, but actually a standalone protocol concluding with both parties sharing a key. Not only does this reduce the difficulty of the analysis, but it also decreases the complexity (and thereby the attack-surface) and allows to update keys less often which reduces the communication and computational load.

In light of the expected duration for which any standard for communication with spacecraft will be used, security against quantum-adversaries is a necessity. While there are some standardization efforts for a Public Key Infrastructure (PKI) for space settings, these are not yet developed to the point, where it would make sense to target anything specifically. Because of this, our protocol is agnostic to how the communicating parties obtain their peers' long-term keys and assume they come pre-installed.

Lastly we note that there is no obvious need to be able to perform dynamic ciphersuite negotiation. Hence, we designed an opinionated protocol with a fixed ciphersuite; changes can be done in new (incompatible) versions of the protocol.

1.2 Related Work

Many widely used key-exchange protocols are based on the Diffie-Hellman Key Exchange (DHKX), which offers a primitive known as Non-Interactive Key Exchange (NIKE) but is vulnerable to attacks with quantum computers. So far, there is no post-quantum NIKE that is commonly considered secure, though first proposals do exist [6,7,9,19]. NIST's post-quantum process did not consider NIKEs and instead requested Key-Encapsulation Mechanisms (KEMs) that have for now become the de-facto standard for asymmetric post-quantum key establishment. In some protocols KEMs are an easy-to-use substitute for NIKEs, but this does not hold universally and needs case-by-case analysis.

Despite this change, there are already several protocols that use KEMs to offer post-quantum security at this point [3,5,13,22]. Our work is heavily based on Noise [17] and post-quantum Noise [13], an extension that incorporated KEMs to provide post-quantum security.

1.3 Design Considerations

We deviate from Noise in the way we derive the final key because we are designing a key exchange rather than a full secure-channel protocol which also transmits data. Firstly, Noise uses its final keys already during the handshake phase to encrypt messages before receiving a key confirmation from the peer. In order to ensure that the resulting keys of the key-update mechanism are truly fresh and can be used without any worries, we instead derive the final keys only once everything in the handshake has been completed by the party in question.

Furthermore, we combine the resulting pre-keys with the handshake hash to improve the robustness against replay attacks. Noise skips this, since its use of the keys in the communication layer provides similar assurances. In our case we treat SDLS as a standalone protocol to which we need to deliver a fresh key.

Lastly, we always insist on key-confirmations. Skipping them is a possibility in signature-based protocols that could potentially save half a round-trip, but would result in a much more fragile protocol.

Due to the difficulty of impersonating a satellite that is physically in orbit, we also provide a variant that does not authenticate the responding party (here: the satellite) in exchange for a slightly more lightweight protocol. While the use of such a protocol requires careful consideration, a scenario in which a channel can be assumed to be partially authenticated can be an instance where the bandwidth-savings may be enough to justify the use of the weaker protocol.

We remark here that such a version assigns trust to whoever provides the out-of-band authentication, which in the motivating example would be the ground-stations, not mission-control. Whether this trust is reasonable is not something that we can comment on, beyond *strongly* advising to thoroughly evaluate that question before any use of protocols that are only partially authenticated.

1.4 Primitives

To choose a specific instantiation to recommend, we evaluated various primitives. Our focus here was on finalists and alternates in NIST's post-quantum competition. For a detailed overview of these schemes we refer to ENISA's report [4], and for NIST's motivation to NIST's announcement [1].

Our primary focus here lay on the KEMs Kyber [21], Frodo [15], and Classic McEliece [2]: Kyber because it was chosen in NIST's competition and its overall high performance-characteristics, Frodo and Classic McEliece because of their more conservative designs and approval by various European bodies, and the latter also for its performance-characteristics when used for long-term keys.

1.5 Reception and ongoing standardization

We provided the results to ESA and presented them to CCSDS which, under the lead of ESA, has now begun work on standardizing our Triple-KEM proposal as a blue book.

2 Proposals

As a baseline, we consider the traditional approach of using signature key pairs as long-term keys and KEM (traditionally public key encryption) key pairs as ephemeral keys. This approach was for example used in TLS up to version 1.2. Most early proposals for post-quantum secure communication focused on TLS and followed this general approach (see for example [8,16,20]). For reference we provide an instantiation of this approach in the full version of this paper [12].

Alternatively it is possible to build protocols that *only* use KEM key pairs and establish authenticity via challenge-response. Since post-quantum KEMs tend to be more efficient than signature-schemes, especially in terms of size, this approach can lead to protocols with lower communication cost. This is also the approach that was used by the PQ protocols PQWireGuard [13], KEM-TLS [22], and PQNoise [3]. For further alternatives see the full version of this paper [12].

2.1 Dual/Triple-KEM Exchanges

If Alice wants to authenticate herself to Bob in a purely KEM-based protocol, she has Bob encapsulate a shared secret for her long-term key and send her the ciphertext. If she is then able to create an AEAD-ciphertext using the shared secret as key, Bob can conclude upon successful decryption that he is talking to Alice. The encapsulated shared secret was only accessible to himself and the owner of the private key (Alice). Since it is (by assumption) not practically possible to create an AEAD-ciphertext for a given key without knowing said key, only Alice or Bob could have created that ciphertext.

Our main proposal follows this idea with three keys – a long term key for each the sender and the receiver, as well as an ephemeral key for the sender, see Figure 1 for a diagram of the protocol. The main differences to previous protocols are that none include a mechanism to update long-term keys and that PQNoise directly proceeds to a messaging-phase, whereas our protocol is a pure key-exchange that outputs keys at the end. Authentication being performed by challenge-response with long-term KEM-keys has the added benefit (besides performance) that it naturally provides replay-security.

We accommodate a situation in which the communicating parties have already a pre-shared key (psk). We use that psk as a symmetric key in authenticated encryption to offer security from the first message on. If no psk exists between initiator and responder it can be initialized with an all-zero bitstring, as it is merely used as a defense-in-depth-measure, as the initial message only

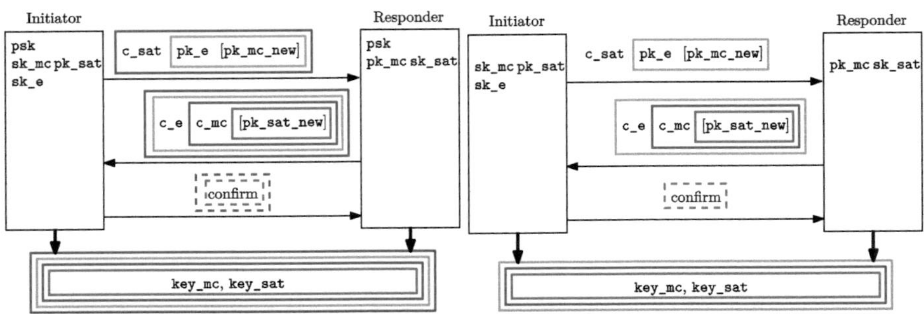

Fig. 1. Overview of the Triple-KEM exchange. Solid boxes indicate that the confidentiality of their content is protected by the same-color secret. Solid blue boxes and boxes in the color of the senders's long-term secret furthermore guarantee authenticity at the time at which they are received. Dashed boxes indicate that only the authenticity (when received), but not the confidentiality is protected. By the time the protocol completes (that is when it outputs `key_mc` and `key_sat`) the entire transcript is authenticated. Values in square-brackets are optionally updated long-term keys and may be skipped. The left diagram depicts the situation in which there is a secure pre-shared key (psk) and the right one the situation where there is not.

sends public-key material and authenticity is derived later for the entire protocol (after the challenge to the long-term key is decrypted correctly). Figure 1 depicts the difference in protection of the transmitted data depending on whether the used psk is secure.

If only the authenticity of the initiator has to be ensured because the authenticity of the responder can be guaranteed out-of-band, Triple-KEM can be simplified into **Dual-KEM**: Dual-KEM differs from Triple-KEM only in that the initiator would not send a ciphertext for the responder's long-term key and that the responder's answer would drop the updated long-term key. The benefit of this approach would lie in a more compact first packet and less computation because a third of the asymmetric operations could be skipped. The disadvantage is that Dual-KEM does not itself guarantee any authenticity of the responder. The full version of this paper [12] includes detailed descriptions of Triple-Kem and Dual-KEM.

2.2 Comparison

The Triple-KEM approach has the potential advantage, that it allows to mix and match different KEMs to protect different properties using different trade-offs. If long-term keys are for example never updated, it would be possible to instantiate them with Classic McEliece to benefit from the small ciphertexts but use Kyber for ephemeral keys where the public key has to be transmitted on every exchange. This would improve the performance, the bandwidth requirements, and potentially even the security. See Table 1 for examples.

An advantage of the signature-based approach on the other hand is that it technically allows to design a protocol that saves half a round-trip because it does not strictly require a key-confirmation message. Assuming that a sufficiently secure replay-protection is in place, the first message in the protocol can be assumed to be authentic by the satellite, because it is by assumption not possible for an attacker to forge the included signature and the replay-protection prevents replays. Similarly, the response could be assumed to be authentic by the receiver for the same reasons. Due to the inherent fragility of non-interactive replay-protection mechanisms, we can already state here, that we do not recommend versions of the signature-based approaches that skip key confirmation.

3 Selection

For a quick summary of the various packet sizes see Table 1 which includes sizes for Triple-KEM with the stated KEMs as well as a comparison with signature-based versions, outlined in the full version [12]. We include Dilithium [14] and FALCON [18], which are selected by NIST. Instead of the third winner, the stateless hash-based scheme SPHINCS+ [10], we included XMSS from RFC 8391 [11] as a standardized stateful signature scheme and its building block, the one-time signature scheme WOTS+.

Table 1. Sizes of different instantiations in bytes. SK = Sign + KEM, SKU = Sign+KEM with update of long-term key, SC = Signature-Chain, TK = Triple-KEM, TKU = Triple-KEM with update of long-term key. P. 1/2/3 = Packet 1/2/3, Sec.-L. = Security-Level of PQC component

Scheme	P. 1	P. 2	P. 3	Sec.-L.
SK(Kyber512+X25519+Dilithium+ECDSA)	3348	3300	16	1
SKU(Kyber512+X25519+Dilithium+ECDSA)	4692	4644	16	1
SK(Kyber512+X25519+Falcon+ECDSA)	1594	1546	16	1
SKU(Kyber512+X25519+Falcon+ECDSA)	2523	2475	16	1
SK(Kyber512+X25519+XMSS-SHA2_10_256)	3364	3316	16	1
SKU(Kyber512+X25519+XMSS-SHA2_10_256)	3428	3380	16	1
SC(Kyber512+X25519,WOTS+(32,16))	3024	2992	16	1
TK(Kyber512+X25519)	1664	1632	16	1
TKU(Kyber512+X25519)	2496	2480	16	1
TK(Kyber512,McEliece348864, both + X25519)	992	960	16	1
TKU(Kyber512,McEliece348864, both + X25519)	2621448	262128	16	1

The hybrid versions assume that a KEM-combiner is used with a KEM version of X25519, but without turning WOTS+ into a hybrid. These numbers would change slightly depending on whether only EKEM, the ephemeral KEM used in the system, should be hybrid or whether the signatures should also be made hybrid. That said, the comparison clearly demonstrates that the use of a hybrid elliptic-curve scheme comes at little cost with regards to packet size compared to using only the post-quantum scheme.

We do not consider instantiating ephemeral KEMs with Classic McEliece due to the large size of the public key, but note that it offers very interesting performance characteristics for long-term keys: As long as there is never a need to update those long-term keys, no other scheme offers competitive size characteristics. The entry TK(Kyber512,McEliece348864, both + X25519) shows a scenario where the long-term keys are instantiated with Classic McEliece and the ephebral keys with Kyber. The corresponding TKU entry shows the impact of updating both long-term keys.

All of these sizes assume the use of an AEAD-scheme that adds a constant 16 bytes to the length of the plaintext; this assumption holds for many widely used schemes, in particular AES-GCM with a full-sized authentication tag. The sizes are however independent of the choices made for the involved hash functions (except for the case of hash-based signatures), as the protocol does not transmit any hashes.

We note that all of these proposals offer forward secrecy, post-compromise security, updateable long-term keys, and some form of hybrid security. This also holds if the network fragments packets, but in the event that fragmentation causes data to arrive out-of order or not at all, the protocol as presented would not be able to reorder or re-request them. Consequently, it needs to assume an attack and drop the connection. The layer handling fragmentation would be required to ensure the correct ordering and re-requesting of lost packets if dropped connections are an issue.

3.1 Our Recommendations

If only one PQ-KEM is used, our primary recommendation is Triple-KEM with Kyber+X25519. The packets are generally smaller than for Sign+KEM (except for Kyber + Falcon without key update), it only requires the implementation of one pair (Kyber and X25519) of cryptographic primitives (reducing attack-surface and simplifying implementations), and can be expected to clearly outperform Sign+KEM with Falcon. Furthermore it avoids the issue of Falcon being notoriously hard to implement securely.

This recommendation also applies to Dual-KEM(Kyber+X25519): While this does sacrifice responder-authenticity, the two variants are otherwise extremely similar and can therefore share most of the implementation burden. While we stress that Dual-KEM should only be used upon very careful analysis of the extent to which the specific mission can afford to skip cryptographic authentication of the responder, it does enable significant bandwidth- and computational savings, by virtue of not sending one Kyber-ciphertext and not performing one encapsulation and one decapsulation.

4 Analysis

We analyzed our protocols in a slightly modified version of the Bellare-Rogaway model, henceforth BR', to prove both confidentiality and authenticity of the resulting keys. We refer to the full version [12] for definitions of the model as well as the proofs and only summarize the core results here.

Intuitively both Triple- and Dual-KEM offer full confidentiality of the resulting keys, even against attackers that can compromise long-term keys. Furthermore both schemes provide authenticity, though Dual-KEM only for the initiator (we formalize this as an assumption that the responder cannot be impersonated and leave it to the instantiating party to evaluate whether this is a reasonable assumption given the specific setting).

More formally:

Theorem 1. *There is no polynomial-time quantum-adversary that can win the BR'-game against Triple-KEM, with more than negligible probability. Specifically, we find for all such adversaries $\mathcal{A}$:*

$$\mathsf{Adv}^{BR'}_{\mathcal{A},\,\mathsf{3KEM}}\left(1^\lambda\right) \leq \left(\begin{array}{rr} & 3 \cdot \mathsf{Adv}^{\textit{coll-res}}_{\mathcal{A}_1,\,\mathsf{H}}\left(1^\lambda\right) \\ + & n_i \cdot n_{s_i} \cdot \mathsf{EKEM}.\delta \\ + & n_i \cdot n_{s_i} \cdot n_r \cdot n_{s_r} \cdot 3 \cdot \mathsf{Adv}^{\textit{IND-CCA}}_{\mathcal{A},\,\mathsf{EKEM}}\left(1^\lambda\right) \\ + & n_{s_r} \cdot n_i \cdot n_r \cdot \frac{1}{1-\mathsf{IKEM}\cdot\delta} \cdot \mathsf{Adv}^{\textit{IND-CCA}}_{\mathcal{A}_4,\,\mathsf{IKEM}}\left(1^\lambda\right) \\ + & n_{s_i} \cdot n_i \cdot n_r \cdot \frac{1}{1-\mathsf{RKEM}\cdot\delta} \cdot \mathsf{Adv}^{\textit{IND-CCA}}_{\mathcal{A}_4,\,\mathsf{RKEM}}\left(1^\lambda\right) \\ + & n_i \cdot n_{s_i} \cdot n_r \cdot n_{s_r} \cdot 3 \cdot \mathsf{Adv}^{\textit{PRHO}}_{\mathcal{A},\,\mathsf{NHO}}\left(1^\lambda\right) \\ + & (n_{s_i} + n_{s_r}) \cdot n_i \cdot n_r \cdot \mathsf{Adv}^{\textit{EUF-CMA}}_{\mathcal{A}_6,\,\mathsf{AEAD}}\left(1^\lambda\right) \\ + & n_i \cdot n_{s_i} \cdot n_r \cdot n_{s_r} \cdot 2 \cdot \mathsf{Adv}^{\textit{PRF}}_{\mathcal{A},\,\mathsf{KDF}}\left(1^\lambda\right) \end{array}\right)$$

Theorem 2. *There is no polynomial-time quantum-adversary that can win the BR'-game against Dual-KEM, with more than negligible probability. Specifically, we find for all such adversaries $\mathcal{A}$:*

$$\mathsf{Adv}^{BR'}_{\mathcal{A},\,\mathsf{2KEM}}\left(1^\lambda\right) \leq \left(\begin{array}{rr} & 2 \cdot \mathsf{Adv}^{\textit{coll-res}}_{\mathcal{A}_1,\,\mathsf{H}}\left(1^\lambda\right) \\ + & n_i \cdot n_{s_i} \cdot \mathsf{EKEM}.\delta \\ + & n_i \cdot n_{s_i} \cdot n_r \cdot n_{s_r} \cdot 3 \cdot \mathsf{Adv}^{\textit{IND-CCA}}_{\mathcal{A},\,\mathsf{EKEM}}\left(1^\lambda\right) \\ + & n_{s_r} \cdot n_i \cdot n_r \cdot \frac{1}{1-\mathsf{IKEM}\cdot\delta} \cdot \mathsf{Adv}^{\textit{IND-CCA}}_{\mathcal{A}_4,\,\mathsf{IKEM}}\left(1^\lambda\right) \\ + & n_i \cdot n_{s_i} \cdot n_r \cdot n_{s_r} \cdot 2 \cdot \mathsf{Adv}^{\textit{PRHO}}_{\mathcal{A},\,\mathsf{NHO}}\left(1^\lambda\right) \\ + & n_{s_r} \cdot n_i \cdot n_r \cdot \mathsf{Adv}^{\textit{EUF-CMA}}_{\mathcal{A}_6,\,\mathsf{AEAD}}\left(1^\lambda\right) \\ + & n_i \cdot n_{s_i} \cdot n_r \cdot n_{s_r} \cdot 2 \cdot \mathsf{Adv}^{\textit{PRF}}_{\mathcal{A},\,\mathsf{KDF}}\left(1^\lambda\right) \\ + & \mathsf{Adv}^{BR'_{\textit{Case A}}}_{\mathcal{A},\,\mathsf{2KEM}}\left(1^\lambda\right) \end{array}\right),$$

where $\mathsf{Adv}^{BR'_{\textit{Case A}}}_{\mathcal{A},\,\mathsf{2KEM}}\left(1^\lambda\right)$ *refers to the maximum achievable advantage for the adversary to cause an unpeered, complete initiator-session.*

Acknowledgements. We'd like to thank Antonios Atlasis, Oana-Alexandra Graur, and Jacob Appelbaum for their helpful comments and feedback. This work was supported by the Dutch Ministry of Education, Culture, and Science through Gravitation project "Challenges in Cyber Security (CiCS) – 024.006.037", by the Dutch Research Council (NWO) under grant VI.Vidi.193.066, by the European Space Agency under project 4000139670/22/NL/CRS, by the Deutsche Forschungsgemeinschaft (DFG, German Research Foundation) under Germanys Excellence Strategy–EXC 2092 CASA–390781972; by the Academia Sinica Grand Challenge Seed Project AS-GCS-113-M07.

References

1. Gorjan Alagic, Daniel Apon, David Cooper, Quynh Dang, Thinh Dang, John Kelsey, Jacob Lichtinger, Yi-Kai Liu, Carl Miller, Dustin Moody, Rene Peralta, Ray Perlner, Angela Robinson, and Daniel Smith-Tone. Status Report on the Third Round of the NIST Post-Quantum Cryptography Standardization Process. Technical report, Sept 2022.
2. Martin R. Albrecht, Daniel J. Bernstein, Tung Chou, Carlos Cid, Jan Gilcher, Tanja Lange, Varun Maram, Ingo von Maurich, Rafael Misoczki, Ruben Niederhagen, Kenneth G. Paterson, Edoardo Persichetti, Christiane Peters, Peter Schwabe, Nicolas Sendrier, Jakub Szefer, Cen Jung Tjhai, Martin Tomlinson, and Wen Wang. Classic McEliece. Technical report, National Institute of Standards and Technology, 2022. available at https://csrc.nist.gov/projects/post-quantum-cryptography/round-4-submissions.
3. Yawning Angel, Benjamin Dowling, Andreas Hülsing, Peter Schwabe, and Fiona Johanna Weber. Post quantum noise. In Heng Yin, Angelos Stavrou, Cas Cremers, and Elaine Shi, editors, *ACM CCS 2022*, pages 97–109. ACM Press, November 2022.
4. Ward Beullens, Jan-Pieter D'Anvers, Andreas Hülsing, Tanja Lange, Lorenz Panny, Cyprien de Saint Guilhem, Nigel P. Smart, Evangelos Rekleitis, Angeliki Aktypi, and Athanasios-Vasileios Grammatopoulos. Post-quantum cryptography: Current state and quantum mitigation, 2021. https://www.enisa.europa.eu/publications/post-quantum-cryptography-current-state-and-quantum-mitigation/@@download/fullReport.
5. Colin Boyd, Bor de Kock, and Lise Millerjord. Modular design of KEM-based authenticated key exchange. In Leonie Simpson and Mir Ali Rezazadeh Baee, editors, *ACISP 23*, volume 13915 of *LNCS*, pages 553–579. Springer, Cham, July 2023.
6. Wouter Castryck, Tanja Lange, Chloe Martindale, Lorenz Panny, and Joost Renes. CSIDH: An efficient post-quantum commutative group action. In Thomas Peyrin and Steven Galbraith, editors, *ASIACRYPT 2018, Part III*, volume 11274 of *LNCS*, pages 395–427. Springer, Cham, December 2018.
7. Jean-Marc Couveignes. Hard homogeneous spaces. Cryptology ePrint Archive, Report 2006/291, 2006.
8. Eric Crockett, Christian Paquin, and Douglas Stebila. Prototyping post-quantum and hybrid key exchange and authentication in TLS and SSH. Cryptology ePrint Archive, Report 2019/858, 2019.
9. Luca De Feo, Jean Kieffer, and Benjamin Smith. Towards practical key exchange from ordinary isogeny graphs. In Thomas Peyrin and Steven Galbraith, editors, *ASIACRYPT 2018, Part III*, volume 11274 of *LNCS*, pages 365–394. Springer, Cham, December 2018.

10. Andreas Hülsing, Daniel J. Bernstein, Christoph Dobraunig, Maria Eichlseder, Scott Fluhrer, Stefan-Lukas Gazdag, Panos Kampanakis, Stefan Kölbl, Tanja Lange, Martin M. Lauridsen, Florian Mendel, Ruben Niederhagen, Christian Rechberger, Joost Rijneveld, Peter Schwabe, Jean-Philippe Aumasson, Bas Westerbaan, and Ward Beullens. SPHINCS$^+$. Technical report, National Institute of Standards and Technology, 2020. available at https://csrc.nist.gov/projects/post-quantum-cryptography/post-quantum-cryptography-standardization/round-3-submissions.
11. Andreas Hülsing, Denise Butin, Stefan-Lukas Gazdag, Joost Rijneveld, and Aziz Mohaisen. XMSS: eXtended Merkle Signature Scheme. RFC 8391, RFC Editor, 05 2018.
12. Andreas Hülsing, Tanja Lange, and Fiona Johanna Weber. A key-update mechanism for the space data link security protocol, 2025.
13. Andreas Hülsing, Kai-Chun Ning, Peter Schwabe, Fiona Johanna Weber, and Philip R. Zimmermann. Post-quantum WireGuard. In *2021 IEEE Symposium on Security and Privacy*, pages 304–321. IEEE Computer Society Press, May 2021.
14. Vadim Lyubashevsky, Léo Ducas, Eike Kiltz, Tancrède Lepoint, Peter Schwabe, Gregor Seiler, Damien Stehlé, and Shi Bai. CRYSTALS-DILITHIUM. Technical report, National Institute of Standards and Technology, 2020. available at https://csrc.nist.gov/projects/post-quantum-cryptography/post-quantum-cryptography-standardization/round-3-submissions.
15. Michael Naehrig, Erdem Alkim, Joppe Bos, Léo Ducas, Karen Easterbrook, Brian LaMacchia, Patrick Longa, Ilya Mironov, Valeria Nikolaenko, Christopher Peikert, Ananth Raghunathan, and Douglas Stebila. FrodoKEM. Technical report, National Institute of Standards and Technology, 2020. available at https://csrc.nist.gov/projects/post-quantum-cryptography/post-quantum-cryptography-standardization/round-3-submissions.
16. Christian Paquin, Douglas Stebila, and Goutam Tamvada. Benchmarking post-quantum cryptography in TLS. In Jintai Ding and Jean-Pierre Tillich, editors, *Post-Quantum Cryptography - 11th International Conference, PQCrypto 2020*, pages 72–91. Springer, Cham, 2020.
17. Trevor Perrin. Noise protocol framework. https://noiseprotocol.org/noise.pdf (Revision 34 vom 2018-07-11).
18. Thomas Prest, Pierre-Alain Fouque, Jeffrey Hoffstein, Paul Kirchner, Vadim Lyubashevsky, Thomas Pornin, Thomas Ricosset, Gregor Seiler, William Whyte, and Zhenfei Zhang. FALCON. Technical report, National Institute of Standards and Technology, 2020. available at https://csrc.nist.gov/projects/post-quantum-cryptography/post-quantum-cryptography-standardization/round-3-submissions.
19. Alexander Rostovtsev and Anton Stolbunov. Public-Key Cryptosystem Based On Isogenies. Cryptology ePrint Archive, Report 2006/145, 2006.
20. John M. Schanck, William Whyte, and Zhenfei Zhang. Quantum-Safe Hybrid (QSH) Ciphersuite for Transport Layer Security (TLS) version 1.2. Internet-Draft draft-whyte-qsh-tls12-02, Internet Engineering Task Force, July 2016. Work in Progress.
21. Peter Schwabe, Roberto Avanzi, Joppe Bos, Léo Ducas, Eike Kiltz, Tancrède Lepoint, Vadim Lyubashevsky, John M. Schanck, Gregor Seiler, Damien Stehlé, and Jintai Ding. CRYSTALS-KYBER. Technical report, National Institute of Standards and Technology, 2022. available at https://csrc.nist.gov/Projects/post-quantum-cryptography/selected-algorithms-2022.
22. Peter Schwabe, Douglas Stebila, and Thom Wiggers. Post-quantum TLS without handshake signatures. In Jay Ligatti, Xinming Ou, Jonathan Katz, and Giovanni Vigna, editors, *ACM CCS 2020*, pages 1461–1480. ACM Press, November 2020.

Automated Verification of Proofs in the Universal Composability Framework with Markov Decision Processes

Maxim Jourenko[1(✉)] and Marcus Völker[2]

[1] Institute of Science Tokyo, Tokyo, Japan
jourenko.m.606a@m.isct.ac.jp
[2] RWTH Aachen University, Aachen, Germany
voelker@embedded.rwth-aachen.de

Abstract. Designing cryptographic protocols and proving these rigorously secure is an arduous and challenging task. Among the methods commonly used to prove security of cryptographic protocols, formalizing it in Canneti's Universal Composability (UC) Framework offers benefits as (1) Modular design, (2) security that remains under composition and concurrent execution. However, working within the UC Framework can be cumbersome, error-prone and requires a long time commitment by the prover. While utilization of proof assistants in Cryptography and IT Security is a prominent research area, proof assistants for UC are still in their infancy. Here we show our ongoing work to utilize model checking for verification of proofs in the UC Framework, which to the best of our knowledge is the first attempt to do so. In this work we (1) formally create a Markov Decision Process (MDP) encoding a given proof in the UC Framework, (2) define and proof notions of soundness and completeness for the constructed MDP, (3) implement a proof of concept and (4) demonstrate practical feasibility through experimental evaluation.

1 Introduction

In the cryptographer's toolkit there are two prominent frameworks for proving security of cryptographic systems and protocols. On the one side, there are game based proofs, where a game is defined based on a cryptographic system and a property it should fulfill. This game is played by an adversary and if they cannot win with more than negligible probability, the cryptographic system fulfills the desired property. An example of a game based security is *existential unforgeability against chosen message attacks* (EU-CMA) for cryptographic signature schemes [16]. On the other side, there are simulation based proofs as Canetti's Universal Composability Framework (UC) [12]. There, the prover creates a specification, called a functionality $\mathcal{F}$, of a cryptographic system they want to prove secure. They then attempt to show that a given protocol Π is indistinguishable

This work was supported by JST CREST Grant Number JPMJCR2113, Japan and Input Output Global.

Y. Kim et al. (Eds.): CANS 2025, LNCS 16351, pp. 612–621, 2026.
https://doi.org/10.1007/978-981-95-4434-9_30

to $\mathcal{F}$ from an outside perspective, called the Environment $\mathcal{Z}$ which is assisted by an adversary $\mathcal{A}$. An example of a functionality is $\mathcal{F}_{sig}$ and it has been shown equivalent to a EU-CMA secure signature scheme [8]. While in this case game based and simulation based notions for security of signature schemes have been shown to be equivalent, this is not the case in general. UC provides more comprehensive guarantees to game based definitions: A system that was shown to implement a functionality is secure in any context, including if multiple instances of a protocol are executed in parallel or under composition of other protocols and attacks not known a-priori. The benefits of the UC framework comes at a cost of a complex formalism where technical mistakes or nuances in the functionalities' design are difficult to spot which is illustrated by the amount of iterations it took to achieve EU-CMA equivalence with a UC functionality [1,7,10,11].

Related Work. With the difficulties researchers face in providing rigorous security proofs, there is a growing body of work to attempt to mechanically prove security [2]. Of note is *EasyCrypt* [4] which is a tool to assist and verify game-based proofs utilizing Hoare logic [17] and variants thereof. However, the outlook regarding proof assistants for UC is rather bleak. Works that attempt to mechanize proofs in UC are EasyUC [12] as well as an approach to reason about adversarial complexity [3] – both based on EasyCrypt. The drawback of these approaches is the significant effort to create a proof for a single cryptographic system that ranges in an order of magnitude of thousands of lines of code (LOC) [3] to tens of thousands [12], making these systems impractical and unscalable. Only recently an implementation of a DSL[1] reduced the effort to about 600 LOC. In this work, we attempt to create a scalable proof assistant that allows formalization of cryptographic systems in the UC framework and mechanically verifies their correctness, utilizing model checking. We aim to lean more heavily on automated exploration of state spaces than the related work, which should offload some of what previously needed to be specified manually in a proof to an automated tool. As proof systems based on automated formal verification, such as model checking [13], usually have a natural way of diagnosing faulty inputs; model checking, for example, is capable of generating counterexamples that encode the precise reason why a system is incorrect. If we can leverage model checking for UC proof verification, we can then report counterexamples back to the user, which allows them to diagnose and fix the proof until it is correct.

Our Contributions. In this work: (1) We formally introduce how to encode a proof in the UC framework as a MDP M_{UC} and provide a property π_{UC} such that, if M_{UC} satisfies π_{UC}, then the UC proof is verified to be correct. (2) We formally define notions of *completeness* and *soundness* and prove that our proof system satisfies these. (3) We implement a proof-of-concept for our approach that

[1] https://github.com/easyuc/EasyUC.

consists of (a) A Domain Specific Language (DSL) that allows formalization of UC proofs and define protocols, functionalities and simulators akin to a pen-and-paper proof and (b) A compiler that synthesizes a MDP written in the PRISM language [18] from a UC proof written in the DSL. (4) We showcase our approach by verifying the EasyUC variation [12] of the Diffie-Hellman based Key Exchange [14] and a Secure Message Communication protocol built on top of it as a use case which has been a common usecase for mechanized UC verification in related work [3,12]. (5) We demonstrate practical feasibility through experimental evaluation of the above use case utilizing the PRISM model checker [18].

2 Background

The Universal Composability Framework [7]. A proof in the UC Framework consists of: (1) a protocol Π which is the cryptographic system to be analyzed, executed betwen $n \in \mathcal{N}$ parties, (2) a functionality $\mathcal{F}$ describing the ideal behavior of the cryptographic system in the form of a trusted third party that executes the cryptographic system on behalf of the parties and (3) a simulator $\mathcal{S}$ that takes a black-box adversary $\mathcal{A}$ as parameter and converts every attempted attack of the adversary onto the protocol into an attack onto the functionality within polynomial time. Formally, all these elements are Interactive Turing Machines (ITMs) which computational resources are polynomially bounded. A Probabilistic Polynomial-Time (PPT) ITM called the *environment* $\mathcal{Z}$ receives access to a black box, either one containing a protocol instance of Π, the *real world* $\mathcal{R}$, or one containing the ideal protocol with $\mathcal{F}$, the *ideal world* $\mathcal{I}$. $\mathcal{Z}$ can interact with this black box, drive its execution, and receive its outputs. In this work, we refer to the outputs received by the environment as the *transcript*. At some point $\mathcal{Z}$ concludes its execution. Only thereafter it reviews the output it received and outputs a value from $\{0,1\}$ to indicate whether it interacted with the real or ideal world and succeeds if it can distinguish $\mathcal{I}$ and $\mathcal{R}$ with at most negligible probability. It is assisted by an adversary $\mathcal{A}$ who can corrupt parties, i.e. make them misbehave and leak information to $\mathcal{Z}$. Let $\mathsf{REAL}_{\Pi,\mathcal{A},\mathcal{Z}}$ be a protocol's Π real execution in presence of adversary $\mathcal{A}$ and $\mathsf{IDEAL}_{\mathcal{F},\mathcal{S},\mathcal{Z}}$ an execution of functionality $\mathcal{F}$ in presence of simulator $\mathcal{S}$. In this work we consider the UC framework with a *dummy* adversary, i.e. an adversary that forwards all messages and instructions from and to $\mathcal{Z}$ directly. It has been shown that this notion is equivalent to the previous notion of arbitrary adversaries in UC 2020 Claim 11 [9]. Executions are controlled by environment $\mathcal{Z}$ given its input z, randomness r and a security parameter κ forming two *binary* ensembles $\mathsf{REAL}_{\Pi,\mathcal{A},\mathcal{Z}} = \{\mathsf{REAL}_{\Pi,\mathcal{A},\mathcal{Z}}(\kappa, z, r)\}_{\kappa\in\mathbb{N},z\in\{0,1\}^*}$ and $\mathsf{IDEAL}_{\mathcal{F},\mathcal{S},\mathcal{Z}} = \{\mathsf{IDEAL}_{\mathcal{F},\mathcal{S},\mathcal{Z}}(\kappa, z, r)\}_{\kappa\in\mathbb{N},z\in\{0,1\}^*}$ which are the outputs for $\mathcal{Z}$ from both executions respectively. It holds that Π realizes $\mathcal{F}$ if $\forall$ PPT $\mathcal{Z}$, $\forall$ PPT $\mathcal{A}$ $\exists$ PPT $\mathcal{S}$ such that for any $c \in \mathbb{N}$ $\exists k, k_0 \in \mathbb{N}$, $\kappa > k_0$ such that $|\mathsf{REAL}_{\Pi,\mathcal{A},\mathcal{Z}} - \mathsf{IDEAL}_{\mathcal{F},\mathcal{S},\mathcal{Z}}| < \kappa^{-c}$ written as $\mathsf{REAL}_{\Pi,\mathcal{A},\mathcal{Z}} \approx_c \mathsf{IDEAL}_{\mathcal{F},\mathcal{S},\mathcal{Z}}$.

Model Checking and Temporal Logic. Model checking is to determine whether the model $\mathcal{M}$ of a system satisfies a given specification φ. Depending on the formalisms used to describe $\mathcal{M}$ and φ, different solvers using different algorithms can be applied [13]. For the specification φ, we use the language of linear temporal logic (LTL) [20] as a formal framework, but we only used two fairly simple kinds of properties for the verification in this paper: In each case, take x to be a formula in propositional logic using atomic symbols from the system. A formula of form G x means that x has to hold *globally*, i.e. in each state of each path through the system. A formula of form F x has to hold *finally*, i.e. in at least one state of each path through the system. To describe the system, we express it as a Markov Decision Process, and use it as input model for the PRISM model checker [18].

Markov Decision Process [5,21]. A *Markov Decision Process* (MDP) can be thought of as a combination of a traditional state transition system and a stochastic process such as a Markov chain [15]. Formally, an MDP is a probabilistic automaton (S, A, P) where S is a finite set of states, A is a finite set of actions, and $P : S \times A \times S \to [0,1]$ is a probabilistic transition function. A describes the external events that cause the system to switch from one state to the next. For each pair of state $s \in S$ and action $a \in A$, there is a discrete probability distribution that describes the probability of the next state $s' \in S$, given by P. That is, $P(s, a, s')$ is the probability that in state s, action a leads to state s'. Consequently, $\forall_{s \in S, a \in A} \sum_{s' \in S} P(s, a, s') = 1$. Other concepts commonly associated with MDPs, such as rewards and policies, are not relevant to our contribution and have been omitted here.

3 Modelling of UC

A TM, including its tape can be simulated within an MDP's statespace, where transitions between states are chosen according to the execution of the TM. We note that UC 2020 shows in Proposition 7 [9] that a system of ITMs can be simulated by a regular TM. Thus, given a system of ITMs, we can create an MDP simulating it. Due to space, we leave details of both to the full version.[2] Now, we consider two *worlds* $\mathcal{I}$ and $\mathcal{R}$ as they would be specified for a UC proof and the MDPs $M_{\mathcal{I}} = (S_{\mathcal{I}}, A_{\mathcal{I}}, P_{\mathcal{I}})$ and $M_{\mathcal{R}} = (S_{\mathcal{R}}, A_{\mathcal{R}}, P_{\mathcal{R}})$ which encode both systems of ITMs. Our aim is to create an MDP M_{UC} representing a UC proof and to use it as input for model checking to verify whether any PPT environment $\mathcal{Z}$ can distinguish between $\mathcal{I}$ and $\mathcal{R}$. This has following challenges: (1) How to model comparison between ideal and real worlds, (2) how to model execution of $\mathcal{I}$ and $\mathcal{R}$ driven by $\mathcal{Z}$, (3) how to quantify over all possible environments, (4) how to address randomness, (5) all while ensuring M_{UC} remains finite and (6) how to construct a property π_{UC} that can be used to prove that there does not exists any environment that can distinguish between $\mathcal{I}$ and $\mathcal{R}$ with more than

[2] https://ia.cr/2025/1454.

negligible probability. We construct MDP M_{UC} by creating intermediary MDPs addressing the above challenges step-by-step and starting with $M_{\mathcal{I}}$ and $M_{\mathcal{R}}$.

Desired Properties. In the following we define two properties M_{UC} and φ_{UC} should fulfill such that model checking can make useful statements about a proof in the UC framework. For one, we require *completeness*, i.e. if an environment exists that can distinguish between two worlds with non-negligible probability, then M_{UC} must not satisfy φ_{UC}. On the flipside, we require *soundness*, i.e. if M_{UC} does not satisfy φ_{UC} there must exist a polynomial time environment that can distinguish between the two worlds simulated in M_{UC}.

Definition 1 (Completeness). *Given a MDP M, property φ and systems of ITMs $\mathcal{I}$ and $\mathcal{R}$ defined according to the UC framework [6] where $\mathcal{I}$ contains functionality $\mathcal{F}$ and simulator $\mathcal{S}$ and where $\mathcal{R}$ contains protocol Π and dummy adversary $\mathcal{A}$, then (M, φ) satisfy completeness if $\exists$ $\mathcal{Z}$ such that* $\mathsf{REAL}_{\Pi,\mathcal{A},\mathcal{Z}} \not\approx_c \mathsf{IDEAL}_{\mathcal{F},\mathcal{S},\mathcal{Z}}$*, then $M \not\models \varphi$.*

Definition 2 (Soundness). *Given a MDP M, property φ and systems of ITMs $\mathcal{I}$ and $\mathcal{R}$ defined according to the UC framework [6] where $\mathcal{I}$ contains functionality $\mathcal{F}$ and simulator $\mathcal{S}$ and where $\mathcal{R}$ contains protocol Π and dummy adversary $\mathcal{A}$, then (M, φ) satisfy Soundness if $M \not\models \varphi$ then $\exists$ $\mathcal{Z}$ such that* $\mathsf{REAL}_{\Pi,\mathcal{A},\mathcal{Z}} \not\approx_c \mathsf{IDEAL}_{\mathcal{F},\mathcal{S},\mathcal{Z}}$.

Comparing two Worlds. To be able to compare executions of both $\mathcal{I}$ and $\mathcal{R}$ we must include both of them within M_{UC}. Let MDP $M_{\mathcal{I},\mathcal{R}} = (S_{\mathcal{I},\mathcal{R}}, A_{\mathcal{I},\mathcal{R}}, P_{\mathcal{I},\mathcal{R}})$ be a union of $M_{\mathcal{I}}$ and $M_{\mathcal{R}}$ as in the standard way of creating unions of automata where $S_{\mathcal{I},\mathcal{R}} = S_{\mathcal{I}} \times S_{\mathcal{R}}$. Note that this MDP is non-deterministic as both $\mathcal{I}$ and $\mathcal{R}$ can be executed in any order resulting in a large state space. We resolve non-determinism by executing $\mathcal{I}$ and $\mathcal{R}$ sequentially: We remove all transitions where $P_{\mathcal{I},\mathcal{R}}$ proceeds to execute $\mathcal{R}$, if there exists any ITM in $\mathcal{I}$ which is active.

A Fixed Environment $\mathcal{Z}$. We extend $M_{\mathcal{I},\mathcal{R}}$ to $M_{\mathcal{I},\mathcal{R},\mathcal{Z}}$ which encodes sequential execution of $\mathcal{I}$ and $\mathcal{R}$, but requires that both system of ITMs include the same $\mathcal{Z}$. We adjust the transition function $P_{\mathcal{I},\mathcal{R},\mathcal{Z}}$ of $M_{\mathcal{I},\mathcal{R},\mathcal{Z}}$ to be as follows. We define $P_{\mathcal{I},\mathcal{R},\mathcal{Z}}$ such that $\mathcal{Z}$'s execution is scheduled when no other ITM is active: (1) If any ITM in $\mathcal{I}$ with the exception of $\mathcal{Z}$ is active, then no ITM in $\mathcal{R}$ can proceed, (2) If any ITM in either $\mathcal{I}$ or $\mathcal{R}$ is active, then $\mathcal{Z}$ cannot proceed. (3) We synchronize executions of both environments: We remove transactions where only one environment issues an instruction, and add transitions such that both environments issue instructions in tandem. To construct $M_{\mathcal{I},\mathcal{R},\mathcal{Z}}$ we only re-arranged transitions in comparison to $M_{\mathcal{I},\mathcal{R}}$ such that $M_{\mathcal{I},\mathcal{R},\mathcal{Z}}$ remains finite.

Quantifying over all Environments. Modelling iteration over all possible environments is practically infeasible resulting in an infinite state space. Thus, we require abstraction: Instead of modeling environments directly, we model that $\mathcal{Z}$ can make arbitrary choices, i.e. send instructions to both $\mathcal{I}$ and $\mathcal{R}$, non-deterministically. Doing so, each state reachable by a polynomial time $\mathcal{Z}$ is reachable in the MDP. However, care must be taken to ensure *soundness*, which we address in the design of ϕ_{UC} later in this section and in Sect. 4. We modify $M_{\mathcal{I},\mathcal{R}}$ to $M_{\mathcal{I},\mathcal{R},\mathcal{Z}} = (S, A, P)$. First, we set $A = \{a, a_0, a_1\} \cup A_{\mathsf{Env}}$ where $A_{\mathsf{Env}} = \{a_{\mathsf{Env}} | a_{\mathsf{Env}} = (m, \mathsf{pid})$ where m is a message identifier and pid is an identifier for an ITM in each $\mathcal{I}$ and $\mathcal{R}$ $\}$. Input a is used to proceed execution if no choice by $\mathcal{Z}$ can be made, whereas $a_b, b \in \{0, 1\}$ represents $\mathcal{Z}$ making a binary choice b. The statespace of $M_{\mathcal{I},\mathcal{R},\mathcal{Z}}$ does not model any environment but instead has a state s_{Env}. We adjust P to now model $\mathcal{Z}$'s choices non-deterministically. There is a transition from s to s_{Env} at action a with probability 1. We further adjust P to create one transition from s_{Env} for each $a'_{\mathsf{Env}} = (m, \mathsf{pid}) \in A_{\mathsf{Env}}$ into state s' on input a'_{Env} with probability 1. Here s' equals s but has an additional message from the environment with message identifier m with the environment as sender on the input tape of the parties with identifier pid in both $M_{\mathcal{I}}$ and $M_{\mathcal{R}}$. Whenever an environment would choose a parameter of length c in state $s \in S$ we proceed as follows: We create a binary tree with s as root where the parameter is specified bit-by-bit. Then P has two transitions from s, one with action a_0 and probability 1 into state s_0 and one with action a_1 and probability 1 to s_1 representing fixing the first bit of the parameter to 0 or 1 respectively.

Randomness. Recall that each ITM accesses an input tape containing bits sampled from a uniform distribution. We derive $M_{\mathsf{UC}} = (S, A, P)$ from $M_{\mathcal{I},\mathcal{R},\mathsf{Env}}$ by modeling reading from these tapes. We modify $M_{\mathcal{I},\mathcal{R},\mathsf{Env}}$ similar to how message parameter are picked by the environment: We modify P such that, whenever in a state $s \in S$ an ITM would read a random bit $i \in \{0, 1\}$ transitioning into s_i respectively, we remove the original transitions replace them with two that go from s into either s_i upon reading input a with probability 0.5 instead.

The Indistinguishability Property. φ_{uc} is defined as an LTL formula such that if it holds true on M_{UC}, then no computationally polynomial bounded environment exists which can distinguish between $\mathcal{I}$ and $\mathcal{R}$ with more than negligible probability. We create an intermediate formula φ_{int} of form Gx where $x = y \vee z$, where y is true in a state $s \in S$ if s is not a dead-end state and z is *true*, if the environment's input tapes containing the outputs of $\mathcal{I}$ and $\mathcal{R}$ are equal. φ_{int} is a rather strict property, modeling an environment that can distinguish $\mathcal{I}$ and $\mathcal{R}$ based on (1) two random values $r_{\mathcal{I}}$, $r_{\mathcal{R}} \in \mathbb{N}$ sampled from the same distribution or (2) based on two values $v_{\mathcal{I}}$, $v_{\mathcal{R}} \in \mathbb{N}$ even if doing so violates computational assumptions. We construct a second intermediate formula $\varphi_{\mathsf{int},2}$ which is of form $G(y \vee z')$. However, here z' requires additional inputs from a human prover namely two additional lists L_R, L_I. (1) L_R contains tuples of form $(r_{\mathcal{I}}, r_{\mathcal{R}})$ where $r_{\mathcal{I}}, r_{\mathcal{R}} \in \mathbb{N}$ are random values sampled from the same distribution in the ideal and real worlds respectively. To account for an environment $\mathcal{Z}$ not being able to distinguish these values, $\varphi_{\mathsf{int},2}$ discards all paths where $r_{\mathcal{I}} \neq r_{\mathcal{R}}$ when evaluating distinguishability. (2) L_I contains tuples of form $(v_{\mathcal{I}}, v_{\mathcal{R}})$ where $v_{\mathcal{I}}, v_{\mathcal{R}} \in \mathbb{N}$ are values in the ideal and real worlds respectively and for which $\mathcal{Z}$ must break a computational assumption to be able to distinguish between them with more than negligible probability. To account for this, $\varphi_{\mathsf{int},2}$ does not consider paths in which $v_{\mathcal{I}} \neq v_{\mathcal{R}}$ distinguishable. Then, $\varphi_{\mathsf{uc}} = \mathsf{Pr}_{\mathsf{min}}(\varphi_{\mathsf{int},2}) \geq 1 - \mathsf{negl}(\kappa)$, where $\mathsf{neg}(\kappa)$ is a negligible term with respect to the security parameter κ. $\mathsf{Pr}_{\mathsf{min}}(\varphi_{\mathsf{int},2})$ is the probability of formula $\varphi_{\mathsf{int},2}$ to be true after resolving all non-deterministic choices in the MDP to minimize its probability[3].

4 Analysis

In the following we provide theoretical analysis of our construction and prove that our construction satisfies properties Completeness and Soundness – with some limitations – as in Definition 2. Due to space constraints we provide summaries of the proofs and refer to the full version for details.

4.1 Theorems and Proofs

Theorem 1 *$(M_{\mathsf{UC}}, \varphi_{\mathsf{UC}})$ satisfies completeness.*

Proof Let $M_{\mathsf{UC}} = (S, A, P)$. Assume there exists an environment $\mathcal{Z}$ that can distinguish between $\mathcal{I}$ and $\mathcal{R}$ with more than negligible probability. We argue through analysis of the reachable states in M_{UC}. By construction M_{UC} models sampling of random bitstrings sampled from a uniform distribution through probabilistic transitions. Moreover, M_{UC} models any choice $\mathcal{Z}$ can make through actions and message parameters chosen bitwise through non-deterministic transitions. Thus, given any randomness and environment choices, a respective state is reachable in M_{UC}. If two transcripts are distinguishable, then it must contain values that are distinguishable with non-negligible probability, thus $M_{\mathsf{UC}} \not\models \varphi_{\mathsf{UC}}$. □

Theorem 2 *$(M_{\mathsf{UC}}, \varphi_{\mathsf{UC}})$ satisfies soundness if $|A|$ is polynomial in security parameter κ and there exists a path in M_{UC} where a distinguishable state is reached after the environment issued at most $\mathcal{O}(1)$ instructions.*

Proof Let $M_{\mathsf{UC}} = (S, A, P)$ and assume that $M_{\mathsf{UC}} \not\models \varphi_{\mathsf{UC}}$. Then, there must exist a set of states S_{dist} reachable in M_{UC} from where an environment can distinguish. As ϕ_{UC} considers lists L_R and L_I it must hold that (1) $\mathcal{Z}$ does not distinguish between two random values $(r_0, r_1) \in L_R$ and does not distinguish based on two values $(v_0, v_1) \in L_I$ that would require breaking a computational assumption.

[3] https://www.prismmodelchecker.org/manual/PropertySpecification/ThePOperator.

Thus, $\mathcal{Z}$ must be able to distinguish with non-negligible probability. We can create a naive environment $\mathcal{Z}_{\mathcal{N}}$ that can reach such a state with non-negligible probability: When $\mathcal{Z}$ reaches a state it can distinguish by executing $\mathcal{A}_{\mathsf{dist}}$, it does so. If $\mathcal{Z}$ is scheduled to execute by issuing an instruction, it picks a random instruction which corresponds to an action $a \in A$. The probability for $\mathcal{Z}$ to reach a state in which it can distinguish is $|\mathsf{REAL}_{\Pi,\mathcal{A},\mathcal{Z}} - \mathsf{IDEAL}_{\mathcal{F},\mathcal{S},\mathcal{Z}}| \geq |A|^{-y} p_s p_a \geq (\kappa^d)^{-y} p_s p_a \geq \kappa^{-dy} \kappa^{-c} = \kappa^{-(c+dy)}$. Thus, for constant $c_s = c + dy \in \mathbb{N}$ it holds that for all $\kappa : |\mathsf{REAL}_{\Pi,\mathcal{A},\mathcal{Z}} - \mathsf{IDEAL}_{\mathcal{F},\mathcal{S},\mathcal{Z}}| \geq \kappa^{-c_s}$. □

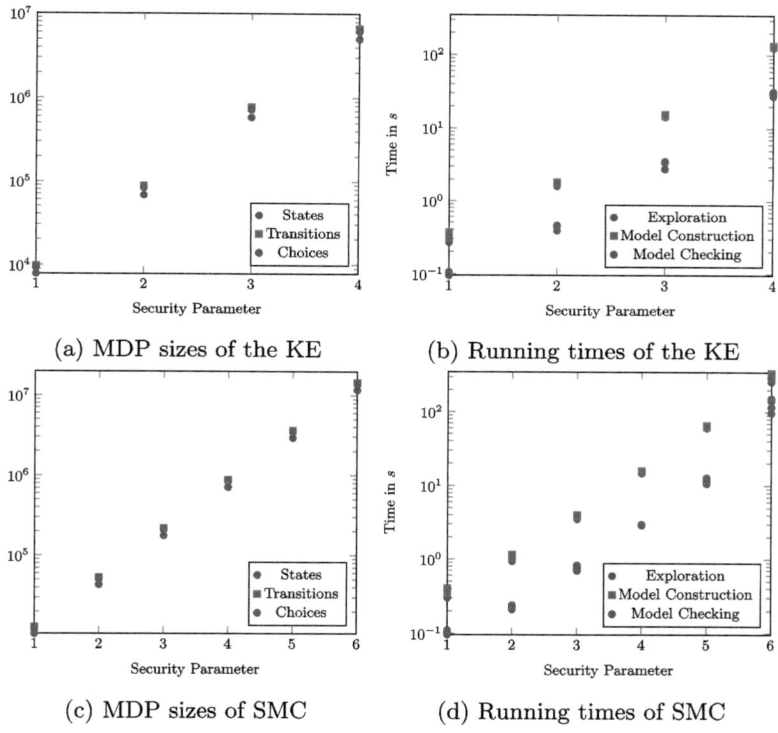

(a) MDP sizes of the KE (b) Running times of the KE

(c) MDP sizes of SMC (d) Running times of SMC

Fig. 1. Experimental evaluation of the Diffie-Hellman Key Exchange 1a, 1b and Secure Message Communication 1c, 1d use cases.

4.2 Experimental Evaluation

We implemented a *proof of concept* to demonstrate practical feasibility. The proof of concept consists of (1) A grammar specifying a Domain Specific Language (DSL) written with ANTLR [19] in which a prover can write a UC proof with notation close to a pen and paper proof, (2) a compiler for UC proofs written in the DSL that sythesizes a corresponding MDP, written in the PRISM language [18]. We showcase our tool by implementing the same uses cases as in related works [3,12], i.e. Diffie-Hellman Key Exchange (KE) and Secure Message Communication (SMC) protocols. We generate PRISM instances with varying security parameters using a timeout of 10 min. The evaluation graphs are split into two per use case: One investigating the size of the MDP and one investigating the run time of PRISM on the MDP. The results can be seen in Figs. 1a to 1d. We can clearly see the exponential relationship between the security parameter and the size of the MDP. The key exchange uses three random numbers the length of the security parameter, while SMC uses two random numbers the length of the security parameter. Consequently, we expect a state space the size of $O(2^{3x}) = O(8^x)$ for the key exchange and $O(2^{2x}) = O(4^x)$ for SMC, which the experimental findings in Figs. 1a and 1c support. Because of the slower scaling of the SMC instance, we were able to evaluate until a security parameter of $\kappa = 6$ compared to the security parameter $\kappa = 4$ for the key exchange. The model checking scales linearly with model size, so we see the same exponential relationships for the run times in Figs. 1b and 1d.

References

1. Backes, M., Hofheinz, D.: How to break and repair a universally composable signature functionality. In: International Conference on Information Security, pp. 61–72. Springer (2004)
2. Barbosa, M., et al.: SoK: computer-aided cryptography. In: 2021 IEEE Symposium on Security and Privacy (SP), pp. 777–795. IEEE (2021)
3. Barbosa, M., Barthe, G., Gregoire, B., Koutsos, A., Strub, P.Y.: Mechanized proofs of adversarial complexity and application to universal composability. In: Proceedings of the 2021 ACM SIGSAC Conference on Computer and Communications Security, pp. 2541–2563 (2021)
4. Barthe, G., Grégoire, B., Heraud, S., Béguelin, S.Z.: Computer-aided security proofs for the working cryptographer. In: Annual Cryptology Conference, pp. 71–90. Springer (2011)
5. Bellman, R.: Dynamic programming and stochastic control processes. Inf. Control **1**(3), 228–239 (1958)
6. Canetti, R.: Universally composable security: a new paradigm for cryptographic protocols. In: Proceedings 42nd IEEE Symposium on Foundations of Computer Science, pp. 136–145 (2001)
7. Canetti, R.: Universally composable security: a new paradigm for cryptographic protocols. In: Proceedings 42nd IEEE Symposium on Foundations of Computer Science, pp. 136–145. IEEE (2001)
8. Canetti, R.: Universally composable signature, certification, and authentication. In: Proceedings. 17th IEEE Computer Security Foundations Workshop, 2004, pp. 219–233. IEEE (2004)
9. Canetti, R.: Universally composable security. J. ACM (JACM) **67**(5), 1–94 (2020)
10. Canetti, R., Krawczyk, H.: Universally composable notions of key exchange and secure channels. In: Advances in Cryptology—EUROCRYPT 2002: International Conference on the Theory and Applications of Cryptographic Techniques Amsterdam, The Netherlands, April 28–May 2 2002 Proceedings 21, pp. 337–351. Springer (2002)

11. Canetti, R., Rabin, T.: Universal composition with joint state. In: Advances in Cryptology-CRYPTO 2003: 23rd Annual International Cryptology Conference, Santa Barbara, California, USA, August 17-21, 2003. Proceedings 23, pp. 265–281. Springer (2003)
12. Canetti, R., Stoughton, A., Varia, M.: EasyUC: using EasyCrypt to mechanize proofs of universally composable security. In: 2019 IEEE 32nd Computer Security Foundations Symposium (CSF), pp. 167–16716. IEEE (2019)
13. Clarke, E.M., Emerson, E.A.: Design and synthesis of synchronization skeletons using branching time temporal logic. In: Kozen, D. (ed.) Logics of Programs, pp. 52–71. Springer, Berlin (1982)
14. Diffie, W., Hellman, M.E.: New directions in cryptography. In: Democratizing Cryptography: The Work of Whitfield Diffie and Martin Hellman, pp. 365–390 (2022)
15. Frigessi, A., Heidergott, B.: Markov Chains, pp. 772–775. Springer, Berlin (2011)
16. Goldwasser, S., Micali, S., Rivest, R.L.: A digital signature scheme secure against adaptive chosen-message attacks. SIAM J. Comput. **17**(2), 281–308 (1988)
17. Hoare, C.A.R.: An axiomatic basis for computer programming. Commun. ACM **12**(10), 576–580 (1969)
18. Kwiatkowska, M., Norman, G., Parker, D.: PRISM 4.0: verification of probabilistic real-time systems. In: Gopalakrishnan, G., Qadeer, S. (eds.) Proc. 23rd International Conference on Computer Aided Verification (CAV'11), volume 6806 of LNCS, pp. 585–591. Springer (2011)
19. Parr, T.: The Definitive ANTLR 4 Reference, 2nd ed. Pragmatic Bookshelf (2013)
20. Pnueli, A.: The temporal logic of programs. In: 18th Annual Symposium on Foundations of Computer Science (SFCS 1977), pp. 46–57, (1977)
21. Schneider, S., Wagner, D.H.: Error detection in redundant systems. In: Papers Presented at the 26–28 February 1957, Western Joint Computer Conference: Techniques for Reliability, IRE-AIEE-ACM '57 (Western), pp. 115–121. Association for Computing Machinery, New York (1957)

Fully Verifiable Ciphertext-Policy Attribute-Based Encryption

Quoc-Bao Ninh[1,2(✉)], Cao Quang Phat[1,2], and Tran Trung Dung[1,2]

[1] Faculty of Information Technology, University of Science, Ho Chi Minh City, Vietnam
{21120004,21120022}@student.hcmus.edu.vn, ttdung@hcmus.edu.vn
[2] Vietnam National University, Ho Chi Minh City, Vietnam

Abstract. Ciphertext-Policy Attribute-Based Encryption (CP-ABE) is a powerful cryptographic mechanism that enables fine-grained access control, making it widely used for secure data management and sharing in cloud environments. However, no existing CP-ABE scheme provides an efficient and comprehensive solution for verifying both key generation and encryption correctness, leaving errors or malicious behavior undetectable. Such vulnerabilities may result in unauthorized access and compromise the reliability and security of the system. In this work, we propose the first Fully Verifiable CP-ABE scheme, introducing mechanisms to verify the correctness of both key generation and encryption outputs. Our approach leverages pairing-based cryptography to allow users to confirm that their private keys correspond to their assigned attributes while enabling public verification that ciphertexts accurately reflect the intended access policies. By introducing verification mechanisms for both the user's private key and ciphertext, our scheme not only ensures that CP-ABE functions as intended, but also significantly enhances system security, accountability, and reliability. Moreover, our construction preserves the efficiency, expressiveness, and security guarantees of the underlying CP-ABE scheme, making it well-suited for real-world applications that require both correctness and efficiency.

Keywords: Fully Verifiable · Pairing-based Crytography · Ciphertext-Policy Attribute-Based Encryption

1 Introduction

In today's interconnected digital landscape, Ciphertext-Policy Attribute-Based Encryption (CP-ABE) is a powerful cryptographic primitive that enables one-to-many encryption while providing fine-grained access control over encrypted data. In CP-ABE, data owners encrypt data under an access policy that defines which attributes are required for decryption. Each user is issued a private key associated with a set of attributes, and decryption is possible only if their attributes satisfy the access policy. CP-ABE allows sensitive information to be managed

Y. Kim et al. (Eds.): CANS 2025, LNCS 16351, pp. 622–630, 2026.
https://doi.org/10.1007/978-981-95-4434-9_31

and shared securely without relying on trusted storage servers for access enforcement.

In CP-ABE, access control is enforced during the key generation and encryption phases. Consequently, errors in the generation of private keys or ciphertext, whether accidental or malicious, can result in unauthorized users gaining access or legitimate users being denied access. Such risks are unacceptable in domains that demand high assurance, such as finance or healthcare. Furthermore, the possibility of a dishonest authority or encryptor must be considered. This concern is a primary motivation for the work of Badrinarayanan et al. [1] on Verifiable Functional Encryption. As illustrated in their examples, such scenarios are plausible in practice. For instance, a dishonest bank employing a CP-ABE system for data management could intentionally issue a private key that does not correspond to the auditor's role, or manipulate the public access policy to prevent a law enforcement auditor from accessing information that might be unfavorable to the bank.

This motivates the design of CP-ABE schemes that support mechanisms to verify whether a user's private key corresponds to their attributes and whether a ciphertext is correctly encrypted under a given public access policy. We refer to such schemes as **Fully Verifiable CP-ABE schemes**. To the best of our knowledge, however, no existing work provides a concrete construction that is both efficient and practical for real-world deployment.

Related Works. Verifiable Functional Encryption (VFE) [1] is closely related to our work, as CP-ABE can be seen as a special case of Functional Encryption (FE). In this work, the authors formally define a *verifiable FE scheme*, of which a Fully Verifiable CP-ABE scheme is a specific instance. Their generic construction addresses a broader problem by enabling verifiability of both ciphertexts and private keys for any FE scheme. However, it requires executing each FE phase, including Setup, Encrypt, and KeyGen, four times, along with the use of the complex technique of non-interactive witness-indistinguishable (NIWI) proofs. This results in substantial computational overhead for both the prover and the verifier, increases implementation complexity, and is not naturally applicable to existing FE-based systems.

Yamada et al. [8] also provide a formal definition of *verifiability* for FE schemes, but their definition only guarantees that an authorized user with a correct private key will obtain the same result upon decryption. It does not verify whether the private key was generated correctly, nor does it address cases where a ciphertext is encrypted with an incorrect ciphertext attribute Y (or an incorrect access policy in the CP-ABE setting) yet still allows all authorized users to decrypt successfully, while potentially enabling some unauthorized users to decrypt as well.

CP-ABE can also be viewed as a specific case of Predicate Encryption (PE). The Verifiable Predicate Encryption (VPE) scheme of [9] similarly provides a formal definition of *verifiability* for PE schemes, but it inherits some of the same limitations as [8] mentioned above. In addition, they define the notion of *pub-*

lic verifiability for PE schemes, which enables verification that a ciphertext is an encryption of a message $\mathcal{M}$ under a specific ciphertext attribute Y. This *public verifiability* directly corresponds to the requirement of verifying whether a ciphertext is correctly encrypted under a given access policy in CP-ABE. Therefore, if verifiability can be integrated for both the private key and the ciphertext in CP-ABE, we can leverage this line of research. This is particularly valuable because [9] also presents a generic transformation from a CPA-secure VPE scheme to a CCA-secure VPE scheme, and constructs Anonymous Deniable Predicate Authentication from a CCA-secure VPE scheme.

Key-Policy ABE (KP-ABE) is the reverse of CP-ABE, where the access policy is embedded in the user's private key, and the attributes are associated with the ciphertext. Tang et al. [5] investigated verifiability in the key generation process of KP-ABE and extended their approach to Multi-Authority ABE, enabling users to verify that their private keys correctly reflect their access policies. This allows users to detect errors in their keys, requiring the authority to resend only the incorrect components rather than regenerating the entire key, thereby improving efficiency. However, their work does not address verification of ciphertext correctness. Nevertheless, their technique of leveraging bilinear pairings to verify the correctness of the secret-sharing process has been a significant source of inspiration for our work.

OpenABE [7] is an open-source library that meets industry standards and is widely used in ABE research. It implements Waters' Large Universe system [6] with an access policy represented as an access tree and uses type-III pairings to ensure security. To ensure our approach can be easily integrated with OpenABE, we adopt its CP-ABE scheme and extend it with a verification mechanism.

Our Contribution. In this work, we propose the first Fully Verifiable CP-ABE scheme built upon Waters' Large Universe system [6]. Our construction leverages pairing-based cryptography to enable verification of both private keys and ciphertexts. Specifically, users can verify that their private keys correspond to their assigned attributes using only the public parameters. Furthermore, any party can verify that a ciphertext was generated according to the intended access policy by using a verification parameter produced during encryption. We formally prove that incorporating this verification parameter does not compromise the security of the scheme; however, due to space limitations, we omit the proof here and refer interested readers to the full version of this work.

Our approach can be seamlessly applied to existing implementations such as OpenABE without requiring a complete system redesign. Only minor adjustments are needed, along with the addition of two new verification mechanisms. Compared to the generic construction in [1], our approach targets a narrower setting but offers a more natural and efficient solution.

Ensuring the correctness of a private key guarantees that an authorized user can always decrypt a properly encrypted ciphertext. Likewise, verifying that a ciphertext is correctly generated according to the access policy ensures that all authorized users with valid private keys can successfully decrypt it. By combining these guarantees, the CP-ABE system can operate reliably and as intended. They also help avoid unnecessary and costly computations, such as pairing operations during decryption, when a ciphertext is invalid or a private key contains errors. Furthermore, our approach enables efficient error correction, allowing only the faulty components to be replaced instead of requiring the regeneration of entire keys or ciphertexts.

Organization. The remainder of this paper is organized as follows. Section 2 introduces the necessary preliminaries. Section 3 describes our construction, building on [6]. Section 4 presents the evaluation of verification costs and discusses the significance and potential applications of our work. Finally, Sect. 5 concludes the paper and outlines open research directions.

2 Preliminaries

2.1 Access Tree

An access tree $\mathcal{T}$ represents an access structure as a boolean formula in tree form. The formal definition of a (monotone) access structure can be found in [2]. In this tree, each leaf node corresponds to an attribute and is satisfied if the given attribute set includes that attribute. Each non-leaf node functions as a threshold gate, defined by its threshold value and its children. A threshold gate is satisfied when at least the threshold number of its children are satisfied. Consequently, the entire access tree is satisfied if the root node is satisfied. For a comprehensive discussion of access trees, we refer the reader to [7].

We now introduce key notations used in the Fully Verifiable CP-ABE scheme. For a non-leaf node u, let num_u denote the number of its children, and k_u its threshold value. The parent of node u is denoted by $parent(u)$. Each non-leaf node maintains an ordered list of its children, and we define $index(u)$ as the position of node u in this list $(1 \leq index(u) \leq num_{parent(u)})$. For the root node, $index(u)$ is defined as 0. We also define an injective function ρ that maps each leaf node to its corresponding attribute and each non-leaf node to its associated threshold gate.

In our construction, the access tree contains a total of $m+1$ nodes, including ℓ leaf nodes. Each node is assigned a unique index based on a bottom-up order: leaf nodes are indexed from 1 to ℓ, non-root inner nodes from $\ell+1$ to m, and the root node is assigned the index $m+1$.

2.2 Secret Sharing

Given an access tree $\mathcal{T}$, the secret sharing process distributes a secret s such that each leaf node (associated with an attribute) receives a share. If the attribute set satisfies the tree, the secret can be reconstructed from these shares.

Each non-leaf node u is assigned a polynomial $q_u(x)$ of degree $d_u = k_u - 1$, where k_u is the node's threshold. The polynomial is defined as $q_u(x) = a_{u,0} + a_{u,1}x + \cdots + a_{u,d_u}x^{d_u}$, with coefficients $a_{u,i} \in \mathbb{Z}_p$.

At the root, $q_{\text{root}}(0)$ is set to the secret s, and the rest of the coefficients are chosen at random. For any non-root node u, its constant term is set as $q_u(0) = q_{\text{parent}(u)}(\text{index}(u))$, and the remaining coefficients are randomized. The value $\lambda_u = q_u(0)$ is the share at node u. For each leaf node t, the share is directly computed as $\lambda_t = q_{\text{parent}(t)}(\text{index}(t))$.

In summary, the secret sharing process assigns a polynomial to each internal node and computes a share λ_u for every non-root node u.

3 Fully Verifiable CP-ABE

We now present our Fully Verifiable CP-ABE scheme. The construction builds upon the Waters Large Universe system [6], but adopts Type-III pairings and uses an access tree to represent the access structure. For simplicity, we assume that encrypted messages are elements of the target group $\mathbb{G}_T$. We use bold letters to denote vectors or sets of values. The notation $\{X_i\}_{i \in S}$ represents a collection of elements X_i indexed by the elements of the set S.

Setup $(\tau) \rightarrow \text{PK}, \text{MSK}$. The setup algorithm takes a security parameter τ and outputs the public parameters PK and the master secret key MSK:

$$\text{PK} = \{g_1, g_2, g_1^a, e(g_1, g_2)^\alpha\}, \quad \text{MSK} = \{\alpha, g_2^a\}$$

Here, g_1 and g_2 are generators of the bilinear groups $\mathbb{G}_1$ and $\mathbb{G}_2$, respectively. The pairing function is defined as $e : \mathbb{G}_1 \times \mathbb{G}_2 \rightarrow \mathbb{G}_T$. The values α and a are randomly selected from $\mathbb{Z}_p$.

Additionally, **Setup** selects a collision-resistant hash function $H : \{0,1\}^* \rightarrow \mathbb{G}_1$ to map arbitrary strings to elements of $\mathbb{G}_1$.

Keygen $(\text{MSK}, \gamma) \rightarrow \text{SK}$. Given the master secret key MSK and an attribute set γ, the algorithm selects a random $t \in \mathbb{Z}_p$ and outputs the secret key:

$$K = g_2^\alpha \cdot g_2^{at}, \quad L = g_2^t, \quad \forall x \in \gamma \; K_x = H(x)^t$$

VerifyKey $(\text{PK}, \text{SK}) \rightarrow 0/1$. The key verification algorithm checks whether a secret key SK is correctly generated for a given attribute set γ, using only the public parameters PK.

1. **VerifyNumComponents**$(\text{SK}, \gamma) = 1$. This function checks whether the private key SK contains the correct number of components as specified by the protocol.
2. $\forall x \in \gamma : \quad e(H(x), L) = e(K_x, g_2)$. This equation verifies that each attribute x in γ has a unique corresponding component K_x, which is generated based on the attribute x and using the same exponent t as in L.
3. $e(g_1, K) = e(g_1^a, L) \cdot e(g_1, g_2)^\alpha$. This equation verifies whether the component K in SK was correctly constructed using α and a as used in PK, and t as used in L.

   If all checks pass, the algorithm returns 1; otherwise, it returns 0.

Encrypt (PK, $\mathcal{M}$, $\mathcal{T}$) $\rightarrow$ CT, V. The encryption algorithm begins by selecting a random secret $s \in \mathbb{Z}p$ and runs a secret sharing process over the access tree $\mathcal{T}$. Let λ_u denote the share at node u, and let $\{a_{u,1}, \ldots, a_{u,d_u}\}$ be the random coefficients assigned to each inner node u. Additionally, choose random values $r_1, \ldots, r_m \in \mathbb{Z}_p$.

The ciphertext structure remains unchanged from the original scheme:

$$\mathrm{CT} = \{C = \mathcal{M} \cdot e(g_1, g_2)^{\alpha s}, \quad C' = g_1^s,$$
$$(C_1 = g_1^{a\lambda_1} H(\rho(1))^{-r_1}, D_1 = g_2^{r_1}), \ldots, (C_\ell = g_1^{a\lambda_\ell} H(\rho(\ell))^{-r_\ell}, D_\ell = g_2^{r_\ell})\Big\}$$

To support ciphertext verification, we introduce the verification parameter:

$$\mathrm{V} = \{C'' = g_2^s,$$
$$(C_{\ell+1} = g_1^{a\lambda_{\ell+1}} H(\rho(\ell+1))^{-r_{\ell+1}}, D_{\ell+1} = g_2^{r_{\ell+1}}), \ldots, (C_m = g_1^{a\lambda_m} H(\rho(m))^{-r_m}, D_m = g_2^{r_m}),$$
$$(\mathbf{E}_{\ell+1} = \{e(g_1, g_2)^{a a_{\ell+1,i}}\}_{i=1..d_{\ell+1}}, \ldots, \mathbf{E}_m = \{e(g_1, g_2)^{a a_{m,i}}\}_{i=1..d_m}),$$
$$\mathbf{E}_{m+1} = \{e(g_1, g_2)^{a a_{m+1,i}}\}_{i=1..d_{m+1}}, \quad h_{m+1} = e(g_1, g_2)^{as}\Big\}$$

VerifyCiphertext (PK, CT, V) $\rightarrow$ 0/1. The ciphertext verification algorithm checks whether the ciphertext is correctly encrypted under the intended access tree $\mathcal{T}$. It first computes the value h_u for all non-root nodes u as follows:

$$\forall u \in \{1, \ldots, m\}: \quad h_u = e(C_u, g_2) \cdot e(H(\rho(u)), D_u).$$

Then, the algorithm verifies the following conditions:

1. Verifies that CT and V contains the precise number of components:

   VerifyNumComponents(CT, $\mathcal{T}$) and **VerifyNumComponents**(V, $\mathcal{T}$).

2. Verifies that each C_u component has the correct corresponding C'_u component.
$$\forall u \in \{1, ..., \ell\}: \quad e(H(\rho(u)), C_u) = e(C'_u, g_2)$$
3. Verifies that the secret sharing process has been correctly applied through the access structure.
$$\forall u \in \{1, \ldots, m\}: \quad C_u = C_{\mathrm{parent}(u)} \cdot \prod_{i=1}^{d_{\mathrm{parent}(u)}} \left(E_{\mathrm{parent}(u),i}\right)^{\mathrm{index}(u)^i}$$
4. Verifies that C_{m+1} and C''_{m+1} are generated using the same exponent "s".
$$e(C''_{m+1}, g_2) = e(g_1, C_{m+1})$$
5. Verifies that C''_{m+1} and C' are generated using the same exponent "s".
$$e(C''_{m+1}, h) = e(g_1, C')$$

If all checks pass, the algorithm returns 1; otherwise, it returns 0.

Decrypt $(\mathrm{CT}, \mathrm{SK}) \rightarrow \mathcal{M}$. The decryption algorithm remains unchanged compared to the original scheme, so we only present the formula here:

$$\frac{e(C', K)}{\prod_{u \in S}(e(C_u, L) \cdot e(K_{\rho(u)}, D_u))^{\omega_u}} = \frac{e(g_1, g_2)^{\alpha s} \cdot e(g_1, g_2)^{ast}}{\prod_{u \in S}(e(g_1, g_2)^{ta\lambda_u \omega_u})} = e(g_1, g_2)^{\alpha s}$$

The decryption algorithm outputs $C/e(g_1, g_2)^{\alpha s}$.

4 Evaluation and Discussion

Table 1. Verifier and prover overhead of Fully Verifiable CP-ABE. Here, θ denotes the number of attributes in the private key's attribute set. m denotes the number of non-root nodes in the access tree, while ℓ represents the number of leaf nodes. π is defined as the sum of the products of the sharing polynomial degrees and the number of child nodes for all inner nodes ($\pi = \sum_{u=\ell+1}^{m+1} d_u \cdot num_u$). δ denotes the total number of sharing polynomial degree for all inner nodes ($\delta = \sum_{u=\ell+1}^{m+1} d_u$).

<table>
<tr><th colspan="5">Verifier Overhead</th><th>Prover Overhead</th></tr>
<tr><th rowspan="2">Verify Algorithm</th><th colspan="4">Number of Operations</th><th rowspan="2">Operations</th></tr>
<tr><th>Hash to $\mathbb{G}_1$</th><th>$\mathbb{G}_T$ Add</th><th>$\mathbb{G}_T$ Exp</th><th>Pairing</th></tr>
<tr><td>VerifyKey</td><td>θ</td><td>1</td><td>0</td><td>$2\theta + 2$</td><td>1 pairing +
$\delta + 1$ $\mathbb{G}_T$ Exp +
$(m - \ell + 1)$ $\mathbb{G}_2$ Exp +</td></tr>
<tr><td>VerifyCiphertext</td><td>m</td><td>$m + \pi$</td><td>π</td><td>$2m + 3$</td><td>$(m - \ell)$ $\mathbb{G}_1$ Add +
$2(m - \ell)$ $\mathbb{G}_1$ Exp +
$(m - \ell)$ Hash to $\mathbb{G}_1$</td></tr>
</table>

Evaluation. Table 1 reports the verification cost for the verifier and the additional overhead for the prover introduced by integrating verifiability into CP-ABE. We focus on the number of pairing operations, as they are the most computationally expensive.

Verifying a private key with θ attributes requires $2\theta+2$ pairings, while verifying a ciphertext whose access tree contains $m+1$ nodes requires $2m+3$ pairings. Both costs scale linearly with θ and m, respectively. However, each verification only needs to be performed once to ensure the correctness of the private key and ciphertext.

A verified private key guarantees that any correctly generated ciphertext can be decrypted by its holder, while a verified ciphertext ensures that all authorized users with valid private keys can decrypt it. Combining both guarantees enforces correct system behavior without assuming trust in any party, making it suitable for deployment in high-security environments.

On the prover side, only one pairing operation is required regardless of access tree size, since the term $e(g_1, g_2)^a$ is computed once and reused. Consequently, the prover's computational overhead remains negligible.

Potential Application. OpenABE [7] is one of the few open-source implementations of attribute-based encryption that meets production standards. It is widely used in research on ABE, especially in cloud computing, IoT, and healthcare [3,4]. Our work can be directly applied to enhance OpenABE by providing verifiability for its CP-ABE scheme.

OpenABE implements a Key Encapsulation Mechanism (KEM) variant of the Waters Large Universe system, which it refers to as the CPA-KEM scheme. This serves as the core building block, encapsulating a component used to derive a symmetric key based on an access tree. The symmetric key is then used to encrypt data with AES. Authorized users can reconstruct the symmetric key from the CPA-KEM output and use it to decrypt the encrypted data.

Our technique can be seamlessly integrated into CPA-KEM to make it fully verifiable without compromising security. By making CPA-KEM verifiable, we ensure that its output is correctly generated from the publicly known policy tree and that every authorized user reconstructs the same symmetric key. This enables a crucial expansion: if one authorized user successfully decrypts the ciphertext using their reconstructed symmetric key, we can confidently conclude that all authorized users will also be able to decrypt it successfully.

5 Conclusion and Open Directions

We presented the first Fully Verifiable Ciphertext-Policy Attribute-Based Encryption construction based on Waters's Large Universe System [6], incorporating mechanisms that allow users to privately verify that their keys correspond to their attribute sets and enabling public verification of whether ciphertexts are correctly encrypted under a given access policy. These verification procedures preserve the original scheme's expressiveness and security while enhancing its reliability. This advancement paves the way for the reliable deployment of CP-ABE in systems requiring high accuracy, such as financial and healthcare applications, as well as in settings involving dishonest authorities or encryptors.

In the future, this work can be extended to CP-ABE schemes that do not employ access trees as their access policy, as well as to more advanced settings such as multi-authority CP-ABE, hidden-policy schemes, and proxy re-encryption.

Acknowledgements. This research is supported by research funding from Faculty of Information Technology, University of Science, Vietnam National University - Ho Chi Minh City.

References

1. Badrinarayanan, S., Goyal, V., Jain, A., Sahai, A.: Verifiable functional encryption. In: International Conference on the Theory and Application of Cryptology and Information Security, pp. 557–587. Springer (2016)
2. Beimel, A.: Secure schemes for secret sharing and key distribution. PhD thesis, Israel Institute of Technology, Technion (1996)
3. Kang, G., Kim, Y.G.: Secure collaborative platform for health care research in an open environment: perspective on accountability in access control. J. Med. Internet Res. **24**(10), e37978 (2022)
4. Roy, S., Crowley, T., Mark, B.L., Zeng, K., Khasawneh, K.N.: Evaluating and optimizing cryptographic offloading for IoT devices: attribute-based encryption case study. In: 2024 IEEE International Conference on Communications Workshops (ICC Workshops), pp. 189–194. IEEE (2024)
5. Tang, Q., Ji, D.: Verifiable attribute-based encryption. Cryptology ePrint Archive (2007)
6. Waters, B.: Ciphertext-policy attribute-based encryption: an expressive, efficient, and provably secure realization. In: International workshop on public key cryptography, pp. 53–70. Springer (2011)
7. Waters, B., Green, M., Waters, S.H., Akinyele, J.A.: Openabe. https://github.com/zeutro/openabe/blob/master/docs/libopenabe-v1.0.0-design-doc.pdf (2018). version 1.0
8. Yamada, S., Attrapadung, N., Hanaoka, G., Kunihiro, N.: Generic constructions for chosen-ciphertext secure attribute based encryption. In: International Workshop on Public Key Cryptography, pp. 71–89. Springer (2011)
9. Yamada, S., Attrapadung, N., Santoso, B., Schuldt, J.C., Hanaoka, G., Kunihiro, N.: Verifiable predicate encryption and applications to CCA security and anonymous predicate authentication. In: International Workshop on Public Key Cryptography, pp. 243–261. Springer (2012)

Few-Shot Retrieval-Augmented LLMs for Anomaly Detection in Network Traffic

Furqan Rustam[1(✉)], Islam Obaidat[2], Davide Di Monda[3], and Anca Delia Jurcut[1]

[1] School of Computer Science, University College Dublin, Dublin, Ireland
furqan.rustam@ucdconnect.ie, anca.jurcut@ucd.ie
[2] Department of CST, North Carolina A&T State University, Greensboro, USA
iaobaidat@ncat.edu
[3] University of Napoli Federico II and IMT School of Advanced Studies Lucca, Naples, Italy
davide.dimonda@unina.it

Abstract. Accurate anomaly detection is essential for protecting heterogeneous *multi-environment* (M-En) networks, where traditional enterprise traffic coexists with *Internet of Things* (IoT) flows. Existing machine learning-based anomaly detection approaches rely on extensive labeled data and frequent retraining, and therefore adapt poorly to unseen attack patterns and few-data settings. In this work, a *Retrieval-Augmented Generation* (RAG) pipeline is introduced in which *Large Language Models* (LLMs) are guided to classify malicious traffic under few-shot settings. Structured packet-level and statistical features are first rendered into natural-language prompts; dense sentence embeddings are then produced and indexed with FAISS (Facebook AI Similarity Search, an approximate-nearest-neighbour vector index) to construct a vector-based knowledge base. At inference time, the embedding of an unseen packet is used to retrieve a specified number of semantically similar, labeled examples, which are supplied as in-context examples to the LLM. This workflow enables learning over heterogeneous traffic without model fine-tuning, improves generalization, and yields human-readable explanations of each decision. When paired with MPNet embeddings and a context of 200 retrieved examples, the 4B-parameter `Gemma3:4b` model reaches 1.0 accuracy, while the 7B `Mistral` model achieves 0.98. Inference takes 23.51 s with `Gemma3:4b` and 66.7 s with `Mistral` for 50 samples, both running on a single NVIDIA GeForce RTX 3090 GPU.

Keywords: LLMs · RAG · Network Security · M-En Networks · Anomaly Detection

1 Introduction

Modern network infrastructures face increasingly complex and evolving cybersecurity threats, including malicious traffic targeting both traditional enterprise

Y. Kim et al. (Eds.): CANS 2025, LNCS 16351, pp. 631–642, 2026.
https://doi.org/10.1007/978-981-95-4434-9_32

systems and *Internet of Things* (IoT) devices [23]. As these diverse traffic sources converge into integrated *multi-environment* (M-En) networks [21,25], the task of accurately detecting cyberattacks becomes more challenging due to heterogeneous traffic patterns, limited labeled data, and the frequent emergence of novel attack variants. Traditional *Machine Learning* (ML) and *Deep Learning* (DL) models typically require extensive labeled datasets and retraining to adapt to new threats, limiting their application in real-time or low-resource scenarios [9].

Recent advances in *Large Language Model* (LLMs) have prompted their exploration in network anomaly detection due to their contextual understanding and adaptability [4,13]. While early studies show that standalone LLMs often underperform compared to traditional models in terms of detection accuracy [14], they offer significant benefits in explainability and incident analysis. Hybrid approaches like IDS-Agent [15] and HuntGPT [3] integrate LLMs with retrieval tools and prompt engineering to enhance detection performance and interpretability. Architectural innovations, e.g., FlowTransformer [16] and BERT-LightGBM combinations [10], deliver satisfactory results, but at the cost of high model complexity. In-context learning with few-shot examples has shown promising performance on zero-day attacks [24], though prior works do not address detection in heterogeneous M-En networks. In parallel, M-En anomaly detection efforts [19,20] rely on ensemble models and automated pipelines to handle mixed traffic from IoT, SDN, and IP-based networks. These approaches achieve robust performance but require extensive offline training and lack contextual reasoning. Furthermore, many rely on synthetic or merged datasets that fail to capture the complexity of real-world M-En environments [21]. Our work addresses these limitations by leveraging real-time NS-3-generated data and a *Retrieval-Augmented Generation* (RAG)-based LLM framework for few-shot, context-aware detection across diverse networks. Further, our proposed framework addresses key challenges in network anomaly detection, namely limited labeled data and generalization across diverse networks. Our experimental results confirm that RAG empowers LLMs to accurately detect anomalies, even in few-shot scenarios. Our findings underscore the potential of prompt-based LLM frameworks as flexible, accurate, and label-efficient solutions for securing heterogeneous network environments.

The **contributions** of our study are as follows: (***i***) We contribute to the security of M-En networks by deploying LLMs capable of distinguishing between normal and malicious traffic. Our approach also incorporates explainability, allowing the model to justify its predictions. (***ii***) We propose a novel few-shot contextual-learning framework based on the RAG paradigm. This framework enables LLMs to leverage relevant contextual data retrieved from a vector database, significantly enhancing performance in scenarios with limited labeled traffic and unseen attack patterns. (***iii***) We integrate a vector database (FAISS) into the RAG pipeline using sentence embeddings, which accelerates retrieval and reduces computational overhead. This design enables real-time or near-real-time threat detection while maintaining high accuracy and scalability.

The paper is structured as follows: Sect. 2 details our LLM-based approach and prompt engineering for M-En networks; Sect. 3 presents results; and Sect. 4 summarizes our findings and proposes future directions.

2 Proposed Methodology

In this work, we propose a RAG pipeline that harnesses the reasoning ability of LLMs to detect anomalies in M-En network traffic under few-shot settings. The overall framework is shown in Fig. 1. At a high level, our approach unfolds as follows: we begin with a real-world M-En dataset; we then extract and normalize packet-level and statistical features, which are later converted into prompts readable by the LLM; for contextual domain knowledge, we use a RAG approach, which leverages a domain-specific database in prompt format. During inference, the input query is first embedded. Relevant contextual information is then retrieved from the database, appended to the query, and passed to the LLM for prediction. We detail this procedure below.

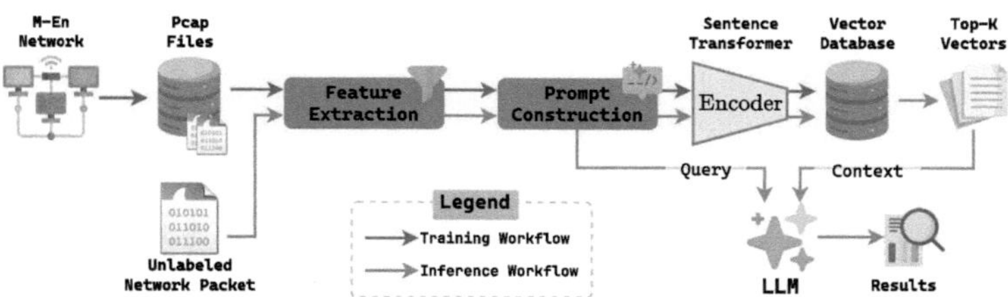

Fig. 1. Our framework consists of two main processes: the *Training Workflow* (blue), which converts labeled packets into embedded natural-language prompts for storage, and the *Inference Workflow* (red), which embeds an unseen packet, retrieves nearest neighbors, and queries an LLM for prediction. (Color figure online)

⇒ **Dataset Description:** We construct a comprehensive M-En dataset that contains benign and malicious traffic captured from both traditional and IoT networks. Every sample corresponds to *one packet.* Its feature vector is a hybrid of (i) 18 packet–level attributes extracted directly from that packet (IP/port fields, protocol flags, sizes, etc.) and (ii) 20 statistical features that summaries all packets observed in the same 1-second aggregation window (packet count, entropy measures, flag frequencies, flow rate, etc.). The label denotes whether the packet is benign (0) or malicious (1). The dataset contains M-En traffic [22], composed of the following sources:

1. **DDoShield-IoT testbed** [7]**:** DDoShield-IoT combines NS-3 and Docker to generate (*i*) benign traditional traffic (FTP, HTTP, RTMP) and (*ii*) malicious IoT traffic produced by Mirai binaries [7]. A Python listener running on a promiscuous Docker node captures and labels every packet in real-time.

2. **External PCAP traces:** Because the testbed does not generate benign IoT or malicious traditional flows, two well-established corpora are injected into the simulation: MQTT-IoT-IDS2020 dataset [1] (benign IoT) and CIC DDoS 2019 dataset [5] (malicious traditional). Packets are replayed through a virtual interface to ensure consistent labeling and feature extraction via the same capture pipeline.

The resulting two-class corpus is shuffled and balanced to avoid source bias and reflect realistic M-En conditions, yielding a final dataset with 38 features.

⇒**Structuring Network Traffic for LLM:** Traffic samples, x_i, have numeric and categorical features. However, LLMs are designed and pre-trained to understand natural language, not raw numbers or feature vectors as traditional ML models. Hence, we transform traffic samples into human-readable token sequences (prompts) using a template function: $\mathcal{Q}(x_i) = q_i$, ready for LLM input.

⇒**Query Embedding:** To enable LLMs to reason over network traffic, we transform the prompts into semantically meaningful embeddings (also called dense vectors) using a pre-trained *Sentence Transformer*, e.g., `all-mpnet-base-v2` [2]. Formally: $\mathbf{e}_i = \text{Encoder}(q_i) \in \mathbb{R}^d$ where d is the embedding dimension (e.g., $d = 768$ for `all-mpnet-base-v2`). These vectors capture the semantic relationships and behavioral similarities between network traffic samples.

⇒**Training Workflow:** After outlining the main components of the framework, we present the offline training workflow as follows. (***i***) *Feature Extraction:* The labeled traffic dataset, $\mathcal{D} = \{(x_i, y_i)\}_{i=1}^{N}$, contains traffic samples x_i, each characterized by 38 features as described earlier, and labels y_i indicating benign (`0`) or malicious (`1`) samples. (***ii***) *Textual Prompt Construction:* Each sample, x_i, is then converted into a structured prompt in natural language, i.e., $\mathcal{Q}(x_i) = q_i$, as explained before. These prompts include packet-based features and the corresponding label. (***iii***) *Embedding Generation and Vector Indexing:* The textual prompts, q_i, are embedded into dense vectors via the Sentence Transformer (i.e., $\mathbf{e}_i = \text{Encoder}(q_i)$), and later stored in a database and indexed using FAISS (*Facebook AI Similarity Search*) [8], a high-performance library for fast similarity search in vector spaces. FAISS constructs an index $\mathcal{I} = \{\mathbf{e}_i\}_{i=1}^{N}$ that enables efficient retrieval of semantically similar samples during inference and supports fast *approximate nearest neighbor* (ANN) queries.

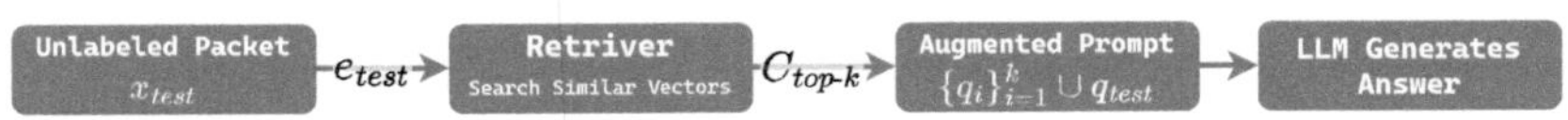

Fig. 2. Inference steps needed to classify an unlabeled packet, x_{test}.

⇒**Inference Workflow & Evaluation:** In the inference workflow (i.e., online phase), the framework follows the steps described hereinafter to classify a new unlabeled packet (x_{test}). (*i*) Retrieval-Augmented Prompting *(RAP):* The test packet is first converted into a natural-language prompt using the same template as in training, q_{test}. Afterwards, its dense vector representation, e_{test}, is used to retrieve the top-$k(=5)$ most similar vectors from the index $\mathcal{I}$ via $L2$ similarity. Formally, $C_{top\text{-}k} = \text{Top}K_{L2}(e_{test}, \mathcal{I}) = \{(q_1, y_1), ..., (q_k, y_k)\}$. Retrieved samples are used to augment the LLM prompt via RAG. (*ii*) *Few-Shot LLM Inference:* A pre-trained LLM (e.g., `Mistral`) is queried using the RAG prompt composed of the natural-language representations of the $k = 5$ retrieved samples, followed by the query q_{test}, which represents the unlabeled packet (see Appendix A for an example). The LLM is instructed to respond with a prediction $\hat{y}_{test}$, which can be "`Attack`" or "`Normal`" based on the given context and features of the query packet. Figure 2 summarizes the LLM and RAG inference steps. (*iii*) *Evaluation:* We evaluate the framework by comparing predictions with ground-truth labels using *Accuracy* as the primary metric. We also assess performance under limited labeled data and class imbalance, measuring GPU, CPU, RAM usage, and testing time. Efficiency is further quantified using Latency-Budget per Parameter (LBP) and Resource Efficiency Ratio (RER), where RER $= \frac{\#\text{Parameters}}{\text{Time}} \times 100$ and LBP $= \frac{\text{Time}}{\#\text{Parameters}} \times 100$.

⇒**Model Overview & Selection Criteria:** In this subsection, we briefly describe the LLMs evaluated in our experiments, chosen for their architectural diversity and suitability for constrained environments. Each model exhibits unique capabilities in terms of instruction following, context window size, positional encoding, and computational efficiency. These factors directly influence their performance in RAG-based cybersecurity tasks, particularly under real-time and M-En constraints. The core architectural characteristics and capabilities of the evaluated models are summarized in Table 1. `Mistral` [17] employs a decoder-only transformer architecture with a *Sliding Window Positional Encoding* (SWPE) [6], enabling a large context window of up to 32k tokens. This makes `Mistral` well-suited for long-sequence reasoning in RAG pipelines. SWPE is defined as $PE(t) = f(t \bmod w)$, where t is the token index and w is the window size, enabling attention to slide within fixed-length segments. `Deepseek-R1` [18] uses a GPT-style decoder transformer with a context range of 4k–8k tokens. It employs *Rotary Positional Encoding* (RoPE), defined as $PE(t) = \cos(\omega t) + \sin(\omega t)$, where ω is a learned frequency matrix [12]. Its limited instruction tuning and moderate context length reduce semantic alignment for cybersecurity-specific inputs. `Phi` is based on a lightweight transformer architecture and uses *Absolute Positional Encoding* with a context length of 2k–4k, making it highly efficient and latency-friendly; however, the encoding (i.e., $PE_t = E_t$) is fixed for each position t, limiting generalization across longer sequences. `Gemma3:4b`, based on Google's decoder architecture, uses RoPE with an 8k token window and is optimized for instruction-following tasks, making it well-suited for RAG workflows. Similarly, both `LLaMA3` and `LLaMA3.2` incorporate RoPE and decoder-only transformer with 8k and 4k context windows, respectively [11]. While `LLaMA3` scales well, `LLaMA3.2` saturates quickly on longer RAG prompts due to limited context size and fewer attention heads.

Table 1. Model capabilities relevant to LLM-based RAG.

Model	Context Window	Instruction Tuning	Positional Encoding	Efficiency
Mistral	32k	●	SWPE	High
Deepseek-R1	4k–8k	◐	RoPE	Medium
Phi	2k–4k	○	Absolute	Very High
Gemma3:4b	8k	●	RoPE	High
LLaMA3	8k	●	RoPE	High
LLaMA3.2	4k	●	RoPE	Medium

3 Framework Evaluation and Result Discussion

We conduct experiments on a Windows 11 Pro (DELL) system with an Intel® Core™ i7-1265U CPU, 64 GB RAM, and an NVIDIA RTX 3090 GPU (24 GB VRAM). We use Python 3.11.7, OLLaMA 0.6.4, TensorFlow and scikit-learn. In this section, we simulate real-world scenarios, benchmark execution times, and assess CPU vs. GPU suitability for deploying LLMs.

Table 2. Resource usage and efficiency metrics.

Model	GPU (MB)	CPU%	RAM%	Time (s)	M. Size	#Param (B)	LBP	RER
Mistral	11521	32.80	33.70	66.70	4.10	7.00	9.53	10.49
Deepseek-R1	5480	19.80	34.20	206.53	4.70	7.00	29.50	3.39
Phi	4972	40.30	42.70	34.57	1.60	2.70	12.80	7.81
Gemma3:4b	4308	33.20	42.80	23.51	3.30	4.00	5.88	17.01
LLaMA3	6120	31.30	37.30	37.78	4.70	8.00	4.72	21.18
LLaMA3.2	3612	25.20	38.30	21.72	2.00	3.00	7.24	13.81

⇒**Resource Consumption Analysis:** Table 2 provides a comparative analysis of the evaluated LLMs for intrusion detection in M-En networks, focusing on latency and efficiency. `LLaMA3` achieves the highest efficiency, with the best RER (21.18) and the lowest LBP (4.72). `Gemma3:4b` follows closely with an RER of 17.01 and LBP of 5.88. `Mistral`, despite its high VRAM usage, remains efficient (RER 10.49, LBP 9.53). In contrast, `Deepseek-R1` shows poor performance due to high latency and a low RER. Lightweight models, i.e., `Phi` and `LLaMA3.2`, are suitable for low-resource environments, though `Phi`'s high LBP limits its per-parameter scalability. `LLaMA3` and `Mistral` are best suited for high-performance needs, `Gemma3:4b` offers an efficient trade-off, and `Phi` and `LLaMA3.2` are ideal for constrained settings. Inference time for LLMs significantly improves with GPU w.r.t. CPU. Figure 3 shows that the average prediction time using GPUs ranges from $\approx$ 21.72 s (`LLaMA3.2`) to $\approx$ 206.53 s (`Deepseek-R1`) for 50 samples.

In contrast, CPU execution times rise drastically, with models like `Mistral` and `LLaMA3` requiring $\approx$ 17,050 s and $\approx$ 20,425 s, respectively, nearly **250**$\times$ slower. Even smaller models, i.e., `Phi` and `LLaMA3.2`, experience significant slowdowns, with GPU inference times of 34.57 s and 21.72 s increasing to $\approx$ 7,900 s and $\approx$ 6,421 s on CPU, respectively. This highlights the critical importance of GPU acceleration for real-time M-En anomaly detection, where low latency is essential.

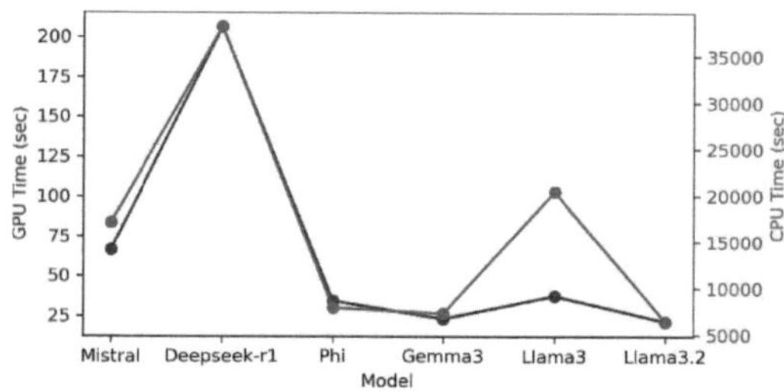

Fig. 3. GPU vs CPU: prediction time for 50 samples.

$\Rightarrow$**Attack Detection in M-En Networks:** In our framework, a packet is first encoded using a Sentence Transformer and then passed through the RAG. We evaluate two pre-trained Sentence Transformers: `all-mpnet-base-v2` (`MPNet` for brevity) and `all-MiniLM-L6-v2` (`MiniLM` for brevity). Table 3 summarizes their main features. Overall, `MPNet` offers rich semantic representations with a 768-dimensional space, enhancing representations for complex traffic patterns. `MiniLM` uses 384-dimensional embeddings and a lighter architecture, enabling $\sim 2\times$ faster encoding and reduced memory usage. As vector search scales with $\mathcal{O}(n \cdot d)$, `MiniLM` is ideal for speed, while `MPNet` favors precision, a trade-off between efficiency and accuracy.

Table 3. Comparison of Sentence Transformers.

Property	MPNet	MiniLM
Tokenizer Vocabulary Size	30,527	30,522
Embedding Length	768	384
Embedding Dimension	768	384
Model Architecture	MPNetForMaskedLM	BertModel
Model Hidden Size	768	384

Table 4 shows the accuracy of the LLMs with RAG using `MiniLM` and `MPNet`. We consider two context sizes (*RAG-200* and *RAG-1000*). `Mistral` and `Gemma3:4b` consistently perform well with `MPNet`, 0.98 and 1.00 for RAG-200, respectively. This improvement is due to the higher embedding dimensionality of `MPNet` (768 vs. 384 of `MiniLM`), which better captures fine-grained features. Larger embeddings enable better alignment between traffic semantics and latent space, leading to improved decision boundaries. However, performance does not increase monotonically with context size (e.g., `Mistral` drops by −0.06 from RAG-200 to RAG-1000 with `MPNet`). This drop likely stems from context window over-saturation: too many samples add noise, especially for models not tuned for long-span reasoning. This highlights a key insight—*retrieval quantity must match the model ability to filter relevant information*, particularly under high-dimensional embeddings. Weaker performance from `Deepseek-R1` and `LLaMA3.2` reflects architectural and compatibility limitations. `Deepseek-R1` suffers from a domain mismatch between its general pre-training and intrusion detection, while `LLaMA3.2` lacks the capacity to generalize over complex embeddings, especially in large RAG contexts. These results indicate that embedding quality alone is insufficient; effective performance relies on architecture and training data alignment. In contrast, `Mistral` and `Gemma3:4b` exhibit strong accuracy and interoperability (Appendix B). `Mistral`'s large context window and efficient attention support precise, context-aware reasoning, while `Gemma3:4b` benefits from instruction tuning and prompt alignment. Both LLMs leverage semantic embeddings and positional encoding to support accurate M-En intrusion detection and explainable outputs.

Table 4. LLMs accuracy using `MiniLM` and `MPNet`.

Model	MiniLM		MPNet	
	RAG-200	RAG-1000	RAG-200	RAG-1000
`Mistral`	0.96	0.94	0.98	0.92
`Deepseek-R1`	0.58	0.44	0.42	0.42
`Phi`	0.58	0.58	0.64	0.64
`Gemma3:4b`	0.94	0.94	1.00	1.00
`LLaMA3`	0.64	0.80	0.64	0.72
`LLaMA3.2`	0.56	0.48	0.44	0.46

⇒**Results without using RAG:** Table 5 shows a significant drop in accuracy without RAG (e.g., `Mistral` drops from 0.98 to 0.56) and a drastic increase in inference time (e.g., from 66.7 to 310.22 seconds). This degradation occurs because, without RAG, LLMs receive no contextual guidance and must rely solely on their pre-trained knowledge to classify complex traffic patterns. RAG improves reasoning by retrieving semantically similar samples via FAISS. RAG simplifies learning from $P(y|x)$ by conditioning on relevant context c, i.e., $P(y|x) \rightarrow P(y|x, c)$, where c is retrieved from the database using embedding similarity. FAISS uses $L2$ distance to enable sub-linear retrieval even in high-dimensional spaces (e.g., $d = 768$ for `MPNet`). This sharply narrows the semantic space, improving both accuracy and latency. Without RAG, inference relies on cold queries, leading to slower, less accurate predictions.

Table 5. Results of LLMs without using RAG.

Metric	Mistral	Deepseek-R1	Phi	Gemma3:4b	LLaMA3	LLaMA3.2
Accuracy	0.56	0.54	0.52	0.56	0.56	0.60
Time (S)	310.22	889.06	126.97	528.49	285.31	216.52

⇒**Limitations:** While LLMs enable rich reasoning, they introduce significant computational overhead. Converting structured telemetry to verbose natural language inflates token counts, adds redundancy, and may obscure anomaly features, especially for LLMs not trained on domain-specific data (e.g., `Mistral` and `Phi`). Inference latency grows with token length ($\mathcal{O}(n)$), raising GPU usage. Embedding models (`MiniLM`, `MPNet`) can introduce bias, weakening detection of subtle threats. FAISS-based retrieval suffers from the curse of dimensionality, semantic drift, and cold-start issues, often leading to imbalanced or irrelevant context retrieval, especially for zero-day attacks.

4 Conclusion and Future Work

This study presents experimental evaluations for attack detection in M-En networks using an LLM-based framework. Through extensive experimentation, we conclude that LLMs can perform effectively under complex scenarios and even in the presence of unseen attacks. LLMs demonstrate strong few-shot learning abilities thanks to their pre-training and generalized skills. Furthermore, we observe that the performance of LLMs without retrieval augmentation (i.e., without RAG and embeddings) is limited, achieving a maximum accuracy of 0.60. However, with the RAG, LLMs achieved significantly higher performance (up to 0.98 with `Mistral` and 1.00 with `Gemma3:4b`). We also conclude that FAISS (vector database) and RAG improve accuracy as well as enhance the inference speed. Although RAG prompts are larger, they provide highly relevant context that simplifies the decision task, reducing computational complexity. This results in faster and more accurate responses compared to shorter, less informative prompts. In our future work, we aim to fine-tune domain-specific LLMs for cybersecurity applications and explore lightweight retrieval frameworks suitable for deployment in real-time and resource-constrained environments.

A Final Prompt

'**Here are examples of network traffic:** Network Traffic Data: - Protocol: TCP - TCP: 1 - UDP: 0 - Packet Size: 60 ...... Label: Attack Network Traffic Data: - Protocol: TCP - TCP: 1 - UDP: 0 - Packet Size: 60 ...... Label: Attack Network Traffic Data: - Protocol: TCP - TCP: 1 - UDP: 0 - Packet Size: 60 .... Label: Attack Network Traffic Data: - Protocol: TCP - TCP: 1 - UDP: 0 - Packet Size: 60 .... Label: Attack Network Traffic Data: - Protocol: TCP - TCP: 1 - UDP: 0 - Packet Size: 78 ..... Label: Attack **Now classify the following sample:** Network Traffic Data: - Protocol: TCP - TCP: 1 - UDP: 0 - Packet Size: 93 ...... **Answer only as:** "Attack" or "Normal".'

B LLM Explainability for Decision Making

Table 6. Sample of Results by LLM (`Mistral`) with Explainability.

Prediction	True Label	Explainability
Attack	Attack	Based on the provided data, it appears that this network traffic could be classified as an "Attack". The high number of SYN packets (118195 out of 119068 total packets), repeated connection attempts, and the significant variance in sequence numbers (1.531506e+18) are indicative of a potential attack, such as a port scan or Denial-of-Service (DoS) attempt. The increased Source Entropy and Destination Port Entropy also suggest unusual activity
Normal	Normal	Based on the provided data, it appears this sample is labeled as "Normal". However, I want to point out that the extremely low payload size of 0 bytes in many packets and a high standard deviation for packet sizes might raise concerns

C Reproducibility

The implementation is available on https://github.com/furqanrustam/Few-Shot-Retrieval-Augmented-LLMs to support reproducibility.

References

1. MQTT-IoT-IDS2020 Dataset. https://paperswithcode.com/dataset/mqtt-iot-ids2020. Accessed 27 July 2025
2. sentence-transformers/all-mpnet-base-v2. https://huggingface.co/sentence-transformers/all-mpnet-base-v2. Accessed 27 July 2025
3. Ali, T., Kostakos, P.: Huntgpt: Integrating Machine Learning-Based Anomaly Detection and Explainable AI With Large Language Models (LLMs). arXiv preprint (2023)
4. Bovenzi, G., et al.: Mapping the landscape of generative AI in network monitoring and management. IEEE Trans. Netw. Serv. Manag. (2025)
5. Canadian Institute for Cybersecurity: CIC-DDoS2019 Dataset. https://www.unb.ca/cic/datasets/ddos-2019.html. Accessed 27 July 2025
6. Child, R., Gray, S., Radford, A., Sutskever, I.: Generating long sequences with sparse transformers. arXiv preprint arXiv:1904.10509 (2019)
7. De Vivo, S., Obaidat, I., Dai, D., Liguori, P.: DDoShield-IoT: a testbed for simulating and lightweight detection of IoT botnet DDoS attacks. In: Proceedings of the 54th Annual IEEE/IFIP International Conference on Dependable Systems and Networks Workshops (DSN-W), pp. 1–8 (2024)
8. Douze, M., et al.: The Faiss Library (2024)
9. Geetha, R., Thilagam, T.: A review on the effectiveness of machine learning and deep learning algorithms for cyber security. Arch. Comput. Methods Eng. **28**(4), 2861–2879 (2021)
10. Ghourabi, A.: A security model based on LightGBM and transformer to protect healthcare systems from cyberattacks. IEEE Access **10**, 48890–48903 (2022)
11. Grattafiori, A., et al.: The llama 3 herd of models. arXiv preprint arXiv:2407.21783 (2024)
12. Guo, D., et al.: Deepseek-r1: incentivizing reasoning capability in LLMs via reinforcement learning. arXiv preprint arXiv:2501.12948 (2025)
13. Halvorsen, J., Izurieta, C., Cai, H., Gebremedhin, A.: Applying generative machine learning to intrusion detection: a systematic mapping study and review. ACM Comput. Surv. **56**(10), 1–33 (2024)
14. Houssel, P.R., Singh, P., Layeghy, S., Portmann, M.: Towards Explainable Network Intrusion Detection Using Large Language Models. arXiv preprint (2024)
15. Li, Y., Xiang, Z., Bastian, N.D., Song, D., Li, B.: IDS-agent: an LLM agent for explainable intrusion detection in IoT networks. In: NeurIPS 2024 Workshop on Open-World Agents (2024)
16. Manocchio, L.D., Layeghy, S., Lo, W.W., Kulatilleke, G.K., Sarhan, M., Portmann, M.: FlowTransformer: a transformer framework for flow-based network intrusion detection systems. Expert Syst. Appl. **241**, 122564 (2024)
17. Mistral AI: Announcing mistral 7b (2023). https://mistral.ai/news/announcing-mistral-7b. Accessed 27 July 2025
18. Ollama / DeepSeek AI: Deepseek-r1 (2025). https://ollama.com/library/deepseek-r1. Accessed 27 July 2025
19. Rustam, F., Aljedaani, W., Elsayed, M.S., Jurcut, A.D.: FAMTDS: a novel MFO-based fully automated malicious traffic detection system for multi-environment networks. Comput. Netw. **251**, 110603 (2024)
20. Rustam, F., Jurcut, A.D.: Malicious traffic detection in multi-environment networks using novel S-DATE and PSO-D-SEM approaches. Comput. Secur. **136**, 103564 (2024)

21. Rustam, F., Jurcut, A.D., Aljedaani, W., Ashraf, I.: Securing multi-environment networks using versatile synthetic data augmentation technique and machine learning algorithms. In: 20th Annual International Conference on Privacy, Security and Trust (PST), pp. 1–10. IEEE (2023). https://doi.org/10.1109/PST58708.2023.10320203
22. Rustam, F., Obaidat, I., Jurcut, A.D.: MULTI-LF: a unified continuous learning framework for real-time DDoS detection in multi-environment networks (2025)
23. Rustam, F., Ranaweera, P., Jurcut, A.D.: AI on the defensive and offensive: securing multi-environment networks from AI agents. In: International Conference on Communications (ICC), pp. 4287–4292. IEEE (2024). https://doi.org/10.1109/ICC51166.2024.10622943
24. Zhang, H., Sediq, A.B., Afana, A., Erol-Kantarci, M.: Large Language Models in Wireless Application Design: In-Context Learning-Enhanced Automatic Network Intrusion Detection. arXiv preprint (2024)
25. Zukaib, U., Cui, X., Zheng, C., Liang, D., Din, S.U.: Meta-fed ids: meta-learning and federated learning based fog-cloud approach to detect known and zero-day cyber attacks in IoMT networks. J. Parallel Distrib. Comput. **192**, 104934 (2024)

Impossible Differential Attack on SAND-128

Nobuyuki Sugio(✉)

Hokkaido University of Science, Sapporo, Japan
sugio-n@hus.ac.jp

Abstract. SAND-128 is an AND-RX-based Feistel cipher proposed by Chen et al. (Designs, Codes and Cryptography 2022). This paper evaluates the security of the lightweight block cipher SAND-128 against impossible differential attacks. We use the bit-level Constraint Programming (CP) model proposed by Hadipour et al., which enables an automatic search for impossible differential distinguishers without requiring fixed input/output differences. Applying this model, we identified $2^{14} \times 7 = 114,688$ distinguishers over 14 rounds. Using one of them, and following the complexity framework established by Boura et al., we show a 21-round key-recovery attack on SAND-128 with data, time, and memory complexities of 2^{126}, $2^{126.33}$, and 2^{122} respectively.

Keyword: Impossible differential attack, lightweight cipher, SAND, Constraint Programming

1 Introduction

Impossible differential attack was independently proposed by Biham et al. [1] and Knudsen [2]. Impossible differential was defined as the differential with probability zero. Boura et al. have formalized the necessary number of data, time, and memory complexities for the impossible differential attacks [3,4].

SAND is proposed by Chen et al. in Designs, Codes and Cryptography 2022 [5]. SAND is a family of lightweight Feistel block ciphers (64- or 128-bit block size with a 128-bit key) designed using only AND, rotation, and XOR (AND-RX) operations, while enabling classical S-box-based cryptanalytic techniques.

For security evaluation, the designers analyzed differential attack [6], linear attack [7], and other cryptanalytical methods using Mixed Integer Linear Programming (MILP). In the previous research on SAND-128, the designers applied the method proposed in [8] to search for impossible differential distinguishers. They fixed the number of active S-boxes in the input and output differences as one, then performed an exhaustive search at nibble level. However, this method limits the search space, overlooking other impossible differential distinguishers.

Hadipour et al. proposed methods to search for impossible differential distinguishers using deterministic differentials [9,10]. These approaches do not require

Y. Kim et al. (Eds.): CANS 2025, LNCS 16351, pp. 643–655, 2026.
https://doi.org/10.1007/978-981-95-4434-9_33

predefined input and output differences, allowing for a more efficient search for impossible differential distinguishers.

Contributions of This Paper: We evaluate the security of SAND-128 against impossible differential attacks. We search for impossible differential distinguishers of SAND-128 using the bit-based Hadipour et al.'s method [10] and reveal 14-round impossible differential distinguishers. The number of 14-round distinguishers is $2^{14} \times 7 = 114,688$. Furthermore, we demonstrate a key recovery attack on 21-round SAND-128. The attack results are summarized in Table 1.

Table 1. Attack Results on SAND-128

Number of rounds	Type	Data	Time	Memory	Method
13	Distinguisher	–	–	–	Impossible Differential [5]
14	Distinguisher	–	–	–	Impossible Differential [13]
14	Distinguisher	–	–	–	Impossible Differential (**Ours**)
16	Distinguisher	2^{127}	–	–	Integral [5]
17	Distinguisher	2^{127}	–	–	Integral [15]
17	Distinguisher	–	–	–	Boomerang [16]
19	Key Recovery	2^{114}	$2^{123.75}$	2^{122}	Boomerang [16]
20	Key Recovery	2^{127}	2^{119}	2^{76}	Integral [15]
21	Key Recovery	2^{124}	$2^{127.2}$	2^{122}	Impossible Differential (**Ours**)
21	Key Recovery	2^{126}	$2^{126.33}$	2^{122}	Impossible Differential (**Ours**)

The structure of this paper is as follows. Section 2 provides related works on SAND-128. Section 3 explains an overview of impossible differential attack. Section 4 introduces constraint programming and the use of deterministic differentials in searching for impossible differential distinguishers. Sections 5 describes the structures of SAND-128. In Sect. 6, we illustrate 14-round impossible differential distinguishers and show a key recovery attack on 21-round SAND-128.

2 Related Works

The designers evaluated SAND's security against various attacks such as impossible differential attack [1], differential attack [6], linear attack [7], integral attack [11], and zero-correlation linear attack [12]. They searched for impossible differentials using a nibble-level search using the method proposed in [8]. As a result, they identified 13-round impossible distinguishers for SAND-128 [5].

Zhang et al. developed a systematic search framework for AND-RX ciphers to find impossible differential distinguishers [13]. Applying their method to SAND, they found 456 types of 14-round impossible differential of SAND-128.

Mirzaie et al. applied the conventional bit-based division property technique [14] to find integral distinguishers on reduced-round SAND-128 [15]. They discovered a 17-round integral distinguisher with nine balanced bits. The data complexity for the distinguisher is 2^{127}. Building on this distinguisher, Mirzaie et al. mounted a key recovery attack on 20-round SAND-128 using the partial sums technique. The time and memory complexities are 2^{119} encryptions and 2^{76} bytes, respectively.

Li and Teh [16] introduced a boomerang-style attack on SAND using a novel AND-specific boomerang connectivity table. Their method led to 19-round key recovery attacks on SAND-128 with 2^{114} data, $2^{123.75}$ time, and 2^{122} memory complexities.

3 Impossible Differential Attack

Impossible differential attack was independently proposed by Biham et al. [1] and Knudsen [2]. Impossible differential was defined as the differential with probability zero. This attack eliminates the key candidates that generate differential with probability zero. In this technique, an attacker searches for an impossible output differential Δ_Y corresponding to a given input differential Δ_X over r-round of the cipher. If such a pair of input-output differentials (Δ_X, Δ_Y) exists, it is termed as an r-round impossible differential distinguisher. It can be used to conduct a distinguishing attack or a key recovery attack against the target cipher.

Boura et al. have formalized the necessary number of data, time, and memory complexities for the impossible differential attacks [3,4]. The following outlines them. For more details, please refer to Refs [3,4].

The notations for an impossible differential attack are as follows. Let Δ_X and Δ_Y be input (resp. output) differences of the impossible differential. Let r_Δ be the number of rounds of the impossible differential. Let Δ_{in} and Δ_{out} be set of all possible input (resp. output) differences of the cipher. Let r_{in} and r_{out} be the number of rounds of the differential paths (Δ_X, Δ_{in}) or (Δ_Y, Δ_{out}).

The differential $(\Delta_X \rightarrow \Delta_{in})$ (resp. $(\Delta_Y \rightarrow \Delta_{out})$) occurs with probability 1 while the differential $(\Delta_{in} \rightarrow \Delta_X)$ (resp. $(\Delta_{out} \rightarrow \Delta_Y)$) is verified with probability $\frac{1}{2^{c_{in}}}$ (resp. $\frac{1}{2^{c_{out}}}$), where c_{in} (resp. c_{out}) is the number of bit-conditions that have to be verified to obtain Δ_X from Δ_{in} (resp. Δ_Y from Δ_{out}).

The probability that for a given key, a pair of inputs already satisfying the differences Δ_{in} and Δ_{out} verifies all the $(c_{in} + c_{out})$ bit-conditions is $2^{-(c_{in}+c_{out})}$. Therefore, the probability that a key trial is kept in the candidate keys set is $p_k = (1 - 2^{-(c_{in}+c_{out})})^N$ with N different input (or output) pairs.

Boura et al. have formalized the smallest value of N, denoted by N_{min}, verifying $p_k = (1 - 2^{-(c_{in}+c_{out})})^{N_{min}} < \frac{1}{2}$ is approximately $N_{min} = 2^{c_{in}+c_{out}}$. The cost of obtaining N pairs of $(\Delta_{in}, \Delta_{out})$ is evaluated as

$$C_N = \max\left\{\min_{\Delta\in\{\Delta_{in},\Delta_{out}\}}\left\{\sqrt{N2^{n+1-|\Delta|}}\right\}, N2^{n+1-|\Delta_{in}|-|\Delta_{out}|}\right\}. \tag{1}$$

The cost C_N also represents the amount of needed data. The time complexity is

$$T = \left(C_N + \left(N + 2^{|k_{in} \cup k_{out}|} \frac{N}{2^{c_{in}+c_{out}}} \right) C'_E + 2^{|K|} p_k \right) C_E, \tag{2}$$

with N such that $p_k = (1 - 2^{-(c_{in}+c_{out})})^N < \frac{1}{2}$, and where C'_E is the ratio of the cost of partial encryption to the full encryption, and where the last term represents the brute-force search complexity. The only elements that need to be stored are the N pairs. Therefore, the memory complexity for the attack is determined by N.

4 Constraint Programming and Its Application to Cryptanalysis

Hadipour et al. proposed the cell-wise model [9] and the bit-wise model [10] to search for impossible differential distinguishers using Constraint Programming. In the bit-wise model, specific constraints are set to track the encryption and decryption processes for each round at the bit level, and an attacker can find bit-wise impossible differential distinguishers of a target cipher. Specifically, Hadipour et al. applied it to ASCON and this method discovered 5-round impossible differential distinguishers [10].

The following outlines the CP models for deterministic differential transitions. For more details, please refer to Refs [9,10]. In the bit-wise models, let integer variables X and Y with the domain of $\{-1, 0, 1\}$ to indicate whether the differential is unknown, zero, or one, respectively.

CP model 1 (Branching) [10]

For $f : \mathbb{F}_2 \to \mathbb{F}_2^n$, $f(x) = (y_0, y_1, \cdots, y_{n-1})$, *where* $y_0 = y_1 = \cdots = y_{n-1} = x$, *the valid transitions for deterministic differential trails satisfy the following:*

$$\texttt{Branch}(X, Y[0], \cdots, Y[n-1]) := \bigwedge_{i=0}^{n-1} (Y[i] = X),$$

where X *and* $Y[i]$ *are integer variables with the domain of* $\{-1, 0, 1\}$ *for all* $0 \le i \le n-1$.

CP model 2 (XOR) [10]

For $f : \mathbb{F}_2^n \to \mathbb{F}_2$, $f(x_0, x_1, \cdots, x_{n-1}) = y$, *where* $y = x_0 \oplus x_1 \oplus \cdots \oplus x_{n-1}$, *the valid transitions for deterministic differential trails satisfy the following:*

$$\texttt{XOR}(X[0], \cdots, X[n-1], Y) := \begin{cases} \text{if } \bigvee_{i=0}^{n-1} (X[i] = -1) \text{ then } Y = -1 \\ \text{else } Y = \sum_{i=0}^{n-1} X[i] \bmod 2 \text{ endif} \end{cases}$$

where $X[i]$ *and* Y *are integer variables with the domain of* $\{-1, 0, 1\}$ *for all* $0 \le i \le n-1$.

CP model 3 (S-box) [10]

CP model for S-box can be derived from the differential distribution table (DDT).

The way how to encode deterministic behaviours of S-box using sbox analyzer is explained in Appendix N of [10].

CP models to search for deterministic differential distinguishers are constructed as follows. We define integer variables XU_r and XL_r, $0 \leq r \leq R$ to represent the differential pattern of the internal state after r rounds of a block cipher whose block size is n in the forward and backward directions. CP models for deterministic differential trails in forward and backward directions over R rounds are independently constructed. The constraints $\sum_{i=0}^{n-1} XU_0[i] \neq 0$ and $\sum_{i=0}^{n-1} XL_R[i] \neq 0$ are added to exclude all trivial solutions. The following constraints are added to ensure the inconsistency between the two deterministic differential propagations at least one point throughout the distinguisher:

$$CSP := \bigvee_{r=0}^{R-1} \left(\bigvee_{i=0}^{n-1} (XU_r[i] + XL_r[i] = 1) \right)$$

If CP models are feasible using a CP-solver, it means that there exist r-round impossible differentials. Otherwise, one can not find any impossible differential at r-round using deterministic differentials.

5 Lightweight Block Cipher SAND-128

SAND is a lightweight block cipher proposed by Chen et al. [5]. It employs an AND-RX structure and has two variants, SAND-64 and SAND-128, depending on the block size. In this paper, we focus on SAND-128 which has a block size of 128 bits and a secret key length of 128 bits. The recommended number of SAND-128 is 54. In the following description, we set $n = 64$.

5.1 Preliminaries

The notations used in the description of SAND-128 are defined as follows:

- $x = (x_{n-1}, x_{n-2}, \ldots, x_0)$: An n-bit variable, where x_{n-1} represents the most significant bit (MSB) and x_0 represents the least significant bit (LSB). The variable x is represented using a $4 \times \frac{n}{4}$ array. $x[i]$ is the i-th nibble (4-bit) of variable x.

$$x = \begin{bmatrix} x_{n-1} & \ldots & x_7 & x_3 \\ x_{n-2} & \ldots & x_6 & x_2 \\ x_{n-3} & \ldots & x_5 & x_1 \\ x_{n-4} & \ldots & x_4 & x_0 \end{bmatrix}, \quad \begin{cases} x[\frac{n}{4} - 1] = (x_{n-1}, x_{n-2}, x_{n-3}, x_{n-4}), \\ \vdots \\ x[1] = (x_7, x_6, x_5, x_4), \\ x[0] = (x_3, x_2, x_1, x_0). \end{cases}$$

- $x||y$: Concatenation of variables x and y
- $x \ll s$: Left shift of variable x by s bits
- $x \lll t$: Left cyclic shift of variable x by t bits
- $x \odot y$: Bitwise AND operation
- $x \oplus y$: Bitwise XOR operation

5.2 Round Function

The round function of SAND-128 is illustrated in Fig. 1. Let (x^r, y^r) denote the input of round r, sk^r denote the round key, and (x^{r+1}, y^{r+1}) denote the output. The round function consists of two types of nonlinear functions, G_0 and G_1, as well as a linear function P_n.

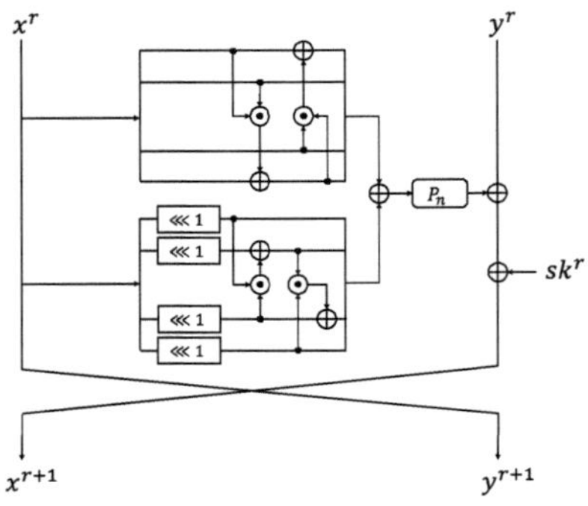

Fig. 1. Round function.

Table 2. Permutation p_{16}.

j	0	1	2	3	4	5	6	7
$p_{16}(j)$	14	15	8	9	2	3	12	13
j	8	9	10	11	12	13	14	15
$p_{16}(j)$	6	7	0	1	10	11	4	5

Let the input to G_0 and G_1 be an n-bit variable $x = x\{3\}||x\{2\}||x\{1\}||x\{0\}$ and the output be $y = y\{3\}||y\{2\}||y\{1\}||y\{0\}$. The function G_0 and G_1 are defined as follows:

$$G_0 := \begin{bmatrix} y\{3\} = y\{0\} \odot x\{1\} \oplus x\{3\} \\ y\{2\} = x\{2\} \\ y\{1\} = x\{1\} \\ y\{0\} = x\{3\} \odot x\{2\} \oplus x\{0\} \end{bmatrix}, \quad G_1 := \begin{bmatrix} y\{3\} = x\{3\} \\ y\{2\} = x\{3\} \odot x\{1\} \oplus x\{2\} \\ y\{1\} = y\{2\} \odot x\{0\} \oplus x\{1\} \\ y\{0\} = x\{0\} \end{bmatrix}.$$

The linear function P_n transforms the input word $x\{i\} = (x_{\frac{n}{4}\cdot i+\frac{n}{4}-1}, \ldots, x_{\frac{n}{4}\cdot i+1}, x_{\frac{n}{4}\cdot i})$ into the output word $y\{i\}$ according to the following equation: $y_{\frac{n}{4}\cdot i+p_{\frac{n}{4}}(j)} = x_{\frac{n}{4}\cdot i+j}$, for $0 \leq j < \frac{n}{4}$, $0 \leq i < 4$. The linear function P_n can be regarded as applying the permutation p_{16} to each of the four $\frac{n}{4}$-bit words in parallel. The permutation p_{16} is defined in Table 2.

5.3 Key Schedule

SAND-128 generates round keys sk^r $(0 \leq r < R)$ from a 128-bit secret key K. The secret key is treated as a concatenation of two 64-bit words: $K = K^1||K^0$. Figures 2 and 3 illustrate the key schedule of SAND-128.

The constant $i+1$ $(0 \leq i < R-2)$ is a round-dependent constant. The update of the linear feedback shift register (LFSR) is defined as $K^{i+2} \leftarrow (A_{16})^3(K^{i+1}) \oplus K^i \oplus (i+1)$. The operation A_{16} processes data in 4-bit units and is applied to

K^{i+1} for three times in succession. The round key sk^r $(0 \leq r < R)$ is loaded from K^r as follows:

$$K^r = \begin{bmatrix} K^r_{63} \dots K^r_7 \; K^r_3 \\ K^r_{62} \dots K^r_6 \; K^r_2 \\ K^r_{61} \dots K^r_5 \; K^r_1 \\ K^r_{60} \dots K^r_4 \; K^r_0 \end{bmatrix}, \quad sk^r = K^r_{63} \dots K^r_3 || K^r_{62} \dots K^r_2 || K^r_{61} \dots K^r_1 || K^r_{60} \dots K^r_0.$$

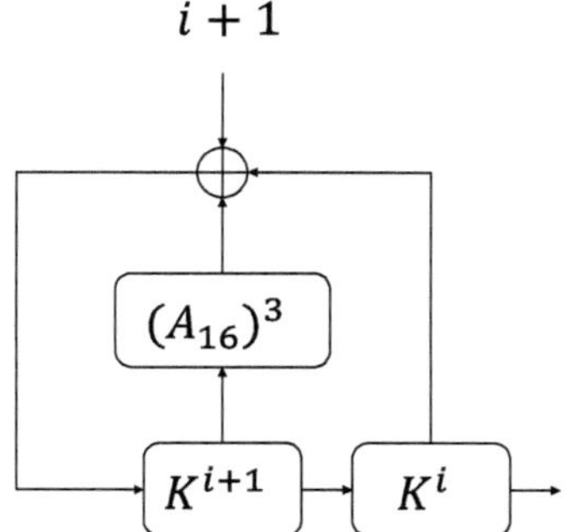

Fig. 2. Key schedule of SAND-128.

Fig. 3. Operation A_{16}.

The operation A_{16} is also nibble-oriented, with the 64-bit input X split into 16 nibbles $X[15]|| \cdots ||X[1]||X[0]$. Then, the output is calculated as follows.

$$(X[15] \lll 1) \oplus X[0]||X[15] \oplus (X[15] \ll 3)||X[14]||X[13]|| \cdots ||X[2]||X[1].$$

6 Impossible Differential Attack on SAND-128

6.1 Construction of the CP Model

We construct a constraint programming (CP) model to search for impossible differential distinguishers of SAND-128 using deterministic differentials. For simplicity, the `StateLoading` process which is linear permutation inserted in the 1st round input and last round output is omitted.

The domain of the following integer variables is defined as $\{-1, 0, 1\}$, where each value represents an unknown, 0, and 1 difference, respectively. Based on the round function illustrated in Fig. 1, we define 32-bit integer variables XU_r and YU_r $(0 \leq r \leq R)$, which represent the internal state differences in the forward (encryption) direction. Similarly, we define 32-bit integer variables XL_r and YL_r $(0 \leq r \leq R)$, which represent the internal state differences in the backward (decryption) direction. The variables XU_0 and YU_0 (as well as XL_0 and YL_0) represent the input differences, while XU_R and YU_R (as well as XL_R and YL_R) represent the output differences after R rounds.

The construction of the CP model in the forward (encryption) direction using XU_r and YU_r is described below. We define 32-bit integer variables G_0U_r and G_1U_r $(1 \leq r \leq R)$ to represent the output differences of the nonlinear functions G_0 and G_1, and impose $G_0U_r = G_0(XU_r)$, $G_1U_r = G_1(XU_r)$ as constraints. The constraints for G_0 and G_1 can be derived from the differential distribution table (DDT). In this paper, we refer to Appendix N of [10] and use the S-box analyzer[1] to derive the constraints for G_0 and G_1.

We define 32-bit integer variables PU_r $(1 \leq r \leq R)$ to represent the output differences of the linear function P_n, and impose $PU_r = P_n(\mathtt{XOR}(G_0U_r, G_1U_r))$ as constraint. For the round function output, the constraints $XU_{r+1} = \mathtt{XOR}(YU_r, PU_r)$, $YU_{r+1} = XU_r$ are imposed.

By constructing these constraints for each round r $(0 \leq r \leq R)$, the CP model for the forward (encryption) direction is completed. Similarly, the CP model for the backward (decryption) direction can be constructed using integer variables XL_r and YL_r. Additionally, we introduce the following constraints to eliminate trivial solutions:

$$\sum_{i=0}^{n-1} XU_0[i] + \sum_{i=0}^{n-1} YU_0[i] \neq 0, \quad \sum_{i=0}^{n-1} XL_R[i] + \sum_{i=0}^{n-1} YL_R[i] \neq 0.$$

Finally, to ensure that there is at least one contradiction between the deterministic difference propagation paths in the forward (encryption) and backward (decryption) directions, we introduce the following constraints:

$$\left\{\bigvee_{r=0}^{R-1}\left(\bigvee_{i=0}^{n-1}(XU_r[i] + XL_r[i] = 1)\right)\right\} \vee \left\{\bigvee_{r=0}^{R-1}\left(\bigvee_{i=0}^{n-1}(YU_r[i] + YL_r[i] = 1)\right)\right\}.$$

If the constructed CP model is satisfiable in a CP solver, it indicates the existence of an r-round impossible differential distinguisher.

6.2 Impossible Differential Distinguishers of SAND-128

We implemented the CP model constructed in the previous section using MiniZinc v2.9.2[2], and employed OR-Tools CP-SAT 9.12.4544[3] as a CP solver. The experiments were conducted using a high-performance system running Windows 11, equipped with an AMD Ryzen™ 5950X 16-core processor, 128 GB RAM, and 1 TB disk space.

As a result of searching for impossible differential distinguishers, we obtained a solution in approximately five minutes, revealing 14-round impossible differential distinguishers of SAND-128. The number of 14-round distinguishers is $2^{14} \times 7 = 114,688$. The results are presented in Tables 3 and 4. In both tables, the nibble-wise symbols **0** and **?** denote **0** = 0000 and **?** =????, respectively.

[1] https://github.com/hadipourh/sboxanalyzer.

[2] https://www.minizinc.org/.

[3] https://developers.google.com/optimization.

Table 3. 14-round Impossible Differentials of SAND-128 (Left 64-bit)

XU_0	0	0	00?0	0	0	0	0	0	0	0	00?0	0	0	0	00?0	0
XU_1	000?	?000	0	?000	000?	0	0	0100	000?	?000	0	?000	000?	?000	0	??00
XU_2	0	?	00?0	0??0	0	??11	0	0?00	0	???0	00?0	0??0	0	?	00?0	0??0
XU_3	?00?	?	??00	?0??	000?	0???	?100	01??	?00?	?	?000	?0??	?00?	?	??00	?
XU_4	?	?	???0	0???	???1	??0?	??00	0???	???0	?	???0	0???	?	?	???0	0???
XU_5	?	?	?	?0??	?	?	?	01??	?	?	?	?0??	?	?	?	?
XU_6	?	?	?	?	?	??1?	?	?	?	?	?	?	?	?	?	?
XL_6	?	?	?	?	?	??0?	?	?	?	?	?	?	?	?	?	?
XL_7	?	?	?	?0??	?	0???	?	00??	?	?	?	?0??	?	?	?	?0??
XL_8	???0	?	???0	0???	??00	??0?	??00	0???	???0	?	???0	0???	???0	?	???0	0???
XL_9	000?	0???	?000	?0??	000?	0???	0	00??	000?	0???	?000	?0??	000?	0???	?000	?0??
XL_{10}	0	???0	00?0	0?00	0	??00	0	0?00	0	???0	00?0	0?00	0	???0	00?0	0?00
XL_{11}	000?	0	0	?000	000?	0	0	0	000?	0	0	?000	000?	0	0	?000
XL_{12}	0	0	00?0	0	0	0	0	0	0	0	00?0	0	0	0	00?0	0
XL_{13}	0	0	0	0	0	0	0	0	0	0	0	0	0	0	0	0
XL_{14}	0	0	00?0	0	0	0	0	0	0	0	00?0	0	0	0	00?0	0

Table 4. 14-round Impossible Differentials of SAND-128 (Right 64-bit)

YU_0	000?	?000	0	?000	000?	0	0	0100	000?	?000	0	?000	000?	?000	0	??00
YU_1	0	0	00?0	0	0	0	0	0	0	0	00?0	0	0	0	00?0	0
YU_2	000?	?000	0	?000	000?	0	0	0100	000?	?000	0	?000	000?	?000	0	??00
YU_3	0	?	00?0	0??0	0	??11	0	0?00	0	???0	00?0	0??0	0	?	00?0	0??0
YU_4	?00?	?	??00	?0??	000?	0???	?100	01??	?00?	?	?000	?0??	?00?	?	??00	?
YU_5	?	?	???0	0???	???1	??0?	??00	0???	???0	?	???0	0???	?	?	???0	0???
YU_6	?	?	?	?0??	?	?	?	01??	?	?	?	?0??	?	?	?	?
YU_7	?	?	?	?	?	??1?	?	?	?	?	?	?	?	?	?	?
YL_7	?	?	?	?	?	??0?	?	?	?	?	?	?	?	?	?	?
YL_8	?	?	?	?0??	?	0???	?	00??	?	?	?	?0??	?	?	?	?0??
YL_9	???0	?	???0	0???	??00	??0?	??00	0???	???0	?	???0	0???	???0	?	???0	0???
YL_{10}	000?	0???	?000	?0??	000?	0???	0	00??	000?	0???	?000	?0??	000?	0???	?000	?0??
YL_{11}	0	???0	00?0	0?00	0	??00	0	0?00	0	???0	00?0	0?00	0	???0	00?0	0?00
YL_{12}	000?	0	0	?000	000?	0	0	0	000?	0	0	?000	000?	0	0	?000
YL_{13}	0	0	00?0	0	0	0	0	0	0	0	00?0	0	0	0	00?0	0
YL_{14}	0	0	0	0	0	0	0	0	0	0	0	0	0	0	0	0

6.3 Key Recovery Attack on 21-Round SAND-128

Using one of the 14-round impossible differential distinguishers shown in Tables 3 and 4, we perform a key recovery attack on 21-round SAND-128, as illustrated in Fig. 4. In Fig. 4, the round function is abbreviated as F and the locations where differences exist are highlighted in red. The data, time, and memory complexities for the key recovery attack are estimated using the method proposed in [3,4].

At $r_{in} = 4$, the bit conditions required to obtain the output difference at the fourth round $(\Delta x^4, \Delta y^4)$ from the plaintext difference $(\Delta x^0, \Delta y^0)$ are $c_{in} = 28+20+12+8 = 68$. Additionally, the number of key bits involved is $k_{in} = 28$ bits ($sk^0 = 16$ bits, $sk^1 = 8$ bits, $sk^2 = 4$ bits). Similarly, at $r_{out} = 3$, the bit conditions required to obtain the output difference at the 18th round $(\Delta x^{18}, \Delta y^{18})$ from the ciphertext difference $(\Delta x^{21}, \Delta y^{21})$ are $c_{out} = 24 + 16 + 8 = 48$. Additionally, the number of key bits involved is $k_{out} = 12$ bits ($sk^{19} = 4$ bits, $sk^{20} = 8$ bits).

To reduce the number of key candidates by at least half, the necessary number of differential pairs $(\Delta_{in}, \Delta_{out})$ is $N_{min} = 2^{68+48} = 2^{116}$. The computational complexity to obtain these differential pairs is estimated from Eq. (1) as follows:

$$C_N = \max\left\{\left\{\sqrt{2^{116}2^{128+1-51}}\right\}, 2^{116}2^{128+1-70-51}\right\} = 2^{124}$$

This computational complexity C_N also represents the necessary number of plaintexts. The total time complexity required for the key recovery attack is estimated from Eq. (2) as follows:

$$T = \left(2^{124} + \left(2^{116} + 2^{28+12}\right) \times \frac{7}{21} + 2^{128} \times \frac{1}{2}\right) \approx 2^{127.2}$$

which corresponds to the number of 21-round SAND-128 encryptions. The memory required to store N_{min} differential pairs is $M = 2^{116} \times 128 \times 4 \times \frac{1}{8} = 2^{122}$ bytes.

We can reduce the time complexity using plenty of plaintexts. For example, if we prepair 2^{126} plaintexts, we can generate at least 4 sets of C_N. Because each data set of C_N can reduce the number of key candidates by at least half, the total time complexity is estimated as follows.

$$T = \left(2^{126} + 2^2 \times \left(2^{116} + 2^{28+12}\right) \times \frac{7}{21} + 2^{128} \times \left(\frac{1}{2}\right)^4\right) = 2^{126.33}$$

Because we can reuse a memory capacity for each data set of C_N, the memory complexity is 2^{122} bytes. The attack result is summarized in Table 1.

6.4 Comparison with Zhang Et Al. [13]

The impossible differential distinguishers revealed in this paper differ from those reported by Zhang et al. [13] in both methodology and practical results. Specifically, the following points clarify why our differentials are either distinct or advantageous:

- **Search Methodology:** While Zhang et al. propose a framework based on differential propagation matrices and matrix threshold XOR-multiplication to evaluate provable and practical bounds, our method utilizes constraint programming (CP) models based on deterministic differentials [9,10].

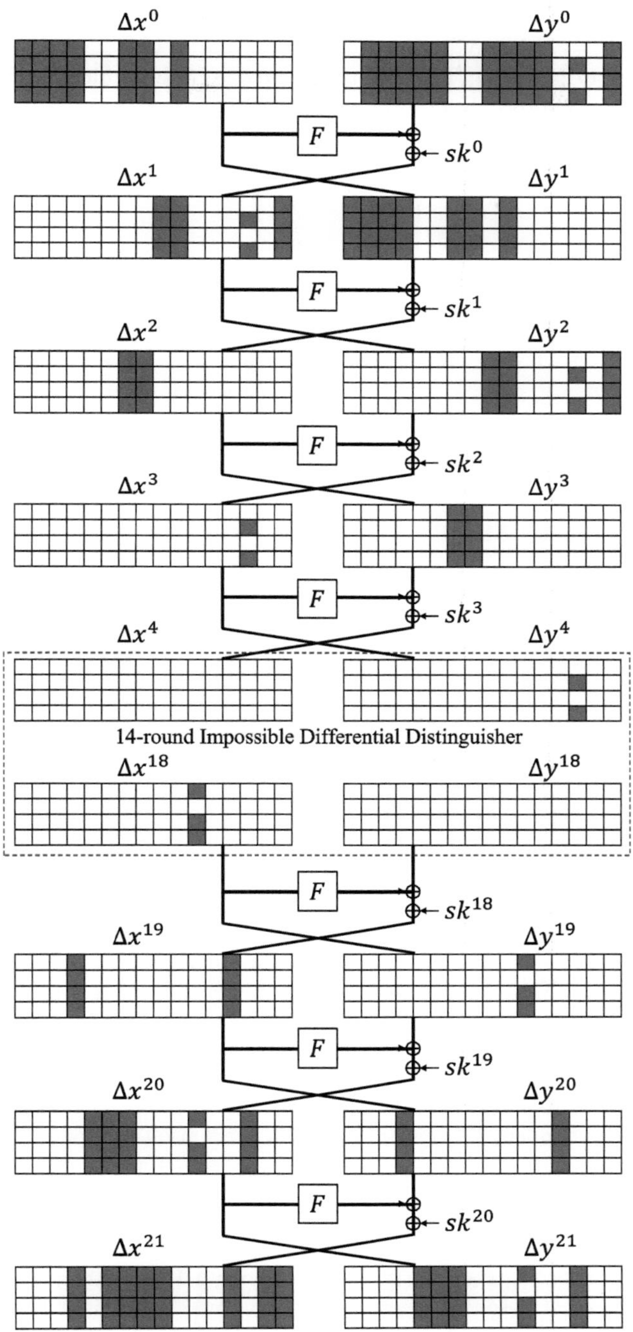

Fig. 4. Key Recovery Attack on 21-Round SAND-128.

– **Distinguisher Coverage:** Zhang et al. report 456 14-round impossible differentials for SAND-128. On the other hand, our method simultaneously identifies $2^{14} \times 7 = 114,688$ distinct 14-round distinguishers using a CP-solver (MiniZinc + OR-Tools). This approach proves highly efficient for discovering various types of impossible differential distinguishers.

References

1. Biham, E., Biryukov, A., Shamir, A.: Cryptanalysis of Skipjack reduced to 31 rounds using impossible differentials. In: Advances in Cryptology-EUROCRYPT'99, vol. 1592 of LNCS, pp. 12–23 (1999)
2. Knudsen L.: DEAL-a 128-bit block cipher. Complexity **258**(2) (1998)
3. Boura, C., Naya-Plasencia, M., Suder, V.: Scrutinizing and improving impossible differential attacks: applications to CLEFIA, Camellia, LBlock and SIMON. In: Sarkar, P., Iwata, T. (eds.) ASIACRYPT 2014. LNCS, vol. 8873, pp. 179–199. Springer, Heidelberg (2014). https://doi.org/10.1007/978-3-662-45611-8_10
4. Boura, C., Lallemand, V., Naya-Plasencia, M., Suder, V.: Making the impossible possible. Cryptology **31**, 101–133. Springer-Verlag (2018)
5. Chen, S., et al.: SAND: an AND-RX Feistel lightweight block cipher supporting S-box-based security evaluations. Des. Codes Crypt. **90**, 155–198 (2022)
6. Biham, E., Shamir, A.: Differential Cryptanalysis of the Data Encryption Standard, pp. 79–88. Springer-Verlag, New York (1993)
7. Matsui, M.: Linear cryptanalysis method for DES cipher. In: Proc. Workshop on the Theory and Application of Cryptographic Techniques, EUROCRYPT '93, vol. 765 of LNCS, pp. 386–397. Springer-Verlag (1993)
8. Cui T., Jia K., Fu K., Chen S., Wang M.: New automatic search tool for impossible differentials and zero-correlation linear approximations. IACR Cryptology ePrint Archive, Report 2016/689 (2016)
9. Hadipour, H., Sadeghi, S. Eichlseder, M.: Finding the impossible: automated search for full impossible differential, zero-correlation, and integral attacks. In: Proc. EUROCRYPT 2023, vol. 14007 of LNCS, pp. 128–157. Springer-Verlag (2023)
10. Hadipour, H., Gerhalter, S., Sadeghi, S., Eichlseder, M.: Improved search for integral, impossible differential and zero-correlation attacks, application to Ascon, ForkSKINNY, SKINNY, MANTIS, PRESENT and QARMAv2. IACR Trans. Symmetric Cryptol. **2024**(1), 234–325 (2024)
11. Knudsen, L., Wagner, D.: Integral cryptanalysis. In: Daemen, J., Rijmen, V. (eds.) FSE 2002. LNCS, vol. 2365, pp. 112–127. Springer, Heidelberg (2002). https://doi.org/10.1007/3-540-45661-9_9
12. Bogdanov, A., Rijmen, V.: Linear hulls with correlation zero and linear cryptanalysis of block ciphers. Des. Codes Crypt. **70**, 369–383 (2014)
13. Zhang, K., Wang, S., Lai, X., Wang, L., Guan, J., Hu, B.: Impossible differential cryptanalysis and a security evaluation framework for AND-RX ciphers. IEEE Trans. Inf. Theory **70**(8), 6025–6040 (2024)
14. Xiang, Z., Zhang, W., Bao, Z., Lin, D.: Applying MILP method to searching integral distinguishers based on division property for 6 lightweight block ciphers. In: Cheon, J.H., Takagi, T. (eds.) ASIACRYPT 2016. LNCS, vol. 10031, pp. 648–678. Springer, Heidelberg (2016). https://doi.org/10.1007/978-3-662-53887-6_24

15. Mirzaie, A., Ahmadi, S., Aref, M.R.: Division property-based integral attack on reduced-round SAND-128. ISC Int. J. Inf. Secur. (ISeCure) **16**(3) (2024)
16. Li, Y., Teh, J.S.: Boomerang cryptanalysis of SAND. J. Inf. Secur. Appl. **92**, 104086 (2025)

Correction to: Lanstree: Cross-Architecture Binary Code Similarity Detection with a Bidirectional Tree-Structured Embedding Model

Congyu Cao, Xiaohan Wang, Shunda Pan, Guohang Shen, and Haipeng Qu

Correction to:
Chapter 21 in: Y. Kim et al. (Eds.): *Cryptology and Network Security*, LNCS 16351, https://doi.org/10.1007/978-981-95-4434-9_21

The original version of chapter 21 was inadvertently published with the incorrect author's name in the references, which have now been corrected (Congyu Cao). The corrections to the book have been updated with the changes.

The updated version of this chapter can be found at
https://doi.org/10.1007/978-981-95-4434-9_21

Y. Kim et al. (Eds.): CANS 2025, LNCS 16351, p. C1, 2026.
https://doi.org/10.1007/978-981-95-4434-9_34

Author Index

Y. Kim et al. (Eds.): CANS 2025, LNCS 16351, pp. 657–658, 2026.
https://doi.org/10.1007/978-981-95-4434-9

MIX
Papier aus verantwortungsvollen Quellen
Paper from responsible sources
FSC® C105338

If you have any concerns about our products,
you can contact us on
ProductSafety@springernature.com

In case Publisher is established outside the EU,
the EU authorized representative is:
Springer Nature Customer Service Center GmbH
Europaplatz 3, 69115 Heidelberg, Germany

Printed by Libri Plureos GmbH
in Hamburg, Germany